CCNA Security Lab Manual Version 1.1

Cisco Networking Academy

Cisco Press
800 East 96th Street
Indianapolis, Indiana 46240 USA

CCNA Security Lab Manual
Version 1.1

Cisco Networking Academy

Published by:
Cisco Press
800 East 96th Street
Indianapolis, IN 46240 USA

Printed in the United States of America

First Printing May 2012

Library of Congress Cataloging-in-Publication Data available upon request.

ISBN-13: 978-1-58713-306-0
ISBN-10: 1-58713-306-7

Warning and Disclaimer

This book is designed to provide information about networking. Every effort has been made to make this book as complete and as accurate as possible, but no warranty or fitness is implied.

The information is provided on an "as is" basis. The authors, Cisco Press, and Cisco Systems, Inc. shall have neither liability nor responsibility to any person or entity with respect to any loss or damages arising from the information contained in this book or from the use of the discs or programs that may accompany it.

The opinions expressed in this book belong to the author and are not necessarily those of Cisco Systems, Inc.

Trademark Acknowledgments

All terms mentioned in this book that are known to be trademarks or service marks have been appropriately capitalized. Cisco Press or Cisco Systems, Inc., cannot attest to the accuracy of this information. Use of a term in this book should not be regarded as affecting the validity of any trademark or service mark.

This book is part of the Cisco Networking Academy® series from Cisco Press. The products in this series support and complement the Cisco Networking Academy curriculum. If you are using this book outside the Networking Academy, then you are not preparing with a Cisco trained and authorized Networking Academy provider.

For more information on the Cisco Networking Academy or to locate a Networking Academy, Please visit www.cisco.com/edu.

Feedback Information

At Cisco Press, our goal is to create in-depth technical books of the highest quality and value. Each book is crafted with care and precision, undergoing rigorous development that involves the unique expertise of members from the professional technical community.

Readers' feedback is a natural continuation of this process. If you have any comments regarding how we could improve the quality of this book, or otherwise alter it to better suit your needs, you can contact us through email at feedback@ciscopress.com. Please make sure to include the book title and ISBN in your message.

We greatly appreciate your assistance.

Publisher	Paul Boger
Associate Publisher	Dave Dusthimer
Cisco Representative	Erik Ullanderson
Cisco Press Program Manager	Anand Sundaram
Executive Editor	Mary Beth Ray
Managing Editor	Sandra Schroeder
Senior Project Editor	Tonya Simpson
Copy Editor	Keith Cline
Editorial Assistant	Vanessa Evans
Cover Designer	Sandra Schroeder

Contents

About This Lab Manual

The only authorized Lab Manual for the Cisco Networking Academy CCNA Security Version 1.1 course

The Cisco® Networking Academy® course on CCNA® Security provides a next step for students who want to expand their CCNA-level skill set to prepare for a career in network security. The CCNA Security course also prepares students for the Implementing Cisco IOS® Network Security (IINS) certification exam (640-554), which leads to the CCNA Security certification.

The CCNA Security Lab Manual provides you with all 16 labs from the course designed as hands-on practice to master the knowledge and skills needed to prepare for entry-level security specialist careers.

All the hands-on labs in the course can be completed on actual physical equipment or in conjunction with the NDG NETLAB+® solution. For current information on labs compatible with NETLAB+® go to http://www.netdevgroup.com/content/cnap/.

Through procedural, skills integration challenges, troubleshooting, and model building labs, this CCNA Security course aims to develop your in-depth understanding of network security principles as well as the tools and configurations used.

Command Syntax Conventions

The conventions used to present command syntax in this book are the same conventions used in the IOS Command Reference. The Command Reference describes these conventions as follows:

- **Boldface** indicates commands and keywords that are entered literally as shown. In actual configuration examples and output (not general command syntax), boldface indicates commands that are manually input by the user (such as a **show** command).
- *Italic* indicates arguments for which you supply actual values.
- Vertical bars (|) separate alternative, mutually exclusive elements.
- Square brackets ([ ]) indicate an optional element.
- Braces ({ }) indicate a required choice.
- Braces within brackets ([{ }]) indicate a required choice within an optional element.

Configuring Devices for Use with Cisco Configuration Professional (CCP) 2.5

Topology

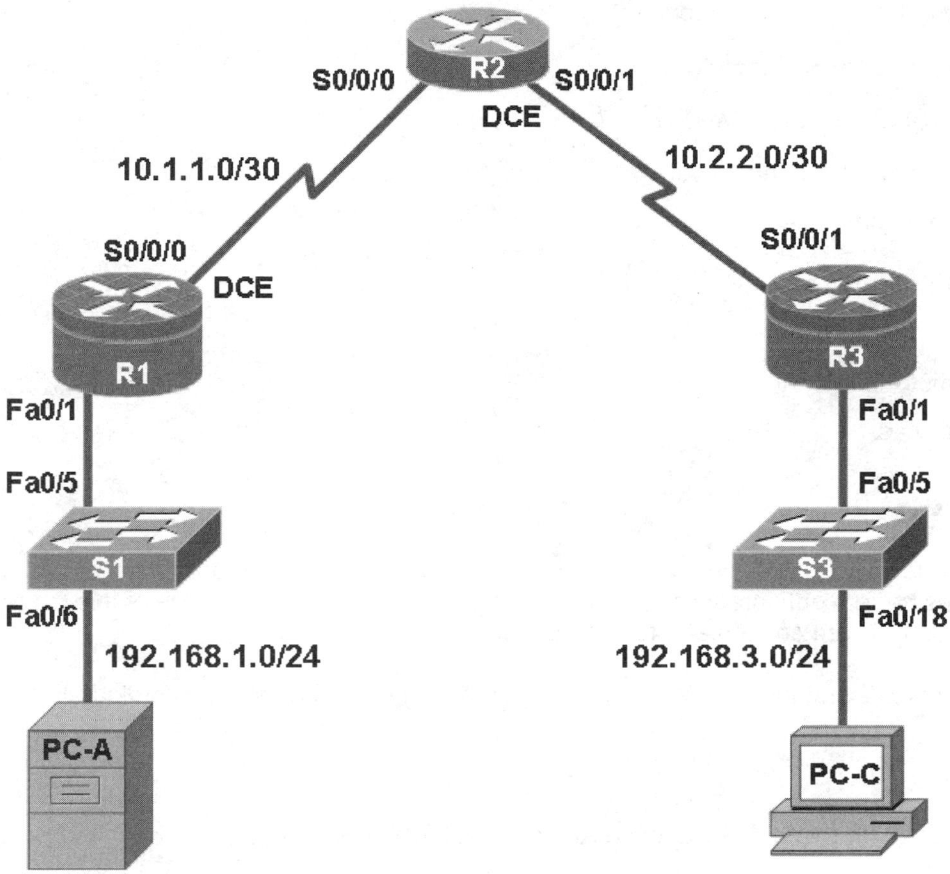

IP Addressing Table

Device	Interface	IP Address	Subnet Mask	Default Gateway	Switch Port
R1	Fa0/1	192.168.1.1	255.255.255.0	N/A	S1 Fa0/5
	S0/0/0 (DCE)	10.1.1.1	255.255.255.252	N/A	N/A
R2	S0/0/0	10.1.1.2	255.255.255.252	N/A	N/A
	S0/0/1 (DCE)	10.2.2.2	255.255.255.252	N/A	N/A
R3	Fa0/1	192.168.3.1	255.255.255.0	N/A	S3 Fa0/5
	S0/0/1	10.2.2.1	255.255.255.252	N/A	N/A
PC-A	NIC	192.168.1.3	255.255.255.0	192.168.1.1	S1 Fa0/6
PC-C	NIC	192.168.3.3	255.255.255.0	192.168.3.1	S3 Fa0/18

Objectives

Part 1: Basic Network Device Configuration

- Cable the network as shown in the topology.
- Configure basic IP addressing for routers and PCs.
- Configure routing.
- Verify connectivity between hosts and routers.

Part 2: Configure CCP Access for Routers

- Enable HTTP/HTTPS server.
- Create a user account with privilege level 15.
- Configure SSH and Telnet access for local login.

Part 3: Basic CCP Configuration

- Install CCP.
- Manage communities.
- Discover router devices.

Background/Scenario

Cisco Configuration Professional (CCP) is a Windows-based device management tool for Integrated Service Routers. CCP simplifies router configurations through easy-to-use wizards. The objective of this lab is to verify that the routers and PC are configured properly for use with CCP.

Note: Ensure that the routers and the switches have been erased and have no startup configurations.

Required Resources

- 3 routers (Cisco 1841 with Cisco IOS Software Release 12.4(20)T1 or comparable)
- 2 switches (Cisco 2960 or comparable)
- PC-A: Windows XP, Vista, or Windows 7
- PC-C: Windows XP, Vista, or Windows 7 with CCP 2.5, Java Version 1.6.0_11 up to 1.6.0_21, Internet Explorer 6.0 or later, and Flash Player Version 10.0.12.36 or later
- Serial and Ethernet cables as shown in the topology
- Rollover cables to configure the routers via the console port

Note: If the PC is running Windows 7, you might need to right-click the Cisco CP icon or menu item and choose **Run as Administrator**.

To run CCP, you might need to temporarily disable antivirus programs and OS firewalls. Make sure to turn off all pop-up blockers in the browser.

Part 1: Basic Router Configuration

In Part 1 of this lab, set up the network topology and configure basic settings such as interface IP addresses and routing.

Step 1: Cable the network.

Attach the devices that are shown in the topology diagram, and cable as necessary.

Step 2: Configure basic settings for each router.

a. Configure hostnames as shown in the topology.

b. Configure interface IP addresses as shown in the IP addressing table.

c. Configure a clock rate for routers with a DCE serial cable attached to their serial interface. Router R1 is shown here as an example:

```
R1(config)# interface S0/0/0
R1(config-if)# clock rate 64000
```

d. To prevent the router from attempting to translate incorrectly entered commands as though they were hostnames, disable DNS lookup. Router R1 is shown here as an example:

```
R1(config)# no ip domain-lookup
```

Step 3: Configure the routing protocol on R1, R2, and R3.

Static and dynamic routing protocols are used in different chapter labs. See the chapter instructions to determine which routing protocol is used in a chapter lab.

Step 4: Configure static default routes on R1, R2, and R3.

a. Configure a static default route from R1 to R2 and from R3 to R2:

```
R1(config)# ip route 0.0.0.0 0.0.0.0 10.1.1.2
R3(config)# ip route 0.0.0.0 0.0.0.0 10.2.2.2
```

b. Configure static routes from R2 to the R1 LAN:

```
R2(config)# ip route 192.168.1.0 255.255.255.0 10.1.1.1
```

c. Configure static routes from R2 to the R3 LAN:

```
R2(config)# ip route 192.168.3.0 255.255.255.0 10.2.2.1
```

Step 5: Configure the EIGRP routing protocol on R1, R2, and R3.

a. On R1, use the following commands:

```
R1(config)# router eigrp 101
R1(config-router)# network 192.168.1.0 0.0.0.255
R1(config-router)# network 10.1.1.0 0.0.0.3
R1(config-router)# no auto-summary
```

b. On R2, use the following commands:

```
R2(config)# router eigrp 101
R2(config-router)# network 10.1.1.0 0.0.0.3
R2(config-router)# network 10.2.2.0 0.0.0.3
R2(config-router)# no auto-summary
```

c. On R3, use the following commands:

```
R3(config)# router eigrp 101
R3(config-router)# network 192.168.3.0 0.0.0.255
```

```
R3(config-router)# network 10.2.2.0 0.0.0.3
R3(config-router)# no auto-summary
```

Step 6: Configure PC host IP settings.

Configure a static IP address, subnet mask, and default gateway for PC-A and PC-C as shown in the IP addressing table.

Step 7: Verify connectivity between the PCs and routers.

a. Ping from R1 to R3.

   Were the ping results successful? _____

   If the pings are not successful, troubleshoot the basic device configurations before continuing.

b. Ping from PC-A on the R1 LAN to PC-C on the R3 LAN.

   Were the ping results successful? _____

   If the pings are not successful, troubleshoot the basic device configurations before continuing.

Note: If you can ping from PC-A to PC-C, you have demonstrated that routing is configured and functioning correctly. If you cannot ping but the device interfaces are up and IP addresses are correct, use the **show run** and **show ip route** commands to help identify routing protocol–related problems.

Part 2: Router Access for CCP

In Part 2 of this lab, you set up a router for use with CCP by enabling an HTTP/HTTPS server, creating a privileged user account, and configuring SSH and Telnet access.

Step 1: Connect to your router through Telnet or SSH or the console.

Enter the global configuration mode using the following commands:

```
Router> enable
Router# configure terminal
```

Step 2: Enable the router HTTP or HTTPS server.

Use the following Cisco IOS Software commands:

```
Router(config)# ip http server
Router(config)# ip http secure-server
Router(config)# ip http authentication local
```

Note: HTTPS is enabled only for cryptography-enabled Cisco IOS Software images.

Step 3: Create a user with privilege level 15.

Use the following command:

```
Router(config)# username admin privilege 15 password cisco12345
```

Step 4: Configure SSH and Telnet for local login.

Use the following commands:

```
Router(config)# line vty 0 4
Router(config-line)# login local
Router(config-line)# transport input telnet
Router(config-line)# transport input telnet ssh
Router(config-line)# exit
```

Part 3: CCP Installation and Initial Setup

Step 1: Install CCP.

Note: You can skip this section if CCP is already installed on your PC.

a. Download CCP 2.5 from the Cisco website:

   http://www.cisco.com/cisco/software/release.html?mdfid=281795035&softwareid=282159854&release=2.5&rellifecycle=&relind=AVAILABLE&reltype=all

b. Choose the file cisco-config-pro-k9-pkg-2_5-en.zip.

Note: Be sure to choose the correct CCP file and not CCP Express. If there is a more current release of CCP, you may choose to download it. However, the labs in this course are based on CCP 2.5.

c. Agree to the terms and conditions and download and save the file to the desired location.

d. Open the zip file and run the CCP executable.

e. Follow the onscreen instructions to install CCP 2.5 on your PC.

Note: If Cisco CP is installed on a PC that uses the Microsoft Windows Vista operating system or the Microsoft Windows 7 operating system, CCP might fail to launch.

Possible Solutions:

1. Compatibility settings:

   a. Right-click the Cisco CP icon or menu item and choose **Properties**.

   b. While in the Properties dialog box, display the **Compatibility** tab. In this tab, check the **Run This Program in Compatibility Mode For** check box. Then in the drop-down menu below, choose **Windows XP (Service Pack 3)**, for example, if it is appropriate for your system.

   c. Click **OK**.

2. Run as Administrator settings:

   a. Right-click the CCP icon or menu item and choose **Properties**.

   b. While in the Properties dialog box, display the **Compatibility** tab. In this tab, check the **Run This Program as Administrator** check box in the Privilege Level section.

   c. Click **OK**.

3. Run as Administrator for each launch:

   a. Right-click the CCP icon or menu item and choose **Run as Administrator**.

   b. For more information, see the *Cisco CP Quick Start Guide* or search on the Internet for "run as administrator" for your operating system.

Note: You might need to temporarily disable antivirus programs and OS firewalls to run CCP.

Step 2: Create/manage communities.

CCP 2.5 can discover up to 10 devices in a community. If desired, the information for both R1 and R3 can be included in one community if the PC has network connectivity to the routers. Only R3 is discovered on PC-C in this section as an example.

a. On PC-C, start CCP: Start > Cisco Configuration Professional.

b. In the Select/Manage Community window, input into the appropriate fields the R3 IP address **192.168.3.1**, the Username **admin**, and the Password **cisco12345**.

c. Click **OK** to continue.

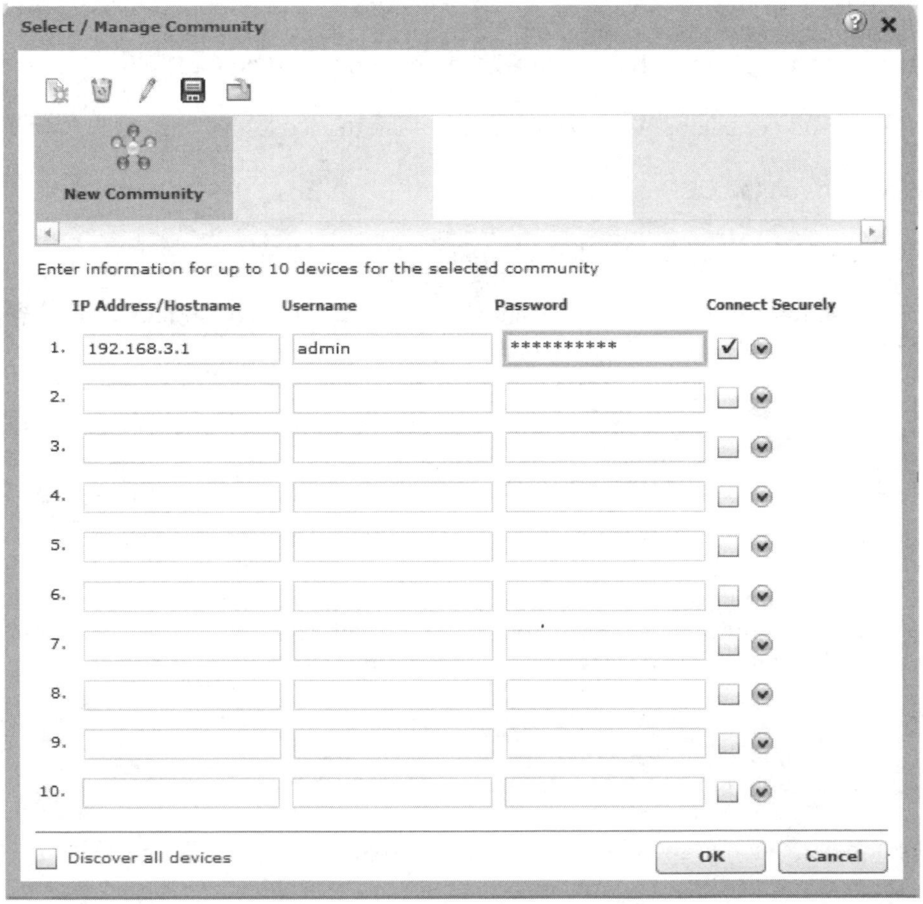

Step 3: Discover router devices.

a. Click **Discover** on the Dashboard to discover and connect to R3. If discovery fails, click the **Discovery Details** button to determine the problem so that you can resolve the issue.

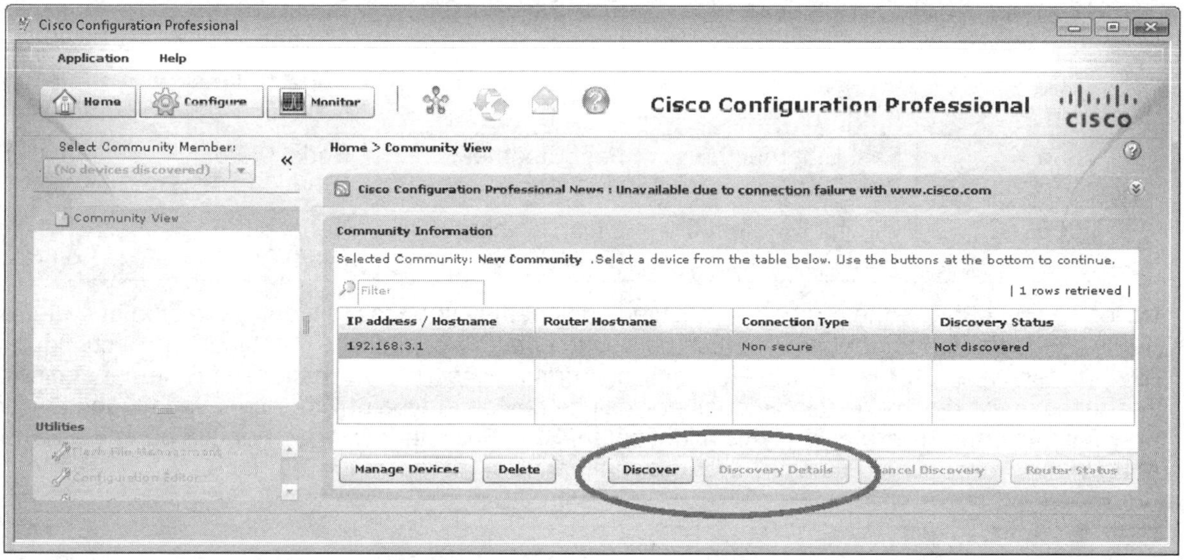

b. After the router has been discovered by CCP, you are ready to configure your Select Community Member. In this example, the Select Community Member is 192.168.3.1.

Router Interface Summary Table

Router Model	Ethernet Interface 1	Ethernet Interface 2	Serial Interface 1	Serial Interface 2
1800	Fast Ethernet 0/0 (Fa0/0)	Fast Ethernet 0/1 (Fa0/1)	Serial 0/0/0 (S0/0/0)	Serial 0/0/1 (S0/0/1)
1900	Gigabit Ethernet 0/0 (Fa0/0)	Gigabit Ethernet 0/1 (Fa0/1)	Serial 0/0/0 (S0/0/0)	Serial 0/0/1 (S0/0/1)
2800	Fast Ethernet 0/0 (Fa0/0)	Fast Ethernet 0/1 (Fa0/1)	Serial 0/0/0 (S0/0/0)	Serial 0/0/1 (S0/0/1)
2900	Gigabit Ethernet 0/0 (Fa0/0)	Gigabit Ethernet 0/1 (Fa0/1)	Serial 0/0/0 (S0/0/0)	Serial 0/0/1 (S0/0/1)

Note: To find out how the router is configured, look at the interfaces to identify the type of router and how many interfaces the router has. There is no way to effectively list all the combinations of configurations for each router class. This table includes identifiers for the possible combinations of Ethernet and serial interfaces in the device. The table does not include any other type of interface, even though a specific router may contain one. An example of this might be an ISDN BRI interface. The string in parentheses is the legal abbreviation that you can use in Cisco IOS commands to represent the interface.

Chapter 1 Lab A: Researching Network Attacks and Security Audit Tools

Objectives

Part 1: Researching Network Attacks

- Research network attacks that have occurred.
- Select a network attack and develop a report for presentation to the class.

Part 2: Researching Security Audit Tools

- Research network security audit tools.
- Select a tool and develop a report for presentation to the class.

Background/Scenario

Network attacks have resulted in the loss of sensitive data and significant network downtime. When a network or the resources within it are inaccessible, worker productivity can suffer, and business income may be lost.

Attackers have developed many tools over the years to attack and compromise the networks of organizations. These attacks take many forms, but in most cases, they seek to obtain sensitive information, destroy resources, or deny legitimate users access to resources.

To understand how to defend a network against attacks, an administrator must first identify network vulnerabilities. Specialized security audit software developed by equipment and software manufacturers can be used to help identify potential weaknesses. In addition, the same tools used by attackers can be used to test the ability of a network to mitigate an attack. After the vulnerabilities are known, you can take steps to help mitigate the network attacks.

This lab provides a structured research project that is divided into two parts: Researching Network Attacks and Researching Security Audit Tools. You can elect to perform Part 1, Part 2, or both. Let your instructor know what you plan to do so that the members of the class report on a variety of network attacks and vulnerability tools.

In Part 1, you research various network attacks that have actually occurred. You select one of these and describe how the attack was perpetrated and how extensive the network outage or damage was. You also investigate how the attack could have been mitigated or what mitigation techniques might have been implemented to prevent future attacks. You prepare a report based on a predefined form included in the lab.

In Part 2, you research network security audit tools and investigate one that can be used to identify host or network device vulnerabilities. You create a one-page summary of the tool based on a predefined form included in the lab. You prepare a short (5 to 10 minute) presentation to present to the class.

You may work in teams of two, with one person reporting on the network attack and the other reporting on the security audit tools. All team members deliver a short overview of their findings. You can use live demonstrations or PowerPoint to summarize your findings.

Required Resources

- Computer with Internet access for research
- Presentation computer with PowerPoint or other presentation software installed
- Video projector and screen for demonstrations and presentations

Part 1: Researching Network Attacks

In Part 1 of this lab, you research various network attacks that have actually occurred and select one on which to report. Fill in the following form based on your findings.

Step 1: Research various network attacks.

List some of the attacks you identified in your search.

____

____

____

Step 2: Fill in the following form for the network attack selected.

Name of attack:	
Type of attack:	
Dates of attacks:	
Computers/organizations affected	
How it works and what it did:	

Mitigation options:
References and info links:
Presentation support graphics (include PowerPoint filename or web links):

Part 2: Researching Security Audit Tools

In Part 2 of this lab, you research network security audit tools and attacker tools and investigate one that can be used to identify host or network device vulnerabilities. Fill in the following report based on your findings.

Step 1: Research various security audit and network attack tools.

List some of the tools that you identified in your search.

____

____

____

____

____

____

____

Step 2: Fill in the following form for the security audit or network attack tool selected.

Name of tool:	
Developer:	
Type of tool (character-based or GUI):	
Used on (network device or computer host):	
Cost:	

Description of key features and capabilities of product or tool:
References and info links:

Reflection

1. How prevalent are network attacks, and what is their impact on the operation of an organization? What key steps can organizations take to help protect their networks and resources?

____
____
____
____
____

2. Have you actually worked for an organization or know of one where the network was compromised? If so, what was the impact to the organization and what did it do about it?

____
____
____
____
____

3. What steps can you take to protect your own PC or laptop computer?

____
____
____
____
____

Chapter 2 Lab A: Securing the Router for Administrative Access

Topology

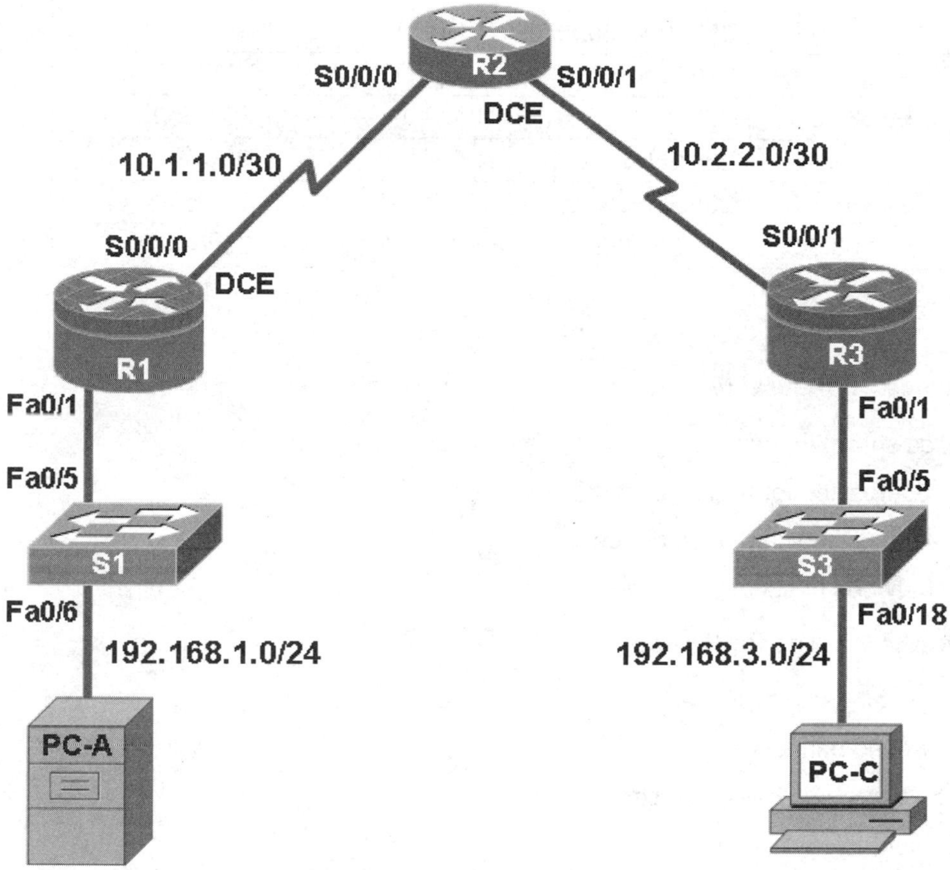

Note: ISR G2 devices use Gigabit Ethernet interfaces rather than FastEthernet interfaces.

IP Addressing Table

Device	Interface	IP Address	Subnet Mask	Default Gateway	Switch Port
R1	Fa0/1	192.168.1.1	255.255.255.0	N/A	S1 Fa0/5
	S0/0/0 (DCE)	10.1.1.1	255.255.255.252	N/A	N/A
R2	S0/0/0	10.1.1.2	255.255.255.252	N/A	N/A
	S0/0/1 (DCE)	10.2.2.2	255.255.255.252	N/A	N/A
R3	Fa0/1	192.168.3.1	255.255.255.0	N/A	S3 Fa0/5
	S0/0/1	10.2.2.1	255.255.255.252	N/A	N/A
PC-A	NIC	192.168.1.3	255.255.255.0	192.168.1.1	S1 Fa0/6
PC-C	NIC	192.168.3.3	255.255.255.0	192.168.3.1	S3 Fa0/18

Objectives

Part 1: Basic Network Device Configuration

- Cable the network as shown in the topology.
- Configure basic IP addressing for routers and PCs.
- Configure static routing, including default routes.
- Verify connectivity between hosts and routers.

Part 2: Control Administrative Access for Routers

- Configure and encrypt all passwords.
- Configure a login warning banner.
- Configure enhanced username password security.
- Configure enhanced virtual login security.
- Configure an SSH server on a router.
- Configure an SSH client and verify connectivity.

Part 3: Configure Administrative Roles

- Create multiple role views and grant varying privileges.
- Verify and contrast views.

Part 4: Configure Cisco IOS Resilience and Management Reporting

- Secure the Cisco IOS image and configuration files.
- Configure a router as a synchronized time source for other devices using NTP.
- Configure syslog support on a router.
- Install a syslog server on a PC and enable it.
- Configure trap reporting on a router using SNMP.
- Make changes to the router and monitor syslog results on the PC.

Part 5: Configure Automated Security Features

- Lock down a router using AutoSecure and verify the configuration.
- Use the CCP Security Audit tool to identify vulnerabilities and to lock down services.
- Contrast the AutoSecure configuration with CCP.

Background/Scenario

The router is a key component that controls the movement of data into and out of the network and between devices within the network. It is particularly important to protect network routers because the failure of a routing device could make sections of the network or the entire network inaccessible. Controlling access to routers and enabling reporting on routers are critical to network security and should be part of a comprehensive security policy.

In this lab, you build a multirouter network and configure the routers and hosts. You use various command-line interface (CLI) and Cisco Configuration Professional (CCP) tools to secure local and remote access to the routers, analyze potential vulnerabilities, and take steps to mitigate them. You also enable management reporting to monitor router configuration changes.

The router commands and output in this lab are from Cisco 1841s using Cisco IOS Software Release 12.4(20)T (advanced IP image). Other routers and Cisco IOS versions can be used. See the Router Interface Summary table at the end of the lab to determine which interface identifiers to use based on the equipment in the lab. Depending on the model of the router, the commands available and output produced may vary from what this lab shows.

Note: Make sure that the routers and the switches have been erased and have no startup configurations.

Required Resources

- 3 routers (Cisco 1841 with Cisco IOS Software Release 12.4(20)T1 or comparable)
- 2 switches (Cisco 2960 or comparable)
- PC-A: Windows XP, Vista, or Windows 7 with CCP 2.5, PuTTy SSH Client (no ACS required)
- PC-C: Windows XP, Vista, or Windows 7 with PuTTy SSH Client and Kiwi or Tftpd32 syslog server
- Serial and Ethernet cables as shown in the topology
- Rollover cables to configure the routers via the console port

CCP Notes

- See Chapter 00 Lab A for instructions on how to install and run CCP. Hardware/software recommendations for CCP include Windows XP, Vista, or Windows 7 with Java Version 1.6.0_11 up to 1.6.0_21, Internet Explorer 6.0 or later, and Flash Player Version 10.0.12.36 or later.
- If the PC on which CCP is installed is running Windows Vista or Windows 7, you might need to right-click the CCP icon or menu item and choose **Run as administrator**.
- To run CCP, you might need to temporarily disable antivirus programs and OS firewalls. Make sure to turn off all pop-up blockers in the browser.

Part 1: Basic Router Configuration

In Part 1 of this lab, you set up the network topology and configure basic settings such as interface IP addresses and static routing.

Step 1: Cable the network.

Attach the devices shown in the topology diagram and cable as necessary.

Step 2: Configure basic settings for each router.

a. Configure hostnames as shown in the topology.

b. Configure interface IP addresses as shown in the IP addressing table.

c. Configure a clock rate for routers with a DCE serial cable attached to their serial interface. Router R1 is shown here as an example:

```
R1(config)# interface S0/0/0
R1(config-if)# clock rate 64000
```

d. To prevent the router from attempting to translate incorrectly entered commands as though they were hostnames, disable DNS lookup. Router R1 is shown here as an example:

```
R1(config)# no ip domain-lookup
```

Step 3: Configure static routing on the routers.

a. Configure a static default route from R1 to R2 and from R3 to R2.

b. Configure a static route from R2 to the R1 LAN and from R2 to the R3 LAN.

Step 4: Configure PC host IP settings.

Configure a static IP address, subnet mask, and default gateway for PC-A and PC-C as shown in the IP addressing table.

Step 5: Verify connectivity between PC-A and R3.

a. Ping from R1 to R3.

Were the ping results successful? __________

If the pings are not successful, troubleshoot the basic device configurations before continuing.

b. Ping from PC-A on the R1 LAN to PC-C on the R3 LAN.

Were the ping results successful? __________

If the pings are not successful, troubleshoot the basic device configurations before continuing.

Note: If you can ping from PC-A to PC-C, you have demonstrated that static routing is configured and functioning correctly. If you cannot ping but the device interfaces are up and IP addresses are correct, use the **`show run`** and **`show ip route`** commands to help identify routing protocol–related problems.

Step 6: Save the basic running configuration for each router.

Use the Transfer > Capture Text option in HyperTerminal or some other method to capture the running configs for each router. Save the three files so that you can use them to restore configs later in the lab.

Part 2: Control Administrative Access for Routers

In Part 2 of this lab, you do the following:

- Configure and encrypt passwords.
- Configure a login warning banner.
- Configure enhanced username password security.
- Configure enhanced virtual login security.
- Configure an SSH server on router R1 using the CLI.
- Research terminal emulation client software and configure the SSH client.

Note: Perform all tasks, on both R1 and R3. The procedures and output for R1 are shown here.

Task 1: Configure and Encrypt Passwords on Routers R1 and R3

Step 1: Configure a minimum password length for all router passwords.

Use the **security passwords** command to set a minimum password length of 10 characters:

```
R1(config)# security passwords min-length 10
```

Step 2: Configure the enable secret password.

Configure the enable secret encrypted password on both routers:

```
R1(config)# enable secret cisco12345
```

How does configuring an enable secret password help protect a router from being compromised by an attack?

____

____

____

Step 3: Configure basic console, auxiliary port, and virtual access lines.

Note: Passwords in this task are set to a minimum of 10 characters, but are relatively simple for the benefit of performing the lab. More-complex passwords are recommended in a production network.

a. Configure a console password and enable login for routers. For additional security, the **exec-timeout** command causes the line to log out after 5 minutes of inactivity. The **logging synchronous** command prevents console messages from interrupting command entry.

Note: To avoid repetitive logins during this lab, you can set the **exec-timeout** command to 0 0, which prevents it from expiring. However, this is not considered a good security practice.

```
R1(config)# line console 0
R1(config-line)# password ciscocon
R1(config-line)# exec-timeout 5 0
R1(config-line)# login
R1(config-line)# logging synchronous
```

When you configured the password for the console line, what message was displayed?

____

b. Configure a new password of **ciscoconpass** for the console.

c. Configure a password for the aux port for router R1:

```
R1(config)# line aux 0
R1(config-line)# password ciscoauxpass
R1(config-line)# exec-timeout 5 0
R1(config-line)# login
```

d. Telnet from R2 to R1:

```
R2> telnet 10.1.1.1
```

Were you able to log in? Why or why not? ______________________________

What messages were displayed?

____
____
____

e. Configure the password on the vty lines for router R1:

```
R1(config)# line vty 0 4
R1(config-line)# password ciscovtypass
R1(config-line)# exec-timeout 5 0
R1(config-line)# login
```

f. Telnet from R2 to R1 again. Were you able to log in this time? ______________________________

g. Enter privileged EXEC mode and issue the show run command. Can you read the enable secret password? Why or why not?

____

Can you read the console, aux, and vty passwords? Why or why not? ______________________________

h. Repeat the configuration portion of steps 3a through 3g on router R3.

Step 4: Encrypt clear-text passwords.

a. Use the **`service password-encryption`** command to encrypt the console, aux, and vty passwords:

```
R1(config)# service password-encryption
```

b. Issue the **`show run`** command. Can you read the console, aux, and vty passwords? Why or why not? ______________________________

c. At what level (number) is the enable secret password encrypted? _____

d. At what level (number) are the other passwords encrypted? _____

e. Which level of encryption is harder to crack and why? ______________________________.

Task 2: Configure a Login Warning Banner on Routers R1 and R3

Step 1: Configure a warning message to display prior to login.

a. Configure a warning to unauthorized users with a message-of-the-day (MOTD) banner using the **banner motd** command. When a user connects to one of the routers, the MOTD banner appears before the login prompt. In this example, the dollar sign ($) is used to start and end the message:

```
R1(config)# banner motd $Unauthorized access strictly prohibited and
prosecuted to the full extent of the law$
R1(config)# exit
```

b. Issue the **show run** command. What does the $ convert to in the output?

____

c. Exit privileged EXEC mode using the **disable** or **exit** command and press **Enter** to get started. Does the MOTD banner look like what you created with the **banner motd** command? _____

Note: If the MOTD banner is not as you wanted it, re-create it using the **banner motd** command.

Task 3: Configure Enhanced Username Password Security on Routers R1 and R3

Step 1: Investigate the options for the username command.

In global configuration mode, enter the following command:

```
R1(config)# username user01 password ?
```

What options are available?

____

____

____

Step 2: Create a new user account using the username command.

a. Create the user01 account, specifying the password with no encryption:

```
R1(config)# username user01 password 0 user01pass
```

b. Use the **show run** command to display the running configuration and check the password that is enabled.

Even though unencrypted (0) was specified, you still cannot read the password for the new user account because the **service password-encryption** command is in effect.

Step 3: Create a new user account with a secret password.

a. Create a new user account with MD5 hashing to encrypt the password:

```
R1(config)# username user02 secret user02pass
```

b. Exit global configuration mode and save your configuration.

c. Display the running configuration. Which hashing method is used for the password?

____

Step 4: Test the new account by logging in to the console.

a. Set the console line to use the locally defined login accounts:

```
R1(config)# line console 0
R1(config-line)# login local
R1(config-line)# end
R1# exit
```

b. Exit to the initial router screen, which displays R1 con0 is now available, Press RETURN to get started.

c. Log in using the user01 account and password previously defined.

What is the difference between logging in at the console now and previously?

____

d. After logging in, issue the **show run** command. Were you able to issue the command? Why or why not?

____

e. Enter privileged EXEC mode using the **enable** command. Were you prompted for a password? Why or why not?

____

Step 5: Test the new account by logging in from a Telnet session.

a. From PC-A, establish a Telnet session with R1:

```
PC-A> telnet 192.168.1.1
```

Were you prompted for a user account? Why or why not?

____

b. Set the vty lines to use the locally defined login accounts:

```
R1(config)# line vty 0 4
R1(config-line)# login local
```

c. From PC-A, telnet to R1 again:

```
PC-A> telnet 192.168.1.1
```

Were you prompted for a user account? Why or why not?

____

d. Log in as **user01** with a password of **user01pass**.

e. While telnetted to R1, access privileged EXEC mode with the **enable** command.

What password did you use? ____

f. For added security, set the aux port to use the locally defined login accounts:

```
R1(config)# line aux 0
```

```
R1(config-line)# login local
```

g. End the Telnet session with the **exit** command.

Task 4: Configure Enhanced Virtual Login Security on Routers R1 and R3

Step 1: Configure the router to protect against login attacks.

Use the **login block-for** command to help prevent brute-force login attempts from a virtual connection, such as Telnet, SSH, or HTTP. This can help slow down dictionary attacks and help protect the router from a possible DoS attack.

a. From the user EXEC or privileged EXEC prompt, issue the **show login** command to see the current router login attack settings:

```
R1# show login
   No login delay has been applied.
   No Quiet-Mode access list has been configured.
   Router NOT enabled to watch for login Attacks
```

b. Use the **login block-for** command to configure a 60 second login shutdown (quiet mode timer) if two failed login attempts are made within 30 seconds:

```
R1(config)# login block-for 60 attempts 2 within 30
```

c. Exit global configuration mode and issue the **show login** command:

```
R1# show login
```

Is the router enabled to watch for login attacks? _____ What is the default login delay?

____

Step 2: Configure the router to log login activity.

a. Configure the router to generate system logging messages for both successful and failed login attempts. The following commands log every successful login and log failed login attempts after every second failed login:

```
R1(config)# login on-success log
R1(config)# login on-failure log every 2
R1(config)# exit
```

b. Issue the **show login** command. What additional information is displayed?

____

____

Step 3: Test the enhanced login security login configuration.

a. From PC-A, establish a Telnet session with R1:

```
PC-A> telnet 10.1.1.1
```

b. Attempt to log in with the wrong user ID or password two times. What message was displayed on PC-A after the second failed attempt?

____

What message was displayed on the router R1 console after the second failed login attempt?

____

____

c. From PC-A, attempt to establish another Telnet session to R1 within 60 seconds. What message was displayed on PC-A after the attempted Telnet connection?

____

____

What message was displayed on router R1 after the attempted Telnet connection?

____

____

d. Issue the **show login** command within 60 seconds. What additional information is displayed?

____

____

____

Task 5: Configure the SSH Server on Router R1 and R3 Using the CLI

In this task, you use the CLI to configure the router to be managed securely using SSH rather than Telnet. Secure Shell (SSH) is a network protocol that establishes a secure terminal emulation connection to a router or other networking device. SSH encrypts all information that passes over the network link and provides authentication of the remote computer. SSH is rapidly replacing Telnet as the remote login tool of choice for network professionals.

Note: For a router to support SSH, it must be configured with local authentication (AAA services or username) or password authentication. In this task, you configure an SSH username and local authentication.

Step 1: Configure a domain name.

Enter global configuration mode and set the domain name:

```
R1# conf t
R1(config)# ip domain-name ccnasecurity.com
```

Step 2: Configure a privileged user for login from the SSH client.

a. Use the `username` command to create the user ID with the highest possible privilege level and a secret password:

```
R1(config)# username admin privilege 15 secret cisco12345
```

b. Exit to the initial router login screen, and log in with this username. What was the router prompt after you entered the password?

____

Step 3: Configure the incoming vty lines.

Specify a privilege level of 15 so that a user with the highest privilege level (15) defaults to privileged EXEC mode when accessing the vty lines. Other users default to user EXEC mode. Use the local user accounts for mandatory login and validation, and accept only SSH connections.

```
R1(config)# line vty 0 4
R1(config-line)# privilege level 15
R1(config-line)# login local
R1(config-line)# transport input ssh
R1(config-line)# exit
```

Note: The login local command should already have been configured in a previous step. It is included here to provide all commands if you were doing this for the first time.

Note: If you add the keyword telnet to the transport input command, users can log in using Telnet and SSH; however, the router will be less secure. If only SSH is specified, the connecting host must have an SSH client installed.

Step 4: Erase existing key pairs on the router.

```
R1(config)# crypto key zeroize rsa
```

Note: If no keys exist, you might receive this message: `% No Signature RSA Keys found in configuration.`

Step 5: Generate the RSA encryption key pair for the router.

The router uses the RSA key pair for authentication and encryption of transmitted SSH data.

Configure the RSA keys with 1024 for the number of modulus bits. The default is 512, and the range is from 360 to 2048.

```
R3(config)# crypto key generate rsa general-keys modulus 1024
The name for the keys will be: R3.ccnasecurity.com

% The key modulus size is 1024 bits
% Generating 1024 bit RSA keys, keys will be non-exportable...[OK]

R3(config)#
*Dec 16 21:24:16.175: %SSH-5-ENABLED: SSH 1.99 has been enabled
R3(config)# exit
```

Note: The details of encryption methods are covered in Chapter 7.

Step 6: Verify the SSH configuration.

a. Use the **`show ip ssh`** command to see the current settings:

```
R1# show ip ssh
```

b. Fill in the following information based on the output of the **`show ip ssh`** command:

SSH version enabled: ____________________

Authentication timeout: ____________________

Authentication retries: ____________________

Step 7: Configure SSH timeouts and authentication parameters.

You can alter the default SSH timeouts and authentication parameters to be more restrictive using the following commands:

```
R1(config)# ip ssh time-out 90
R1(config)# ip ssh authentication-retries 2
```

Step 8: Save the running-config to the startup-config.

```
R1# copy running-config startup-config
```

Task 6: Research Terminal Emulation Client Software and Configure the SSH Client

Step 1: Research terminal emulation client software.

Conduct a web search for freeware terminal emulation client software, such as TeraTerm or PuTTy. What are some capabilities of each?

____

____

____

Step 2: Install an SSH client on PC-A and PC-C.

a. If the SSH client is not already installed, download either TeraTerm or PuTTY.

b. Save the application to the desktop.

Note: The procedure described here is for PuTTY and pertains to PC-A.

Step 3: Verify SSH connectivity to R1 from PC-A.

a. Launch PuTTY by double-clicking the putty.exe icon.

b. Input the R1 Fa0/1 IP address 192.168.1.1 in the **Host Name or IP Address** field.

c. Verify that the **SSH** radio button is selected.

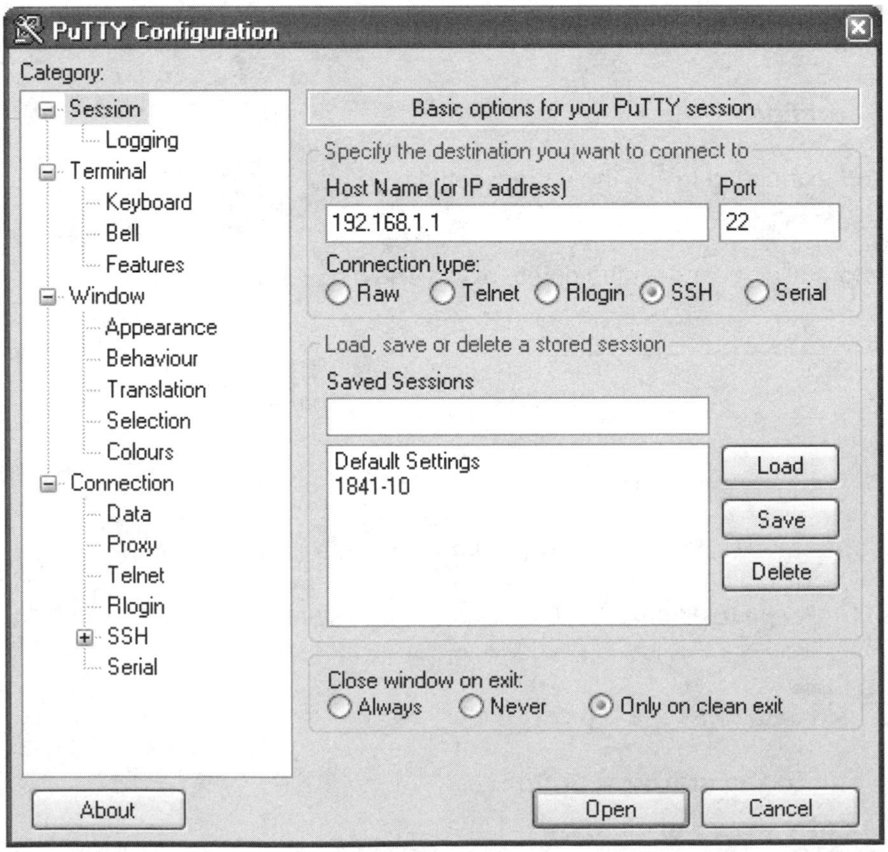

d. Click **Open**.

e. In the PuTTY Security Alert window, click **Yes**.

f. Enter the **admin** username and password **cisco12345** in the PuTTY window.

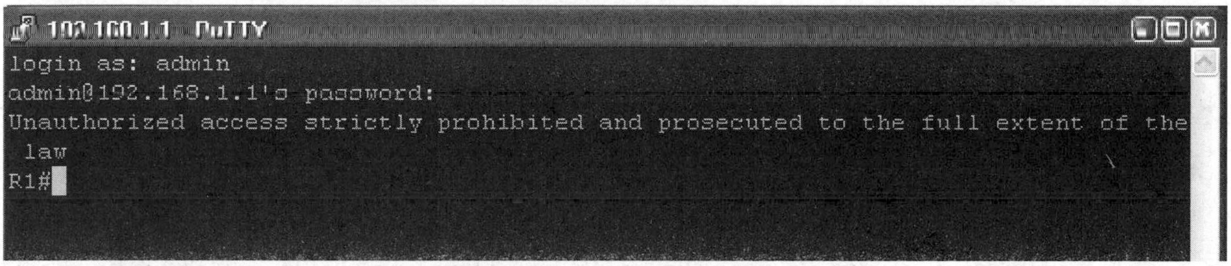

g. At the R1 privileged EXEC prompt, enter the `show users` command:

```
R1# show users
```

What users are connected to router R1 at this time?

____

____

____

h. Close the PuTTY SSH session window.

i. Try to open a Telnet session to your router from PC-A. Were you able to open the Telnet session? Why or why not? ______________________________

j. Open a PuTTY SSH session to the router from PC-A. Enter the user01 username and password user01pass in the PuTTY window to try connecting for user who does not have privilege level of 15. Were you able to log in? _____ What was the prompt? ______________________

k. Use the `enable` command to enter privilege EXEC mode and enter the enable secret password **cisco12345**.

l. Disable the generation of system logging messages for successful login attempts:

```
R1(config)# no login on-success log
```

Step 4: Save the configuration.

Save the running configuration to the startup configuration from the privileged EXEC prompt:

```
R1# copy running-config startup-config
```

Note: Complete steps 3 and 4 between PC-C and router R3.

Part 3: Configure Administrative Roles

In Part 3 of this lab, you do the following:

- Create multiple administrative roles or views on routers R1 and R3.
- Grant each view varying privileges.
- Verify and contrast the views.

The role-based CLI access feature enables the network administrator to define views, which are a set of operational commands and configuration capabilities that provide selective or partial access to Cisco IOS EXEC and configuration (config) mode commands. Views restrict user access to the Cisco IOS CLI and configuration information. A view can define which commands are accepted and what configuration information is visible.

Note: Perform all tasks on both R1 and R3. The procedures and output for R1 are shown here.

Task 1: Enable Root View on R1 and R3

If an administrator wants to configure another view to the system, the system must be in root view. When a system is in root view, the user has the same access privileges as a user who has level-15 privileges, but the root view user can also configure a new view and add or remove commands from the view. When you are in a CLI view, you have access only to the commands that have been added to that view by the root view user.

Step 1: Enable AAA on router R1.

To define views, AAA must be enabled:

```
R1# config t
R1(config)# aaa new-model
R1(config)# exit
```

Note: AAA is covered in Chapter 3.

Step 2: Enable the root view.

Use the command **enable view** to enable the root view. Use the enable secret password cisco12345. If the router does not have an enable secret password, create one now:

```
R1# enable view
Password: cisco12345
*Dec 16 22:41:17.483: %PARSER-6-VIEW_SWITCH: successfully set to view 'root'.
```

Task 2: Create New Views for the Admin1, Admin2, and Tech Roles on R1 and R3

Step 1: Create the admin1 view, establish a password, and assign privileges.

a. The admin1 user is the top-level user below root that is allowed to access this router. It has the most authority. The admin1 user can use all show, config, and debug commands. Use the following command to create the admin1 view while in the root view:

```
R1(config)# parser view admin1
R1(config-view)#
*Dec 16 22:45:27.587: %PARSER-6-VIEW_CREATED: view 'admin1'
successfully created.
R1(config-view)#
```

Note: To delete a view, use the command **no parser view** *viewname*.

b. Associate the admin1 view with an encrypted password:

```
R1(config-view)# secret admin1pass
R1(config-view)#
```

c. Review the commands that can be configured in the admin1 view. Use the **commands ?** command to see available commands. The following is a partial listing of the available commands:

```
R1(config-view)# commands ?
  RITE-profile            Router IP traffic export profile command mode
  RMI Node Config         Resource Policy Node Config mode
  RMI Resource Group      Resource Group Config mode
  RMI Resource Manager    Resource Manager Config mode
  RMI Resource Policy     Resource Policy Config mode
  SASL-profile            SASL profile configuration mode
  aaa-attr-list           AAA attribute list config mode
  aaa-user                AAA user definition
  accept-dialin           VPDN group accept dialin configuration mode
  accept-dialout          VPDN group accept dialout configuration mode
  address-family          Address Family configuration mode
<output omitted>
```

d. Add all **config**, **show**, and **debug** commands to the admin1 view, and then exit from view configuration mode:

```
R1(config-view)# commands exec include all show
R1(config-view)# commands exec include all config terminal
R1(config-view)# commands exec include all debug
R1(config-view)# end
```

e. Verify the admin1 view:

```
R1# enable view admin1
Password:admin1pass
*Dec 16 22:56:46.971: %PARSER-6-VIEW_SWITCH: successfully set to view
'admin1'

R1# show parser view
R1# Current view is 'admin1'
```

f. Examine the commands available in the admin1 view:

```
R1# ?
Exec commands:
  configure   Enter configuration mode
  debug       Debugging functions (see also 'undebug')
  enable      Turn on privileged commands
  exit        Exit from the EXEC
  show        Show running system information
```

g. Examine the **show** commands available in the admin1 view:

```
R1# show ?
  aaa            Show AAA values
  accounting     Accounting data for active sessions
  adjacency      Adjacent nodes
  alignment      Show alignment information
  appfw          Application Firewall information
  archive        Archive of the running configuration information
  arp            ARP table
<output omitted>
```

Step 2: Create the admin2 view, establish a password, and assign privileges.

The admin2 user is a junior administrator in training who is allowed to view all configurations but is not allowed to configure the routers or use **debug** commands.

a. Use the `enable view` command to enable the root view, and enter the enable secret password **cisco12345**:

```
R1# enable view
Password:cisco12345
```

b. Use the following command to create the admin2 view:

```
R1(config)# parser view admin2
R1(config-view)#
*Dec 16 23:02:27.587: %PARSER-6-VIEW_CREATED: view 'admin2'
successfully created.
R1(config-view)#
```

c. Associate the admin2 view with a password:

```
R1(config-view)# secret admin2pass
R1(config-view)#
```

d. Add all **show** commands to the view, and then exit from view configuration mode:

```
R1(config-view)# commands exec include all show
R1(config-view)# end
```

e. Verify the admin2 view:

```
R1# enable view admin2
Password: admin2pass
*Dec 16 23:05:46.971: %PARSER-6-VIEW_SWITCH: successfully set to view
'admin2'
R1# show parser view
R1# Current view is 'admin2'
```

f. Examine the commands available in the admin2 view:

```
R1# ?
Exec commands:
  enable      Turn on privileged commands
  exit        Exit from the EXEC
  show        Show running system information
```

What is missing from the list of admin2 commands that is present in the admin1 commands?

____

Step 3: Create the tech view, establish a password, and assign privileges.

a. The tech user typically installs end-user devices and cabling. Tech users are only allowed to use selected show commands.

b. Use the `enable view` command to enable the root view, and enter the enable secret password **cisco12345**:

```
R1# enable view
Password:cisco12345
```

c. Use the following command to create the tech view:

```
R1(config)# parser view tech
R1(config-view)#
*Dec 16 23:10:27.587: %PARSER-6-VIEW_CREATED: view 'tech' successfully
created.
```

d. Associate the tech view with a password:

```
R1(config-view)# secret techpasswd
R1(config-view)#
```

e. Add the following **show** commands to the view, and then exit from view configuration mode:

```
R1(config-view)# commands exec include show version
R1(config-view)# commands exec include show interfaces
R1(config-view)# commands exec include show ip interface brief
R1(config-view)# commands exec include show parser view
R1(config-view)# end
```

f. Verify the tech view:

```
R1# enable view tech
Password:techpasswd
*Dec 16 23:13:46.971: %PARSER-6-VIEW_SWITCH: successfully set to view
'tech'
R1# show parser view
R1# Current view is 'tech'
```

g. Examine the commands available in the tech view:

```
R1# ?
Exec commands:
  enable      Turn on privileged commands
  exit        Exit from the EXEC
  show        Show running system information
```

h. Examine the **show** commands available in the tech view:

```
R1# show ?
  flash:      display information about flash: file system
  interfaces  Interface status and configuration
  ip          IP information
  parser      Show parser commands
  version     System hardware and software status
```

i. Issue the **show ip interface brief** command. Were you able to do it as the tech user? Why or why not? ______________________________

j. Issue the **show ip route** command. Were you able to do it as the tech user? ______________

k. Return to root view with the **enable view** command:

```
R1# enable view
Password: cisco12345
```

l. Issue the **show run** command to see the views you created. For tech view, why are the **show** and **show ip** commands listed as well as **show ip interface** and **show ip interface brief**?

____

Step 4: Save the configuration on routers R1 and R3.

Save the running configuration to the startup configuration from the privileged EXEC prompt.

Part 4: Configure IOS Resilience and Management Reporting

In Part 4 of this lab, you do the following:

- Secure the Cisco IOS image and configuration files.
- Using NTP, configure a router as a synchronized time source for other devices.
- Configure syslog support on a router.

- Install a syslog server on a PC and enable it.
- Configure the logging trap level on a router.
- Make changes to the router and monitor syslog results on the PC.

Note: Perform all tasks on both R1 and R3. The procedure and output for R1 is shown here.

Task 1: Secure Cisco IOS Image and Configuration Files on R1 and R3

The Cisco IOS Resilient Configuration feature enables a router to secure the running image and maintain a working copy of the configuration so that those files can withstand malicious attempts to erase the contents of persistent storage (NVRAM and flash). The feature secures the smallest working set of files to preserve persistent storage space. No extra space is required to secure the primary Cisco IOS image file. In this task, you configure the Cisco IOS Resilient Configuration feature.

Step 1: Display the files in flash memory for R1.

```
R1# show flash
-# - --length-- -----date/time------ path
1     37081324 Dec 16 2008 21:57:10 c1841-advipservicesk9-mz.124-20.T1.bin
2      6389760 Dec 16 2008 22:06:56 sdm.tar
3      1505280 Dec 16 2008 22:08:52 common.tar
4       527849 Dec 16 2008 17:13:40 128MB.sdf
5         1821 Dec 16 2008 00:11:30 sdmconfig-18xx.cfg
6       931840 Dec 16 2008 17:14:42 es.tar
7       112640 Dec 16 2008 17:15:06 home.tar
8         1038 Dec 16 2008 17:15:22 home.shtml
9      1697952 Dec 16 2008 17:17:54 securedesktop-ios-3.1.1.45-k9.pkg
10      415956 Dec 16 2008 17:21:16 sslclient-win-1.1.4.176.pkg

14815232 bytes available (49197056 bytes used)
```

Step 2: Secure the Cisco IOS image and archive a copy of the running configuration.

a. The **secure boot-image** command enables Cisco IOS image resilience, which hides the file from **dir** and **show** commands. The file cannot be viewed, copied, modified, or removed using EXEC mode commands. (It can be viewed in ROMMON mode.) When turned on for the first time, the running image is secured.

```
R1(config)# secure boot-image
.Dec 17 25:40:13.170: %IOS_RESILIENCE-5-IMAGE_RESIL_ACTIVE: Successfully
secured running image
```

b. The **secure boot-config** command takes a snapshot of the router running configuration and securely archives it in persistent storage (flash):

```
R1(config)# secure boot-config
.Dec 17 25:42:18.691: %IOS_RESILIENCE-5-CONFIG_RESIL_ACTIVE:
Successfully secured config archive [flash:.runcfg-20081219-224218.ar]
```

Step 3: Verify that your image and configuration are secured.

You can use only the **show secure bootset** command to display the archived filename. Display the status of configuration resilience and the primary bootset filename:

```
R1# show secure bootset
IOS resilience router id FTX1111W0QF
```

```
IOS image resilience version 12.4 activated at 25:40:13 UTC Wed Dec 17 2008
Secure archive flash:c1841-advipservicesk9-mz.124-20.T1.bin type is image
(elf)
[]
  file size is 37081324 bytes, run size is 37247008 bytes
  Runnable image, entry point 0x8000F000, run from ram

IOS configuration resilience version 12.4 activated at 25:42:18 UTC Wed Dec
17 2008
Secure archive flash:.runcfg-20081219-224218.ar type is config
configuration archive size 1986 bytes
```

What is the name of the archived running config file and on what is the name based?

____

Step 4: Display the files in flash memory for R1.

Display the contents of flash using the **show flash** command:

```
R1# show flash
-# - --length-- -----date/time------ path
1       6389760 Dec 16 2008 22:06:56 sdm.tar
2       1505280 Dec 16 2008 22:08:52 common.tar
3        527849 Dec 16 2008 17:13:40 128MB.sdf
4          1821 Dec 16 2008 00:11:30 sdmconfig-18xx.cfg
5        512000 Dec 16 2008 17:14:24 dg_sdm.tar
6        931840 Dec 16 2008 17:14:42 es.tar
7        112640 Dec 16 2008 17:15:06 home.tar
8          1038 Dec 16 2008 17:15:22 home.shtml
10      1697952 Dec 16 2008 17:17:54 securedesktop-ios-3.1.1.45-k9.pkg
11       415956 Dec 16 2008 17:21:16 sslclient-win-1.1.4.176.pkg

14807040 bytes available (49205248 bytes used)
```

Is the Cisco IOS image or the archived running config file listed? ____________________________

How can you tell that the Cisco IOS image is still there?

____

Step 5: Disable the IOS Resilient Configuration feature.

a. Disable the Resilient Configuration feature for the Cisco IOS image:

```
R1# config t
R1(config)# no secure boot-image
.Dec 17 25:48:23.009: %IOS_RESILIENCE-5-IMAGE_RESIL_INACTIVE: Disabled
secure image archival
```

b. Disable the Resilient Configuration feature for the running config file:

```
R1(config)# no secure boot-config
.Dec 17 25:48:47.972: %IOS_RESILIENCE-5-CONFIG_RESIL_INACTIVE: Disabled
secure config archival [removed flash:.runcfg-20081219-224218.ar]
```

Step 6: Verify that the Cisco IOS image is now visible in flash.

```
R1# show flash
```

```
-# - --length-- -----date/time------ path
1     37081324 Dec 16 2008 21:57:10 c1841-advipservicesk9-mz.124-20.T1.bin
2      6389760 Dec 16 2008 22:06:56 sdm.tar
3      1505280 Dec 16 2008 22:08:52 common.tar
4       527849 Dec 16 2008 17:13:40 128MB.sdf
5         1821 Dec 16 2008 00:11:30 sdmconfig-18xx.cfg
6       931840 Dec 16 2008 17:14:42 es.tar
7       112640 Dec 16 2008 17:15:06 home.tar
8         1038 Dec 16 2008 17:15:22 home.shtml
9      1697952 Dec 16 2008 17:17:54 securedesktop-ios-3.1.1.45-k9.pkg
10      415956 Dec 16 2008 17:21:16 sslclient-win-1.1.4.176.pkg

14815232 bytes available (49197056 bytes used)
```

Step 7: Save the configuration on both routers.

Save the running configuration to the startup configuration from the privileged EXEC prompt.

Task 2: Configure a Synchronized Time Source Using NTP

Router R2 will be the master Network Time Protocol (NTP) clock source for routers R1 and R3.

Note: R2 could also be the master clock source for switches S1 and S3, but it is not necessary to configure them for this lab.

Step 1: Set up the NTP master using Cisco IOS commands.

R2 is the master NTP server in this lab. All other routers and switches learn the time from it, either directly or indirectly. For this reason, you must ensure that R2 has the correct coordinated universal time set.

Note: If you are using CCP to configure R2 to support NTP, skip this step and go to Step 2.

a. Use the **`show clock`** command to display the current time set on the router:

```
R2# show clock
*01:19:02.331 UTC Mon Dec 15 2008
```

b. To set the time on the router, use the **`clock set`** *`time`* command:

```
R2# clock set 20:12:00 Dec 17 2008
R2#
*Dec 17 20:12:18.000: %SYS-6-CLOCKUPDATE: System clock has been updated
from 01:20:26 UTC Mon Dec 15 2008 to 20:12:00 UTC Wed Dec 17 2008,
configured from console by admin on console.
```

c. Configure R2 as the NTP master using the **`ntp master`** *`stratum-number`* command in global configuration mode. The stratum number indicates the distance from the original source. For this lab, use a stratum number of 3 on R2. When a device learns the time from an NTP source, its stratum number becomes one greater than the stratum number of its source.

```
R2(config)# ntp master 3
```

Step 2: Configure R1 and R3 as NTP clients using the CLI.

a. R1 and R3 will become NTP clients of R2. To configure R1, use the global configuration command **`ntp server`** ***`hostname`***. The hostname can also be an IP address. The command **`ntp update-calendar`** periodically updates the calendar with the NTP time:

```
R1(config)# ntp server 10.1.1.2
R1(config)# ntp update-calendar
```

b. Verify that R1 has made an association with R2 with the **show ntp associations** command. You can also use the more verbose version of the command by adding the **detail** argument. It might take some time for the NTP association to form.

```
R1# show ntp associations

address      ref clock      st   when   poll reach   delay  offset    disp
~10.1.1.2    127.127.1.1     3     14     64     3   0.000  -280073   3939.7
*sys.peer, # selected, +candidate, -outlyer, x falseticker, ~
configured
```

c. Issue the **debug ntp all** command to see NTP activity on R1 as it synchronizes with R2:

```
R1# debug ntp all
NTP events debugging is on
NTP core messages debugging is on
NTP clock adjustments debugging is on
NTP reference clocks debugging is on
NTP packets debugging is on

Dec 17 20.12:18.554: NTP message sent to 10.1.1.2, from interface
'Serial0/0/0' (10.1.1.1).
Dec 17 20.12:18.574: NTP message received from 10.1.1.2 on interface
'Serial0/0/0' (10.1.1.1).
Dec 17 20:12:18.574: NTP Core(DEBUG): ntp_receive: message received
Dec 17 20:12:18.574: NTP Core(DEBUG): ntp_receive: peer is 0x645A3120,
next action is 1.
Dec 17 20:12:18.574: NTP Core(DEBUG): receive: packet given to
process_packet
Dec 17 20:12:18.578: NTP Core(INFO): system event
'event_peer/strat_chg' (0x04)
status 'sync_alarm, sync_ntp, 5 events, event_clock_reset' (0xC655)
Dec 17 20:12:18.578: NTP Core(INFO): synchronized to 10.1.1.2, stratum
3
Dec 17 20:12:18.578: NTP Core(INFO): system event 'event_sync_chg'
(0x03) status
 'leap_none, sync_ntp, 6 events, event_peer/strat_chg' (0x664)
Dec 17 20:12:18.578: NTP Core(NOTICE): Clock is synchronized.
Dec 17 20:12:18.578: NTP Core(INFO): system event
'event_peer/strat_chg' (0x04)
status 'leap_none, sync_ntp, 7 events, event_sync_chg' (0x673)
Dec 17 20:12:23.554: NTP: Calendar updated.
```

d. Issue the **undebug all** or the **no debug ntp all** command to turn off debugging:

```
R1# undebug all
```

e. Verify the time on R1 after it has made an association with R2:

```
R1# show clock
*20:12:24.859 UTC Wed Dec 17 2008
```

Step 3: (Optional) Configure R1 and R3 as NTP clients using CCP.

You can also use CCP to configure the router to support NTP. If you configured R1 as an NTP client using Cisco IOS commands in Step 2, you can skip this step. However, read through it to become familiar with the process. If you configured R1 and R3 as NTP clients using Cisco IOS commands in Step 2, you can still perform this step, but you need to issue the following commands first on each router:

```
R1(config)# no ntp server 10.1.1.2
R1(config)# no ntp update-calendar
```

a. From the CLI, enable the http server on R1:

```
R1(config)# ip http server
R1(config)# username admin privilege 15 secret cisco12345
R1(config)# ip http authentication local
```

b. Start CCP on PC-A. In the Mange Devices window, enter the R1 IP address 192.168.1.1 in the first IP address field. Enter admin in the **Username** field, and cisco12345 in the **Password** field. Click the **OK** button.

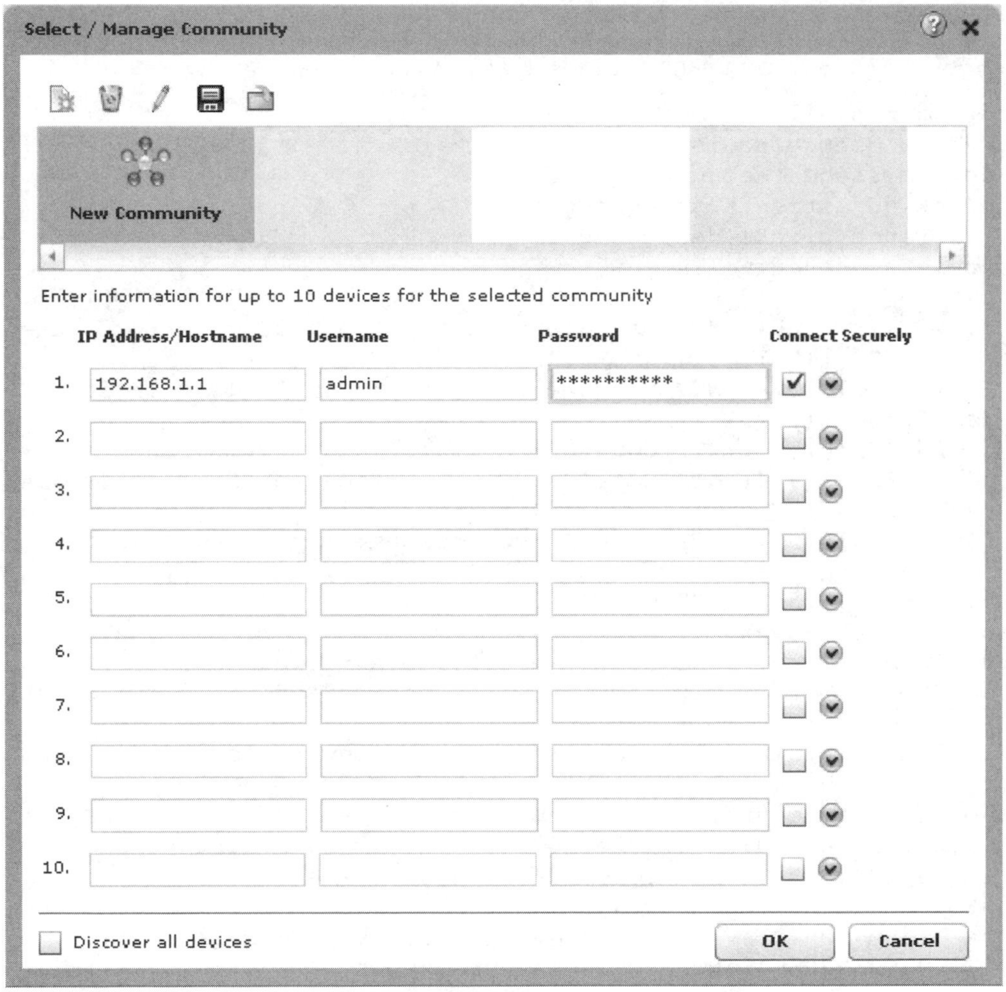

c. At the CCP Dashboard, click the **Discover** button to discover and connect to R1. If discovery fails, use the **Discovery Details** button to determine what the problem is. Resolve it.

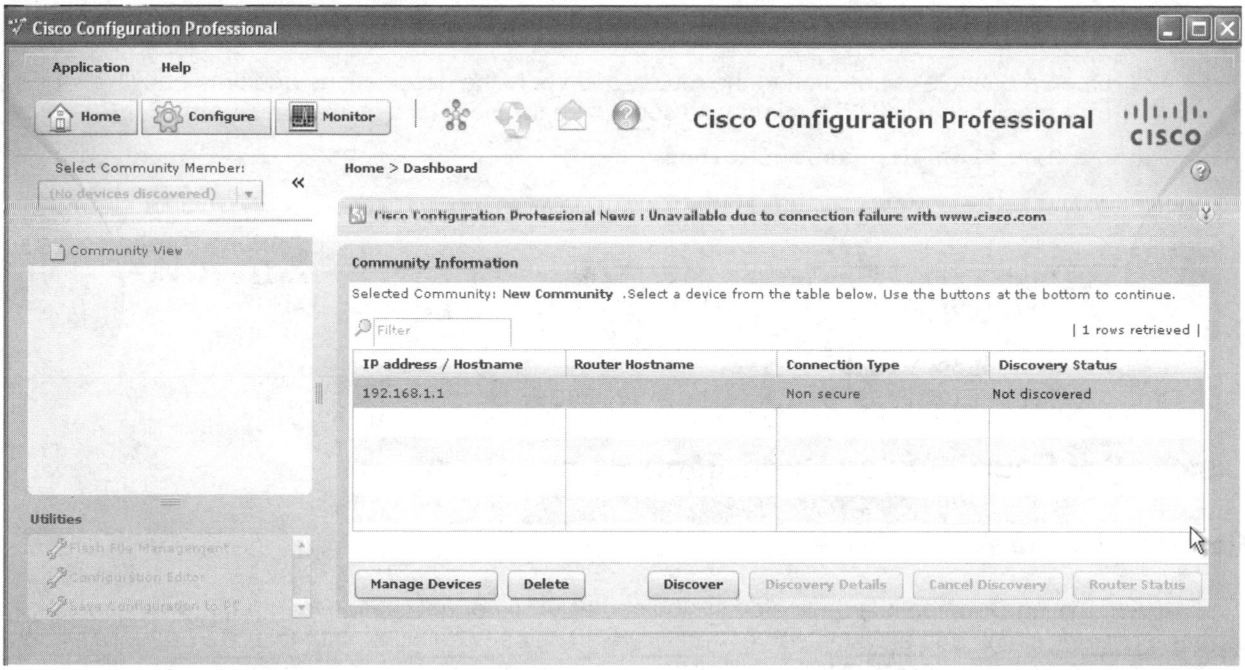

d. To configure an NTP server, click the **Configure** button and choose **Router > Time > NTP and SNTP**. Click **Add**.

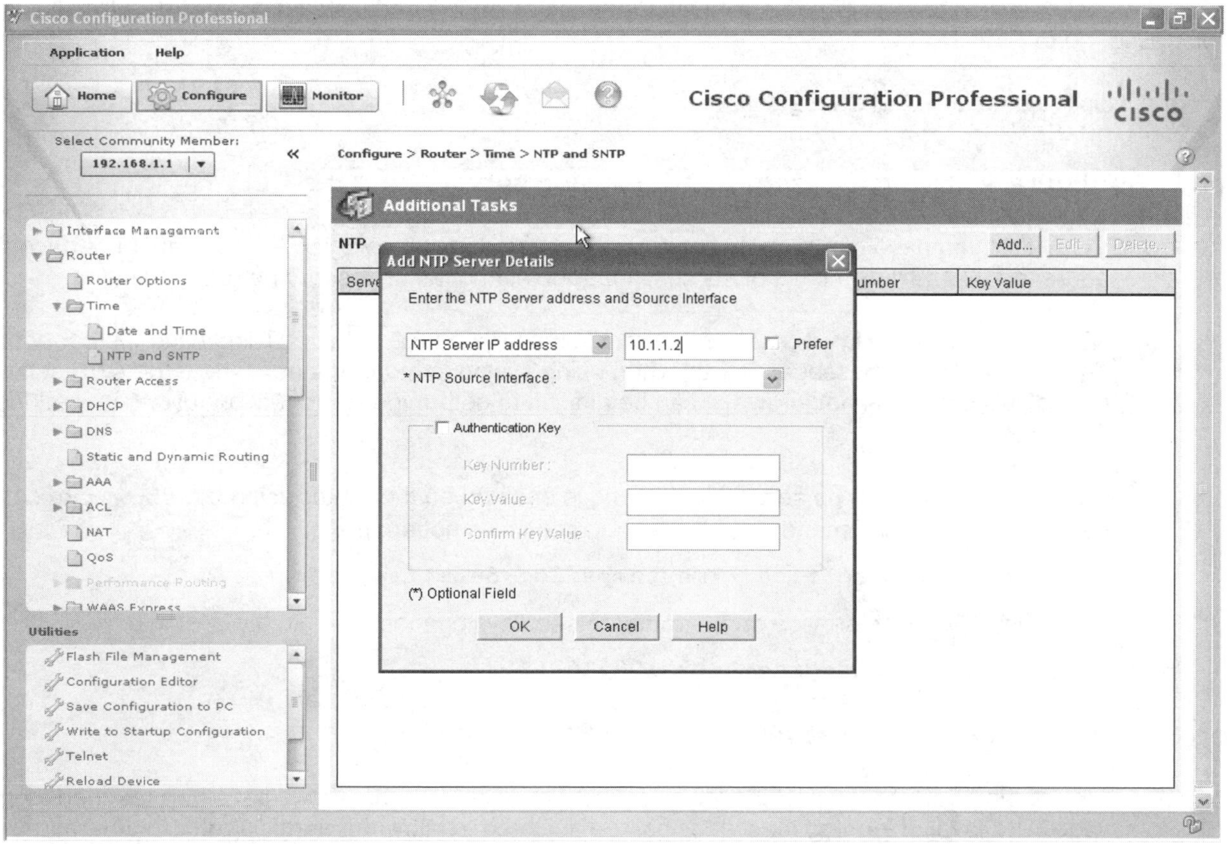

e. In the NTP Server IP Address field, enter the IP address of the R2 master NTP router (10.1.1.2) and click **OK**.

f. In the Deliver Configuration to Router window, make sure that the **Save running config to router's startup config** check box is checked and click **Deliver**.

g. Click **OK** in the Commands Delivery Status window.

h. Open a console connection to the router, and verify the associations and time on R1 after it has made an association with R2. It might take some time for the NTP association to form.

```
R1# show ntp associations

address       ref clock      st   when   poll reach  delay  offset    disp
~10.1.1.2    127.127.1.1     3     14     64     3  0.000  -280073  3939.7
*sys.peer, # selected, +candidate, -outlyer, x falseticker, ~
configured

R1# show clock
*20:12:24.859 UTC Wed Dec 17 2008
```

Task 3: Configure Syslog Support on R1 and PC-A

Step 1: Install the syslog server.

The Kiwi Syslog Daemon is a dedicated syslog server. Another application is Tftpd32, which includes a TFTP server, TFTP client, and a syslog server and viewer. You can use either with this lab. Both are available as a free version and run with Microsoft Windows.

If a syslog server is not currently installed on the host, download the latest version of Kiwi from http://www.kiwisyslog.com or Tftpd32 from http://tftpd32.jounin.net and install it on your desktop. If it is already installed, go to Step 2.

Note: This lab uses the Kiwi syslog server.

Step 2: Configure R1 to log messages to the syslog server using the CLI.

a. Verify that you have connectivity between R1 and the host by pinging the R1 Fa0/1 interface IP address 192.168.1.1. If it is not successful, troubleshoot as necessary before continuing.

b. NTP was configured in Task 2 to synchronize the time on the network. Displaying the correct time and date in syslog messages is vital when using syslog to monitor a network. If the correct time and date of a message is not known, it can be difficult to determine what network event caused the message.

   Verify that the timestamp service for logging is enabled on the router using the **show run** command. Use the following command if the timestamp service is not enabled:

```
R1(config)# service timestamps log datetime msec
```

c. Configure the syslog service on the router to send syslog messages to the syslog server:

```
R1(config)# logging host 192.168.1.3
```

Step 3: Configure the logging severity level on R1.

You can set logging traps to support the logging function. A trap is a threshold that when reached triggers a log message. The level of logging messages can be adjusted to allow the administrator to determine what kinds of messages are sent to the syslog server. Routers support different levels of logging. The eight levels range from 0 (emergencies), indicating that the system is unstable, to 7 (debugging), which sends messages that include router information.

Note: The default level for syslog is 6, informational logging. The default for console and monitor logging is 7, debugging.

a. Use the **logging trap** command to determine the options for the command and the various trap levels available:

```
R1(config)# logging trap ?
<0-7>            Logging severity level
alerts           Immediate action needed              (severity=1)
critical         Critical conditions                  (severity=2)
debugging        Debugging messages                   (severity=7)
emergencies      System is unusable                   (severity=0)
errors           Error conditions                     (severity=3)
informational    Informational messages               (severity=6)
notifications    Normal but significant conditions    (severity=5)
warnings         Warning conditions                   (severity=4)
<cr>
```

b. Define the level of severity for messages sent to the syslog server. To configure the severity levels, use either the keyword or the severity level number (0–7).

Severity Level Keyword Description

Severity Level	Keyword	Meaning
0	emergencies	System unusable
1	alerts	Immediate action required
2	critical	Critical conditions
3	errors	Error conditions
4	warnings	Warning conditions
5	notifications	Normal but significant condition
6	informational	Informational messages
7	debugging	Debugging messages

Note: The severity level includes the level specified and anything with a lower severity number. If you set the level to 4 or use the keyword **warnings**, you capture messages with severity level 4, 3, 2, 1, and 0.

c. Use the **logging trap** command to set the severity level for R1:

```
R1(config)# logging trap warnings
```

d. What is the problem with setting the level of severity too high or too low?

____

____

____

e. If the command **logging trap critical** were issued, which severity levels of messages would be logged? ____

Step 4: Display the current status of logging for R1.

Use the **show logging** command to see the type and level of logging enabled:

```
R1# show logging
Syslog logging: enabled (0 messages dropped, 1 messages rate-limited,
                0 flushes, 0 overruns, xml disabled, filtering disabled)
```

```
No Active Message Discriminator.
No Inactive Message Discriminator.

    Console logging: level debugging, 271 messages logged, xml disabled,
                     filtering disabled
    Monitor logging: level debugging, 0 messages logged, xml disabled,
                     filtering disabled
    Buffer logging:  disabled, xml disabled,
                     filtering disabled
    Logging Exception size (4096 bytes)
    Count and timestamp logging messages: disabled
    Persistent logging: disabled

No active filter modules.

ESM: 0 messages dropped

    Trap logging: level warnings, 0 message lines logged
        Logging to 192.168.1.3  (udp port 514,  audit disabled,
              authentication disabled, encryption disabled, link up),
              0 message lines logged,
              0 message lines rate-limited,
              0 message lines dropped-by-MD,
              xml disabled, sequence number disabled
              filtering disabled
```

At what level is console logging enabled? ______________________

At what level is trap logging enabled? _________________________

What is the IP address of the syslog server? ___________________

What port is syslog using? __________________________________

Step 5: (Optional) Use CCP to configure R1 to log messages to the syslog server.

You can also use CCP to configure the router for syslog support. If you previously configured R1 for syslog and trap levels, you can skip this step. If you used Cisco IOS commands in Step 4 to configure R1 syslog and trap levels, you can still perform this step, but you must issue the following commands first on the router:

```
R1(config)# no logging 192.168.1.3
R1(config)# no logging trap warnings
```

a. Open CCP and discovery R1 by entering the R1 IP address 192.168.1.1 in the Address field. Use admin for the username and cisco12345 for the password.

b. Choose Configure > Router > Logging, and double-click Syslog.

c. In the Logging window, click **Add** and enter the IP address of the syslog server, PC-A (192.168.1.3). Click **OK**.

d. From the Logging Level drop-down menu, choose the logging level of **Warnings (4)**.

e. Uncheck **Logging Buffer**, and then click **OK**.

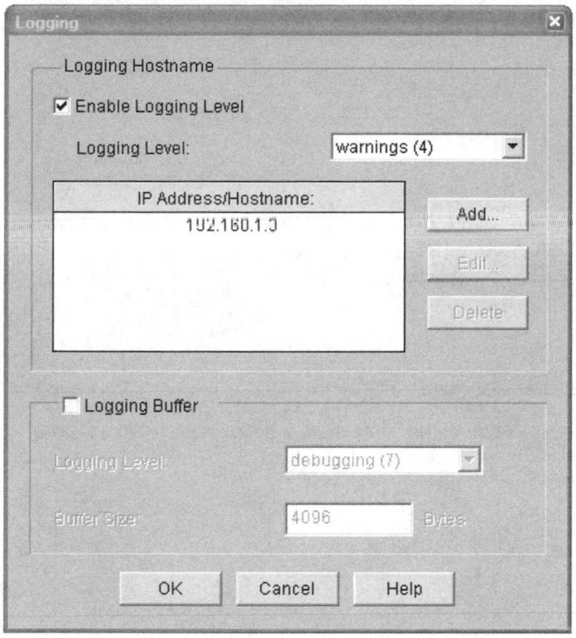

f. Click **Yes** in the CCP Warning dialog box.

g. In the Deliver Configuration to Router window, click **Deliver**. Click **OK** in the Commands Delivery Status window.

h. Click **Save** on the toolbar. Click **Yes** in the CCP Write to Startup Config Warning window.

Step 6: Start the Kiwi Syslog Server.

Open the Kiki Syslog Daemon application on your desktop or click the **Start** button and choose **Programs > Kiwi Enterprises > Kiwi Syslog Daemon**.

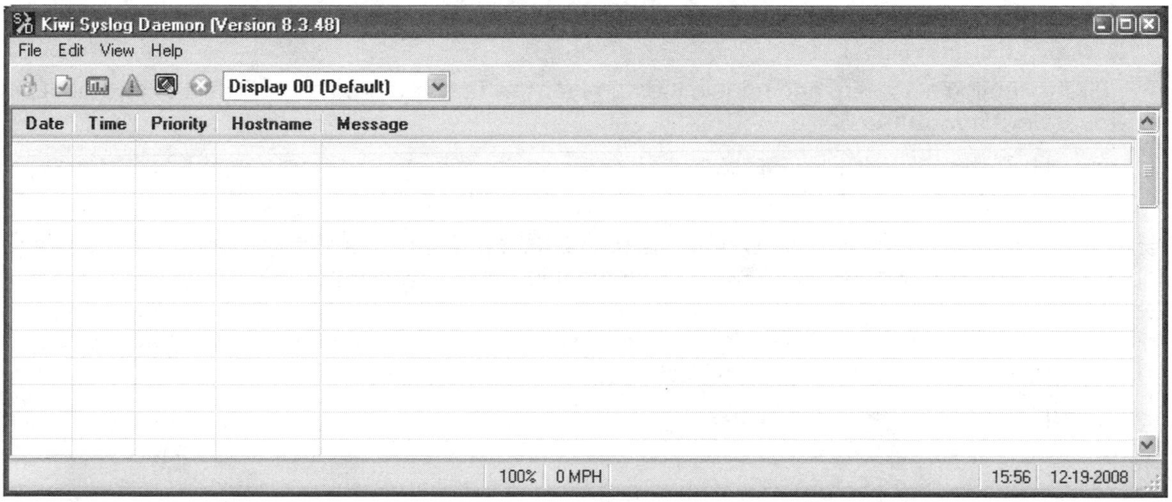

Step 7: Verify that logging to the syslog server is occurring.

On the syslog server host PC-A, observe messages as they are sent from R1 to the syslog server.

a. Send a test log message to the Kiwi Syslog Server by choosing **File > Send test message to local host**.

b. Generate a logging message by shutting down the Serial 0/0/0 interface on R1 or R2 and then reenabling it:

```
R1(config)# interface S0/0/0
R1(config-if)# shutdown
R1(config-if)# no shutdown
```

The Kiwi Syslog Daemon screen should look similar to the one here.

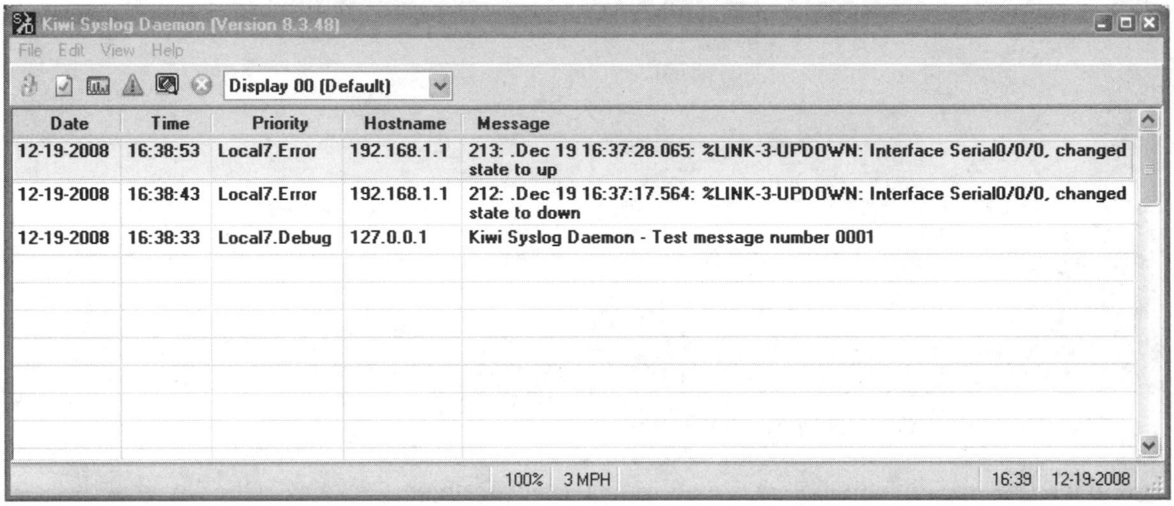

c. What would happen if you shut down the Fa0/1 interface on R1? (Do not actually perform this action.)

____

d. From the R1 global configuration mode, enable the logging of user info when enabling privileged mode and reset the trap level to informational:

```
R1(config)# logging userinfo
R1(config)# logging trap informational
```

e. On the Kiwi Syslog Daemon, choose **View > Clear Display** to clear the log display.

f. Exit to the login screen, and enable the admin1 view that you created in Part 3 of this lab. Enter the password **admin1pass**:

```
R1> enable view admin1
Password:
```

Note: You can enable the desired view from the user EXEC prompt. This allows different users to log in without having to know the privileged EXEC mode enable secret password.

g. Exit to the login screen again, and enable the admin1 view. This time enter the password incorrectly. What message was displayed on the syslog server?

```
R1> enable view admin1
Password:
```

Your screen should look similar to the one here.

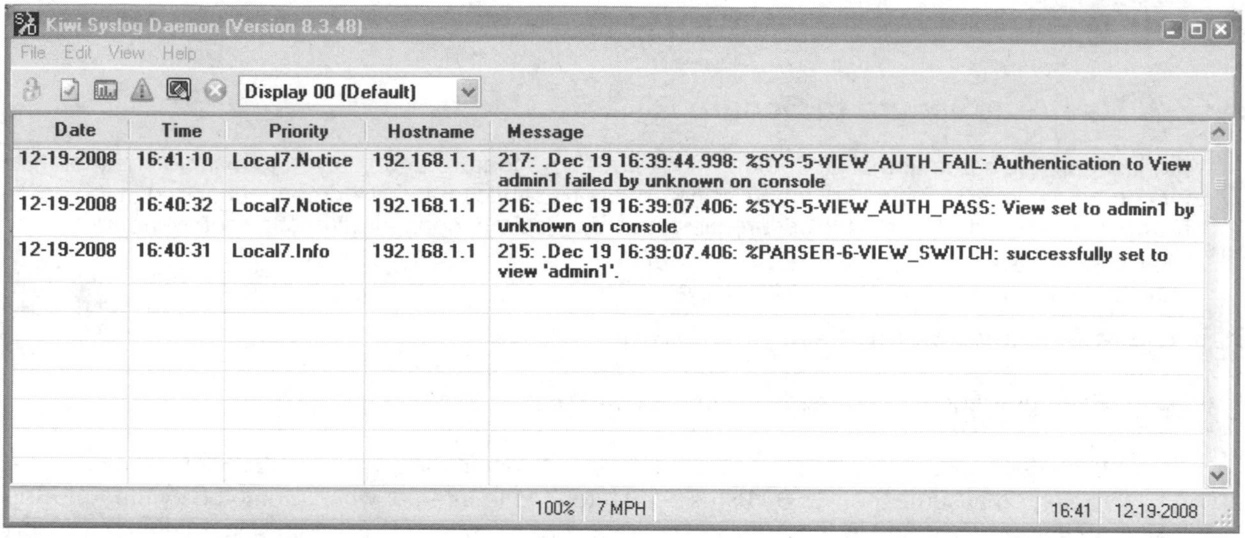

Part 5: Configure Automated Security Features

In Part 5 of this lab, you do the following:

- Restore routers R1 and R3 to their basic configuration.
- Use AutoSecure to secure R3.
- Use the CCP Security Audit tool on router R1 to identify security risks.
- Fix security problems on R1 using the Security Audit tool.
- Review router security configurations with CCP and the CLI.

Task 1: Restore Router R3 to Its Basic Configuration

To avoid confusion as to what was already entered and what AutoSecure provides for the router configuration, start by restoring router R3 to its basic configuration.

Step 1: Erase and reload the router.

a. Connect to the R3 console and log in as admin.

b. Enter privileged EXEC mode.

c. Erase the startup config and then reload the router.

Step 2: Restore the basic configuration.

a. When the router restarts, restore the basic configuration for R3 that was created and saved in Part 1 of this lab.

b. Issue the **`show run`** command to view the current running configuration. Are there any security related commands? ______________________________

c. Test connectivity by pinging from host PC-A on the R1 LAN to PC-C on the R3 LAN. If the pings are not successful, troubleshoot the router and PC configurations until they are.

d. Save the running config to the startup config using the **copy run start** command.

Task 2: Use AutoSecure to Secure R3

With just a single command in CLI mode, the AutoSecure feature enables you to disable common IP services that can be exploited for network attacks and enable IP services and features that can aid in the defense of a network when under attack. AutoSecure simplifies the security configuration of a router and hardens the router configuration.

Step 1: Use the AutoSecure Cisco IOS feature.

a. Enter privileged EXEC mode using the **enable** command.

b. Issue the **auto secure** command on R3 to lock down the router. Router R2 represents an ISP router, so assume that R3 S0/0/1 is connected to the Internet when prompted by the AutoSecure questions. Respond to the AutoSecure questions as shown in the following output. The responses are bolded.

```
R3# auto secure
                --- AutoSecure Configuration ---

*** AutoSecure configuration enhances the security of the router, but
it will not make it absolutely resistant to all security attacks ***

AutoSecure will modify the configuration of your device. All
configuration changes will be shown. For a detailed explanation of how
the configuration changes enhance security and any possible side
effects, please refer to Cisco.com for
Autosecure documentation.
At any prompt you may enter '?' for help.
Use ctrl-c to abort this session at any prompt.

Gathering information about the router for AutoSecure

Is this router connected to internet? [no]:  yes
Enter the number of interfaces facing the internet [1]:  Press ENTER to
accept the default of 1 in square brackets.

Interface          IP-Address   OK?  Method Status
Protocol
FastEthernet0/0    unassigned   YES  NVRAM  administratively down    down
FastEthernet0/1    192.168.3.1  YES  NVRAM  up                       up
Serial0/0/0        unassigned   YES  NVRAM  administratively down    down
Serial0/0/1        10.2.2.1     YES  NVRAM  up                       up

Enter the interface name that is facing the internet: serial0/0/1

Securing Management plane services...

Disabling service finger
Disabling service pad
Disabling udp & tcp small servers
Enabling service password encryption
Enabling service tcp-keepalives-in
Enabling service tcp-keepalives-out
Disabling the cdp protocol
```

```
Disabling the bootp server
Disabling the http server
Disabling the finger service
Disabling source routing
Disabling gratuitous arp

Here is a sample Security Banner to be shown
at every access to device. Modify it to suit your
enterprise requirements.

Authorized Access only
  This system is the property of So-&-So-Enterprise.
  UNAUTHORIZED ACCESS TO THIS DEVICE IS PROHIBITED.
  You must have explicit permission to access this
  device. All activities performed on this device
  are logged. Any violations of access policy will result
  in disciplinary action.

Enter the security banner {Put the banner between
k and k, where k is any character}:

#  Unauthorized Access Prohibited #

Enable secret is either not configured or
 is the same as enable password
Enter the new enable secret: cisco12345
Confirm the enable secret : cisco12345
Enter the new enable password: cisco67890
Confirm the enable password: cisco67890

Configuration of local user database
Enter the username: admin
Enter the password: cisco12345
Confirm the password: cisco12345
Configuring AAA local authentication
Configuring Console, Aux and VTY lines for
local authentication, exec-timeout, and transport
Securing device against Login Attacks
Configure the following parameters

Blocking Period when Login Attack detected: 60

Maximum Login failures with the device: 2

Maximum time period for crossing the failed login attempts: 30

Configure SSH server? [yes]: Press ENTER to accept the default of yes

Enter the domain-name: ccnasecurity.com

Configuring interface specific AutoSecure services
Disabling the following ip services on all interfaces:

 no ip redirects
 no ip proxy-arp
 no ip unreachables
 no ip directed-broadcast
 no ip mask-reply
```

```
Disabling mop on Ethernet interfaces

Securing Forwarding plane services...

Enabling CEF (This might impact the memory requirements for your
platform)
Enabling unicast rpf on all interfaces connected
to internet

Configure CBAC Firewall feature? [yes/no]: no
Tcp intercept feature is used prevent tcp syn attack
on the servers in the network. Create autosec_tcp_intercept_list
to form the list of servers to which the tcp traffic is to
be observed


Enable tcp intercept feature? [yes/no]: yes

This is the configuration generated:

no service finger
no service pad
no service udp-small-servers
no service tcp-small-servers
service password-encryption
service tcp-keepalives-in
service tcp-keepalives-out
no cdp run
no ip bootp server
no ip http server
no ip finger
no ip source-route
no ip gratuitous-arps
no ip identd
banner motd ^C Unauthorized Access Prohibited ^C
security passwords min-length 6
security authentication failure rate 10 log
enable secret 5 $1$FmV1$.xZUegmNYFJwJv/oFwwvG1
enable password 7 045802150C2E181B5F
username admin password 7 01100F175804575D72
aaa new-model
aaa authentication login local_auth local
line con 0
 login authentication local_auth
 exec-timeout 5 0
 transport output telnet
line aux 0
 login authentication local_auth
 exec-timeout 10 0
 transport output telnet
line vty 0 4
 login authentication local_auth
 transport input telnet
line tty 1
 login authentication local_auth
 exec-timeout 15 0
login block-for 60 attempts 2 within 30
ip domain-name ccnasecurity.com
```

```
crypto key generate rsa general-keys modulus 1024
ip ssh time-out 60
ip ssh authentication-retries 2
line vty 0 4
 transport input ssh telnet
service timestamps debug datetime msec localtime show-timezone
service timestamps log datetime msec localtime show-timezone
logging facility local2
logging trap debugging
service sequence-numbers
logging console critical
logging buffered
interface FastEthernet0/0
 no ip redirects
 no ip proxy-arp
 no ip unreachables
 no ip directed-broadcast
 no ip mask-reply
 no mop enabled
interface FastEthernet0/1
 no ip redirects
 no ip proxy-arp
 no ip unreachables
 no ip directed-broadcast
 no ip mask-reply
 no mop enabled
interface Serial0/0/0
 no ip redirects
 no ip proxy-arp
 no ip unreachables
 no ip directed-broadcast
 no ip mask-reply
interface Serial0/0/1
 no ip redirects
 no ip proxy-arp
 no ip unreachables
 no ip directed-broadcast
 no ip mask-reply
interface Vlan1
 no ip redirects
 no ip proxy-arp
 no ip unreachables
 no ip directed-broadcast
 no ip mask-reply
 no mop enabled
ip cef
access-list 100 permit udp any any eq bootpc
interface Serial0/0/1
 ip verify unicast source reachable-via rx allow-default 100
ip tcp intercept list autosec_tcp_intercept_list
ip tcp intercept drop-mode random
ip tcp intercept watch-timeout 15
ip tcp intercept connection-timeout 3600
ip tcp intercept max-incomplete low 450
ip tcp intercept max-incomplete high 550
!
end
```

```
Apply this configuration to running-config? [yes]: <ENTER>

Applying the config generated to running-config
The name for the keys will be: R3.ccnasecurity.com

% The key modulus size is 1024 bits
% Generating 1024 bit RSA keys, keys will be non-exportable...[OK]

R3#
000037: *Dec 19 21:18:52.495 UTC: %AUTOSEC-1-MODIFIED: AutoSecure
configuration
has been Modified on this device
```

Step 2: Establish an SSH connection from PC-C to R3.

a. Start PuTTy or another SSH client, and log in with the **admin** account and password **cisco12345** created when AutoSecure was run. Enter the IP address of the R3 Fa0/1 interface, 192.168.3.1.

b. Because AutoSecure configured SSH on R3, you receive a PuTTY security warning. Click **Yes** to connect anyway.

c. Enter privileged EXEC mode, and verify the R3 configuration using the **`show run`** command.

d. Issue the **`show flash`** command. Is there a file that might be related to AutoSecure, and if so, what is its name and when was it created?

____.

e. Issue the command **`more flash:pre_autosec.cfg`**. What are the contents of this file, and what is its purpose?

____

f. How can you restore this file if AutoSecure does not produce the desired results?

____

____

Step 3: Contrast the AutoSecure-generated configuration of R3 with the manual configuration of R1.

a. What security-related configuration changes were performed on R3 by AutoSecure that were not performed in previous sections of the lab on R1?

____

____

____

____

____

____

b. What security-related configuration changes were performed in previous sections of the lab that were not performed by AutoSecure?

____

____

c. Identify at least five unneeded services that were locked down by AutoSecure and at least three security measures applied to each interface.

Note: Some of the services listed as being disabled in the AutoSecure output above might not appear in the **`show running-config`** output because they are already disabled by default for this router and Cisco IOS version.

Services disabled include the following:

____
____
____
____
____

For each interface, the following were disabled:

____
____
____

Step 4: Test connectivity.

Ping from PC-A on the R1 LAN to PC-C on the router R3 LAN. Were the pings successful? _____

If pings from PC-A to PC-C are not successful, troubleshoot before continuing.

Task 3: Restore R1 to Its Basic Configuration

To avoid confusion as to what was previously configured and what CCP Security Audit tool provides for the router configuration, start by restoring router R1 to its basic configuration.

Step 1: Erase and reload the router.

a. Connect to the R1 console and log in as admin.

b. Enter privileged EXEC mode.

c. Erase the startup config and then reload the router.

Step 2: Restore the basic config.

a. When the router restarts, cut and paste the basic startup config for R1 that was created and saved in Part 1 of this lab.

b. Test connectivity by pinging from host PC-A to R1. If the pings are not successful, troubleshoot the router and PC configurations to verify connectivity before continuing.

c. Save the running config to the startup config using the **`copy run start`** command.

Task 4: Use the CCP Security Audit Tool on R1 to Identify Security Risks

In this task, you use the CCP graphical user interface to analyze security vulnerabilities on router R1. CCP is faster than typing each command and provides greater control than the AutoSecure feature.

Step 1: Verify that CCP is installed on Host PC.

Note: CCP can only be run from a host PC. If CCP is not installed on the PC, consult your instructor for directions.

Step 2: Create a CCP user and enable the HTTP secure server on R1.

a. Create a privilege-level 15 username and password on R1:

```
R1(config)# username admin privilege 15 secret 0 cisco12345
```

b. Enable the HTTP secure server on R1:

```
R1(config)# ip http secure-server
% Generating 1024 bit RSA keys, keys will be non-exportable...[OK]
R1(config)#
*Dec 19 17:01:07.763: %SSH-5-ENABLED: SSH 1.99 has been enabled
*Dec 19 17:01:08.731: %PKI-4-NOAUTOSAVE: Configuration was modified.
Issue
"write memory" to save new certificate
```

c. Enable local HTTP authentication on R1:

```
R1(config)# ip http authentication local
R1(config)# end
```

d. Save the running config to the startup config:

```
R1# copy run start
```

Step 3: Start CCP.

a. From PC-A, run the CCP application.

Note: Make sure that all pop-up blockers are turned off in the browser, and make sure that Java is installed and updated.

b. In the Manage Devices window, enter the R1 IP address 192.168.1.1 in the first IP address field. Enter **admin** in the username field, and enter **cisco12345** in the password field. Click the **Connect Securely** check box to use secure server for your connection. Check the **Discover All Devices** check box, and then click the **OK** button.

c. When the Security Certification Alert is displayed, click **Yes**.

d. If the Discovery fails, use the **Discovery Details** button to determine the problem and resolve it.

Step 4: Back up the current router configuration using CCP.

a. Back up the router configuration from within CCP by choosing **Utilities > Save Configuration to PC**.

b. Save the configuration on the desktop using the default name of RunningConfig_192.168.1.1.txt.

Step 5: Begin the security audit.

a. Choose **Configure > Security > Security Audit**.

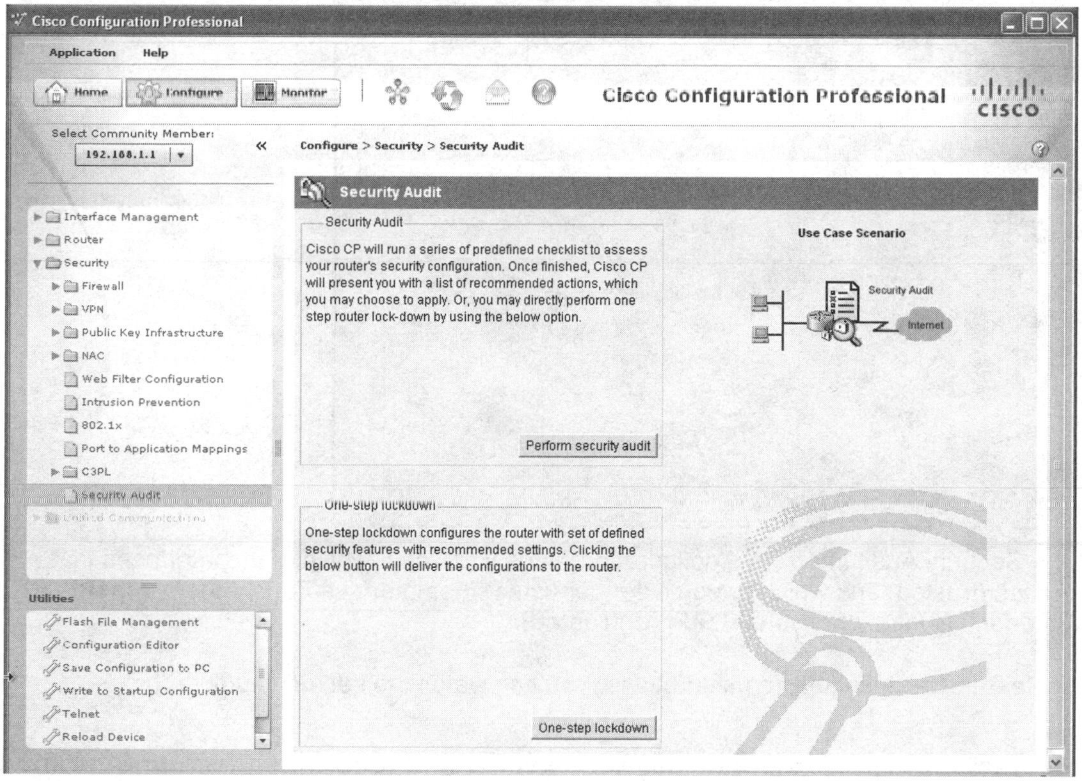

b. Click the **Perform security audit** button to start the Security Audit Wizard, which analyzes potential vulnerabilities. This helps you become familiar with the types of vulnerabilities that **Security Audit** can identify. You are given an opportunity to fix all or selected security problems after the audit finishes.

Note: The Security Audit tool also provides a **One-step lockdown** option that performs a function similar to AutoSecure but does not prompt the user for input.

c. After you have familiarized yourself with the wizard instructions, click **Next**.

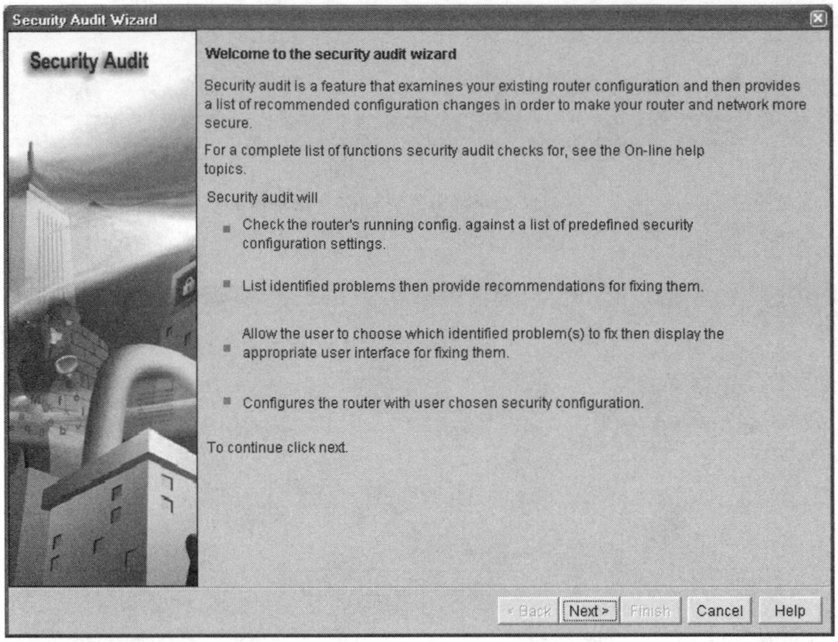

d. On the Security Audit Interface Configuration window, indicate which of the interfaces that are shown are inside (trusted) and which are outside (untrusted). For interface Fa0/1, choose **Inside (trusted)**. For interface S0/0/0, choose **Outside (untrusted)**.

e. Click **Next** to check security configurations. You can watch the security audit progress.

Step 6: Review the Security Audit unneeded services list and recommended configurations.

a. Scroll through the Security Audit results screen. What are some of the major vulnerabilities listed as Not Passed?

____

____

____

b. After reviewing the Security Audit report, click **Save Report**. Save the report to the desktop using the default name CPSecurityAuditReportCard.html.

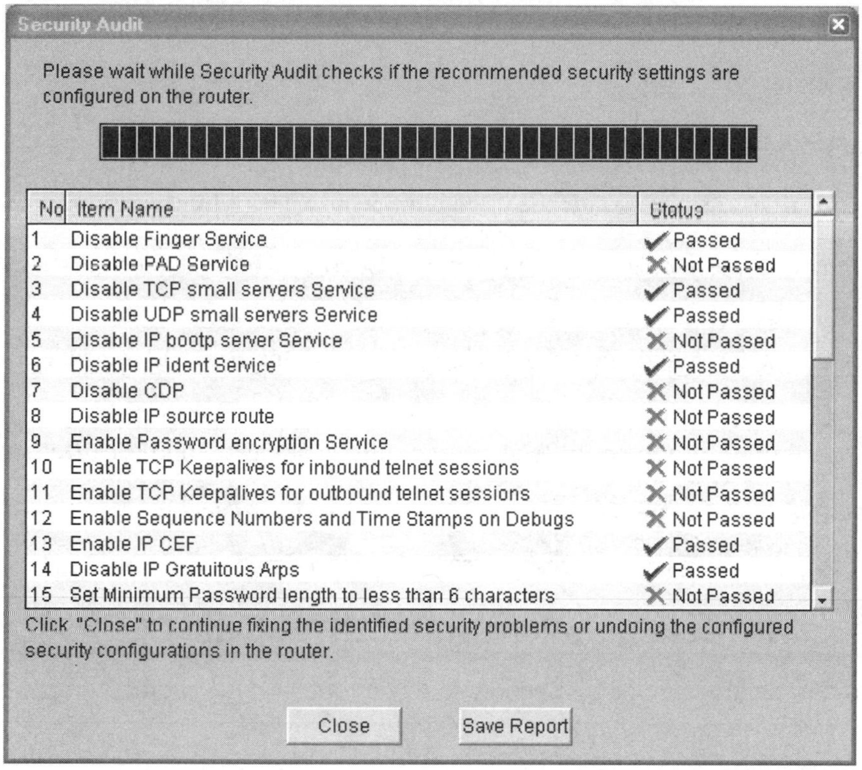

c. Open the report card HTML document you saved on the desktop to view the contents, and then close it.

Task 5: Fix Security Problems on R1 Using the Security Audit Tool

In this task, you use the Security Audit Wizard to make the necessary changes to the router configuration.

Step 1: Review the Security Problems Identified window for potential items to fix.

a. In the Security Audit window, click **Close**.

b. A window appears listing the items that did not pass the security audit. Click **Next** without choosing any items. What message did you get? ______________________________

c. Click **OK** to remove the message.

Step 2: Fix security problems.

With the Security Audit tool, you can fix selected problems or all security problems identified.

a. Click **Fix All** and then click **Next** to fix all security problems.

b. When prompted, enter an enable secret password of **cisco12345** and confirm it.

c. Enter the text for the login banner: Unauthorized Access Prohibited. Click **Next**.

d. Add the logging host IP address **192.168.1.3** and accept the logging defaults. Click **Next**.

Note: The Advanced Firewall Configuration Wizard window appears. Click **Next**.

e. Accept the default security settings for inside and outside interfaces and click **Next**.

Note: Click **OK** to accept the warning.

f. For the security level, select **Low Security** and click **Next**.

g. At the Firewall Configuration Summary, review the configuration and click **Finish**.

h. Scroll through the Summary screen. This screen shows what Security Audit will configure for the router.

i. Click **Finish** to see the actual commands that are delivered to the router. Scroll to review the commands.

j. Make sure that **Save running config to router's startup config** is selected, and click **Deliver**.

k. Click **OK** in the Commands Delivery Status window to exit the Security Audit tool. How many commands were delivered to the router? ______________________

Task 6: Review Router Security Configurations with CCP and the CLI

In this task, you use CCP to review changes made by Security Audit on router R1 and compare them to those made by AutoSecure on R3.

Step 1: View the running configs for R1 and R3.

a. From the PC-A CCP session with R1, in the utilities area at the bottom-left corner, click **View > Running Configuration**.

b. Using PuTTY, open an SSH connection to router R3 and log in as admin.

c. Enter privileged EXEC mode and issue the `show run` command.

Step 2: Contrast AutoSecure with CCP Security Audit.

a. Compare the function and ease of use between AutoSecure and CCP Security Audit. What are some similarities and differences?

____
____
____
____
____
____
____

b. Refer to the AutoSecure configuration on R3 and the CCP Security Audit configuration on R1. What are some similarities and differences between the configurations that are generated by AutoSecure and Security Audit?

____
____
____

Step 3: Test connectivity.

a. Ping from router R1 to the router R3 S0/0/1 interface (10.2.2.1). Were the pings successful? Why or why not? ______________________________

Note: Firewalls are covered in detail in Chapter 4.

b. Ping from PC-A on the R1 LAN to PC-C on the router R3 LAN. Were the pings successful? Why or why not? ______________________________

c. Ping from router R3 to the router R2 S0/0/0 interface (10.1.1.2). Were the pings successful? Why or why not? ______________________________

d. Ping from router R3 to the router R1 S0/0/0 interface (10.1.1.1). Were the pings successful? Why or why not? ______________________________

e. Ping from PC-C on the R3 LAN to PC-A on the router R1 LAN. Were the pings successful? Why or why not? ______________________________

Reflection

1. How important is securing router access and monitoring network devices to ensure responsibility and accountability and for thwarting potentially malicious activity?

____
____
____

2. What advantages does SSH have over Telnet?

____

3. What advantages does Telnet have over SSH?

____

4. How scalable is setting up usernames and using the local database for authentication?

____
____

5. Why it is better to have centralized logging servers rather than only have the routers log locally?

____
____

6. What are some advantages to using automated security mechanisms like AutoSecure and CCP Security Audit?

____
____
____

Router Interface Summary Table

Router Model	Ethernet Interface 1	Ethernet Interface 2	Serial Interface 1	Serial Interface 2
1800	Fast Ethernet 0/0 (Fa0/0)	Fast Ethernet 0/1 (Fa0/1)	Serial 0/0/0 (S0/0/0)	Serial 0/0/1 (S0/0/1)
1900	Gigabit Ethernet 0/0 (G0/0)	Gigabit Ethernet 0/1 (G0/1)	Serial 0/0/0 (S0/0/0)	Serial 0/0/1 (S0/0/1)
2800	Fast Ethernet 0/0 (Fa0/0)	Fast Ethernet 0/1 (Fa0/1)	Serial 0/0/0 (S0/0/0)	Serial 0/0/1 (S0/0/1)
2900	Gigabit Ethernet 0/0 (G0/0)	Gigabit Ethernet 0/1 (G0/1)	Serial 0/0/0 (S0/0/0)	Serial 0/0/1 (S0/0/1)

Note: To find out how the router is configured, look at the interfaces to identify the type of router and how many interfaces the router has. There is no way to effectively list all the combinations of configurations for each router class. This table includes identifiers for the possible combinations of Ethernet and serial interfaces in the device. The table does not include any other type of interface, even though a specific router may contain one. An example of this might be an ISDN BRI interface. The string in parentheses is the legal abbreviation that can be used in Cisco IOS commands to represent the interface.

Chapter 3 Lab A: Securing Administrative Access Using AAA and RADIUS

Topology

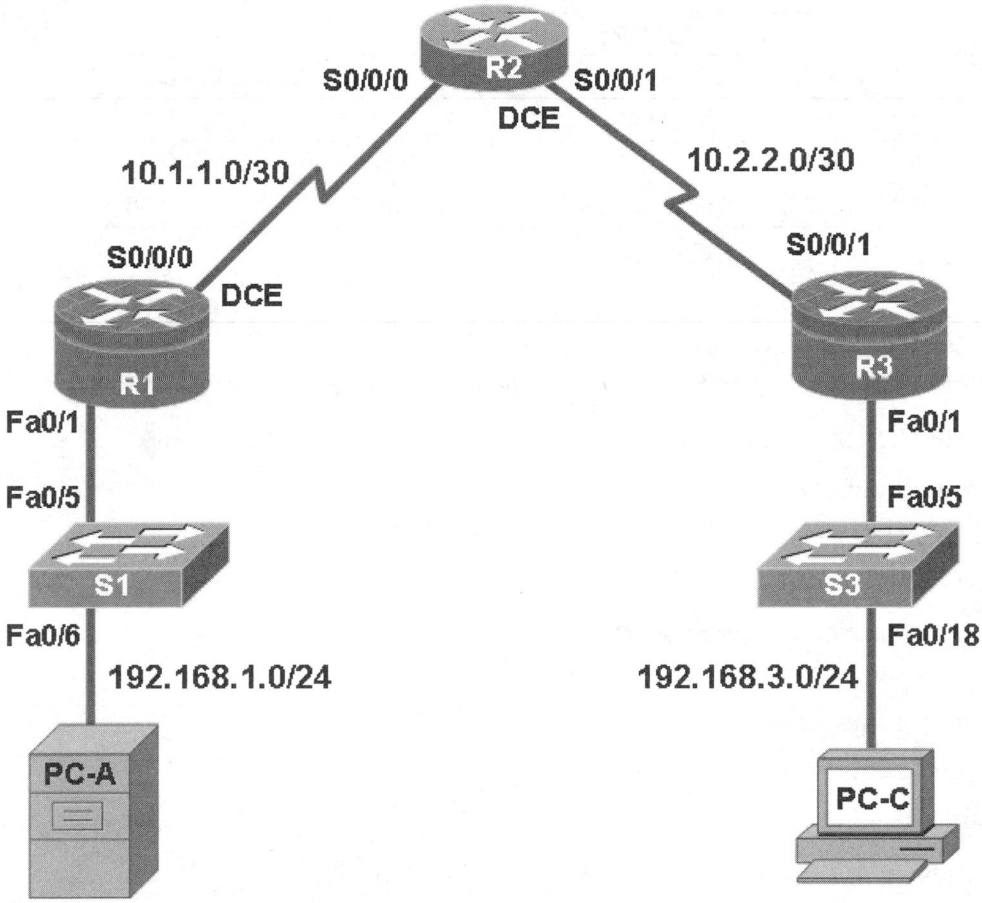

Note: ISR G2 devices have Gigabit Ethernet interfaces rather than Fast Ethernet interfaces.

IP Addressing Table

Device	Interface	IP Address	Subnet Mask	Default Gateway	Switch Port
R1	Fa0/1	192.168.1.1	255.255.255.0	N/A	S1 Fa0/5
	S0/0/0 (DCE)	10.1.1.1	255.255.255.252	N/A	N/A
R2	S0/0/0	10.1.1.2	255.255.255.252	N/A	N/A
	S0/0/1 (DCE)	10.2.2.2	255.255.255.252	N/A	N/A
R3	Fa0/1	192.168.3.1	255.255.255.0	N/A	S3 Fa0/5
	S0/0/1	10.2.2.1	255.255.255.252	N/A	N/A
PC-A	NIC	192.168.1.3	255.255.255.0	192.168.1.1	S1 Fa0/6
PC-C	NIC	192.168.3.3	255.255.255.0	192.168.3.1	S3 Fa0/18

Objectives

Part 1: Basic Network Device Configuration

- Configure basic settings such as hostname, interface IP addresses, and access passwords.
- Configure static routing.

Part 2: Configure Local Authentication

- Configure a local database user and local access for the console, vty, and aux lines.
- Test the configuration.

Part 3: Configure Local Authentication Using AAA

- Configure the local user database using Cisco IOS.
- Configure AAA local authentication using Cisco IOS.
- Configure AAA local authentication using CCP.
- Test the configuration.

Part 4: Configure Centralized Authentication Using AAA and RADIUS

- Install a RADIUS server on a computer.
- Configure users on the RADIUS server.
- Use Cisco IOS to configure AAA services on a router to access the RADIUS server for authentication.
- Use CCP to configure AAA services on a router to access the RADIUS server for authentication.
- Test the AAA RADIUS configuration.

Background

The most basic form of router access security is to create passwords for the console, vty, and aux lines. A user is prompted for only a password when accessing the router. Configuring a privileged EXEC mode enable secret password further improves security, but still only a basic password is required for each mode of access.

In addition to basic passwords, you can define specific usernames or accounts with varying privilege levels in the local router database that can apply to the router as a whole. When the console, vty, or aux lines are configured to refer to this local database, the user is prompted for a username and a password when using any of these lines to access the router.

Additional control over the login process can be achieved using authentication, authorization, and accounting (AAA). For basic authentication, AAA can be configured to access the local database for user logins, and fallback procedures can also be defined. However, this approach is not very scalable because it must be configured on every router. To take full advantage of AAA and achieve maximum scalability, AAA is used in conjunction with an external TACACS+ or RADIUS server database. When a user attempts to log in, the router references the external server database to verify that the user is logging in with a valid username and password.

In this lab, you build a multirouter network and configure the routers and hosts. You then use command-line interface (CLI) commands and Cisco Configuration Professional (CCP) tools to configure routers with basic local authentication by means of AAA. You install RADIUS software on an external computer and use AAA to authenticate users with the RADIUS server.

Note: The router commands and output in this lab are from a Cisco 1841 with Cisco IOS Software Release 12.4(20)T (advanced IP image). Other routers and Cisco IOS versions can be used. See the Router Interface Summary table at the end of the lab to determine which interface identifiers to use based on the equipment in the lab. Depending on the router model and Cisco IOS version, the commands available and output produced might vary from what this lab shows.

Note: Make sure that the routers and switches have been erased and have no startup configurations.

Required Resources

- 3 routers (Cisco 1841 with Cisco IOS Software Release 12.4(20)T1 or comparable)
- 2 switches (Cisco 2960 or comparable)
- PC-A: Windows XP, Vista, or Windows 7 with CCP 2.5 and RADIUS server software available
- PC-C: Windows XP, Vista, or Windows 7 with CCP 2.5
- Serial and Ethernet cables as shown in the topology
- Rollover cables to configure the routers via the console

CCP Notes

- See Chapter 00 Lab A for instructions on how to install and run CCP. Hardware/software recommendations for CCP include Windows XP, Vista, or Windows 7 with Java Version 1.6.0_11 up to 1.6.0_21, Internet Explorer 6.0 or later and Flash Player Version 10.0.12.36 or later.
- If the PC on which CCP is installed is running Windows Vista or Windows 7, you might need to right-click the CCP icon or menu item and choose **Run as administrator**.
- To run CCP, you might need to temporarily disable antivirus programs and OS firewalls. Make sure to turn off all pop-up blockers in the browser.

Part 1: Basic Network Device Configuration

In Part 1 of this lab, you set up the network topology and configure basic settings, such as the interface IP addresses, static routing, device access, and passwords.

Perform all steps on routers R1 and R3. Only steps 1, 2, 3 and 6 need to be performed on R2. The procedure for R1 is shown here as an example.

Step 1: Cable the network as shown in the topology.

Attach the devices shown in the topology diagram, and cable as necessary.

Step 2: Configure basic settings for each router.

a. Configure hostnames as shown in the topology.

b. Configure the interface IP addresses as shown in the IP addressing table.

c. Configure a clock rate for the routers with a DCE serial cable attached to their serial interface:

```
R1(config)# interface S0/0/0
R1(config-if)# clock rate 64000
```

d. To prevent the router from attempting to translate incorrectly entered commands as though they were hostnames, disable DNS lookup:

```
R1(config)# no ip domain-lookup
```

Step 3: Configure static routing on the routers.

a. Configure a static default route from R1 to R2 and from R3 to R2.

b. Configure a static route from R2 to the R1 LAN and from R2 to the R3 LAN.

Step 4: Configure PC host IP settings.

Configure a static IP address, subnet mask, and default gateway for PC-A and PC-C, as shown in the IP addressing table.

Step 5: Verify connectivity between PC-A and R3.

a. Ping from R1 to R3.

   Were the ping results successful? _____

   If the pings are not successful, troubleshoot the basic device configurations before continuing.

b. Ping from PC-A on the R1 LAN to PC-C on the R3 LAN.

   Were the ping results successful? _____

   If the pings are not successful, troubleshoot the basic device configurations before continuing.

Note: If you can ping from PC-A to PC-C, you have demonstrated that static routing is configured and functioning correctly. If you cannot ping but the device interfaces are up and IP addresses are correct, use the **`show run`** and **`show ip route`** commands to help identify routing protocol-related problems.

Step 6: Save the basic running configuration for each router.

Use the **Transfer > Capture text** option in HyperTerminal or some other method to capture the running configs for each router. Save the three files so that you can use them to restore configs later in the lab.

Step 7: Configure and encrypt passwords on R1 and R3.

Note: Passwords in this task are set to a minimum of 10 characters but are relatively simple for the benefit of performing the lab. More complex passwords are recommended in a production network.

For this step, configure the same settings for R1 and R3. Router R1 is shown here as an example.

a. Configure a minimum password length.

   Use the **security passwords** command to set a minimum password length of 10 characters:

```
R1(config)# security passwords min-length 10
```

b. Configure the enable secret password on both routers:

```
R1(config)# enable secret cisco12345
```

c. Configure the basic console, auxiliary port, and vty lines.

d. Configure a console password and enable login for router R1. For additional security, the **exec-timeout** command causes the line to log out after 5 minutes of inactivity. The **logging synchronous** command prevents console messages from interrupting command entry.

Note: To avoid repetitive logins during this lab, you can set the **exec-timeout** command to 0 0, which prevents it from expiring. However, this is not considered a good security practice.

```
R1(config)# line console 0
R1(config-line)# password ciscoconpass
R1(config-line)# exec-timeout 5 0
R1(config-line)# login
R1(config-line)# logging synchronous
```

e. Configure a password for the aux port for router R1:

```
R1(config)# line aux 0
R1(config-line)# password ciscoauxpass
R1(config-line)# exec-timeout 5 0
R1(config-line)# login
```

f. Configure the password on the vty lines for router R1:

```
R1(config)# line vty 0 4
R1(config-line)# password ciscovtypass
R1(config-line)# exec-timeout 5 0
R1(config-line)# login
```

g. Encrypt the console, aux, and vty passwords:

```
R1(config)# service password-encryption
```

h. Issue the **show run** command. Can you read the console, aux, and vty passwords? Why or why not? ____

Step 8: Configure a login warning banner on routers R1 and R3.

a. Configure a warning to unauthorized users using a message-of-the-day (MOTD) banner with the **banner motd** command. When a user connects to the router, the MOTD banner appears before the login prompt. In this example, the dollar sign ($) is used to start and end the message:

```
R1(config)# banner motd $Unauthorized access strictly prohibited and
prosecuted to the full extent of the law$
R1(config)# exit
```

b. Issue the **show run** command. What does the $ convert to in the output?

____

c. Exit privileged EXEC mode by using the **disable** or **exit** command and press **Enter** to get started. Does the MOTD banner look like what you expected? ______

Note: If it does not, just re-create it using the **banner motd** command.

Step 9: Save the basic configurations.

Save the running configuration to the startup configuration from the privileged EXEC prompt:

```
R1# copy running-config startup-config
```

Part 2: Configure Local Authentication

In Part 2 of this lab, you configure a local username and password and change the access for the console, aux, and vty lines to reference the router's local database for valid usernames and passwords. Perform all steps on R1 and R3. The procedure for R1 is shown here.

Step 1: Configure the local user database.

a. Create a local user account with MD5 hashing to encrypt the password:

```
R1(config)# username user01 secret user01pass
```

b. Exit global configuration mode and display the running configuration. Can you read the user's password? ____

Step 2: Configure local authentication for the console line and login.

a. Set the console line to use the locally defined login usernames and passwords:

```
R1(config)# line console 0
R1(config-line)# login local
```

b. Exit to the initial router screen that displays:

```
R1 con0 is now available. Press RETURN to get started.
```

c. Log in using the user01 account and password previously defined.

d. What is the difference between logging in at the console now and previously?

____

e. After logging in, issue the **show run** command. Were you able to issue the command? Why or why not?

____

f. Enter privileged EXEC mode using the **enable** command. Were you prompted for a password? Why or why not?

____

Step 3: Test the new account by logging in from a Telnet session.

a. From PC-A, establish a Telnet session with R1:

```
PC-A> telnet 192.168.1.1
```

b. Were you prompted for a user account? Why or why not?

____

c. What password did you use to log in? _______________________________

d. Set the vty lines to use the locally defined login accounts:

```
R1(config)# line vty 0 4
R1(config-line)# login local
```

e. From PC-A, telnet R1 to R1 again:

```
PC-A> telnet 192.168.1.1
```

f. Were you prompted for a user account? Why or why not? ___________________

g. Log in as **user01** with a password of **user01pass**.

h. While connected to R1 via Telnet, access privileged EXEC mode with the **enable** command.

i. What password did you use? _______________________________

j. For added security, set the aux port to use the locally defined login accounts:

```
R1(config)# line aux 0
R1(config-line)# login local
```

k. End the Telnet session with the **exit** command.

Step 4: Save the configuration on R1.

a. Save the running configuration to the startup configuration from the privileged EXEC prompt:

```
R1# copy running-config startup-config
```

b. Use HyperTerminal or another means to save the R1 running configuration from Parts 1 and 2 of this lab and edit it so that you can use it to restore the R1 configuration later in the lab.

Note: Remove all occurrences of "- - More - -." Remove any commands that are not related to the items you configured in Parts 1 and 2 of the lab, such as the Cisco IOS version number, no service pad, and so on. Many commands are entered automatically by the Cisco IOS software. Also replace the encrypted passwords with the correct ones specified previously.

Step 5: Perform steps 1 through 4 on R3 and save the configuration.

a. Save the running configuration to the startup configuration from the privileged EXEC prompt:

```
R3# copy running-config startup-config
```

b. Use HyperTerminal or another means to save the R3 running configuration from Parts 1 and 2 of this lab and edit it so that you can use it to restore the R3 configuration later in the lab.

Part 3: Configure Local Authentication Using AAA on R3

Task 1: Configure the Local User Database Using Cisco IOS

Note: To configure AAA using CCP, skip to Task 3.

Step 1: Configure the local user database.

a. Create a local user account with MD5 hashing to encrypt the password:

```
R3(config)# username Admin01 privilege 15 secret Admin01pass
```

b. Exit global configuration mode and display the running configuration. Can you read the user's password? ______________________________

Task 2: Configure AAA Local Authentication Using Cisco IOS

Step 1: Enable AAA services.

a. On R3, enable services with the global configuration command **`aaa new-model`**. Because you are implementing local authentication, use local authentication as the first method, and no authentication as the secondary method.

   If you were using an authentication method with a remote server, such as TACACS+ or RADIUS, you would configure a secondary authentication method for fallback if the server is unreachable. Normally, the secondary method is the local database. In this case, if no usernames are configured in the local database, the router allows all users login access to the device.

b. Enable AAA services:

```
R3(config)# aaa new-model
```

Step 2: Implement AAA services for console access using the local database.

a. Create the default login authentication list by issuing the `aaa authentication login default method1[`*`method2`*`][`*`method3`*`]` command with a method list using the **`local`** and **`none`** keywords:

```
R3(config)# aaa authentication login default local none
```

Note: If you do not set up a default login authentication list, you could get locked out of the router and be forced to use the password recovery procedure for your specific router.

b. Exit to the initial router screen that displays: `R3 con0 is now available, Press RETURN to get started.`

c. Log in to the console as **Admin01** with a password of **Admin01pass**. Remember that passwords are case sensitive. Were you able to log in? Why or why not?

   ____

Note: If your session with the console port of the router times out, you might have to log in using the default authentication list.

d. Exit to the initial router screen that displays: R3 con0 is now available, Press RETURN to get started.

e. Attempt to log in to the console as **baduser** with any password. Were you able to log in? Why or why not? ____

f. If no user accounts are configured in the local database, which users are permitted to access the device? ____

Step 3: Create a AAA authentication profile for Telnet using the local database.

a. Create a unique authentication list for Telnet access to the router. This does not have the fallback of no authentication, so if no usernames are in the local database, Telnet access is disabled. To create an authentication profile that is not the default, specify a list name of TELNET_LINES and apply it to the vty lines:

```
R3(config)# aaa authentication login TELNET_LINES local
R3(config)# line vty 0 4
R3(config-line)# login authentication TELNET_LINES
```

b. Verify that this authentication profile is used by opening a Telnet session from PC-C to R3:

```
PC-C> telnet 192.168.3.1
Trying 192.168.3.1 ... Open
```

c. Log in as **Admin01** with a password of **Admin01pass**. Were you able to log in? Why or why not?

____

d. Exit the Telnet session with the **`exit`** command, and telnet to R3 again.

e. Attempt to log in as **baduser** with any password. Were you able to log in? Why or why not?

____

____

Task 3: (Optional) Configure AAA Local Authentication Using Cisco CCP

You can also use CCP to configure the router to support AAA.

Note: If you configured R3 AAA authentication using Cisco IOS commands in Tasks 1 and 2, you can skip this task. If you performed Tasks 1 and 2 and you want to perform this task, you should restore R3 to its basic configuration. See Part 4, Step 1 for the procedure to restore R3 to its basic configuration.

Even if you do not perform this task, read through the steps to become familiar with the CCP process.

Step 1: Implement AAA services and HTTP router access before starting CCP.

a. From the CLI global config mode, enable a new AAA model:

```
R3(config)# aaa new-model
```

b. Enable the HTTP server on R3 for CCP access:

```
R3(config)# ip http server
```

Note: For maximum security, enable the secure HTTP server by using the ip http secure-server command.

c. Add a user named admin to the local database:

```
R3(config)# username admin privilege 15 secret cisco12345
```

d. Have CCP use the local database to authenticate web sessions:

```
R3(config)# ip http authentication local
```

Step 2: Access CCP and discover R3.

a. Start CCP on PC-C. In the Manage Devices window, enter R3 IP address 192.168.3.1 in the first IP Address field. Enter **admin** in the Username field, and **cisco12345** in the Password field.

b. At the CCP Dashboard, click the **Discover** button to discover and connect to R3. If discovery fails, click the **Discovery Details** button to determine the problem.

Step 3: Use CCP to create an administrative user.

a. Click the **Configure** button at the top of the screen.

b. Choose **Router > Router Access > User Accounts/View**.

c. In the User Accounts/View window, click **Add**.

d. In the Add an Account window, enter **Admin01** in the Username field.

e. Enter the password **Admin01pass** in the New Password and Confirm New Password fields. (Remember, passwords are case sensitive.)

f. Confirm that the **Encrypt password using MD5 hash algorithm** check box is checked.

g. Select **15** from the Privilege Level drop-down list and click **OK**.

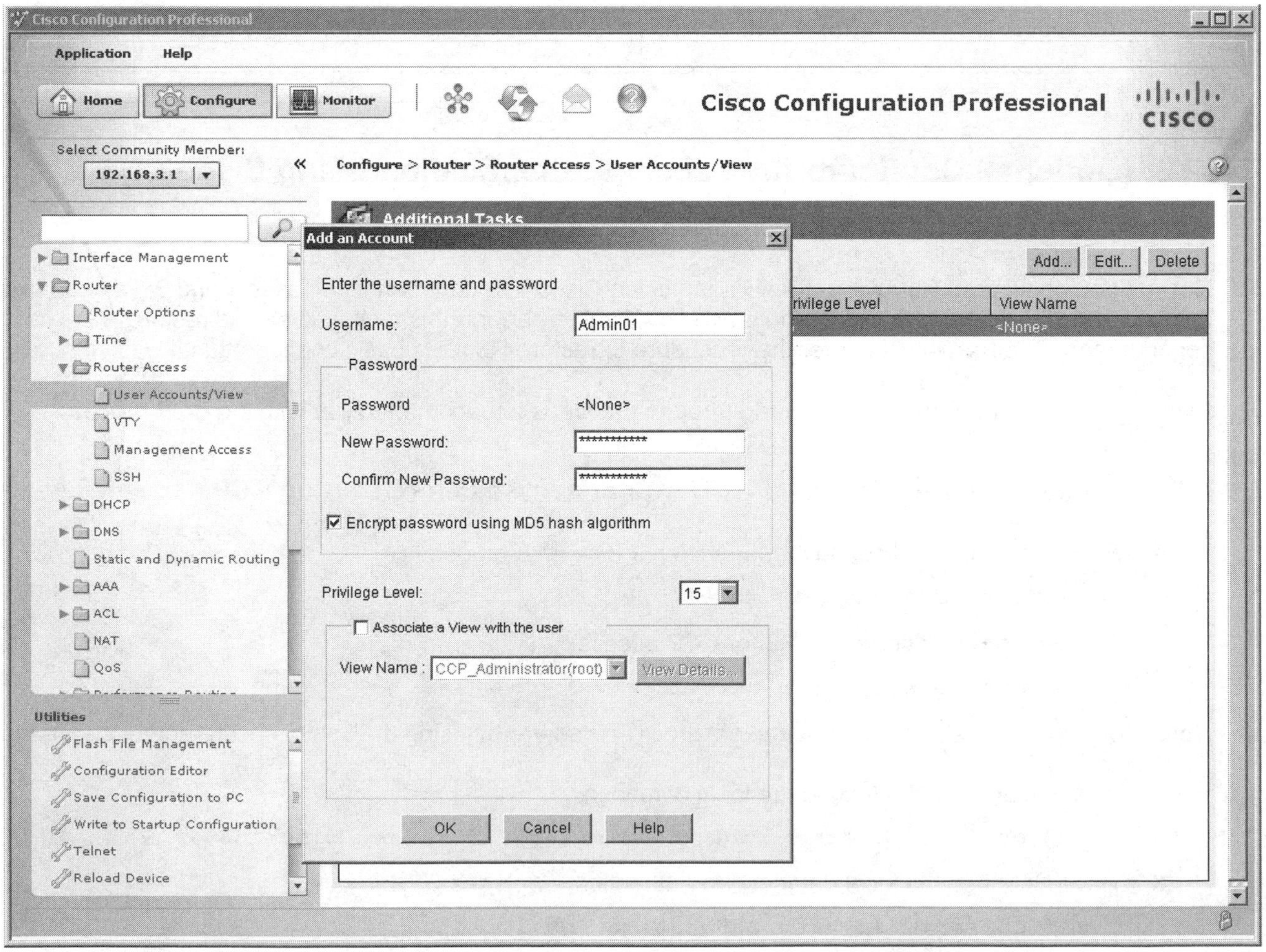

h. In the Deliver Configuration to Router window, make sure that the Save Running Config to Router's Startup Config check box is checked, and click **Deliver**.

i. In the Commands Delivery Status window, click **OK**.

Step 4: Create AAA method list for login.

a. Click the **Configure** button at the top of the screen.

b. Choose **Router > AAA > Authentication Policies > Login**.

c. In the Authentication Login window, click **Add**.

d. In the Add a Method List for Authentication Login window, verify that **Default** is in the Name field.

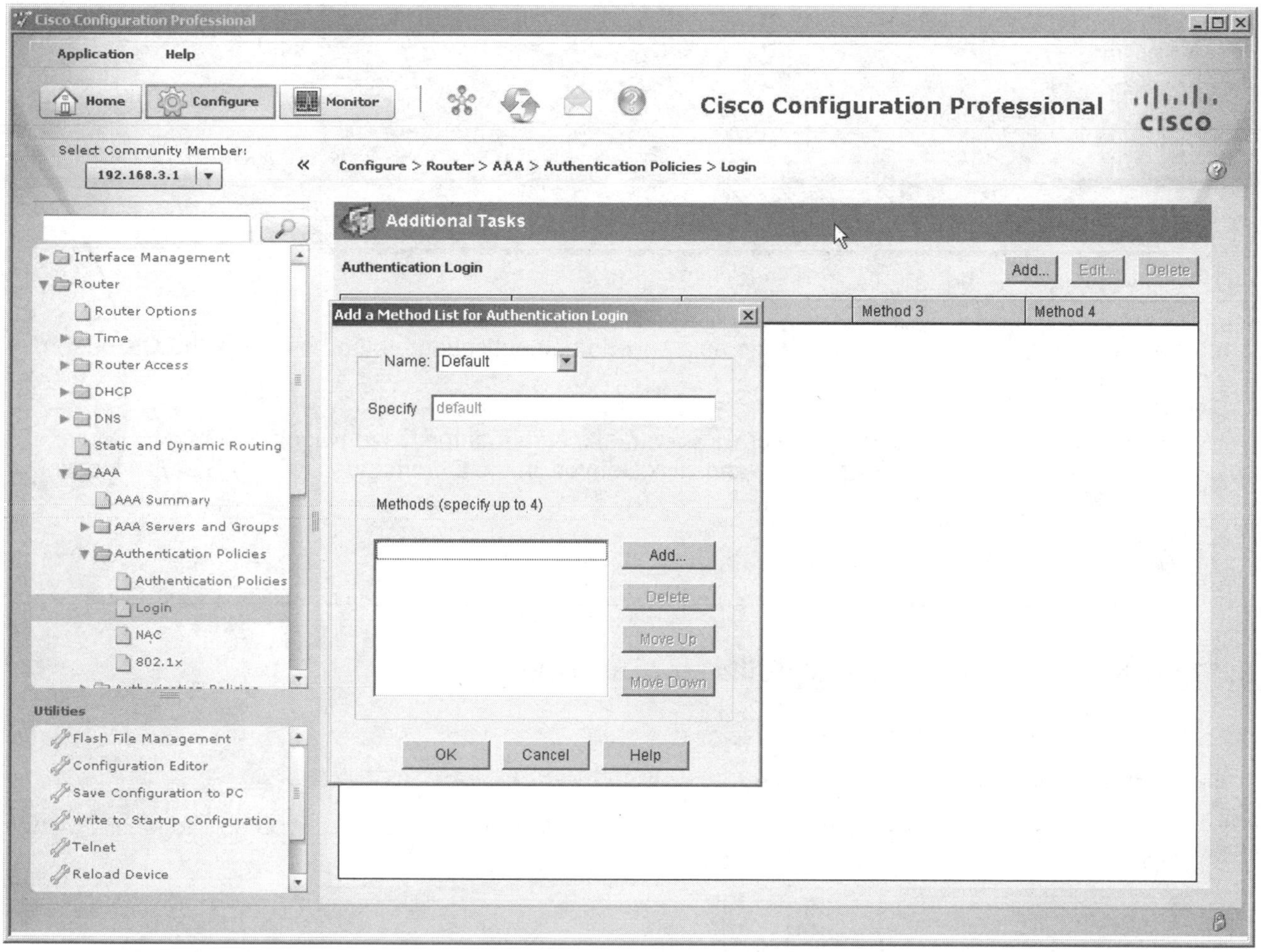

e. Click **Add** in the Methods section.

f. In the Select Method List(s) for Authentication Login window, choose **local** and click **OK**. Take note of the other methods listed, which include RADIUS (group radius) and TACACS+ (group tacacs+).

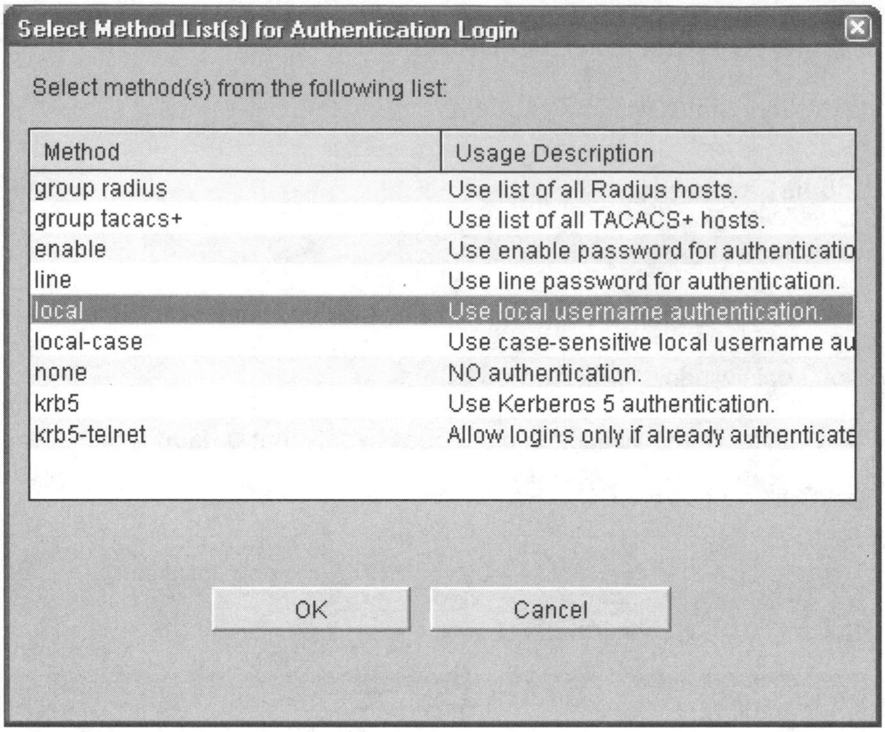

g. Click **OK** to close the window.

h. Repeat steps 4f and 4g. Choose **none** as a second authentication method and click the **OK** button when done.

i. In the Deliver Configuration to Router window, make sure that the Save Running Config to Router's Startup Config checkbox is checked, and click **Deliver**. In the Commands Delivery Status window, click **OK**.

j. What command was delivered to the router?

____

Step 5: Verify the AAA username and profile for console login.

a. Exit to the initial router screen that displays:

```
R3 con0 is now available, Press RETURN to get started.
```

b. Log in to the console as **Admin01** with a password of **Admin01pass**. Were you able to log in? Why or why not?

____

c. Exit to the initial router screen that displays:

```
R3 con0 is now available, Press RETURN to get started.
```

d. Attempt to log in to the console as **baduser**. Were you able to log in? Why or why not?

____

If no user accounts are configured in the local database, which users are permitted to access the device? ____

e. Log in to the console as **Admin01** with a password of **Admin01pass**. Access privileged EXEC mode using the enable secret password **cisco12345** and then show the running config. What commands are associated with the CCP session?

____

____

Task 4: Observe AAA Authentication Using Cisco IOS Debug

In this task, you use the **debug** command to observe successful and unsuccessful authentication attempts.

Step 1: Verify that the system clock and debug time stamps are configured correctly.

a. From the R3 user or privileged EXEC mode prompt, use the **show clock** command to determine what the current time is for the router. If the time and date are incorrect, set the time from privileged EXEC mode with the command **clock set HH:MM:SS DD month YYYY.** An example is provided here for R3:

```
R3# clock set 14:15:00 26 December 2008
```

b. Verify that detailed time-stamp information is available for your debug output using the **show run** command. This command displays all lines in the running config that include the word *timestamps*:

```
R3# show run | include timestamps

service timestamps debug datetime msec
service timestamps log datetime msec
```

c. If the **service timestamps debug** command is not present, enter it in global config mode:

```
R3(config)# service timestamps debug datetime msec
R3(config)# exit
```

d. Save the running configuration to the startup configuration from the privileged EXEC prompt:

```
R3# copy running-config startup-config
```

Step 2: Use debug to verify user access.

a. Activate debugging for AAA authentication:

```
R3# debug aaa authentication
AAA Authentication debugging is on
```

b. Start a Telnet session from PC-C to R3.

c. Log in with username Admin01 and password Admin01pass. Observe the AAA authentication events in the console session window. Debug messages similar to the following should be displayed:

```
R3#
Dec 26 14:36:42.323: AAA/BIND(000000A5): Bind i/f
Dec 26 14:36:42.323: AAA/AUTHEN/LOGIN (000000A5): Pick method list
'default'
```

d. From the Telnet window, enter privileged EXEC mode. Use the enable secret password of **cisco12345**. Debug messages similar to the following should be displayed. In the third entry, note the username (Admin01), virtual port number (tty194), and remote Telnet client address (192.168.3.3). Also note that the last status entry is PASS.

```
R3#
Dec 26 14:40:54.431: AAA: parse name=tty194 idb type=-1 tty=-1
```

```
Dec 26 14:40:54.431: AAA: name=tty194 flags=0x11 type=5 shelf=0 slot=0
adapter=0 port=194 channel=0
Dec 26 14:40:54.431: AAA/MEMORY: create_user (0x64BB5510)
user='Admin01' ruser=' NULL' ds0=0 port='tty194' rem_addr='192.168.3.3'
authen_type=ASCII service=ENABLE priv=15 initial_task_id='0', vrf=
(id=0)
Dec 26 14:40:54.431: AAA/AUTHEN/START (2467624222): port='tty194'
list='' action=LOGIN service=ENABLE
Dec 26 14:40:54.431: AAA/AUTHEN/START (2467624222): non-console enable
– default to enable password
Dec 26 14:40:54.431: AAA/AUTHEN/START (2467624222): Method=ENABLE
R3#
Dec 26 14:40:54.435: AAA/AUTHEN(2467624222): Status=GETPASS
R3#
Dec 26 14:40:59.275: AAA/AUTHEN/CONT (2467624222): continue_login
(user='(undef)')
Dec 26 14:40:59.275: AAA/AUTHEN(2467624222): Status=GETPASS
Dec 26 14:40:59.275: AAA/AUTHEN/CONT (2467624222): Method=ENABLE
Dec 26 14:40:59.287: AAA/AUTHEN(2467624222): Status=PASS
Dec 26 14:40:59.287: AAA/MEMORY: free_user (0x64BB5510) user='NULL'
ruser='NULL' port='tty194' rem_addr='192.168.3.3' authen_type=ASCII
service=ENABLE priv=15 v
rf= (id=0)
```

e. From the Telnet window, exit privileged EXEC mode using the **disable** command. Try to enter privileged EXEC mode again, but use a bad password this time. Observe the debug output on R3, noting that the status is FAIL this time:

```
Dec 26 15:46:54.027: AAA/AUTHEN(2175919868): Status=GETPASS
Dec 26 15:46:54.027: AAA/AUTHEN/CONT (2175919868): Method=ENABLE
Dec 26 15:46:54.039: AAA/AUTHEN(2175919868): password incorrect
Dec 26 15:46:54.039: AAA/AUTHEN(2175919868): Status=FAIL
Dec 26 15:46:54.039: AAA/MEMORY: free_user (0x6615BFE4) user='NULL'
ruser='NULL'
 port='tty194' rem_addr='192.168.3.3' authen_type=ASCII service=ENABLE
priv=15 v
rf= (id=0)
```

f. From the Telnet window, exit the Telnet session to the router. Then try to open a Telnet session to the router again, but this time try to log in with the username **Admin01** and a bad password. From the console window, the debug output should look similar to the following:

```
Dec 26 15:49:32.339: AAA/AUTHEN/LOGIN (000000AA): Pick method list
'default'
```

What message was displayed on the Telnet client screen? ______________________

g. Turn off all debugging using the **undebug all** command at the privileged EXEC prompt.

Part 4: Configure Centralized Authentication Using AAA and RADIUS

In Part 4 of the lab, you install RADIUS server software on PC-A. You then configure router R1 to access the external RADIUS server for user authentication. The freeware server WinRadius is used for this section of the lab.

Task 1: Restore Router R1 to Its Basic Settings

To avoid confusion as to what was already entered and the AAA RADIUS configuration, start by restoring router R1 to its basic configuration as performed in Parts 1 and 2 of this lab.

Step 1: Erase and reload the router.

a. Connect to the R1 console, and log in with the username **Admin01** and password **Admin01pass**.

b. Enter privileged EXEC mode with the password **cisco12345**.

c. Erase the startup config, and then issue the **`reload`** command to restart the router.

Step 2: Restore the basic configuration.

a. When the router restarts, enter privileged EXEC mode with the **`enable`** command, and then enter global config mode. Use the HyperTerminal **Transfer > Send File** function, cut and paste, or use another method to load the basic startup config for R1 that was created and saved in Part 2 of this lab.

b. Test connectivity by pinging from host PC-A to PC-C. If the pings are not successful, troubleshoot the router and PC configurations until they are.

c. If you are logged out of the console, log in again as **user01** with password **user01pass**, and access privileged EXEC mode with the password **cisco12345**.

d. Save the running config to the startup config using the **`copy run start`** command.

Task 2: Download and Install a RADIUS Server on PC-A

A number of RADIUS servers are available, both freeware and for cost. This lab uses WinRadius, a freeware standards-based RADIUS server that runs on Windows XP and most other Windows operating systems. The free version of the software can support only five usernames.

Step 1: Download the WinRadius software.

a. Create a folder named WinRadius on your desktop or other location in which to store the files.

b. Download the latest version from http://www.suggestsoft.com/soft/itconsult2000/winradius/, http://winradius.soft32.com, http://www.brothersoft.com/winradius-20914.html.

c. Save the downloaded zip file in the folder you created in Step 1a, and extract the zipped files to the same folder. There is no installation setup. The extracted WinRadius.exe file is executable.

d. You may create a shortcut on your desktop for WinRadius.exe.

Note: If WinRadius is used on a PC that uses the Microsoft Windows Vista operating system or the Microsoft Windows 7 operating system, ODBC may fail to create successfully because it cannot write to the Registry.

Possible Solutions

1. Compatibility settings:

    a. Right-click the WinRadius.exe icon and choose **Properties**.

    b. In the **Properties** dialog box, select the **Compatibility** tab. In this tab, check the **Run this program in compatibility mode for** check box. Then in the drop-down menu below, choose **Windows XP (Service Pack 3)**, for example, if it is appropriate for your system.

    c. Click **OK**.

2. Run as Administrator settings:

    a. Right-click the WinRadius.exe icon and choose **Properties**.

    b. While in the **Properties** dialog box, select the **Compatibility** tab. In this tab, check the **Run This Program as Administrator** check box in the Privilege Level section.

    c. Click **OK**.

3. Run as Administrator for each launch:

    a. Right-click the WinRadius.exe icon and choose **Run as Administrator**.

    b. When WinRadius launches, click **Yes** in the User Account Control dialog box.

Step 2: Configure the WinRadius server database.

a. Start the WinRadius.exe application. WinRadius uses a local database in which it stores user information. When the application is started for the first time, the following messages are displayed:

```
Please go to "Settings/Database and create the ODBC for your RADIUS
database.

Launch ODBC failed.
```

b. From the main menu, choose **Settings > Database**. The following screen is displayed. Click the **Configure ODBC Automatically** button, and then click **OK**. You should see a message that the ODBC was created successfully. Exit WinRadius and restart the application for the changes to take effect.

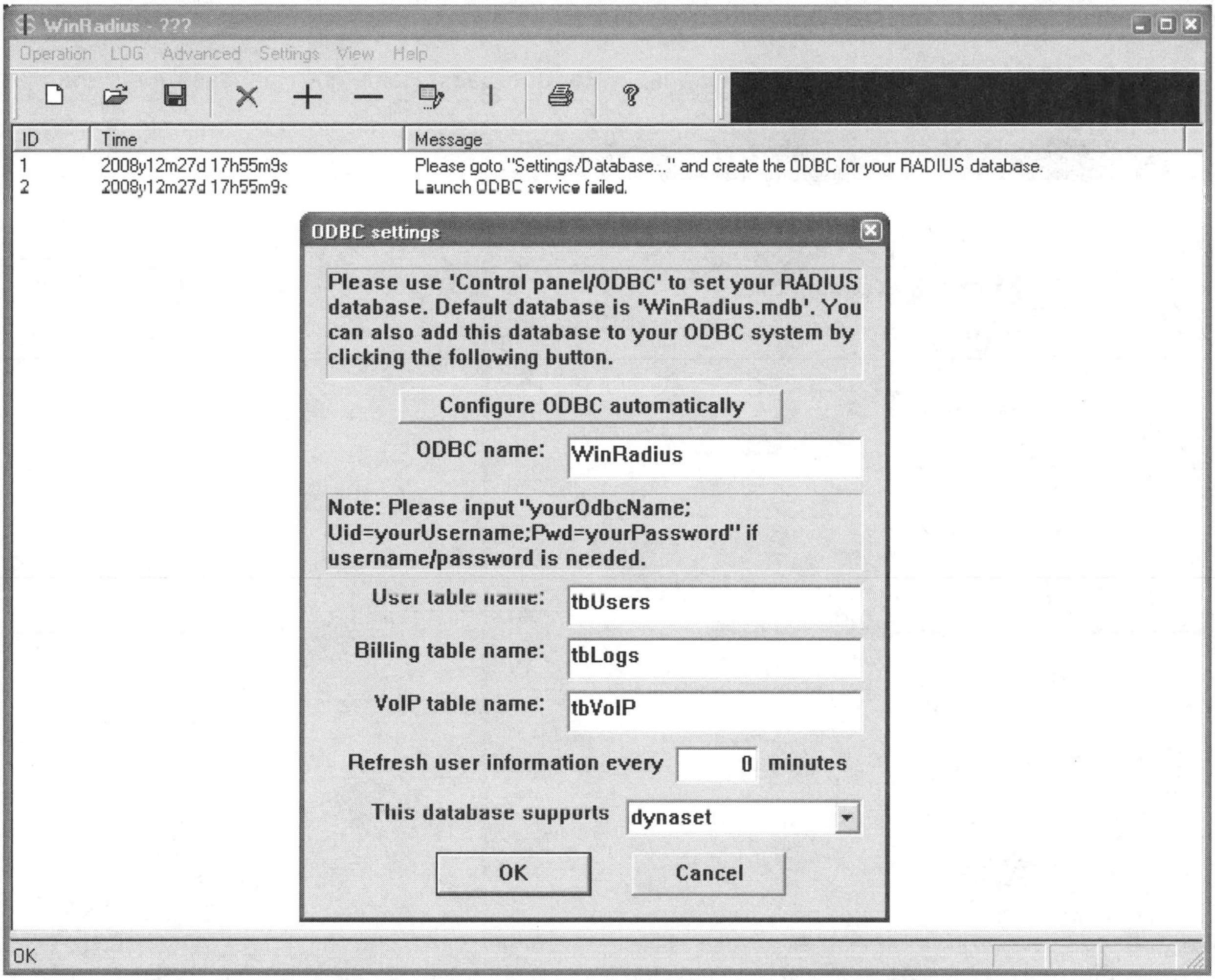

When WinRadius starts again, you should see messages similar to the following displayed.

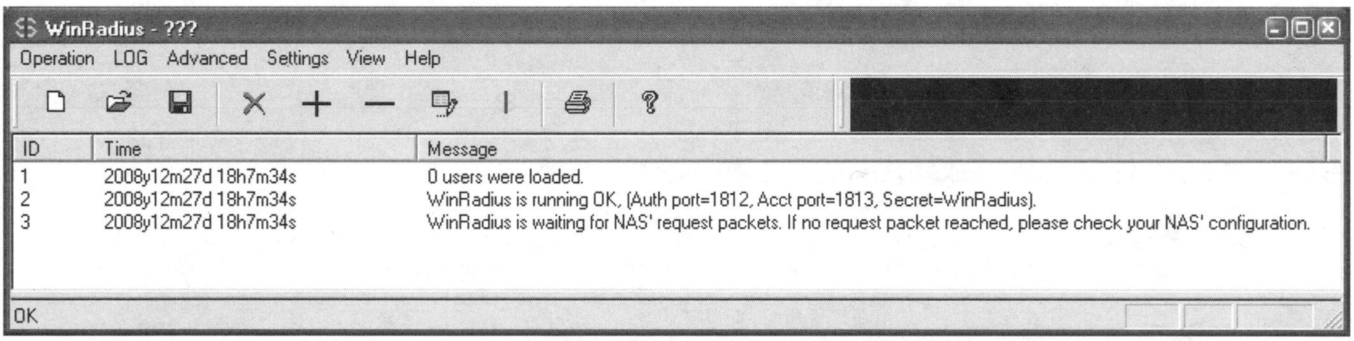

On which ports is WinRadius listening for authentication and accounting?

____

Step 3: Configure users and passwords on the WinRadius server.

Note: The free version of WinRadius can support only five usernames. The usernames are lost if you exit the application and restart it. Any usernames created in previous sessions must be re-created. Note that the first message in the previous screen shows that zero users were loaded. No users had been created prior to this, but this message is displayed each time WinRadius is started, regardless of whether users were created.

a. From the main menu, choose **Operation > Add User**.

b. Enter the username **RadUser** with a password of **RadUserpass**. Remember that passwords are case sensitive.

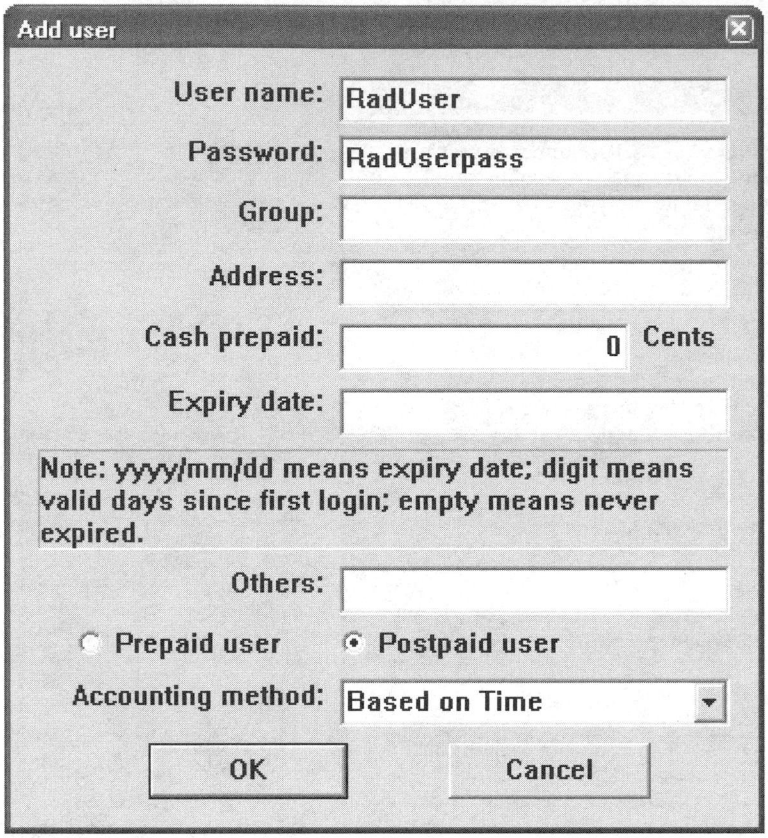

c. Click **OK**. You should see a message on the log screen that the user was added successfully.

Step 4: Clear the log display.

From the main menu, choose **Log > Clear**.

Step 5: Test the new user added using the WinRadius test utility.

a. A WinRadius testing utility is included in the downloaded zip file. Navigate to the folder where you unzipped the WinRadius.zip file and locate the file named RadiusTest.exe.

b. Start the RadiusTest application, and enter the IP address of this RADIUS server (192.168.1.3), username **RadUser**, and password **RadUserpass** as shown. Do not change the default RADIUS port number of 1813 and the RADIUS password of WinRadius.

c. Click **Send** and you should see a Send Access_Request message indicating the server at 192.168.1.3, port number 1813, received 44 hexadecimal characters. On the WinRadius log display, you should also see a message indicating that user RadUser was authenticated successfully.

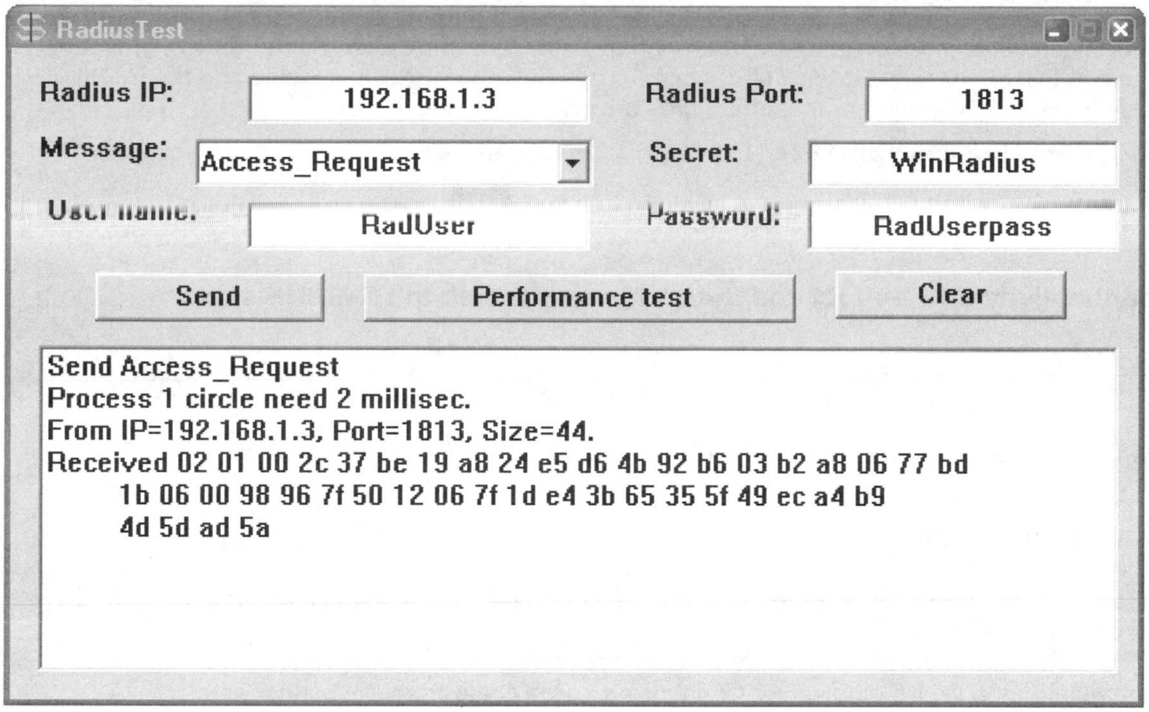

d. Close the RadiusTest application.

Task 3: Configure R1 AAA Services and Access the RADIUS Server Using Cisco IOS

Note: To configure AAA using CCP, proceed to Task 5.

Step 1: Enable AAA on R1.

Use the **aaa new-model** command in global configuration mode to enable AAA:

```
R1(config)# aaa new-model
```

Step 2: Configure the default login authentication list.

a. Configure the list to first use RADIUS for the authentication service, and then none. If no RADIUS server can be reached and authentication cannot be performed, the router globally allows access without authentication. This is a safeguard measure in case the router starts up without connectivity to an active RADIUS server.

```
R1(config)# aaa authentication login default group radius none
```

b. You could alternatively configure local authentication as the backup authentication method instead.

Note: If you do not set up a default login authentication list, you could get locked out of the router and need to use the password recovery procedure for your specific router.

Step 3: Specify a RADIUS server.

Use the **radius-server host *hostname* key *key*** command to point to the RADIUS server. The *hostname* argument accepts either a hostname or an IP address. Use the IP address of the RADIUS server, PC-A (192.168.1.3). The key is a secret password shared between the RADIUS server and the RADIUS client

(R1, in this case) and used to authenticate the connection between the router and the server before the user authentication process takes place. The RADIUS client may be a Network Access Server (NAS), but router R1 plays that role in this lab. Use the default NAS secret password of WinRadius specified on the RADIUS server (see Task 2, Step 5). Remember that passwords are case sensitive.

```
R1(config)# radius-server host 192.168.1.3 key WinRadius
```

Task 4: Test the AAA RADIUS Configuration

Step 1: Verify connectivity between R1 and the computer running the RADIUS server.

Ping from R1 to PC-A:

```
R1# ping 192.168.1.3
```

If the pings were not successful, troubleshoot the PC and router configuration before continuing.

Step 2: Test your configuration.

a. If you restarted the WinRadius server, you must re-create the user **RadUser** with a password of **RadUserpass** by choosing **Operation > Add User**.

b. Clear the log on the WinRadius server by choosing **Log > Clear** from the main menu.

c. On R1, exit to the initial router screen that displays:

```
R1 con0 is now available, Press RETURN to get started.
```

d. Test your configuration by logging in to the console on R1 using the username **RadUser** and the password of **RadUserpass**. Were you able to gain access to the user EXEC prompt and, if so, was there any delay? ____

e. Exit to the initial router screen that displays:

```
R1 con0 is now available, Press RETURN to get started.
```

f. Test your configuration again by logging in to the console on R1 using the nonexistent username of **Userxxx** and the password of **Userxxxpass**. Were you able to gain access to the user EXEC prompt? Why or why not? ____

g. Were any messages displayed on the RADIUS server log for either login? _______

h. Why was a nonexistent username able to access the router and no messages are displayed on the RADIUS server log screen? ____

i. When the RADIUS server is unavailable, messages similar to the following are typically displayed after attempted logins:

```
*Dec 26 16:46:54.039: %RADIUS-4-RADIUS_DEAD: RADIUS server
192.168.1.3:1645,1646 is not responding.
*Dec 26 15:46:54.039: %RADIUS-4-RADIUS_ALIVE: RADIUS server
192.168.1.3:1645,1646 is being marked alive.
```

Step 3: Troubleshoot router-to-RADIUS server communication.

a. Check the default Cisco IOS RADIUS UDP port numbers used on R1 with the **radius-server host** command and the Cisco IOS Help function:

```
R1(config)# radius-server host 192.168.1.3 ?
```

```
acct-port   UDP port for RADIUS accounting server (default is 1646)
alias         1-8 aliases for this server (max. 8)
auth-port   UDP port for RADIUS authentication server (default is 1645)
 < Output omitted >
```

b. Check the R1 running configuration for lines containing the command **radius**. The following command displays all running config lines that include the word *radius*:

```
R1# show run | incl radius
aaa authentication login default group radius none
radius-server host 192.168.1.3 auth-port 1645 acct-port 1646 key 7
097B47072B04131B1E1F
< Output omitted >
```

c. What are the default R1 Cisco IOS UDP port numbers for the RADIUS server? ________________

Step 4: Check the default port numbers on the WinRadius server on PC-A.

a. From the WinRadius main menu, choose **Settings > System**.

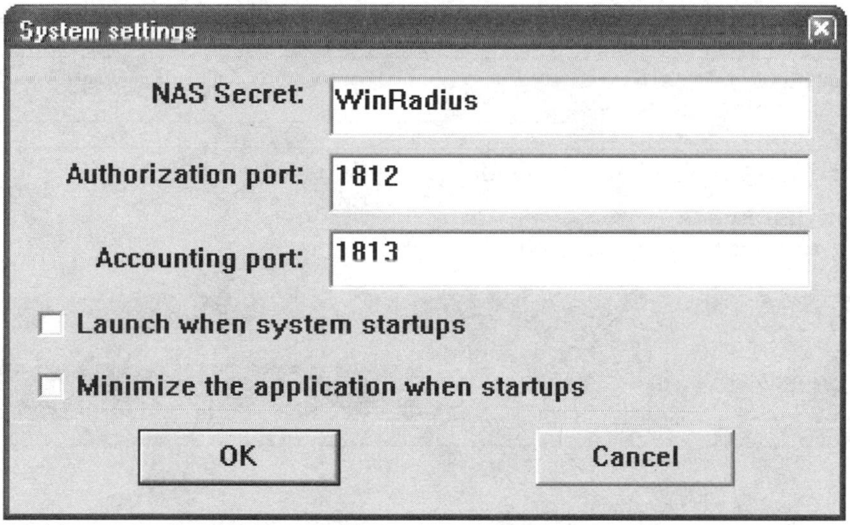

b. What are the default WinRadius UDP port numbers? ________________________________

Note: The early deployment of RADIUS was done using UDP port number 1645 for authentication and 1646 for accounting, which conflicts with the datametrics service. Because of this conflict, RFC 2865 officially assigned port numbers 1812 and 1813 for RADIUS.

Step 5: Change the RADIUS port numbers on R1 to match the WinRadius server.

Unless specified otherwise, the Cisco IOS RADIUS configuration defaults to UDP port numbers 1645 and 1646. Either the router Cisco IOS port numbers must be changed to match the port number of the RADIUS server or the RADIUS server port numbers must be changed to match the port numbers of the Cisco IOS router. In this step, you modify the IOS port numbers to those of the RADIUS server, which are specified in RFC 2865.

a. Remove the previous configuration using the following command:

```
R1(config)# no radius-server host 192.168.1.3 auth-port 1645 acct-port
1646
```

b. Issue the **radius-server host** command again and this time specify port numbers 1812 and 1813, along with the IP address and secret key for the RADIUS server:

```
R1(config)# radius-server host 192.168.1.3 auth-port 1812 acct-port
1813 key WinRadius
```

Step 6: Test your configuration by logging in to the console on R1.

a. Exit to the initial router screen that displays:

```
R1 con0 is now available, Press RETURN to get started.
```

b. Log in again with the username of **RadUser** and password of **RadUserpass**. Were you able to log in? Was there any delay this time?

____

c. The following message should display on the RADIUS server log:

```
User (RadUser) authenticate OK.
```

d. Exit to the initial router screen that displays:

```
R1 con0 is now available, Press RETURN to get started.
```

e. Log in again using an invalid username of Userxxx and the password of Userxxxpass. Were you able to log in? ____

What message was displayed on the router? ____

The following messages should display on the RADIUS server log:

```
Reason: Unknown username
User (Userxxx) authenticate failed
```

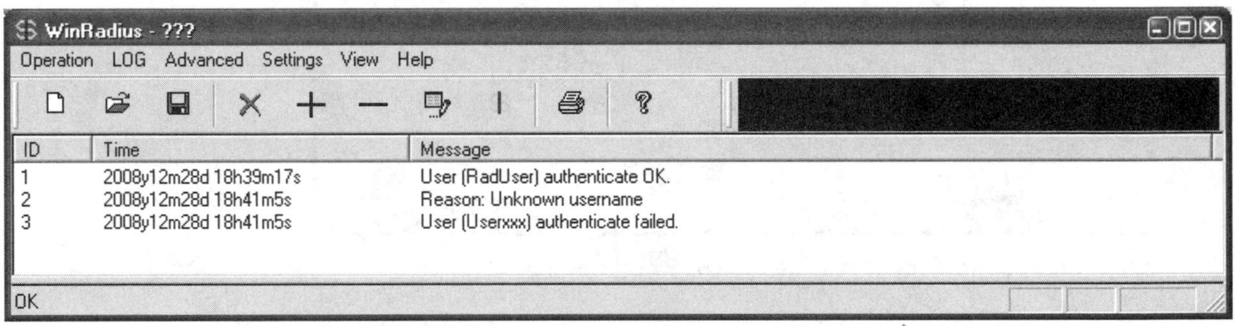

Step 7: Create an authentication method list for Telnet and test it.

a. Create a unique authentication method list for Telnet access to the router. This does not have the fallback of no authentication, so if there is no access to the RADIUS server, Telnet access is disabled. Name the authentication method list **TELNET_LINES**:

```
R1(config)# aaa authentication login TELNET_LINES group radius
```

b. Apply the list to the vty lines on the router using the login authentication command:

```
R1(config)# line vty 0 4
R1(config-line)# login authentication TELNET_LINES
```

c. Telnet from PC-A to R1, and log in with the username **RadUser** and the password of **RadUserpass**. Were you able to gain access to log in?

____

d. Exit the Telnet session, and telnet from PC-A to R1 again. Log in with the username **Userxxx** and the password of **Userxxxpass**. Were you able to log in?

____

Task 5: (Optional) Configure R1 AAA Services and Access the RADIUS Server Using CCP

You can also use CCP to configure the router to access the external RADIUS server.

Note: If you configured R1 to access the external RADIUS server using Cisco IOS in Task 3, you can skip this task. If you performed Task 3 and you want to perform this task, restore the router to its basic configuration as described Task 1 of this part, except log in initially as RadUser with the password RadUserpass. If the RADIUS server is unavailable at this time, you can still log in to the console.

If you do not perform this task, read through the steps to become familiar with the CCP process.

Step 1: Implement AAA services and HTTP router access before starting CCP.

a. From the CLI global config mode, enable a new AAA model:

```
R1(config)# aaa new-model
```

b. Enable the HTTP server on R1:

```
R1(config)# ip http server
```

c. Add a user named admin to the local database:

```
R1(config)# username admin privilege 15 secret cisco12345
```

d. Have CCP use the local database to authenticate web sessions:

```
R1(config)# ip http authentication local
```

Step 2: Access CCP and discover R1.

a. Start CCP on PC-C. In the Manage Devices window, add R1 IP address 192.168.1.1 in the first IP Address field. Enter **admin** in the Username field, and **cisco12345** in the Password field.

b. At the CCP Dashboard, click the **Discover** button to discover and connect to R3. If discovery fails, click the **Discovery Details** button to determine the problem.

Step 3: Configure R1 AAA to access the WinRADIUS server.

a. Click the **Configure** button at the top of the screen.

b. Choose **Router > AAA > AAA Servers and Groups > Servers**.

c. In the AAA Servers window, click **Add**.

d. In the Add AAA Server window, verify that **RADIUS** is in the Server Type field.

e. In the Server IP or Host field, enter the IP address of PC-A, **192.168.1.3**.

f. Change the **Authorization Port** from 1645 to 1812, and change the **Accounting Port** from 1646 to 1813 to match the RADIUS server port number settings.

g. Check the **Configure Key** check box.

h. Enter **WinRadius** in both the New Key and Confirm Key fields.

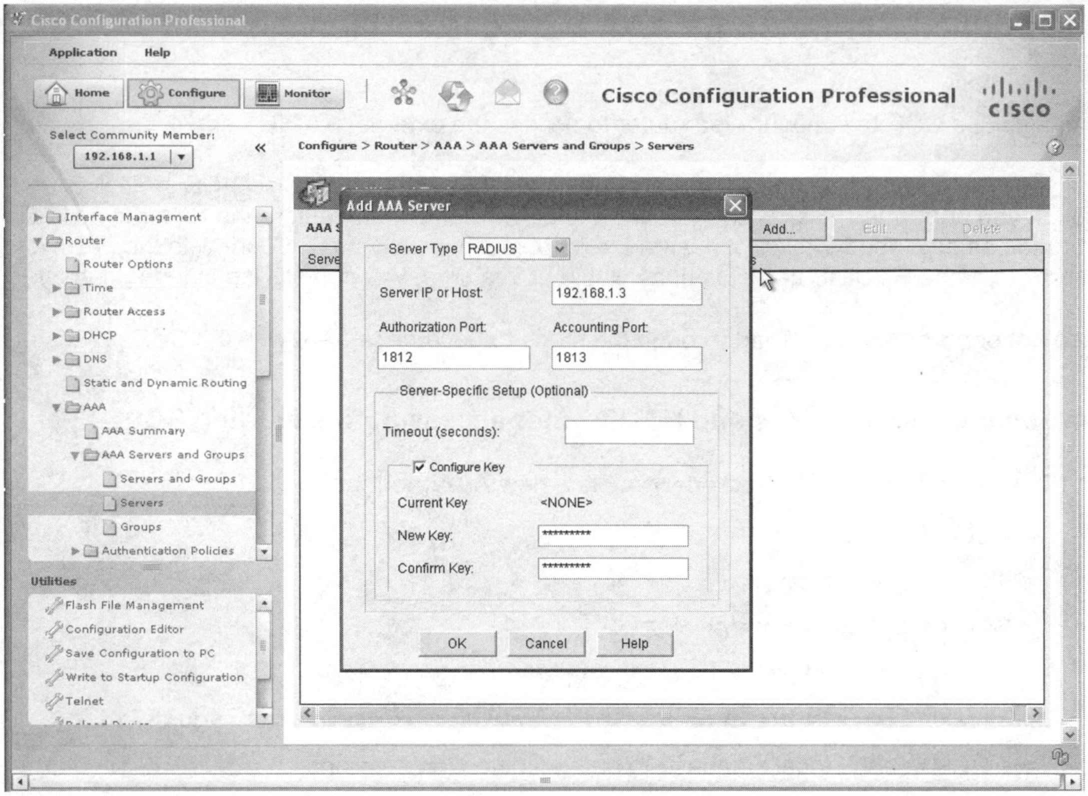

i. In the Deliver Configuration to Router window, click **Deliver**, and in the Commands Delivery Status window, click **OK**.

j. What command was delivered to the router?

____

____

Step 4: Configure the R1 AAA login method list for RADIUS.

a. Click the **Configure** button at the top of the screen.

b. Choose **Router > AAA > Authentication Policies > Login**.

c. In the Authentication Login window, click **Add**.

d. In the Select Method List(s) for Authentication Login window, choose **group radius** and click **OK**.

e. In the Select Method List(s) for Authentication Login window, choose **local** as a second method and click **OK**.

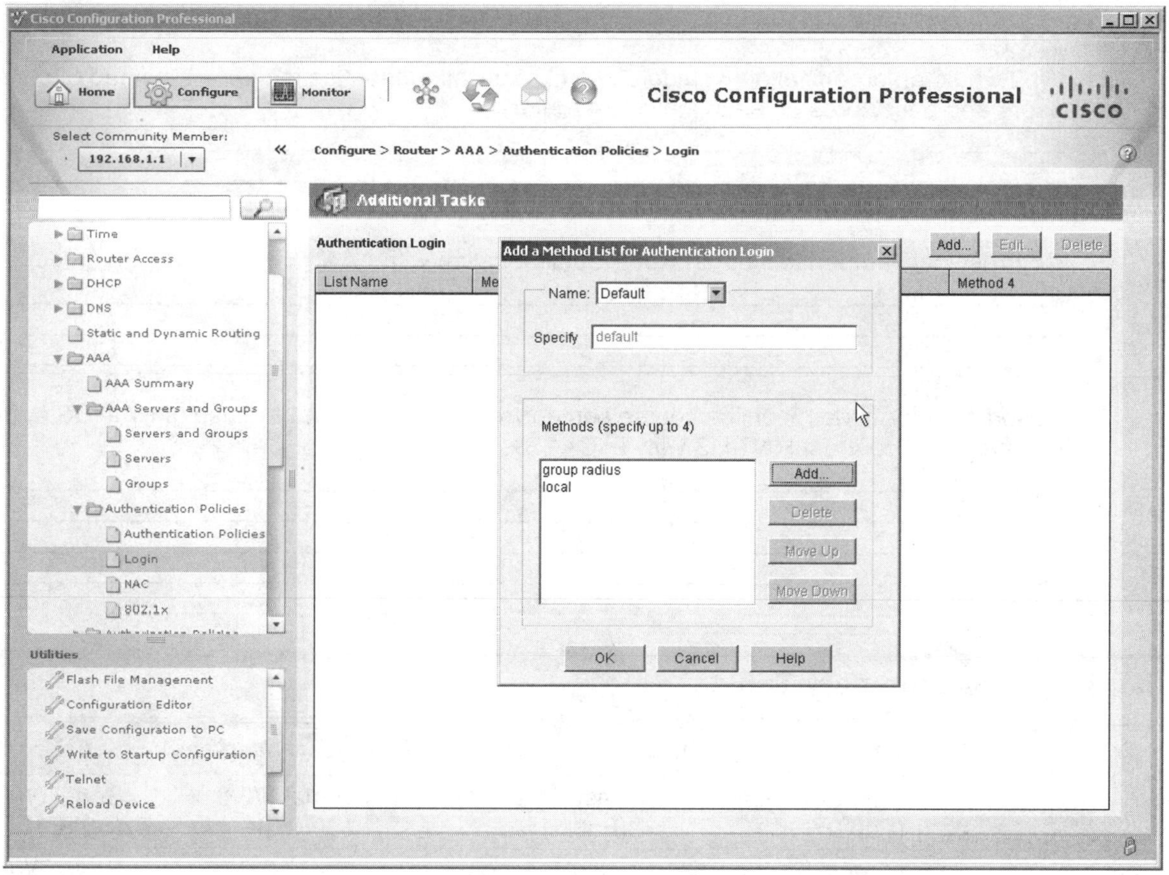

f. In the Deliver Configuration to Router window, click **Deliver** and in the Commands Delivery Status window, click **OK**.

g. What command(s) were delivered to the router?

____

____

Step 5: Test your configuration.

a. If you restarted the RADIUS server, you must re-create the user **RadUser** with a password of **RadUserpass** by choosing **Operation > Add User**.

b. Clear the log on the WinRadius server by choosing **Log > Clear**.

c. Test your configuration by opening a Telnet session from PC-A to R1:

```
C:> telnet 192.168.1.1
```

d. At the login prompt, enter the username **RadUser** defined on the RADIUS server and a password of **RadUserpass**.

Were you able to log in to R1? _____

Reflection

1. Why would an organization want to use a centralized authentication server instead of configuring users and passwords on each individual router?

____
____
____

2. Contrast local authentication and local authentication with AAA.

____
____
____

3. Based on the Academy online course content, web research, and the use of RADIUS in this lab, compare and contrast RADIUS with TACACS+.

____
____
____
____
____

Router Interface Summary Table

Router Model	Ethernet Interface 1	Ethernet Interface 2	Serial Interface 1	Serial Interface 2
1800	Fast Ethernet 0/0 (Fa0/0)	Fast Ethernet 0/1 (Fa0/1)	Serial 0/0/0 (S0/0/0)	Serial 0/0/1 (S0/0/1)
1900	Gigabit Ethernet 0/0 (G0/0)	Gigabit Ethernet 0/1 (G0/1)	Serial 0/0/0 (S0/0/0)	Serial 0/0/1 (S0/0/1)
2800	Fast Ethernet 0/0 (Fa0/0)	Fast Ethernet 0/1 (Fa0/1)	Serial 0/0/0 (S0/0/0)	Serial 0/0/1 (S0/0/1)
2900	Gigabit Ethernet 0/0 (G0/0)	Gigabit Ethernet 0/1 (G0/1)	Serial 0/0/0 (S0/0/0)	Serial 0/0/1 (S0/0/1)

Note: To find out how the router is configured, look at the interfaces to identify the type of router and how many interfaces the router has. There is no way to effectively list all the combinations of configurations for each router class. This table includes identifiers for the possible combinations of Ethernet and serial interfaces in the device. The table does not include any other type of interface, even though a specific router may contain one. An example of this might be an ISDN BRI interface. The string in parentheses is the legal abbreviation that can be used in Cisco IOS commands to represent the interface.

Chapter 4 Lab A: Configuring CBAC and Zone-Based Firewalls

Topology

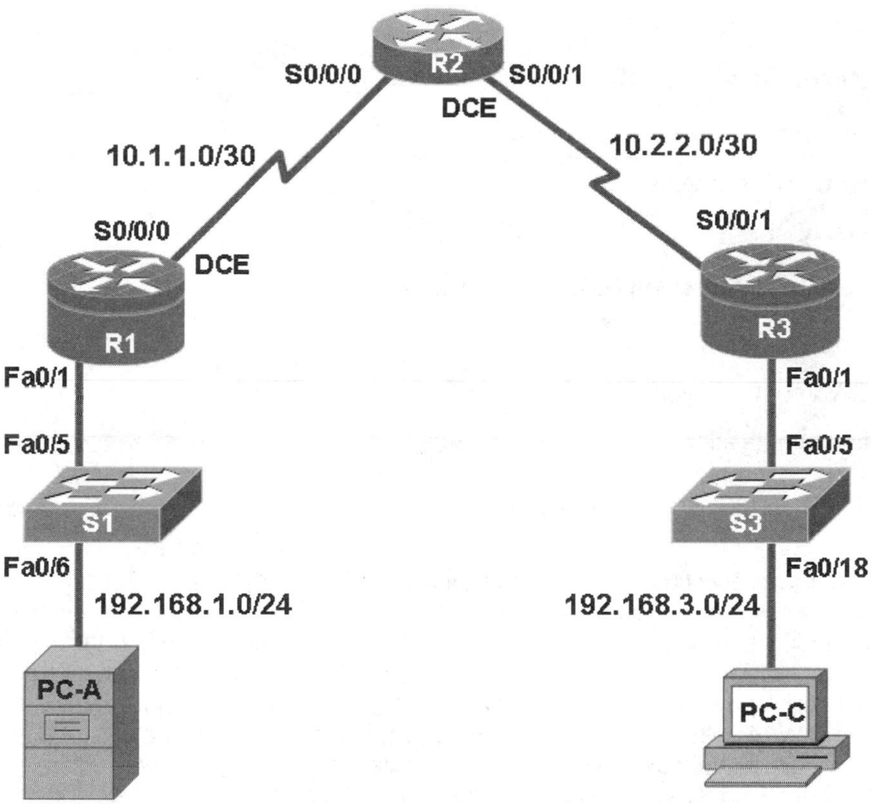

Note: ISR G2 devices have Gigabit Ethernet interfaces rather than Fast Ethernet interfaces.

IP Addressing Table

Device	Interface	IP Address	Subnet Mask	Default Gateway	Switch Port
R1	Fa0/1	192.168.1.1	255.255.255.0	N/A	S1 Fa0/5
	S0/0/0 (DCE)	10.1.1.1	255.255.255.252	N/A	N/A
R2	S0/0/0	10.1.1.2	255.255.255.252	N/A	N/A
	S0/0/1 (DCE)	10.2.2.2	255.255.255.252	N/A	N/A
R3	Fa0/1	192.168.3.1	255.255.255.0	N/A	S3 Fa0/5
	S0/0/1	10.2.2.1	255.255.255.252	N/A	N/A
PC-A	NIC	192.168.1.3	255.255.255.0	192.168.1.1	S1 Fa0/6
PC-C	NIC	192.168.3.3	255.255.255.0	192.168.3.1	S3 Fa0/18

Objectives

Part 1: Basic Router Configuration

- Configure hostnames, interface IP addresses, and access passwords.
- Configure the EIGRP dynamic routing protocol.
- Use the Nmap port scanner to test for router vulnerabilities

Part 2: Configuring a Context-Based Access Control (CBAC) Firewall

- Configure CBAC using AutoSecure.
- Examine the resulting CBAC configuration.
- Verify the firewall functionality.

Part 3: Configuring a Zone-Based Policy Firewall (ZBF, ZPF, or ZFW)

- Use CCP to configure a zone-based policy firewall.
- Examine the resulting CBAC configuration.
- Use CCP Monitor to verify configuration.

Background

The most basic form of a Cisco IOS firewall uses access control lists (ACLs) with filtering IP traffic and monitoring established traffic patterns. This is referred to as a traditional Cisco IOS firewall. In more recent Cisco IOS versions, this approach has evolved into a method called context-based access control (CBAC) or Inspect/CBAC, which is based on stateful packet inspection (SPI). CBAC makes creating firewalls easier and gives the administrator greater control over various types of application traffic originating from inside and outside of the protected network. When Cisco IOS AutoSecure is run, it prompts to create a CBAC firewall and generates a basic configuration. For simple networks with a single inside and outside interface, CBAC is easier to configure than traditional Cisco IOS firewalls. Configurations with multiple interfaces and demilitarized zone (DMZ) requirements can become complex and difficult to manage using CBAC.

The current method used with CCP for securing routers is called a zone-based policy firewall (may be abbreviated as ZBF, ZPF, or ZFW). A zone-based policy firewall provides the same type of functionality as CBAC, but is better suited for multiple interfaces that have similar or varying security requirements. Whereas AutoSecure generates a CBAC firewall, CCP generates a ZBF firewall by default.

In this lab, you build a multirouter network and configure the routers and hosts. You use AutoSecure to configure a CBAC firewall and CCP to configure a zone-based policy firewall.

Note: The router commands and output in this lab are from a Cisco 1841 with Cisco IOS Software Release 12.4(20)T (Advanced IP image). Other routers and Cisco IOS versions can be used. See the Router Interface Summary table at the end of the lab to determine which interface identifiers to use based on the equipment in the lab. Depending on the router model and Cisco IOS version, the commands available and output produced might vary from what this lab shows.

Note: Make sure that the routers and the switches have been erased and have no startup configurations.

Required Resources

- 3 routers (Cisco 1841 with Cisco IOS Software Release 12.4(20)T1 or comparable)
- 2 switches (Cisco 2960 or comparable)

- PC-A: Windows XP, Vista, or Windows 7
- PC-C: Windows XP, Vista, or Windows 7 with CCP 2.5
- Serial and Ethernet cables as shown in the topology
- Rollover cables to configure the routers via the console

CCP Notes

- Refer to Chapter 00 Lab A for instructions on how to install CCP. Hardware/software recommendations for CCP include Windows XP, Vista, or Windows 7 with Java version 1.6.0_11 up to 1.6.0_21, Internet Explorer 6.0 or later, and Flash Player Version 10.0.12.36 or later.
- If the PC on which CCP is installed is running Windows Vista or 7, you might need to right-click the CCP icon or menu item and choose Run as Administrator.
- To run CCP, you might need to temporarily disable antivirus programs and OS firewalls. Make sure to turn off all pop-up blockers in the browser.

Part 1: Basic Router Configuration

In Part 1 of this lab, you set up the network topology and configure basic settings, such as the interface IP addresses, dynamic routing, device access, and passwords.

Note: All tasks should be performed on routers R1, R2 and R3. The procedure for R1 is shown here as an example.

Task 1: Configure Basic Router Settings

Step 1: Cable the network as shown in the topology.

Attach the devices shown in the topology diagram, and cable as necessary.

Step 2: Configure basic settings for each router.

a. Configure hostnames as shown in the topology.

b. Configure the interface IP addresses as shown in the IP addressing table.

c. Configure a clock rate for the serial router interfaces with a DCE serial cable attached:

```
R1(config)# interface S0/0/0
R1(config-if)# clock rate 64000
```

Step 3: Disable DNS lookup.

To prevent the router from attempting to translate incorrectly entered commands, disable DNS lookup:

```
R1(config)# no ip domain-lookup
```

Step 4: Configure the EIGRP routing protocol on R1, R2, and R3.

a. On R1, use the following commands:

```
R1(config)# router eigrp 101
```

```
R1(config-router)# network 192.168.1.0 0.0.0.255
R1(config-router)# network 10.1.1.0 0.0.0.3
R1(config-router)# no auto-summary
```

b. On R2, use the following commands:

```
R2(config)# router eigrp 101
R2(config-router)# network 10.1.1.0 0.0.0.3
R2(config-router)# network 10.2.2.0 0.0.0.3
R2(config-router)# no auto-summary
```

c. On R3, use the following commands:

```
R3(config)# router eigrp 101
R3(config-router)# network 192.168.3.0 0.0.0.255

R3(config-router)# network 10.2.2.0 0.0.0.3
R3(config-router)# no auto-summary
```

Step 5: Configure PC host IP settings.

a. Configure a static IP address, subnet mask, and default gateway for PC-A, as shown in the IP addressing table.

b. Configure a static IP address, subnet mask, and default gateway for PC-C, as shown in the IP addressing table.

Step 6: Verify basic network connectivity.

a. Ping from R1 to R3.

   Were the results successful? _____

   If the pings are not successful, troubleshoot the basic device configurations before continuing.

b. Ping from PC-A on the R1 LAN to PC-C on the R3 LAN.

   Were the results successful? _____

   If the pings are not successful, troubleshoot the basic device configurations before continuing.

Note: If you can ping from PC-A to PC-C, you have demonstrated that the EIGRP routing protocol is configured and functioning correctly. If you cannot ping but the device interfaces are up and IP addresses are correct, use the show run and show ip route commands to help identify routing protocol-related problems.

Step 7: Configure a minimum password length.

Note: Passwords in this lab are set to a minimum of 10 characters but are relatively simple for the benefit of performing the lab. More complex passwords are recommended in a production network.

Use the security passwords command to set a minimum password length of 10 characters:

```
R1(config)# security passwords min-length 10
```

Step 8: Configure basic console, auxiliary port, and vty lines.

a. Configure a console password and enable login for router R1. For additional security, the **exec-timeout** command causes the line to log out after 5 minutes of inactivity. The **logging synchronous** command prevents console messages from interrupting command entry.

Note: To avoid repetitive logins during this lab, you can set the **exec-timeout** command to 0 0, which prevents it from expiring. However, this is not considered a good security practice.

```
R1(config)# line console 0
R1(config-line)# password ciscoconpass
R1(config-line)# exec-timeout 5 0
R1(config-line)# login
R1(config-line)# logging synchronous
```

b. Configure a password for the aux port for router R1:

```
R1(config)# line aux 0
R1(config-line)# password ciscoauxpass
R1(config-line)# exec-timeout 5 0
R1(config-line)# login
```

c. Configure the password on the vty lines for router R1:

```
R1(config)# line vty 0 4
R1(config-line)# password ciscovtypass

R1(config-line)# exec-timeout 5 0
R1(config-line)# login
```

d. Repeat these configurations on both R2 and R3.

Step 9: Enable HTTP server and HTTP server secure.

Enabling these services allows the router to be managed using the GUI and a web browser:

```
R1(config)# ip http server
```

Step 10: Encrypt clear text passwords.

a. Use the **service password-encryption** command to encrypt the console, aux, and vty passwords:

```
R1(config)# service password-encryption
```

b. Issue the **show run** command. Can you read the console, aux, and vty passwords? Why or why not? ____

c. Repeat this configuration on both R2 and R3.

Step 11: Save the basic running configuration for all three routers.

Save the running configuration to the startup configuration from the privileged EXEC prompt:

```
R1# copy running-config startup-config
```

Task 2: Use the Nmap Port Scanner to Determine Router Vulnerabilities

In this task, you determine open ports or services running on R1 using Nmap, before configuring a firewall.

Step 1: (Optional) Download and install Nmap and the Zenmap GUI front end.

Nmap (Network Mapper) is a free and open source utility for network exploration or security auditing.

a. If Nmap is already installed on PC-A and PC-C, go to Step 2. Otherwise, download the latest Windows version from http://nmap.org/download.html.

b. On PC-A and PC-C, run the Nmap setup utility and install all components listed, including the Zenmap GUI front end. Click **Next** to accept the defaults when prompted.

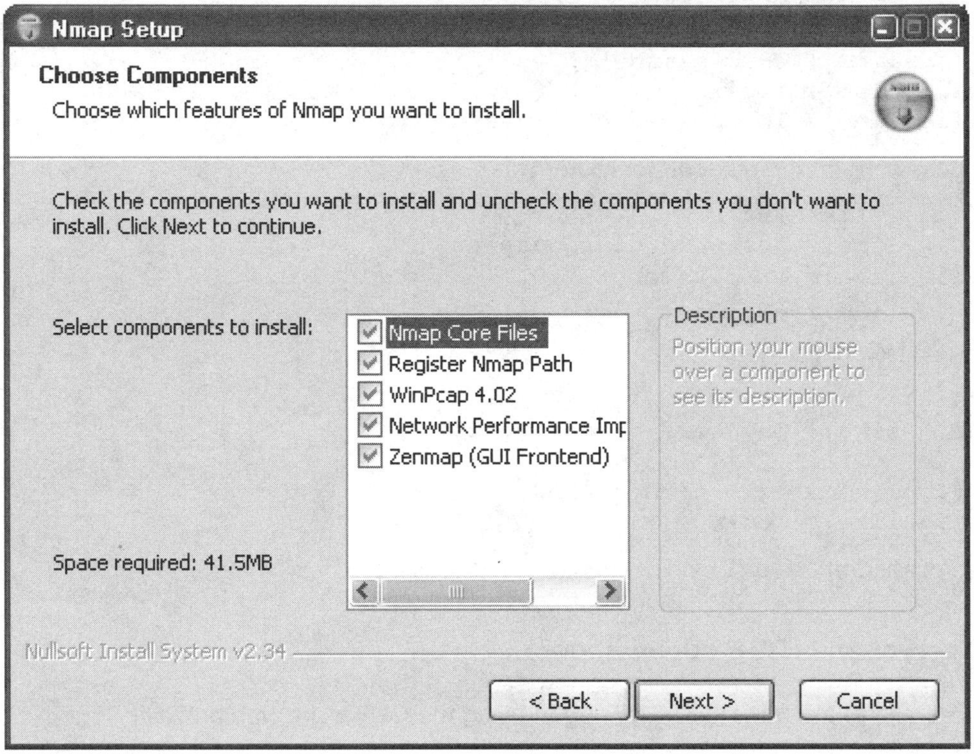

Step 2: Scan for open ports on R1 using Nmap from internal host PC-A.

a. From internal host PC-A, start the Nmap-Zenmap application and enter the IP address of the default gateway, R1 Fa0/1 (192.168.1.1), as the **Target**. Accept the default Nmap command entered for you in the **Command** window and use the **Intense scan** profile.

Note: If the PC is running a personal firewall you might need to turn it off temporarily to obtain accurate test results.

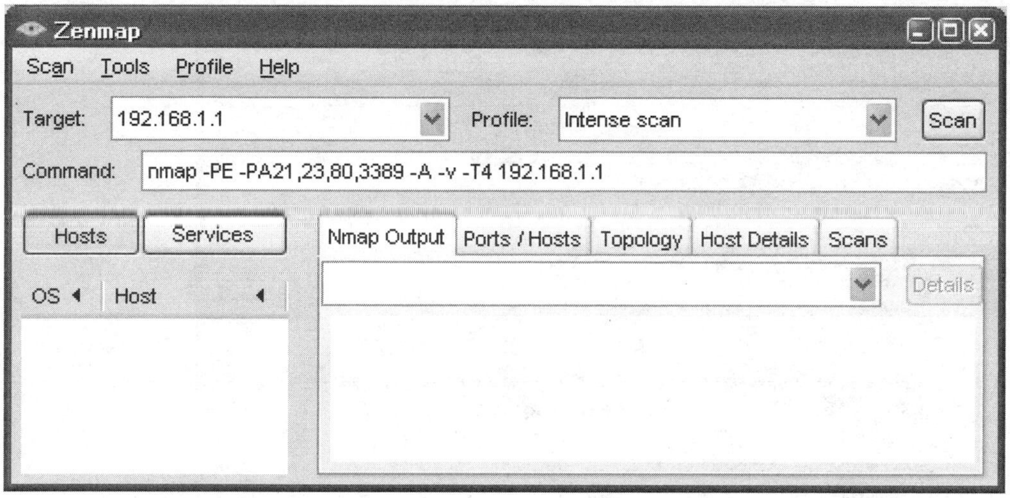

b. Click the **Scan** button to begin the scan of R1 from internal host PC-A. Allow some time for the scan to complete. The next two screens show the entire output of the scan after scrolling.

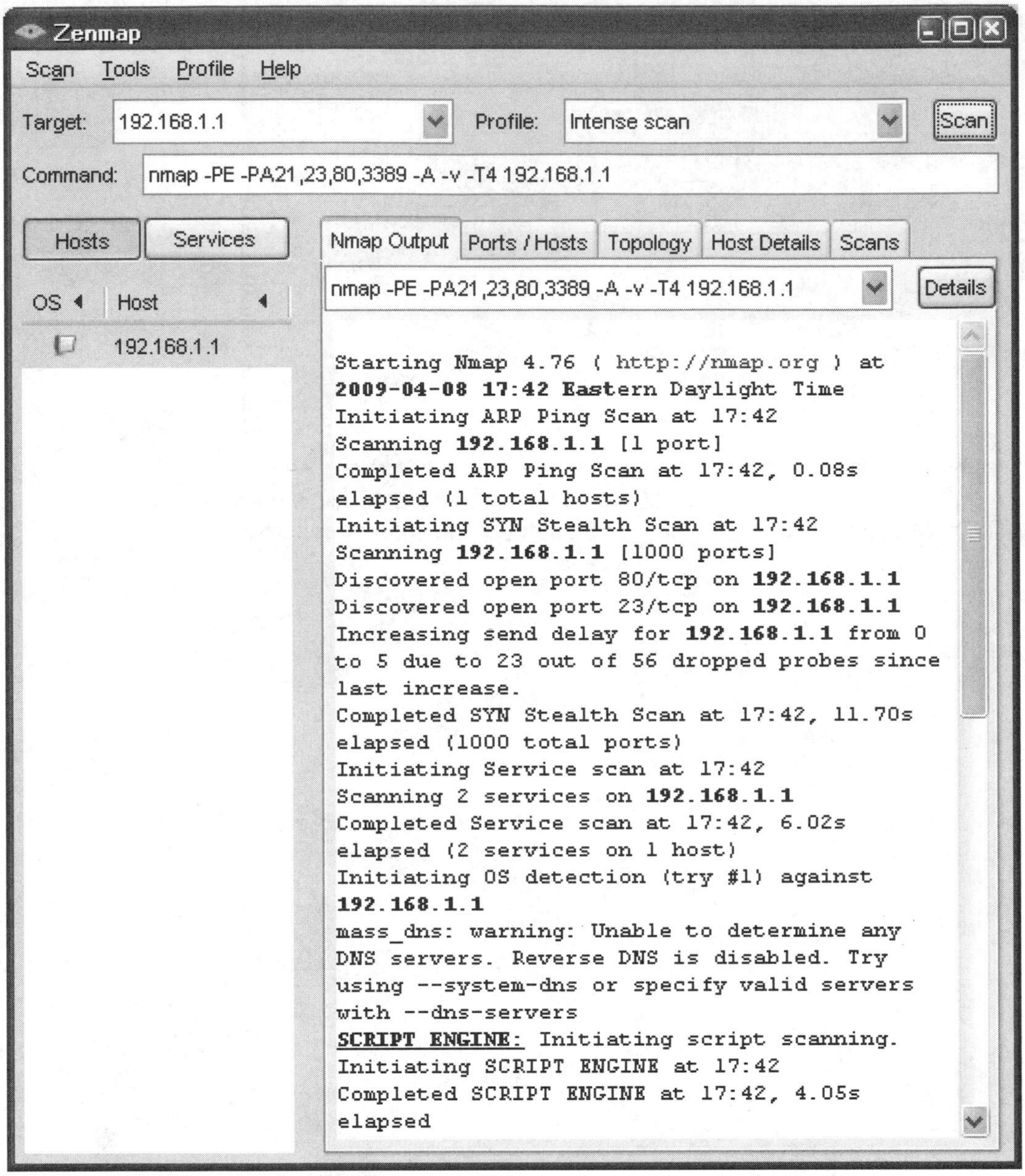
Zenmap
Scan Tools Profile Help
Target: 192.168.1.1
Profile: Intense scan
Scan
Command: nmap -PE -PA21,23,80,3389 -A -v -T4 192.168.1.1
Hosts
Services
OS
Host
192.168.1.1
Nmap Output
Ports / Hosts
Topology
Host Details
Scans
nmap -PE -PA21,23,80,3389 -A -v -T4 192.168.1.1
Details
Starting Nmap 4.76 (http://nmap.org) at
2009-04-08 17:42 Eastern Daylight Time
Initiating ARP Ping Scan at 17:42
Scanning 192.168.1.1 [1 port]
Completed ARP Ping Scan at 17:42, 0.08s
elapsed (1 total hosts)
Initiating SYN Stealth Scan at 17:42
Scanning 192.168.1.1 [1000 ports]
Discovered open port 80/tcp on 192.168.1.1
Discovered open port 23/tcp on 192.168.1.1
Increasing send delay for 192.168.1.1 from 0
to 5 due to 23 out of 56 dropped probes since
last increase.
Completed SYN Stealth Scan at 17:42, 11.70s
elapsed (1000 total ports)
Initiating Service scan at 17:42
Scanning 2 services on 192.168.1.1
Completed Service scan at 17:42, 6.02s
elapsed (2 services on 1 host)
Initiating OS detection (try #1) against
192.168.1.1
mass_dns: warning: Unable to determine any
DNS servers. Reverse DNS is disabled. Try
using --system-dns or specify valid servers
with --dns-servers
SCRIPT ENGINE: Initiating script scanning.
Initiating SCRIPT ENGINE at 17:42
Completed SCRIPT ENGINE at 17:42, 4.05s
elapsed

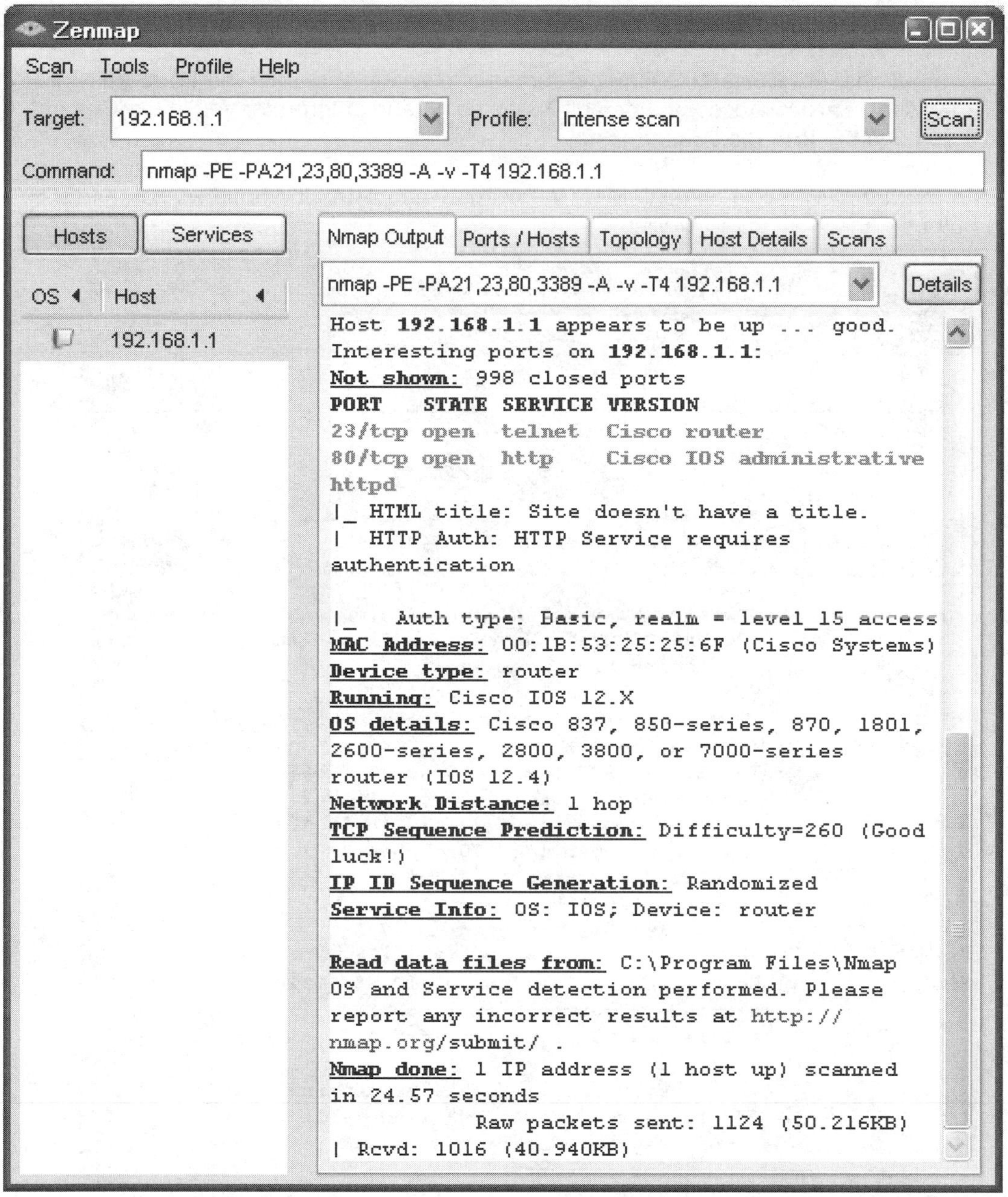

c. Click the **Service** button in the upper-left side of the screen.

What ports are open on R1 Fa0/1 from the perspective of internal host PC-A?

____

What is the MAC address of the R1 Fa0/1 interface?

____

For R1, what type of device and what OS version does Nmap detect?

____

Step 3: Scan for open ports on R1 using Nmap from external host PC-C.

a. From external host PC-C, start the Nmap-Zenmap application and enter the IP address of R1 S0/0/0 (10.1.1.1) as the **Target**. Accept the default Nmap command entered for you in the Command window and use the **Intense scan** profile.

b. Click the **Scan** button. Allow some time for the scan to complete. The next two screens show the entire output of the scan after scrolling.

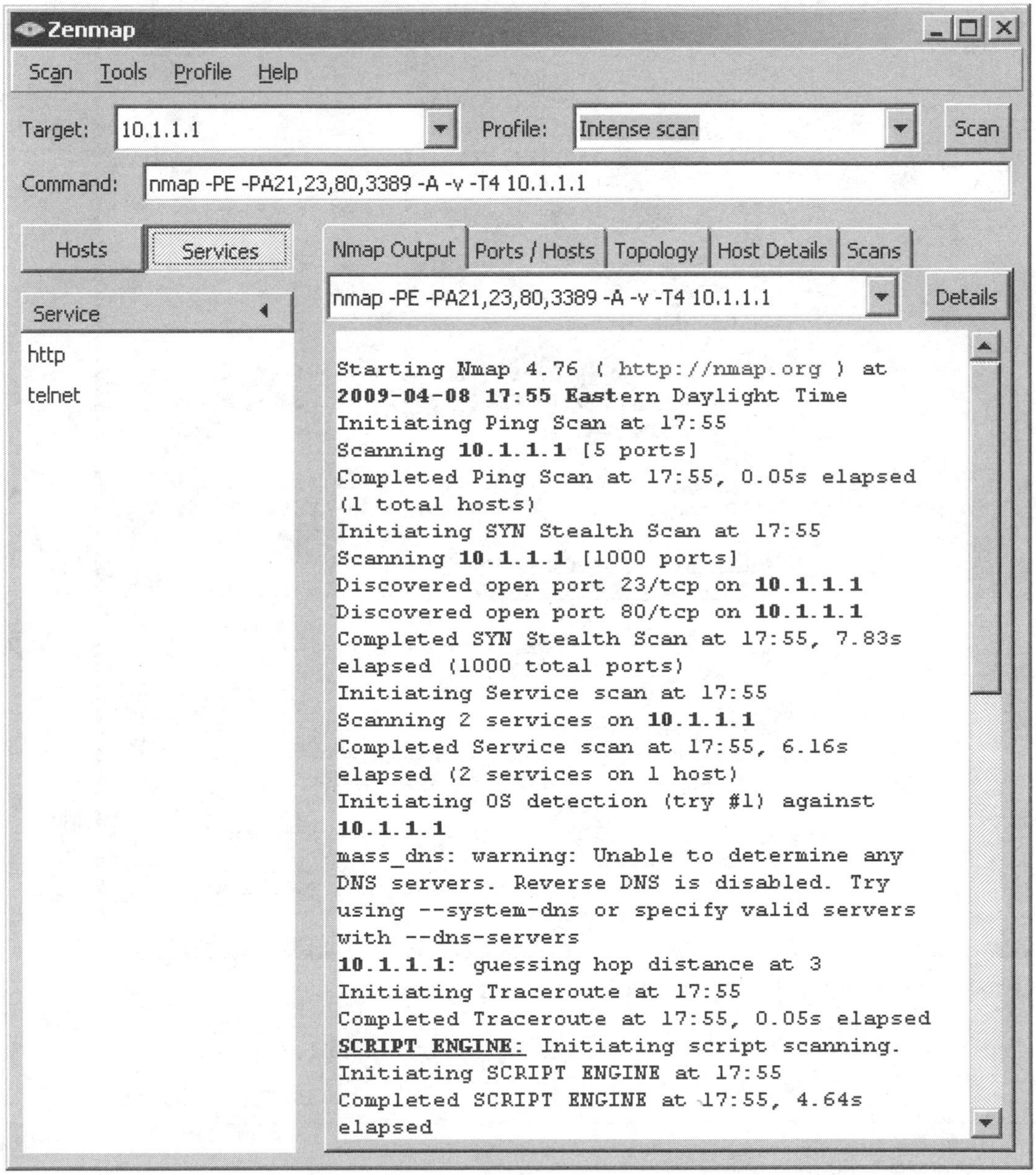

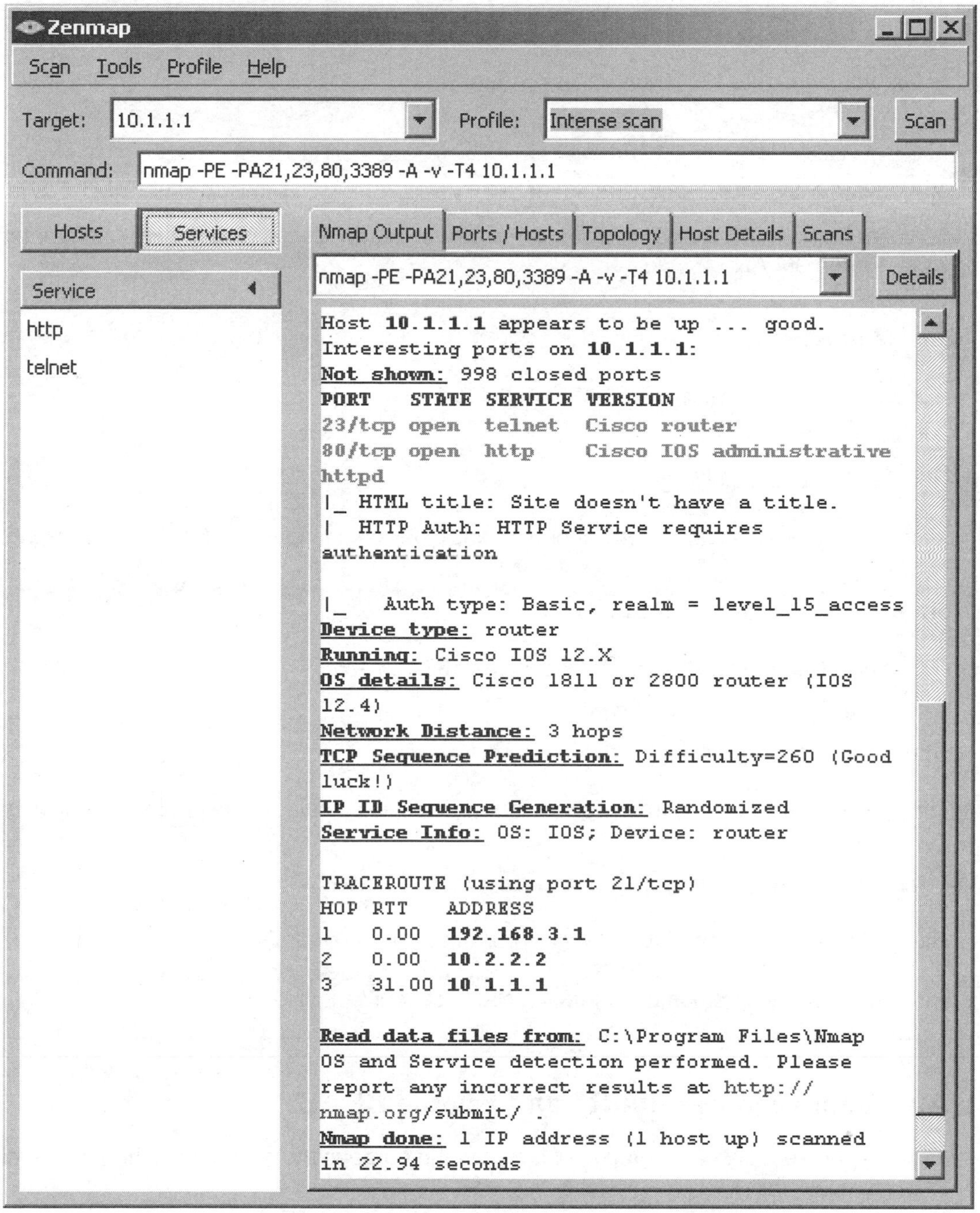

c. Click the **Services** button below the Command entry field. What services are running and available on R1 from the perspective of PC-C? ______________________________

d. In the Nmap scan output, refer to the TRACEROUTE information. How many hops are between PC-C and R1 and through what IP addresses did the scan have to go to reach R1?

____

Note: In Part 2 of this lab, you configure a CBAC firewall on R1 and then run Nmap again to test access from external host PC-C to R1.

Part 2: Configuring a Context-Based Access Control (CBAC) Firewall

In Part 2 of this lab, you configure CBAC on R1 using AutoSecure. You then review and test the resulting configuration.

Task 1: Verify Access to the R1 LAN from R2

In this task, you verify that with no firewall in place, the external router R2 can ping the R1 S0/0/0 interface and PC-A on the R1 internal LAN.

Step 1: Ping from R2 to R1.

a. From R2, ping the R1interface S0/0/0 at IP address 10.1.1.1:

```
R2# ping 10.1.1.1
```

b. Were the results successful? _____

If the pings are not successful, troubleshoot the basic device configurations before continuing.

Step 2: Ping from R2 to PC-A on the R1 LAN.

a. From R2, ping PC-A on the R1 LAN at IP address 192.168.1.3:

```
R2# ping 192.168.1.3
```

b. Were the results successful? _____

If the pings are not successful, troubleshoot the basic device configurations before continuing.

Step 3: Display the R1 running config prior to using AutoSecure.

a. Issue the **show run** command to review the current basic configuration on R1.

b. Are there any security commands related to access control?

____

Task 2: Use AutoSecure to Secure R1 and Enable CBAC

AutoSecure simplifies the security configuration of a router and hardens the router configuration. In this task, you run AutoSecure and enable CBAC during the process.

Step 1: Use the AutoSecure IOS feature to enable CBAC.

a. On R1, enter privileged EXEC mode using the **enable** command.

b. Issue the **auto secure** command on R1. Respond as shown in the following AutoSecure output to the AutoSecure questions and prompts. The responses are bolded.

Note: The focus here is the commands generated by AutoSecure for CBAC, so you do not enable all the potential security features that AutoSecure can provide, such as SSH access. Be sure to respond yes to the prompt Configure CBAC Firewall feature?.

```
R1# auto secure
                  --- AutoSecure Configuration ---
```

```
*** AutoSecure configuration enhances the security of the router, but
it will not make it absolutely resistant to all security attacks ***

AutoSecure will modify the configuration of your device. All
configuration changes will be shown. For a detailed explanation of how
the configuration changes enhance security and any possible side
effects, please refer to Cisco.com for
Autosecure documentation.
At any prompt you may enter '?' for help.
Use ctrl-c to abort this session at any prompt.

Gathering information about the router for AutoSecure

Is this router connected to internet? [no]:  yes
Enter the number of interfaces facing the internet [1]: 1
Interface          IP-Address     OK? Method Status
Protocol
FastEthernet0/0    unassigned     YES unset  administratively down down

FastEthernet0/1    192.168.1.1    YES manual up                    up

Serial0/0/0        10.1.1.1       YES SLARP  up                    up

Serial0/0/1        unassigned     YES unset  administratively down down

Enter the interface name that is facing the internet: serial0/0/0

Securing Management plane services...

Disabling service finger
Disabling service pad
Disabling udp & tcp small servers
Enabling service password encryption
Enabling service tcp-keepalives-in
Enabling service tcp-keepalives-out
Disabling the cdp protocol

Disabling the bootp server
Disabling the http server
Disabling the finger service
Disabling source routing
Disabling gratuitous arp

Here is a sample Security Banner to be shown
at every access to device. Modify it to suit your
enterprise requirements.

Authorized Access only
  This system is the property of So-&-So-Enterprise.
  UNAUTHORIZED ACCESS TO THIS DEVICE IS PROHIBITED.
  You must have explicit permission to access this
  device. All activities performed on this device
  are logged. Any violations of access policy will result
  in disciplinary action.

Enter the security banner {Put the banner between
k and k, where k is any character}:
```

```
$ Unauthorized Access Prohibited $

Enable secret is either not configured or
 is the same as enable password
Enter the new enable secret: cisco12345
Confirm the enable secret : cisco12345
Enter the new enable password: cisco67890
Confirm the enable password: cisco67890

Configuration of local user database
Enter the username: admin
Enter the password: cisco12345
Confirm the password: cisco12345
Configuring AAA local authentication
Configuring Console, Aux and VTY lines for
local authentication, exec-timeout, and transport
Securing device against Login Attacks
Configure the following parameters

Blocking Period when Login Attack detected: 60

Maximum Login failures with the device: 2

Maximum time period for crossing the failed login attempts: 30

Configure SSH server? [yes]: no

Configuring interface specific AutoSecure services
Disabling the following ip services on all interfaces:

 no ip redirects
 no ip proxy-arp
 no ip unreachables
 no ip directed-broadcast
 no ip mask-reply
Disabling mop on Ethernet interfaces

Securing Forwarding plane services...

Enabling CEF (This might impact the memory requirements for your
platform)
Enabling unicast rpf on all interfaces connected
to internet

Configure CBAC Firewall feature? [yes/no]: yes

This is the configuration generated:

no service finger
no service pad
no service udp-small-servers
no service tcp-small-servers
service password-encryption
service tcp-keepalives-in
service tcp-keepalives-out
no cdp run
no ip bootp server
```

```
no ip http server
no ip finger
no ip source-route
no ip gratuitous-arps
no ip identd
banner motd ^C Unauthorized Access Prohibited ^C
security authentication failure rate 10 log
enable secret 5 $1$m.de$Mp5tQr/I8W5VhuQoG6AoA1
enable password 7 05080F1C2243185E415C47
username admin password 7 02050D4808095E731F1A5C
aaa new-model
aaa authentication login local_auth local
line con 0
 login authentication local_auth
 exec-timeout 5 0
 transport output telnet
line aux 0
 login authentication local_auth
 exec-timeout 10 0
 transport output telnet
line vty 0 4
 login authentication local_auth
 transport input telnet
line tty 1
 login authentication local_auth
 exec-timeout 15 0
login block-for 60 attempts 2 within 30
service timestamps debug datetime msec localtime show-timezone
service timestamps log datetime msec localtime show-timezone
logging facility local2
logging trap debugging
service sequence-numbers
logging console critical
logging buffered
interface FastEthernet0/0
 no ip redirects
 no ip proxy-arp
 no ip unreachables
 no ip directed-broadcast
 no ip mask-reply
 no mop enabled
interface FastEthernet0/1
 no ip redirects
 no ip proxy-arp
 no ip unreachables
 no ip directed-broadcast
 no ip mask-reply
 no mop enabled
interface Serial0/0/0
 no ip redirects
 no ip proxy-arp
 no ip unreachables
 no ip directed-broadcast
 no ip mask-reply
interface Serial0/0/1
 no ip redirects
 no ip proxy-arp
 no ip unreachables
```

```
 no ip directed-broadcast
 no ip mask-reply
interface Vlan1
 no ip redirects
 no ip proxy-arp
 no ip unreachables
 no ip directed-broadcast
 no ip mask-reply
 no mop enabled
access-list 100 permit udp any any eq bootpc
interface Serial0/0/0
 ip verify unicast source reachable-via rx allow-default 100
ip inspect audit-trail
ip inspect dns-timeout 7
ip inspect tcp idle-time 14400
ip inspect udp idle-time 1800
ip inspect name autosec_inspect cuseeme timeout 3600
ip inspect name autosec_inspect ftp timeout 3600
ip inspect name autosec_inspect http timeout 3600
ip inspect name autosec_inspect rcmd timeout 3600
ip inspect name autosec_inspect realaudio timeout 3600
ip inspect name autosec_inspect smtp timeout 3600
ip inspect name autosec_inspect tftp timeout 30
ip inspect name autosec_inspect udp timeout 15
ip inspect name autosec_inspect tcp timeout 3600
ip access-list extended autosec_firewall_acl
 permit udp any any eq bootpc
 deny ip any any
interface Serial0/0/0
 ip inspect autosec_inspect out
 ip access-group autosec_firewall_acl in
!
end

Apply this configuration to running-config? [yes]: yes

Applying the config generated to running-config

R1#
000043: *Dec 29 21:28:59.223 UTC: %AUTOSEC-1-MODIFIED: AutoSecure
configuration has been Modified on this device
```

Step 2: Configure the R1 firewall to allow EIGRP updates.

The AutoSecure CBAC firewall on R1 does not permit EIGRP hellos and neighbor associations to occur and, therefore, no updates can be sent or received. Because EIGRP updates are blocked, R1 does not know of the 10.2.2.0/30 or the 192.168.3.0/24 networks, and R2 does not know of the 192.168.1.0/24 network.

Note: When you configure the ZBF firewall on R3 in Part 3 of this lab, CCP gives the option of allowing EIGRP routing updates to be received by R3.

a. Display the Extended ACL named **autosec_firewall_acl**, which is applied to S0/0/0 inbound:

```
R1# show access-list autosec_firewall_acl
Extended IP access list autosec_firewall_acl
    10 permit udp any any eq bootpc
    20 deny ip any any (10 matches)
```

b. Notice the 10 matches (this number may vary) on ACL line 20. What is this a result of?

____

c. Configure R1 to allow EIGRP updates by adding a statement to the Extended ACL autosec_firewall_acl that permits the EIGRP protocol:

```
R1(config)# ip access-list extended autosec_firewall_acl
R1(config-ext-nacl)# 15 permit eigrp any any
R1(config-ext-nacl)# end
```

d. Display the Extended ACL autosec_firewall_acl again:

```
R1# show access-list autosec_firewall_acl
Extended IP access list autosec_firewall_acl
    10 permit udp any any eq bootpc
    15 permit eigrp any any (5)
    20 deny ip any any (10)
```

Notice that there is now some EIGRP packet activity for ACL statement 15.

Note: You can use the **`ip access-list`** command to create and edit both named and numbered ACLs (both standard and extended). The use of this command allows for the insertion of entries in the ACL by specifying unused line numbers (as shown in Step 3c). Also, you can remove existing lines in the ACL by specifying the name or number of the ACL and the then the line number of the entry to be deleted using the **`no`** version of the ACL command.

The **`ip access-list`** command provides greater flexibility than the earlier **`access-list`** command and is the preferred method of creating ACLs, in most cases. With the **`access-list`** command, a new ACL entry is, by default, appended to the end of the ACL and the ACL is not editable. In addition, the **`access-list`** command cannot be used with named ACLs.

Step 3: Save the running configuration.

Enter privileged EXEC mode using the **`enable`** command and provide the enable password **cisco12345**:

```
R1# copy run start
```

Step 4: Scan for open ports on R1 using Nmap from external host PC-C.

a. From external host PC-C, use Nmap-Zenmap to scan R1 at target IP address 10.1.1.1. Accept the default **`Nmap`** command entered for you in the Command window. Use the **Intense scan** profile.

b. Click the **Scan** button to being scanning R1.

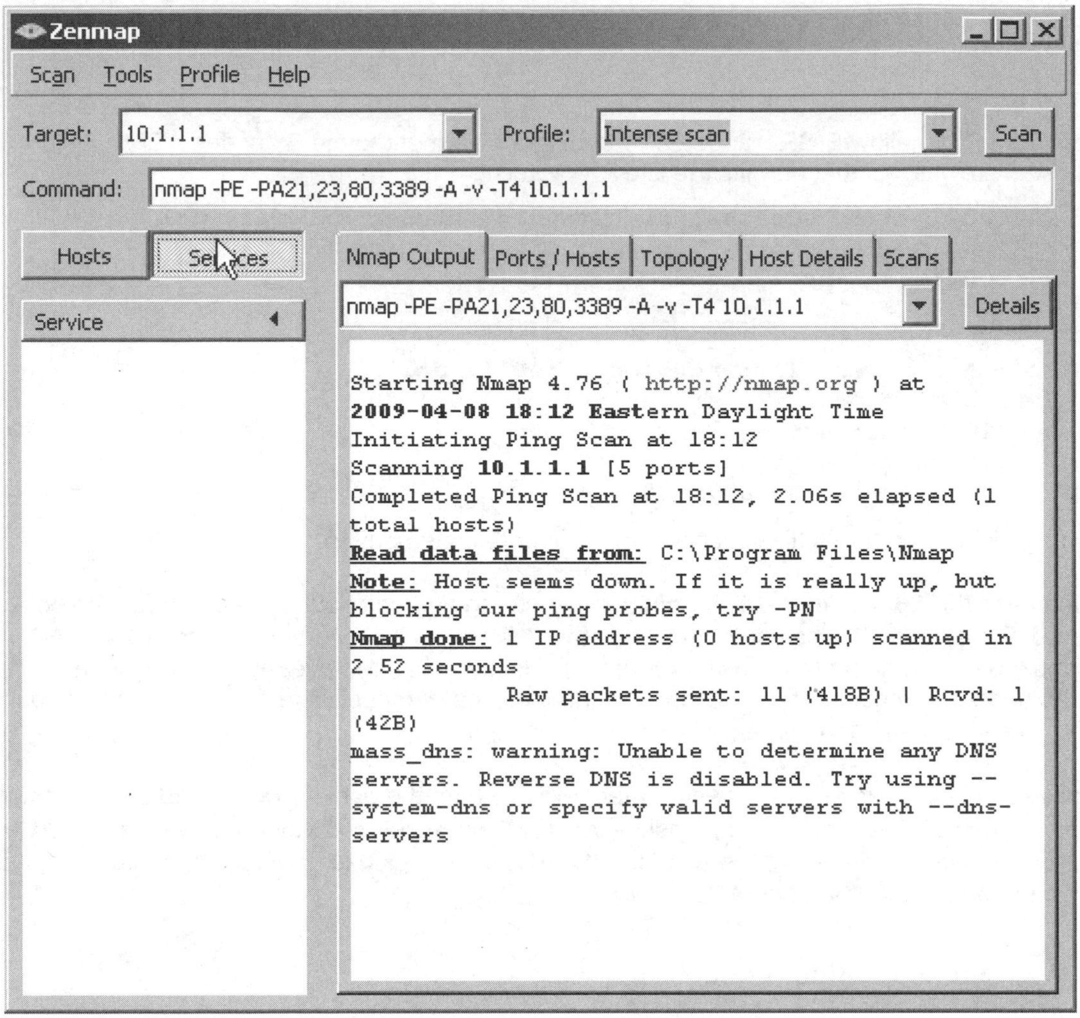

Now that the R1 CBAC firewall is in place, what services are available on R1 and what is the status of R1 from the perspective of external PC-C?

____

Task 3: Review the AutoSecure CBAC Configuration

Step 1: Review the commands that were delivered to router R1.

a. Display the running configuration for R1. The AutoSecure output should look similar to that shown in Task 2, Step 1.

b. What is the most common command issued that is related to CBAC?

____

c. CBAC creates rules to track TCP and UDP flows using the **`ip inspect name name protocol`** command. To what interface is the autosec_inspect name applied and in what direction?

____

Step 2: Display the protocols available with the `ip inspect` command.

To see the protocols available, enter the **ip inspect name** *name* command in global config mode, followed by a question mark (?).

Note: Most of the protocols listed are application layer protocols. Newer Cisco IOS versions have more protocols listed.

```
R1(config)# ip inspect name autosec_inspect ?
802-11-iapp          IEEE 802.11 WLANs WG IAPP
ace-svr              ACE Server/Propagation
appfw                Application Firewall
appleqtc             Apple QuickTime
bgp                  Border Gateway Protocol
biff                 Bliff mail notification
bittorrent           bittorrent
<Output Omitted>
```

How many protocols can be configured for inspection? ______________________________

Refer to the running configuration output or the AutoSecure output in Task 2, Step 1. Which protocols did AutoSecure configure to be inspected as they leave the S0/0/0 interface?

____

To which interface is the ACL autosec_firewall_acl applied and in which direction? ______________

What is the purpose of the ACL autosec_firewall_acl?

____

Task 4: Verify CBAC Functionality

For the protocols identified to be inspected, the CBAC firewall allows return traffic for connections initiated from the inside, but blocks all other connections from the outside.

Step 1: From PC-A, ping the R1 internal LAN interface.

From PC-A, ping R1 interface Fa0/1 at IP address 192.168.1.1:

```
C:\> ping 192.168.1.1
```

Were the pings successful? Why or why not?

____

Step 2: From PC-A, ping the R2 external WAN interface.

From PC-A, ping the R2 interface S0/0/0 at IP address 10.1.1.2:

```
C:\> ping 10.1.1.2
```

Were the pings successful? Why or why not?

____

Step 3: Add ICMP to the autosec_inspect list.

From global config mode, configure R1 to inspect ICMP and allow ICMP echo replies from outside hosts:

```
R1(config)# ip inspect name autosec_inspect icmp timeout 5
```

Step 4: From PC-A, ping the R2 external WAN interface.

a. From PC-A, ping the R2 interface S0/0/0 at IP address 10.1.1.2:

```
C:\> ping 10.1.1.2
```

Were the pings successful? Why or why not?

____

b. Remove ICMP from the inspect list. This restores the CBAC configuration to the one generated by AutoSecure.

```
R1(config)# no ip inspect name autosec_inspect icmp timeout 5
```

Step 5: Test Telnet access from R2 to R1.

From external router R2, telnet to R1 at IP address 10.1.1.1:

```
R2> telnet 10.1.1.1
Trying 10.1.1.1 ...
% Connection timed out; remote host not responding
```

Was the telnetting successful? Why or why not?

____

Step 6: Configure R1 to allow Telnet access from external hosts.

a. Display the Extended ACL named **autosec_firewall_acl** that is applied to S0/0/0 inbound:

```
R1# show access-list autosec_firewall_acl
Extended IP access list autosec_firewall_acl
    10 permit udp any any eq bootpc
    15 permit eigrp any any (15)
    20 deny ip any any (57 matches)
```

b. Notice the 57 matches on ACL line 20. What is this a result of?

____

c. Configure R1 to allow Telnet access by adding a statement to the Extended ACL autosec_firewall_acl that permits TCP port 23 (Telnet):

```
R1(config)# ip access-list extended autosec_firewall_acl
R1(config-ext-nacl)# 18 permit tcp any any eq 23
R1(config-ext-nacl)# end
```

d. From external router R2, telnet again to R1 at IP address 10.1.1.1:

```
R2> telnet 10.1.1.1
Trying 10.1.1.1 ... Open

Unauthorized Access Prohibited
```

```
User Access Verification

Username: admin
Password: cisco12345

R1>
```

e. From the Telnet session on R1, display the modified Extended ACL autosec_firewall_acl:

```
R1> show access-list autosec_firewall_acl
Extended IP access list autosec_firewall_acl
    10 permit udp any any eq bootpc
    15 permit eigrp any any (25)
    18 permit tcp any any eq telnet (12 matches)
    20 deny ip any any (57 matches)
```

f. Notice the new line 18 in the ACL and the 12 matches. What is this a result of?

____

g. Remove Telnet external access from the R1 firewall ACL:

```
R1(config)# ip access-list extended autosec_firewall_acl
R1(config-ext-nacl)# no 18 permit tcp any any eq telnet
R1(config-ext-nacl)# end
```

Note: SSH is recommended instead of Telnet because it provides a more secure way to allow remote administration access to a router or other networking devices. SSH provides encrypted communication; however, some additional configuration is required to support the SSH connection. See Chapter 2 Lab A for the procedure to enable SSH. For added security, configure SSH as the only input transport on the vty lines and remove Telnet as an input transport. Allowing SSH access to R1 from external hosts also requires adding a statement to the Extended ACL autosec_firewall_acl that permits TCP port 22 (SSH).

Step 7: Test Telnet access from internal PC-A to external router R2.

a. From PC-A, telnet to R2 at IP address 10.1.1.2:

```
C:\> telnet 10.1.1.2
```

Was the Telnet attempt successful? Why or why not?

____

b. Log in to R2 by providing the vty password of ciscovtypass.

Leave the Telnet session open.

Task 5: Verify CBAC Configuration and Operation

Step 1: Display CBAC inspection information.

a. Use the **show ip inspect all** command to see the configuration and inspection status.

Note: The end of the command output shows the established sessions and the inspected TCP Telnet connection between PC-A and R2.

```
R1# show ip inspect all
Session audit trail is enabled
Session alert is enabled
```

```
one-minute (sampling period) thresholds are [unlimited : unlimited]
connections
max-incomplete sessions thresholds are [unlimited : unlimited]
max-incomplete tcp connections per host is unlimited. Block-time 0
minute.
tcp synwait-time is 30 sec -- tcp finwait-time is 5 sec
tcp idle-time is 14400 sec -- udp idle-time is 1800 sec
tcp reassembly queue length 16; timeout 5 sec; memory-limit 1024 kilo
bytes
dns-timeout is 7 sec
Inspection Rule Configuration
 Inspection name autosec_inspect
    cuseeme alert is on audit-trail is on timeout 3600
    ftp alert is on audit-trail is on timeout 3600
    http alert is on audit-trail is on timeout 3600
    rcmd alert is on audit-trail is on timeout 3600
    rcmd alert is on audit-trail is on timeout 3600
    smtp max-data 20000000 alert is on audit-trail is on timeout 3600
    tftp alert is on audit-trail is on timeout 30
    udp alert is on audit-trail is on timeout 15
    tcp alert is on audit-trail is on timeout 3600

Interface Configuration
 Interface Serial0/0/0
  Inbound inspection rule is not set
  Outgoing inspection rule is autosec_inspect
    cuseeme alert is on audit-trail is on timeout 3600
    ftp alert is on audit-trail is on timeout 3600
    http alert is on audit-trail is on timeout 3600
    rcmd alert is on audit-trail is on timeout 3600
    realaudio alert is on audit-trail is on timeout 3600
    smtp max-data 20000000 alert is on audit-trail is on timeout 3600
    tftp alert is on audit-trail is on timeout 30
    udp alert is on audit-trail is on timeout 15
    tcp alert is on audit-trail is on timeout 3600
  Inbound access list is autosec_firewall_acl
  Outgoing access list is not set

Established Sessions
 Session 6556C128 (192.168.1.3:1185)=>(10.1.1.2:23) tcp SIS_OPEN
```

In the Established Sessions section, what is the source IP address and port number for Session 655C128? ____________________

What is the destination IP address and port number for Session 655C128?

____

Step 2: View detailed session information.

a. View detailed session information using the **show ip inspect sessions detail** command on R1:

```
R1# show ip inspect sessions detail
Established Sessions
 Session 6556C128 (192.168.1.3:1185)=>(10.1.1.2:23) tcp SIS_OPEN
  Created 00:00:09, Last heard 00:00:02
  Bytes sent (initiator:responder) [45:154]
```

```
    In  SID 10.1.1.2[23:23]=>192.168.1.3[1185:1185] on ACL
  autosec_firewall_acl  (19 matches)
```

b. Close the Telnet connection when you finish verifying CBAC operation.

Part 3: Configuring a Zone-Based Firewall (ZBF) Using CCP

In Part 3 of this lab, you configure a zone-based firewall (ZBF) on R3 by using CCP.

Task 1: Verify Access to the R3 LAN from R2

In this task, you verify that with no firewall in place, external router R2 can access the R3 S0/0/1 interface and PC-C on the R3 internal LAN.

Step 1: Ping from R2 to R3.

From R2, ping the R3 interface S0/0/1 at IP address 10.2.2.1:

```
R2# ping 10.2.2.1
```

Were the results successful? _____

If the pings are not successful, troubleshoot the basic device configurations before continuing.

Step 2: Ping from R2 to PC-C on the R3 LAN.

From R2, ping PC-C on the R3 LAN at IP address 192.168.3.3:

```
R2# ping 192.168.3.3
```

Were the results successful? _____

If the pings are not successful, troubleshoot the basic device configurations before continuing.

Step 3: Display the R3 running config before starting CCP.

a. Issue the **show run** command to review the current basic configuration on R3.

b. Verify the R3 basic configuration as performed in Part 1 of the lab. Are there any security commands related to access control? ______________________________

Task 2: Create a Zone-Based Policy Firewall

In this task, you use CCP to create a zone-based policy firewall on R3.

Step 1: Configure the enable secret password and HTTP router access before starting CCP.

a. From the CLI, configure the enable secret password for use with CCP on R3:

```
R3(config)# enable secret cisco12345
```

b. Enable the HTTP server on R3:

```
R3(config)# ip http server
```

c. Add admin user to the local database:

```
R3(config)# username admin privilege 15 secret cisco12345
```

d. Have CCP use the local database to authenticate web sessions:

```
R3(config)# ip http authentication local
```

Step 2: Access CCP and discover R3.

a. Start CCP on PC-C. In the Manage Devices window, enter R3 IP address **192.168.3.1** in the first IP Address field. Enter **admin** in the Username field, and **cisco12345** in the Password field.

b. At the CCP Dashboard, click the **Discover** button to discover and connect to R3. If discovery fails, click the **Discovery Details** button to determine the problem.

Step 3: Use the CCP Firewall wizard to configure a zone-based firewall.

a. Click **Monitor > Security > Firewall Status**. What is the state of the Firewall Policies?

____

b. Click **Configure > Security > Firewall > Firewall** and read through the overview descriptions for the Basic and Advanced Firewall options. What are some of the key differences?

____

____

____

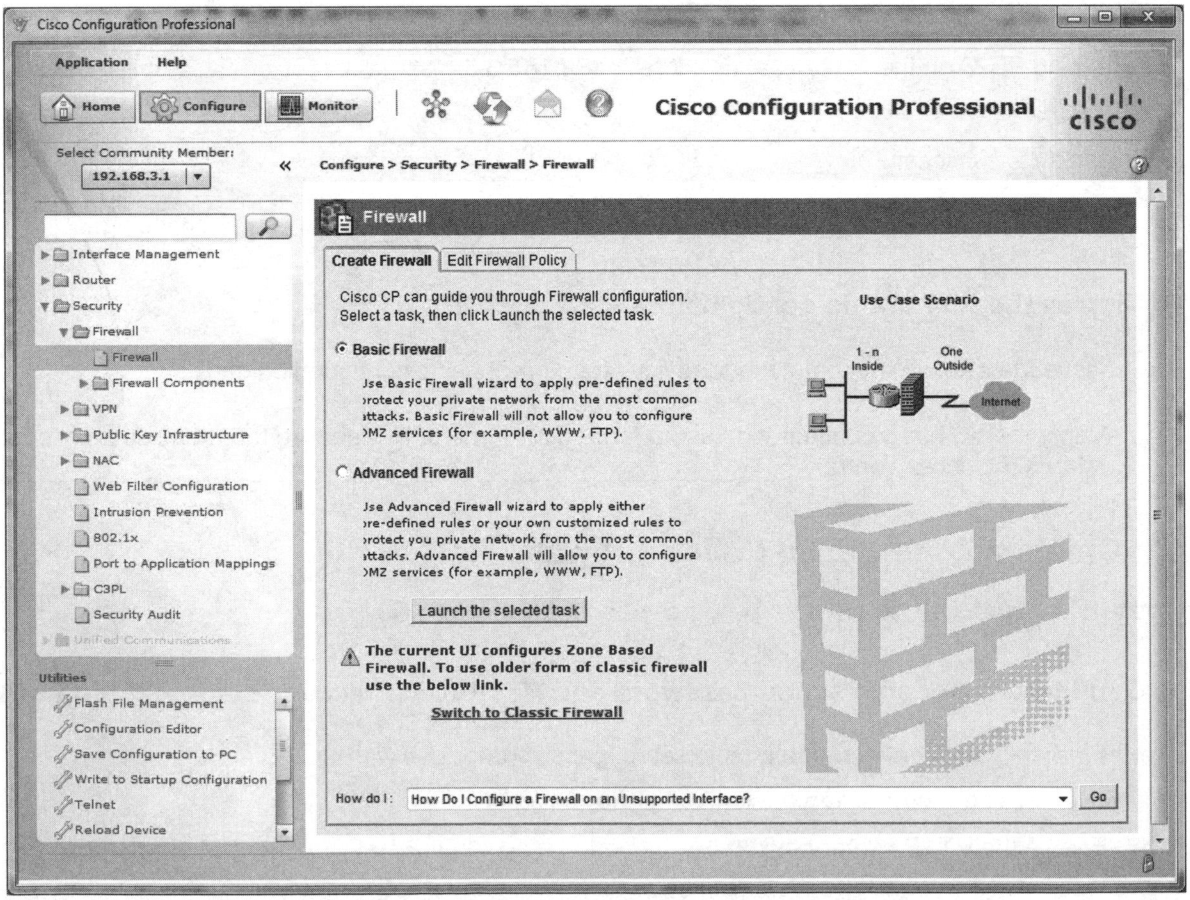

c. Choose **Basic Firewall** and click the **Launch the Selected Task** button.

d. In the Basic Firewall Configuration Wizard window, familiarize yourself with what the Basic Firewall does. What does the Basic Firewall do with traffic from outside zones to inside zones? _________

e. Click **Next** to continue.

f. Check the **Inside (Trusted)** check box for **FastEthernet0/1** and the **Outside (Untrusted)** check box for **Serial0/0/1**. Click **Next**.

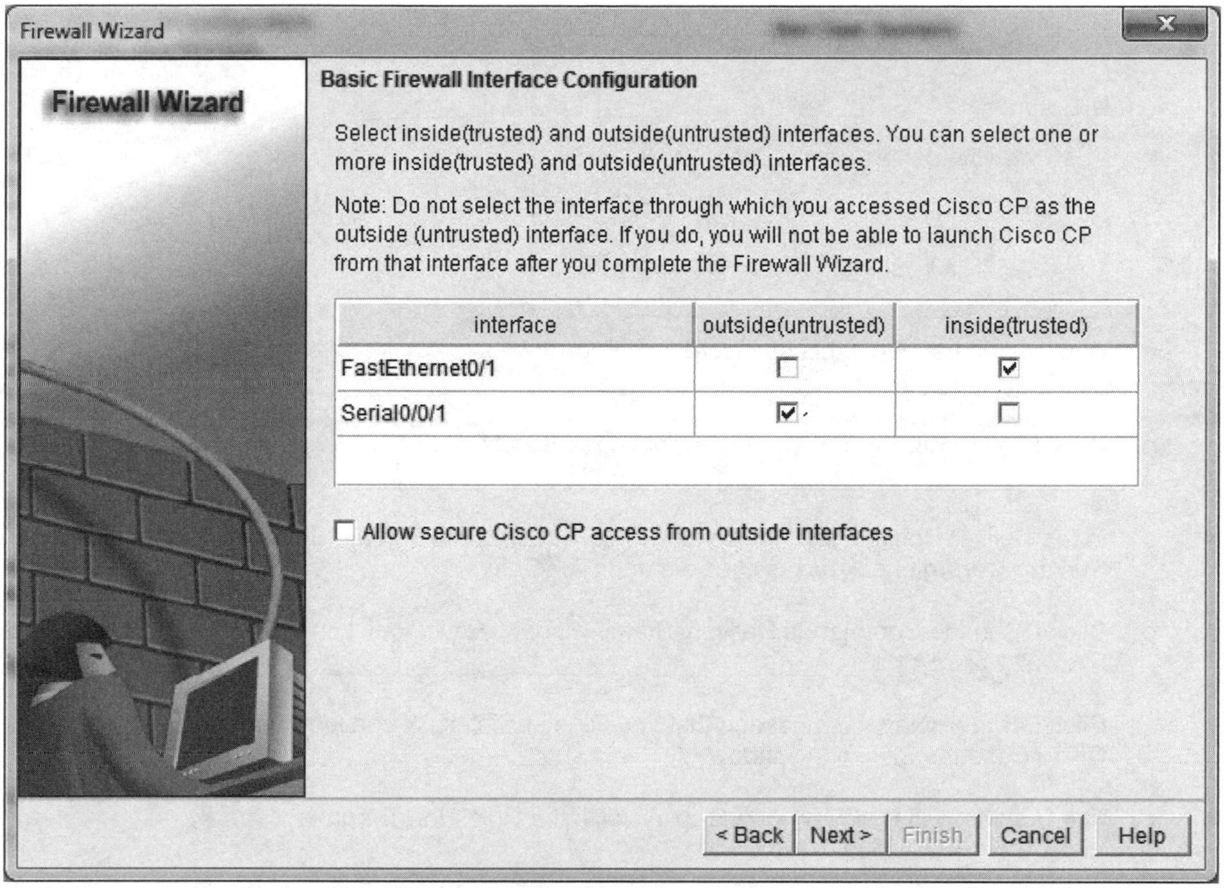

g. Click **OK** when the warning is displayed informing you that you cannot launch CCP from the S0/0/1 interface after the Firewall wizard completes.

h. Move the slider between High, Medium, and Low security to familiarize yourself with what each provides. What is the main difference between High security and Medium or Low security?

____

____

____

i. Move the slider to Low Security and click the **Preview Commands** button to preview the commands that are delivered to the router. When you are finished reviewing the commands, click **Close** and then click **Next**.

j. Review the Firewall Configuration Summary. What does this display provide?

____

k. Click **Finish** to complete the Firewall wizard.

l. When the Routing traffic configuration window displays, ensure that the check box **Allow EIGRP updates come through the firewall** is checked and click **OK**.

Note: This screen displays only if a dynamic routing protocol is configured.

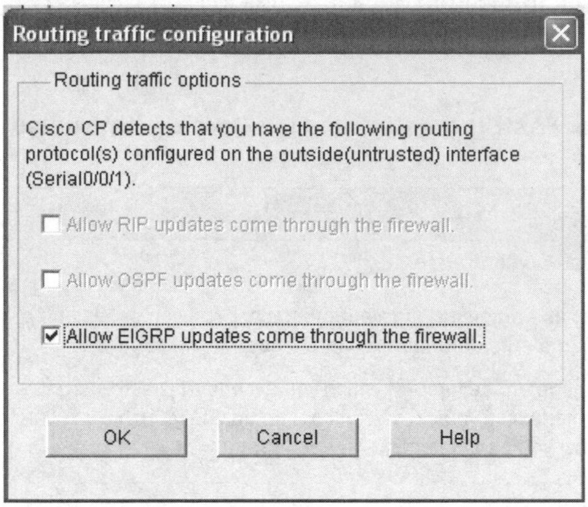

m. What would happen if this box were not checked?

____

n. In addition to EIGRP, for what other routing protocols does the firewall allow updates?

____

o. In the Deliver Configuration to Router window, make sure that the **Save Running Config to Router's Startup Config** check box is checked and click **Deliver**.

p. Click **OK** in the Commands Delivery Status window. How many commands were generated by the Firewall wizard? ____

q. Click **OK** to display the message that you have successfully configured a firewall on the router. Click **OK** to close the message window.

r. The Edit Firewall Policy window displays with the Rule Flow Diagram.

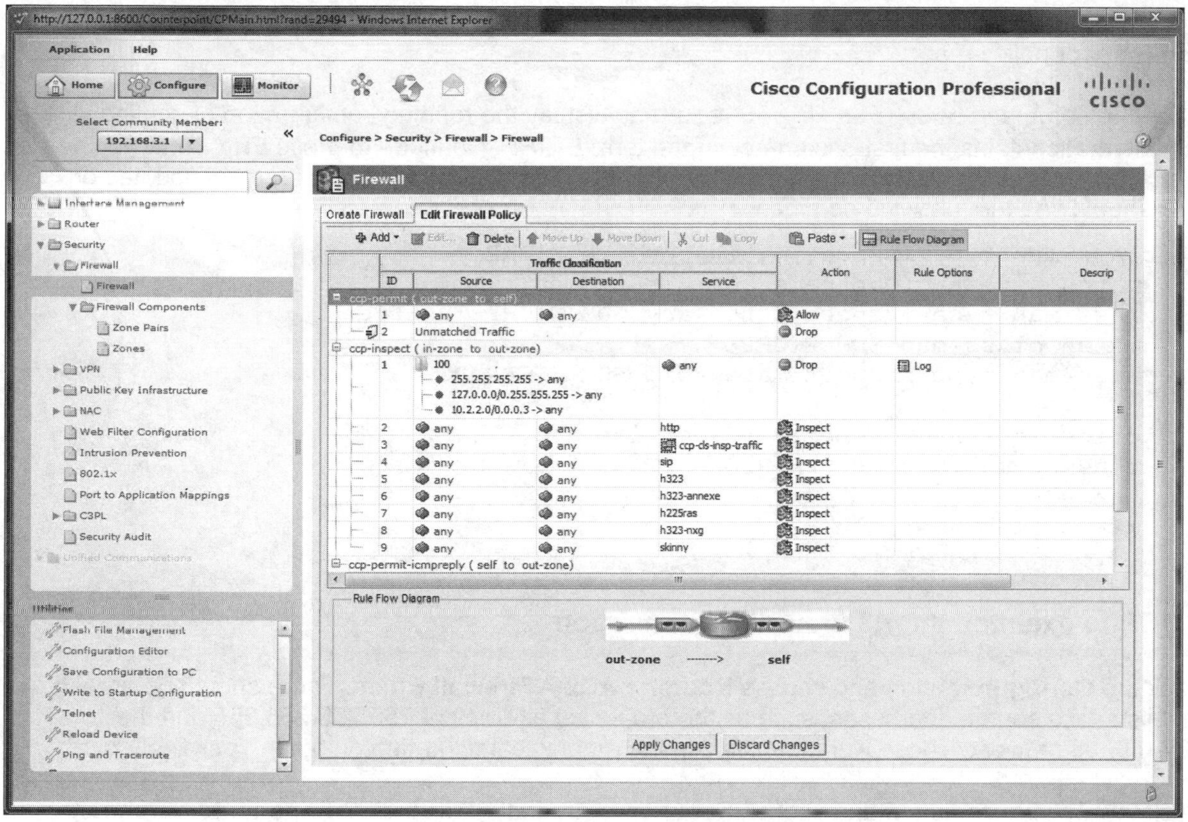

s. In the Rule Flow Diagram, locate access list 100 (folder icon). What action is taken and what rule options are applied for traffic with an invalid source address in the 127.0.0.0/8 address range?

____

Task 3: Review the Zone-Based Firewall Configuration

Step 1: Examine the R3 running configuration with the CLI.

a. From the R3 CLI, display the running configuration to view the changes that the CCP Basic Firewall wizard made to the router.

   The following commands are related to ACL 100 and class-map ccp-invalid-source:

```
class-map type inspect match-all ccp-invalid-src
 match access-group 100

policy-map type inspect ccp-inspect
 class type inspect ccp-invalid-src
  drop log
<output omitted>

access-list 100 remark CCP_ACL Category=128
access-list 100 permit ip host 255.255.255.255 any
access-list 100 permit ip 127.0.0.0 0.255.255.255 any
access-list 100 permit ip 10.2.2.0 0.0.0.3 any
```

b. In ACL 100, notice that the source addresses listed are permitted. The ACL uses **permit** statements to identify these addresses as a group so that they can be matched with the **class-map type inspect match-all ccp-invalid-src** command and then dropped and logged by the **class**

type inspect ccp-invalid-src command, which is one of the class types specified for the **ccp-inspect** policy-map.

c. Issue the command **show run | beg EIGRP** to display the running configuration beginning with the line that contains the first occurrence of the term *EIGRP*. Continue to press **Enter** until you see all the commands in the firewall configuration that are related to EIGRP routing protocol updates on R3. You should see the following commands:

```
class-map type inspect match-any SDM_EIGRP
 match access-group name SDM_EIGRP
class-map type inspect match-any SDM_EIGRP_TRAFFIC
 match class-map SDM_EIGRP
class-map type inspect match-all SDM_EIGRP_PT

policy-map type inspect ccp-permit
 class type inspect SDM_EIGRP_PT
  pass
 class class-default
  drop
```

Step 2: Use CCP to examine the R3 firewall configuration.

a. Click the **Configure** button and choose **Router > ACL > Firewall Rules**. There should be an ACL that lists fake source addresses, such as the broadcast address of 255.255.255.255 and the 127.0.0.0/8 network. These were identified in the running configuration output in Task 3, Step 1b.

b. Click the **Configure** button and choose **Security > Firewall > Firewall Components > Zones** to verify the zones configuration. What interfaces are listed and in what zone is each?

____

c. Click **Configure** and choose **Security > Firewall > Firewall Components > Zones Pairs** to verify zone pair configuration. Fill in the following information.

Zone Pair	Source	Destination	Policy

d. What is C3PL short for? ____

e. Click **Configure** and choose **Security > C3PL > Class Map > Inspection**. How many class maps were created by the CCP Firewall wizard? _____

f. Choose **Security > C3PL > Policy Map > Protocol Inspection**. How many policy maps were created by the CCP Firewall Wizard? _____

g. Examine the details for the policy map ccp-permit that is applied to the ccp-zp-out-self zone pair. Fill in the following information. List the action for the traffic matching each of the class maps referenced within the ccp-permit policy map.

Match Class Name: ____________________ Action: ___________

Match Class Name: ____________________ Action: ___________

Task 4: Verify EIGRP Routing Functionality on R3

Step 1: Display the R3 routing table using the CLI.

In Task 2, Step 3, the Firewall Wizard configured the router to allow EIGRP updates. Verify that EIGRP messages are still being exchanged using the **show ip route** command and verify that there are still EIGRP learned routes in the routing table:

```
R3# show ip route
Codes: C - connected, S - static, R - RIP, M - mobile, B - BGP
       D - EIGRP, EX - EIGRP external, O - OSPF, IA - OSPF inter area
<Output omitted>

Gateway of last resort is not set

        10.0.0.0/30 is subnetted, 2 subnets
C          10.2.2.0 is directly connected, Serial0/0/1
D          10.1.1.0 [90/21024000] via 10.2.2.2, 00:34:12, Serial0/0/1
D       192.168.1.0/24 [90/21026560] via 10.2.2.2, 00:32:16, Serial0/0/1
C       192.168.3.0/24 is directly connected, FastEthernet0/1
```

Which networks has R3 learned via the EIGRP routing protocol? ______________________________

Task 5: Verify Zone-Based Firewall Functionality

Step 1: From PC-C, ping the R3 internal LAN interface.

From PC-C, ping the R3 interface Fa0/1 at IP address 192.168.3.1:

C:\> **ping 192.168.3.1**

Were the pings successful? Why or why not?

____

Step 2: From PC-C, ping the R2 external WAN interface.

From PC-C, ping the R2 interface S0/0/1 at IP address 10.2.2.2:

C:\> **ping 10.2.2.2**

Were the pings successful? Why or why not?

____

Step 3: From R2 ping PC-C.

From external router R2, ping PC-C at IP address 192.168.3.3:

R2# **ping 192.168.3.3**

Were the pings successful? Why or why not?

____

Step 4: Telnet from R2 to R3.

From router R2, telnet to R3 at IP address 10.2.2.1:

R2# **telnet 10.2.2.1**

```
Trying 10.2.2.1 ... Open

Trying 10.2.2.1 ...
% Connection timed out; remote host not responding
```

Why was telnetting unsuccessful? ______________________________

Step 5: Telnet from internal PC-C to external router R2.

a. From PC-C on the R3 internal LAN, telnet to R2 at IP address 10.2.2.2 and log in:

```
C:\> telnet 10.2.2.2

User Access verification
Password: ciscovtypass
```

b. With the Telnet session open from PC-C to R2, enter privileged EXEC mode with the **enable** command and password cisco12345.

c. Issue the command **show policy-map type inspect zone-pair session** on R3. Continue pressing **Enter** until you see an Inspect Established session section toward the end. Your output should look similar to the following:

```
Inspect

   Number of Established Sessions = 1
   Established Sessions
     Session 657344C0 (192.168.3.3:1274)=>(10.2.2.2:23) tacacs:tcp
SIS_OPEN
       Created 00:01:20, Last heard 00:01:13
       Bytes sent (initiator:responder) [45:65]
```

In the Established Sessions in the output, what is the source IP address and port number for Session 657344C0? ______________________________

What is the destination IP address and port number for Session 657344C0?

____

Step 6: Use CCP Monitor to verify the ZBF function.

a. From CCP, click the **Monitor** button at the top of the screen and choose **Security > Firewall Status**.

b. Choose the **ccp-zp-out-self** policy from the list of policies. This policy applies to traffic from the outside zone to the router (self) zone.

c. Verify that Active Sessions is selected and that the view interval is set to Real-time data every 10 sec. Click the **Monitor Policy** button to start monitoring traffic from outside the zone to inside the zone.

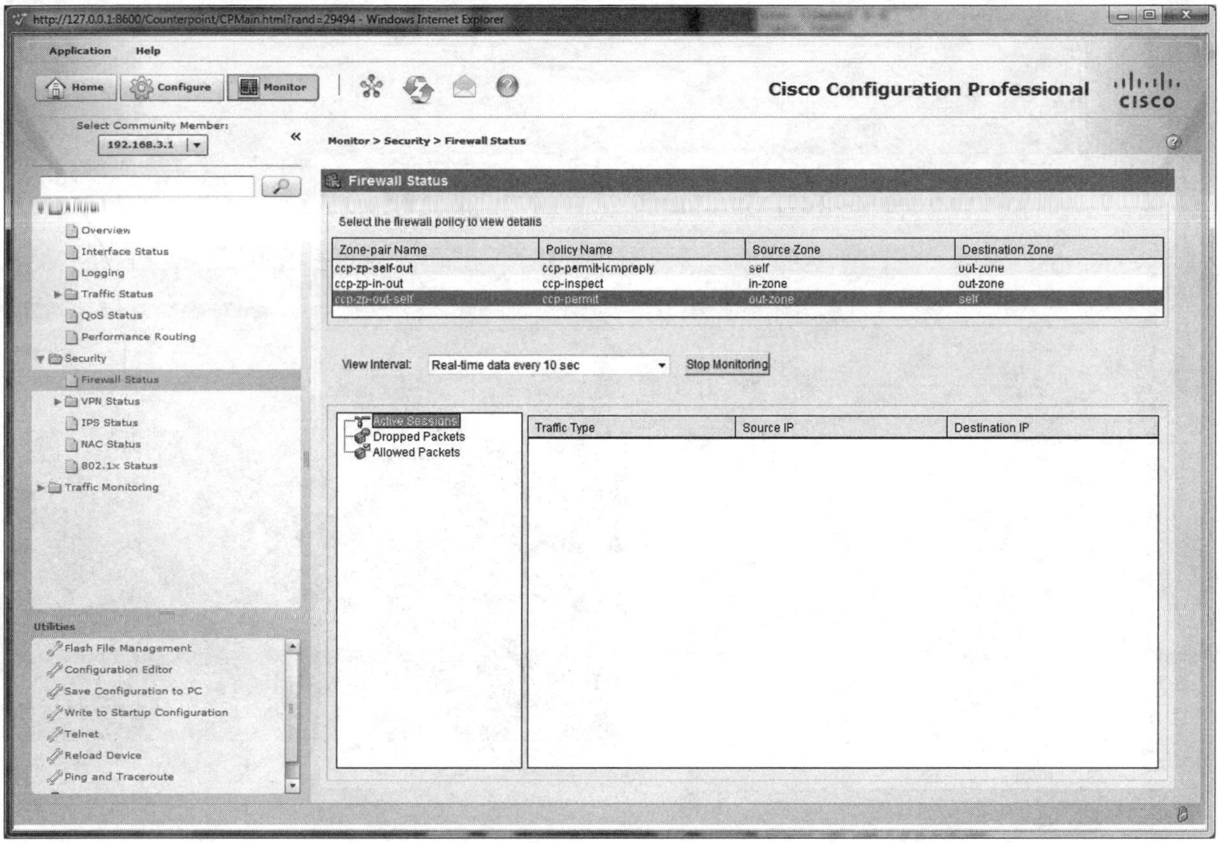

d. From the R2 CLI, ping the R3 S0/0/1 interface at IP address 10.2.2.1. The pings should fail.

e. From the R2 CLI, telnet to the R3 S0/0/1 interface at IP address 10.2.2.1. The Telnet attempt should fail.

f. Click the **Dropped Packets** option and observe the graph showing the number of dropped packets resulting from the failed ping and Telnet attempts. Your screen should look similar to the one shown here.

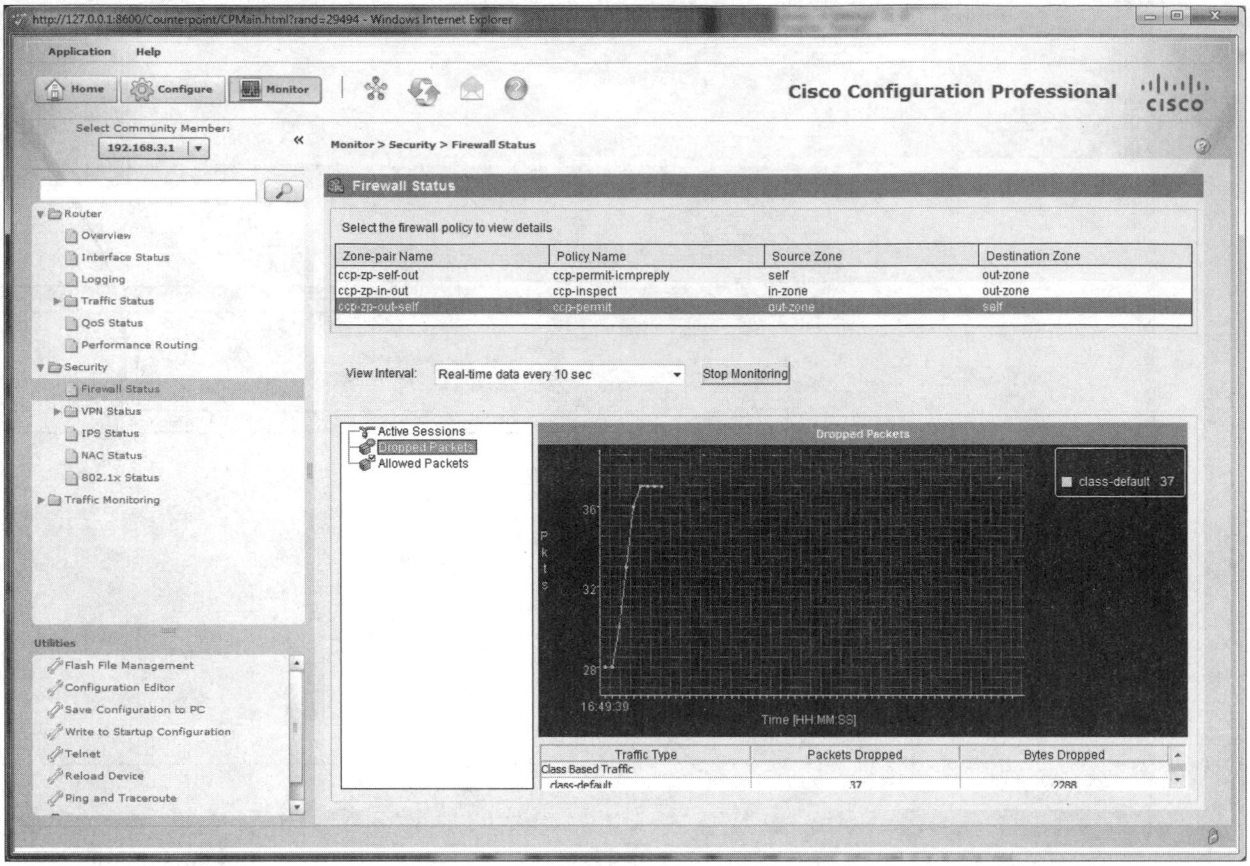

g. Click the **Allowed Packets** option and observe the graph showing the number of EIGRP packets received from router R3. This number continues to grow at a steady pace as EIGRP updates are received from R2.

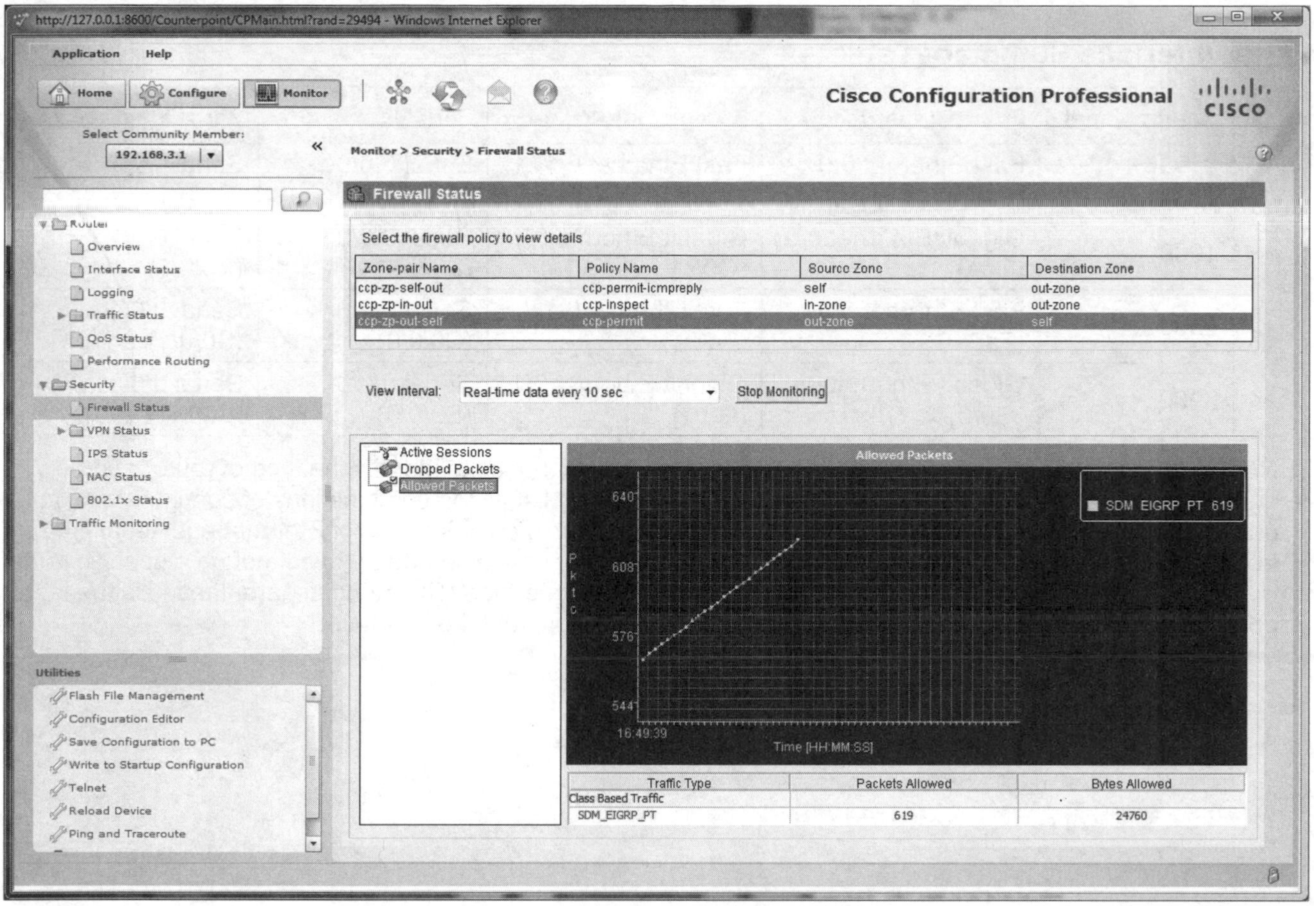

h. Click the **Stop Monitoring** button and close CCP.

Reflection

What are some factors to consider when configuring firewalls using traditional manual CLI methods compared to using the automated AutoSecure CBAC and the CCP Firewall Wizard GUI methods?

Router Interface Summary Table

Router Model	Ethernet Interface 1	Ethernet Interface 2	Serial Interface 1	Serial Interface 2
1800	Fast Ethernet 0/0 (Fa0/0)	Fast Ethernet 0/1 (Fa0/1)	Serial 0/0/0 (S0/0/0)	Serial 0/0/1 (S0/0/1)
1900	Gigabit Ethernet 0/0 (G0/0)	Gigabit Ethernet 0/1 (G0/1)	Serial 0/0/0 (S0/0/0)	Serial 0/0/1 (S0/0/1)
2800	Fast Ethernet 0/0 (Fa0/0)	Fast Ethernet 0/1 (Fa0/1)	Serial 0/0/0 (S0/0/0)	Serial 0/0/1 (S0/0/1)
2900	Gigabit Ethernet 0/0 (G0/0)	Gigabit Ethernet 0/1 (G0/1)	Serial 0/0/0 (S0/0/0)	Serial 0/0/1 (S0/0/1)

Note: To find out how the router is configured, look at the interfaces to identify the type of router and how many interfaces the router has. There is no way to effectively list all the combinations of configurations for each router class. This table includes identifiers for the possible combinations of Ethernet and serial interfaces in the device. The table does not include any other type of interface, even though a specific router may contain one. An example of this might be an ISDN BRI interface. The string in parentheses is the legal abbreviation that can be used in Cisco IOS commands to represent the interface.

Chapter 5 Lab A: Configuring an Intrusion Prevention System (IPS) Using the CLI and CCP

Topology

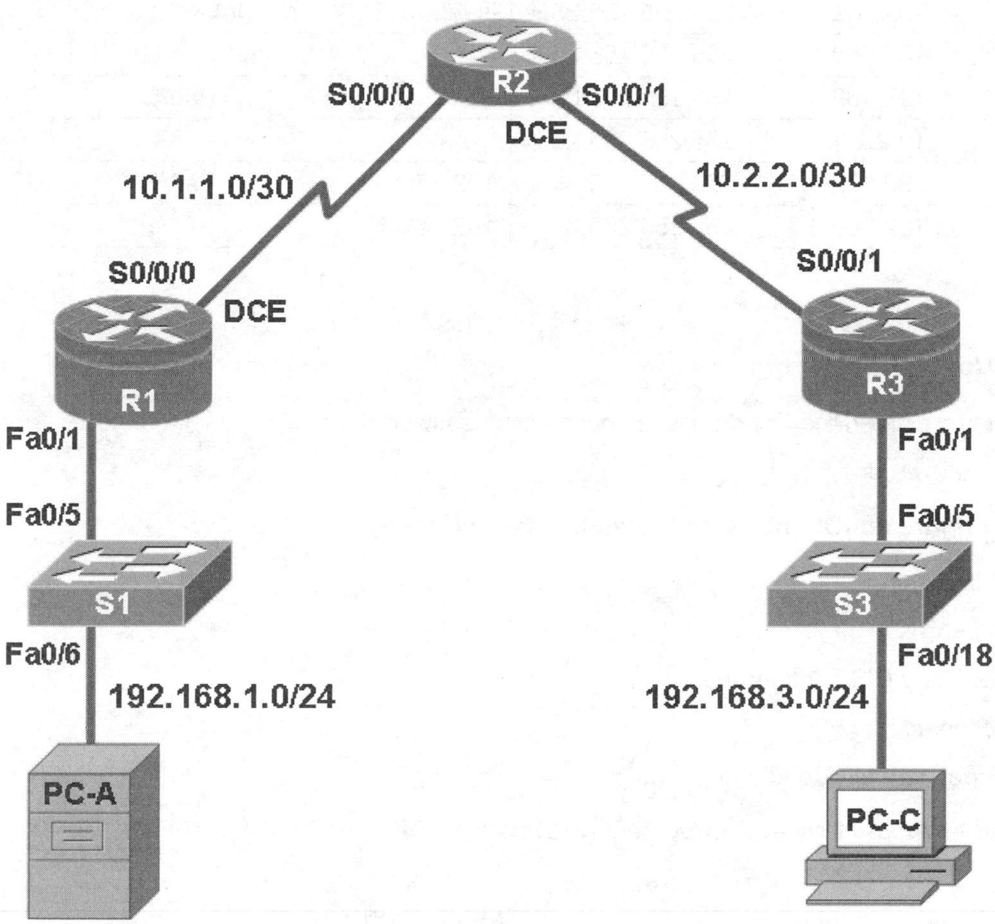

Note: ISR G2 devices have Gigabit Ethernet interfaces rather than Fast Ethernet interfaces.

IP Addressing Table

Device	Interface	IP Address	Subnet Mask	Default Gateway	Switch Port
R1	Fa0/1	192.168.1.1	255.255.255.0	N/A	S1 Fa0/5
	S0/0/0 (DCE)	10.1.1.1	255.255.255.252	N/A	N/A
R2	S0/0/0	10.1.1.2	255.255.255.252	N/A	N/A
	S0/0/1 (DCE)	10.2.2.2	255.255.255.252	N/A	N/A
R3	Fa0/1	192.168.3.1	255.255.255.0	N/A	S3 Fa0/5
	S0/0/1	10.2.2.1	255.255.255.252	N/A	N/A
PC-A	NIC	192.168.1.3	255.255.255.0	192.168.1.1	S1 Fa0/6
PC-C	NIC	192.168.3.3	255.255.255.0	192.168.3.1	S3 Fa0/18

Objectives

Part 1: Basic Router Configuration

- Configure hostname, interface IP addresses and access passwords.
- Configure the static routing.

Part 2: Use CLI to Configure an IOS Intrusion Prevention System (IPS)

- Configure IOS IPS using CLI.
- Modify IPS signatures.
- Examine the resulting IPS configuration.
- Verify IPS functionality.
- Log IPS messages to a syslog server.

Part 3: Configuring an Intrusion Prevention System (IPS) Using CCP

- Configure IPS using CCP.
- Modify IPS signatures.
- Examine the resulting IPS configuration.
- Use a scanning tool to simulate an attack.
- Use the CCP Monitor to verify IPS functionality.

Background

In this lab, you configure the Cisco IOS Intrusion Prevention System (IPS), which is part of the Cisco IOS Firewall feature set. IPS examines certain attack patterns and alerts or mitigates when those patterns occur. IPS alone is not enough to make a router into a secure Internet firewall, but in addition to other security features, it can be a powerful defense.

You configure IPS using the Cisco IOS CLI on one router and CCP on another router, and then test IPS functionality on both routers. You load the IPS signature package from a TFTP server and configure the public crypto key using the Cisco IOS CLI and CCP.

Note: The router commands and output in this lab are from a Cisco 1841 using Cisco IOS Software Release 12.4(20)T (Advanced IP image). Other routers and Cisco IOS versions can be used. See the Router Interface Summary table at the end of the lab to determine which interface identifiers to use based on the equipment in the lab. Depending on the model of the router and Cisco IOS version, the available commands and the output produced might vary from what this lab shows.

Note: Make sure that the routers and the switches have been erased and have no startup configurations.

Required Resources

- 2 routers (Cisco 1841 with Cisco IOS Software Release 12.4(20)T1 and 192 MB DRAM or comparable routers)
- 1 router (R2) Cisco 1841 with Cisco IOS Software Release 12.4(20)T1 or comparable
- 2 switches (Cisco 2960 or comparable)
- PC-A: Windows XP, Vista, or Windows 7 with syslog and TFTP servers and the SuperScan tool (optional)
- PC-C: Windows XP, Vista, or Windows 7 with Java 6 Standard Edition, CCP 2.5, syslog, and TFTP servers, and the SuperScan tool (optional)
- Serial and Ethernet cables as shown in the topology
- Rollover cables to configure the routers via the console
- IPS signature package and public crypto key files on PC-A and PC-C (provided by instructor)

CCP Notes

- See Chapter 00 Lab A for instructions on how to install CCP. Hardware/software recommendations for CCP include Windows XP, Vista, or Windows 7 with Java Version 1.6.0_11 up to 1.6.0_21, Internet Explorer 6.0 or later, and Flash Player Version 10.0.12.36 or later.
- If the PC on which CCP is installed is running Windows Vista or Windows 7, you might need to right-click the CCP icon or menu item and choose **Run as Administrator**.
- To run CCP, you might need to temporarily disable antivirus programs and OS firewalls. Make sure to turn off all pop-up blockers in the browser.

Part 1: Basic Router Configuration

In Part 1 of this lab, you set up the network topology and configure basic settings such as hostnames, interface IP addresses, static routing, device access, and passwords.

Note: Perform all tasks on routers R1, R2, and R3. The procedure for R1 is shown here as an example.

Step 1: Cable the network as shown in the topology.

Attach the devices shown in the topology diagram and cable as necessary.

Step 2: Configure the basic settings for each router.

a. Configure the hostnames as shown in the topology.

b. Configure the interface IP addresses as shown in the IP addressing table.

c. Configure a clock rate for serial router interfaces with a DCE serial cable attached:

```
R1(config)# interface S0/0/0
R1(config-if)# clock rate 64000
```

d. To prevent the router from attempting to translate incorrectly entered commands, disable DNS lookup:

```
R1(config)# no ip domain-lookup
```

Step 3: Configure static routing on the routers.

a. Configure a static default route from R1 to R2 and from R3 to R2.

b. Configure a static route from R2 to the R1 LAN and from R2 to the R3 LAN.

Step 4: Configure PC host IP settings.

Configure a static IP address, subnet mask, and default gateway for PC-A and PC-C, as shown in the IP addressing table.

Step 5: Verify basic network connectivity.

a. Ping from R1 to R3.

Were the results successful? _____

If the pings are not successful, troubleshoot the basic device configurations before continuing.

b. Ping from PC-A on the R1 LAN to PC-C on the R3 LAN.

Were the results successful? _____

If the pings are not successful, troubleshoot the basic device configurations before continuing.

Note: If you can ping from PC-A to PC-C, you have demonstrated that the static routing protocol is configured and functioning correctly. If you cannot ping but the device interfaces are up and IP addresses are correct, use the **show run** and **show ip route** commands to identify routing protocol-related problems.

Step 6: Configure and encrypt passwords.

Note: Passwords in this task are set to a minimum of 10 characters, but are relatively simple for the benefit of performing the lab. More complex passwords are recommended in a production network.

a. Configure a minimum password length using the **security passwords** command to set a minimum password length of 10 characters:

```
R1(config)# security passwords min-length 10
```

b. Configure a console password and enable login for router R1. For additional security, the **exec-timeout** command causes the line to log out after 5 minutes of inactivity. The **logging synchronous** command prevents console messages from interrupting command entry.

Note: To avoid repetitive logins during this lab, you can set the **exec-timeout** command to 0 0, which prevents it from expiring. However, this is not considered to be a good security practice.

```
R1(config)# line console 0
R1(config-line)# password ciscoconpass
R1(config-line)# exec-timeout 5 0
R1(config-line)# login
R1(config-line)# logging synchronous
```

c. Configure a password for the aux port for router R1:

```
R1(config)# line aux 0
R1(config-line)# password ciscoauxpass
R1(config-line)# exec-timeout 5 0
R1(config-line)# login
```

d. Configure the password on the vty lines for router R1:

```
R1(config)# line vty 0 4
R1(config-line)# password ciscovtypass
R1(config-line)# exec-timeout 5 0
R1(config-line)# login
```

e. Encrypt the console, aux, and vty clear-text passwords:

```
R1(config)# service password-encryption
```

f. Issue the **show run** command. Can you read the console, aux, and vty passwords? Why or why not? ____

Step 7: Save the basic configurations for all three routers.

Save the running configuration to the startup configuration from the privileged EXEC prompt:

```
R1# copy running-config startup-config
```

Part 2: Configuring IPS Using the Cisco IOS CLI

In Part 2 of this lab, you configure IPS on R1 using the Cisco IOS CLI. You then review and test the resulting configuration.

Task 1: Verify Access to the R1 LAN from R2

In this task, you verify that without IPS configured, the external router R2 can ping the R1 S0/0/0 interface and PC-A on the R1 internal LAN.

Step 1: Ping from R2 to R1.

From R2, ping R1 interface S0/0/0 at IP address 10.1.1.1.

```
R2# ping 10.1.1.1
```

Were the results successful? _____

If the pings are not successful, troubleshoot the basic device configurations before continuing.

Step 2: Ping from R2 to PC-A on the R1 LAN.

From R2, ping PC-A on the R1 LAN at IP address 192.168.1.3.

```
R2# ping 192.168.1.3
```

Were the results successful? _____

If the pings are not successful, troubleshoot the basic device configurations before continuing.

Step 3: Display the R1 running config before configuring IPS.

Issue the **show run** command to review the current basic configuration on R1.

Are there any security commands related to IPS?

____

Task 2: Prepare the Router and TFTP Server

Step 1: Verify the availability of Cisco IOS IPS files.

To configure Cisco IOS IPS 5.x, the IOS IPS signature package file and public crypto key file must be available on PC-A. Check with your instructor if these files are not on the PC. These files can be downloaded from Cisco.com with a valid user account that has proper authorization.

a. Verify that the IOS-S*xxx*-CLI.pkg file is in a TFTP folder. This is the signature package. The *xxx* is the version number and varies depending on which file was downloaded.

b. Verify that the realm-cisco.pub.key.txt file is available and note its location on PC-A. This is the public crypto key used by IOS IPS.

Step 2: Verify or create the IPS directory in router flash on R1.

In this step, you verify the existence of, or create a directory in, the router flash memory where the required signature files and configurations will be stored.

Note: Alternatively, you can use a USB flash drive connected to the router USB port to store the signature files and configurations. The USB flash drive needs to remain connected to the router USB port if it is used as the IOS IPS configuration directory location. IOS IPS also supports any Cisco IOS file system as its configuration location with proper write access.

a. From the R1 CLI, display the contents of flash memory using the **show flash** command and check for the ipsdir directory:

```
R1# show flash
```

b. If the ipsdir directory is not listed, create it in privileged EXEC mode:

```
R1# mkdir ipsdir
Create directory filename [ipsdir]? Press Enter
Created dir flash:ipsdir
```

Note: If the directory already exists, the following message displays.

```
%Error Creating dir flash:ipsdir (Can't create a file that exists)
```

c. From the R1 CLI, verify that the directory is present using the **dir flash:** or **dir flash:ipsdir** command:

```
R1# dir flash:
Directory of flash:/

    5  -rw-    37081324  Dec 17 2008 21:57:10 +00:00  c1841-
advipservicesk9-mz.124-20.T1.bin
    6  drw-           0   Jan 6 2009 11:19:14 +00:00  ipsdir
```

or

```
R1# dir flash:ipsdir

Directory of flash:/ipsdir/

No files in directory
```

Note: The directory exists, but there are currently no files in it.

Task 3: Configuring the IPS Crypto Key

The crypto key verifies the digital signature for the master signature file (sigdef-default.xml). The contents are signed by a Cisco private key to guarantee the authenticity and integrity at every release.

Note: The following instructions use Notepad as the text editor and HyperTerminal as the terminal emulation program. Another text editor and terminal emulation program can be used.

Step 1: Locate and open the crypto key file.

On PC-A, locate the crypto key file named realm-cisco.pub.key.txt and open it using Notepad or another text editor. The contents should look similar to the following:

```
crypto key pubkey-chain rsa
 named-key realm-cisco.pub signature
  key-string
   30820122 300D0609 2A864886 F70D0101 01050003 82010F00 3082010A 02820101
   00C19E93 A8AF124A D6CC7A24 5097A975 206BE3A2 06FBA13F 6F12CB5B 4E441F16
   17E630D5 C02AC252 912BE27F 37FDD9C8 11FC7AF7 DCDD81D9 43CDABC3 6007D128
   B199ABCB D34ED0F9 085FADC1 359C189E F30AF10A C0EFB624 7E0764BF 3E53053E
5B2146A9 D7A5EDE3 0298AF03 DED7A5B8 9479039D 20F30663 9AC64B93 C0112A35
FE3F0C87 89BCB7BB 994AE74C FA9E481D F65875D6 85EAF974 6D9CC8E3 F0B08B85
   50437722 FFBE85B9 5E4189FF CC189CB9 69C46F9C A84DFBA5 7A0AF99E AD768C36
   006CF498 079F88F8 A3B3FB1F 9FB7B3CB 5539E1D1 9693CCBB 551F78D2 892356AE
   2F56D826 8918EF3C 80CA4F4D 87BFCA3B BFF668E9 689782A5 CF31CB6E B4B094D3
   F3020301 0001
  quit
```

Step 2: Copy the contents of the text file.

a. From the Notepad menu bar, choose **Edit > Select All**.

b. Choose **Edit > Copy** (or press Ctrl+C).

Step 3: Apply the contents of the text file to the router.

a. At the R1 privileged EXEC prompt, enter global config mode using the config t command.

b. With the cursor at the R1(config)# prompt, paste the text file contents from HyperTerminal by right-clicking and selecting Paste to Host from the context menu. Alternatively, you can select Edit > Paste to Host from the HyperTerminal menu bar.

c. Exit global config mode and issue the show run command to confirm that the crypto key is configured.

Task 4: Configure IPS

Step 1: Create an IPS rule.

a. On R1, create an IPS rule name using the **ip ips name** *name* command in global configuration mode. Name the IPS rule **iosips**. This will be used later on an interface to enable IPS.

```
R1(config)# ip ips name iosips
```

b. You can specify an optional extended or standard access control list (ACL) to filter the traffic that will be scanned by this rule name. All traffic that is permitted by the ACL is subject to inspection by the IPS. Traffic that is denied by the ACL is not inspected by the IPS.

c. To see the options available for specifying an ACL with the rule name, use the **ip ips name** command and the CLI help function (**?**):

```
R1(config)# ip ips name ips list ?
  <1-199>  Numbered access list
  WORD     Named access list
```

Step 2: Configure the IPS Signature storage location in router flash memory.

The IPS files are stored in the ipsdir directory that was created in Task 2, Step 2. Configure the location using the **ip ips config location** command:

```
R1(config)# ip ips config location flash:ipsdir
```

Step 3: Enable IPS SDEE event notification.

The Cisco Security Device Event Exchange (SDEE) server is a Simple Object Access Protocol (SOAP)-based, intrusion detection system (IDS) alert format and transport protocol specification. SDEE replaces Cisco RDEP.

To use SDEE, the HTTP server must be enabled with the **ip http server** command. If the HTTP server is not enabled, the router cannot respond to the SDEE clients because it cannot see the requests. SDEE notification is disabled by default and must be explicitly enabled.

Note: CCP Monitor uses HTTP and SDEE to capture IPS events.

To enable SDEE, use the following command:

```
R1(config)# ip ips notify sdee
```

Step 4: Enable IPS syslog support.

IOS IPS also supports the use of syslog to send event notification. SDEE and syslog can be used independently or enabled at the same time to send IOS IPS event notification. Syslog notification is enabled by default.

a. If console logging is enabled, you see IPS syslog messages. Enable syslog if it is not enabled.

```
R1(config)# ip ips notify log
```

b. Use the **show clock** command to verify the current time and date for the router. Use the **clock set** command from privileged EXEC mode to reset the clock if necessary. The following is an example of how to set the clock:

```
R1# clock set 01:20:00 6 january 2009
```

c. Verify that the timestamp service for logging is enabled on the router using the **show run** command. Enable the timestamp service if it is not enabled:

```
R1(config)# service timestamps log datetime msec
```

d. To send log messages to the syslog server on PC-A, use the following command:

```
R1(config)# logging 192.168.1.3
```

e. To see the type and level of logging enabled on R1, use the **show logging** command.

```
R1# show logging
```

Note: Verify that you have connectivity between R1 and PC-A by pinging from PC-A to the R1 Fa0/1 interface IP address 192.168.1.1. If it is not successful, troubleshoot as necessary before continuing.

The next step describes how to download one of the freeware syslog servers if one is not available on PC-A.

Step 5: (Optional) Download and start the syslog server.

If a syslog server is not currently available on PC-A, you can download the latest version of Kiwi from http://www.kiwisyslog.com or Tftpd32 from http://tftpd32.jounin.net/. If the syslog server is available on the PC, go to Step 6.

Note: This lab uses the Tftpd32 syslog server.

Start the syslog server software on PC-A if you want to send log messages to it.

Step 6: Configure IOS IPS to use one of the pre-defined signature categories.

IOS IPS with Cisco 5.x format signatures operates with signature categories, just like Cisco IPS appliances do. All signatures are pregrouped into categories, and the categories are hierarchical. This helps classify signatures for easy grouping and tuning.

Warning: The "all" signature category contains *all* signatures in a signature release. Because IOS IPS cannot compile and use all the signatures contained in a signature release at one time, do not unretire the "all" category. Otherwise, the router will run out of memory.

Note: When configuring IOS IPS, it is required to first retire all the signatures in the "all" category and then unretire selected signature categories.

In the following example, all signatures in the "all" category are retired, and then the ios_ips basic category is unretired:

```
R1(config)# ip ips signature-category
R1(config-ips-category)# category all
R1(config-ips-category-action)# retired true
R1(config-ips-category-action)# exit
R1(config-ips-category)# category ios_ips basic
R1(config-ips-category-action)# retired false
R1(config-ips-category-action)# exit
R1(config-ips-category)# exit
Do you want to accept these changes? [confirm] <Enter>

Jan  6 01:32:37.983: Applying Category configuration to signatures ...
```

Step 7: Apply the IPS rule to an interface.

a. Apply the IPS rule to an interface with the **`ip ips`** *`name direction`* command in interface configuration mode. Apply the rule you just created inbound on the S0/0/0 interface. After you enable IPS, some log messages will be sent to the console line indicating that the IPS engines are being initialized.

Note: The direction **`in`** means that IPS inspects only traffic going into the interface. Similarly, **`out`** means only traffic going out the interface. To enable IPS to inspect both in and out traffic, enter the IPS rule name for in and out separately on the same interface.

```
R1(config)# interface serial0/0/0
R1(config-if)# ip ips iosips in

Jan  6 03:03:30.495: %IPS-6-ENGINE_BUILDS_STARTED:  03:03:30 UTC Jan 6
2008
Jan  6 03:03:30.495: %IPS-6-ENGINE_BUILDING: atomic-ip - 3 signatures - 1
of 13 engines
Jan  6 03:03:30.511: %IPS-6-ENGINE_READY: atomic-ip - build time 16 ms –
packets for this engine will be scanned
Jan  6 03:03:30.511: %IPS-6-ALL_ENGINE_BUILDS_COMPLETE: elapsed time 16 ms
```

The message also displays on the syslog server if it is enabled. The Tftpd32 syslog server is shown here.

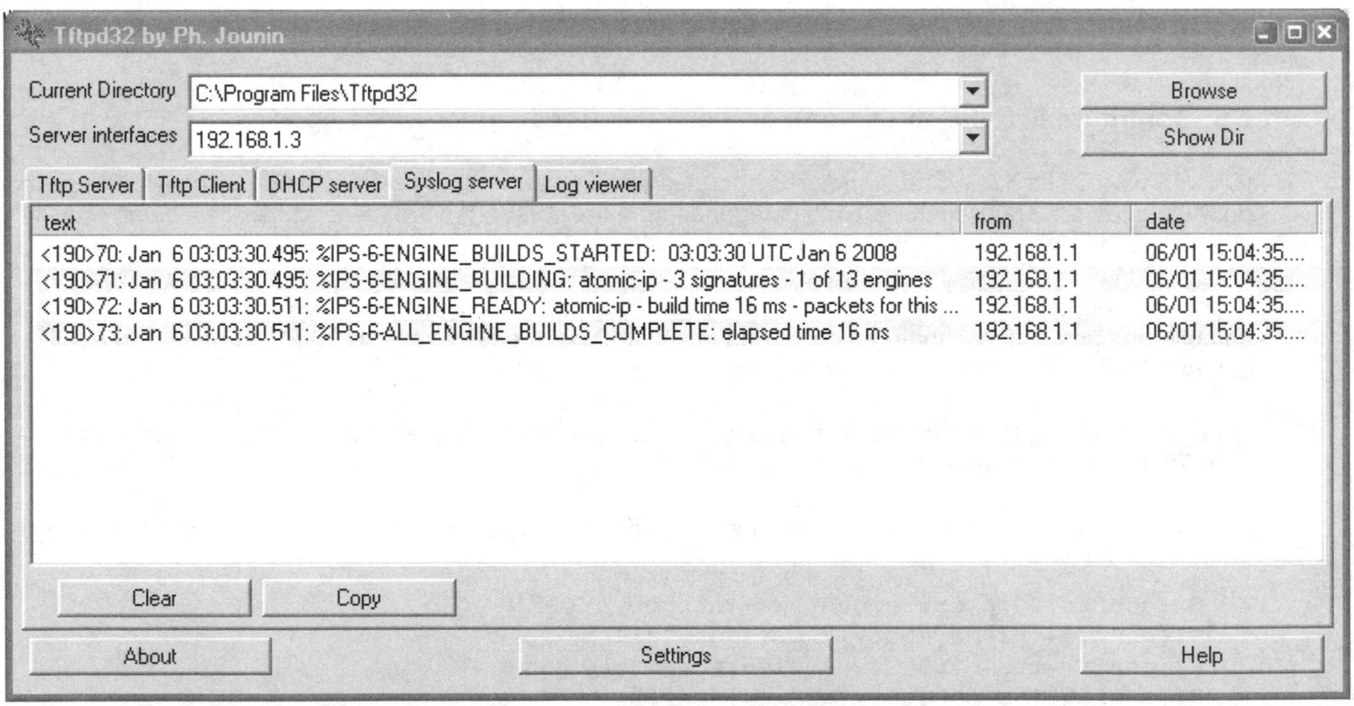

b. Although the R1 Fa0/1 interface is an internal interface, it might be desirable to configure it with IPS to respond to internal attacks. Apply the IPS rule to the R1 Fa0/1 interface in the inbound direction.

```
R1(config)# interface fa0/1
R1(config-if)# ip ips iosips in
```

Step 8: Save the running configuration.

Enter privileged EXEC mode using the **`enable`** command and provide the enable password **cisco12345**:

```
R1# copy run start
```

Task 5: Load the IOS IPS Signature Package to the Router

The most common way to load the signature package to the router is to use TFTP. See Step 4 for alternative methods for loading the IOS IPS signature package. The alternative methods include the use of FTP and a USB flash drive.

Step 1: (Optional) Download the TFTP server.

The Tftpd32 freeware TFTP server is used in this task. Many other free TFTP servers are also available. If a TFTP server is not currently available on PC-A, you can download the latest version of Tftpd32 from http://tftpd32.jounin.net/. If it is already installed, go to Step 2.

Note: This lab uses the Tftpd32 TFTP server. This software also includes a syslog server, which runs simultaneously with the TFTP server.

Step 2: Start the TFTP server on PC-A and verify the IPS file directory.

a. Verify connectivity between R1 and PC-A, the TFTP server, using the **`ping`** command.

b. Verify that the PC has the IPS signature package file in a directory on the TFTP server. This file is typically named IOS-S*xxx*-CLI.pkg, where *xxx* is the signature file version.

Note: If this file is not present, contact your instructor before continuing.

c. Start Tftpd32 or another TFTP server and set the default directory to the one with the IPS signature package in it. The Tftpd32 screen is shown here with the C:\Program Files\Tftpd32\IPS directory contents displayed. Take note of the filename for use in the next step.

Note: It is recommended to use the latest signature file available in a production environment. However, if the amount of router flash memory is an issue in a lab environment, you may use an older version 5.x signature, which requires less memory. The S364 file is used with this lab for demonstration purposes, although newer versions are available. Consult CCO to determine the latest version.

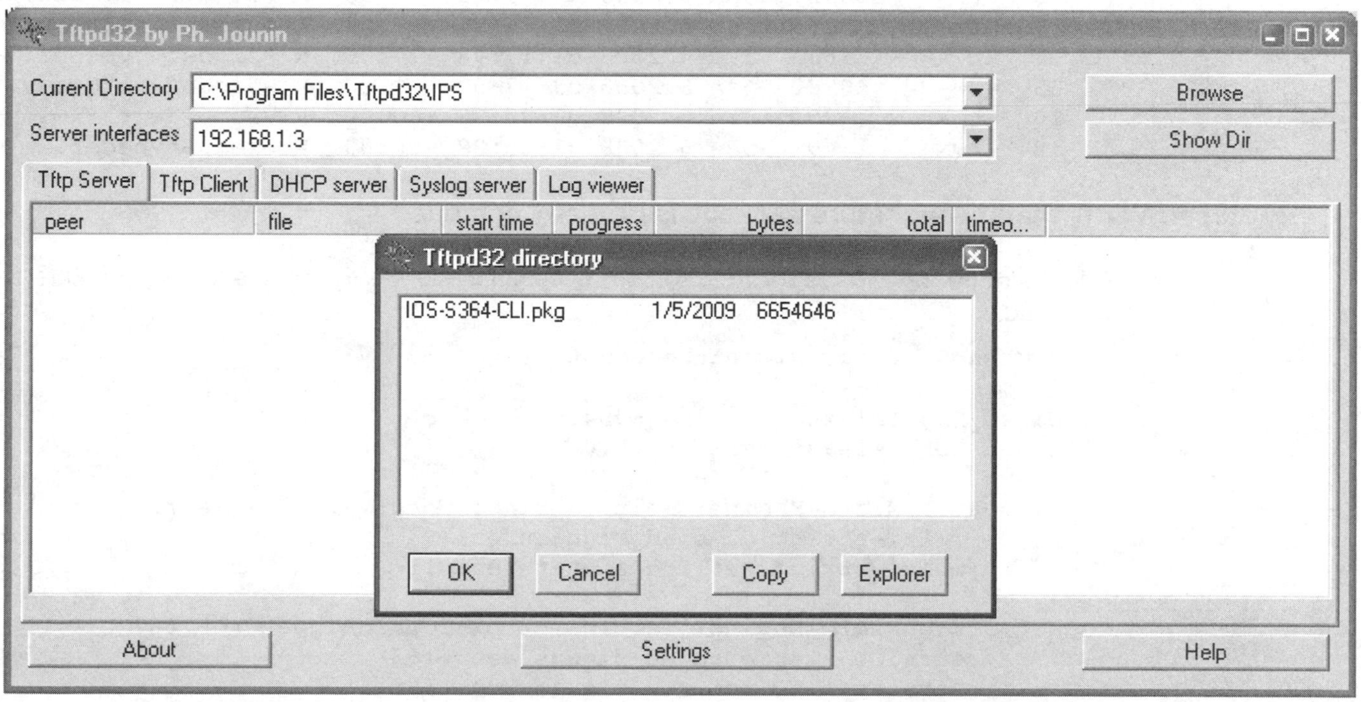

Step 3: Copy the signature package from the TFTP server to the router.

If you do not have a TFTP server available and are using a router with a USB port, you can go to Step 5 and use the procedure described there.

a. Use the **copy tftp** command to retrieve the signature file. Be sure to use the **idconf** keyword at the end of the **copy** command.

Note: Immediately after the signature package is loaded to the router, signature compiling begins. You can see the messages on the router with logging level 6 or above enabled.

```
R1# copy tftp://192.168.1.3/IOS-S364-CLI.pkg idconf

Loading IOS-S364-CLI.pkg from 192.168.1.3 (via FastEthernet0/1):
!!!!!!!!!!!!!!!!!!!!!!!!!!
[OK - 6654646 bytes]

Jan  6 03:18:36.799: %IPS-6-ENGINE_BUILDS_STARTED:  03:18:36 UTC Jan 6
2008
Jan  6 03:18:36.799: %IPS-6-ENGINE_BUILDING: multi-string - 8
signatures - 1 of 13 engines
Jan  6 03:18:36.811: %IPS-6-ENGINE_READY: multi-string - build time 12
ms - packets for this engine will be scanned
Jan  6 03:18:36.831: %IPS-6-ENGINE_BUILDING: service-http - 629
signatures - 2 of 13 engines
Jan  6 03:18:46.755: %IPS-6-ENGINE_READY: service-http - build time
9924 ms - packets for this engine will be scanned
<Output omitted>
```

b. Use the **dir flash** command to see the contents of the ipsdir directory created earlier. There should be six files, as shown here:

```
R1# dir flash:ipsdir
Directory of flash:/ipsdir/

16  -rw-   230621  Jan 6 2008 03:19:42 +00:00  R1-sigdef-default.xml
15  -rw-      255  Jan 6 2008 01:35:26 +00:00  R1-sigdef-delta.xml
14  -rw-     6632  Jan 6 2008 03:17:48 +00:00  R1-sigdef-typedef.xml
13  -rw-    28282  Jan 6 2008 03:17:52 +00:00  R1-sigdef-category.xml
10  -rw-      304  Jan 6 2008 01:35:28 +00:00  R1-seap-delta.xml
18  -rw-      491  Jan 6 2008 01:35:28 +00:00  R1-seap-typedef.xml
```

Step 4: Verify that the signature package is properly compiled.

a. Use the **show ip ips signature count** command to see the counts for the signature package compiled:

```
R1# show ip ips signature count

Cisco SDF release version S364.0
Trend SDF release version V0.0

Signature Micro-Engine: multi-string: Total Signatures 11
      multi-string enabled signatures: 9
      multi-string retired signatures: 11

Signature Micro-Engine: service-http: Total Signatures 662
      service-http enabled signatures: 163
      service-http retired signatures: 565
```

```
        service-http compiled signatures: 97
        service-http obsoleted signatures: 1

  Signature Micro-Engine: string-tcp: Total Signatures 1148
        string-tcp enabled signatures: 622
        string-tcp retired signatures: 1031
        string-tcp compiled signatures: 117
        string-tcp obsoleted signatures: 21

  <Output Omitted>

  Total Signatures: 2435
     Total Enabled Signatures: 1063
     Total Retired Signatures: 2097
     Total Compiled Signatures: 338
     Total Obsoleted Signatures: 25
```

Note: If you see an error message during signature compilation, such as `%IPS-3-INVALID_DIGITAL_SIGNATURE: Invalid Digital Signature found (key not found)`, it means the public crypto key is invalid. See Task 3, Configuring the IPS Crypto Key, to reconfigure the public crypto key.

b. Use the **`show ip ips all`** command to see an IPS configuration status summary. To which interfaces and in which direction is the iosips rule applied? ______________________________

```
R1# show ip ips all

IPS Signature File Configuration Status
    Configured Config Locations: flash:ipsdir/
    Last signature default load time: 18:47:52 UTC Jan 6 2009
    Last signature delta load time: 20:11:35 UTC Jan 6 2009
    Last event action (SEAP) load time: -none-

    General SEAP Config:
    Global Deny Timeout: 3600 seconds
    Global Overrides Status: Enabled
    Global Filters Status: Enabled

IPS Auto Update is not currently configured

IPS Syslog and SDEE Notification Status
    Event notification through syslog is enabled
    Event notification through SDEE is enabled

IPS Signature Status
    Total Active Signatures: 339
    Total Inactive Signatures: 2096

IPS Packet Scanning and Interface Status
    IPS Rule Configuration
      IPS name iosips
    IPS fail closed is disabled
    IPS deny-action ips-interface is false
    Interface Configuration
      Interface Serial0/0/0
        Inbound IPS rule is iosips
        Outgoing IPS rule is not set
      Interface FastEthernet0/1
              Inbound IPS rule is iosips
```

```
                    Outgoing IPS rule is not set

        IPS Category CLI Configuration:
            Category all:
                Retire: True
            Category ios_ips basic:
                Retire: False
```

Step 5: (Optional) Alternative methods of copying the signature package to the router.

If you used TFTP to copy the file and do not intend to use one of these alternative methods, read through the procedures described here to become familiar with them. If you use one of these methods instead of TFTP, return to Step 4 to verify that the signature package loaded properly.

FTP method: Although the TFTP method is generally adequate, the signature file is rather large and FTP provides a more positive method of copying the file. You can use an FTP server to copy the signature file to the router with this command:

```
copy ftp://<ftp_user:password@Server_IP_address>/<signature_package> idconf
```

In the following example, the user **admin** must be defined on the FTP server with a password of **cisco**:

```
R1# copy ftp://admin:cisco@192.168.1.3/IOS-S364-CLI.pkg idconf
Loading IOS-S364-CLI.pkg !!!!!!!!!!!!!!!!!!!!!!!!!!!!!!!
[OK - 7608873/4096 bytes]
```

USB method: If there is no access to a FTP or TFTP server, you can use a USB flash drive to load the signature package to the router.

a. Copy the signature package onto the USB drive.

b. Connect the USB drive to one of the USB ports on the router.

c. Use the **show file systems** command to see the name of the USB drive. In the following output, a 4-GB USB drive is connected to the USB port on the router as file system usbflash0:

```
R1# show file systems
File Systems:

       Size(b)       Free(b)      Type  Flags  Prefixes
             -             -    opaque     rw   archive:
             -             -    opaque     rw   system:
             -             -    opaque     rw   tmpsys:
             -             -    opaque     rw   null:
             -             -   network     rw   tftp:
        196600        185972     nvram     rw   nvram:
*     64012288      14811136      disk     rw   flash:#
             -             -    opaque     wo   syslog:
             -             -    opaque     rw   xmodem:
             -             -    opaque     rw   ymodem:
             -             -   network     rw   rcp:
             -             -   network     rw   pram:
             -             -   network     rw   http:
             -             -   network     rw   ftp:
             -             -   network     rw   scp:
             -             -    opaque     ro   tar:
             -             -   network     rw   https:
             -             -    opaque     ro   cns:
    4001378304    3807461376  usbflash     rw   usbflash0:
```

d. Verify the contents of the flash drive using the **dir** command:

```
R1# dir usbflash0:
Directory of usbflash0:/
90   -rw-   6654646  Jan 5 2009 14:49:34 +00:00  IOS-S364-CLI.pkg
91   -rw-       805  Jan 5 2009 14:49:34 +00:00  realm-cisco.pub.key.txt
```

e. Use the **copy** command with the **idconf** keyword to copy the signature package to the router:

```
R1# copy usbflash0:IOS-S364-CLI.pkg idconf
```

The USB copy process can take 60 seconds or more, and no progress indicator is displayed. When the copy process is completed, numerous engine building messages display. These must finish before the command prompt returns.

Task 6: Test the IPS Rule and Modify a Signature

You can work with signatures in many ways. They can be retired and unretired, enabled and disabled, and their characteristics and actions can be changed. In this task, you first test the default behavior of IOS IPS by pinging it from the outside.

Step 1: Ping from R2 to the R1 Serial 0/0/0 interface.

From the CLI on R2, ping R1 S0/0/0 at IP address 10.1.1.1. The pings are successful because the ICMP Echo Request signature 2004:0 is retired.

Step 2: Ping from R2 to PC-A.

From the CLI on R2, ping PC-A at IP address 192.168.1.3. These pings are also successful because of the retired signature. This is the default behavior of the IPS signatures.

```
R2# ping 192.168.1.3

Type escape sequence to abort.
Sending 5, 100-byte ICMP Echos to 192.168.1.3, timeout is 2 seconds:
!!!!!
Success rate is 100 percent (5/5), round-trip min/avg/max = 1/1/4 ms
```

Step 3: Modify the signature.

You can use Cisco IOS CLI to change signature status and actions for one signature or a group of signatures based on signature categories.

The following example shows how to unretire the echo request signature, enable it, change the signature action to alert, and drop and reset for signature 2004 with a subsig ID of 0:

```
R1(config)# ip ips signature-definition
R1(config-sigdef)# signature 2004 0
R1(config-sigdef-sig)#status
R1(config-sigdef-sig-status)# retired false
R1(config-sigdef-sig-status)# enabled true
R1(config-sigdef-sig-status)# engine
R1(config-sigdef-sig-engine)# event-action produce-alert
R1(config-sigdef-sig-engine)# event-action deny-packet-inline
R1(config-sigdef-sig-engine)# event-action reset-tcp-connection
R1(config-sigdef-sig-engine)# exit
R1(config-sigdef-sig)# exit
R1(config-sigdef)# exit
```

```
Do you want to accept these changes? [confirm] <Enter>

*Jan  6 19:36:56.459: %IPS-6-ENGINE_BUILDS_STARTED:  19:36:56 UTC Jan 6 2009
*Jan  6 19:36:56.891: %IPS-6-ENGINE_BUILDING: atomic-ip - 306 signatures - 1
of 13 engines
*Jan  6 19:36:57.599: %IPS-6-ENGINE_READY: atomic-ip - build time 704 ms -
packets for this engine will be scanned
*Jan  6 19:36:57.979: %IPS-6-ALL_ENGINE_BUILDS_COMPLETE: elapsed time 1520 ms
```

Step 4: Ping from R2 to R1 Serial 0/0/0 interface.

a. Start the syslog server.

b. From the CLI on R2, ping R1 S0/0/0 at IP address 10.1.1.1. Where the pings successful? Why or why not? ____________________

Step 5: Ping from R2 to PC-A.

a. From the CLI on R2, ping R1 S0/0/0 at IP address 192.168.1.3. Were the pings successful?

____

```
R2# ping 192.168.1.3

Type escape sequence to abort.
Sending 5, 100-byte ICMP Echos to 192.168.1.3, timeout is 2 seconds:
.....
Success rate is 0 percent (0/5)
```

b. Notice the IPS messages from R1 on the following syslog server screen. How many messages were generated from the R2 pings to R1 and PC-A? ____________________

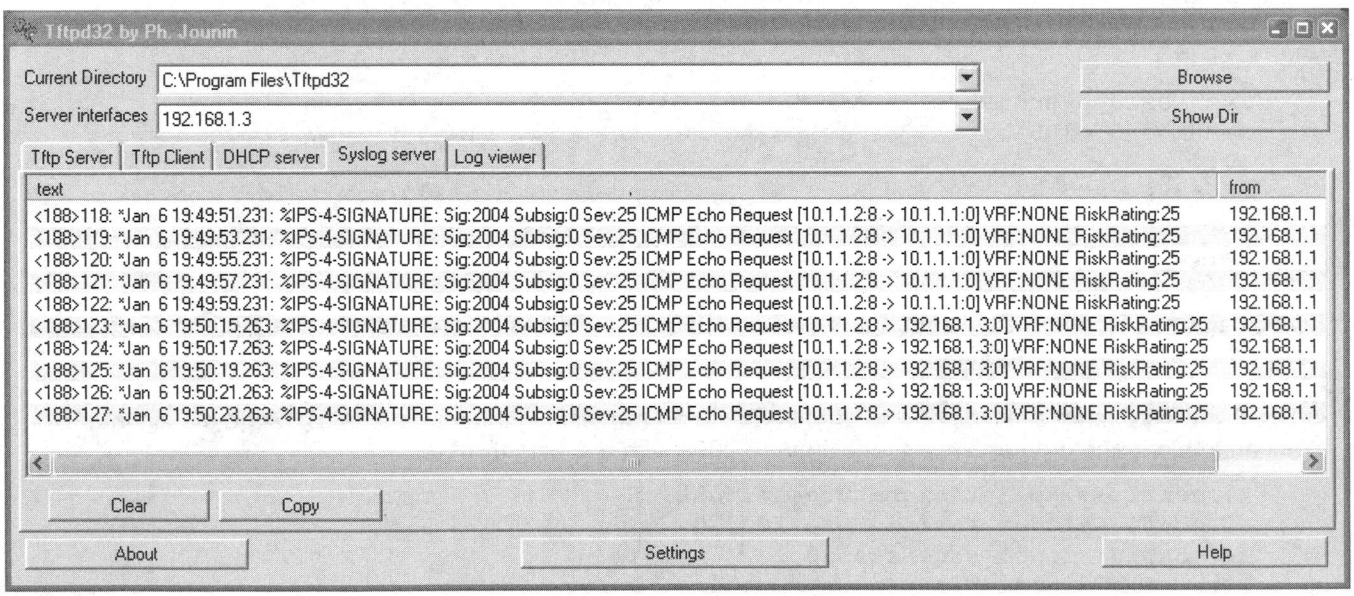

Note: The ICMP echo request IPS risk rating (severity level) is relatively low at 25. Risk rating can range from 0 to 100.

Task 7: (Optional) Test IPS with SuperScan

SuperScan is a freeware scanning tool that runs with Windows XP. It can detect open TCP and UDP ports on a target host. If the SuperScan program is available on PC-A or can be downloaded, you can perform this task.

SuperScan tests the IPS capabilities on R1. You run the scanning program from PC-A and attempt to scan open ports on router R2. The IPS rule iosips, which is set on R1 F0/1 inbound, should intercept the scanning attempts and send messages to the R1 console and syslog server.

Step 1: Download the SuperScan program.

a. If SuperScan is not on PC-A, download the SuperScan 4.0 tool from the Scanning Tools group at http://www.foundstone.com.

b. Unzip the file into a folder. The SuperScan4.exe file is executable and installation is not required.

Step 2: Run SuperScan and set scanning options.

a. Start the SuperScan program on PC-A.

b. Display the **Host and Service Discovery** tab. Check the **Timestamp Request** check box, and uncheck the **Echo Request** check box.

c. Scroll through the UDP and TCP port selection lists and notice the range of ports that will be scanned.

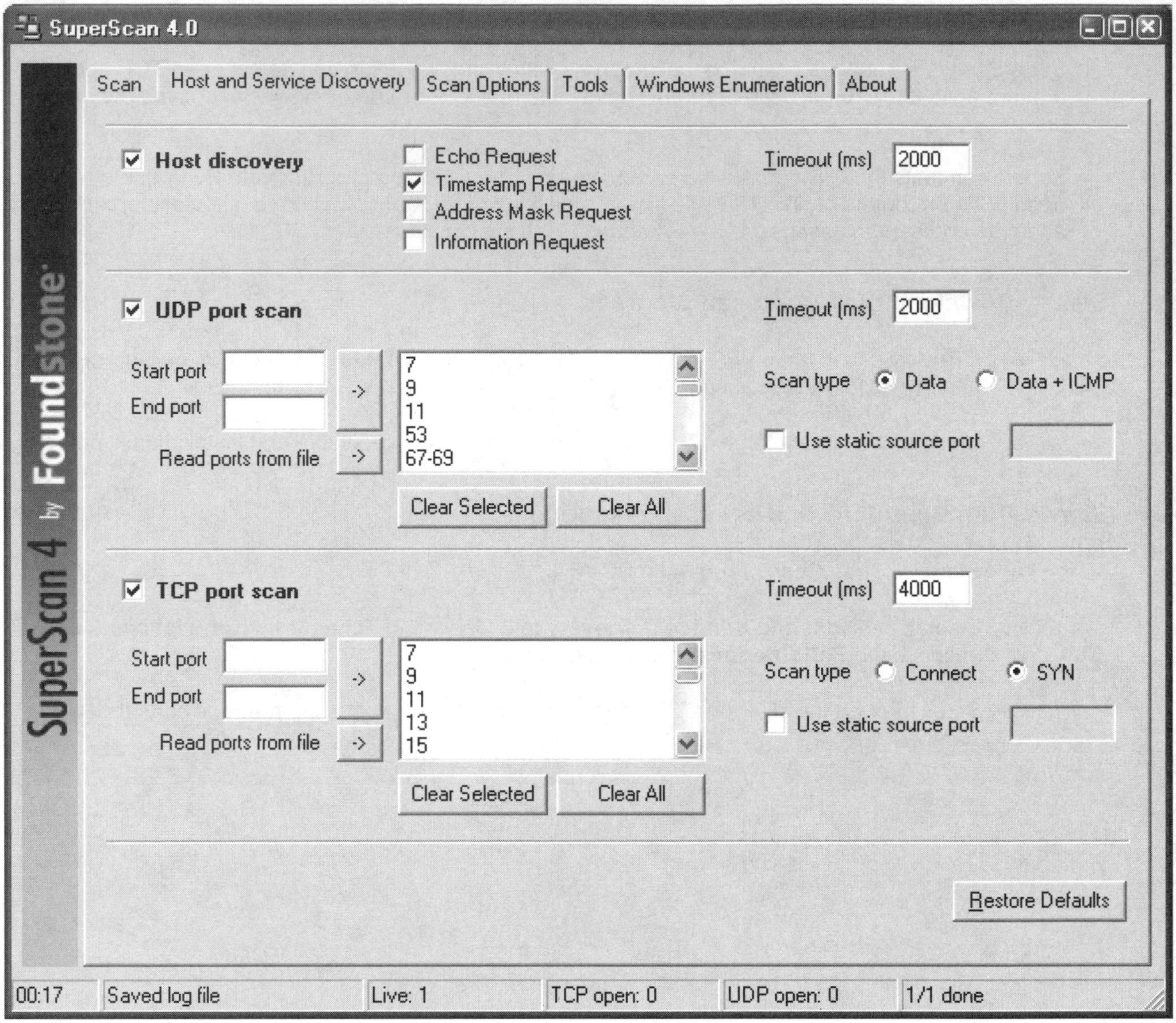

d. Click the **Scan** tab and enter the IP address of R2 S0/0/0 (**10.1.1.2**) in the Hostname/IP field.

Note: You can also specify an address range, such as 10.1.1.1 to 10.1.1.254, by entering an address in the Start IP and End IP fields. The program scans all hosts with addresses in the range specified.

e. To start the scan, click the button with the blue arrow at the bottom left of the screen. Results of the scan are shown in the SuperScan window.

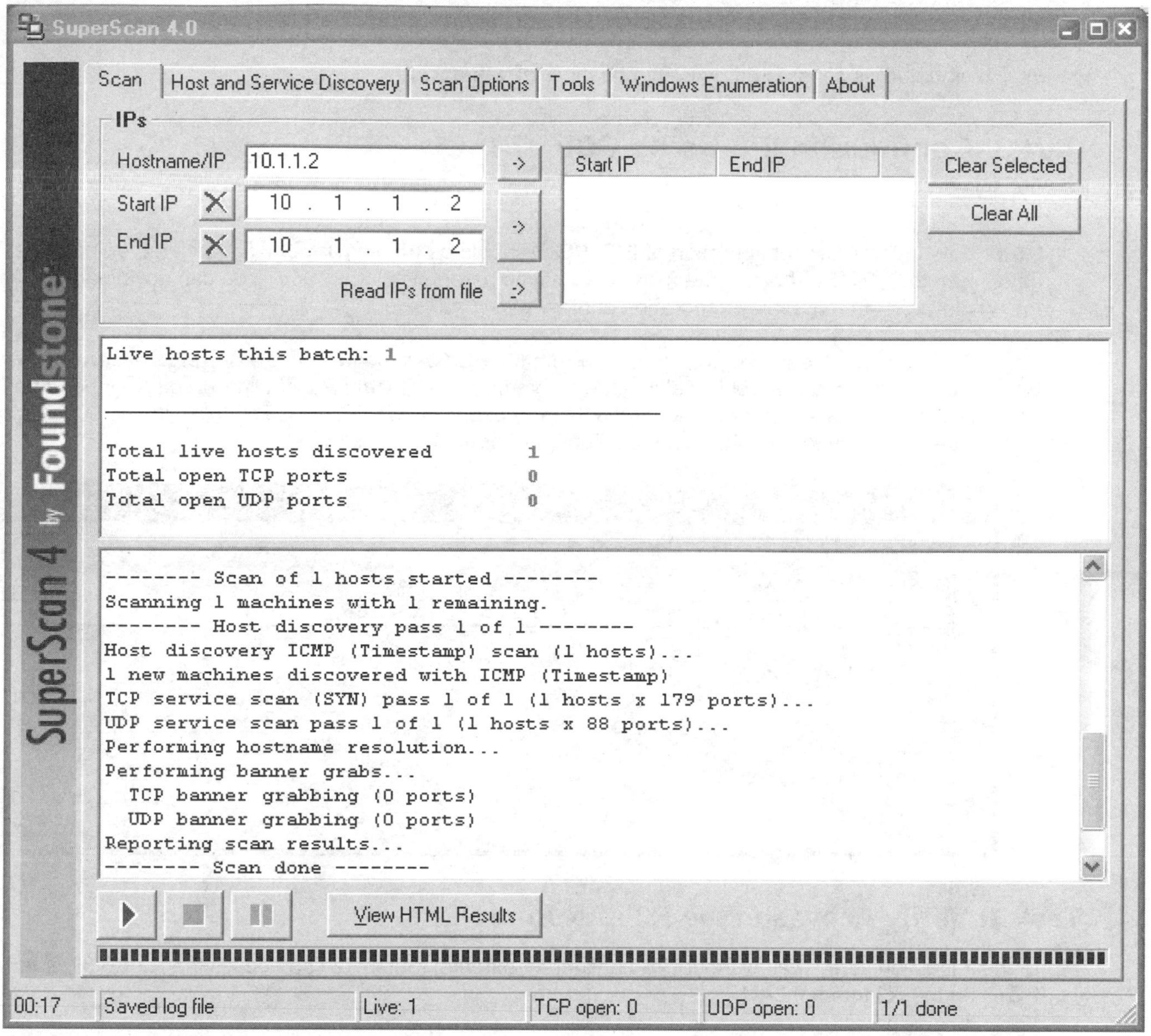

How many open TCP and UDP ports did SuperScan find on R2? Why do you think this is?

____

f. Exit SuperScan.

Step 3: Observe the syslog messages on R1.

You should see syslog entries on the R1 console and on the syslog server if it is enabled. The descriptions should include phrases such as "`Invalid DHCP Packet`" and "`DNS Version Request`."

```
R1#
*Jan  6 19:43:35.611: %IPS-4-SIGNATURE: Sig:6054 Subsig:0 Sev:50 DNS Version
Request [192.168.1.3:1076 -> 10.1.1.2:53] VRF:NONE RiskRating:50
*Jan  6 19:43:35.851: %IPS-4-SIGNATURE: Sig:4619 Subsig:0 Sev:75 Invalid DHCP
Packet [192.168.1.3:1096 -> 10.1.1.2:67] VRF:NONE RiskRating:75
```

What is the IPS risk rating or severity level (Sev:) of the DNS version request, signature 6054? ___

What is the IPS risk rating or severity level (Sev:) of the Invalid DHCP Packet, signature 4619? ___

Which signature is considered by IPS to be more of a threat? ______________________

Part 3: Configuring IPS Using CCP

In Part 3 of this lab, you configure IOS IPS on R3 using CCP.

Note: To support CCP configuration of IPS, PC-C should be running Java JRE Version 6 or later to set the Java heap to 256 MB. This is done using the runtime parameter `–Xmx256m`. You can download the latest JRE for Windows XP from Oracle Corporation at http://www.oracle.com/.

The PC must have at least 512 MB of RAM. From the PC Start menu, choose **Settings > Control Panel > Java** to open the Java Control Panel window. From the Java Control Panel window, display the **Java** tab and click the **View** button to enter or change the Java Applet Runtime Settings. The following screenshot shows setting the heap size to 256 MB using the Runtime Parameter `–Xmx256m`.

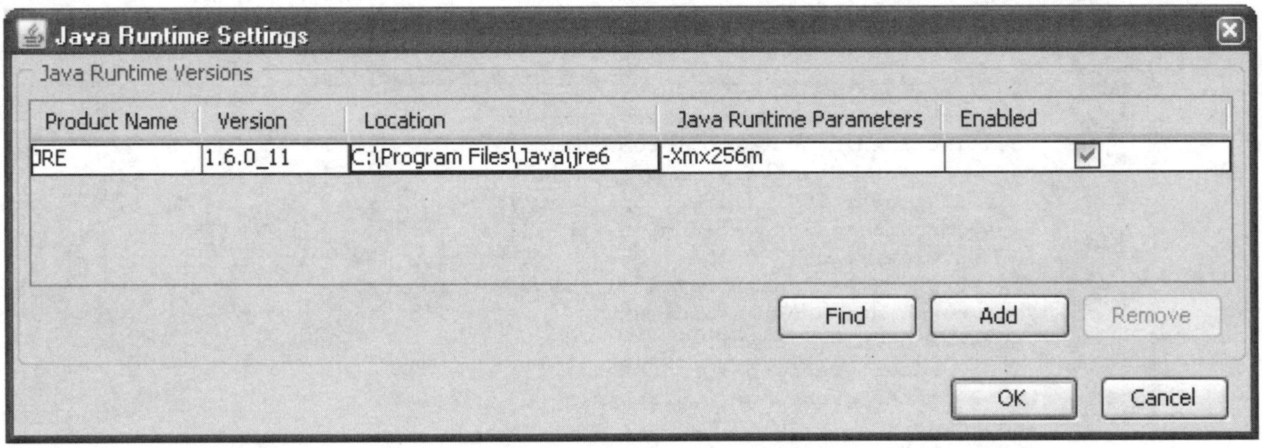

Task 1: Verify Access to the R3 LAN from R2

In this task, you verify that, without IPS configured, external router R2 can access the R3 S0/0/1 interface and PC-C on the R3 internal LAN.

Step 1: Ping from R2 to R3.

From R2, ping the R3 interface S0/0/1 at IP address 10.2.2.1

```
R2# ping 10.2.2.1
```

Were the results successful? ______

If the pings are not successful, troubleshoot the basic device configurations before continuing.

Step 2: Ping from R2 to PC-C on the R3 LAN.

From R2, ping PC-C on the R3 LAN at IP address 192.168.3.3

```
R2# ping 192.168.3.3
```

Were the results successful? _____

If the pings are not successful, troubleshoot the basic device configurations before continuing.

Step 3: Display the R3 running config before starting CCP.

Issue the **show run** command to review the current basic configuration on R3.

Verify the R3 basic configuration as performed in Part 1 of the lab. Are there any security commands related to IPS? ____

Task 2: Prepare the Router for CCP and IPS

Step 1: Configure the enable secret password and HTTP router access before starting CCP.

a. From the CLI, configure the enable secret password for use with CCP on R3:

```
R3(config)# enable secret cisco12345
```

b. Enable the HTTP server on R3:

```
R3(config)# ip http server
```

c. Add admin user to the local database:

```
R3(config)# username admin privilege 15 secret cisco12345
```

d. Have CCP use the local database to authenticate web sessions:

```
R3(config)# ip http authentication local
```

Step 2: Verify or create the IPS directory in router flash.

a. From the R3 CLI, display the content of flash memory using the **show flash** command and check for the ipsdir directory:

```
R3# show flash
```

b. If this directory is not listed, create it by entering the command **mkdir ipsdir** in privileged EXEC mode:

```
R3# mkdir ipsdir
Create directory filename [ipsdir]?
Created dir flash:ipsdir
```

c. From the R3 CLI, verify that the directory is present using the **dir flash:ipsdir** command:

```
R3# dir flash:ipsdir

Directory of flash:/ipsdir/

No files in directory
```

Note: The directory exists, but there are currently no files in it.

Task 3: Prepare the TFTP Server

Step 1: Download the TFTP server.

The Tftp32 freeware TFTP server is used in this task. Many other free TFTP servers are also available. If a TFTP server is not currently available on PC-C, you can download the latest version of Tftpd32 from http://tftpd32.jounin.net/. If it is already installed, go to Step 2.

This lab uses the Tftpd32 TFTP server. This software also includes a syslog server that runs simultaneously with the TFTP server.

Step 2: Start the TFTP server on PC-C and verify the IPS file directory.

a. Verify connectivity between R3 and PC-C, the TFTP server, using the ping command.

b. Verify that the PC has the IPS signature package file in a directory on the TFTP server. This file is typically named IOS-S*xxx*-CLI.pkg, where *xxx* is the signature file version.

Note: If this file is not present, contact your instructor before continuing.

c. Start Tftpd32 or another TFTP server and set the default directory to the one with the IPS signature package. The Tftpd32 screen is shown here with the C:\Program Files\Tftpd32\IPS directory contents displayed. Take note of the filename for use in the next step.

What is the name of the signature file? ____________________

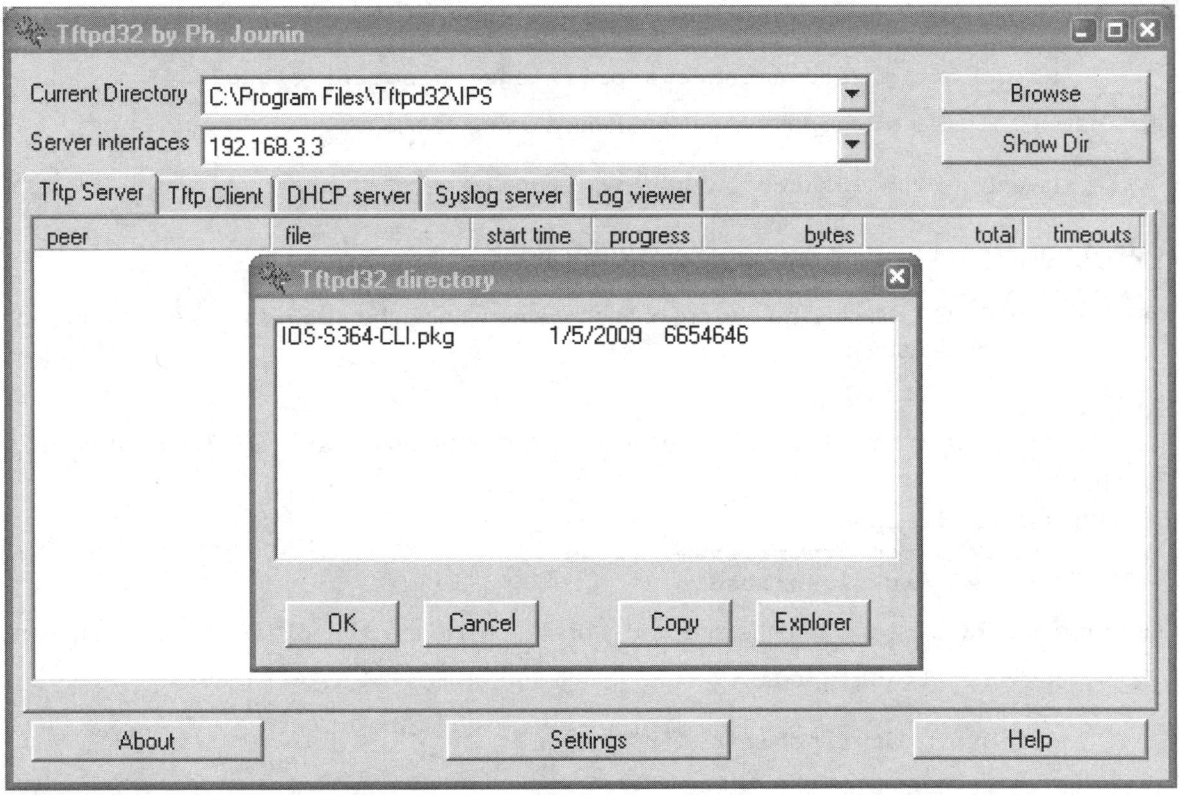

Task 4: Use CCP to Configure IPS

Step 1: Access CCP and discover R3.

a. Start CCP on PC-C. In the Manage Devices window, add R3 IP address 192.168.3.1 in the first IP Address field. Enter **admin** in the Username field and **cisco12345** in the Password field.

b. At the CCP Dashboard, click the **Discover** button to discover and connect to R3. If discovery fails, click the **Discovery Details** button to determine the problem.

Note: If you are using Java Version 1.6 or later, the Java console displays by default when CCP is run. If the Java console displays, you can close it. You can also start the Java plug-in application and choose **Advanced > Java Console > Do not start console**. The Java console does not appear again unless you change the setting.

Step 2: Use the CCP IPS Wizard to configure Cisco IOS IPS.

a. Click the **Configure** button at the top of the CCP screen and then choose **Security** > **Intrusion Prevention > Create IPS**.

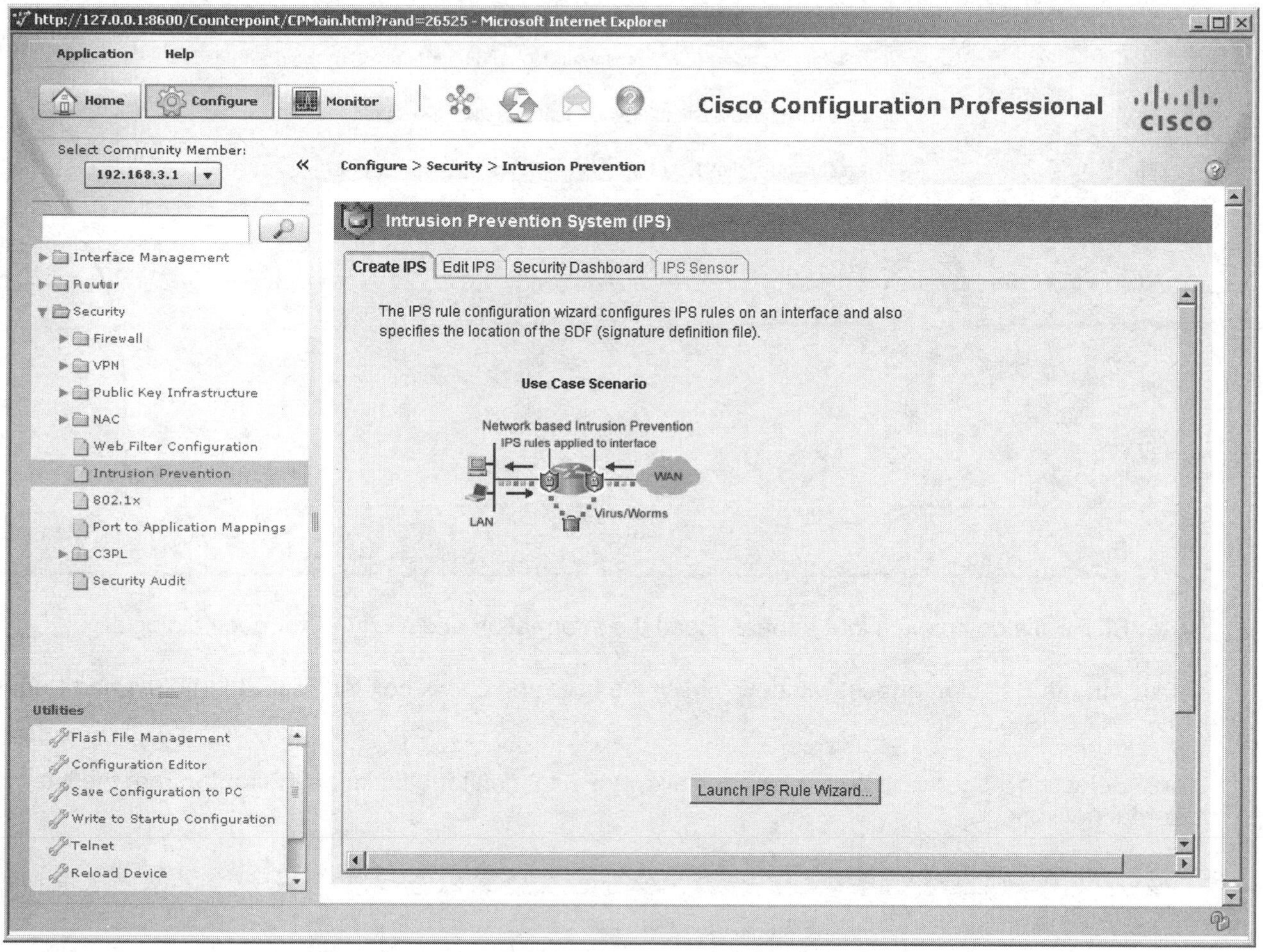

b. Click the **Launch IPS Rule Wizard** button to open the Welcome to the IPS Policies Wizard window.

c. Read the information on the IPS Policies Wizard screen to become familiar with what the wizard does. Click **Next**.

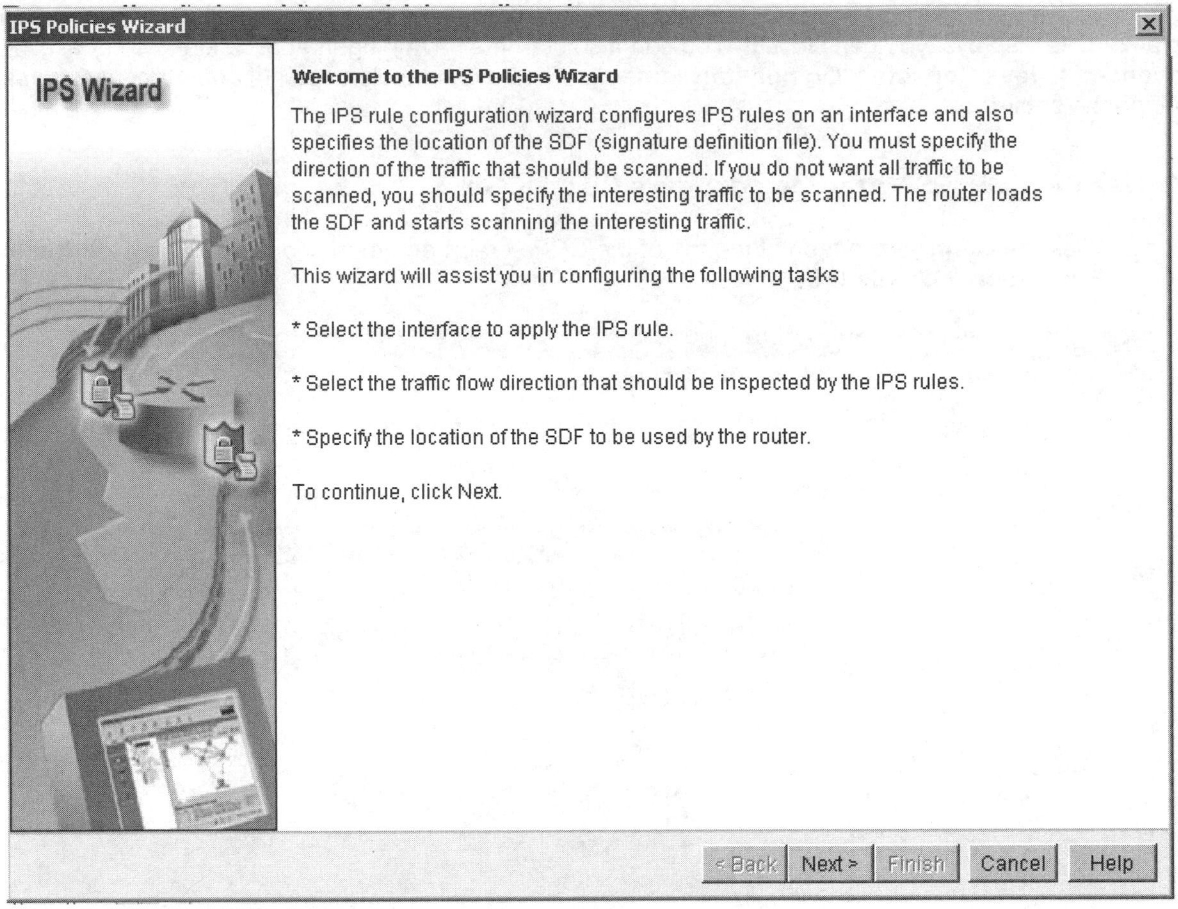

Note: SDEE dialog boxes might appear. Read the information and click **OK** for each dialog box.

d. In the Select Interfaces window, check the **Inbound** check box for Fast Ethernet0/1 and Serial0/0/1. Click **Next**.

Note: Selecting inbound on both interfaces allows IPS to monitor attacks on the router from the internal and external network.

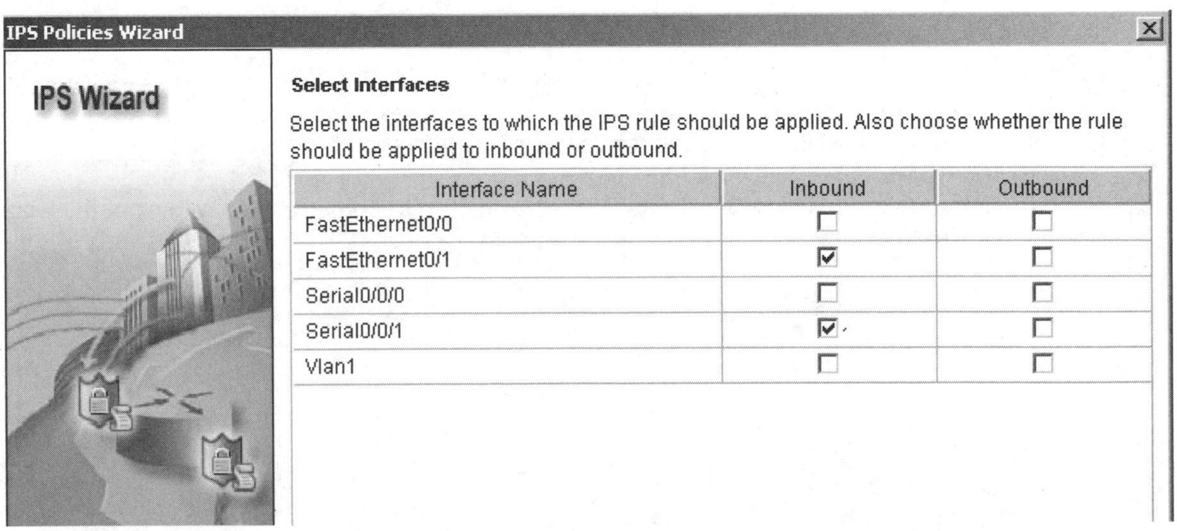

e. In the Signature File and Public Key window, click the ellipsis (**...**) button next to Specify the Signature File You Want to Use with IOS IPS to open the Specify Signature File window. Confirm that the **Specify signature file using URL** option is chosen.

f. For Protocol, choose **tftp** from the drop-down menu. Enter the IP address of the PC-C TFTP server and the filename (for example, 192.168.3.3/IOS-S364-CLI.pkg).

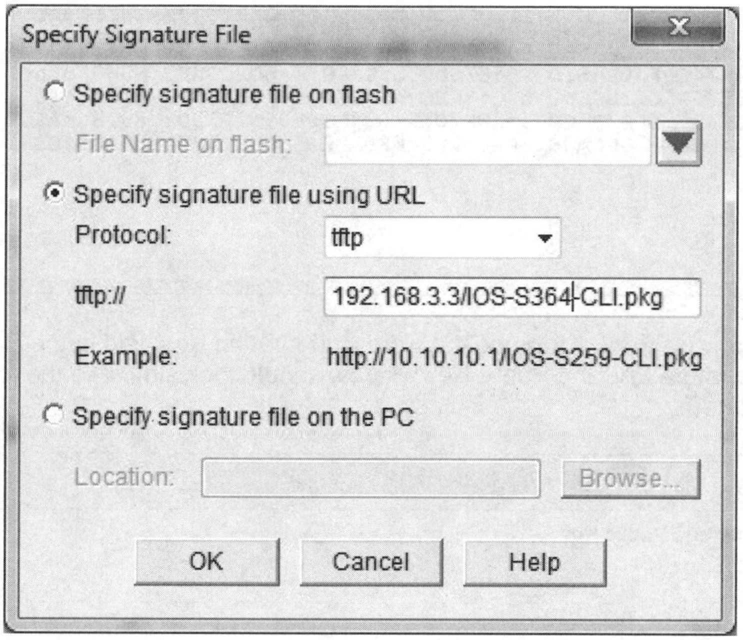

What other options can be specified as a source for the Signature File?

____

g. Click **OK** to return to the Signature File and Public Key window. In the Configure Public Key section of the Signature File and Public Key window, enter **realm-cisco.pub** in the Name field.

h. Each change to the signature configuration is saved in a delta file. This file must be digitally signed with a public key. You can obtain a key from Cisco.com and paste the information in the Name and Key fields. In this lab, you copy and paste the key from a text file on PC-C.

i. Open the realm-cisco-pub-key.txt file located on the PC-C desktop. The following is an example from the realm-cisco-pub-key.txt file.

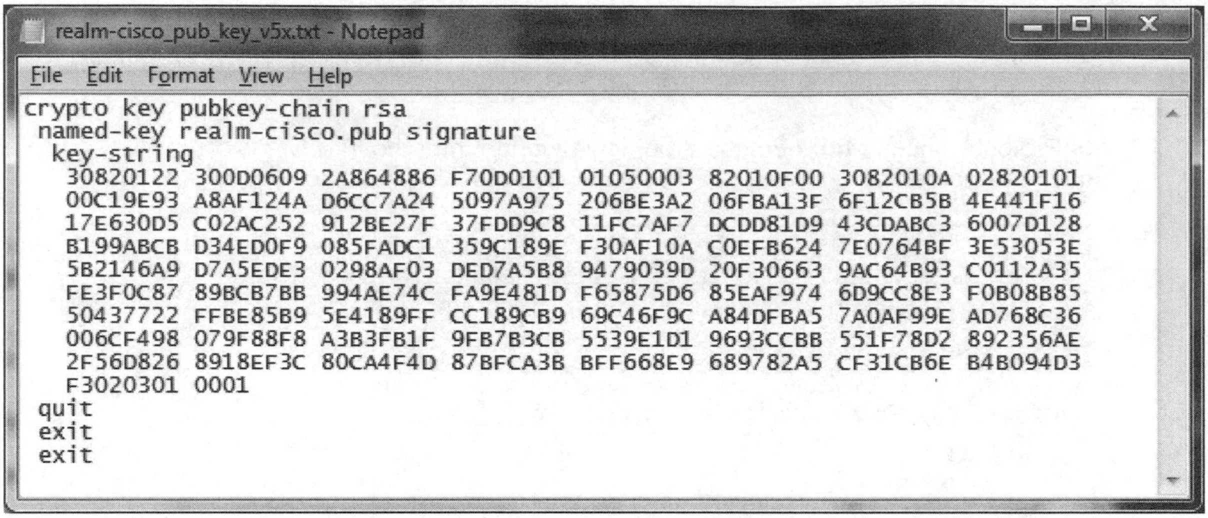


```
crypto key pubkey-chain rsa
 named-key realm-cisco.pub signature
  key-string
   30820122 300D0609 2A864886 F70D0101 01050003 82010F00 3082010A 02820101
   00C19E93 A8AF124A D6CC7A24 5097A975 206BE3A2 06FBA13F 6F12CB5B 4E441F16
   17E630D5 C02AC252 912BE27F 37FDD9C8 11FC7AF7 DCDD81D9 43CDABC3 6007D128
   B199ABCB D34ED0F9 085FADC1 359C189E F30AF10A C0EFB624 7E0764BF 3E53053E
   5B2146A9 D7A5EDE3 0298AF03 DED7A5B8 9479039D 20F30663 9AC64B93 C0112A35
   FE3F0C87 89BCB7BB 994AE74C FA9E481D F65875D6 85EAF974 6D9CC8E3 F0B08B85
   50437722 FFBE85B9 5E4189FF CC189CB9 69C46F9C A84DFBA5 7A0AF99E AD768C36
   006CF498 079F88F8 A3B3FB1F 9FB7B3CB 5539E1D1 9693CCBB 551F78D2 892356AE
   2F56D826 8918EF3C 80CA4F4D 87BFCA3B BFF668E9 689782A5 CF31CB6E B4B094D3
   F3020301 0001
 quit
 exit
 exit
```

j. Copy the text between the phrase **key-string** and the word **quit** into the Key field in the Configure Public Key section. The Signature File and Public Key window should look similar to the following when the entries are completed.

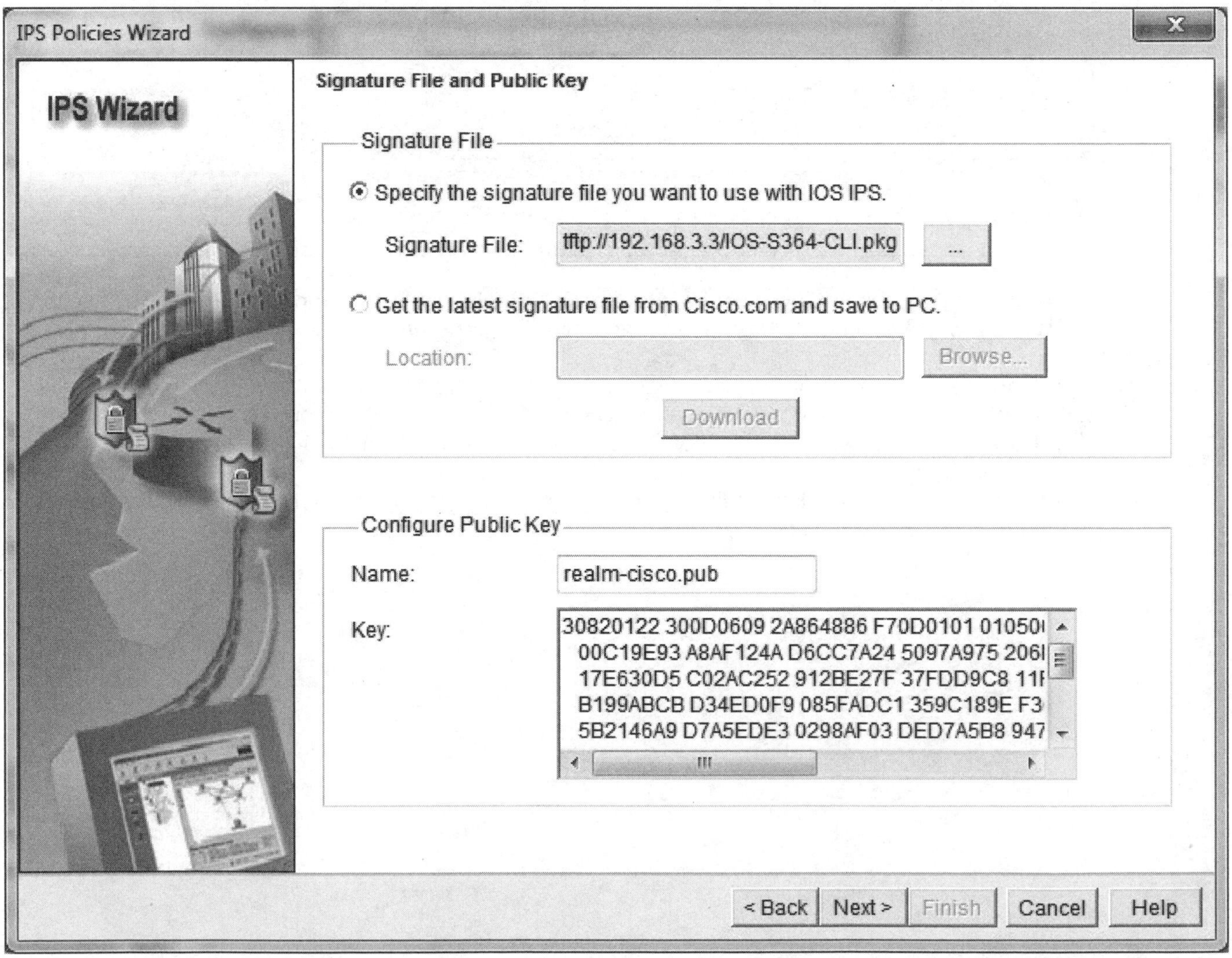

k. Click **Next** to display the Config Location and Category window. This is used to specify where to store the signature information. This file is used by the Cisco IOS IPS for detecting attacks from coming into the Fast Ethernet0/1 or Serial0/0/1 interfaces.

l. In the Config Location and Category window in the Config Location section, click the ellipsis (**...**) button next to **Config Location** to add the location.

m. Verify that **Specify the config location on this router** is selected. Click the ellipsis (**...**) button. Click the plus sign (**+**) next to flash. Choose **ipsdir**, and then click **OK**.

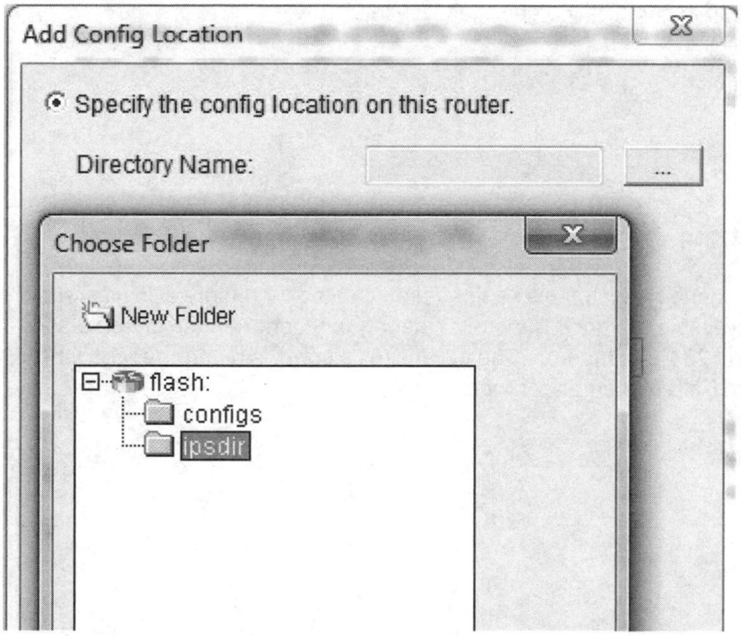

n. Because router memory and resource constraints might prevent using all the available signatures, there are two categories of signatures: basic and advanced. In the Choose Category field of the Config Location and Category window, choose **Basic**. The Config Location and Category window should look similar to the following when the entries are completed.

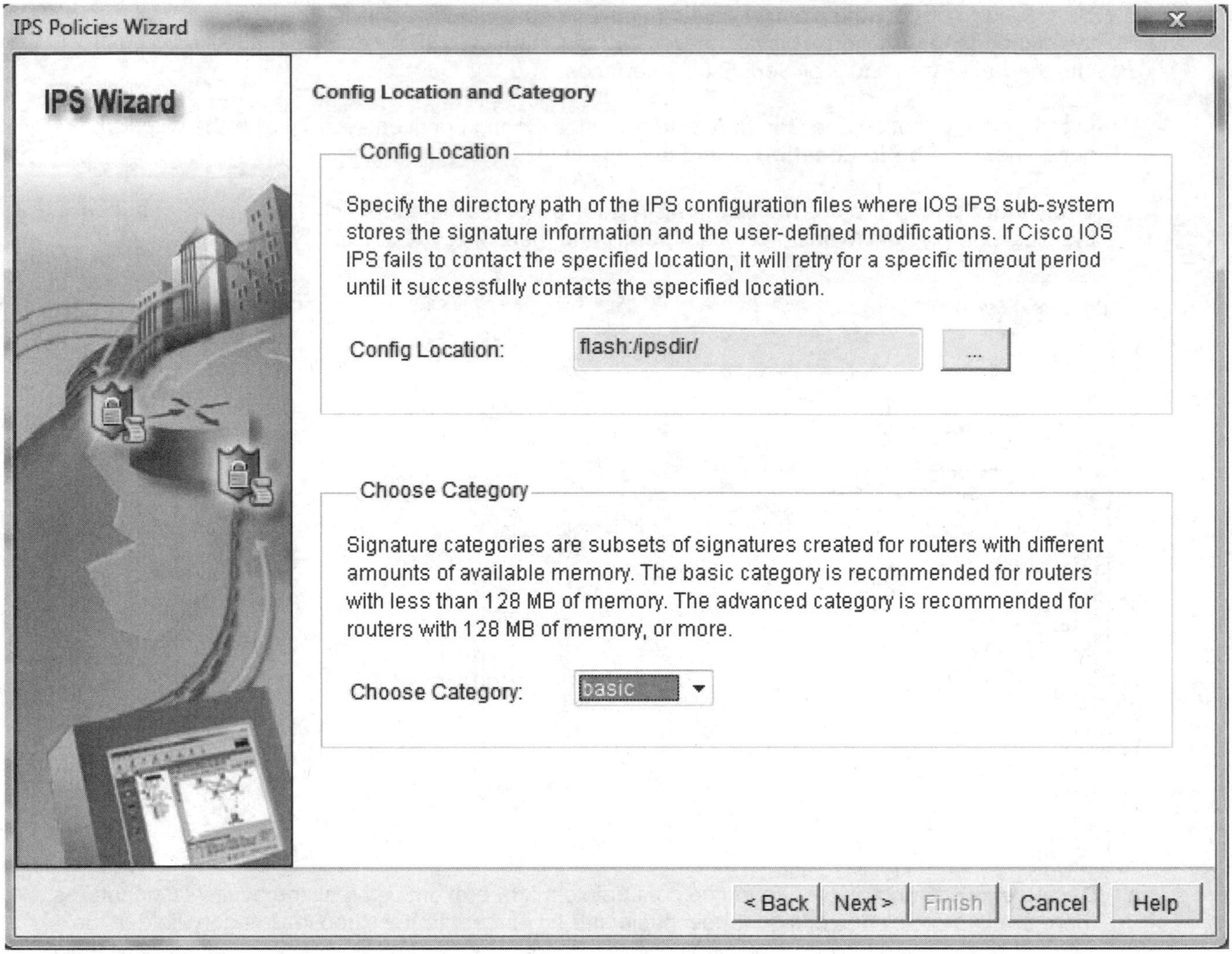

o. Click **Next** in the CCP IPS Policies Wizard window. The Summary window appears. Examine the IPS configuration information shown.

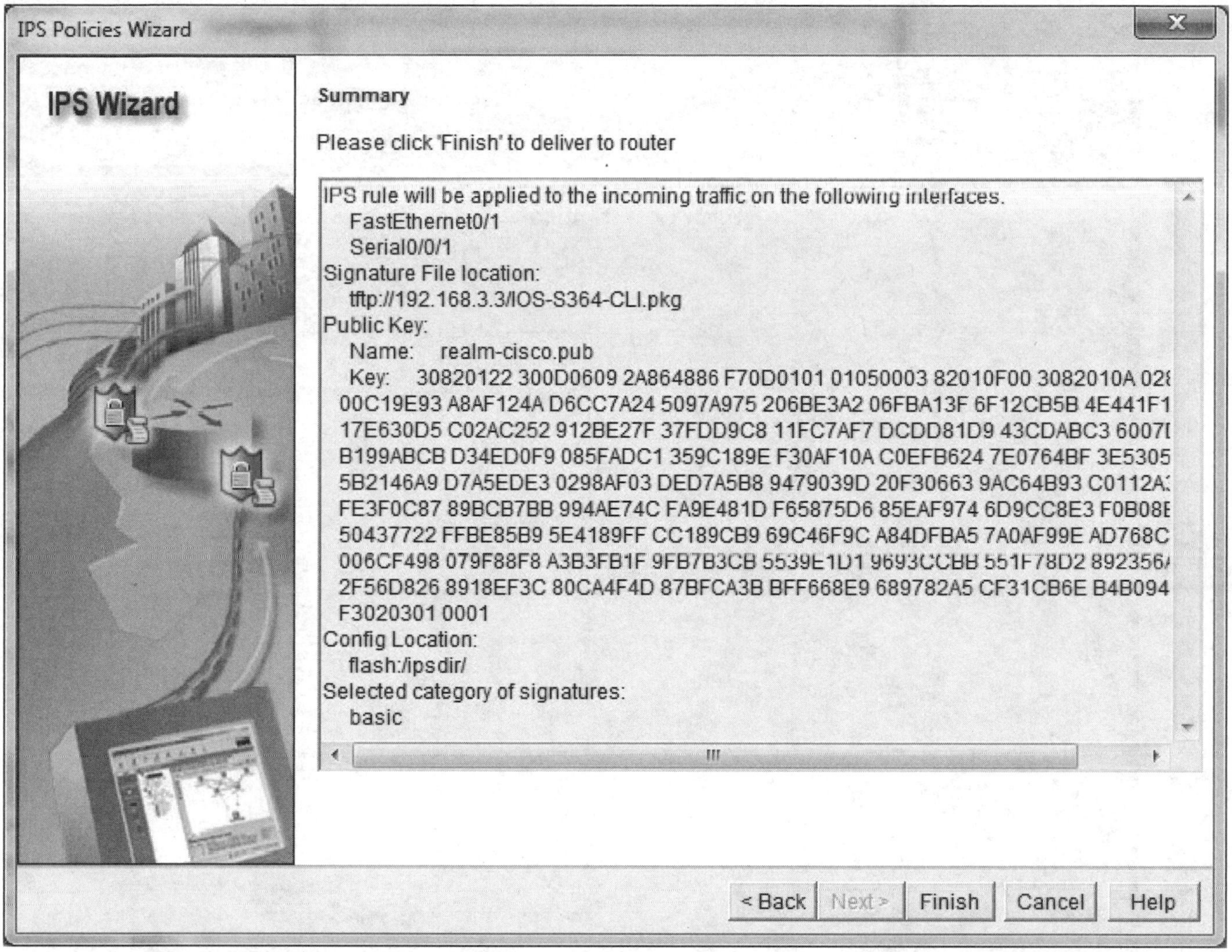

p. Click **Finish** in the IPS Policies Wizard window and review the commands that are delivered to the router.

q. Click **Deliver**. How many commands were delivered to the router? ______________________________

r. When the Commands Deliver Status window is ready, click **OK**. The IOS IPS Configuration Status window opens stating that it can take several minutes for the signatures to be configured.

s. When the signature configuration process has completed, you return to the IPS window with the Edit IPS tab selected. Your screen should look similar to the following.

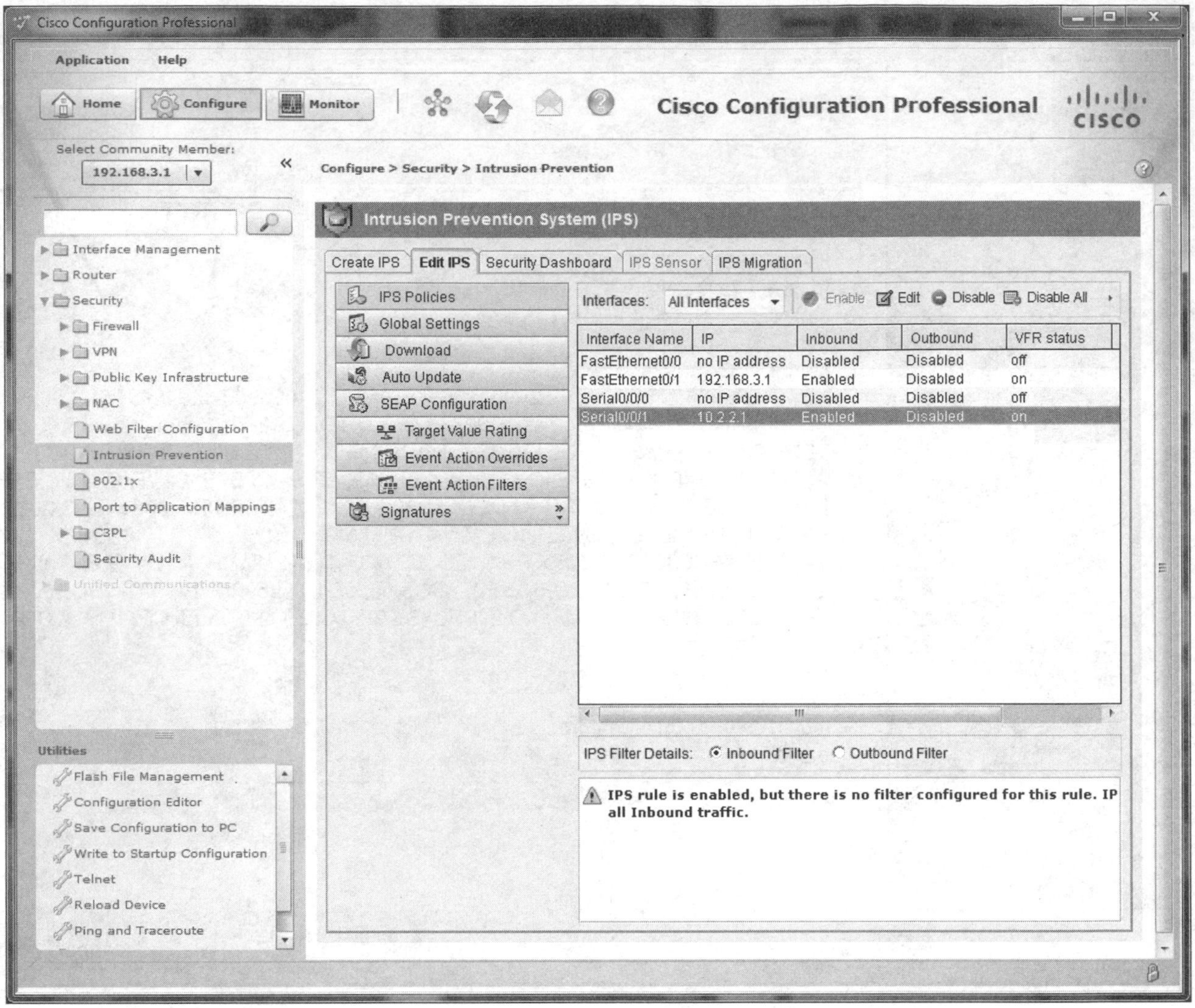

t. Select interface Serial0/0/1 from the list. What information is displayed at the bottom of the screen?

____

Task 5: Modify Signature Settings

Step 1: Verify connectivity.

From PC-C, ping R3. The pings should be successful.

Step 2: Configure the IPS application to drop ping (echo request) traffic.

a. From CCP, click **Configure** and choose **Security > Intrusion Prevention > Edit IPS > Signatures**. How many total signatures are there? ______________________________

Are all of them enabled? _____

b. In the View By drop-down list, choose **Sig ID**.

c. In the **Sig ID** field, enter **2004**, and then click **Go**. What is Sig ID 2004?

____

d. Do you know why the pings from PC-C in Step 1 were successful?

____

e. Select signature **2004**, click the **Unretire** button, and then click the **Enable** button.

f. Right-click the signature and choose **Actions** from the context menu.

g. Choose **Deny Packet Inline** and leave the **Produce Alert** check box checked. Click **OK**.

h. Click **Apply Changes**. It might take some time for the changes to take effect.

CCP 2.5 lists all the signatures again. Once again, choose **Sig ID** in the View By drop-down list, enter **2004** in the **Sig ID** field, and then click **Go**. Your screen should look similar to the following.

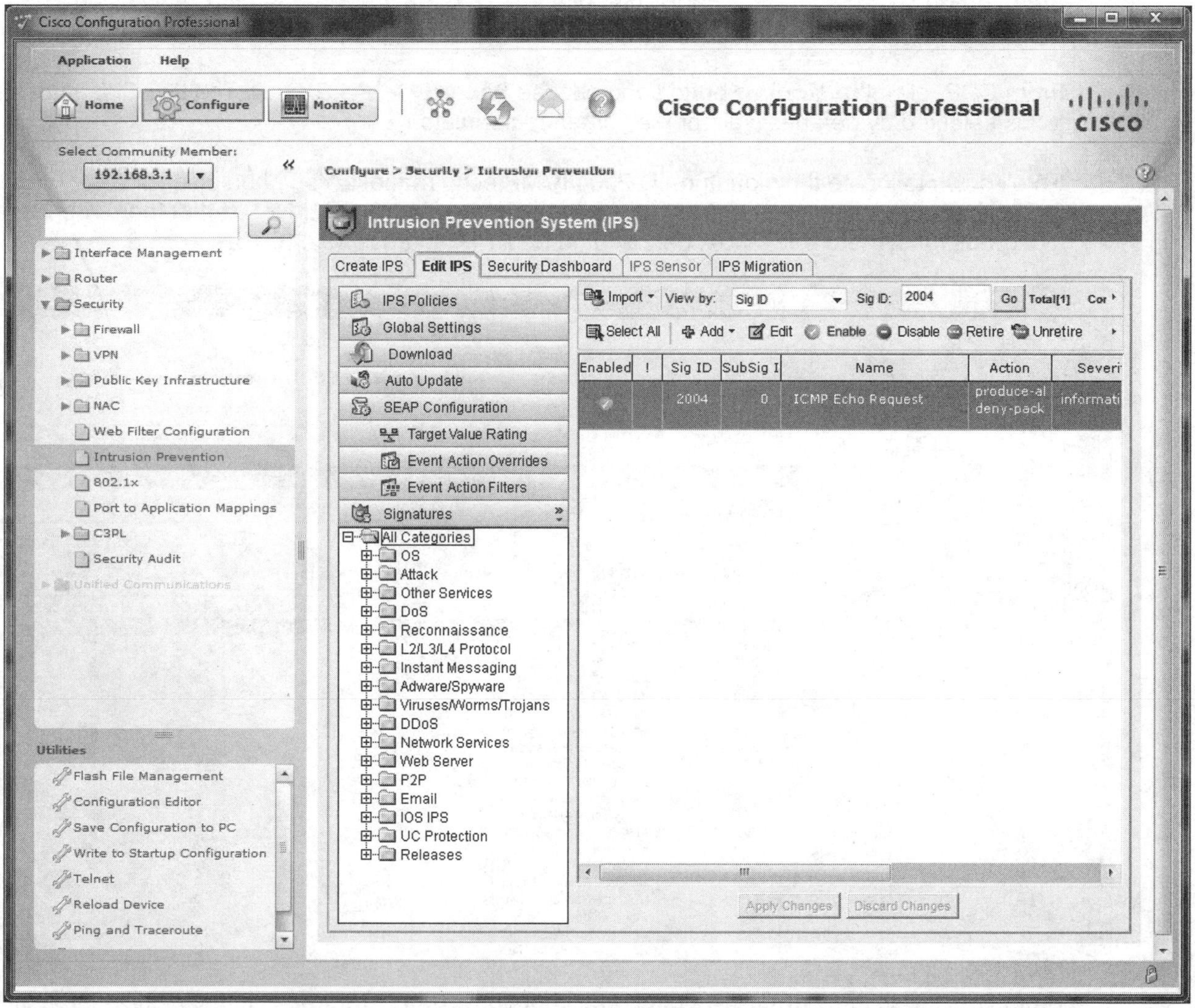

i. Return to PC-C and ping R3 again. Were the pings successful this time?

____

Task 6: Configure IPS Global Settings Using CCP

In this task, you enable the syslog and SDEE global settings using the CCP GUI.

a. From CCP, click **Configure** and choose **Security > Intrusion Prevention > Edit IPS > Global Settings**.

b. Verify that the syslog and SDEE options are enabled.

Note: Even if the Syslog and SDEE options are already enabled, click the **Edit** button and explore the options available in the Edit Global Settings dialog box. Examine the options to learn whether Cisco IOS IPS has set the default to fail opened or to fail closed.

Task 7: Verify IPS Functionality with CCP Monitor and Ping

In this task, you demonstrate how the Cisco IOS IPS protects against an external attacker using ping.

a. From the R2 CLI, ping the R3 Fa0/1 interface at 192.168.3.1. Were the pings successful?

____

b. From CCP, click the **Monitor** button and choose **Security > IPS Status**. The IPS Signature Statistics tab is selected by default. Wait for the screen to populate.

c. Scroll down to locate the signature ID 2004 ICMP echo request. You should see an entry similar to the one here indicating that IPS identified the ping attempt from R2. Notice that there are five hits and five drops for signature ID 2004, detected on Fa0/1 IP address 192.168.3.1.

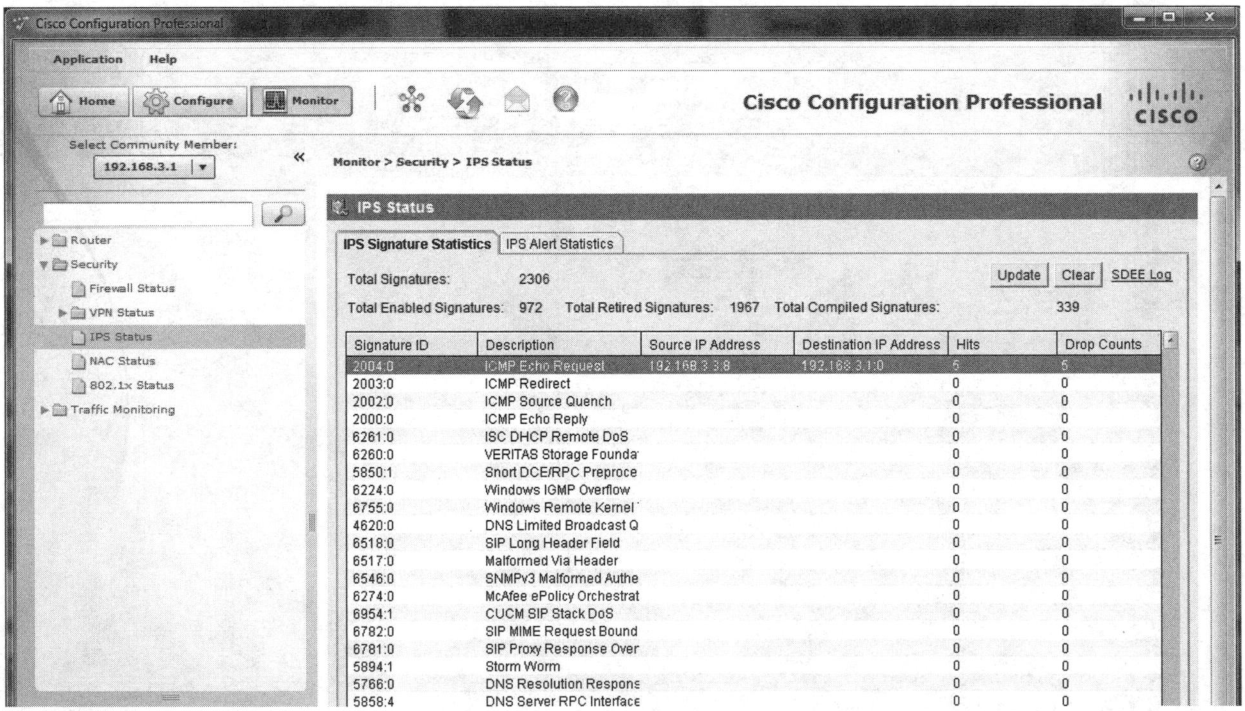

d. From CCP, click the **Configure** button and choose **Router > Logging**. In the Additional Tasks window, ensure that syslog is running on R3 by clicking the **Edit** button. The window should be similar to the following Logging dialog.

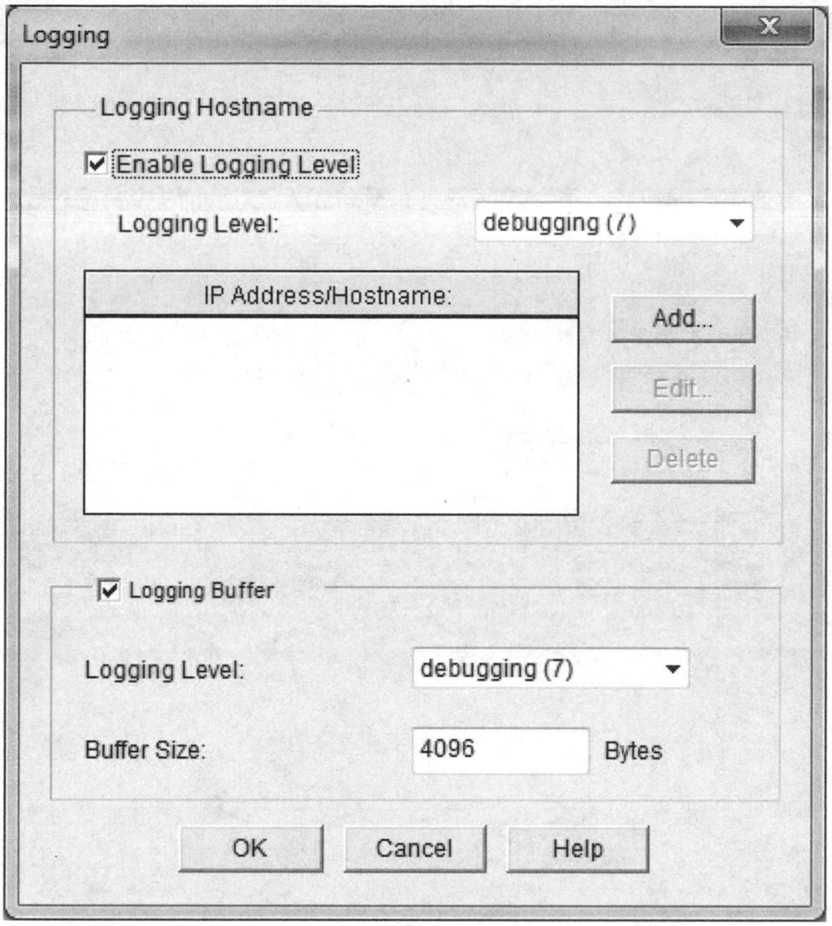

e. From CCP, click the **Monitor** button and choose **Router > Logging**.

f. A number of syslog messages are displayed. Click the **Clear** button to clear the log.

g. From the R2 CLI, ping the R3 Fa0/1 interface at 192.168.3.1 again.

h. Click the **Update** button. You will see that the Cisco IOS IPS logged the ping attempts from R2.

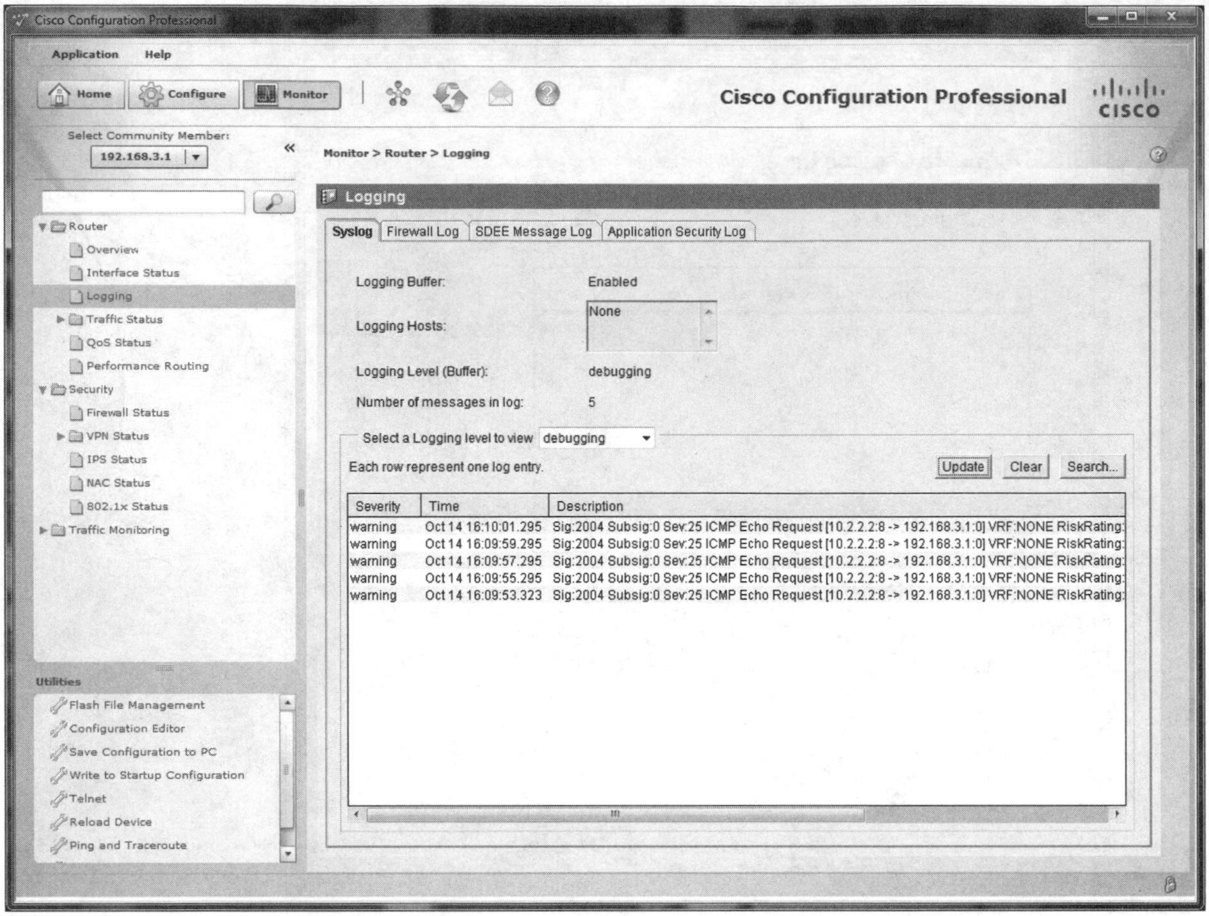

Task 8: (Optional) Verify IPS Functionality with CCP Monitor and SuperScan

In this task, you demonstrate how the Cisco IOS IPS protects against an internal attacker that is using SuperScan. SuperScan is a freeware scanning tool that runs with Windows XP that can detect open TCP and UDP ports on a target host. You can perform this task if the SuperScan program is available on PC-C or if it can be downloaded.

SuperScan tests the IPS capabilities on R3. You run the scanning program from PC-C and attempt to scan open ports on router R2. The IPS rule iosips, which is set on R3 Fa0/1 inbound, should intercept the scanning attempts and send messages to the R3 console and CCP syslog.

Step 1: Download the SuperScan program.

a. If SuperScan is not on PC-C, download the SuperScan 4.0 tool from the Scanning Tools group at http://www.foundstone.com.

b. Unzip the file into a folder. The SuperScan4.exe file is executable and installation is not required.

Step 2: Run SuperScan and set scanning options.

a. Start SuperScan on PC-C. Display the **Host and Service Discovery** tab. Check the **Timestamp Request** check box, and uncheck the **Echo Request** check box. Scroll through the UDP and TCP port selection lists and notice the range of ports that will be scanned.

b. Display the **Scan** tab and enter the IP address of R2 S0/0/1 (**10.2.2.2**) in the Hostname/IP field.

Note: You can also specify an address range, such as 10.2.2.1 to 10.2.2.254, by entering an address in the Start IP and End IP fields. The program will scan all hosts with addresses in the range specified.

c. Click the button with the blue arrow in the lower-left corner of the screen to start the scan.

Step 3: Check the results with CCP logging.

a. From CCP, choose **Monitor > Router > Logging**.

b. Click the **Update** button. You see that the Cisco IOS IPS has been logging the port scans generated by SuperScan.

c. You should see syslog messages on R3 and entries in the CCP Monitor Log with descriptions that include one of these phrases: `Invalid DHCP Packet` or `DNS Version Request`.

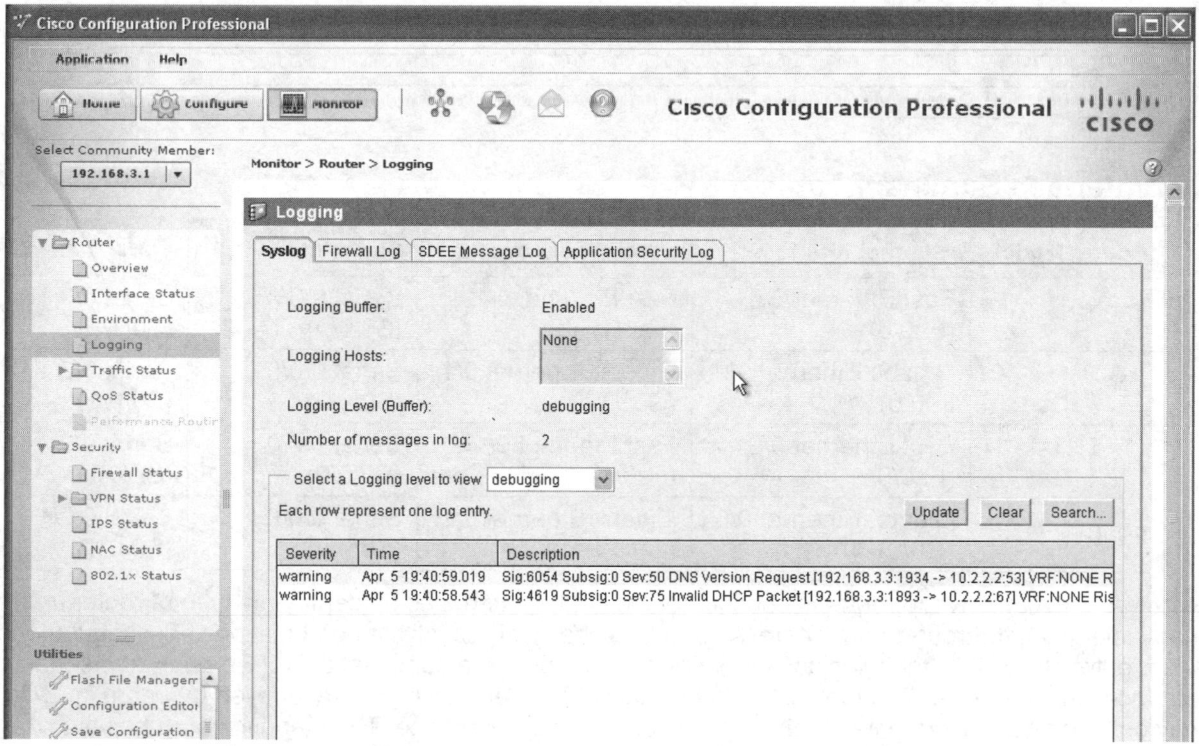

d. Close the SuperScan window.

Task 9: Compare the Results for Different IPS Configuration Methods.

a. On R1, display the running configuration after IPS was configured with IOS CLI commands. Note the commands related to IPS.

b. On R3, from the menu bar, choose **Utilities > View** > **Show Running Config** to display the running configuration after IPS was configured with the CCP GUI. Note the commands related to IPS.

What differences are there between the CLI-based running configuration and the CCP-based running configuration?

____

Reflection

1. What are some advantages and disadvantages to using CLI or CCP to configure IPS?

2. With Version 5.x signature files, if changes are made to a signature, are they visible in the router running configuration?

Router Interface Summary Table

Router Model	Ethernet Interface 1	Ethernet Interface 2	Serial Interface 1	Serial Interface 2
1800	Fast Ethernet 0/0 (Fa0/0)	Fast Ethernet 0/1 (Fa0/1)	Serial 0/0/0 (S0/0/0)	Serial 0/0/1 (S0/0/1)
1900	Gigabit Ethernet 0/0 (G0/0)	Gigabit Ethernet 0/1 (G0/1)	Serial 0/0/0 (S0/0/0)	Serial 0/0/1 (S0/0/1)
2800	Fast Ethernet 0/0 (Fa0/0)	Fast Ethernet 0/1 (Fa0/1)	Serial 0/0/0 (S0/0/0)	Serial 0/0/1 (S0/0/1)
2900	Gigabit Ethernet 0/0 (G0/0)	Gigabit Ethernet 0/1 (G0/1)	Serial 0/0/0 (S0/0/0)	Serial 0/0/1 (S0/0/1)

Note: To find out how the router is configured, look at the interfaces to identify the type of router and how many interfaces the router has. There is no way to effectively list all the combinations of configurations for each router class. This table includes identifiers for the possible combinations of Ethernet and serial interfaces in the device. The table does not include any other type of interface, even though a specific router may contain one. An example of this might be an ISDN BRI interface. The string in parentheses is the legal abbreviation that can be used in Cisco IOS commands to represent the interface.

Chapter 6 Lab A: Securing Layer 2 Switches

Topology

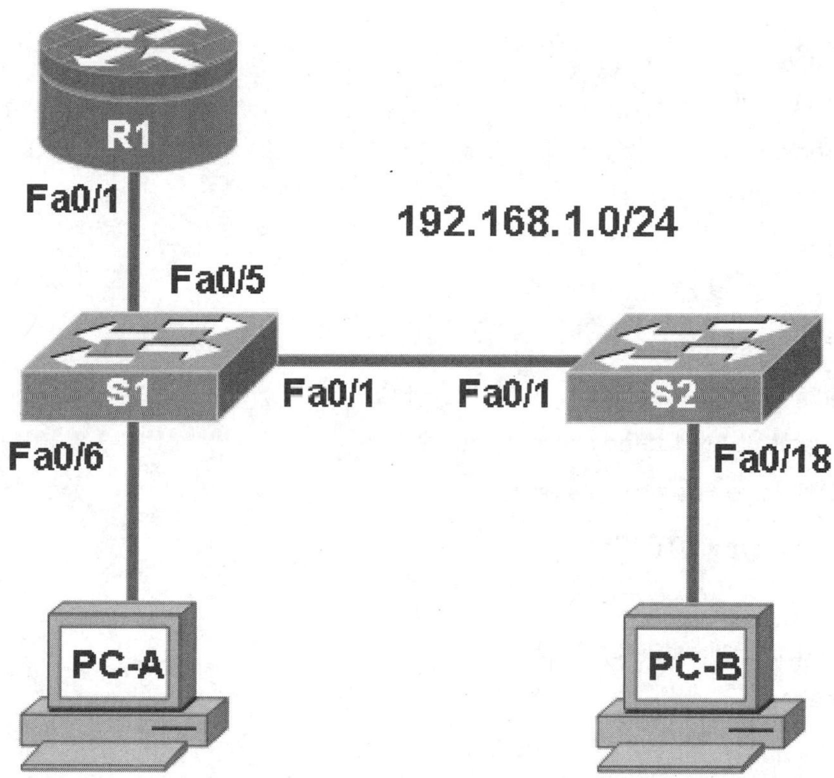

IP Addressing Table

Device	Interface	IP Address	Subnet Mask	Default Gateway	Switch Port
R1	Fa0/1	192.168.1.1	255.255.255.0	N/A	S1 Fa0/5
S1	VLAN 1	192.168.1.2	255.255.255.0	N/A	N/A
S2	VLAN 1	192.168.1.3	255.255.255.0	N/A	N/A
PC-A	NIC	192.168.1.10	255.255.255.0	192.168.1.1	S1 Fa0/6
PC-B	NIC	192.168.1.11	255.255.255.0	192.168.1.1	S2 Fa0/18

Objectives

Part 1: Configure Basic Switch Settings

- Build the topology.
- Configure the hostname, IP address, and access passwords.

Part 2: Configure SSH Access to the Switches

- Configure SSH access on the switch.

- Configure an SSH client to access the switch.
- Verify the configuration.

Part 3: Secure Trunks and Access Ports

- Configure trunk port mode.
- Change the native VLAN for trunk ports.
- Verify trunk configuration.
- Enable storm control for broadcasts.
- Configure access ports.
- Enable PortFast and BPDU guard.
- Verify BPDU guard.
- Enable root guard.
- Configure and verify port security.
- Disable unused ports.
- Move ports from default VLAN 1 to an alternate VLAN.
- Configure the PVLAN Edge Feature on a port.

Part 4: Configure SPAN and Monitor Traffic

- Configure Switched Port Analyzer (SPAN).
- Monitor port activity using Wireshark.
- Analyze a sourced attack.

Background

The Layer 2 infrastructure consists mainly of interconnected Ethernet switches. Most end-user devices, such as computers, printers, IP phones, and other hosts, connect to the network via Layer 2 access switches. As a result, switches can present a network security risk. Similar to routers, switches are subject to attack from malicious internal users. The switch Cisco IOS software provides many security features that are specific to switch functions and protocols.

In this lab, you configure Secure Shell (SSH) access and Layer 2 security for switches S1 and S2. You also configure various switch protection measures, including access port security, switch storm control, and Spanning Tree Protocol (STP) features such as BPDU guard and root guard. Finally, you use Cisco Switched Port Analyzer (SPAN) to monitor traffic to specific ports on the switch.

Note: The router commands and output in this lab are from a Cisco 1841 with Cisco IOS Software Release 12.4(20)T (advanced IP image). The switch commands and output are from a Cisco WS-C2960-24TT-L with Cisco IOS Software Release 12.2(46)SE (C2960-LANBASEK9-M image). Other routers, switches, and IOS versions may be used. See the Router Interface Summary table at the end of the lab to determine which interface identifiers to use based on the equipment in the lab. Depending on the router or switch model and IOS version, the commands available and output produced might vary from what is shown in this lab.

Note: Make sure that the router and the switches have been erased and have no startup configurations.

Required Resources

- 1 router (Cisco 1841 with Cisco IOS Software Release 12.4(20)T1 or comparable)
- 2 switches (Cisco 2960 or comparable with cryptography IOS image for SSH support – Release 12.2(46)SE or comparable)
- PC-A: Windows XP, Vista, or Windows 7 with PuTTY SSH client and Wireshark
- PC-B: Windows XP, Vista, or Windows 7 with PuTTY SSH client and SuperScan (optional)
- Ethernet cables as shown in the topology
- Rollover cables to configure the switches via the console

Part 1: Basic Device Configuration

In Part 1 of this lab, you set up the network topology and configure basic settings such as the hostnames, IP addresses, and device access passwords.

Note: Perform all tasks on router R1 and switches S1 and S2. The procedure for S1 is shown here as an example.

Step 1: Cable the network as shown in the topology.

Attach the devices shown in the topology diagram and cable as necessary.

Step 2: Configure basic settings for the router and each switch.

a. Configure hostnames as shown in the topology.

b. Configure interface IP addresses as shown in the IP addressing table. The configuration of the VLAN 1 management interface on switch S1 is shown here:

```
S1(config)# interface vlan 1
S1(config-if)# ip address 192.168.1.2 255.255.255.0
S1(config-if)# no shutdown
```

c. Configure the enable secret and console passwords:

```
S1(config)# enable secret cisco12345
S1(config)# line console 0
S1(config-line)# password ciscoconpass
S1(config-line)# exec-timeout 5 0
S1(config-line)# login
S1(config-line)# logging synchronous
```

Note: Do not configure the switch vty access at this time. The vty lines are configured on the switches in Part 2 for SSH access.

d. Configure the vty lines and password on R1:

```
R1(config)# line vty 0 4
R1(config-line)# password ciscovtypass
R1(config-line)# exec-timeout 5 0
R1(config-line)# login
```

e. To prevent the router or switch from attempting to translate incorrectly entered commands, disable DNS lookup. Router R1 is shown here as an example:

```
R1(config)# no ip domain-lookup
```

f. HTTP access to the switch is enabled by default. To prevent HTTP access, disable the HTTP server and HTTP secure server:

```
S1(config)# no ip http server
S1(config)# no ip http secure-server
```

Note: The switch must have a cryptography IOS image to support the **ip http secure-server** command. HTTP access to the router is disabled by default.

Step 3: Configure PC host IP settings.

Configure a static IP address, subnet mask, and default gateway for PC-A and PC-B as shown in the IP Addressing Table.

Step 4: Verify basic network connectivity.

Ping from PC-A and PC-B to the R1 Fa0/1 interface at IP address 192.168.1.1. Were the results successful?

_____

If the pings are not successful, troubleshoot the basic device configurations before continuing.

Ping from PC-A to PC-B. Were the results successful? _____

If the pings are not successful, troubleshoot the basic device configurations before continuing.

Step 5: Save the basic configurations for the router and both switches.

Save the running configuration to the startup configuration from the privileged EXEC prompt:

```
S1# copy running-config startup-config
```

Part 2: SSH Configuration

In Part 2 of this lab, you configure switches S1 and S2 to support SSH connections and install SSH client software on the PCs.

Note: A switch IOS image that supports encryption is required to configure SSH. Otherwise, you cannot specify SSH as an input protocol for the vty lines and the **crypto** commands are not available.

Task 1: Configure the SSH Server on Switch S1 and S2 Using the CLI

In this task, use the CLI to configure the switch to be managed securely using SSH instead of Telnet. Secure Shell (SSH) is a network protocol that establishes a secure terminal emulation connection to a switch or other networking device. SSH encrypts all information that passes over the network link and provides authentication of the remote computer. SSH is rapidly replacing Telnet as the remote login tool of choice for network professionals. It is strongly recommended that SSH be used in place of Telnet on production networks.

Note: For a switch to support SSH, it must be configured with local authentication or AAA. In this task, you configure an SSH username and local authentication on S1 and S2. S1 is shown here as an example.

Step 1: Configure a domain name.

Enter global configuration mode and set the domain name:

```
S1# conf t
S1(config)# ip domain-name ccnasecurity.com
```

Step 2: Configure a privileged user for login from the SSH client.

a. Use the **username** command to create the user ID with the highest possible privilege level and a secret password.

```
S1(config)#username admin privilege 15 secret cisco12345
```

b. Exit to the initial switch login screen, and log in with this username. What was the switch prompt after you entered the password? ______________________________

Step 3: Configure the incoming vty lines.

a. Configure vty access on lines 0 through 4. Specify a privilege level of 15 so that a user with the highest privilege level (15) defaults to privileged EXEC mode when accessing the vty lines. Other users default to user EXEC mode. Specify the use of local user accounts for mandatory login and validation, and accept only SSH connections:

```
S1(config)# line vty 0 4
S1(config-line)# privilege level 15
S1(config-line)# exec-timeout 5 0
S1(config-line)# login local
S1(config-line)# transport input ssh
S1(config-line)# exit
```

b. Disable login for switch vty lines 5 through 15 by allowing no transport input:

```
S1(config)# line vty 5 15
S1(config-line)# transport input none
```

Step 4: Generate the RSA encryption key pair for the router.

The switch uses the RSA key pair for authentication and encryption of transmitted SSH data.

Configure the RSA keys with 1024 for the number of modulus bits. The default is 512, and the range is from 360 to 2048.

```
S1(config)# crypto key generate rsa general-keys modulus 1024
The name for the keys will be: S1.ccnasecurity.com

% The key modulus size is 1024 bits
% Generating 1024 bit RSA keys, keys will be non-exportable...[OK]

S1(config)#
00:15:36: %SSH-5-ENABLED: SSH 1.99 has been enabled
```

Step 5: Verify the SSH configuration.

a. Use the **show ip ssh** command to see the current settings:

```
S1# show ip ssh
```

b. Fill in the following information based on the output of the **`show ip ssh`** command:

SSH version enabled: ____________________

Authentication timeout: ____________________

Authentication retries: ____________________

Step 6: Configure SSH timeouts and authentication parameters.

You can alter the default SSH timeouts and authentication parameters to be more restrictive using the following commands:

```
S1(config)# ip ssh time-out 90
S1(config)# ip ssh authentication-retries 2
```

Step 7: Save the running-config to the startup-config.

```
S1# copy running-config startup-config
```

Task 2: Configure the SSH Client

TeraTerm and PuTTY are two terminal emulation programs that can support SSHv2 client connections. This lab uses PuTTY.

Step 1: (Optional) Download and install an SSH client on PC-A and PC-B.

If the SSH client is not already installed, download either TeraTerm or PuTTY.

Note: The procedure described here is for PuTTY and pertains to PC-A.

Step 2: Verify SSH connectivity to S1 from PC-A.

a. Launch PuTTY by double-clicking the putty.exe icon (and clicking **Run** if prompted).

b. Input the S1 IP address **192.168.1.2** in the Host Name (or IP address) field.

c. Verify that the **SSH** radio button is selected. PuTTY defaults to SSH Version 2.

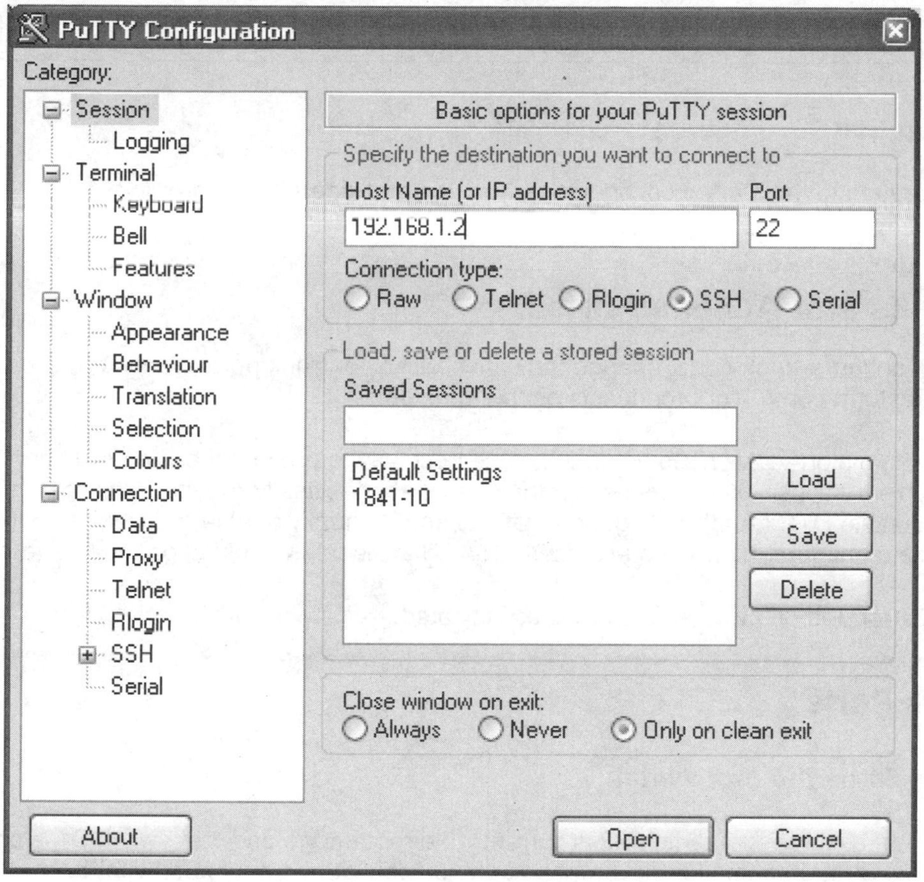

d. Click **Open**.

Note: Upon first connection, the user is prompted with a PuTTY Security Alert stating that the server's host key is not cached in the Registry.

e. In the PuTTY Security Alert window, click **Yes** to cache the server's host key.

f. Enter the admin username and password **cisco12345** in the PuTTY window.

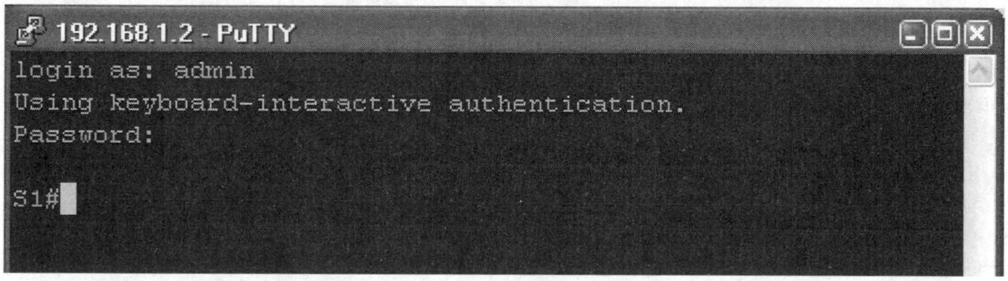

g. At the S1 privileged EXEC prompt, enter the **`show users`** command:

```
S1# show users
```

What users are connected to switch S1 at this time?

____

____

h. Close the PuTTy SSH session window with the **`exit`** or **`quit`** command.

i. Try to open a Telnet session to switch S1 from PC-A. Were you able to open the Telnet session? Why or why not? ____________________

Step 3: Save the configuration.

Save the running configuration to the startup configuration from the privileged EXEC prompt:

```
R1# copy running-config startup-config
```

Part 3: Secure Trunks and Access Ports

In Part 3 of this lab, you configure trunk ports, change the native VLAN for trunk ports, verify trunk configuration, and enable storm control for broadcasts on the trunk ports.

Securing trunk ports can help stop VLAN hopping attacks. The best way to prevent a basic VLAN hopping attack is to explicitly disable trunking on all ports except the ones that specifically require trunking. On the required trunking ports, disable DTP (autotrunking) negotiations and manually enable trunking. If no trunking is required on an interface, configure the port as an access port. This disables trunking on the interface.

Note: Tasks should be performed on switches S1 or S2 as indicated.

Task 1: Secure Trunk Ports

Step 1: Configure switch S1 as the root switch.

For the purposes of this lab, assume that switch S2 is currently the root bridge and that switch S1 is preferred as the root switch. To force S1 to become the new root bridge, you configure a new priority for it.

a. From the console on S1, enter privileged EXEC mode and then global configuration mode.

b. The default priority for switches S1 and S2 is 32769 (32768 + 1 with System ID Extension). Set S1 priority to 0 so that it becomes the root switch:

```
S1(config)# spanning-tree vlan 1 priority 0
S1(config)# exit
```

Note: You can also use the **spanning-tree vlan 1 root primary** command to make S1 the root switch for VLAN 1.

c. Issue the **show spanning-tree** command to verify that S1 is the root bridge and to see the ports in use and their status.

```
S1# show spanning-tree

VLAN0001
  Spanning tree enabled protocol ieee
  Root ID     Priority    1
              Address     001d.4635.0c80
              This bridge is the root
              Hello Time   2 sec  Max Age 20 sec  Forward Delay 15 sec

  Bridge ID   Priority    1        (priority 0 sys-id-ext 1)
              Address     001d.4635.0c80
              Hello Time   2 sec  Max Age 20 sec  Forward Delay 15 sec
              Aging Time 300

Interface          Role Sts Cost      Prio.Nbr Type
```

```
---------------- ---- --- --------- -------- --------------------------
------
Fa0/1            Desg FWD 19        128.1    P2p
Fa0/5            Desg FWD 19        128.5    P2p
Fa0/6            Desg FWD 19        128.6    P2p
```

What is the S1 priority? ____________________

What ports are in use and what is their status? ____________________

Step 2: Configure trunk ports on S1 and S2.

a. Configure port Fa0/1 on S1 as a trunk port:

```
S1(config)# interface FastEthernet 0/1
S1(config-if)# switchport mode trunk
```

Note: If performing this lab using NetLab with a 3560 switch, the user must first enter the command **switchport trunk encapsulation dot1q**.

b. Configure port Fa0/1 on S2 as a trunk port:

```
S2(config)# interface FastEthernet 0/1
S2(config-if)# switchport mode trunk
```

c. Verify that S1 port Fa0/1 is in trunking mode with the **show interfaces trunk** command:

```
S1# show interfaces trunk

Port      Mode         Encapsulation  Status        Native vlan
Fa0/1     on           802.1q         trunking      1

Port      Vlans allowed on trunk
Fa0/1     1-4094

Port      Vlans allowed and active in management domain
Fa0/1     1

Port      Vlans in spanning tree forwarding state and not pruned
Fa0/1     1
```

Step 3: Change the native VLAN for the trunk ports on S1 and S2.

Changing the native VLAN for trunk ports to an unused VLAN helps prevent VLAN hopping attacks.

From the output of the **show interfaces trunk** in the previous step, what is the current native VLAN for the S1 Fa0/1 trunk interface? ____________________

a. Set the native VLAN on the S1 Fa0/1 trunk interface to an unused VLAN 99:

```
S1(config)# interface Fa0/1
S1(config-if)# switchport trunk native vlan 99
S1(config-if)# end
```

The following message should be displayed after a brief period of time:

```
02:16:28: %CDP-4-NATIVE_VLAN_MISMATCH: Native VLAN mismatch discovered
on FastEthernet0/1 (99), with S2 FastEthernet0/1 (1).
```

What does the message mean? ____________________

b. Set the native VLAN on the S2 Fa0/1 trunk interface to VLAN 99:

```
S2(config)# interface Fa0/1
S2(config-if)# switchport trunk native vlan 99
S2(config-if)# end
```

Step 4: Prevent the use of DTP on S1 and S2.

Setting the trunk port to not negotiate also helps to mitigate VLAN hopping by turning off the generation of DTP frames:

```
S1(config)# interface Fa0/1
S1(config-if)# switchport nonegotiate

S2(config)# interface Fa0/1
S2(config-if)# switchport nonegotiate
```

Step 5: Verify the trunking configuration on port Fa0/1.

```
S1# show interface fa0/1 trunk

Port        Mode          Encapsulation  Status        Native vlan
Fa0/1       on            802.1q         trunking      99

Port        Vlans allowed on trunk
Fa0/1       1-4094

Port        Vlans allowed and active in management domain
Fa0/1       1

Port        Vlans in spanning tree forwarding state and not pruned
Fa0/1       1

S1# show interface fa0/1 switchport

Name: Fa0/1
Switchport: Enabled
Administrative Mode: trunk
Operational Mode: trunk
Administrative Trunking Encapsulation: dot1q
Operational Trunking Encapsulation: dot1q
Negotiation of Trunking: Off
Access Mode VLAN: 1 (default)
Trunking Native Mode VLAN: 99 (Inactive)
Administrative Native VLAN tagging: enabled
Voice VLAN: none
Administrative private-vlan host-association: none
Administrative private-vlan mapping: none
Administrative private-vlan trunk native VLAN: none
Administrative private-vlan trunk Native VLAN tagging: enabled
Administrative private-vlan trunk encapsulation: dot1q
Administrative private-vlan trunk normal VLANs: none
Administrative private-vlan trunk private VLANs: none
Operational private-vlan: none
Trunking VLANs Enabled: ALL
Pruning VLANs Enabled: 2-1001
Capture Mode Disabled
Capture VLANs Allowed: ALL
```

```
Protected: false
Unknown unicast blocked: disabled
Unknown multicast blocked: disabled
Appliance trust: none
```

Step 6: Enable storm control for broadcasts.

Enable storm control for broadcasts on the trunk port with a 50 percent rising suppression level using the **storm-control broadcast** command:

```
S1(config)# interface FastEthernet 0/1
S1(config-if)# storm-control broadcast level 50

S2(config)# interface FastEthernet 0/1
S2(config-if)# storm-control broadcast level 50
```

Step 7: Verify your configuration with the show run command.

Use the **show run** command to display the running configuration, beginning with the first line that has the text string "0/1" in it:

```
S1# show run | beg 0/1
interface FastEthernet0/1
 switchport trunk native vlan 99
 switchport mode trunk
 switchport nonegotiate
 storm-control broadcast level 50.00

<Output omitted>
```

Task 2: Secure Access Ports

By manipulating the STP root bridge parameters, network attackers hope to spoof their system, or a rogue switch that they add to the network, as the root bridge in the topology. If a port that is configured with PortFast receives a bridge protocol data unit (BPDU), STP can put the port into the blocking state by using a feature called BPDU guard.

Step 1: Disable trunking on S1 access ports.

a. On S1, configure Fa0/5, the port to which R1 is connected, as access mode only:

```
S1(config)# interface FastEthernet 0/5
S1(config-if)# switchport mode access
```

b. On S1, configure Fa0/6, the port to which PC-A is connected, as access mode only:

```
S1(config)# interface FastEthernet 0/6
S1(config-if)# switchport mode access
```

c. On S2, configure Fa0/18, the port to which PC-B is connected, as access mode only:

```
S2(config)# interface FastEthernet 0/18
S2(config-if)# switchport mode access
```

Task 3: Protect Against STP Attacks

The topology has only two switches and no redundant paths, but STP is still active. In this step, you enable some switch security features that can help reduce the possibility of an attacker manipulating switches via STP-related methods.

Step 1: Enable PortFast on S1 and S2 access ports.

PortFast is configured on access ports that connect to a single workstation or server to enable them to become active more quickly.

a. Enable PortFast on the S1 Fa0/5 access port:

```
S1(config)# interface FastEthernet 0/5
S1(config-if)# spanning-tree portfast
```

The following Cisco IOS warning message is displayed:

```
%Warning: portfast should only be enabled on ports connected to a
single host. Connecting hubs, concentrators, switches, bridges, etc...
to this interface when portfast is enabled, can cause temporary
bridging loops. Use with CAUTION

%Portfast has been configured on FastEthernet0/5 but will only
 have effect when the interface is in a non-trunking mode.
```

b. Enable PortFast on the S1 Fa0/6 access port:

```
S1(config)# interface FastEthernet 0/6
S1(config-if)# spanning-tree portfast
```

c. Enable PortFast on the S2 Fa0/18 access ports:

```
S2(config)# interface FastEthernet 0/18
S2(config-if)# spanning-tree portfast
```

Step 2: Enable BPDU guard on the S1 and S2 access ports.

BPDU guard is a feature that can help prevent rogue switches and spoofing on access ports.

a. Enable BPDU guard on the switch ports previously configured as access only:

```
S1(config)# interface FastEthernet 0/5
S1(config-if)# spanning-tree bpduguard enable

S1(config)# interface FastEthernet 0/6
S1(config-if)# spanning-tree bpduguard enable

S2(config)# interface FastEthernet 0/18
S2(config-if)# spanning-tree bpduguard enable
```

PortFast and BPDU guard can also be enabled globally with the **spanning-tree portfast default** and **spanning-tree portfast bpduguard** commands in global configuration mode.

Note: BPDU guard can be enabled on all access ports that have PortFast enabled. These ports should never receive a BPDU. BPDU guard is best deployed on user-facing ports to prevent rogue switch network extensions by an attacker. If a port enabled with BPDU guard receives a BPDU, it is disabled and must be manually reenabled. An err-disable timeout can be configured on the port so that it can recover automatically after a specified time period.

b. Verify that BPDU guard is configured by using the **show spanning-tree interface fa0/5 detail** command on switch S1:

```
S1# show spanning-tree interface fa0/5 detail

Port 5 (FastEthernet0/5) of VLAN0001 is designated forwarding
   Port path cost 19, Port priority 128, Port Identifier 128.5.
```

```
Designated root has priority 1, address 001d.4635.0c80
Designated bridge has priority 1, address 001d.4635.0c80
Designated port id is 128.5, designated path cost 0
Timers: message age 0, forward delay 0, hold 0
Number of transitions to forwarding state: 1
The port is in the portfast mode
Link type is point-to-point by default
Bpdu guard is enabled
BPDU: sent 3349, received 0
```

Step 3: (Optional) Enable root guard.

Root guard is another option in helping to prevent rogue switches and spoofing. You can enable root guard on all ports on a switch that are not root ports. It is normally enabled only on ports connecting to edge switches where a superior BPDU should never be received. Each switch should have only one root port, which is the best path to the root switch.

a. The following command configures root guard on S2 interface Gi0/1. Normally, this is done if another switch is attached to this port. Root guard is best deployed on ports that connect to switches that should not be the root bridge. In the lab topology, S1 Fa0/1 would be the most logical candidate for root guard. However, S2 Gi0/1 is shown here as an example, as Gigabit ports are more commonly used for inter-switch connections:

```
S2(config)# interface gigabitEthernet 0/1
S2(config-if)# spanning-tree guard root
```

b. Issue the **show run** command to verify that root guard is configured:

```
S2# sh run | beg Gig
interface GigabitEthernet0/1
 spanning-tree guard root
```

Note: The S2 Gi0/1 port is not currently up, so it is not participating in STP. Otherwise, you could use the **show spanning-tree interface Gi0/1 detail** command.

c. If a port that is enabled with BPDU guard receives a superior BPDU, it goes into a root-inconsistent state. Use the **show spanning-tree inconsistentports** command to determine whether there are any ports currently receiving superior BPDUs that should not be.

```
S2# show spanning-tree inconsistentports

Name                 Interface              Inconsistency
-------------------- ---------------------- ------------------
Number of inconsistent ports (segments) in the system : 0
```

Note: Root guard allows a connected switch to participate in STP as long as the device does not try to become the root. If root guard blocks the port, subsequent recovery is automatic. If the superior BPDUs stop, the port returns to the forwarding state.

Task 4: Configure Port Security and Disable Unused Ports

Switches can also be subject to CAM table (also known as MAC address table) overflow, MAC spoofing attacks, and unauthorized connections to switch ports. In this task, you configure port security to limit the number of MAC addresses that can be learned on a switch port and disable the port if that number is exceeded.

Step 1: Record the R1 Fa0/0 MAC address.

a. From the router R1 CLI, use the **show interface** command and record the MAC address of the interface:

```
R1# show interface fa0/1

FastEthernet0/1 is up, line protocol is up
  Hardware is Gt96k FE, address is 001b.5325.256f (bia 001b.5325.256f)
  Internet address is 192.168.1.1/24
  MTU 1500 bytes, BW 100000 Kbit/sec, DLY 100 usec,
     reliability 255/255, txload 1/255, rxload 1/255
  Encapsulation ARPA, loopback not set
  Keepalive set (10 sec)
  Full-duplex, 100Mb/s, 100BaseTX/FX
```

What is the MAC address of the R1 Fa0/1 interface? ______________________________

Step 2: Configure basic port security.

This procedure should be performed on all access ports that are in use. Switch S1 port Fa0/5 is shown here as an example.

Note: A switch port must be configured as an access port to enable port security.

a. From the switch S1 CLI, enter interface configuration mode for the port that connects to the router (FastEthernet 0/5):

```
S1(config)# interface FastEthernet 0/5
```

b. Shut down the switch port:

```
S1(config-if)# shutdown
```

c. Enable port security on the port:

```
S1(config-if)# switchport port-security
```

Note: Entering just the **switchport port-security** command sets the maximum MAC addresses to 1 and the violation action to shutdown. The **switchport port-security maximum** and **switchport port-security violation** commands can be used to change the default behavior.

d. Configure a static entry for the MAC address of R1 Fa0/1/ interface recorded in Step 1:

```
S1(config-if)# switchport port-security mac-address xxxx.xxxx.xxxx
```

(*xxxx.xxxx.xxxx* is the actual MAC address of the router FastEthernet 0/1 interface.)

Note: Optionally, you can use the **switchport port-security mac-address sticky** command to add all the secure MAC addresses that are dynamically learned on a port (up to the maximum set) to the switch running configuration.

e. Bring up the switch port:

```
S1(config-if)# no shutdown
```

Step 3: Verify port security on S1 Fa0/5.

a. On S1, issue the **show port-security** command to verify that port security has been configured on S1 Fa0/5:

```
S1# show port-security interface f0/5
Port Security              : Enabled
Port Status                : Secure-up
Violation Mode             : Shutdown
Aging Time                 : 0 mins
Aging Type                 : Absolute
SecureStatic Address Aging : Disabled
Maximum MAC Addresses      : 1
Total MAC Addresses        : 1
Configured MAC Addresses   : 1
Sticky MAC Addresses       : 0
Last Source Address:Vlan   : 001b.5325.256f:1
Security Violation Count   : 0
```

What is the status of the Fa0/5 port? ______________________________

What is the Last Source Address and VLAN?

____

b. From the router R1 CLI, ping PC-A to verify connectivity. This also ensures that the R1 Fa0/1 MAC address is learned by the switch.

```
R1# ping 192.168.1.10
```

c. You will now violate security by changing the MAC address on the router interface. Enter interface configuration mode for the FastEthernet 0/1 interface and shut it down:

```
R1(config)# interface FastEthernet 0/1
R1(config-if)# shutdown
```

d. Configure a MAC address for the interface on the interface, using aaaa.bbbb.cccc as the address:

```
R1(config-if)# mac-address aaaa.bbbb.cccc
```

e. Enable the Fast Ethernet 0/1 interface:

```
R1(config-if)# no shutdown
R1(config-if)# end
```

Note: You could also change the PC MAC address attached to S1 Fa0/6 and achieve similar results to those shown here.

f. From the router R1 CLI, ping PC-A. Was the ping successful? Why or why not?

____

g. On switch S1 console, observe the messages when port Fa0/5 detects the violating MAC address:

```
*Jan 14 01:34:39.750: %PM-4-ERR_DISABLE: psecure-violation error
detected on Fa0/5, putting Fa0/5 in err-disable state
*Jan 14 01:34:39.750: %PORT_SECURITY-2-PSECURE_VIOLATION: Security
violation occurred, caused by MAC address aaaa.bbbb.cccc on port
FastEthernet0/5.
*Jan 14 01:34:40.756: %LINEPROTO-5-UPDOWN: Line protocol on Interface
FastEthernet0/5, changed state to down
*Mar  1 01:34:41.755: %LINK-3-UPDOWN: Interface FastEthernet0/5,
changed state to down
```

h. On the switch, use the various **show port-security** commands to verify that port security has been violated:

```
S1# show port-security
Secure Port MaxSecureAddr CurrentAddr SecurityViolation Security Action
               (Count)       (Count)          (Count)
---------------------------------------------------------------------------
      Fa0/5             1           1                  1         Shutdown
---------------------------------------------------------------------------

S1# show port-security interface fastethernet0/5
Port Security              : Enabled
Port Status                : Secure-shutdown
Violation Mode             : Shutdown
Aging Time                 : 0 mins
Aging Type                 : Absolute
SecureStatic Address Aging : Disabled
Maximum MAC Addresses      : 1
Total MAC Addresses        : 1
Configured MAC Addresses   : 1
Sticky MAC Addresses       : 0
Last Source Address:Vlan   : aaaa.bbbb.cccc:1
Security Violation Count   : 1

S1#show port-security address
          Secure Mac Address Table
------------------------------------------------------------------------
-
Vlan  Mac Address       Type                     Ports   Remaining Age
                                                            (mins)
----  -----------       ----                     -----   -------------
  1   001b.5325.256f    SecureConfigured         Fa0/5          -
------------------------------------------------------------------------
```

i. On the router, shut down the FastEthernet 0/1 interface, remove the hard-coded MAC address from the router, and reenable the FastEthernet 0/1 interface:

```
R1(config)# interface FastEthernet 0/1
R1(config-if)# shutdown
R1(config-if)# no mac-address aaaa.bbbb.cccc
R1(config-if)# no shutdown
```

Note: This will restore the original Fast Ethernet interface MAC address.

j. From R1, try to ping the PC-A again at 192.168.1.10. Was the ping successful? Why or why not?

____

Step 4: Clear the S1 Fa0/5 error disabled status.

a. From the S1 console, clear the error and re-enable the port using the following commands. This will change the port status from Secure-shutdown to Secure-up.

```
S1(config)# interface FastEthernet 0/5
S1(config-if)# shutdown
S1(config-if)# no shutdown
```

Note: This assumes the device/interface with the violating MAC address has been removed and replaced with the one originally configured.

b. From R1, ping PC-A again. You should be successful this time.

```
R1#ping 192.168.1.10
```

Step 5: Remove basic port security on S1 Fa0/5.

a. From the S1 console, remove port security on Fa0/5. This procedure can also be used to reenable the port but port security commands will need to be reconfigured.

```
S1(config)# interface FastEthernet 0/5
S1(config-if)# shutdown
S1(config-if)# no switchport port-security
S1(config-if)# no switchport port-security mac-address 001b.5325.256f
S1(config-if)# no shutdown
```

b. You can also use the following commands to reset the interface to its default settings:

```
S1(config)# interface FastEthernet 0/5
S1(config-if)# shutdown
S1(config-if)# exit
S1(config)# default interface fastethernet 0/5
S1(config)# interface FastEthernet 0/5
S1(config-if)# no shutdown
```

Note: This default interface command also requires you to reconfigure the port as an access port to reenable the security commands.

Step 6: (Optional) Configure port security for VoIP.

The following example shows a typical port security configuration for a voice port. Three MAC addresses are allowed, and they are to be learned dynamically. One MAC address is for the IP phone, one is for the switch, and the third IP address is for the PC connected to the IP phone. Violations of this policy result in the port being shut down. The aging timeout for the learned MAC addresses is set to two hours.

This example is shown for switch S2 port Fa0/18:

```
S2(config)# interface Fa0/18
S2(config-if)# switchport mode access
S2(config-if)# switchport port-security
S2(config-if)# switchport port-security maximum 3
S2(config-if)# switchport port-security violation shutdown
S2(config-if)# switchport port-security aging time 120
```

Step 7: Disable unused ports on S1 and S2.

As a further security measure, disable any ports not being used on the switch.

a. Ports Fa0/1, Fa0/5, and Fa0/6 are used on switch S1. The remaining Fast Ethernet ports and the two Gigabit Ethernet ports will be shut down.

```
S1(config)# interface range Fa0/2 - 4
S1(config-if-range)# shutdown
S1(config-if-range)# interface range Fa0/7 - 24
S1(config-if-range)# shutdown
S1(config-if-range)# interface range gigabitethernet0/1 - 2
S1(config-if-range)# shutdown
```

b. Ports Fa0/18 and Gi0/1 are used on switch S2. The remaining Fast Ethernet ports and the Gigabit Ethernet ports will be shut down.

```
S2(config)# interface range Fa0/2 - 17
S2(config-if-range)# shutdown
```

```
S2(config-if-range)# interface range Fa0/19 - 24
S2(config-if-range)# shutdown
S2(config-if-range)# exit
S2(config)# interface gigabitethernet0/2
S2(config-if)# shutdown
```

Step 8: (Optional) Move active ports to a VLAN other than the default VLAN 1.

As a further security measure, you can move all active end user and router ports to a VLAN other than the default VLAN 1 on both switches.

a. Configure a new VLAN for users on each switch using the following commands:

```
S1(config)# vlan 20
S1(config-vlan)# name Users

S2(config)# vlan 20
S2(config-vlan)# name Users
```

b. Add the current active access (non-trunk) ports to the new VLAN:

```
S1(config)# interface range fa0/5 - 6
S1(config-if)# switchport access vlan 20

S2(config)# interface fa0/18
S2(config-if)# switchport access vlan 20
```

Note: This prevents communication between end-user hosts and the management VLAN IP address of the switch, which is currently VLAN 1. The switch can still be accessed and configured using the console connection.

If you need to provide Telnet or SSH access to the switch, a specific port can be designated as the management port and added to VLAN 1 with a specific management workstation attached. A more elaborate solution is to create a new VLAN for switch management (or use the existing native trunk VLAN 99) and configure a separate subnet for the management and user VLANs. Enable trunking with subinterfaces on R1 to route between the management and user VLAN subnets.

Step 9: Configure a port with the PVLAN Edge feature.

Some applications require that no traffic be forwarded at Layer 2 between ports on the same switch so that one neighbor does not see the traffic generated by another neighbor. In such an environment, the use of the Private VLAN (PVLAN) Edge feature, also known as protected ports, ensures that there is no exchange of unicast, broadcast, or multicast traffic between these ports on the switch. The PVLAN Edge feature can be implemented only for ports on the same switch and is locally significant.

For example, to prevent traffic between host PC-A on switch S1 (port Fa0/6) and a host on another S1 port (for example, port Fa0/7, which was previously shut down), you could use the **`switchport protected`** command to activate the PVLAN Edge feature on these two ports. To disable protected port, use the **`no switchport protected`** interface configuration command.

a. Configure the PVLAN Edge feature in interface configuration mode using the following commands:

```
S1(config)# interface fastEthernet 0/6
S1(config-if)# switchport protected

S1(config-if)# interface fastEthernet 0/7
S1(config-if)# switchport protected
S1(config-if)# no shut
S1(config-if)# end
```

b. Verify that the PVLAN Edge Feature (protected port) is enabled on Fa0/6:

```
S1# show interfaces fa0/6 switchport
Name: Fa0/6
Switchport: Enabled
Administrative Mode: dynamic auto
Operational Mode: static access
Administrative Trunking Encapsulation: dot1q
Negotiation of Trunking: On
Access Mode VLAN: 1 (default)
Trunking Native Mode VLAN: 1 (default)
Administrative Native VLAN tagging: enabled
Voice VLAN: none
Administrative private-vlan host-association: none
Administrative private-vlan mapping: none
Administrative private-vlan trunk native VLAN: none
Administrative private-vlan trunk Native VLAN tagging: enabled
Administrative private-vlan trunk encapsulation: dot1q
Administrative private-vlan trunk normal VLANs: none
Administrative private-vlan trunk private VLANs: none
Operational private-vlan: none
Trunking VLANs Enabled: ALL
Pruning VLANs Enabled: 2-1001
Capture Mode Disabled
Capture VLANs Allowed: ALL

Protected: true
Unknown unicast blocked: disabled
Unknown multicast blocked: disabled
Appliance trust: none
```

c. Deactivate protected port on interfaces Fa0/6 and Fa0/7 using the following commands:

```
S1(config)# interface fastEthernet 0/6
S1(config-if)# no switchport protected

S1(config-if)# interface fastEthernet 0/7
S1(config-if)# no switchport protected
```

Part 4: Configure SPAN and Monitor Traffic

Note: There are two tasks in this part of the lab, Task 1: Option 1 is to be performed using hands-on equipment. Task 2: Option 2 is modified to be compatible with the NETLAB+ system but can also be performed using hands-on equipment.

Cisco IOS provides a feature that can be used to monitor traffic in general and network attacks in particular, called Switched Port Analyzer (SPAN). Cisco IOS supports local SPAN and remote SPAN (RSPAN). With local SPAN, the source VLANs, source switch ports, and the destination switch ports are on the same physical switch.

In this part of the lab, you configure a local SPAN to copy traffic from one port where a host is connected to another port where a monitoring station is connected. The monitoring station will run the Wireshark packet sniffer application to analyze traffic.

Note: SPAN enables you to select and copy traffic from one or more source switch ports or source VLANs onto one or more destination ports.

Task 1: Option 1 - Configure a SPAN Session Using Hands-on Equipment

Note: Option 1 assumes you have physical access to the devices shown in the topology for this lab. NETLAB+ users accessing lab equipment remotely should proceed to Task 2: Option 2.

Step 1: Configure a SPAN session on S1 with a source and destination.

a. Set the SPAN source interface using the **`monitor session`** command in global configuration mode. The following configures a SPAN source port on FastEthernet 0/5 for ingress and egress traffic. Traffic copied on the source port can be ingress only, egress only or both. Switch S1 port Fa0/5 is connected to router R1, so ingress traffic from R1 and egress to R1 on switch port Fa0/5 will be monitored.

```
S1(config)# monitor session 1 source interface fa0/5 both
```

Note: You can specify monitor tx (transmit) or rx (receive) traffic. The keyword **`both`** includes tx and rx. The source can be a single interface, a range of interfaces, a single VLAN, or a range of VLANs.

b. Set the SPAN destination interface:

```
S1(config)# monitor session 1 destination interface fa0/6
```

All traffic from S1 Fa0/5, where R1 is connected, will be copied to the SPAN destination port Fa0/6, where PC-A with Wireshark is connected.

Note: The destination can be an interface or a range of interfaces.

Step 2: Verify the setup of the SPAN session on S1.

Confirm the SPAN session setup:

```
S1# show monitor session 1
Session 1
---------
Type                    : Local Session
Source Ports            :
    Both                : Fa0/5
Destination Ports       : Fa0/6
    Encapsulation       : Native
          Ingress       : Disabled
```

Step 3: (Optional) Download and install Wireshark on PC-A.

a. Wireshark is a network protocol analyzer (also called a packet sniffer) that runs with Windows XP and Vista. If Wireshark is not currently available on PC-A, you can download the latest version from http://www.wireshark.org/download.html. This lab uses Wireshark Version 1.0.5. The initial Wireshark installation screen is shown here.

b. Click **I Agree** to the License agreement and accept the defaults by clicking **Next** when prompted.

Note: On the Install WinPcap screen, choose the install WinPcap options, and choose the **Start WinPcap service** option if you want to have other users besides those with administrative privileges run Wireshark.

Step 4: Monitor switch S1 port Fa0/5 ping activity using Wireshark on PC-A.

a. If Wireshark is available, start the application.

b. From the main menu, choose **Capture > Interfaces**.

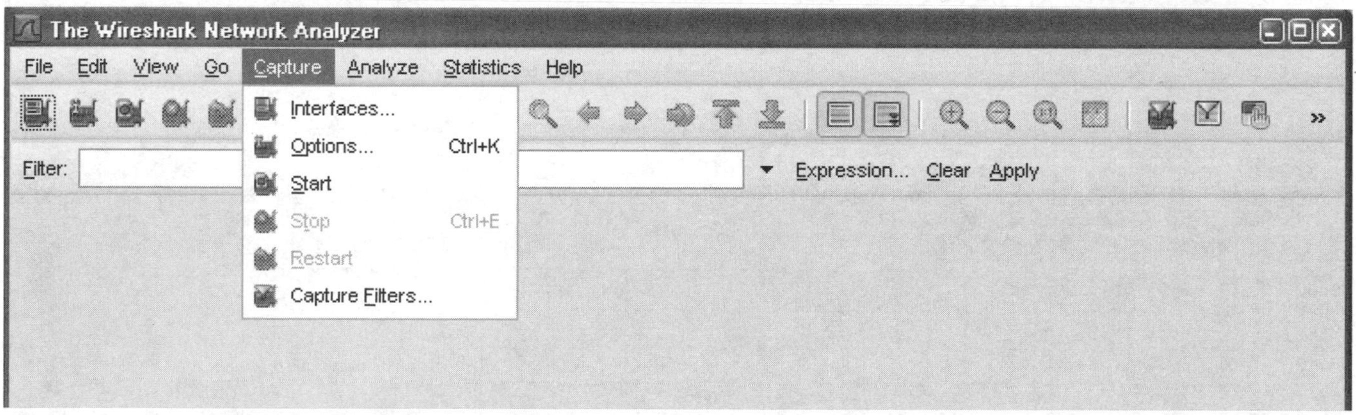

c. Click the **Start** button for the local-area network interface adapter with IP address 192.168.1.10.

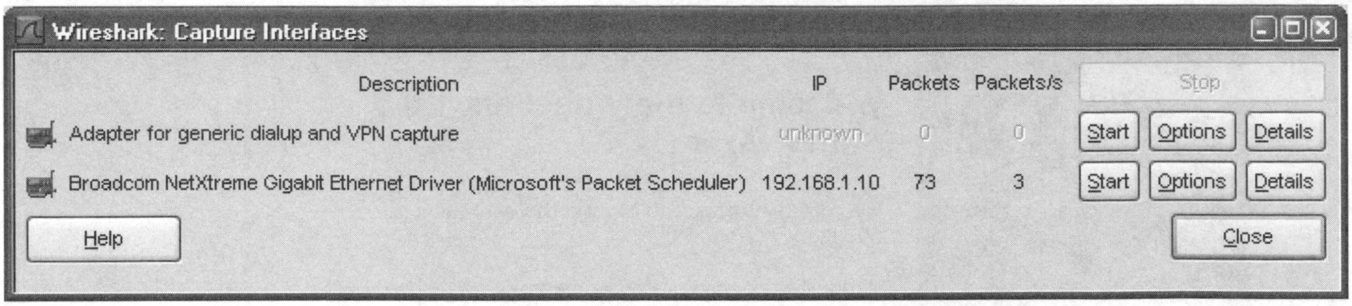

d. Generate some traffic from PC-B (192.168.1.11) to R1 interface Fa0/1 (192.168.1.1) using the **ping** command. This traffic goes from S2 port Fa0/18 to S2 port Fa0/1 across the trunk link to S1 port Fa0/1 and then exits interface Fa0/5 on S1 to reach R1.

```
PC-B:\>ping 192.168.1.1
```

e. Observe the results in Wireshark on PC-A. If you have not pinged 192.168.1.1 before, you will see the initial ARP request broadcast from PC-B (Intel NIC) to determine the MAC address of the R1 Fa0/1 interface with IP address 192.168.1.1 and the ARP reply from the R1 Cisco Ethernet interface. After the ARP request, the pings (echo request and replies) can be seen going from PC-B to R1 and from R1 to PC-B through the switch.

Note: Your screen should look similar to the one shown here. Some additional packets might be captured in addition to the pings, such as the R1 Fa0/1 LOOP reply.

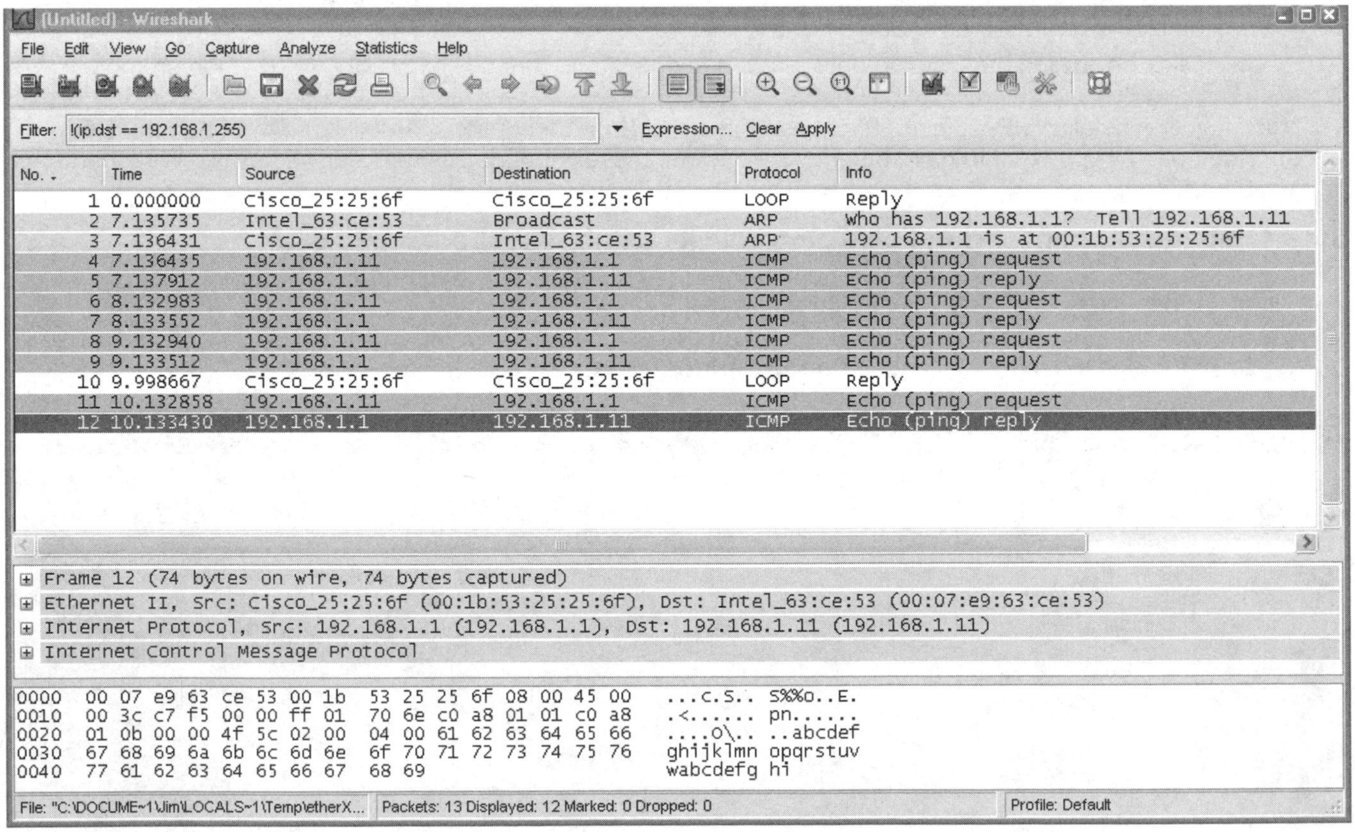

Step 5: Monitor switch S1 port Fa0/5 SuperScan activity using Wireshark on PC-A.

a. If SuperScan is not on PC-B, download the SuperScan 4.0 tool from the Scanning Tools group at http://www.foundstone.com. Unzip the file into a folder. The SuperScan4.exe file is executable and installation is not required.

b. Start the SuperScan program on PC-B. Display the **Host and Service Discovery** tab. Check the **Timestamp Request** check box, and uncheck the **Echo Request** check box. Scroll through the UDP and TCP port selection lists and notice the range of ports that will be scanned.

c. In the SuperScan program, display the **Scan** tab and enter the IP address R1 Fa0/1 (**192.168.1.1**) in the Hostname/IP field.

d. Click the right arrow to populate the Start IP and End IP fields.

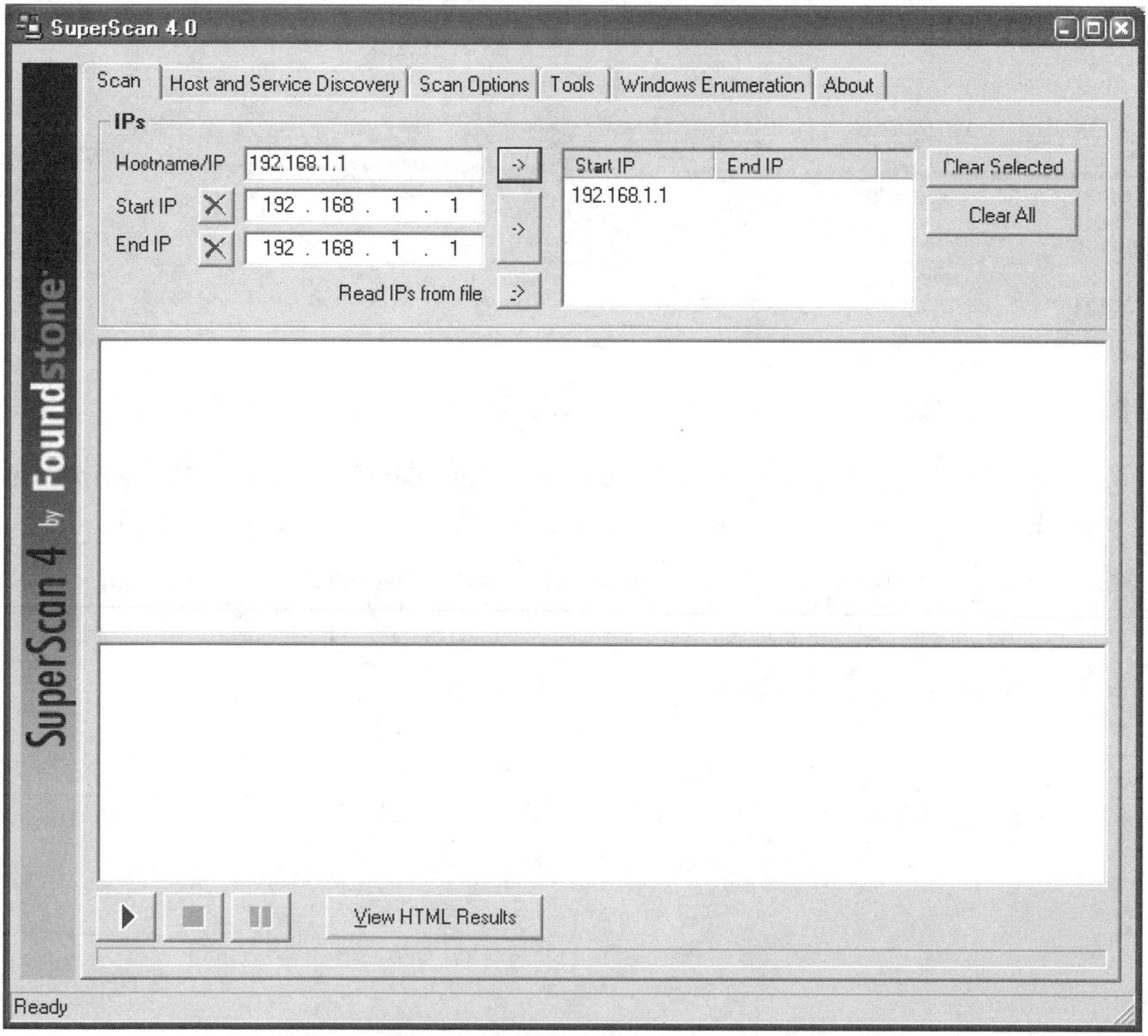

e. Clear the previous capture in Wireshark and start a new capture by clicking **Capture > Start**. When prompted, click the **Continue without saving** button.

f. In the SuperScan program, click the blue arrow button in the lower left to start the scan.

g. Observe the results in the Wireshark window on PC-A. Notice the number and types of ports tried by the simulated SuperScan attack from PC-B (192.168.1.11) to R1 Fa0/1 (192.168.1.1). Your screen should look similar to the following.

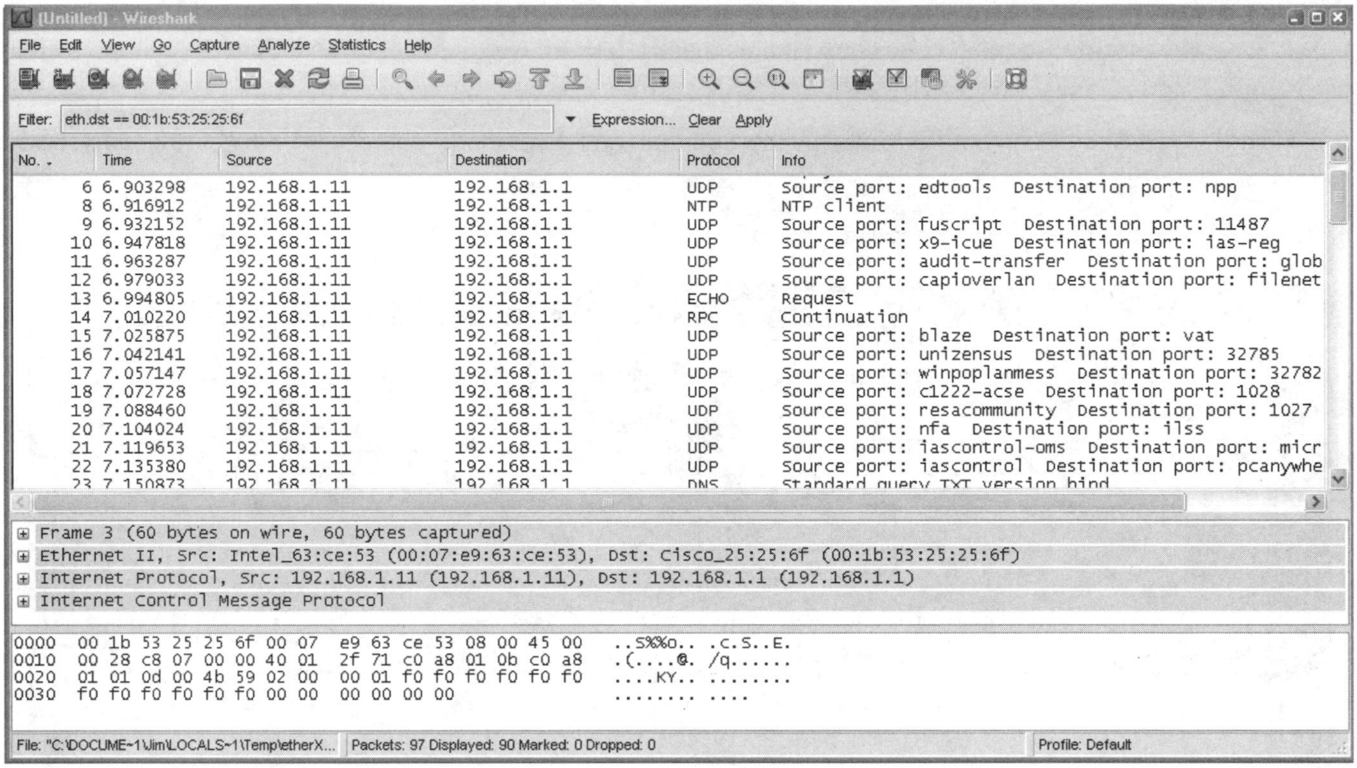

Task 2: Option 2 - Configure a SPAN Session Using NETLAB+ Remote Equipment

Note: This portion of the lab has been rewritten to enhance compatibility with the NETLAB+ system.

On switch S1, you configure a local SPAN to reflect the traffic exiting Port Fa0/5 (in this case, the traffic from PC-A to R1's Fa0/1). This traffic should be received by switch S2, and forwarded to PC-B, where Wireshark is capturing the packets. See the following diagram, which illustrates the SPAN traffic flow.

Note: To perform this task, Wireshark should be installed on PC-B.

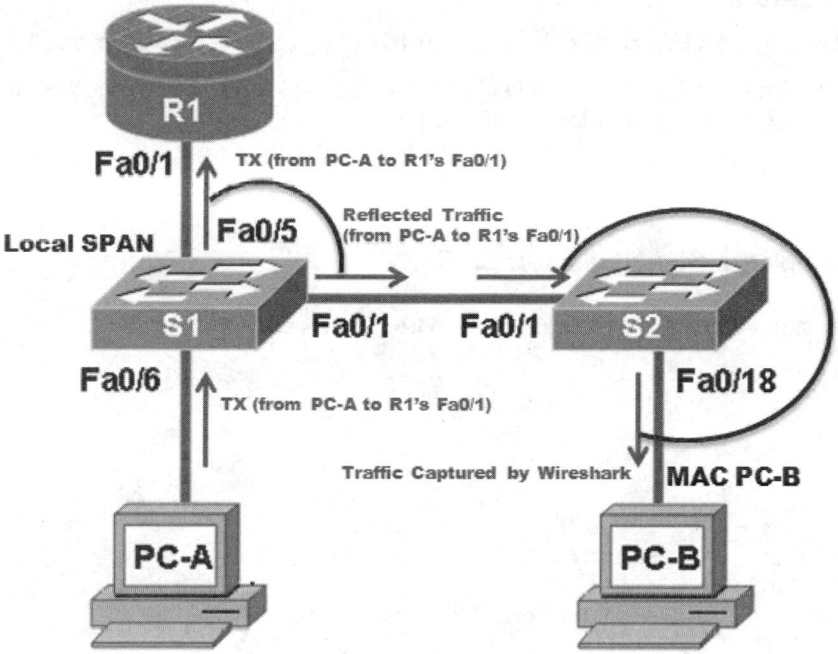

Note: Switch S2 is acting as a regular switch, forwarding frames based on destination MAC addresses and switch ports. The traffic entering S2 through Port Fa0/1 uses the R1's MAC address as the destination for the Ethernet frame Therefore, to forward those packets to PC-B, the R1's MAC address must be the same as PC-B. To accomplish this, R1's Fa0/1 MAC address is modified using the IOS CLI to simulate PC-B's MAC address. This requirement is specific to the NETLAB+ environment.

Step 1: Configure a SPAN session on S1 with source and destination.

a. Return the Fa0/1 on S1 and S2 to its default configuration. This link S1 Fa0/1 to S2 Fa0/1 is going to be used to carry the traffic being monitored.

```
S1(config)# default interface fastethernet 0/1
S2(config)# default interface fastethernet 0/1
```

b. Write down the MAC address for PC-B:

PC-B's MAC address: ______________________________

PC-B's MAC address in this example is 000c-299a-e61a.

c. Configure the PC-B's MAC address on R1's Fa0/1:

```
R1(config)# interface fa0/1
R1(config-if)# mac-address 000c.299a.e61a
```

d. Set the SPAN Source Interface using the `monitor session` command in global configuration mode. The following configures a SPAN source port on FastEthernet0/5 for egress traffic. Traffic copied on the source port can be ingress only, egress only, or both. In this case, the egress traffic is the only one analyzed. On switch S1 port Fa0/5 is connected to router R1, so traffic to the switch port Fa0/5 to R1 will be monitored.

```
S1(config)# monitor session 1 source interface fa0/5 tx
```

Note: The source can be a single interface, a range of interfaces, a single VLAN, or a range of VLANs.

e. Set the SPAN destination interface:

```
S1(config)# monitor session 1 destination interface fa0/1
```

All egress traffic from S1 Fa0/5, where R1 is connected, will be copied to the SPAN destination port Fa0/1, where PC-B with Wireshark is connected.

Note: The destination can be an interface or a range of interfaces.

Step 2: Verify the setup of the SPAN session on S1.

Confirm the SPAN session setup using the **show monitor session 1** command:

```
S1# show monitor session 1
Session 1
---------
Type                   : Local Session
Source Ports           :
    TX Only            : Fa0/5
Destination Ports      : Fa0/1
    Encapsulation      : Native
          Ingress      : Disabled
```

Step 3: (Optional) Download and install Wireshark on PC-B.

Wireshark is a network protocol analyzer (also called a packet sniffer) that runs with Windows XP and Vista. If Wireshark is not currently available on PC-B, you may download the latest version from http://www.wireshark.org/download.html and install it as described in Part 4, Task 1, Step 3.

Step 4: Monitor Switch S1 port Fa0/5 ping activity using Wireshark on PC-B.

a. If Wireshark is available, start the application.

b. From the main menu, choose **Capture > Interfaces**.

c. Click the **Start** button for the local-area network interface adapter.

d. Before pinging, delete the ARP table on PC-A so that an ARP request will be generated:

```
C:\>arp –d *
```

e. Generate some traffic from PC-A (192.168.1.10) to R1 interface Fa0/1 (192.168.1.1) using ping. This traffic goes from S1 port Fa0/6 to S1 port Fa0/5. In addition, the traffic going from PC-A to R1 interface Fa0/1 is forwarded across the link between S1 and S2, and then S2 forwards this traffic to PC-B, where Wireshark is capturing the packets. Note that the SPAN session is configured only on S1, and S2 is operating as a normal switch.

```
C:\>ping 192.168.1.1
```

f. Observe the results in Wireshark on PC-B. Notice the initial ARP request broadcast from PC-A to determine the MAC address of the R1 Fa0/1 interface with IP address 192.168.1.1 and the ARP reply from the R1 Cisco Ethernet interface. After the ARP request, the pings (echo requests) can be seen going from PC-A to R1 through the switch.

Note: Your screen should look similar to the one shown here. Some addition packets might be captured, in addition to the pings, such as the R1 Fa0/1 LOOP Reply and Spanning Tree Packets.

Note: The NetLab VM NICs must be configured for promiscuous mode for the capture part of this lab to work.

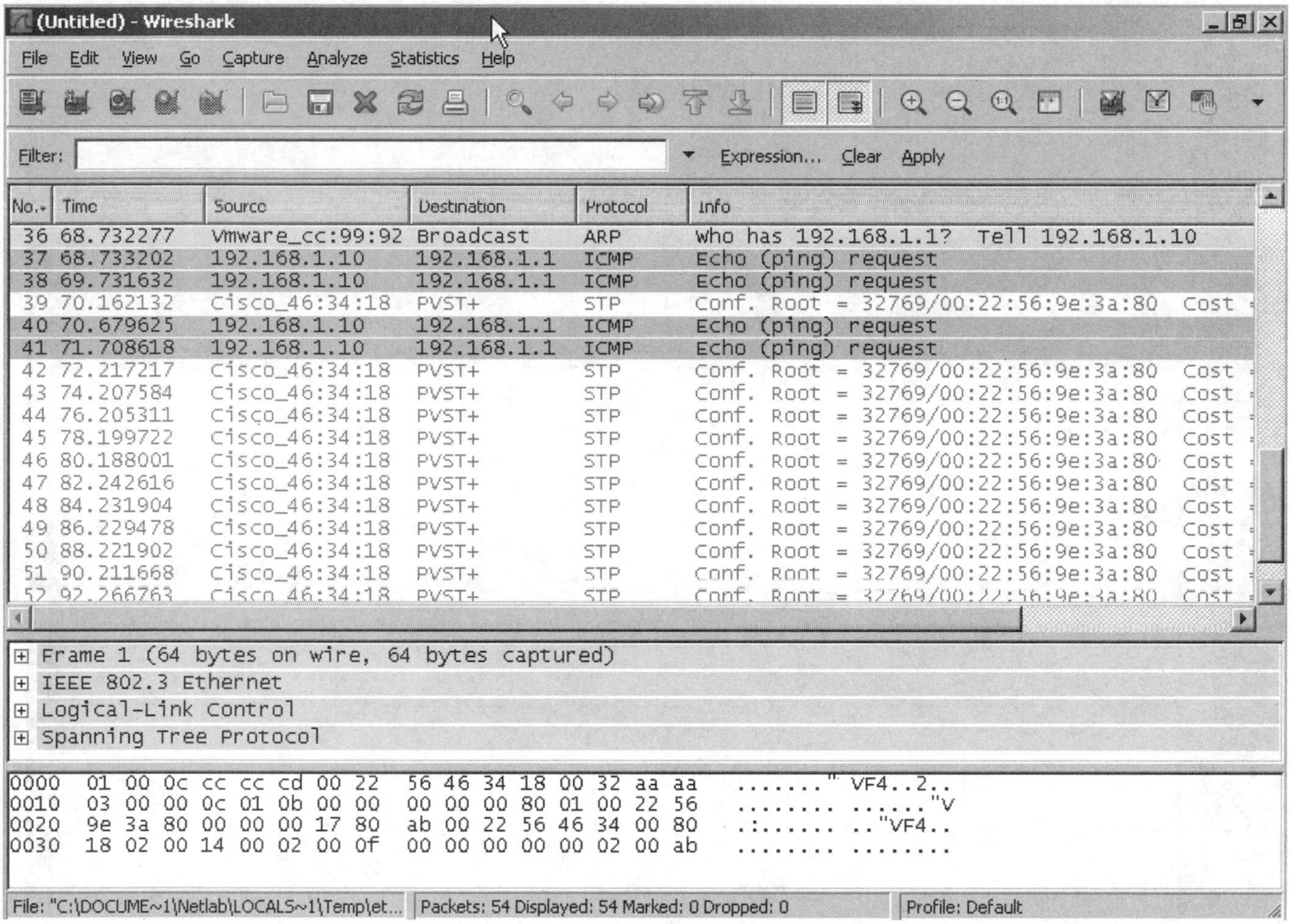

Step 5: Monitor Switch S1 port Fa0/5 SuperScan activity using Wireshark on PC-B.

a. If SuperScan is not on PC-A, download the SuperScan 4.0 tool from the Scanning Tools group at http://www.foundstone.com. Unzip the file into a folder. The SuperScan4.exe file is executable and installation is not required.

b. Start the SuperScan program on PC-A. Display the **Host and Service Discovery** tab. Check the **Timestamp Request** check box, and uncheck the **Echo Request** check box. Scroll the UDP and TCP port selection lists and notice the range of ports that will be scanned.

c. In the SuperScan program, display the **Scan** tab and enter the IP address of R1 Fa0/1 (**192.168.1.1**) in the Hostname/IP field.

d. Click the right-facing arrow to populate the Start and End IP fields.

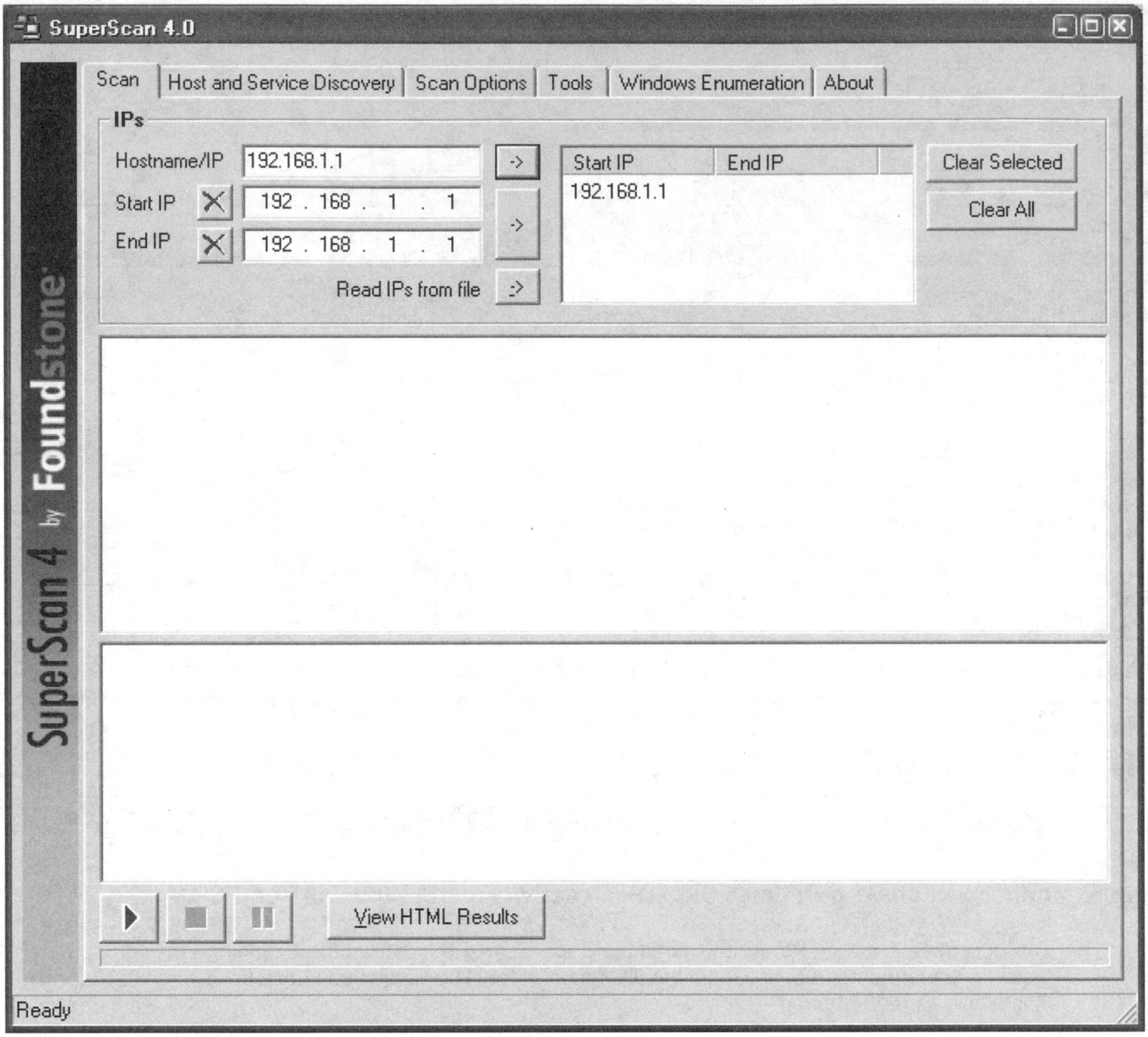

e. Clear the previous capture in Wireshark and start a new capture by clicking **Capture > Start** and when prompted click the **Continue without saving** button.

f. In the SuperScan program click the blue arrow button in the lower left to start the scan.

g. Observe the results on the Wireshark window on PC-B. Notice the number and types of ports tried by the simulated SuperScan attack from PC-A (192.168.1.11) to R1 Fa0/1 (192.168.1.1). Your screen should look similar the following.

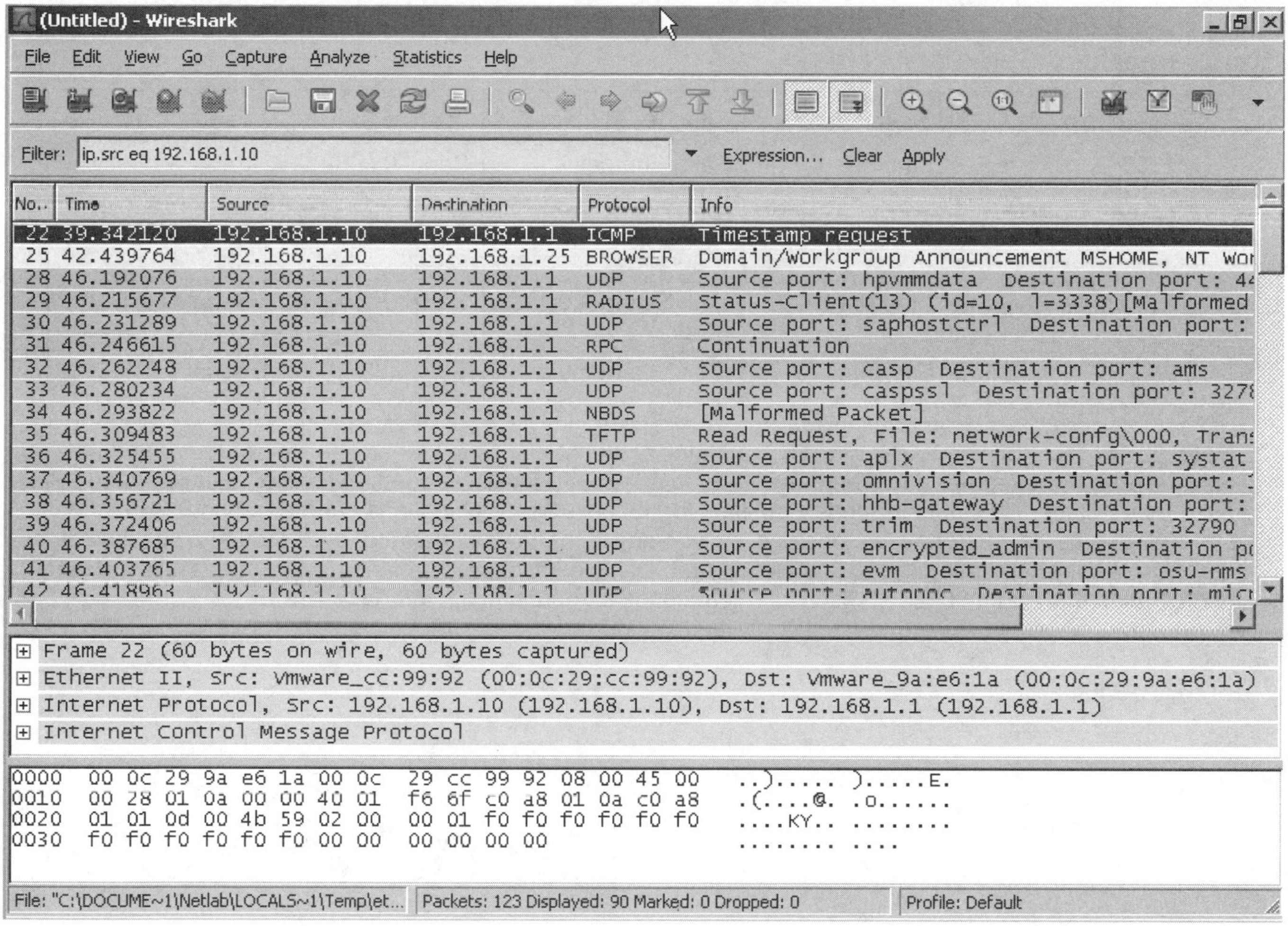

Reflection

1. Why should port security be enabled on switch access ports?

____

____

2. Why should port security be enabled on switch trunk ports?

____

____

3. Why should unused ports on a switch be disabled?

____

____

Router Interface Summary Table

Router Model	Ethernet Interface 1	Ethernet Interface 2	Serial Interface 1	Serial Interface 2
1700	Fast Ethernet 0 (Fa0)	Fast Ethernet 1 (Fa1)	Serial 0 (S0)	Serial 1 (S1)
1800	Fast Ethernet 0/0 (Fa0/0)	Fast Ethernet 0/1 (Fa0/1)	Serial 0/0/0 (S0/0/0)	Serial 0/0/1 (S0/0/1)
2600	Fast Ethernet 0/0 (Fa0/0)	Fast Ethernet 0/1 (Fa0/1)	Serial 0/0 (S0/0)	Serial 0/1 (S0/1)
2800	Fast Ethernet 0/0 (Fa0/0)	Fast Ethernet 0/1 (Fa0/1)	Serial 0/0/0 (S0/0/0)	Serial 0/0/1 (S0/0/1)

Note: To find out how the router is configured, look at the interfaces to identify the type of router and how many interfaces the router has. There is no way to effectively list all the combinations of configurations for each router class. This table includes identifiers for the possible combinations of Ethernet and serial interfaces in the device. The table does not include any other type of interface, even though a specific router may contain one. An example of this might be an ISDN BRI interface. The string in parentheses is the legal abbreviation that can be used in Cisco IOS commands to represent the interface.

Chapter 7 Lab A: Exploring Encryption Methods

Topology

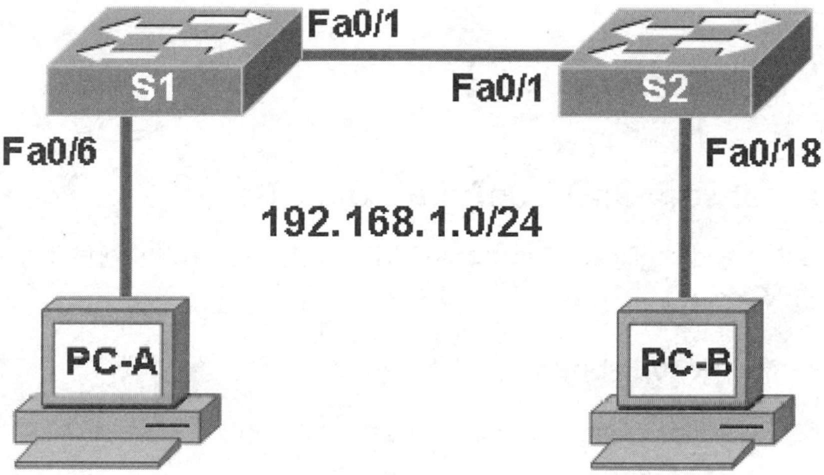

Objectives

Part 1: (Optional) Build the Network and Configure the PCs

- Connect the PCs and configure IP addresses.

Part 2: Decipher a Pre-encrypted Message Using the Vigenere Cipher

- Given an encrypted message, a cipher key, and the Vigenere cipher square, decipher the message.

Part 3: Create a Vigenere Cipher Encrypted Message and Decrypt It

- Work with a lab partner and agree on a secret password.
- Create a secret message using the Vigenere cipher and the key.
- Exchange messages and decipher them using the pre-shared key.
- Use an interactive Vigenere decoding tool to verify decryption.

Part 4: Use Steganography to Embed a Secret Message in a Graphic

- Create a secret message and save it as a .txt file.
- Use S-Tools to embed the secret text message into a .bmp graphic.
- Send the graphic to a lab partner to reveal the embedded message.

Background

The Cisco IOS password encryption service uses a Cisco-proprietary algorithm that is based on the Vigenere cipher. Vigenere is an example of a common type of cipher mechanism called polyalphabetic substitution. Although not a strong encryption technique, Vigenere serves to illustrate a commonly used encryption and decryption process.

Note: Students can work in teams of two for this lab.

Required Resources

- 2 switches (Cisco 2960 or comparable)
- PC-A (Windows XP or Vista)
- PC-B (Windows XP or Vista)
- Ethernet cables as necessary

Part 1: (Optional) Build the Network and Configure the PCs

In Part 1 of this lab, you connect the PCs and configure IP addresses. This is not required to perform the lab, unless you want to copy files between PCs.

Step 1: Cable the network as shown in the topology.

Attach the devices shown in the topology diagram, and cable as necessary.

Note: The switches in the topology can be omitted and the PCs connected directly together using a crossover cable, if desired. This is necessary only if the files used in the lab are to be exchanged by copying them from one PC to the other. If files are to be exchanged using removable media, such as a flash drive or floppy disk, no cabling is required.

Step 2: Configure PC host IP settings.

Configure a static IP address and subnet mask for PC-A and PC-B as shown here. A default gateway is not required because the PCs are on the same local network.

- PC-A IP address: 192.168.1.1, subnet mask 255.255.255.0
- PC-B IP address: 192.168.1.2, subnet mask 255.255.255.0

Step 3: Verify connectivity between PC-A and PC-B.

Ping from PC-A to PC-B.

Are the ping results successful? _____

If the pings are not successful, troubleshoot the basic device configurations before continuing.

Part 2: Decipher a Pre-encrypted Message Using the Vigenere Cipher

In Part 2 of this lab, you analyze an encrypted message and decrypt it using a cipher key and the Vigenere cipher square.

Step 1: Review the encrypted message.

The following message has been encrypted using the Vigenere cipher.

VECIHXEJZXMA

Can you tell what the message says? ________________

Step 2: Review the cipher keyword.

The cipher keyword **TCPIP** was used to encrypt the message. The same keyword will be used to decrypt or decipher the message.

Step 3: Review the structure of the Vigenere square.

A standard Vigenere square or table is used with the keyword to decipher the message.

	A	B	C	D	E	F	G	H	I	J	K	L	M	N	O	P	Q	R	S	T	U	V	W	X	Y	Z
A	A	B	C	D	E	F	G	H	I	J	K	L	M	N	O	P	Q	R	S	T	U	V	W	X	Y	Z
B	B	C	D	E	F	G	H	I	J	K	L	M	N	O	P	Q	R	S	T	U	V	W	X	Y	Z	A
C	C	D	E	F	G	H	I	J	K	L	M	N	O	P	Q	R	S	T	U	V	W	X	Y	Z	A	B
D	D	E	F	G	H	I	J	K	L	M	N	O	P	Q	R	S	T	U	V	W	X	Y	Z	A	B	C
E	E	F	G	H	I	J	K	L	M	N	O	P	Q	R	S	T	U	V	W	X	Y	Z	A	B	C	D
F	F	G	H	I	J	K	L	M	N	O	P	Q	R	S	T	U	V	W	X	Y	Z	A	B	C	D	E
G	G	H	I	J	K	L	M	N	O	P	Q	R	S	T	U	V	W	X	Y	Z	A	B	C	D	E	F
H	H	I	J	K	L	M	N	O	P	Q	R	S	T	U	V	W	X	Y	Z	A	B	C	D	E	F	G
I	I	J	K	L	M	N	O	P	Q	R	S	T	U	V	W	X	Y	Z	A	B	C	D	E	F	G	H
J	J	K	L	M	N	O	P	Q	R	S	T	U	V	W	X	Y	Z	A	B	C	D	E	F	G	H	I
K	K	L	M	N	O	P	Q	R	S	T	U	V	W	X	Y	Z	A	B	C	D	E	F	G	H	I	J
L	L	M	N	O	P	Q	R	S	T	U	V	W	X	Y	Z	A	B	C	D	E	F	G	H	I	J	K
M	M	N	O	P	Q	R	S	T	U	V	W	X	Y	Z	A	B	C	D	E	F	G	H	I	J	K	L
N	N	O	P	Q	R	S	T	U	V	W	X	Y	Z	A	B	C	D	E	F	G	H	I	J	K	L	M
O	O	P	Q	R	S	T	U	V	W	X	Y	Z	A	B	C	D	E	F	G	H	I	J	K	L	M	N
P	P	Q	R	S	T	U	V	W	X	Y	Z	A	B	C	D	E	F	G	H	I	J	K	L	M	N	O
Q	Q	R	S	T	U	V	W	X	Y	Z	A	B	C	D	E	F	G	H	I	J	K	L	M	N	O	P
R	R	S	T	U	V	W	X	Y	Z	A	B	C	D	E	F	G	H	I	J	K	L	M	N	O	P	Q
S	S	T	U	V	W	X	Y	Z	A	B	C	D	E	F	G	H	I	J	K	L	M	N	O	P	Q	R
T	T	U	V	W	X	Y	Z	A	B	C	D	E	F	G	H	I	J	K	L	M	N	O	P	Q	R	S
U	U	V	W	X	Y	Z	A	B	C	D	E	F	G	H	I	J	K	L	M	N	O	P	Q	R	S	T
V	V	W	X	Y	Z	A	B	C	D	E	F	G	H	I	J	K	L	M	N	O	P	Q	R	S	T	U
W	W	X	Y	Z	A	B	C	D	E	F	G	H	I	J	K	L	M	N	O	P	Q	R	S	T	U	V
X	X	Y	Z	A	B	C	D	E	F	G	H	I	J	K	L	M	N	O	P	Q	R	S	T	U	V	W
Y	Y	Z	A	B	C	D	E	F	G	H	I	J	K	L	M	N	O	P	Q	R	S	T	U	V	W	X
Z	Z	A	B	C	D	E	F	G	H	I	J	K	L	M	N	O	P	Q	R	S	T	U	V	W	X	Y

Step 4: Decrypt the message using the keyword and Vigenere square.

a. Use the following table to help you decrypt the message. Start by entering the letters of the encrypted message in the second row of cells, from left to right.

b. Enter the keyword TCPIP in the top row, repeating the letters until there is a keyword letter for each letter of the encrypted message, even if the keyword letters at the end do not represent the complete keyword.

c. Refer to the Vigenere square or table shown in Step 3 and find the horizontal row that starts with the first letter of the keyword (the letter T). Scan across that row and locate the first letter of the encrypted message in the row (the letter V). The letter at the top of the column where the encrypted message letter appears is the first letter of the decrypted message (the letter C).

d. Continue this process until you have decrypted the entire message and enter it in the following table.

Cipher Keyword												
Encrypted Message												
Decrypted Message												

Part 3: Create a Vigenere Cipher Encrypted Message and Decrypt It

In Part 3 of this lab, you work with a lab partner and agree on a secret password, referred to as the pre-shared key. Each lab partner creates a secret message using the Vigenere cipher and the key. Partners exchange messages and decipher them using their pre-shared key.

Note: If you do not have a partner, you can perform the steps by yourself.

Step 1: Determine the cipher keyword.

With your partner, establish a cipher keyword and enter it here. ____________________________________

Step 2: Create a plain-text message and encrypt it (both partners).

a. Create a plain-text (decrypted) message to be encrypted by your partner. ______________________

b. You can use the following table to help you encrypt the message. You can enter the unencrypted message and cipher keyword here, but do not let your partner see it.

c. In the Vigenere table, locate the row that starts with the first letter of the cipher keyword. Next locate the first letter to be encrypted at the top of the column in the table. The point (cell) at which the table row (key letter) and column (message letter) intersect is the first letter of the encrypted message. Continue this process until you have encrypted the entire message.

Note: This table is limited to messages of 12 characters. You can create longer messages if desired. Message encryption and decryption is not case sensitive.

Cipher Keyword												
Encrypted Message												
Decrypted Message												

Step 3: Decrypt the message from your partner.

a. You can use the following table to help you decrypt your partner's encrypted message. Enter the encrypted message from your partner and the cipher keyword.

b. Use the same procedure described in Part 2, Step 4.

Note: This table is limited to messages of 12 characters. You can create longer messages if desired.

Cipher Keyword												
Encrypted Message												
Decrypted Message												

Step 4: Use an interactive decryption tool to confirm decryption.

a. A search for "vigenere decode" on the Internet shows that various cipher encryption and decryption tools are available. Many of these are interactive.

b. One interactive tool is located at http://sharkysoft.com/misc/vigenere/. Go to this URL. Enter the encrypted message from your partner in the top part of the screen and the cipher key in the middle. Click the **Decode** button to see the clear text version of the message. You can also use this tool to encrypt messages.

c. The following example shows using Sharky's Vigenere Cipher tool for decoding the encrypted message from Part 1 of the lab.

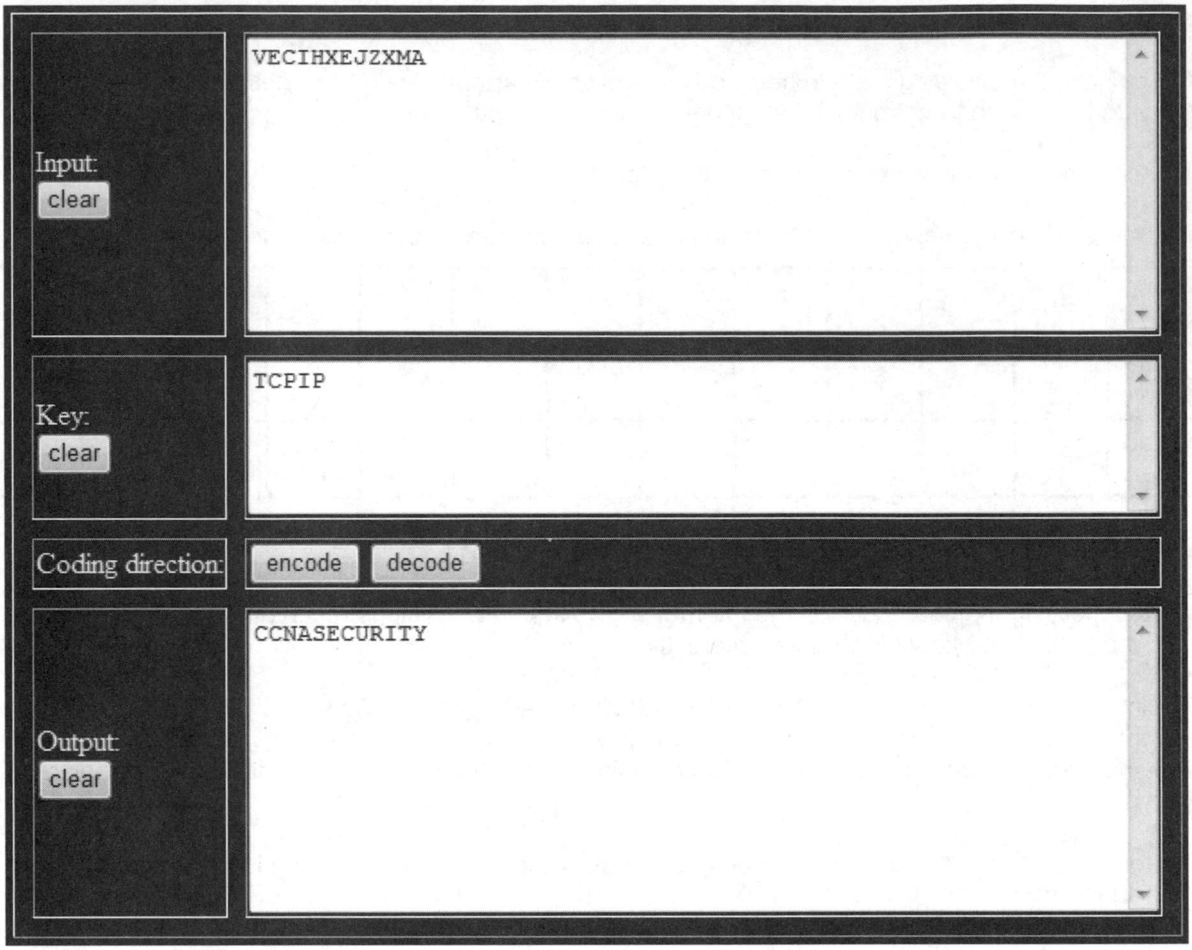

Part 4: Use Steganography to Embed a Secret Message in a Graphic

In Part 4 of this lab, you create a secret message for your partner, embed it into a graphic file, and then give it to your partner to retrieve it. You embed the message in a graphic file using S-Tools. S-Tools is a steganography tool that hides files in BMP, GIF, and WAV files. You start by opening S-Tools, and then drag you graphics and sounds into the blank window. To hide files, you drag them into open graphics or sound windows. Data is compressed before being encrypted and then hidden.

Note: The following steps should be performed by both partners, one at PC-A and the other at PC-B. If you do not have a partner, you can perform the steps by yourself.

Step 1: (Optional) Download and install S-Tools.

If the S-Tools application is not installed on the PC, download it from http://www.spychecker.com/program/stools.html or another site and unzip the files to a folder.

Step 2: Create a secret message text file (both partners).

a. On PC-A or PC-B, open the Windows Notepad application and create a message.

b. Save the message in a folder on the desktop and name it **secret.txt**.

c. Close the Notepad application.

Step 3: Create a simple .bmp graphic file.

a. Open the Windows Paint application and create a simple graphic. For example, you can write your first name using the pencil tool or text tool and apply some color using the spray can or fill tool.

b. Save the graphic as a .bmp file in a folder on the desktop and name it **graphic.bmp**.

c. Close the Paint application.

Step 4: Create a secret password using the Vigenere cipher.

a. Choose a passphrase to be encrypted using the Vigenere cipher and record it here. ____________ Do not share the passphrase with your partner. This passphrase will be used later to protect the text file when it is embedded in the graphic file.

b. Choose a cipher keyword to be used when encrypting and decrypting the passphrase and record it here. ____________________

c. Encrypt the passphrase using the cipher keyword and the procedure described in Part 3, Step 2. Record the encrypted passphrase here. ____

Step 5: Embed the message into a graphic image file.

a. Open the S-Tools.exe application.

b. Locate the file named **graphic.bmp**, which you saved previously. Determine its size by right-clicking the file and choosing **Properties**. Record the file size (for example, 2,359,350 bytes).

____

c. Drag the **graphic.bmp** file into the S-Tools window.

d. Drag the file **secret.txt**, which you created in Step 2, and place it inside the **graphic.bmp** window. The image should still be displayed. A dialog box is displayed showing the number of bytes being hidden. You can enter a passphrase and choose the encryption algorithm to be used. The default algorithm is IDEA.

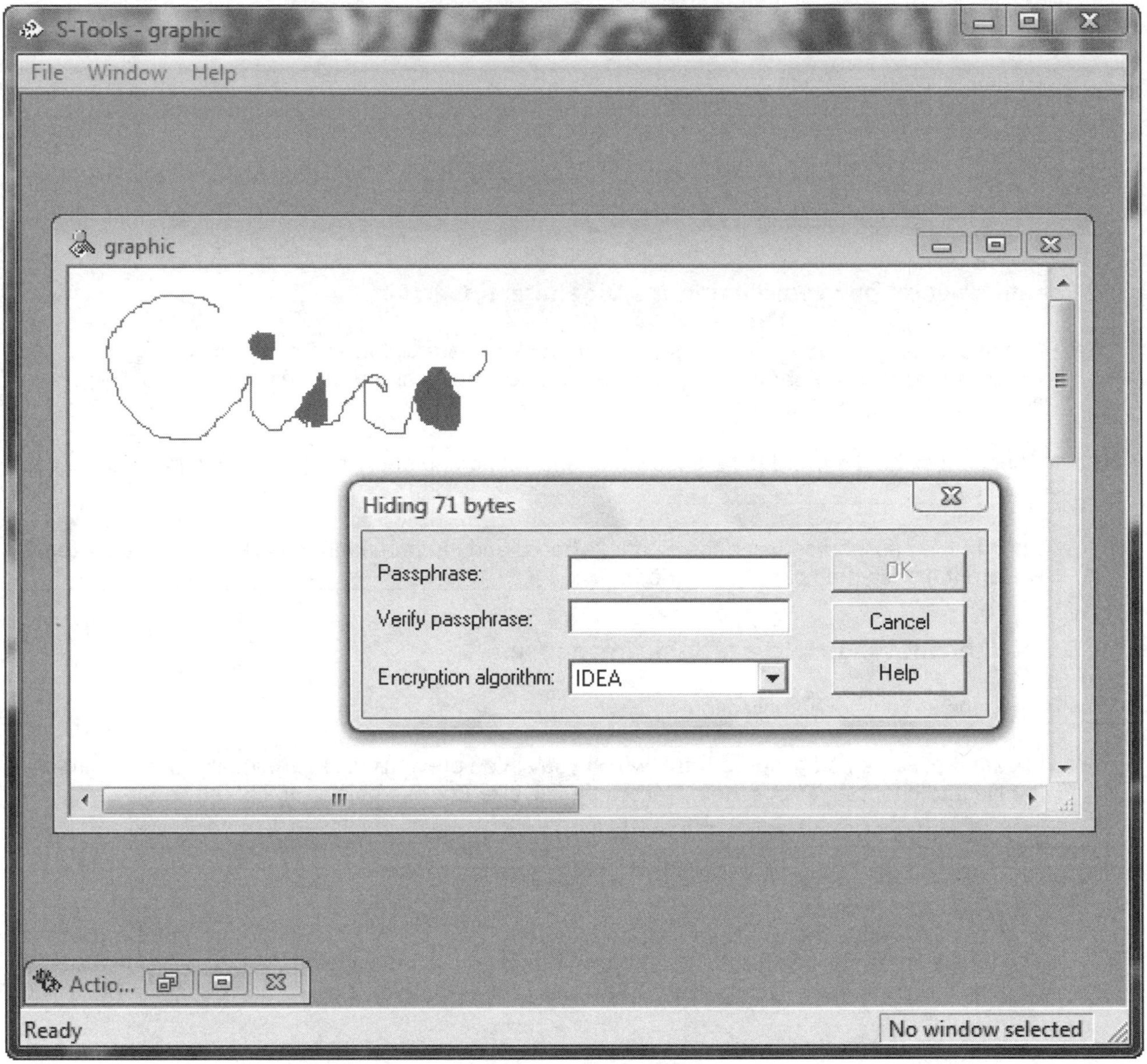

Step 6: Use the unencrypted passphrase to protect the embedded text file.

a. Enter the unencrypted passphrase from Step 4 in the **Passphrase** and **Verify passphrase** fields.

b. Choose **Triple DES** from the **Encryption Algorithm** field and click **OK**. This creates a second image with the name **hidden data**.

c. Right-click the hidden data graphics image and choose **Save As** from the menu. Name the file **graphic2** and save it as a .bmp file.

d. Close the S-Tools application.

Step 7: Provide the graphic2.bmp file to your partner.

a. Provide a copy of your **graphic2.bmp** file to your partner. You can do this by sharing folders (if PCs were cabled together and IP addresses were assigned in Part 1 of the lab). You can also copy the file onto a removable drive (flash drive or floppy disk), or send it as an email attachment if you are performing the lab remotely.

b. Provide your partner with the Vigenere-encrypted passphrase from Step 4 and the cipher keyword that you used to create it.

Step 8: Decrypt the Vigenere password from your partner.

Decrypt your partner's passphrase using the procedure described in Part 1, Step 4. This is done so that you can use it with S-Tools to reveal the hidden message embedded in your partner's graphic.

Step 9: Reveal the embedded message from your partner.

a. Open the S-Tools application.

b. Locate the **graphic2.bmp** file from your partner, and determine how large it is using the same method as in Step 5. Record the file size here. ______________________________

Has the file size changed? _____

c. Drag the file into the S-Tools window. The image should be displayed. Can you tell that there is a secret message embedded in the graphics image? ______________

d. Right-click the image and choose **Reveal** from the menu.

e. Enter the Vigenere passphrase decrypted in Step 8 into the **Passphrase** field.

f. Choose **Triple DES** from the **Encryption Algorithm** field and click **OK**. This displays a revealed archive.

g. Right-click the hidden message file and choose **Save As** from the menu. Name the file **secret2.txt**.

h. Close the S-Tools application.

i. Open the **secret2.txt** file from your partner to reveal the hidden message and write it here.

____

Reflection

1. Could the Vigenere cipher be used to decode messages in the field without a computer?

____

2. Do an Internet search for Vigenere cipher cracking tools. Is the Vigenere cipher considered a strong encryption system that is difficult to crack? ______________________________

Chapter 8 Lab A: Configuring a Site-to-Site VPN Using Cisco IOS and CCP

Topology

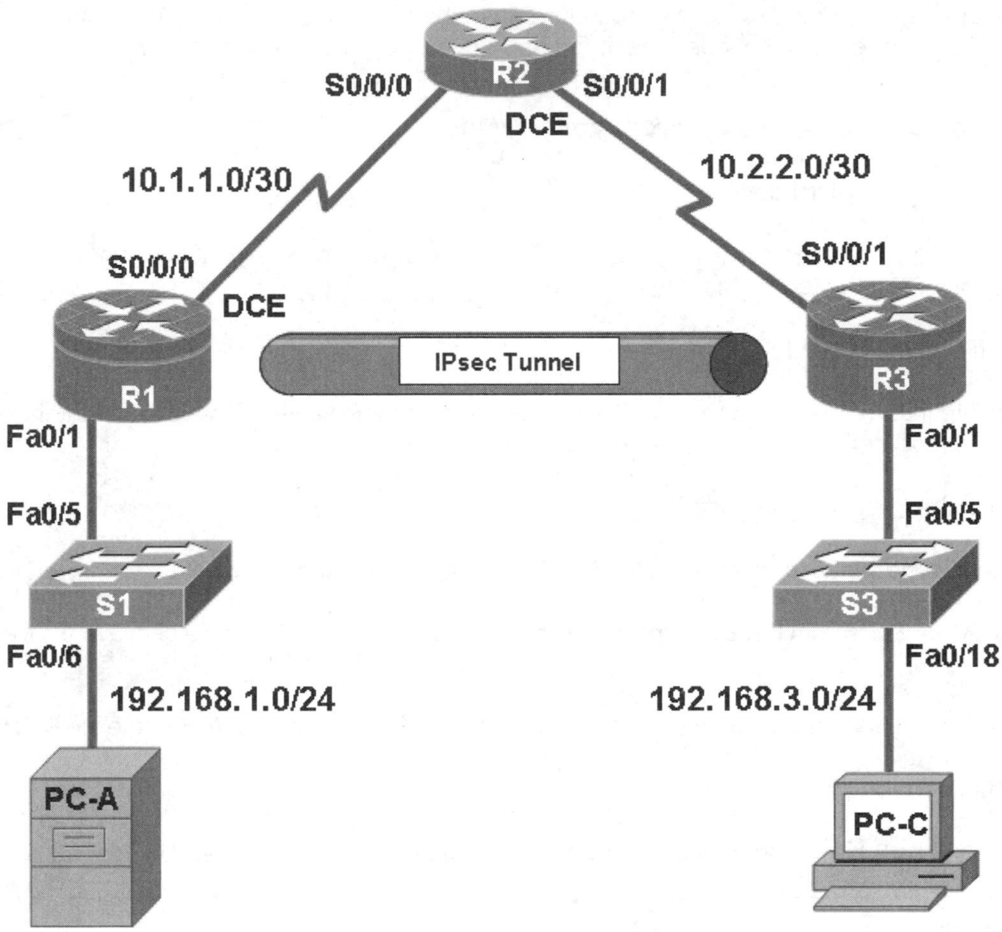

Note: ISR G2 devices have Gigabit Ethernet interfaces rather than FastEthernet interfaces.

IP Addressing Table

Device	Interface	IP Address	Subnet Mask	Default Gateway	Switch Port
R1	Fa0/1	192.168.1.1	255.255.255.0	N/A	S1 Fa0/5
	S0/0/0 (DCE)	10.1.1.1	255.255.255.252	N/A	N/A
R2	S0/0/0	10.1.1.2	255.255.255.252	N/A	N/A
	S0/0/1 (DCE)	10.2.2.2	255.255.255.252	N/A	N/A
R3	Fa0/1	192.168.3.1	255.255.255.0	N/A	S3 Fa0/5
	S0/0/1	10.2.2.1	255.255.255.252	N/A	N/A
PC-A	NIC	192.168.1.3	255.255.255.0	192.168.1.1	S1 Fa0/6
PC-C	NIC	192.168.3.3	255.255.255.0	192.168.3.1	S3 Fa0/18

Objectives

Part 1: Basic Router Configuration

- Configure hostnames, interface IP addresses, and access passwords.
- Configure the EIGRP dynamic routing protocol.

Part 2: Configure a Site-to-Site VPN Using Cisco IOS

- Configure IPsec VPN settings on R1 and R3.
- Verify site-to-site IPsec VPN configuration.
- Test IPsec VPN operation.

Part 3: Configure a Site-to-Site VPN Using CCP

- Configure IPsec VPN settings on R1.
- Create a mirror configuration for R3.
- Apply the mirror configuration to R3.
- Verify the configuration.
- Test the VPN configuration using CCP

Background

Virtual Private Networks (VPN) can provide a secure method of transmitting data over a public network, such as the Internet. VPN connections can help reduce the costs associated with leased lines. Site-to-site VPNs typically provide a secure (IPsec or other) tunnel between a branch office and a central office. Another common implementation that uses VPN technology is remote access to a corporate office from a telecommuter location such as a small office or home office.

In this lab, you build and configure a multirouter network, and then use Cisco IOS and CCP to configure a site-to-site IPsec VPN and then test it. The IPsec VPN tunnel is from router R1 to router R3 via R2. R2 acts as a pass-through and has no knowledge of the VPN. IPsec provides secure transmission of sensitive information over unprotected networks such as the Internet. IPsec acts at the network layer, protecting and authenticating IP packets between participating IPsec devices (peers), such as Cisco routers.

Note: The router commands and output in this lab are from a Cisco 1841 with Cisco IOS Software Release 12.4(20)T (advanced IP image). Other routers and Cisco IOS versions can be used. See the Router Interface Summary table at the end of the lab to determine which interface identifiers to use based on the equipment in the lab. Depending on the router model and Cisco IOS version, the commands available and the output produced might vary from what this lab shows.

Note: Make sure that the routers and the switches have been erased and have no startup configurations.

Required Resources

- 3 routers with (Cisco 1841 with Cisco IOS Software Release 12.4(20)T1 or comparable)
- 2 switches (Cisco 2960 or comparable)
- PC-A: Windows XP, Vista, or Windows 7 with CCP 2.5 installed
- PC-C: Windows XP, Vista, or Windows 7 with CCP 2.5 installed
- Serial and Ethernet cables as shown in the topology
- Rollover cables to configure the routers via the console

CCP Notes

- See Chapter 00 Lab A for instructions on how to install CCP. Hardware/software recommendations for CCP include Windows XP, Vista, or Windows 7 with Java Version 1.6.0_11 up to 1.6.0_21, Internet Explorer 6.0 or later, and Flash Player Version 10.0.12.36 or later.
- If the PC on which CCP is installed is running Windows Vista or Windows 7, you might need to right-click the CCP icon or menu item and choose **Run as Administrator**.
- To run CCP, you might need to temporarily disable antivirus programs and OS firewalls. Make sure to turn off all pop-up blockers in the browser.

Part 1: Basic Router Configuration

In Part 1 of this lab, you set up the network topology and configure basic settings, such as the interface IP addresses, dynamic routing, device access, and passwords.

Note: All tasks should be performed on routers R1, R2, and R3. The procedure for R1 is shown here as an example.

Step 1: Cable the network as shown in the topology.

Attach the devices shown in the topology diagram, and cable as necessary.

Step 2: Configure basic settings for each router.

a. Configure hostnames as shown in the topology.

b. Configure the interface IP addresses as shown in the IP addressing table.

c. Configure a clock rate for the serial router interfaces with a DCE serial cable attached:

```
R1(config)# interface S0/0/0
R1(config-if)# clock rate 64000
```

Step 3: Disable DNS lookup.

To prevent the router from attempting to translate incorrectly entered commands, disable DNS lookup:

```
R1(config)# no ip domain-lookup
```

Step 4: Configure the EIGRP routing protocol on R1, R2, and R3.

a. On R1, use the following commands:

```
R1(config)# router eigrp 101
R1(config-router)# network 192.168.1.0 0.0.0.255
R1(config-router)# network 10.1.1.0 0.0.0.3
R1(config-router)# no auto-summary
```

b. On R2, use the following commands:

```
R2(config)# router eigrp 101
R2(config-router)# network 10.1.1.0 0.0.0.3
R2(config-router)# network 10.2.2.0 0.0.0.3
R2(config-router)# no auto-summary
```

c. On R3, use the following commands:

```
R3(config)# router eigrp 101
R3(config-router)# network 192.168.3.0 0.0.0.255
R3(config-router)# network 10.2.2.0 0.0.0.3
R3(config-router)# no auto-summary
```

Step 5: Configure PC host IP settings.

a. Configure a static IP address, subnet mask, and default gateway for PC-A, as shown in the IP addressing table.

b. Configure a static IP address, subnet mask, and default gateway for PC-C, as shown in the IP addressing table.

Step 6: Verify basic network connectivity.

a. Ping from R1 to the R3 Fa0/1 interface at IP address 192.168.3.1.

Were the results successful? _____

If the pings are not successful, troubleshoot the basic device configurations before continuing.

b. Ping from PC-A on the R1 LAN to PC-C on the R3 LAN.

Were the results successful? _____

If the pings are not successful, troubleshoot the basic device configurations before continuing.

Note: If you can ping from PC-A to PC-C, you have demonstrated that the EIGRP routing protocol is configured and functioning correctly. If you cannot ping but the device interfaces are up and IP addresses are correct, use the **`show run`** and **`show ip route`** commands to help identify routing protocol-related problems.

Step 7: Configure a minimum password length.

Note: Passwords in this lab are set to a minimum of 10 characters but are relatively simple for the benefit of performing the lab. More complex passwords are recommended in a production network.

Use the **security passwords** command to set a minimum password length of 10 characters.

```
R1(config)# security passwords min-length 10
```

Step 8: Configure the basic console and vty lines.

a. Configure a console password and enable login for router R1. For additional security, the **exec-timeout** command causes the line to log out after 5 minutes of inactivity. The **logging synchronous** command prevents console messages from interrupting command entry.

Note: To avoid repetitive logins during this lab, you can set the **exec-timeout** command to 0 0, which prevents it from expiring. However, this is not considered a good security practice.

```
R1(config)# line console 0
R1(config-line)# password ciscoconpass
R1(config-line)# exec-timeout 5 0
R1(config-line)# login
R1(config-line)# logging synchronous
```

b. Configure the password on the vty lines for router R1:

```
R1(config)# line vty 0 4
R1(config-line)# password ciscovtypass
R1(config-line)# exec-timeout 5 0
R1(config-line)# login
```

c. Repeat these configurations on both R2 and R3.

Step 9: Encrypt clear-text passwords.

a. Use the **service password-encryption** command to encrypt the console, aux, and vty passwords:

```
R1(config)# service password-encryption
```

b. Issue the **show run** command. Can you read the console, aux, and vty passwords? Why or why not? ____________________

c. Repeat this configuration on both R2 and R3.

Step 10: Save the basic running configuration for all three routers.

Save the running configuration to the startup configuration from the privileged EXEC prompt:

```
R1# copy running-config startup-config
```

Step 11: Save the configuration on R1 and R3 for later restoration.

Using a program such as HyperTerminal, copy/paste functions, or TFTP, save the R1 and R3 running configurations from Part 1 of this lab. These can be used later, in Part 3 of this lab, to restore the routers to configure the VPN with CCP.

Note: When editing the captured running config text, remove all occurrences of "- - More - -." Remove any commands that are not related to the items you configured in Part 1 of the lab, such as the Cisco IOS version number, no service pad, and so on. Many commands are entered automatically by the Cisco IOS software. Also replace the encrypted passwords with the correct ones specified previously and be sure to use the no shutdown command for interfaces that need to be enabled.

Part 2: Configure a Site-to-Site VPN with Cisco IOS

In Part 2 of this lab, you configure an IPsec VPN tunnel between R1 and R3 that passes through R2. You configure R1 and R3 using the Cisco IOS CLI. You then review and test the resulting configuration.

Task 1: Configure IPsec VPN Settings on R1 and R3

Step 1: Verify connectivity from the R1 LAN to the R3 LAN.

In this task, you verify that with no tunnel in place, the PC-A on the R1 LAN can ping the PC-C on R3 LAN.

a. From PC-A, ping the PC-C IP address of 192.168.3.3:

```
PC-A:\> ping 192.168.3.3
```

b. Are the results successful? _____

If the pings are not successful, troubleshoot the basic device configurations before continuing.

Step 2: Enable IKE policies on R1 and R3.

IPsec is an open framework that allows the exchange of security protocols as new technologies, such as encryption algorithms, are developed.

There are two central configuration elements to the implementation of an IPsec VPN:

- Implement Internet Key Exchange (IKE) parameters
- Implement IPsec parameters

a. Verify that IKE is supported and enabled.

IKE Phase 1 defines the key exchange method used to pass and validate IKE policies between peers. In IKE Phase 2, the peers exchange and match IPsec policies for the authentication and encryption of data traffic.

IKE must be enabled for IPsec to function. IKE is enabled by default on IOS images with cryptographic feature sets. If it is disabled for some reason, you can enable it with the command **crypto isakmp enable**. Use this command to verify that the router IOS supports IKE and that it is enabled:

```
R1(config)# crypto isakmp enable

R3(config)# crypto isakmp enable
```

Note: If you cannot execute this command on the router, you need to upgrade the IOS image to one with a feature set that includes the Cisco cryptographic services.

b. Establish an Internet Security Association and Key Management Protocol (ISAKMP) policy and view the available options.

To allow IKE Phase 1 negotiation, you must create an ISAKMP policy and configure a peer association involving that ISAKMP policy. An ISAKMP policy defines the authentication and encryption algorithms and hash function used to send control traffic between the two VPN endpoints. When an ISAKMP security association has been accepted by the IKE peers, IKE Phase 1 has been completed. IKE Phase 2 parameters are configured later.

Issue the **crypto isakmp policy** *number* configuration command on R1 for policy 10:

```
R1(config)# crypto isakmp policy 10
```

c. View the various IKE parameters available using Cisco IOS help by typing a question mark (?):

```
R1(config-isakmp)# ?
ISAKMP commands:
  authentication  Set authentication method for protection suite
  default         Set a command to its defaults
  encryption      Set encryption algorithm for protection suite
  exit            Exit from ISAKMP protection suite configuration mode
  group           Set the Diffie-Hellman group
  hash            Set hash algorithm for protection suite
  lifetime        Set lifetime for ISAKMP security association
  no              Negate a command or set its defaults
```

Step 3: Configure ISAKMP policy parameters on R1 and R3.

Your choice of an encryption algorithm determines how confidential the control channel between the endpoints is. The hash algorithm controls data integrity, ensuring that the data received from a peer has not been tampered with in transit. The authentication type ensures that the packet was indeed sent and signed by the remote peer. The Diffie-Hellman group is used to create a secret key shared by the peers that has not been sent across the network.

a. Configure an authentication type of pre-shared keys. Use AES 256 encryption, SHA as your hash algorithm, and Diffie-Hellman group 5 key exchange for this IKE policy.

b. Give the policy a lifetime of 3600 seconds (1 hour). Configure the same policy on R3. Older versions of Cisco IOS do not support AES 256 encryption and SHA as a hash algorithm. Substitute whatever encryption and hashing algorithm your router supports. Be sure the same changes are made on the other VPN endpoint so that they are in sync.

Note: You should be at the R1(config-isakmp)# at this point. The **crypto isakmp policy 10** command is repeated here for clarity:

```
R1(config)# crypto isakmp policy 10
R1(config-isakmp)# authentication pre-share
R1(config-isakmp)# encryption aes 256
R1(config-isakmp)# hash sha
R1(config-isakmp)# group 5
R1(config-isakmp)# lifetime 3600
R1(config-isakmp)# end

R3(config)# crypto isakmp policy 10
R3(config-isakmp)# authentication pre-share
R3(config-isakmp)# encryption aes 256
R3(config-isakmp)# hash sha
R3(config-isakmp)# group 5
R3(config-isakmp)# lifetime 3600
R3(config-isakmp)# end
```

c. Verify the IKE policy with the **show crypto isakmp policy** command:

```
R1# show crypto isakmp policy
Global IKE policy
Protection suite of priority 10
   encryption algorithm: AES - Advanced Encryption Standard (256 bit
   keys).
   hash algorithm:              Secure Hash Standard
   authentication method:       Pre-Shared Key
   Diffie-Hellman group:        #5 (1536 bit)
   lifetime:                    3600 seconds, no volume limit
```

Step 4: Configure pre-shared keys.

a. Because pre-shared keys are used as the authentication method in the IKE policy, configure a key on each router that points to the other VPN endpoint. These keys must match for authentication to be successful. The global configuration command **crypto isakmp key** *key-string* **address** *address* is used to enter a pre-shared key. Use the IP address of the remote peer, the remote interface that the peer would use to route traffic to the local router.

   Which IP addresses should you use to configure the IKE peers, given the topology diagram and IP addressing table?

   ____

   ____

b. Each IP address that is used to configure the IKE peers is also referred to as the IP address of the remote VPN endpoint. Configure the pre-shared key of cisco123 on router R1 using the following command. Production networks should use a complex key. This command points to the remote peer R3 S0/0/1 IP address:

```
R1(config)# crypto isakmp key cisco123 address 10.2.2.1
```

c. The command for R3 points to the R1 S0/0/0 IP address. Configure the pre-shared key on router R1 using the following command:

```
R3(config)# crypto isakmp key cisco123 address 10.1.1.1
```

Step 5: Configure the IPsec transform set and lifetimes.

a. The IPsec transform set is another crypto configuration parameter that routers negotiate to form a security association. To create an IPsec transform set, use the **crypto ipsec transform-set** *tag* parameters. Use **?** to see which parameters are available.

```
R1(config)# crypto ipsec transform-set 50 ?
  ah-md5-hmac    AH-HMAC-MD5 transform
  ah-sha-hmac    AH-HMAC-SHA transform
  comp-lzs       IP Compression using the LZS compression algorithm
  esp-3des       ESP transform using 3DES(EDE) cipher (168 bits)
  esp-aes        ESP transform using AES cipher
  esp-des        ESP transform using DES cipher (56 bits)
  esp-md5-hmac   ESP transform using HMAC-MD5 auth
  esp-null       ESP transform w/o cipher
  esp-seal       ESP transform using SEAL cipher (160 bits)
  esp-sha-hmac   ESP transform using HMAC-SHA auth
```

b. On R1 and R3, create a transform set with tag 50 and use an Encapsulating Security Protocol (ESP) transform with an AES 256 cipher with ESP and the SHA hash function. The transform sets must match.

```
R1(config)# crypto ipsec transform-set 50 esp-aes 256 esp-sha-hmac
R1(cfg-crypto-trans)#exit

R3(config)# crypto ipsec transform-set 50 esp-aes 256 esp-sha-hmac
R3(cfg-crypto-trans)#exit
```

c. What is the function of the IPsec transform set?

____

____

d. You can also change the IPsec security association lifetimes from the default of 3600 seconds or 4,608,000 KB, whichever comes first. On R1 and R3, set the IPsec security association lifetime to 30 minutes, or 1800 seconds:

```
R1(config)# crypto ipsec security-association lifetime seconds 1800

R3(config)# crypto ipsec security-association lifetime seconds 1800
```

Step 6: Define interesting traffic.

To make use of the IPsec encryption with the VPN, it is necessary to define extended access lists to tell the router which traffic to encrypt. A packet that is permitted by an access list used for defining IPsec traffic is encrypted if the IPsec session is configured correctly. A packet that is denied by one of these access lists is not dropped, but sent unencrypted. Also, like any other access list, there is an implicit deny at the end, which, in this case, means the default action is to not encrypt traffic. If there is no IPsec security association correctly configured, no traffic is encrypted, and traffic is forwarded as unencrypted.

In this scenario, the traffic you want to encrypt is traffic going from R1's Ethernet LAN to R3's Ethernet LAN, or vice versa. These access lists are used outbound on the VPN endpoint interfaces and must mirror each other.

a. Configure the IPsec VPN interesting traffic ACL on R1:

```
R1(config)# access-list 101 permit ip 192.168.1.0 0.0.0.255 192.168.3.0
0.0.0.255
```

b. Configure the IPsec VPN interesting traffic ACL on R3:

```
R3(config)# access-list 101 permit ip 192.168.3.0 0.0.0.255 192.168.1.0
0.0.0.255
```

Does IPsec evaluate whether the access lists are mirrored as a requirement to negotiate its security association? ____

Step 7: Create and apply a crypto map.

A crypto map associates traffic that matches an access list to a peer and various IKE and IPsec settings. After the crypto map is created, it can be applied to one or more interfaces. The interfaces that it is applied to should be the ones facing the IPsec peer.

a. To create a crypto map, use the global configuration command **`crypto map`** *`name sequence-num type`* to enter the crypto map configuration mode for that sequence number. Multiple crypto map statements can belong to the same crypto map and are evaluated in ascending numerical order. Enter the crypto map configuration mode on R1. Use a type of **`ipsec-isakmp`**, which means IKE is used to establish IPsec security associations.

b. Create the crypto map on R1, name it **CMAP**, and use 10 as the sequence number. A message displays after you issue the command.

```
R1(config)# crypto map CMAP 10 ipsec-isakmp
% NOTE: This new crypto map will remain disabled until a peer
and a valid access list have been configured.
```

c. Use the **match address** *access-list* command to specify which access list defines which traffic to encrypt:

```
R1(config-crypto-map)# match address 101
```

d. To view the list of possible **set** commands that you can do in a crypto map, use the help function:

```
R1(config-crypto-map)# set ?
Identity                Identity restriction.
Ip                      Interface Internet Protocol config commands
isakmp-profile          Specify isakmp Profile
nat                     Set NAT translation
peer                    Allowed Encryption/Decryption peer.
pfs                     Specify pfs settings
security-association    Security association parameters
transform-set           Specify list of transform sets in priority order
```

e. Setting a peer IP or hostname is required, so set it to R3's remote VPN endpoint interface using the following command.

```
R1(config-crypto-map)# set peer 10.2.2.1
```

f. Hard code the transform set to be used with this peer, using the **set transform-set** *tag* command. Set the perfect forwarding secrecy type using the **set pfs** *type* command, and also modify the default IPsec security association lifetime with the **set security-association lifetime seconds** *seconds* command:

```
R1(config-crypto-map)# set pfs group5
R1(config-crypto-map)# set transform-set 50
R1(config-crypto-map)# set security-association lifetime seconds 900
R1(config-crypto-map)# exit
```

g. Create a mirrored matching crypto map on R3:

```
R3(config)# crypto map CMAP 10 ipsec-isakmp
R3(config-crypto-map)# match address 101
R3(config-crypto-map)# set peer 10.1.1.1
R3(config-crypto-map)# set pfs group5
R3(config-crypto-map)# set transform-set 50
R3(config-crypto-map)# set security-association lifetime seconds 900
R3(config-crypto-map)# exit
```

The last step is applying the maps to interfaces. Note that the security associations (SAs) will not be established until the crypto map has been activated by interesting traffic. The router will generate a notification that crypto is now on.

h. Apply the crypto maps to the appropriate interfaces on R1 and R3.

```
R1(config)# interface S0/0/0
R1(config-if)# crypto map CMAP
*Jan 28 04:09:09.150: %CRYPTO-6-ISAKMP_ON_OFF: ISAKMP is ON
R1(config)# end

R3(config)# interface S0/0/1
R3(config-if)# crypto map CMAP
*Jan 28 04:10:54.138: %CRYPTO-6-ISAKMP_ON_OFF: ISAKMP is ON
R3(config)# end
```

Task 2: Verify Site-to-Site IPsec VPN Configuration

Step 1: Verify the IPsec configuration on R1 and R3.

a. Previously, you used the **show crypto isakmp policy** command to show the configured ISAKMP policies on the router. Similarly, the **show crypto ipsec transform-set** command displays the configured IPsec policies in the form of the transform sets:

```
R1# show crypto ipsec transform-set
Transform set 50: { esp-256-aes esp-sha-hmac }
will negotiate = { Tunnel, },

Transform set #$!default_transform_set_1: { esp-aes esp-sha-hmac  }
   will negotiate = { Transport,  },

Transform set #$!default_transform_set_0: { esp-3des esp-sha-hmac  }
   will negotiate = { Transport,  },


R3# show crypto ipsec transform-set
Transform set 50: { esp-256-aes esp-sha-hmac }
will negotiate = { Tunnel, },

Transform set #$!default_transform_set_1: { esp-aes esp-sha-hmac  }
   will negotiate = { Transport,  },

Transform set #$!default_transform_set_0: { esp-3des esp-sha-hmac  }
   will negotiate = { Transport,  },
```

b. Use the **show crypto map** command to display the crypto maps that will be applied to the router:

```
R1# show crypto map
Crypto Map "CMAP" 10 ipsec-isakmp
  Peer = 10.2.2.1
  Extended IP access list 101
  access-list 101 permit ip 192.168.1.0 0.0.0.255 192.168.3.0 0.0.0.255

  Current peer: 10.2.2.1
  Security association lifetime: 4608000 kilobytes/900 seconds
  PFS (Y/N): Y
  DH group:  group5
  Transform sets={
         50: { esp-256-aes esp-sha-hmac  } ,
        }
  Interfaces using crypto map MYMAP: Serial0/0/0

R3# show crypto map
Crypto Map "CMAP" 10 ipsec-isakmp
  Peer = 10.1.1.1
  Extended IP access list 101
  access-list 101 permit ip 192.168.3.0 0.0.0.255 192.168.1.0 0.0.0.255

  Current peer: 10.1.1.1
  Security association lifetime: 4608000 kilobytes/900 seconds
  PFS (Y/N): Y
  DH group:  group5
  Transform sets={
```

```
                50: { esp-256-aes esp-sha-hmac  } ,
               }
        Interfaces using crypto map MYMAP: Serial0/0/1
```

Note: The output of these **show** commands does not change if interesting traffic goes across the connection. You test various types of traffic in the next task.

Task 3: Verify IPsec VPN Operation

Step 1: Display isakmp security associations.

The show crypto isakmp sa command reveals that no IKE SAs exist yet. When interesting traffic is sent, this command output changes:

```
R1# show crypto isakmp sa

dst   src   state     conn-id slot status
```

Step 2: Display IPsec security associations.

The **show crypto ipsec sa** command shows the unused SA between R1 and R3. Note the number of packets sent across and the lack of any security associations listed toward the bottom of the output. The output for R1 is shown here:

```
R1# show crypto ipsec sa

interface: Serial0/0/0
    Crypto map tag: CMAP, local addr 10.1.1.1

   protected vrf: (none)
   local  ident (addr/mask/prot/port): (192.168.1.0/255.255.255.0/0/0)
   remote ident (addr/mask/prot/port): (192.168.3.0/255.255.255.0/0/0)
   current_peer 10.2.2.1 port 500
     PERMIT, flags={origin_is_acl,}
    #pkts encaps: 0, #pkts encrypt: 0, #pkts digest: 0
    #pkts decaps: 0, #pkts decrypt: 0, #pkts verify: 0
    #pkts compressed: 0, #pkts decompressed: 0
    #pkts not compressed: 0, #pkts compr. failed: 0
    #pkts not decompressed: 0, #pkts decompress failed: 0
    #send errors 0, #recv errors 0

     local crypto endpt.: 10.1.1.1, remote crypto endpt.: 10.2.2.1
     path mtu 1500, ip mtu 1500, ip mtu idb Serial0/0/0
     current outbound spi: 0x0(0)

     inbound esp sas:
     inbound ah sas:
     inbound pcp sas:
     outbound esp sas:
     outbound ah sas:
     outbound pcp sas:
```

Why have no security associations (SAs) been negotiated?

____

Step 3: Generate some uninteresting test traffic and observe the results.

a. Ping from R1 to the R3 S0/0/1 interface IP address 10.2.2.1. Were the pings successful? ______

b. Issue the **show crypto isakmp sa** command. Was an SA created between R1 and R3? ____

c. Ping from R1 to the R3 Fa01 interface IP address 192.168.3.1. Were the pings successful? ____

d. Issue the **show crypto isakmp sa** command again. Was an SA created for these pings? Why or why not?

____

____

e. Issue the command **debug eigrp packets**. You should see EIGRP hello packets passing between R1 and R3.

```
R1# debug eigrp packets
EIGRP Packets debugging is on
    (UPDATE, REQUEST, QUERY, REPLY, HELLO, IPXSAP, PROBE, ACK, STUB,
SIAQUERY, SIAREPLY)
R1#
*Jan 29 16:05:41.243: EIGRP: Received HELLO on Serial0/0/0 nbr 10.1.1.2
*Jan 29 16:05:41.243:   AS 101, Flags 0x0, Seq 0/0 idbQ 0/0 iidbQ
un/rely 0/0 pe
erQ un/rely 0/0
*Jan 29 16:05:41.887: EIGRP: Sending HELLO on Serial0/0/0
*Jan 29 16:05:41.887:   AS 101, Flags 0x0, Seq 0/0 idbQ 0/0 iidbQ
un/rely 0/0
R1#
*Jan 29 16:05:43.143: EIGRP: Sending HELLO on FastEthernet0/1
*Jan 29 16:05:43.143:   AS 101, Flags 0x0, Seq 0/0 idbQ 0/0 iidbQ
un/rely 0/0
R1#
```

f. Turn off debugging with the **no debug eigrp packets** or **undebug all** command.

g. Issue the **show crypto isakmp sa** command again. Was an SA created between R1 and R3? Why or why not?

____

____

Step 4: Generate some interesting test traffic and observe the results.

a. Use an extended ping from R1 to the R3 Fa01 interface IP address 192.168.3.1. Extended ping enables you to control the source address of the packets. Respond as shown in the following example. Press **Enter** to accept the defaults, except where a specific response is indicated.

```
R1# ping
Protocol [ip]:
Target IP address: 192.168.3.1
Repeat count [5]:
Datagram size [100]:
Timeout in seconds [2]:
Extended commands [n]: y
Source address or interface: 192.168.1.1
Type of service [0]:
Set DF bit in IP header? [no]:
```

```
Validate reply data? [no]:
Data pattern [0xABCD]:
Loose, Strict, Record, Timestamp, Verbose[none]:
Sweep range of sizes [n]:
Type escape sequence to abort.
Sending 5, 100-byte ICMP Echos to 192.168.3.1, timeout is 2 seconds:

Packet sent with a source address of 192.168.1.1
!!!!!
Success rate is 100 percent (5/5), round-trip min/avg/max = 92/92/92 ms
```

b. Issue the **show crypto isakmp sa** command again:

```
R1# show crypto isakmp sa
IPv4 Crypto ISAKMP SA
dst             src             state          conn-id slot status
10.2.2.1        10.1.1.1        QM_IDLE           1001    0 ACTIVE
```

Why was an SA created between R1 and R3 this time?

____

What are the endpoints of the IPsec VPN tunnel? ______________________________

c. Ping from PC-A to PC-C. Were the pings successful? _____

d. Issue the **show crypto ipsec sa** command. How many packets have been transformed between R1 and R3?

____

```
R1# show crypto ipsec sa

interface: Serial0/0/0
    Crypto map tag: CMAP, local addr 10.1.1.1

   protected vrf: (none)
   local  ident (addr/mask/prot/port): (192.168.1.0/255.255.255.0/0/0)
   remote ident (addr/mask/prot/port): (192.168.3.0/255.255.255.0/0/0)
   current_peer 10.2.2.1 port 500
     PERMIT, flags={origin_is_acl,}
    #pkts encaps: 9, #pkts encrypt: 9, #pkts digest: 9
    #pkts decaps: 9, #pkts decrypt: 9, #pkts verify: 9
    #pkts compressed: 0, #pkts decompressed: 0
    #pkts not compressed: 0, #pkts compr. failed: 0
    #pkts not decompressed: 0, #pkts decompress failed: 0
    #send errors 0, #recv errors 0

     local crypto endpt.: 10.1.1.1, remote crypto endpt.: 10.2.2.1
     path mtu 1500, ip mtu 1500, ip mtu idb Serial0/0/0
     current outbound spi: 0xC1DD058(203280472)

     inbound esp sas:
      spi: 0xDF57120F(3747025423)
        transform: esp-256-aes esp-sha-hmac ,
        in use settings ={Tunnel, }
        conn id: 2005, flow_id: FPGA:5, crypto map: CMAP
        sa timing: remaining key lifetime (k/sec): (4485195/877)
        IV size: 16 bytes
        replay detection support: Y
        Status: ACTIVE
```

```
inbound ah sas:

inbound pcp sas:

outbound esp sas:
 spi: 0xC1DD058(203280472)
   transform: esp-256-aes esp-sha-hmac ,
   in use settings ={Tunnel, }
   conn id: 2006, flow_id: FPGA:6, crypto map: CMAP
   sa timing: remaining key lifetime (k/sec): (4485195/877)
   IV size: 16 bytes
   replay detection support: Y
   Status: ACTIVE

outbound ah sas:

outbound pcp sas:
```

The previous example used pings to generate interesting traffic. What other types of traffic would result in an SA forming and tunnel establishment?

____

____

Part 3: Configure a Site-to-Site IPsec VPN with CCP

In Part 3 of this lab, configure an IPsec VPN tunnel between R1 and R3 that passes through R2. Task 1 restores the router to the basic settings using your saved configurations. In Task 2, configure R1 using CCP. In Task 3, mirror those settings to R3 using CCP utilities. Finally, review and test the resulting configuration.

Task 1: Restore Router R1 and R3 to the Basic Settings

To avoid confusion as to what was entered in Part 2 of the lab, start by restoring R1 and R3 to the basic configuration as described in Part 1 of this lab.

Step 1: Erase and reload the router.

a. Connect to the router console, and enter privileged EXEC mode.

b. Erase the startup config and then issue the **`reload`** command to restart the router.

Step 2: Restore the basic configuration.

a. When the router restarts, enter privileged EXEC mode with the **`enable`** command, and then enter global config mode. Use the HyperTerminal **Transfer > Send File** function, copy and paste, or use another method to load the basic startup config for R1 and R3 that was created and saved in Part 1 of this lab.

b. Save the running config to the startup config for R1 and R3 using the **`copy run start`** command.

c. Test connectivity by pinging from host PC-A to PC-C. If the pings are not successful, troubleshoot the router and PC configurations before continuing.

Task 2: Configure IPsec VPN Settings on R1 Using CCP

Step 1: Configure a username and password pair and enable HTTP router access.

a. From the CLI, configure a username and password for use with CCP on R1 and R3:

```
R1(config)# username admin privilege 15 secret cisco12345

R3(config)# username admin privilege 15 secret cisco12345
```

b. Enable the HTTP server on R1 and R3:

```
R1(config)#ip http server

R3(config)#ip http server
```

c. Configure local database authentication of web sessions to support CCP connectivity:

```
R1(config)# ip http authentication local
R3(config)# ip http authentication local
```

Step 2: Access CCP and discover R1.

a. Run the CCP application on PC-A. In the Select/Manage Community window, input the R1 IP address **192.168.1.1** in the Hostname/Address field, **admin** in the Username field, and **cisco12345** in the Password field. Click the **OK** button.

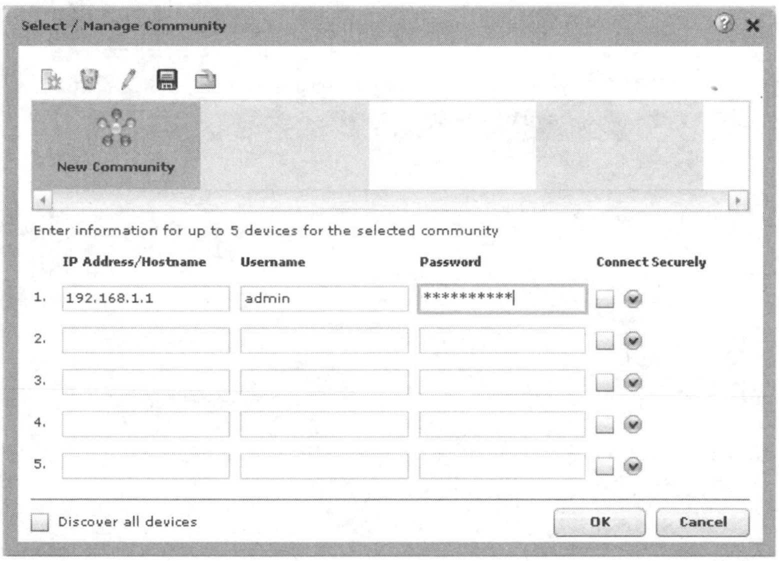

b. At the CCP Dashboard, click the **Discovery** button to discover and connect to R1. If the discovery process fails, use the **Discover Details** button to determine the problem so that you can resolve the issue.

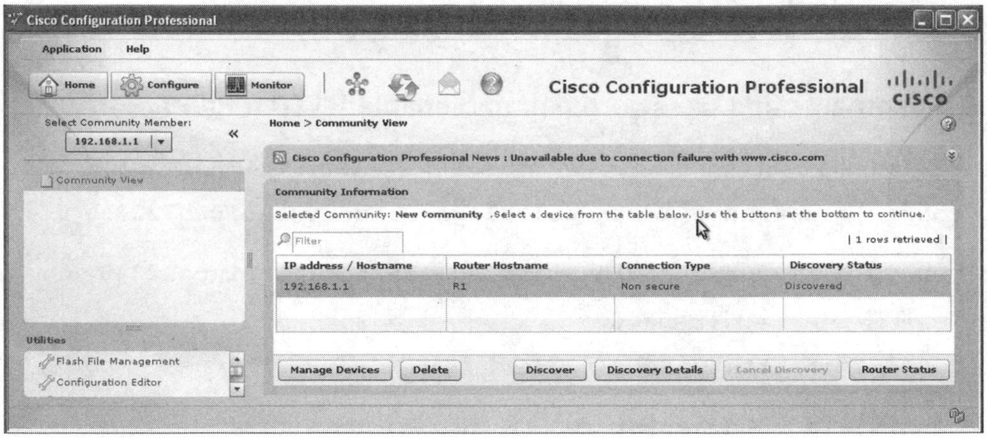

Step 3: Start the CCP VPN Wizard to configure R1.

a. Click the **Configure** button at the top of the CCP screen and choose **Security > VPN > Site-to-Site VPN**. Read through the description of this option.

What must you know to complete the configuration?

____

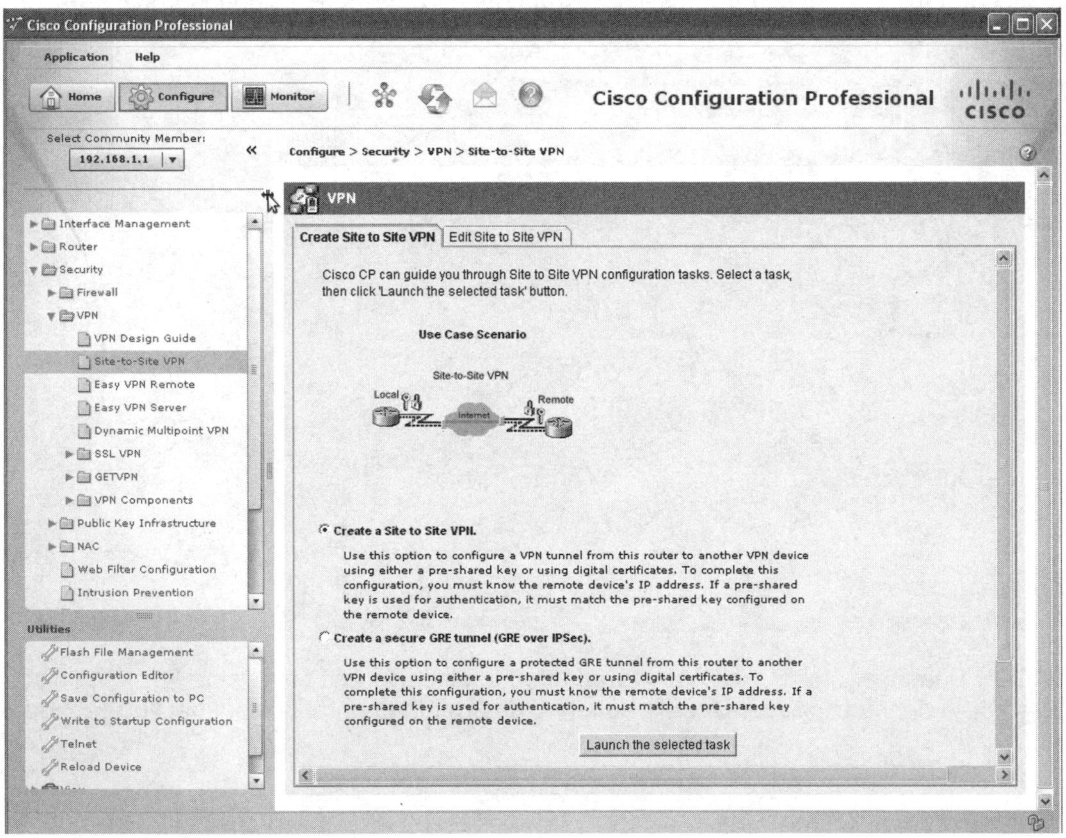

b. Click the **Launch the Selected Task** button to begin the CCP Site-to-Site VPN Wizard.

c. On the initial Site-to-Site VPN Wizard window, the Quick Setup option is selected by default. Click the **View Defaults** button to see what settings this option uses. What type of encryption does the default transform set use? ____________________

d. From the initial Site-to-Site VPN Wizard window, choose the **Step by Step Wizard**, and then click **Next**. Why would you use this option over the Quick setup option?

____

Step 4: Configure basic VPN connection information settings.

a. From the VPN Connection Information window, choose the interface for the connection, which should be R1 **Serial0/0/0**.

b. In the Peer Identity section, choose **Peer with Static IP Address** and enter the IP address of remote peer R3 S0/0/1 (**10.2.2.1**).

c. In the Authentication section, click **Pre-shared Keys**, and enter the pre-shared VPN key **cisco12345**. Reenter the key for confirmation. This key authenticates the initial exchange to establish the security association between devices. When finished, your screen should look similar to the following. After you have entered these settings correctly, click **Next**.

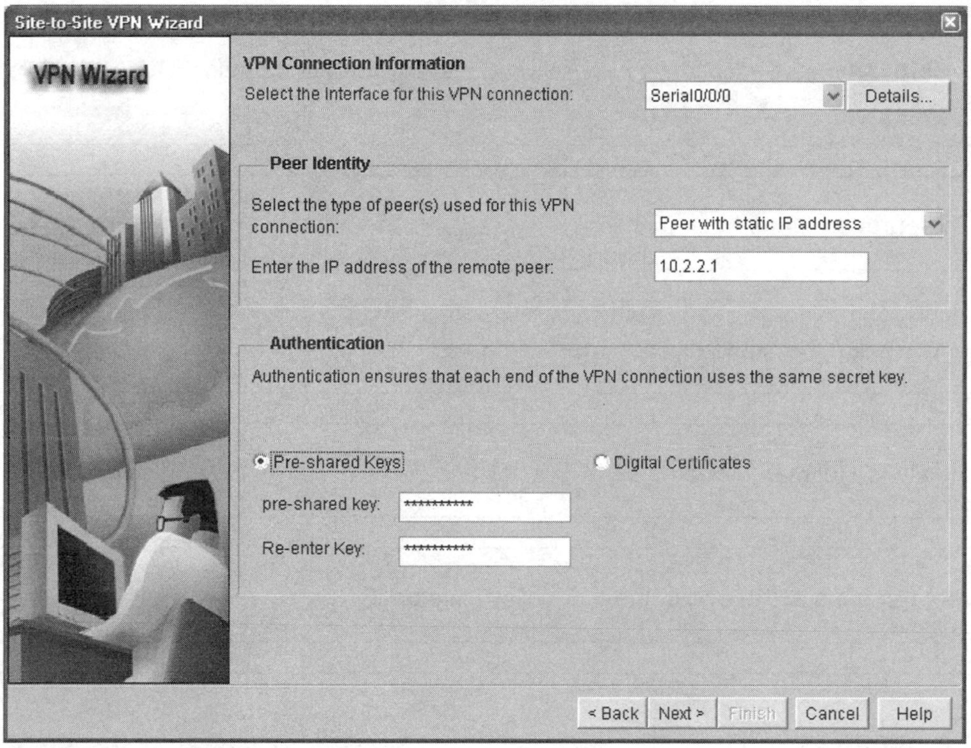

Step 5: Configure IKE policy parameters.

IKE policies are used while setting up the control channel between the two VPN endpoints for key exchange. This is also referred to as the IKE secure association (SA). In contrast, the IPsec policy is used during IKE Phase 2 to negotiate an IPsec security association to pass target data traffic.

In the IKE Proposals window, a default policy proposal is displayed. You can use this one or create a new one. What function does this IKE proposal serve?

____

a. Click the **Add** button to create a new IKE policy.

b. Set up the security policy as shown in the Add IKE Policy dialog box. These settings are matched later on R3. When finished, click **OK** to add the policy. Then click **Next**.

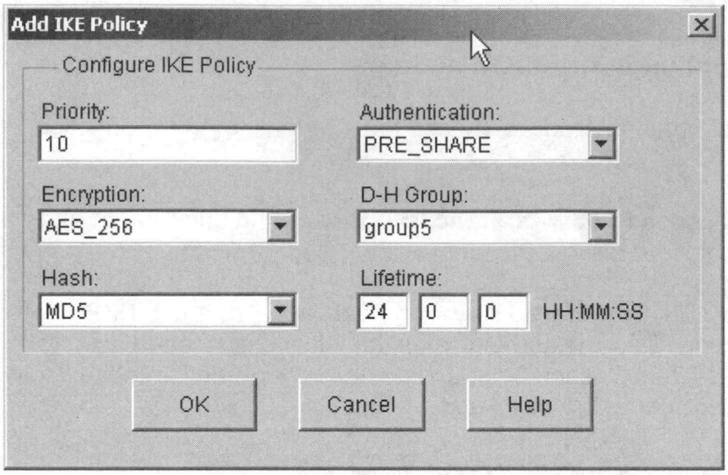

c. Click the **Help** button for assistance in answering the following questions. What is the function of the encryption algorithm in the IKE policy?

____

____

What is the purpose of the hash function?

____

____

What function does the authentication method serve?

____

____

How is the Diffie-Hellman group in the IKE policy used?

____

____

What event happens at the end of the IKE policy's lifetime?

____

____

Step 6: Configure a transform set.

The transform set is the IPsec policy used to encrypt, hash, and authenticate packets that pass through the tunnel. The transform set is the IKE Phase 2 policy.

a. A CCP default transform set is displayed. Click the **Add** button to create a new transform set.

b. Set up the transform set as shown in the Transform Set dialog box. These settings are matched later on R3. When finished, click **OK** to add the transform set. Then click **Next**.

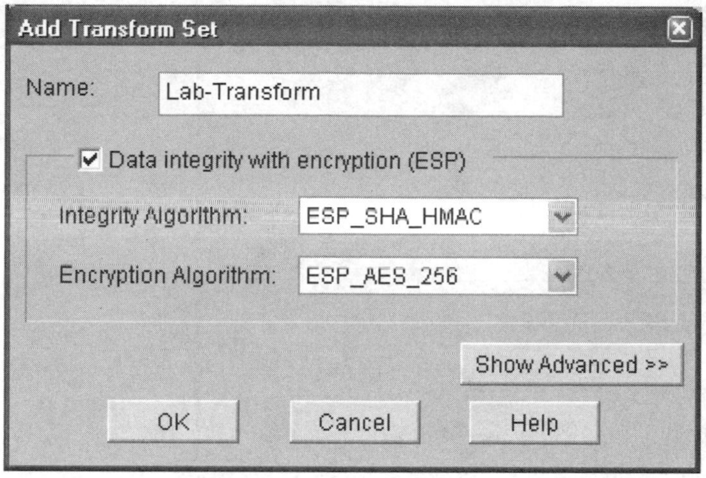

Step 7: Define interesting traffic.

You must define interesting traffic to be protected through the VPN tunnel. Interesting traffic is defined through an access list applied to the router. When you enter the source and destination subnets that you want to protect through the VPN tunnel, CCP generates the appropriate simple access list for you.

In the Traffic to Protect window, enter the information as shown here. These are the opposite of the settings configured on R3 later in the lab. When finished, click Next.

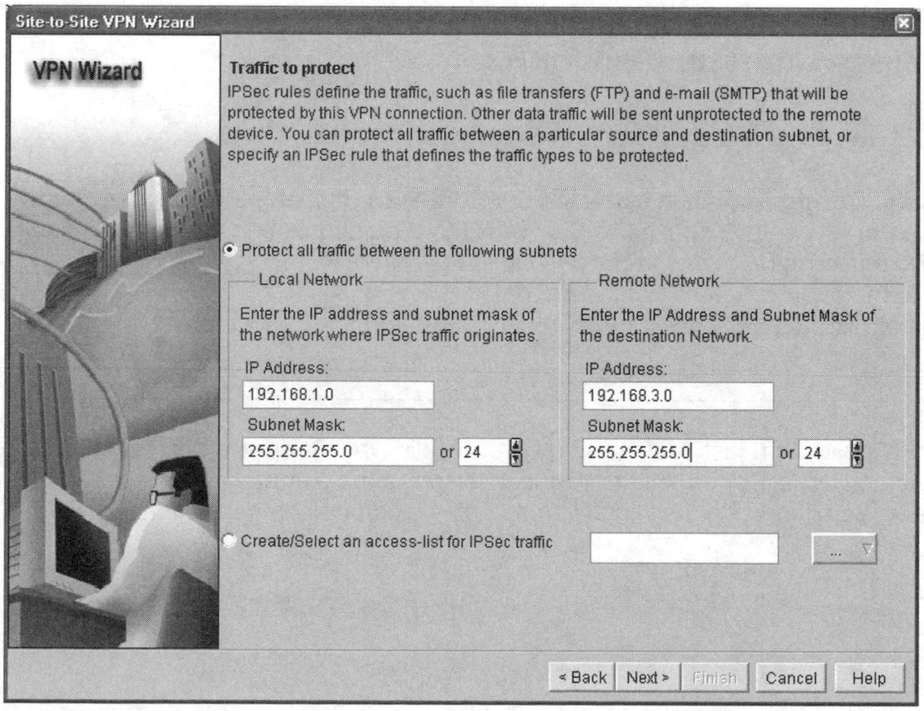

Step 8: Review the summary configuration and deliver commands to the router.

a. Review the Summary of the Configuration window. It should look similar to the one here. Do not check the Test VPN Connectivity After Configuring check box. This is done after configuring R3.

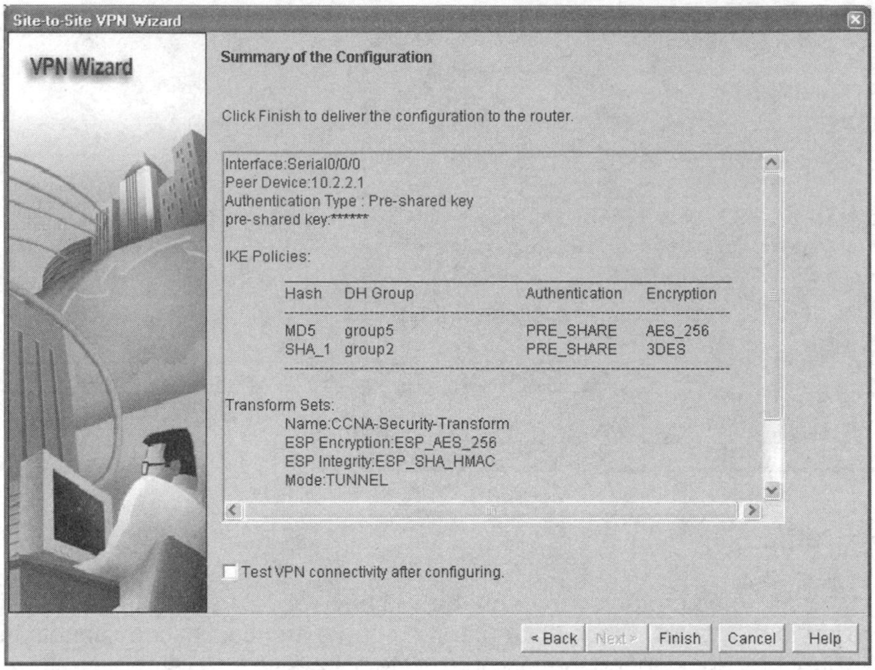

b. In the Deliver Configuration to router window, choose **Save Running Config to Router's Startup Config** and click the **Deliver** button. After the commands have been delivered, click **OK**. How many commands were delivered? ______________________________

Task 3: Create a Mirror Configuration for R3

Step 1: Use CCP on R1 to generate a mirror configuration for R3.

a. On R1, click the **Configure** button at the top of the CCP screen, and then choose **Security > VPN > Site-to-Site VPN**. Click the **Edit Site to Site VPN** tab. You should see the VPN configuration listed that you just created on R1. What is the description of the VPN? ______________________________

What is the status of the VPN and why?

____

____

b. Select the VPN policy you just configured on R1 and click the **Generate Mirror** button in the lower right of the window. The Generate Mirror window displays the commands necessary to configure R3 as a VPN peer. Scroll through the window to see all the commands generated.

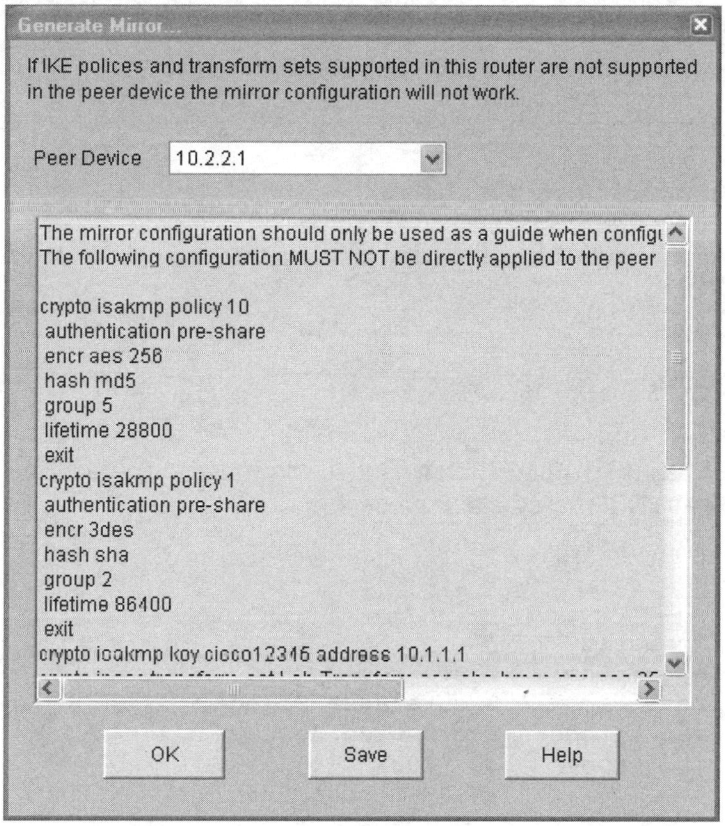

c. The text at the top of the window states that the configuration generated should only be used as a guide for setting up a site-to-site VPN. What commands are missing to allow this crypto policy to function on R3? ____

Hint: Look at the description entry following the **`crypto map SDM_CMAP_1`** command.

Step 2: Save the configuration commands for R3.

a. Click the **Save** button to create a text file for use in the next task.

b. Save the commands to the desktop or other location and name it **VPN-Mirror-Cfg-for-R3.txt**.

Note: You can also copy the commands directly from the Generate Mirror window.

c. (Optional) Edit the file to remove the explanation text at the beginning and the description entry following the **`crypto map SDM_CMAP_1`** command.

Task 4: Apply the Mirror Configuration to R3 and Verify the Configuration

Step 1: Access the R3 CLI and copy the mirror commands.

Note: You can also use CCP on R3 to create the appropriate VPN configuration, but copying and pasting the mirror commands generated from R1 is easier.

a. On R3, enter privileged EXEC mode and then global config mode.

b. Copy the commands from the text file into the R3 CLI.

Step 2: Apply the crypto map to the R3 S0/0/1 interface.

```
R3(config)# interface S0/0/1
R3(config-if)# crypto map SDM_CMAP_1
*Jan 30 13:00:38.184: %CRYPTO-6-ISAKMP_ON_OFF: ISAKMP is ON
```

Step 3: Verify the VPN configuration on R3 using Cisco IOS.

a. Display the running config beginning with the first line that contains the string "0/0/1" to verify that the crypto map is applied to S0/0/1:

```
R3# sh run | beg 0/0/1
interface Serial0/0/1
 ip address 10.2.2.1 255.255.255.252
 crypto map SDM_CMAP_1
```

b. On R3, use the **show crypto isakmp policy** command to show the configured ISAKMP policies on the router. Note that the default CCP policy is also present.

```
R3# show crypto isakmp policy

Global IKE policy
Protection suite of priority 1
        encryption algorithm:   Three key triple DES
        hash algorithm:         Secure Hash Standard
        authentication method:  Pre-Shared Key
        Diffie-Hellman group:   #2 (1024 bit)
        lifetime:               86400 seconds, no volume limit

Protection suite of priority 10
        encryption algorithm:   AES - Advanced Encryption Standard (256
bit keys
).
        hash algorithm:         Message Digest 5
        authentication method:  Pre-Shared Key
        Diffie-Hellman group:   #5 (1536 bit)
        lifetime:               28800 seconds, no volume limit
```

In the preceding output, how many ISAKMP policies are there?

____

____

c. Issue the **show crypto ipsec transform-set** command to display the configured IPsec policies in the form of the transform sets:

```
R3# show crypto ipsec transform-set
Transform set Lab-Transform: { esp-256-aes esp-sha-hmac  }
   will negotiate = { Tunnel,  },

Transform set #$!default_transform_set_1: { esp-aes esp-sha-hmac  }
   will negotiate = { Transport,  },

Transform set #$!default_transform_set_0: { esp-3des esp-sha-hmac  }
   will negotiate = { Transport,  },
```

d. Use the **show crypto map** command to display the crypto maps that will be applied to the router:

```
R3# show crypto map
Crypto Map "SDM_CMAP_1" 1 ipsec-isakmp
        Description: Apply the crypto map on the peer router's
interface having
```

```
IP address 10.2.2.1 that connects to this router.
        Peer = 10.1.1.1
        Extended IP access list SDM_1
            access-list SDM_1 permit ip 192.168.3.0 0.0.0.255
192.168.1.0 0.0.0.255
        Current peer: 10.1.1.1
        Security association lifetime: 4608000 kilobytes/3600 seconds
        PFS (Y/N): N
        Transform sets={
                Lab-Transform:  { esp-256-aes esp-sha-hmac  } ,
        }
        Interfaces using crypto map SDM_CMAP_1:
                Serial0/0/1
```

e. In the preceding output, the ISAKMP policy being used by the crypto map is the CCP default policy with sequence number priority 1, indicated by the number 1 in the first output line: `Crypto Map "SDM_CMAP_1" 1 ipsec-isakmp`. Why is it not using the one you created in the CCP session (the one shown with priority 10 in Step 3b above)?

____

f. (Optional) You can force the routers to use the more stringent policy that you created by changing the crypto map references in the R1 and R3 router configs as shown here. If this is done, you can remove the default ISAKMP policy 1 from both routers.

```
R1(config)# interface S0/0/1
R1(config-if)# no crypto map SDM_CMAP_1
R1(config-if)# exit
*Jan 30 17:01:46.099: %CRYPTO-6-ISAKMP_ON_OFF: ISAKMP is OFF
R1(config)# no crypto map SDM_CMAP_1 1
R1(config)# crypto map SDM_CMAP_1 10 ipsec-isakmp
% NOTE: This new crypto map will remain disabled until a peer
        and a valid access list have been configured.
R1(config-crypto-map)# description Tunnel to 10.2.2.1
R1(config-crypto-map)# set peer 10.2.2.1
R1(config-crypto-map)# set transform-set Lab-Transform
R1(config-crypto-map)# match address 100
R1(config-crypto-map)# exit
R1(config)#int S0/0/1
R1(config-if)# crypto map SDM_CMAP_1
R1(config-if)#e
*Jan 30 17:03:16.603: %CRYPTO-6-ISAKMP_ON_OFF: ISAKMP is ON

R3(config)# interface S0/0/1
R3(config-if)# no crypto map SDM_CMAP_1
R3(config-if)# exit
R3(config)# no crypto map SDM_CMAP_1 1
R3(config)# crypto map SDM_CMAP_1 10 ipsec-isakmp
% NOTE: This new crypto map will remain disabled until a peer
        and a valid access list have been configured.
R3(config-crypto-map)# description Tunnel to 10.1.1.1
R3(config-crypto-map)# set peer 10.1.1.1
R3(config-crypto-map)# set transform-set Lab-Transform
R3(config-crypto-map)# match address 100
R3(config-crypto-map)# exit
R3(config)# int S0/0/1
R3(config-if)# crypto map SDM_CMAP_1
R3(config-if)#
*Jan 30 22:18:28.487: %CRYPTO-6-ISAKMP_ON_OFF: ISAKMP is ON
```

Task 5: Test the VPN Configuration Using CCP on R1

a. On R1, use CCP to test the IPsec VPN tunnel between the two routers. Choose the folder **Security > VPN > Site-to-Site VPN** and display the **Edit Site-to-Site VPN** tab.

b. From the Edit Site to Site VPN tab, choose the VPN and click **Test Tunnel**.

c. When the VPN Troubleshooting window displays, click the **Start** button to have CCP start troubleshooting the tunnel.

d. When the CCP Warning window displays indicating that CCP will enable router debugs and generate some tunnel traffic, click **Yes** to continue.

e. In the next VPN Troubleshooting window, the IP address of the R1 Fa0/1 interface in the source network is displayed by default (192.168.1.1). Enter the IP address of the R3 Fa0/1 interface in the destination network field (**192.168.3.1**) and click **Continue** to begin the debugging process.

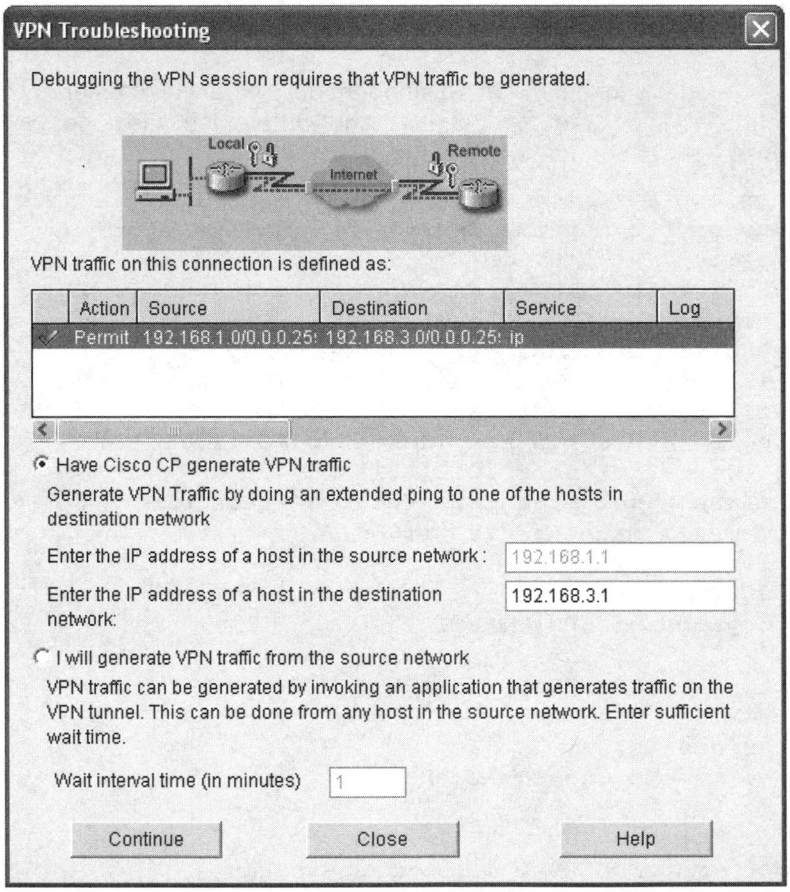

f. If the debug is successful and the tunnel is up, you should see the following screen. If the testing fails, CCP displays failure reasons and recommended actions. Click **OK** to remove the window.

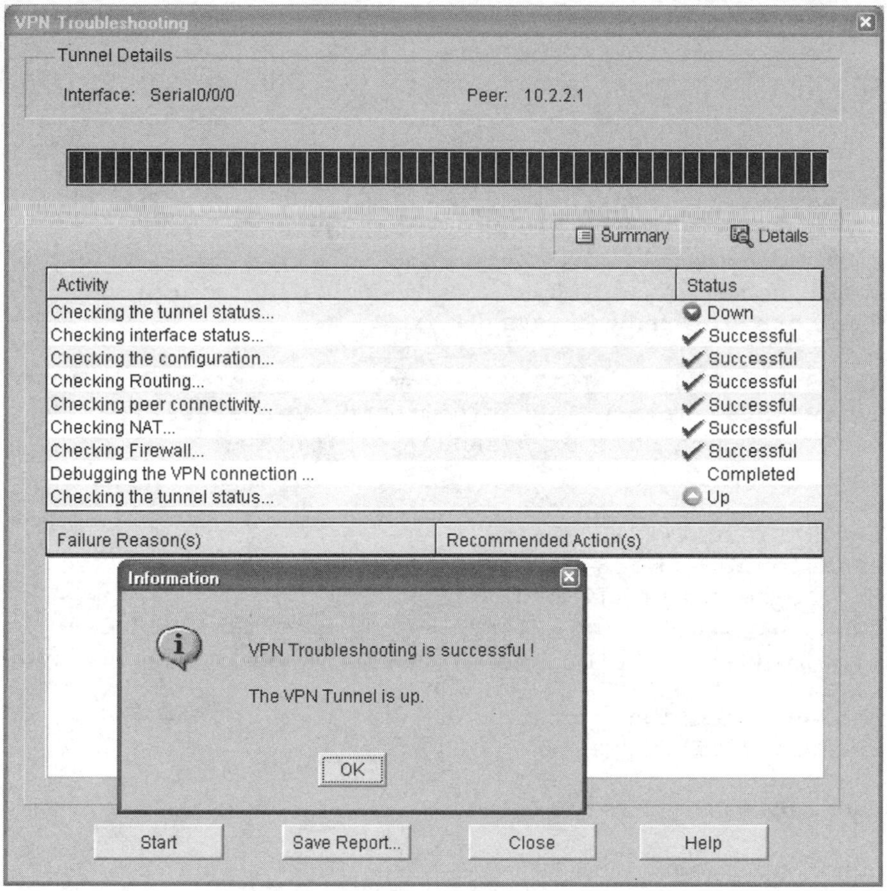

g. You can save the report if desired; otherwise, click **Close**.

Note: If you want to reset the tunnel and test again, you can click the **Clear Connection** button from the Edit Suite-to-Site VPN window. This can also be accomplished at the CLI using the **`clear crypto session`** command.

h. Display the running config for R3 beginning with the first line that contains the string "0/0/1" to verify that the crypto map is applied to S0/0/1:

```
R3# sh run | beg 0/0/1
interface Serial0/0/1
 ip address 10.2.2.1 255.255.255.252
 crypto map SDM_CMAP_1
<output omitted>
```

i. Issue the **`show crypto isakmp sa`** command on R3 to view the security association created:

```
R3# show crypto isakmp sa
IPv4 Crypto ISAKMP SA
dst             src             state          conn-id slot status
10.2.2.1        10.1.1.1        QM_IDLE           1001    0 ACTIVE
```

j. Issue the **`show crypto ipsec sa`** command. How many packets have been transformed between R1 and R3? ______________________________

```
R3# show crypto ipsec sa

interface: Serial0/0/1
    Crypto map tag: SDM_CMAP_1, local addr 10.2.2.1
```

```
protected vrf: (none)
local  ident (addr/mask/prot/port): (192.168.3.0/255.255.255.0/0/0)
remote ident (addr/mask/prot/port): (192.168.1.0/255.255.255.0/0/0)
current_peer 10.1.1.1 port 500
  PERMIT, flags={origin_is_acl,}
 #pkts encaps: 116, #pkts encrypt: 116, #pkts digest: 116
 #pkts decaps: 116, #pkts decrypt: 116, #pkts verify: 116
 #pkts compressed: 0, #pkts decompressed: 0
 #pkts not compressed: 0, #pkts compr. failed: 0
 #pkts not decompressed: 0, #pkts decompress failed: 0
 #send errors 0, #recv errors 0

  local crypto endpt.: 10.2.2.1, remote crypto endpt.: 10.1.1.1
  path mtu 1500, ip mtu 1500, ip mtu idb Serial0/0/1
  current outbound spi: 0x207AAD8A(544910730)

  inbound esp sas:
   spi: 0xAF102CAE(2937072814)
     transform: esp-256-aes esp-sha-hmac ,
     in use settings ={Tunnel, }
     conn id: 2007, flow_id: FPGA:7, crypto map: SDM_CMAP_1
     sa timing: remaining key lifetime (k/sec): (4558294/3037)
     IV size: 16 bytes
     replay detection support: Y
     Status: ACTIVE

  inbound ah sas:

  inbound pcp sas:

  outbound esp sas:
   spi: 0x207AAD8A(544910730)
     transform: esp-256-aes esp-sha-hmac ,
     in use settings ={Tunnel, }
     conn id: 2008, flow_id: FPGA:8, crypto map: SDM_CMAP_1
     sa timing: remaining key lifetime (k/sec): (4558294/3037)
     IV size: 16 bytes
     replay detection support: Y
     Status: ACTIVE

  outbound ah sas:

  outbound pcp sas:
```

Reflection

1. Would traffic on the Fast Ethernet link between PC-A and the R1 Fa0/0 interface be encrypted by the site-to-site IPsec VPN tunnel? Why or why not?

   ____
   ____
   ____

2. Compared to using the CCP VPN Wizard GUI, what are some factors to consider when configuring site-to-site IPsec VPNs using the manual CLI?

   ____
   ____
   ____
   ____

Router Interface Summary Table

Router Model	Ethernet Interface 1	Ethernet Interface 2	Serial Interface 1	Serial Interface 2
1800	Fast Ethernet 0/0 (Fa0/0)	Fast Ethernet 0/1 (Fa0/1)	Serial 0/0/0 (S0/0/0)	Serial 0/0/1 (S0/0/1)
1900	Gigabit Ethernet 0/0 (G0/0)	Gigabit Ethernet 0/1 (G0/1)	Serial 0/0/0 (S0/0/0)	Serial 0/0/1 (S0/0/1)
2800	Fast Ethernet 0/0 (Fa0/0)	Fast Ethernet 0/1 (Fa0/1)	Serial 0/0/0 (S0/0/0)	Serial 0/0/1 (S0/0/1)
2900	Gigabit Ethernet 0/0 (G0/0)	Gigabit Ethernet 0/1 (G0/1)	Serial 0/0/0 (S0/0/0)	Serial 0/0/1 (S0/0/1)

Note: To find out how the router is configured, look at the interfaces to identify the type of router and how many interfaces the router has. There is no way to effectively list all the combinations of configurations for each router class. This table includes identifiers for the possible combinations of Ethernet and serial interfaces in the device. The table does not include any other type of interface, even though a specific router may contain one. An example of this might be an ISDN BRI interface. The string in parentheses is the legal abbreviation that can be used in Cisco IOS commands to represent the interface.

Chapter 8 Lab B: Configuring a Remote Access VPN Server and Client

Topology

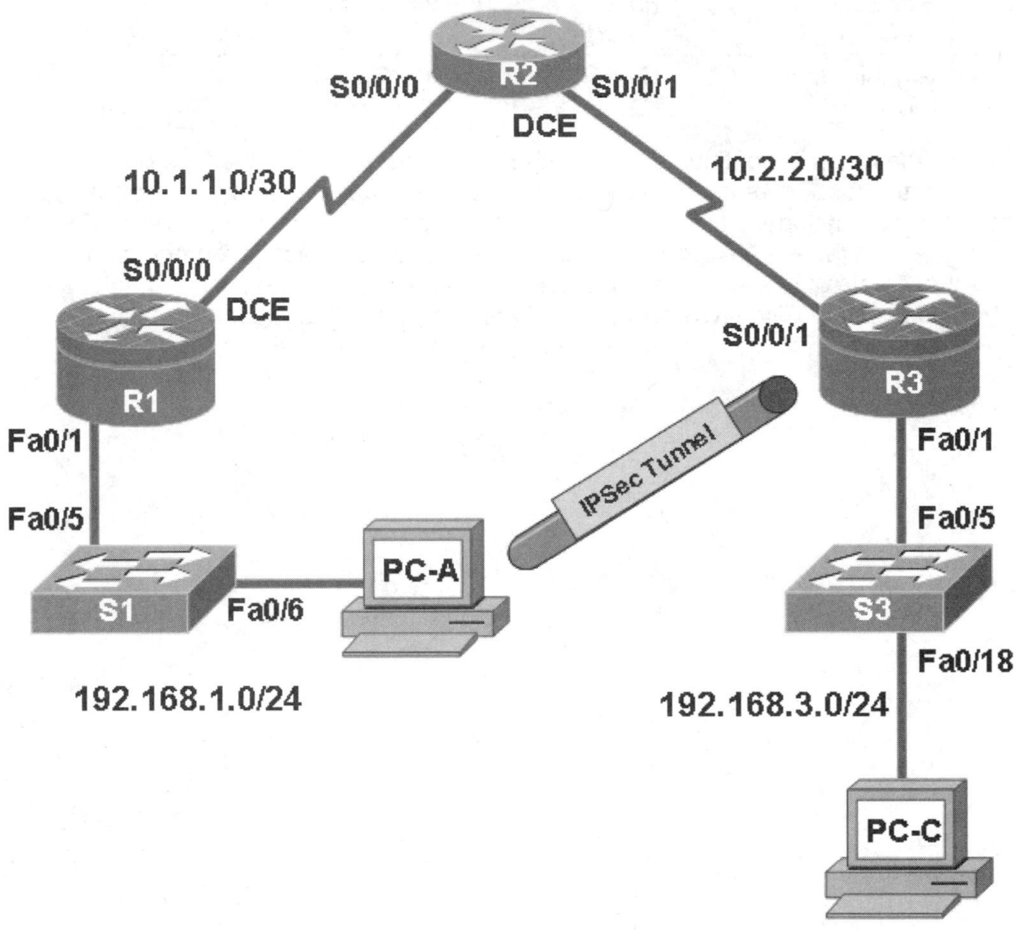

Note: ISR G2 devices have Gigabit Ethernet interfaces rather than Fast Ethernet interfaces.

IP Addressing Table

Device	Interface	IP Address	Subnet Mask	Default Gateway	Switch Port
R1	Fa0/1	192.168.1.1	255.255.255.0	N/A	S1 Fa0/5
	S0/0/0 (DCE)	10.1.1.1	255.255.255.252	N/A	N/A
R2	S0/0/0	10.1.1.2	255.255.255.252	N/A	N/A
	S0/0/1 (DCE)	10.2.2.2	255.255.255.252	N/A	N/A
R3	Fa0/1	192.168.3.1	255.255.255.0	N/A	S3 Fa0/5
	S0/0/1	10.2.2.1	255.255.255.252	N/A	N/A
PC-A	NIC	192.168.1.3	255.255.255.0	192.168.1.1	S1 Fa0/6
PC-C	NIC	192.168.3.3	255.255.255.0	192.168.3.1	S3 Fa0/18

Objectives

Part 1: Basic Router Configuration

- Configure hostnames, interface IP addresses, and access passwords.
- Configure static routing.

Part 2: Configuring a Remote Access VPN

- Configure a zone-based firewall (ZBF) on R3 using CCP.
- Configure Router R3 to support Cisco Easy VPN Server using CCP.
- Configure the Cisco VPN Client on PC-A and connect to R3.
- Verify the configuration.
- Test VPN functionality.

Background

Virtual private networks (VPN) can provide a secure method of transmitting data over a public network, such as the Internet. A common VPN implementation is used for remote access to a corporate office from a telecommuter location such as a small office/home office (SOHO).

In this lab, you build a multirouter network and configure the routers and hosts. You configure a remote-access IPsec VPN between a client computer and a simulated corporate network. You start by using CCP to configure a zoned-based firewall (ZBF) to prevent connections from outside the corporate network. You next use CCP to configure a Cisco Easy VPN Server on the corporate gateway router. Finally, you configure the Cisco VPN Client on a host and connect to the corporate network through a simulated Internet service provider (ISP) router.

The Cisco VPN Client enables organizations to establish end-to-end, encrypted (IPsec) VPN tunnels for secure connectivity for mobile employees or teleworkers. It supports Cisco Easy VPN, which allows the client to receive security policies upon a VPN tunnel connection from the central site VPN device (Cisco Easy VPN Server), minimizing configuration requirements at the remote location. Easy VPN is a scalable solution for remote-access deployments for which it is impractical to individually configure policies for multiple remote PCs.

Router R1 represents a remote site, and R3 represents the corporate headquarters. Host PC-A simulates an employee connecting from home or a small office over the Internet. Router R2 simulates an Internet ISP router and acts as a passthrough with no knowledge of the VPN connection running through it.

Note: The router commands and output in this lab are from a Cisco 1841 with Cisco IOS Software Release 12.4(20)T (advanced IP image). Other routers and Cisco IOS versions can be used. See the Router Interface Summary table at the end of the lab to determine which interface identifiers to use based on the equipment in the lab. Depending on the router model and Cisco IOS version, the commands available and the output produced might vary from what this lab shows.

Note: Make sure that the routers and the switches have been erased and have no startup configurations.

Required Resources

- 3 routers with Cisco 1841 with Cisco IOS Software Release 12.4(20)T1 or comparable
- 2 switches (Cisco 2960 or comparable)
- PC-A: Windows XP, Vista, or Windows 7 with Cisco VPN Client
- PC-C: Windows XP, Vista, or Windows 7 with CCP 2.5 installed
- Serial and Ethernet cables as shown in the topology
- Rollover cables to configure the routers via the console

CCP Notes

- See Chapter 00 Lab A for instructions on how to install CCP. Hardware/software recommendations for CCP include Windows XP, Vista, or Windows 7 with Java Version 1.6.0_11 up to 1.6.0_21, Internet Explorer 6.0 or later, and Flash Player Version 10.0.12.36 or later.
- If the PC on which CCP is installed is running Windows Vista or Windows 7, you might need to right-click the CCP icon or menu item and choose Run as Administrator.
- To run CCP, you might need to temporarily disable antivirus programs and OS firewalls. Make sure to turn off all pop-up blockers in the browser.

Part 1: Basic Router Configuration

In Part 1, you set up the network topology and configure basic settings, such as the interface IP addresses and static routing. Perform the steps on the routers as indicated.

Step 1: Cable the network as shown in the topology.

Attach the devices shown in the topology diagram, and cable as necessary.

Step 2: Configure basic settings for all routers.

a. Configure hostnames as shown in the topology.

b. Configure the physical interface IP addresses as shown in the IP addressing table.

c. Configure a clock rate for the routers with a DCE serial cable attached to their serial interface:

```
R1(config)# interface S0/0/0
R1(config-if)# clock rate 64000
```

d. Disable DNS lookup to prevent the router from attempting to translate incorrectly entered commands as though they were hostnames:

```
R1(config)# no ip domain-lookup
```

Step 3: Configure static default routes on R1 and R3.

Configure a static default route from R1 to R2 and from R3 to R2.

```
R1(config)# ip route 0.0.0.0 0.0.0.0 10.1.1.2

R3(config)# ip route 0.0.0.0 0.0.0.0 10.2.2.2
```

Step 4: Configure static routes on R2.

a. Configure a static route from R2 to the R1 LAN:

```
R2(config)# ip route 192.168.1.0 255.255.255.0 10.1.1.1
```

b. Configure a static route from R2 to the R3 LAN:

```
R2(config)# ip route 192.168.3.0 255.255.255.0 10.2.2.1
```

Step 5: Configure PC host IP settings.

Configure a static IP address, subnet mask, and default gateway for PC-A and PC-C, as shown in the IP addressing table.

Step 6: Verify connectivity between PC-A and R3.

From PC-A, ping the R3 S0/0/1 interface at IP address 10.2.2.1:

```
PC-A:\> ping 10.2.2.1
```

Are the results successful? _____

If the pings are not successful, troubleshoot the basic device configurations before continuing.

Step 7: Configure a minimum password length.

Note: Passwords in this lab are set to a minimum of 10 characters, but are relatively simple for the benefit of performing the lab. More complex passwords are recommended in a production network.

Use the **`security passwords`** command to set a minimum password length of 10 characters:

```
R1(config)# security passwords min-length 10
```

Step 8: Configure the enable secret password and console and vty lines.

a. Configure the enable secret password **cisco12345** on R1:

```
R1(config)# enable secret cisco12345
```

b. Configure a console password and enable login for router R1. For additional security, the **`exec-timeout`** command causes the line to log out after 5 minutes of inactivity. The **`logging synchronous`** command prevents console messages from interrupting command entry.

Note: To avoid repetitive logins during this lab, you can set the **`exec-timeout`** command to 0 0, which prevents it from expiring. However, this is not considered a good security practice.

```
R1(config)# line console 0
R1(config-line)# password ciscoconpass
R1(config-line)# exec-timeout 5 0
R1(config-line)# login
R1(config-line)# logging synchronous
```

c. Configure the password on the vty lines for router R1:

```
R1(config)# line vty 0 4
R1(config-line)# password ciscovtypass
R1(config-line)# exec-timeout 5 0
R1(config-line)# login
```

d. Repeat these configurations on R2 and R3.

Step 9: Encrypt clear-text passwords.

a. Use the **service password-encryption** command to encrypt the console, aux, and vty passwords:

```
R1(config)# service password-encryption
```

b. Issue the **show run** command. Can you read the console, aux, and vty passwords? Why or why not? ____

c. Repeat this configuration on R2 and R3.

Step 10: Configure a login warning banner on routers R1 and R3.

Configure a message-of-the-day (MOTD) warning banner to unauthorized users:

```
R1(config)# banner motd $Unauthorized access strictly prohibited and
prosecuted to the full extent of the law$
```

Step 11: Save the basic running configuration for all three routers.

Save the running configuration to the startup configuration from the privileged EXEC prompt:

```
R1# copy running-config startup-config
```

Part 2: Configuring a Remote Access VPN

In Part 2 of this lab, configure a firewall and a remote-access IPsec VPN. You use CCP to configure R3 as a VPN server. On PC-C, you enable and configure the Cisco VPN Client.

Task 1: Prepare R3 for CCP Access

Step 1: Configure HTTP router access and a AAA user.

a. Enable the HTTP server on R3:

```
R3(config)# ip http server
```

Note: For added security, you can enable the HTTP secure server on R3 using the ip **http secure-server** command. The HTTP server and the HTTP secure server are disabled by default.

b. Create an **admin01** account on R3 with privilege level **15** and a password of **admin01pass** for use with AAA:

```
R3(config)# username admin01 privilege 15 password 0 admin01pass
```

c. Configure R3 so that CCP use the local database to authenticate web sessions:

```
R3(config)# ip http authentication local
```

Step 2: Access CCP and discover R3.

a. Run the CCP application on PC-C. In the Select/Manage Community window, input the R1 IP address **192.168.3.1** in the Hostname/Address field, **admin01** in the Username field, and **admin01pass** in the Password field. Click the **OK** button.

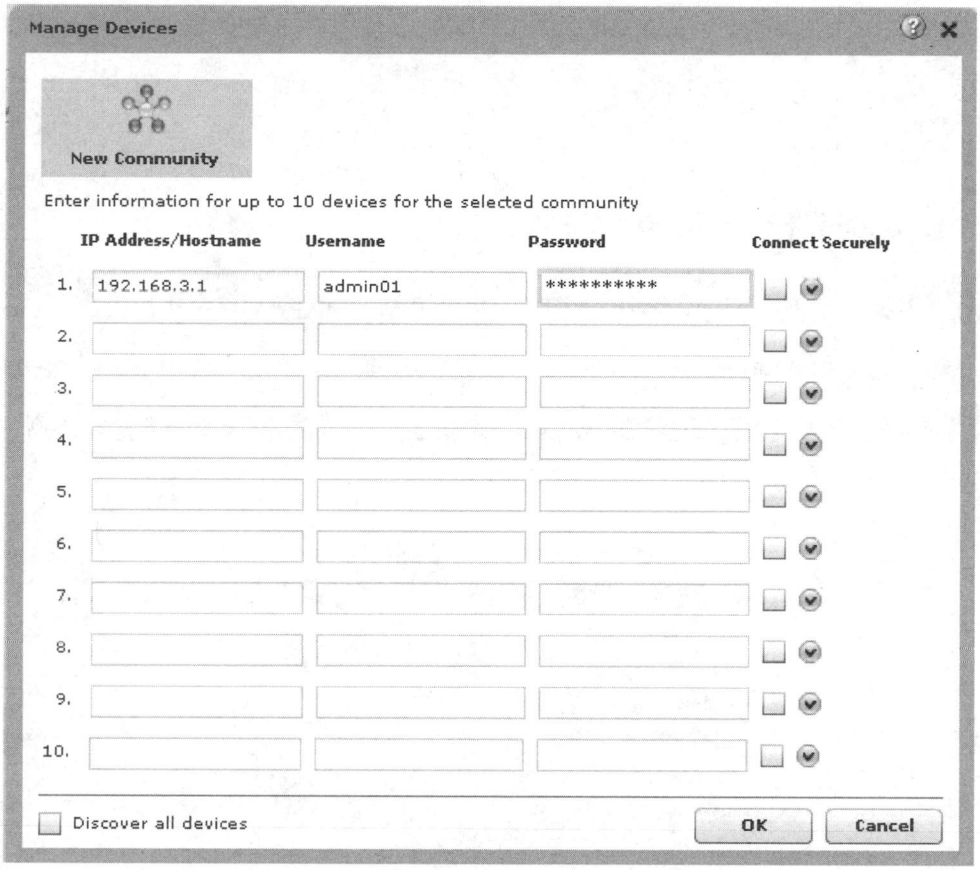

b. At the CCP Dashboard, click the **Discovery** button to discover and connect to R3. If the discovery process fails, click the **Discover Details** button to determine the problem to resolve the issue.

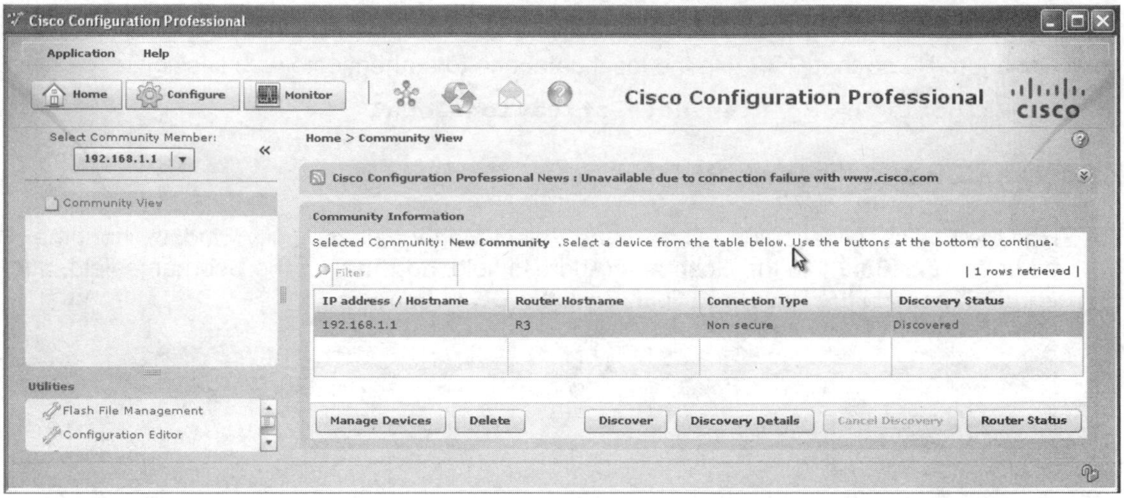

Task 2: Configure a ZBF Firewall on R3

Step 1: Use the CCP firewall wizard to configure a zone-based firewall (ZBF) on R3.

a. Click the **Configure** button at the top of the CCP screen, and choose **Security** > **Firewall > Firewall**.

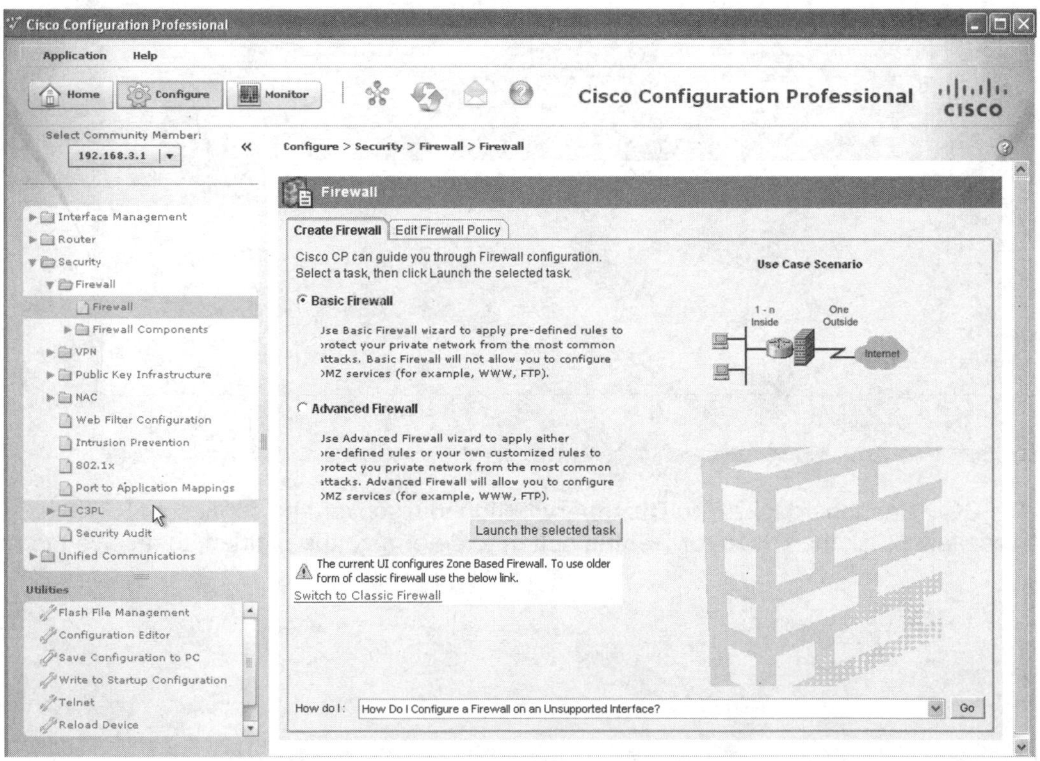

b. Choose **Basic Firewall** and click the **Launch the selected task** button. On the Basic Firewall Configuration Wizard screen, click **Next**.

c. Check the **Inside (Trusted)** check box for FastEthernet0/1 and the **Outside (Untrusted)** check box for Serial0/0/1. Click **Next**. Click **OK** when the CCP launch warning for Serial0/0/1 is displayed.

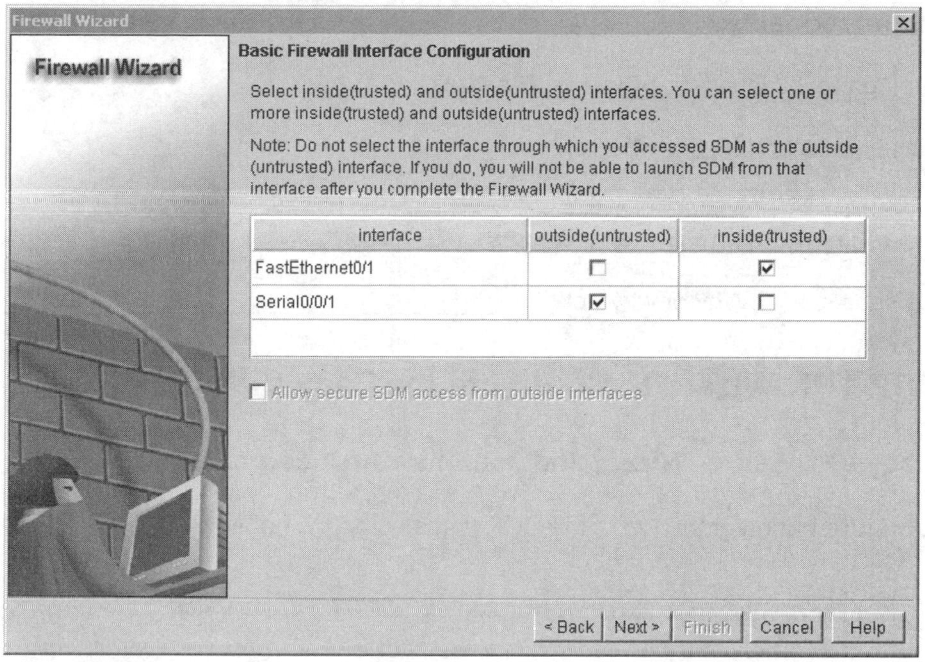

d. In the next window, choose **Low Security** for the security level and click **Next**.

e. In the Summary window, click **Finish**.

f. Click **Deliver** to send the commands to the router. Click **OK** in the Commands Delivery Status window. Click **OK** on the Information window. You are returned to the Edit Firewall Policy tab, as shown here.

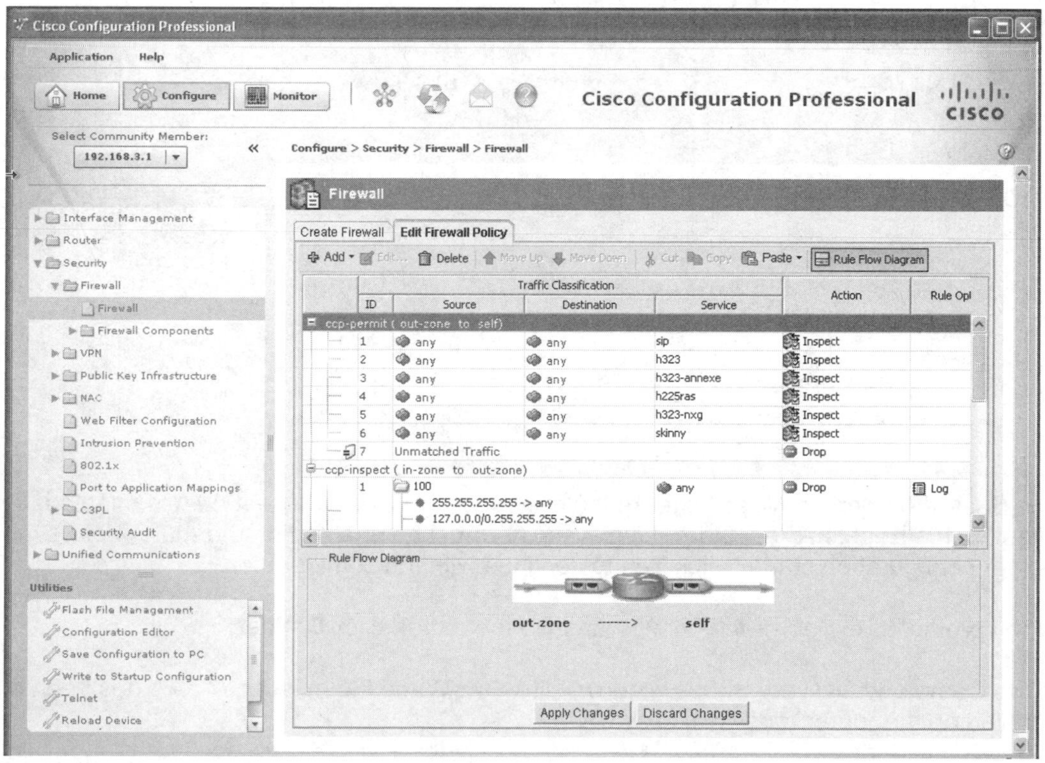

Step 2: Verify firewall functionality.

a. From PC-C, ping the R2 interface S0/0/1 at IP address 10.2.2.2:

Are the pings successful? Why or why not?

____

b. From external router R2, ping PC-C at IP address 192.168.3.3.

Are the pings successful? Why or why not? ________________________________

Task 3: Use the CCP VPN Wizard to Configure the Easy VPN Server

Step 1: Launch the Easy VPN Server Wizard and configure AAA services.

a. Click the **Configure** button at the top of the CCP home screen. Choose **Security > VPN > Easy VPN Server**.

b. Click the **Launch Easy VPN Server Wizard** button.

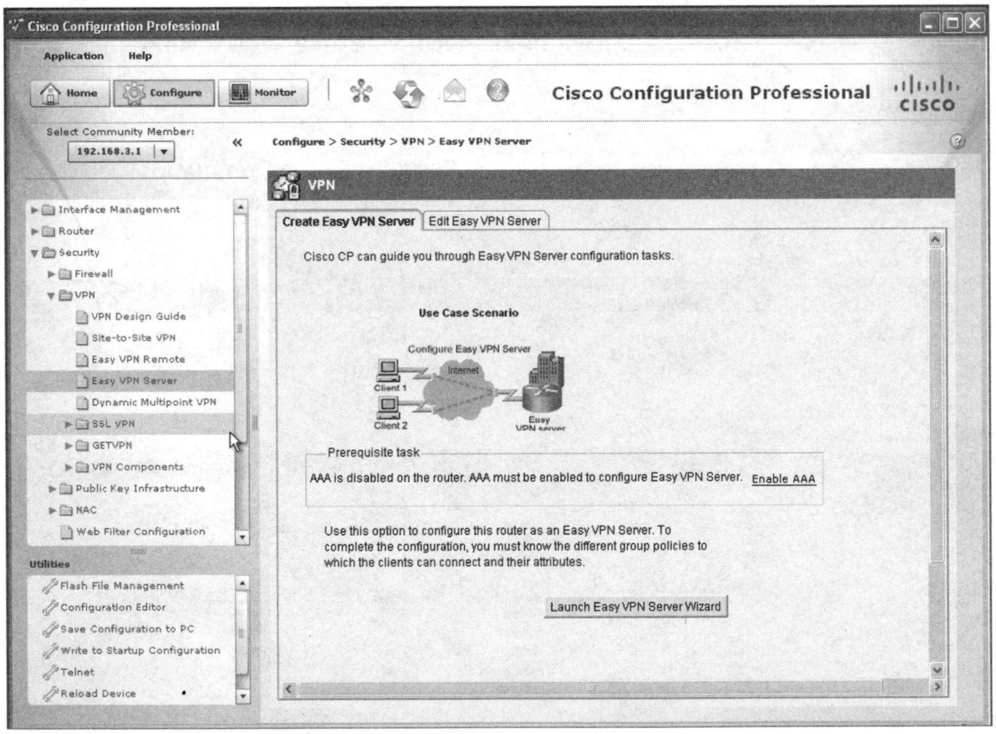

c. The Easy VPN Server Wizard checks the router configuration to see if AAA is enabled. If AAA is not enabled, the Enable AAA window displays. AAA must be enabled on the router before the Easy VPN Server configuration starts. Click **Yes** to continue with the configuration.

d. When prompted to deliver the configuration to the router, click **Deliver**.

e. In the Command Delivery Status window, click **OK**. When the message "AAA has been successfully enabled on the router" displays, click **OK**.

f. When returned to the Easy VPN Server Wizard window, click **Next**.

g. Now that AAA is enabled, you can start the Easy VPN Server Wizard by clicking the **Launch Easy VPN Server Wizard** button. Read through the descriptions of the tasks that the wizard guides you through.

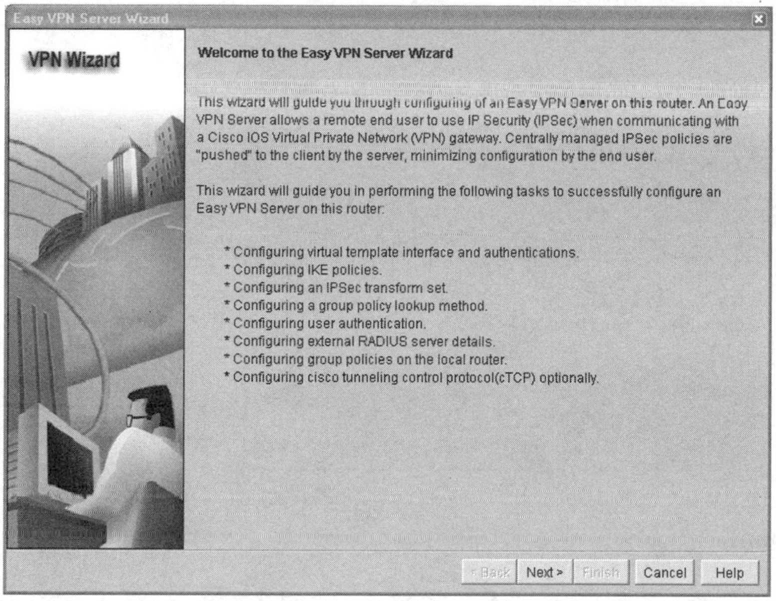

How does the client receive the IPsec policies?

____

How does the Easy VPN remote server configuration differ from the site-to-site configuration?

____

____

____

h. Click **Next** when you have finished answering the questions.

Step 2: Configure the virtual tunnel interface and authentication.

a. Select the interface on which the client connections terminate. Click the **Unnumbered to** radio button and choose the **Serial0/0/1** interface from the pull-down menu.

b. Choose **Pre-shared Keys** for the authentication type and click **Next** to continue.

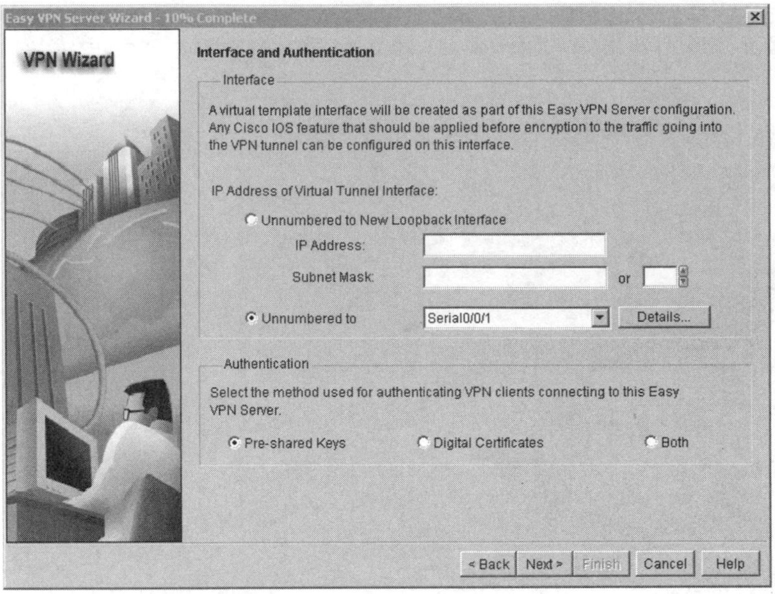

Step 3: Select an IKE proposal.

a. In the IKE Proposals window, the default IKE proposal is used for R3.

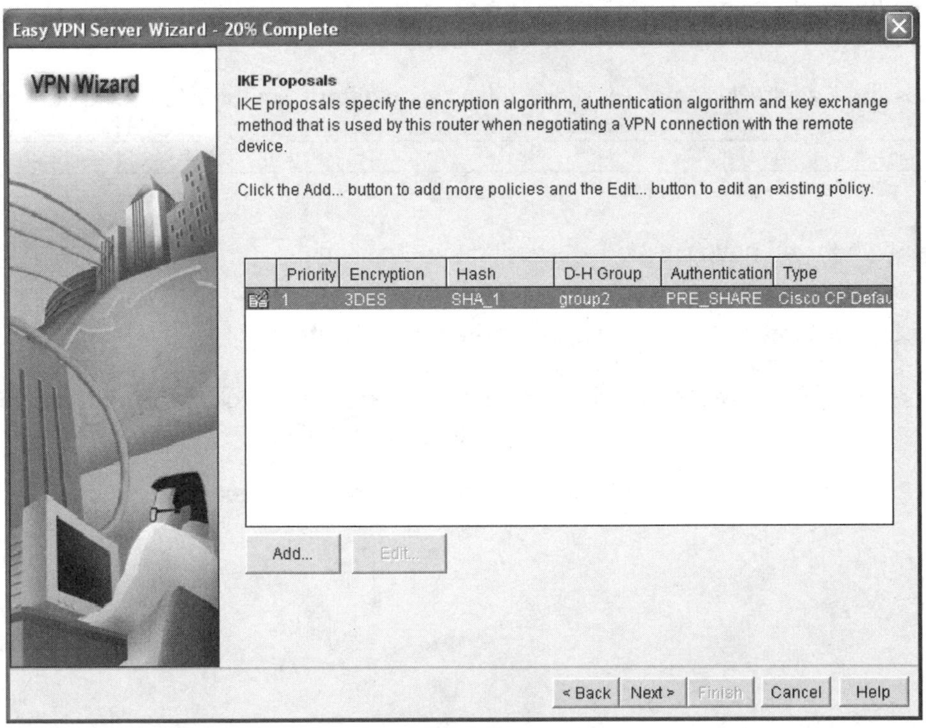

What is the encryption method used with the default IKE policy? ____________

What is the hash algorithm used to ensure that the keys have not been tampered with?

____

b. Click **Next** to accept the default IKE policy.

Note: Configurations on both sides of the tunnel must match exactly. The Cisco VPN Client automatically selects the proper configuration for itself. Therefore, an IKE configuration is not necessary on the client PC.

Step 4: Select the transform set.

a. In the Transform Set window, the default CCP transform set is used. What ESP encryption method is used with the default transform set? ____________________

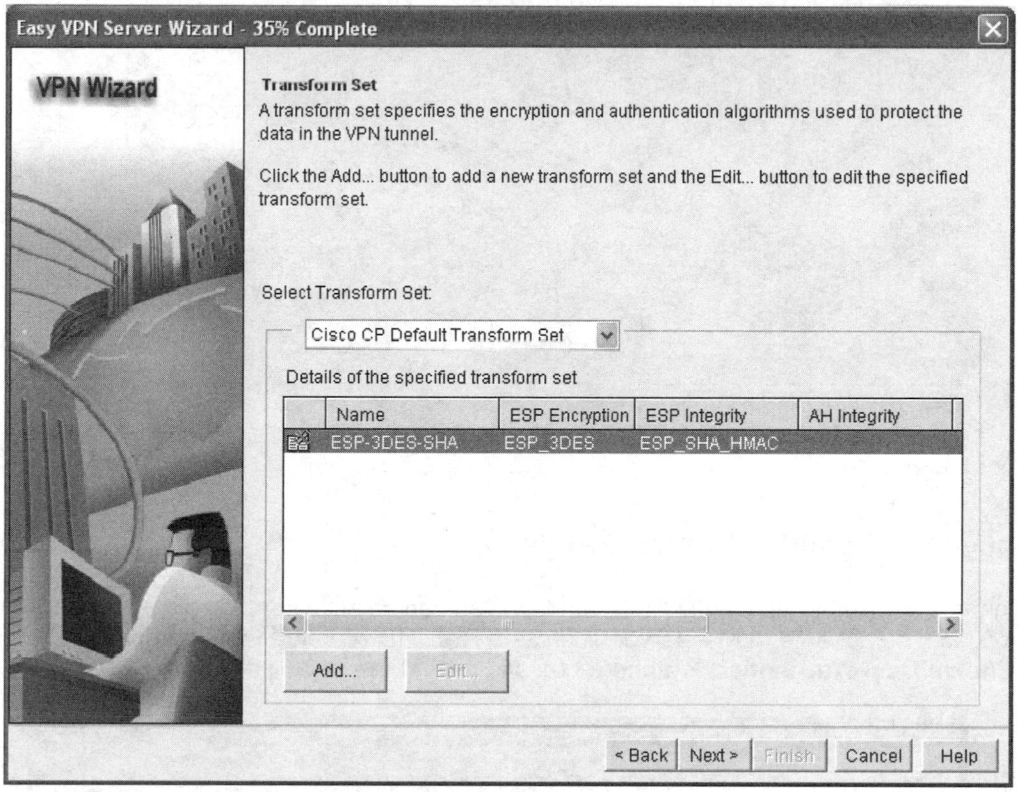

b. Click **Next** to accept the default transform set.

Step 5: Specify group authorization and group policy lookup.

a. In the Group Authorization and Group Policy Lookup window, choose the **Local** option.

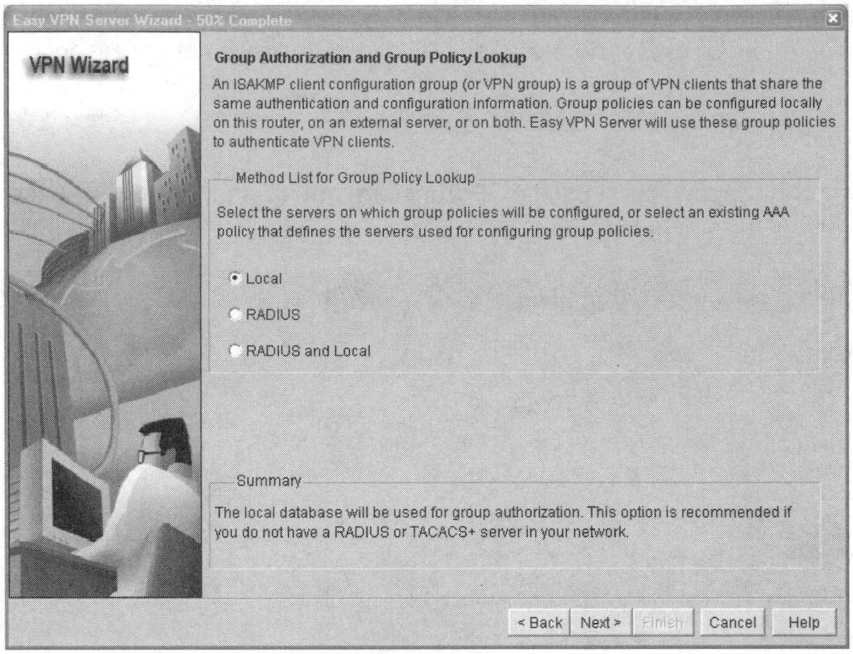

b. Click **Next** to create a new AAA method list for group policy lookup that uses the local router database.

Step 6: Configure user authentication (XAuth).

a. In the User Authentication (XAuth) window, you can select where user credentials will be configured. You can select an external server, such as a RADIUS server, a local database, or both. Check the **Enable User Authentication** check box and accept the default of **Local Only**.

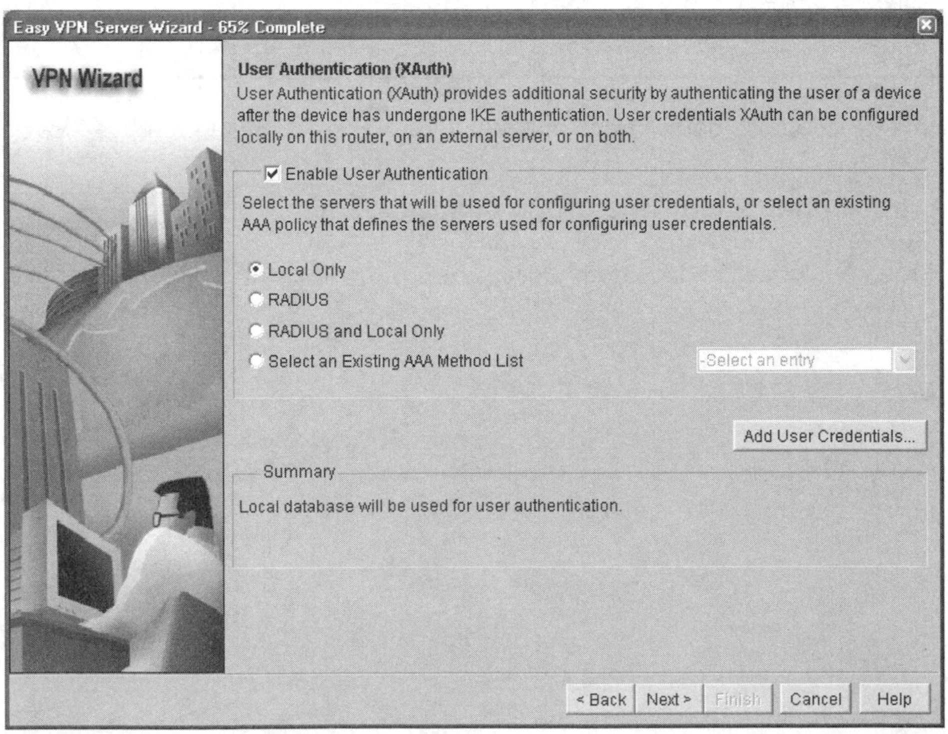

Where does the router look for valid user accounts and passwords to authenticate remote VPN users when they attempt to log in? ____

b. Click the **Add User Credentials** button. In the User Accounts window, you can view currently defined users or add new users.

What is the name of the user currently defined and what is the user privilege level? ____

How was this user defined? ____

c. In the User Accounts window, click the **Add** button to add another user. Enter the username **VPNuser1** with a password of **VPNuser1pass**. Check the check box for encrypting the password using the MD5 hash algorithm. Leave the privilege level at 1.

What range of privilege level can you set for a user? ______________________________

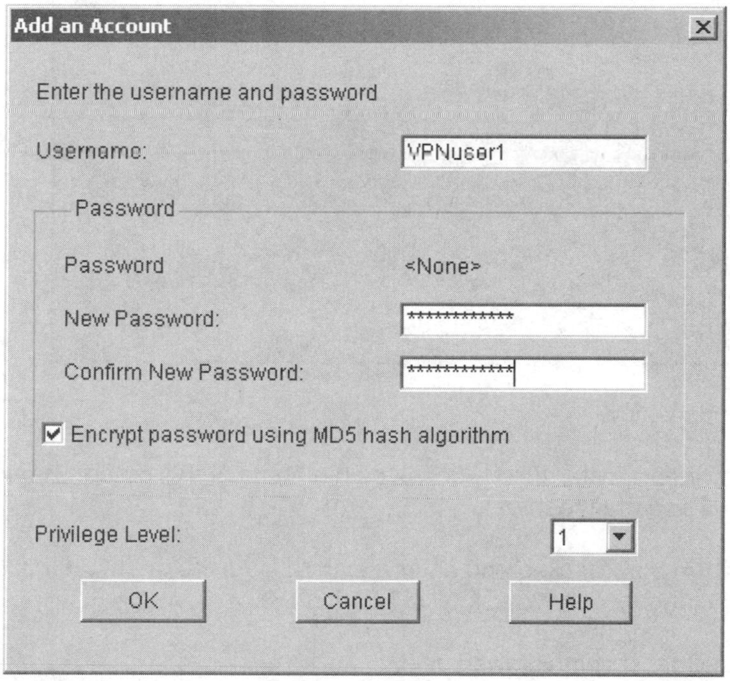

d. Click **OK** to accept the VPNuser1 entries, and then click **OK** to close the User Accounts window.

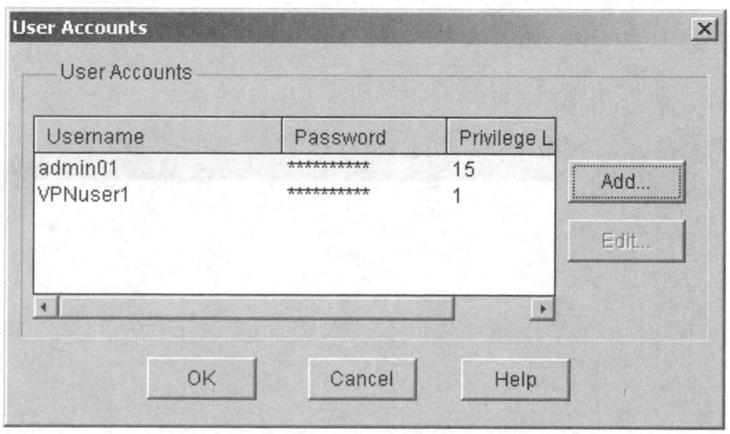

e. In the User Authentication (XAuth) window, click **Next** to continue.

Step 7: Specify group authorization and user group policies.

a. In the Group Authorization and User Group Policies window, you must create at least one group policy for the VPN server.

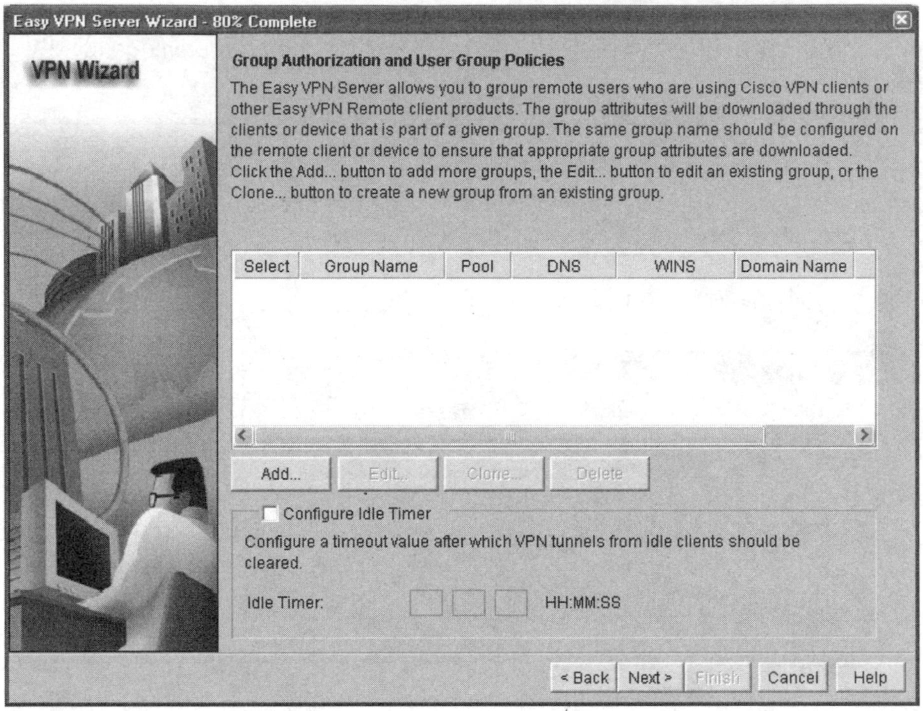

b. Click **Add** to create a group policy.

c. In the Add Group Policy window, enter **VPN-Access** as the name of this group. Enter a new pre-shared key of **cisco12345** and then reenter it.

d. Leave the **Pool Information** box checked and enter a starting address of **192.168.3.100**, an ending address of **192.168.3.150**, and a subnet mask of **255.255.255.0**.

e. Enter **50** in the Maximum Connections Allowed field.

f. Click **OK** to accept the entries.

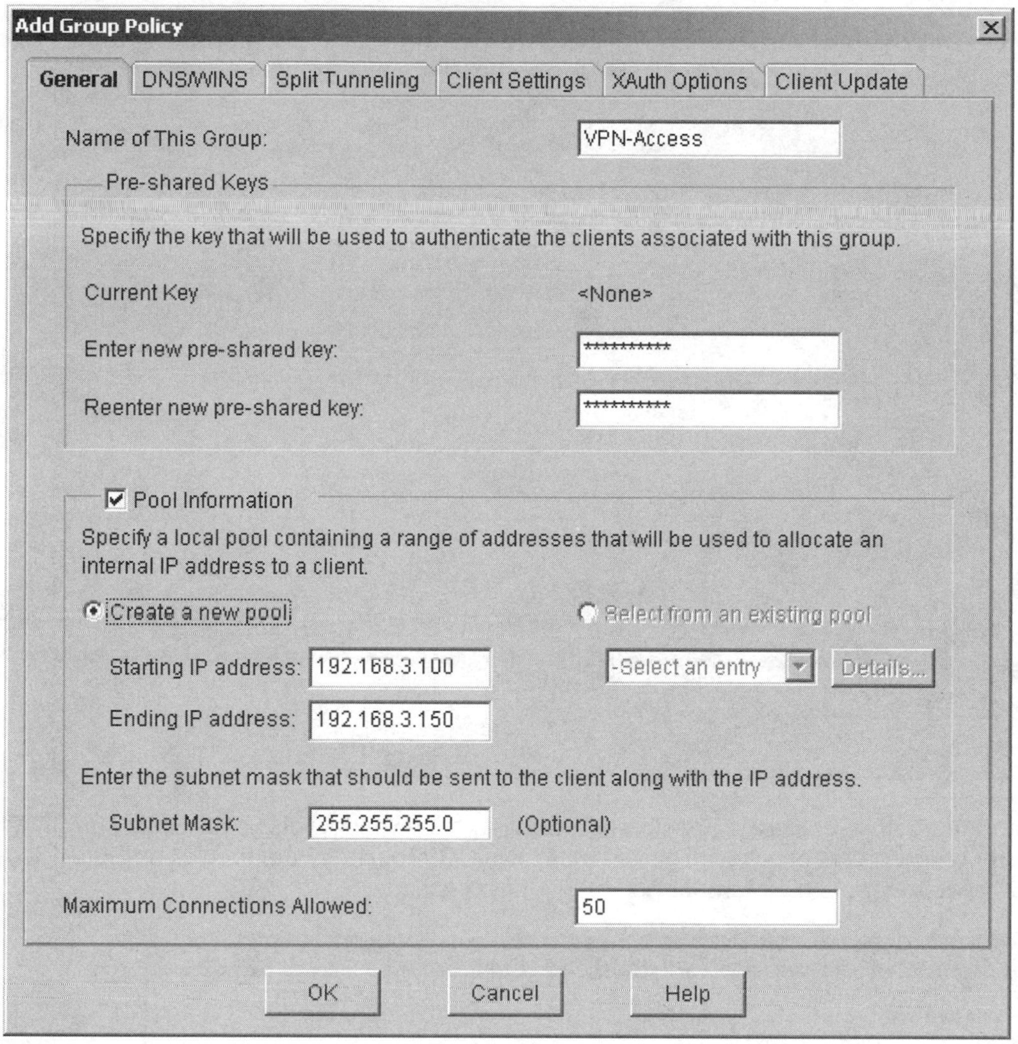

g. A CCP warning message displays indicating that the IP addresses in the pool and the IP address of the Fast Ethernet0/1 interface are in the same subnet. Click **Yes** to continue.

h. When you return to the Group Authorization window, check the **Configure Idle Timer** check box and enter one hour (**1**). This disconnects idle users if there is no activity for one hour and allows others to connect. Click **Next** to continue.

i. When the Cisco Tunneling Control Protocol (cTCP) window displays, do not enable cTCP. Click **Next** to continue.

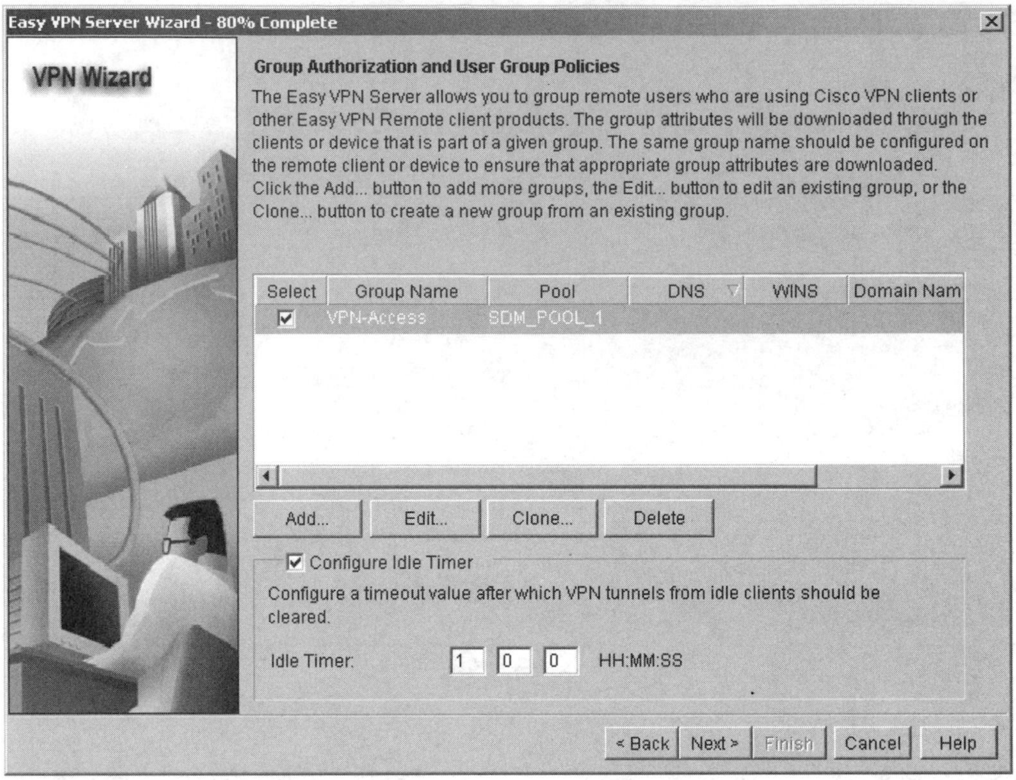

j. When the Easy VPN Server Passthrough Configuration window displays, make sure that the **Action Modify** check box is checked. This option allows CCP to modify the firewall on S0/0/1 to allow IPsec VPN traffic to reach the internal LAN. Click **OK** to continue.

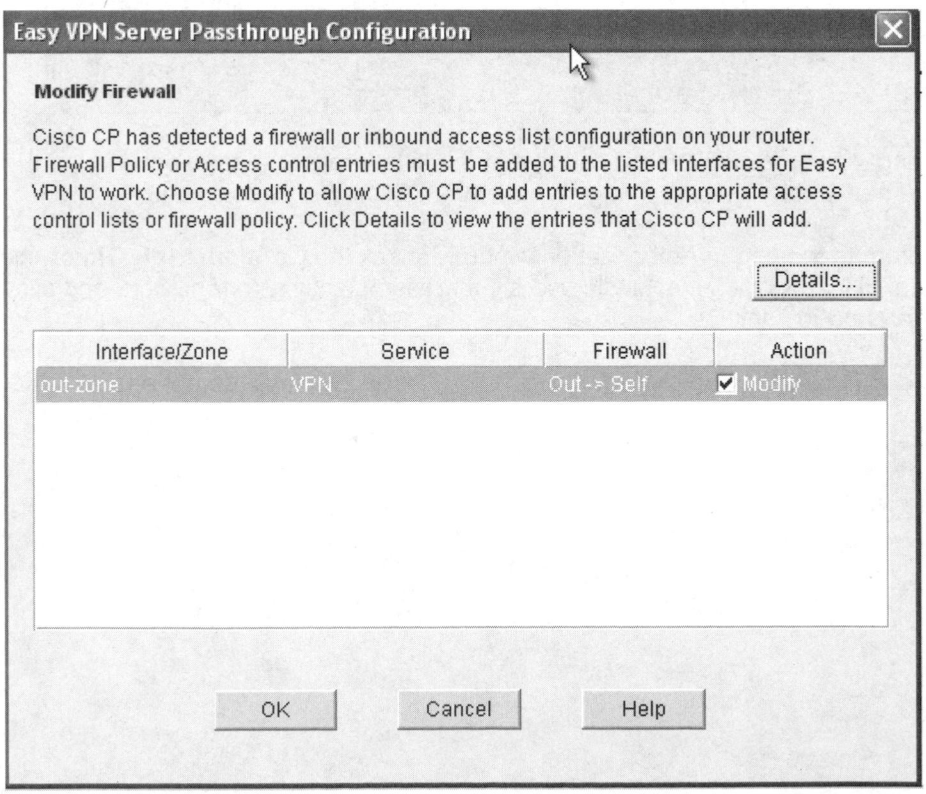

Step 8: Review the configuration summary and deliver the commands.

a. Scroll through the commands that CCP will send to the router. Do not check the check box to test the VPN. Click **Finish**.

b. When prompted to deliver the configuration to the router, click **Deliver**.

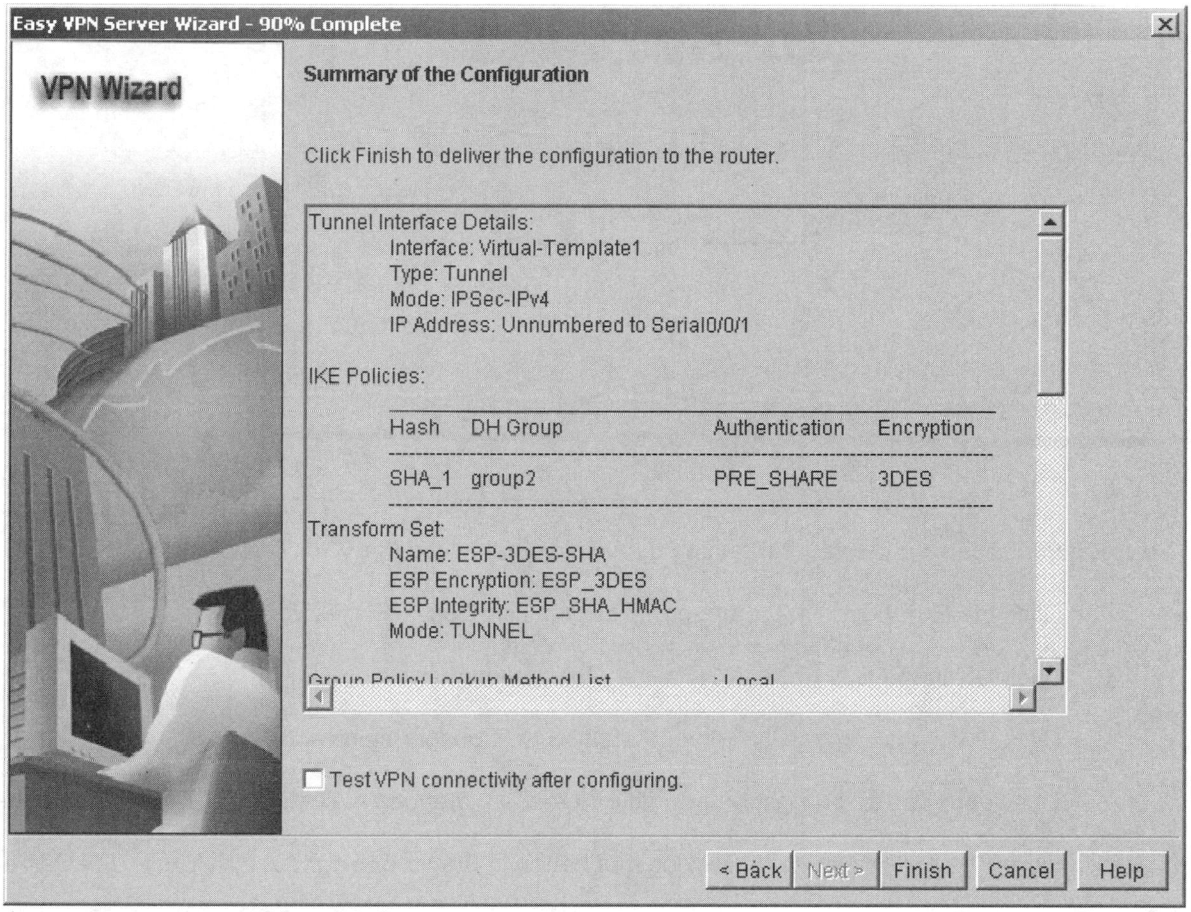

c. In the Command Delivery Status window, click **OK**. How many commands are delivered? ________

Step 9: Test the VPN Server.

a. You are returned to the main VPN window with the Edit Easy VPN Server tab displayed. Click the **Test VPN Server** button in the lower-right corner of the screen.

b. In the VPN Troubleshooting window, click the **Start** button.

c. Your screen should look similar to the one here. Click **OK** to close the Information window. Click **Close** to exit the VPN Troubleshooting window.

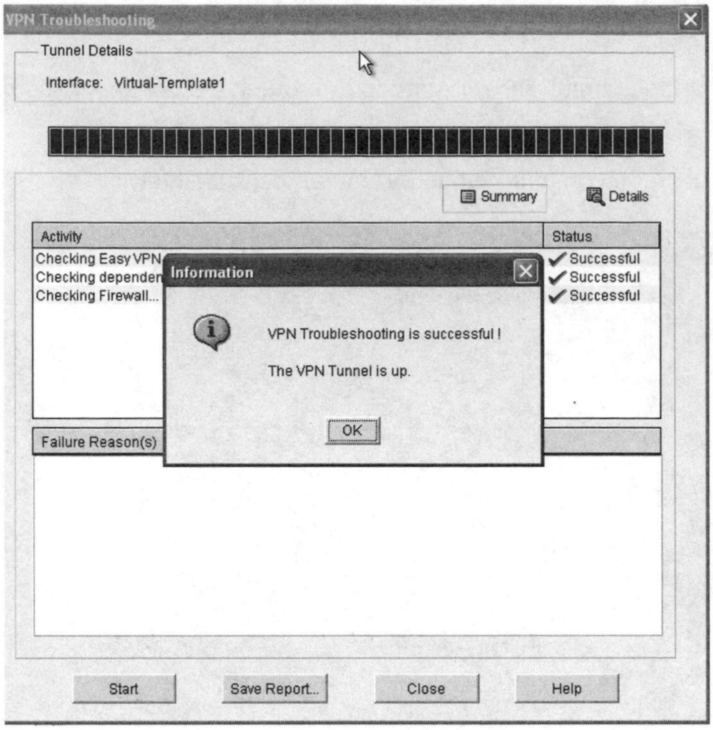

Note: If you receive a failure after testing the VPN server, close the VPN Troubleshooting window.

1. Click the **Edit** button in the upper right of the Edit Easy VPN Server tab.
2. Click **OK** in the Edit Easy VPN Server Connection window.
3. Click **OK** in the Easy VPN Server Passthrough Configuration window.
4. Check the box to the right of the FastEthernet0/1 interface indicating that it is inside (trusted).
5. Rerun Test VPN Server by clicking that button in the bottom right of Edit Easy VPN Server tab.
6. Click the **Start** button. The test should pass this time.

Task 4: Use the Cisco VPN Client to Test the Remote Access VPN

Step 1: (Optional) Install the Cisco VPN Client.

If the Cisco VPN Client software on host PC-A is not installed, install it now. If you do not have the Cisco VPN Client software, contact your instructor.

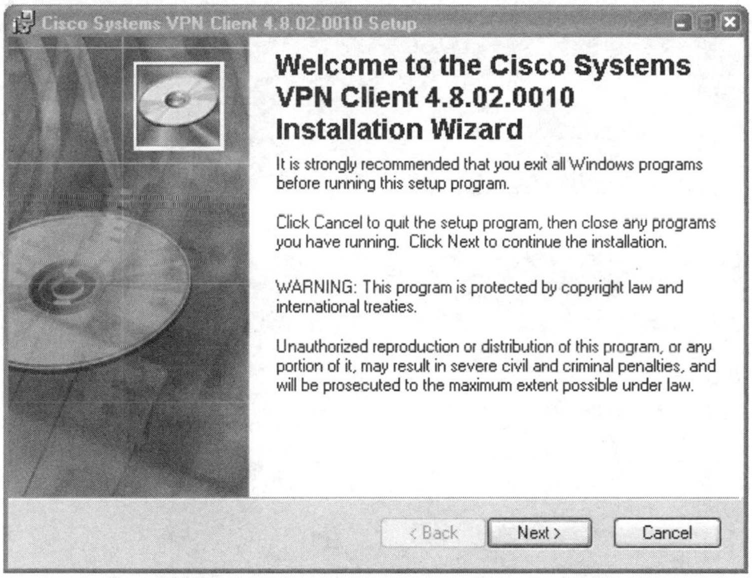

Step 2: Configure PC-A as a VPN client to access the R1 VPN server.

a. Start the Cisco VPN Client and choose **Connection Entries > New,** or click the **New** icon with the red plus sign (+) on it.

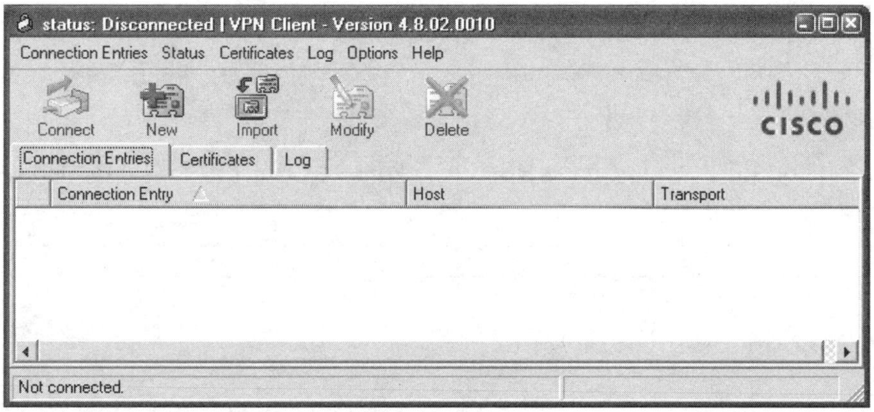

b. Enter the following information to define the new connection entry. Click **Save** when you are finished.

Connection Entry: **VPN-R3**

Description: **Connection to R3 internal network**

Host: **10.2.2.1** (IP address of the R3 S0/0/1 interface)

Group Authentication Name: **VPN-Access** (defines the address pool configured in Task 2)

Password: **cisco12345** (pre-shared key configured in Task 2)

Confirm Password: **cisco12345**

Note: The group authentication name and password are case sensitive and must match the ones created on the VPN server.

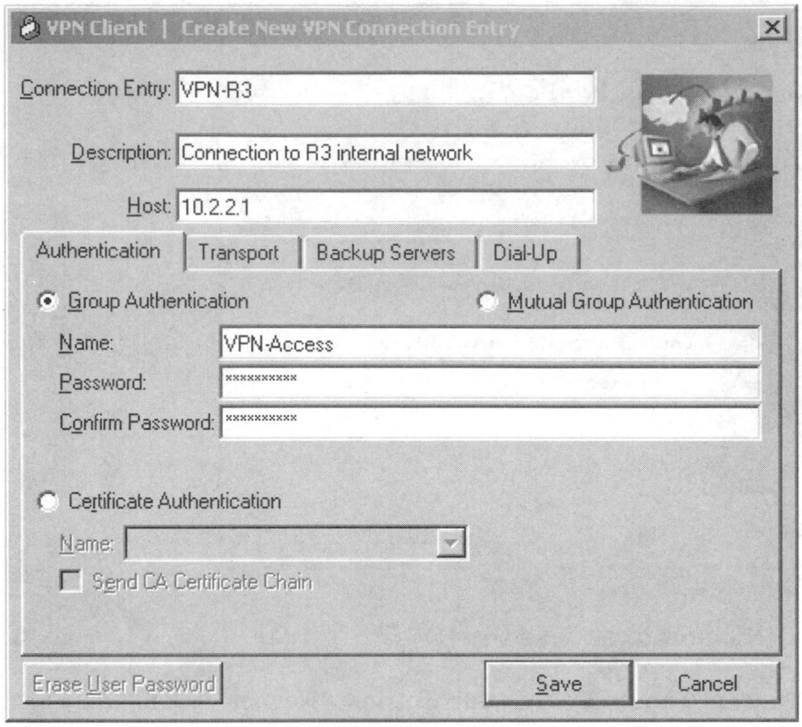

Step 3: Test access from PC-A without a VPN connection.

In the previous step, you created a VPN connection entry on the VPN client computer PC-A but have not activated it, so the VPN tunnel is not yet up.

Open a command prompt on PC-A and ping the PC-C IP address at 192.168.3.3 on the R3 LAN. Are the pings successful? Why or why not?

____

____

Step 4: Establish a VPN connection and log in.

a. Select the newly created connection VPN-R3 and click the **Connect** icon. You can also double-click the connection entry.

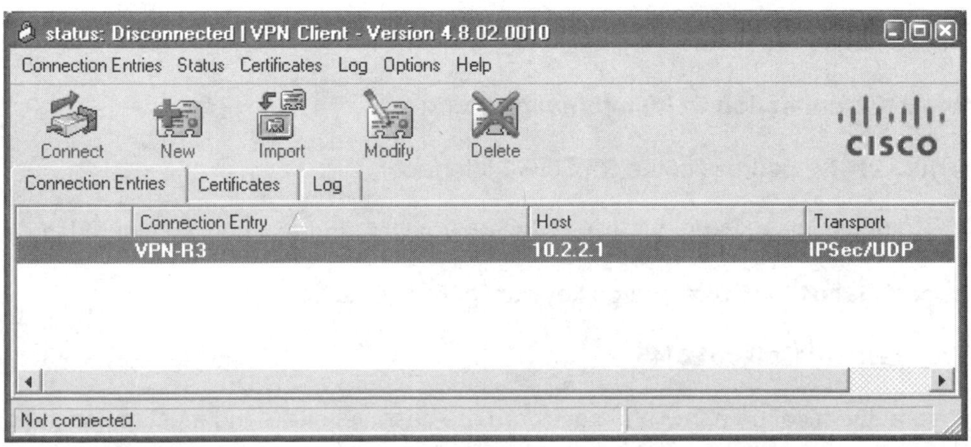

b. Enter the previously created username **VPNuser1** in the VPN Client User Authentication dialog box and enter the password **VPNuser1pass**. Click **OK** to continue. The VPN Client window minimizes to a lock icon in the tools tray of the taskbar. When the lock is closed, the VPN tunnel is up. When it is open, the VPN connection is down.

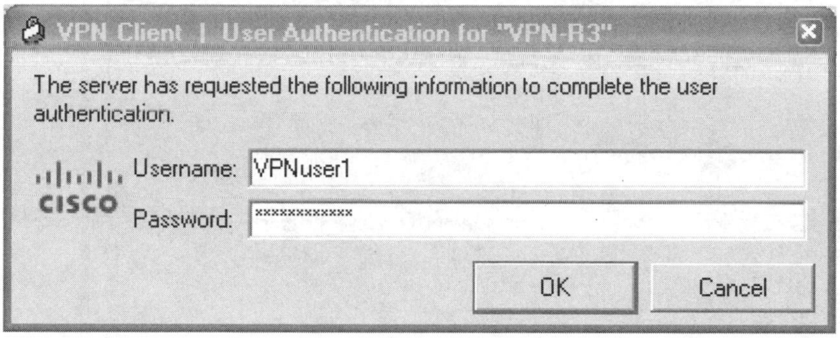

Task 5: Verify the VPN Tunnel Between the Client, Server, and Internal Network

Step 1: Open the VPN Client icon.

a. Double-click the VPN lock icon to expand the VPN Client window.

What does it say about the connection status at the top of the window?

____

b. From the PC-A command line, issue the **`ipconfig`** command.

What is the IP address of the first Local Area Connection?

____

What is the IP address of Local Area Connection 2?

____

Step 2: Close the VPN connection and reopen it.

a. Click the **Disconnect** icon in the VPN Client window to close the VPN-R3 connection.

b. Click the **Connect** icon and log in again as VPNuser1.

What is the IP address of Local Area Connection 2 now?

____

Note: Each time you disconnect and reconnect to the VPN server, you receive a new IP address until the limit is reached.

Step 3: Check the tunnel statistics.

a. Choose **Status > Statistics**. Display the Tunnel Details tab.

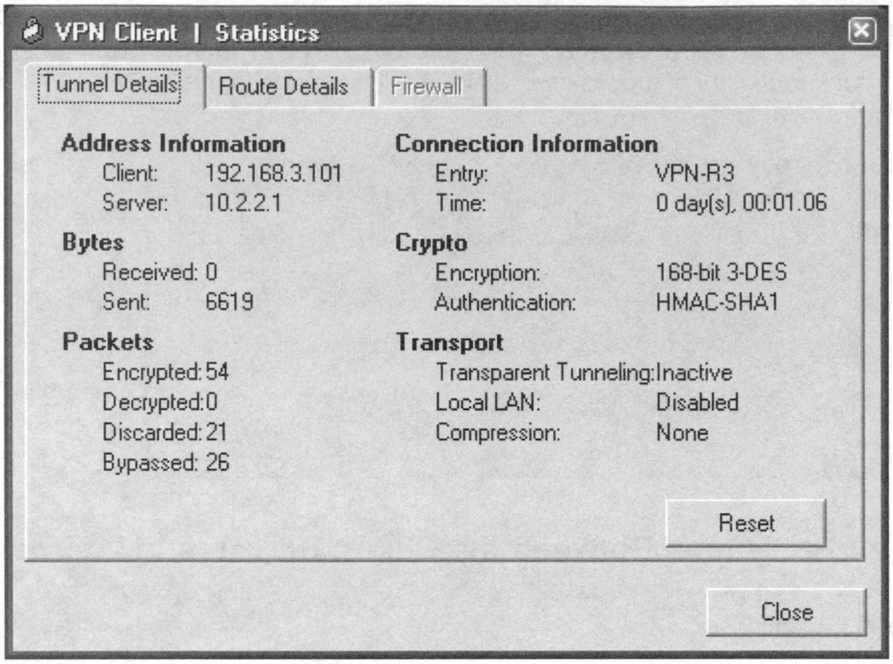

What is the current address obtained from the R3 VPN server and what is the range of addresses that can be assigned?

____

What is the VPN server address? ______________________

How many packets have been encrypted? ______________

What is the encryption method? ______________________

What is the authentication method? ___________________

b. Leave the VPN Client Statistics window open.

Step 4: Test access from the client PC-A using the VPN connection.

a. With the VPN connection from computer PC-A to router R3 activated, open a command prompt on PC-A and ping the PC-C IP address at 192.168.3.3 on the R3 LAN. Are the pings successful?

____

b. How many packets have now been encrypted? ____________________________________

Step 5: Check the Cisco IOS message on R3 when the tunnel is created.

Open the console connection for R3 and locate the message displayed indicating that the virtual interface came up when the VPN Client connection was made.

What is the name of the interface on R3 that is activated for the VPN? ___________________________

Step 6: Verify the VPN connection information for PC-A.

a. From the PC-A command prompt, issue the `ipconfig /all` command to see the network connections.

b. What is the configuration for the first Local Area Connection?

IP address: ____________________

Subnet mask: ____________________

Default gateway: ____________________

Description: ____________________

c. What is the configuration for Local Area Connection 2?

IP address: ____________________

Subnet mask: ____________________

Default gateway: ____________________

Description: ____________________

Step 7: Telnet from PC-A to R3.

a. From the PC-A command prompt, telnet to R3 at the Fa0/1 IP address 192.168.3.1. Log in as **admin01** with a password of **admin01pass**. What is the router command prompt and why is this?

____

b. Issue the `show run` command to view the various commands generated by CCP to configure the VPN server.

c. Issue the `show users` command to see connections to router R3. What connections are present?

____

d. Close the Telnet connection using the `quit` or `exit` command.

Reflection

Why is VPN a good option for remote users?

____

____

____

Router Interface Summary Table

Router Model	Ethernet Interface 1	Ethernet Interface 2	Serial Interface 1	Serial Interface 2
1800	Fast Ethernet 0/0 (Fa0/0)	Fast Ethernet 0/1 (Fa0/1)	Serial 0/0/0 (S0/0/0)	Serial 0/0/1 (S0/0/1)
1900	Gigabit Ethernet 0/0 (G0/0)	Gigabit Ethernet 0/1 (G0/1)	Serial 0/0/0 (S0/0/0)	Serial 0/0/1 (S0/0/1)
2800	Fast Ethernet 0/0 (Fa0/0)	Fast Ethernet 0/1 (Fa0/1)	Serial 0/0/0 (S0/0/0)	Serial 0/0/1 (S0/0/1)
2900	Gigabit Ethernet 0/0 (G0/0)	Gigabit Ethernet 0/1 (G0/1)	Serial 0/0/0 (S0/0/0)	Serial 0/0/1 (S0/0/1)

Note: To find out how the router is configured, look at the interfaces to identify the type of router and how many interfaces the router has. There is no way to effectively list all the combinations of configurations for each router class. This table includes identifiers for the possible combinations of Ethernet and serial interfaces in the device. The table does not include any other type of interface, even though a specific router may contain one. An example of this might be an ISDN BRI interface. The string in parentheses is the legal abbreviation that can be used in Cisco IOS commands to represent the interface.

Chapter 8 Lab C (Optional): Configuring a Remote Access VPN Server and Client

Topology

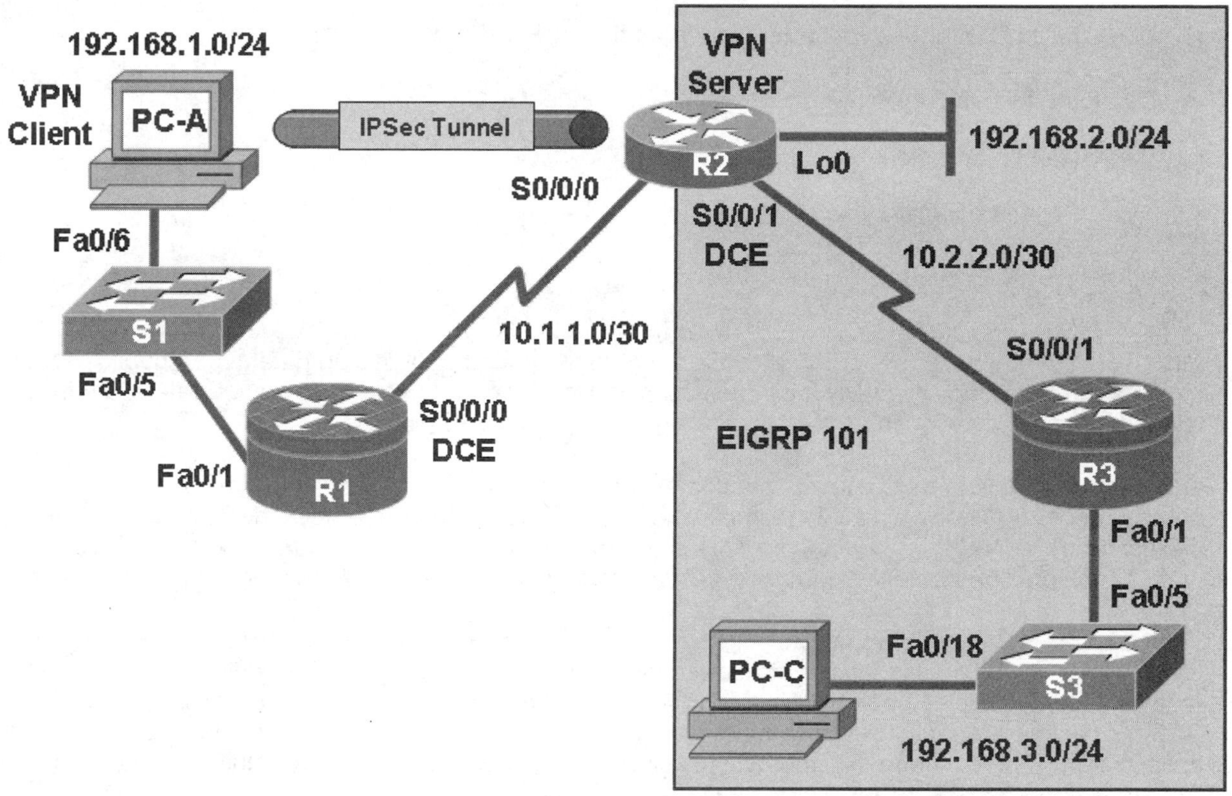

Note: ISR G2 devices have Gigabit Ethernet interfaces rather than FastEthernet interfaces.

IP Addressing Table

Device	Interface	IP Address	Subnet Mask	Default Gateway	Switch Port
R1	Fa0/1	192.168.1.1	255.255.255.0	N/A	S1 Fa0/5
	S0/0/0 (DCE)	10.1.1.1	255.255.255.252	N/A	N/A
R2	S0/0/0	10.1.1.2	255.255.255.252	N/A	N/A
	S0/0/1 (DCE)	10.2.2.2	255.255.255.252	N/A	N/A
	Loopback 0	192.168.2.1	255.255.255.0	N/A	N/A
R3	Fa0/1	192.168.3.1	255.255.255.0	N/A	S3 Fa0/5
	S0/0/1	10.2.2.1	255.255.255.252	N/A	N/A
PC-A	NIC	192.168.1.3	255.255.255.0	192.168.1.1	S1 Fa0/6
PC-C	NIC	192.168.3.3	255.255.255.0	192.168.3.1	S3 Fa0/18

Objectives

Part 1: Basic Router Configuration

- Configure hostnames, interface IP addresses, and access passwords.
- Configure the EIGRP dynamic routing protocol on R2 and R3.

Part 2: Configuring a Remote Access VPN

- Use CCP to configure a router to support an Easy VPN server.
- Configure the Cisco VPN Client on PC-A and connect to R2.
- Verify the configuration.
- Test VPN functionality.

Background

Virtual private networks (VPN) can provide a secure method of transmitting data over a public network, such as the Internet. A common VPN implementation is used for remote access to a corporate office from a telecommuter location such as a small office/home office (SOHO).

In this lab, you build a multirouter network and configure the routers and hosts. You configure a remote access IPsec VPN between a client computer and a simulated corporate network. You use CCP to configure a Cisco Easy VPN Server on the corporate edge gateway router and configure the Cisco VPN Client on a host. Then you connect to the corporate network through a simulated Internet service provider (ISP) router.

The Cisco VPN Client allows organizations to establish end-to-end, encrypted (IPsec) VPN tunnels for secure connectivity for mobile employees or teleworkers. It supports Cisco Easy VPN, which allows the client to receive security policies upon a VPN tunnel connection from the central site VPN device (Cisco Easy VPN Server), minimizing configuration requirements at the remote location. This is a scalable solution for remote access deployments where it is impractical to individually configure policies for multiple remote PCs.

Note: The router commands and output in this lab are from a Cisco 1841 with Cisco IOS Software Release 12.4(20)T (advanced IP image). Other routers and Cisco IOS versions can be used. See the Router Interface Summary table at the end of the lab to determine which interface identifiers to use based on the equipment in the lab. Depending on the router model and Cisco IOS version, the commands available and the output produced might vary from what this lab shows.

Note: Make sure that the routers and the switches have been erased and have no startup configurations.

Required Resources

- 3 routers (Cisco 1841 with Cisco IOS Software Release 12.4(20)T1 or comparable)

Note: This lab requires that R2 have a comparable IOS and hardware characteristics to R1 and R3 for it to play the role of the VPN server.

- 2 switches (Cisco 2960 or comparable)
- PC-A: Windows XP, Vista, or Windows 7 with Cisco VPN Client and CCP 2.5 installed
- PC-C: Windows XP, Vista, or Windows 7

- Serial and Ethernet cables as shown in the topology
- Rollover cables to configure the routers via the console

CCP Notes

- See Chapter 00 Lab A for instructions on how to install CCP. Hardware/software recommendations for CCP include Windows XP, Vista, or Windows 7 with Java Version 1.6.0_11 up to 1.6.0_21, Internet Explorer 6.0 or later, and Flash Player Version 10.0.12.36 or later.
- If the PC on which CCP is installed is running Windows Vista or Windows 7, you might need to right-click the CCP icon or menu item and choose **Run as Administrator**.
- To run CCP, you might need to temporarily disable antivirus programs and OS firewalls. Make sure to turn off all pop-up blockers in the browser.

Part 1: Basic Router Configuration

In Part 1 of this lab, you set up the network topology and configure basic settings, such as the interface IP addresses, dynamic routing, device access, and passwords.

Note: Perform all tasks on routers R1, R2, and R3. The procedure for R1 is shown here as an example.

Step 1: Cable the network as shown in the topology.

Attach the devices shown in the topology diagram, and cable as necessary.

Step 2: Configure basic settings for each router.

a. Configure hostnames as shown in the topology.

b. Configure the physical interface IP addresses as shown in the IP addressing table.

c. Configure the logical loopback 0 interface on R2. This simulates the network from which the remote access clients receive addresses (192.168.2.0/24). Because loopback interfaces are up by default, it is not necessary to use the **no shutdown** command.

```
R2(config)# interface Loopback 0
R2(config-if)# ip address 192.168.2.1 255.255.255.0
```

d. Configure a clock rate for the serial router interfaces with a DCE serial cable attached:

```
R1(config)# interface S0/0/0
R1(config-if)# clock rate 64000
```

Step 3: Disable DNS lookup.

To prevent the router from attempting to translate incorrectly entered commands, disable DNS lookup:

```
R1(config)# no ip domain-lookup
```

Step 4: Configure the EIGRP routing protocol on R2 and R3.

Note: R2 and R3 exchange routes in EIGRP AS 101. R1 is acting as an ISP router and does not participate in the EIGRP routing process.

a. On R2, use the following commands:

```
R2(config)# router eigrp 101
```

```
R2(config-router)# network 10.1.1.0 0.0.0.3
R2(config-router)# network 10.2.2.0 0.0.0.3
R2(config-router)# network 192.168.2.0 0.0.0.255
R2(config-router)# no auto-summary
```

b. On R3, use the following commands:

```
R3(config)# router eigrp 101
R3(config-router)# network 192.168.3.0 0.0.0.255
R3(config-router)# network 10.2.2.0 0.0.0.3
R3(config-router)# no auto-summary
```

Step 5: Configure a static default route on R2.

Router R1 represents a connection to the Internet. A default route is configured on R2 for all traffic whose destination network does not exist in the R2 routing table.

Note: Without the default route configured on R2, R2 cannot respond to the CCP HTTP connection from PC-A later in the lab. Because R1 is not part of the EIGRP domain and is not advertising the PC-A LAN, R2 does not know about the 192.168.1.0/24 network.

a. Configure a static default route on R2 that points to the R1 S0/0/0 interface IP address:

```
R2(config)# ip route 0.0.0.0 0.0.0.0 10.1.1.1
```

b. Redistribute the static default into EIGRP so that R3 also learns the route:

```
R2(config)# router eigrp 101
R2(config-router)# redistribute static
```

Step 6: Configure PC host IP settings.

a. Configure a static IP address, subnet mask, and default gateway for PC-A, as shown in the IP addressing table.

b. Configure a static IP address, subnet mask, and default gateway for PC-C, as shown in the IP addressing table.

Step 7: Verify basic network connectivity.

a. Ping from PC-A to the R2 S0/0/0 interface at IP address 10.1.1.2. Are the results successful? _____

If the pings are not successful, troubleshoot the basic device configurations before continuing.

Note: PC-A should be able to ping external R2 interface S0/0/0 but is not able to ping any of the internal EIGRP network IP addresses on R2 and R3.

b. Ping from R2 to PC-C on the R3 LAN. Are the results successful? _____

If the pings are not successful, troubleshoot the basic device configurations before continuing.

Note: If you can ping from R2 to PC-C, you have demonstrated that the EIGRP routing protocol is configured and functioning correctly. If you cannot ping but the device interfaces are up and IP addresses are correct, use the **show run** and **show ip route** commands to help identify routing protocol-related problems.

Step 8: Configure a minimum password length.

Note: Passwords in this lab are set to a minimum of 10 characters but are relatively simple for the benefit of performing the lab. More complex passwords are recommended in a production network.

Use the **security passwords** command to set a minimum password length of 10 characters:

```
R1(config)# security passwords min-length 10
```

Step 9: Configure the basic console and vty lines.

a. Configure a console password and enable login for router R1. For additional security, the **exec-timeout** command causes the line to log out after 5 minutes of inactivity. The **logging synchronous** command prevents console messages from interrupting command entry.

Note: To avoid repetitive logins during this lab, you can set the **exec-timeout** command to 0 0, which prevents it from expiring. However, this is not considered a good security practice.

```
R1(config)# line console 0
R1(config-line)# password ciscoconpass
R1(config-line)# exec-timeout 5 0
R1(config-line)# login
R1(config-line)# logging synchronous
```

b. Configure the password on the vty lines for router R1:

```
R1(config)# line vty 0 4
R1(config-line)# password ciscovtypass
R1(config-line)# exec-timeout 5 0
R1(config-line)# login
```

c. Repeat these configurations on both R2 and R3.

Step 10: Encrypt clear-text passwords.

a. Use the **service password-encryption** command to encrypt the console, aux, and vty passwords:

```
R1(config)# service password-encryption
```

b. Issue the **show run** command. Can you read the console, aux, and vty passwords? Why or why not? ____

c. Repeat this configuration on both R2 and R3.

Step 11: Save the basic running configuration for all three routers.

Save the running configuration to the startup configuration from the privileged EXEC prompt:

```
R1# copy running-config startup-config
```

Part 2: Configuring a Remote Access VPN

In Part 2 of this lab, you configure a remote access IPsec VPN. You use CCP to configure R2 as an Easy VPN Server and configure the Cisco VPN Client on PC-A. The PC-A host simulates an employee connecting from home over the Internet. Router R1 simulates an Internet ISP router.

Task 1: Prepare R2 for CCP Access and Easy VPN Server Setup

Step 1: Configure user credentials for HTTP router access before starting CCP.

a. Enable the HTTP server on R2:

```
R2(config)# ip http server
```

b. Create an admin account on R2 with privilege level 15 for use with AAA and CCP:

```
R2(config)# username admin privilege 15 password 0 cisco12345
```

c. Have CCP use the local database to authenticate web sessions:

```
R2(config)# ip http authentication local
```

Step 2: Access CCP and discover R2.

a. Run the CCP application on PC-A. In the Select/Manage Community window, input the R2 IP address **10.1.1.2** in the IP Address/Hostname field, **admin** in the Username field, and **cisco12345** in the Password field. Click the **OK** button.

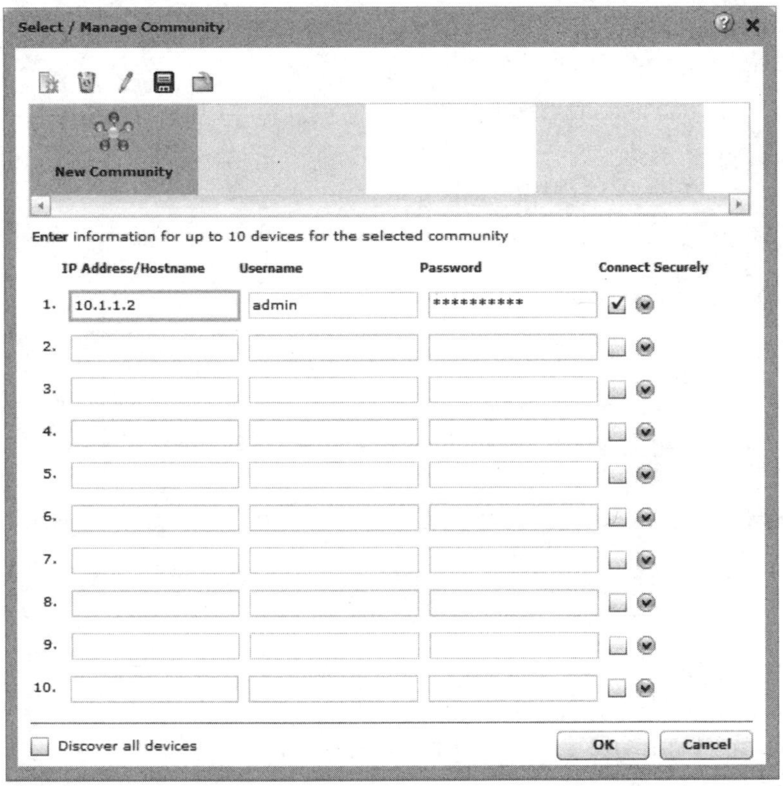

b. At the CCP Dashboard, click the **Discover** button to discover and connect to R1. If the discovery process fails, use the **Discover Details** button to determine the possible problem to resolve the issue.

Task 2: Use the CCP VPN Wizard to Configure the Easy VPN Server

Step 1: Launch the Easy VPN Server Wizard and configure AAA services.

a. Click the **Configure** button at the top of the CCP home screen. Choose **Security > VPN > Easy VPN Server**

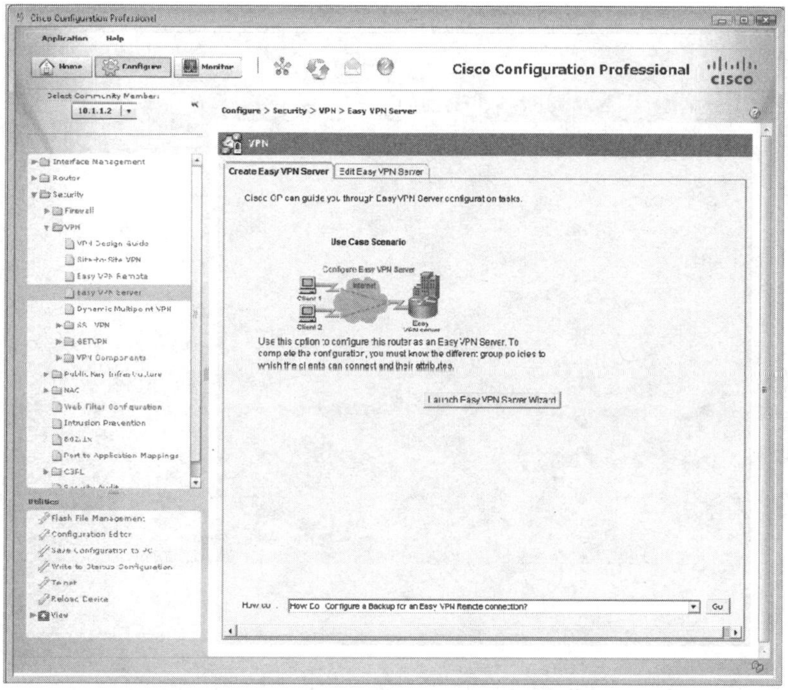

b. Click **Launch Easy VPN Server Wizard**.

c. The Easy VPN Server Wizard checks the router configuration to see whether AAA is enabled. If not, the Enable AAA window displays. AAA must be enabled on the router before the Easy VPN Server configuration starts. Click **Yes** to continue with the configuration.

d. If prompted to deliver the configuration to the router, click **Deliver**.

e. In the Command Delivery Status window, click **OK**. When the message "AAA has been successfully enabled on the router" displays, click **OK**.

f. Now that AAA is enabled, you can start the Easy VPN Server Wizard by clicking Next in the Welcome window. Read through the descriptions of the tasks that the wizard guides you through.

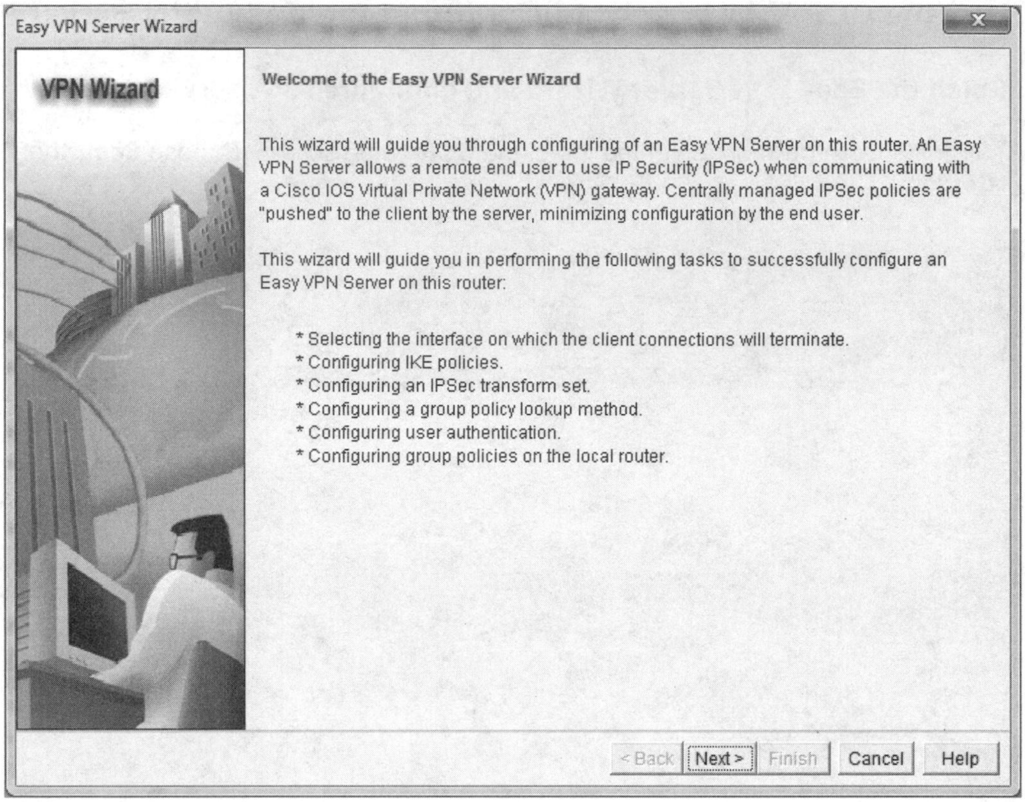

How does the client receive the IPsec policies? ____

How does the Easy VPN remote server configuration differ from the site-to-site?

____

g. Click **Next** when you are finished answering the above questions.

Step 2: Configure the virtual tunnel interface and authentication

a. Select the Serial0/0/0 interface from the pull-down menu as the interface for the Easy VPN Server. This is the interface on which the client connections terminate.

b. Select **Pre-shared Keys** for the authentication type and click **Next** to continue.

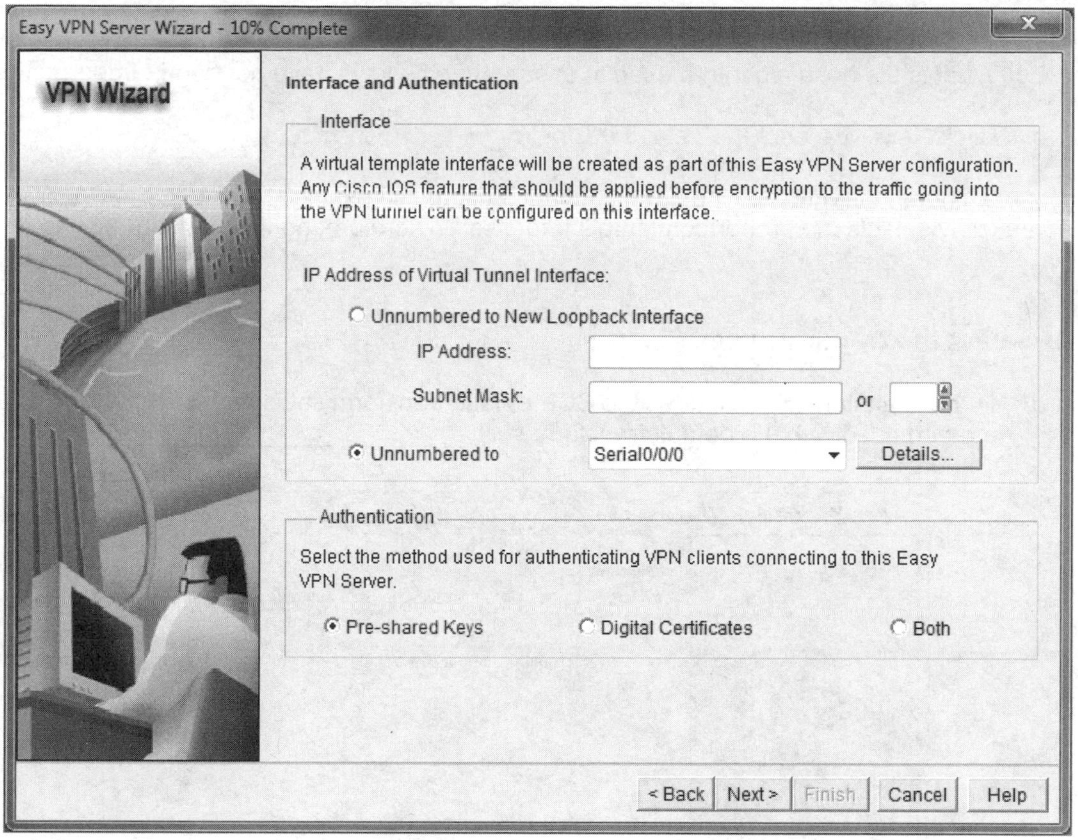

Step 3: Select the IKE proposal.

a. In the Internet Key Exchange (IKE) Proposals window, the default IKE proposal is used for R2.

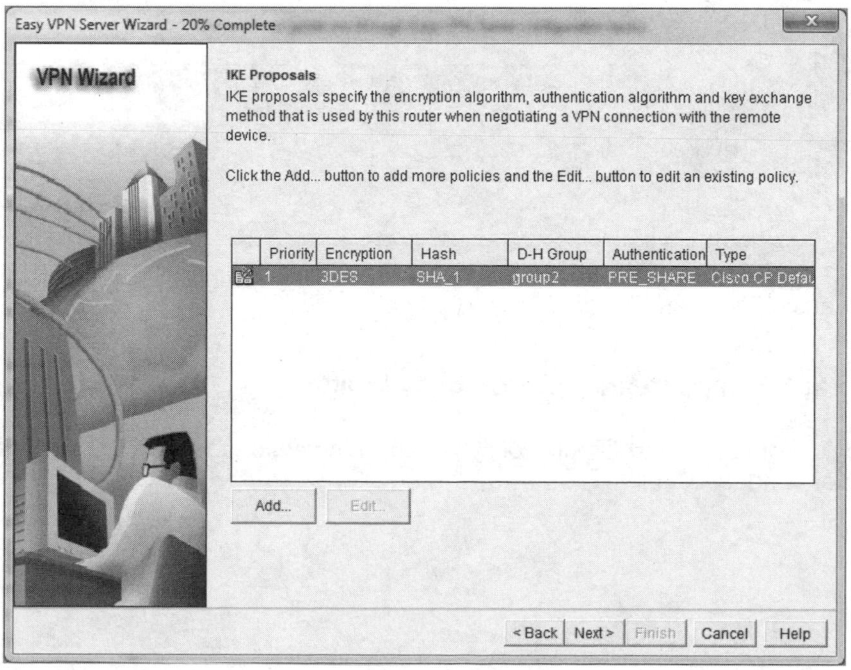

What is the encryption method used with the default IKE policy? ______

What is the hash algorithm used to ensure that the keys have not been tampered with? _____

b. Click **Next** to accept the default IKE policy.

Note: Configurations on both sides of the tunnel must match exactly. However, the Cisco VPN Client automatically selects the proper configuration for itself. Therefore, no IKE configuration is necessary on the client PC.

Step 4: Select the transform set.

a. In the Transform Set window, the CCP default transform set is used. What is the ESP encryption method used with the default transform set? ________________________________

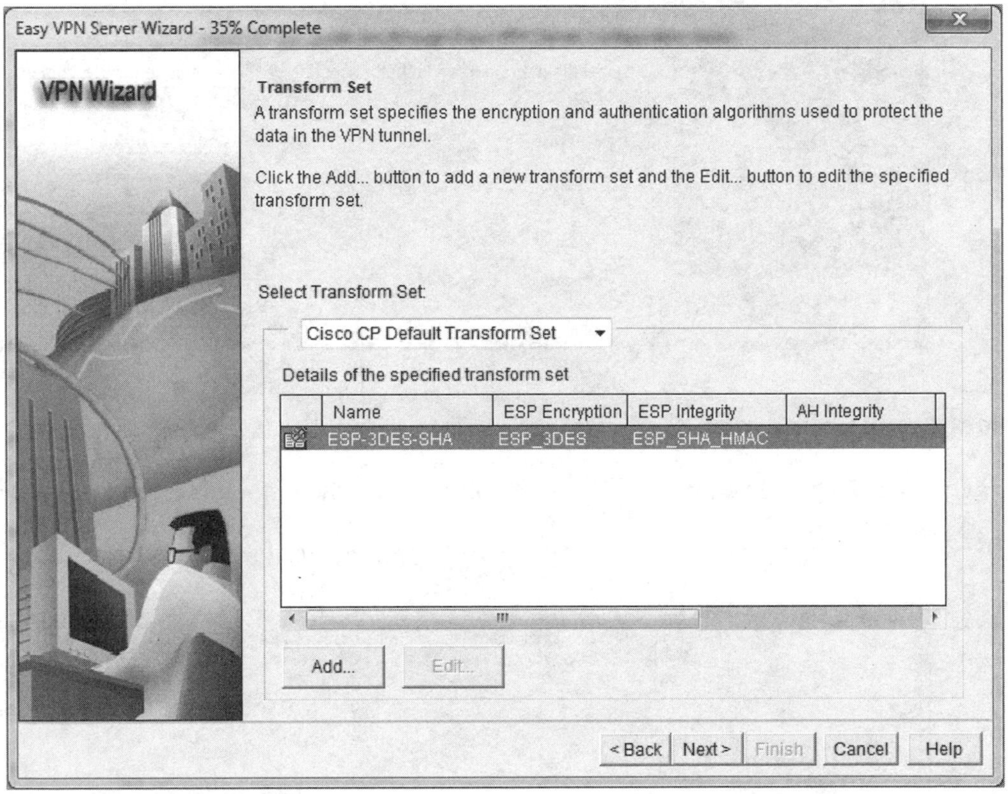

b. Click **Next** to accept the default transform set.

Step 5: Specify group authorization and group policy lookup.

a. In the Group Authorization and Group Policy Lookup window, choose the **Local** option because a RADIUS server is not available.

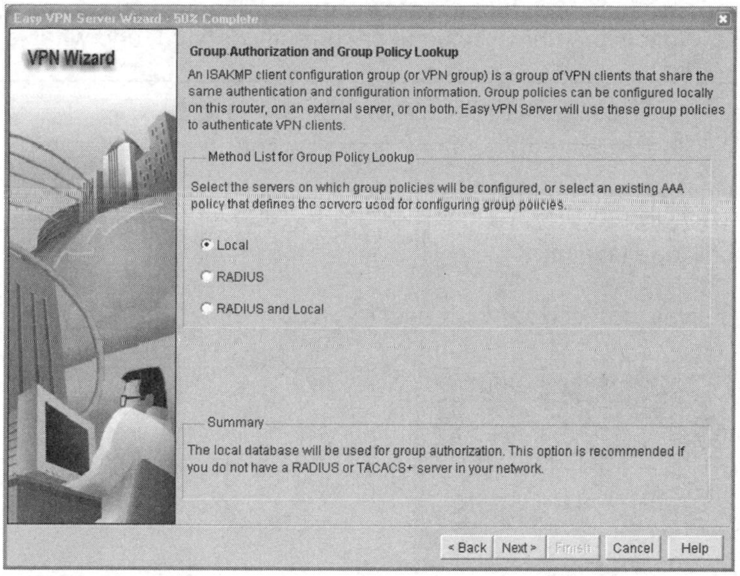

b. Click **Next** to create a new AAA method list for the group policy lookup that uses the local router database.

Step 6: Configure User Authentication (XAuth).

a. In the User Authentication (XAuth) window, you can specify where user information will be configured. Choices include an external server, such as a RADIUS server, a local database or both. Check the **Enable User Authentication** check box and accept the default of **Local Only**.

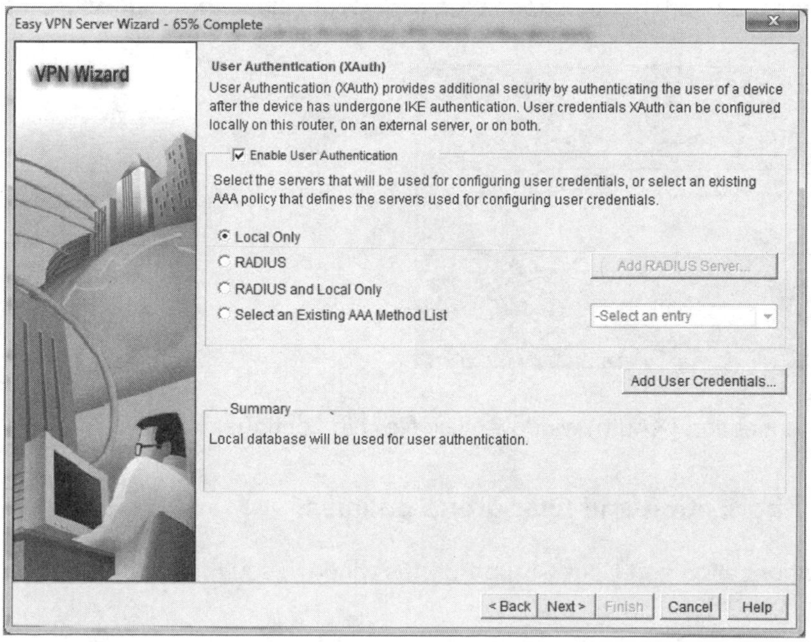

Where does the router look for valid user account and passwords to authenticate remote VPN users when they attempt to log in? ______________________________

b. Click the **Add User Credentials** button. In the User Accounts window, you can view currently defined users or add new users. What is the name of the user currently defined, and what is the user privilege level? ______________________________

How was this user defined? ______________________________

c. In the User Accounts window, click the **Add** button to add another user. Enter the username **user01** with a password of **user01pass**, and check the **Encrypt Password Using MD5 Hash Algorithm** check box. Leave the privilege level at 1.

What range of privilege levels can you set for a user? ____________________

d. Click **OK** to accept the user01 entries, and then click **OK** to close the User Accounts window.

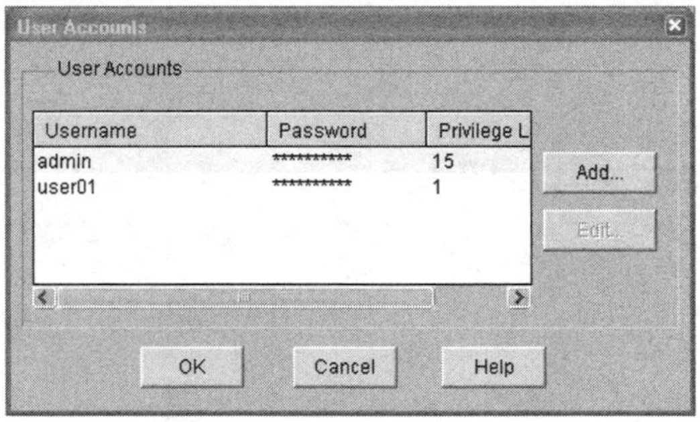

e. In the User Authentication (XAuth) window, click **Next** to continue.

Step 7: Specify group authorization and user group policies.

a. In the Group Authorization and User Group Policies window, you must create at least one group policy for the VPN server.

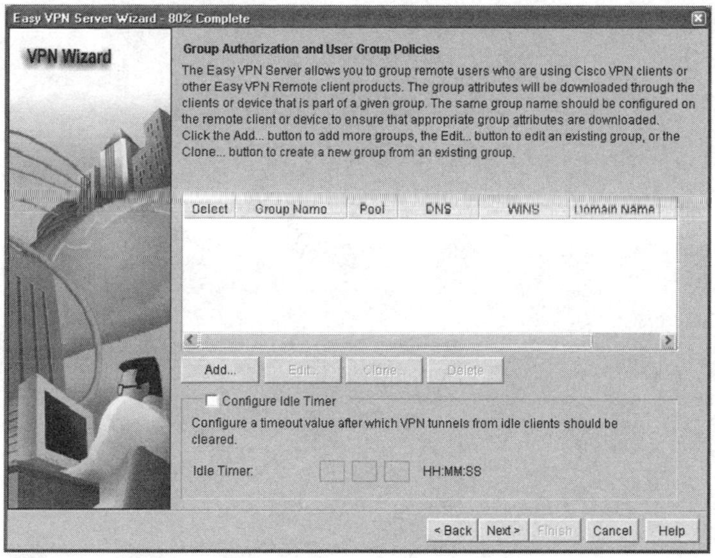

b. Click **Add** to create a group policy.

c. In the Add Group Policy window, enter **VPN-Access** as the name of this group. Enter a new pre-shared key of **cisco12345**, and then reenter it.

d. Leave the **Pool Information** box checked. Enter a starting address of **192.168.2.101**, an ending address of **192.168.2.150**, and a subnet mask of **255.255.255.0**.

e. Enter **50** in the Maximum Connections Allowed field.

f. Click **OK** to accept the entries.

g. A CCP warning message displays indicating that the IP addresses in the pool and the IP address of the Loopback0 interface are in the same subnet. Click **Yes** to confirm.

Why use an IP network for the VPN clients pool that is associated with a loopback interface?

____

How does R3 route traffic to the VPN clients?

____

h. When you return to the Group Authorization window, check the **Configure Idle Timer** check box and enter one hour (**1**). This disconnects idle users if there is no activity for one hour and allows others to connect. Click **Next** to continue.

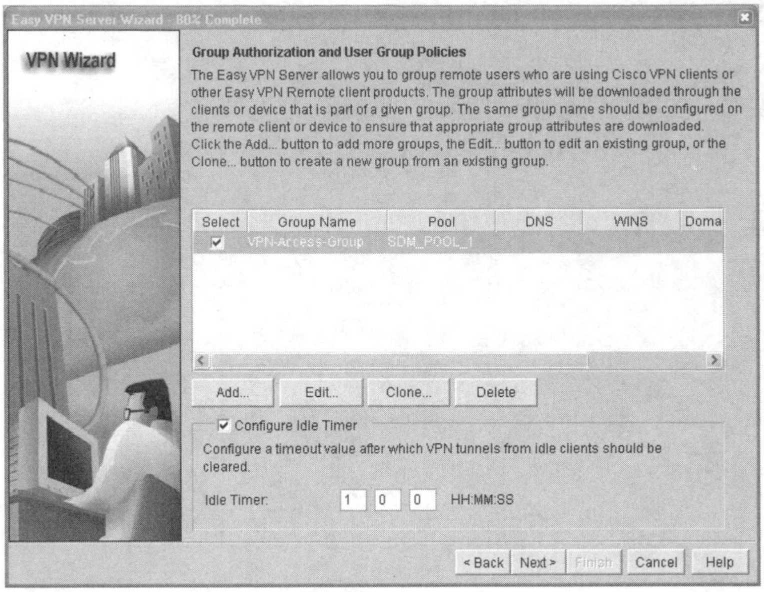

i. If the Cisco Tunneling Control Protocol (cTCP) window displays, do not enable cTCP. Click **Next** to continue.

Step 8: Review the configuration summary and deliver the commands.

a. Scroll through the commands that CCP will send to the router. Do not check the Test VPN Connectivity After Configuring check box. Click **Finish**.

b. If prompted to deliver the configuration to the router, click **Deliver**.

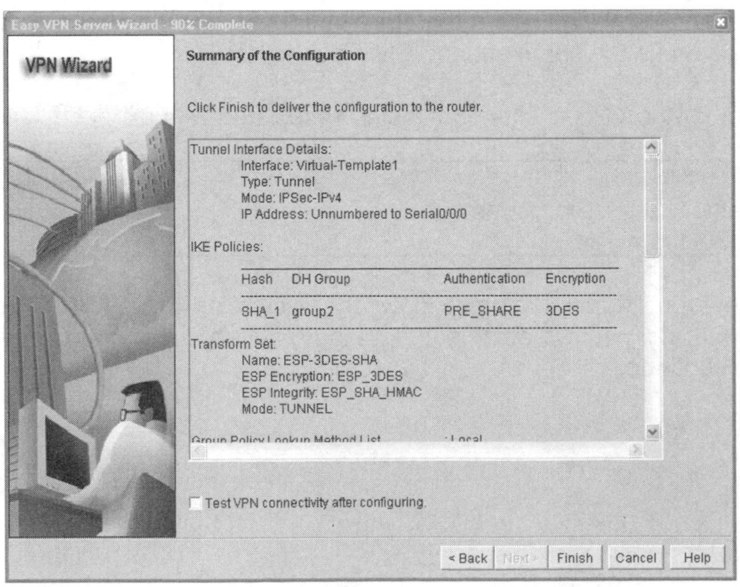

c. In the Command Delivery Status window, click **OK**. How many commands were delivered? ________

Step 9: Test the VPN server.

a. You are returned to the main VPN window with the **Edit Easy VPN Server** tab displayed. Click the **Test VPN Server** button in the lower-right corner of the screen.

b. In the VPN Troubleshooting window, click the **Start** button.

c. Your screen should look similar to the one here. Click **OK** to close the Information window. Click **Close** to exit the VPN Troubleshooting window.

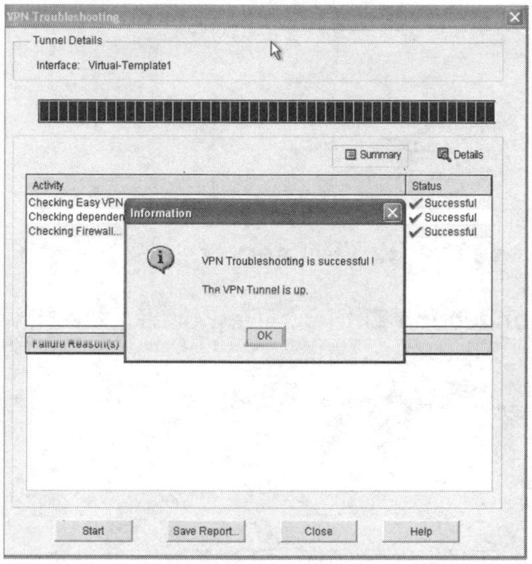

Note: If you receive a failure after testing the VPN server, close the VPN Troubleshooting window:

1. Click the Edit button in the upper right of Edit Easy VPN Server tab.
2. Click OK in the Edit Easy VPN Server Connection window.
3. Click OK in the Easy VPN Server Passthrough Configuration window.
4. Check the box to the right of the FastEthernet0/1 interface indicating that it is inside (trusted).
5. Rerun Test VPN Server by clicking that button in the lower right of Edit Easy VPN Server tab.
6. Click the Start button. The test should pass this time.

Task 3: Use the Cisco VPN Client to Test the Remote Access VPN

Step 1: (Optional) Install the Cisco VPN Client.

If not already installed, install Cisco VPN Client software on host PC-A. If you do not have the Cisco VPN Client software, contact your instructor.

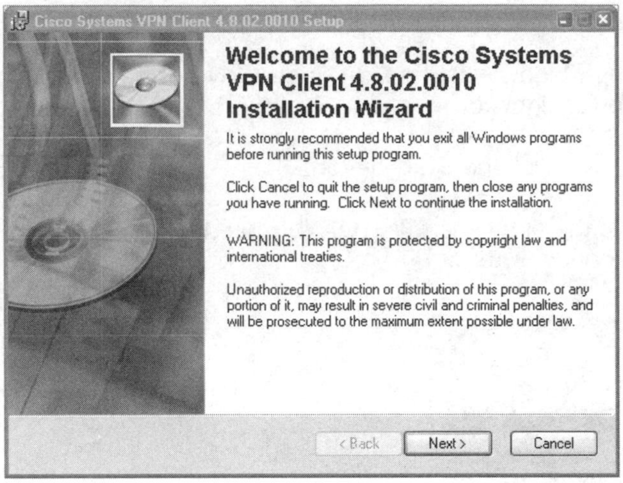

Step 2: Configure PC-A as a VPN client to access the R2 VPN server.

a. Start the Cisco VPN Client and choose **Connection Entries > New** or click the **New** icon.

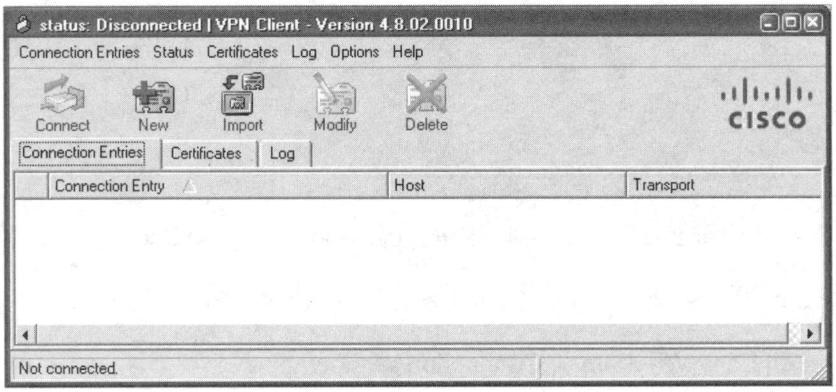

b. Enter the following information to define the new connection entry. Click **Save** when you are finished.

Connection Entry: **VPN-R2**

Description: **Connection to R2 internal network**

Host: **10.1.1.2** (IP address of the R2 S0/0/0 interface)

Group Authentication Name: **VPN-Access** (Defines the address pool configured in Task 2)

Password: **cisco12345** (Pre-shared key configured in Task 2)

Confirm Password: **cisco12345**

Note: The group authentication name and password are case sensitive and must match the ones created on the VPN server.

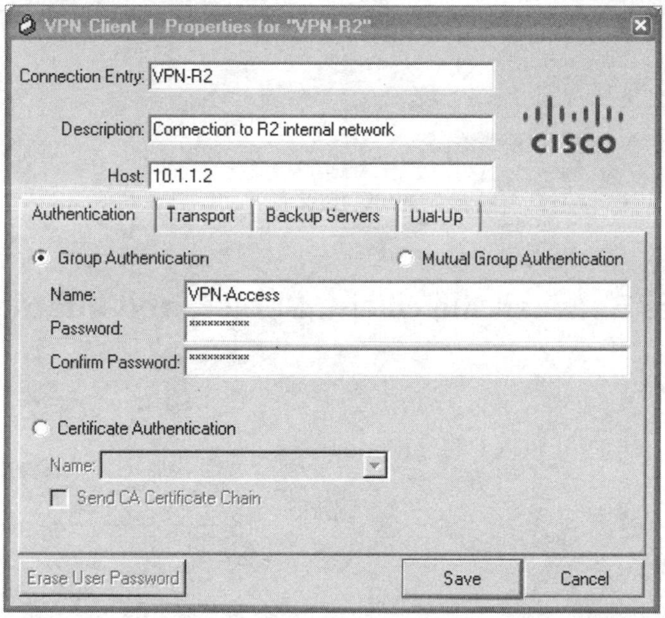

Step 3: Test access from PC-A without a VPN connection.

Open a command prompt on PC-A, and ping the PC-C IP address at 192.168.3.3 on the R3 LAN. Are the pings successful? Why or why not?

____

____

Note: After creating a VPN connection entry, you must activate it. Currently, the VPN tunnel is not up.

Step 4: Establish a VPN connection and log in

a. Select the newly created connection VPN-R2 and click the **Connect** icon. You can also double-click the connection entry.

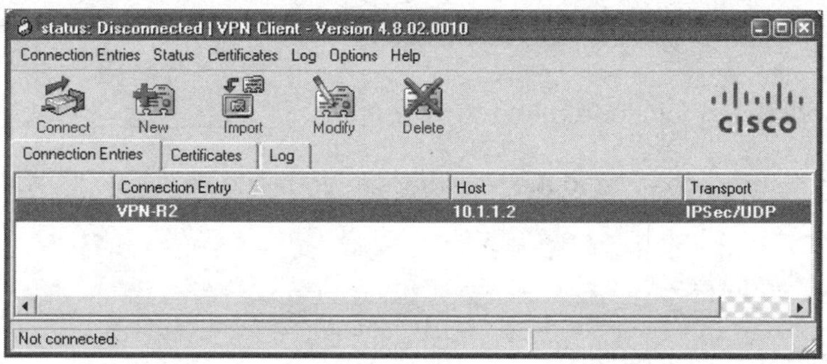

b. Enter the username **admin** created previously on the VPN router, and enter the password **cisco12345**.

c. Click **OK** to continue. The VPN Client window minimizes to a lock icon in the tools tray of the taskbar. When the lock is closed, the VPN tunnel is up. When it is open, the VPN connection is down.

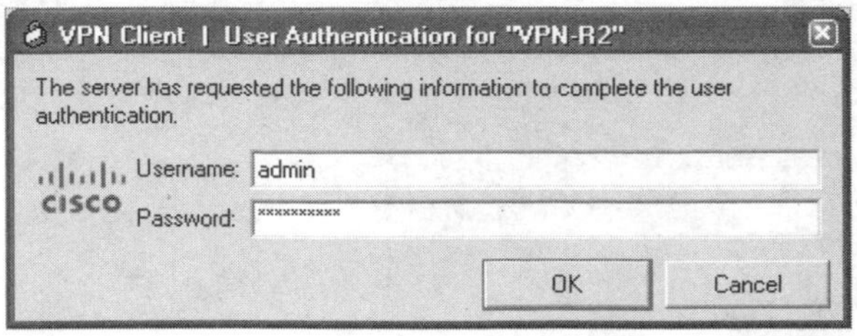

Task 4: Verify the VPN Tunnel Between the Client, Server, and Internal Network

Step 1: Check the VPN Client status.

Double-click the VPN lock icon to expand the VPN Client window.

What does it say about the connection status at the top of the window? ______________________

Step 2: Check the tunnel statistics.

a. Choose **Status > Statistics** to display the Tunnel Details tab.

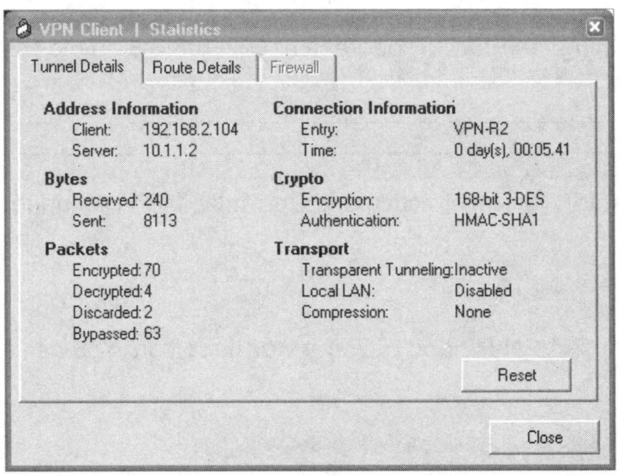

What is the client IP address obtained from the VPN server? ______________________

Note: Each time you disconnect and reconnect to the VPN server, you receive a new IP address until the limit is reached.

What is the VPN server address? ____________________

How many packets have been encrypted? ______________

What is the encryption method being used? ______________

What is the authentication being used? ________________

Step 3: Check the Cisco IOS messages on R2 when the tunnel is created.

Open the console connection for R2 and locate the message displayed indicating that the virtual interface came up when the VPN Client connection was made:

```
R2#
*Feb  3 16:09:08.907: %LINEPROTO-5-UPDOWN: Line protocol on Interface
Virtual-Access2, changed state to up
R2#
```

Step 4: Verify the VPN connection.

a. From the PC-A command prompt, issue the **ipconfig /all** command to see the network connections currently in use.

b. What is the configuration for the first local area connection?

IP address: ________________________________

Subnet mask: ________________________________

Default gateway: ________________________________

Description: ________________________________

c. What is the configuration for Local Area Connection 2?

IP address: ________________________________

Subnet mask: ________________________________

Default gateway: ________________________________

Description: ________________________________

Step 5: Test the access from the client with the VPN connection.

With the VPN connection from computer PC-A to router R2 activated, open a command prompt on PC-A and ping the PC-C IP address at 192.168.3.3 on the R3 LAN. Are the pings successful? Why or why not?

Step 6: Telnet to R2 from PC-A.

a. From the PC-A command prompt, telnet to R2 at the Lo0 IP address 192.168.2.1. Log in as **admin** with the password **cisco12345**. What is the router command prompt and why?

____

b. Issue the **show run** command to view the various commands generated by CCP to configure the VPN server.

c. Issue the **show users** command to see the connections to router R2. What connections are present? ____

d. Exit the Telnet session with the **quit** or **exit** command.

e. Right-click the VPN Client icon in the tools tray and choose **Disconnect**, or click the VPN-R2 connection and click the **Disconnect** icon.

f. Open the VPN client connection again but this time log in as **user01** with the password **user01pass**.

g. Telnet from PC-A to R2 again at the Lo0 IP address 192.168.2.1. Log in as **user01** with the password **user01pass**. What is the router command prompt and why is this?

____

Note: You could have telnetted to R2 from the first VPN session and logged in as user01, but this process demonstrates the VPN disconnect and connect process and verifies that user01 is set up properly.

Reflection

Why is VPN a good option for remote users?

____
____
____
____

Router Interface Summary Table

Router Model	Ethernet Interface 1	Ethernet Interface 2	Serial Interface 1	Serial Interface 2
1800	Fast Ethernet 0/0 (Fa0/0)	Fast Ethernet 0/1 (Fa0/1)	Serial 0/0/0 (S0/0/0)	Serial 0/0/1 (S0/0/1)
1900	Gigabit Ethernet 0/0 (G0/0)	Gigabit Ethernet 0/1 (G0/1)	Serial 0/0/0 (S0/0/0)	Serial 0/0/1 (S0/0/1)
2800	Fast Ethernet 0/0 (Fa0/0)	Fast Ethernet 0/1 (Fa0/1)	Serial 0/0/0 (S0/0/0)	Serial 0/0/1 (S0/0/1)
2900	Gigabit Ethernet 0/0 (G0/0)	Gigabit Ethernet 0/1 (G0/1)	Serial 0/0/0 (S0/0/0)	Serial 0/0/1 (S0/0/1)

Note: To find out how the router is configured, look at the interfaces to identify the type of router and how many interfaces the router has. There is no way to effectively list all the combinations of configurations for each router class. This table includes identifiers for the possible combinations of Ethernet and serial interfaces in the device. The table does not include any other type of interface, even though a specific router may contain one. An example of this might be an ISDN BRI interface. The string in parentheses is the legal abbreviation that can be used in Cisco IOS commands to represent the interface.

Chapter 9 Lab A: Security Policy Development and Implementation

Topology

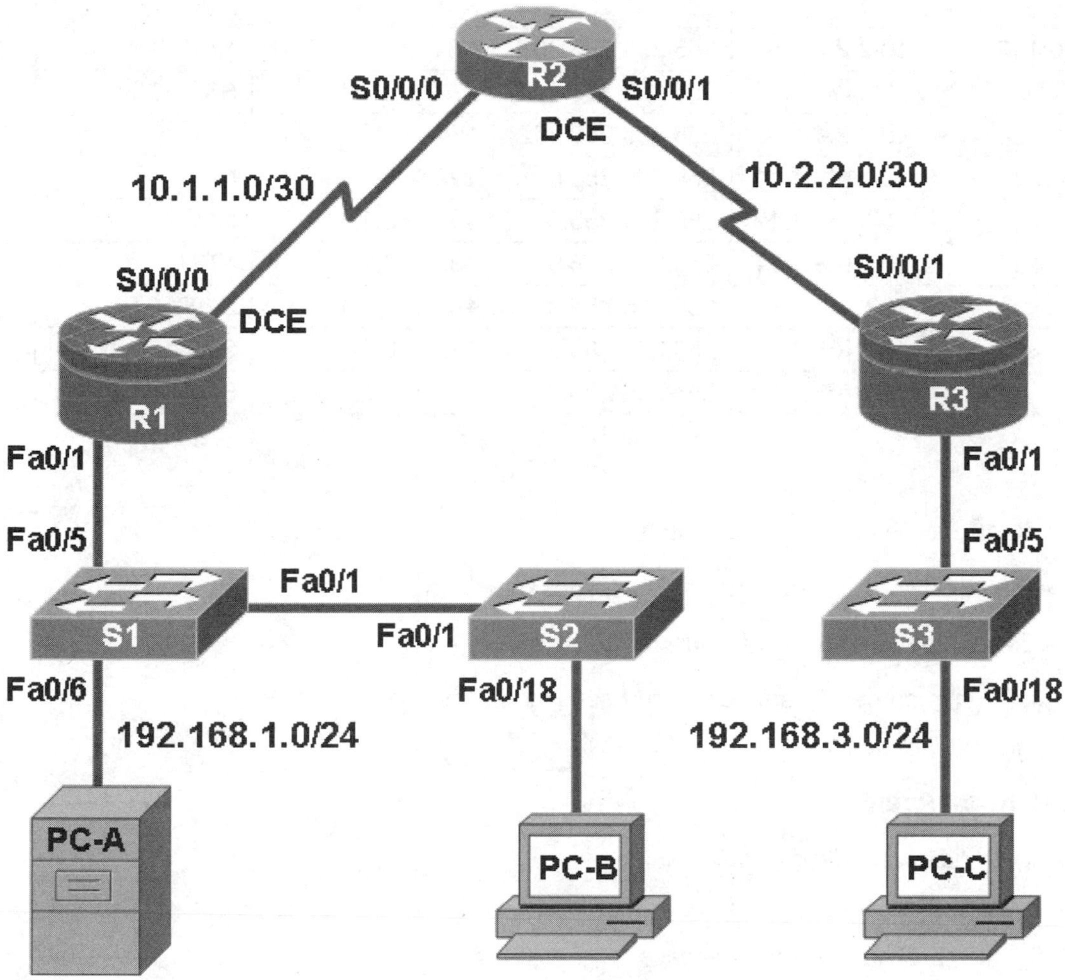

Note: ISR G2 devices have Gigabit Ethernet interfaces rather than FastEthernet interfaces.

IP Addressing Table

Device	Interface	IP Address	Subnet Mask	Default Gateway	Switch Port
R1	FA0/1	192.168.1.1	255.255.255.0	N/A	S1 FA0/5
	S0/0/0 (DCE)	10.1.1.1	255.255.255.252	N/A	N/A
R2	S0/0/0	10.1.1.2	255.255.255.252	N/A	N/A
	S0/0/1 (DCE)	10.2.2.2	255.255.255.252	N/A	N/A
R3	FA0/1	192.168.3.1	255.255.255.0	N/A	S3 FA0/5
	S0/0/1	10.2.2.1	255.255.255.252	N/A	N/A
S1	VLAN 1	192.168.1.11	255.255.255.0	192.168.1.1	N/A
S2	VLAN 1	192.168.1.12	255.255.255.0	192.168.1.1	N/A
S3	VLAN 1	192.168.3.11	255.255.255.0	192.168.3.1	N/A
PC-A	NIC	192.168.1.3	255.255.255.0	192.168.1.1	S1 FA0/6
PC-B	NIC	192.168.1.2	255.255.255.0	192.168.1.1	S2 FA0/18
PC-C	NIC	192.168.3.3	255.255.255.0	192.168.3.1	S3 FA0/18

Objectives

Part 1: Create a Basic Technical Security Policy

- Develop a Network Device Security Guidelines document.

Part 2: Basic Network Device Configuration

- Configure hostnames, interface IP addresses, and passwords.
- Configure static routing.

Part 3: Secure Network Routers

- Configure passwords and a login banner.
- Configure SSH access and disable Telnet.
- Configure HTTP secure server access.
- Configure a synchronized time source using NTP.
- Configure router syslog support.
- Configure centralized authentication using AAA and RADIUS.
- Use Cisco IOS to disable unneeded services and secure against login attacks.
- Use CCP to disable unneeded services.
- Configure a CBAC firewall.
- Configure a ZBF firewall.
- Configure intrusion prevention system (IPS) using Cisco IOS and CCP.
- Back up and secure the Cisco IOS image and configuration files.

Part 4: Secure Network Switches

- Configure passwords, and a login banner.
- Configure management VLAN access.
- Configure a synchronized time source using NTP.
- Configure syslog support.
- Configure SSH access.
- Configure AAA and RADIUS.
- Secure trunk ports.
- Secure access ports.
- Protect against STP attacks.
- Configure port security and disable unused ports.

Part 5: Configure VPN Remote Access

- Use CCP to configure Easy VPN Server.
- Use the Cisco VPN Client to test the remote access VPN.

Background

A comprehensive security policy covers three main areas: governing policies, end-user policies, and technical policies. Technical policies can include email, remote access, telephony, applications, and network policies, such as device access controls and logging. The focus of this lab is the creation of a technical network policy that specifies security measures to be configured for network devices and implementation of those measures.

In Part 1 of this lab, you create a basic Network Device Security Guidelines document that can serve as part of a comprehensive policy. This document addresses specific router and switch security measures and describes the security requirements to be implemented on the infrastructure equipment. The Network Device Security Guidelines document is presented to your instructor for review before starting Part 2 of the lab.

In Part 2, you build the network and configure basic device settings. In Parts 3 and 4, you secure routers and switches. In Part 5, you configure a router for VPN remote access. The Network Device Security Guidelines policy is used as the guiding document.

The company you are working for has two locations connected by an Internet service provider (ISP). Router R1 represents a remote site, and R3 represents the corporate headquarters. Router R2 represents the ISP.

Note: The router commands and output in this lab are from a Cisco 1841 with Cisco IOS Software Release 12.4(20)T (advanced IP image). The switch commands and output are from a Cisco WS-C2960-24TT-L with Cisco IOS Software Release 12.2(46)SE (C2960-LANBASEK9-M image). Other routers, switches, and Cisco IOS versions can be used. See the Router Interface Summary table at the end of the lab to determine which interface identifiers to use based on the equipment in the lab. Depending on the router or switch model and Cisco IOS version, the commands available and output produced might vary from what is shown in this lab.

Note: Make sure that the routers and switches have been erased and have no startup configurations.

Required Resources

- 2 routers (Cisco 1841 with Cisco IOS Software Release 12.4(20)T1 Advanced IP Service or comparable)
- 1 router (Cisco 1841 with Cisco IOS Software Release 12.4(20)T1 IP Base or comparable)

- 3 switches (Cisco 2960 with Cisco IOS Release 12.2(46)SE C2960-LANBASEK9-M image or comparable)
- PC-A: Windows XP, Vista, or Windows 7 with CCP 2.5, RADIUS, TFTP, and syslog servers plus PuTTY and Cisco VPN Client software available
- PC-B: Windows XP, Vista, or Windows 7
- PC-C: Windows XP, Vista, or Windows 7 with CCP 2.5, RADIUS, TFTP, and syslog servers plus PuTTY software available and SuperScan (optional)
- Serial and Ethernet cables as shown in the topology
- Rollover cables to configure the routers via the console

CCP Notes

- See Chapter 00 Lab A for instructions on how to install and run CCP. Hardware/software recommendations for CCP include Windows XP, Vista, or Windows 7 with Java Version 1.6.0_11 up to 1.6.0_21, Internet Explorer 6.0 or later, and Flash Player Version 10.0.12.36 or later.
- If the PC on which CCP is installed is running Windows Vista or Windows 7, you might need to right-click the CCP icon or menu item and choose Run as Administrator.
- To run CCP, you might need to temporarily disable antivirus programs and OS firewalls. Make sure to turn off all pop-up blockers in the browser.

Part 1: Create a Basic Technical Security Policy

In Part 1, you create a Network Device Security Guidelines document that can serve as part of a comprehensive network security policy. This document addresses specific router and switch security measures and describes the security requirements to be implemented on the infrastructure equipment.

Task 1: Identify Potential Sections of a Basic Network Security Policy (Chapter 9)

A network security policy should include several key sections that can address potential issues for users, network access, device access, and other areas. List some key sections you think could be part of good basic security policy.

____
____
____
____
____
____
____

Task 2: Create Network Equipment Security Guidelines as a Supplement to a Basic Security Policy (Chapter 9)

Step 1: Review the objectives from previous CCNA Security labs.

a. Open each of the previous labs completed from Chapters 1 through 8 and review the objectives listed for each one.

b. Copy the objectives to a separate document for use as a starting point. Focus mainly on those objectives that involve security practices and device configuration.

Step 2: Create a Network Device Security Guidelines document for router and switch security.

Create a high-level list of tasks to include for network access and device security. This document should reinforce and supplement the information presented in a basic Security Policy. It is based on the content of previous CCNA Security labs and on the networking devices present in the course lab topology.

Note: The Network Device Security Guidelines document should be no more than two pages and is the basis for the equipment configuration in the remaining parts of the lab.

Step 3: Submit the Network Device Security Guidelines to your instructor.

Provide the Network Device Security Guidelines documents to your instructor for review before starting Part 2 of the lab. You can send them as email attachments or put them on removable storage media, such as a flash drive.

Part 2: Basic Network Device Configuration (Chapters 2 and 6)

In Part 2, you set up the network topology and configure basic settings, such as the interface IP addresses and static routing. Perform steps on routers and switches as indicated.

Step 1: Cable the network as shown in the topology.

Attach the devices shown in the topology diagram, and cable as necessary.

Step 2: Configure basic settings for all routers.

a. Configure hostnames as shown in the topology.

b. Configure the interface IP addresses as shown in the IP addressing table.

c. Configure a clock rate for the routers with a DCE serial cable attached to their serial interface.

d. Disable DNS lookup to prevent the router from attempting to translate incorrectly entered commands as though they were hostnames.

Step 3: Configure static default routes on R1 and R3.

Configure a static default route from R1 to R2 and from R3 to R2.

Step 4: Configure static routes on R2.

Configure a static route from R2 to the R1 LAN and from R2 to the R3 LAN.

Step 5: Configure basic settings for each switch.

a. Configure hostnames as shown in the topology.

b. Configure the VLAN 1 management addresses as shown in the IP addressing table.

c. Configure the IP default gateway for each of the three switches. The gateway for the S1 and S2 switches is the R1 Fa0/1 interface IP address. The gateway for the S3 switch is the R3 Fa0/1 interface IP address.

d. Disable DNS lookup to prevent the switches from attempting to translate incorrectly entered commands as though they were hostnames.

Step 6: Configure PC host IP settings.

Configure a static IP address, subnet mask, and default gateway for PC-A, PC-B, and PC-C, as shown in the IP addressing table.

Step 7: Verify connectivity between PC-A and PC-C.

Step 8: Save the basic running configuration for each router.

Part 3: Secure Network Routers

In Part 3, you configure device access, passwords, firewalls, and intrusion prevention. Perform steps on routers as indicated.

Task 1: Configure Passwords and a Login Banner (Chapter 2)

Step 1: Configure a minimum password length of 10 characters on all routers.

Step 2: Configure the enable secret password on all routers.

Use an enable secret password of **cisco12345**.

Step 3: Encrypt plain-text passwords.

Step 4: Configure the console lines on all routers.

Configure a console password of **ciscoconpass** and enable login. Set the exec-timeout to log out after 5 minutes of inactivity. Prevent console messages from interrupting command entry.

Step 5: Configure the vty lines on R2.

Configure a vty lines password of **ciscovtypass** and enable login. Set the exec-timeout to log out after 5 minutes of inactivity.

Note: The vty lines for R1 and R3 are configured for SSH in Task 2.

Step 6: Configure a login warning banner on routers R1 and R3.

Configure a warning to unauthorized users with a message-of-the-day (MOTD) banner that says "Unauthorized access strictly prohibited and prosecuted to the full extent of the law."

Task 2: Configure the SSH Server on Routers R1 and R3 (Chapter 2)

Step 1: Configure a privileged user for login from the SSH client.

Create the user Admin01 account with a privilege level of **15** and a secret password of **Admin01pa55**.

Step 2: Configure the domain name ccnasecurity.com.

Step 3: Configure the incoming vty lines.

Specify a privilege level of 15 so that a user with the highest privilege level (15) defaults to privileged EXEC mode when accessing the vty lines. Other users default to user EXEC mode. Specify local user accounts for mandatory login and validation, and accept only SSH connections.

Step 4: Generate the RSA encryption key pair for the router.

Configure the RSA keys with 1024 for the number of modulus bits.

Step 5: Verify SSH connectivity to R1 from PC-A.

a. If the SSH client is not already installed, download either TeraTerm or PuTTY.

b. Launch the SSH client, enter the Fa0/1 IP address, and enter the **Admin01** username and password **Admin01pa55**.

Task 3: Configure a Synchronized Time Source Using NTP (Chapter 2)

Step 1: Set up the NTP master using Cisco IOS commands.

R2 will be the master Network Time Protocol (NTP) server. All other routers and switches learn their time from it, either directly or indirectly.

a. Ensure that R2 has the correct coordinated universal time. Set the time if it is not correct.

b. Configure R2 as the NTP master with a stratum number of 3.

Step 2: Configure R1 and R3 as NTP clients.

a. Configure R1 and R3 to become NTP clients of R2.

b. Verify that R1 and R3 have made an association with R2 using the **`show ntp associations`** command.

Task 4: Configure Router Syslog Support (Chapter 2)

Step 1: (Optional) Install the syslog server on PC-A and PC-C.

If a syslog server is not currently installed on the host, download the latest version of Kiwi from http://www.kiwisyslog.com or Tftpd32 from http://tftpd32.jounin.net and install it on your desktop. If it is already installed, go to Step 2.

Step 2: Configure R1 to log messages to the PC-A syslog server.

a. Verify that you have connectivity between R1 and host PC-A by pinging the R1 Fa0/1 interface IP address 192.168.1.1 from PC-A. If the pings are not successful, troubleshoot as necessary before continuing.

b. Configure logging on the router to send syslog messages to the syslog server.

Step 3: Configure R3 to log messages to the PC-C syslog server.

a. Verify that you have connectivity between R3 and the host PC-C by pinging the R3 Fa0/1 interface IP address 192.168.3.1 from PC-C. If the pings are not successful, troubleshoot as necessary before continuing.

b. Configure logging on the router to send syslog messages to the syslog server.

Task 5: Configure Authentication Using AAA and RADIUS (Chapter 3)

PC-A serves as the local RADIUS server for the remote site, and R1 accesses the external RADIUS server for user authentication. The freeware RADIUS server WinRadius is used for this section of the lab.

Step 1: (Optional) Download and configure the WinRadius software.

a. If WinRadius is not currently installed on PC-A, download the latest version from http://www.suggestsoft.com/soft/itconsult2000/winradius/, http://winradius.soft32.com, http://www.brothersoft.com/winradius-20914.html. There is no installation setup. The extracted WinRadius.exe file is executable.

b. Start the WinRadius.exe application. If the application is being started for the first time, follow the instructions to configure the WinRadius server database.

Note: If WinRadius is used on a PC that uses the Microsoft Windows Vista operating system or the Microsoft Windows 7 operating system, ODBC may fail to create successfully because it cannot write to the Registry.

Possible Solutions

1. Compatibility settings:

    a. Right-click the WinRadius.exe icon and choose **Properties**.

    b. While in the Properties dialog box, display the **Compatibility** tab. In this tab, check the **Run This Program in Compatibility Mode For** check box. Then in the drop-down menu below, choose **Windows XP (Service Pack 3)**, for example, if it is appropriate for your system.

    c. Click **OK**.

2. Run as Administrator settings:

    a. Right-click the WinRadius.exe icon and choose **Properties**.

    b. While in the Properties dialog box, display the **Compatibility** tab. In this tab, check the **Run This Program as Administrator** check box in the Privilege Level section.

    c. Click **OK**.

3. Run as Administrator for each launch:

   a. Right-click the WinRadius.exe icon and choose **Run as Administrator**.

   b. When WinRadius launches, click **Yes** in the User Account Control dialog box.

Step 2: Configure users and passwords on the WinRadius server.

a. Add username **RadAdmin** with a password of **RadAdminpa55**.

b. Add username **RadUser** with a password of **RadUserpa55**.

Step 3: Enable AAA on R1.

Use the `aaa new-model` command to enable AAA.

Step 4: Configure the default login authentication list.

Configure the list to first use **radius** for the authentication service and then **local** to allow access based on the local router database if a RADIUS server cannot be reached.

Step 5: Verify connectivity between R1 and the PC-A RADIUS server.

Ping from R1 to PC-A. If the pings are not successful, troubleshoot the PC and router configuration before continuing.

Step 6: Specify a RADIUS server on R1.

Configure the router to access the RADIUS server at the PC-A IP address. Specify port numbers **1812** and **1813**, along with the default secret key of **WinRadius** for the RADIUS server.

Step 7: Test your configuration by logging in to the console on R1.

a. Exit to the initial router screen that displays `R1 con0 is now available.`

b. Log in with the username **RadAdmin** and password **RadAdminpa55**. Are you able to log in with minimal delay? ______________________________

Note: If you close the WinRadius server and restart it, you must re-create the user accounts from Step 2.

Step 8: Test your configuration by connecting to R1 with SSH.

a. Clear the log display for the WinRadius server by choosing **Log > Clear**.

b. Use PuTTY or another terminal emulation client to open an SSH session from PC-A to R1.

c. At the login prompt, enter the username **RadAdmin** defined on the RADIUS server and the password **RadAdminpa55**.

   Are you able to log in to R1? _______

d. Exit the SSH session.

e. Stop the WinRadius server on PC-A by choosing **Operation > Exit**.

f. Open an SSH session and attempt to log in again as **RadAdmin**.

Are you able to log in to R1? ______________________________

g. Close the SSH client and open another SSH session to R1 and attempt to log in as **Admin01** with a password of **Admin01pa55**.

With the WinRadius server unavailable, are you able to log in to R1? Why or why not?

____

____

Step 9: Configure RADIUS support on R3.

Repeat steps 1 through 6 to configure R3 to access PC-C as a RADIUS server.

Task 6: Use CLI to Disable Unneeded Services on R1 and Secure Against Login Attacks (Chapter 2)

Step 1: Use CLI to disable common IP services that can be exploited for network attacks.

Tip: You can issue the **`auto secure management`** command to see the management related commands that would be generated. When prompted with `Apply this configuration to running-config? [yes]:` respond **NO**, and then selectively copy the desired commands to a text file for editing and application to the router.

a. Disable the following global services on the router:

```
service finger
service pad
service udp-small-servers
service tcp-small-servers
cdp run
ip bootp server
ip http server
ip finger
ip source-route
ip gratuitous-arps
ip identd
```

Note: Disabling the HTTP server prevents web-based access to the router via CCP. If you want secure access to the router via CCP, you can enable it using the command **`ip http secure-server`**.

b. For each serial interface, disable the following interface services:

```
ip redirects
ip proxy-arp
ip unreachables
ip directed-broadcast
ip mask-reply
```

c. For each Fast Ethernet interface, disable the following interface services:

```
ip redirects
ip proxy-arp
ip unreachables
ip directed-broadcast
ip mask-reply
mop enabled
```

Step 2: Secure against login attacks on R1 and R3.

Configure the following parameters:

- Blocking period when login attack detected: 60
- Maximum login failures with the device: 2
- Maximum time period for crossing the failed login attempts: 30

Step 3: Save the running configuration to the startup configuration for R1 and R3.

Task 7: Use CCP to Disable Unneeded Services on R3 (Chapter 2)

Step 1: Configure user credentials for HTTP router access before starting CCP.

a. Enable the HTTP server on R3.

   Or enable the HTTP secure server to connect securely.

b. Create an admin account on R3 with privilege level 15 and password **cisco12345** for use with AAA and CCP.

c. Have CCP use the local database to authenticate web sessions.

Step 2: Access CCP and discover R3.

a. Run the CCP application on PC-C. In the Select/Manage Community window, input the R3 IP address **192.168.3.1** in the first IP Address/Hostname field. Enter **admin** in the Username field, and **cisco12345** in the Password field. Click the **OK** button.

b. At the CCP Dashboard, click the **Discovery** button to discover and connect to R3. If the discovery process fails, use the **Discover Details** button to determine the problem to resolve the issue.

Step 3: Begin the security audit.

a. Choose **Configure > Security > Security Audit** and click the **Perform Security Audit** button. Click **Next** at the welcome screen

b. Choose **FastEthernet 0/1** as the Inside Trusted interface and **Serial 0/0/1** as the Outside Untrusted interface.

c. View the Security Audit report and note which services did not pass. Click **Close**.

d. In the Fix It window, click **Fix It** to disable the following global and interface services:

```
Global services to disable:
service pad
```

```
cdp run
ip bootp server
ip source-route

Per-interface service to disable:
ip redirects
ip unreachables
mop enabled
```

Note: Do not fix (disable) Proxy ARP because this disables ARP on all R3 interfaces and causes a problem, specifically with interface Fa0/1, and pings to the R3 VPN server LAN. The VPN server is configured in Part 5 of the lab.

e. Click **Next** to view a summary of the problems that will be fixed. Click **Finish** and deliver the commands to the router.

Task 8: Configure a CBAC Firewall on R1 (Chapter 4)

Step 1: Use the Cisco IOS AutoSecure feature to enable a CBAC firewall on R1.

a. To configure only the Context Based Access Control (CBAC) firewall on R1, use the **auto secure** command and specify the **firewall** option. Respond as shown in the following AutoSecure output to the AutoSecure questions and prompts. The responses are in bold.

```
R1# auto secure firewall
                --- AutoSecure Configuration ---

*** AutoSecure configuration enhances the security of the router, but
it will not make it absolutely resistant to all security attacks ***

AutoSecure will modify the configuration of your device. All
configuration changes will be shown. For a detailed explanation of how
the configuration changes enhance security and any possible side
effects, please refer to Cisco.com for
Autosecure documentation.
At any prompt you may enter '?' for help.
Use ctrl-c to abort this session at any prompt.

Gathering information about the router for AutoSecure

Is this router connected to internet? [no]: yes
Enter the number of interfaces facing the internet [1]: 1
Interface          IP-Address     OK? Method Status
Protocol
FastEthernet0/0    unassigned     YES unset  administratively down down

FastEthernet0/1    192.168.1.1    YES manual up                    up

Serial0/0/0        10.1.1.1       YES SLARP  up                    up

Serial0/0/1        unassigned     YES unset  administratively down down

Enter the interface name that is facing the internet: serial0/0/0
Configure CBAC Firewall feature? [yes/no]: yes

This is the configuration generated:
```

```
ip inspect audit-trail
ip inspect dns-timeout 7
ip inspect tcp idle-time 14400
ip inspect udp idle-time 1800
ip inspect name autosec_inspect cuseeme timeout 3600
ip inspect name autosec_inspect ftp timeout 3600
ip inspect name autosec_inspect http timeout 3600
ip inspect name autosec_inspect rcmd timeout 3600
ip inspect name autosec_inspect realaudio timeout 3600
ip inspect name autosec_inspect smtp timeout 3600
ip inspect name autosec_inspect tftp timeout 30
ip inspect name autosec_inspect udp timeout 15
ip inspect name autosec_inspect tcp timeout 3600
ip access-list extended autosec_firewall_acl
 permit udp any any eq bootpc
 deny ip any any
interface Serial0/0/0
 ip inspect autosec_inspect out
 ip access-group autosec_firewall_acl in
!
end

Apply this configuration to running-config? [yes]: yes

Applying the config generated to running-config

R1#
Feb 12 18:34:58.040: %AUTOSEC-5-ENABLED: AutoSecure is configured on
the device
```

Step 2: Review the AutoSecure CBAC configuration.

To which interface is the autosec_inspect name applied and in what direction? ________________

To which interface is the ACL autosec_firewall_acl applied and in which direction? ______________

What is the purpose of the ACL autosec_firewall_acl?

____

Step 3: From PC-A, ping the R2 external WAN interface.

From PC-A, ping the R2 interface S0/0/0 at IP address 10.1.1.2.

Are the pings successful? Why or why not?

____

Step 4: Add ICMP to the autosec_inspect list.

Configure R1 to inspect ICMP and allow ICMP echo replies from outside hosts with a timeout of 60 seconds.

Step 5: From PC-A, ping the R2 external WAN interface.

From PC-A, ping the R2 interface S0/0/0 at IP address 10.1.1.2.

Are the pings successful? Why or why not? ______________________________

Step 6: From R2, ping PC-A.

From R2 ping PC-A.

Are the pings successful? Why or why not? ______________________________

Step 7: Test SSH access from PC-C to R1.

From external host PC-C, start a PuTTY session to R1.

Is the SSH session connection successful? Why or why not? ______________________

Step 8: Configure the R1 firewall to allow SSH access from external hosts on the 192.168.3.0/24 network.

a. Display the extended ACL named autosec_firewall_acl that is applied to S0/0/0 inbound:

```
R1# show access-list autosec_firewall_acl
Extended IP access list autosec_firewall_acl
    10 permit udp any any eq bootpc
    20 deny ip any any (57 matches)
```

b. Configure R1 to allow SSH access by adding a statement to the extended ACL autosec_firewall_acl that permits the SSH TCP port 22:

```
R1(config)# ip access-list extended autosec_firewall_acl
R1(config-ext-nacl)# 13 permit tcp 192.168.3.0 0.0.0.255 any eq 22
R1(config-ext-nacl)# end
```

c. From external host PC-C, start a PuTTY SSH session to R1 at IP address 10.1.1.1 and log in as RADIUS user RadAdmin with a password of RadAdminpa55.

d. From the SSH session on R1, display the modified extended ACL autosec_firewall_acl:

```
R1# show access-list autosec_firewall_acl
Extended IP access list autosec_firewall_acl
    10 permit udp any any eq bootpc
    13 permit tcp 192.168.3.0 0.0.0.255 any eq 22 (16 matches)
    20 deny ip any any (60 matches)
```

Step 9: Configure the R1 firewall to allow NTP and VPN traffic.

a. Configure R1 to allow NTP updates from R2 by adding a statement to the extended ACL autosec_firewall_acl that permits the NTP (UDP port 123):

```
R1(config)# ip access-list extended autosec_firewall_acl
R1(config-ext-nacl)# 15 permit udp host 10.1.1.2 host 10.1.1.1 eq ntp
```

b. Configure R1 to allow IPsec VPN traffic between PC-A and R3 by adding a statement to the extended ACL autosec_firewall_acl that permits the IPsec Encapsulating Security Protocol (ESP).

Note: In Part 5 of the lab, R3 is configured as a VPN server and PC-A is the remote client.

```
R1(config-ext-nacl)# 18 permit esp any any
R1(config-ext-nacl)# end
```

c. Display the modified extended ACL autosec_firewall_acl:

```
R1# show access-list autosec_firewall_acl
Extended IP access list autosec_firewall_acl
    10 permit udp any any eq bootpc
    13 permit tcp 192.168.3.0 0.0.0.255 any eq 22 (67 matches)
    15 permit udp host 10.1.1.2 host 10.1.1.1 eq ntp (3 matches)
    18 permit esp any any
    20 deny ip any any (21 matches)
```

Step 10: Test Telnet access from internal PC-A to external router R2.

a. From PC-A, Telnet to R2 at IP address **10.1.1.2** using the vty line password **ciscovtypass**:

```
C:\> telnet 10.1.1.2
```

Is the Telnet attempt successful? Why or why not? ______________________________

b. Leave the Telnet session open.

Step 11: Display CBAC inspection sessions.

Display the IP inspect session to see the active Telnet session from PC-A to R2.

Task 9: Configure a ZBF Firewall on R3 (Chapter 4)

Step 1: Use CCP to discover R3.

a. Run the CCP application on PC-C. In the Select/Manage Community window, input the R3 IP address **192.168.3.1** in the first IP Address/Hostname field. Enter **admin** in the Username field, and **cisco12345** in the Password field. Click the **OK** button.

b. At the CCP Dashboard, click the **Discovery** button to discover and connect to R3. If the discovery process fails, use the **Discover Details** button to determine the problem to resolve the issue.

Step 2: Use the CCP Firewall Wizard to configure a ZBF on R3.

a. Click the **Configure** button at the top of the CCP screen, and then click **Security > Firewall > Firewall**.

b. Select **Basic Firewall** and click the **Launch the selected task** button. On the Basic Firewall Configuration Wizard screen, click **Next**.

c. Check the **Inside (Trusted)** check box for **FastEthernet0/1** and the **Outside (Untrusted)** check box for **Serial0/0/1**. Click **Next**. Click **OK** when the CCP access warning is displayed.

d. Choose **Low Security** and click **Next**. In the Summary window, click **Finish** and deliver the commands to the router.

e. Click **OK** in the Commands Delivery Status window.

Step 3: Verify ZBF functionality.

a. From PC-C, ping the R2 interface S0/0/1 at IP address 10.2.2.2.

Are the pings successful? Why or why not? ______________________________

b. From external router R2, ping PC-C at IP address 192.168.3.3.

Are the pings successful? Why or why not? ______________________________

c. From router R2, Telnet to R3 at IP address 10.2.2.1.

Is the Telnet attempt successful? Why or why not?

____

d. From PC-C on the R3 internal LAN, Telnet to R2 at IP address **10.2.2.2** and use password **ciscovtypass**.

e. With the Telnet session open from PC-C to R2, issue the command **`show policy-map type inspect zone-pair session`** on R3. Continue pressing **Enter** until you see an Inspect Established session section toward the end.

Step 4: Save the running configuration to the startup configuration.

Task 10: Configure Intrusion Prevention System (IPS) on R1 Using Cisco IOS (Chapter 5)

Step 1: (Optional) Install the TFTP server on PC-A.

If a TFTP server is not currently installed on PC-A, download Tftpd32 from http://tftpd32.jounin.net and install it on your desktop. If it is already installed, go to Step 2.

Step 2: Prepare the router and TFTP server.

To configure Cisco IOS IPS 5.x, the IOS IPS signature package file and public crypto key files must be available on PC-A. Check with your instructor if these files are not on the PC. These files can be downloaded from Cisco.com with a valid user account that has proper authorization.

a. Verify that the IOS-S*xxx*-CLI.pkg signature package file is in a TFTP folder. The *xxx* is the version number and varies depending on which file was downloaded.

b. Verify that the realm-cisco.pub.key.txt file is available and note its location on PC-A. This is the public crypto key used by IOS IPS.

c. Verify or create the IPS directory in router flash on R1. From the R1 CLI, display the content of flash memory using the **`show flash`** command. Check whether the ipsdir directory exists and if it has files in it.

d. If the **ipsdir** directory is not listed, create it:

```
R1# mkdir ipsdir
Create directory filename [ipsdir]? Press Enter
Created dir flash:ipsdir
```

e. If the ipsdir directory exists and the signature files are in it, you must remove the files to perform this part of the lab. Switch to the ipsdir directory and verify that you are in the directory. Remove the files from the directory, and then return to the flash root directory when you have finished.

```
R1# cd ipsdir

R1# pwd
flash:/ipsdir/

R1# delete R1*
Delete filename [/ipsdir/R1*]?
Delete flash:/ipsdir/R1-sigdef-typedef.xml? [confirm]
Delete flash:/ipsdir/R1-sigdef-category.xml? [confirm]
Delete flash:/ipsdir/R1-sigdef-default.xml? [confirm]
Delete flash:/ipsdir/R1-sigdef-delta.xml? [confirm]
Delete flash:/ipsdir/R1-seap-delta.xml? [confirm]
Delete flash:/ipsdir/R1-seap-typedef.xml? [confirm]

R1# cd flash:/
R1# pwd
flash:/
```

Step 3: Open the IPS crypto key file and copy the contents to the router.

On PC-A, locate the crypto key file named realm-cisco.pub.key.txt and open it using Notepad or another text editor. On R1, enter global config mode, copy the contents of the file, and paste the contents to the router.

Step 4: Create an IPS rule.

On R1, create an IPS rule named **iosips**. This rule is used later on an interface to enable IPS.

Step 5: Configure the IPS signature storage location in router flash memory.

Specify the location **flash:ipsdir** where the signature files will be stored.

Step 6: Configure Cisco IOS IPS to use a predefined signature category.

Retire all signatures in the "all" category, and then unretire the **ios_ips basic** category.

Step 7: Apply the IPS rule to interfaces S0/0/0 and Fa0/1.

a. Apply the **iosips** rule that you created on the **S0/0/0** interface in the **inbound** direction.

b. Apply the IPS rule to the R1 **Fa0/1** interface in the **inbound** direction.

Step 8: Verify the IOS IPS signature package location and TFTP server setup.

a. Verify connectivity between R1 and PC-A, the TFTP server.

b. Verify that the PC has the IPS signature package file in a directory on the TFTP server. This file is typically named IOS-S*xxx*-CLI.pkg, where *xxx* is the signature file version.

Note: Use the newest signature file available if the router memory can support it. If a signature file is not present, contact your instructor before continuing.

c. Start the TFTP server and set the default directory to the one that contains the IPS signature package.

Step 9: Copy the signature package from the TFTP server to the router.

a. Use the **copy tftp** command to retrieve the signature file. Be sure to use the **idconf** keyword at the end of the **copy** command.

Note: Immediately after the signature package is loaded to the router, signature compiling begins. Allow time for this process to complete. It can take several minutes.

b. Display the contents of the ipsdir directory created earlier.

c. Use the **show ip ips all** command to see an IPS configuration status summary. To which interfaces and in which direction is the iosips rule applied? ______________________________

Step 10: Save the running configuration to the startup configuration.

Task 11: Configure IPS on R3 Using CCP (Chapter 5)

Step 1: (Optional) Install the TFTP server on PC-C.

If a TFTP server is not currently installed on PC-C, download Tftpd32 from http://tftpd32.jounin.net and install it on your desktop. If it is already installed, go to Step 2.

Step 2: Prepare the router and TFTP server.

To configure Cisco IOS IPS 5.x, the IOS IPS signature package file and public crypto key files must be available on PC-C. Check with your instructor if these files are not on the PC. These files can be downloaded from Cisco.com with a valid user account that has proper authorization.

a. Verify that the IOS-S*xxx*-CLI.pkg signature package file is in a TFTP folder. The *xxx* is the version number and varies depending on which file was downloaded.

Note: Use the newest signature file available if the router memory can support it. If a signature file is not present, contact your instructor before continuing.

b. Verify that the realm-cisco.pub.key.txt file is available and note its location on PC-C. This is the public crypto key used by Cisco IOS IPS.

c. Verify or create the IPS directory in router flash on R1. From the R1 CLI, display the content of flash memory and check to see whether the ipsdir directory exists.

d. If the **ipsdir** directory is not listed, create it in privileged EXEC mode.

Step 3: Verify the IOS IPS signature package and TFTP server setup.

a. Verify connectivity between R3 and PC-C, the TFTP server, using the **ping** command.

b. Verify that the PC has the IPS signature package file in a directory on the TFTP server. This file is typically named IOS-S*xxx*-CLI.pkg, where *xxx* is the signature file version number.

Note: If this file is not present, contact your instructor before continuing.

c. Start Tftpd32 or another TFTP server and set the default directory to the one with the IPS signature package in it. Take note of the filename for use in the next step.

Step 4: Configure R3 to allow CCP Access and Discovery.

a. Run the CCP application on PC-C. In the Select/Manage Community window, input R3 IP address **192.168.3.1** in the first IP Address/Hostname field. Enter **admin** in the Username field, and **cisco12345** in the Password field. Click the **OK** button.

b. At the CCP Dashboard, click the **Discovery** button to discover and connect to R3. If the discovery process fails, use the **Discover Details** button to determine the problem to resolve the issue.

Step 5: Use the CCP IPS Wizard to configure IPS.

a. Click the **Configure** button at the top of the CCP screen and then choose **Security > Intrusion Prevention > Create IPS**. Click the **Launch IPS Rule Wizard** button to begin the IPS configuration. If prompted about SDEE notification, click **OK**. Click **Next** at the welcome screen.

b. Apply the IPS rule in the inbound direction for FastEthernet0/1 and Serial0/0/1. Click **Next**.

c. In the Signature File and Public Key window, specify the signature file with a URL and use TFTP to retrieve the file from PC-C. Enter the IP address of the PC-C TFTP server and the filename. Click **OK**.

d. In the Signature File and Public Key window, enter the name of the public key file **realm-cisco.pub**.

e. Open the public key file and copy the text that is between the phrase *key-string* and the word *quit*" Paste the text into the Key field in the Configure Public Key section. Click **Next**.

f. In the Config Location and Category window, specify **flash:/ipsdir** as the location to store the signature information. Click **OK**.

g. In the Choose Category field of the Config Location and Category window, choose **basic**.

h. Click **Next** to display the Summary window, and click **Finish** and deliver the commands to the router. Click **OK**.

Note: Allow the signature configuration process to complete. This can take several minutes.

Step 6: (Optional) Verify IPS functionality with CCP Monitor and SuperScan.

a. If SuperScan is not on PC-C, download the SuperScan 4.0 tool from the Scanning Tools group at http://www.foundstone.com.

b. Start SuperScan on PC-C. Display the **Host and Service Discovery** tab. Check the **Timestamp Request** check box, and uncheck the **Echo Request** check box. Scroll the UDP and TCP port selection lists and notice the range of ports that will be scanned.

c. Display the **Scan** tab and enter the IP address of R2 S0/0/1 (**10.2.2.2**) in the Hostname/IP field.

Note: You can also specify an address range, such as 10.1.1.1 to 10.1.1.254, by entering an address in the Start IP and End IP fields. The program scans all hosts with addresses in the range specified.

d. Click the button with the blue arrow in the lower-left corner of the screen to start the scan.

Step 7: Check the results with CCP logging.

a. Enter the logging buffered command in config mode on R3.

b. From CCP, choose **Monitor > Router > Logging**.

c. Click the **Update** button. You will see that Cisco IOS IPS has been logging the port scans generated by SuperScan.

What syslog messages did you see?

____

____

Step 8: Save the running configuration to the startup configuration.

Task 12: Back Up and Secure the Cisco Router IOS Image and Configuration Files (Chapter 2)

Note: The procedures described here can also be used to back up the switch IOS images and configuration files.

Step 1: Back up the IOS Image from R1 and R3 to a TFTP server.

a. Create a directory for the IOS images on PC-A and PC-C.

b. Start the TFTP server on PC-A and choose the IOS images directory as the default directory.

c. Copy the R1 IOS image to the PC-A TFTP server as a backup in case the current image becomes corrupted.

d. Start the TFTP server on PC-C and choose the IOS images directory as the default directory.

e. Copy the R3 IOS image to the TFTP server as a backup in case the current image becomes corrupted.

Note: The IOS image on R1 should be the same as the one for R3, so a single backup could suffice for both routers.

Step 2: Back up the configuration files from R1 and R3 to a TFTP server.

a. Create a directory for configurations on PC-A and PC-C.

b. Start the TFTP server on PC-A and choose the Configs directory as the default directory.

c. Copy the R1 startup-config file to the PC-A TFTP server as a backup.

Note: If changes have been made to the running config, you can save them to the startup config before backing up the config file.

d. Start the TFTP server on PC-C and choose the Configs directory as the default directory.

e. Copy the R3 startup-config file to the PC-C TFTP server as a backup.

Step 3: Secure the Cisco IOS image and archive a copy of the running configuration for R1 and R3.

a. Secure the IOS boot image to enable Cisco IOS image resilience and hide the file from **`dir`** and **`show`** commands.

b. Secure the router running configuration and securely archive it in persistent storage (flash).

Step 4: Verify that the image and configuration are secured.

Display the status of configuration resilience and the primary bootset filename.

Part 4: Secure Network Switches (Chapter 6)

Task 1: Configure Passwords and a Login Banner on All Switches (Chapter 2)

Step 1: Configure the enable secret password.

Use an enable secret password of **cisco12345**.

Step 2: Encrypt a plain-text password.

Step 3: Configure the console line.

Configure a console password of **ciscoconpass** and enable login. Set the exec-timeout to log out after 5 minutes of inactivity. Prevent console messages from interrupting command entry.

Note: The vty lines for the switches are configured for SSH in Task 2.

Step 4: Configure a login warning banner.

Configure a warning to unauthorized users with a message-of-the-day (MOTD) banner that says "Unauthorized access strictly prohibited and prosecuted to the full extent of the law".

Step 5: Disable HTTP access.

HTTP access to the switch is enabled by default. To prevent HTTP access, disable the HTTP server and HTTP secure server.

Task 2: Configure Switches as NTP Clients (Chapter 2)

Note: Router R2 is the master NTP server. All other routers and switches learn their time from it, either directly or indirectly.

Step 1: Configure S1, S2, and S3 to become NTP clients of R2.

Step 2: Verify that S1 has made an association with R2.

Task 3: Configure Syslog Support on All Switches (Chapter 2)

Step 1: (Optional) Install the syslog server on PC-A and PC-C.

If a syslog server is not currently installed on the host, download the latest version of Kiwi from http://www.kiwisyslog.com or Tftpd32 from http://tftpd32.jounin.net and install it on your desktop. If it is already installed, go to Step 2.

Step 2: Configure S1 to log messages to the PC-A syslog server.

a. Verify that you have connectivity between S1 and host PC-A by pinging the S1 VLAN 1 interface IP address 192.168.1.11 from PC-A. If the pings are not successful, troubleshoot as necessary before continuing.

b. Configure the syslog service on the switch to send syslog messages to the syslog server.

Task 4: Configure the SSH Server on All Switches (Chapter 2)

Step 1: Configure a domain name.

Enter global configuration mode and set the domain name.

Step 2: Configure a privileged user for login from the SSH client.

Use the **`username`** command to create the user ID with the highest possible privilege level and a secret password.

Step 3: Configure the incoming vty lines.

Configure vty access on lines 0 through 15. Specify that a privilege level of 15 is required to access the vty lines, use the local user accounts for mandatory login and validation, and accept only SSH connections.

Step 4: Generate the RSA encryption key pair.

The switch uses the RSA key pair for authentication and encryption of transmitted SSH data. Configure the RSA keys with 1024 for the number of modulus bits.

Step 5: Verify SSH connectivity to S1 from the SSH client PC-A.

a. If the SSH client is not already installed, download either TeraTerm or PuTTY.

b. Launch the client, enter the VLAN 1 IP address, and enter the **Admin01** username and password.

c. Close the PuTTY SSH session window with the **`exit`** or **`quit`** command.

d. Try to open a Telnet session to switch S1 from PC-A. Are you able to open the Telnet session? Why or why not? ____

Task 5: Configure Authentication Using AAA and RADIUS on All Switches (Chapter 3)

Step 1: (Optional) Download and configure the WinRadius software.

a. If WinRadius is not currently installed on PC-A and PC-C, download the latest version from http://www.suggestsoft.com/soft/itconsult2000/winradius/, http://winradius.soft32.com, http://www.brothersoft.com/winradius-20914.html. There is no installation setup. The extracted WinRadius.exe file is executable.

b. Start the WinRadius.exe application. If the application is being started for the first time, follow the instructions to configure the WinRadius server database.

Step 2: Configure users and passwords on the WinRadius server.

Note: If the RADIUS user accounts were previously configured, you can skip this step. If the RADIUS server has been shut down and restarted, you must re-create the user accounts.

a. Add username **RadAdmin** with a password of **RadAdminpa55**.

b. Add username **RadUser** with a password of **RadUserpa55**.

Step 3: Enable AAA.

Create a AAA new model to enable AAA.

Step 4: Configure the default login authentication list.

Configure the list to first use RADIUS for the authentication service and then local, to allow access based on the local switch database if a RADIUS server cannot be reached.

Step 5: Verify connectivity between S1 and the PC-A RADIUS server.

Ping from S1 to PC-A.

If the pings are not successful, troubleshoot the PC and switch configuration before continuing.

Step 6: Specify a RADIUS server.

Configure the switch to access the RADIUS server at PC-A. Specify **auth-port 1812** and **acct-port 1813**, along with the IP address and secret key of WinRadius for the RADIUS server.

Step 7: Test the RADIUS configuration by logging in to the console on S1.

a. Exit to the initial switch screen that displays `S1 con0 is now available. Press RETURN to get started.`

b. Log in with the username **RadAdmin** and password **RadAdminpa55**. Can you log in with minimal delay? ____________________

Note: If you exit the WinRadius server and restart it, you must re-create the user accounts from Step 2.

Step 8: Test your configuration by connecting to S1 with SSH.

a. Clear the log on the WinRadius server by choosing **Log > Clear**.

b. Use PuTTY or another terminal emulation client to open an SSH session from PC-A to S1.

c. At the login prompt, enter the username **RadAdmin** defined on the RADIUS server and a password of **RadAdminpa55**.

   Are you able to log in to S1? ______

Task 6: Secure Trunk Ports (Chapter 6)

Step 1: Configure trunk ports on S1 and S2.

a. Configure port Fa0/1 on S1 as a trunk port.

b. Configure port Fa0/1 on S2 as a trunk port.

c. Verify that S1 port Fa0/1 is in trunking mode.

Step 2: Change the native VLAN for the trunk ports on S1 and S2.

Changing the native VLAN for trunk ports to an unused VLAN helps prevent VLAN hopping attacks.

a. Set the native VLAN on the S1 Fa0/1 trunk interface to an unused **VLAN 99**.

b. Set the native VLAN on the S2 Fa0/1 trunk interface to **VLAN 99**.

Step 3: Prevent the use of DTP on S1 and S2.

Set the trunk ports on S1 and S2 so that they do not negotiate by turning off the generation of DTP frames.

Step 4: Verify the trunking configuration on port Fa0/1.

Step 5: Enable storm control for broadcasts.

Enable storm control for broadcasts on the trunk port `with a 50 percent rising suppression level` using the **`storm-control broadcast`** command.

Step 6: Verify the configuration with the `show run` command.

Task 7: Secure Access Ports (Chapter 6)

By manipulating the Spanning Tree Protocol (STP) root bridge parameters, network attackers hope to spoof his or her system as the root bridge in the topology. Alternatively, they can spoof a rogue switch that they added to the network as the root bridge. If a port that is configured with PortFast receives a bridge protocol data unit (BPDU), STP can put the port into the blocking state by using a feature called BPDU guard.

Step 1: Disable trunking on S1, S2, and S3 access ports.

a. On S1, configure ports Fa0/5 and F0/6 as access mode only.

b. On S2, configure Fa0/18 as access mode only.

c. On S3, configure ports Fa0/5 and Fa0/18 as access mode only.

Task 8: Protect Against STP Attacks (Chapter 6)

The topology has only two switches and no redundant paths, but STP is still active. In this step, you enable some switch security features that can help reduce the possibility of an attacker manipulating switches via STP-related methods.

Step 1: Enable PortFast on S1, S2, and S3 access ports.

PortFast is configured on access ports that connect to a single workstation or server to enable them to become active more quickly.

a. Enable PortFast on the S1 Fa0/5 and Fa0/6 access ports.

b. Enable PortFast on the S2 Fa0/18 access port.

c. Enable PortFast on the S3 Fa0/5 and Fa0/18 access port.

Step 2: Enable BPDU guard on the S1, S2, and S3 access ports.

BPDU guard is a feature that can help prevent rogue switches and spoofing on access ports. Enable BPDU guard on the switch ports previously configured as access only.

Task 9: Configure Port Security and Disable Unused Ports (Chapter 6)

Step 1: Configure basic port security.

Shut down all end-user access ports that are in use and enable basic default port security. This sets the maximum MAC addresses to 1 and the violation action to shutdown. Reissue the port security command using the **`sticky`** option to allow the secure MAC address that is dynamically learned on a port, to be added to the switch running configuration. Reenable each access port to which port security was applied.

Step 2: Disable unused ports on S1 and S2.

As a further security measure, disable any ports not being used on the switch.

a. Ports Fa0/1, Fa0/5, and Fa0/6 are used on switch S1. Shut down the remaining Fast Ethernet ports and the two Gigabit Ethernet ports.

b. Ports Fa01/ and Fa0/18 are used on switch S2. Shut down the remaining Fast Ethernet ports and the two Gigabit Ethernet ports.

c. Ports Fa0/5 and Fa0/18 are used on switch S3. Shut down the remaining Fast Ethernet ports and the two Gigabit Ethernet ports.

Step 3: (Optional) Move active ports to another VLAN and change the management VLAN.

As a further security measure, you can move all active end-user and router ports to a VLAN other than the default VLAN 1 on the switches. You can also change the management VLAN from VLAN 1 to another VLAN, but you must have at least one end-user host port in that VLAN to manage the switch remotely using Telnet, SSH, or HTTP.

Note: The following configuration allows you to manage either switch remotely from either PC-A or PC-B. You can only access the switches remotely using SSH, because Telnet and HTTP have been disabled. The procedure for switch S3 is also shown.

a. Configure a new VLAN for users on each switch using the following commands.

Note: You could also configure VLAN 10 on switch S3, but it would not communicate with VLAN 10 on switches S1 and S2.

b. Add the current active access (non-trunk) ports to the new VLAN.

c. On each switch, remove the management VLAN IP address from VLAN 1 (configured in Part 1 of the lab) and shut it down.

d. Configure a management VLAN IP address for the VLAN 10 interface on S1 and S2 and enable it.

e. Configure a management VLAN IP address for the VLAN 30 interface on S3 and enable it.

Step 4: Save the running-config to the startup-config.

Part 5: Configuring VPN Remote Access

In Part 5, configure a remote access IPsec VPN. R3 is configured via CCP as an Easy VPN Server, and the Cisco VPN Client is configured on PC-A. The PC-A host simulates an employee connecting from home or a remote office over the Internet. Router R2 simulates an Internet ISP router.

Task 1: Use the CCP VPN Wizard to Configure the Easy VPN Server (Chapter 8)

Step 1: Configure R3 to allow CCP Access and Discovery.

a. Enable the HTTP server on R3.

   Or enable the HTTP secure server to connect securely.

b. Create an admin account on R3 with privilege level 15 for use with AAA and CCP.

c. Have CCP use the local database to authenticate web sessions.

d. Run the CCP application on PC-C. In the Select/Manage Community window, input the R3 IP address **192.168.3.1** in the first IP Address/Hostname field. Enter **admin** in the Username field and **cisco12345** in the Password field. Click the **OK** button.

e. At the CCP Dashboard, click the **Discovery** button to discover and connect to R3. If the discovery process fails, click the **Discover Details** button to determine the problem to resolve the issue.

Step 2: Launch the Easy VPN Server Wizard.

Click the **Configure** button at the top of the CCP home screen and choose **Security > VPN > Easy VPN Server**, and then click **Launch Easy VPN Server Wizard**. Click **Next** on the Welcome Screen to continue.

Note: The Easy VPN Server Wizard checks the router configuration to see whether AAA is enabled. If AAA is not enabled, the Enable AAA window displays. AAA was enabled on the router previously.

Step 3: Configure the virtual tunnel interface and authentication.

a. Choose the interface on which the client connections terminate. Click the **Unnumbered To** radio button, and choose the **Serial0/0/1** interface from the drop down menu.

b. Choose **Pre-shared Keys** for the authentication type and click **Next** to continue.

Step 4: Select an IKE proposal.

In the Internet Key Exchange (IKE) Proposals window, the default IKE proposal is used for R3. Click **Next** to accept the default IKE policy.

Step 5: Select the transform set.

In the Transform Sets window, the default CCP transform set is used. Click **Next** to accept the default transform set.

Step 6: Specify the group authorization and group policy lookup.

a. In the Group Authorization and Group Policy Lookup window, choose the **Local** option.

b. Click **Next** to create a new AAA method list for group policy lookup that uses the local router database.

Step 7: Configure user authentication (XAuth).

a. In the User Authentication (XAuth) window, check the **Enable User Authentication** check box and choose **Local Only**.

b. Click the **Add User Credentials** button. In the User Accounts window, you can view currently defined local users or add new users. Which user account is currently defined locally? ____________________

c. Add the new user **VPNUser1** with a password of **VPNUser1pa55** and click **OK**.

d. Click **OK** to close the User Accounts window. Click **Next**.

Step 8: Specify group authorization and user group policies.

In the Group Authorization and User Group Policies window, you must create at least one group policy for the VPN server.

a. Click **Add** to create a group policy.

b. In the Add Group Policy window, enter **VPN-Access** in the **Name of This Group** field. Enter a new pre-shared key of **cisco12345**, and then reenter it. Leave the **Pool Information** box checked. Enter a starting address of **192.168.3.200**, an ending address of **192.168.3.250**, and a subnet mask of **255.255.255.0**.

c. Click **OK** to accept the entries.

d. A CCP warning message displays indicating that the IP address pool and the Fast Ethernet 0/1 address are in the same subnet. Click **Yes** to continue.

e. Check the **Configure Idle Timer** check box and enter 1 hour, 0 minutes, and 0 seconds.

f. When the Cisco Tunneling Control Protocol (cTCP) window displays, do not enable cTCP. Click **OK** if a firewall warning message displays. Click **Next** to continue.

g. When the Easy VPN Server Passthrough Configuration window displays, make sure that the **Action Modify** check box is checked. This option allows CCP to modify the firewall on S0/0/1 to allow IPsec VPN traffic to reach the internal LAN.

Step 9: Review the configuration summary and deliver the commands.

Scroll through the commands that CCP will send to the router. Click **Finish**.

Step 10: Test the VPN Server

You are returned to the main VPN window with the Edit VPN Server tab displayed. Click the **Test VPN Server** button in the lower-right corner of the screen. In the VPN Troubleshooting window, click the **Start** button. Click **Close** to exit the VPN Troubleshooting window.

Task 2: Use the Cisco VPN Client to Test the Remote Access VPN (Chapter 8)

Step 1: (Optional) Install the Cisco VPN Client.

If the Cisco VPN Client software is not already installed on host PC-A, install it now. If you do not have the Cisco VPN Client software or are unsure of the process, contact your instructor.

Step 2: Configure PC-A as a VPN client to access the R3 VPN server

a. Start the Cisco VPN Client. Select **Connection Entries > New** or click the **New** icon with the plus sign (+) on it.

b. Enter the following information to define the new connection entry. Click **Save** when you are finished.

   Connection Entry: **VPN-Corp**

   Description: **Connection to R3 corporate network**

Host: **10.2.2.1** (IP address of the R3 S0/0/1 interface)

Group Authentication Name: **VPN-Access** (specifies the address pool configured in Task 2)

Password: **cisco12345** (pre-shared key configured in Task 2)

Confirm Password: **cisco12345**

Note: The group authentication name and password are case sensitive and must match the ones created on the VPN Server.

Step 3: Test access from PC-A without a VPN connection.

Note: In the previous step, you created a VPN connection entry on the VPN client computer PC-A, but have not activated it yet.

Open a command prompt on PC-A and ping the PC-C IP address at 192.168.3.3 on the R3 LAN. Are the pings successful? Why or why not? ____

Step 4: Establish a VPN connection and log in.

a. Choose the newly created connection **VPN-Corp** and click the **Connect** icon. You can also double-click the connection entry.

b. When the VPN Client User Authentication dialog box displays, enter the username **VPNUser1** created previously on the VPN router R3, and enter the password of **VPNUser1pa55**. Click **OK** to continue. The VPN Client window minimizes to a lock icon in the tools tray of the taskbar. When the lock is closed, the VPN tunnel is up. When it is open, the VPN connection is down.

Step 5: Test access from the client with the VPN connection.

With the VPN connection from computer PC-A to router R3 activated, open a command prompt on PC-A and ping the R3 default gateway at 192.168.3.1. Then ping the PC-C IP address at 192.168.3.3 on the R3 LAN. Are the pings successful? Why or why not?

____

____

Router Interface Summary Table

Router Model	Ethernet Interface 1	Ethernet Interface 2	Serial Interface 1	Serial Interface 2
1800	Fast Ethernet 0/0 (Fa0/0)	Fast Ethernet 0/1 (Fa0/1)	Serial 0/0/0 (S0/0/0)	Serial 0/0/1 (S0/0/1)
1900	Gigabit Ethernet 0/0 (G0/0)	Gigabit Ethernet 0/1 (G0/1)	Serial 0/0/0 (S0/0/0)	Serial 0/0/1 (S0/0/1)
2800	Fast Ethernet 0/0 (Fa0/0)	Fast Ethernet 0/1 (Fa0/1)	Serial 0/0/0 (S0/0/0)	Serial 0/0/1 (S0/0/1)
2900	Gigabit Ethernet 0/0 (G0/0)	Gigabit Ethernet 0/1 (G0/1)	Serial 0/0/0 (S0/0/0)	Serial 0/0/1 (S0/0/1)

Note: To find out how the router is configured, look at the interfaces to identify the type of router and how many interfaces the router has. There is no way to effectively list all the combinations of configurations for each router class. This table includes identifiers for the possible combinations of Ethernet and serial interfaces in the device. The table does not include any other type of interface, even though a specific router may contain one. An example of this might be an ISDN BRI interface. The string in parentheses is the legal abbreviation that can be used in Cisco IOS commands to represent the interface.

Chapter 10 Lab A: Configuring ASA Basic Settings and Firewall Using CLI

Topology

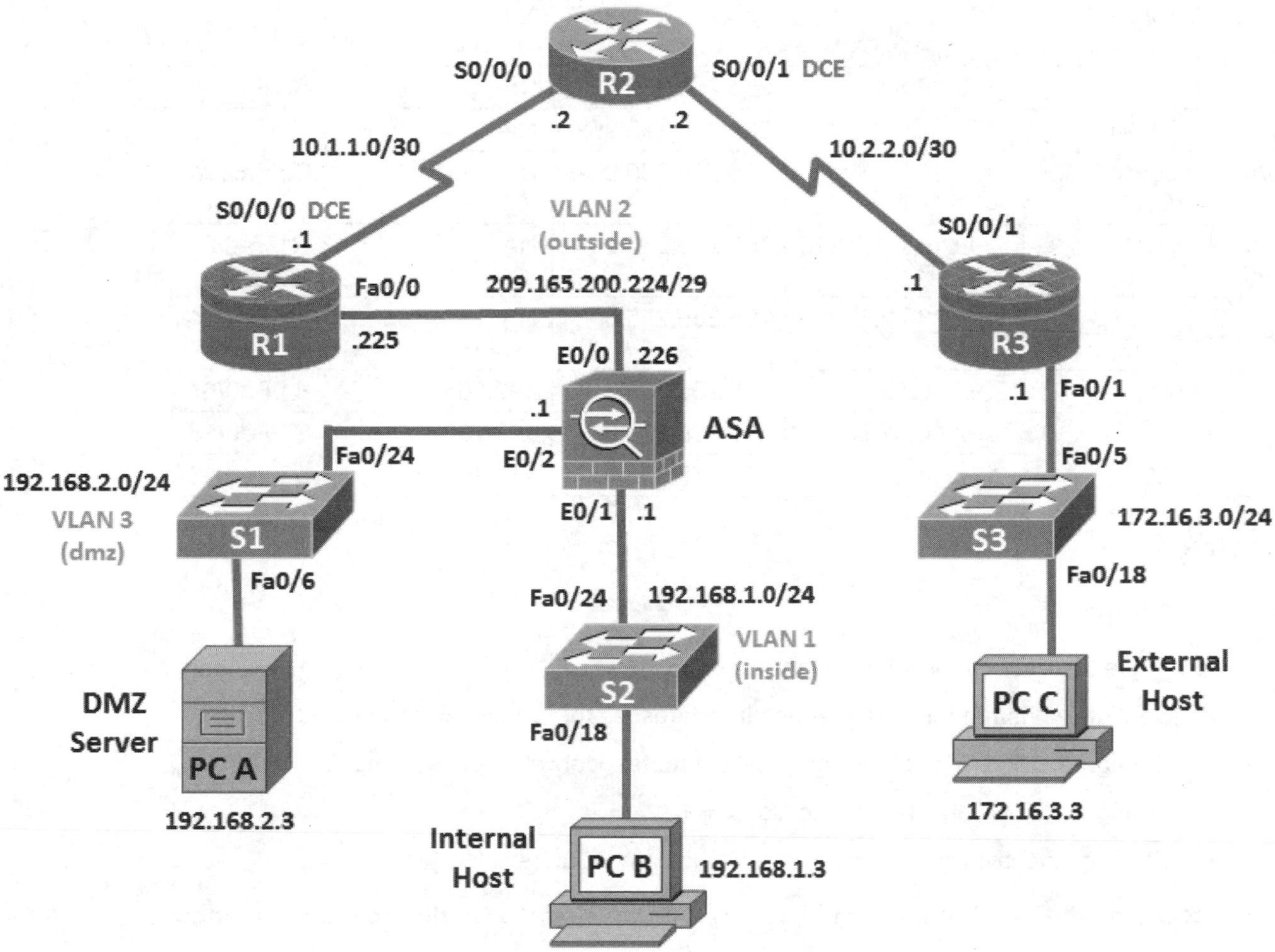

Note: ISR G2 devices have Gigabit Ethernet interfaces rather than FastEthernet interfaces.

IP Addressing Table

Device	Interface	IP Address	Subnet Mask	Default Gateway	Switch Port
R1	Fa0/0	209.165.200.225	255.255.255.248	N/A	ASA E0/0
	S0/0/0 (DCE)	10.1.1.1	255.255.255.252	N/A	N/A
R2	S0/0/0	10.1.1.2	255.255.255.252	N/A	N/A
	S0/0/1 (DCE)	10.2.2.2	255.255.255.252	N/A	N/A
R3	Fa0/1	172.16.3.1	255.255.255.0	N/A	S3 Fa0/5
	S0/0/1	10.2.2.1	255.255.255.252	N/A	N/A
ASA	VLAN 1 (E0/1)	192.168.1.1	255.255.255.0	NA	S2 Fa0/24
ASA	VLAN 2 (E0/0)	209.165.200.226	255.255.255.248	NA	R1 Fa0/0
ASA	VLAN 3 (E0/2)	192.168.2.1	255.255.255.0	NA	S1 Fa0/24
PC-A	NIC	192.168.2.3	255.255.255.0	192.168.2.1	S1 Fa0/6
PC-B	NIC	192.168.1.3	255.255.255.0	192.168.1.1	S2 Fa0/18
PC-C	NIC	172.16.3.3	255.255.255.0	172.16.3.1	S3 Fa0/18

Objectives

Part 1: Lab Setup

- Cable the network as shown in the topology.
- Configure hostnames and interface IP addresses for routers, switches, and PCs.
- Configure static routing, including default routes, between R1, R2, and R3.
- Configure HTTP and Telnet access for R1.
- Verify connectivity between hosts, switches, and routers.

Part 2: Accessing the ASA Console and Using CLI Setup Mode to Configure Basic Settings

- Access the ASA console and view hardware, software, and configuration settings.
- Clear previous configuration settings.
- Use CLI Setup mode to configure basic settings (hostname, passwords, clock, and so on).

Part 3: Configuring Basic ASA Settings and Interface Security Levels Using CLI

- Configure the hostname and domain name.
- Configure the login and enable passwords.
- Set the date and time.
- Configure the inside and outside interfaces.
- Test connectivity to the ASA.
- Configure remote management with Telnet.

- Configure HTTPS access to the ASA for ASDM.

Part 4: Configuring Routing, Address Translation, and Inspection Policy Using CLI

- Configure a static default route for the ASA.
- Configure port address translation (PAT) for the inside network.
- Modify the MPF application inspection policy.

Part 5: Configuring DHCP, AAA, and SSH

- Configure the ASA as a DHCP server/client.
- Configure Local AAA user authentication.
- Configure remote management with SSH.

Part 6: Configuring a DMZ, Static NAT, and ACLs

- Configure static NAT for the DMZ server.
- Configure an ACL on the ASA to allow access to the DMZ for Internet users.
- Verify access to the DMZ server for external and internal users.

Background/Scenario

The Cisco Adaptive Security Appliance (ASA) is an advanced network security device that integrates a stateful firewall and VPN and other capabilities. This lab employs an ASA 5505 to create a firewall and protect an internal corporate network from external intruders while allowing internal hosts access to the Internet. The ASA creates three security interfaces: Outside, Inside, and DMZ. It provides outside users limited access to the DMZ and no access to inside resources. Inside users can access the DMZ and outside resources.

The focus of this lab is on the configuration of the ASA as a basic firewall. Other devices receive minimal configuration to support the ASA portion of the lab. This lab uses the ASA CLI, which is similar to the IOS CLI, to configure basic device and security settings.

In Part 1 of the lab, you configure the topology and non-ASA devices. In Parts 2 through 4, you configure basic ASA settings and the firewall between the inside and outside networks. In Part 5, you configure the ASA for additional services such as Dynamic Host Configuration Protocol (DHCP); authentication, authorization, and accounting (AAA); and Secure Shell (SSH). In Part 6, you configure a demilitarized zone (DMZ) on the ASA and provide access to a server in the DMZ.

Your company has one location connected to an Internet service provider (ISP). Router R1 represents a customer premise equipment (CPE) device managed by the ISP. Router R2 represents an intermediate Internet router. Router R3 represents an ISP that connects an administrator from a network management company, who has been hired to manage your network remotely. The ASA is an edge CPE security device that connects the internal corporate network and DMZ to the ISP while providing NAT and DHCP services to inside hosts. The ASA is configured for management by an administrator on the internal network as well as by the remote administrator. Layer 3 VLAN interfaces provide access to the three areas created in the lab: inside, outside, and DMZ. The ISP has assigned the public IP address space of 209.165.200.224/29, which will be used for address translation on the ASA.

Note: The routers used with this lab are Cisco 1841 with Cisco IOS Software Release 12.4(20)T (advanced IP image). The switches are Cisco WS-C2960-24TT-L with Cisco IOS Software Release 12.2(46)SE (C2960-LANBASEK9-M image). Other routers, switches, and Cisco IOS versions can be used. However, results and output may vary.

The ASA used with this lab is a Cisco model 5505 with an eight-port integrated switch, running OS version 8.4(2) and ASDM version 6.4(5) and comes with a Base license that allows a maximum of three VLANs.

Note: Make sure that the routers and switches have been erased and have no startup configurations.

Required Resources

- 3 routers (Cisco 1841 with Cisco IOS Software Release 12.4(20)T1 or comparable)
- 3 switches (Cisco 2960 or comparable)
- 1 ASA 5505 (OS Version 8.4(2) and ASDM Version 6.4(5) and Base license or comparable)
- PC-A: Windows XP, Vista, or Windows 7 with CCP, PuTTy SSH client
- PC-B: Windows XP, Vista, or Windows 7 with PuTTy SSH client (ASDM optional)
- PC-C: Windows XP, Vista, or Windows 7 with CCP, PuTTy SSH client
- Serial and Ethernet cables as shown in the topology
- Rollover cables to configure the routers and ASA via the console

Part 1: Basic Router/Switch/PC Configuration

In Part 1 of this lab, you set up the network topology and configure basic settings on the routers, such as interface IP addresses and static routing.

Note: Do not configure any ASA settings at this time.

Step 1: Cable the network and clear previous device settings.

Attach the devices that are shown in the topology diagram and cable as necessary. Make sure that the routers and switches have been erased and have no startup configurations.

Step 2: Configure basic settings for routers and switches.

a. Configure hostnames as shown in the topology for each router.

b. Configure router interface IP addresses as shown in the IP addressing table.

c. Configure a clock rate for routers with a DCE serial cable attached to their serial interface. Router R1 is shown here as an example.

```
R1(config)# interface S0/0/0
R1(config-if)# clock rate 64000
```

d. Configure the hostname for the switches. Other than the hostname, the switches can be left in their default configuration state. Configuring the VLAN management IP address for the switches is optional.

Step 3: Configure static routing on the routers.

a. Configure a static default route from R1 to R2 and from R3 to R2:

```
R1(config)# ip route 0.0.0.0 0.0.0.0 Serial0/0/0
R3(config)# ip route 0.0.0.0 0.0.0.0 Serial0/0/1
```

b. Configure a static route from R2 to the R1 Fa0/0 subnet (connected to ASA interface E0/0) and a static route from R2 to the R3 LAN:

```
R2(config)# ip route 209.165.200.224 255.255.255.248 Serial0/0/0
R2(config)# ip route 172.16.3.0 255.255.255.0 Serial0/0/1
```

Step 4: Enable the HTTP server on R1 and set the enable and vty passwords.

a. Enable HTTP access to R1 using the **ip http server** command in global config mode. Also set the console and VTY passwords to **cisco**. This provides web and Telnet targets for testing later in the lab.

```
R1(config)# ip http server
R1(config)# enable password class

R1(config)# line vty 0 4
R1(config-line)# password cisco
R1(config-line)# login

R1(config)# line con 0
R1(config-line)# password cisco
R1(config-line)# login
```

b. On routers R2 and R3, set the same enable, console and vty passwords as with R1

Step 5: Configure PC host IP settings.

Configure a static IP address, subnet mask, and default gateway for PC-A, PC-B, and PC-C as shown in the IP Addressing Table.

Step 6: Verify connectivity.

Because the ASA is the focal point for the network zones and it has not yet been configured, there will be no connectivity between devices that are connected to it. However, PC-C should be able to ping the R1 interface. From PC-C, ping the R1 Fa0/0 IP address (209.165.200.225). If these pings are not successful, troubleshoot the basic device configurations before continuing.

Note: If you can ping from PC-C to R1 Fa0/0 and S0/0/0 you have demonstrated that static routing is configured and functioning correctly.

Step 7: Save the basic running configuration for each router and switch.

Part 2: Accessing the ASA Console and Using Setup to Configure Basic Settings

In Part 2 of this lab, you access the ASA via the console and use various **show** commands to determine hardware, software, and configuration settings. You clear the current configuration and use the CLI interactive Setup utility to configure basic ASA settings.

Note: Do not configure any ASA settings at this time.

Step 1: Access the ASA Console.

a. Accessing the ASA via the console port is the same as with a Cisco router or switch. Connect to the ASA console port with a rollover cable.

b. Use a terminal emulation program such as TeraTerm or HyperTerminal to access the CLI. Then use the serial port settings of 9600 baud, 8 data bits, no parity, 1 stop bit, and no flow control.

c. Enter privileged mode with the **enable** command and password (if set). By default, the password is blank, so you can just press **Enter**. If the password has been changed to that specified in this lab, enter the word **class**. The default ASA hostname and prompt is ciscoasa>.

```
ciscoasa> enable
Password: class (or press Enter if none set)
```

Step 2: Determine the ASA version, interfaces, and license.

The ASA 5505 comes with an integrated eight-port Ethernet switch. Ports E0/0 though E0/5 are normal Fast Ethernet ports and ports E0/6 and E0/7 are Power over Ethernet (PoE) ports for use with PoE devices such as IP phones or network cameras.

a. Use the **show version** command to determine various aspects of this ASA device:

```
ciscoasa# show version

Cisco Adaptive Security Appliance Software Version 8.4(2)
Device Manager Version 6.4(5)

Compiled on Wed 15-Jun-11 18:17 by builders
System image file is "disk0:/asa842-k8.bin"
Config file at boot was "startup-config"

ciscoasa up 23 hours 0 mins

Hardware:   ASA5505, 512 MB RAM, CPU Geode 500 MHz
Internal ATA Compact Flash, 128MB
BIOS Flash M50FW016 @ 0xfff00000, 2048KB

Encryption hardware device : Cisco ASA-5505 on-board accelerator
(revision 0x0)
                    Boot microcode        : CN1000-MC-BOOT-2.00
                    SSL/IKE microcode     : CNLite-MC-SSLm-PLUS-2.03
                    IPSec microcode       : CNlite-MC-IPSECm-MAIN-2.06
                         Number of accelerators: 1

 0: Int: Internal-Data0/0     : address is 0007.7dbf.5645, irq 11
 1: Ext: Ethernet0/0          : address is 0007.7dbf.563d, irq 255
 2: Ext: Ethernet0/1          : address is 0007.7dbf.563e, irq 255

<output omitted>
```

What software version is this ASA running? ______________________________

What is the name of the system image file and from where was it loaded?

____

The ASA can be managed using a built-in GUI known as the Adaptive Security Device Manager (ASDM). What version of ASDM is this ASA running? ______________________________

How much RAM does this ASA have? ______________________________

How much flash memory does this ASA have? ______________________________

How many Ethernet ports does this ASA have? ____________________

What type of license does this ASA have? ____________________

How many VLANs can be created with this license? ____________________

Step 3: Determine the file system and contents of flash memory.

a. Display the ASA file system using the **show file system** command to determine what prefixes are supported:

```
ciscoasa# show file system

File Systems:

     Size(b)      Free(b)       Type      Flags  Prefixes
* 128573440     55664640        disk      rw       disk0: flash:
              -             -   network   rw       tftp:
              -             -   opaque    rw       system:
              -             -   network   ro       http:
              -             -   network   ro       https:
              -             -   network   rw       ftp:
  -           -     network   rw      smb:
```

What is another name for flash:? __________

b. Display the contents of flash memory using one of these commands: **show flash, show disk0, dir flash:** or **dir disk0**:

```
ciscoasa# show flash:
--#--  --length--  -----date/time------  path
  168  25159680    Aug 29 2011 13:00:52  asa842-k8.bin
  122  0           Aug 29 2011 13:09:32  nat_ident_migrate
   13  2048        Aug 29 2011 13:02:14  coredumpinfo
   14  59          Aug 29 2011 13:02:14  coredumpinfo/coredump.cfg
  169  16280544    Aug 29 2011 13:02:58  asdm-645.bin
    3  2048        Aug 29 2011 13:04:42  log
    6  2048        Aug 29 2011 13:05:00  crypto_archive
  171  34816       Jan 01 1980 00:00:00  FSCK0000.REC
  173  36864       Jan 01 1980 00:00:00  FSCK0001.REC
  174  12998641    Aug 29 2011 13:09:22  csd_3.5.2008-k9.pkg
  175  2048        Aug 29 2011 13:09:24  sdesktop
  211  0           Aug 29 2011 13:09:24  sdesktop/data.xml
  176  6487517     Aug 29 2011 13:09:26  anyconnect-macosx-i386-
2.5.2014-k9.pkg
  177  6689498     Aug 29 2011 13:09:30  anyconnect-linux-2.5.2014-
k9.pkg
  178  4678691     Aug 29 2011 13:09:32  anyconnect-win-2.5.2014-k9.pkg
  <output omitted>
```

What is the name of the ASDM file in flash:? ______________

Step 4: Determine the current running configuration.

The ASA 5505 is commonly used as an edge security device that connects a small business or teleworker to an ISP device, such as a DSL or cable modem, for access to the Internet. The default factory configuration for the ASA 5505 includes the following:

- An inside VLAN 1 interface is configured that includes the Ethernet 0/1 through 0/7 switch ports. The VLAN 1 IP address and mask are 192.168.1.1 and 255.255.255.0.
- An outside VLAN 2 interface is configured that includes the Ethernet 0/0 switch port. By default, VLAN 2 derives its IP address from the ISP using DHCP.
- The default route is also derived from the DHCP default gateway.
- All inside IP addresses are translated when accessing the outside, using interface PAT on the VLAN 2 interface.
- By default, inside users can access the outside with an access list, and outside users are prevented from accessing the inside.
- The DHCP server is enabled on the security appliance, so a PC connecting to the VLAN 1 interface receives an address between 192.168.1.5 and 192.168.1.36 (base license), although the actual range may vary.
- The HTTP server is enabled for ASDM and is accessible to users on the 192.168.1.0/24 network.
- No console or enable passwords are required and the default hostname is **ciscoasa**.

Note: In this lab, you manually configure settings similar to those listed above, as well as some additional ones, using the ASA CLI.

a. Display the current running configuration using the **show running-config** command:

```
ciscoasa# show running-config
: Saved
:
ASA Version 8.4(2)
!
hostname ciscoasa
enable password 8Ry2YjIyt7RRXU24 encrypted
passwd 2KFQnbNIdI.2KYOU encrypted
names
!
interface Ethernet0/0
 switchport access vlan 2
!
interface Ethernet0/1
!
interface Ethernet0/2

<output omitted>
```

Note: To stop the output from a command using the CLI, press **Q**.

If you see VLANs 1 and 2 and other settings as described previously, the device is most likely configured with the default factory configuration. You may also see other security features such as a global policy that inspects selected application traffic, which the ASA inserts by default, if the original startup configuration has been erased. The actual output will vary depending on the ASA model, version, and configuration status.

b. You can restore the ASA to its factory default settings by using the command **configure factory-default**, as shown here:

```
ciscoasa# conf t
ciscoasa(config)# configure factory-default

WARNING: The boot system configuration will be cleared.
The first image found in disk0:/ will be used to boot the
```

```
system on the next reload.
Verify there is a valid image on disk0:/ or the system will
not boot.

Begin to apply factory-default configuration:
Clear all configuration
WARNING: DHCPD bindings cleared on interface 'inside', address pool
removed
Executing command: interface Ethernet 0/0
Executing command: switchport access vlan 2
Executing command: no shutdown
Executing command: exit
Executing command: interface Ethernet 0/1
Executing command: switchport access vlan 1
Executing command: no shutdown
Executing command: exit

<output omitted>
```

c. Review this output and pay particular attention to the VLAN interfaces, and NAT and DHCP related sections. You configure these later in this lab using the CLI.

d. You might want to capture and print the factory-default configuration as a reference. Use the terminal emulation program to copy it from the ASA and paste it into a text document. You can then edit this file, if desired, so that it contains only valid commands. You should also remove password commands and enter the **no shut** command to bring up the desired interfaces.

Step 5: Clear the previous ASA configuration settings.

a. Use the **write erase** command to remove the **startup-config** file from flash memory:

```
ciscoasa# write erase
Erase configuration in flash memory? [confirm]
[OK]
ciscoasa#

ciscoasa# show start
No Configuration
```

Note: The IOS command **erase startup-config** is not supported on the ASA.

b. Use the **reload** command to restart the ASA. This will cause the ASA to come up in CLI Setup mode. If prompted that the config has been modified, asking if you want to save it, respond with **N**.

```
ciscoasa# reload
Proceed with reload? [confirm]
ciscoasa#
***
*** --- START GRACEFUL SHUTDOWN ---
Shutting down isakmp
Shutting down File system
***
*** --- SHUTDOWN NOW ---
Process shutdown finished
Rebooting.....
CISCO SYSTEMS
Embedded BIOS Version 1.0(12)13 08/28/08 15:50:37.45
<output omitted>
```

Step 6: Use the Setup interactive CLI mode to configure basic settings.

When the ASA completes the reload process, it should detect that the startup-config file is missing and present a series of interactive prompts to configure basic ASA settings. If it does not come up in this mode, repeat Step 5. As an alternative, you can run the **setup** command at the global configuration prompt, but you must first create a VLAN interface (VLAN 1), name the VLAN **management** (using the **nameif** command), and assign the VLAN an IP address.

Note: The interactive prompt mode does not configure the ASA with factory defaults as described in Step 4. This mode can be used to configure minimal basic settings such as hostname, clock, passwords, and so on. You can also bypass this mode and go directly to the CLI to configure the ASA settings, as described in Part 3 of this lab.

a. Respond to the Setup interactive prompts as shown here, after the ASA reloads:

```
Pre-configure Firewall now through interactive prompts [yes]? <enter>
Firewall Mode [Routed]: <enter>
Enable password [<use current password>]: cisco
Allow password recovery [yes]? <enter>
Clock (UTC):
  Year [2011]: <enter>
  Month [Oct]: <enter>
  Day [01]: <enter>
  Time [12:24:42]: <enter>
Management IP address: 192.168.1.1 <enter>
Management network mask: 255.255.255.0 <enter>
Host name: ASA-Init
Domain name: generic.com
IP address of host running Device Manager: <enter>

The following configuration will be used:
Enable password: cisco
Allow password recovery: yes
Clock (UTC): 12:24:42 Sep 25 2011
Firewall Mode: Routed
Management IP address: 192.168.1.1
Management network mask: 255.255.255.0
Host name: ASA-Init
Domain name: generic.com
IP address of host running Device Manager: <enter>

Use this configuration and write to flash? yes

INFO: Security level for "management" set to 0 by default.
WARNING: http server is not yet enabled to allow ASDM access.
Cryptochecksum: c8a535f0 e273d49e 5bddfd19 e12566b1

2070 bytes copied in 0.940 secs
Type help or '?' for a list of available commands.
ASA-Init#
```

Note: In the above configuration, the IP address of the host running ASDM was left blank. It is not necessary to install ASDM on a host. It can be run from the flash memory of the ASA device itself using the browser of the host. This process is described in Chapter 10, Lab B, "Configuring ASA Basic Settings and Firewall Using ASDM."

You may also see the warning above stating that the ASA HTTP server has not yet been enabled. This is done in a subsequent step.

Note: The responses to the prompts are automatically stored in the startup-config and the running config. However, additional security related commands, such as a global default inspection service policy, are inserted into the running-config by the ASA OS.

b. Issue the **show run** command to see the additional security related configuration commands that are inserted by the ASA.

c. Issue the **copy run start** command to capture the additional security related commands in the startup config.

d. Issue the **reload** command to restart the ASA and load the startup configuration:

```
ASA-Init# reload
Proceed with reload? [confirm] <enter>

<output omitted>
```

e. Enter privileged EXEC mode with the **enable** command. Provide the password set in Step 6a (cisco). Issue the **show running-config** command. You should see the entries you provided in the interactive configuration process.

Part 3: Configuring ASA Settings and Interface Security Using the CLI

In Part 3 of this lab, you configure basic settings by using the ASA CLI, even though some of them were already configured using the Setup mode interactive prompts in Part 2. In this part, you start with the settings configured in Part 2 and add to or modify them to create a more complete basic configuration.

Tip: You will find that many ASA CLI commands are similar to if not the same as those used with the Cisco IOS CLI. In addition, moving between configuration modes and submodes is essentially the same.

Note: You must complete Part 2 before beginning Part 3.

Step 1: Configure the hostname and domain name.

a. Enter global configuration mode using the **config t** command. The first time you enter configuration mode after running Setup you are asked whether you want to enable anonymous reporting. Respond with **N**:

```
ASA-Init# conf t
ASA-Init(config)#

***************************** NOTICE *****************************

Help to improve the ASA platform by enabling anonymous reporting,
which allows Cisco to securely receive minimal error and health
information from the device. To learn more about this feature,
please visit: http://www.cisco.com/go/smartcall

Would you like to enable anonymous error reporting to help improve
the product? [Y]es, [N]o, [A]sk later: n

In the future, if you would like to enable this feature,
issue the command "call-home reporting anonymous".

Please remember to save your configuration.
```

b. Configure the ASA hostname using the **hostname** command:

```
ASA-Init(config)# hostname CCNAS-ASA
```

c. Configure the domain name using the **domain-name** command:

```
CCNAS-ASA(config)# domain-name ccnasecurity.com
```

Step 2: Configure the login and enable mode passwords.

a. The login password is used for Telnet connections (and SSH before ASA version 8.4). By default, it is set to cisco. You can change the login password using the **passwd** or **password** command. For this lab, leave it set to the default of cisco.

b. Configure the privileged EXEC mode (enable) password using the **enable password** command:

```
CCNAS-ASA(config)# enable password class
```

Step 3: Set the date and time.

You can set the date and time manually using the **clock set** command. The syntax for the clock set command is **clock set** *hh:mm:ss* {*month day* | *day month*} *year*. The following is an example of how to set the date and time using a 24-hour clock:

```
CCNAS-ASA(config)# clock set 14:25:00 october 1 2011
```

Step 4: Configure the inside and outside interfaces.

ASA 5505 Interface Notes

The 5505 is different from the other 5500 series ASA models. With other ASAs, the physical port can be assigned a Layer 3 IP address directly, much like a Cisco router. With the ASA 5505, the eight integrated switch ports are Layer 2 ports. To assign Layer 3 parameters, you must create a switch virtual interface (SVI) or logical VLAN interface and then assign one or more of the physical layer 2 ports to it. All eight switch ports are initially assigned to VLAN 1, unless the factory default config is present, in which case port E0/0 is assigned to VLAN 2. In this step, you create internal and external VLAN interfaces, name them, assign IP addresses, and set the interface security level.

If you completed the initial configuration Setup utility, interface VLAN 1 is configured as the management VLAN with an IP address of 192.168.1.1. You configure it as the inside interface for this lab. You configure only the VLAN 1 (inside) and VLAN 2 (outside) interfaces at this time. You configure the VLAN 3 (DMZ) interface in Part 6 of the lab.

a. Configure a logical VLAN 1 interface for the inside network, 192.168.1.0/24, and set the security level to the highest setting of 100:

```
CCNAS-ASA(config)# interface vlan 1
CCNAS-ASA(config-if)# nameif inside
CCNAS-ASA(config-if)# ip address 192.168.1.1 255.255.255.0
CCNAS-ASA(config-if)# security-level 100
```

b. Create a logical VLAN 2 interface for the outside network, 209.165.200.224/29, set the security level to the lowest setting of 0 and bring up the VLAN 2 interface:

```
CCNAS-ASA(config-if)# interface vlan 2
CCNAS-ASA(config-if)# nameif outside
INFO: Security level for "outside" set to 0 by default.

CCNAS-ASA(config-if)# ip address 209.165.200.226 255.255.255.248
CCNAS-ASA(config-if)# no shutdown
```

Interface Security Level Notes

You might receive a message that the security level for the inside interface was set automatically to 100 and the outside interface was set to 0. The ASA uses interface security levels from 0 to 100 to enforce the security policy. Security Level 100 (inside) is the most secure, and level 0 (outside) is the least secure.

By default, the ASA applies a policy where traffic from a higher security level interface to one with a lower level is permitted and traffic from a lower security level interface to one with a higher security level is denied. The ASA default security policy permits outbound traffic, which is inspected by default. Returning traffic is allowed because of stateful packet inspection. This default "routed mode" firewall behavior of the ASA allows packets to be routed from the inside network to the outside network but not vice versa. In Part 4 of this lab, you configure NAT to increase the firewall protection.

c. Use the **show interface** command to ensure that ASA Layer 2 ports E0/0 (for VLAN 2) and E0/1 (for VLAN 1) are both up. An example is shown for E0/0. If either port is shown as down/down, check the physical connections. If either port is administratively down, bring it up with the **no shutdown** command.

```
CCNAS-ASA# show interface e0/0
Interface Ethernet0/0 "", is administratively down, line protocol is up
  Hardware is 88E6095, BW 100 Mbps, DLY 100 usec
        Auto Duplex(Full-duplex), Auto-Speed(100 Mbps)
<output omitted>
```

d. Assign ASA Layer 2 port E0/1 to VLAN 1 and port E0/0 to VLAN 2 and use the **no shutdown** command to ensure they are up:

```
CCNAS-ASA(config)# interface e0/1
CCNAS-ASA(config-if)# switchport access vlan 1
CCNAS-ASA(config-if)# no shutdown
CCNAS-ASA(config-if)# interface e0/0
CCNAS-ASA(config-if)# switchport access vlan 2
CCNAS-ASA(config-if)# no shutdown
```

Note: Even though E0/1 is in VLAN 1 by default, the commands are provided above.

e. Display the status for all ASA interfaces using the **show interface ip brief** command. Note that this command is different from the IOS command **show ip interface brief**. If any of the physical or logical interfaces previously configured are not UP/UP, troubleshoot as necessary before continuing.

Tip: Most ASA **show** commands, as well as **ping**, **copy** and others, can be issued from within any config mode prompt without the do command required with IOS.

```
CCNAS-ASA(config)# show interface ip brief
Interface            IP-Address      OK? Method Status        Protocol
Ethernet0/0          unassigned      YES unset  up            up
Ethernet0/1          unassigned      YES unset  up            up
Ethernet0/2          unassigned      YES unset  up            up
Ethernet0/3          unassigned      YES unset  down          down
Ethernet0/4          unassigned      YES unset  down          down
Ethernet0/5          unassigned      YES unset  down          down
Ethernet0/6          unassigned      YES unset  down          down
Ethernet0/7          unassigned      YES unset  down          down
Internal-Data0/0     unassigned      YES unset  up            up
Internal-Data0/1     unassigned      YES unset  up            up
Vlan1                192.168.1.1     YES manual up            up
Vlan2                209.165.200.226 YES manual up            up
Virtual0             127.0.0.1       YES unset  up            up
```

f. Display the information for the Layer 3 VLAN interfaces using the **show ip address** command:

```
CCNAS-ASA(config)# show ip address
System IP Addresses:
Interface      Name         IP address        Subnet mask       Method
Vlan1          inside       192.168.1.1       255.255.255.0     manual
Vlan2          outside      209.165.200.226   255.255.255.248   manual

Current IP Addresses:
Interface      Name         IP address        Subnet mask       Method
Vlan1          inside       192.168.1.1       255.255.255.0     manual
Vlan2          outside      209.165.200.226   255.255.255.248   manual
```

g. Use the **show switch vlan** command to display the inside and outside VLANs configured on the ASA and to display the assigned ports:

```
CCNAS-ASA# show switch vlan
VLAN Name                           Status     Ports
---- -------------------------- --------- -----------------------------
1    inside                         up         Et0/1, Et0/2, Et0/3, Et0/4
                                               Et0/5, Et0/6, Et0/7
2    outside                        up         Et0/0
```

h. You may also use the command **show running-config interface type/number** to display the configuration for a particular interface from the running config:

```
CCNAS-ASA# show run interface vlan 1
!
interface Vlan1
 nameif inside
 security-level 100
 ip address 192.168.1.1 255.255.255.0
```

Step 5: Test connectivity to the ASA.

a. Ensure that PC-B has a static IP address of 192.168.1.3 along with subnet mask 255.255.255.0 and default gateway 192.168.1.1 (the IP address of ASA VLAN 1 inside interface).

b. You should be able to ping from PC-B to the ASA inside interface address and ping from the ASA to PC-B. If the pings fail, troubleshoot the configuration as necessary.

```
CCNAS-ASA# ping 192.168.1.3
Type escape sequence to abort.
Sending 5, 100-byte ICMP Echos to 192.168.1.3, timeout is 2 seconds:
!!!!!
Success rate is 100 percent (5/5), round-trip min/avg/max = 1/1/1 ms
```

c. From PC-B, ping the VLAN 2 (outside) interface at IP address 209.165.200.226. You should not be able to ping this address.

d. From PC-B, telnet to the ASA using address 192.168.1.1. Were you able to make the connection? Why or why not?

____

Step 6: Configure Telnet access to the ASA from the inside network.

a. You can configure the ASA to accept Telnet connections from a single host or a range of hosts on the inside network. Configure the ASA to allow Telnet connections from any host on the inside network 192.168.1.0/24 and set the Telnet timeout to 10 minutes (the default is 5 minutes):

```
CCNAS-ASA(config)# telnet 192.168.1.0 255.255.255.0 inside
CCNAS-ASA(config)# telnet timeout 10
```

b. From PC-B, telnet to the ASA using address 192.168.1.1 to verify the Telnet access. Use the remote access login password **cisco** to access the ASA CLI prompt. Exit the Telnet session using the **`quit`** command.

Note: You cannot use Telnet to the lowest security interface (outside) from the outside unless you use Telnet inside an IPsec tunnel. Telnet is not the preferred remote access tool because of its lack of encryption. In Part 5 of this lab, you configure SSH access from the internal and external network.

Step 7: Configure ASDM access to the ASA.

a. You can configure the ASA to accept HTTPS connections using the **`http`** command. This allows access to the ASA GUI (ASDM). Configure the ASA to allow HTTPS connections from any host on the inside network 192.168.1.0/24:

```
CCNAS-ASA(config)# http server enable
CCNAS-ASA(config)# http 192.168.1.0 255.255.255.0 inside
```

b. Open a browser on PC-B and test the HTTPS access to the ASA by entering **https://192.168.1.1**. You are prompted with a security certificate warning. Click **Continue** to this website. Click **Yes** for the other security warnings. You should see the Cisco ASDM-IDM Launcher where you can enter a username and password. Leave the username blank and enter the password **cisco**, which was configured when you ran the Setup utility.

Note: Be sure to specify the HTTPS protocol in the URL.

c. Close the browser. In the next lab, you use ASDM extensively to configure the ASA. The objective here is not to use the ASDM configuration screens, but to verify HTTP/ASDM connectivity to the ASA. If you are unable to access ASDM, check your configurations or contact your instructor or do both.

Part 4: Configuring Routing, Address Translation, and Inspection Policy Using the CLI

In Part 4 of this lab, you provide a default route for the ASA to reach external networks. You configure address translation using network objects to enhance firewall security. You then modify the default application inspection policy to allow specific traffic.

Note: You must complete Part 3 before going on to Part 4.

Step 1: Configure a static default route for the ASA.

In Part 3, you configured the ASA outside interface with a static IP address and subnet mask. However, the ASA does not have a gateway of last resort defined. To enable the ASA to reach external networks, you configure a default static route on the ASA outside interface.

Note: If the ASA outside interface were configured as a DHCP client, it could obtain a default gateway IP address from the ISP. However, in this lab, the outside interface is configured with a static address.

a. Ping from the ASA to R1 Fa0/0 IP address 209.165.200.225. Was the ping successful?

____

b. Ping from the ASA to R1 S0/0/0 IP address 10.1.1.1. Was the ping successful?

____

c. Create a "quad zero" default route using the **route** command, associate it with the ASA outside interface, and point to the R1 Fa0/0 IP address 209.165.200.225 as the gateway of last resort. The default administrative distance is 1 by default.

```
CCNAS-ASA(config)# route outside 0.0.0.0 0.0.0.0 209.165.200.225
```

d. Issue the **show route** command to display the ASA routing table and the static default route just created:

```
CCNAS-ASA# show route
Codes: C - connected, S - static, I - IGRP, R - RIP, M - mobile, B -
BGP
       D - EIGRP, EX - EIGRP external, O - OSPF, IA - OSPF inter area
       N1 - OSPF NSSA external type 1, N2 - OSPF NSSA external type 2
       E1 - OSPF external type 1, E2 - OSPF external type 2, E - EGP
       i - IS-IS, L1 - IS-IS level-1, L2 - IS-IS level-2, ia - IS-IS
inter area
       * - candidate default, U - per-user static route, o - ODR
       P - periodic downloaded static route

Gateway of last resort is 209.165.200.225 to network 0.0.0.0

C    192.168.10.0 255.255.255.0 is directly connected, inside
C    209.165.200.224 255.255.255.248 is directly connected, outside
S*   0.0.0.0 0.0.0.0 [1/0] via 209.165.200.225, outside
```

e. Ping from the ASA to R1 S0/0/0 IP address 10.1.1.1. Was the ping successful? _______________

Step 2: Configure address translation using PAT and network objects.

Note: Beginning with ASA version 8.3, network objects are used to configure all forms of NAT. A network object is created and it is within this object that NAT is configured. In Step 2a a network object inside-net is used to translate the inside network addresses 192.168.10.0/24 to the global address of the outside ASA interface. This type of object configuration is called Auto-NAT.

a. Create network object inside-net and assign attributes to it using the **subnet** and **nat** commands. In Version 8.3 and later only the **nat** command is used and the **static** and **global** commands are no longer supported.

```
CCNAS-ASA(config)# object network inside-net
CCNAS-ASA(config-network-object)# subnet 192.168.1.0 255.255.255.0
CCNAS-ASA(config-network-object)# nat (inside,outside) dynamic
interface
CCNAS-ASA(config-network-object)# end
```

b. The ASA splits the configuration into the object portion that defines the network to be translated and the actual **nat** command parameters. These appear in two different places in the running config. Display the NAT object configuration using the **show run object** and **show run nat** commands:

```
CCNAS-ASA# show run object
object network inside-net
 subnet 192.168.1.0 255.255.255.0

CCNAS-ASA# show run nat
!
object network inside-net
 nat (inside,outside) dynamic interface
```

c. From PC-B, attempt to ping the R1 Fa0/0 interface at IP address 209.165.200.225. Were the pings successful? _____

d. Issue the **show nat** command on the ASA to see the translated and untranslated hits. Notice that, of the pings from PC-B, four were translated and four were not. This is because ICMP is not being inspected by the global inspection policy. The outgoing pings (echos) were translated, the returning echo replies were blocked by the firewall policy. You configure the default inspection policy to allow ICMP in the next step.

```
CCNAS-ASA# show nat

Auto NAT Policies (Section 2)
1 (inside) to (outside) source dynamic inside-net interface
    translate_hits = 4, untranslate_hits = 4
```

e. Ping from PC-B to R1 again and quickly issue the **show xlate** command to see the actual addresses being translated:

```
CCNAS-ASA# show xlate
1 in use, 28 most used
Flags: D - DNS, i - dynamic, r - portmap, s - static, I - identity, T -
twice

ICMP PAT from inside:192.168.1.3/512 to outside:209.165.200.226/21469
flags ri idle 0:00:03 timeout 0:00:30
```

Note: The flags (`r` and `i`) indicate that the translation was based on a port map (`r`) and was done dynamically (`i`).

f. Open a browser on PC-B and enter the IP address of R1 Fa0/0 (209.165.200.225). You should be prompted by R1 for SDM or CCP GUI login. TCP-based HTTP traffic is permitted by default by the firewall inspection policy.

g. On the ASA use the **show nat and show xlate** commands again to see the hits and addresses being translated for the HTTP connection.

Step 3: Modify the default MPF application inspection global service policy.

For application layer inspection, as well as other advanced options, the Cisco Modular Policy

Framework (MPF) is available on ASAs. Cisco MPF uses three configuration objects to define modular, object-oriented, hierarchical policies:

- **Class maps:** Define a match criterion
- **Policy maps:** Associate actions to the match criteria
- **Service policies:** Attach the policy map to an interface, or globally to all interfaces of the appliance.

a. Display the default MPF policy map that performs the inspection on inside-to-outside traffic. Only traffic that was initiated from the inside is allowed back in to the outside interface. Notice that ICMP is missing.

```
CCNAS-ASA# show run
<output omitted>

class-map inspection_default
 match default-inspection-traffic
!
policy-map type inspect dns preset_dns_map
 parameters
  message-length maximum client auto
  message-length maximum 512
```

```
policy-map global_policy
 class inspection_default
  inspect dns preset_dns_map
  inspect ftp
  inspect h323 h225
  inspect h323 ras
  inspect ip-options
  inspect netbios
  inspect rsh
  inspect rtsp
  inspect skinny
  inspect esmtp
  inspect sqlnet
  inspect sunrpc
  inspect tftp
  inspect sip
  inspect xdmcp
!
service-policy global_policy global
```

b. Add the inspection of ICMP traffic to the policy map list using the following commands:

```
CCNAS-ASA(config)# policy-map global_policy
CCNAS-ASA(config-pmap)# class inspection_default
CCNAS-ASA(config-pmap-c)# inspect icmp
```

c. From PC-B attempt to ping the R1 Fa0/0 interface at IP address 209.165.200.225. The pings should be successful this time because ICMP traffic is now being inspected and legitimate return traffic is being allowed.

Part 5: Configuring DHCP, AAA, and SSH

In Part 5 of this lab, you configure ASA features, such as DHCP and enhanced login security, using AAA and SSH.

Note: You must complete Part 4 before beginning Part 5.

Step 1: Configure the ASA as a DHCP server.

The ASA can be both a DHCP server and a DHCP client. In this step you configure the ASA as a DHCP server to dynamically assign IP addresses for DHCP clients on the inside network.

a. Configure a DHCP address pool and enable it on the ASA inside interface. This is the range of addresses to be assigned to inside DHCP clients. Attempt to set the range from 192.168.1.5 through 192.168.1.100:

```
CCNAS-ASA(config)# dhcpd address 192.168.1.5-192.168.1.100 inside
Warning, DHCP pool range is limited to 32 addresses, set address range
as: 192.1
68.1.5-192.168.1.36
```

Were you able to do this on this ASA? ______________________________

Repeat the **dhcpd** command and specify the pool as **192.168.1.5-192.168.1.36**:

```
CNAS-ASA(config)# dhcpd address 192.168.1.5-192.168.1.36 inside
```

b. (Optional) Specify the IP address of the DNS server to be given to clients:

```
CCNAS-ASA(config)# dhcpd dns 209.165.201.2
```

Note: You can specify other parameters for clients, such as WINS server, lease length, and domain name.

c. Enable the DHCP daemon within the ASA to listen for DHCP client requests on the enabled interface (inside):

```
CCNAS-ASA(config)# dhcpd enable inside
```

d. Verify the DHCP daemon configuration by using the **show run dhcpd** command:

```
CCNAS-ASA(config)# show run dhcpd
dhcpd address 192.168.1.5-192.168.1.36 inside
dhcpd enable inside
```

e. Access the Network Connection IP Properties for PC-B and change it from a static IP address to a DHCP client so that it obtains an IP address automatically from the ASA DHCP server. The procedure to do this varies depending on the PC operating system. You might need to issue the **ipconfig /renew** command on PC-B to force it obtain a new IP address from the ASA.

Step 2: Configure AAA to use the local database for authentication.

a. Define a local user named **admin** by entering the **username** command. Specify a password of **cisco123**.

```
CCNAS-ASA(config)# username admin password cisco123
```

b. Configure AAA to use the local ASA database for Telnet and SSH user authentication:

```
CCNAS-ASA(config)# aaa authentication ssh console LOCAL
CCNAS-ASA(config)# aaa authentication telnet console LOCAL
```

Note: For added security, starting in ASA version 8.4(2), it is necessary to configure AAA authentication to support SSH connections. The Telnet/SSH default login is not supported. You can no longer connect to the ASA using SSH with the default username and the login password.

Step 3: Configure SSH remote access to the ASA.

You can configure the ASA to accept SSH connections from a single host or a range of hosts on the inside or outside network.

a. Generate an RSA key pair, which is required to support SSH connections. The modulus (in bits) can be 512, 768, 1024, or 2048. The larger the key modulus size you specify, the longer it takes to generate an RSA. Specify a modulus of 1024 using the **crypto key** command:

```
CCNAS-ASA(config)# crypto key generate rsa modulus 1024
INFO: The name for the keys will be: <Default-RSA-Key>
Keypair generation process begin. Please wait...
```

b. Save the RSA keys to persistent flash memory using either the **copy run start** or **write mem** command:

```
CCNAS-ASA# write mem
Building configuration...
Cryptochecksum: 3c845d0f b6b8839a f9e43be0 33feb4ef
3270 bytes copied in 0.890 secs
[OK]
```

c. Configure the ASA to allow SSH connections from any host on the inside network 192.168.1.0/24 and from the remote management host at the branch office (172.16.3.3) on the outside network. Set the SSH timeout to 10 minutes (the default is 5 minutes):

```
CCNAS-ASA(config)# ssh 192.168.1.0 255.255.255.0 inside
CCNAS-ASA(config)# ssh 172.16.3.3  255.255.255.255 outside
CCNAS-ASA(config)# ssh timeout 10
```

d. On PC-C, use an SSH client, such as PuTTY, to connect to the ASA outside interface at IP address 209.165.200.226. The first time you connect you may be prompted by the SSH client to accept the RSA host key of the ASA SSH server. Log in as user admin and provide the password cisco123. You can also connect to the ASA inside interface from a PC-B SSH client using IP address 192.168.1.1.

Part 6: Configuring a DMZ, Static NAT, and ACLs

In Part 4 of this lab, you configured address translation using PAT for the inside network. In this part, you create a DMZ on the ASA, configure static NAT to a DMZ server, and apply ACLs to control access to the server.

To accommodate the addition of a DMZ and a web server, you use another address from the ISP range assigned, 209.165.200.224/29 (.224-.231). Router R1 Fa0/0 and the ASA outside interface are already using 209.165.200.225 and .226, respectively. You use public address 209.165.200.227 and static NAT to provide address translation access to the server.

Step 1: Configure the DMZ interface VLAN 3 on the ASA.

a. Configure DMZ VLAN 3, which is where the public access web server will reside. Assign it IP address 192.168.2.1/24, name it **dmz**, and assign it a security level of 70.

Note: If you are working with the ASA 5505 base license, you get the error message shown in the following output. The ASA 5505 base license allows for the creation of up to three named VLAN interfaces. However, you must disable communication between the third interface and one of the other interfaces using the **`no forward`** command. This is not an issue if the ASA has a Security Plus license, which allows 20 named VLANs.

b. Because the server does not need to initiate communication with the inside users, disable forwarding to interface VLAN 1:

```
CCNAS-ASA(config)# interface vlan 3
CCNAS-ASA(config-if)# ip address 192.168.2.1 255.255.255.0
CCNAS-ASA(config-if)# nameif dmz

ERROR: This license does not allow configuring more than 2 interfaces
with nameif and without a "no forward" command on this interface or on
1 interface(s) with nameif already configured.

CCNAS-ASA(config-if)# no forward interface vlan 1
CCNAS-ASA(config-if)# nameif dmz
INFO: Security level for "dmz" set to 0 by default.

CCNAS-ASA(config-if)# security-level 70
CCNAS-ASA(config-if)# no shut
```

c. Assign ASA physical interface E0/2 to DMZ VLAN 3 and enable the interface:

```
CCNAS-ASA(config-if)# interface Ethernet0/2
CCNAS-ASA(config-if)# switchport access vlan 3
CCNAS-ASA(config-if)# no shut
```

d. Display the status for all ASA interfaces using the **show interface ip brief** command:

```
CCNAS-ASA # show interface ip brief
Interface            IP-Address       OK? Method Status     Protocol
Ethernet0/0          unassigned       YES unset  up         up
Ethernet0/1          unassigned       YES unset  up         up
Ethernet0/2          unassigned       YES unset  up         up
Ethernet0/3          unassigned       YES unset  down       down
Ethernet0/4          unassigned       YES unset  down       down
Ethernet0/5          unassigned       YES unset  down       down
Ethernet0/6          unassigned       YES unset  down       down
Ethernet0/7          unassigned       YES unset  down       down
Internal-Data0/0     unassigned       YES unset  up         up
Internal-Data0/1     unassigned       YES unset  up         up
Vlan1                192.168.1.1      YES manual up         up
Vlan2                209.165.200.226  YES manual up         up
Vlan3                192.168.2.1      YES manual up         up
Virtual0             127.0.0.1        YES unset  up         up
```

e. Display the information for the Layer 3 VLAN interfaces using the **show ip address** command:

```
CCNAS-ASA # show ip address
System IP Addresses:
Interface      Name        IP address        Subnet mask       Method
Vlan1          inside      192.168.1.1       255.255.255.0     manual
Vlan2          outside     209.165.200.226   255.255.255.248   manual
Vlan3          dmz         192.168.2.1       255.255.255.0     manual
<output omitted>
```

f. Display the VLANs and port assignments on the ASA using the **show switch vlan** command:

```
CCNAS-ASA(config)# show switch vlan
VLAN Name                             Status     Ports
---- -------------------------------- ---------  -----------------------------
1    inside                            up         Et0/1, Et0/3, Et0/4, Et0/5
                                                  Et0/6, Et0/7
2    outside                           up         Et0/0
3    dmz                               up         Et0/2
```

Step 2: Configure static NAT to the DMZ server using a network object.

Configure a network object named **dmz-server** and assign it the static IP address of the DMZ server (192.168.2.3). While in object definition mode, use the **nat** command to specify that this object is used to translate a DMZ address to an outside address using static NAT and specify a public translated address of 209.165.200.227:

```
CCNAS-ASA(config)# object network dmz-server
CCNAS-ASA(config-network-object)# host 192.168.2.3
CCNAS-ASA(config-network-object)# nat (dmz,outside) static 209.165.200.227
```

Step 3: Configure an ACL to allow access to the DMZ server from the Internet.

Configure a named access list OUTSIDE-DMZ that permits any IP protocol from any external host to the internal IP address of the DMZ server. Apply the access list to the ASA outside interface in the "IN" direction:

```
CCNAS-ASA(config)# access-list OUTSIDE-DMZ permit ip any host 192.168.2.3
CCNAS-ASA(config)# access-group OUTSIDE-DMZ in interface outside
```

Note: Unlike IOS ACLs, the ASA ACL **permit** statement must permit access to the internal private DMZ address. External hosts access the server using its public static NAT address, and the ASA translates it to the internal host IP address and applies the ACL.

You can modify this ACL to allow only services that you want to be exposed to external hosts, such as web (HTTP) or file transfer (FTP).

Step 4: Test access to the DMZ server.

a. Create a loopback 0 interface on Internet router R2 representing an external host. Assign Lo0 IP address 172.30.1.1 and a mask of 255.255.255.0. Ping the DMZ server public address from R2 using the loopback interface as the source of the ping. The pings should be successful.

```
R2(config-if)# interface Lo0
R2(config-if)# ip address 172.30.1.1 255.255.255.0

R2# ping 209.165.200.227 source lo0

Type escape sequence to abort.
Sending 5, 100-byte ICMP Echos to 209.165.200.227, timeout is 2
seconds:
Packet sent with a source address of 172.30.1.1
!!!!!
Success rate is 100 percent (5/5), round-trip min/avg/max = 1/2/4 ms
```

b. Clear the NAT counters using the **clear nat counters** command:

```
CCNAS-ASA# clear nat counters
```

c. Ping from PC-C to the DMZ server at the public address 209.165.200.227. The pings should be successful.

d. Issue the **show nat** and **show xlate** commands on the ASA to see the effect of the pings. Both the PAT (inside to outside) and static NAT (DMZ to outside) policies are shown:

```
CCNAS-ASA# show nat

Auto NAT Policies (Section 2)
1 (dmz) to (outside) source static dmz-server 209.165.200.227
    translate_hits = 0, untranslate_hits = 4

2 (inside) to (outside) source dynamic inside-net interface
    translate_hits = 4, untranslate_hits = 0
```

Note: Pings from inside to outside are translated hits. Pings from outside host PC-C to the DMZ are considered untranslated hits.

```
CCNAS-ASA# show xlate
1 in use, 3 most used
Flags: D - DNS, i - dynamic, r - portmap, s - static, I - identity, T -
twice
NAT from dmz:192.168.2.3 to outside:209.165.200.227 flags s idle
0:22:58 timeout 0:00:00
```

Note that the flag this time is `s`, indicating a static translation.

e. Because the ASA inside interface (VLAN 1) is set to security level of 100 (the highest) and the DMZ interface (VLAN 3) is set to 70, you can also access the DMZ server from a host on the inside network. The ASA acts like a router between the two networks. Ping the DMZ server (PC-A) internal address (192.168.2.3) from inside network host PC-B (192.168.1.X). The pings should be successful because of the interface security level and the fact that ICMP is being inspected on the inside interface by the global inspection policy. The pings from PC-B to PC-A do not affect the NAT translation counts because both PC-B and PC-A are behind the firewall and no translation takes place.

f. The DMZ server cannot ping PC-B on the inside network. This is because the DMZ interface VLAN 3 has a lower security level and the fact that, when the VLAN 3 interface was created, it was necessary to specify the **no forward** command. Try to ping from the DMZ server PC-A to PC-B at IP address 192.168.1.X. The pings should not be successful.

g. Use the **show run** command to display the configuration for VLAN 3:

```
CCNAS-ASA# show run interface vlan 3
!
interface Vlan3
 no forward interface Vlan1
 nameif dmz
 security-level 70
 ip address 192.168.2.1 255.255.255.0
```

Note: An access list can be applied to the inside interface if it is desired to control the type of access to be permitted or denied to the DMZ server from inside hosts.

Reflection

1. How does the configuration of the ASA firewall differ from that of an ISR?

____

____

2. What does the ASA use to define address translation and what is the benefit?

____

____

3. How does the ASA 5505 use logical and physical interfaces to manage security and how does this differ from other ASA models?

____

____

____

____

Router Interface Summary Table

Router Model	Ethernet Interface 1	Ethernet Interface 2	Serial Interface 1	Serial Interface 2
1800	Fast Ethernet 0/0 (Fa0/0)	Fast Ethernet 0/1 (Fa0/1)	Serial 0/0/0 (S0/0/0)	Serial 0/0/1 (S0/0/1)
1900	Gigabit Ethernet 0/0 (G0/0)	Gigabit Ethernet 0/1 (G0/1)	Serial 0/0/0 (S0/0/0)	Serial 0/0/1 (S0/0/1)
2800	Fast Ethernet 0/0 (Fa0/0)	Fast Ethernet 0/1 (Fa0/1)	Serial 0/0/0 (S0/0/0)	Serial 0/0/1 (S0/0/1)
2900	Gigabit Ethernet 0/0 (G0/0)	Gigabit Ethernet 0/1 (G0/1)	Serial 0/0/0 (S0/0/0)	Serial 0/0/1 (S0/0/1)

Note: To find out how the router is configured, look at the interfaces to identify the type of router and how many interfaces the router has. There is no way to effectively list all the combinations of configurations for each router class. This table includes identifiers for the possible combinations of Ethernet and serial interfaces in the device. The table does not include any other type of interface, even though a specific router may contain one. An example of this might be an ISDN BRI interface. The string in parentheses is the legal abbreviation that can be used in Cisco IOS commands to represent the interface.

Chapter 10 Lab B: Configuring ASA Basic Settings and Firewall Using ASDM

Topology

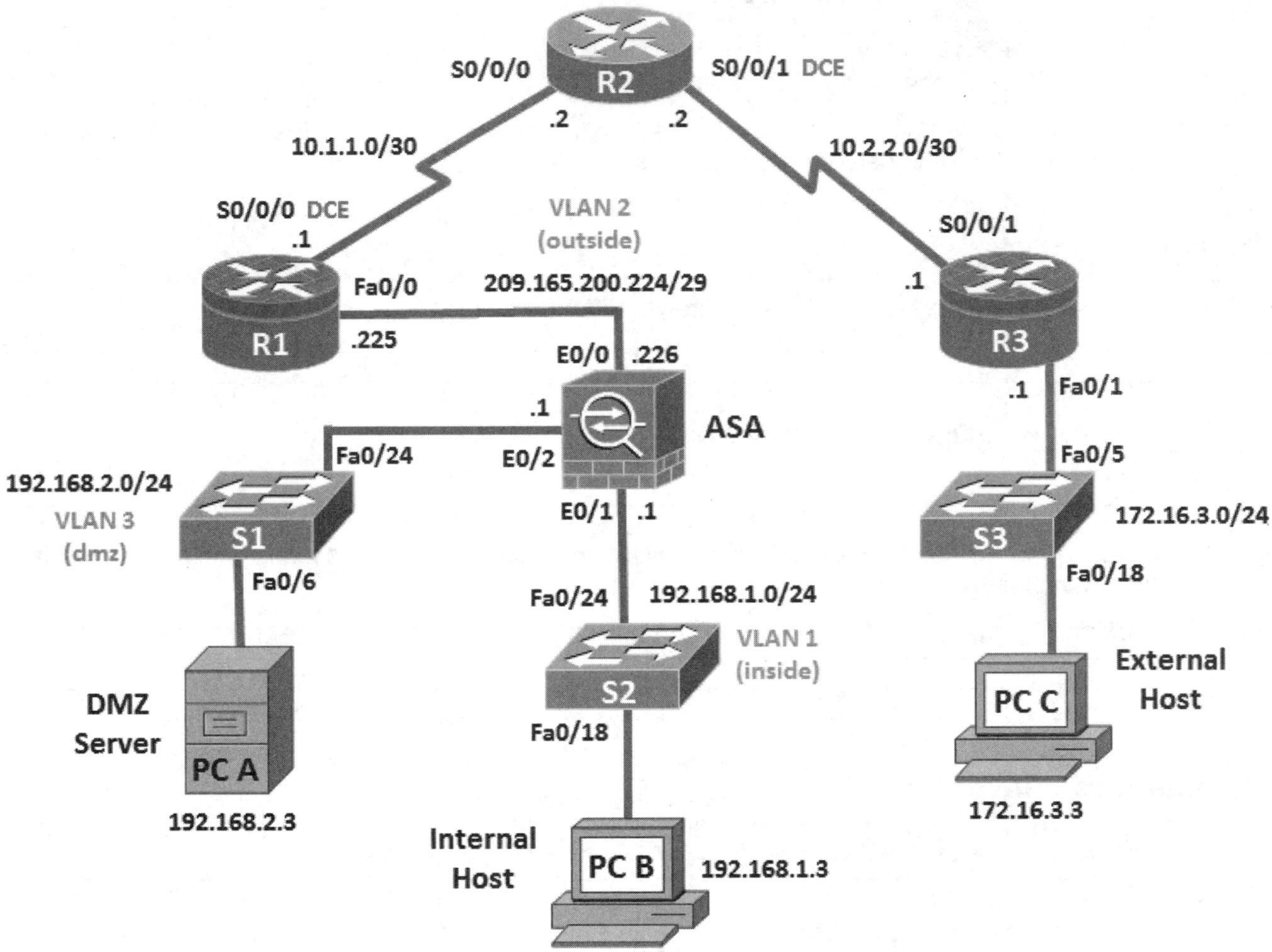

Note: ISR G2 devices have Gigabit Ethernet interfaces rather than FastEthernet interfaces.

IP Addressing Table

Device	Interface	IP Address	Subnet Mask	Default Gateway	Switch Port
R1	Fa0/0	209.165.200.225	255.255.255.248	N/A	ASA E0/0
	S0/0/0 (DCE)	10.1.1.1	255.255.255.252	N/A	N/A
R2	S0/0/0	10.1.1.2	255.255.255.252	N/A	N/A
	S0/0/1 (DCE)	10.2.2.2	255.255.255.252	N/A	N/A
R3	Fa0/1	172.16.3.1	255.255.255.0	N/A	S3 FA0/5
	S0/0/1	10.2.2.1	255.255.255.252	N/A	N/A
ASA	VLAN 1 (E0/1)	192.168.1.1	255.255.255.0	NA	S2 Fa0/24
ASA	VLAN 2 (E0/0)	209.165.200.226	255.255.255.248	NA	R1 Fa0/0
ASA	VLAN 3 (E0/2)	192.168.2.1	255.255.255.0	NA	S1 Fa0/24
PC-A	NIC	192.168.2.3	255.255.255.0	192.168.2.1	S1 Fa0/6
PC-B	NIC	192.168.1.3	255.255.255.0	192.168.1.1	S2 Fa0/18
PC-C	NIC	172.16.3.3	255.255.255.0	172.16.3.1	S3 Fa0/18

Objectives

Part 1: Lab Setup

- Cable the network as shown in the topology.
- Configure hostnames and interface IP addresses for routers, switches, and PCs.
- Configure static routing, including default routes, between R1, R2, and R3.
- Configure HTTP and Telnet access for R1.
- Verify connectivity between hosts, switches, and routers.

Part 2: Accessing the ASA Console and ASDM

- Access the ASA console and view hardware, software, and configuration settings.
- Clear previous configuration settings.
- Use the CLI to configure settings for ASDM access.
- Test Ethernet connectivity to the ASA.
- Access the ASDM GUI and explore major windows and options.

Part 3: Configuring ASA Settings and Firewall Using the ASDM Startup Wizard

- Configure the hostname, domain name, and enable password.
- Configure the inside and outside VLAN interfaces.
- Configure DHCP for the inside network.

- Configure port address translation (PAT) for the inside network.
- Configure Telnet and SSH administrative access.

Part 4: Configuring ASA Settings from the ASDM Configuration Menu

- Set the date and time.
- Configure a static default route for the ASA.
- Test connectivity using ASDM Ping and Traceroute.
- Configure Local AAA user authentication.
- Modify the MPF application inspection policy.

Part 5: Configuring a DMZ, Static NAT, and ACLs

- Configure static NAT for the DMZ server.
- Configure an ACL on the ASA to allow access to the DMZ for Internet users.
- Verify access to the DMZ server for external and internal users.
- Use ASDM Monitor to graph traffic.

Background/Scenario

The Cisco Adaptive Security Appliance (ASA) is an advanced network security device that integrates a stateful firewall and VPN and other capabilities. This lab employs an ASA 5505 to create a firewall and protect an internal corporate network from external intruders while allowing internal hosts access to the Internet. The ASA creates three security interfaces: Outside, inside, and demilitarized zone (DMZ). It provides outside users limited access to the DMZ and no access to internal resources. Inside users can access the DMZ and outside resources.

The focus of this lab is on the configuration of the ASA as a basic firewall. Other devices receive minimal configuration to support the ASA portion of the lab. This lab uses the ASA GUI interface ASDM, which is similar to the SDM and CCP used with Cisco ISRs, to configure basic device and security settings.

In Part 1 of the lab, you configure the topology and non-ASA devices. In Part 2, you prepare the ASA for ADSM access. In Part 3, you use the ASDM Startup Wizard to configure basic ASA settings and the firewall between the inside and outside networks. In Part 4, you configure additional settings via the ASDM configuration menu. In Part 5, you configure a DMZ on the ASA and provide access to a server in the DMZ.

Your company has one location connected to an ISP. Router R1 represents a customer premise equipment (CPE) device managed by the Internet service provider (ISP). Router R2 represents an intermediate Internet router. Router R3 connects an administrator from a network management company, who has been hired to manage your network remotely. The ASA is an edge CPE security device that connects the internal corporate network and DMZ to the ISP while providing Network Address Translation (NAT) and Dynamic Host Configuration Protocol (DHCP) services to inside hosts. The ASAs are configured for management by an administrator on the internal network and the remote administrator. Layer 3 VLAN interfaces provide access to the three areas created in the lab: Inside, Outside, and DMZ. The ISP has assigned the public IP address space of 209.165.200.224/29, which is used for address translation on the ASA.

Note: The routers used with this lab are Cisco 1841 with Cisco IOS Software Release 12.4(20)T (advanced IP image). The switches are Cisco WS-C2960-24TT-L with Cisco IOS Software Release 12.2(46)SE (C2960-LANBASEK9-M image). Other routers, switches, and Cisco IOS versions can be used. However, results and output may vary.

The ASA use with this lab is a Cisco model 5505 with an eight-port integrated switch, running OS version 8.4(2) and ASDM version 6.4(5) and comes with a Base license that allows a maximum of three VLANs.

Note: Make sure that the routers and switches have been erased and have no startup configurations.

Required Resources

- 3 routers (Cisco 1841 with Cisco IOS Software Release 12.4(20)T1 or comparable)
- 3 switches (Cisco 2960 or comparable)
- 1 ASA 5505 (OS version 8.4(2) and ASDM version 6.4(5) and Base license or comparable)
- PC-A: Windows XP, Vista, or Windows 7 with CCP, PuTTy SSH client (web and FTP server optional)
- PC-B: Windows XP, Vista, or Windows 7 with PuTTy SSH client and Java version 6.x or later (ASDM loaded on the PC is optional)
- PC-C: Windows XP, Vista, or Windows 7 with CCP, PuTTy SSH client
- Serial and Ethernet cables as shown in the topology
- Rollover cables to configure the routers and ASA via the console

Part 1: Basic Router/Switch/PC Configuration

In Part 1 of this lab, you set up the network topology and configure basic settings on the routers, such as interface IP addresses and static routing.

Note: Do not configure any ASA settings at this time.

Step 1: Cable the network and clear previous device settings.

Attach the devices that are shown in the topology diagram and cable as necessary. Make sure that the routers and switches have been erased and have no startup configurations.

Step 2: Configure basic settings for routers and switches.

a. Configure hostnames as shown in the topology for each router.

b. Configure router interface IP addresses as shown in the IP Addressing Table.

c. Configure a clock rate for routers with a DCE serial cable attached to the serial interface. Router R1 is shown here as an example:

```
R1(config)# interface S0/0/0
R1(config-if)# clock rate 64000
```

d. Configure the hostname for the switches. With the exception of the hostname, the switches can be left in their default configuration state. Configuring the VLAN management IP address for the switches is optional.

Step 3: Configure static routing on the routers.

a. Configure a static default route from R1 to R2 and from R3 to R2:

```
R1(config)# ip route 0.0.0.0 0.0.0.0 Serial0/0/0
R3(config)# ip route 0.0.0.0 0.0.0.0 Serial0/0/1
```

b. Configure a static route from R2 to the R1 Fa0/0 subnet (connected to ASA interface E0/0) and a static route from R2 to the R3 LAN:

```
R2(config)# ip route 209.165.200.224 255.255.255.248 Serial0/0/0
R2(config)# ip route 172.16.3.0 255.255.255.0 Serial0/0/1
```

Step 4: Enable the HTTP server on R1 and set the enable and vty passwords.

a. Enable HTTP access to R1 using the **ip http server** command in global config mode. Configure an enable password of **class**. Also set the vty and console passwords to **cisco**. This provides web and Telnet targets for testing later in the lab.

```
R1(config)# ip http server
R1(config)# enable password class

R1(config)# line vty 0 4
R1(config-line)# password cisco
R1(config-line)# login

R1(config)# line con 0
R1(config-line)# password cisco
R1(config-line)# login
```

Step 5: Configure PC host IP settings.

Configure a static IP address, subnet mask, and default gateway for PC-A, PC-B, and PC-C, as shown in the IP addressing table.

Step 6: Verify connectivity.

Because the ASA is the focal point for the network zones and it has not yet been configured, there will be no connectivity between devices that are connected to it. However, PC-C should be able to ping the R1 interface Fa0/0. From PC-C, ping the R1 Fa0/0 IP address (209.165.200.225). If these pings are not successful, troubleshoot the basic device configurations before continuing.

Note: If you can ping from PC-C to R1 Fa0/0 and S0/0/0, you have demonstrated that static routing is configured and functioning correctly.

Step 7: Save the basic running configuration for each router and switch.

Part 2: Accessing the ASA Console and ASDM

In Part 2 of this lab, you access the ASA via the console and use various **show** commands to determine hardware, software, and configuration settings. You prepare the ASA for ASDM access and explore some of the ASDM screens and options.

Step 1: Access the ASA console.

a. Accessing the ASA via the console port is the same as with a Cisco router or switch. Connect to the ASA console port with a rollover cable.

b. Use a terminal emulation program such as TeraTerm or HyperTerminal to access the CLI. Use the serial port settings of 9600 baud, 8 data bits, no parity, 1 stop bit, and no flow control.

c. If prompted to enter Interactive Firewall configuration (Setup mode), answer **no**.

d. Enter privileged mode with the **enable** command and password (if set). By default, the password is blank, so you can just press **Enter**. If the password has been changed to that specified in this lab, enter the password **class**. The default ASA hostname and prompt is ciscoasa>.

```
ciscoasa> enable
Password: class (or press Enter if no password is set)
```

Step 2: Determine the ASA version, interfaces, and license.

The ASA 5505 comes with an integrated eight-port Ethernet switch. Ports E0/0 though E0/5 are normal Fast Ethernet ports, and ports E0/6 and E0/7 are Power over Ethernet (PoE) ports for use with PoE devices such as IP phones or network cameras.

Use the **show version** command to determine various aspects of this ASA device:

```
ciscoasa# show version

Cisco Adaptive Security Appliance Software Version 8.4(2)
Device Manager Version 6.4(5)

Compiled on Wed 15-Jun-11 18:17 by builders
System image file is "disk0:/asa842-k8.bin"
Config file at boot was "startup-config"

ciscoasa up 23 hours 0 mins

Hardware:   ASA5505, 512 MB RAM, CPU Geode 500 MHz
Internal ATA Compact Flash, 128MB
BIOS Flash M50FW016 @ 0xfff00000, 2048KB

Encryption hardware device : Cisco ASA-5505 on-board accelerator (revision
0x0)
                             Boot microcode        : CN1000-MC-BOOT-2.00
                             SSL/IKE microcode     : CNLite-MC-SSLm-PLUS-2.03
                             IPSec microcode       : CNlite-MC-IPSECm-MAIN-
2.06
                             Number of accelerators: 1

 0: Int: Internal-Data0/0    : address is 0007.7dbf.5645, irq 11
 1: Ext: Ethernet0/0         : address is 0007.7dbf.563d, irq 255
 2: Ext: Ethernet0/1         : address is 0007.7dbf.563e, irq 255

<output omitted>
```

What software version is this ASA running? ______________________________

What is the name of the system image file and from where was it loaded?

____

The ASA can be managed using a built-in GUI known as the Adaptive Security Device Manager (ASDM). What version of ASDM is this ASA running? ______________________________

How much RAM does this ASA have? ______________________________

How much flash memory does this ASA have? ______________________________

How many Ethernet ports does this ASA have? ______________________________

What type of license does this ASA have? ______________________________

How many VLANs can be created with this license? ______________________________

Step 3: Determine the file system and contents of flash memory.

a. Display the ASA file system using the **show file system** command to determine what prefixes are supported:

```
ciscoasa# show file system

File Systems:

     Size(b)      Free(b)       Type      Flags  Prefixes
* 128573440     55664640        disk      rw       disk0: flash:
                   -          - network   rw       tftp:
                   -          - opaque    rw       system:
                   -          - network   ro       http:
                   -          - network   ro       https:
                   -          - network   rw       ftp:
  -                - network   rw       smb:
```

What is another name for flash:? _______

b. Display the contents of flash memory using one of these commands: **show flash, show disk0, dir flash:** or **dir disk0**:

```
ciscoasa# show flash:
--#--  --length--  -----date/time------  path
  168  25159680    Aug 29 2011 13:00:52  asa842-k8.bin
  122  0           Aug 29 2011 13:09:32  nat_ident_migrate
   13  2048        Aug 29 2011 13:02:14  coredumpinfo
   14  59          Aug 29 2011 13:02:14  coredumpinfo/coredump.cfg
  169  16280544    Aug 29 2011 13:02:58  asdm-645.bin
    3  2048        Aug 29 2011 13:04:42  log
    6  2048        Aug 29 2011 13:05:00  crypto_archive
  171  34816       Jan 01 1980 00:00:00  FSCK0000.REC
  173  36864       Jan 01 1980 00:00:00  FSCK0001.REC
  174  12998641    Aug 29 2011 13:09:22  csd_3.5.2008-k9.pkg
  175  2048        Aug 29 2011 13:09:24  sdesktop
  211  0           Aug 29 2011 13:09:24  sdesktop/data.xml
  176  6487517     Aug 29 2011 13:09:26  anyconnect-macosx-i386-
2.5.2014-k9.pkg
  177  6689498     Aug 29 2011 13:09:30  anyconnect-linux-2.5.2014-
k9.pkg
  178  4678691     Aug 29 2011 13:09:32  anyconnect-win-2.5.2014-k9.pkg
  <output omitted>
```

What is the name of the ASDM file in flash:? _______________

Step 4: Determine the current running configuration.

The ASA may be configured with the default factory configuration or may have a configuration remaining from a previous lab. The default factory configuration for the ASA 5505 includes the following:

- An inside VLAN 1 interface is configured and by default, Ethernet 0/1 through 0/7 switch ports are assigned to it. The VLAN 1 IP address and mask are 192.168.1.1 and 255.255.255.0.

- An outside VLAN 2 interface is configured that includes the Ethernet 0/0 switch port. By default, VLAN 2 derives its IP address from the upstream device (usually the ISP) using DHCP.
- The default route is also derived from the upstream DHCP default gateway.
- All inside IP addresses are translated when accessing the outside interface using Port Address Translation (PAT) on the VLAN 2 interface.
- By default, an access list allows inside users to access the outside, and outside users are prevented from accessing the inside.
- The DHCP server is enabled on the security appliance. Therefore, a PC connecting to any VLAN 1 interface receives an address between 192.168.1.5 and 192.168.1.36 (Base license).
- The HTTP server is enabled for ASDM and is accessible to users on the 192.168.1.0/24 network.
- No console or enable passwords are required and the default hostname is ciscoasa.

Note: In this lab, you use ASDM to configure settings similar to those listed above, as well as some additional ones.

Display the current running configuration using the **`show running-config`** command:

```
ciscoasa# show running-config
: Saved
:
ASA Version 8.4(2)
!
hostname ciscoasa
enable password 8Ry2YjIyt7RRXU24 encrypted
passwd 2KFQnbNIdI.2KYOU encrypted
names
!
interface Ethernet0/0
 switchport access vlan 2
!
interface Ethernet0/1
!
interface Ethernet0/2

<output omitted>
```

Note: To stop the output from a command using the CLI, press **Q**.

If you see VLANs 1 and 2 configured and other settings as described previously, the device is most likely configured with the default factory configuration. You may also see other security features such as a global policy that inspects selected application traffic, which the ASA inserts by default, if the original startup configuration has been erased. The actual output will vary depending on the ASA model, version and configuration status.

Step 5: Clear the previous ASA configuration settings.

a. Use the **`write erase`** command to remove the startup-config file from flash memory:

```
ciscoasa# write erase
Erase configuration in flash memory? [confirm]
[OK]
ciscoasa#

ciscoasa# show start
No Configuration
```

Note: The IOS command **erase startup-config** is not supported on the ASA.

b. Use the **reload** command to restart the ASA:

```
ciscoasa# reload
Proceed with reload? [confirm] <enter>
ciscoasa#
***
*** --- START GRACEFUL SHUTDOWN ---
Shutting down isakmp
Shutting down File system
***
*** --- SHUTDOWN NOW ---
Process shutdown finished
Rebooting.....
CISCO SYSTEMS
Embedded BIOS Version 1.0(12)13 08/28/08 15:50:37.45
<output omitted>
```

Step 6: Bypass setup mode and configure the ASDM VLAN interfaces.

When the ASA completes the reload process, it should detect that the startup-config file is missing and present a series of interactive prompts to configure basic ASA settings. If it does not come up in this mode, repeat Step 5.

a. When prompted to preconfigure the firewall through interactive prompts (Setup mode), respond with **no**:

```
Pre-configure Firewall now through interactive prompts [yes]?  no
```

b. Enter privileged EXEC mode with the **enable** command. The password should be blank (no password) at this point.

c. Enter global configuration mode using the command **config t**. The first time you enter configuration mode after reloading, you are asked whether you want to enable anonymous reporting. Respond with **no**.

d. Configure the inside interface VLAN 1 to prepare for ASDM access. The Security Level should be automatically set to the highest level of 100. The VLAN 1 logical interface will be used by PC-B to access ASDM on ASA physical interface E0/1.

```
ciscoasa(config)# interface vlan 1
ciscoasa(config-if)# nameif inside
INFO: Security level for "inside" set to 100 by default.
ciscoasa(config-if)# ip address 192.168.1.1 255.255.255.0
ciscoasa(config-if)# exit
```

PC-B is connected to switch S2 which is connected to ASA port E0/1. Why is it not necessary to add physical interface E0/1 to this VLAN? ______________________________

ASA 5505 Interface Notes

The 5505 is different from the other 5500 series ASA models. With other ASAs, the physical port can be assigned a Layer 3 IP address directly, much like a Cisco router. With the ASA 5505, the eight integrated switch ports are Layer 2 ports. To assign Layer 3 parameters, you must create a switch virtual interface (SVI) or logical VLAN interface and then assign one or more of the physical Layer 2 ports to it.

e. By default, all ASA physical interfaces are administratively down, unless the Setup utility has been run or the factory defaults have been reset. Because no physical interface in VLAN 1 has been enabled, the VLAN 1 status is down/down. Use the **show interface ip brief** command to verify this:

```
ciscoasa(config)# show interface ip brief
Interface          IP-Address      OK? Method Status
Protocol
Ethernet0/0        unassigned      YES unset  administratively down up
Ethernet0/1        unassigned      YES unset  administratively down up
Ethernet0/2        unassigned      YES unset  administratively down up
Ethernet0/3        unassigned      YES unset  administratively down up
Ethernet0/4        unassigned      YES unset  administratively down down
Ethernet0/5        unassigned      YES unset  administratively down down
Ethernet0/6        unassigned      YES unset  administratively down down
Ethernet0/7        unassigned      YES unset  administratively down down
Internal-Data0/0 unassigned        YES unset  up                    up
Internal-Data0/1 unassigned        YES unset  up                    up
Vlan1              192.168.1.1     YES manual down                  down
Virtual0           127.0.0.1       YES unset  up                    up
```

f. Enable the E0/1 interface using the **no shutdown** command and verify the E0/1 and VLAN 1 interface status. The status and protocol for interface E0/1 and VLAN 1 should be up/up.

```
ciscoasa(config)# interface e0/1
ciscoasa(config-if)# no shut
ciscoasa(config-if)# exit

ciscoasa(config)# show interface ip brief
Interface          IP-Address      OK? Method Status                Protocol
Ethernet0/0        unassigned      YES unset  administratively down up
Ethernet0/1        unassigned      YES unset  up                    up
Ethernet0/2        unassigned      YES unset  administratively down up
Ethernet0/3        unassigned      YES unset  administratively down up
Ethernet0/4        unassigned      YES unset  administratively down down
Ethernet0/5        unassigned      YES unset  administratively down down
Ethernet0/6        unassigned      YES unset  administratively down down
Ethernet0/7        unassigned      YES unset  administratively down down
Internal-Data0/0 unassigned        YES unset  up                    up
Internal-Data0/1 unassigned        YES unset  up                    up
Vlan1              192.168.1.1     YES manual up                    up
Virtual0           127.0.0.1       YES unset  up                    up
```

g. Also preconfigure outside interface VLAN 2, add physical interface E0/0 to VLAN 2, and bring up the E0/0 interface. You assign the IP address using ASDM.

```
ciscoasa(config)# interface vlan 2
ciscoasa(config-if)# nameif outside
INFO: Security level for "outside" set to 0 by default.

ciscoasa(config-if)# interface e0/0
ciscoasa(config-if)# switchport access vlan 2
ciscoasa(config-if)# no shut
ciscoasa(config-if)# exit
```

h. Test connectivity to the ASA by pinging from PC-B to ASA interface VLAN 1 IP address 192.168.1.1. The pings should be successful.

Step 7: Configure ASDM and verify access to the ASA.

a. Configure the ASA to accept HTTPS connections using the **http** command to allow access to ASDM from any host on the inside network 192.168.1.0/24:

```
ciscoasa(config)# http server enable
ciscoasa(config)# http 192.168.1.0 255.255.255.0 inside
```

b. Open a browser on PC-B and test the HTTPS access to the ASA by entering **https://192.168.1.1**.

Note: Be sure to specify the HTTPS protocol in the URL.

Step 8: Access ASDM and explore the GUI.

a. After entering the URL above, you should see a security warning about the website security certificate. Click **Continue to This Website**. The ASDM Welcome page will display. From this screen, you can run ASDM as a local application on the PC (installs ASDM on the PC), run ASDM as a browser-based Java applet directly from the ASA, or run the Startup Wizard.

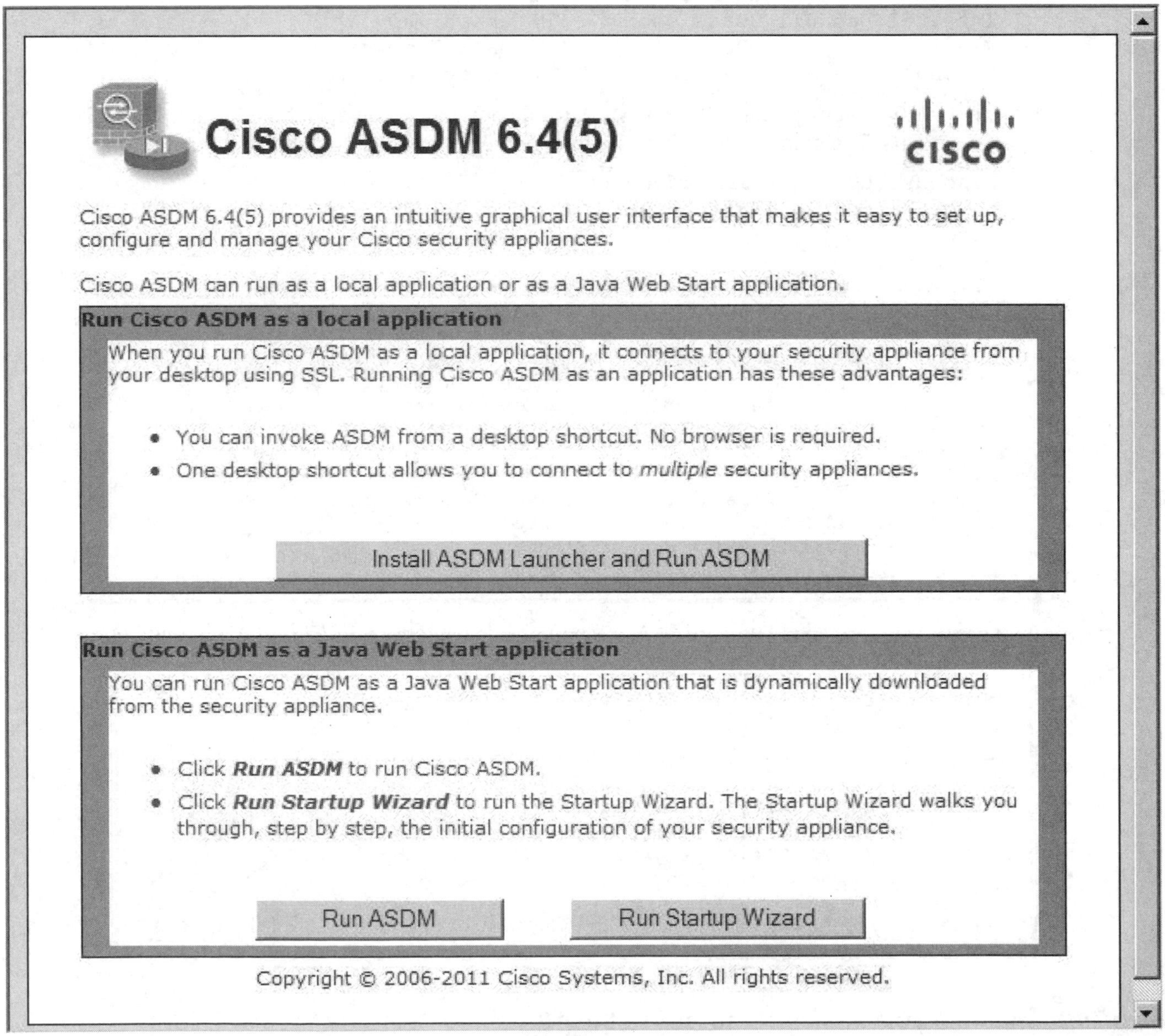

b. Click the **Run ASDM** button.

c. Click **Yes** for any other security warnings. You should see the Cisco ASDM-IDM Launcher dialog box, where you can enter a username and password. Leave these fields blank because they have not yet been configured.

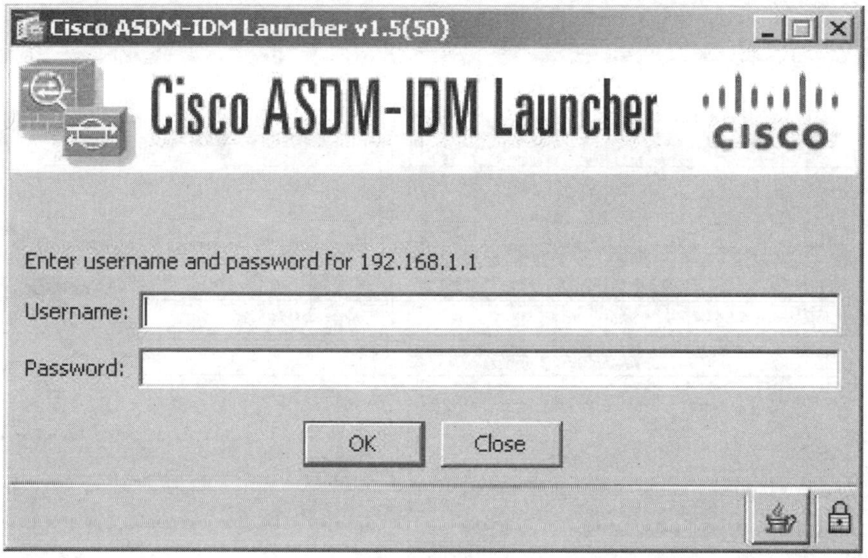

d. Click **OK** to continue. ASDM will load the current configuration into the GUI.

The initial GUI screen is displayed with various areas and options. The main menu at the top left of the screen contains three main sections; Home, Configuration, and Monitoring. The Home section is the default and has two dashboards: Device and Firewall. The Device dashboard is the default screen and shows device information such as Type (ASA 5505), ASA and ASDM version, amount of memory and firewall mode (routed). There are five areas on the Device Dashboard.

- Device Information
- Interface Status
- VPN Sessions
- System Resources Status
- Traffic Status

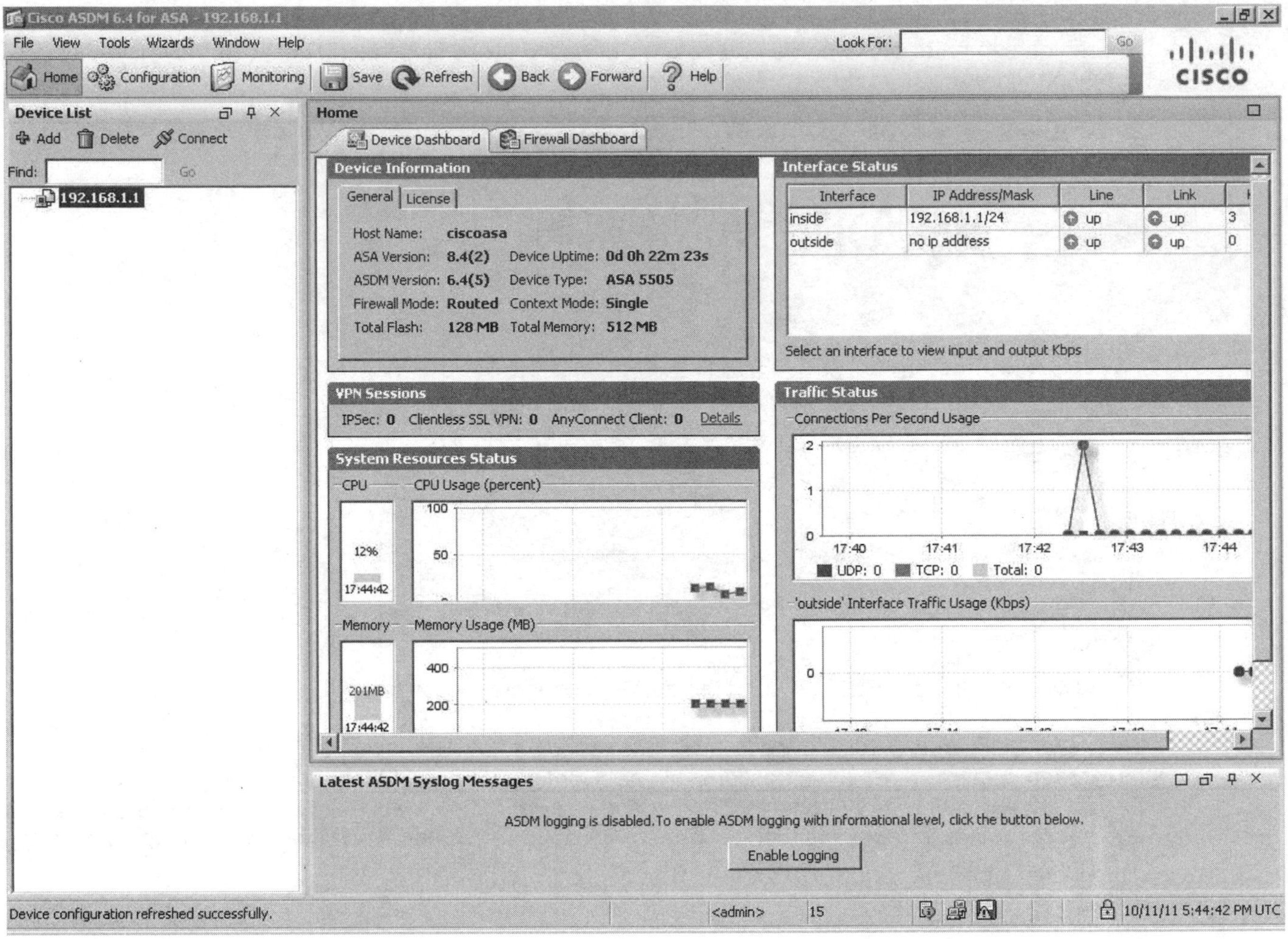

e. Display the Configuration and Monitoring tabs to become familiar with their layout and to see what options are available.

Part 3: Configuring Basic ASA Settings and Firewall Using the ASDM Startup Wizard

Step 1: Access the Configuration menu and launch the Startup Wizard.

a. Click the **Configuration** button at the top left of the screen. There are five main configuration areas:

- Device Setup
- Firewall
- Remote Access VPN
- Site-to-Site VPN
- Device Management

b. The Device Setup Startup Wizard is the first option available and displays by default. Read through the onscreen text describing the Startup Wizard, and then click the **Launch Startup Wizard** button.

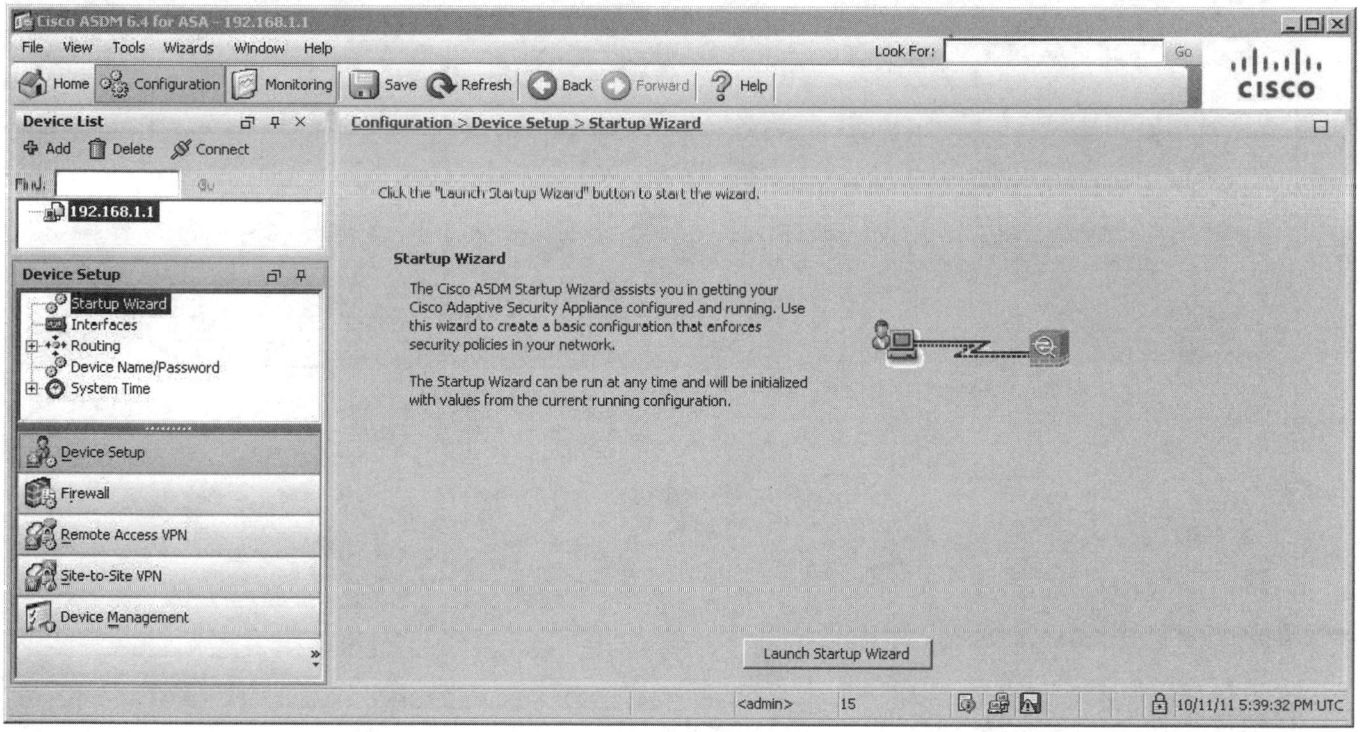

Step 2: Configure the hostname, domain name, and enable password.

a. On the first Startup Wizard screen, you have a choice of modifying the existing configuration or resetting the ASA to the factory defaults. With the **Modify Existing Configuration** option selected, click **Next** to continue.

b. On the Startup Wizard Step 2 screen, configure the ASA hostname **CCNAS-ASA** and domain name of **ccnasecurity.com**. Check the check box for changing the enable mode password and change it from blank (no password) to **class** and enter it again to confirm. When the entries are completed, click **Next** to continue.

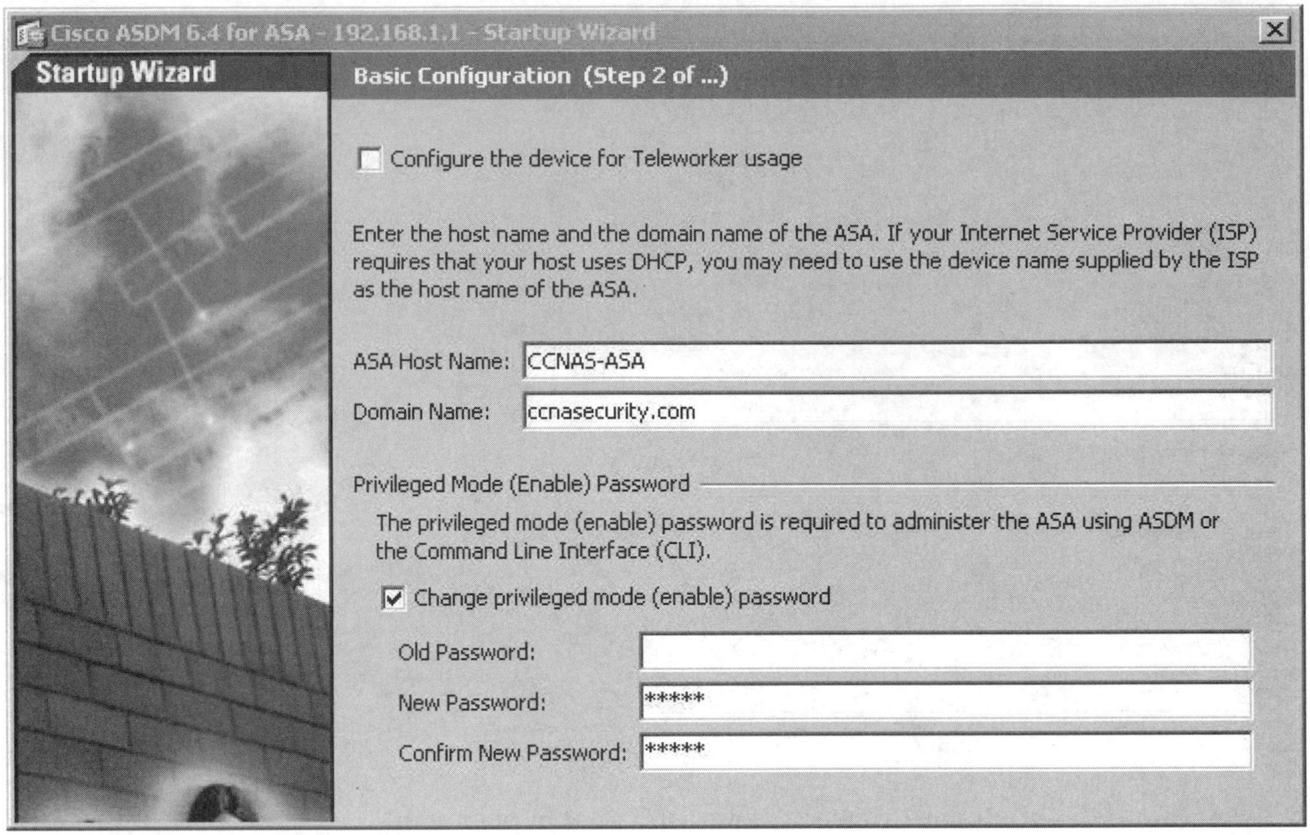

Step 3: Configure the inside and outside VLAN interfaces.

a. On the Startup Wizard Step 3 screen, Interface Selection, for the Outside and Inside VLANs, do not change the current settings because these were previously defined using the CLI. The inside VLAN is named inside, and the security level is set to 100 (highest). The Outside VLAN interface is named outside, and the security level set to 0 (lowest). For the DMZ VLAN, click the **Do Not Configure** button and uncheck the **Enable VLAN** check box. The DMZ VLAN is configured later. Click **Next** to continue.

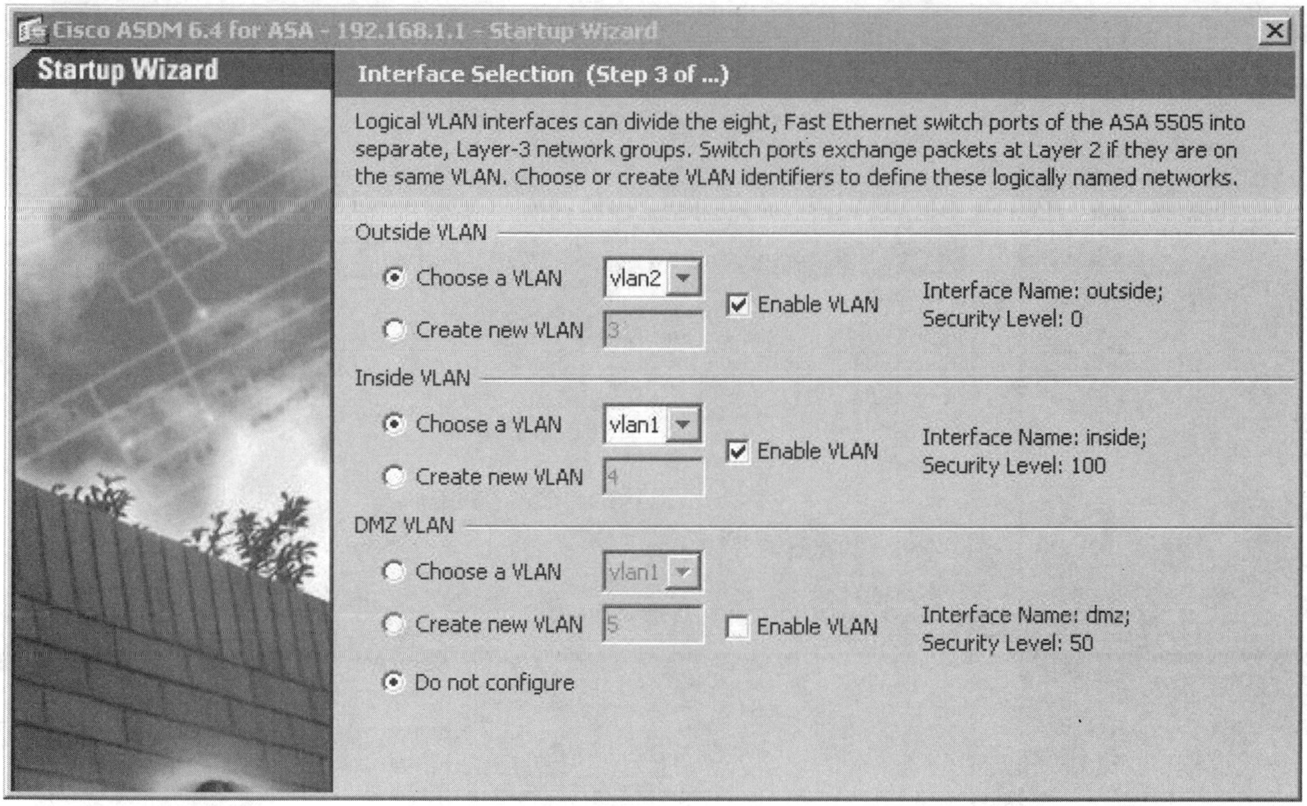

b. On the Startup Wizard Step 4 screen, Switch Port Allocation, verify that port Ethernet1 is in inside VLAN 1 and that port Ethernet0 is in outside VLAN 2.

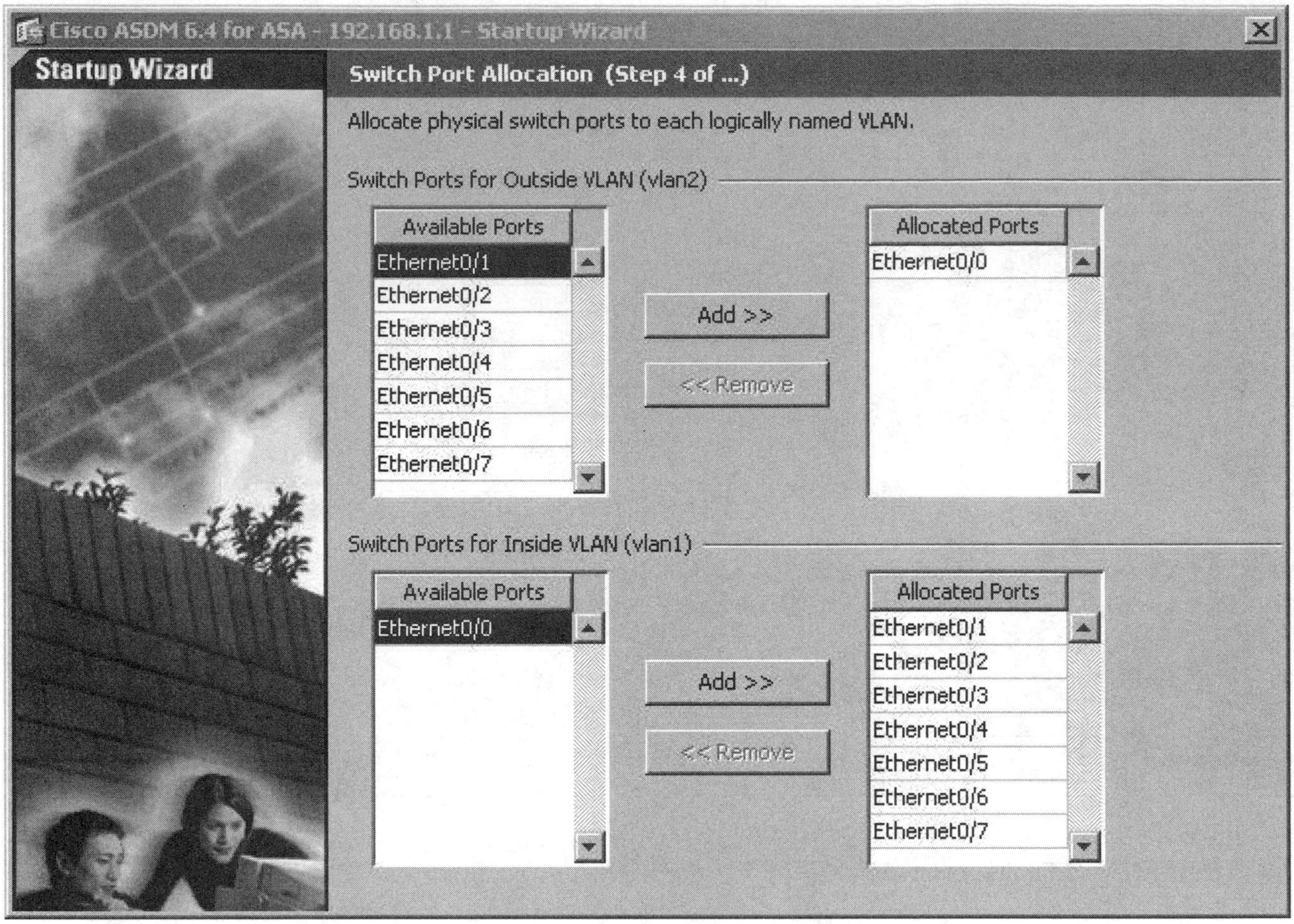

c. On the Startup Wizard Step 5 screen, Interface IP Address Configuration, enter an outside IP address of **209.165.200.226** and mask of **255.255.255.248**. You can use the pull-down menu to select the mask. Leave the inside interface IP address as 192.168.1.1 with a mask of 255.255.255.0. Click **Next** to continue.

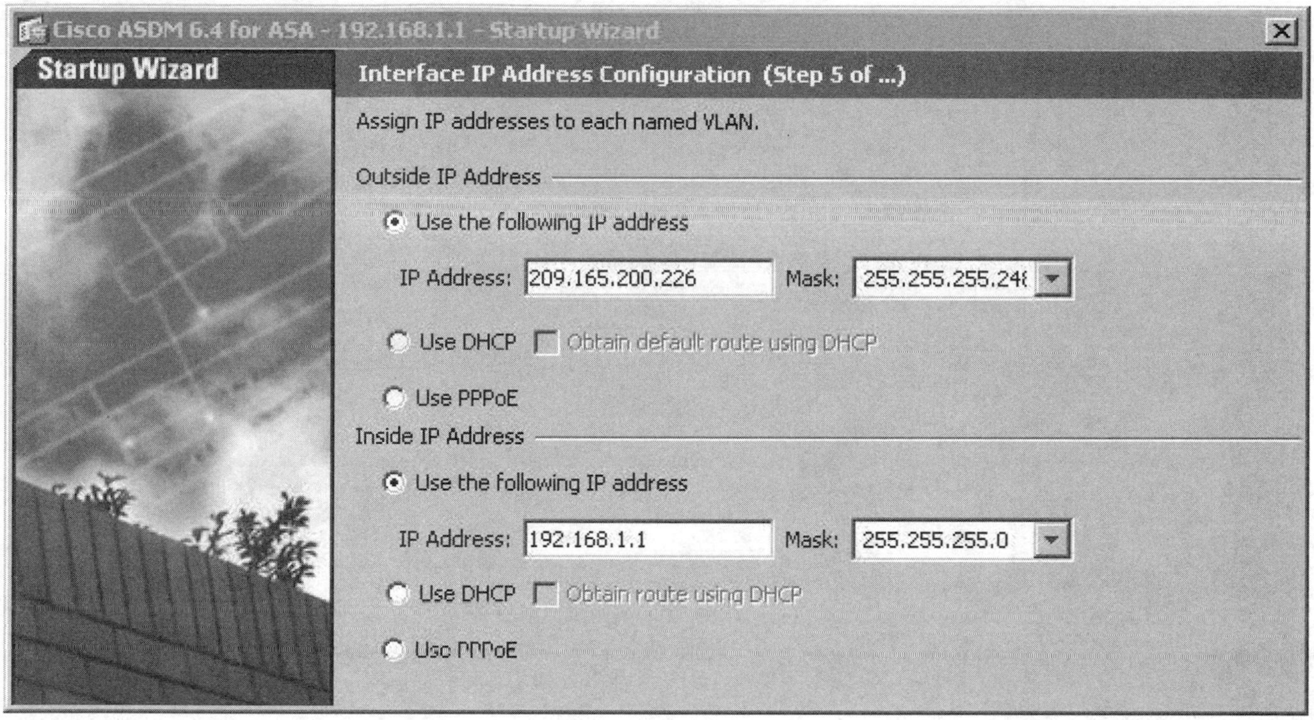

Step 4: Configure DHCP, address translation and administrative access.

a. On the Startup Wizard Step 6 screen, DHCP Server, check the **Enable DHCP Server on the Inside Interface** check box. Enter a starting IP address of **192.168.1.3** and ending IP address of **192.168.1.30**. Enter the DNS Server 1 address of **10.20.30.40** and Domain Name **ccnasecurity.com**. Do *not* check the Enable Auto-configuration from Interface check box. Click **Next** to continue.

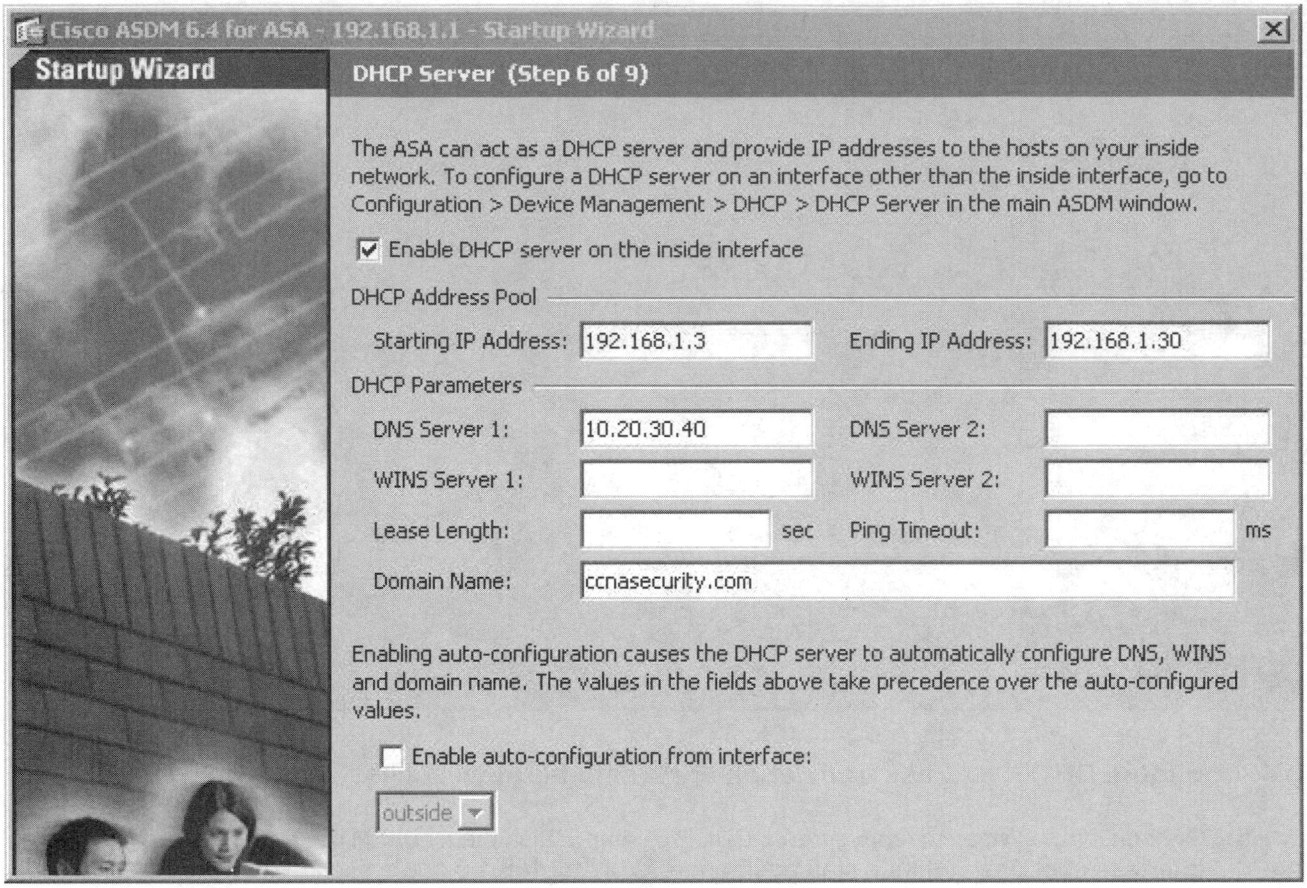

b. On the Startup Wizard Step 7 screen, Address Translation (NAT/PAT), click the **Use Port Address Translation (PAT)** button. The default is to use the IP address of the outside interface. Note that you can also specify a particular IP address for PAT or a range of addresses with NAT. Click **Next** to continue.

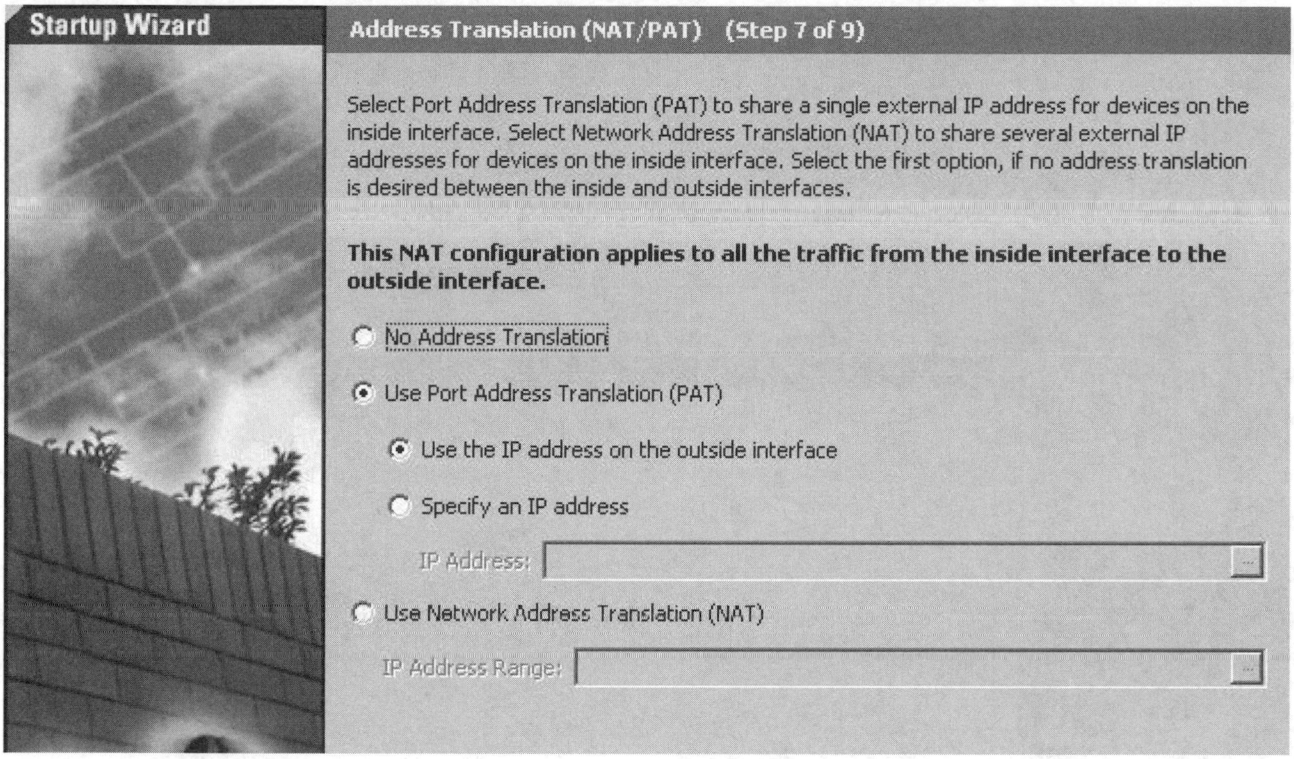

c. On the Startup Wizard Step 8 screen, Administrative Access, HTTPS/ASDM access is currently configured for hosts on inside network 192.168.1.0/24. Add Telnet access to the ASA for the inside network 192.168.1.0 with a subnet mask of 255.255.255.0. Add SSH access to the ASA from host 172.16.3.3 on the outside network. Make sure the **Enable HTTP Server for HTTPS/ASDM Access** check box is checked. Click **Next** to continue.

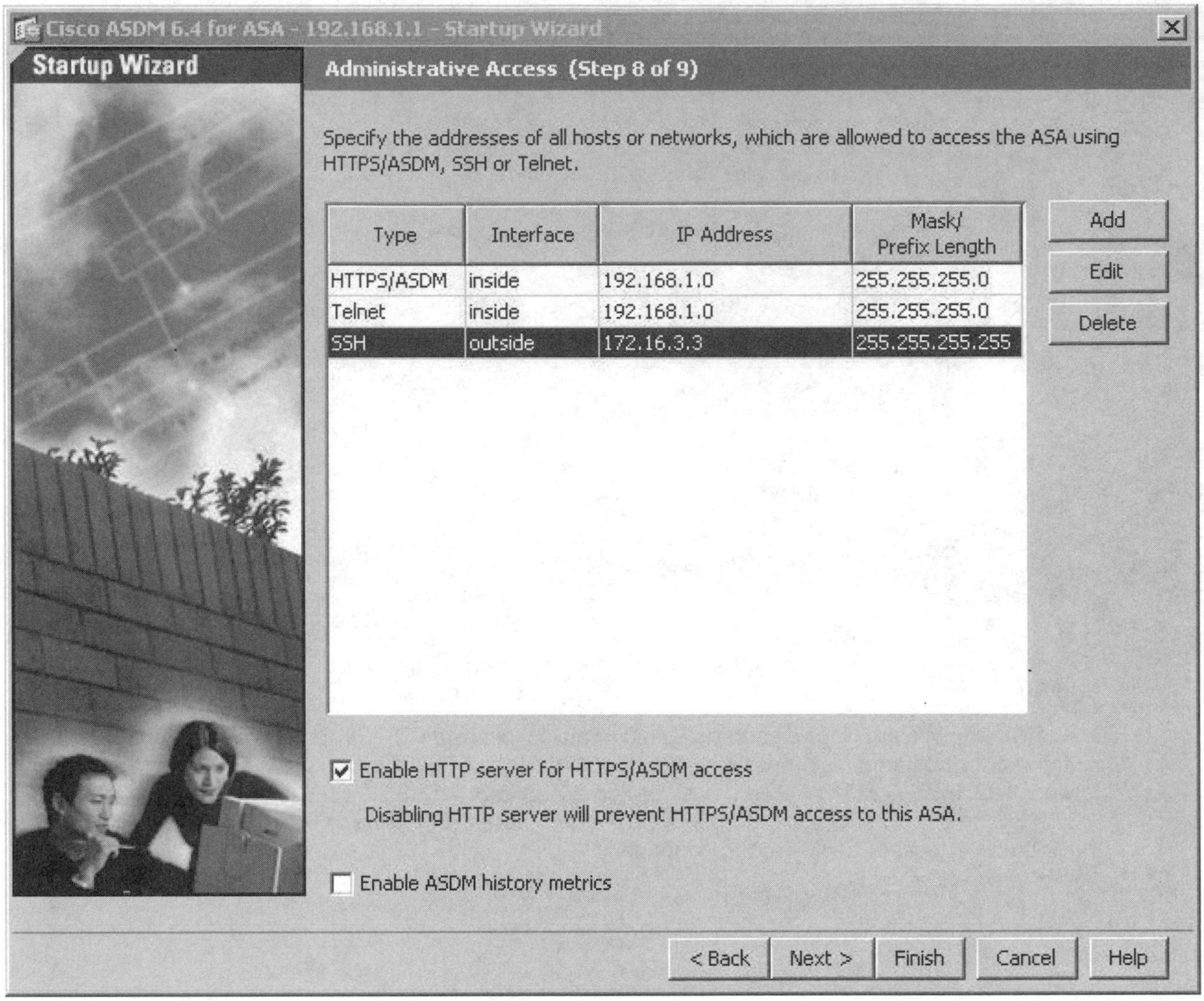

Step 5: Review the summary and deliver the commands to the ASA.

a. On the Startup Wizard Step 9 screen, Startup Wizard Summary, review the Configuration Summary and click **Finish**. ASDM delivers the commands to the ASA device and then reloads the modified configuration.

Note: If the GUI dialog box stops responding during the reload process, close it, exit ASDM, and restart the browser and ASDM. If prompted to save the configuration to flash memory, respond with **Yes**. Even though ASDM may not appear to have reloaded the configuration, the commands were delivered. If errors are encountered as ASDM delivers the commands, you are notified with a list of commands that succeeded and those that failed.

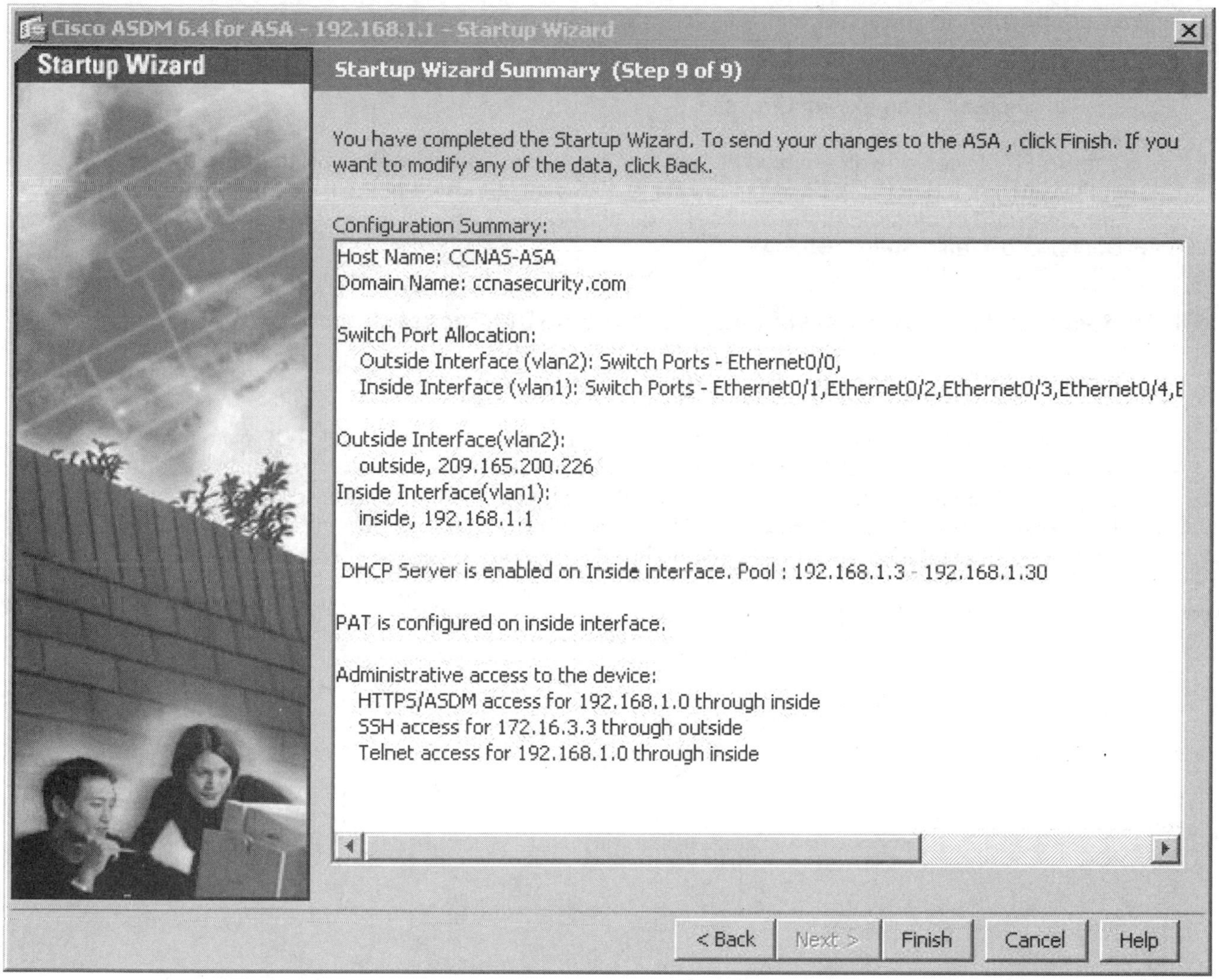

b. Restart ASDM and provide the new enable password **class** with no username. Return to the Device Dashboard and check the Interface Status window. You should see the inside and outside interfaces with IP address and status. The inside interface should show some number of Kbps. The Traffic Status window may show the ASDM access as TCP traffic spike.

Step 6: Test Telnet and SSH access to the ASA.

a. From a command prompt or GUI Telnet client on PC-B, telnet to the ASA inside interface at IP address 192.168.1.1.

b. Log in to the ASA using the default login password of **cisco**. Enter privileged EXEC mode by using the `enable` command and provide the password **class**. Exit the Telnet session by using the `quit` command.

c. In Lab Step 4, SSH access was configured using the Startup Wizard to allow access to the ASA from outside PC-C (172.16.3.3). From PC-C, open an SSH client such as PuTTY and attempt to connect to the ASA outside interface at 209.165.200.226. You cannot establish the connection because SSH access (ASA version 8.4(2) or later) requires that you also configure AAA and provide an authenticated user name. You configure AAA in Part 4 of the lab.

Step 7: Test access to an external website from PC-B.

a. Open a browser on PC-B and enter the IP address of the R1 Fa0/0 interface (**209.165.200.225**) to simulate access to an external website.

b. The R1 HTTP server was enabled in Part 1 of the lab, so you should be prompted with a user authentication login dialog box from the R1 GUI device manger. Leave the username blank and enter the password of **class**. Exit the browser. You should see TCP activity in the ASDM Device Dashboard Traffic Status window.

Step 8: Test access to an external website using the ASDM Packet Tracer utility.

a. From the ASDM Home page, choose **Tools > Packet Tracer**.

b. Choose the **Inside** interface from the Interface drop-down menu and click **TCP** from the Packet Type radio buttons. From the Source drop-down menu, choose **IP Address** and enter the address **192.168.1.3** (PC-B) with a source port of **1500**. From the Destination drop-down menu, choose **IP Address** and enter **209.165.200.225** (R1 Fa0/0) with a destination port of **HTTP**. Click **Start** to begin the trace of the packet. The packet should be permitted.

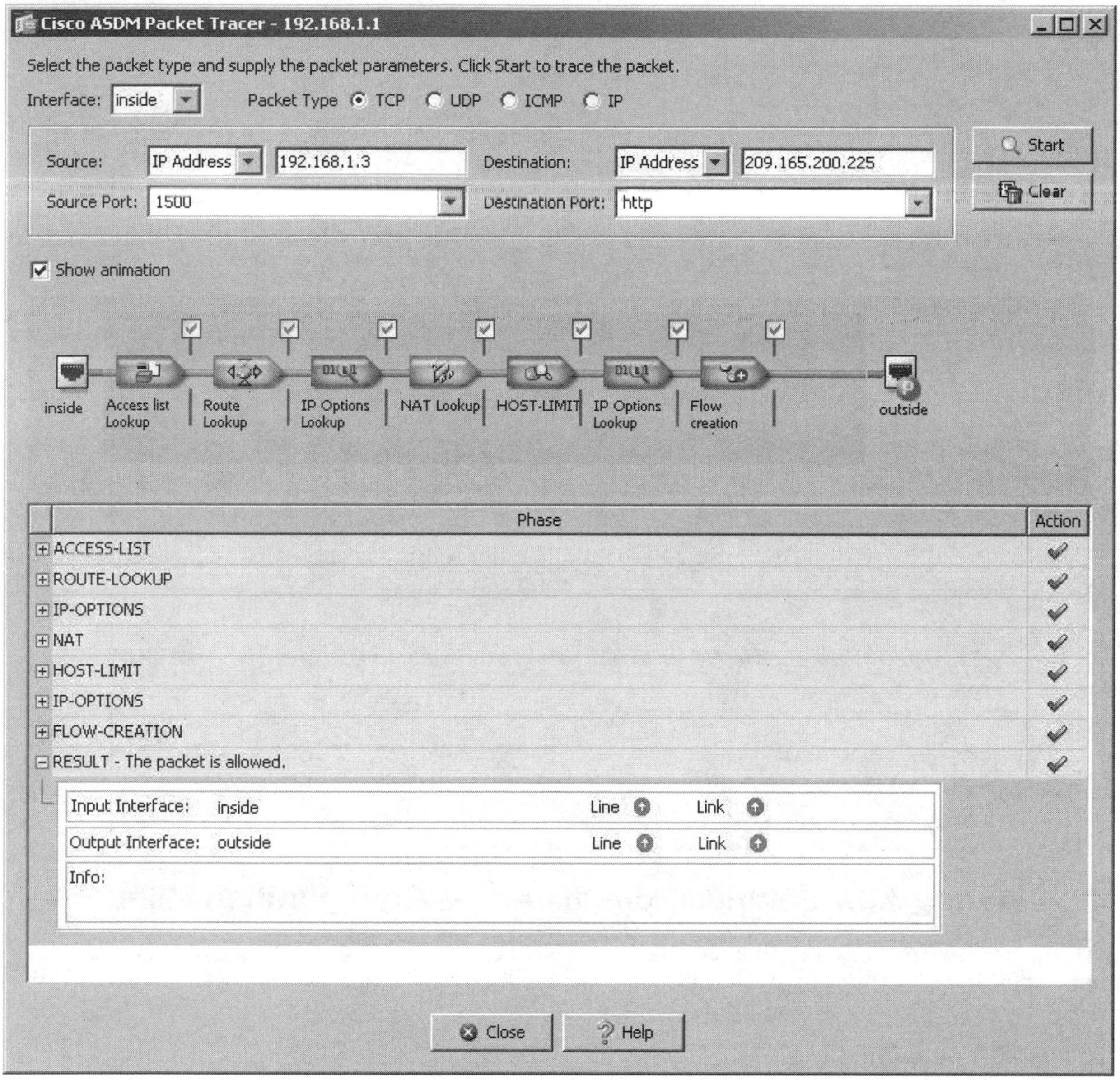

c. Reset the entries by clicking **Clear**. Try another trace and choose outside from the Interface drop-down menu and leave **TCP** as the packet type. From the Sources drop-down menu, choose **IP Address** and enter **209.165.200.225** (R1 Fa0/0) and a source port of **1500**. From the Destination drop-down menu, choose **IP Address** and enter the address **209.165.200.226** (ASA outside interface) with a destination port of **telnet**. Click **Start** to begin the trace of the packet. The packet should be dropped. Click **Close** to continue.

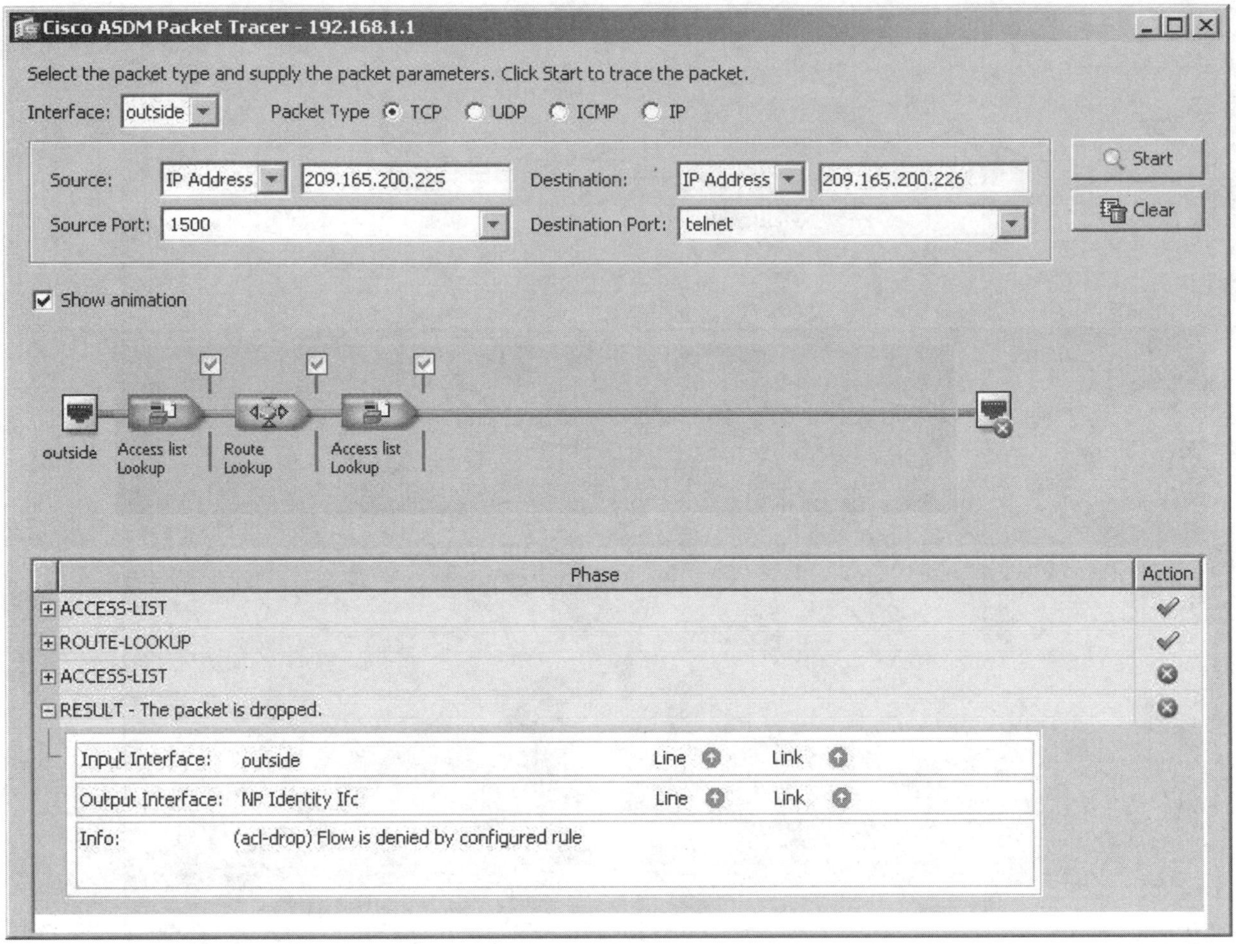

Part 4: Configuring ASA Settings from the ASDM Configuration Menu

In Part 4, you set the ASA clock, configure a default route, test connectivity using ASDM tools Ping and Traceroute, configure Local AAA user authentication, and modify the MPF application inspection policy.

Step 1: Set the ASA date and time.

a. From the Configuration screen, Device Setup menu, choose **System Time > Clock**.

b. Select your Time Zone from the drop-down menu and enter the current date and time in the fields provided. The clock is a 24-hour clock. Click **Apply** to send the commands to the ASA.

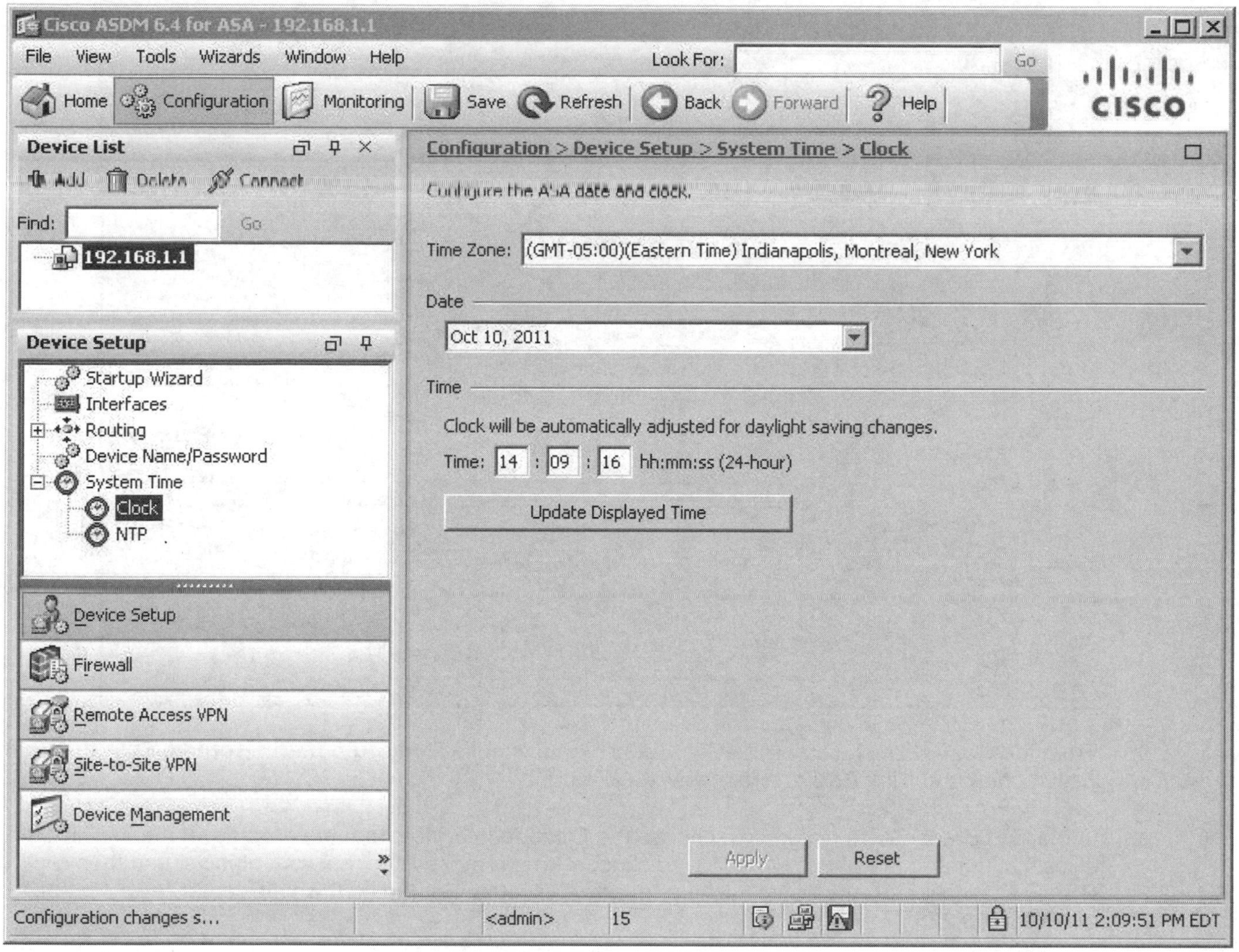

Step 2: Configure a static default route for the ASA.

a. From the ASDM Tools menu, choose **Ping** and enter the IP address of router R1 S0/0/0 (**10.1.1.1**). The ASA does not have a default route to unknown external networks. The ping should fail because the ASA has no route to 10.1.1.1. Click **Close** to continue.

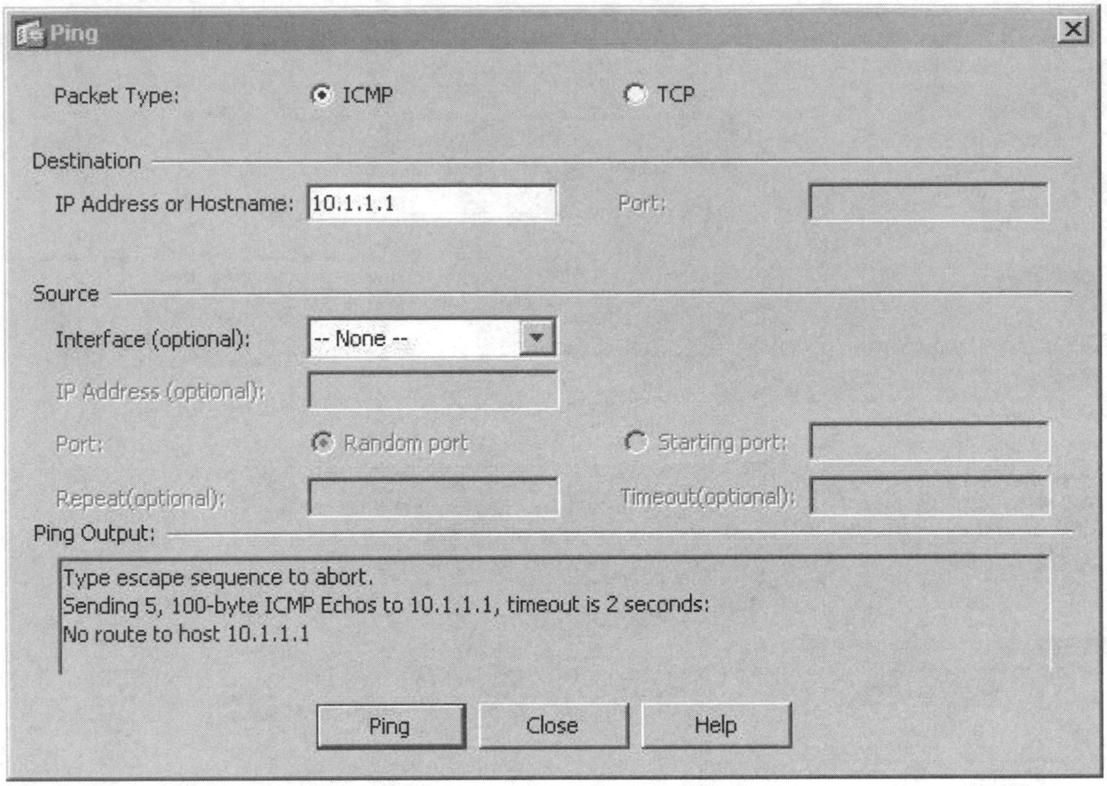

b. From the Configuration screen, Device Setup menu, choose **Routing > Static Routes**. Click the **IPv4 Only** button and click **Add** to add a new static route.

c. In the Add Static Route dialog box, choose the **Outside** interface from the drop-down menu. Click the ellipsis button to the right of Network and choose **Any** from the list of network objects, and then click **OK**. The selection of Any translates to a "quad zero" route. For the Gateway IP, enter **209.165.200.225** (R1 Fa0/0).

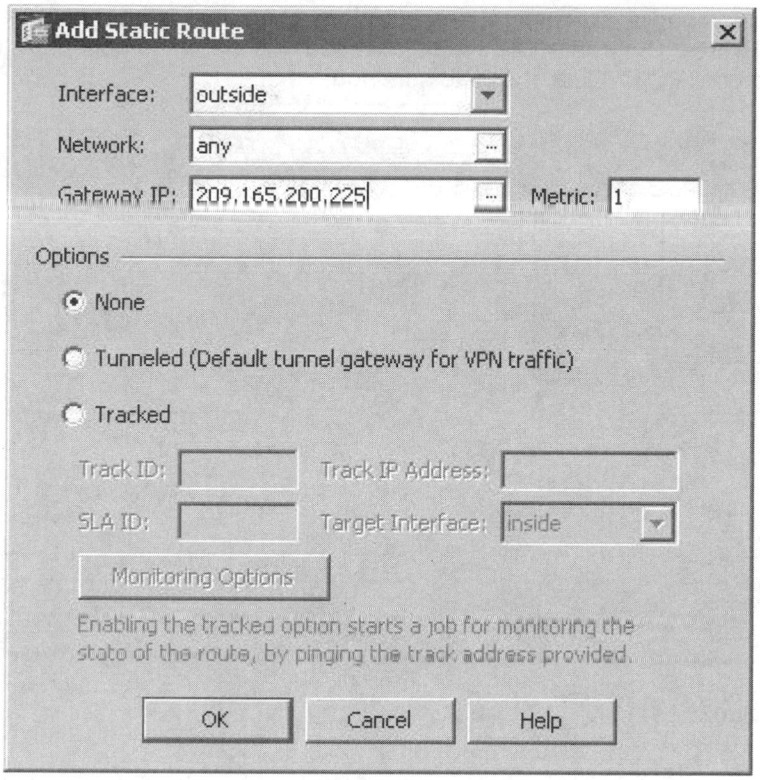

d. Click **OK** and click **Apply** to send the commands to the ASA.

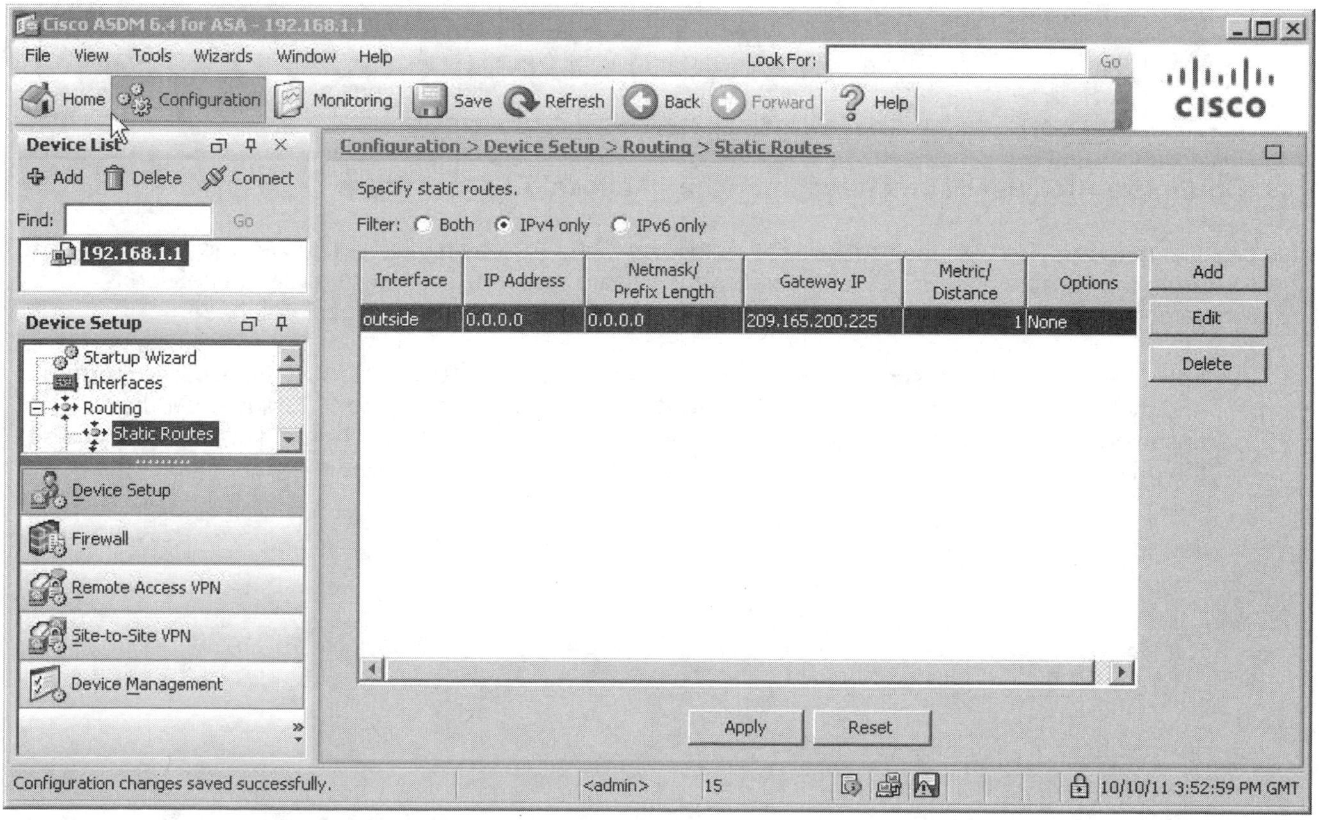

e. From the ASDM Tools menu, choose **Ping** and enter the IP address of router R1 S0/0/0 (10.1.1.1). The ping should succeed this time. Click **Close** to continue.

f. From the ASDM Tools menu, choose **Traceroute** and enter the IP address of external host PC-C (**172.16.3.3**). Click **Trace Route**. The traceroute should succeed and show the hops from the ASA through R1, R2, and R3 to host PC-C. Click **Close** to continue.

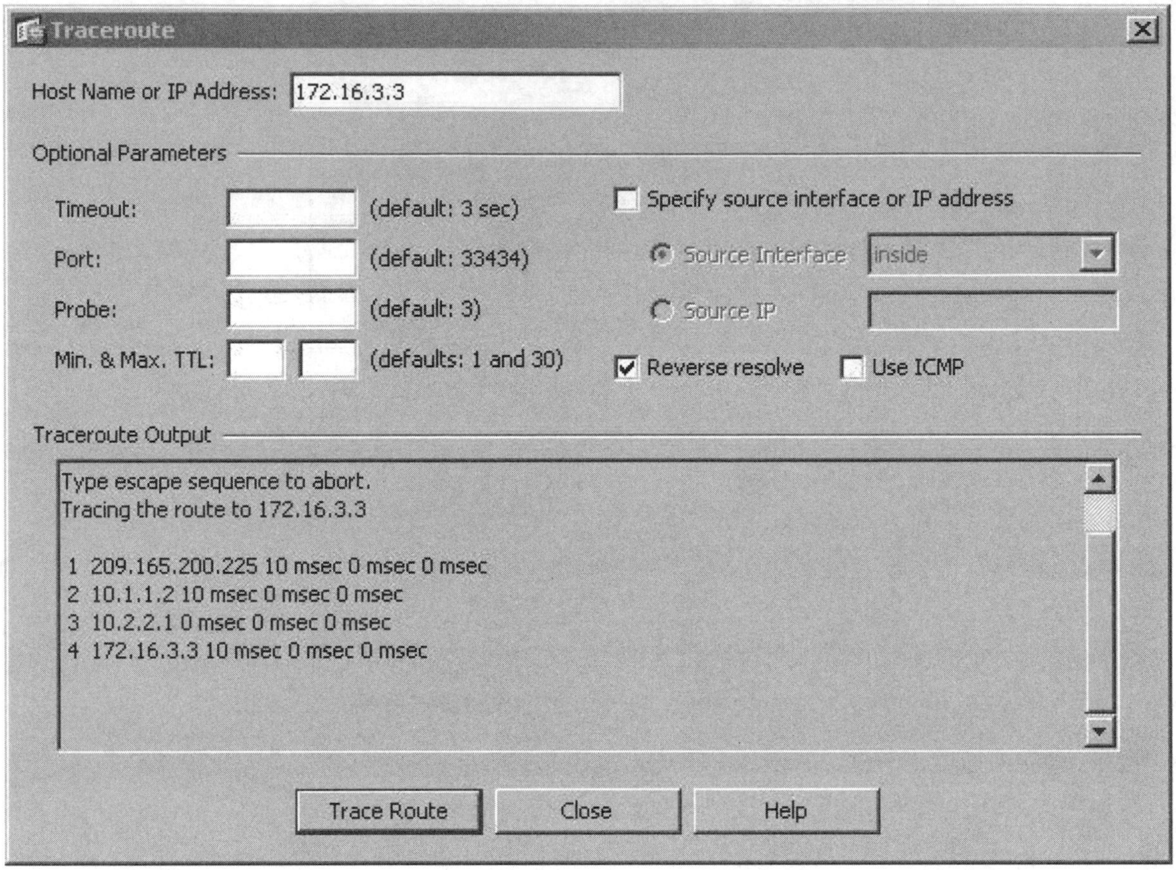

Step 3: Configure AAA user authentication using the local ASA database.

It is necessary to enable AAA user authentication to access the ASA using SSH. You allowed SSH access to the ASA from the outside host PC-C when the Startup Wizard was run. To allow the remote network administrator at PC-C to have SSH access to the ASA, you create a user in the local database.

a. From the Configuration screen, Device Management area, click **Users/AAA**. Click **User Accounts** and then **Add**. Create a new user named **admin** with a password of **cisco123** and enter the password again to confirm it. Allow this user **Full access** (ASDM, SSH, Telnet, and console) and set the privilege level to **15**. Click **OK** to add the user and click **Apply** to send the command to the ASA.

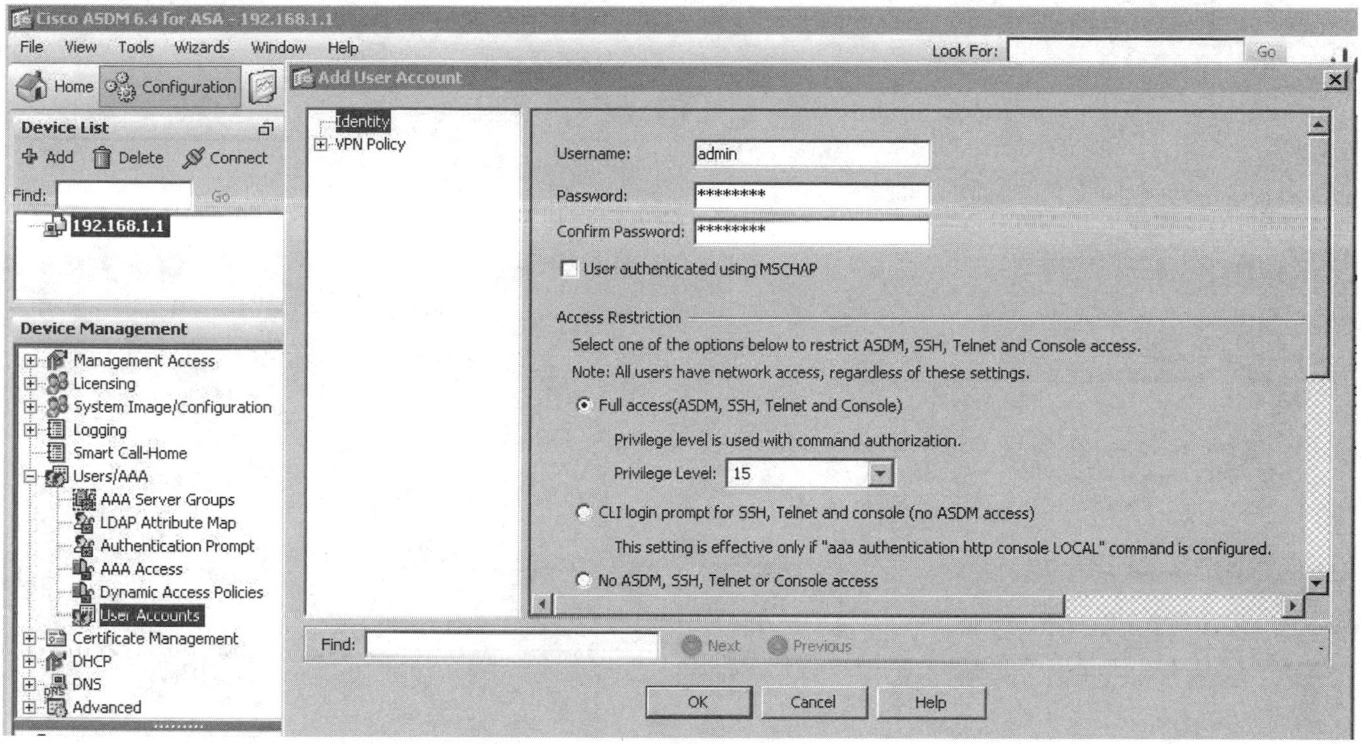

b. From the Configuration screen, Device Management area, click **Users/AAA**. Click **AAA Access**. On the Authentication tab, check the check box to require authentication for HTTP/ASDM, SSH, and Telnet connections and specify the **LOCAL** server group for each connection type. Click **Apply** to send the commands to the ASA.

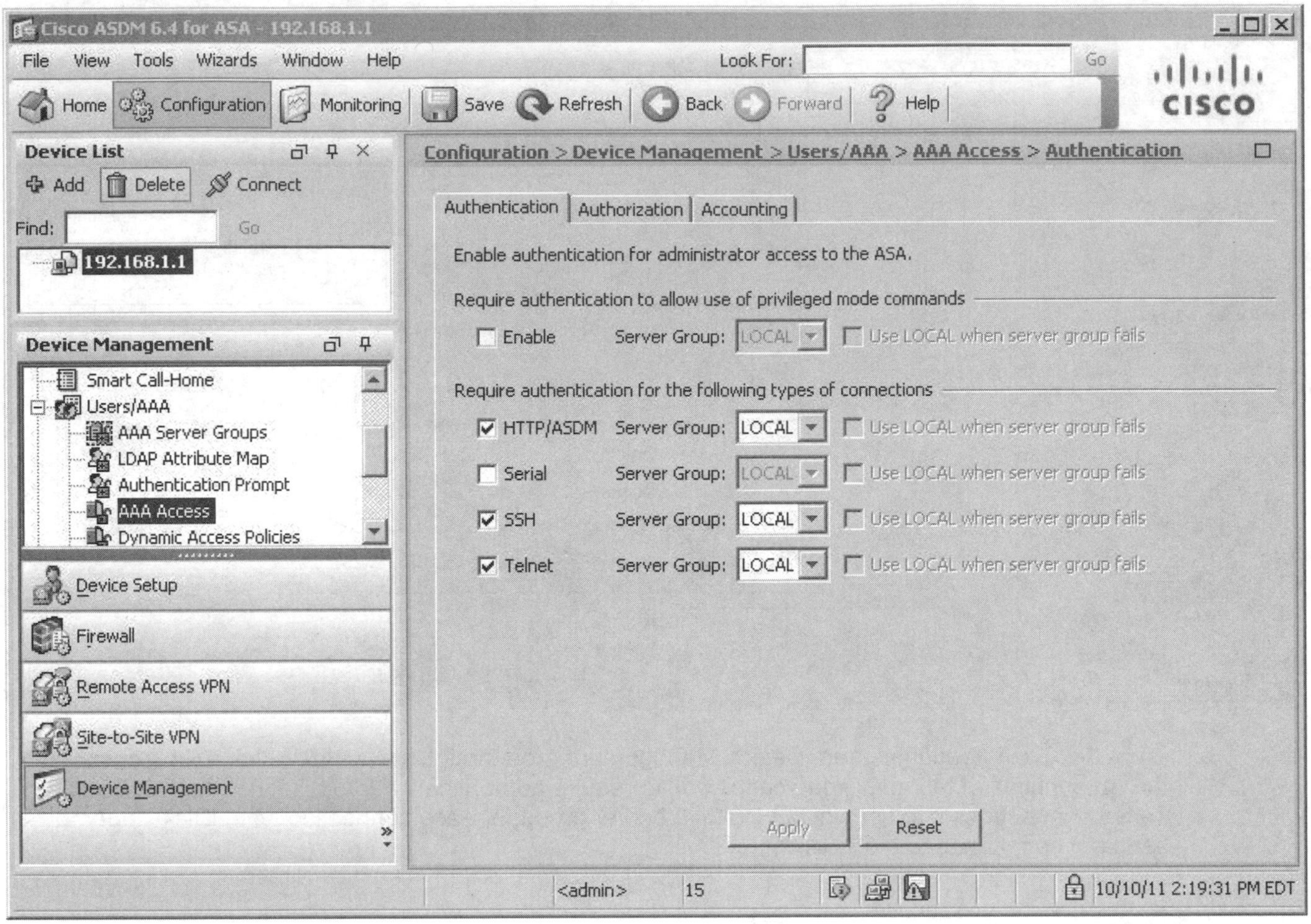

Note: The next action you attempt within ASDM will require you to log in as **admin** with password **cisco123**.

c. From PC-C, open an SSH client such as PuTTY and attempt to access the ASA outside interface at 209.165.200.226. You should be able to establish the connection. When prompted to log in, enter user name **admin** and password **cisco123**.

d. After logging in to the ASA using SSH, enter the **`enable`** command and provide the password **class**. Issue the **`show run`** command to display the current configuration you have created using ASDM.

Note: The default timeout for Telnet and SSH is 5 minutes. You can increase this setting using the CLI as described in Lab 10A or by going to ASDM **Device Management > Management Access > ASDM/HTTP/Telnet/SSH**.

Step 4: Modify the MPF application inspection policy.

For application layer inspection and other advanced options, the Cisco Modular Policy Framework (MPF) is available on ASAs.

a. The default global inspection policy does not inspect ICMP. To enable hosts on the internal network to ping external hosts and receive replies, ICMP traffic must be inspected. From the Configuration screen, Firewall area menu, click **Service Policy Rules**.

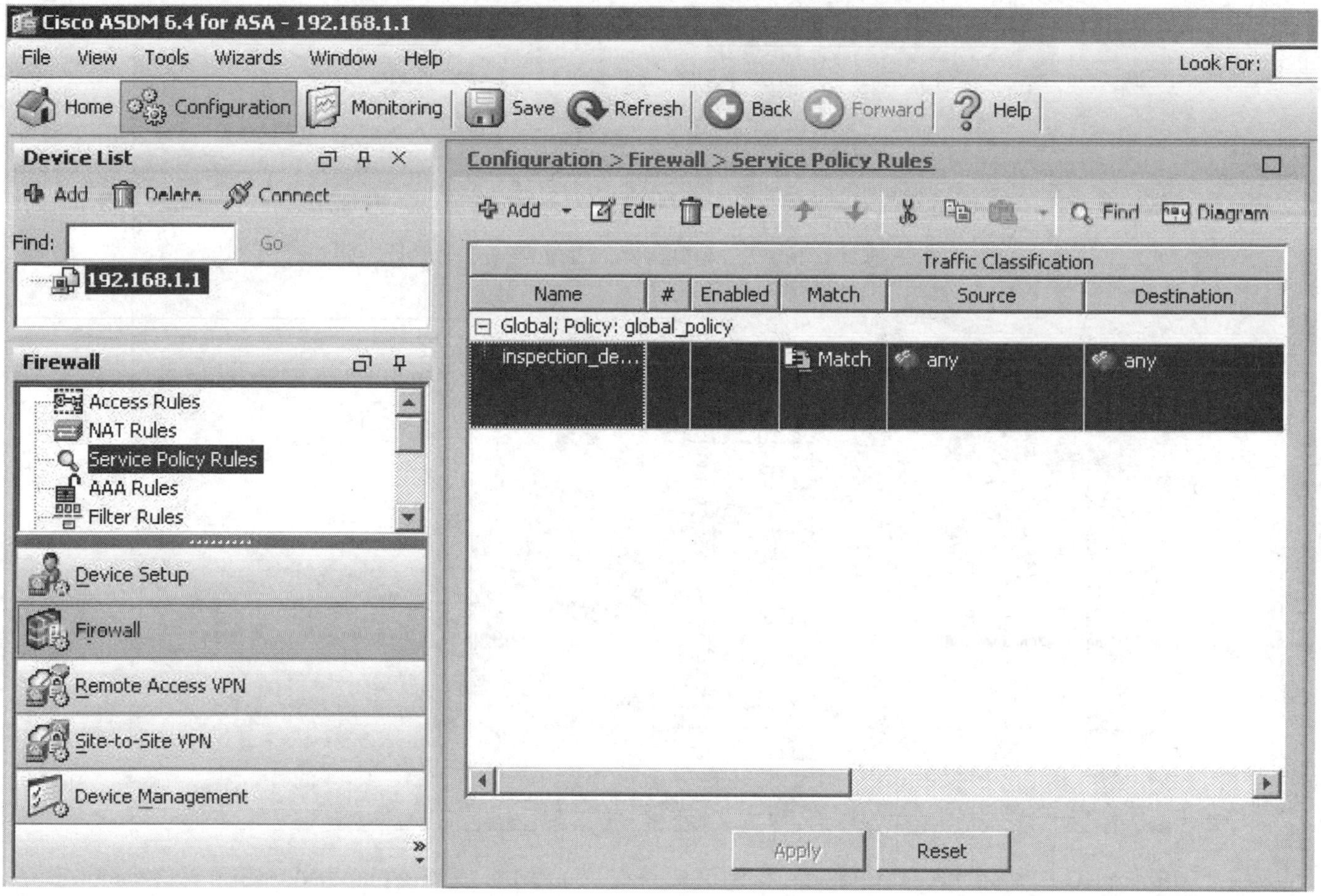

b. Select the inspection_default policy and click **Edit** to modify the default inspection rules. On the Edit Service Policy Rule window, display the **Rule Actions** tab and check the **ICMP** check box. Do not change the other default protocols that are checked. Click **OK** and then click **Apply** to send the commands to the ASA. If prompted, log in again as **admin** with a password of **cisco123**.

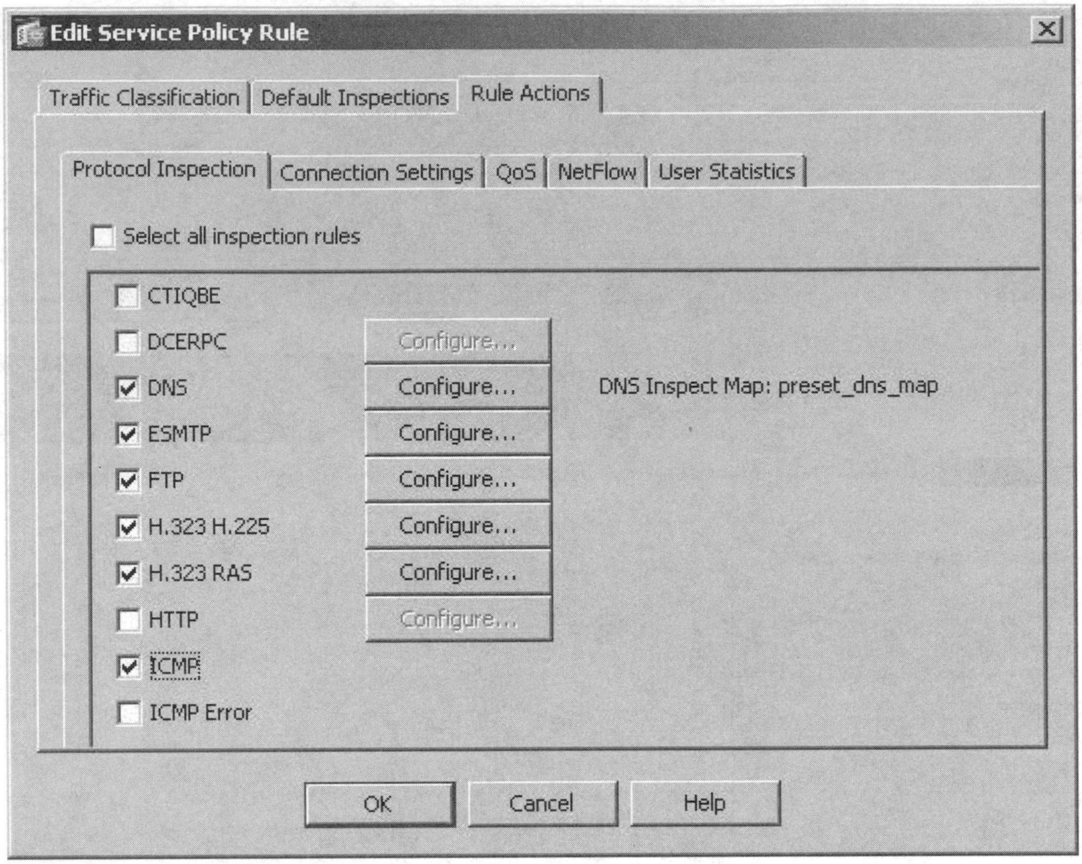

c. From PC-B, ping the external interface of R1 S0/0/0 (10.1.1.1). The pings should be successful.

Part 5: Configuring a DMZ, Static NAT, and ACLs

In Part 3 of this lab, you configured address translation using PAT for the inside network. In this part, you create a DMZ on the ASA, configure static NAT to a DMZ server, and apply an ACL to control access to the server.

Step 1: Configure the ASA DMZ VLAN 3 interface.

In this step, you create a new interface VLAN 3 named **dmz**, assign physical interface E0/2 to the VLAN, set the security level to 70, and limit communication from this interface to the inside (VLAN1) interface.

a. From the Configuration screen, Device Setup menu, click **Interfaces**. Click **Add** to define a new interface. The General tab is displayed by default, and currently defined inside (VLAN 1, E0/1) and outside (VLAN 2, E0/0) interfaces are listed. Click **Add** to create a new interface.

b. In the Add Interface dialog box, choose port **Ethernet0/2** and click **Add**. You are prompted to change the interface from the inside network. Click **OK** for the message to remove the port from the inside interface and add it to this new interface. In the Interface Name box, name the interface **dmz**, assign it a security level of **70**, and make sure the **Enable Interface** check box is checked.

c. Ensure that the **Use Static IP** button is selected and enter an IP address of 192.168.2.1 with a subnet mask of 255.255.255.0. Do *not* click OK at this time.

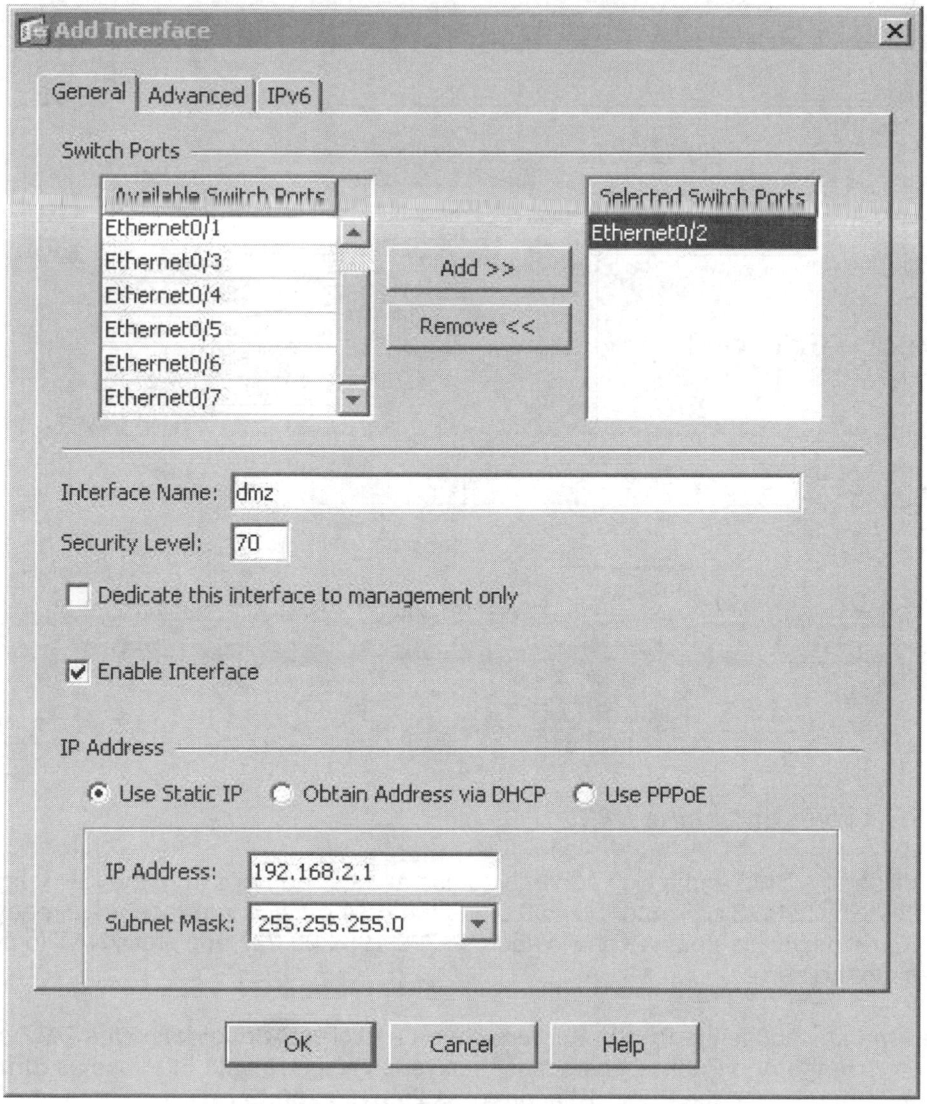

d. ASDM configures this interface as VLAN ID 12 by default. Before clicking OK to add the interface, click the **Advanced** tab and specify this interface as VLAN ID 3.

Note: If you are working with the ASA 5505 base license, you are allowed to create up to three named interfaces. However, you must disable communication between the third interface and one of the other interfaces. Because the DMZ server does not need to initiate communication with the inside users, you can disable forwarding to interfaces VLAN 1.

e. On the Advanced tab, you also need to block traffic from this interface VLAN 3 (DMZ) to the VLAN 1 (inside) interface. From the Block Traffic area, choose **vlan1 (inside)** from the drop-down menu. Click **OK** to return to the Interfaces window. You should see the new interface named **dmz**, in addition to the inside and outside interfaces. Click **Apply** to send the commands to the ASA.

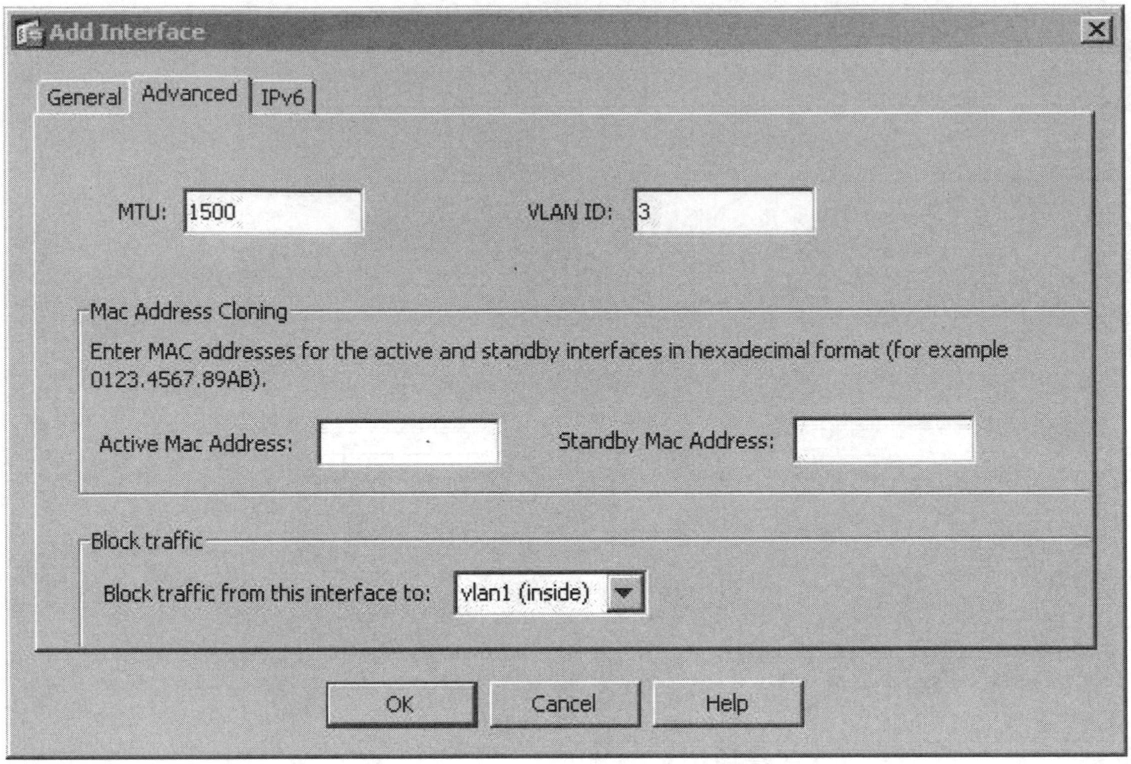

Step 2: Configure the DMZ server and static NAT.

To accommodate the addition of a DMZ and a web server, you use another address from the ISP range assigned, 209.165.200.224/29 (.224-.231). Router R1 Fa0/0 and the ASA outside interface are already using 209.165.200.225 and .226, respectively. You use public address 209.165.200.227 and static NAT to provide address translation access to the server.

a. From the Firewall menu, choose the **Public Servers** option and click **Add** to define the DMZ server and services offered. In the Add Public Server dialog box, specify the Private Interface as **dmz**, the Public Interface as **outside**, and the Public IP address as **209.165.200.227**.

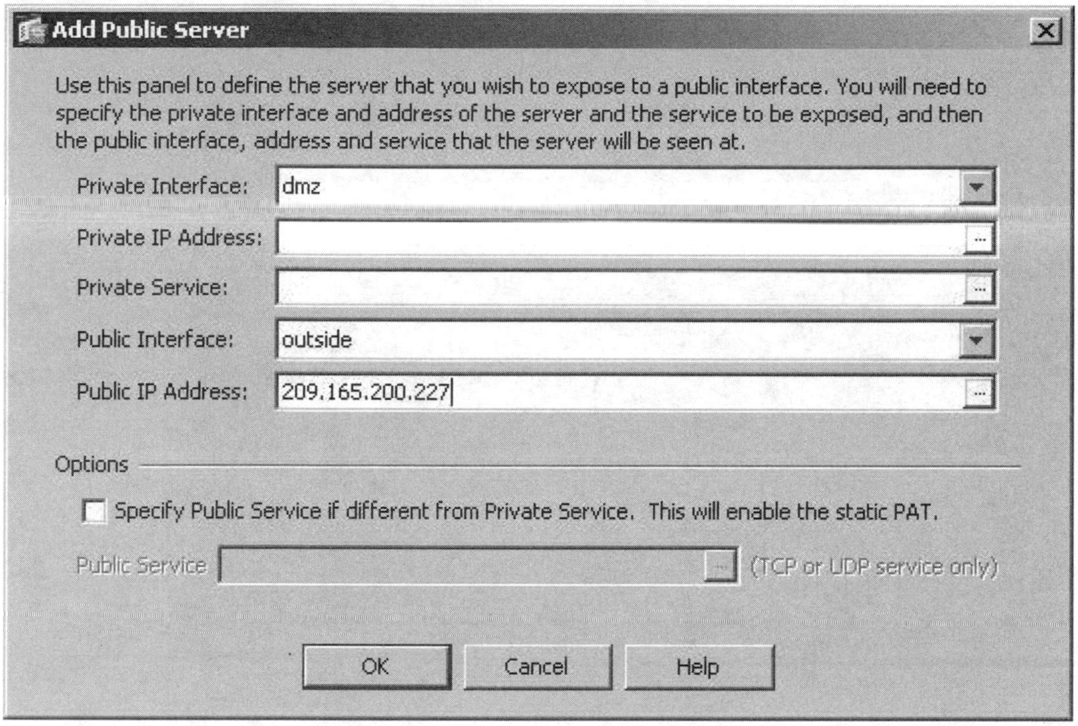

b. Click the ellipsis button to the right of Private IP Address. In the Browse Private IP Address window, click **Add** to define the server as a **Network Object**. Enter the name **DMZ-Server**, with a type of **Host** and the private IP address of **192.168.2.3**.

c. While in the Add Network Object dialog box, click the double-down arrow button for NAT. Check the **Add Automatic Address Translation Rules** check box, and enter the type as **Static**. Enter **209.165.200.227** as the Translated Address. When the screen looks like the following, click **OK** to add the server network object. From the Browse Private IP Address window, click **OK**. You return to the Add Public Server dialog box.

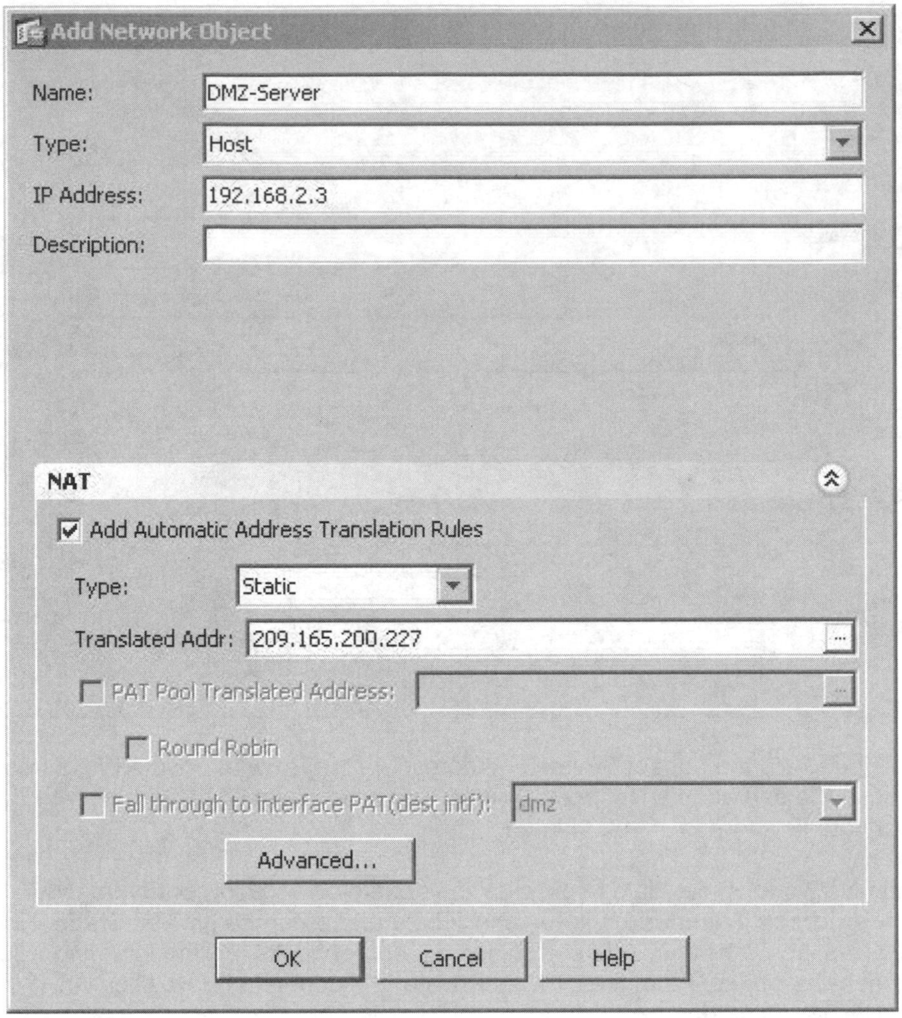

d. In the Add Public Server dialog, click the ellipsis button to the right of Private Service. In the Browse Private Service window, double-click to select the following services: **tcp/http**, **tcp/ftp**, **icmp/echo** and **icmp/echo-reply** (scroll down to see all services). Click **OK** to continue and return to the Add Public Server dialog.

Note: You can specify public services, if different from the private services, using the option on this screen.

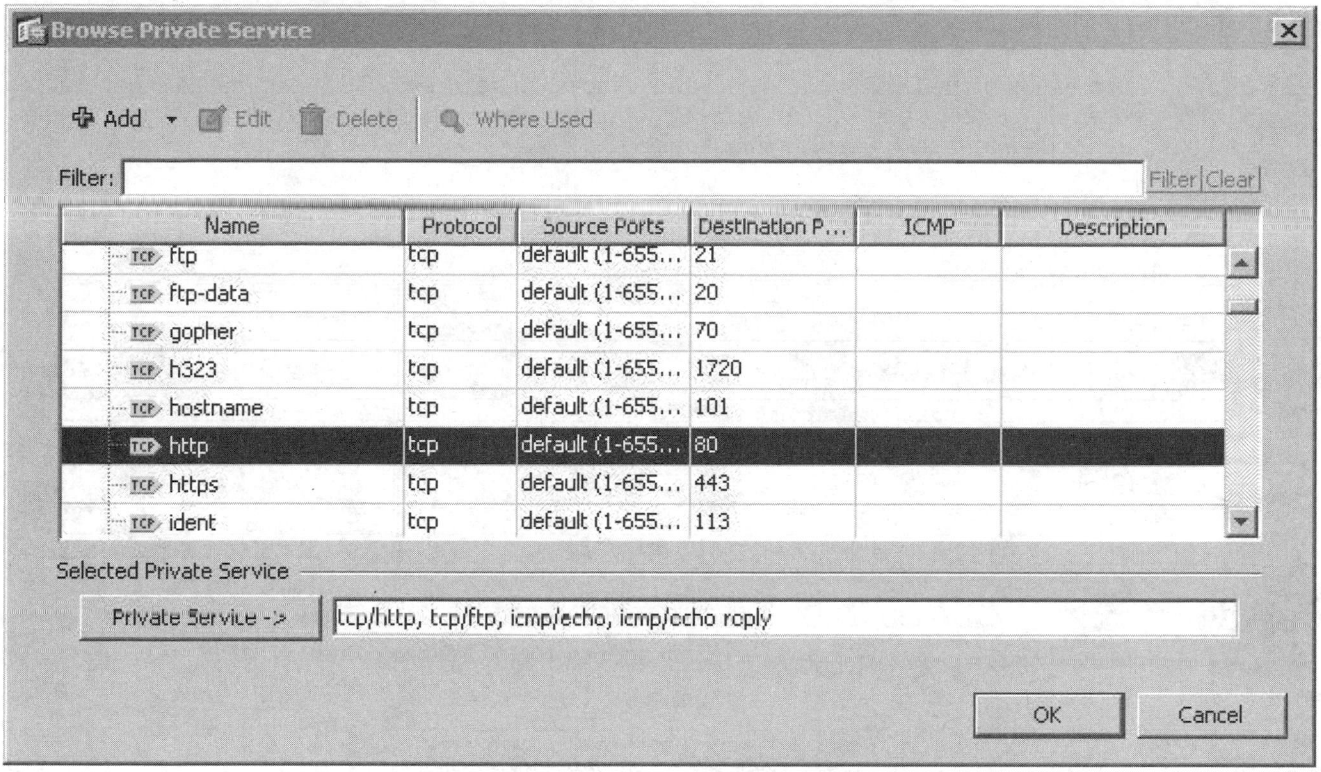

e. When you have completed all information in the Add Public Server dialog box, it should look like the one shown here. Click **OK** to add the server. Click **Apply** at the Public Servers screen to send the commands to the ASA.

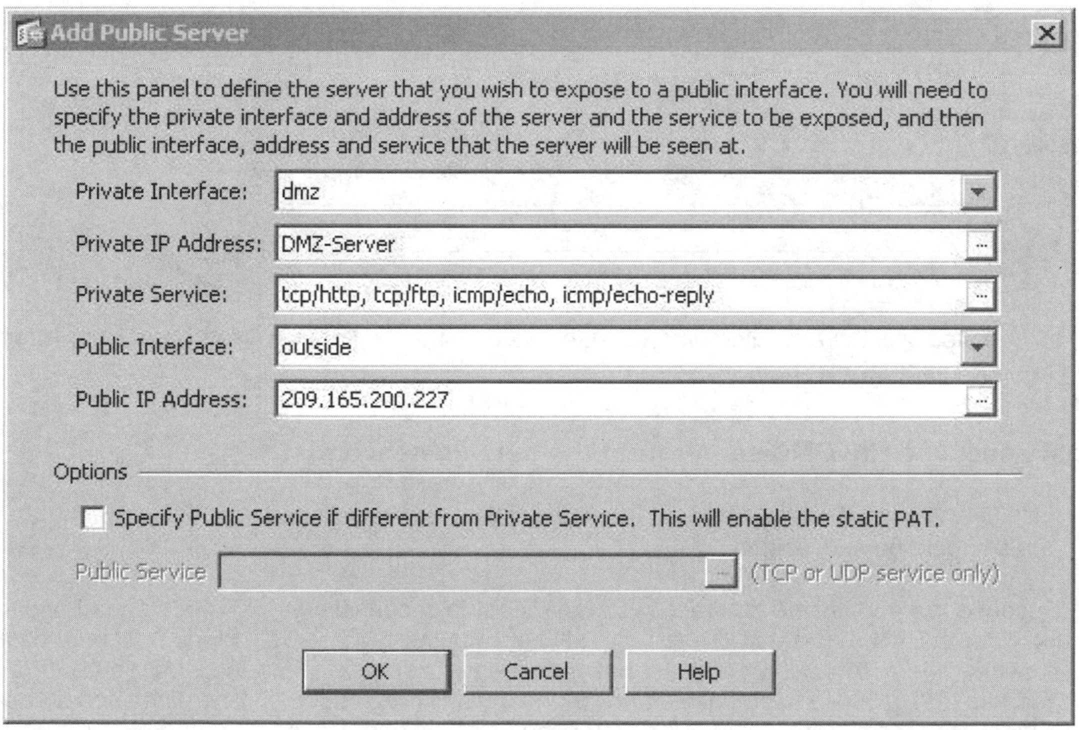

Step 3: View the DMZ Access Rule (ACL) generated by ASDM.

a. With the creation of the DMZ server object and selection of services, ASDM automatically generates an access rule (access control list, or ACL) to permit the appropriate access to the server and applies it to the outside interface in the incoming direction.

b. View this Access Rule in ASDM by choosing **Configuration > Firewall > Access Rules**. It appears as an outside incoming rule. You can select the rule and use the horizontal scroll bar to see all the components.

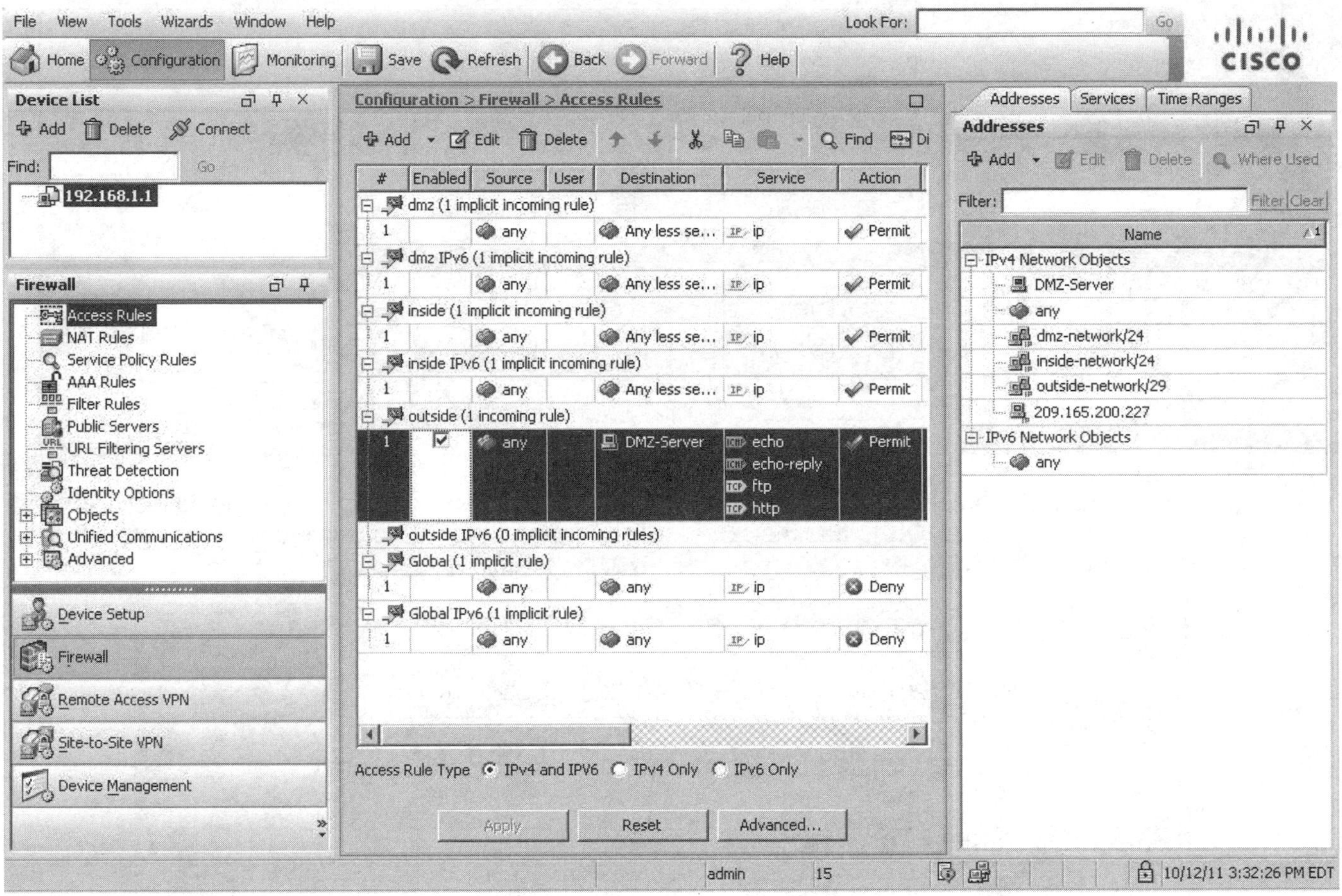

Note: You can also see the actual commands generated using the **Tools > Command Line Interface** and entering the command **`show run`**.

Step 4: Test access to the DMZ server from the outside network.

a. From PC-C, ping the IP address of the static NAT public server address (209.165.200.227). The pings should be successful.

b. Because the ASA inside interface (VLAN 1) is set to security level 100 (the highest) and the DMZ interface (VLAN 3) is set to 70, you can also access the DMZ server from a host on the inside network. The ASA acts like a router between the two networks. Ping the DMZ server (PC-A) internal address (192.168.2.3) from inside network host PC-B (192.168.1.X). The pings should be successful due to interface security level and the fact that ICMP is being inspected on the inside interface by the global inspection policy.

c. The DMZ server cannot ping PC-B on the inside network. This is because the DMZ interface VLAN 3 has a lower security level and the fact that, when the VLAN 3 interface was created, it was necessary to specify the **no forward** command. Try to ping from the DMZ server PC-A to PC-B at IP address 192.168.1.X. The pings should not be successful.

Step 5: Use ASDM Monitoring to graph packet activity.

You can monitor a number of aspects of the ASA using the Monitoring screen. The main categories on this screen are Interfaces, VPN, Routing, Properties, and Logging. In this step, you create a graph to monitor packet activity for the outside interface.

a. From the Monitoring screen, Interfaces menu, choose **Interface Graphs > outside**. Choose **Packet Counts** and click **Add** to add the graph. The following figure shows Packet Counts added.

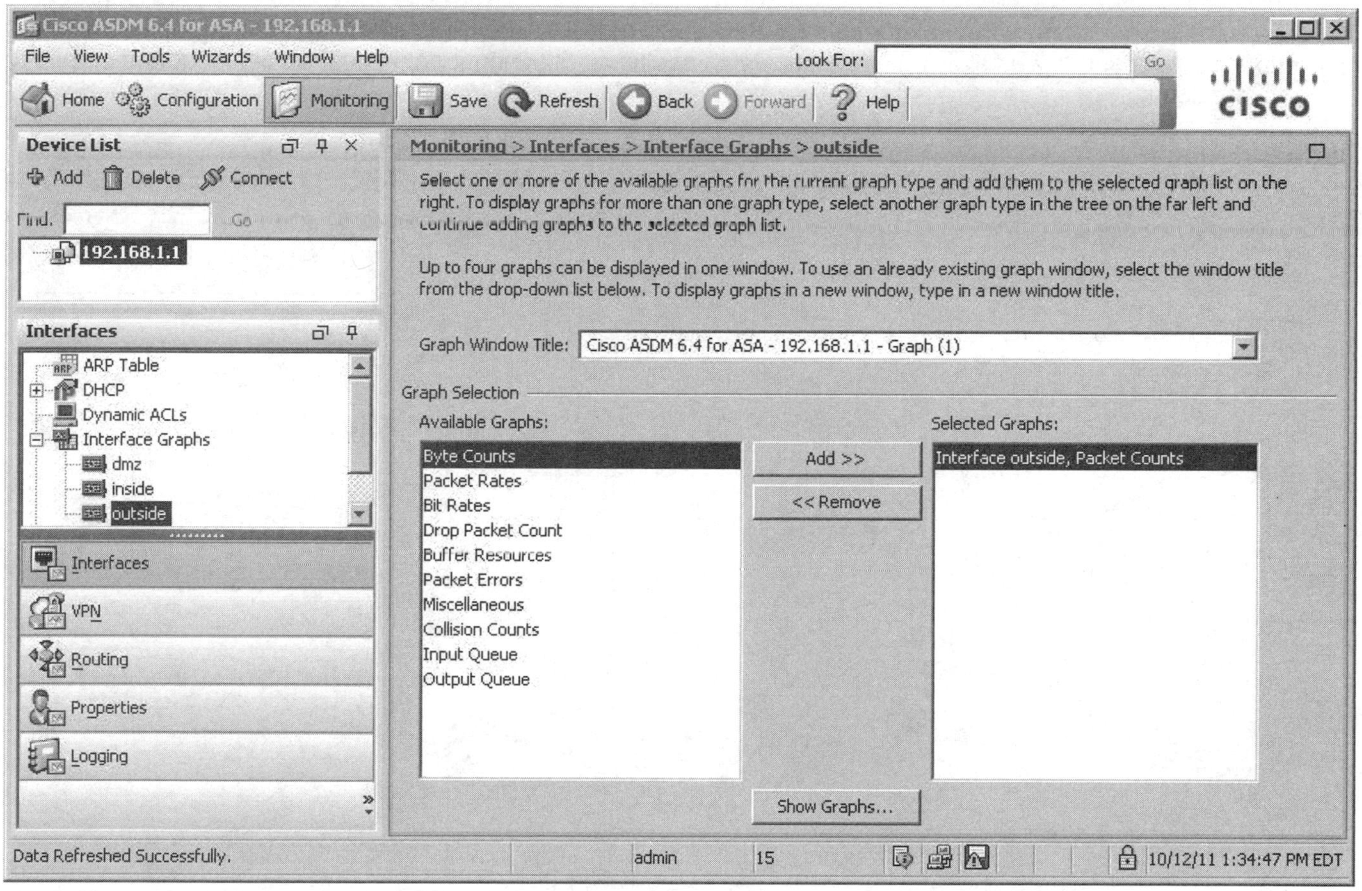

b. Click the **Show Graphs** button to display the graph. Initially there is no traffic displayed.

c. From a privileged mode command prompt on R2, simulate Internet traffic to the ASA by pinging the DMZ server public address with a repeat count of 1000. You can increase the number of pings if desired.

```
R2# ping 209.165.200.227 repeat 1000

Type escape sequence to abort.
Sending 1000, 100-byte ICMP Echos to 209.165.200.227, timeout is 2
seconds:
!!!!!!!!!!!!!!!!!!!!!!!!!!!!!!!!!!!!!!!!!!!!!!!!!!!!!!!!!!!!!!!!!!!!!!
!!!!!!!!!!!!!!!!!!!!!!!!!!!!!!!!!!!!!!!!!!!!!!!!!!!!!!!!!!!!!!!!!!!!!!
<output omitted>
```

```
!!!!!!!!!!!!!!!!!!!!!!!!!!!!!!!!!!!!!!!!!!!!!!!!!!!!!!!!!!!!!!!!!!!!!!!
!!!!!!!!!!!!!!!!!!!!
Success rate is 100 percent (1000/1000), round-trip min/avg/max =
1/2/12 ms
```

d. You should see the results of the pings from R2 on the graph as an Input Packet Count. The scale of the graph is automatically adjusted depending on the volume of traffic. You can also view the data in tabular form by clicking the **Table** tab. Notice that the View selected at the bottom left of the Graph screen is real-time data every 10 seconds. Click the pull-down menu to see the other options available.

e. Ping from PC-B to R1 Fa0/0 at 209.165.200.225 using the –n option (number of packets) to specify 1000 packets:

C:>\ **ping 209.165.200.225 –n 1000**

Note: The response from the PC is relatively slow and it may take a while to show up on the graph as an output packet count. The following figure shows an additional 5000 input packets and both input and output packet counts.

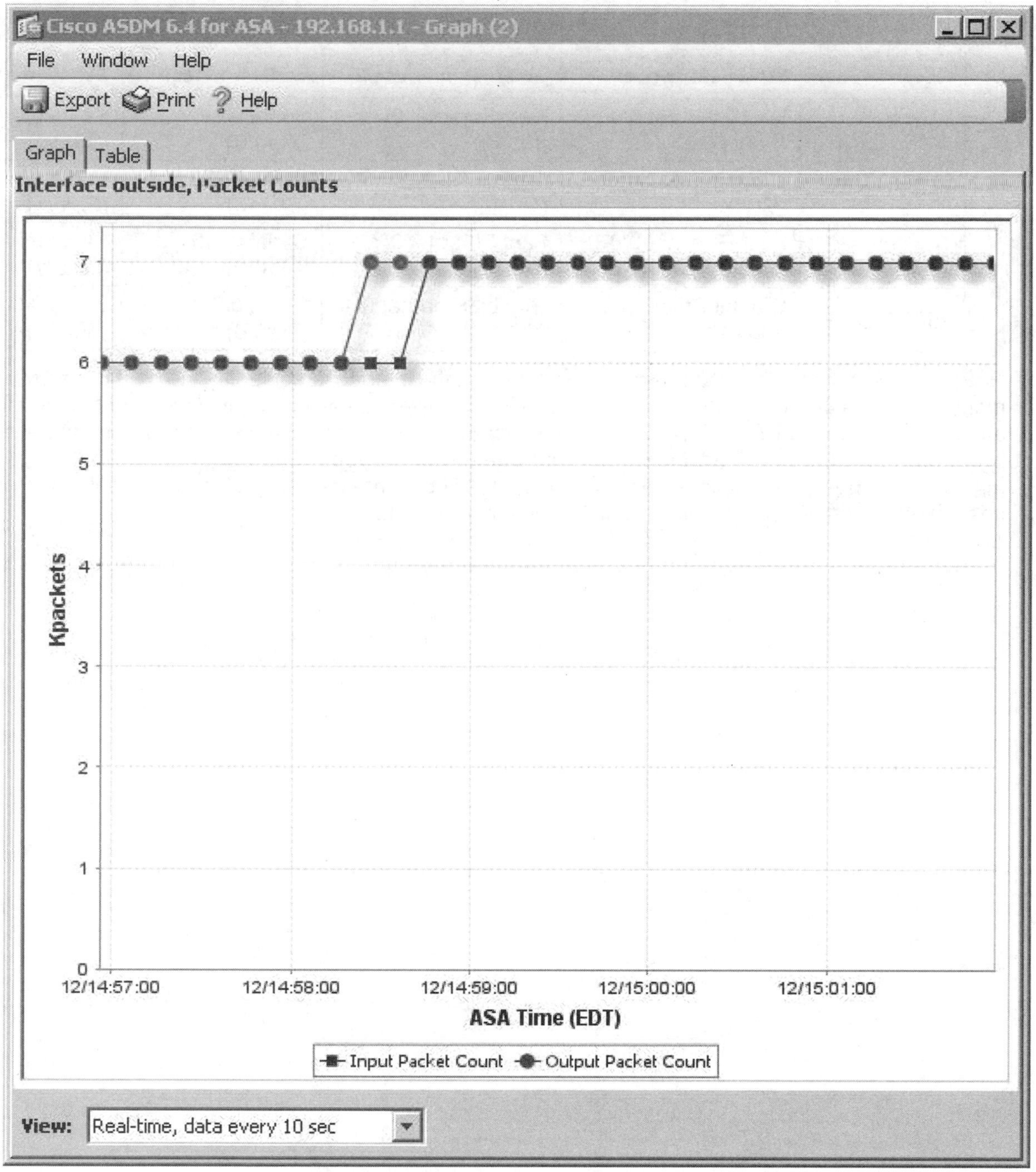

Reflection

1. What are some benefits to using ASDM over the CLI?

____

____

2. What are some benefits to using the CLI over ASDM?

____

____

Router Interface Summary Table

Router Model	Ethernet Interface 1	Ethernet Interface 2	Serial Interface 1	Serial Interface 2
1800	Fast Ethernet 0/0 (Fa0/0)	Fast Ethernet 0/1 (Fa0/1)	Serial 0/0/0 (S0/0/0)	Serial 0/0/1 (S0/0/1)
1900	Gigabit Ethernet 0/0 (G0/0)	Gigabit Ethernet 0/1 (G0/1)	Serial 0/0/0 (S0/0/0)	Serial 0/0/1 (S0/0/1)
2800	Fast Ethernet 0/0 (Fa0/0)	Fast Ethernet 0/1 (Fa0/1)	Serial 0/0/0 (S0/0/0)	Serial 0/0/1 (S0/0/1)
2900	Gigabit Ethernet 0/0 (G0/0)	Gigabit Ethernet 0/1 (G0/1)	Serial 0/0/0 (S0/0/0)	Serial 0/0/1 (S0/0/1)

Note: To find out how the router is configured, look at the interfaces to identify the type of router and how many interfaces the router has. There is no way to effectively list all the combinations of configurations for each router class. This table includes identifiers for the possible combinations of Ethernet and serial interfaces in the device. The table does not include any other type of interface, even though a specific router may contain one. An example of this might be an ISDN BRI interface. The string in parentheses is the legal abbreviation that can be used in Cisco IOS commands to represent the interface.

Chapter 10 Lab C: Configuring Clientless and AnyConnect Remote Access SSL VPNs Using ASDM

Topology

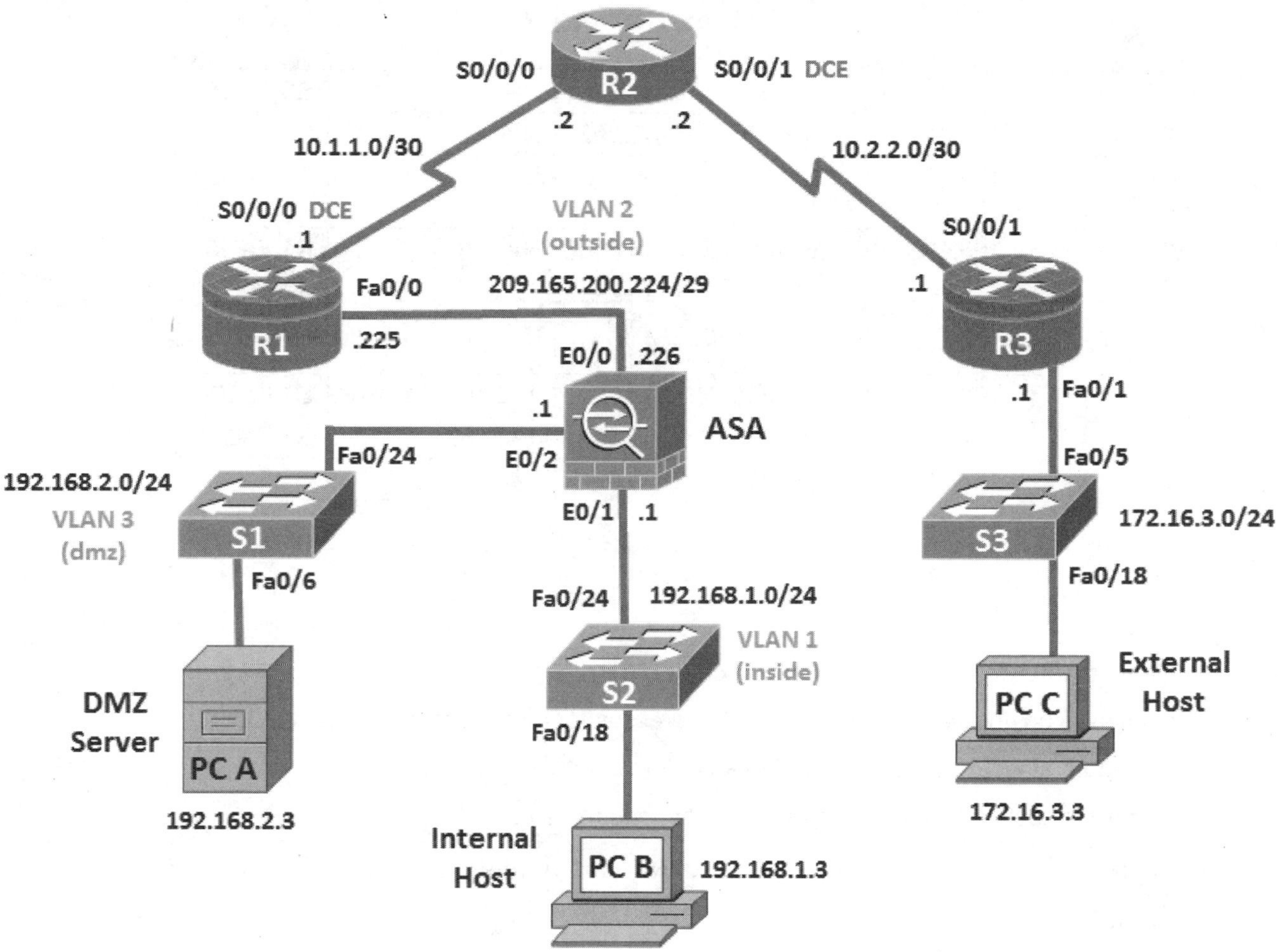

Note: ISR G2 devices have Gigabit Ethernet interfaces rather than FastEthernet interfaces.

IP Addressing Table

Device	Interface	IP Address	Subnet Mask	Default Gateway	Switch Port
R1	Fa0/0	209.165.200.225	255.255.255.248	N/A	ASA E0/0
	S0/0/0 (DCE)	10.1.1.1	255.255.255.252	N/A	N/A
R2	S0/0/0	10.1.1.2	255.255.255.252	N/A	N/A
	S0/0/1 (DCE)	10.2.2.2	255.255.255.252	N/A	N/A
R3	Fa0/1	172.16.3.1	255.255.255.0	N/A	S3 Fa0/5
	S0/0/1	10.2.2.1	255.255.255.252	N/A	N/A
ASA	VLAN 1 (E0/1)	192.168.1.1	255.255.255.0	NA	S2 Fa0/24
ASA	VLAN 2 (E0/0)	209.165.200.226	255.255.255.248	NA	R1 Fa0/0
ASA	VLAN 3 (E0/2)	192.168.2.1	255.255.255.0	NA	S1 Fa0/24
PC-A	NIC	192.168.2.3	255.255.255.0	192.168.2.1	S1 Fa0/6
PC-B	NIC	192.168.1.3	255.255.255.0	192.168.1.1	S2 Fa0/18
PC-C	NIC	172.16.3.3	255.255.255.0	172.16.3.1	S3 Fa0/18

Objectives

Part 1: Lab Setup

- Cable the network as shown in the topology.
- Configure hostnames, and interface IP addresses for routers, switches, and PCs.
- Configure static routing, including default routes, between R1, R2, and R3.
- Verify connectivity between hosts, switches, and routers.

Part 2: Access the ASA Console and Prepare for VPN Configuration

- Access the ASA console.
- Clear previous configuration settings.
- Load the ASA CLI command script to configure basic settings.
- Access ASDM.

Part 3: Configuring Clientless SSL VPN Remote Access Using ASDM

- Configure the SSL VPN interface connection profile.
- Configure Local AAA user authentication.
- Configure the group policy.
- Configure a bookmark list for intranet URLs.
- Verify access to the VPN portal.
- Monitor the clientless SSL VPN connection.

Part 4: Configuring AnyConnect Client SSL VPN Remote Access Using ASDM

- Clear Clientless SSL VPN configuration from Part 3.
- Configure the SSL VPN interface connection profile.
- Configure the VPN encryption protocol.
- Configure the AnyConnect client image to upload.
- Configure Local AAA user authentication.
- Configure the client address pool.
- Configure the DNS server and NAT exempt.
- Configure AnyConnect client deployment.
- Verify VPN access and AnyConnect client upload.
- Monitor the AnyConnect SSL VPN connection.

Background/Scenario

In addition to stateful firewall and other security features, the ASA can provide both site-to-site and remote access virtual private network (VPN) functionality. The ASA provides two main deployment modes that are found in Cisco SSL remote access VPN solutions.

- **Clientless SSL VPN:** Clientless, browser-based VPN that lets users establish a secure, remote-access VPN tunnel to the ASA using a web browser and built-in Secure Sockets Layer (SSL) to protect VPN traffic. After authentication, users are presented with a portal page and can access specific, predefined internal resources from the portal.
- **Client-Based SSL VPN:** Provides full-tunnel SSL VPN connection but requires a VPN client application to be installed on the remote host. After authentication, users can access any internal resource as if they were physically on the local network. The ASA supports both SSL and IPsec client-based VPNs.

In Part 1 of the lab, you configure the topology and non-ASA devices. In Part 2, you prepare the ASA for ADSM access. In Part 3, you use the ASDM VPN Wizard to configure a clientless SSL remote access VPN and verify access using a remote PC with a browser. In Part 4, you configure an AnyConnect client-based SSL remote access VPN and verify connectivity.

Your company has two locations connected to an Internet service provider (ISP). Router R1 represents a CPE device managed by the ISP. Router R2 represents an intermediate Internet router. Router R3 connects users at the remote branch office to the ISP. The ASA is an edge CPE security device that connects the internal corporate network and demilitarized zone (DMZ) to the ISP while providing Network Address Translation (NAT) services to inside hosts.

Management has asked you to provide VPN access, using the ASA as a VPN concentrator, to teleworkers. They want you to test both the clientless access model, using SSL and a browser for client access, and the client-based model using SSL and the Cisco AnyConnect client.

Note: The routers used with this lab are Cisco 1841 with Cisco IOS Software Release 12.4(20)T (advanced IP image). The switches are Cisco WS-C2960-24TT-L with Cisco IOS Software Release 12.2(46)SE (C2960-LANBASEK9-M image). Other routers, switches, and Cisco IOS versions can be used. However, results and output may vary.

The ASA used with this lab is a Cisco model 5505 with an eight-port integrated switch, running OS version 8.4(2) and ASDM version 6.4(5) and comes with a Base license that allows a maximum of three VLANs.

Note: Make sure that the routers and switches have been erased and have no startup configurations.

Required Resources

- 3 routers (Cisco 1841 with Cisco IOS Software Release 12.4(20)T1 or comparable)
- 3 switches (Cisco 2960 or comparable)
- 1 ASA 5505 (OS version 8.4(2) and ASDM version 6.4(5) and Base license or comparable)
- PC-A: Windows XP, Vista, or Windows 7 with CCP, PuTTy SSH client (web server optional)
- PC-B: Windows XP, Vista, or Windows 7 with PuTTy SSH client and Java 6 (ASDM loaded on the PC is optional)
- PC-C: Windows XP, Vista, or Windows 7 with Internet Explorer, CCP, PuTTy SSH client
- Serial and Ethernet cables as shown in the topology
- Rollover cables to configure the routers and ASA via the console

Note: Use of a browser other than Internet Explorer 7 or later on remote PC-C may produce results different from those shown in this lab. You might need to create an exception when connecting to the ASA over the remote access VPN.

Part 1: Basic Router/Switch/PC Configuration

In Part 1 of this lab, you set up the network topology and configure basic settings on the routers such as interface IP addresses and static routing.

Note: Do not configure any ASA settings at this time.

Step 1: Cable the network and clear previous device settings.

Attach the devices shown in the topology diagram and cable as necessary. Make sure that the routers and switches have been erased and have no startup configurations.

Step 2: Configure basic settings for routers and switches.

a. Configure hostnames as shown in the topology for each router.

b. Configure router interface IP addresses as shown in the IP Addressing Table.

c. Configure a clock rate for routers with a DCE serial cable attached to their serial interface. Router R1 is shown here as an example:

```
R1(config)# interface S0/0/0
R1(config-if)# clock rate 64000
```

d. Configure the hostname for the switches. Other than hostname, the switches can be left in their default configuration state. Configuring the VLAN management IP address for the switches is optional.

Step 3: Configure static routing on the routers.

a. Configure a static default route from R1 to R2 and from R3 to R2:

```
R1(config)# ip route 0.0.0.0 0.0.0.0 Serial0/0/0
R3(config)# ip route 0.0.0.0 0.0.0.0 Serial0/0/1
```

b. Configure a static route from R2 to the R1 Fa0/0 subnet (connected to ASA interface E0/0) and a static route from R2 to the R3 LAN:

```
R2(config)# ip route 209.165.200.224 255.255.255.248 Serial0/0/0
R2(config)# ip route 172.16.3.0 255.255.255.0 Serial0/0/1
```

Step 4: Enable the HTTP server on R1 and set the enable and vty passwords.

a. Enable HTTP access to R1 using the `ip http server` command in global config mode. Also set the vty password to **cisco**.

b. Configure the same settings on R2 and R3. Router R1 is shown here as an example:

```
R1(config)# ip http server
R1(config)# enable password class

R1(config)# line vty 0 4
R1(config-line)# password cisco
R1(config-line)# login

R1(config)# line con 0
R1(config-line)# password cisco
R1(config-line)# login
```

Step 5: Configure PC host IP settings.

Configure a static IP address, subnet mask, and default gateway for PC-A, PC-B, and PC-C, as shown in the IP addressing table.

Step 6: Verify connectivity.

Because the ASA is the focal point for the network zones and it has not yet been configured, there will be no connectivity between devices connected to it. However, PC-C should be able to ping the R1 interface Fa0/0. From PC-C, ping the R1 Fa0/0 IP address (209.165.200.225). If these pings are not successful, troubleshoot the basic device configurations before continuing.

Note: If you can ping from PC-C to R1 Fa0/0 you have demonstrated that static routing is configured and functioning correctly.

Step 7: Save the basic running configuration for each router and switch.

Part 2: Accessing the ASA Console and ASDM

Step 1: Access the ASA console.

a. Accessing the ASA via the console port is the same as with a Cisco router or switch. Connect to the ASA Console port with a rollover cable.

b. Use a terminal emulation program such as TeraTerm or HyperTerminal to access the CLI, and use the serial port settings of 9600 baud, 8 data bits, no parity, 1 stop bit, and no flow control.

c. If prompted to enter Interactive Firewall configuration (Setup mode), answer **no**.

d. Enter privileged mode with the **enable** command and password (if set). By default the password is blank, so you can just press **Enter**. If the password has been changed to that specified in this lab, the password will be **class**. In addition, the hostname and prompt is CCNAS-ASA>, as shown here. The default ASA hostname and prompt is ciscoasa>.

```
CCNAS-ASA> enable
Password: class (or press Enter if none set)
```

Step 2: Clear the previous ASA configuration settings.

a. Use the **write erase** command to remove the **startup-config** file from flash memory:

```
CCNAS-ASA# write erase
Erase configuration in flash memory? [confirm]
[OK]
CCNAS-ASA#
```

Note: The IOS command **erase startup-config** is not supported on the ASA.

b. Use the **reload** command to restart the ASA. This causes the ASA to come up in CLI Setup mode. If you see the message `System config has been modified. Save? [Y]es/[N]o:`, respond with **N**.

```
CCNAS-ASA# reload
Proceed with reload? [confirm] <enter>
CCNAS-ASA#
***
*** --- START GRACEFUL SHUTDOWN ---
Shutting down isakmp
Shutting down File system
***
*** --- SHUTDOWN NOW ---
Process shutdown finished
Rebooting.....
CISCO SYSTEMS
Embedded BIOS Version 1.0(12)13 08/28/08 15:50:37.45
<output omitted>
```

Step 3: Bypass setup mode.

When the ASA completes the reload process, it should detect that the startup config file is missing and go into Setup mode. If it does not come up in this mode, repeat Step 2.

a. When prompted to preconfigure the firewall through interactive prompts (Setup mode), respond with **no**.

```
Pre-configure Firewall now through interactive prompts [yes]?  no
```

b. Enter privileged EXEC mode with the **enable** command. The password should be blank (no password) at this point.

c. The first time you enter configuration mode after running reloading you are asked whether you want to enable anonymous reporting. Respond with **no**.

Step 4: Configure the ASA by using the CLI script.

In this step, you use the modified running-config from Lab 10A to preconfigure basic settings, the firewall and DMZ.

a. Other than the defaults that the ASA automatically inserts, ensure with the use of the **show run** command that there is no previous configuration in the ASA.

b. Enter CLI global configuration mode. When prompted to enable anonymous call-home reporting, respond with **no**.

```
ciscoasa> enable
Password: <enter>

ciscoasa# conf t
ciscoasa(config)#
```

c. Copy and paste the Pre-VPN Configuration Script commands listed below at the ASA global config mode prompt to bring it to the point where you can start configuring the SSL VPNs.

d. Observe the messages as the commands are applied to ensure that there are no warnings or errors. If prompted to replace the RSA key pair, respond with **yes**.

e. Issue the **write mem** (or **copy run start**) command to save the running configuration to the startup configuration and the RSA keys to nonvolatile memory.

Lab 10C Pre-VPN Configuration Script

```
hostname CCNAS-ASA
!
domain-name ccnasecurity.com
!
enable password class
passwd cisco
!
interface Ethernet0/0
 switchport access vlan 2
 no shut
!
interface Ethernet0/1
 switchport access vlan 1
 no shut
!
interface Ethernet0/2
 switchport access vlan 3
 no shut
!
interface Vlan1
 nameif inside
 security-level 100
 ip address 192.168.1.1 255.255.255.0
!
interface Vlan2
 nameif outside
 security-level 0
 ip address 209.165.200.226 255.255.255.248
!
interface Vlan3
 no forward interface Vlan1
 nameif dmz
 security-level 70
 ip address 192.168.2.1 255.255.255.0
!
```

```
object network inside-net
 subnet 192.168.1.0 255.255.255.0
!
object network dmz-server
 host 192.168.2.3
!
access-list OUTSIDE-DMZ extended permit ip any host 192.168.2.3
!
object network inside-net
 nat (inside,outside) dynamic interface
!
object network dmz-server
 nat (dmz,outside) static 209.165.200.227
!
access-group OUTSIDE-DMZ in interface outside
!
route outside 0.0.0.0 0.0.0.0 209.165.200.225 1
!
username admin password cisco123
!
aaa authentication telnet console LOCAL
aaa authentication ssh console LOCAL
aaa authentication http console LOCAL
!
http server enable
http 192.168.1.0 255.255.255.0 inside
ssh 192.168.1.0 255.255.255.0 inside
telnet 192.168.1.0 255.255.255.0 inside
telnet timeout 10
ssh timeout 10
!
class-map inspection_default
 match default-inspection-traffic
policy-map type inspect dns preset_dns_map
 parameters
  message-length maximum client auto
  message-length maximum 512
policy-map global_policy
 class inspection_default
   inspect icmp
!
prompt hostname context
no call-home reporting anonymous
!
crypto key generate rsa modulus 1024
```

Step 5: Access ASDM.

a. Open a browser on PC-B and test the HTTPS access to the ASA by entering **https://192.168.1.1**.

Note: Be sure to specify the HTTPS protocol in the URL.

b. After entering the URL, you should see a security warning about the website security certificate. Click **Continue to this website**. Click **Yes** for any other security warnings. At the ASDM welcome page, click the **Run ASDM** button. The ASDM-IDM Launcher will display. Log in as user **admin** with password **cisco123**. ASDM loads the current configuration into the GUI.

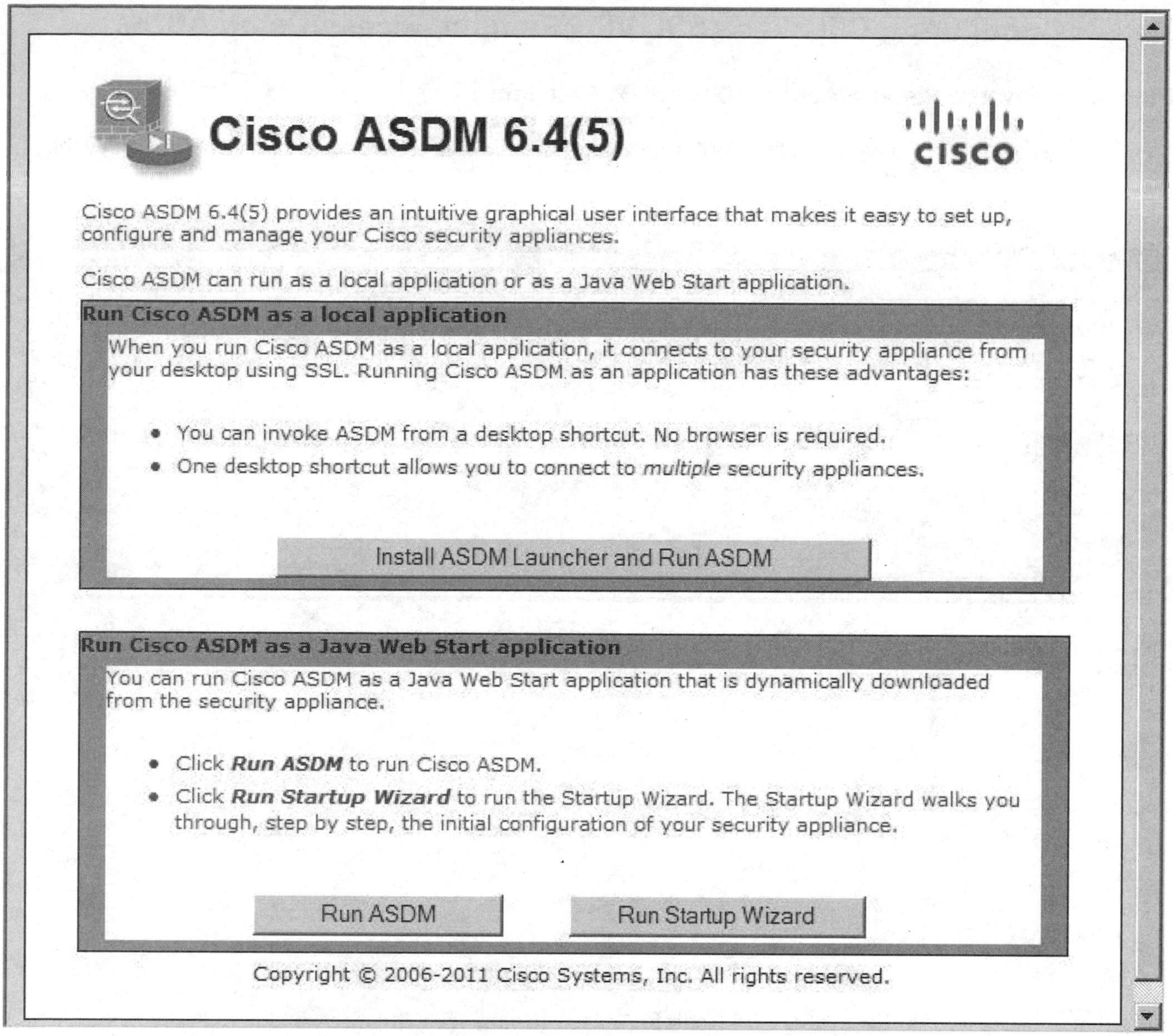
Cisco ASDM 6.4(5)
CISCO
Cisco ASDM 6.4(5) provides an intuitive graphical user interface that makes it easy to set up, configure and manage your Cisco security appliances.
Cisco ASDM can run as a local application or as a Java Web Start application.
Run Cisco ASDM as a local application
When you run Cisco ASDM as a local application, it connects to your security appliance from your desktop using SSL. Running Cisco ASDM as an application has these advantages:
You can invoke ASDM from a desktop shortcut. No browser is required.
One desktop shortcut allows you to connect to multiple security appliances.
Install ASDM Launcher and Run ASDM
Run Cisco ASDM as a Java Web Start application
You can run Cisco ASDM as a Java Web Start application that is dynamically downloaded from the security appliance.
Click Run ASDM to run Cisco ASDM.
Click Run Startup Wizard to run the Startup Wizard. The Startup Wizard walks you through, step by step, the initial configuration of your security appliance.
Run ASDM
Run Startup Wizard
Copyright © 2006-2011 Cisco Systems, Inc. All rights reserved.

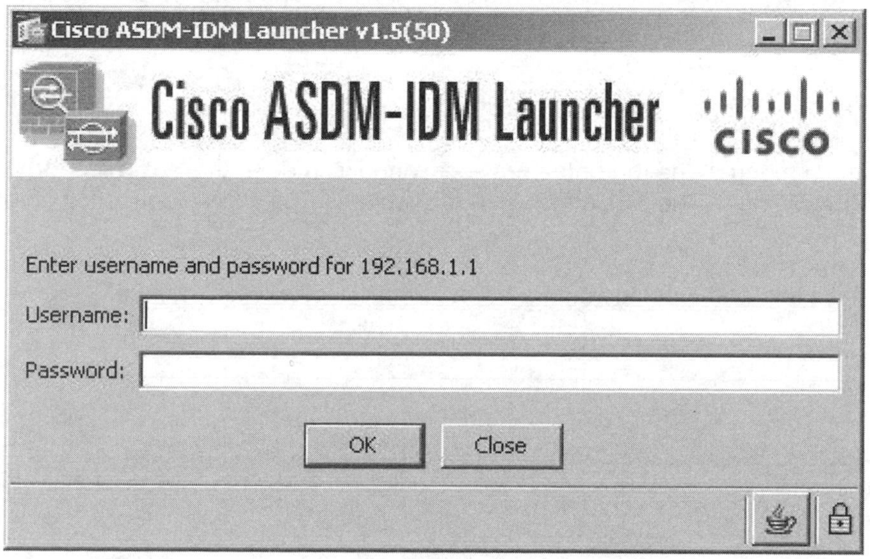
Cisco ASDM-IDM Launcher v1.5(50)
Cisco ASDM-IDM Launcher
CISCO
Enter username and password for 192.168.1.1
Username:
Password:
OK
Close

Part 3: Configuring Clientless SSL VPN Remote Access Using ASDM

Step 1: Review the Remote Access VPN ASDM Assistant.

a. From the menu bar, click the **Configuration** button, and click **Remote Access VPN** to display the Introduction screen. From here, you can access information on how to create any of the three types of remote access VPNs.

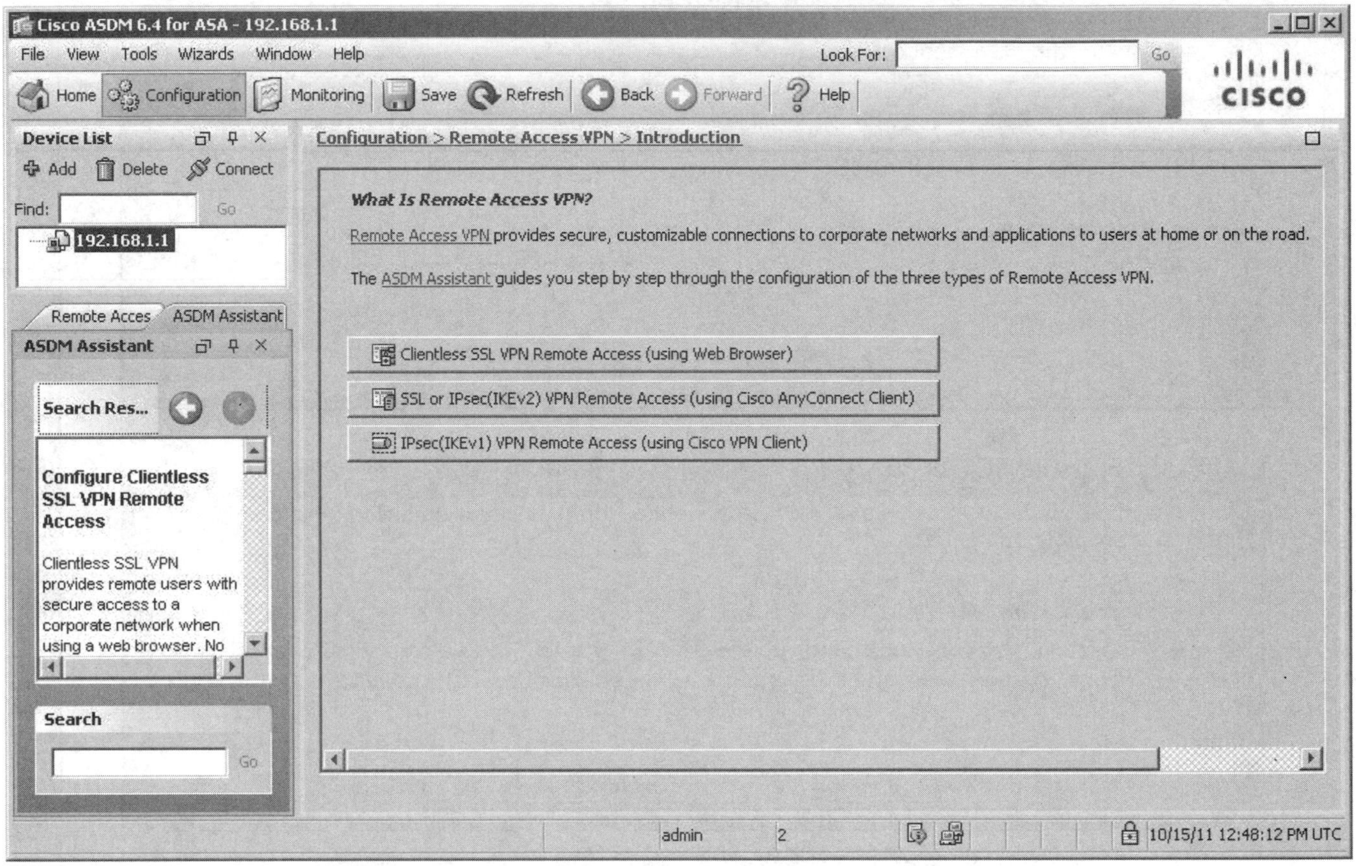

b. Click the **Clientless SSL VPN Remote Access (Using Web Browser)** button to access the ASDM Assistant. Read through the information provided to get a better understanding of the process for creating this type of VPN.

Step 2: Start the VPN Wizard.

a. From the ASDM main menu at the top of the browser window, choose the **Wizards > VPN Wizards > Clientless SSL VPN Wizard**. The SSL VPN Wizard Clientless SSL VPN Connection screen is displayed.

b. Review the onscreen text and topology diagram, and then click **Next** to continue.

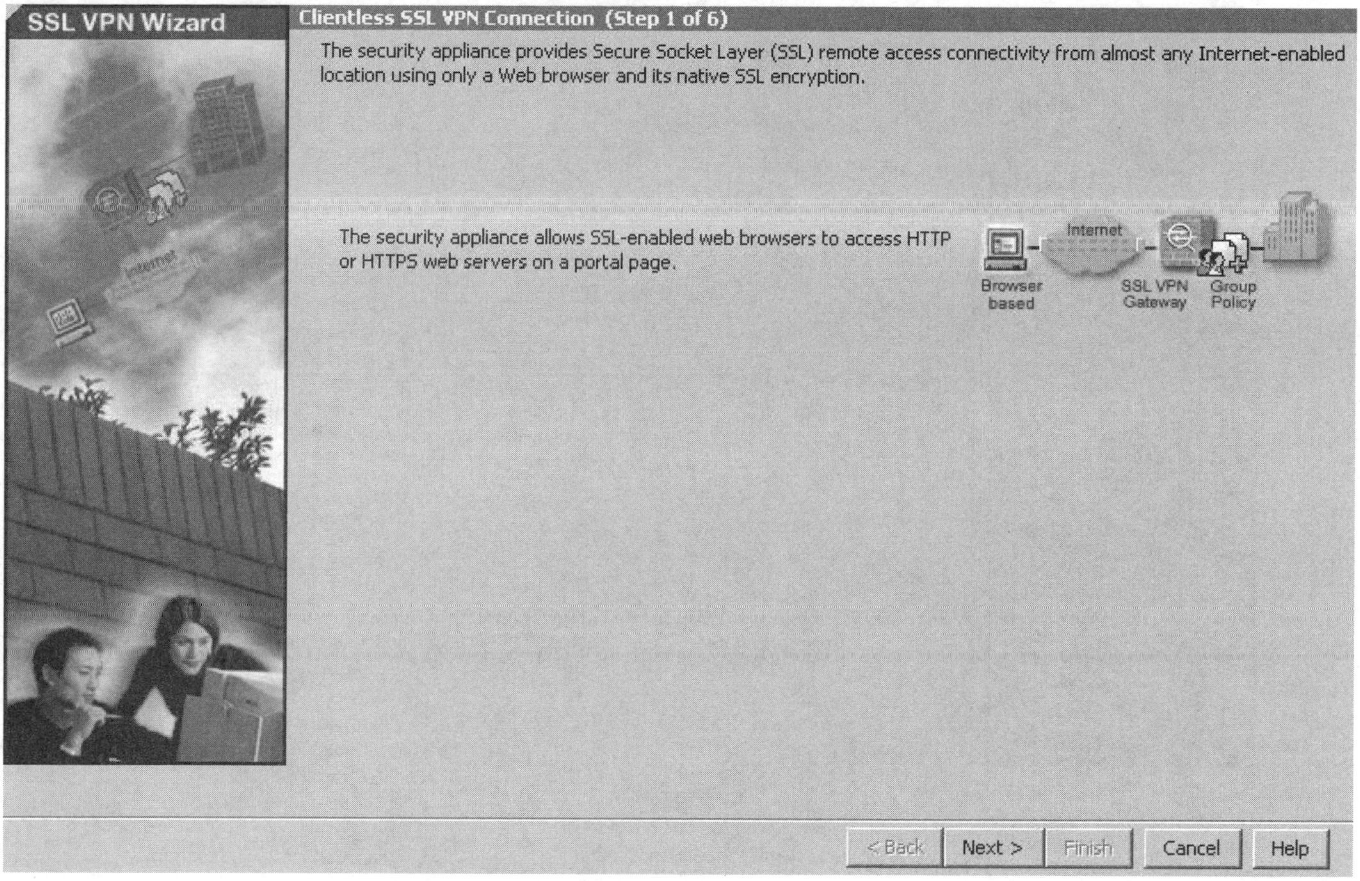

Step 3: Configure the SSL VPN user interface.

a. On the SSL VPN Interface screen, configure **ClientlessVPN-Con-Prof** as the **Connection Profile Name**, and specify **outside** as the interface to which outside users will connect.

Note: By default, the ASA uses a self-signed certificate to send to the client for authentication. Optionally, the ASA may be configured to use a third-party certificate that is purchased from a well-known certificate authority, such as VeriSign, to connect clients. In the event that a certificate is purchased, it may be selected in the Digital Certificate drop-down menu.

The SSL VPN Interface screen provides links in the Information section. These links identify the URLs that need to be used for the SSL VPN service access (login) and for Cisco ASDM access (to access the Cisco ASDM software).

b. Click **Next** to continue.

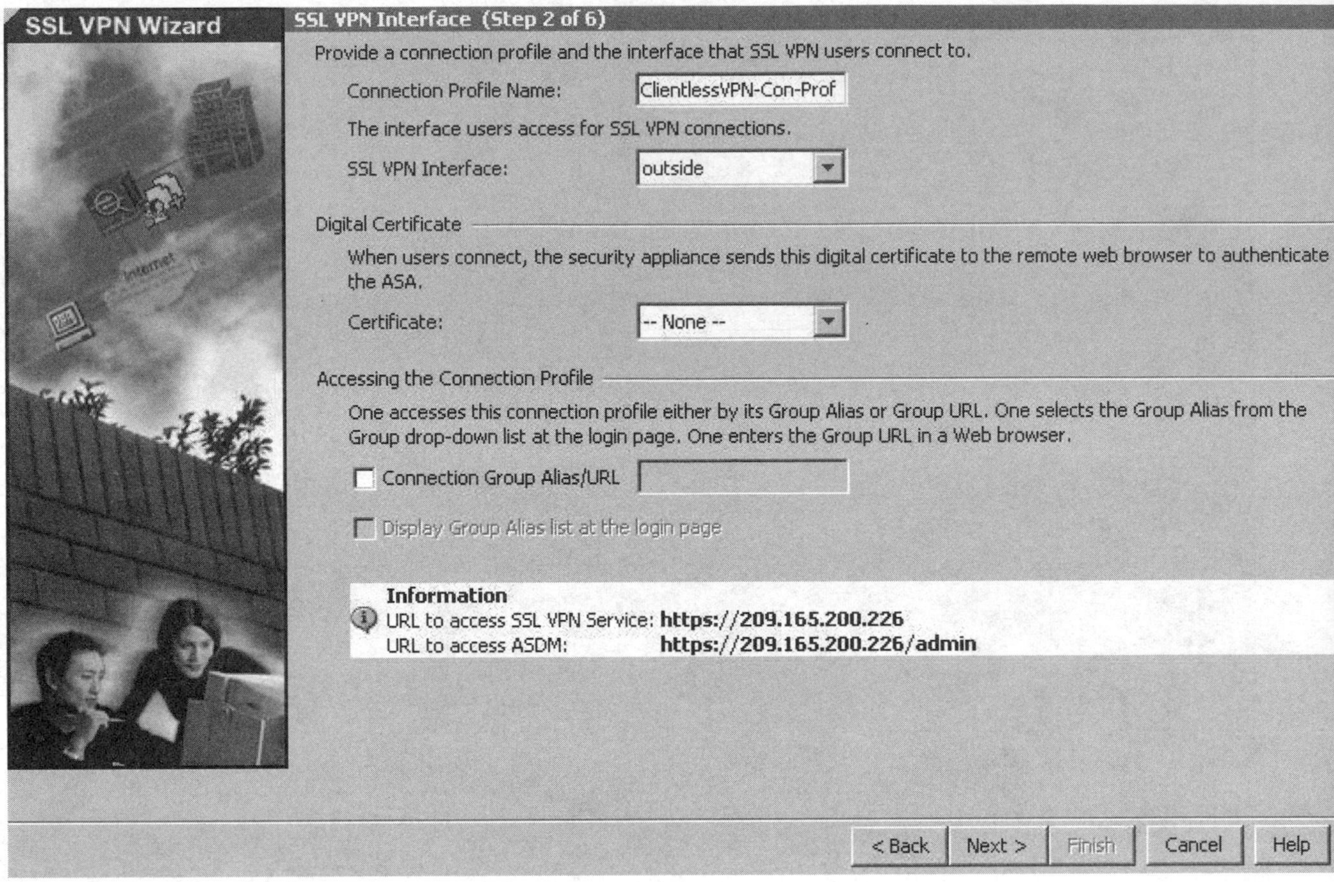

Step 4: Configure AAA user authentication.

On the User Authentication screen, click **Authenticate Using the Local User Database** and enter the username **VPN-User** with a password of **remote**. Click **Add** to create the new user, and then click **Next** to continue.

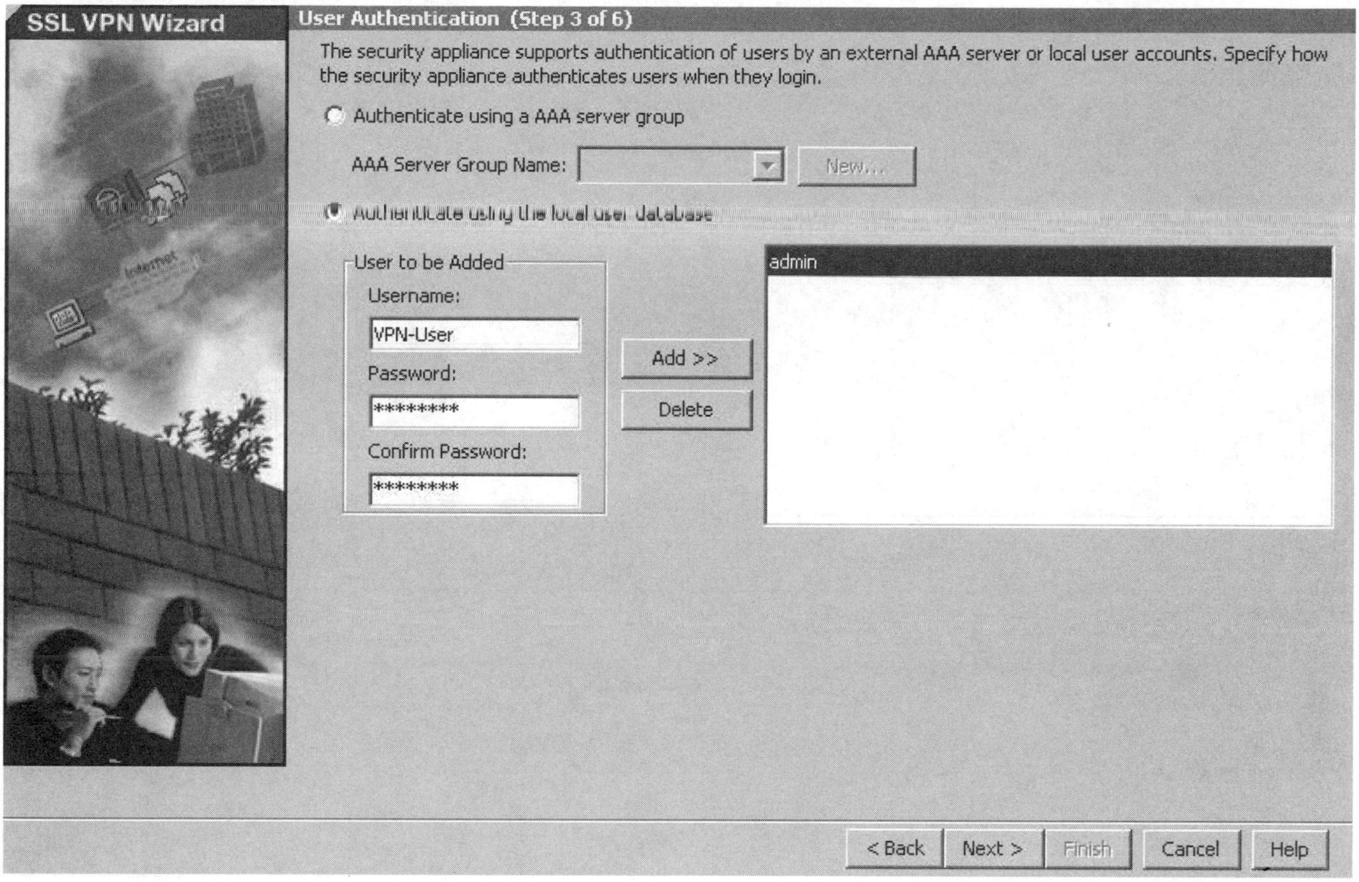

Step 5: Configure the VPN group policy.

On the Group Policy screen, create a new group policy named **ClientlessVPN-Grp-Pol**. When you are configuring a new policy, the policy name cannot contain any spaces. Click **Next** to continue.

Note: By default, the created user group policy inherits its settings from the DfltGrpPolicy. These settings may be modified after the wizard has been completed by navigating to the **Configuration > Remote Access VPN > Clientless SSL VPN Access > Group Policies** submenu.

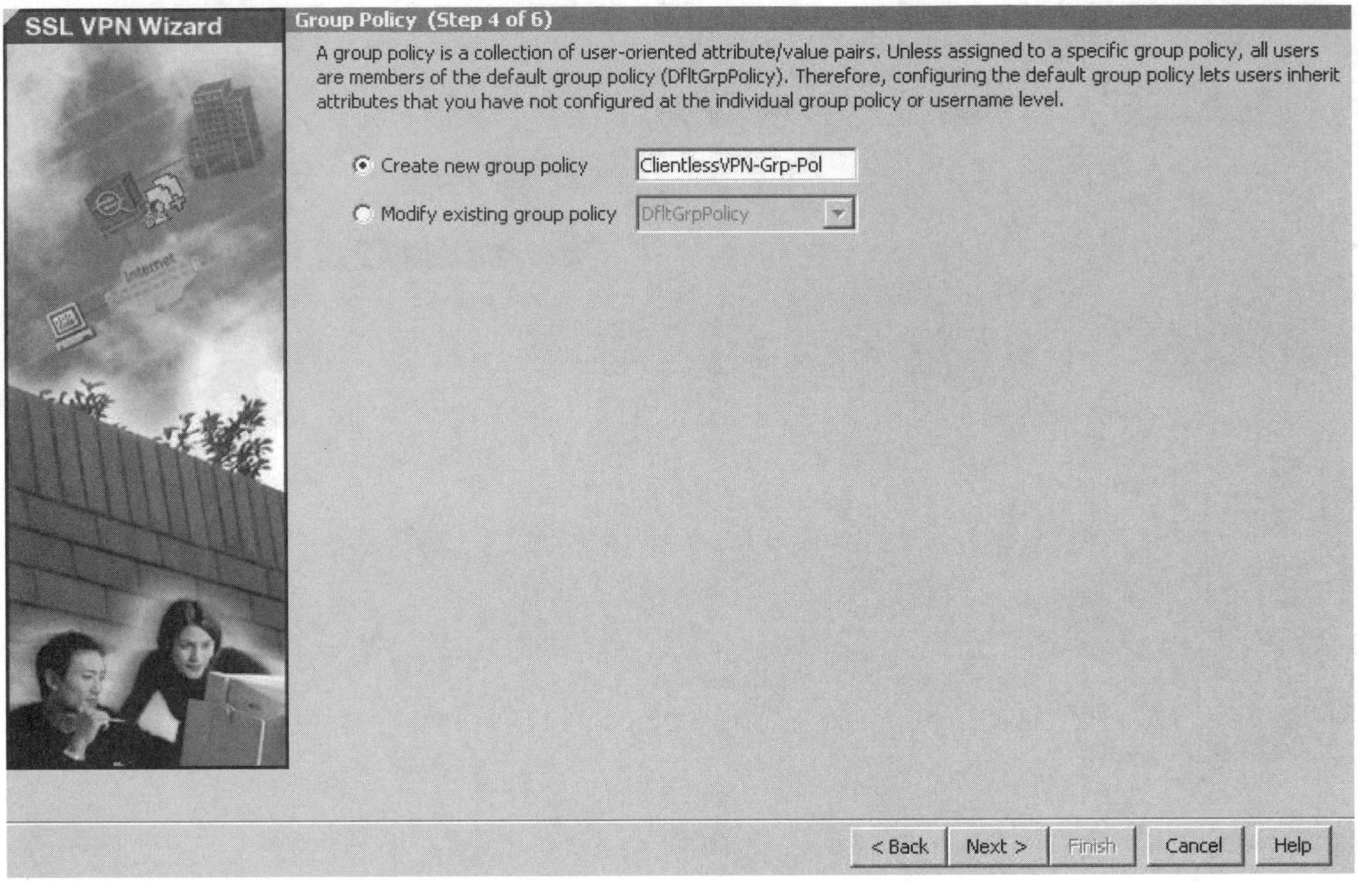

Step 6: Configure the bookmark list (clientless connections only).

A bookmark list is a set of URLs that is configured to be used in the clientless SSL VPN web portal. If there are bookmarks already listed, use the Bookmark List drop-down menu, choose the bookmark of choice, and click **Next** to continue with the SSL VPN Wizard. However, there are no configured bookmark lists by default, and therefore they must be configured by the network administrator.

a. From the Clientless Connections Only – Bookmark List screen, click the **Manage** button to create an HTTP server bookmark in the bookmark list. In the Configure GUI Customization Objects window, click **Add** to open the Add Bookmark List window. Name the list **Web-Server**.

Note: If the Web-Server bookmark list is shown as available from a previous configuration, you can delete it in ASDM and re-create it.

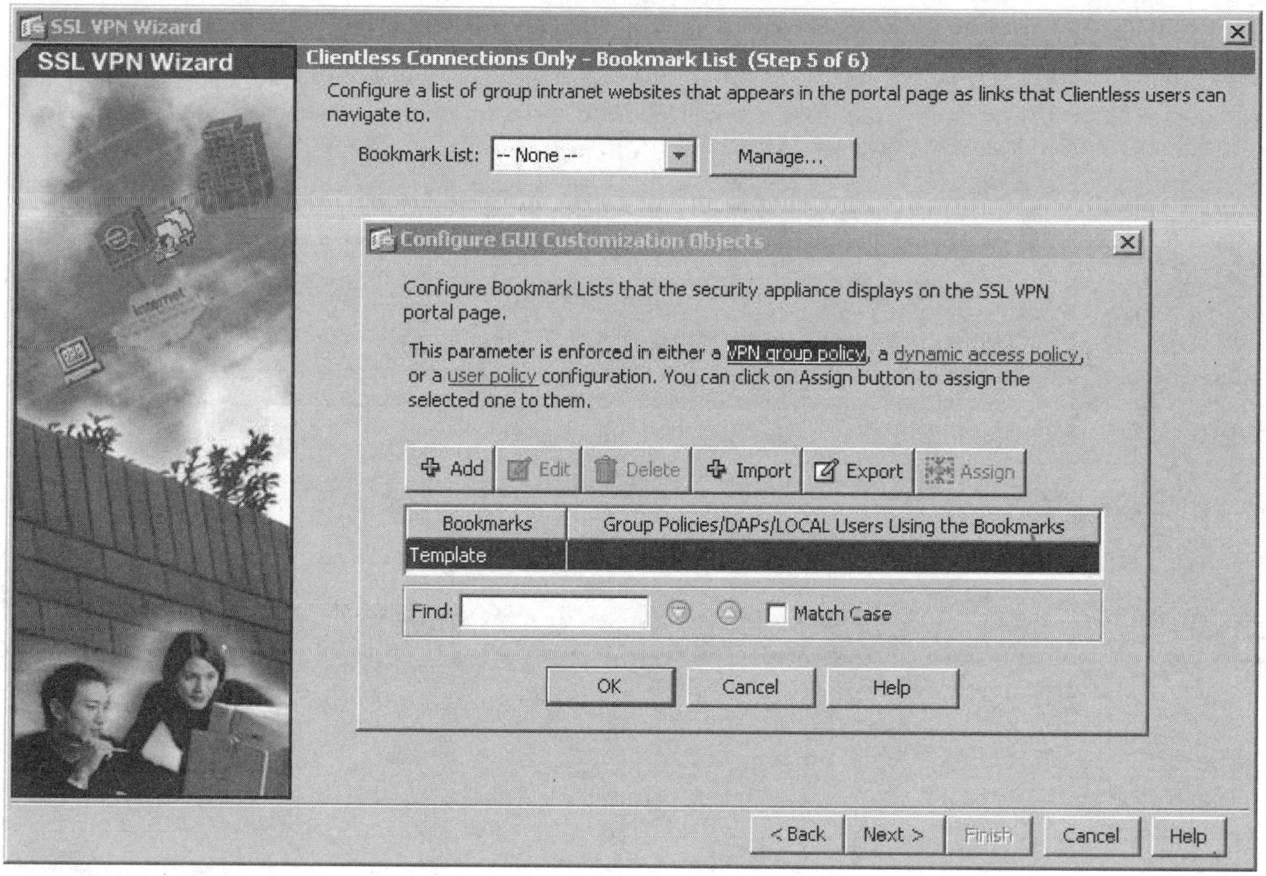
SSL VPN Wizard
SSL VPN Wizard
Clientless Connections Only - Bookmark List (Step 5 of 6)
Configure a list of group intranet websites that appears in the portal page as links that Clientless users can navigate to.
Bookmark List: -- None --
Manage...
Configure GUI Customization Objects
Configure Bookmark Lists that the security appliance displays on the SSL VPN portal page.
This parameter is enforced in either a VPN group policy, a dynamic access policy, or a user policy configuration. You can click on Assign button to assign the selected one to them.
Add
Edit
Delete
Import
Export
Assign
Bookmarks
Group Policies/DAPs/LOCAL Users Using the Bookmarks
Template
Find:
Match Case
OK
Cancel
Help
< Back
Next >
Finish
Cancel
Help

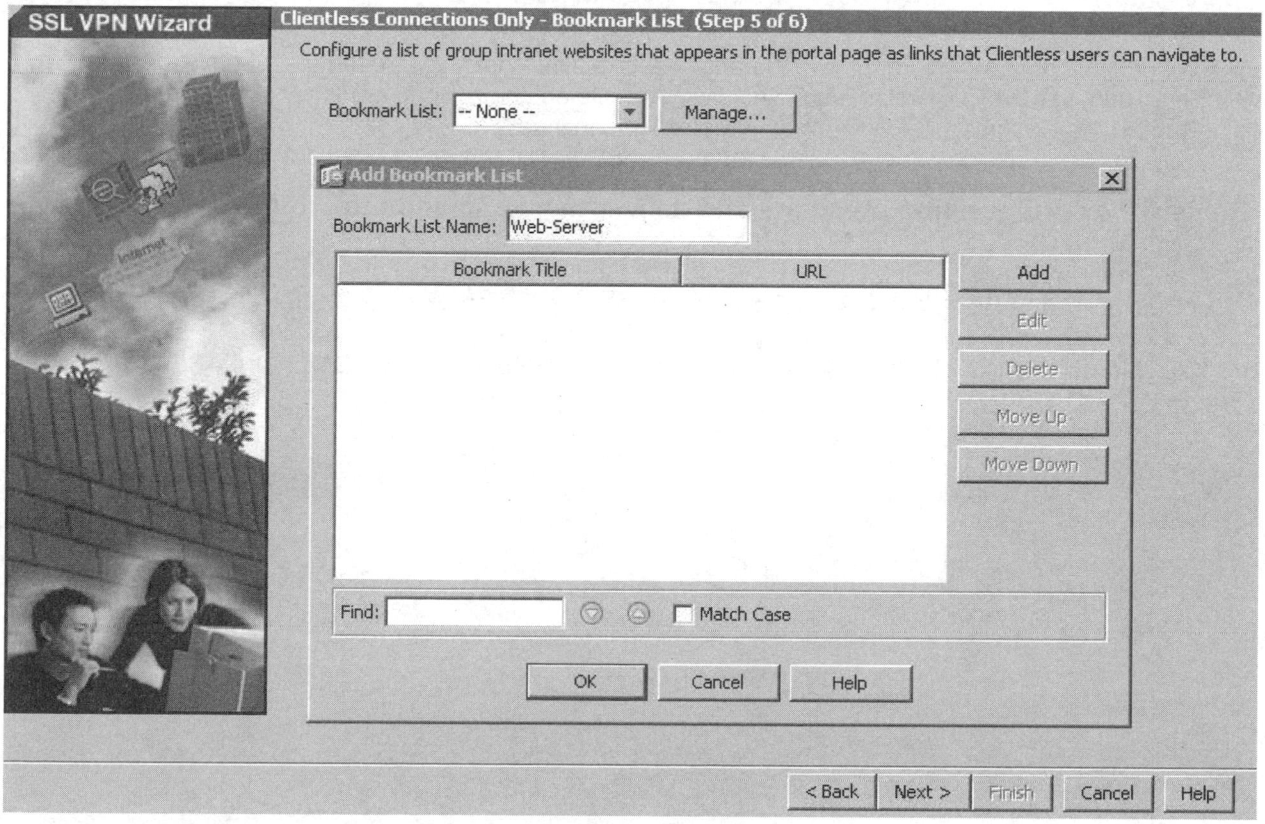
SSL VPN Wizard
Clientless Connections Only - Bookmark List (Step 5 of 6)
Configure a list of group intranet websites that appears in the portal page as links that Clientless users can navigate to.
Bookmark List: -- None --
Manage...
Add Bookmark List
Bookmark List Name: Web-Server
Bookmark Title
URL
Add
Edit
Delete
Move Up
Move Down
Find:
Match Case
OK
Cancel
Help
< Back
Next >
Finish
Cancel
Help

b. From the Add Bookmark List window, click **Add** to open the Add Bookmark window. Enter **Web Mail** as the Bookmark Title. Enter the server destination IP address or hostname as the URL to be used with the bookmark entry. In this example, the internal IP address of the DMZ server is specified. If this server has HTTP web services and web mail installed and functional, the outside users can access the server from the ASA portal when they connect.

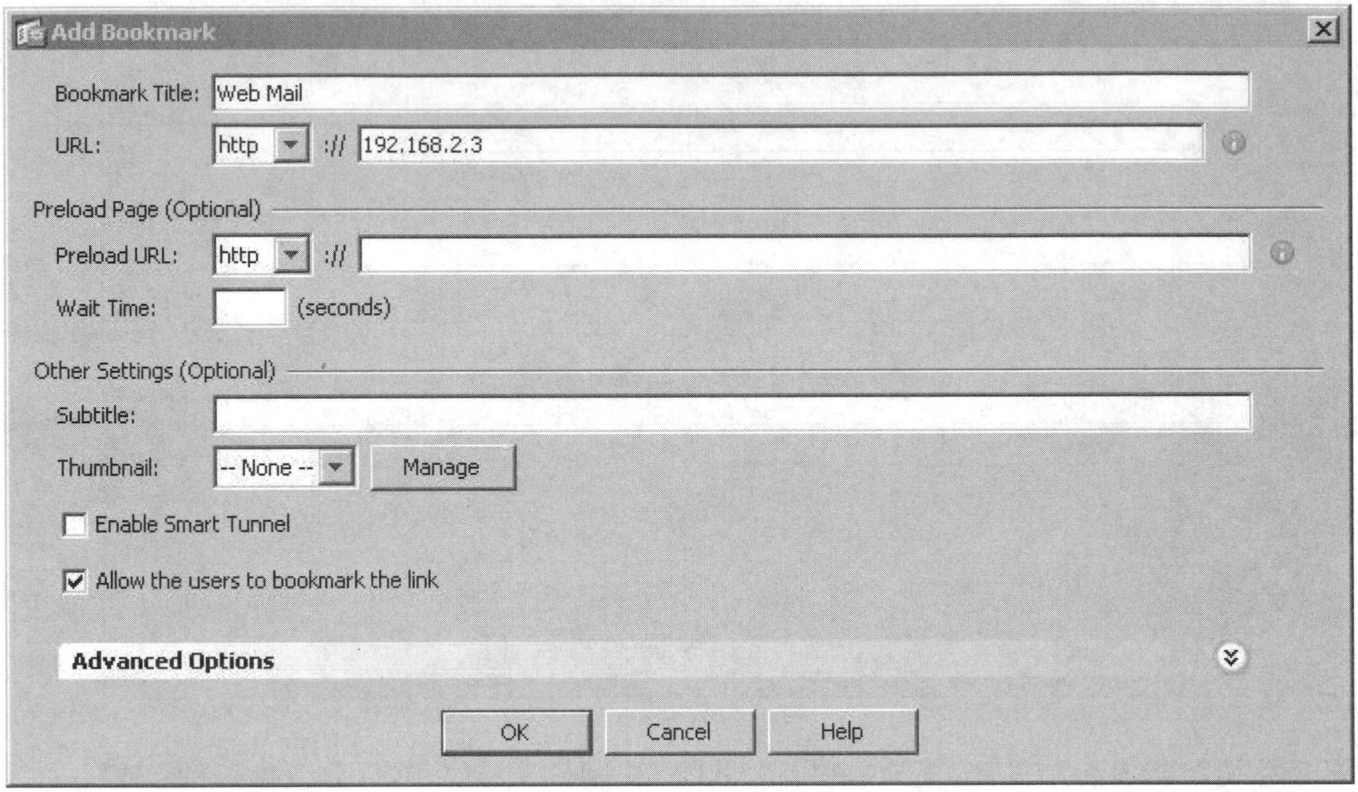

c. When the Bookmark Title and URL are entered, click **OK** in the Add Bookmark window to return to the Configure GUI Customization Objects window. Select the desired bookmark and click **OK** to return to the Bookmark List window. Click **Next** to continue.

Step 7: Review the configuration summary and deliver the commands to the ASA.

a. The Summary page is displayed next. Verify that the information configured in the SSL VPN Wizard is correct. Click the **Back** button to make changes, or click **Cancel** and restart the VPN Wizard.

b. Click **Finish** to complete the process and deliver the commands to the ASA.

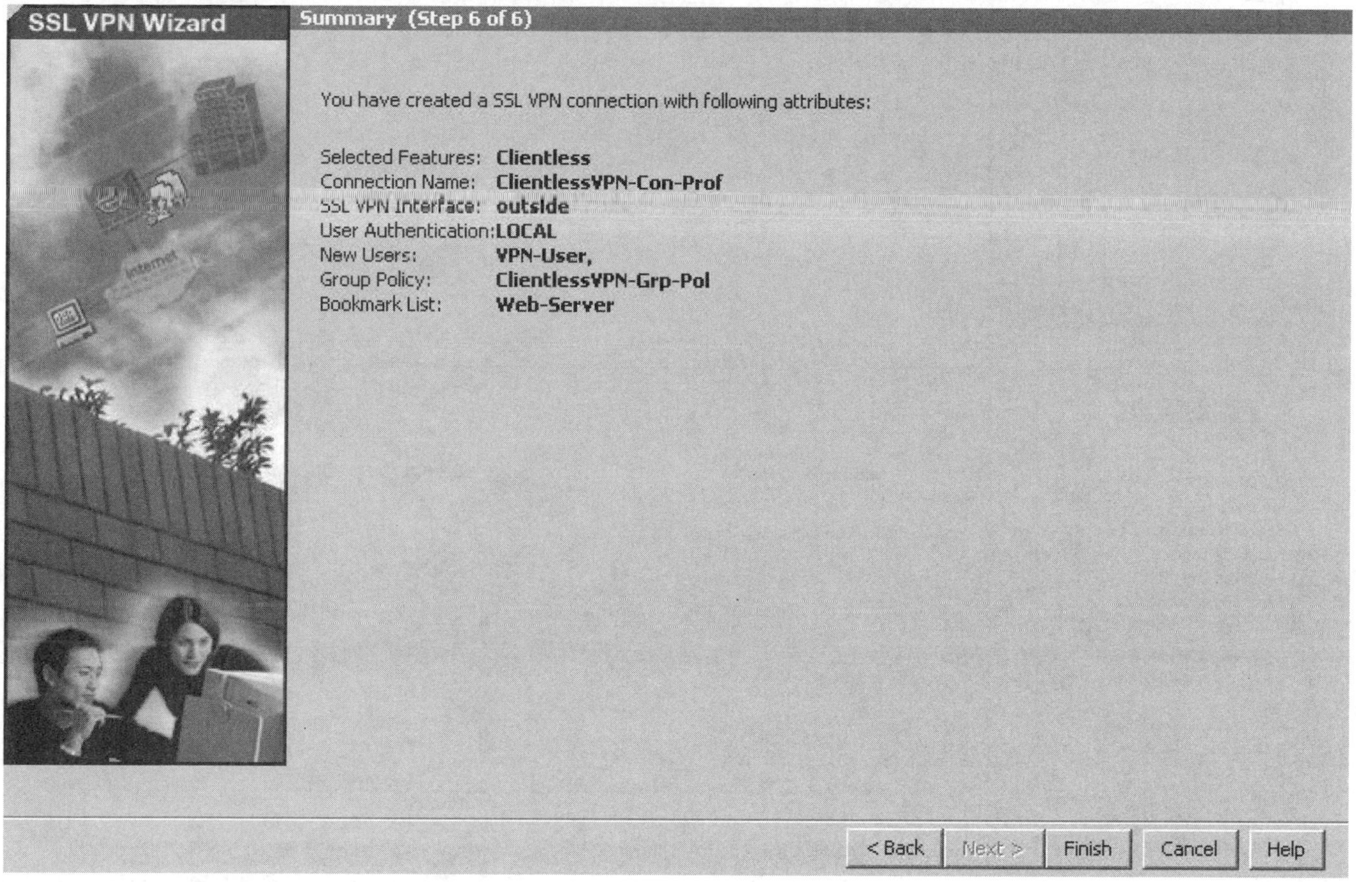

Step 8: Verify the ASDM SSL VPN connection profile.

In ASDM, choose **Configuration > Remote Access VPN > Clientless SSL VPN Access > Connection Profiles**. From this window, you can verify and edit the VPN configuration.

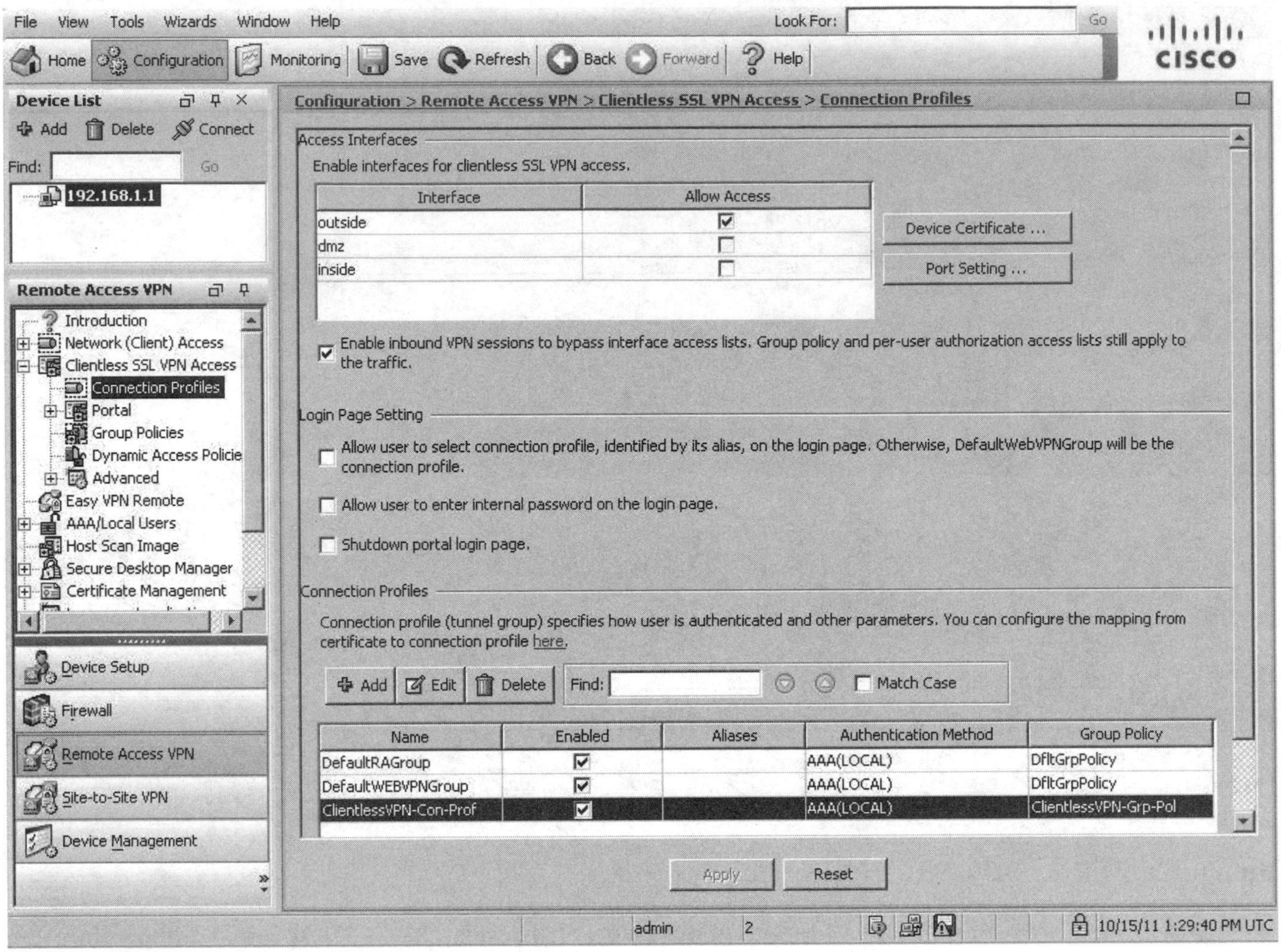

Step 9: Verify VPN access from the remote host.

a. Open the browser on PC-C and enter the login URL for the SSL VPN into the Address field (**https://209.165.200.226**). Be sure to use secure HTTP (HTTPS) because SSL is required to connect to the ASA.

b. The Logon window should appear. Enter the previously configured username **VPN-User** and password **remote**, and click **Logon** to continue.

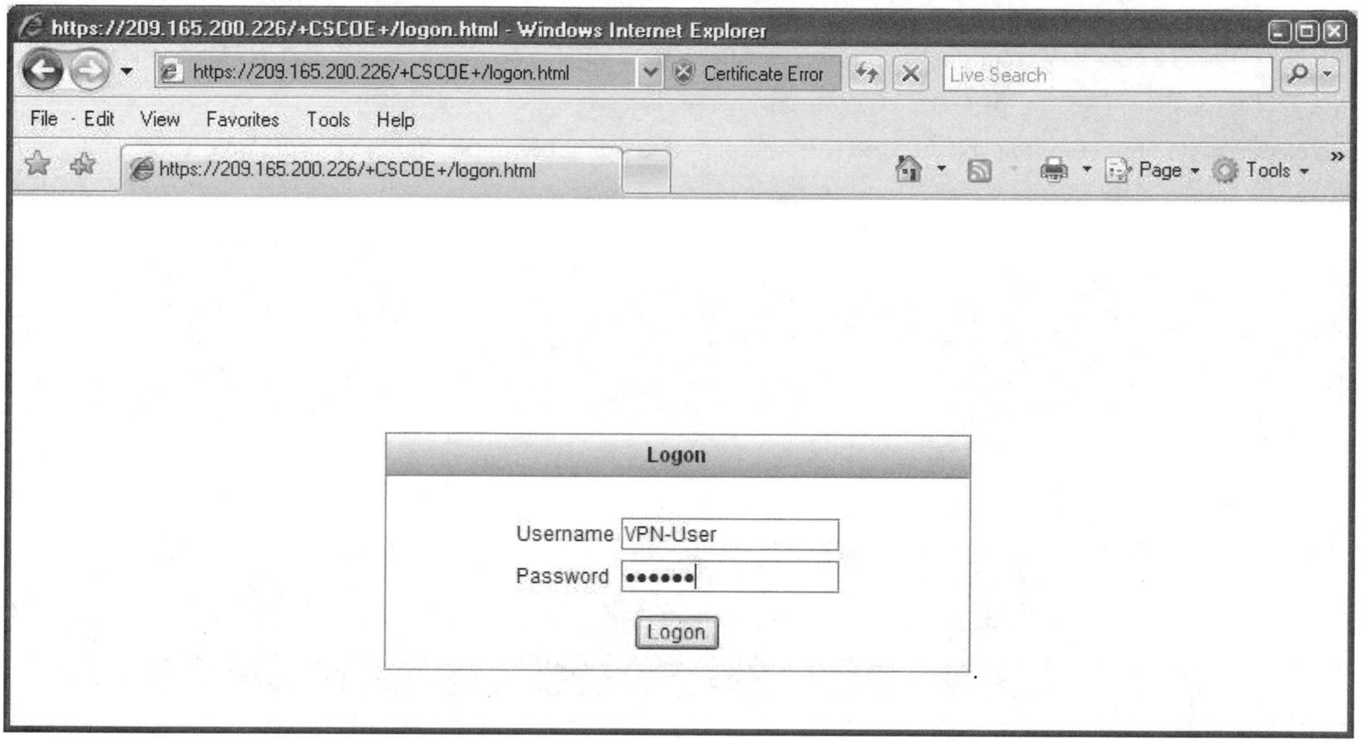

Step 10: Access the Web Portal window.

Once the user authenticates, the ASA SSL Web portal web page will be displayed listing the various bookmarks previously assigned to the profile. If the Bookmark points to a valid server IP address or hostname that has HTTP web services installed and functional, the outside user can access the server from the ASA portal. In this lab, the web mail server is not installed.

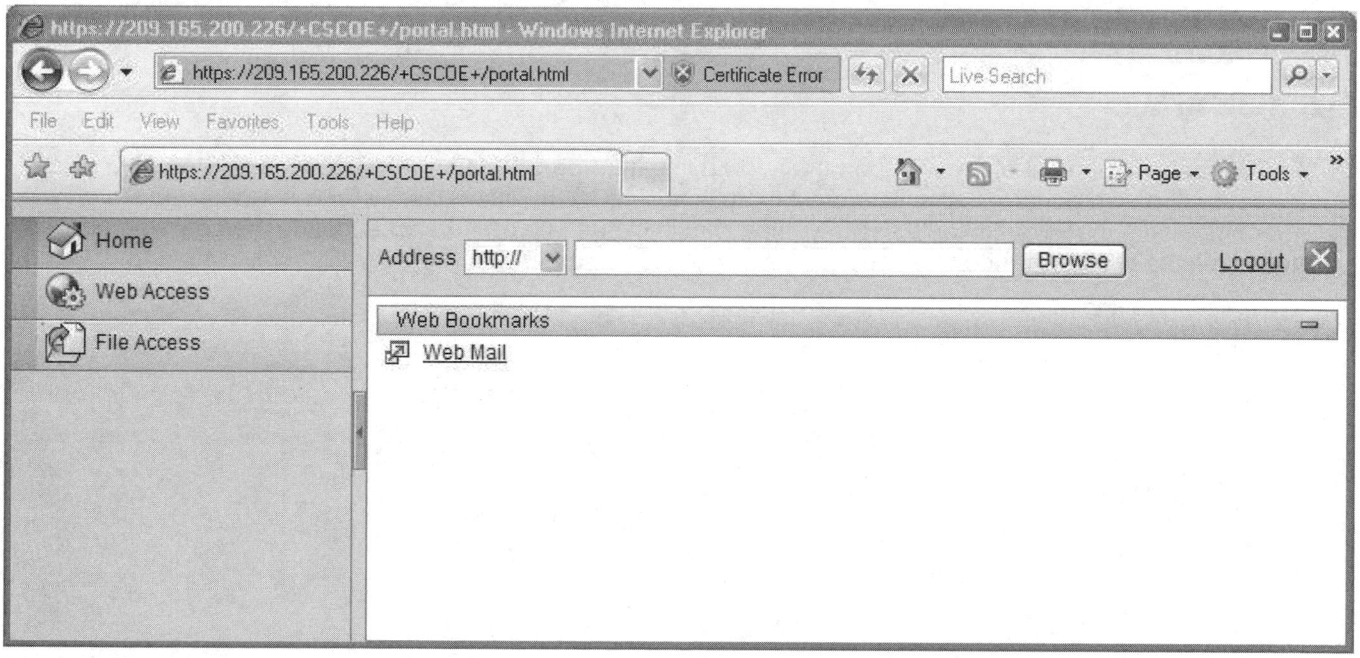

Step 11: View the clientless remote user session using ASDM Monitor.

While the remote user at PC-C is still logged in and on the ASA portal page, you can view the session statistics using ASDM Monitor.

From the menu bar, click the **Monitoring** button, and then choose **VPN** > **VPN Statistics** > **Sessions**. Click the **Filter By** pull-down menu and choose **Clientless SSL VPN**. You should see the VPN-User session logged in from PC-C (172.16.3.3).

Note: You might need to click the **Refresh** button on the menu bar to display the remote user session.

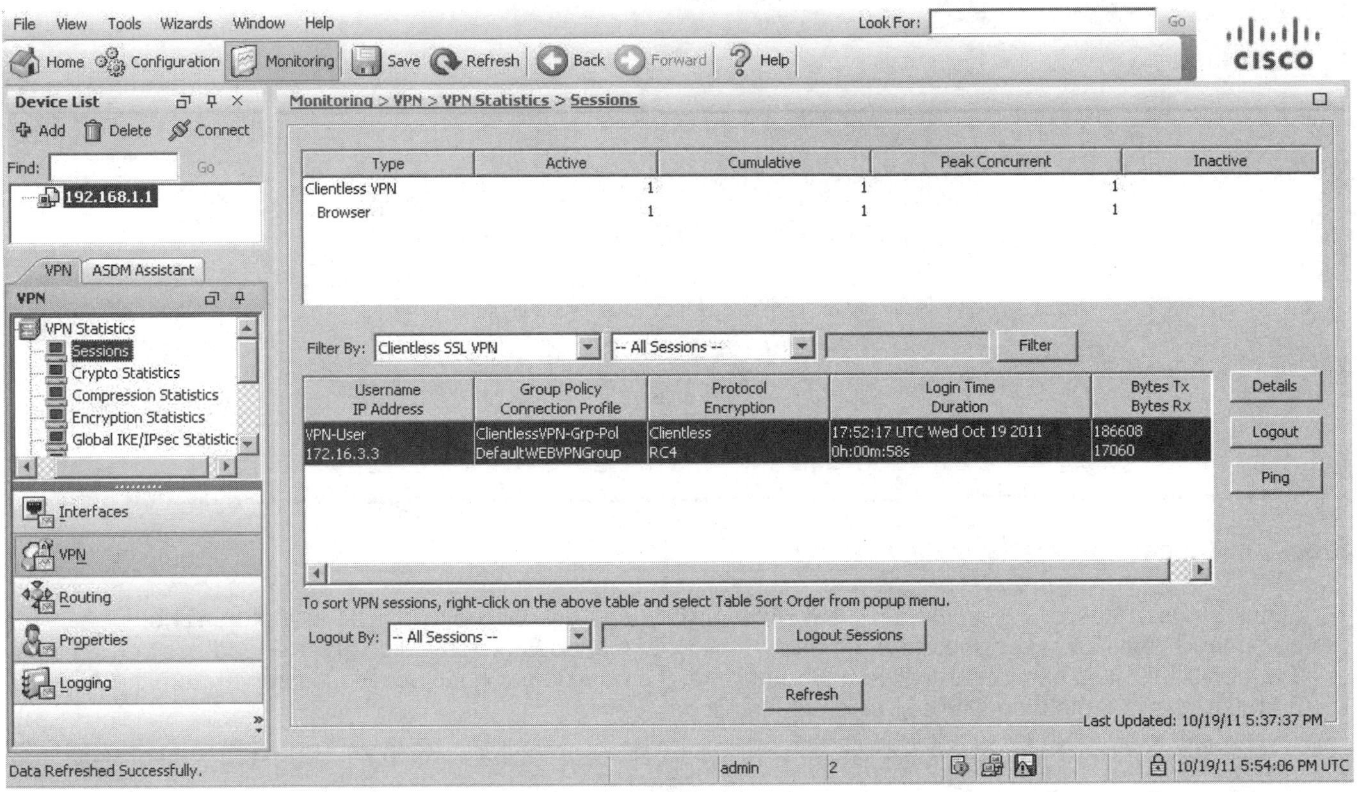

Step 12: Log out.

The user should log out of the web portal window using the **Logout** button when done (see Step 10). However, the web portal will also time out if there is no activity. In either case, a logout window appears informing users that for additional security, they should clear the browser cache, delete the downloaded files, and close the browser window.

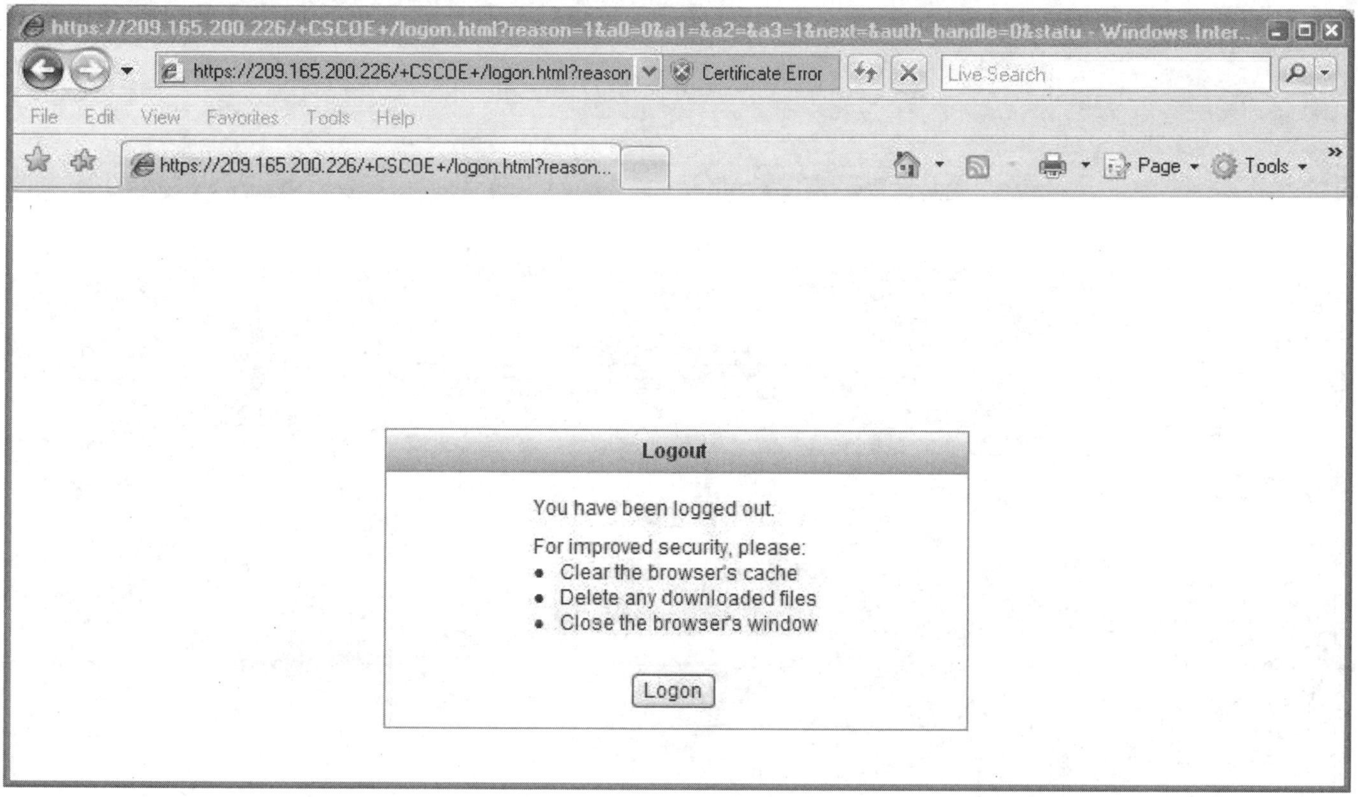

Part 4: Configuring AnyConnect SSL VPN Remote Access Using ASDM

Step 1: Clear the ASA configuration and access ASDM.

a. Before beginning Part 4 of this lab, use the procedure that is described in Part 2 to remove the current VPN settings, return the ASA to its base configuration, and verify ASDM access.

b. Open a browser on PC-B and test the HTTPS access to the ASA by entering **https://192.168.1.1**.

Note: Be sure to specify the HTTPS protocol in the URL.

c. After entering the URL, you should see a security warning about the security certificate of the website. Click **Continue to this website**. The ASDM welcome page will display. Click the **Run ASDM** button and login as **admin** with a password of **cisco123**.

Step 2: Review the Remote Access VPN ASDM Assistant.

a. From the ASDM menu bar, click the **Configuration** button and choose **Remote Access VPN** to display the Introduction screen. From here you can access information on how to create each of the three types of remote access VPNs that are supported by the ASA.

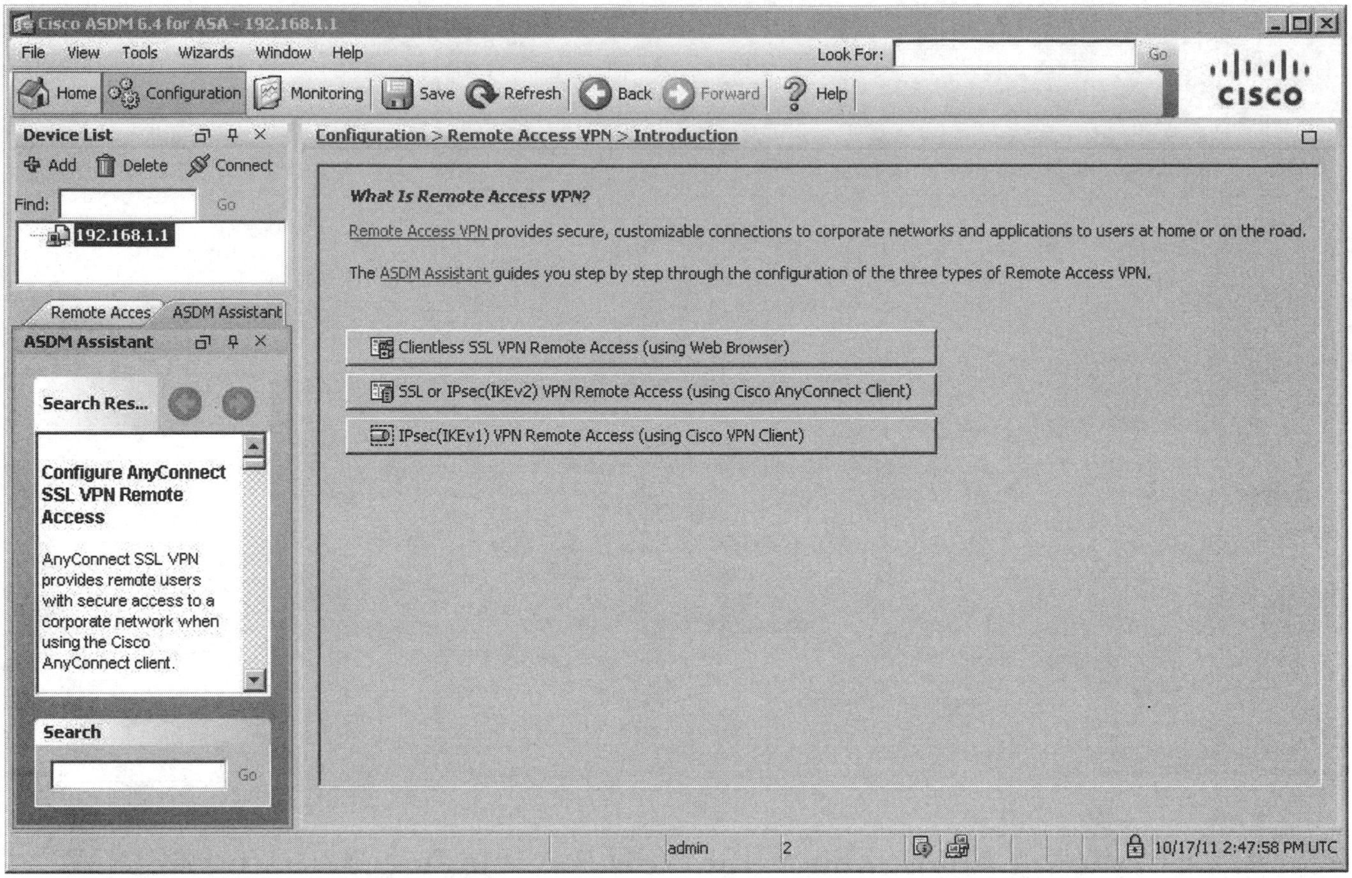

b. Click the button **SSL or IPsec(IKEv2) VPN Remote Access (using Cisco AnyConnect Client)** to access the ASDM Assistant. Read through the information provided to get a better understanding of the process for creating this type of VPN.

Step 3: Start the VPN Wizard.

a. From the ASDM main menu, choose **Wizards > VPN Wizards > AnyConnect VPN Wizard**.

b. Review the onscreen text and topology diagram, and then click **Next** to continue.

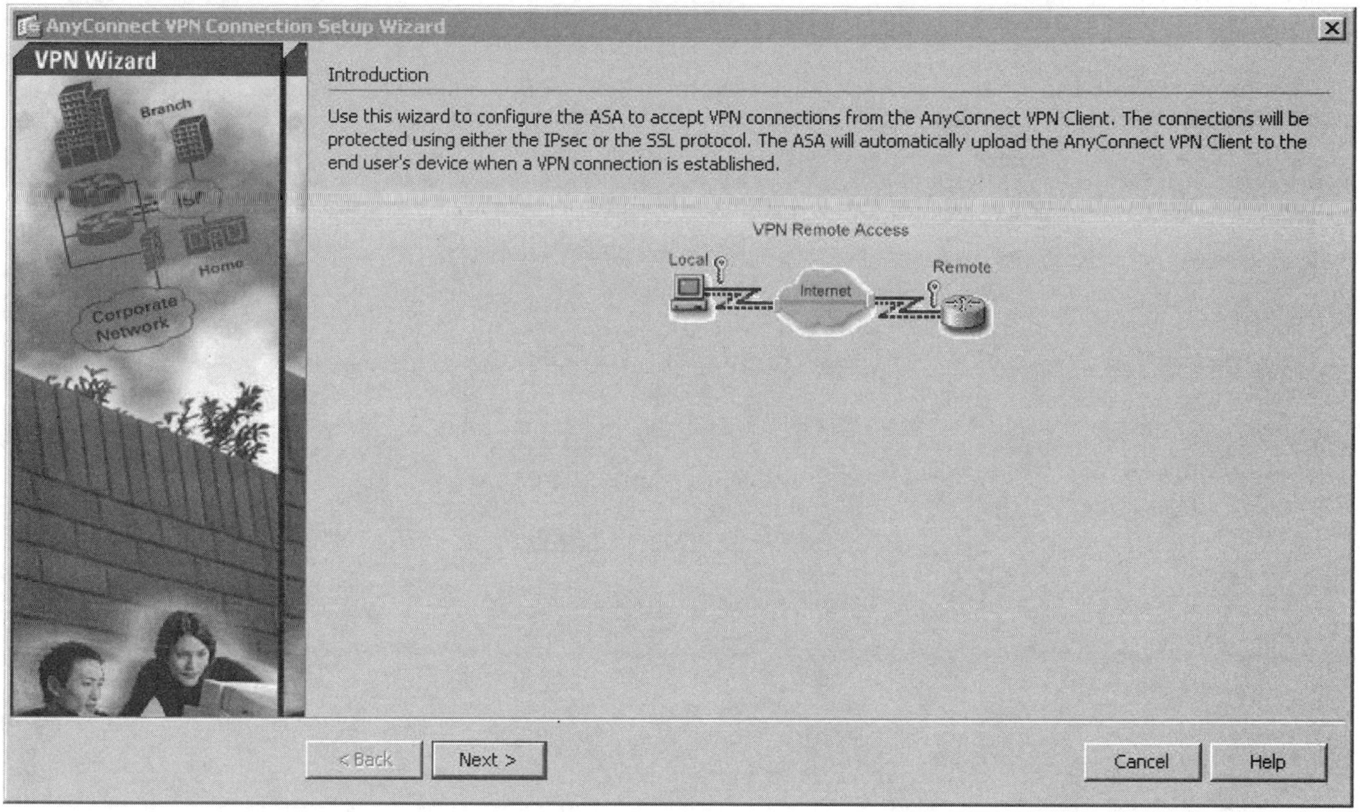

Step 4: Configure the connection profile.

On the Connection Profile Identification screen, enter **AnyC-SSL-VPN-Con-Prof** as the Connection Profile Name and specify the **outside** interface as the VPN Access Interface. Click **Next** to continue.

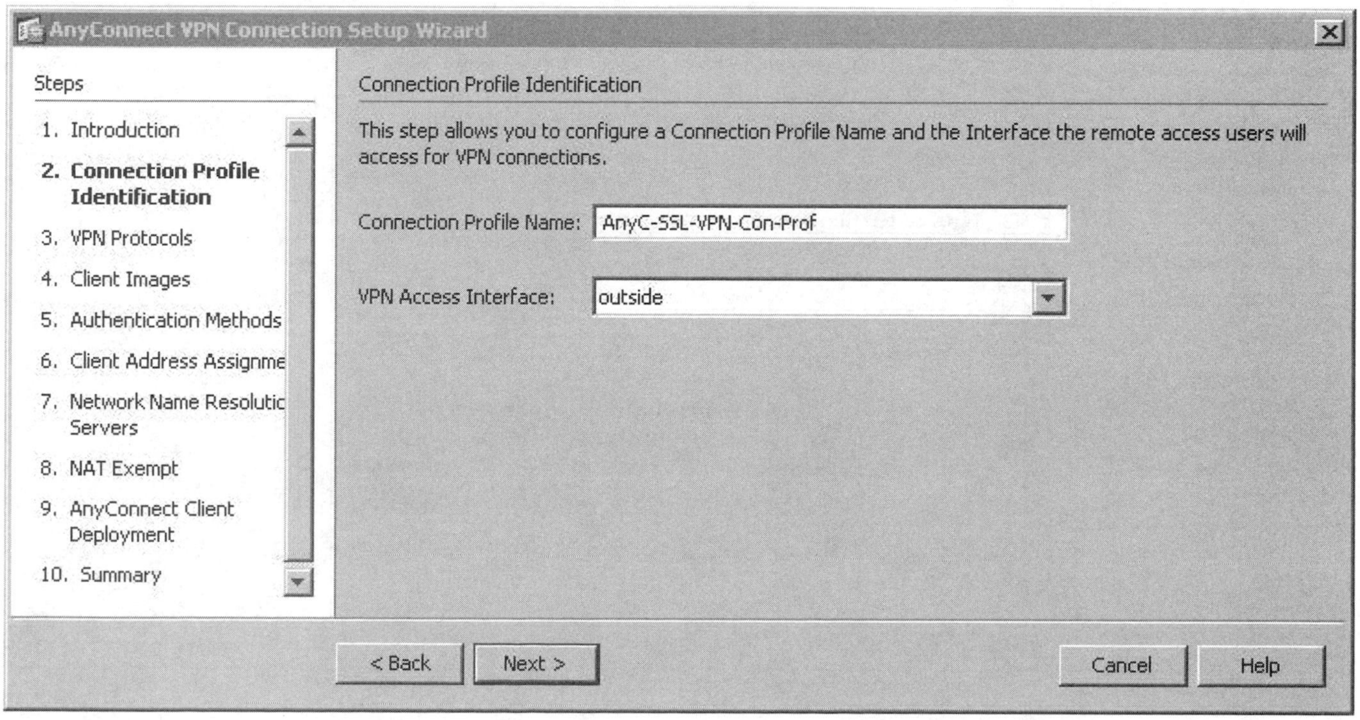

Step 5: Specify the VPN encryption protocol.

On the VPN Protocols screen, uncheck the IPsec protocol check box and leave the **SSL** check box checked. Do not specify a device certificate. Click **Next** to continue.

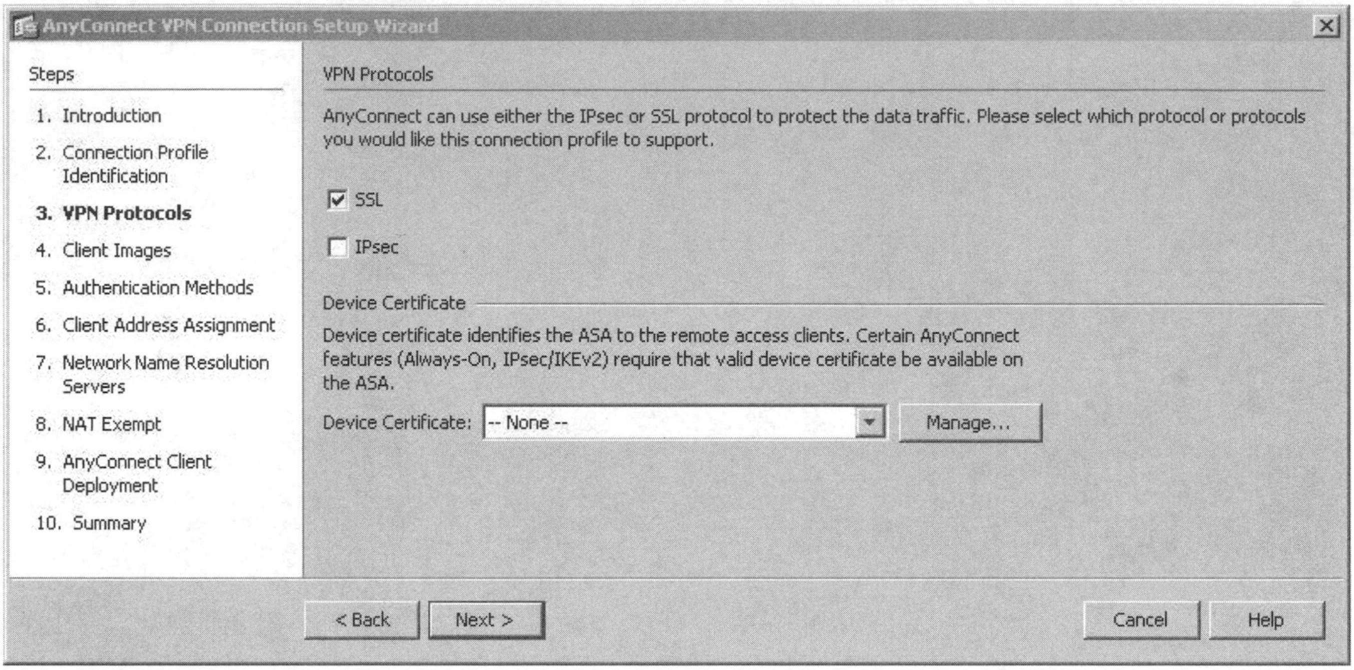

Step 6: Specify the client image to upload to AnyConnect users.

a. On the Client Images screen, click **Add** to specify the AnyConnect client image filename. In the Add AnyConnect Client Image window, click the **Browse Flash** button.

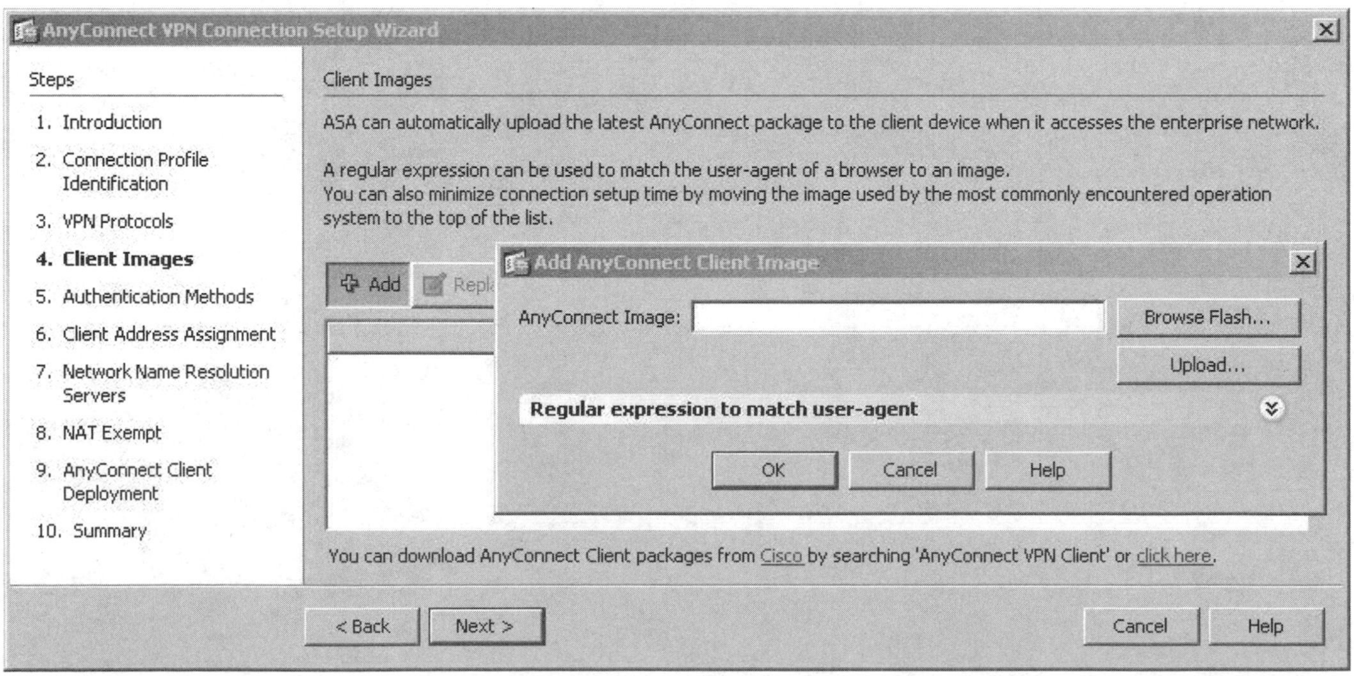

b. From the Browse Flash window, choose the AnyConnect package file for Windows (anyconnect-win-2.5.2014-k9.pkg, in this case). Click **OK** to return to the AnyConnect Client Images window, and then click **OK** again. On the Client Images screen, click **Next** to continue.

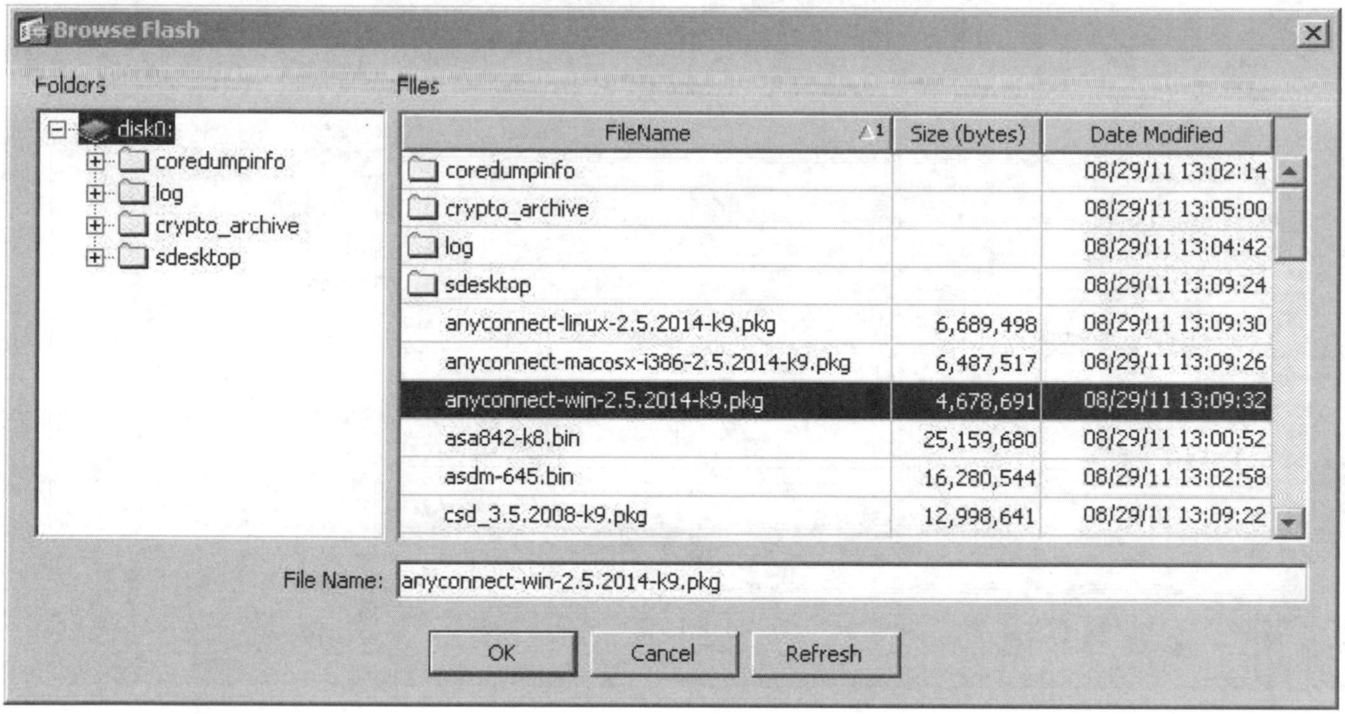

Step 7: Configure AAA local authentication.

a. On the Authentication Methods screen, ensure that the AAA Server Group is specified as **LOCAL**.

b. Enter a new user named **VPN-User** with a password of **remote**. Click **Add** to create the new user. Click **Next** to continue.

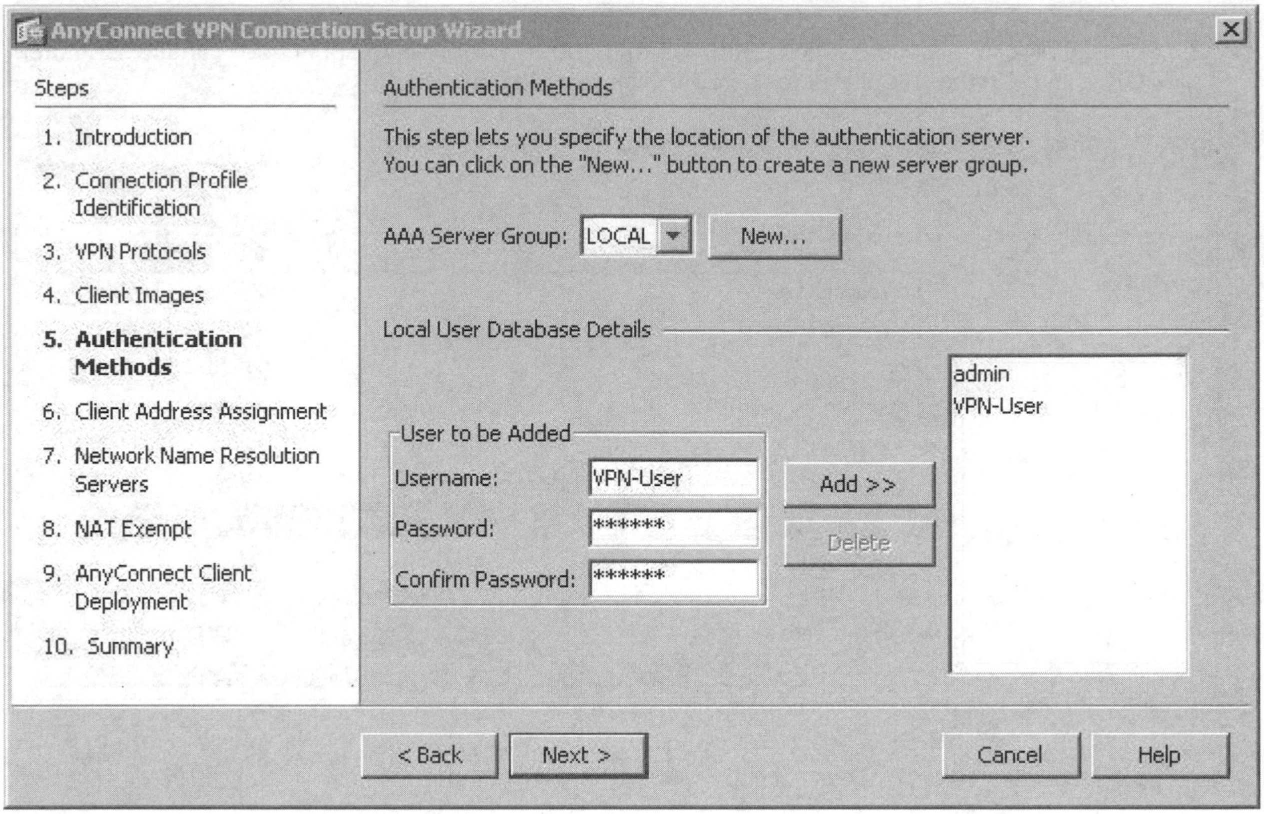

Step 8: Configure the client address assignment.

a. On the Client Address Assignment screen, click **New** to create an IPv4 address pool named **AnyC-VPN-Client-Pool**. Enter a starting IP address of **192.168.1.33**, an ending IP address of **192.168.1.62**, and subnet mask of **255.255.255.224**.

b. Click **Next** to continue.

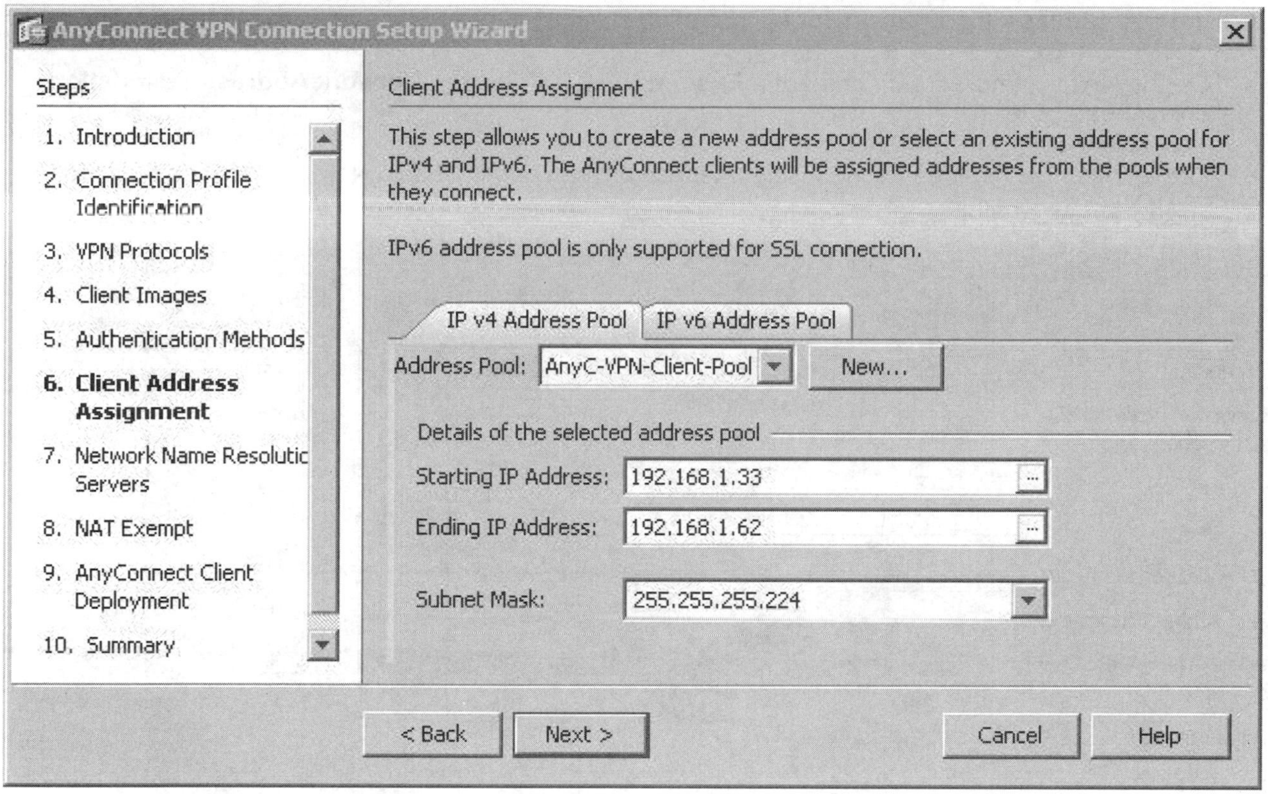

Step 9: Configure network name resolution.

On the Network Name Resolution Servers screen, enter the IP address of a DNS server. Leave the current domain name as ccnasecurity. Click **Next** to continue.

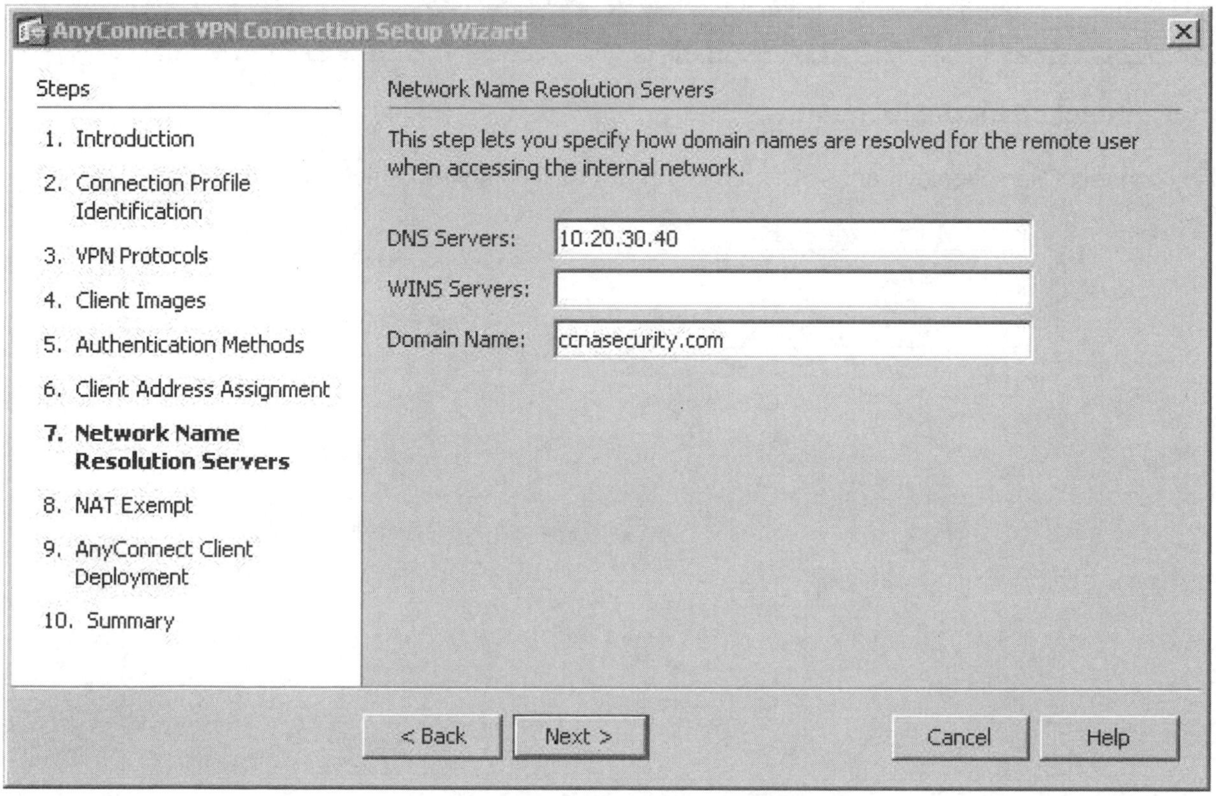

Step 10: Exempt address translation for VPN traffic.

a. On the NAT Exempt screen, check the **Exempt VPN Traffic from Network Address Translation** check box.

b. Leave the default entries for the Inside Interface (inside) and the Local Network (any) as they are. Click **Next** to continue.

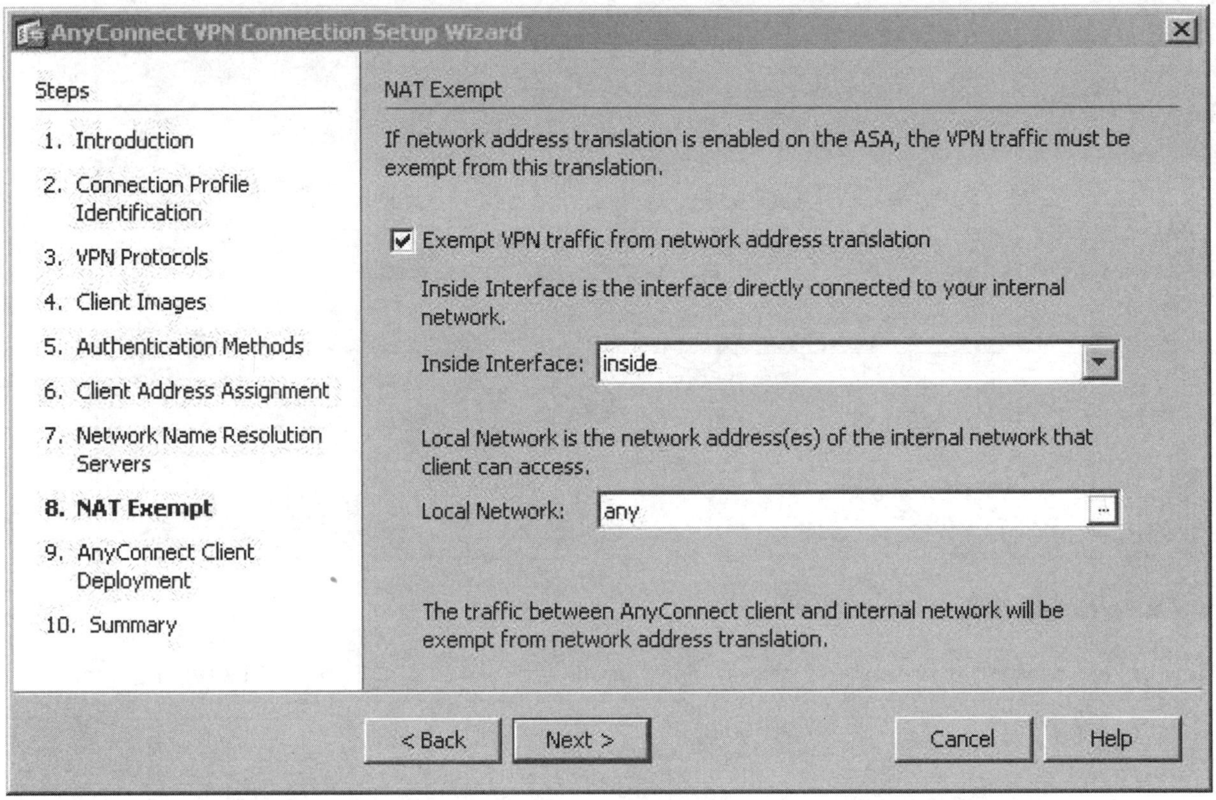

Step 11: AnyConnect client deployment.

On the AnyConnect Client Deployment screen, read the text describing the options, and then click **Next** to continue.

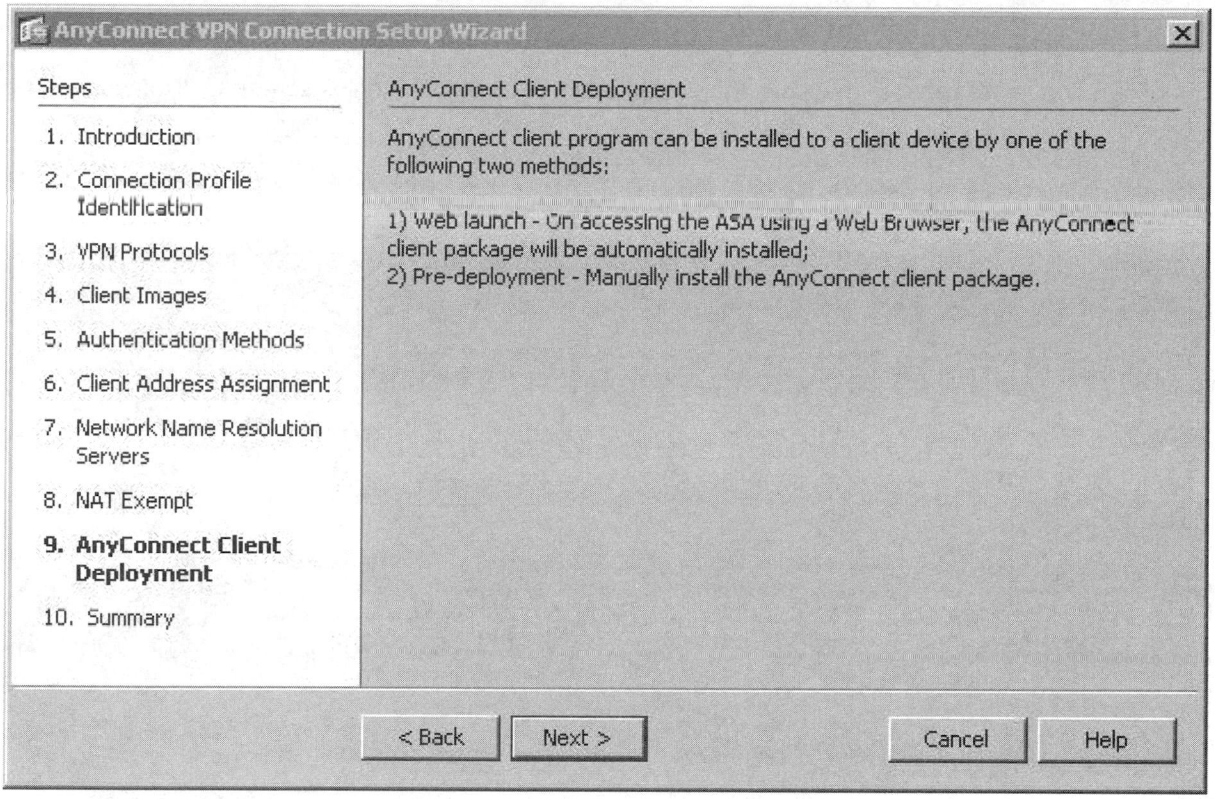

Step 12: Review the Summary screen and apply the configuration to the ASA.

On the Summary screen, review the configuration description, and then click **Finish** to send the commands to the ASA.

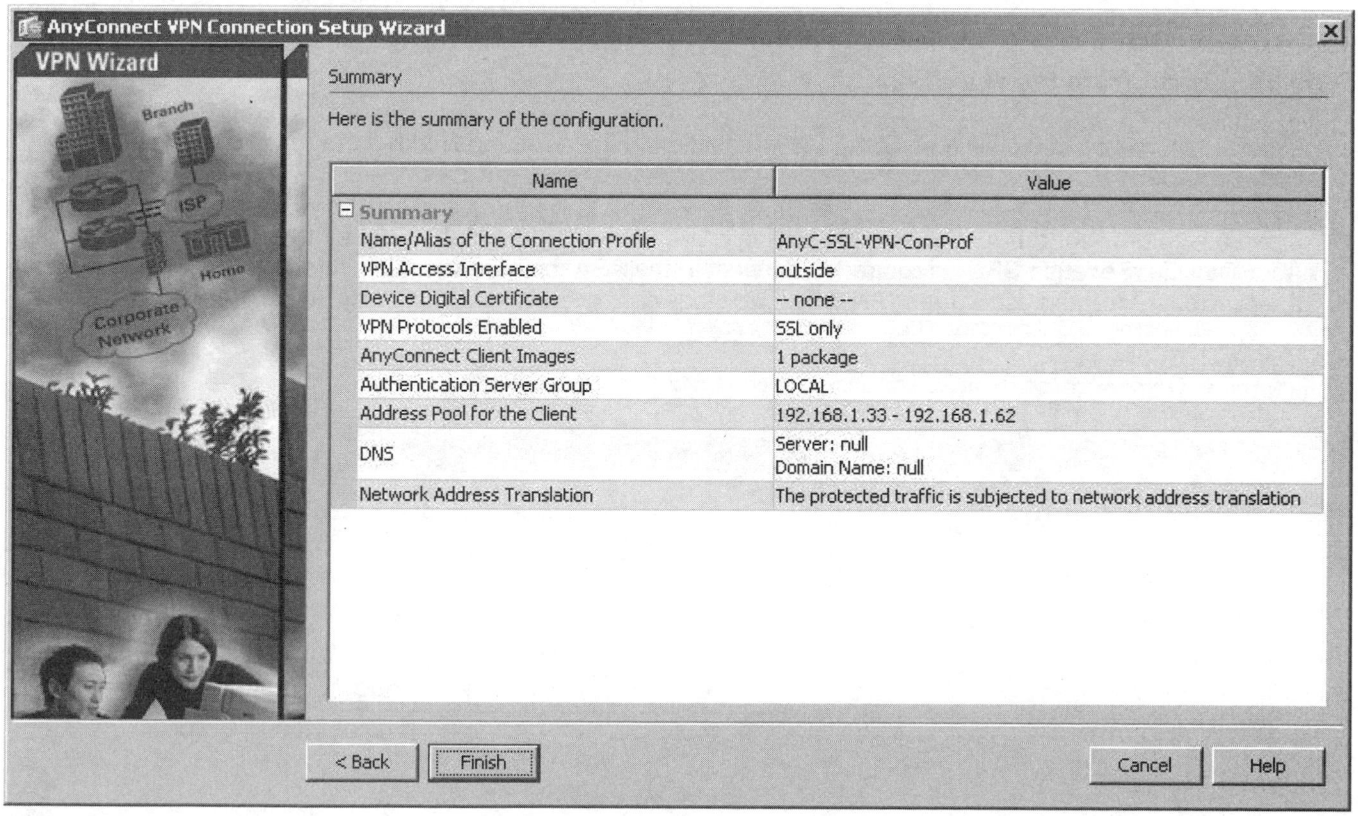

Step 13: Verify the AnyConnect client profile.

After the configuration is delivered to the ASA, the AnyConnect Connection Profiles screen is displayed.

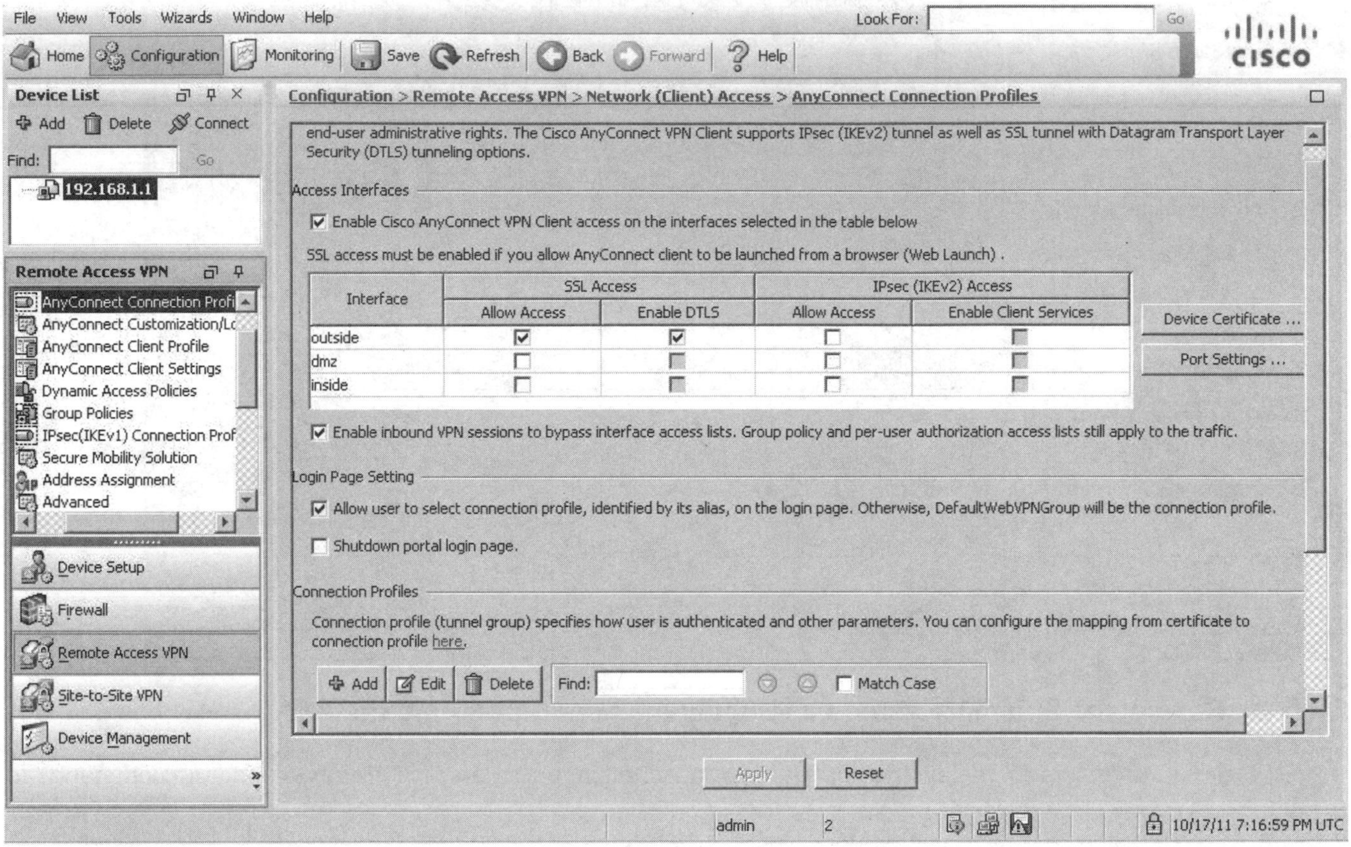

Step 14: Log in from the remote host.

Initially, you establish a clientless SSL VPN connection to the ASA to download the AnyConnect client software.

Open a web browser on PC-C and enter the login URL **https://209.165.200.226** for the SSL VPN into the Address field. Because SSL is required to connect to the ASA, be sure to use secure HTTP (HTTPS). Enter the previously created username **VPN-User** with password **remote** and click **Logon** to continue.

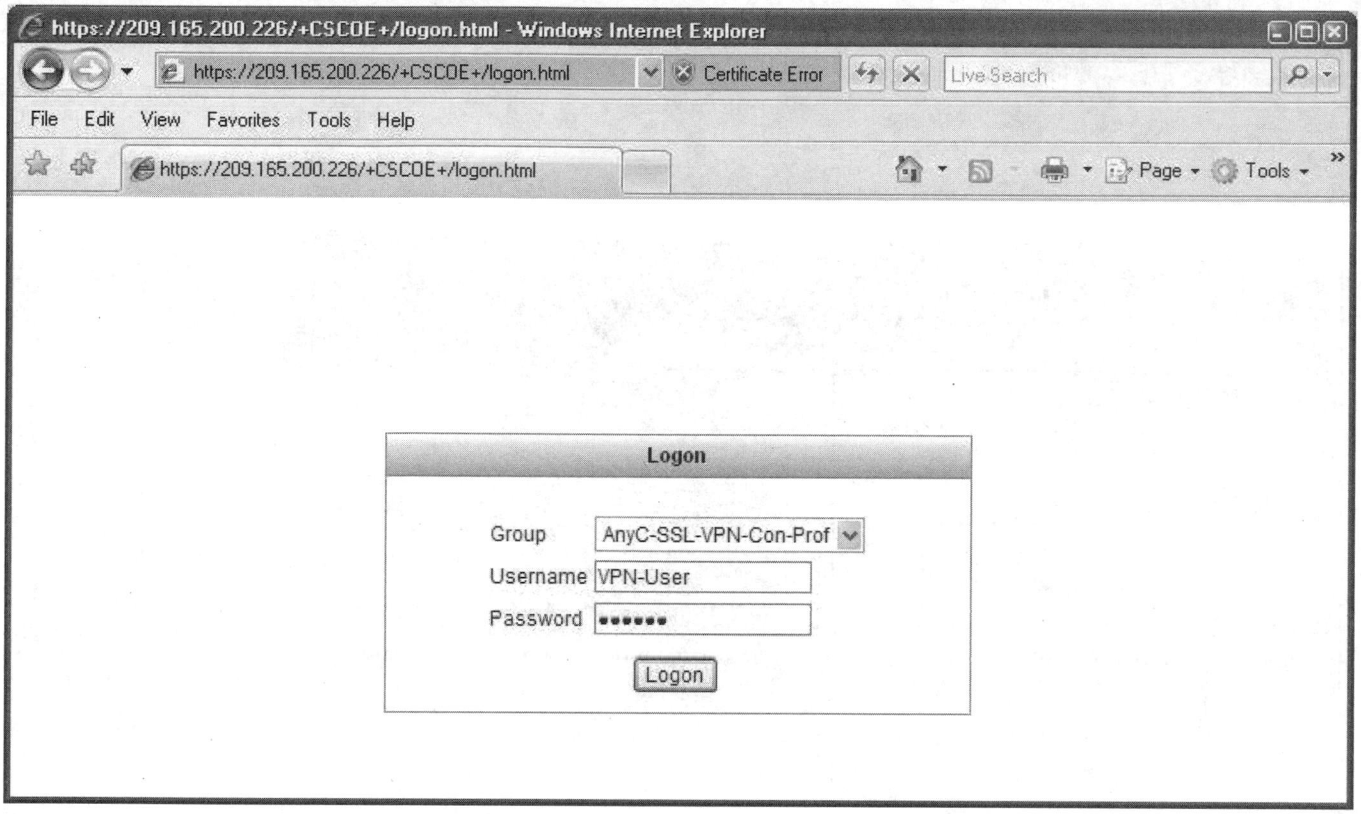

Step 15: Accept the security certificate (if required).

The ASA may request confirmation that this is a trusted site. If requested, then click **Yes** to proceed.

Step 16: Perform platform detection (if required).

The ASA begins a software autodownload process consisting of a series of compliance checks for the target system. The ASA performs the platform detection by querying the client system in an attempt to identify the type of client connecting to the security appliance. Based on the platform that is identified, the proper software package may be autodownloaded.

Step 17: Install AnyConnect (if required)

If the AnyConnect client must be downloaded, a security warning displays on the remote host. Then the ASA detects whether ActiveX is available on the host system. For ActiveX to operate properly with the Cisco ASA, it is important that the security appliance is added as a trusted network site. ActiveX is used for client download if a web portal is not in use.

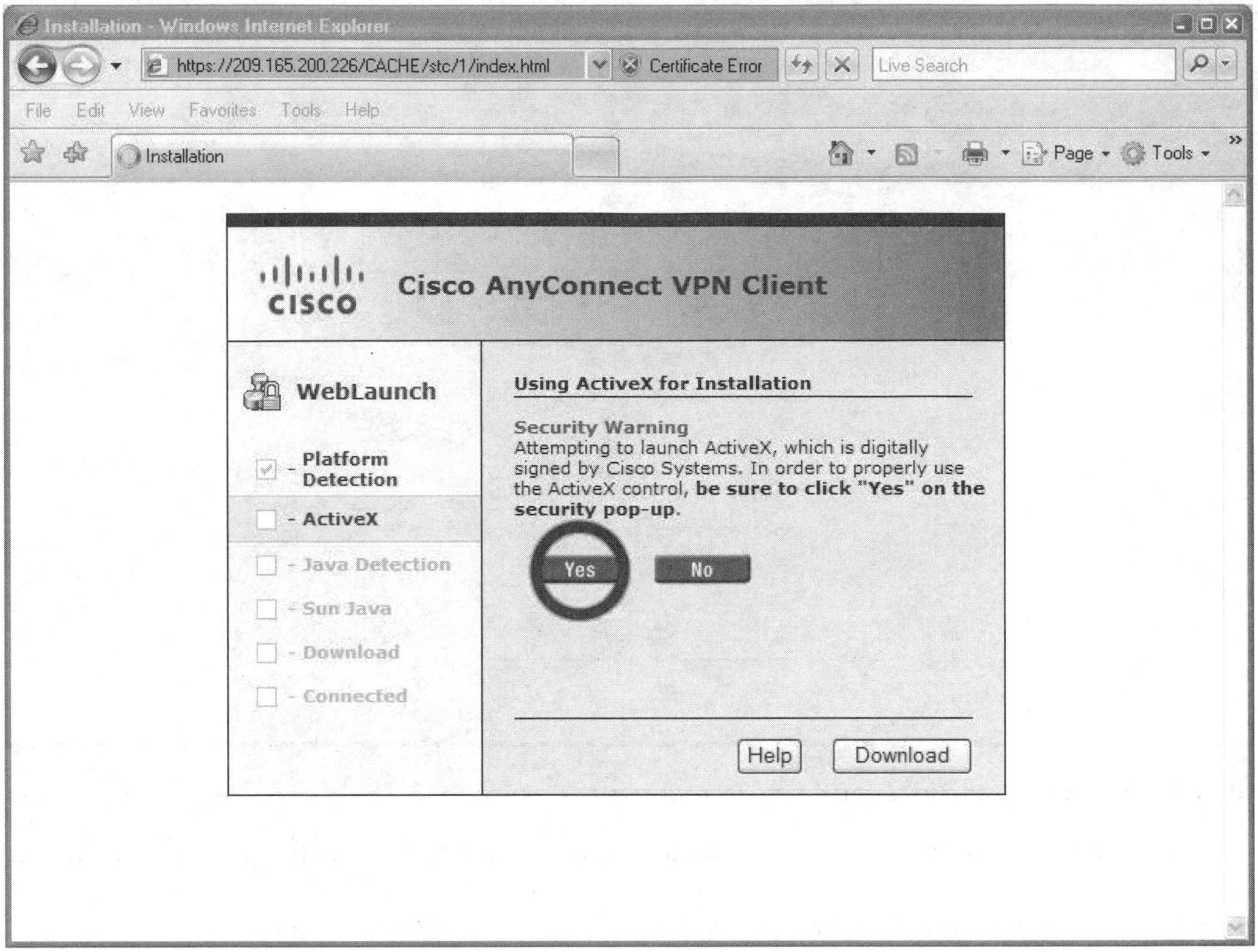

To continue, choose **Install**. If requested, click **Yes**. The VPN Client Installer begins, and another security alert window might appear. If required, click **Yes** to continue and accept the security certificate.

Step 18: Client connection is established with the ASA.

When the client completes the autodownload of the Cisco AnyConnect SSL VPN Client, the web session automatically launches the Cisco AnyConnect SSL VPN Client and attempts to log in the user to the network using the same credentials that are supplied when logging in to the web portal.

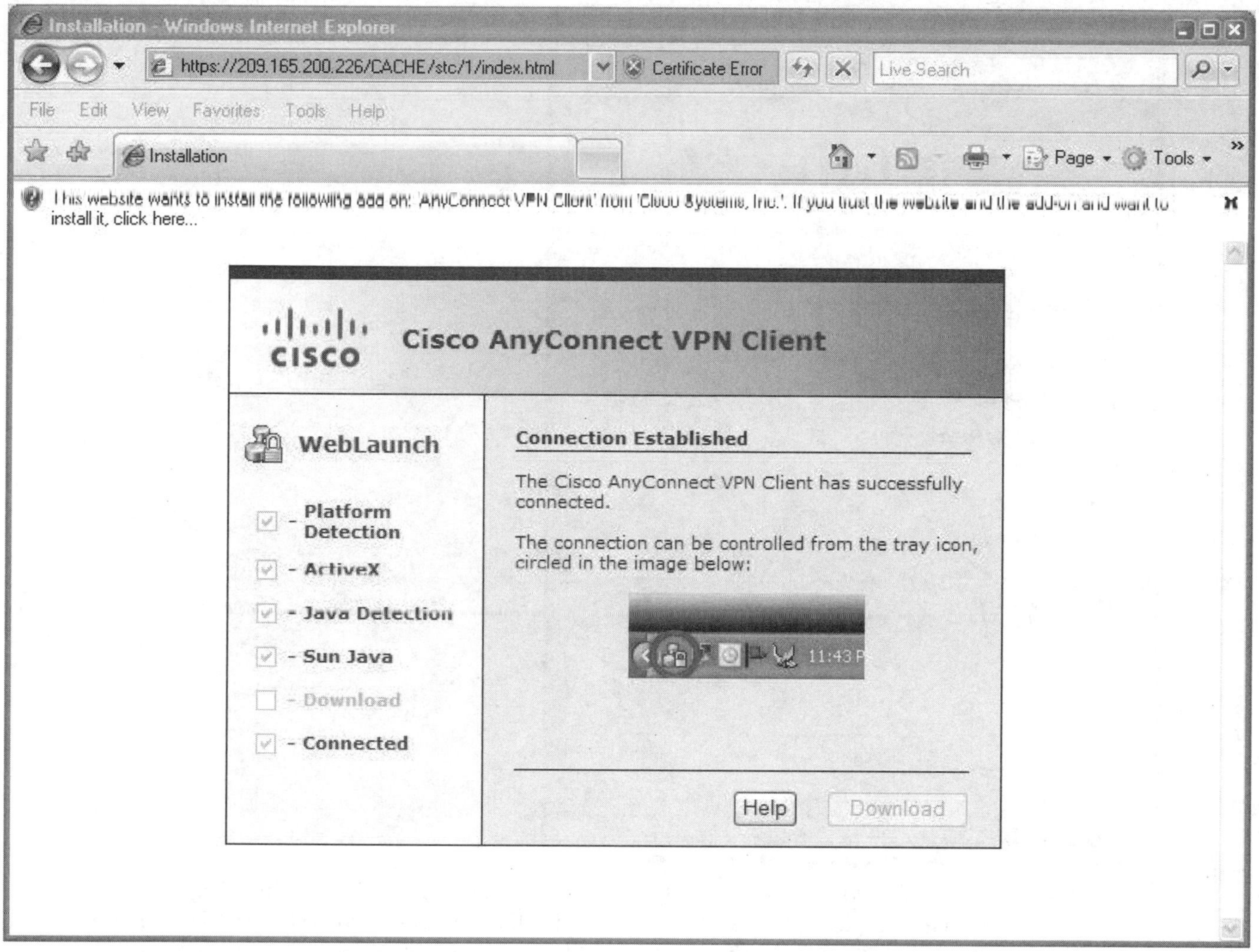

Step 19: Confirm VPN connectivity.

When the full tunnel SSL VPN connection is established, an icon appears in the system tray that signifies that the client has successfully connected to the SSL VPN network.

a. Display connection statistics and information by double-clicking the **AnyConnect** icon in the system tray. This client interface may also be used to log out the user. Note the inside IP address that is assigned to the client from the VPN pool (192.168.1.33-.62).

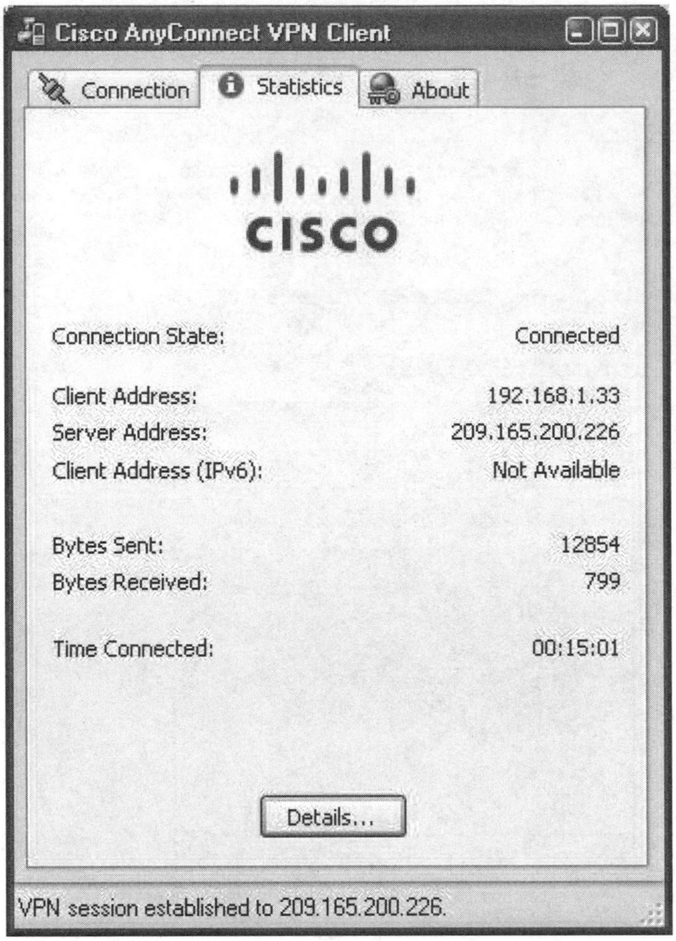

b. From a command prompt on remote host PC-C, verify the IP addressing using the **ipconfig** command. Two IP addresses should be listed. One is for the PC-C remote host local IP address (172.16.3.3), and the other is the IP address assigned for the SSL VPN tunnel (192.168.1.33).

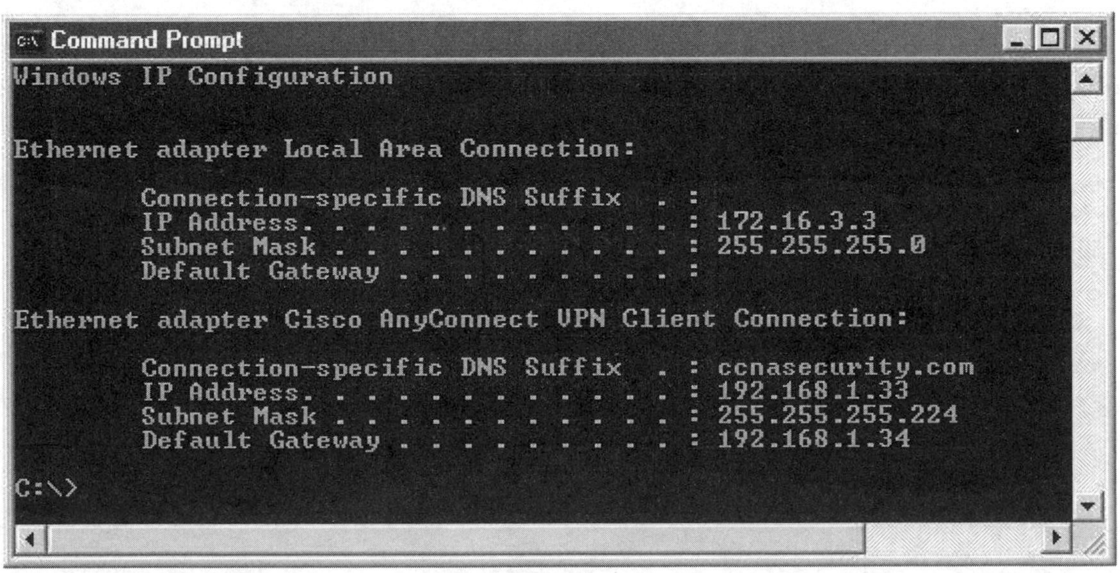

c. From remote host PC-C, ping inside host PC-B (192.168.1.3) to verify connectivity.

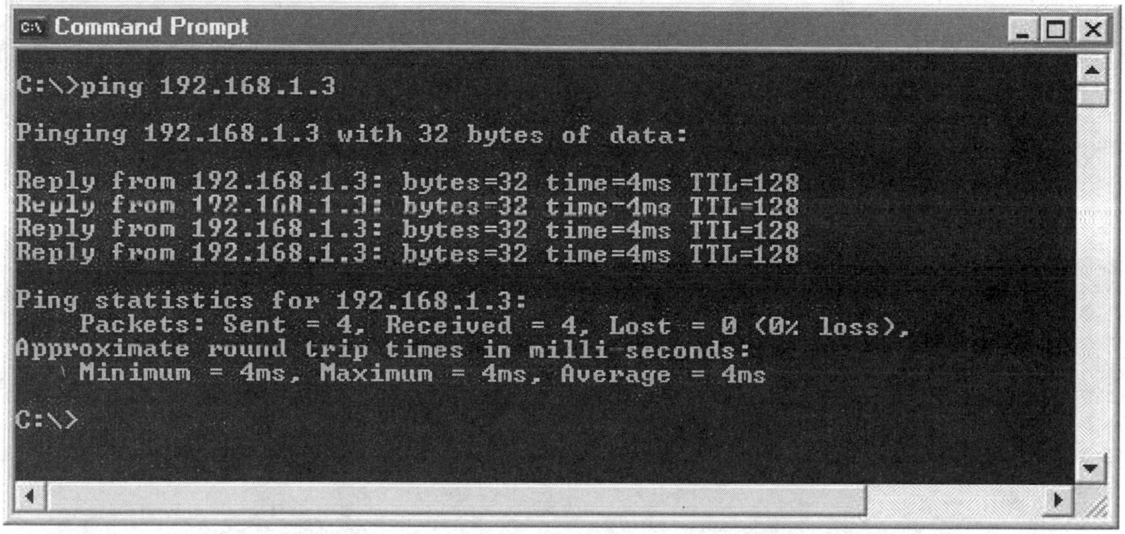

Note: Future SSL VPN sessions may be launched through the web portal or through the installed Cisco AnyConnect SSL VPN Client.

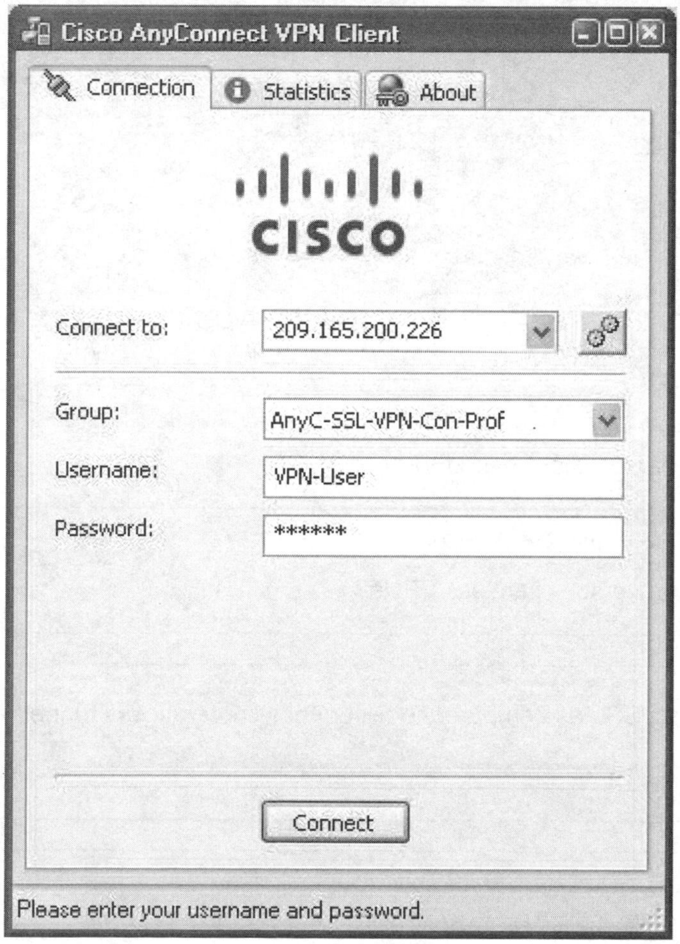

Step 20: Use the ASDM Monitor to view the AnyConnect remote user session.

While the remote user at PC-C is still logged in using the AnyConnect client, you can view the session statistics using ASDM Monitor.

From the menu bar, click the **Monitoring** button, and then choose **VPN** > **VPN Statistics** > **Sessions**. Click the **Filter By** pull-down menu and choose **AnyConnect Client**. You should see the VPN-User session logged in from PC-C, which has been assigned an inside network IP address of 192.168.1.33 by the ASA.

Note: You might need to click the **Refresh** button on the menu bar to display the remote user session.

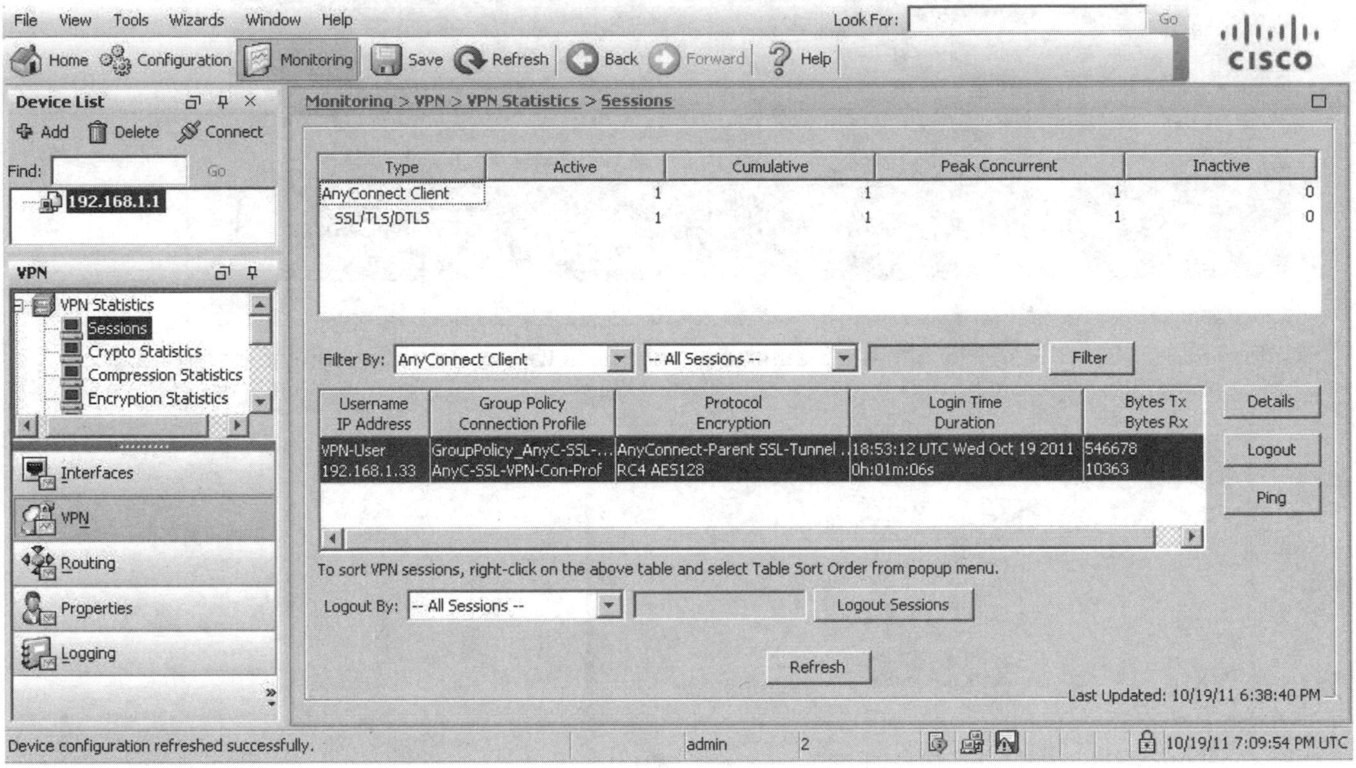

Reflection

1. What are some benefits of clientless versus client-based VPNs?

____

____

2. What are some benefits of client-based versus clientless VPNs?

____

____

3. What are some differences when using SSL as compared to IPsec for remote access tunnel encryption?

____

____

____

Router Interface Summary Table

Router Model	Ethernet Interface 1	Ethernet Interface 2	Serial Interface 1	Serial Interface 2
1800	Fast Ethernet 0/0 (Fa0/0)	Fast Ethernet 0/1 (Fa0/1)	Serial 0/0/0 (S0/0/0)	Serial 0/0/1 (S0/0/1)
1900	Gigabit Ethernet 0/0 (G0/0)	Gigabit Ethernet 0/1 (G0/1)	Serial 0/0/0 (S0/0/0)	Serial 0/0/1 (S0/0/1)
2800	Fast Ethernet 0/0 (Fa0/0)	Fast Ethernet 0/1 (Fa0/1)	Serial 0/0/0 (S0/0/0)	Serial 0/0/1 (S0/0/1)
2900	Gigabit Ethernet 0/0 (G0/0)	Gigabit Ethernet 0/1 (G0/1)	Serial 0/0/0 (S0/0/0)	Serial 0/0/1 (S0/0/1)

Note: To find out how the router is configured, look at the interfaces to identify the type of router and how many interfaces the router has. There is no way to effectively list all the combinations of configurations for each router class. This table includes identifiers for the possible combinations of Ethernet and serial interfaces in the device. The table does not include any other type of interface, even though a specific router may contain one. An example of this might be an ISDN BRI interface. The string in parentheses is the legal abbreviation that can be used in Cisco IOS commands to represent the interface.

Chapter 10 Lab D: Configuring a Site-to-Site IPsec VPN Using CCP and ASDM

Topology

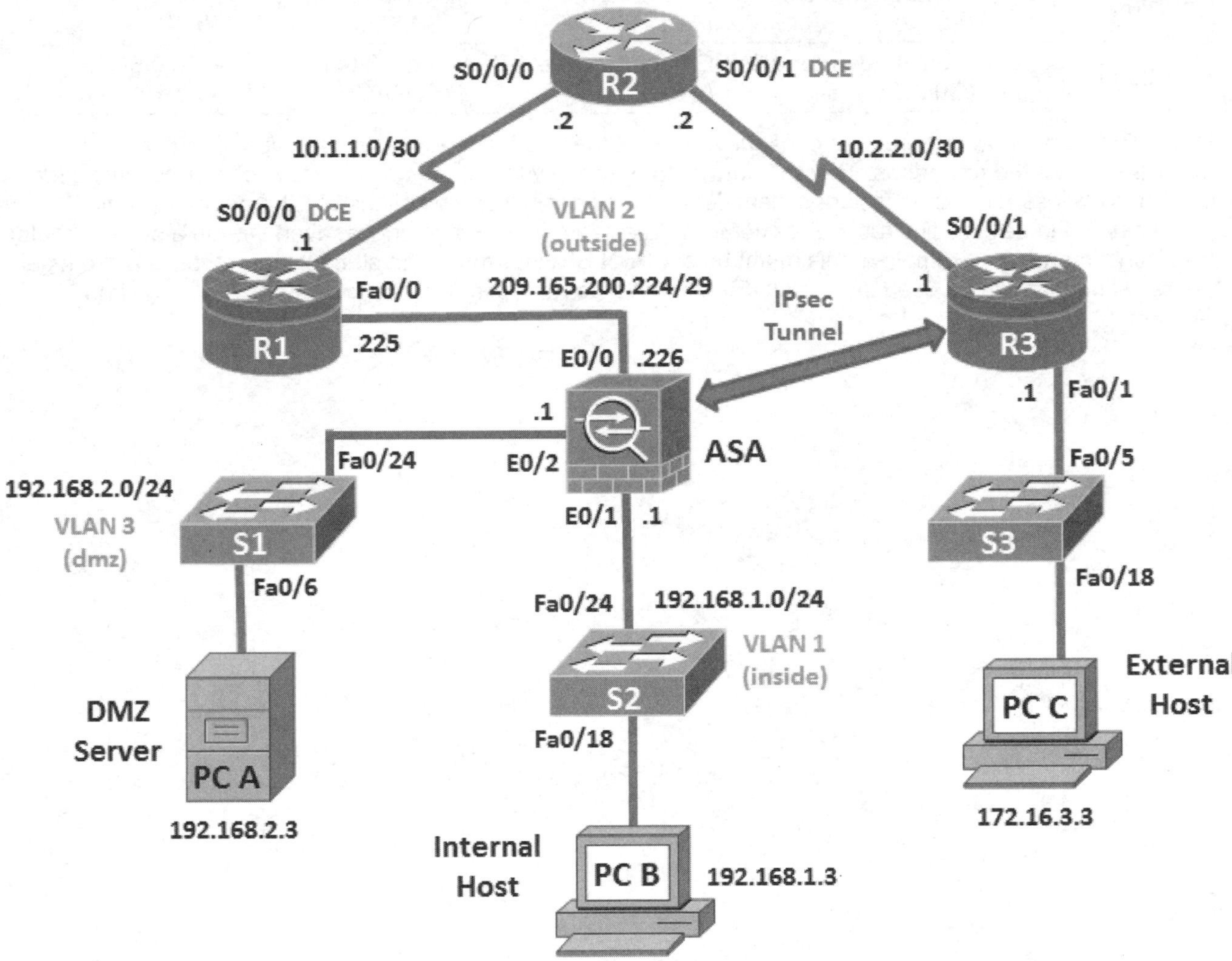

Note: ISR G2 devices have Gigabit Ethernet interfaces rather than FastEthernet interfaces.

IP Addressing Table

Device	Interface	IP Address	Subnet Mask	Default Gateway	Switch Port
R1	Fa0/0	209.165.200.225	255.255.255.248	N/A	ASA E0/0
	S0/0/0 (DCE)	10.1.1.1	255.255.255.252	N/A	N/A
R2	S0/0/0	10.1.1.2	255.255.255.252	N/A	N/A
	S0/0/1 (DCE)	10.2.2.2	255.255.255.252	N/A	N/A
R3	Fa0/1	172.16.3.1	255.255.255.0	N/A	S3 Fa0/5
	S0/0/1	10.2.2.1	255.255.255.252	N/A	N/A
ASA	VLAN 1 (E0/1)	192.168.1.1	255.255.255.0	NA	S2 Fa0/24
ASA	VLAN 2 (E0/0)	209.165.200.226	255.255.255.248	NA	R1 Fa0/0
ASA	VLAN 3 (E0/2)	192.168.2.1	255.255.255.0	NA	S1 Fa0/24
PC-A	NIC	192.168.2.3	255.255.255.0	192.168.2.1	S1 Fa0/6
PC-B	NIC	192.168.1.3	255.255.255.0	192.168.1.1	S2 Fa0/18
PC-C	NIC	172.16.3.3	255.255.255.0	172.16.3.1	S3 Fa0/18

Objectives

Part 1: Basic Router/Switch/PC Configuration

- Cable the network as shown in the topology.
- Configure hostnames, interface IP addresses for routers, switches and PCs.
- Configure static routing, including default routes, between R1, R2 and R3.
- Configure R3 HTTP access to enable CCP management.
- Verify connectivity between hosts, switches and routers.

Part 2: Basic ASA Configuration

- Access the ASA console.
- Clear previous configuration settings.
- Load the ASA CLI command script to configure basic settings.
- Verify access to ASA/ASDM.

Part 3: Configuring the ISR as a Site-to-Site IPsec VPN Endpoint Using CCP

- Configure basic VPN connection information settings.
- Configure IKE policy parameters.
- Configure a transform set.
- Define traffic to protect.
- Verify the VPN configuration on R3.

Part 4: Configuring the ASA as a Site-to-Site IPsec VPN Endpoint Using ASDM

- Identify peer device and access interface.
- Specify IKE version.
- Specify traffic to protect.
- Configure authentication methods.
- Specify encryption algorithm.
- Verify VPN functionality.
- Monitor the VPN connection and traffic.

Background/Scenario

In addition to acting as a remote access virtual private network (VPN) concentrator, the ASA can provide Site-to-Site IPsec VPN tunneling. The tunnel can be configured between two ASAs or between an ASA and another IPsec VPN-capable device such as an Integrated Services Router (ISR), as is the case with this lab.

Your company has two locations connected to an Internet service provider (ISP). Router R1 represents a customer premise equipment (CPE) device managed by the ISP. Router R2 represents an intermediate Internet router. Router R3 connects users at the remote branch office to the ISP. The ASA is an edge CPE security device that connects the internal corporate network and demilitarized zone (DMZ) to the ISP while providing Network Address Translation (NAT) services to inside hosts.

Management has asked you to provide a dedicated Site-to-Site IPsec VPN tunnel between the ISR router at the remote branch office and the ASA device at the corporate site. This tunnel will protect traffic between the branch office LAN and the corporate LAN, as it passes through the Internet. The Site-to-Site VPN does not require a VPN client on the remote or corporate site host computers. Traffic from either LAN to other Internet destinations is routed by the ISP and is not protected by the VPN tunnel. The VPN tunnel will pass through R1 and R2, which are not aware of its existence.

In Part 1 of the lab, you configure the topology and non-ASA devices. In Part 2, you prepare the ASA for ASDM access. In Part 3, you use the CCP VPN Wizard to configure the R3 ISR as a Site-to-Site IPsec VPN endpoint. In Part 4, you configure the ASA as a Site-to-Site IPsec VPN endpoint using the ASDM VPN Wizard.

Note: The routers used with this lab are Cisco 1841 with Cisco IOS Software Release 12.4(20)T (advanced IP image). The switches are Cisco WS-C2960-24TT-L with Cisco IOS Software Release 12.2(46)SE (C2960-LANBASEK9-M image). Other routers, switches, and Cisco IOS versions can be used. However, results and output may vary.

The ASA that is used with this lab is a Cisco model 5505 with an eight-port integrated switch, running OS Version 8.4(2) and ASDM Version 6.4(5) and comes with a Base license that allows a maximum of three VLANs.

Note: Make sure that the routers and switches have been erased and have no startup configurations.

Required Resources

- 3 routers (Cisco 1841 with Cisco IOS Software Release 12.4(20)T1 or comparable)
- 3 switches (Cisco 2960 or comparable)
- 1 ASA 5505 (OS version 8.4(2) and ASDM version 6.4(5) and Base license or comparable)
- PC-A: Windows XP, Vista, or Windows 7 with PuTTy SSH client (Web server optional)

- PC-B: Windows XP, Vista, or Windows 7 with PuTTy SSH client and Java 6 (ASDM loaded on the PC is optional)
- PC-C: Windows XP, Vista, or Windows 7 with PuTTy SSH client, Java 6 and CCP version 2.5.
- Serial and Ethernet cables as shown in the topology
- Rollover cables to configure the routers and ASA via the console

CCP Notes

- See Chapter 00 Lab A for instructions on how to install and run CCP. Hardware/software recommendations for CCP include Windows XP, Vista, or Windows 7 with Java Version 1.6.0_11 up to 1.6.0_21, Internet Explorer 6.0 or later, and Flash Player Version 10.0.12.36 or later.
- If the PC on which CCP is installed is running Windows Vista or Windows 7, you might need to right-click the CCP icon or menu item and choose **Run as Administrator**.
- To run CCP, you might need to temporarily disable antivirus programs and OS firewalls. Make sure to turn off all pop-up blockers in the browser.

Part 1: Basic Router/Switch/PC Configuration

In Part 1 of this lab, you set up the network topology and configure basic settings on the routers such as interface IP addresses and static routing.

Note: Do not configure any ASA settings at this time.

Step 1: Cable the network and clear previous device settings.

Attach the devices shown in the topology diagram and cable as necessary. Make sure that the routers and switches have been erased and have no startup configurations.

Step 2: Configure basic settings for routers and switches.

a. Configure hostnames as shown in the topology for each router.

b. Configure router interface IP addresses as shown in the IP addressing table.

c. Configure a clock rate for routers with a DCE serial cable attached to their serial interface. Router R1 is shown here as an example:

```
R1(config)# interface S0/0/0
R1(config-if)# clock rate 64000
```

d. Configure the hostname for the switches. Other than hostname, the switches can be left in their default configuration state. Configuring the VLAN management IP address for the switches is optional.

Step 3: Configure static routing on the routers.

a. Configure a static default route from R1 to R2 and from R3 to R2:

```
R1(config)# ip route 0.0.0.0 0.0.0.0 Serial0/0/0
R3(config)# ip route 0.0.0.0 0.0.0.0 Serial0/0/1
```

b. Configure a static route from R2 to the R1 Fa0/0 subnet (connected to ASA interface E0/0) and a static route from R2 to the R3 LAN:

```
R2(config)# ip route 209.165.200.224 255.255.255.248 Serial0/0/0
R2(config)# ip route 172.16.3.0 255.255.255.0 Serial0/0/1
```

Step 4: Configure the enable and VTY passwords on R3.

On R3, set the enable password to **class** and the console and VTY passwords to **cisco**. Configure these settings on R1 and R2. R3 is shown here as an example:

```
R3(config)# enable secret class

R3(config)# line vty 0 4
R3(config-line)# password cisco
R3(config-line)# login

R3(config)# line con 0
R3(config-line)# password cisco
R3(config-line)# login
```

Step 5: Configure HTTP access, a username, and local authentication before starting CCP.

a. From the CLI, configure a username and password for use with CCP on R3:

```
R3(config)# ip http server
R3(config)# username admin privilege 15 secret cisco123
```

b. Use the local database to authenticate web sessions with CCP:

```
R3(config)# ip http authentication local
```

Step 6: Configure PC host IP settings.

Configure a static IP address, subnet mask, and default gateway for PC-A, PC-B, and PC-C, as shown in the IP Addressing Table.

Step 7: Verify connectivity.

From PC-C, ping the R1 Fa0/0 IP address (209.165.200.225). If these pings are not successful, troubleshoot the basic device configurations before continuing.

Note: If you can ping from PC-C to R1 Fa0/0 you have demonstrated that static routing is configured and functioning correctly.

Step 8: Save the basic running configuration for each router and switch.

Part 2: Basic ASA Configuration

Step 1: Access the ASA console.

a. Accessing the ASA via the console port is the same as with a Cisco router or switch. Connect to the ASA Console port with a rollover cable.

b. Use a terminal emulation program such as TeraTerm or HyperTerminal to access the CLI, and use the serial port settings of 9600 baud, 8 data bits, no parity, 1 stop bit, and no flow control.

c. If prompted to enter Interactive Firewall configuration (Setup mode), answer **no**.

d. Enter privileged mode with the **enable** command and password (if set). By default, the password is blank, so you can just press **Enter**. If the password has been changed to that specified in this lab, the password will be **class**. In addition, the hostname and prompt will be CCNAS-ASA>, as shown here. The default ASA hostname and prompt is ciscoasa>.

```
CCNAS-ASA> enable
Password: class (or press Enter if none set)
```

Step 2: Clear the previous ASA configuration settings.

a. Use the **write erase** command to remove the **startup-config** file from flash memory:

```
CCNAS-ASA# write erase
Erase configuration in flash memory? [confirm]
[OK]
CCNAS-ASA#
```

Note: The IOS command **erase startup-config** is not supported on the ASA.

b. Use the **reload** command to restart the ASA. This causes the ASA to come up in CLI Setup mode. If you see the message `System config has been modified. Save? [Y]es/[N]o:`, respond with **N**.

```
CCNAS-ASA# reload
Proceed with reload? [confirm] <enter>
CCNAS-ASA#
***
*** --- START GRACEFUL SHUTDOWN ---
Shutting down isakmp
Shutting down File system
***
*** --- SHUTDOWN NOW ---
Process shutdown finished
Rebooting.....
CISCO SYSTEMS
Embedded BIOS Version 1.0(12)13 08/28/08 15:50:37.45
<output omitted>
```

Step 3: Bypass Setup Mode.

When the ASA completes the reload process, it should detect that the startup config file is missing and go into Setup mode. If it does not come up in this mode, repeat Step 2.

a. When prompted to preconfigure the firewall through interactive prompts (Setup mode), respond with **no**.

```
Pre-configure Firewall now through interactive prompts [yes]?  no
```

b. Enter privileged EXEC mode with the **enable** command. The password should be blank (no password) at this point.

Step 4: Use the CLI script to configure the ASA.

In this step, you use the modified running config from Lab 10A to preconfigure basic settings, the firewall and DMZ:

a. Ensure that there is no previous configuration in the ASA, other than the defaults that the ASA automatically inserts, using the **show run** command.

b. Enter CLI global configuration mode. When prompted to enable anonymous call-home reporting, respond with **no**.

```
ciscoasa> enable
Password: <enter>

ciscoasa# conf t
ciscoasa(config)#
```

c. The first time you enter configuration mode after running reload, you are asked whether you want to enable anonymous reporting. Respond with **no**.

d. Copy and paste the **Pre-VPN Configuration Script** commands listed below at the ASA global config mode prompt to bring it to the point where you can start configuring the SSL VPNs.

e. Observe the messages as the commands are applied to ensure that there are no warnings or errors. If prompted to replace the RSA key pair, respond with **yes**.

f. Issue the **`write mem`** (or **`copy run start`**) command to save the running configuration to the startup configuration and the RSA keys to nonvolatile memory.

Lab 10D Pre-VPN ASA Configuration Script

```
hostname CCNAS-ASA
!
domain-name ccnasecurity.com
!
enable password class
passwd cisco
!
interface Ethernet0/0
 switchport access vlan 2
 no shut
!
interface Ethernet0/1
 switchport access vlan 1
 no shut
!
interface Ethernet0/2
 switchport access vlan 3
 no shut
!
interface Vlan1
 nameif inside
 security-level 100
 ip address 192.168.1.1 255.255.255.0
!
interface Vlan2
 nameif outside
 security-level 0
 ip address 209.165.200.226 255.255.255.248
!
interface Vlan3
 no forward interface Vlan1
 nameif dmz
 security-level 70
 ip address 192.168.2.1 255.255.255.0
!
```

```
object network inside-net
 subnet 192.168.1.0 255.255.255.0
!
object network dmz-server
 host 192.168.2.3
!
access-list OUTSIDE-DMZ extended permit ip any host 192.168.2.3
!
object network inside-net
 nat (inside,outside) dynamic interface
!
object network dmz-server
 nat (dmz,outside) static 209.165.200.227
!
access-group OUTSIDE-DMZ in interface outside
!
route outside 0.0.0.0 0.0.0.0 209.165.200.225 1
!
username admin password cisco123
!
aaa authentication telnet console LOCAL
aaa authentication ssh console LOCAL
aaa authentication http console LOCAL
!
http server enable
http 192.168.1.0 255.255.255.0 inside
ssh 192.168.1.0 255.255.255.0 inside
telnet 192.168.1.0 255.255.255.0 inside
telnet timeout 10
ssh timeout 10
!
class-map inspection_default
 match default-inspection-traffic
policy-map type inspect dns preset_dns_map
 parameters
  message-length maximum client auto
  message-length maximum 512
policy-map global_policy
 class inspection_default
   inspect icmp
!
prompt hostname context
no call-home reporting anonymous
!
crypto key generate rsa modulus 1024
```

Step 5: Verify HTTPS ASDM access.

This step is intended to verify HTTPS connectivity from PC-B to the ASA. You configure ASDM settings in Part 4 of the lab.

a. Open a browser on PC-B and test the HTTPS access to the ASA by entering **https://192.168.1.1**.

Note: Be sure to specify the HTTPS protocol in the URL.

b. After entering the URL, you should see a security warning about the website's security certificate. Click **Continue to this website**. The ASDM welcome page will display. From this screen, you can install ASDM on the PC, Run ASDM as browser-based Java applet directly from the ASA, or run the Startup Wizard. Click the **Run ASDM** button.

Note: The process may vary depending on the browser used. This example is for Internet Explorer.

Part 3: Configuring the ISR as a Site-to-Site IPsec VPN Endpoint Using CCP

In Part 3 of this lab, you configure R3 as an IPsec VPN endpoint for the tunnel between R3 and the ASA. Routers R1 and R2 are unaware of the tunnel.

Note: If the PC on which CCP is installed is running Windows 7, you might need to right-click the CCP icon or menu item and choose **Run as Administrator**.

You might need to temporarily disable antivirus programs and OS firewalls to run CCP. The minimum recommended Windows PC requirements to run CCP are as follows:

- Internet Explorer with Java 6 plug-in Version 1.6.0-11
- Adobe Flash Player Version 10
- 1 GB RAM
- Screen resolution of 1024 x 768

Note: If you receive the following Java-related error message from CCP during the VPN configuration process, perform the steps indicated in the message:

Security component has failed. In order to work on Router or Security features, do the following. Go to **Java Control panel > Advanced tab > Java Plug-in** tree Entry. Uncheck the check box for **Enable next-generation Java Plug-in**. Relaunch CCP after this.

Step 1: Run the CCP application on PC-C and discover R3.

a. Run the CCP application on PC-C. In the Select/Manage Community window, enter the R3 Fa0/0 IP address **172.16.3.1**, username **admin**, and **cisco123** as the **Password**. Click the **OK** button.

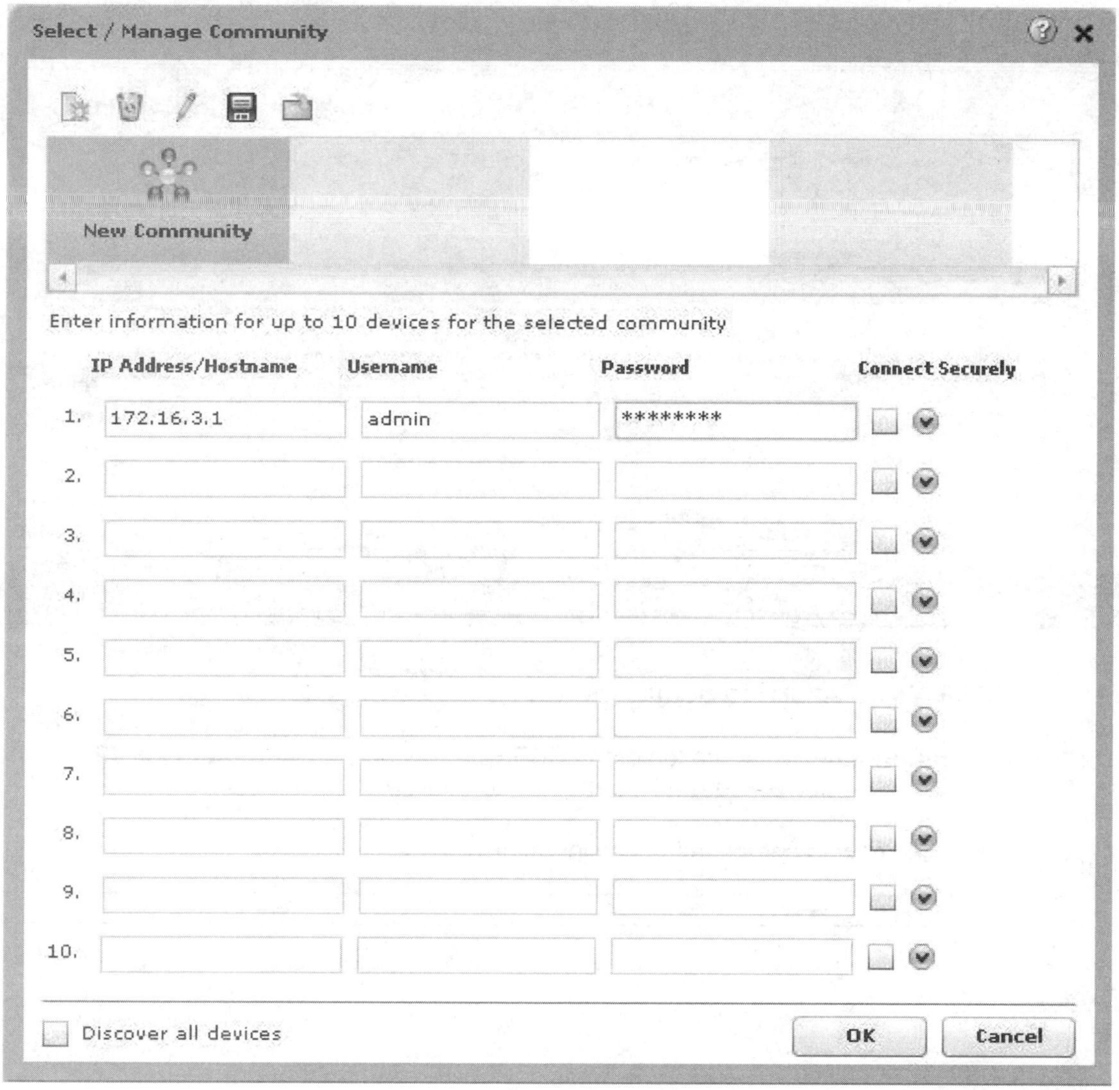

b. In the Community Information panel, click the **Discover** button to discover and connect to R3. If the PC-C CCP application can make an HTTP connection to R3, the **Discovery Status** changes to Discovered. If the discovery process fails, click the **Discover Details** button to determine the problem so that you can resolve the issue.

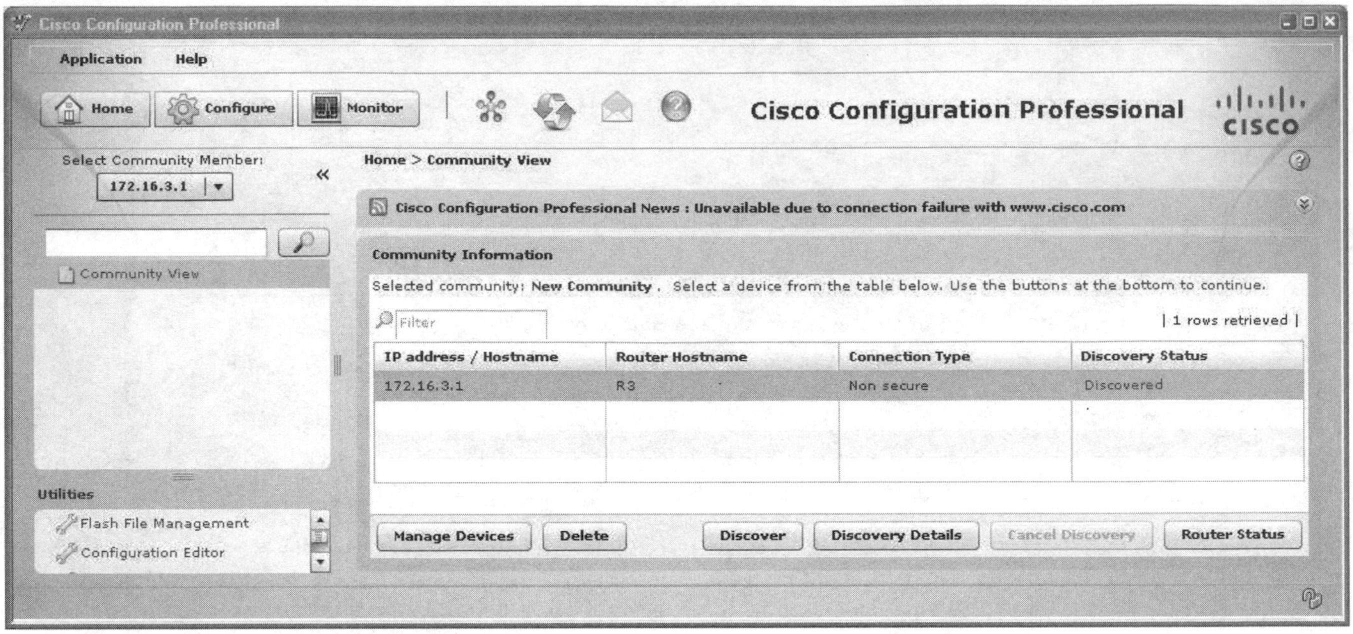

Step 2: Start the CCP VPN Wizard to configure R3.

a. Click the **Configure** button at the top of the CCP screen, and choose **Security > VPN > Site-to-Site VPN**. Read the onscreen text describing the Site-to-Site VPN.

   What must you know to complete the configuration?

   ____

   ____

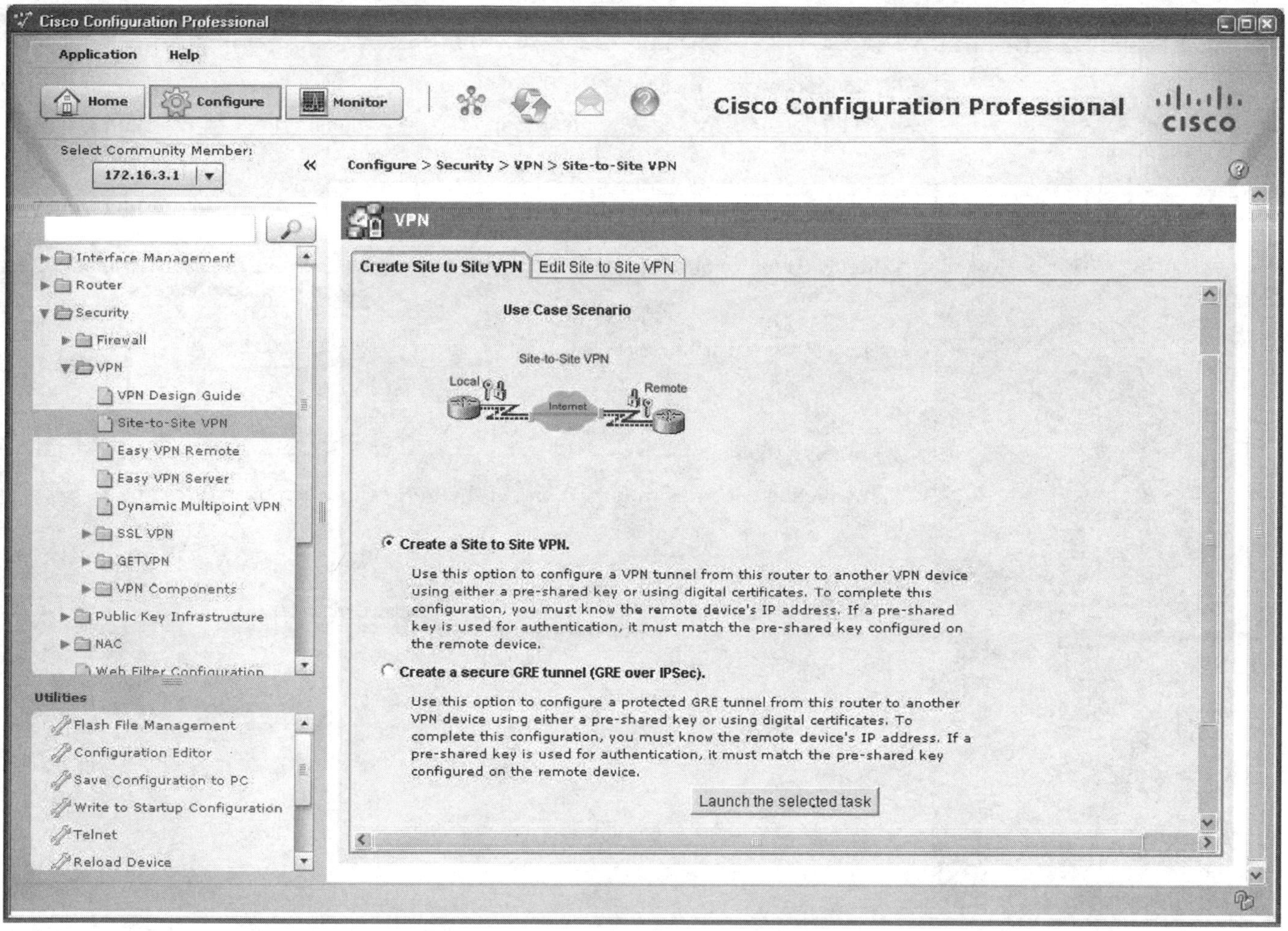

b. Click the **Launch the Selected Task** button to begin the CCP Site-to-Site VPN Wizard.

c. From the initial Site-to-Site VPN Wizard screen, choose the Step by Step Wizard, and then click **Next**.

Step 3: Configure basic VPN connection information settings.

a. On the VPN Connection Information screen, choose the interface for the connection, which should be R3 **Serial0/0/1**.

b. In the Peer Identity section, choose **Peer with static IP address** and enter the IP address of the remote peer, ASA VLAN 2 interface E0/0 (**209.165.200.226**).

c. In the Authentication section, click **Pre-shared Keys**, and enter the pre-shared VPN key **cisco12345**. Reenter the key for confirmation. This key authenticates the initial exchange to establish the security association between devices. When finished, your screen should look similar to the following. After you have entered these settings correctly, click **Next**.

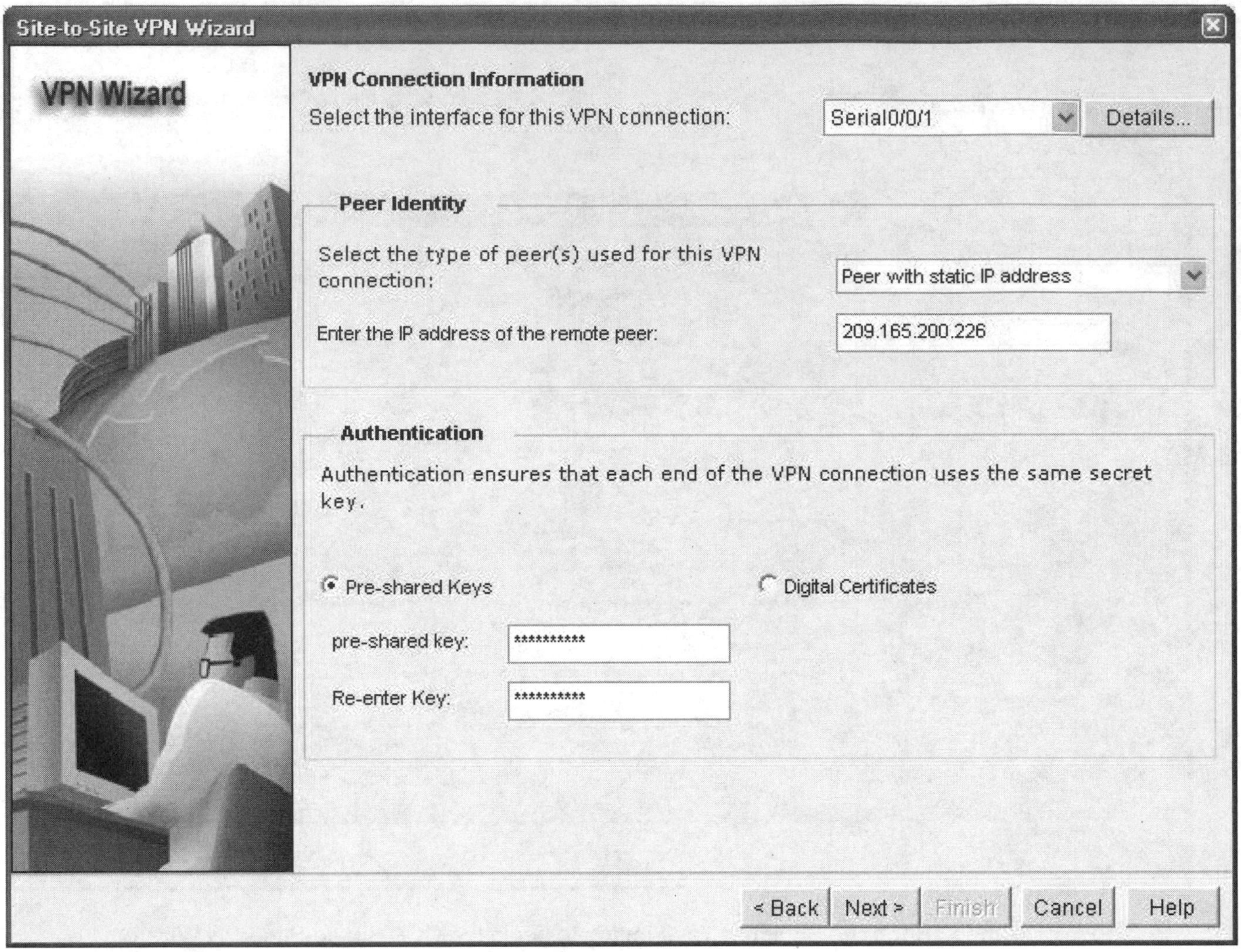

Step 4: Specify the IKE Policy.

IKE policies are used while setting up the control channel between the two VPN endpoints for key exchange. This is also referred to as the IKE secure association (SA). In contrast, the IPsec policy is used during IKE Phase 2 to negotiate an IPsec security association to pass target data traffic.

On the IKE Proposals screen, a default policy proposal is displayed with a priority of 1. You can use this one or create a new one, if necessary. In this lab, you configure the R3 end of the VPN tunnel using the default IKE proposal. Click **Next** to continue.

Settings for the CCP default IKE Phase 1 policy for this ISR are as follows:

- Priority = 1
- Encryption = 3DES
- Hash = SHA_1
- D-H Group = group2
- Authentication = PRE_SHARE

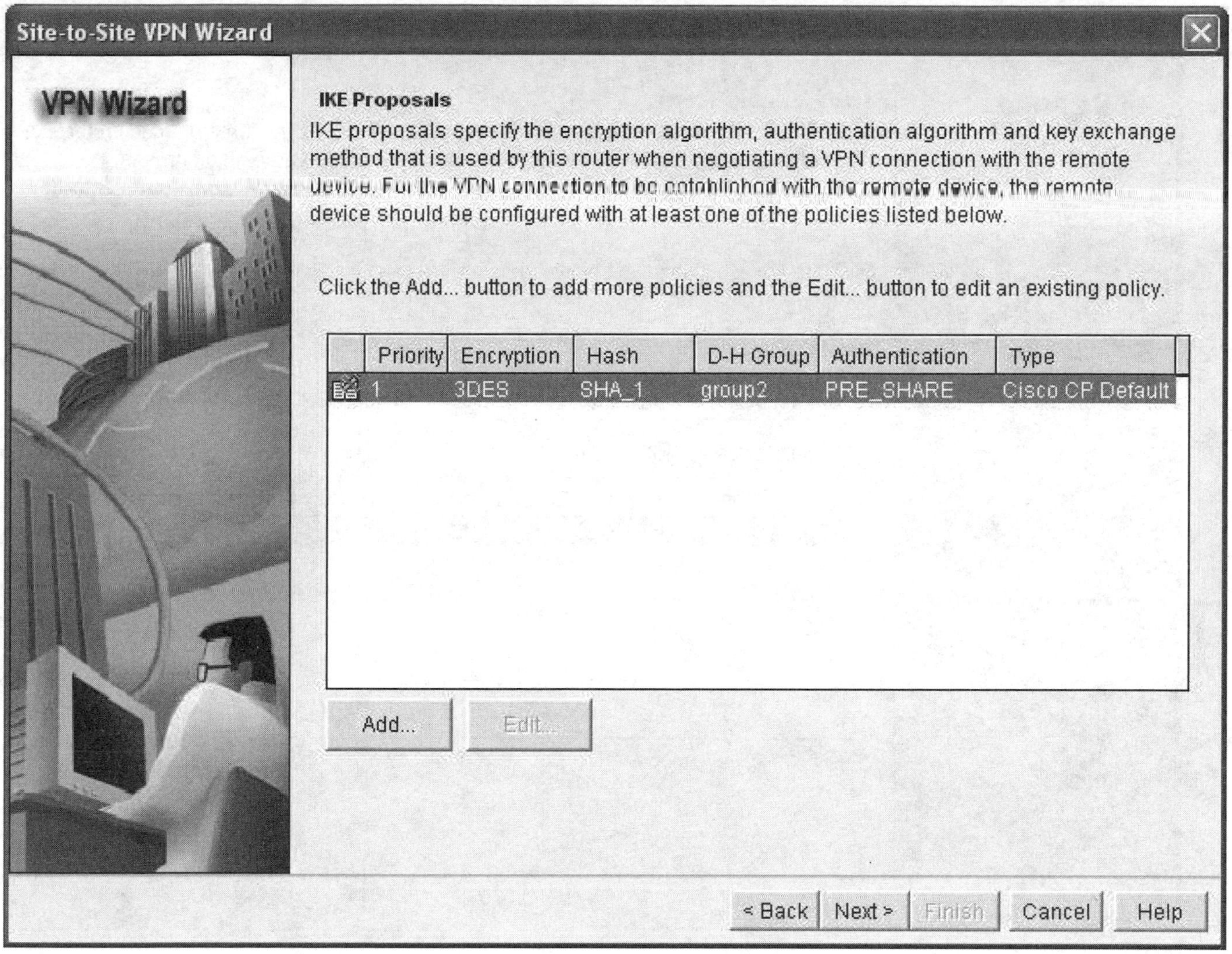

Step 5: Configure a transform set.

The transform set is the IPsec policy used to encrypt, hash, and authenticate packets that pass through the tunnel. The transform set is the IKE Phase 2 policy.

On the Transform Set screen, a default transform set is displayed. You can use this one or create a new one, if necessary. In this lab, you configure the R3 end of the VPN tunnel using the default transform set. Click **Next** to continue.

Settings for the CCP default IKE Phase 2 policy transform set for this ISR are as follows:

- Name = ESP-3DES-SHA
- ESP Encryption = ESP_3DES
- ESP Integrity = ESP_SHA_HMAC
- Mode = Tunnel

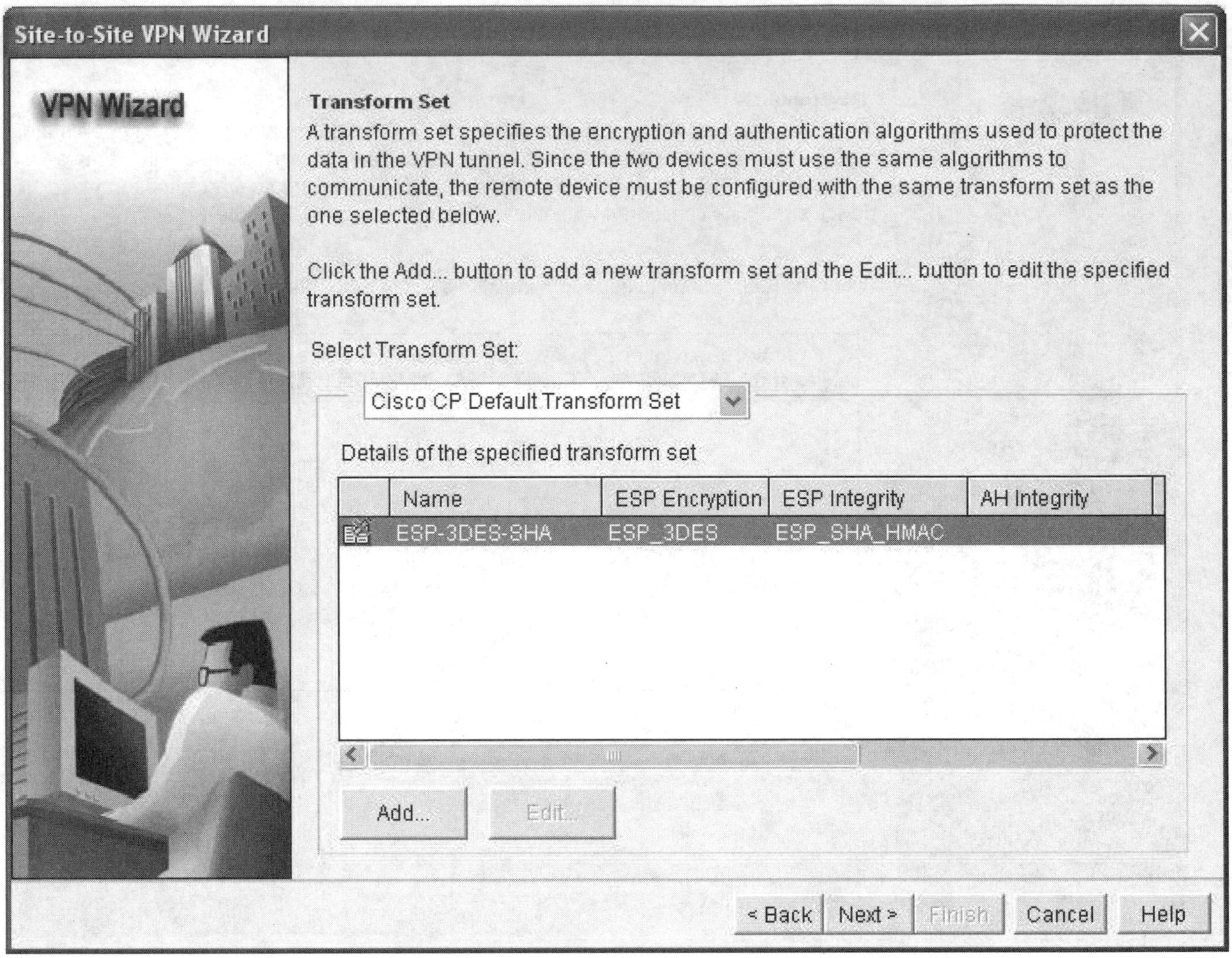

Step 6: Specify traffic to protect.

You must define "interesting" traffic to be protected through the VPN tunnel. Interesting traffic is defined through an access list that is applied to the router. When you enter the source and destination subnets that you want to protect through the VPN tunnel, CCP generates the appropriate simple access list for you.

On the Traffic to Protect screen, enter the information shown below. These are the opposite of the settings configured on the ASA later in the lab. When finished, click **Next**.

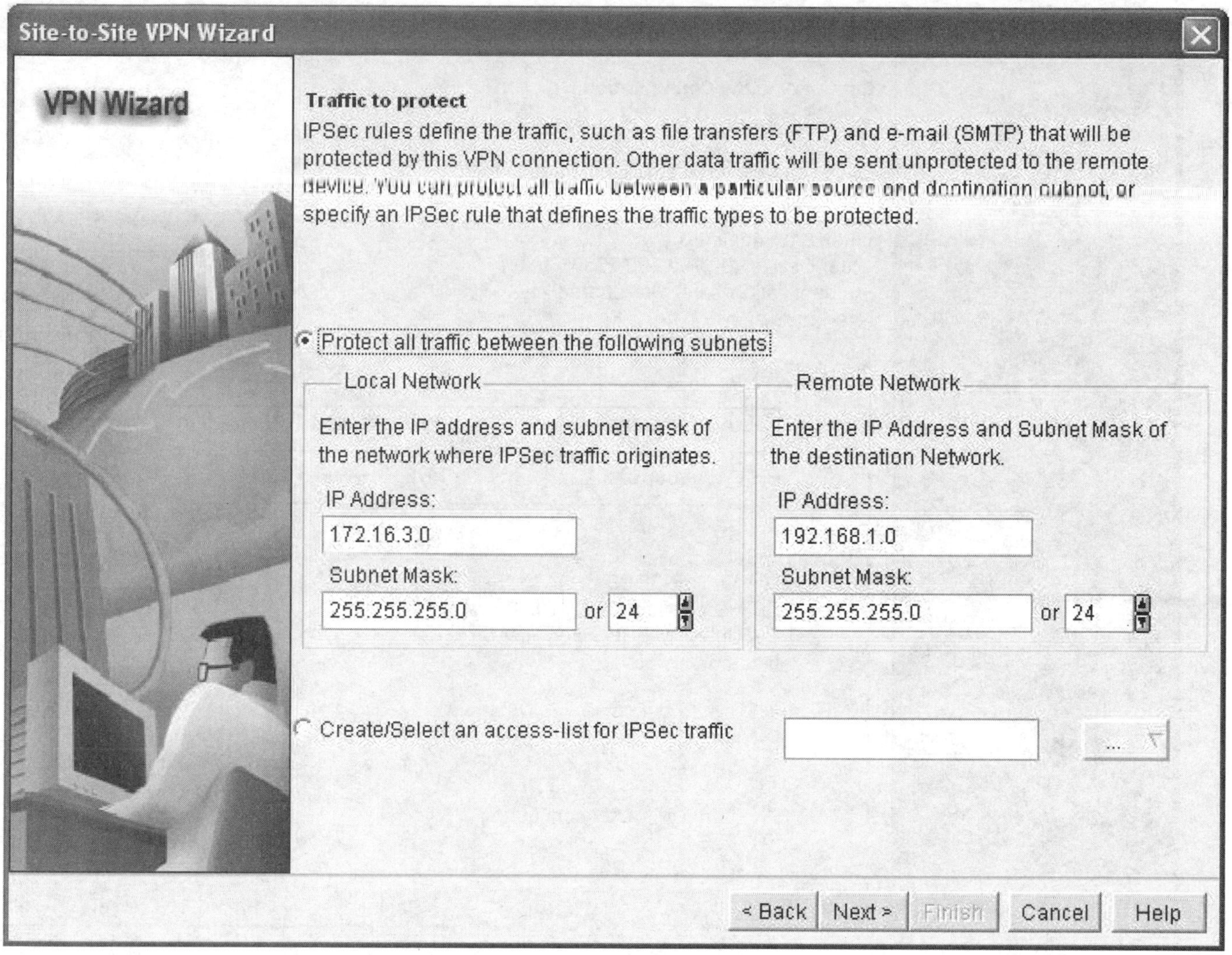

Step 7: Review the summary of the configuration.

a. Review the Summary of the Configuration screen. It should look similar to the one below. You can scroll down to see the IPsec rule (ACL) that CCP creates for R3, which permits all traffic from network 172.16.3.0/24 to network 192.168.1.0/24.

b. Do not check the Test VPN Connectivity After Configuring check box. This is done after you configure the ASA side of the VPN tunnel.

Click **Finish** to go to the Deliver Configuration to Device screen.

Note: Pay particular attention to the IKE Policies and Transform Set because you configure the ASA to match these settings in the next part of the lab.

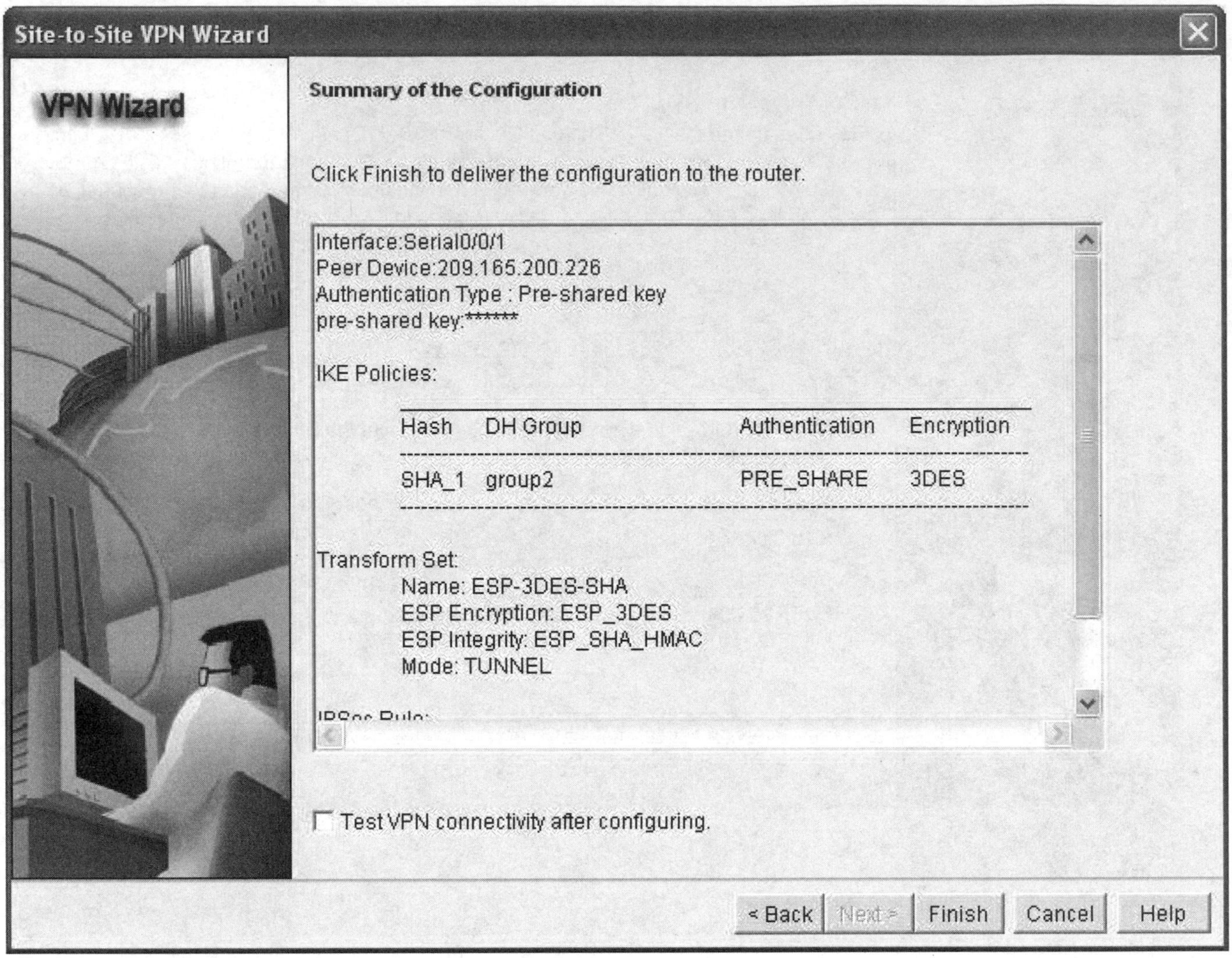

c. On the Deliver Configuration to Device screen, choose **Save Running Config to Device's Startup Config** and click the **Deliver** button. After the commands have been delivered, click **OK**.

d. You can also save these configuration commands for later editing or documentation purposes by clicking the **Save to File** button.

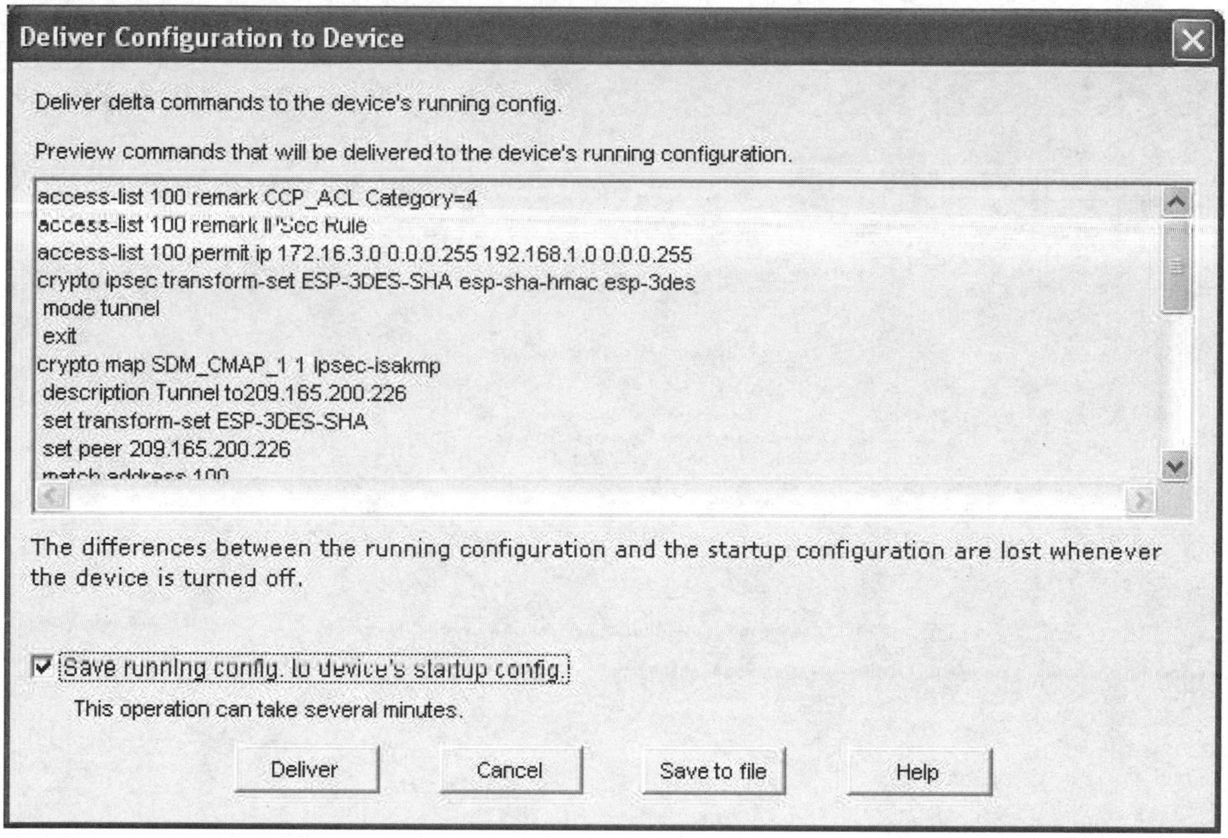

Note: If you receive an error message that CCP was unable to copy the running config to the startup config, you can verify that the commands were delivered by using the **`show startup-config`** CLI command on R3. If the startup config has not been updated, use the **`copy run start`** command on R3.

e. You can view the running config and startup config from within CCP. To view the running config, click the **Home** button, and under the Utilities section at the bottom left of the screen, click **View > Running Configuration**. The running config will display.

f. To view the startup config, click the **Home > Utilities > View > IOS Show Commands**. Click the pull-down menu next to the command window, choose the **`show startup-config`** command, and then click the **Show** button. The startup configuration will display.

Note: Several predefined **`show`** commands are listed in the pull-down menu, but you can also enter any valid IOS command, such as **`show ip interface brief`**, and then click the **Show** button.

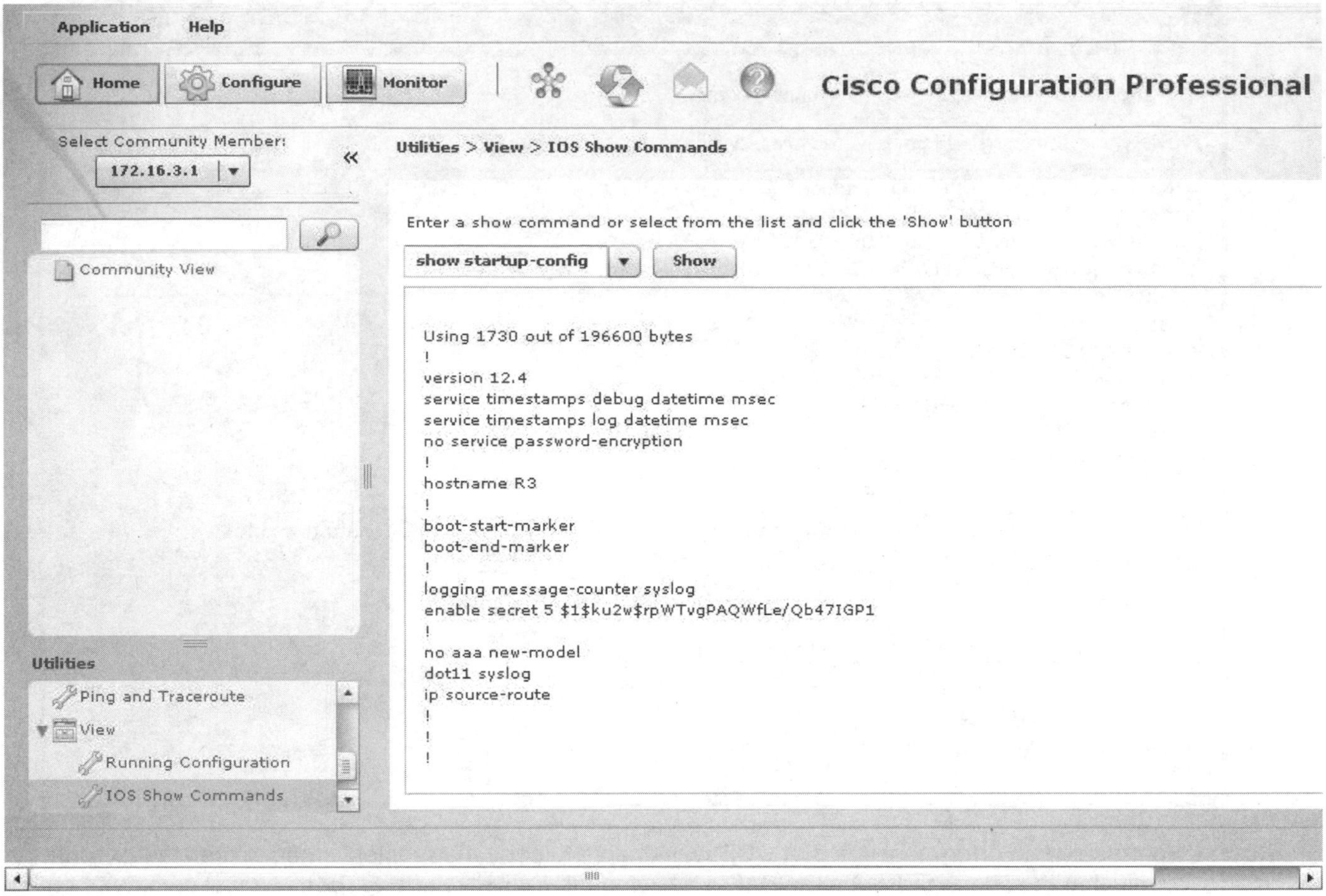

Step 8: Review the Site-to-Site VPN tunnel configuration.

a. The Edit Site-to-Site VPN screen is displayed after the commands are delivered. Use the scroll buttons to examine the configuration. The tunnel status is down at this point because the ASA end of the tunnel is not yet configured.

Note: Leave CCP running and connected to R3 on PC-C. You click the **Test Tunnel** button on this screen to verify VPN functionality after configuring the ASA end of the tunnel.

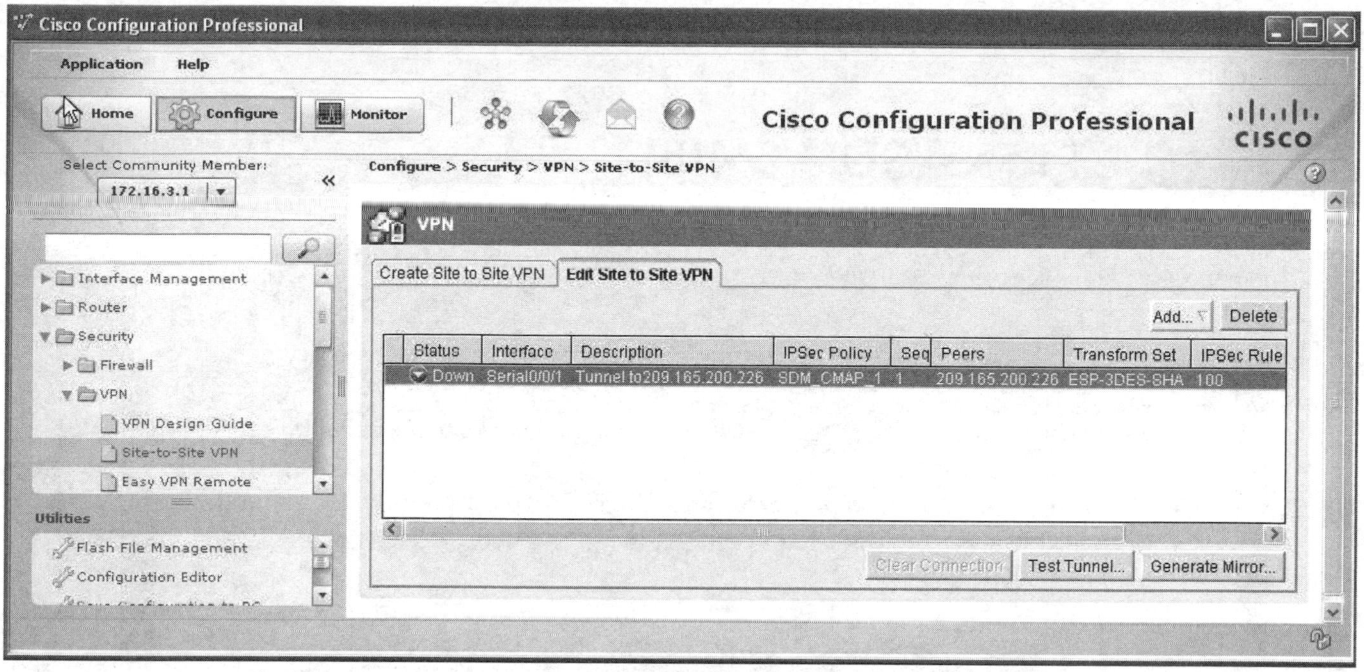

Part 4: Configuring the ASA as a Site-to-Site IPsec VPN Endpoint Using ASDM

In Part 4 of this lab, you configure the ASA as an IPsec VPN tunnel endpoint. The tunnel between the ASA and R3 passes through R1 and R2.

Step 1: Access ASDM.

a. Open a browser on PC-B and test the HTTPS access to the ASA by entering **https://192.168.1.1**.

Note: Be sure to specify the HTTPS protocol in the URL.

b. After entering the URL, you should see a security warning about the website security certificate. Click **Continue to This Website**. Click **Yes** for any other security warnings. At the ASDM welcome page, click the **Run ASDM** button. The ASDM-IDM Launcher will display. Log in as user **admin** with password **cisco123**. ASDM loads the current configuration into the GUI.

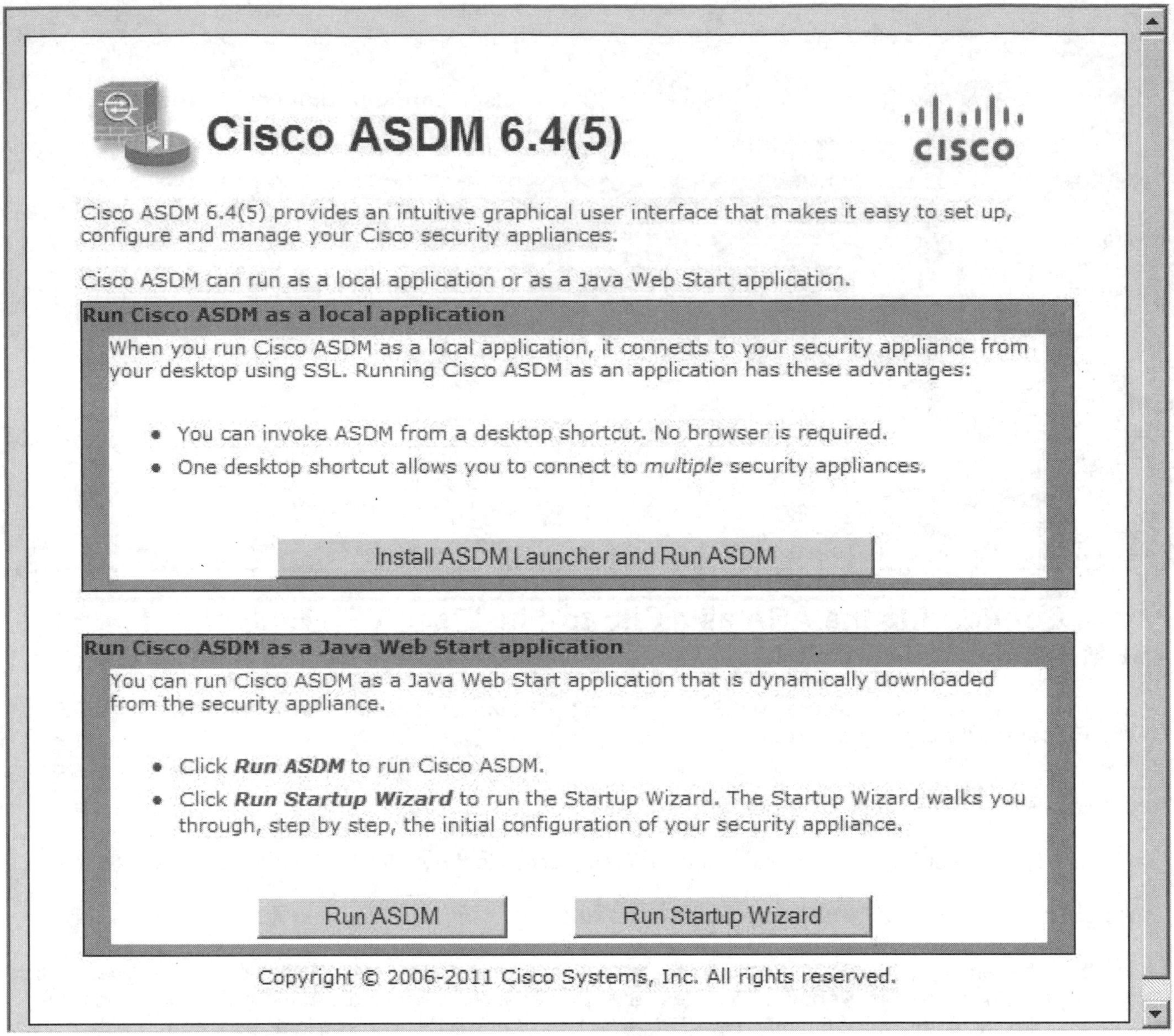
Cisco ASDM 6.4(5)
CISCO
Cisco ASDM 6.4(5) provides an intuitive graphical user interface that makes it easy to set up, configure and manage your Cisco security appliances.
Cisco ASDM can run as a local application or as a Java Web Start application.
Run Cisco ASDM as a local application
When you run Cisco ASDM as a local application, it connects to your security appliance from your desktop using SSL. Running Cisco ASDM as an application has these advantages:
• You can invoke ASDM from a desktop shortcut. No browser is required.
• One desktop shortcut allows you to connect to multiple security appliances.
Install ASDM Launcher and Run ASDM
Run Cisco ASDM as a Java Web Start application
You can run Cisco ASDM as a Java Web Start application that is dynamically downloaded from the security appliance.
• Click Run ASDM to run Cisco ASDM.
• Click Run Startup Wizard to run the Startup Wizard. The Startup Wizard walks you through, step by step, the initial configuration of your security appliance.
Run ASDM
Run Startup Wizard
Copyright © 2006-2011 Cisco Systems, Inc. All rights reserved.

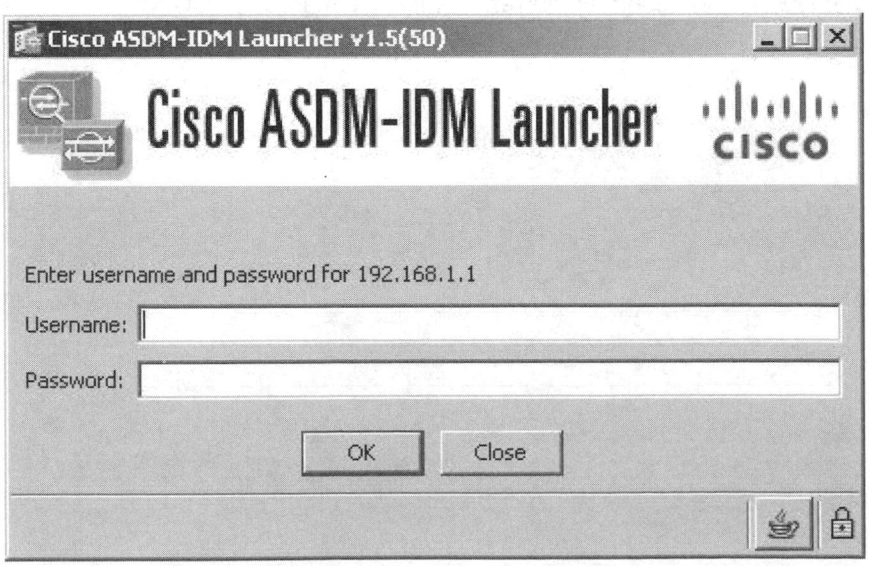
Cisco ASDM-IDM Launcher v1.5(50)
Cisco ASDM-IDM Launcher
CISCO
Enter username and password for 192.168.1.1
Username:
Password:
OK
Close

Step 2: Review the ASDM Home screen.

The Home screen displays showing the current ASA device configuration and some traffic flow statistics. Note the inside, outside, and DMZ interfaces, which were configured in Part 2.

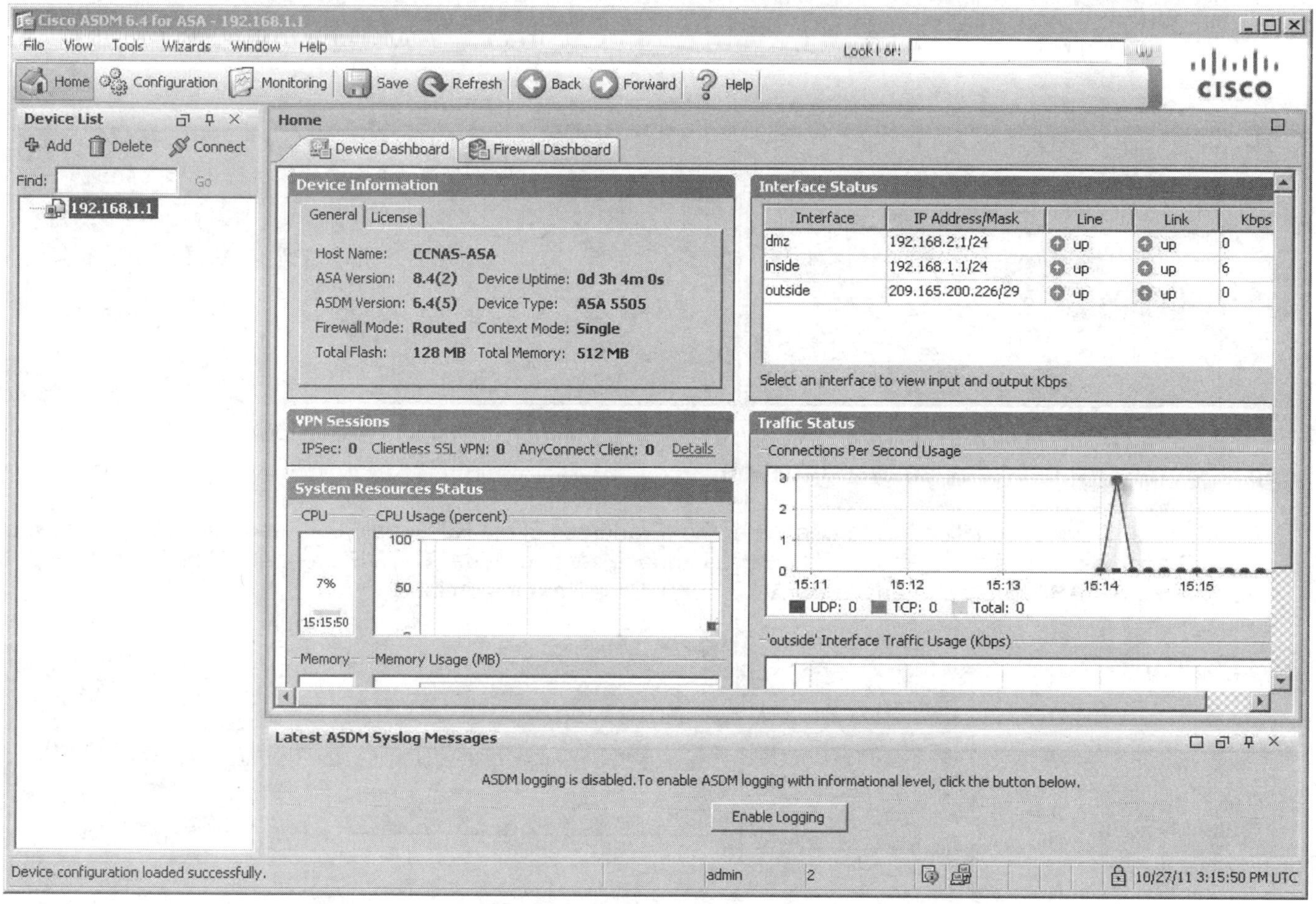

Step 3: Start the VPN Wizard.

a. From the ASDM main menu, choose the **Wizards > VPN Wizards > Site-to-Site VPN Wizard**. The Site-to-Site VPN Connection Setup Wizard Introduction screen is displayed.

b. Review the onscreen text and topology diagram, and then click **Next** to continue.

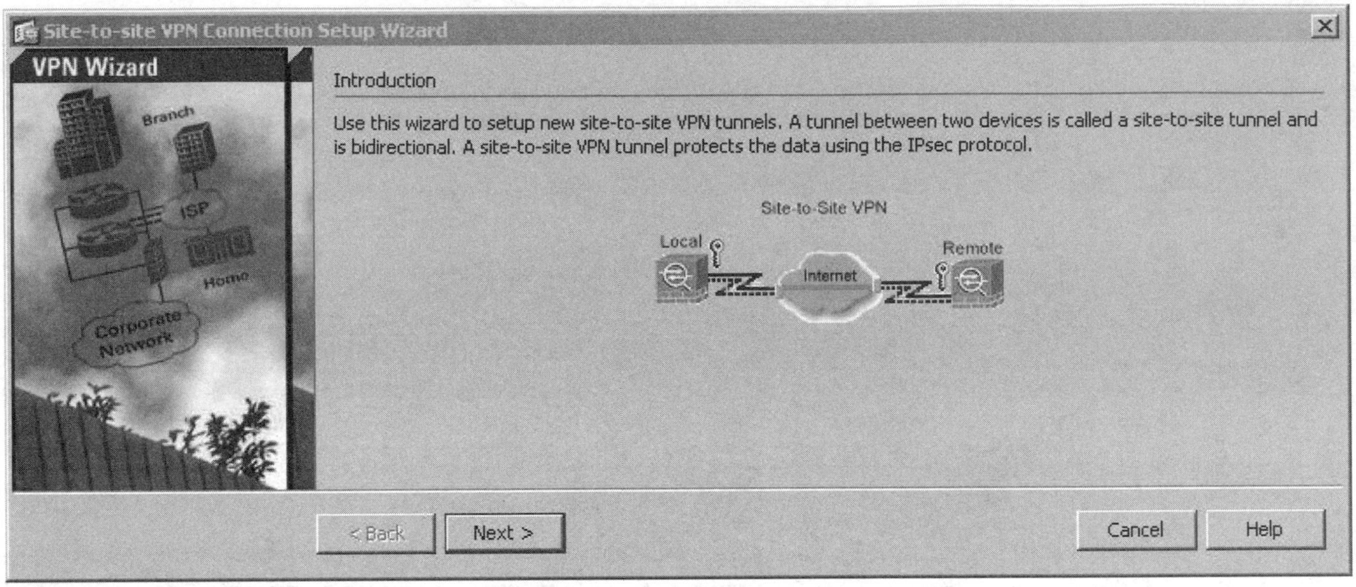

Step 4: Configure peer device identification.

On the Peer Device Identification screen, enter the IP address of the R3 Serial0/0/1 interface (10.2.2.1) as the peer IP address. Leave the default VPN access interface set to outside. The VPN tunnel will be between R3 S0/0/1 and the ASA outside interface (VLAN 2 E0/0). Click **Next** to continue.

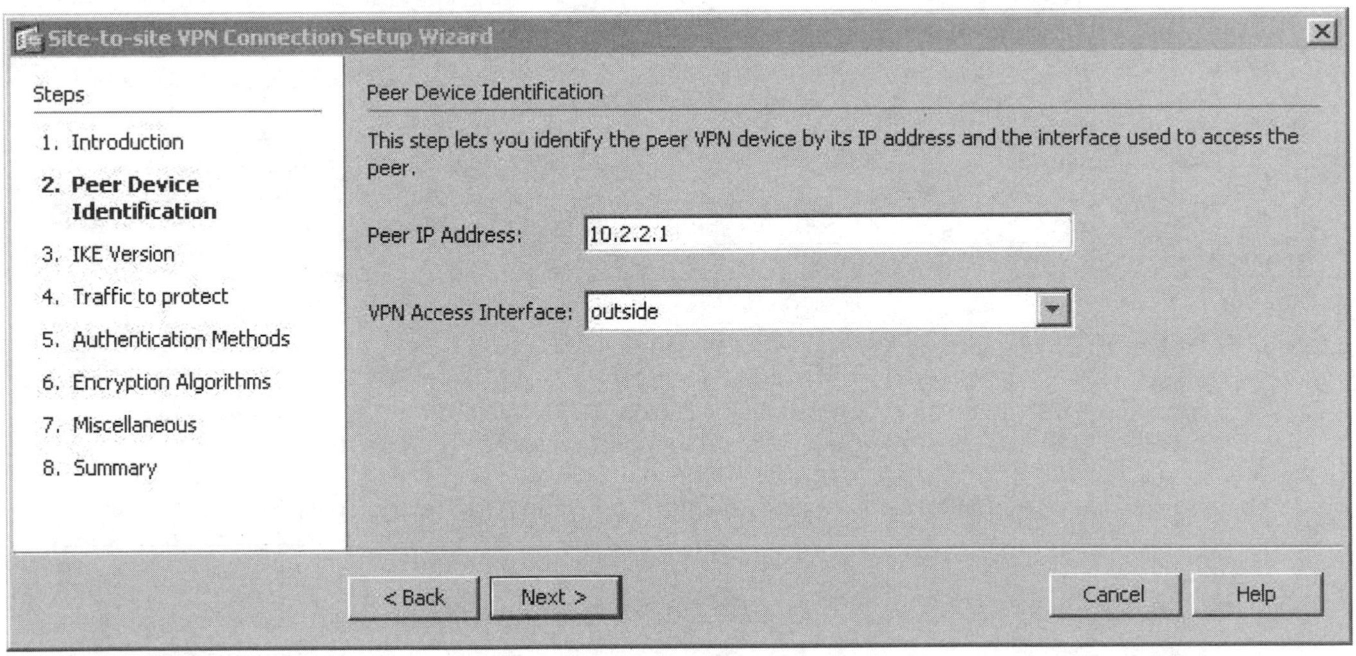

Step 5: Specify the IKE version.

IKE V1 simple pre-shared keys will be used. On the IKE Version screen, uncheck the **IKE Version 2** check box and leave **IKE Version 1** checked. Click **Next** to continue.

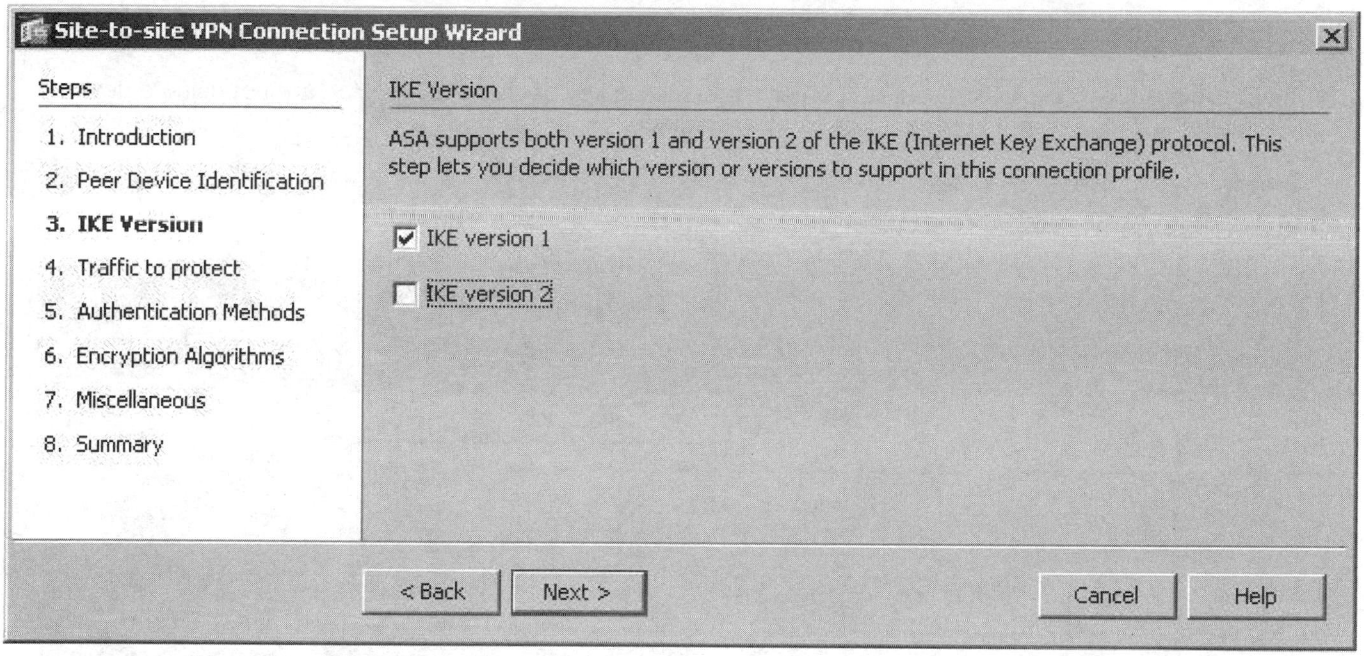

Step 6: Specify the traffic to protect.

On the Traffic to Protect screen, click **IPv4** and enter the inside network **192.168.1.0/24** as the local network and the R3 LAN **172.16.3.0/24** as the remote network. Click **Next** to continue. A message displays that the certificate information is being retrieved.

Note: If the ASA does not respond, you might need to close the window and continue to the next step. If prompted to authenticate, log in again as **admin** with the password **cisco123**.

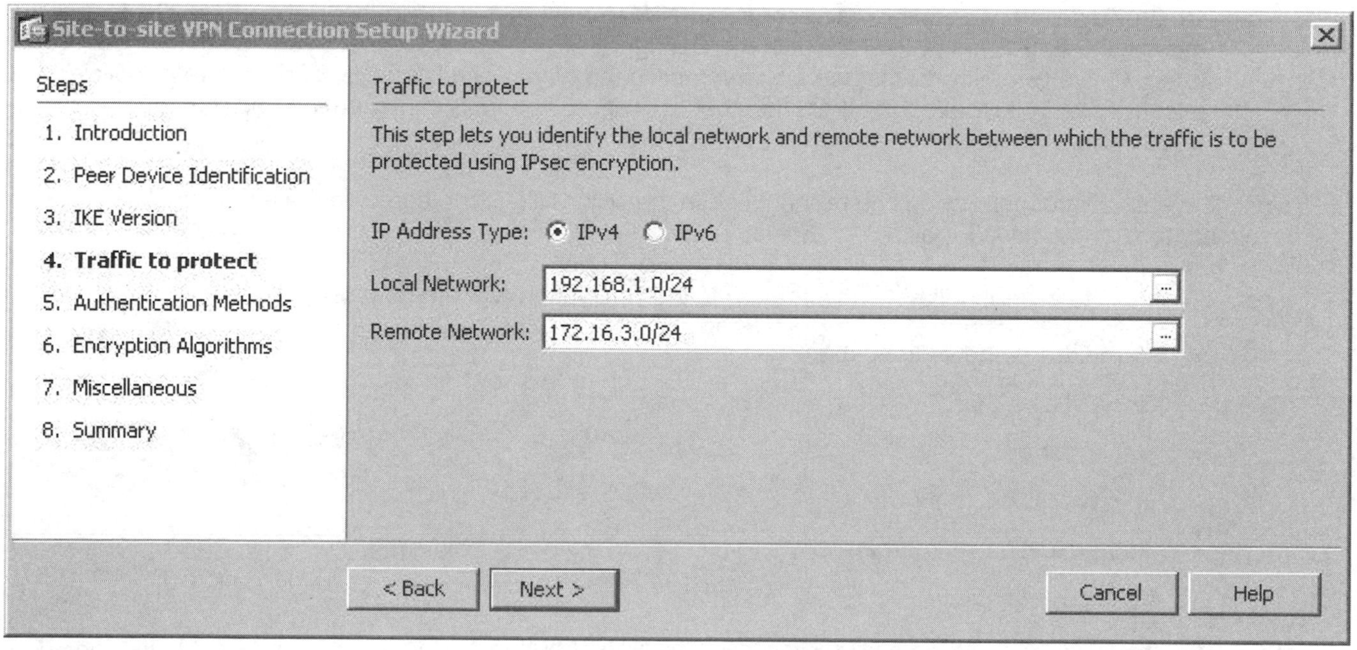

Step 7: Configure authentication.

On the Authentication Methods screen, enter a pre-shared key of **cisco12345**. You are not using a device certificate, so leave it set to **None**. Click **Next** to continue.

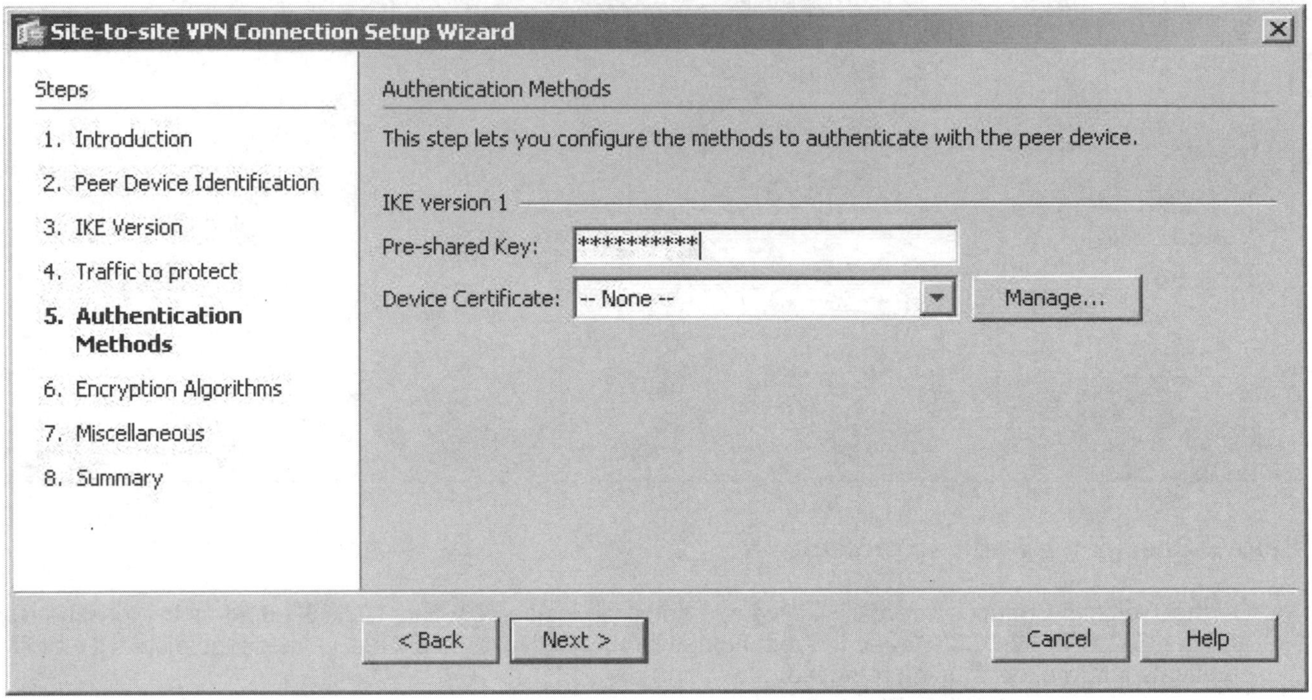

Step 8: Configure Encryption Algorithms (IKE policy and IPsec transform sets).

a. On the Encryption Algorithms screen, click the **Manage** button next to IKE Policy. Click **OK** to the message that IKE policy is global. On the Configure IKEv1 Policies screen, you see many policies listed. Only IKE policy 120 is needed to establish the tunnel with R3, so you can delete all policies except 120. If you leave the others they become part of the ASA configuration and are unnecessary. Select and click **Delete** for all policies except 120.

Note: The entire list of policies will be repopulated in the wizard if it is run again, in the event that it is necessary to change the IKE policy.

b. Click **OK** to accept policy 120 and return to the Encryption Algorithms screen.

- Name = pre-share-3des-sha
- Encryption = 3DES
- Hash = sha
- D-H Group = 2
- Authentication = pre-share
- Lifetime = 86400.

c. On the Encryption Algorithms screen, click the **Select** button next to IPsec Proposal. On the Select IPsec Proposals (Transform Sets) screen, remove all the IPsec proposal entries from the Assigned entry field, except for ESP-3DES-SHA, because this is the one R3 is using. All the transform sets listed will still be inserted into the final configuration, but the crypto map only draws on the specific transform set identified.

- Name = ESP-3DES-SHA
- Mode = Tunnel
- ESP Encryption = 3DES
- ESP Authentication = SHA

d. Click **OK** to assign the IPsec proposal and return to the Encryption Algorithms screen. When finished, the screen should look like the one shown here. Click **Next** to continue.

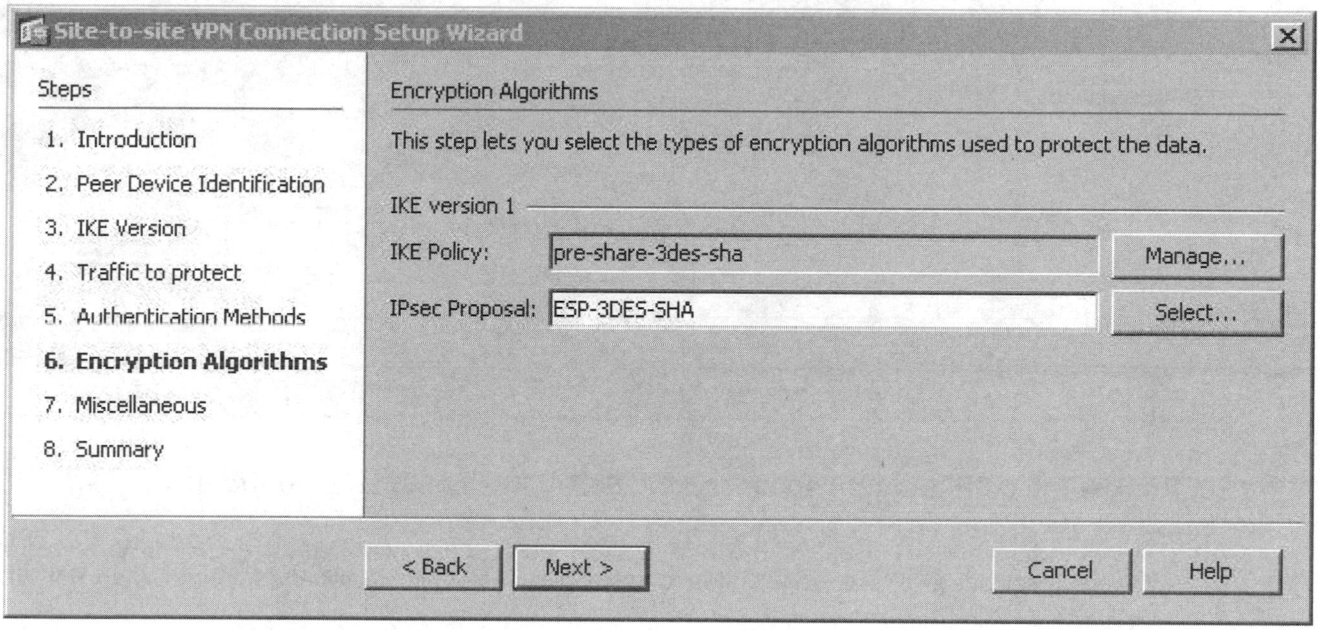

Step 9: Configure miscellaneous settings.

On the Miscellaneous screen, check the **Enable Inbound IPsec Sessions to Bypass Interface Access Lists** check box. Check the **Exempt ASA Side Host/Network from Address Translation** check box for the inside interface. Click **Next** to continue.

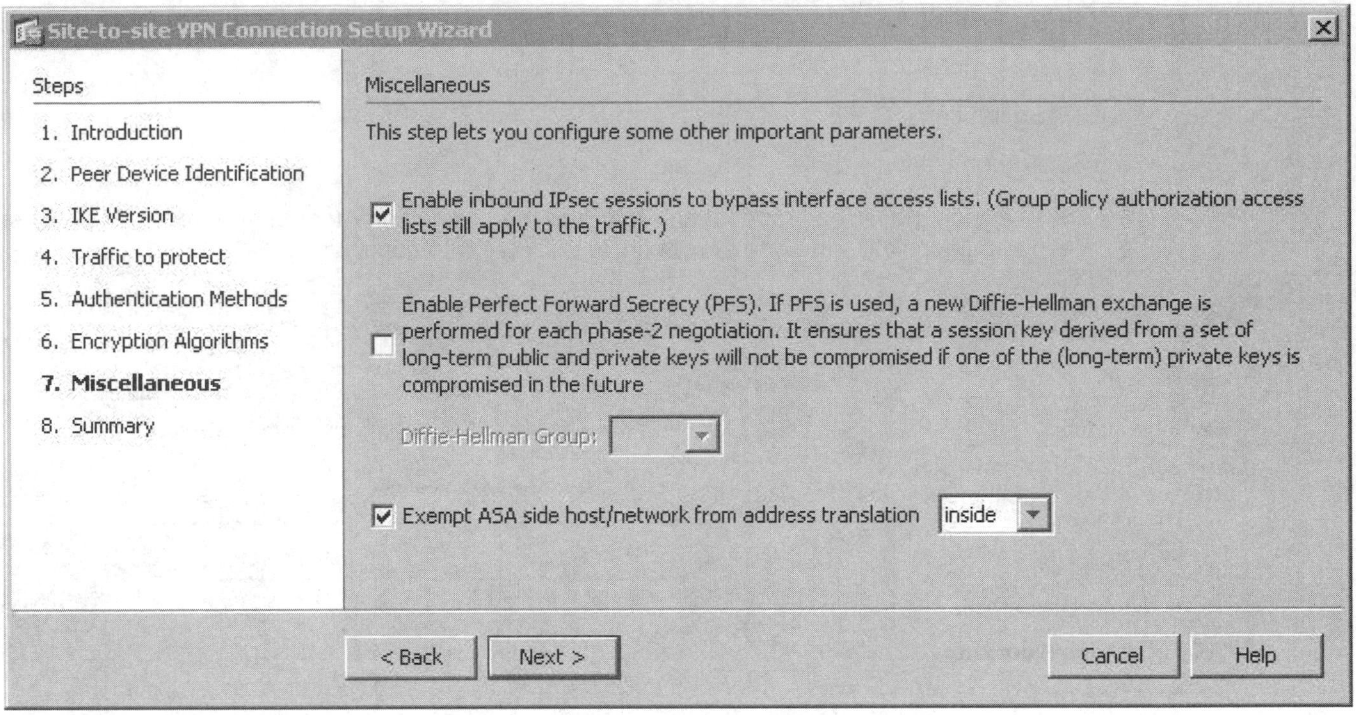

Step 10: Review the configuration summary and deliver the commands to the ASA.

a. The Summary page is displayed next. Verify that the information configured in the Site-to-Site VPN Wizard is correct. Click the **Back** button to make changes or click **Cancel** and restart the VPN Wizard (recommended).

b. Click **Finish** to complete the process and deliver the commands to the ASA. If prompted to authenticate, log in again as **admin** with a password of **cisco123**.

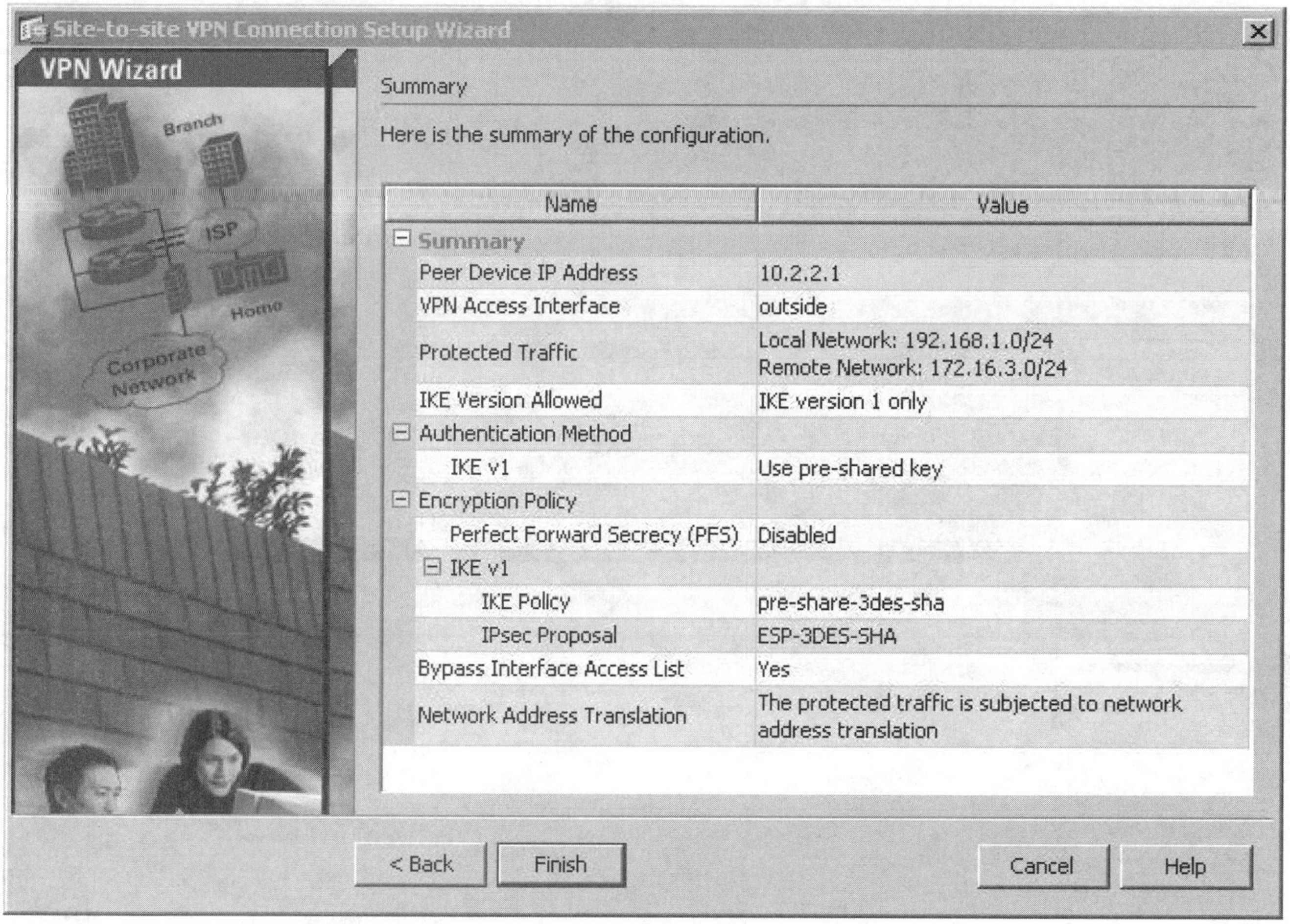

Step 11: Verify the ASDM VPN connection profile.

The ASDM **Configurations > Site-to-Site VPN > Connection Profiles** screen displays showing the settings you just configured. From this window, you can verify and edit the VPN configuration.

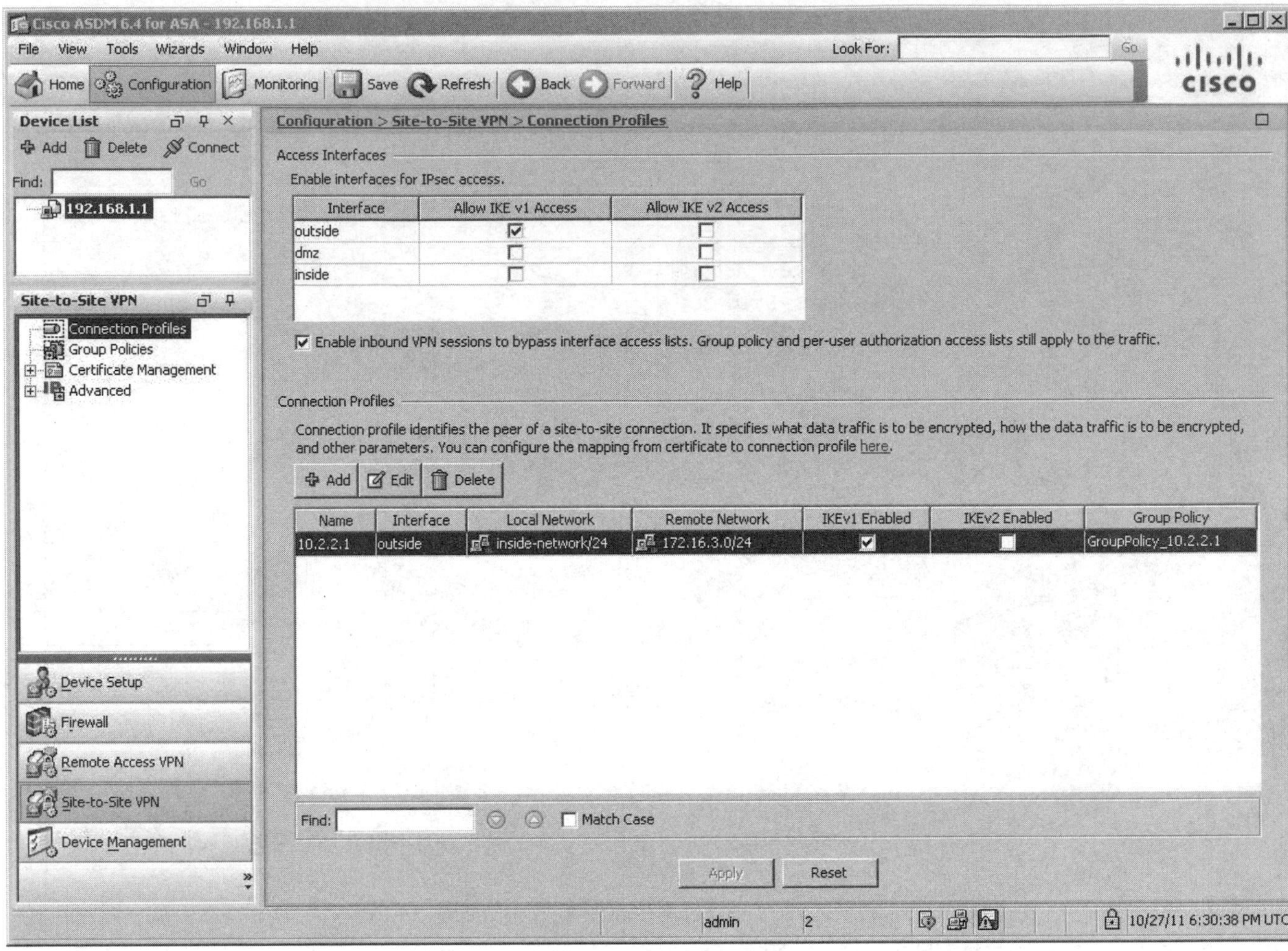

Step 12: Test the VPN configuration from R3 using CCP.

a. On PC-C, use CCP to test the IPsec VPN tunnel between the R3 ISR and the ASA. Choose **Configure > Security > VPN > Site-to-Site VPN** and display the **Edit Site-to-Site VPN** tab.

b. From the Edit Site-to-Site VPN tab, click **Test Tunnel**.

c. When the VPN Troubleshooting window displays, click the **Start** button to have CCP start troubleshooting the tunnel.

d. When the CCP warning window displays indicating that CCP will enable router debugs and generate some tunnel traffic, click **Yes** to continue.

e. On the next VPN Troubleshooting screen, the IP address of the host in the source network is displayed by default (R3 Fa0/1 = 172.16.3.1). Enter the IP address of host PC-B in the destination network field (**192.168.1.3**) and click **Continue** to begin the debugging process.

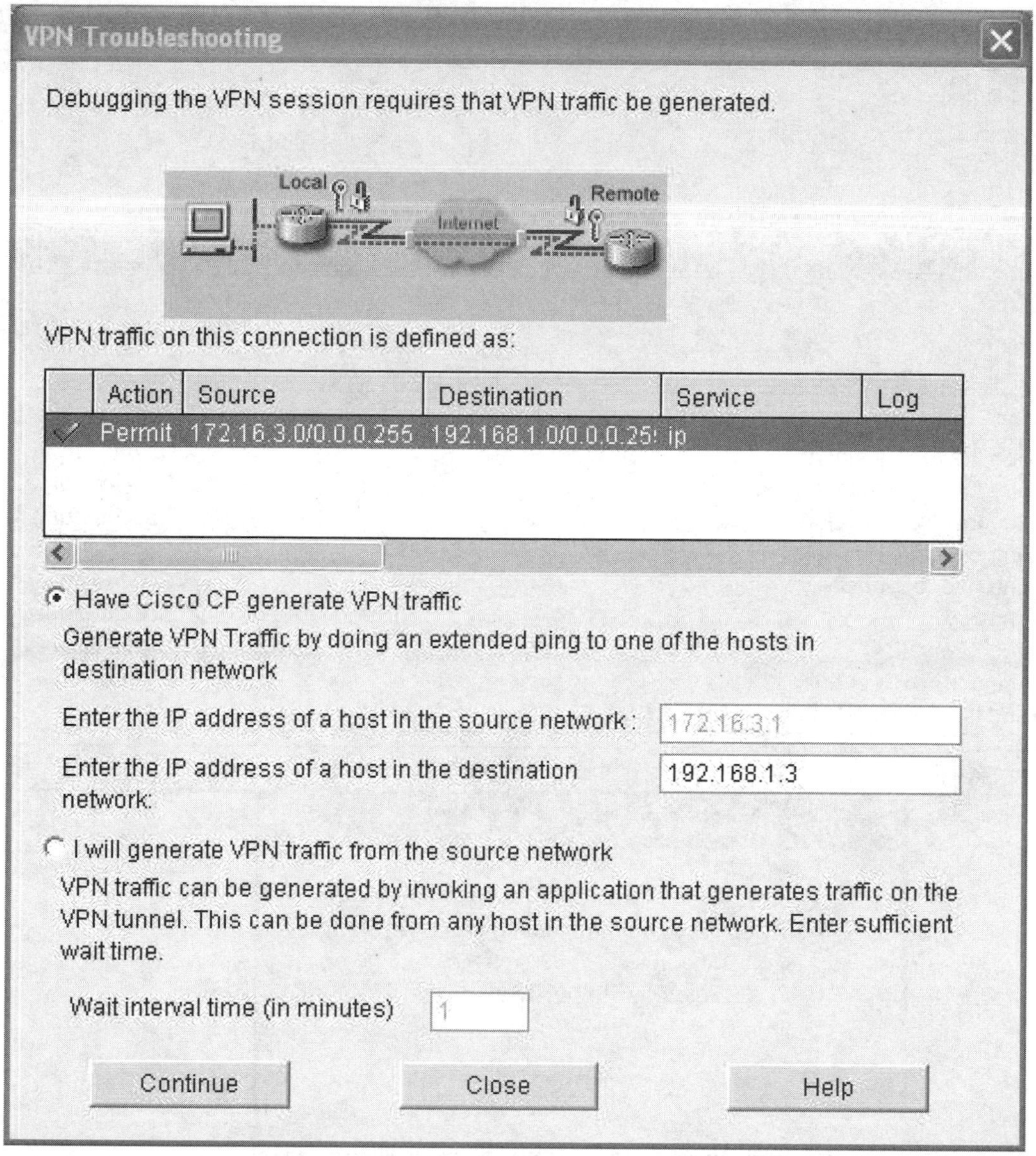

f. If the debug is successful and the tunnel is up, you should see the following screen. If the testing fails, CCP displays failure reasons and recommended actions. Click **OK** to remove the window.

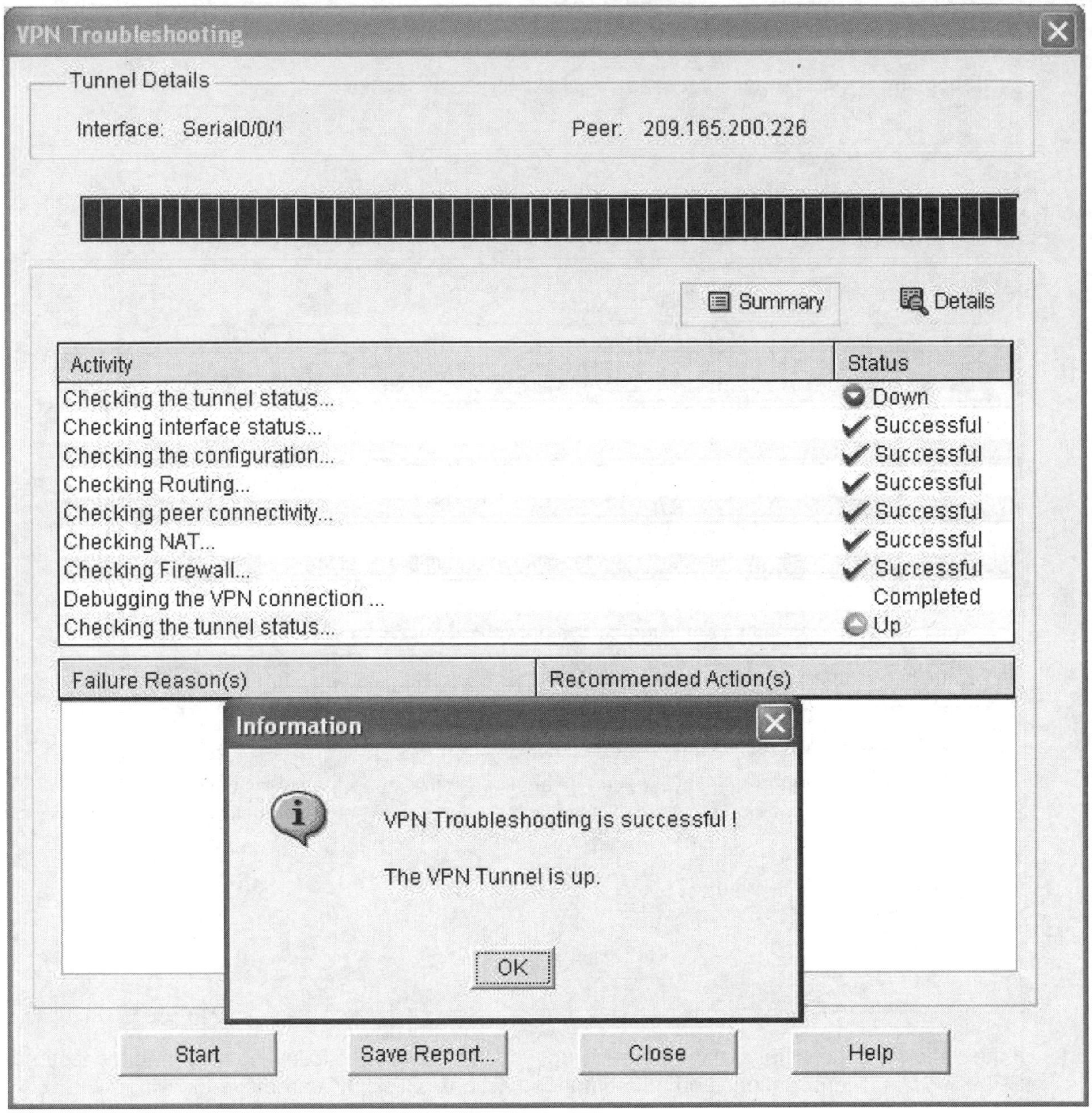

g. You can save the report if desired; otherwise, click **OK** and then **Close**.

h. On R3, choose **Configure > Security > VPN > Site-to-Site VPN** and display the **Edit Site-to-Site VPN** tab. The tunnel Status should now be **up**.

Note: If you want to reset the tunnel and test again, you can click the **Clear Connection** button from the Edit Site-to-Site VPN window.

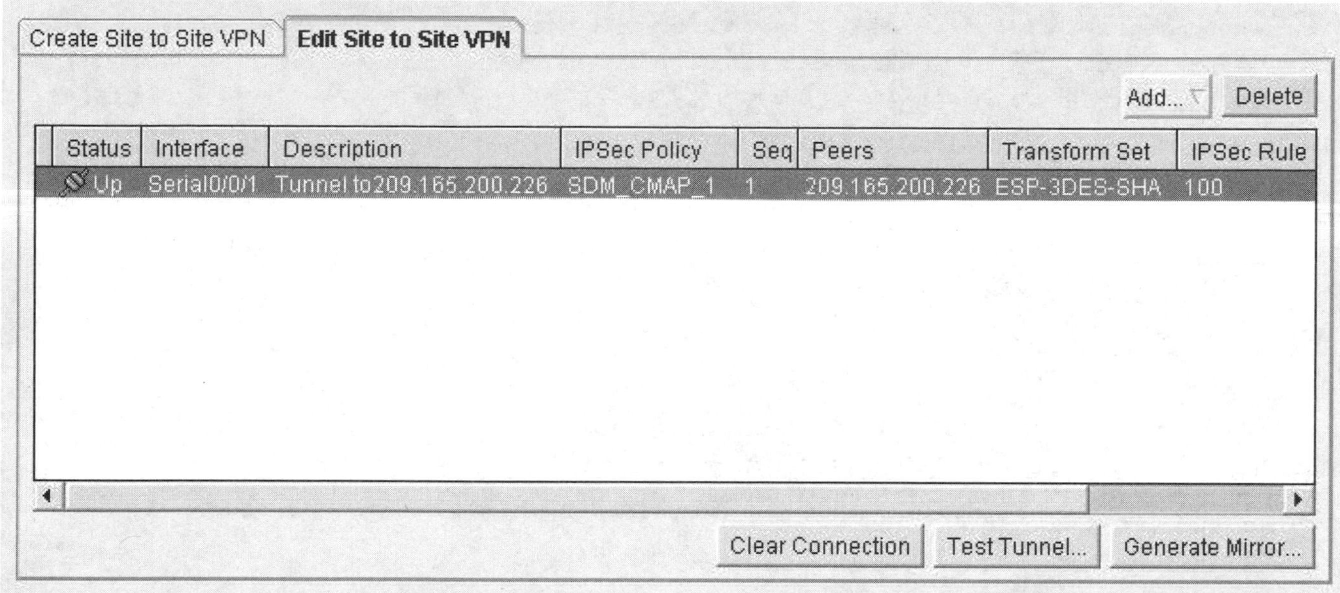

i. You can further verify tunnel functionality by pinging from branch office PC-C to PC-B on the internal network. The pings should be successful.

Note: Without the tunnel in place and bypassing NAT, it would be impossible for PC-C on the external network to ping PC-B on the private internal network.

Step 13: Use ASDM monitoring to verify the tunnel.

a. From the ASDM menu bar, choose **Monitoring** and click **VPN** from the panels at the lower left of the screen. Click **VPN Statistics > Sessions**. You should see the Site-to-Site IPsec VPN tunnel listed and Active.

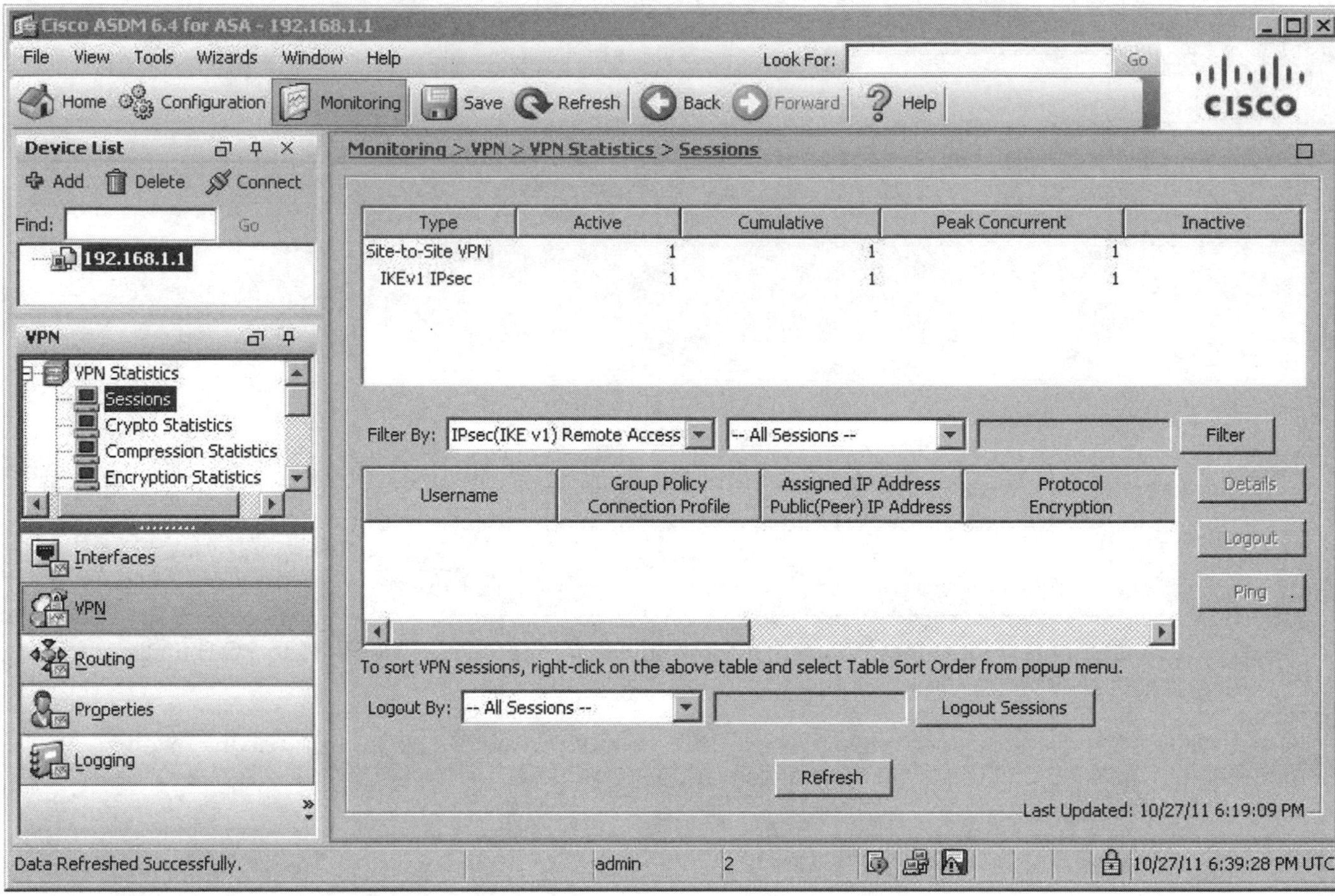

b. Click **Encryption Statistics**. You should see one or more sessions using the 3DES encryption algorithm.

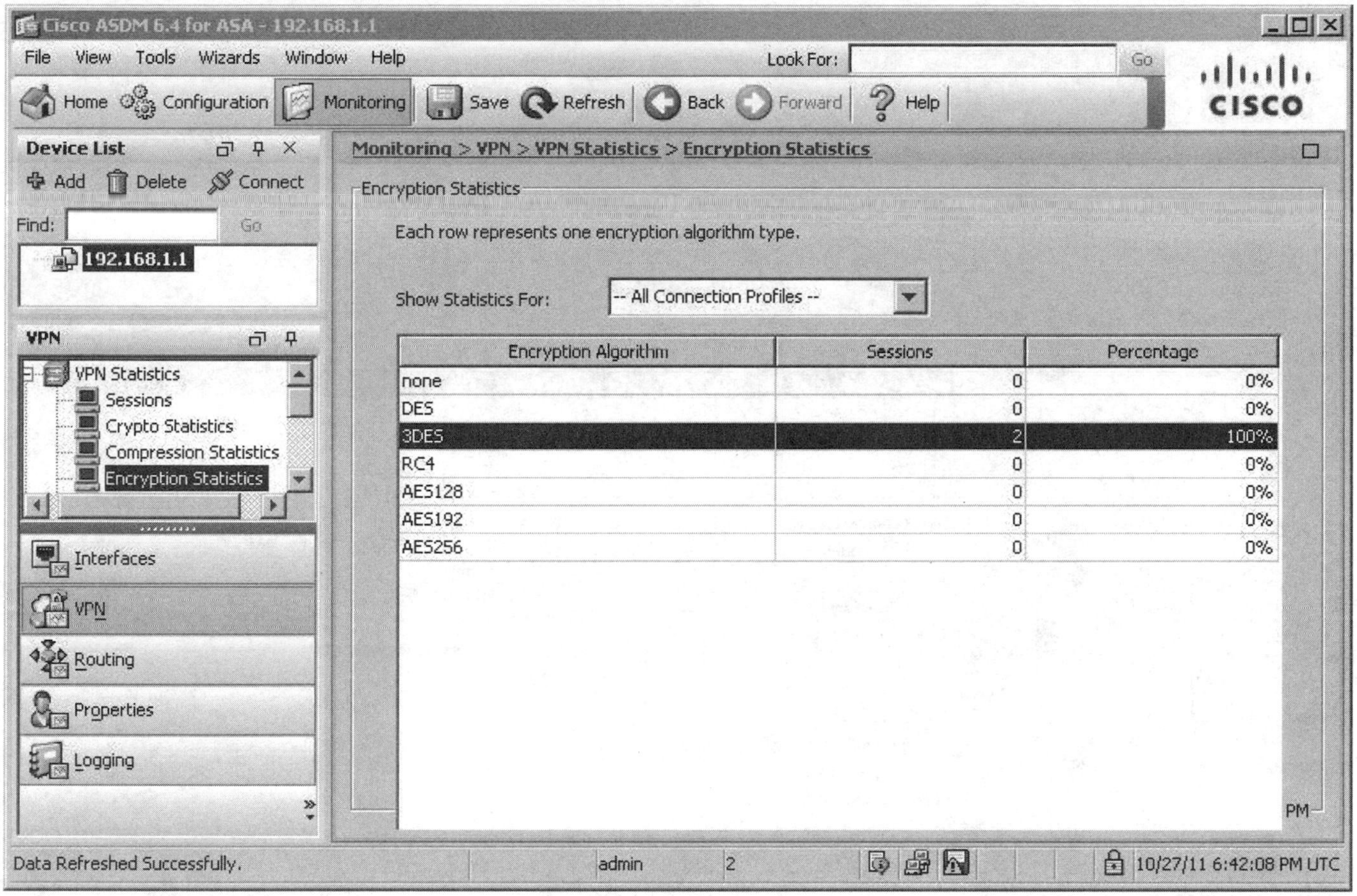

c. Click **Crypto Statistics**. You should see values for the number of packets encrypted and decrypted, security association (SA) requests, and so on.

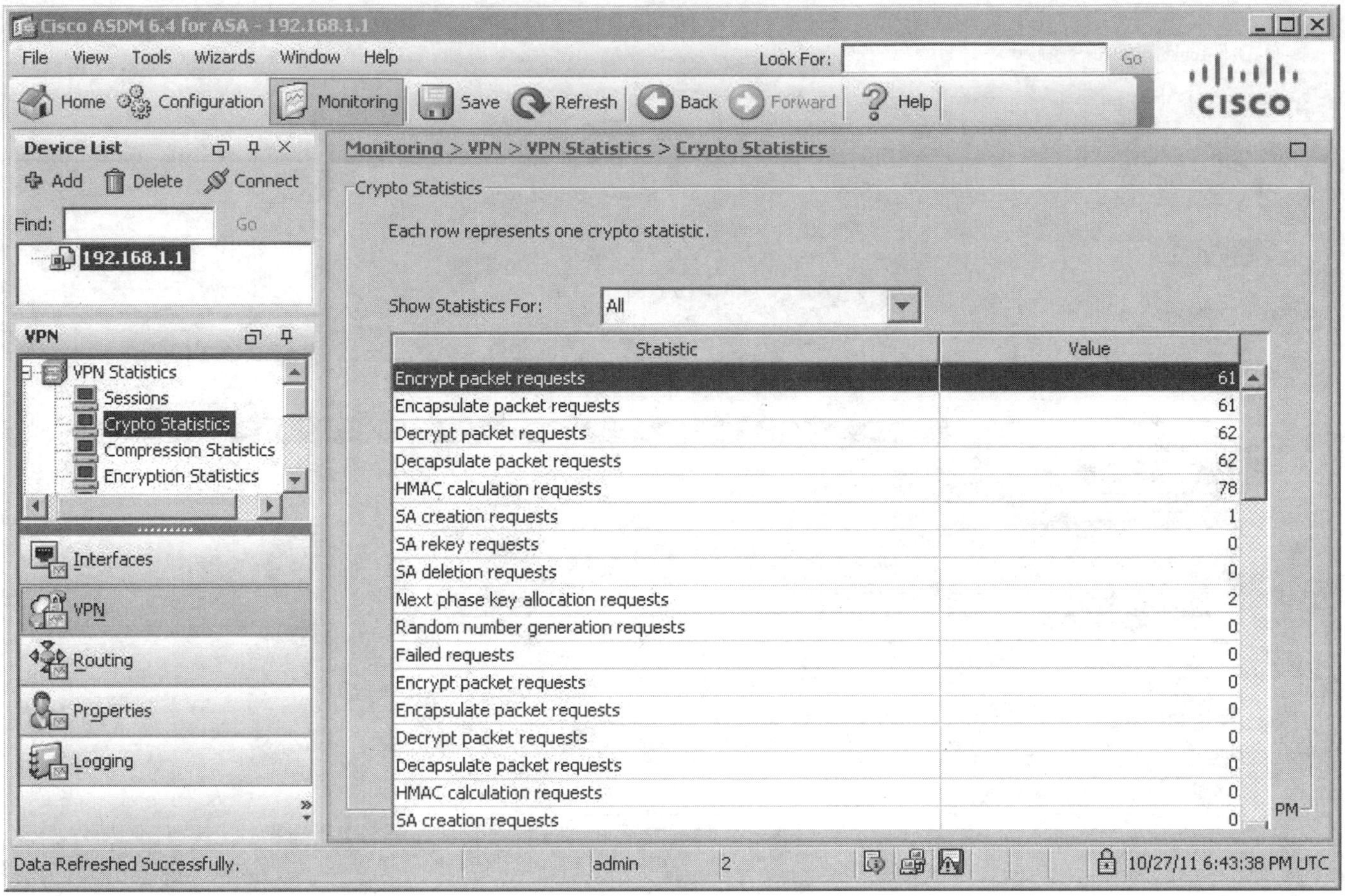

Reflection

1. What are some situations where a site-to-site IPsec VPN would be preferable as compared to a remote access SSL VPN?

____

____

____

____

____

2. What are some situations where a remote access VPN would be preferable as compared to site-to-site VPN?

____

____

____

____

____

Router Interface Summary Table

Router Model	Ethernet Interface 1	Ethernet Interface 2	Serial Interface 1	Serial Interface 2
1800	Fast Ethernet 0/0 (Fa0/0)	Fast Ethernet 0/1 (Fa0/1)	Serial 0/0/0 (S0/0/0)	Serial 0/0/1 (S0/0/1)
1900	Gigabit Ethernet 0/0 (G0/0)	Gigabit Ethernet 0/1 (G0/1)	Serial 0/0/0 (S0/0/0)	Serial 0/0/1 (S0/0/1)
2800	Fast Ethernet 0/0 (Fa0/0)	Fast Ethernet 0/1 (Fa0/1)	Serial 0/0/0 (S0/0/0)	Serial 0/0/1 (S0/0/1)
2900	Gigabit Ethernet 0/0 (G0/0)	Gigabit Ethernet 0/1 (G0/1)	Serial 0/0/0 (S0/0/0)	Serial 0/0/1 (S0/0/1)

Note: To find out how the router is configured, look at the interfaces to identify the type of router and how many interfaces the router has. There is no way to effectively list all the combinations of configurations for each router class. This table includes identifiers for the possible combinations of Ethernet and serial interfaces in the device. The table does not include any other type of interface, even though a specific router may contain one. An example of this might be an ISDN BRI interface. The string in parentheses is the legal abbreviation that can be used in Cisco IOS commands to represent the interface.

Appendix: ASA 5510 Supplemental Lab Manual

The four labs in this appendix are alternative Chapter 10 labs for Academies that are using the ASA 5510.

- Chapter 10 Lab E: Configuring ASA 5510 Basic Settings and Firewall Using CLI
- Chapter 10 Lab F: Configuring ASA 5510 Basic Settings and Firewall Using ASDM
- Chapter 10 Lab G: Configuring ASA 5510 Clientless and AnyConnect Remote Access SSL VPNs Using ASDM
- Chapter 10 Lab H: Configuring a Site-to-Site IPsec VPN Using CCP on an ISR and ASDM on an ASA 5510

Chapter 10 Lab E: Configuring ASA 5510 Basic Settings and Firewall Using CLI

Topology

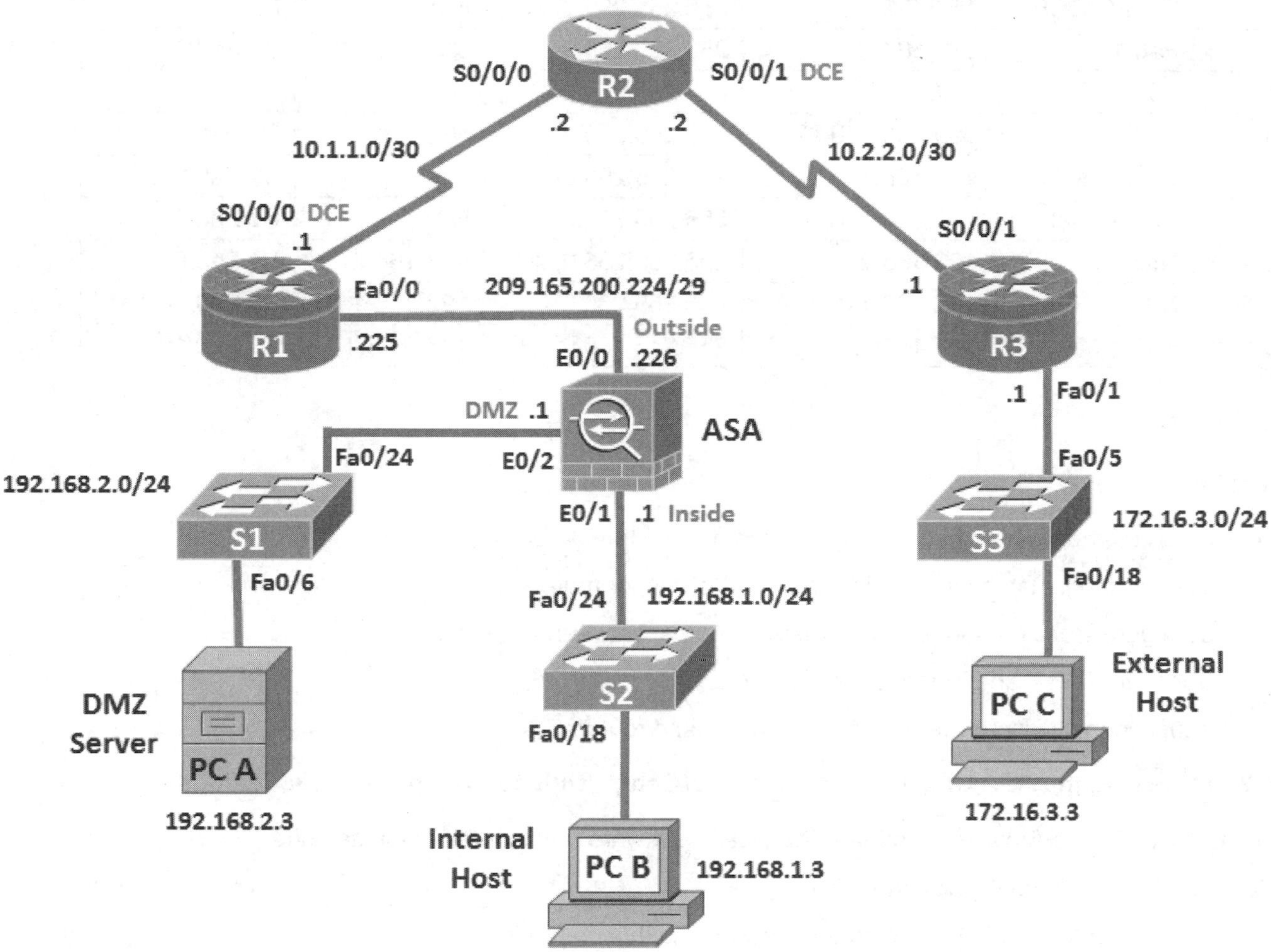

Note: ISR G2 devices have Gigabit Ethernet interfaces rather than FastEthernet interfaces.

IP Addressing Table

Device	Interface	IP Address	Subnet Mask	Default Gateway	Switch Port
R1	Fa0/0	209.165.200.225	255.255.255.248	N/A	ASA E0/0
	S0/0/0 (DCE)	10.1.1.1	255.255.255.252	N/A	N/A
R2	S0/0/0	10.1.1.2	255.255.255.252	N/A	N/A
	S0/0/1 (DCE)	10.2.2.2	255.255.255.252	N/A	N/A
R3	Fa0/1	172.16.3.1	255.255.255.0	N/A	S3 Fa0/5
	S0/0/1	10.2.2.1	255.255.255.252	N/A	N/A
ASA	E0/0 (outside)	209.165.200.226	255.255.255.248	NA	R1 Fa0/0
	E0/1 (inside)	192.168.1.1	255.255.255.0	NA	S2 Fa0/24
	E0/2 (dmz)	192.168.2.1	255.255.255.0	NA	S1 Fa0/24
PC-A	NIC	192.168.2.3	255.255.255.0	192.168.2.1	S1 Fa0/6
PC-B	NIC	192.168.1.3	255.255.255.0	192.168.1.1	S2 Fa0/18
PC-C	NIC	172.16.3.3	255.255.255.0	172.16.3.1	S3 Fa0/18

Objectives

Part 1: Lab Setup

- Cable the network as shown in the topology.
- Configure hostnames and interface IP addresses for routers, switches, and PCs.
- Configure static routing, including default routes, between R1, R2, and R3.
- Configure HTTP and Telnet access for R1.
- Verify connectivity between hosts, switches, and routers.

Part 2: Accessing the ASA Console and Using CLI Setup Mode to Configure Basic Settings

- Access the ASA console and view hardware, software, and configuration settings.
- Clear previous configuration settings.
- Use CLI Setup mode to configure basic settings (hostname, passwords, clock, etc.).

Part 3: Configuring Basic ASA Settings and Interface Security Levels Using CLI

- Configure the hostname and domain name.
- Configure the login and enable passwords.
- Set the date and time.
- Configure the inside and outside interfaces.
- Test connectivity to the ASA.
- Configure remote management with Telnet.
- Configure HTTPS access to the ASA for ASDM.

Part 4: Configuring Routing, Address Translation, and Inspection Policy Using CLI

- Configure a static default route for the ASA.
- Configure port address translation (PAT) for the inside network.
- Modify the MPF application inspection policy.

Part 5: Configuring DHCP, AAA, and SSH

- Configure the ASA as a DHCP server/client.
- Configure Local AAA user authentication.
- Configure remote management with SSH.

Part 6: Configuring a DMZ, Static NAT, and ACLs

- Configure static NAT for the DMZ server.
- Configure an ACL on the ASA to allow access to the DMZ for Internet users.
- Verify access to the DMZ server for external and internal users.

Background/Scenario

The Cisco Adaptive Security Appliance (ASA) is an advanced network security device that integrates a stateful firewall as well as VPN and other capabilities. This lab employs an ASA 5510 to create a firewall and protect an internal corporate network from external intruders while allowing internal hosts access to the Internet. The ASA creates three security interfaces: Outside, Inside, and DMZ. It provides outside users limited access to the DMZ and no access to inside resources. Inside users can access the DMZ and outside resources.

The focus of this lab is on the configuration of the ASA as a basic firewall. Other devices will receive minimal configuration to support the ASA portion of the lab. This lab uses the ASA CLI, which is similar to the IOS CLI, to configure basic device and security settings.

In part 1 of the lab, you configure the topology and non-ASA devices. In Parts 2 through 4, you configure basic ASA settings and the firewall between the inside and outside networks. In part 5, you configure the ASA for additional services such as DHCP, AAA, and SSH. In Part 6, you configure a DMZ on the ASA and provide access to a server in the DMZ.

Your company has one location connected to an ISP. Router R1 represents a CPE device managed by the ISP. Router R2 represents an intermediate Internet router. Router R3 represents an ISP that connects an administrator from a network management company, who has been hired to manage your network remotely. The ASA is an edge CPE security device that connects the internal corporate network and DMZ to the ISP while providing NAT and DHCP services to inside hosts. The ASA will be configured for management by an administrator on the internal network as well as by the remote administrator. ASA Layer 3 routed interfaces provide access to the three areas created in the lab: Inside, Outside, and DMZ. The ISP has assigned the public IP address space of 209.165.200.224/29, which will be used for address translation on the ASA.

Note: The routers used with this lab are Cisco 1841 with Cisco IOS Software Release 12.4(20)T (advanced IP image). The switches are Cisco WS-C2960-24TT-L with Cisco IOS Software Release 12.2(46)SE (C2960-LANBASEK9-M image). Other routers, switches, and Cisco IOS versions can be used. However, results and output may vary.

The ASA used with this lab is a Cisco model 5510 with four FastEthernet routed interfaces running OS Version 8.4(2) and ASDM Version 6.4(5) and comes with a Base license that allows a maximum of 50 VLANs.

Note: Make sure that the routers and switches have been erased and have no startup configurations.

Required Resources

- 3 routers (Cisco 1841 with Cisco IOS Software Release 12.4(20)T1 or comparable)
- 3 switches (Cisco 2960 or comparable)
- 1 ASA 5510 (OS Version 8.4(2) and ASDM Version 6.4(5) and Base license or comparable)
- PC-A: Windows XP, Vista, or Windows 7 with CCP, PuTTy SSH client
- PC-B: Windows XP, Vista, or Windows 7 with PuTTy SSH client (ASDM optional)
- PC-C: Windows XP, Vista, or Windows 7 with CCP, PuTTy SSH client
- Serial and Ethernet cables as shown in the topology
- Rollover cables to configure the routers and ASA via the console

Part 1: Basic Router/Switch/PC Configuration

In Part 1 of this lab, you set up the network topology and configure basic settings on the routers, such as interface IP addresses and static routing.

Note: Do not configure any ASA settings at this time.

Step 1: Cable the network and clear previous device settings.

Attach the devices that are shown in the topology diagram, and cable as necessary. Make sure the routers and switches have been erased and have no startup configurations.

Step 2: Configure basic settings for routers and switches.

a. Configure hostnames as shown in the topology for each router.

b. Configure router interface IP addresses as shown in the IP addressing table.

c. Configure a clock rate for routers with a DCE serial cable attached to their serial interface.

d. Configure the hostname for the switches. Other than the hostname, the switches can be left in their default configuration state. Configuring the VLAN management IP address for the switches is optional.

Step 3: Configure static routing on the routers.

a. Configure a static default route from R1 to R2 and from R3 to R2.

```
R1(config)# ip route 0.0.0.0 0.0.0.0 Serial0/0/0
R3(config)# ip route 0.0.0.0 0.0.0.0 Serial0/0/1
```

b. Configure a static route from R2 to the R1 Fa0/0 subnet (connected to ASA interface E0/0) and a static route from R2 to the R3 LAN.

```
R2(config)# ip route 209.165.200.224 255.255.255.248 Serial0/0/0
R2(config)# ip route 172.16.3.0 255.255.255.0 Serial0/0/1
```

Step 4: Enable the HTTP server on R1 and set the enable and vty passwords.

a. Enable HTTP access to R1 using the **`ip http server`** command in global config mode. Also set the console and VTY passwords to **cisco**. This will provide web and Telnet targets for testing later in the lab.

```
R1(config)# ip http server
R1(config)# enable password class

R1(config)# line vty 0 4
R1(config-line)# password cisco
R1(config-line)# login

R1(config)# line con 0
R1(config-line)# password cisco
R1(config-line)# login
```

b. On routers R2 and R3, set the same enable, console and vty passwords as with R1.

Step 5: Configure PC host IP settings.

Configure a static IP address, subnet mask, and default gateway for PC-A, PC-B, and PC-C as shown in the IP addressing table.

Step 6: Verify connectivity.

Because the ASA is the focal point for the network zones and it has not yet been configured, there will be no connectivity between devices that are connected to it. However, PC-C should be able to ping the Fa0/0 interface of R1. From PC-C, ping the R1 Fa0/0 IP address (209.165.200.225). If these pings are not successful, troubleshoot the basic device configurations before continuing.

Note: If you can ping from PC-C to R1 Fa0/0 and S0/0/0 you have demonstrated that static routing is configured and functioning correctly.

Step 7: Save the basic running configuration for each router and switch.

Part 2: Accessing the ASA Console and Using Setup to Configure Basic Settings

In Part 2 of this lab, you access the ASA via the console and use various **`show`** commands to determine hardware, software, and configuration settings. You clear the current configuration and use the CLI interactive Setup utility to configure basic ASA settings.

Note: Do not configure any ASA settings at this time.

Step 1: Access the ASA console.

a. Accessing the ASA via the console port is the same as with a Cisco router or switch. Connect to the ASA console port with a rollover cable.

b. Use a terminal emulation program, such as TeraTerm or HyperTerminal, to access the CLI. Then, use the serial port settings of 9600 baud, eight data bits, no parity, one stop bit, and no flow control.

c. Enter privileged mode with the **`enable`** command and password (if set). By default, the password is blank, so you can just press **Enter**. If the password has been changed to that specified in this lab, the password will be **class**. In addition, the hostname and prompt will be CCNAS-ASA>, as shown here. The default ASA hostname and prompt is ciscoasa>.

```
CCNAS-ASA> enable
Password: class (or press Enter if none set)
```

Step 2: Determine the ASA version, interfaces, and license.

The ASA 5510 used in this lab has four integrated 10/100 FastEthernet interfaces (E0/0–E0/3). Unlike the 5505 model, these are Layer 3 routed interfaces similar to those in an ISR. In addition, a special Management FastEthernet interface (M0/0) is also provided, which is not present on the ASA 5505.

Use the **show version** command to determine various aspects of this ASA device.

```
CCNAS-ASA# show version

Cisco Adaptive Security Appliance Software Version 8.4(2)
Device Manager Version 6.4(5)

Compiled on Wed 15-Jun-11 18:17 by builders
System image file is "disk0:/asa842-k8.bin"
Config file at boot was "startup-config"

CCNAS-ASA up 24 mins 5 secs

Hardware:   ASA5510, 1024 MB RAM, CPU Pentium 4 Celeron 1599 MHz
Internal ATA Compact Flash, 256MB
BIOS Flash M50FW016 @ 0xfff00000, 2048KB

Encryption hardware device : Cisco ASA-55x0 on-board accelerator (revision
0x0)
                             Boot microcode        : CN1000-MC-BOOT-2.00
                             SSL/IKE microcode     : CNLite-MC-SSLm-PLUS-2.03
                             IPSec microcode       : CNlite-MC-IPSECm-MAIN-
2.06
                             Number of accelerators: 1

 0: Ext: Ethernet0/0         : address is 44d3.cafd.986c, irq 9
 1: Ext: Ethernet0/1         : address is 44d3.cafd.986d, irq 9
 2: Ext: Ethernet0/2         : address is 44d3.cafd.986e, irq 9
 3: Ext: Ethernet0/3         : address is 44d3.cafd.986f, irq 9
 4: Ext: Management0/0       : address is 44d3.cafd.986b, irq 11
 5: Int: Not used            : irq 11
 6: Int: Not used            : irq 5

Licensed features for this platform:
Maximum Physical Interfaces      : Unlimited      perpetual
Maximum VLANs                    : 50             perpetual
Inside Hosts                     : Unlimited      perpetual
Failover                         : Disabled       perpetual
VPN-DES                          : Enabled        perpetual
VPN-3DES-AES                     : Enabled        perpetual
Security Contexts                : 0              perpetual
GTP/GPRS                         : Disabled       perpetual
AnyConnect Premium Peers         : 2              perpetual
AnyConnect Essentials            : Disabled       perpetual
Other VPN Peers                  : 250            perpetual
Total VPN Peers                  : 250            perpetual
```

```
Shared License                      : Disabled       perpetual
AnyConnect for Mobile               : Disabled       perpetual
AnyConnect for Cisco VPN Phone      : Disabled       perpetual
Advanced Endpoint Assessment        : Disabled       perpetual
UC Phone Proxy Sessions             : 2              perpetual
Total UC Proxy Sessions             : 2              perpetual
Botnet Traffic Filter               : Disabled       perpetual
Intercompany Media Engine           : Disabled       perpetual

This platform has a Base license.

<output omitted>
```

What software version is this ASA 5510 running? ______________________________

What is the name of the system image file, and from where was it loaded? ______________________________

____

The ASA can be managed using a built-in GUI known as the Adaptive Security Device Manager (ASDM). What version of ASDM is this ASA running? ______________________________

How much RAM does this ASA have? ______________________________

How much flash memory does this ASA have? ______________________________

How many Ethernet interfaces does this ASA have? ______________________________

What type of license does this ASA have? ______________________________

How many VLANs can be created with this license? ______________________________

Step 3: Determine the file system and contents of flash memory.

a. Display the ASA file system using the **show file system** command to determine what prefixes are supported:

```
CCNAS-ASA# show file system

File Systems:

     Size(b)      Free(b)      Type      Flags  Prefixes
* 260034560     198070272      disk      rw      disk0: flash:
          -             -      disk      rw      disk1:
          -             -      network   rw      tftp:
          -             -      opaque    rw      system:
          -             -      network   ro      http:
          -             -      network   ro      https:
          -             -      network   rw      ftp:
          -             -      network   rw      smb:
```

What is another name for flash:? __________

b. Display the contents of flash memory using one of these commands: **show flash**, **show disk0**, **dir flash:** or **dir disk0**:

```
CCNAS-ASA# show flash:
--#--  --length--  -----date/time------  path
```

```
  124  15390720    Oct 19 2011 15:49:48  asa842-k8.bin
  125  16280544    Oct 19 2011 18:22:24  asdm-645.bin
    3  4096        Jan 01 2003 00:03:32  log
   10  4096        Jan 01 2003 00:04:00  crypto_archive
   11  4096        Jan 01 2003 00:04:04  coredumpinfo
   12  43          Jan 01 2003 00:04:04  coredumpinfo/coredump.cfg
  127  12105313    Oct 19 2011 18:07:50  csd_3.5.841-k9.pkg
  128  4096        Oct 19 2011 18:07:52  sdesktop
  135  1462        Oct 19 2011 18:07:52  sdesktop/data.xml
  129  2857568     Oct 19 2011 18:07:54  anyconnect-wince-ARMv4I-
2.4.1012-k9.pkg
  130  3203909     Oct 19 2011 18:07:54  anyconnect-win-2.4.1012-k9.pkg
  131  4832344     Oct 19 2011 18:07:58  anyconnect-macosx-i386-
2.4.1012-k9.pkg
  132  5209423     Oct 19 2011 18:08:00  anyconnect-linux-2.4.1012-
k9.pkg

260034560 bytes total (198070272 bytes free)
```

What is the name of the ASDM file in flash:? ________________

Step 4: Determine the current running configuration.

The ASA 5510 is commonly used as an edge security device that connects a medium-sized business to an ISP for access to the Internet. The default factory configuration for the ASA 5510 includes the following:

- The management interface, Management 0/0, is configured. If you did not set the IP address using the **configure factory-default** command, the IP address and mask are 192.168.1.1 and 255.255.255.0.

Note: The Management 0/0 interface is a separate physical FastEthernet interface on the ASA 5510. This interface is not present on the ASA 5505.

- The DHCP server is enabled on the security appliance, so a PC connecting to the Management 0/0 interface receives an address between 192.168.1.2 and 192.168.1.254.

Note: With the default factory configuration, it is assumed that the PC connected to Management 0/0 is a DHCP client and will be used to configure the 5510 using the ASDM GUI embedded in flash.

- The HTTP server is enabled for ASDM and is accessible to users on the 192.168.1.0 network.
- No console or enable passwords are required, and the default hostname is **ciscoasa**.

Note: The default factory configuration only configures the Management 0/0 interface and does not configure an inside or outside network interface.

The configuration consists of the commands listed below.

Note: Do not use these commands to configure the ASA at this time.

```
interface management 0/0
   ip address 192.168.1.1 255.255.255.0
   nameif management
   security-level 100
   no shutdown
logging asdm informational 100
asdm history enable
http server enable
http 192.168.1.0 255.255.255.0 management
```

```
dhcpd address 192.168.1.2-192.168.1.254 management
dhcpd lease 3600
dhcpd ping_timeout 750
dhcpd enable management
```

a. Display the current running configuration using the **show running-config** command. Output will vary depending on the current state of the ASA configuration.

```
CCNAS-ASA# show running-config
: Saved
:
ASA Version 8.4(2)
!
hostname CCNAS-ASA
enable password 8Ry2YjIyt7RRXU24 encrypted
passwd 2KFQnbNIdI.2KYOU encrypted
names
!
interface Ethernet0/0
 shutdown
 no nameif
 no security-level
 no ip address

<output omitted>
```

Tip: To stop the output from a command using the CLI, press the letter **Q**.

If you see the Management interface configured, and other settings as described previously, the device is most likely configured with the default factory configuration. You also might see other security features, such as a global policy that inspects selected application traffic, which the ASA inserts by default if the original startup configuration has been erased. The actual output will vary depending on the ASA model, version, and configuration status.

b. You can restore the ASA to its factory default settings by using the **configure factory-default** command from global configuration mode, as shown here:

```
CCNAS-ASA# conf t
CCNAS-ASA(config)# configure factory-default

WARNING: The boot system configuration will be cleared.
The first image found in disk0:/ will be used to boot the
system on the next reload.
Verify there is a valid image on disk0:/ or the system will
not boot.

Begin to apply factory-default configuration:
Clear all configuration
WARNING: DHCPD bindings cleared on interface 'inside', address pool removed
Executing command: interface management0/0
Executing command: nameif management
INFO: Security level for "management" set to 0 by default.
Executing command: ip address 192.168.1.1 255.255.255.0
Executing command: security-level 100
Executing command: no shutdown
Executing command: exit
Executing command: http server enable
Executing command: http 192.168.1.0 255.255.255.0 management
Executing command: dhcpd address 192.168.1.2-192.168.1.254 management
Executing command: dhcpd enable management
Executing command: logging asdm informational
Factory-default configuration is completed
```

c. Review this output. You might want to capture and print the factory-default configuration as a reference.

Note: Restoring the ASA to factory default settings resets the hostname and prompt to **ciscoasa>**.

Step 5: Clear the previous ASA configuration settings.

a. Use the **write erase** command to remove the startup-config file from flash memory:

```
ciscoasa# write erase
Erase configuration in flash memory? [confirm]
[OK]
ciscoasa#

ciscoasa# show start
No Configuration
```

Note: The IOS command **erase startup-config** is not supported on the ASA.

b. Use the **reload** command to restart the ASA. This causes the ASA to come up in CLI Setup mode. If you're prompted that the config has been modified, and are asked whether you want to save it, respond N.

```
ciscoasa# reload
Proceed with reload? [confirm]
ciscoasa#
***
*** --- START GRACEFUL SHUTDOWN ---
Shutting down isakmp
Shutting down File system
***
*** --- SHUTDOWN NOW ---
Process shutdown finished
Rebooting.....
CISCO SYSTEMS
Embedded BIOS Version 1.0(12)13 08/28/08 15:50:37.45
<output omitted>
```

Step 6: Use the Setup interactive CLI mode to configure basic settings.

When the ASA completes the reload process, it should detect that the startup-config file is missing and present a series of interactive prompts to configure basic ASA settings. If it does not come up in this mode, repeat Step 5. As an alternative, you can run the **setup** command at the global configuration prompt, but you must first configure an inside interface. To configure the inside, name it “inside” (using the **nameif** command), assign it an IP address and subnet mask, and use the **no shutdown** command to enable it.

Note: The interactive prompt mode does not configure the ASA with factory defaults as described in Step 4. This mode can be used to configure minimal basic settings, such as hostname, clock, passwords, inside interface, and so on. You can bypass this mode and go directly to the CLI to configure the ASA settings, as described in Part 3 of this lab.

a. Respond to the Setup interactive prompts as shown here, after the ASA reloads:

```
Pre-configure Firewall now through interactive prompts [yes]? <Enter>
Firewall Mode [Routed]: <Enter>
Enable password [<use current password>]: cisco
Allow password recovery [yes]? <Enter>
Clock (UTC):
```

```
    Year [2012]: <Enter>
    Month [Jan]: <Enter>
    Day [16]: <Enter>
    Time [12:24:42]: <Enter>
Management IP address: 192.168.1.1 <Enter>
Management network mask: 255.255.255.0 <Enter>
Host name: ASA-Init
Domain name: generic.com
IP address of host running Device Manager: <Enter>

The following configuration will be used:
Enable password: cisco
Allow password recovery: yes
Clock (UTC): 12:24:42 Sep Jan 16 2012
Firewall Mode: Routed
Management IP address: 192.168.1.1
Management network mask: 255.255.255.0
Host name: ASA-Init
Domain name: generic.com

Use this configuration and write to flash? Yes <enter>

INFO: Security level for "management" set to 0 by default.
WARNING: http server is not yet enabled to allow ASDM access.
Cryptochecksum: c8a535f0 e273d49e 5bddfd19 e12566b1

2070 bytes copied in 0.940 secs

Type help or '?' for a list of available commands.
ASA-Init#
```

Note: In the above configuration, the IP address of the host running ASDM was left blank. It is not necessary to install ASDM on a host. It can be run from the flash memory of the ASA device itself using the browser of the host.

You also might see the warning above stating that the ASA HTTP server has not yet been enabled. This will be done in a subsequent step.

Note: The responses to the prompts are automatically stored in the startup-config and running config files. However, additional security-related commands, such as a global default inspection service policy, are inserted into the running-config by the ASA OS.

b. Issue the **show run** command to see the additional security related configuration commands that are inserted by the ASA.

c. Issue the **copy run start** command to capture the additional security related commands in the startup-config.

d. Issue the **reload** command to restart the ASA and load the startup configuration.

```
ASA-Init# reload
Proceed with reload? [confirm] <Enter>

<output omitted>
```

e. Enter privileged EXEC mode with the **enable** command. Provide the password set in Step 6a (class). Issue the **show running-config** command. You should see the entries you provided in the interactive configuration process.

Part 3: Configuring ASA Settings and Interface Security Using the CLI

In Part 3 of this lab, you configure basic settings by using the ASA CLI, even though some of them were already configured using the Setup mode interactive prompts in Part 2. In this part, you start with the settings configured in Part 2 and add to or modify them to create a more complete basic configuration.

Tip: You will find that many ASA CLI commands are similar to, if not the same as, those used with Cisco IOS CLI. In addition, moving between configuration modes and submodes is essentially the same.

Note: You must complete Part 2 before beginning Part 3.

Step 1: Configure the hostname and domain name.

a. Enter global configuration mode using the **config t** command. The first time you enter configuration mode after running Setup, you might be asked whether you want to enable anonymous reporting. Respond with **no**.

b. Configure the ASA hostname using the **hostname** command:

```
ASA-Init(config)# hostname CCNAS-ASA
```

c. Configure the domain name using the **domain-name** command:

```
CCNAS-ASA(config)# domain-name ccnasecurity.com
```

Step 2: Configure the login and enable mode passwords.

a. The login password is used for Telnet connections (and SSH prior to ASA version 8.4). By default, it is set to **cisco**. You can change the login password using the **passwd** or **password** command. For this lab, leave it set to the default of **cisco**.

b. Configure the privileged EXEC mode (enable) password using the **enable password** command:

```
CCNAS-ASA(config)# enable password class
```

Step 3: Set the date and time.

You can set the date and time manually using the **clock set** command. The syntax for the clock set command is **clock set** *hh:mm:ss {month day | day month} year*. The following is an example of how to set the date and time using a 24-hour clock:

```
CCNAS-ASA(config)# clock set 14:25:00 January 16 2012
```

Step 4: Configure the inside and outside interfaces.

ASA 5510 interface notes: The 5510 and other higher-end 5500 series ASA models are different from the ASA 5505. With the 5510 model, a physical FastEthernet interface can be assigned a Layer 3 IP address directly, much like a Cisco router. With the ASA 5505 model, the eight integrated switch ports are Layer 2 ports, and VLANs must be created. This is not the case with the 5510. The four FastEthernet interfaces on the 5510 are routed interfaces.

Note: If you finished the initial configuration Setup utility, Management interface M0/0 is configured with an IP address of 192.168.1.1. You will need to remove the IP address from the M0/0 interface to assign it to the inside interface E0/1. Instructions are provided here to configure both the inside (E0/1) and outside (E0/0) interface at this time. The DMZ interface (E0/2) will be configured in Part 6 of the lab.

a. Remove the configuration from the M0/0 interface and shut it down (if required):

```
CCNAS-ASA(config)# interface m0/0
CCNAS-ASA(config-if)# shutdown
CCNAS-ASA(config-if)# no nameif
CCNAS-ASA(config-if)# no security-level
CCNAS-ASA(config-if)# no ip address
```

b. Configure interface E0/1 for the inside network, 192.168.1.0/24. Name the Interface **inside**, set the security level to the highest setting of **100**, and bring it up.

```
CCNAS-ASA(config)# interface e0/1
CCNAS-ASA(config-if)# nameif inside
CCNAS-ASA(config-if)# ip address 192.168.1.1 255.255.255.0
CCNAS-ASA(config-if)# security-level 100
CCNAS-ASA(config-if)# no shutdown
```

c. Configure interface E0/0 for the outside network, 209.165.200.224/29. Name the interface **outside**, set the security level to the lowest setting of **0**, and bring it up.

```
CCNAS-ASA(config-if)# interface e0/0
CCNAS-ASA(config-if)# nameif outside
CCNAS-ASA(config-if)# ip address 209.165.200.226 255.255.255.248
CCNAS-ASA(config-if)# security-level 0
CCNAS-ASA(config-if)# no shutdown
```

Interface security level notes: You might receive a message that the security level for the inside interface was set automatically to 100 and the outside interface was set to 0. The ASA uses interface security levels from 0 to 100 to enforce the security policy. Security Level 100 (inside) is the most secure, and level 0 (outside) is the least secure.

By default, the ASA applies a policy where traffic from a higher security level interface to one with a lower level is permitted, and traffic from a lower security level interface to one with a higher security level is denied. The ASA default security policy permits outbound traffic, which is inspected by default. Returning traffic is allowed because of stateful packet inspection. This default "routed mode" firewall behavior of the ASA enables packets to be routed from the inside network to the outside network but not vice versa. In Part 4 of this lab, you configure NAT to increase the firewall protection.

d. Use the **show interface ip brief** command to ensure that ASA interfaces E0/0 and E0/1 are both up/up. Note that this command is different from the IOS command **show ip interface brief**. If either port is shown as down/down, check the physical connections. If either port is administratively down, bring it up with the **no shutdown** command.

```
CCNAS-ASA(config-if)# show interface ip brief
Interface         IP-Address        OK?  Method Status
Protocol
Ethernet0/0       209.165.200.226   YES  manual up                        up
Ethernet0/1       192.168.1.1       YES  manual up                        up
Ethernet0/2       unassigned        YES  unset  administratively down up
Ethernet0/3       unassigned        YES  unset  administratively down down
Management0/0     unassigned        YES  unset  administratively down down
```

Tip: Most ASA **show** commands, as well as **ping**, **copy**, and others, can be issued from within any config mode prompt without the **do** command required with IOS.

e. Display the Layer 3 interface information using the **show ip address** command:

```
CCNAS-ASA(config)# show ip address
<output omitted>

Current IP Addresses:
```

```
Interface      Name       IP address        Subnet mask       Method
Ethernet0/0    outside    209.165.200.226   255.255.255.248   manual
Ethernet0/1    inside     192.168.1.1       255.255.255.0     Manual
```

f. You may also use the **show running-config interface** command to display the configuration for a particular interface from the running-config:

```
CCNAS-ASA# show run interface e0/0
!
interface Ethernet0/0
 nameif outside
 security-level 0
 ip address 209.165.200.226 255.255.255.248
```

Step 5: Test connectivity to the ASA.

a. Ensure that PC-B has a static IP address of 192.168.1.3 along with subnet mask 255.255.255.0 and default gateway 192.168.1.1 (the IP address of the ASA E0/1 inside interface).

b. You should be able to ping from PC-B to the ASA inside interface address and ping from the ASA to PC-B. If the pings fail, troubleshoot the configuration as necessary.

```
CCNAS-ASA# ping 192.168.1.3
Type escape sequence to abort.
Sending 5, 100-byte ICMP Echos to 192.168.1.3, timeout is 2 seconds:
!!!!!
Success rate is 100 percent (5/5), round-trip min/avg/max = 1/1/1 ms
```

c. From PC-B, ping the outside interface at IP address 209.165.200.226. You should not be able to ping this address.

d. From PC-B, Telnet to the ASA using address 192.168.1.1. Were you able to make the connection? Why or why not? ____

Step 6: Configure Telnet access to the ASA from the inside network.

a. You can configure the ASA to accept Telnet connections from a single host or a range of hosts on the inside network. Configure the ASA to allow Telnet connections from any host on the inside network 192.168.1.0/24, and set the Telnet timeout to 10 minutes (the default is 5 minutes).

```
CCNAS-ASA(config)# telnet 192.168.1.0 255.255.255.0 inside
CCNAS-ASA(config)# telnet timeout 10
```

b. From PC-B, Telnet to the ASA using address 192.168.1.1 to verify the Telnet access. Use the remote access login password **cisco** to access the ASA CLI prompt. Exit the Telnet session using the **quit** command.

Note: You cannot use Telnet to the lowest security interface (outside) from the outside unless you use Telnet inside an IPsec tunnel. Telnet is not the preferred remote access tool because of its lack of encryption. In Part 5 of this lab, you configure SSH access from the internal and external network.

Step 7: Configure HTTP and verify ASDM access to the ASA.

a. You can configure the ASA to accept HTTPS connections using the **http** command. This allows access to the ASA GUI (ASDM). Configure the ASA to allow HTTPS connections from any host on the inside network 192.168.1.0/24:

```
CCNAS-ASA(config)# http server enable
CCNAS-ASA(config)# http 192.168.1.0 255.255.255.0 inside
```

b. Open a browser on PC-B, and test the HTTPS access to the ASA by entering https://192.168.1.1. You are prompted with a security certificate warning. Click **Continue** to this website. On the ASDM home page, click the **Run ASDM** button and click **Yes** for the other security warnings. You should see the Cisco ASDM-IDM Launcher, where you can enter a username and password. Leave the username blank and enter the enable password **class**, which was configured previously.

Note: Be sure to specify the HTTPS protocol in the URL.

c. Close the browser. In the next lab, you use ASDM extensively to configure the ASA. The objective here is not to use the ASDM configuration screens, but to verify HTTP/ASDM connectivity to the ASA. If you are unable to access ASDM, check your configurations or contact your instructor, or do both.

Part 4: Configuring Routing, Address Translation, and Inspection Policy Using the CLI

In Part 4 of this lab, you provide a default route for the ASA to reach external networks. You configure address translation using network objects to enhance firewall security. You then modify the default application inspection policy to allow specific traffic.

Note: You must complete Part 3 before going on to Part 4.

Step 1: Configure a static default route for the ASA.

In Part 3, you configured the ASA outside interface with a static IP address and subnet mask. However, the ASA does not have a gateway of last resort defined. To enable the ASA to reach external networks, you will configure a default static route on the ASA outside interface.

Note: If the ASA outside interface were configured as a DHCP client, it could obtain a default gateway IP address from the ISP. However, in this lab, the outside interface is configured with a static address.

a. Ping from the ASA to R1 Fa0/0 IP address 209.165.200.225. Was the ping successful?

____

b. Ping from the ASA to the R1 S0/0/0 IP address 10.1.1.1. Was the ping successful?

____

c. Create a "quad zero" default route using the **`route`** command, associate it with the ASA outside interface, and point to the R1 Fa0/0 IP address 209.165.200.225 as the gateway of last resort. The administrative distance is 1 by default.

```
CCNAS-ASA(config)# route outside 0.0.0.0 0.0.0.0 209.165.200.225
```

d. Issue the **`show route`** command to display the ASA routing table and the static default route just created:

```
CCNAS-ASA# show route
Codes: C - connected, S - static, I - IGRP, R - RIP, M - mobile, B -
BGP
       D - EIGRP, EX - EIGRP external, O - OSPF, IA - OSPF inter area
       N1 - OSPF NSSA external type 1, N2 - OSPF NSSA external type 2
       E1 - OSPF external type 1, E2 - OSPF external type 2, E - EGP
       i - IS-IS, L1 - IS-IS level-1, L2 - IS-IS level-2, ia - IS-IS
inter area
       * - candidate default, U - per-user static route, o - ODR
```

```
        P - periodic downloaded static route

Gateway of last resort is 209.165.200.225 to network 0.0.0.0

C    192.168.10.0 255.255.255.0 is directly connected, inside
C    209.165.200.224 255.255.255.248 is directly connected, outside
S*   0.0.0.0 0.0.0.0 [1/0] via 209.165.200.225, outside
```

e. Ping from the ASA to the R1 S0/0/0 IP address 10.1.1.1. Was the ping successful?

____

Step 2: Configure address translation using PAT and network objects.

Note: Beginning with ASA Version 8.3, network objects are used to configure all forms of NAT. A network object is created, and NAT is configured within this object. In Step 2a, a network object **inside-net** is used to translate the inside network addresses 192.168.1.0/24 to the global address of the outside ASA interface. This type of object configuration is called Auto-NAT.

a. Create network object **inside-net** and assign attributes to it using the **subnet** and **nat** commands. In Version 8.3 and newer, only the **nat** command is used and the **static** and **global** commands are no longer supported.

```
CCNAS-ASA(config)# object network inside-net
CCNAS-ASA(config-network-object)# subnet 192.168.1.0 255.255.255.0
CCNAS-ASA(config-network-object)# nat (inside,outside) dynamic
interface
CCNAS-ASA(config-network-object)# end
```

b. The ASA splits the configuration into the object portion that defines the network to be translated and the actual **nat** command parameters. These appear in two different places in the running-config. Display the NAT object configuration using the **show run object** and **show run nat** commands.

```
CCNAS-ASA# show run object
object network inside-net
 subnet 192.168.1.0 255.255.255.0

CCNAS-ASA# show run nat
!
object network inside-net
 nat (inside,outside) dynamic interface
```

c. From PC-B, attempt to ping the R1 Fa0/0 interface at IP address 209.165.200.225. Were the pings successful? ____________

d. Issue the **show nat** command on the ASA to see the translated and untranslated hits. Notice that, of the pings from PC-B, four were translated and four were not. This is because that ICMP is not being inspected by the global inspection policy. The outgoing pings (echos) were translated and the returning echo replies were blocked by the firewall policy. You configure the default inspection policy to allow ICMP in the next step.

```
CCNAS-ASA# show nat

Auto NAT Policies (Section 2)
1 (inside) to (outside) source dynamic inside-net interface
    translate_hits = 4, untranslate_hits = 4
```

e. Ping from PC-B to R1 again, and quickly issue the **show xlate** command to see the actual addresses being translated:

```
CCNAS-ASA# show xlate
1 in use, 28 most used
Flags: D - DNS, i - dynamic, r - portmap, s - static, I - identity, T -
twice

ICMP PAT from inside:192.168.1.3/512 to outside:209.165.200.226/21469
flags ri idle 0:00:03 timeout 0:00:30
```

Note: The flags (r and i) indicate that the translation was based on a port map (r) and was done dynamically (i).

f. Open a browser on PC-B, and enter the IP address of R1 Fa0/0 (209.165.200.225). You should be prompted by R1 for SDM or CCP GUI login. TCP-based HTTP traffic is permitted by default by the firewall inspection policy.

g. On the ASA, use the **show nat** and **show xlate** commands again to see the hits and addresses being translated for the HTTP connection.

Step 3: Modify the default MPF application inspection global service policy.

For application layer inspection, as well as other advanced options, the Cisco Modular Policy Framework (MPF) is available on ASAs. Cisco MPF uses three configuration objects to define modular, object-oriented, hierarchical policies:

- **Class maps:** Define a match criterion.
- **Policy maps:** Associate actions to the match criteria.
- **Service policies:** Attach the policy map to an interface, or globally to all interfaces of the appliance.

a. Display the default MPF policy map that performs the inspection on inside-to-outside traffic. Only traffic that was initiated from the inside is allowed back in to the outside interface. Notice that the ICMP protocol is missing.

```
CCNAS-ASA# show run
<output omitted>

class-map inspection_default
 match default-inspection-traffic
!
policy-map type inspect dns preset_dns_map
 parameters
  message-length maximum client auto
  message-length maximum 512

policy-map global_policy
 class inspection_default
  inspect dns preset_dns_map
  inspect ftp
  inspect h323 h225
  inspect h323 ras
  inspect ip-options
  inspect netbios
  inspect rsh
  inspect rtsp
  inspect skinny
  inspect esmtp
  inspect sqlnet
  inspect sunrpc
```

```
    inspect tftp
    inspect sip
    inspect xdmcp
  !
  service-policy global_policy global
```

b. Add the inspection of ICMP traffic to the policy map list using the following commands:

```
CCNAS-ASA(config)# policy-map global_policy
CCNAS-ASA(config-pmap)# class inspection_default
CCNAS-ASA(config-pmap-c)# inspect icmp
```

c. From PC-B, attempt to ping the R1 Fa0/0 interface at IP address 209.165.200.225. The pings should be successful this time because ICMP traffic is now being inspected, and legitimate return traffic is being allowed.

Part 5: Configuring DHCP, AAA, and SSH

In Part 5 of this lab, you configure ASA features, such as DHCP and enhanced login security, using AAA and SSH.

Note: You must complete Part 4 before beginning Part 5.

Step 1: Configure the ASA as a DHCP server.

The ASA can be both a DHCP server and a DHCP client. In this step, you configure the ASA as a DHCP server to dynamically assign IP addresses for DHCP clients on the inside network.

a. Configure a DHCP address pool and enable it on the ASA inside interface. This is the range of addresses to be assigned to inside DHCP clients. Set the range from 192.168.1.5 through 192.168.1.100.

```
CCNAS-ASA(config)# dhcpd address 192.168.1.5-192.168.1.100 inside
```

Were you able to do this on this ASA? ____

____

b. (Optional) Specify the IP address of the DNS server to be given to clients:

```
CCNAS-ASA(config)# dhcpd dns 209.165.201.2
```

Note: Other parameters can be specified for clients, such as WINS server, lease length, and domain name.

c. Enable the DHCP daemon within the ASA to listen for DHCP client requests on the enabled interface (inside):

```
CCNAS-ASA(config)# dhcpd enable inside
```

d. Verify the DHCP daemon configuration by using the **`show run dhcpd`** command:

```
CCNAS-ASA(config)# show run dhcpd
dhcpd address 192.168.1.5-192.168.1.36 inside
dhcpd enable inside
```

e. Access the network connection IP properties for PC-B and change it from a static IP address to a DHCP client so that it obtains an IP address automatically from the ASA DHCP server. The procedure to do this varies depending on the PC operating system. It might be necessary to issue the **`ipconfig /renew`** command on PC-B to force it obtain a new IP address from the ASA.

Step 2: Configure AAA to use the local database for authentication.

a. Define a local user named **admin** by entering the **username** command. Specify a password of **cisco123**.

```
CCNAS-ASA(config)# username admin password cisco123
```

b. Configure AAA to use the local ASA database for Telnet and SSH user authentication:

```
CCNAS-ASA(config)# aaa authentication ssh console LOCAL
CCNAS-ASA(config)# aaa authentication telnet console LOCAL
```

Note: For added security, starting in ASA Version 8.4(2), it is necessary to configure AAA authentication to support SSH connections. The Telnet/SSH default login is not supported. You can no longer connect to the ASA using SSH with the default username and the login password.

Step 3: Configure SSH remote access to the ASA.

You can configure the ASA to accept SSH connections from a single host or a range of hosts on the inside or outside network.

a. Generate an RSA key pair, which is required to support SSH connections. The modulus (in bits) can be 512, 768, 1024, or 2048. The larger the key modulus size you specify, the longer it takes to generate an RSA. Specify a modulus of 1024 using the **crypto key** command:

```
CCNAS-ASA(config)# crypto key generate rsa modulus 1024
INFO: The name for the keys will be: <Default-RSA-Key>
Keypair generation process begin. Please wait...
```

b. Save the RSA keys to persistent flash memory using either the **copy run start** or **write mem** command.

```
CCNAS-ASA# write mem
Building configuration...
Cryptochecksum: 3c845d0f b6b8839a f9e43be0 33feb4ef
3270 bytes copied in 0.890 secs
[OK]
```

c. Configure the ASA to allow SSH connections from any host on the inside network 192.168.1.0/24 and from the remote management host at the branch office (172.16.3.3) on the outside network. Set the SSH timeout to 10 minutes (the default is 5 minutes).

```
CCNAS-ASA(config)# ssh 192.168.1.0 255.255.255.0 inside
CCNAS-ASA(config)# ssh 172.16.3.3 255.255.255.255 outside
CCNAS-ASA(config)# ssh timeout 10
```

d. On PC-C, use an SSH client, such as PuTTY, to connect to the ASA outside interface at IP address 209.165.200.226. The first time you connect, you might be prompted by the SSH client to accept the RSA host key of the ASA SSH server. Log in as user admin and provide the password **cisco123**. You also can connect to the ASA inside interface from a PC-B SSH client using IP address 192.168.1.1.

Part 6: Configuring a DMZ, Static NAT, and ACLs

In Part 4 of this lab, you configured address translation using PAT for the inside network. In this part, you create a DMZ on the ASA, configure static NAT to a DMZ server, and apply ACLs to control access to the server.

To accommodate the addition of a DMZ and a web server, you will use another address from the ISP range assigned, 209.165.200.224/29 (.224–.231). Router R1 Fa0/0 and the ASA outside interface are already using

209.165.200.225 and .226, respectively. You will use public address 209.165.200.227 and static NAT to provide address translation access to the DMZ web server.

Step 1: Configure the DMZ interface on the ASA.

a. Configure DMZ interface E0/2, which is on the LAN where the public access web server will reside. Assign the interface IP address **192.168.2.1/24**, name it **dmz**, assign it a security level of **70** and bring it up.

Note: If you are working with the ASA 5510 base license, you will not get an error message as with the 5505 base license, which is DMZ-restricted. This is not an issue if you are working with the ASA 5510.

```
CCNAS-ASA(config)# interface e0/2
CCNAS-ASA(config-if)# ip address 192.168.2.1 255.255.255.0
CCNAS-ASA(config-if)# nameif dmz
INFO: Security level for "dmz" set to 0 by default.

CCNAS-ASA(config-if)# security-level 70
CCNAS-ASA(config-if)# no shut
```

b. Display the status for all ASA interfaces using the **show interface ip brief** command:

```
CCNAS-ASA # show interface ip brief
Interface        IP-Address        OK?  Method Status
Protocol
Ethernet0/0      209.165.200.226   YES  manual up                    up
Ethernet0/1      192.168.1.1       YES  manual up                    up
Ethernet0/2      192.168.2.1       YES  manual up                    up
Ethernet0/3      unassigned        YES  unset  administratively down down
Management0/0    unassigned        YES  unset  administratively down down
```

c. Display the information for the Layer 3 interfaces using the **show ip address** command:

```
CCNAS-ASA # show ip address
<output omitted>

Current IP Addresses:
Interface        Name          IP address         Subnet mask        Method
Ethernet0/0      outside       209.165.200.226    255.255.255.248    manual
Ethernet0/1      inside        192.168.1.1        255.255.255.0      manual
Ethernet0/2      dmz           192.168.2.1        255.255.255.0      manual
```

Step 2: Configure static NAT to the DMZ server using a network object.

Configure a network object named **dmz-server** and assign it the static IP address of the DMZ server (192.168.2.3). While in object definition mode, use the **nat** command to specify that this object is used to translate a DMZ address to an outside address using static NAT and specify a public translated address of 209.165.200.227.

```
CCNAS-ASA(config)# object network dmz-server
CCNAS-ASA(config-network-object)# host 192.168.2.3
CCNAS-ASA(config-network-object)# nat (dmz,outside) static 209.165.200.227
```

Step 3: Configure an ACL to allow access to the DMZ server from the Internet.

Configure a named access list OUTSIDE-DMZ that permits any IP protocol from any external host to the internal IP address of the DMZ server. Apply the access list to the ASA outside interface in the "IN" direction.

```
CCNAS-ASA(config)# access-list OUTSIDE-DMZ permit ip any host 192.168.2.3
CCNAS-ASA(config)# access-group OUTSIDE-DMZ in interface outside
```

Note: Unlike IOS ACLs, the ASA ACL **`permit`** statement must permit access to the internal private DMZ address. External hosts access the server using its public static NAT address, and the ASA translates it to the internal host IP address and applies the ACL.

You can modify this ACL to allow only services that you want to be exposed to external hosts, such as web (HTTP) or file transfer (FTP).

Step 4: Test access to the DMZ server.

a. Create a loopback 0 interface on Internet router R2 representing an external host. Assign Lo0 IP address 172.30.1.1 and a mask of 255.255.255.0. Ping the DMZ server public address from R2 using the loopback interface as the source of the ping. The pings should be successful.

```
R2(config-if)# interface Lo0
R2(config-if)# ip address 172.30.1.1 255.255.255.0

R2# ping 209.165.200.227 source lo0

Type escape sequence to abort.
Sending 5, 100-byte ICMP Echos to 209.165.200.227, timeout is 2
seconds:
Packet sent with a source address of 172.30.1.1
!!!!!
Success rate is 100 percent (5/5), round-trip min/avg/max = 1/2/4 ms
```

b. Clear the NAT counters using the **`clear nat counters`** command:

```
CCNAS-ASA# clear nat counters
```

c. Ping from PC-C to the DMZ server at the public address 209.165.200.227. The pings should be successful.

d. Issue the **`show nat`** and **`show xlate`** commands on the ASA to see the effect of the pings. Both the PAT (inside to outside) and static NAT (dmz to outside) policies are shown.

```
CCNAS-ASA# show nat

Auto NAT Policies (Section 2)
1 (dmz) to (outside) source static dmz-server 209.165.200.227
    translate_hits = 0, untranslate_hits = 4

2 (inside) to (outside) source dynamic inside-net interface
    translate_hits = 4, untranslate_hits = 0
```

Note: Pings from inside to outside are translated hits. Pings from outside host PC-C to the DMZ are considered untranslated hits.

```
CCNAS-ASA# show xlate
1 in use, 3 most used
Flags: D - DNS, i - dynamic, r - portmap, s - static, I - identity, T -
twice
NAT from dmz:192.168.2.3 to outside:209.165.200.227 flags s idle
0:22:58 timeout 0:00:00
```

Note that the flag this time is **s**, indicating a static translation.

e. Because the ASA inside interface E0/1 is set to a security level of 100 (the highest) and the DMZ interface E0/2 is set to 70, you can also access the DMZ server from a host on the inside network. The ASA acts like a router between the two networks. Ping the DMZ server (PC-A) internal address (192.168.2.3) from inside network host PC-B (192.168.1.X). The pings should be successful due to the interface security level and the fact that ICMP is being inspected on the inside interface by the global inspection policy. The pings from PC-B to PC-A will not affect the NAT translation counts because both PC-B and PC-A are behind the firewall, and no translation takes place.

f. The DMZ server cannot ping PC-B on the inside network because the DMZ interface E0/2 has a lower security level (70) than inside interface E0/1 (100). Try to ping from the DMZ server PC-A to PC-B at IP address 192.168.1.X. The pings should not be successful.

g. Use the **show run** command to display the configuration for interface E0/2:

```
CCNAS-ASA# show run interface e0/2
!
interface Ethernet0/2
 nameif dmz
 security-level 70
 ip address 192.168.2.1 255.255.255.0
```

Note: An access list can be applied to the inside interface to control the type of access to be permitted or denied to the DMZ server from inside hosts.

Reflection

1. How does the configuration of the ASA firewall differ from that of an ISR?

____

____

2. What does the ASA use to define address translation, and what is the benefit?

____

____

3. How does the ASA 5510 use logical and physical interfaces to manage security, and how does this differ from the 5505 model?

____

____

____

Router Interface Summary Table

Router Model	Ethernet Interface 1	Ethernet Interface 2	Serial Interface 1	Serial Interface 2
1800	Fast Ethernet 0/0 (Fa0/0)	Fast Ethernet 0/1 (Fa0/1)	Serial 0/0/0 (S0/0/0)	Serial 0/0/1 (S0/0/1)
1900	Gigabit Ethernet 0/0 (G0/0)	Gigabit Ethernet 0/1 (G0/1)	Serial 0/0/0 (S0/0/0)	Serial 0/0/1 (S0/0/1)
2800	Fast Ethernet 0/0 (Fa0/0)	Fast Ethernet 0/1 (Fa0/1)	Serial 0/0/0 (S0/0/0)	Serial 0/0/1 (S0/0/1)
2900	Gigabit Ethernet 0/0 (G0/0)	Gigabit Ethernet 0/1 (G0/1)	Serial 0/0/0 (S0/0/0)	Serial 0/0/1 (S0/0/1)

Note: To find out how the router is configured, look at the interfaces to identify the type of router and how many interfaces the router has. There is no way to effectively list all the combinations of configurations for each router class. This table includes identifiers for the possible combinations of Ethernet and serial interfaces in the device. The table does not include any other type of interface, even though a specific router may contain one. An example of this might be an ISDN BRI interface. The string in parenthesis is the legal abbreviation that can be used in Cisco IOS commands to represent the interface.

Chapter 10 Lab F: Configuring ASA 5510 Basic Settings and Firewall Using ASDM

Topology

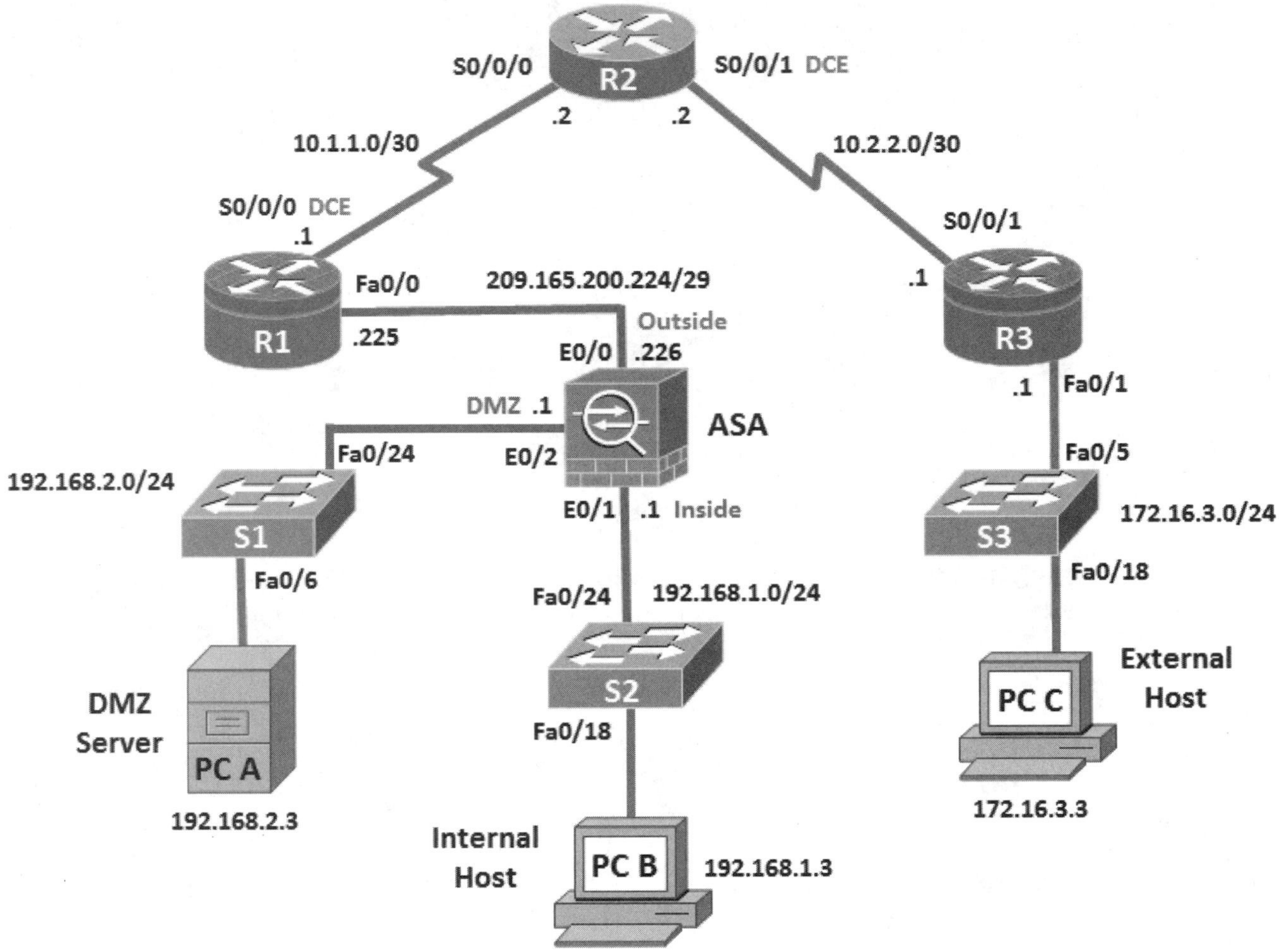

Note: ISR G2 devices have Gigabit Ethernet interfaces rather than FastEthernet interfaces.

IP Addressing Table

Device	Interface	IP Address	Subnet Mask	Default Gateway	Switch Port
R1	Fa0/0	209.165.200.225	255.255.255.248	N/A	ASA E0/0
	S0/0/0 (DCE)	10.1.1.1	255.255.255.252	N/A	N/A
R2	S0/0/0	10.1.1.2	255.255.255.252	N/A	N/A
	S0/0/1 (DCE)	10.2.2.2	255.255.255.252	N/A	N/A
R3	Fa0/1	172.16.3.1	255.255.255.0	N/A	S3 Fa0/5
	S0/0/1	10.2.2.1	255.255.255.252	N/A	N/A
ASA	E0/0 (outside)	209.165.200.226	255.255.255.248	NA	R1 Fa0/0
	E0/1 (inside)	192.168.1.1	255.255.255.0	NA	S2 Fa0/24
	E0/2 (dmz)	192.168.2.1	255.255.255.0	NA	S1 Fa0/24
PC-A	NIC	192.168.2.3	255.255.255.0	192.168.2.1	S1 Fa0/6
PC-B	NIC	192.168.1.3	255.255.255.0	192.168.1.1	S2 Fa0/18
PC-C	NIC	172.16.3.3	255.255.255.0	172.16.3.1	S3 Fa0/18

Objectives

Part 1: Lab Setup

- Cable the network as shown in the topology.
- Configure hostnames and interface IP addresses for routers, switches, and PCs.
- Configure static routing, including default routes, between R1, R2, and R3.
- Configure HTTP and Telnet access for R1.
- Verify connectivity between hosts, switches, and routers.

Part 2: Accessing the ASA Console and ASDM

- Access the ASA console and view hardware, software, and configuration settings.
- Clear previous configuration settings.
- Use CLI to configure settings for ASDM access.
- Test Ethernet and Layer 3 connectivity to the ASA.
- Access the ASDM GUI and explore major windows and options.

Part 3: Configuring ASA Settings and Firewall Using the ASDM Startup Wizard

- Configure the hostname, domain name, and enable password.
- Configure the inside and outside interfaces.
- Configure DHCP for the inside network.
- Configure port address translation (PAT) for the inside network.
- Configure Telnet and SSH administrative access.

Part 4: Configuring ASA Settings from the ASDM Configuration Menu

- Set the date and time.
- Configure a static default route for the ASA.
- Test connectivity using ASDM Ping and Traceroute.
- Configure Local AAA user authentication.
- Modify the MPF application inspection policy.

Part 5: Configuring a DMZ, Static NAT and ACLs

- Configure static NAT for the DMZ server.
- Configure an ACL on the ASA to allow access to the DMZ for Internet users.
- Verify access to the DMZ server for external and internal users.
- Use ASDM Monitor to graph traffic.

Background/Scenario

The Cisco Adaptive Security Appliance (ASA) is an advanced network security device that integrates a stateful firewall as well as VPN and other capabilities. This lab employs an ASA 5510 to create a firewall and protect an internal corporate network from external intruders while allowing internal hosts access to the Internet. The ASA creates three security interfaces: Outside, Inside, and DMZ. It provides outside users limited access to the DMZ and no access to internal resources. Inside users can access the DMZ and outside resources.

The focus of this lab is on the configuration of the ASA as a basic firewall. Other devices will receive minimal configuration to support the ASA portion of the lab. This lab uses the ASA GUI interface ASDM, which is similar to the SDM and CCP used with Cisco ISRs, to configure basic device and security settings.

In Part 1 of the lab you configure the topology and non-ASA devices. In Part 2, you prepare the ASA for ADSM access. In Part 3, you use the ASDM Startup Wizard to configure basic ASA settings and the firewall between the inside and outside networks. In Part 4, you configure additional settings via the ASDM configuration menu. In Part 5, you configure a DMZ on the ASA and provide access to a server in the DMZ.

Your company has one location connected to an ISP. Router R1 represents a CPE device managed by the ISP. Router R2 represents an intermediate Internet router. Router R3 connects an administrator from a network management company who has been hired to manage your network remotely. The ASA is an edge CPE security device that connects the internal corporate network and DMZ to the ISP while providing NAT and DHCP services to inside hosts. The ASA will be configured for management by an administrator on the internal network as well as the remote administrator. ASA Layer 3 routed interfaces provide access to the three areas created in the lab: Inside, Outside, and DMZ. The ISP has assigned the public IP address space of 209.165.200.224/29, which will be used for address translation on the ASA.

Note: The routers used with this lab are Cisco 1841 with Cisco IOS Software Release 12.4(20)T (advanced IP image). The switches are Cisco WS-C2960-24TT-L with Cisco IOS Software Release 12.2(46)SE (C2960-LANBASEK9-M image). Other routers, switches, and Cisco IOS versions can be used; however, results and output might vary.

The ASA used with this lab is a Cisco model 5510 with four FastEthernet routed interfaces running OS Version 8.4(2) and ASDM Version 6.4(5) and comes with a Base license that allows a maximum of 50 VLANs.

Note: Make sure that the routers and switches have been erased and have no startup configurations.

Required Resources

- 3 routers (Cisco 1841 with Cisco IOS Software Release 12.4(20)T1 or comparable)
- 3 switches (Cisco 2960 or comparable)
- 1 ASA 5510 (OS Version 8.4(2) and ASDM Version 6.4(5) and Base license or comparable)
- PC-A: Windows XP, Vista, or Windows 7 with CCP, PuTTy SSH client (Web and FTP server optional)
- PC-B: Windows XP, Vista, or Windows 7 with PuTTy SSH client and Java Version 6.x or higher (ASDM loaded on the PC is optional)
- PC-C: Windows XP, Vista, or Windows 7 with CCP, PuTTy SSH client
- Serial and Ethernet cables as shown in the topology
- Rollover cables to configure the routers and ASA via the console

Part 1: Basic Router/Switch/PC Configuration

In Part 1 of this lab, you set up the network topology and configure basic settings on the routers such as interface IP addresses and static routing.

Note: Do not configure any ASA settings at this time.

Step 1: Cable the network and clear previous device settings.

Attach the devices that are shown in the topology diagram, and cable as necessary. Make sure that the routers and switches have been erased and have no startup configurations.

Step 2: Configure basic settings for routers and switches.

a. Configure hostnames as shown in the topology for each router.

b. Configure router interface IP addresses as shown in the IP addressing table.

c. Configure a clock rate for routers with a DCE serial cable attached to the serial interface.

d. Configure the hostname for the switches. With the exception of the hostname, the switches can be left in their default configuration state. Configuring the VLAN management IP address for the switches is optional.

Step 3: Configure static routing on the routers.

a. Configure a static default route from R1 to R2 and from R3 to R2:

```
R1(config)# ip route 0.0.0.0 0.0.0.0 Serial0/0/0
R3(config)# ip route 0.0.0.0 0.0.0.0 Serial0/0/1
```

b. Configure a static route from R2 to the R1 Fa0/0 subnet (connected to ASA interface E0/0) and a static route from R2 to the R3 LAN:

```
R2(config)# ip route 209.165.200.224 255.255.255.248 Serial0/0/0
R2(config)# ip route 172.16.3.0 255.255.255.0 Serial0/0/1
```

Step 4: Enable the HTTP server on R1 and set the enable and vty passwords.

a. Enable HTTP access to R1 using the **ip http server** command in global config mode. Configure an enable password of **class**. Also set the vty and console passwords to **cisco**. This will provide web and Telnet targets for testing later in the lab.

```
R1(config)# ip http server
R1(config)# enable password class

R1(config)# line vty 0 4
R1(config-line)# password cisco
R1(config-line)# login

R1(config)# line con 0
R1(config-line)# password cisco
R1(config-line)# login
```

b. On routers R2 and R3, set the same enable, console and vty passwords as with R1.

Step 5: Configure PC host IP settings.

Configure a static IP address, subnet mask, and default gateway for PC-A, PC-B, and PC-C as shown in the IP addressing table.

Step 6: Verify connectivity.

Because the ASA is the focal point for the network zones and it has not yet been configured, there will be no connectivity between devices that are connected to it. However, PC-C should be able to ping the Fa0/0 interface of R1. From PC-C, **ping** the R1 Fa0/0 IP address (209.165.200.225). If these pings are not successful, troubleshoot the basic device configurations before continuing.

Note: If you can ping from PC-C to R1 Fa0/0 and S0/0/0, you have demonstrated that static routing is configured and functioning correctly.

Step 7: Save the basic running configuration for each router and switch.

Part 2: Accessing the ASA Console and ASDM

In Part 2 of this lab, you access the ASA via the console and use various **show** commands to determine hardware, software, and configuration settings. You prepare the ASA for ASDM access and explore some of the ASDM screens and options.

Step 1: Access the ASA console.

a. Accessing the ASA via the console port is the same as with a Cisco router or switch. Connect to the ASA console port with a rollover cable.

b. Use a terminal emulation program, such as TeraTerm or HyperTerminal, to access the CLI. Use the serial port settings of 9600 baud, 8 data bits, no parity, 1 stop bit, and no flow control.

c. If prompted to enter interactive firewall configuration (Setup mode), answer **no**.

d. Enter privileged mode with the **enable** command and password (if set). By default, the password is blank, so you can just press **Enter**. If the password has been changed to that specified in this lab, the password will be **class**. In addition, the hostname and prompt will be `CCNAS-ASA>`, as shown here. The default ASA hostname and prompt is `ciscoasa>`.

```
CCNAS-ASA> enable
Password: class (or press Enter if none set)
```

Step 2: Determine the ASA version, interfaces, and license.

The ASA 5510 used in this lab has four integrated 10/100 FastEthernet interfaces (E0/0–E0/3). Unlike the 5505 model, these are Layer 3 routed interfaces similar to those in an ISR. In addition, a special Management FastEthernet interface (M0/0) is also provided, which is not present on the ASA 5505.

Use the **show version** command to determine various aspects of this ASA device.

```
CCNAS-ASA# show version

Cisco Adaptive Security Appliance Software Version 8.4(2)
Device Manager Version 6.4(5)

Compiled on Wed 15-Jun-11 18:17 by builders
System image file is "disk0:/asa842-k8.bin"
Config file at boot was "startup-config"

CCNAS-ASA up 24 mins 5 secs

Hardware:   ASA5510, 1024 MB RAM, CPU Pentium 4 Celeron 1599 MHz
Internal ATA Compact Flash, 256MB
BIOS Flash M50FW016 @ 0xfff00000, 2048KB

Encryption hardware device : Cisco ASA-55x0 on-board accelerator (revision
0x0)
                             Boot microcode        : CN1000-MC-BOOT-2.00
                             SSL/IKE microcode     : CNLite-MC-SSLm-PLUS-2.03
                             IPSec microcode       : CNlite-MC-IPSECm-MAIN-
2.06
                             Number of accelerators: 1

 0: Ext: Ethernet0/0         : address is 44d3.cafd.986c, irq 9
 1: Ext: Ethernet0/1         : address is 44d3.cafd.986d, irq 9
 2: Ext: Ethernet0/2         : address is 44d3.cafd.986e, irq 9
 3: Ext: Ethernet0/3         : address is 44d3.cafd.986f, irq 9
 4: Ext: Management0/0       : address is 44d3.cafd.986b, irq 11
 5: Int: Not used            : irq 11
 6: Int: Not used            : irq 5

Licensed features for this platform:
Maximum Physical Interfaces       : Unlimited      perpetual
Maximum VLANs                     : 50             perpetual
Inside Hosts                      : Unlimited      perpetual
Failover                          : Disabled       perpetual
VPN-DES                           : Enabled        perpetual
VPN-3DES-AES                      : Enabled        perpetual
Security Contexts                 : 0              perpetual
GTP/GPRS                          : Disabled       perpetual
AnyConnect Premium Peers          : 2              perpetual
AnyConnect Essentials             : Disabled       perpetual
Other VPN Peers                   : 250            perpetual
Total VPN Peers                   : 250            perpetual
```

```
Shared License                    : Disabled       perpetual
AnyConnect for Mobile             : Disabled       perpetual
AnyConnect for Cisco VPN Phone    : Disabled       perpetual
Advanced Endpoint Assessment      : Disabled       perpetual
UC Phone Proxy Sessions           : 2              perpetual
Total UC Proxy Sessions           : 2              perpetual
Botnet Traffic Filter             : Disabled       perpetual
Intercompany Media Engine         : Disabled       perpetual

This platform has a Base license.

<output omitted>
```

What software version is this ASA 5510 running? ____________________

What is the name of the system image file, and from where was it loaded? ____________________

____

The ASA can be managed using a built-in GUI known as the Adaptive Security Device Manager (ASDM). Which version of ASDM is this ASA running? ____________________

How much RAM does this ASA have? ____________________

How much flash memory does this ASA have? ____________________

How many Ethernet interfaces does this ASA have? ____________________

What type of license does this ASA have? ____________________

How many VLANs can be created with this license? ____________________

Step 3: Determine the file system and contents of flash memory.

a. Display the ASA file system using the **show file system** command to determine what prefixes are supported:

```
CCNAS-ASA# show file system

File Systems:

      Size(b)     Free(b)      Type      Flags  Prefixes
* 260034560     198070272      disk      rw      disk0: flash:
            -              -   disk      rw      disk1:
            -              -   network   rw      tftp:
            -              -   opaque    rw      system:
            -              -   network   ro      http:
            -              -   network   ro      https:
            -              -   network   rw      ftp:
            -              -   network   rw      smb:
```

What is another name for flash:? ____________

b. Display the contents of flash memory using one of these commands: **show flash**, **show disk0**, **dir flash:** or **dir disk0:**

```
CCNAS-ASA# show flash:
--#--  --length--  -----date/time------  path
```

```
   124   15390720     Oct 19 2011 15:49:48  asa842-k8.bin
   125   16280544     Oct 19 2011 18:22:24  asdm-645.bin
     3   4096         Jan 01 2003 00:03:32  log
    10   4096         Jan 01 2003 00:04:00  crypto_archive
    11   4096         Jan 01 2003 00:04:04  coredumpinfo
    12   43           Jan 01 2003 00:04:04  coredumpinfo/coredump.cfg
   127   12105313     Oct 19 2011 18:07:50  csd_3.5.841-k9.pkg
   128   4096         Oct 19 2011 18:07:52  sdesktop
   135   1462         Oct 19 2011 18:07:52  sdesktop/data.xml
   129   2857568      Oct 19 2011 18:07:54  anyconnect-wince-ARMv4I-
2.4.1012-k9.pkg
   130   3203909      Oct 19 2011 18:07:54  anyconnect-win-2.4.1012-k9.pkg
   131   4832344      Oct 19 2011 18:07:58  anyconnect-macosx-i386-
2.4.1012-k9.pkg
   132   5209423      Oct 19 2011 18:08:00  anyconnect-linux-2.4.1012-
k9.pkg

260034560 bytes total (198070272 bytes free)
```

What is the name of the ASDM file in flash:? ____________________

Step 4: Determine the current running configuration.

The ASA 5510 is commonly used as an edge security device that connects a medium-sized business to an ISP for access to the Internet. The default factory configuration for the ASA 5510 includes the following:

- The management interface, Management 0/0, is configured. If you did not set the IP address using the **configure factory-default** command, the IP address and mask are 192.168.1.1 and 255.255.255.0.

Note: The Management 0/0 interface is a separate physical FastEthernet interface on the ASA 5510. This interface is not present on the ASA 5505.

- The DHCP server is enabled on the security appliance, so a PC connecting to the Management 0/0 interface receives an address between 192.168.1.2 and 192.168.1.254.

Note: With the default factory configuration, it is assumed that the PC connected to Management 0/0 is a DHCP client and will be used to configure the 5510 using the ASDM GUI embedded in flash.

- The HTTP server is enabled for ASDM and is accessible to users on the 192.168.1.0 network.
- No console or enable passwords are required, and the default hostname is ciscoasa.

Note: The default factory configuration only configures the Management 0/0 interface and does not configure an inside or outside network interface.

The configuration consists of the commands listed below.

Note: Do not use these commands to configure the ASA at this time.

```
interface management 0/0
   ip address 192.168.1.1 255.255.255.0
   nameif management
   security-level 100
   no shutdown
logging asdm informational 100
asdm history enable
http server enable
http 192.168.1.0 255.255.255.0 management
```

```
dhcpd address 192.168.1.2-192.168.1.254 management
dhcpd lease 3600
dhcpd ping_timeout 750
dhcpd enable management
```

a. Display the current running configuration using the **show running-config** command. Output will vary depending on the current state of the ASA configuration

```
CCNAS-ASA# show running-config
: Saved
:
ASA Version 8.4(2)
!
hostname CCNAS-ASA
enable password 8Ry2YjIyt7RRXU24 encrypted
passwd 2KFQnbNIdI.2KYOU encrypted
names
!
interface Ethernet0/0
 shutdown
 no nameif
 no security-level
 no ip address
!
<output omitted>
```

Tip: To stop the output from a command using the CLI, press the letter **Q**.

If you see the Management interface configured, and other settings as described previously, the device is most likely configured with the default factory configuration. You might also see other security features, such as a global policy that inspects selected application traffic, which the ASA inserts by default, if the original startup configuration has been erased. The actual output will vary depending on the ASA model, version, and configuration status.

b. You can restore the ASA to its factory default settings by using the **configure factory-default** command from global configuration mode, as shown here:

```
CCNAS-ASA# conf t
CCNAS-ASA(config)# configure factory-default

WARNING: The boot system configuration will be cleared.
The first image found in disk0:/ will be used to boot the
system on the next reload.
Verify there is a valid image on disk0:/ or the system will
not boot.

Begin to apply factory-default configuration:
Clear all configuration
Executing command: interface management0/0
Executing command: nameif management
INFO: Security level for "management" set to 0 by default.
Executing command: ip address 192.168.1.1 255.255.255.0
Executing command: security-level 100
Executing command: no shutdown
Executing command: exit
Executing command: http server enable
Executing command: http 192.168.1.0 255.255.255.0 management
Executing command: dhcpd address 192.168.1.2-192.168.1.254 management
Executing command: dhcpd enable management
```

```
Executing command: logging asdm informational
Factory-default configuration is completed
```

c. Review this output. You might want to capture and print the factory-default configuration as a reference.

Note: Restoring the ASA to factory default settings resets the hostname and prompt to `ciscoasa>`.

Step 5: Clear the previous ASA configuration settings.

a. Use the **`write erase`** command to remove the startup-config file from flash memory.

```
ciscoasa# write erase
Erase configuration in flash memory? [confirm]
[OK]
ciscoasa#

ciscoasa# show start
No Configuration
```

Note: The Cisco IOS command **`erase startup-config`** is not supported on the ASA.

b. Use the **`reload`** command to restart the ASA. If prompted to save the configuration, respond with **no**.

```
ciscoasa# reload
Proceed with reload? [confirm] <Enter>
ciscoasa#
***
*** --- START GRACEFUL SHUTDOWN ---
Shutting down isakmp
Shutting down File system
***
*** --- SHUTDOWN NOW ---
Process shutdown finished
Rebooting.....
CISCO SYSTEMS
Embedded BIOS Version 1.0(12)13 08/28/08 15:50:37.45
<output omitted>
```

Step 6: Bypass setup mode and configure the ASA interfaces.

When the ASA completes the reload process, it should detect that the startup-config file is missing and present a series of interactive prompts to configure basic ASA settings. If it does not come up in this mode, repeat Step 5.

a. When prompted to preconfigure the firewall through interactive prompts (Setup mode), respond with **no**.

```
Pre-configure Firewall now through interactive prompts [yes]? no
```

b. Enter privileged EXEC mode with the **`enable`** command and press Enter. The password should be blank (no password) at this point.

c. Enter global configuration mode using the **`config t`** command. The first time you enter configuration mode after reloading, you are asked whether you want to enable anonymous reporting. Respond with **no**.

ASA 5510 interface notes: The 5510 and other higher-end 5500 series ASA models are different from the ASA 5505 model. With the 5510 model, a physical FastEthernet interface can be assigned a Layer 3 IP address directly, much like a Cisco router. With the ASA 5505 model, the eight integrated switch ports are Layer 2 ports, and VLANs must be created. This is not the case with the 5510. The four FastEthernet interfaces on the 5510 are routed interfaces.

Note: If you completed the initial configuration Setup utility, Management interface M0/0 is configured with an IP address of 192.168.1.1. You will need to remove the IP address from the M0/0 interface to assign it to the inside interface E0/1. Instructions are provide here to configure both the inside (E0/1) and outside (E0/0) interface at this time. The DMZ interface (E0/2) is configured in Part 6 of the lab.

d. Remove the configuration from the M0/0 interface and shut it down (if required):

```
ciscoasa(config)# interface m0/0
ciscoasa(config-if)# shutdown
ciscoasa(config-if)# no nameif
ciscoasa(config-if)# no security-level
ciscoasa(config-if)# no ip address
```

e. Configure interface E0/1 for the inside network, 192.168.1.0/24. Name the interface **inside**, set the security level to the highest setting of **100**, and bring it up:

```
ciscoasa(config)# interface e0/1
ciscoasa(config-if)# nameif inside
ciscoasa(config-if)# ip address 192.168.1.1 255.255.255.0
ciscoasa(config-if)# security-level 100
ciscoasa(config-if)# no shutdown
```

f. Configure interface E0/0 for the outside network, 209.165.200.224/29. Name the interface **outside**, set the security level to the lowest setting of **0**, and bring it up:

```
ciscoasa(config-if)# interface e0/0
ciscoasa(config-if)# nameif outside
ciscoasa(config-if)# ip address 209.165.200.226 255.255.255.248
ciscoasa(config-if)# security-level 0
ciscoasa(config-if)# no shutdown
```

Interface security level notes: You might receive a message that the security level for the inside interface was set automatically to 100 and the outside interface was set to 0. The ASA uses interface security levels from 0 to 100 to enforce the security policy. Security Level 100 (inside) is the most secure, and level 0 (outside) is the least secure.

By default, the ASA applies a policy where traffic from a higher security level interface to one with a lower level is permitted, and traffic from a lower security level interface to one with a higher security level is denied. The ASA default security policy permits outbound traffic, which is inspected by default. Returning traffic is allowed because of stateful packet inspection. This default "routed mode" firewall behavior of the ASA enables packets to be routed from the inside network to the outside network but not vice versa. In Part 3 of this lab, you configure NAT to increase the firewall protection.

g. Use the **`show interface ip brief`** command to ensure that ASA interfaces E0/0 and E0/1 are both up/up. Note that this command is different from the IOS command **`show ip interface brief`**. If either port is shown as down/down, check the physical connections. If either port is administratively down, bring it up with the **`no shutdown`** command.

```
ciscoasa(config-if)# show interface ip brief
Interface          IP-Address        OK?  Method Status
Protocol
Ethernet0/0        209.165.200.226   YES  manual up                        up
Ethernet0/1        192.168.1.1       YES  manual up                        up
Ethernet0/2        unassigned        YES  unset  administratively down up
Ethernet0/3        unassigned        YES  unset  administratively down down
Management0/0      unassigned        YES  unset  administratively down down
```

Tip: Most ASA **show** commands, as well as **ping**, **copy**, and others, can be issued from within any config mode prompt without the **do** command required with IOS.

h. Display the Layer 3 interface information using the **show ip address** command:

```
ciscoasa(config)# show ip address

<output omitted>

Current IP Addresses:
Interface        Name            IP address         Subnet mask          Method
Ethernet0/0      outside         209.165.200.226    255.255.255.248      manual
Ethernet0/1      inside          192.168.1.1        255.255.255.0        Manual
```

i. You also may use the **show running-config interface** command to display the configuration for a particular interface from the running-config:

```
ciscoasa# show run interface e0/0
!
interface Ethernet0/0
 nameif outside
 security-level 0
 ip address 209.165.200.226 255.255.255.248
```

j. Test basic connectivity to the ASA by pinging from PC-B to ASA interface E0/1 IP address 192.168.1.1. The pings should be successful.

Step 7: Configure HTTP and verify ASDM access to the ASA.

a. Configure the ASA to accept HTTPS connections using the **http** command to allow access to ASDM from any host on the inside network 192.168.1.0/24:

```
ciscoasa(config)# http server enable
ciscoasa(config)# http 192.168.1.0 255.255.255.0 inside
```

b. Open a browser on PC-B and test the HTTPS access to the ASA by entering https://192.168.1.1.

Note: Be sure to specify the HTTPS protocol in the URL.

Step 8: Access ASDM and explore the GUI.

a. After entering the URL above, you should see a security warning about the website security certificate. Click **Continue to this website**. The ASDM Welcome page displays. From this screen, you can run ASDM as a local application on the PC (installs ASDM on the PC), run ASDM as a browser-based Java applet directly from the ASA, or run the Startup Wizard.

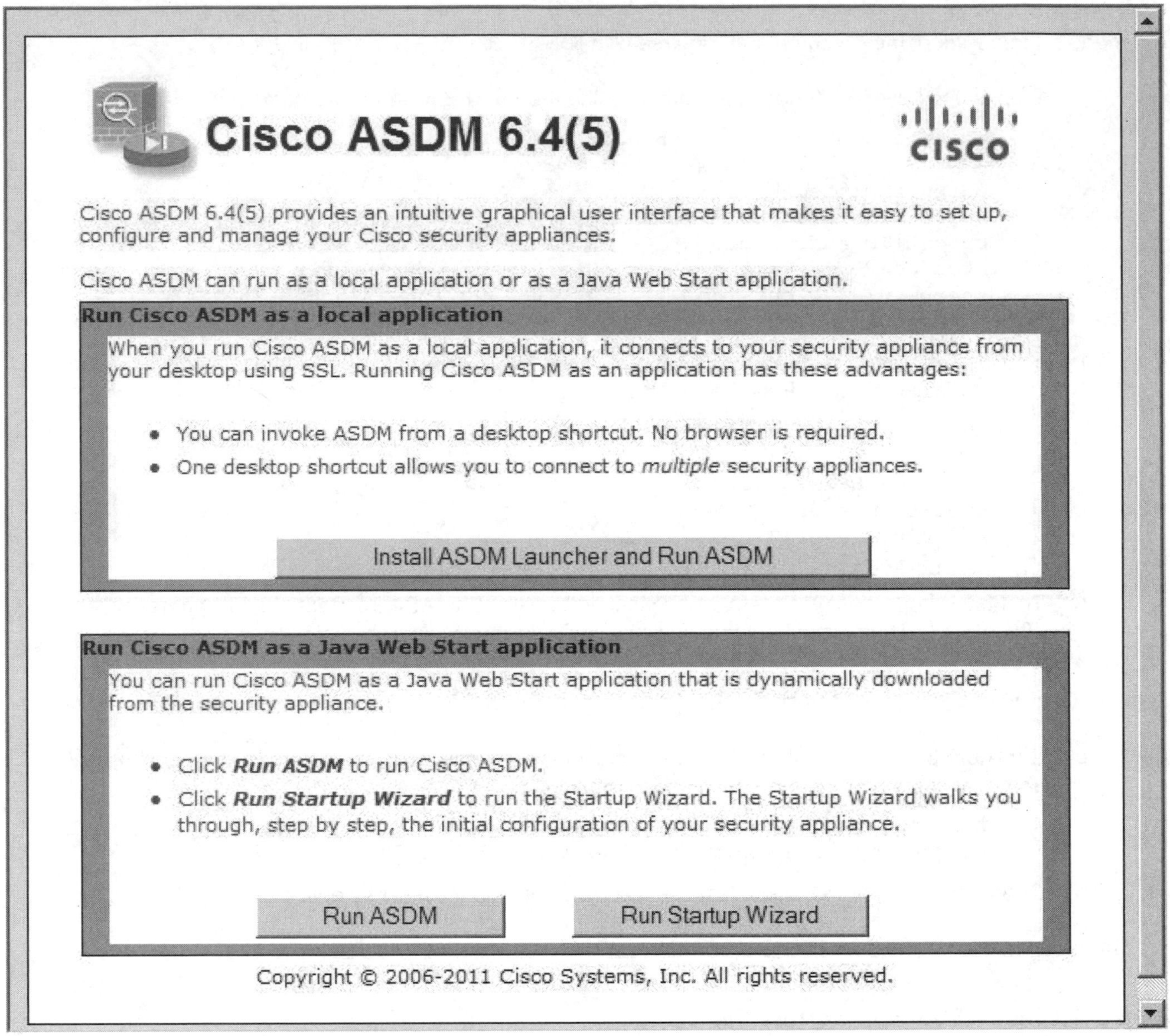

b. Click the **Run ASDM** button.

c. Click **Yes** for any other security warnings. You should see the **Cisco ASDM-IDM Launcher** dialog box, where you can enter a username and password. Leave these fields blank because they have not yet been configured.

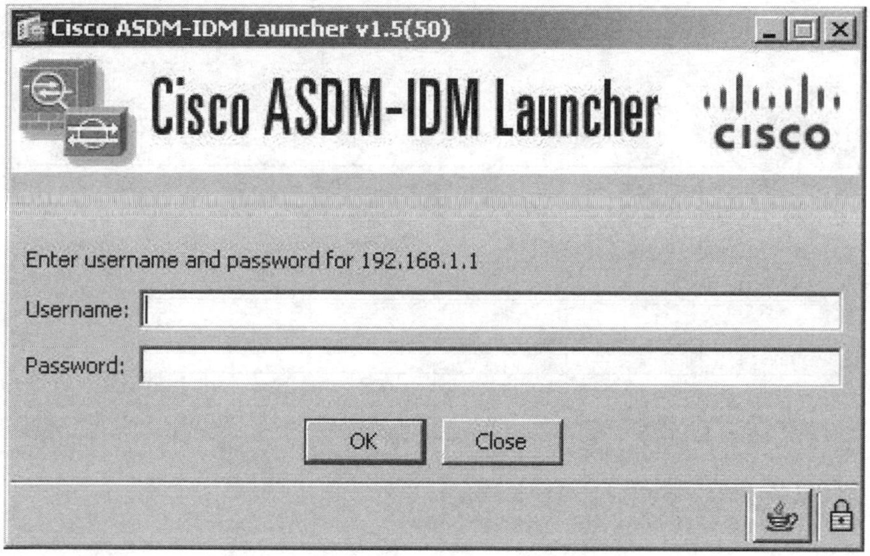

d. Click **OK** to continue. ASDM loads the current configuration into the GUI.

e. The initial GUI screen is displayed with various areas and options. The main menu at the top left of the screen contains three main sections: Home, Configuration, and Monitoring. The Home section is the default and has two dashboards: Device and Firewall. The Device dashboard is the default screen and shows device information such as Type (ASA 5510), ASA and ASDM version, amount of memory, and firewall mode (routed). There are five areas on the Device Dashboard:

- Device Information
- Interface Status
- VPN Sessions
- System Resources Status
- Traffic Status

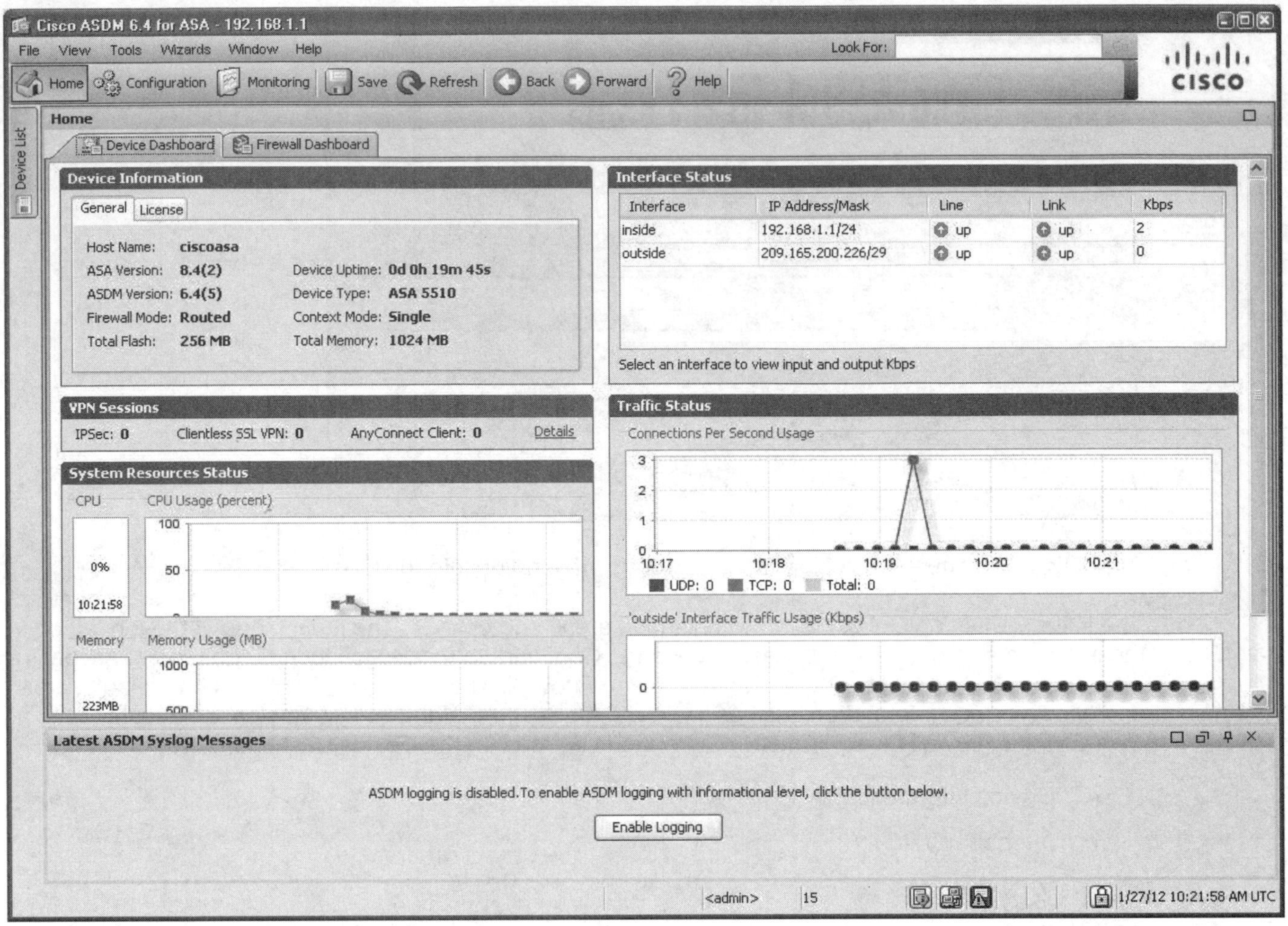

f. Click the **Configuration** and **Monitoring** tabs to become familiar with their layout and to see what options are available.

Part 3: Configuring Basic ASA Settings and Firewall Using the ASDM Startup Wizard

Step 1: Access the Configuration menu and launch the Startup wizard.

a. Click the **Configuration** button at the top left of the screen. There are five main configuration areas:

- Device Setup
- Firewall
- Remote Access VPN
- Site-to-Site VPN
- Device Management

b. The Device Setup Startup Wizard is the first option available and displays by default. Read through the on-screen text describing the Startup Wizard, and then click the **Launch Startup Wizard** button.

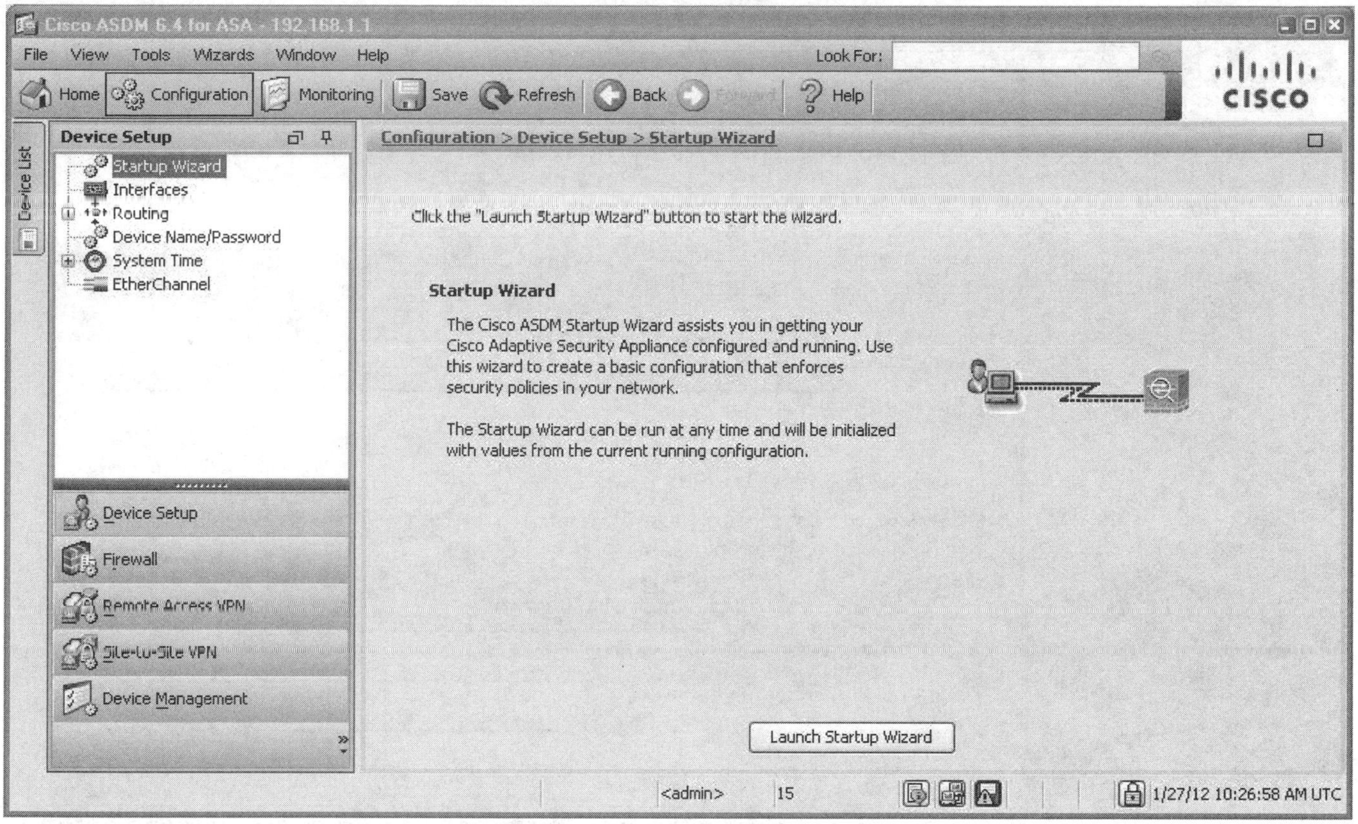

Step 2: Configure hostname, domain name, and enable password.

a. On the first Startup Wizard screen, you have a choice of modifying the existing configuration or resetting the ASA to the factory defaults. With the **Modify Existing Configuration** option selected, click **Next** to continue.

b. On the Startup Wizard Step 2 screen, Basic Configuration, configure the ASA hostname CCNAS-ASA and the domain name of ccnasecurity.com. Click the **Change Privileged Mode (Enable) Password** checkbox and change it from blank (no password) to **class**. Enter it again to confirm. When the entries are completed, click **Next** to continue.

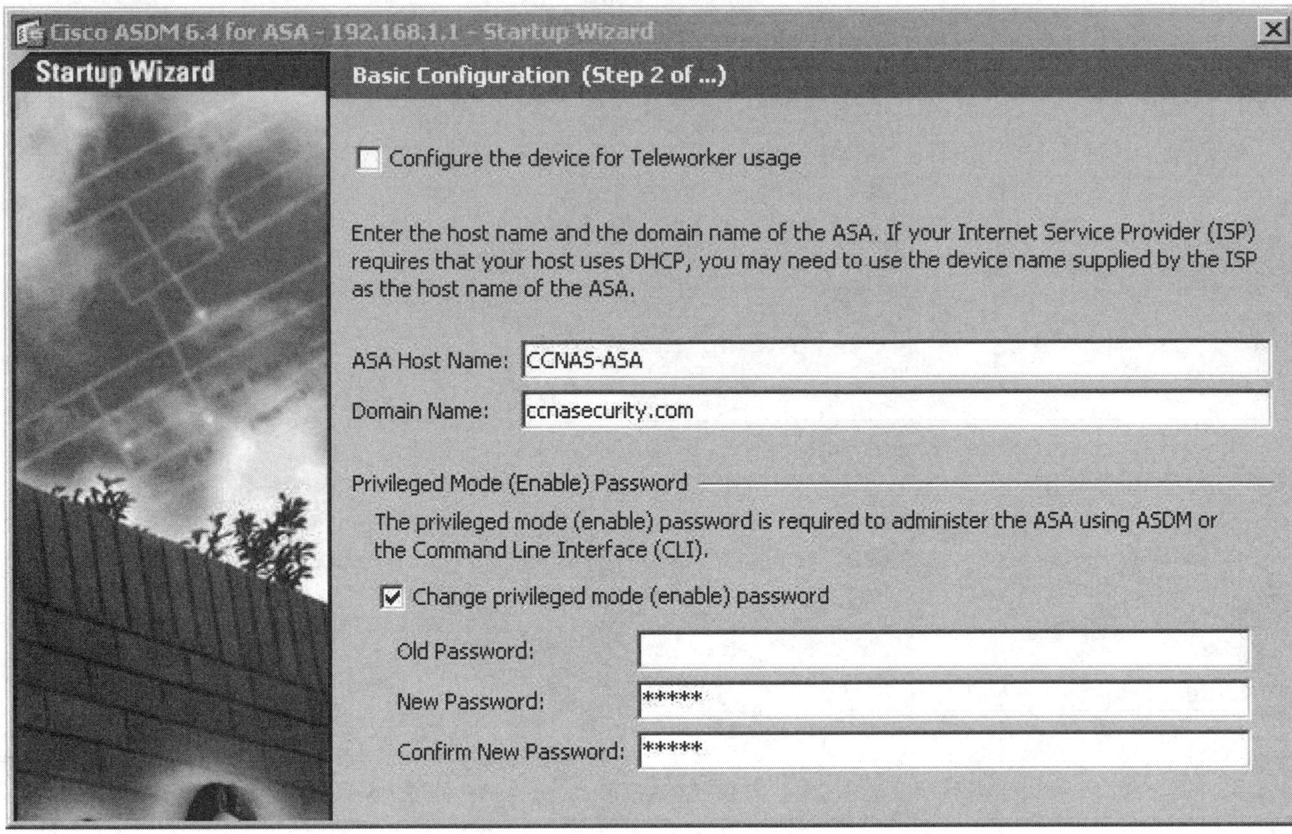

Step 3: Configure the outside interface.

a. On the Startup Wizard Step 3 screen (Outside Interface Configuration) Interface Settings tab, review the interface properties shown. Do not change the current settings because these were previously defined using the CLI. Click **Next** to continue.

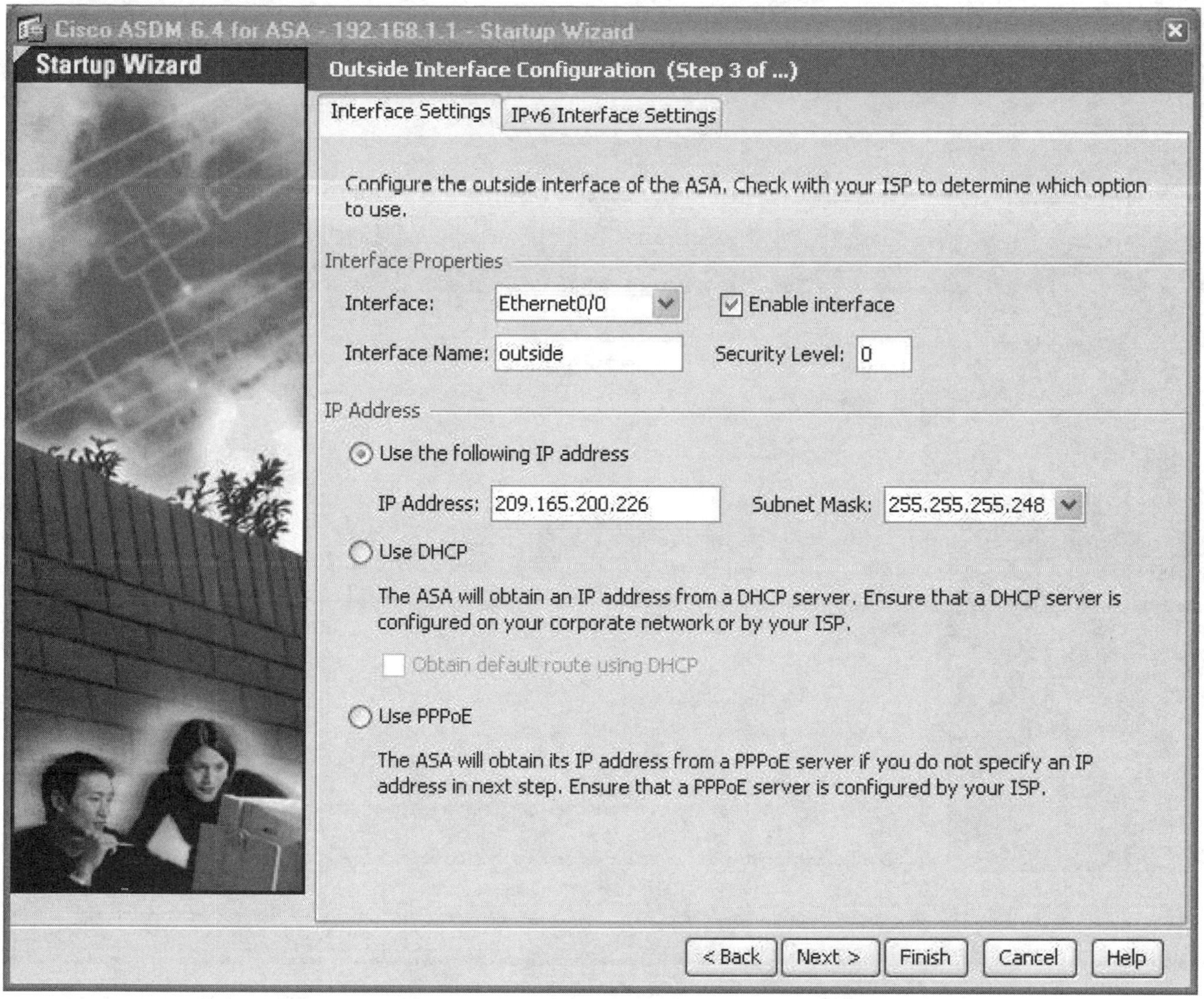

b. On the Startup Wizard Step 4 screen (Other Interface Configuration), verify the settings for the inside interface, which were previously configured via the CLI. You can edit the settings for any of the interfaces from this screen.

Note: Do not check the two boxes for enabling traffic between interfaces of the same security level and hosts on the same interface.

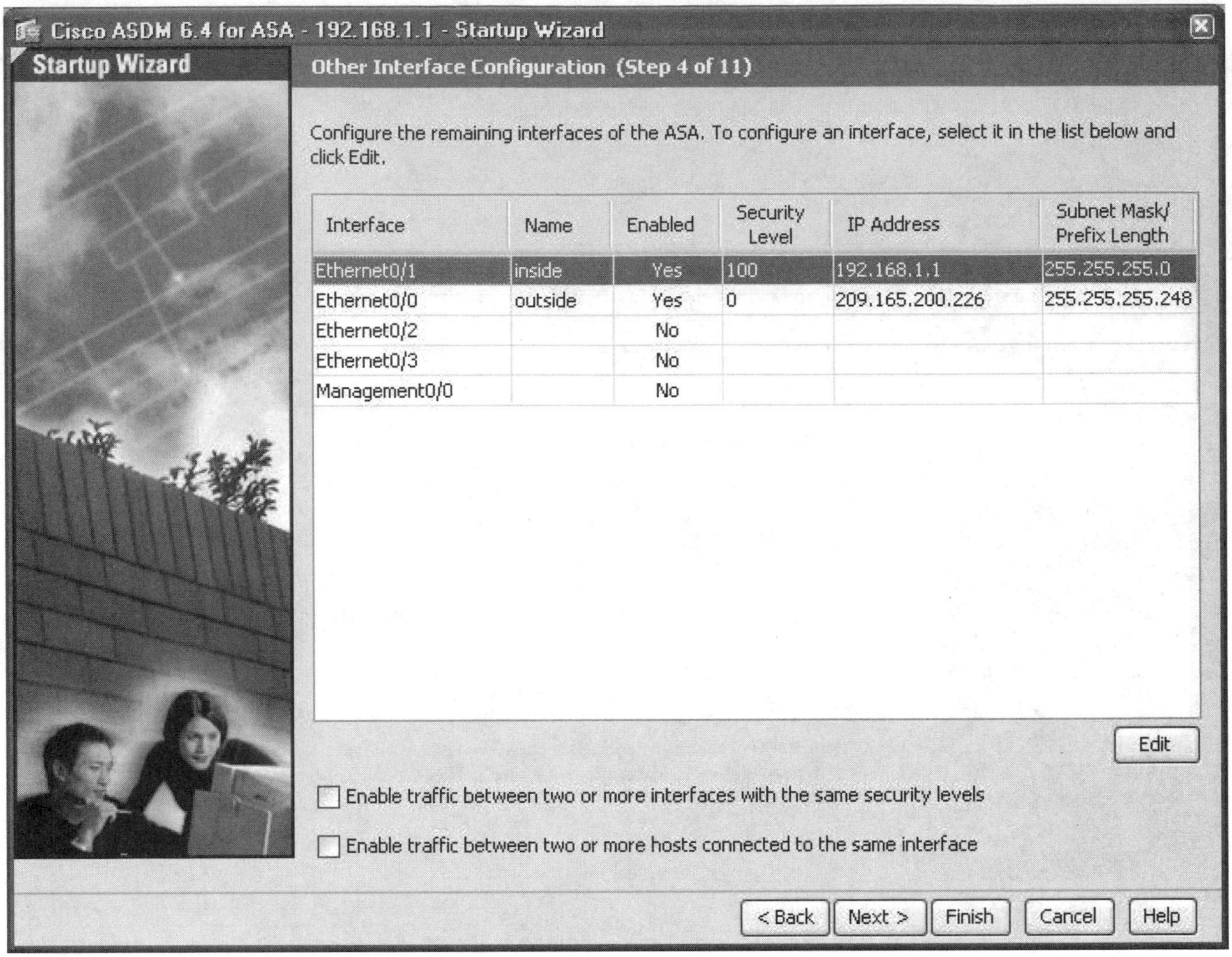

c. On the Startup Wizard Step 5 screen (Static Routes), click **Next** to bypass this wizard option at this time. You configure a static route for the ASA later using the Configuration menu.

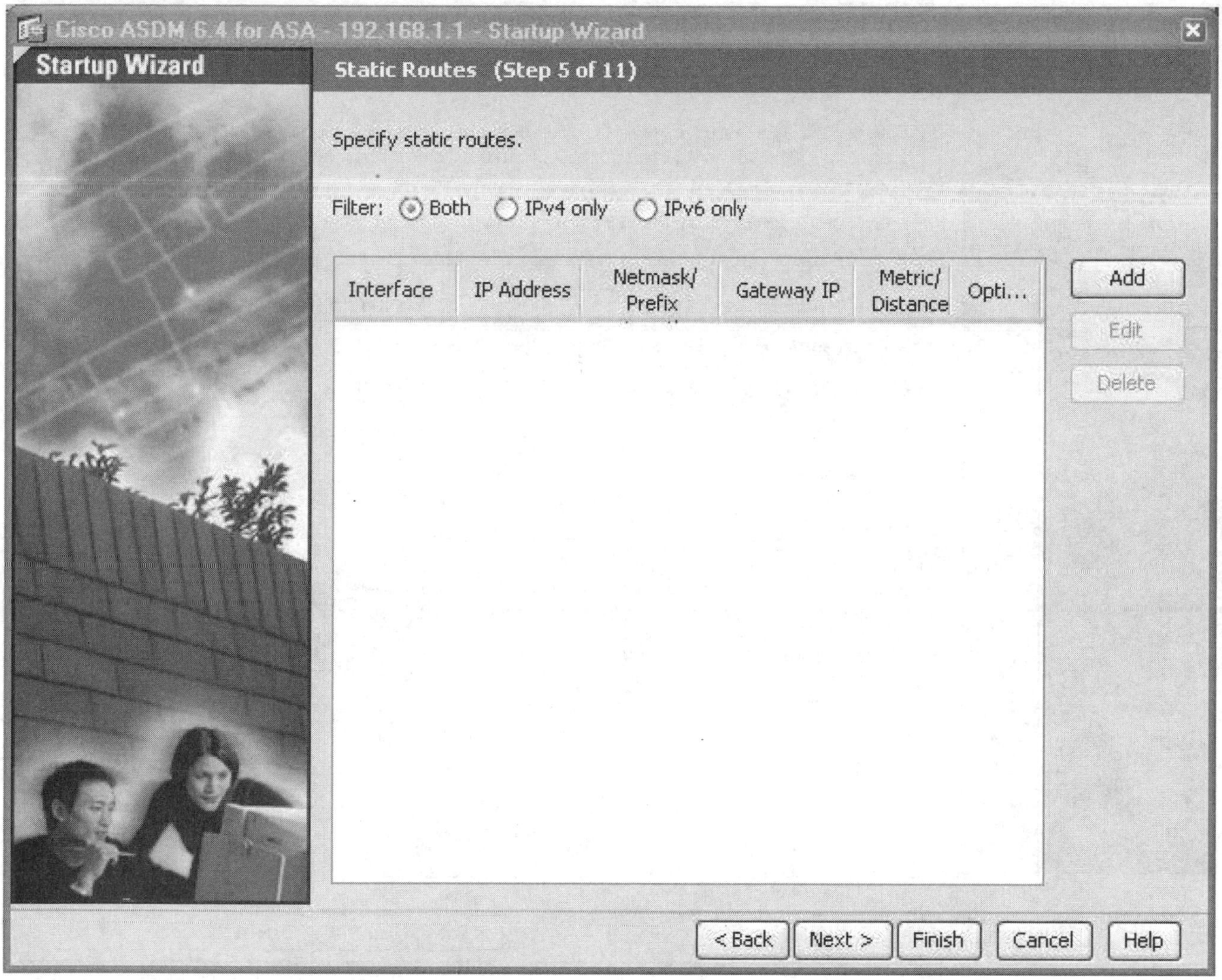

Step 4: Configure DHCP, address translation, and administrative access.

a. On the Startup Wizard Step 6 screen (DHCP Server), select the **Enable DHCP Server on the Inside Interface** checkbox. Enter a starting IP address of **192.168.1.5** and ending IP address of **192.168.1.50**. Enter the DNS server 1 address of **10.20.30.40** and the domain name **ccnasecurity.com**. Do *not* check the Enable Autoconfiguration from Interface box. Click **Next** to continue.

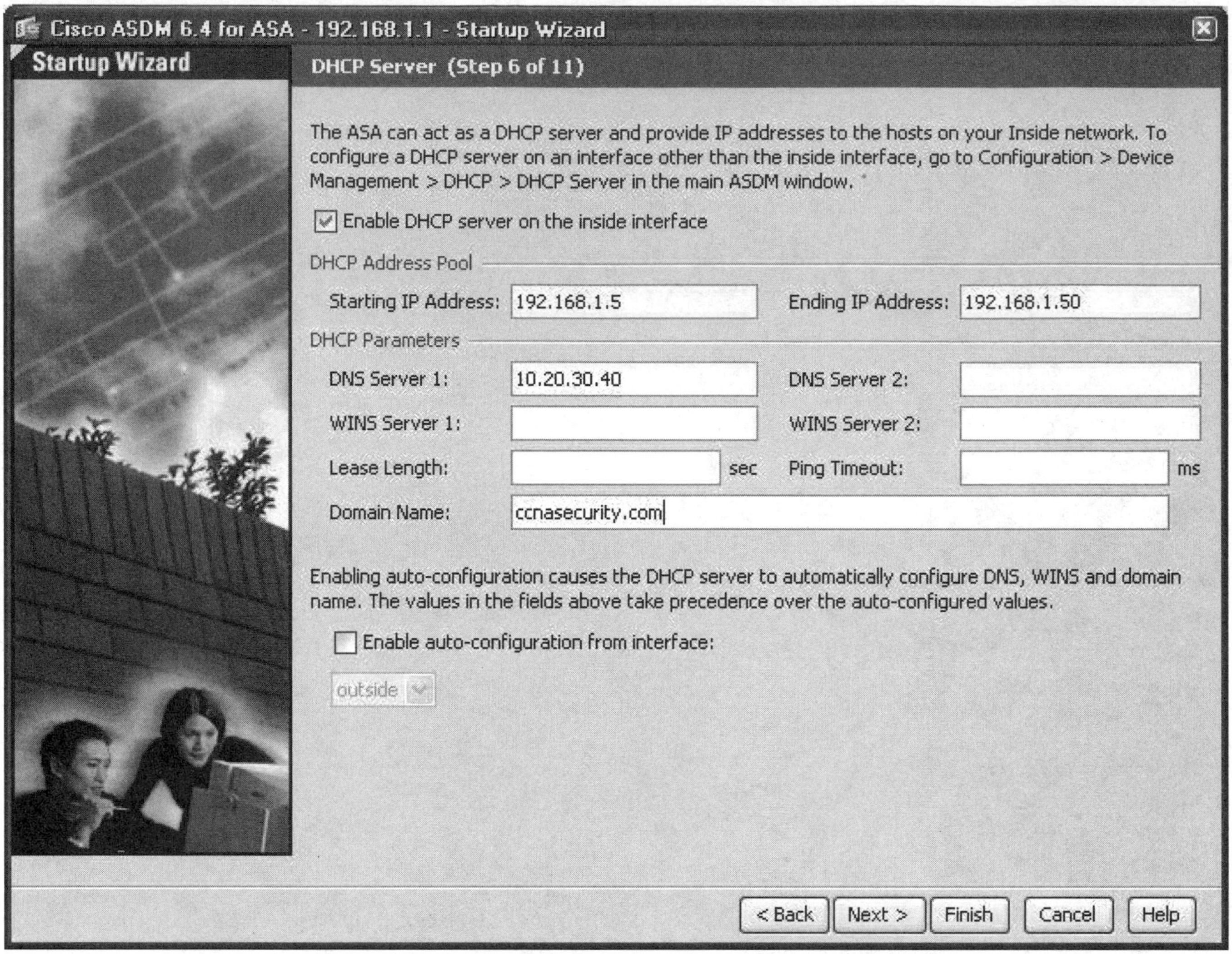

b. On the Startup Wizard Step 7 screen (Address Translation [NAT/PAT]), click the **Use Port Address Translation (PAT)** button. The default is to use the IP address of the outside interface. Note that you can also specify a particular IP address for PAT or a range of addresses with NAT. Click **Next** to continue.

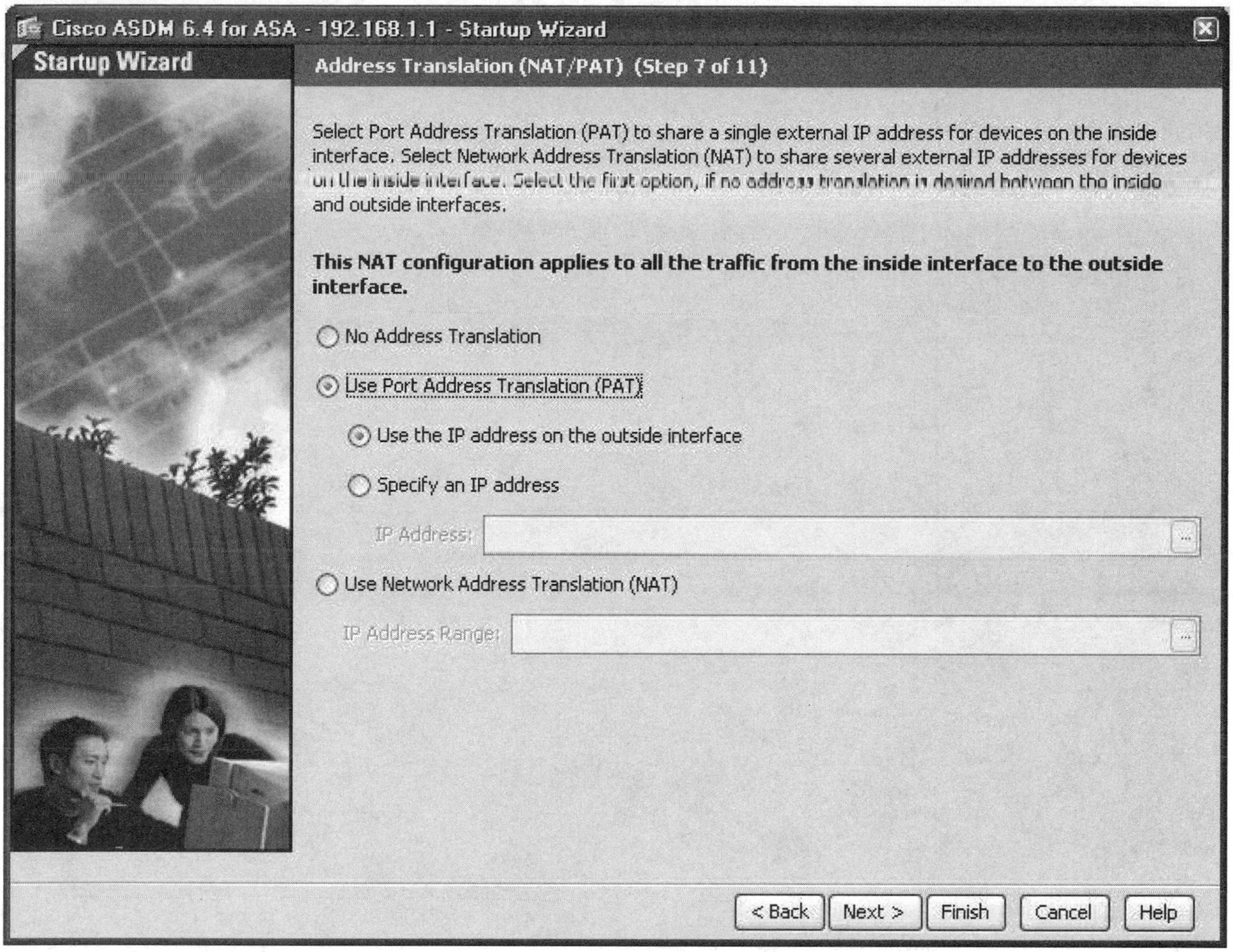

c. On the Startup Wizard Step 8 screen (Administrative Access), HTTPS/ASDM access is currently configured for hosts on inside network 192.168.1.0/24. Add Telnet access to the ASA for the inside network 192.168.1.0 with a subnet mask of 255.255.255.0. Add SSH access to the ASA from host 172.16.3.3 on the outside network. Make sure the **Enable HTTP Server for HTTPS/ASDM Access** box is checked. Click **Next** to continue.

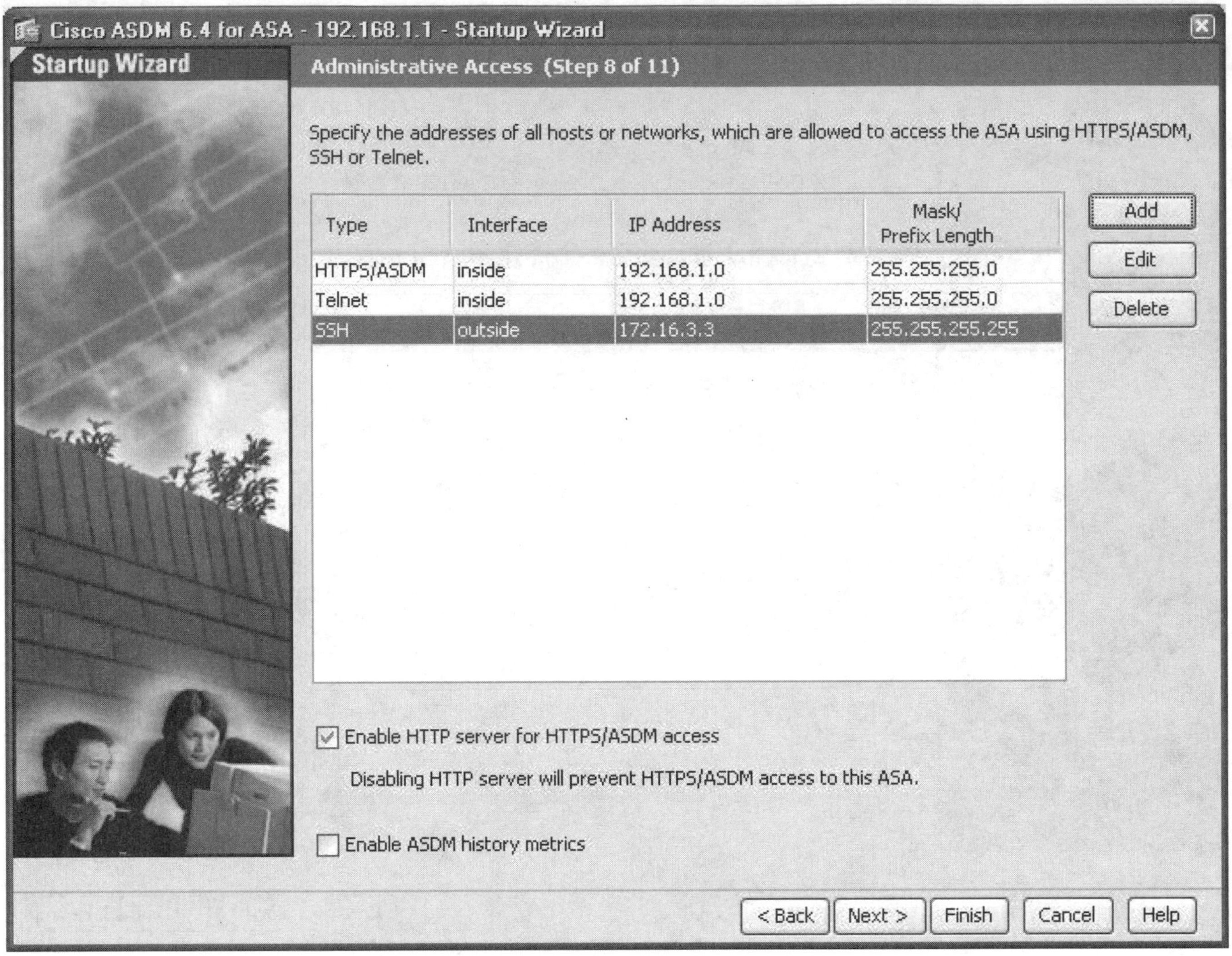

d. On the Startup Wizard Step 9 screen (Auto Update Server), review the on-screen text describing the function of Auto Update, but do not check the Enable Auto Update ASA box. Click **Next** to continue.

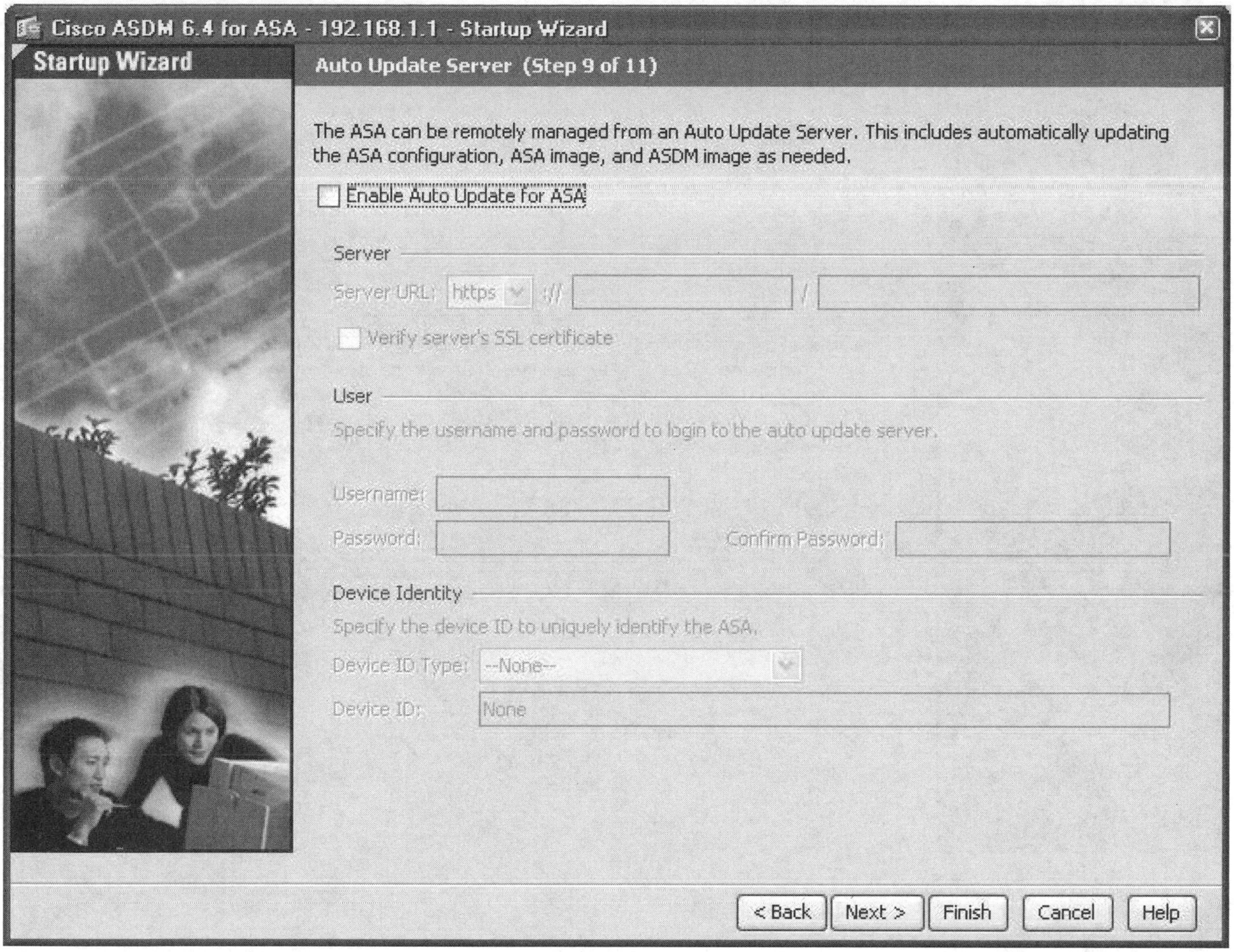

e. On the Startup Wizard Step 10 screen (Cisco Smart Call Home Enrollment), review the on-screen text describing the function of Smart Call Home and leave the default radio button selected to not enable this feature. Click **Next** to continue.

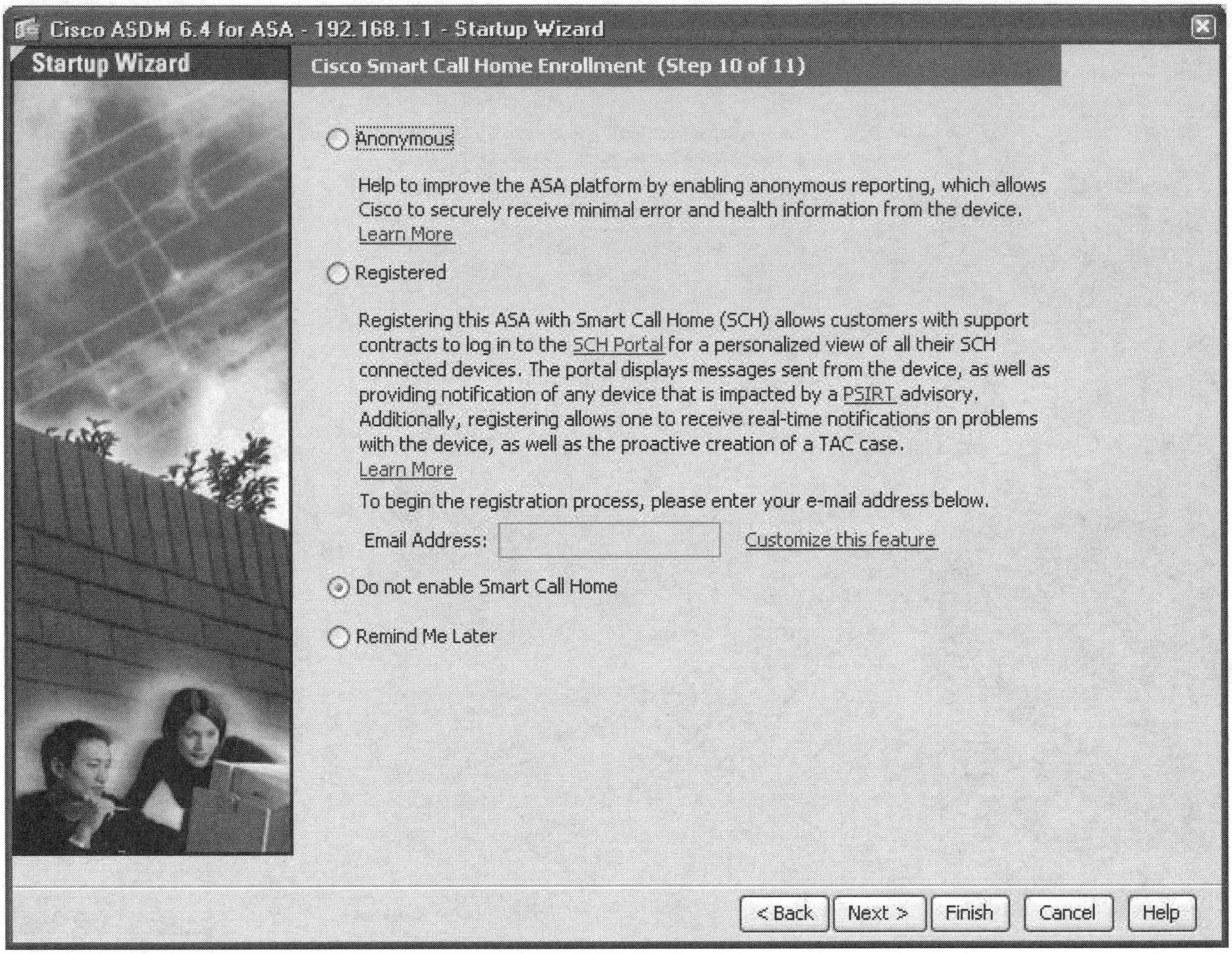

Step 5: Review the summary and deliver the commands to the ASA.

a. On the Startup Wizard Step 11 screen (Startup Wizard Summary), review the Configuration Summary and click **Finish**. ASDM will deliver the commands to the ASA device and then reload the modified configuration.

Note: If the GUI dialog box stops responding during the reload process, close it, exit ASDM, and restart the browser and ASDM. If prompted to save the configuration to flash memory, respond with **Yes**. Even though ASDM might not appear to have reloaded the configuration, the commands were delivered. If errors are encountered as ASDM delivers the commands, you will be notified with a list of commands that succeeded and those that failed.

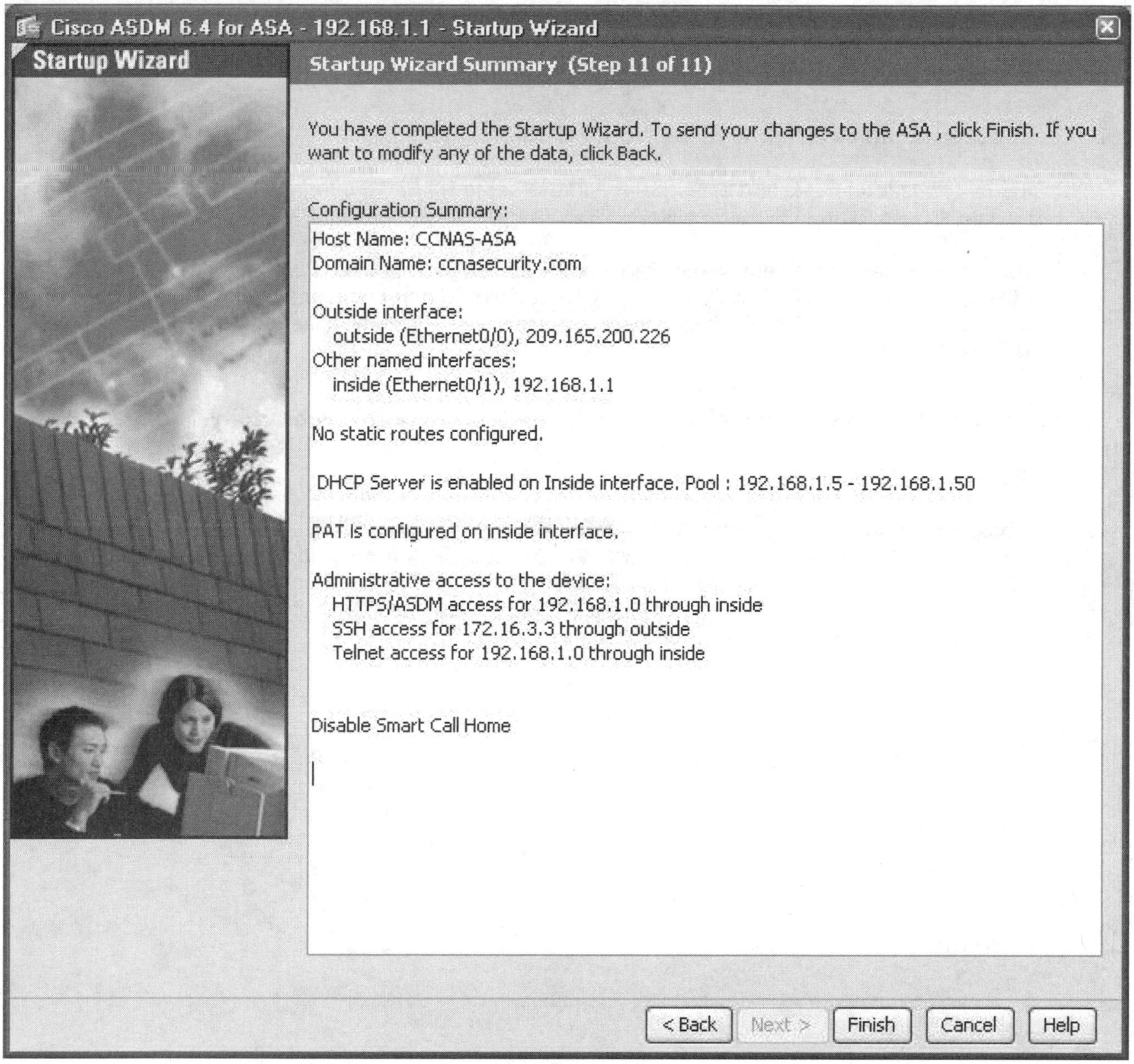

b. Restart ASDM and provide the new enable password **class** with no username. Return to the Device Dashboard and check the Interface Status window. You should see the inside and outside interfaces with IP address and status. The inside interface should show some number of Kb/s. The Traffic Status window might show the ASDM access as TCP traffic spike.

Step 6: Test Telnet and SSH access to the ASA.

a. From a command prompt or GUI Telnet client on PC-B, Telnet to the ASA inside interface at IP address 192.168.1.1.

b. Log in to the ASA using the default login password of **cisco**. Enter privileged EXEC mode by using the `enable` command and provide the password **class**. Exit the Telnet session by using the `quit` command.

c. In Part 3, Step 4, SSH access was configured using the Startup Wizard to allow access to the ASA from outside PC-C (172.16.3.3). From PC-C, open an SSH client, such as PuTTY, and attempt to connect to the ASA outside interface at 209.165.200.226. You will not be able to establish the connection because SSH access (ASA Version 8.4(2) and later) requires you to also configure AAA and provide an authenticated username. AAA is configured in Part 4 of the lab.

Step 7: Test access to an external website from PC-B.

a. Open a browser on PC-B and enter the IP address of the R1 Fa0/0 interface (209.165.200.225) to simulate access to an external website.

b. The R1 HTTP server was enabled in Part 1 of the lab, so you should be prompted with a user authentication login dialog box from the R1 GUI device manger. Leave the username blank and enter the password of **class**. Exit the browser. You should see TCP activity in the ASDM Device Dashboard Traffic Status window.

Step 8: Test access to an external website using the ASDM Packet Tracer utility.

a. From the ASDM Home page, choose **Tools > Packet Tracer**.

b. Choose the **Inside** interface from the Interface drop-down menu and click **TCP** from the Packet Type radio buttons. From the Source drop-down menu, choose **IP Address** and enter the address **192.168.1.3** (PC-B) with a source port of **1500**. From the Destination drop-down menu, choose **IP Address** and enter **209.165.200.225** (R1 Fa0/0) with a destination port of **HTTP**. Click **Start** to begin the trace of the packet. The packet should be permitted.

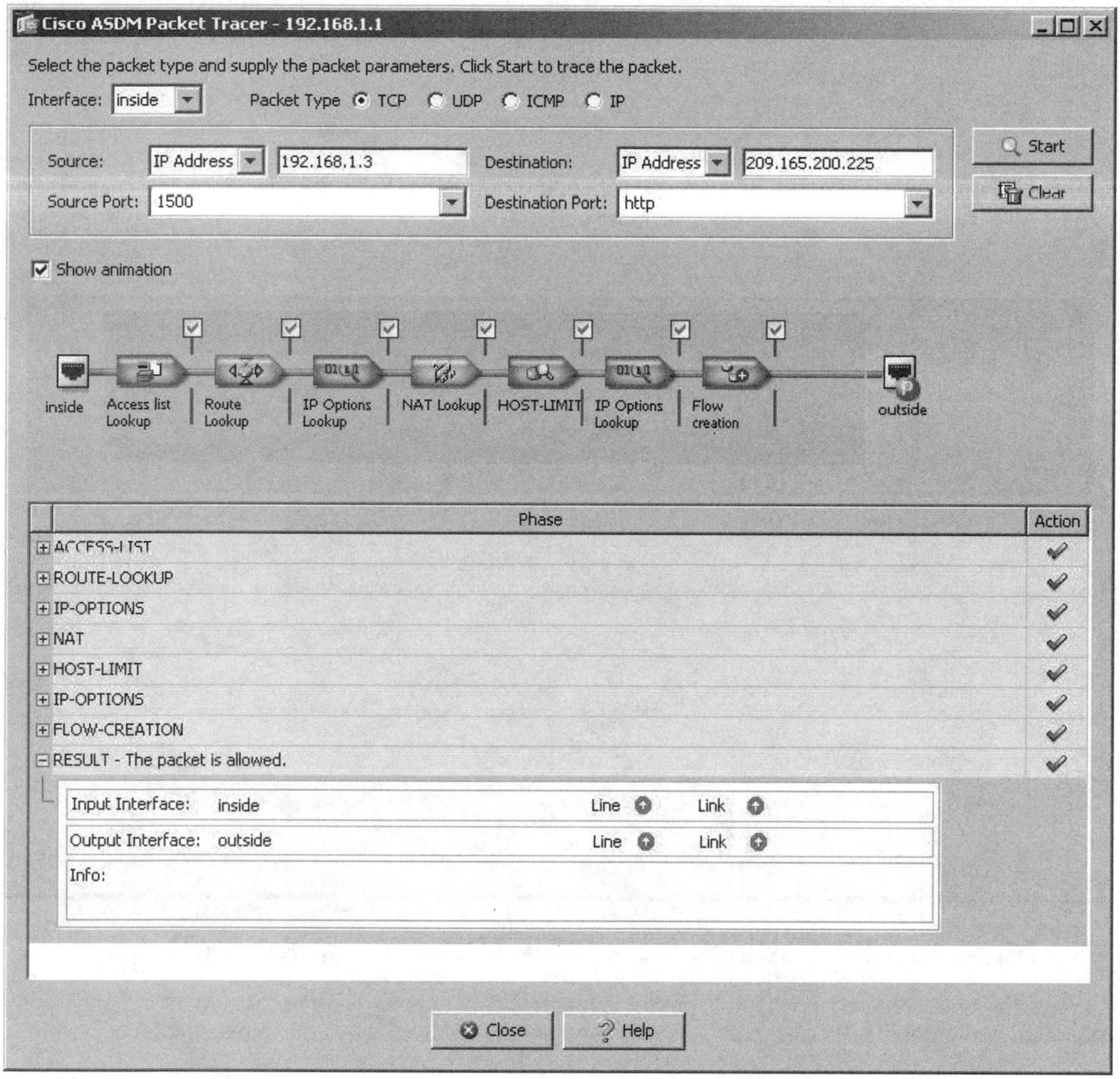

c. Reset the entries by clicking the **Clear** button. Try another trace, and choose **Outside** from the Interface drop-down menu; leave **TCP** as the packet type. From the Source drop-down menu, choose **IP Address** and enter **209.165.200.225** (R1 Fa0/0) and a source port of **1500**. From the Destination drop-down menu, choose **IP Address** and enter the address **209.165.200.226** (ASA outside interface) with a destination port of telnet. Click **Start** to begin the trace of the packet. The packet should be dropped. Click **Close** to continue.

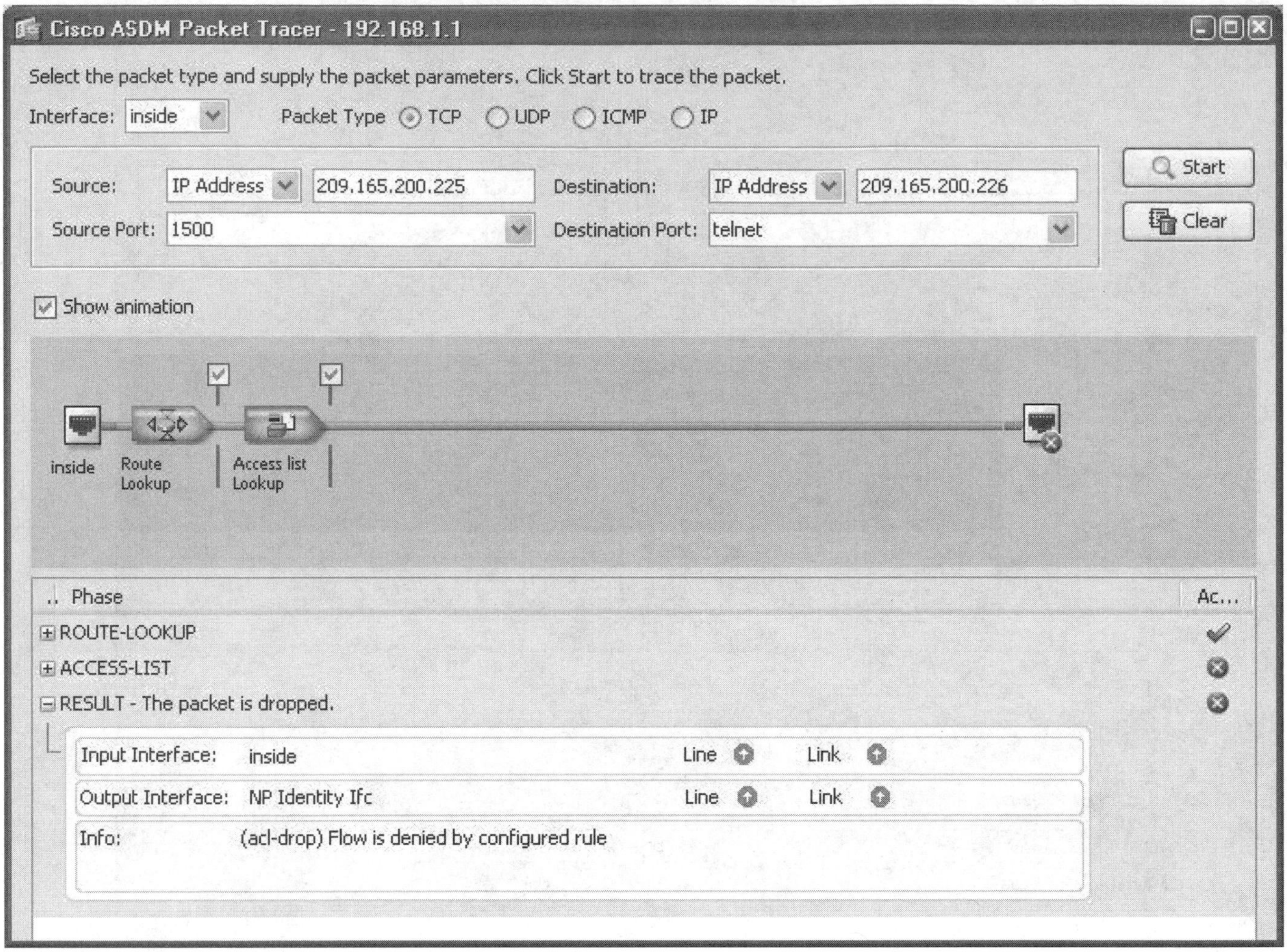

Part 4: Configuring ASA Settings from the ASDM Configuration Menu

In Part 4, you set the ASA clock, configure a default route, test connectivity using ASDM tools Ping and Traceroute, configure Local AAA user authentication, and modify the MPF application inspection policy.

Step 1: Set the ASA date and time.

a. From the Configuration screen, Device Setup menu, choose **System Time > Clock**.

b. Select your time zone from the drop-down menu, and enter the current date and time in the fields provided. The clock is a 24-hour clock. Click **Apply** to send the commands to the ASA.

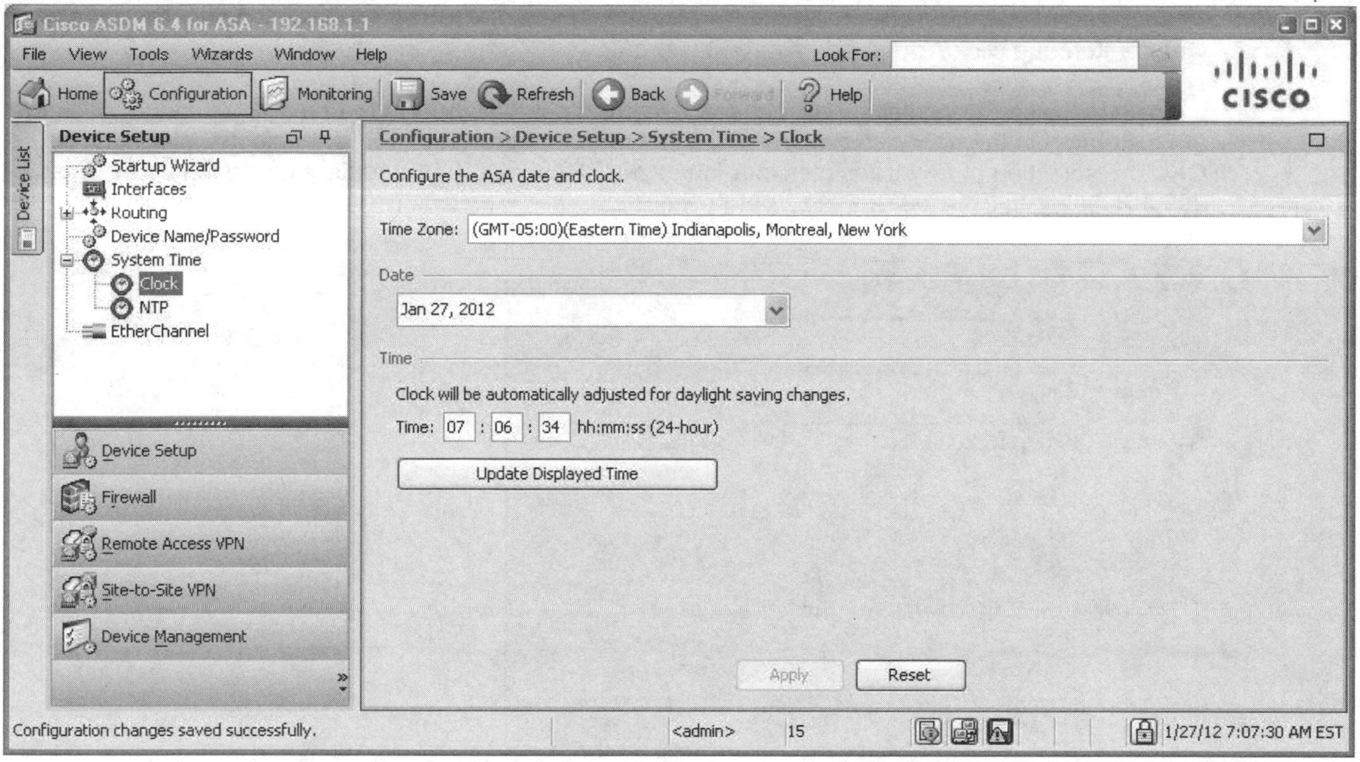

Step 2: Configure a static default route for the ASA.

a. From the ASDM Tools menu, select **Ping** and enter the IP address of router R1 S0/0/0 (10.1.1.1). The ASA does not have a default route to unknown external networks. The ping should fail because the ASA has no route to 10.1.1.1. Click **Close** to continue.

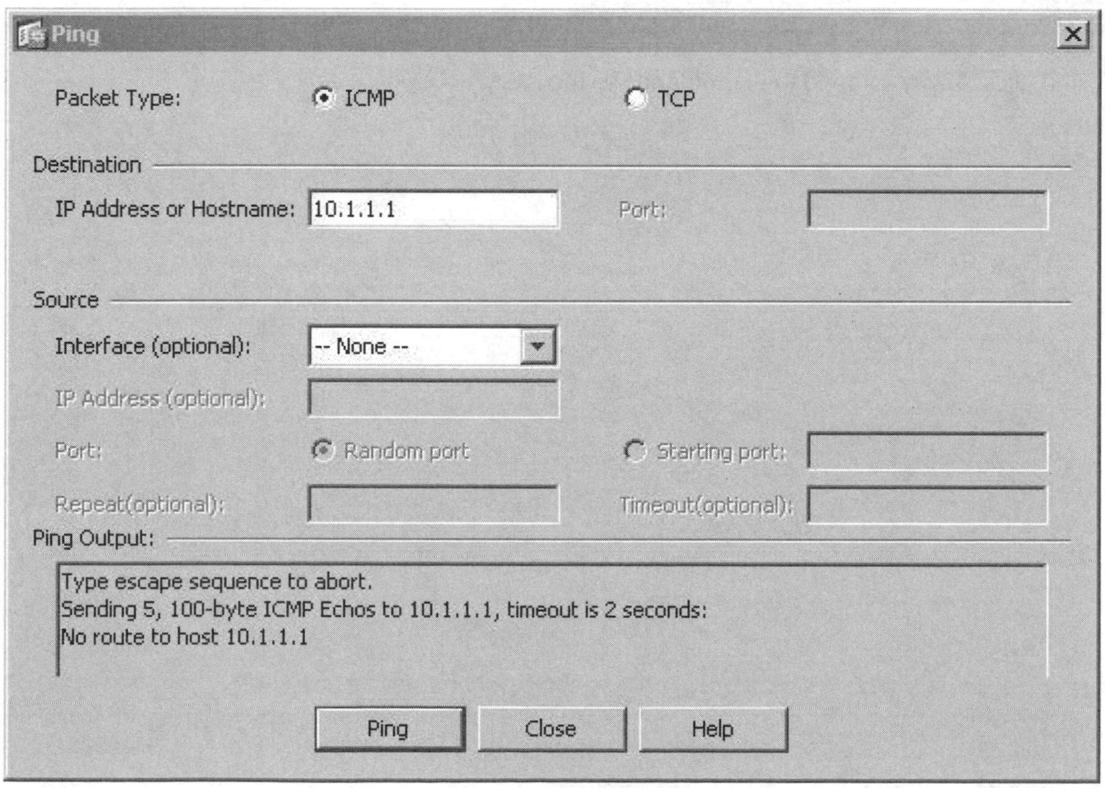

b. From the Configuration screen, Device Setup menu, choose **Routing > Static Routes**. Click the **IPv4 Only** button and click **Add** to add a new static route.

c. In the Add Static Route dialog box, choose the **outside** interface from the drop-down menu. Click the ellipsis button to the right of **Network** and select **any** from the list of network objects, and then click **OK**. The selection of **any** translates to a "quad zero" (0.0.0.0 0.0.0.0) route. For the Gateway IP, enter **209.165.200.225** (R1 Fa0/0).

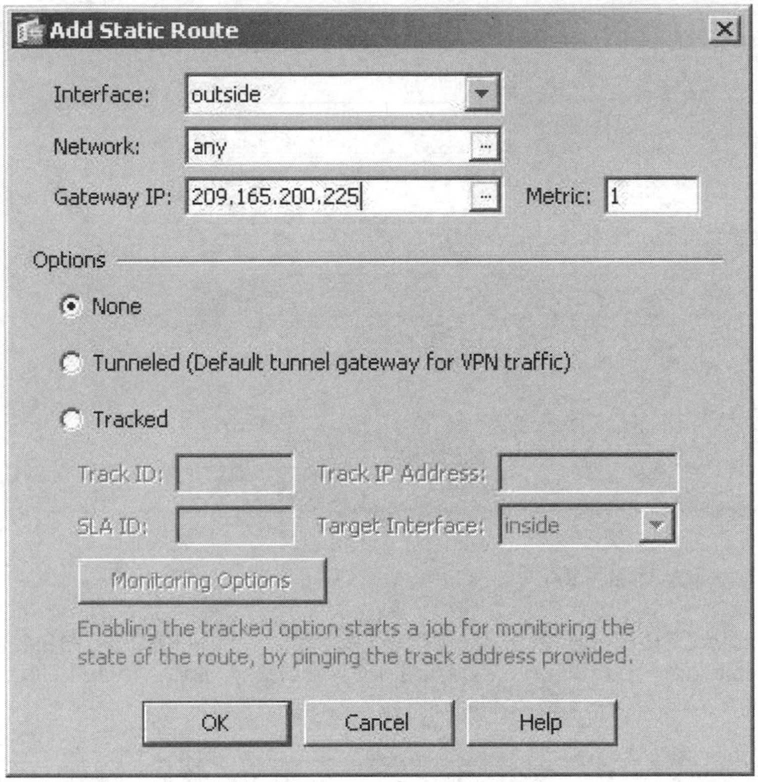

d. Click **OK**, and click **Apply** to send the commands to the ASA.

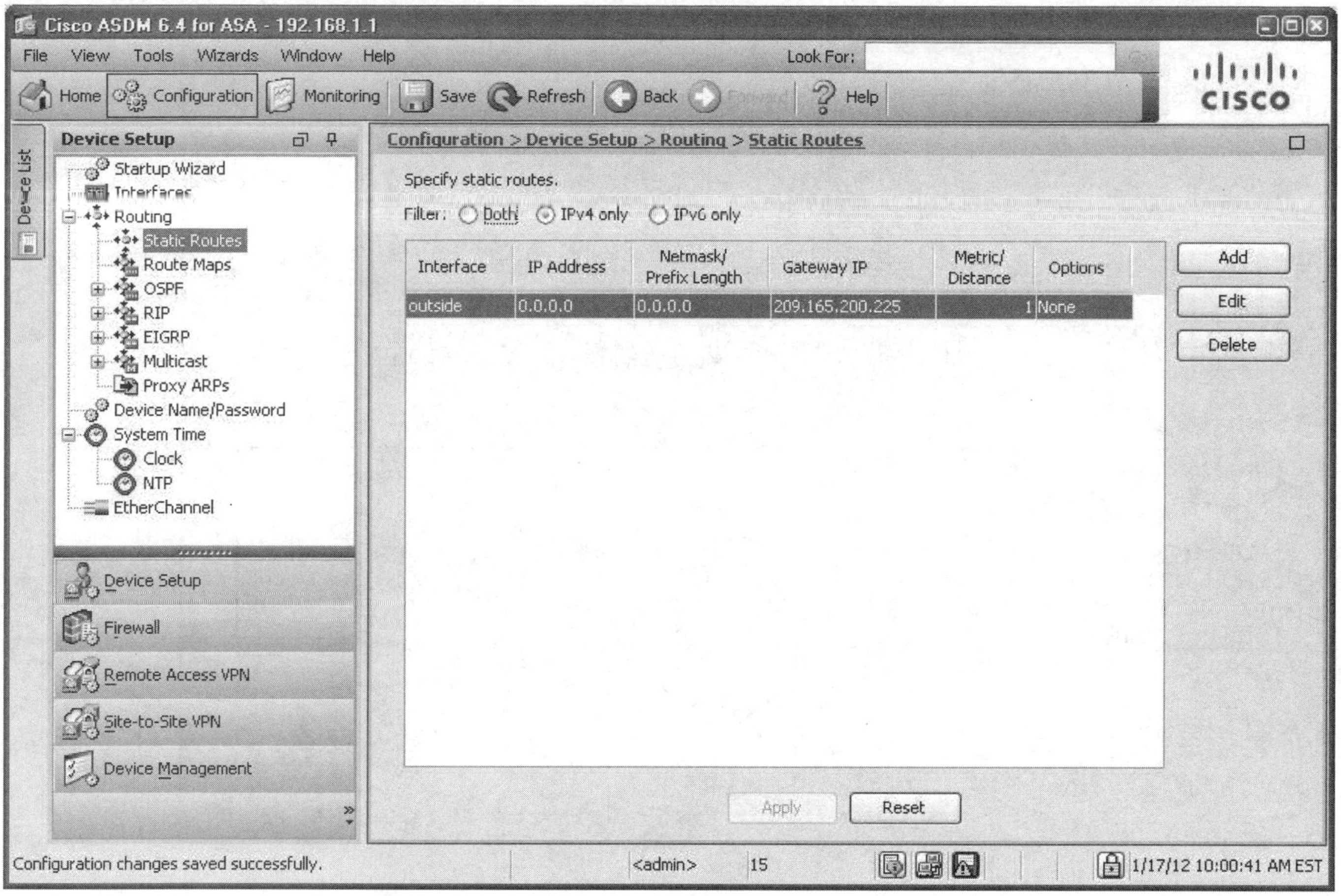

e. From the ASDM Tools menu, select **Ping** and enter the IP address of router R1 S0/0/0 (10.1.1.1). The ping should succeed this time. Click **Close** to continue.

f. From the ASDM Tools menu, select **Traceroute** and enter the IP address of external host PC-C (172.16.3.3). Click **Trace Route**. The traceroute should succeed and show the hops from the ASA through R1, R2, and R3 to host PC-C. Click **Close** to continue.

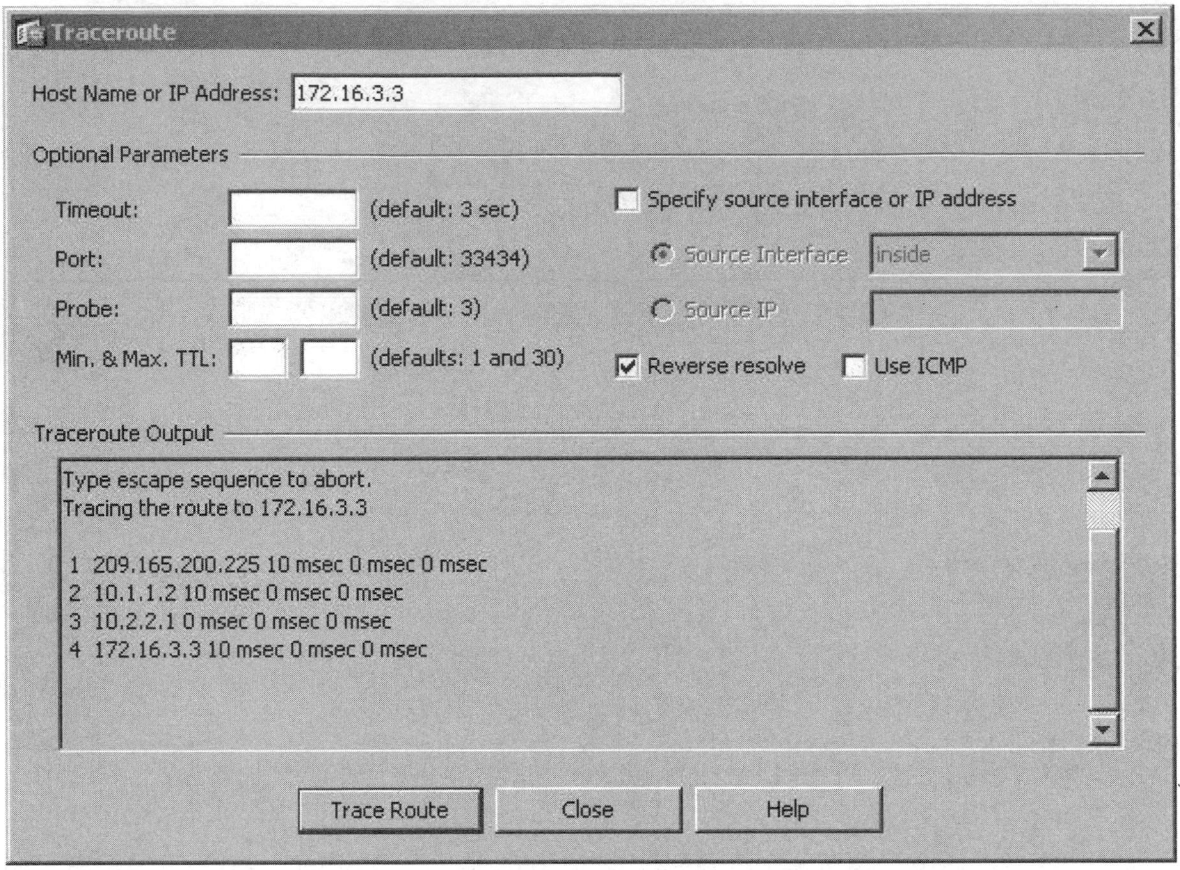

Step 3: Configure AAA user authentication using the local ASA database.

It is necessary to enable AAA user authentication to access the ASA using SSH. You allowed SSH access to the ASA from the outside host PC-C when the Startup Wizard was run. To allow the remote network administrator at PC-C to have SSH access to the ASA, you will create a user in the local database.

a. From the Configuration screen, Device Management area, click **Users/AAA**. Click **User Accounts** and then **Add**. Create a new user named **admin** with a password of **cisco123**, and enter the password again to confirm it. Allow this user Full access (ASDM, SSH, Telnet, and console) and set the privilege level to **15**. Click **OK** to add the user, and click **Apply** to send the commands to the ASA.

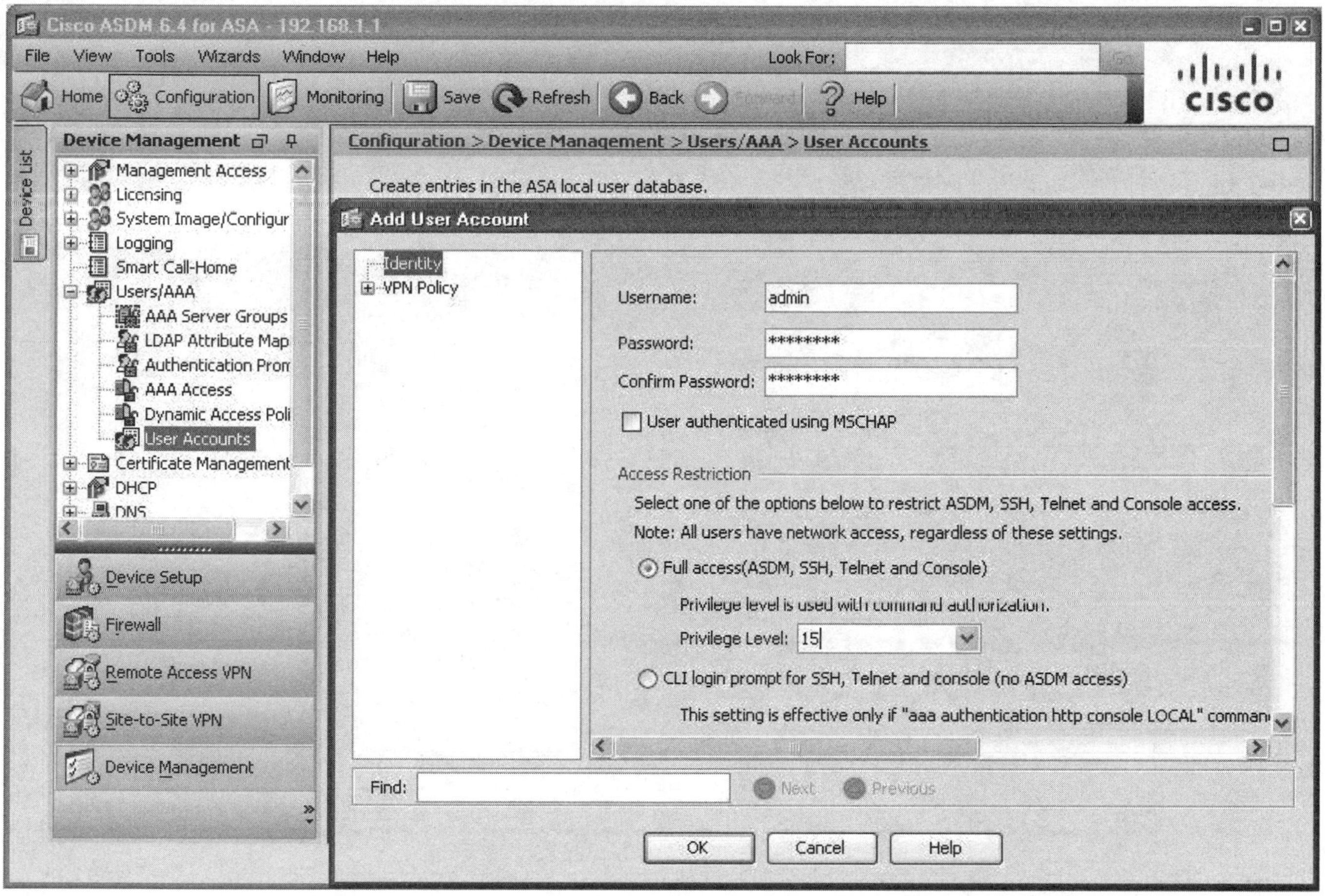

b. From the Configuration screen, Device Management area, click **Users/AAA**. Click **AAA Access**. On the Authentication tab, select the checkboxes to require authentication for HTTP/ASDM, SSH, and Telnet connections, and specify the LOCAL server group for each connection type. Click **Apply** to send the commands to the ASA.

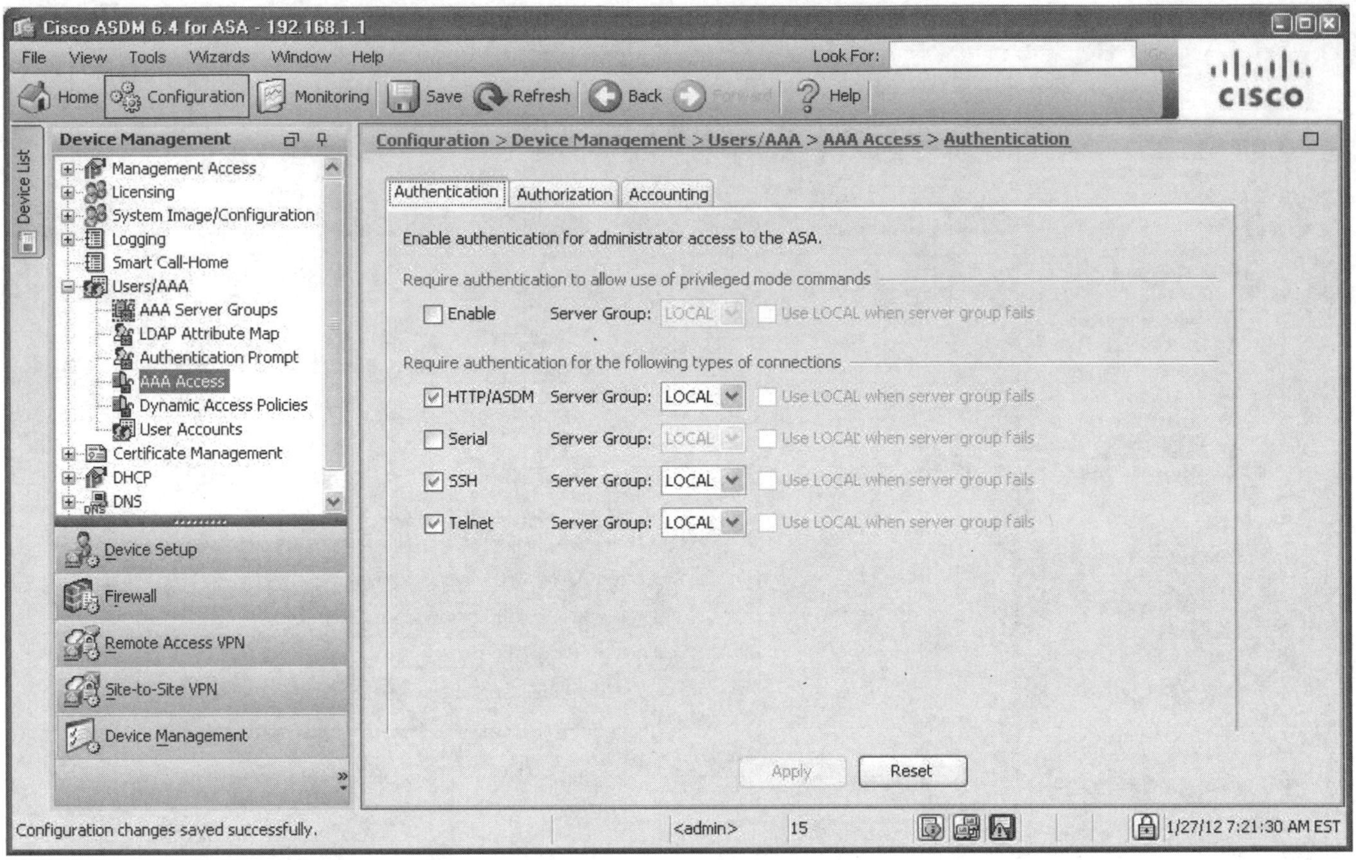

Note: The next action you attempt within ASDM will require you to log in as admin with password cisco123.

c. From PC-C, open an SSH client, such as PuTTY, and attempt to access the ASA outside interface at 209.165.200.226. You should be able to establish the connection. When prompted to log in, enter user name **admin** and password **cisco123**.

d. After logging in to the ASA using SSH, enter the **`enable`** command and provide the password **class**. Issue the **`show run`** command to display the current configuration you have created using ASDM.

Note: The default timeout for Telnet and SSH is 5 minutes. You can increase this setting using the CLI as described in Lab 10A, or go to ASDM **Device Management > Management Access > ASDM/HTTP/Telnet/SSH**.

Step 4: Modify the MPF application inspection policy.

For application layer inspection, as well as other advanced options, the Cisco Modular Policy Framework (MPF) is available on ASAs.

a. The default global inspection policy does not inspect ICMP. To enable hosts on the internal network to ping external hosts and receive replies, ICMP traffic must be inspected. From the Configuration screen, click the **Firewall** area menu, and click **Service Policy Rules**.

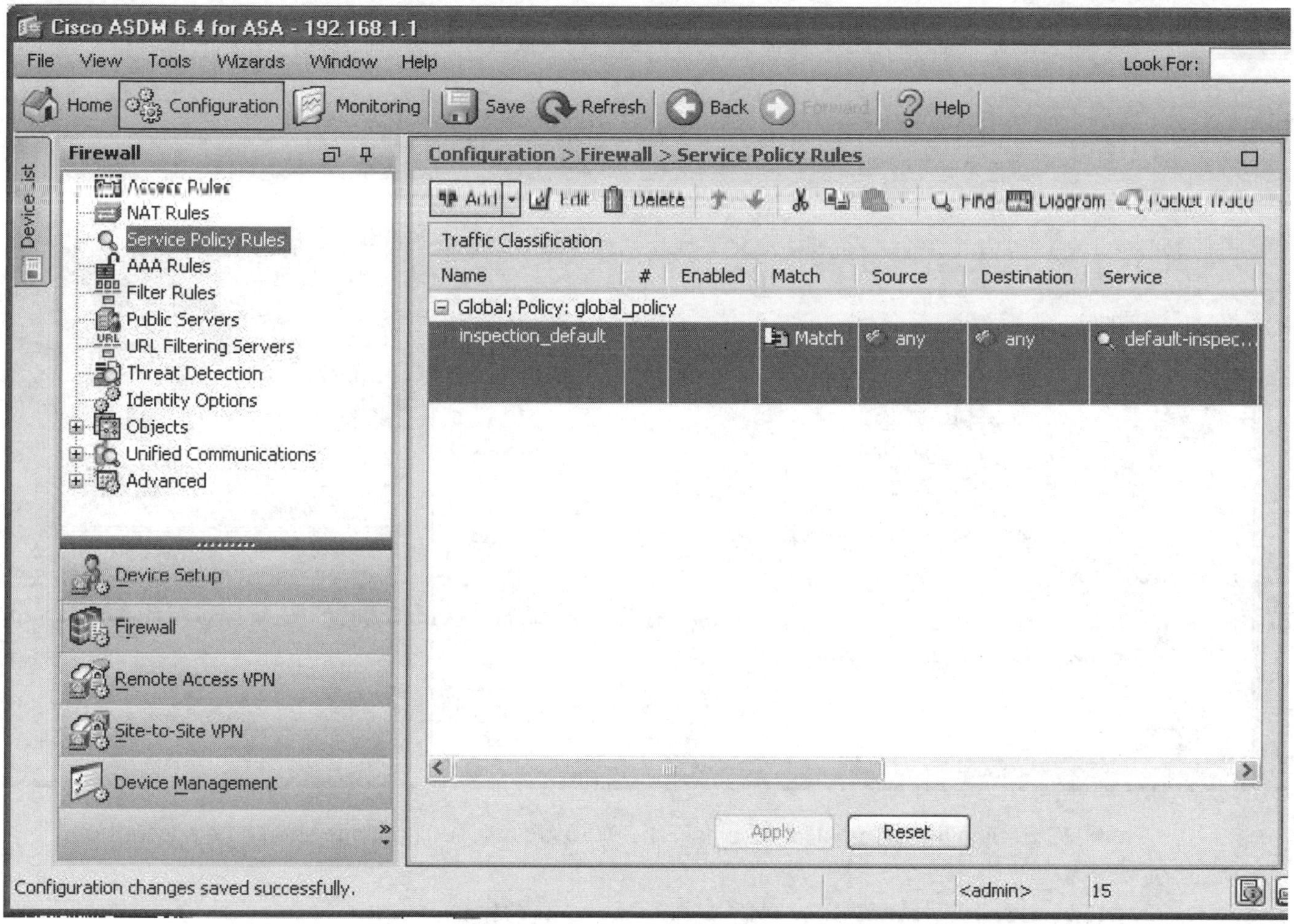

b. Select the **inspection_default** policy, and click **Edit** to modify the default inspection rules. On the Edit Service Policy Rule window, click the **Rule Actions** tab and check the **ICMP** box. Do not change the other default protocols that are checked. Click **OK**, and then click **Apply** to send the commands to the ASA. If prompted, log in as again admin with a password of cisco123.

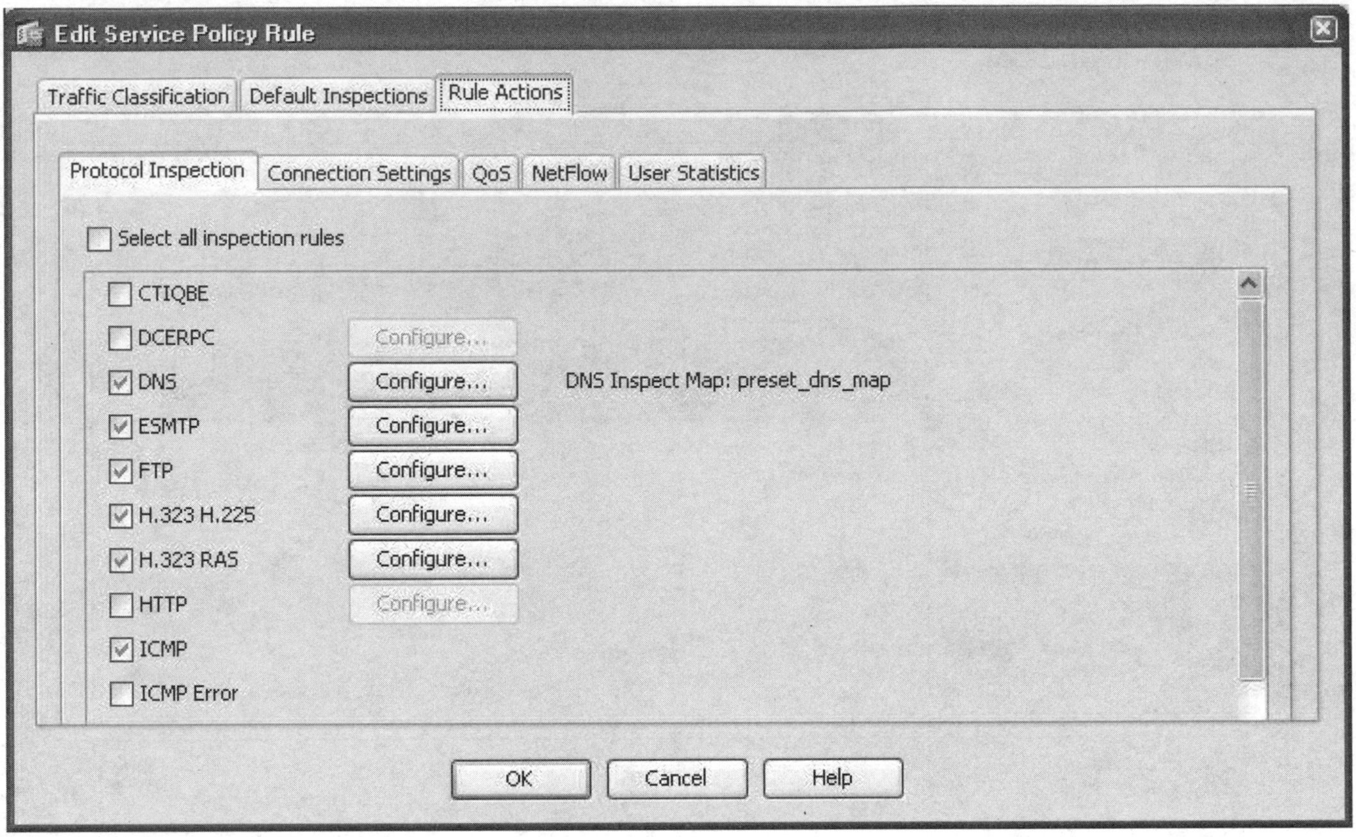

c. From PC-B, ping the external interface of R1 S0/0/0 (10.1.1.1). The pings should be successful.

Part 5: Configuring a DMZ, Static NAT, and ACLs

In Part 3 of this lab, you configured address translation using PAT for the inside network. In this part, you create a DMZ on the ASA, configure static NAT to a DMZ server, and apply an ACL to control access to the server.

Step 1: Configure the ASA DMZ interface.

In this step, you configure a new interface E0/2 named dmz, set the security level to 70, and bring the interface up:

a. From the Device Setup menu on the Configuration screen, click **Interfaces**. Select interface Ethernet0/2 and click **Edit**.

b. In the Edit Interface dialog box, the General tab is displayed by default. Name the interface **dmz**, assign it a security level of **70**, and make sure the **Enable Interface** box is checked.

c. Ensure that the **Use Static IP** button is selected, and enter an IP address of **192.168.2.1** with a subnet mask of **255.255.255.0**. Click **OK**. When the Security Level Change warning is displayed, read it, and then click **OK** again. On the Interfaces screen, click **Apply** to send the commands to the ASA.

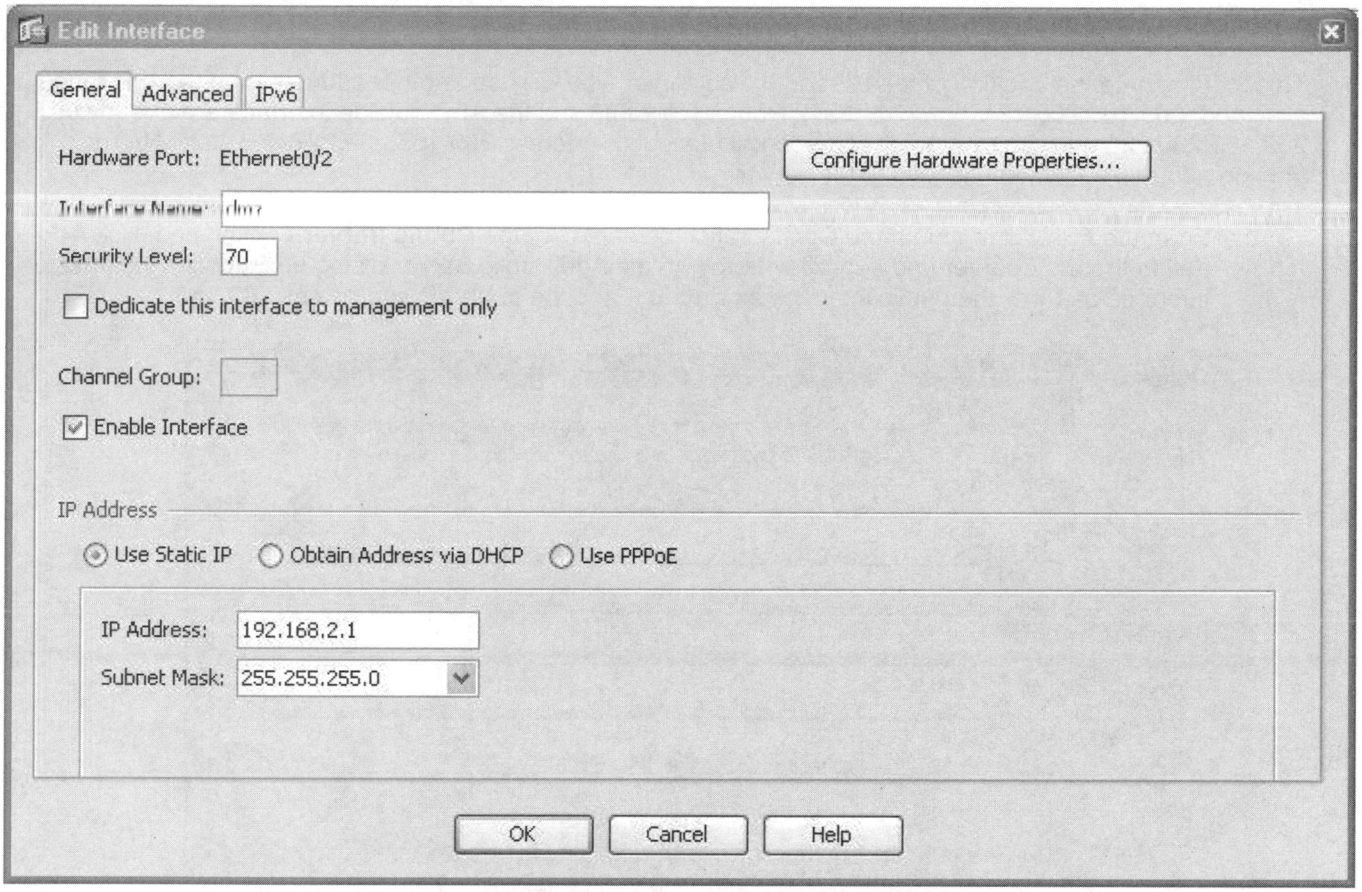
Edit Interface
General
Advanced
IPv6
Hardware Port: Ethernet0/2
Configure Hardware Properties...
Interface Name: dmz
Security Level: 70
Dedicate this interface to management only
Channel Group:
Enable Interface
IP Address
Use Static IP
Obtain Address via DHCP
Use PPPoE
IP Address: 192.168.2.1
Subnet Mask: 255.255.255.0
OK
Cancel
Help

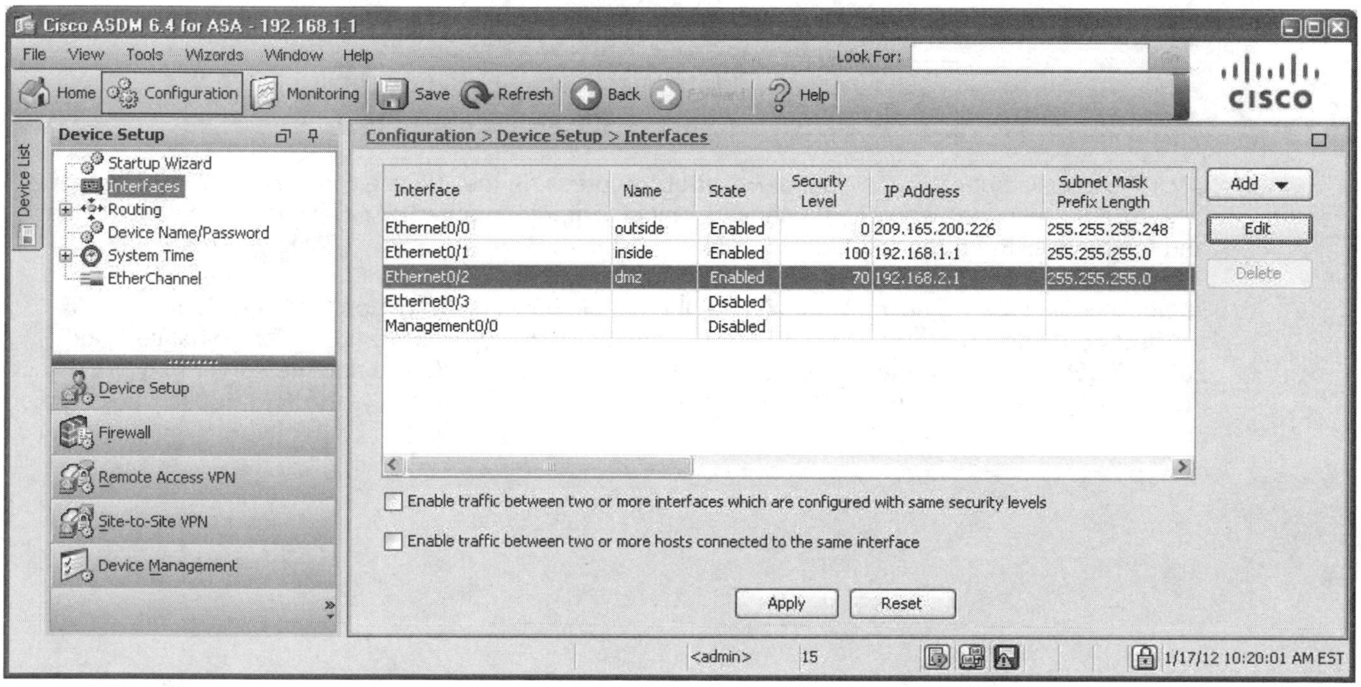
Cisco ASDM 6.4 for ASA - 192.168.1.1
File View Tools Wizards Window Help
Look For:
Home Configuration Monitoring Save Refresh Back Forward Help
cisco
Device Setup
Startup Wizard
Interfaces
Routing
Device Name/Password
System Time
EtherChannel
Configuration > Device Setup > Interfaces
Interface | Name | State | Security Level | IP Address | Subnet Mask Prefix Length
Ethernet0/0 | outside | Enabled | 0 | 209.165.200.226 | 255.255.255.248
Ethernet0/1 | inside | Enabled | 100 | 192.168.1.1 | 255.255.255.0
Ethernet0/2 | dmz | Enabled | 70 | 192.168.2.1 | 255.255.255.0
Ethernet0/3 | | Disabled
Management0/0 | | Disabled
Add
Edit
Delete
Enable traffic between two or more interfaces which are configured with same security levels
Enable traffic between two or more hosts connected to the same interface
Apply
Reset
Device Setup
Firewall
Remote Access VPN
Site-to-Site VPN
Device Management
<admin> 15
1/17/12 10:20:01 AM EST

Step 2: Configure the DMZ server and static NAT.

To accommodate the addition of a DMZ and a web server, you will use another address from the ISP range assigned, 209.165.200.224/29 (.224–.231). Router R1 Fa0/0 and the ASA outside interface are already using 209.165.200.225 and .226, respectively. You will use public address 209.165.200.227 and static NAT to provide address translation access to the server.

a. From the Firewall menu on the Configuration screen, click the **Public Servers** option and click **Add** to define the DMZ server and services offered. In the Add Public Server dialog box, specify the private interface as **dmz**, the public interface as **outside**, and the public IP address as **209.165.200.227**.

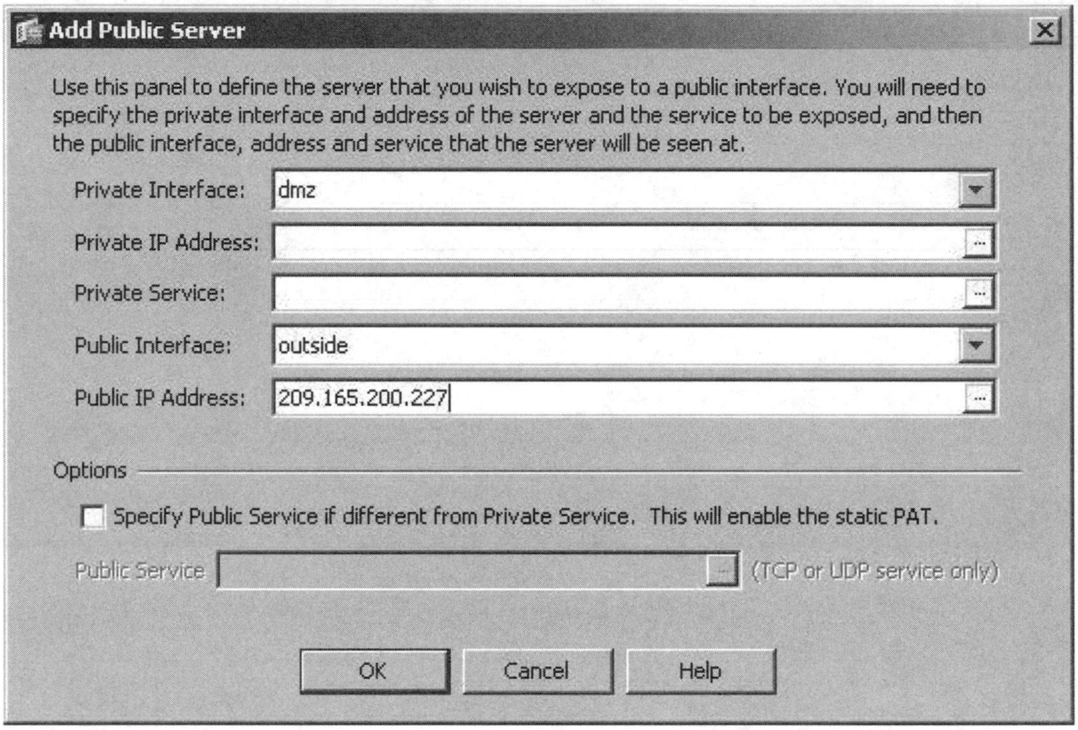

b. Click the ellipsis button to the right of Private IP Address. In the Browse Private IP Address window, click **Add** to define the server as a network object. Enter the name **DMZ-Server** with a type of Host and the private IP address of 192.168.2.3.

c. In the Add Network Object dialog box, click the double down arrow button for **NAT**. Click the **Add Automatic Address Translation Rules** box, and enter the type as **Static**. Enter Translated Addr: **209.165.200.227**. When the screen looks like the following, click **OK** to add the server network object. From the Browse Private IP Address window, click **OK**. You will return to the Add Public Server dialog box.

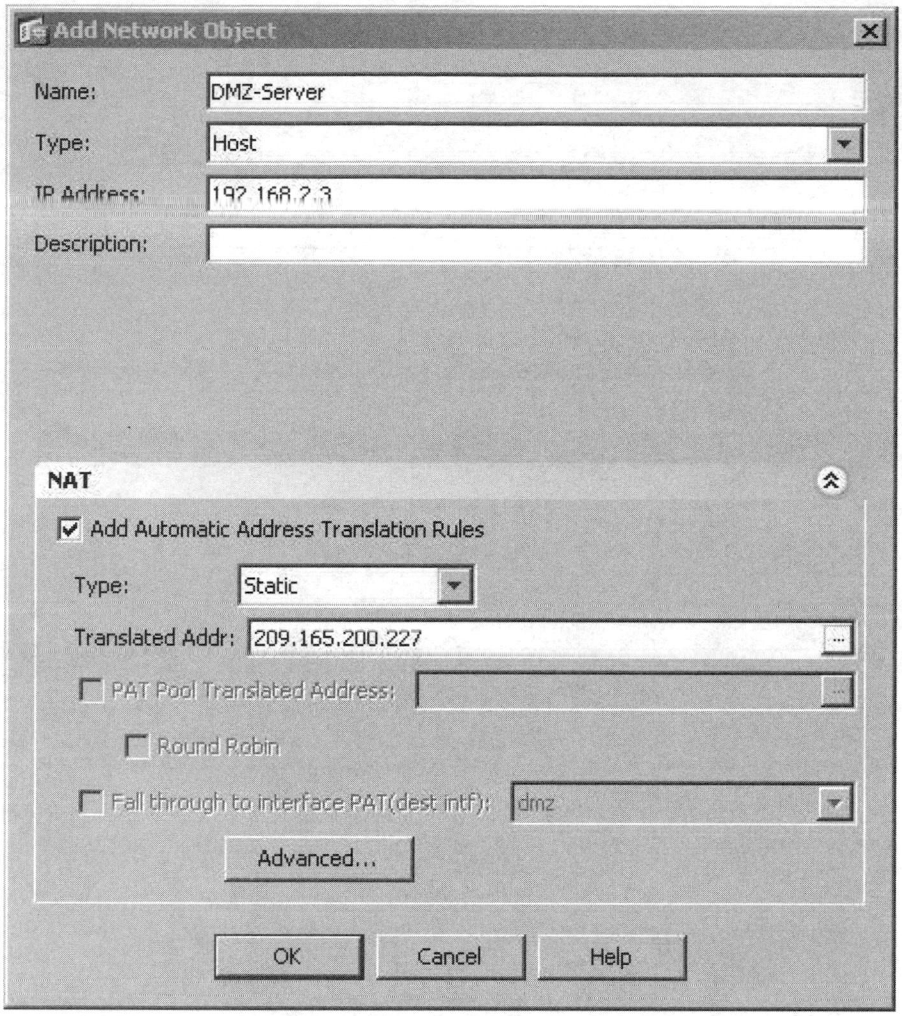

d. In the Add Public Server dialog, click the ellipsis button to the right of Private Service. In the Browse Private Service window, double-click to select the following services: **tcp/http**, **tcp/ftp**, **icmp/echo**, and **icmp/echo-reply** (scroll down to see all services). Click **OK** to continue and return to the Add Public Server dialog.

Note: You can specify public services if different from the private services using the option on this screen.

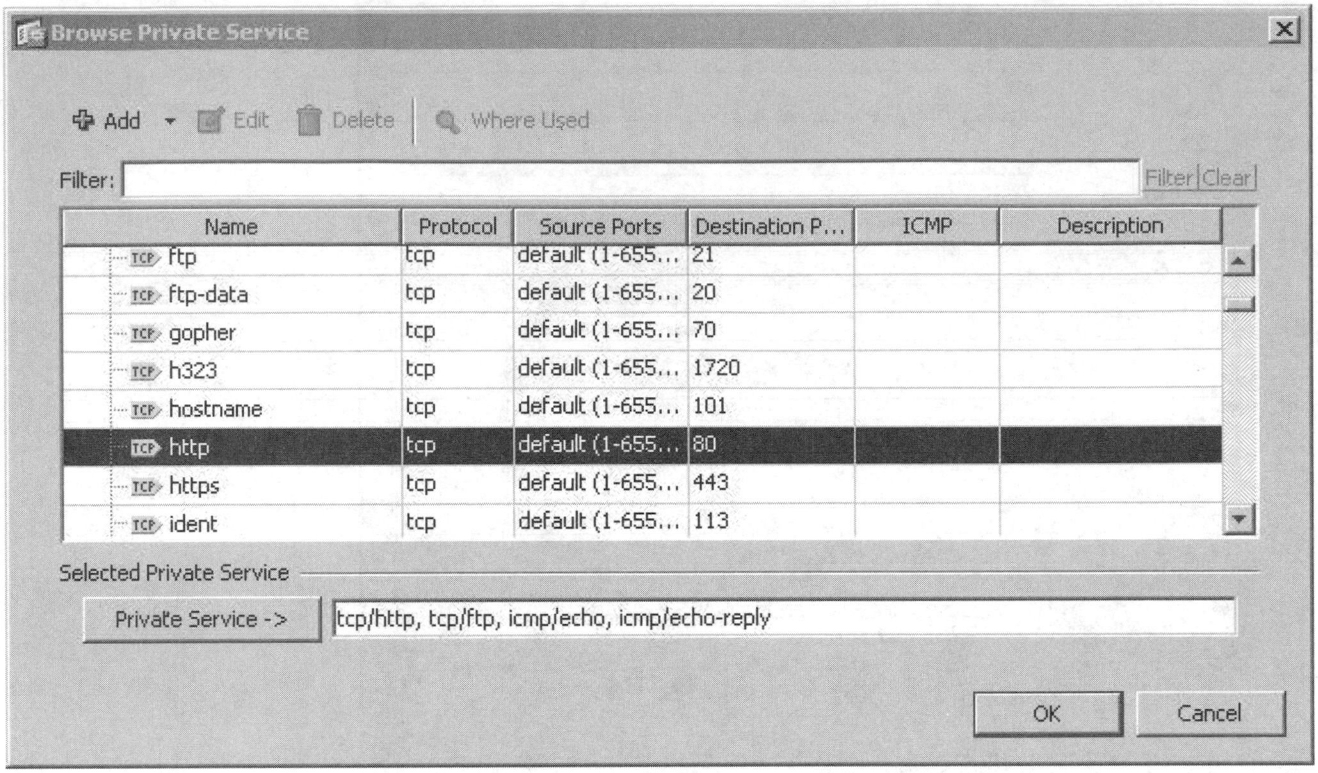

e. When you have completed all information in the Add Public Server dialog box, it should look like the following. Click **OK** to add the server. Click **Apply** at the Public Servers screen to send the commands to the ASA.

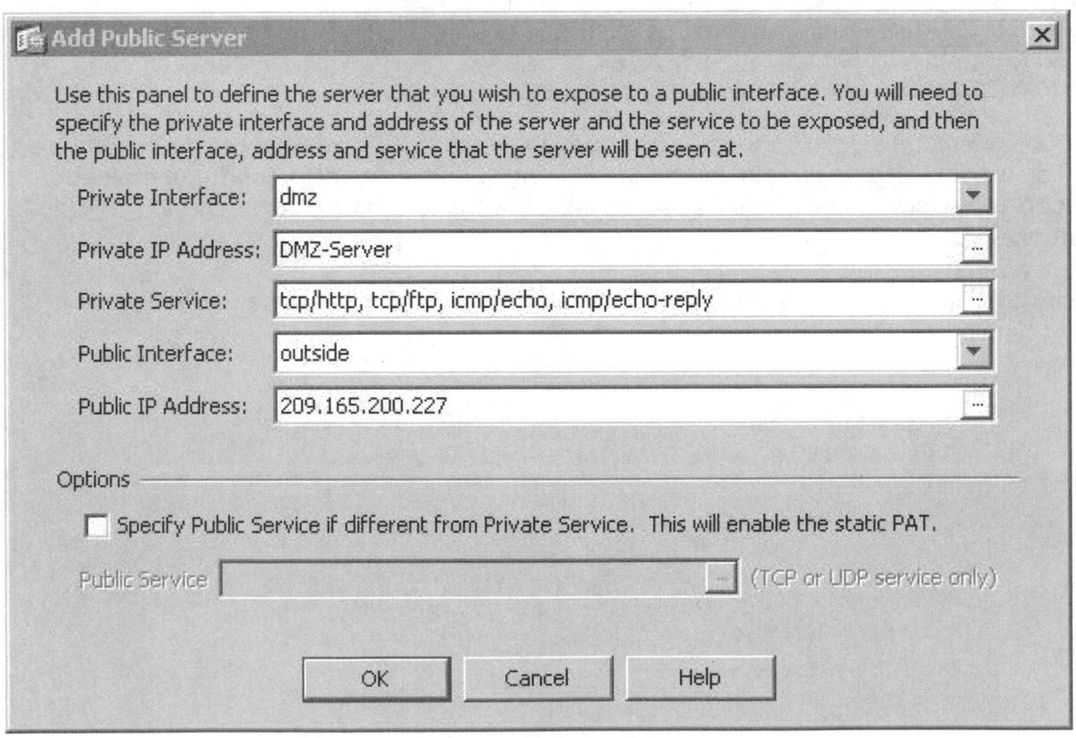

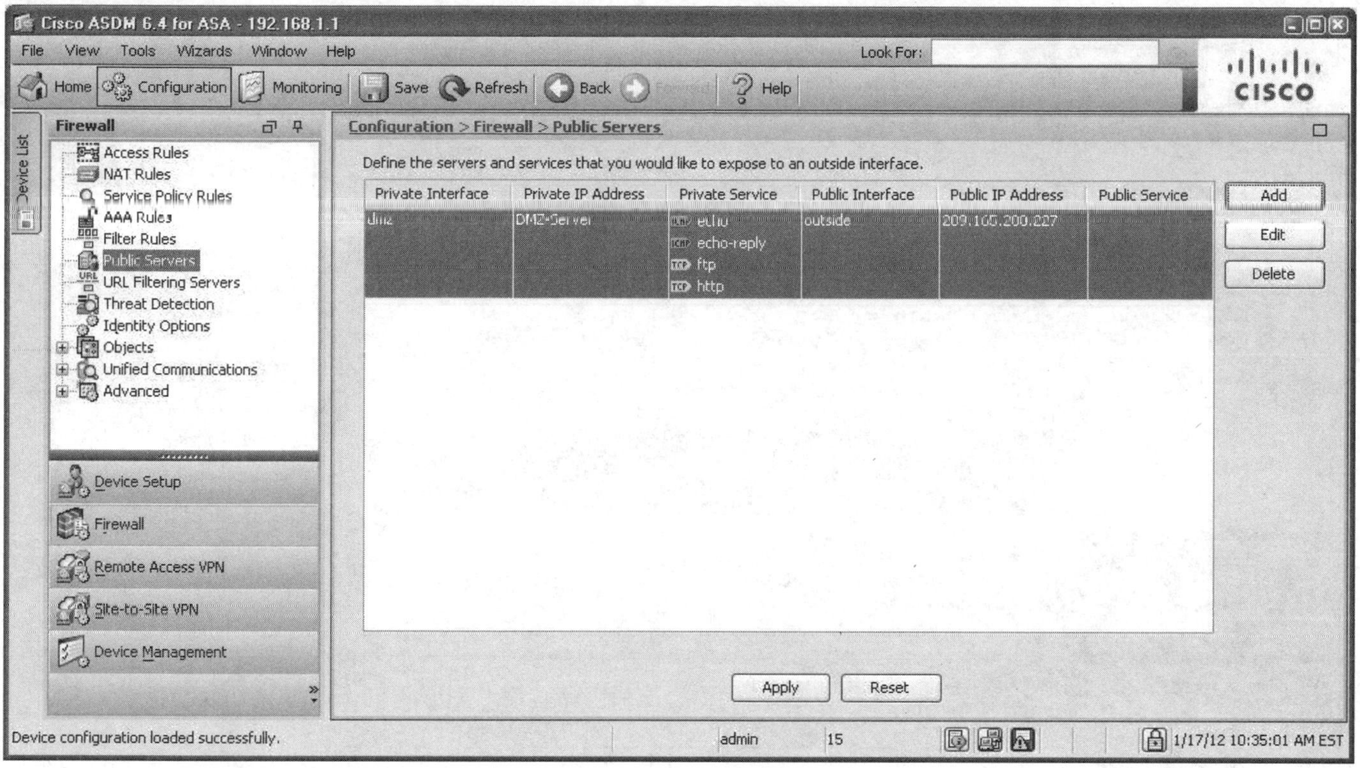

Step 3: View the DMZ Access Rule (ACL) generated by ASDM.

With the creation of the DMZ server object and selection of services, ASDM automatically generates an access rule (ACL) to permit the appropriate access to the server and applies it to the outside interface in the incoming direction.

View this access rule in ASDM by choosing **Configuration > Firewall > Access Rules**. It appears as an outside incoming rule. You can select the rule and use the horizontal scrollbar to see all the components.

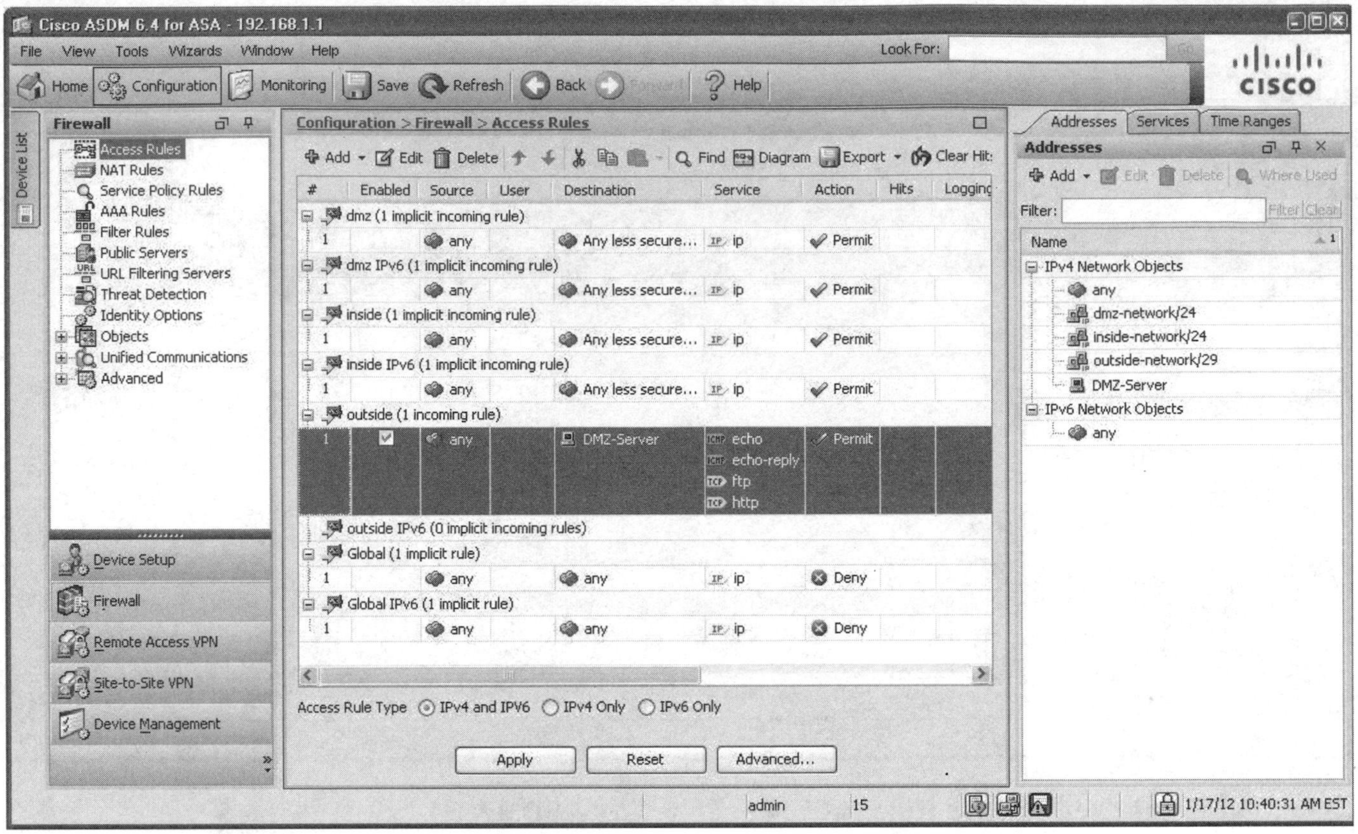

Note: You can also see the actual IOS commands generated using the **ASDM Tools > Command Line Interface** and entering the command `show run`.

Step 4: Test access to the DMZ server from the outside network.

a. From PC-C, ping the IP address of the static NAT public server address (209.165.200.227). The pings should be successful.

b. Because the ASA inside interface E0/1 is set to security level 100 (the highest) and the DMZ interface E0/2 is set to 70, you can also access the DMZ server from a host on the inside network. The ASA acts like a router between the two networks. Ping the DMZ server (PC-A) internal address (192.168.2.3) from inside network host PC-B (192.168.1.3 or DHCP assigned address). The pings should be successful due to interface security level and the fact that ICMP is being inspected on the inside interface by the global inspection policy.

c. The DMZ server cannot ping PC-B on the inside network because the DMZ interface E0/2 has a lower security level (70) than the inside interface E0/1 (100). Try to ping from the DMZ server PC-A to PC-B at IP address 192.168.1.X. The pings should not be successful.

Step 5: Use ASDM monitoring to graph packet activity.

A number of aspects of the ASA can be monitored using the Monitoring screen. The main categories on this screen are Interfaces, VPN, Routing, Properties, and Logging. In this step, you create a graph to monitor packet activity for the ASA outside interface.

a. From the Interfaces menu of the Monitoring screen, click **Interface Graphs > outside**. Select **Packet Counts** and click **Add** to add the graph. The following figure shows Packet Counts added.

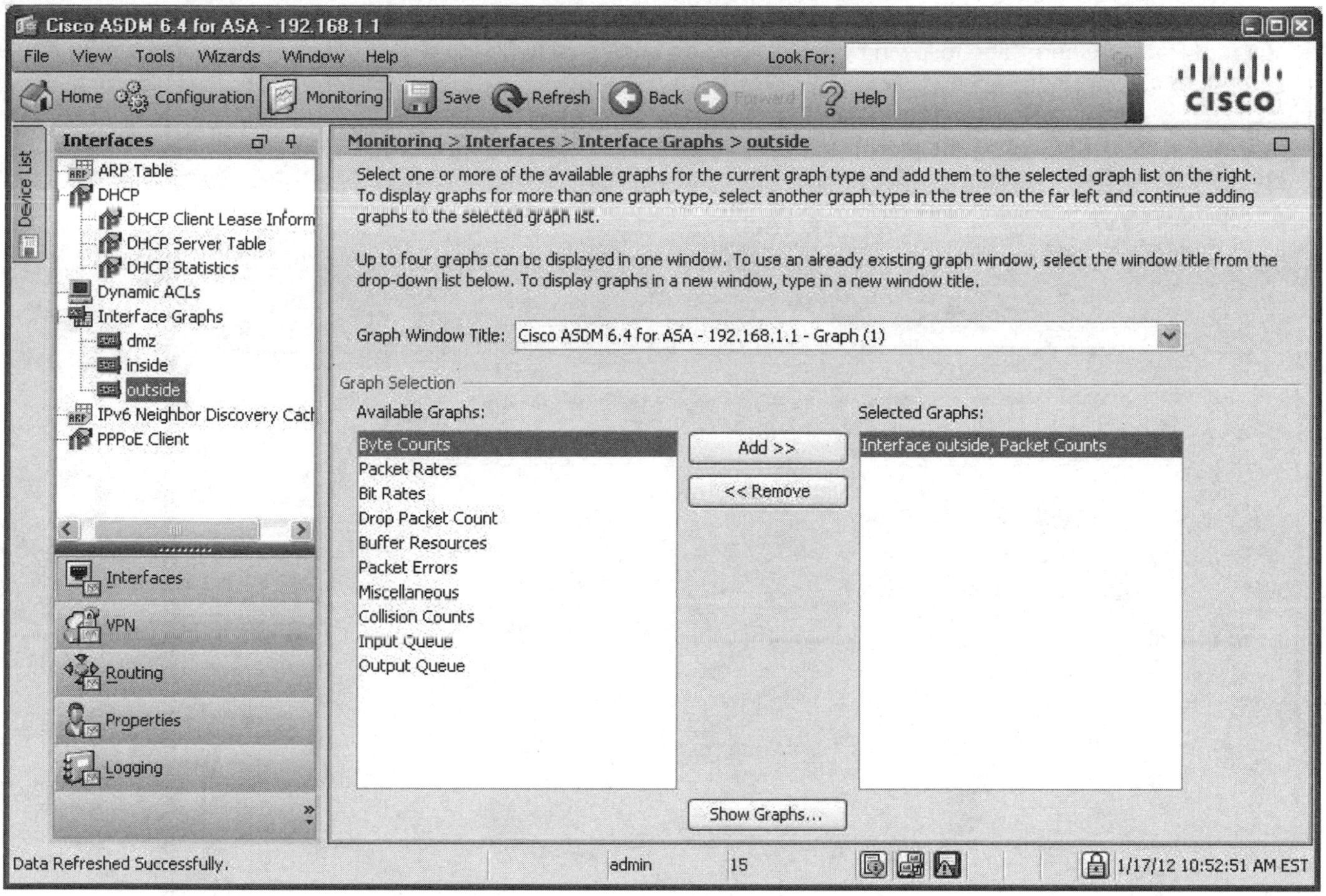

b. Click the **Show Graphs** button to display the graph. Initially, no traffic is displayed.

c. From a privileged mode command prompt on R2, simulate Internet traffic to the ASA by pinging the DMZ server public address with a repeat count of 1000. You can increase the number of pings.

```
R2# ping 209.165.200.227 repeat 1000

Type escape sequence to abort.
Sending 1000, 100-byte ICMP Echos to 209.165.200.227, timeout is 2
seconds:
!!!!!!!!!!!!!!!!!!!!!!!!!!!!!!!!!!!!!!!!!!!!!!!!!!!!!!!!!!!!!!!!!!!!!!
!!!!!!!!!!!!!!!!!!!!!!!!!!!!!!!!!!!!!!!!!!!!!!!!!!!!!!!!!!!!!!!!!!!!!!
<output omitted>
!!!!!!!!!!!!!!!!!!!!!!!!!!!!!!!!!!!!!!!!!!!!!!!!!!!!!!!!!!!!!!!!!!!!!!
!!!!!!!!!!!!!!!!!!!!
Success rate is 100 percent (1000/1000), round-trip min/avg/max =
1/2/12 ms
```

d. You should see the results of the pings from R2 on the graph as an Input Packet Count. The scale of the graph is automatically adjusted depending on the volume of traffic. You can also view the data in tabular form by clicking the **Table** tab. Notice that the view selected at the bottom left of the Graph screen is Real-time, data every 10 seconds. Click the pull-down menu to see the other options available.

e. Ping from PC-B to R1 Fa0/0 at 209.165.200.225 using the –n option (number of packets) to specify 1000 packets:

```
C:>\ ping 209.165.200.225 –n 1000
```

Note: The response from the PC is relatively slow, and it might take a while to show up on the graph as Output Packet Count. The following graph shows an additional 5000 input packets as well as both input and output packet counts.

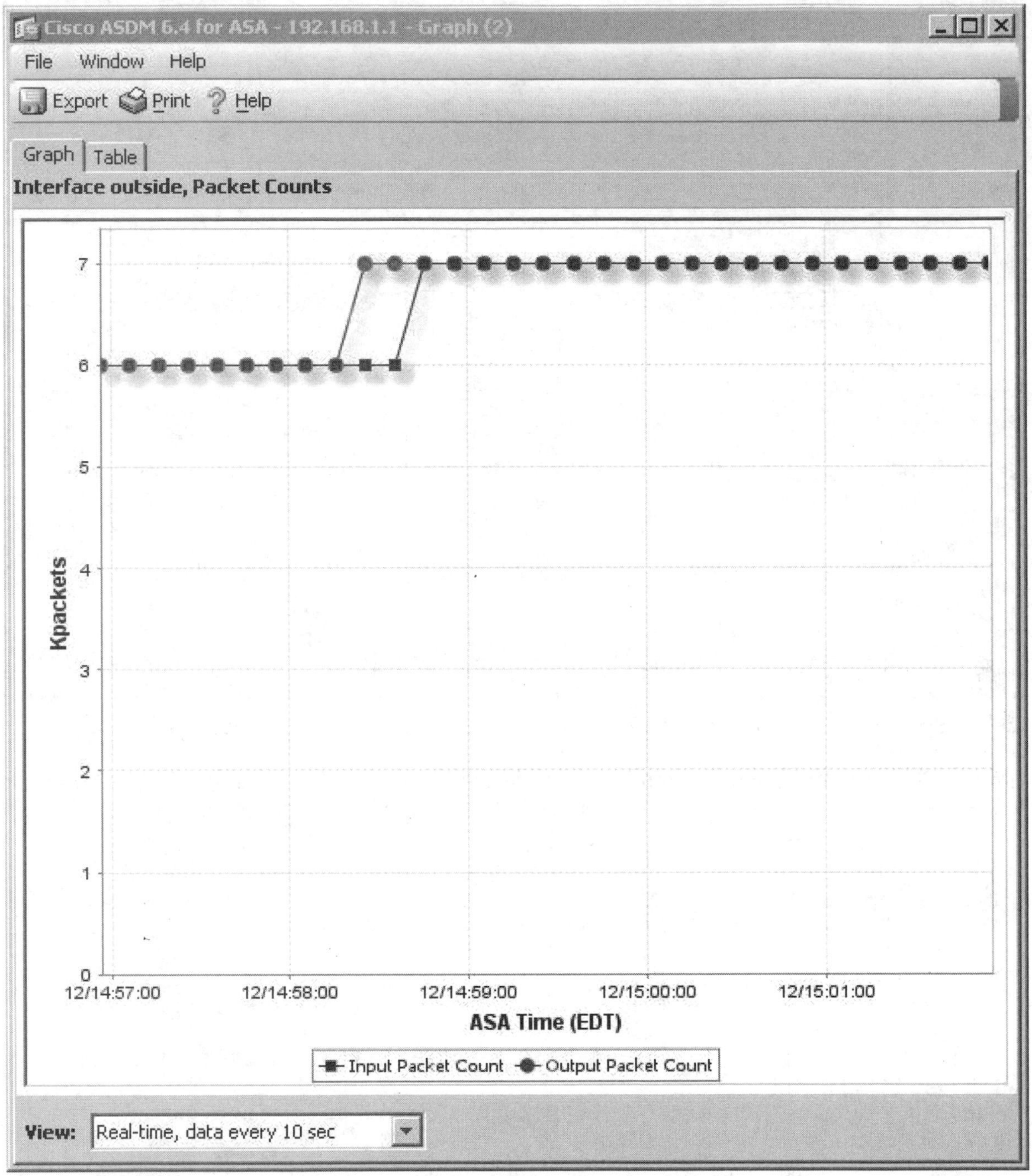

Reflection

1. What are some benefits to using ASDM over the CLI?

____

____

____

2. What are some benefits to using the CLI over ASDM?

____
____
____

Router Interface Summary Table

Router Model	Ethernet Interface 1	Ethernet Interface 2	Serial Interface 1	Serial Interface 2
1800	Fast Ethernet 0/0 (Fa0/0)	Fast Ethernet 0/1 (Fa0/1)	Serial 0/0/0 (S0/0/0)	Serial 0/0/1 (S0/0/1)
1900	Gigabit Ethernet 0/0 (G0/0)	Gigabit Ethernet 0/1 (G0/1)	Serial 0/0/0 (S0/0/0)	Serial 0/0/1 (S0/0/1)
2800	Fast Ethernet 0/0 (Fa0/0)	Fast Ethernet 0/1 (Fa0/1)	Serial 0/0/0 (S0/0/0)	Serial 0/0/1 (S0/0/1)
2900	Gigabit Ethernet 0/0 (G0/0)	Gigabit Ethernet 0/1 (G0/1)	Serial 0/0/0 (S0/0/0)	Serial 0/0/1 (S0/0/1)

Note: To find out how the router is configured, look at the interfaces to identify the type of router and how many interfaces the router has. There is no way to effectively list all the combinations of configurations for each router class. This table includes identifiers for the possible combinations of Ethernet and serial interfaces in the device. The table does not include any other type of interface, even though a specific router may contain one. An example of this might be an ISDN BRI interface. The string in parentheses is the legal abbreviation that can be used in Cisco IOS commands to represent the interface.

Chapter 10 Lab G: Configuring ASA 5510 Clientless and AnyConnect Remote Access SSL VPNs Using ASDM

Topology

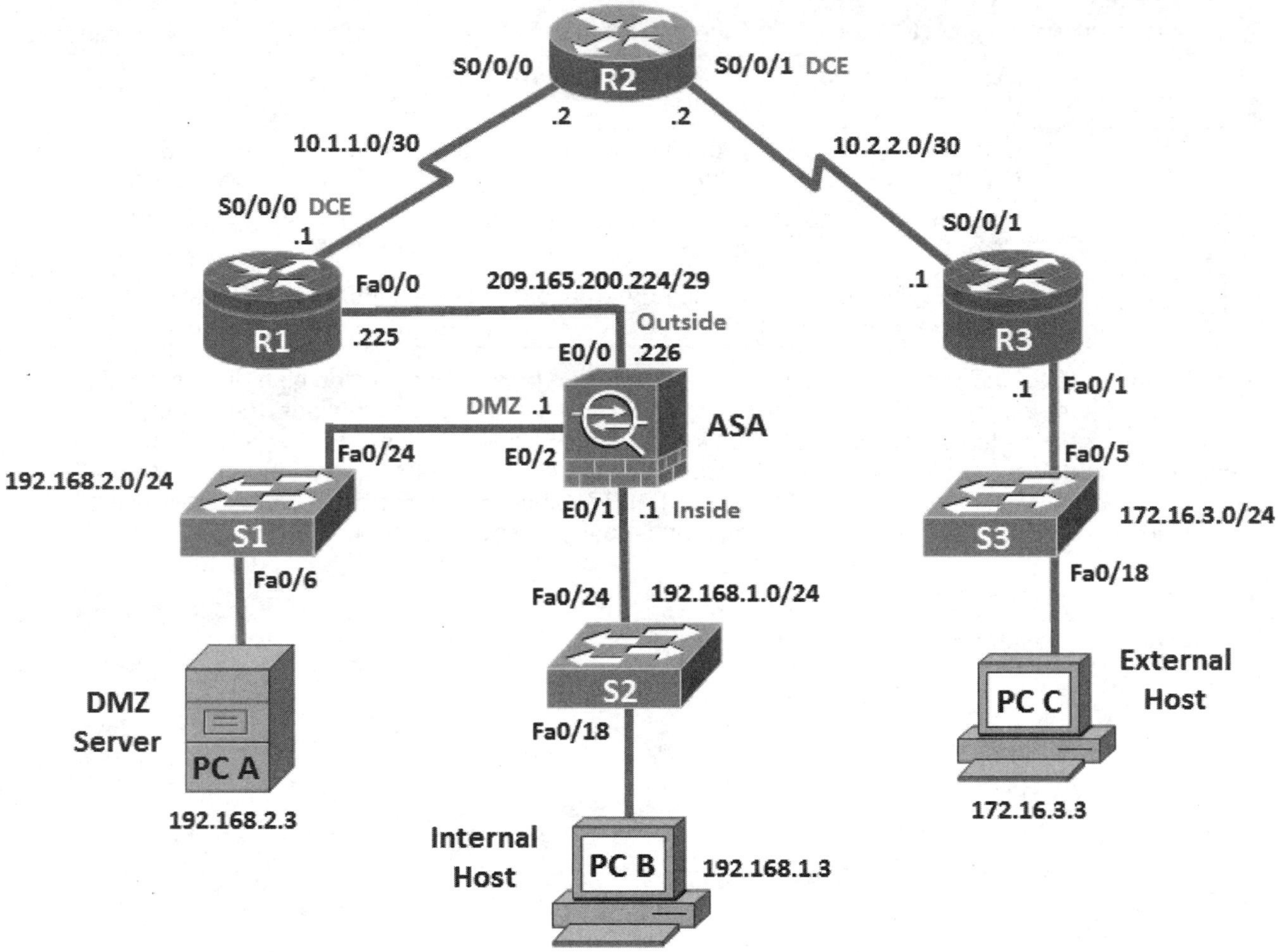

Note: ISR G2 devices have Gigabit Ethernet interfaces rather than FastEthernet interfaces.

IP Addressing Table

Device	Interface	IP Address	Subnet Mask	Default Gateway	Switch Port
R1	Fa0/0	209.165.200.225	255.255.255.248	N/A	ASA E0/0
	S0/0/0 (DCE)	10.1.1.1	255.255.255.252	N/A	N/A
R2	S0/0/0	10.1.1.2	255.255.255.252	N/A	N/A
	S0/0/1 (DCE)	10.2.2.2	255.255.255.252	N/A	N/A
R3	Fa0/1	172.16.3.1	255.255.255.0	N/A	S3 Fa0/5
	S0/0/1	10.2.2.1	255.255.255.252	N/A	N/A
ASA	E0/0 (outside)	209.165.200.226	255.255.255.248	NA	R1 Fa0/0
	E0/1 (inside)	192.168.1.1	255.255.255.0	NA	S2 Fa0/24
	E0/2 (dmz)	192.168.2.1	255.255.255.0	NA	S1 Fa0/24
PC-A	NIC	192.168.2.3	255.255.255.0	192.168.2.1	S1 Fa0/6
PC-B	NIC	192.168.1.3	255.255.255.0	192.168.1.1	S2 Fa0/18
PC-C	NIC	172.16.3.3	255.255.255.0	172.16.3.1	S3 Fa0/18

Objectives

Part 1: Lab Setup

- Cable the network as shown in the topology.
- Configure hostnames and interface IP addresses for routers, switches, and PCs.
- Configure static routing, including default routes, between R1, R2, and R3.
- Verify connectivity between hosts, switches, and routers.

Part 2: Accessing the ASA Console and Preparing for VPN Configuration

- Access the ASA console.
- Clear previous configuration settings.
- Load the ASA CLI command script to configure basic settings.
- Access ASDM.

Part 3: Configuring Clientless SSL VPN Remote Access Using ASDM

- Configure the SSL VPN interface connection profile.
- Configure Local AAA user authentication.
- Configure the group policy.
- Configure a bookmark list for intranet URLs.
- Verify access to the VPN portal.
- Monitor the clientless SSL VPN connection.

Part 4: Configuring AnyConnect Client SSL VPN Remote Access Using ASDM

- Clear Clientless SSL VPN configuration from Part 3.

- Configure the SSL VPN interface connection profile.
- Configure the VPN encryption protocol.
- Configure the AnyConnect client image to upload.
- Configure Local AAA user authentication.
- Configure the client address pool.
- Configure the DNS server and NAT exempt.
- Configure AnyConnect client deployment.
- Verify VPN access and AnyConnect client upload.
- Monitor the AnyConnect SSL VPN connection.

Background/Scenario

In addition to stateful firewall and other security features, the ASA can provide both site-to-site and remote access VPN functionality. The ASA provides two main deployment modes that are found in Cisco SSL remote access VPN solutions:

- **Clientless SSL VPN:** Clientless, browser-based VPN that lets users establish a secure, remote-access VPN tunnel to the ASA using a web browser and built-in SSL to protect VPN traffic. After authentication, users are presented with a portal page and can access specific, predefined internal resources from the portal.
- **Client-Based SSL VPN:** Provides full-tunnel SSL VPN connection but requires a VPN client application to be installed on the remote host. After authentication, users can access any internal resource as if they were physically on the local network. The ASA supports both SSL and IPsec client–based VPNs.

In Part 1 of the lab, you configure the topology and non-ASA devices. In Part 2, you prepare the ASA for ADSM access. In Part 3, you use the ASDM VPN Wizard to configure a clientless SSL remote access VPN and verify access using a remote PC with a browser. In Part 4, you configure an AnyConnect client-based SSL remote access VPN and verify connectivity.

Your company has two locations connected to an ISP. Router R1 represents a CPE device managed by the ISP. Router R2 represents an intermediate Internet router. Router R3 connects users at the remote branch office to the ISP. The ASA is an edge CPE security device that connects the internal corporate network and DMZ to the ISP while providing NAT services to inside hosts.

Management has asked you to provide VPN access, using the ASA as a VPN concentrator, to teleworkers. They want you to test both the clientless access model, using SSL and a browser for client access, and the client-based model using SSL and the Cisco AnyConnect client.

Note: The routers used with this lab are Cisco 1841 with Cisco IOS Software Release 12.4(20)T (advanced IP image). The switches are Cisco WS-C2960-24TT-L with Cisco IOS Software Release 12.2(46)SE (C2960-LANBASEK9-M image). Other routers, switches, and Cisco IOS versions can be used; however, results and output may vary.

The ASA used with this lab is a Cisco model 5510 with four FastEthernet routed interfaces running OS Version 8.4(2) and ASDM Version 6.4(5) and comes with a Base license that allows a maximum of 50 VLANs.

Note: Make sure the routers and switches have been erased and have no startup configurations.

Required Resources

- 3 routers (Cisco 1841 with Cisco IOS Software Release 12.4(20)T1 or comparable)

- 3 switches (Cisco 2960 or comparable)
- 1 ASA 5510 (OS Version 8.4(2) and ASDM Version 6.4(5) and Base license or comparable)
- PC-A: Windows XP, Vista, or Windows 7 with CCP, PuTTy SSH client (Web server optional)
- PC-B: Windows XP, Vista, or Windows 7 with PuTTy SSH client and Java 6 (ASDM loaded on the PC is optional)
- PC-C: Windows XP, Vista, or Windows 7 with Internet Explorer, CCP, PuTTy SSH client
- Serial and Ethernet cables as shown in the topology
- Rollover cables to configure the routers and ASA via the console

Note: Use of a browser other than Internet Explorer 7 or newer on remote PC-C may produce results different from those shown in this lab. It might be necessary to create an exception when connecting to the ASA over the remote access VPN.

Part 1: Basic Router/Switch/PC Configuration

In Part 1 of this lab, you set up the network topology and configure basic settings on the routers, such as interface IP addresses and static routing.

Note: Do not configure any ASA settings at this time.

Step 1: Cable the network and clear previous device settings.

Attach the devices shown in the topology diagram, and cable as necessary. Make sure the routers and switches have been erased and have no startup configurations.

Step 2: Configure basic settings for routers and switches.

a. Configure hostnames as shown in the topology for each router.

b. Configure router interface IP addresses as shown in the IP addressing table.

c. Configure a clock rate for routers with a DCE serial cable attached to their serial interface.

d. Configure the hostname for the switches. Other than hostname, the switches can be left in their default configuration state. Configuring the VLAN management IP address for the switches is optional.

Step 3: Configure static routing on the routers.

a. Configure a static default route from R1 to R2 and from R3 to R2:

```
R1(config)# ip route 0.0.0.0 0.0.0.0 Serial0/0/0
R3(config)# ip route 0.0.0.0 0.0.0.0 Serial0/0/1
```

b. Configure a static route from R2 to the R1 Fa0/0 subnet (connected to ASA interface E0/0) and a static route from R2 to the R3 LAN:

```
R2(config)# ip route 209.165.200.224 255.255.255.248 Serial0/0/0
R2(config)# ip route 172.16.3.0 255.255.255.0 Serial0/0/1
```

Step 4: Enable the HTTP server on R1 and set the enable and vty passwords.

a. Enable HTTP access to R1 using the **ip http server** command in global config mode. Also, set the VTY password to **cisco**.

b. Configure the same settings on R2 and R3. Router R1 is shown here as an example:

```
R1(config)# ip http server
R1(config)# enable password class

R1(config)# line vty 0 4
R1(config-line)# password cisco
R1(config-line)# login

R1(config)# line con 0
R1(config-line)# password cisco
R1(config-line)# login
```

Step 5: Configure PC host IP settings.

Configure a static IP address, subnet mask, and default gateway for PC-A, PC-B, and PC-C as shown in the IP addressing table.

Step 6: Verify connectivity.

Because the ASA is the focal point for the network zones and it has not yet been configured, there will be no connectivity between devices connected to it; however, PC-C should be able to ping the R1 interface Fa0/0. From PC-C, ping the R1 Fa0/0 IP address (209.165.200.225). If these pings are not successful, troubleshoot the basic device configurations before continuing.

Note: If you can ping from PC-C to R1 Fa0/0, you have demonstrated that static routing is configured and functioning correctly.

Step 7: Save the basic running configuration for each router and switch.

Part 2: Accessing the ASA Console and ASDM

Step 1: Access the ASA console.

a. Accessing the ASA via the console port is the same as with a Cisco router or switch. Connect to the ASA Console port with a rollover cable.

b. Use a terminal emulation program, such as TeraTerm or HyperTerminal, to access the CLI, and use the serial port settings of 9600 baud, 8 data bits, no parity, 1 stop bit, and no flow control.

c. If prompted to enter interactive Firewall configuration (Setup mode), answer **no**.

d. Enter privileged mode with the **enable** command and password (if set). By default, the password is blank, so you can just press **Enter**. If the password has been changed to that specified in this lab, the password will be **class**. In addition, the hostname and prompt will be `CCNAS-ASA>`, as shown here. The default ASA hostname and prompt is `ciscoasa>`.

```
CCNAS-ASA> enable
Password: class (or press Enter if none set)
```

Step 2: Clear the previous ASA configuration settings.

a. Use the **write erase** command to remove the **startup-config** file from flash memory:

```
CCNAS-ASA# write erase
Erase configuration in flash memory? [confirm]
[OK]
CCNAS-ASA#
```

Note: The IOS command **erase startup-config** is not supported on the ASA.

b. Use the **reload** command to restart the ASA. This causes the ASA to come up in CLI Setup mode. If you see the message **System config has been modified. Save? [Y]es/[N]o:**, respond with **N**.

```
CCNAS-ASA# reload
Proceed with reload? [confirm] <enter>
CCNAS-ASA#
***
*** --- START GRACEFUL SHUTDOWN ---
Shutting down isakmp
Shutting down File system
***
*** --- SHUTDOWN NOW ---
Process shutdown finished
Rebooting.....
CISCO SYSTEMS
Embedded BIOS Version 1.0(12)13 08/28/08 15:50:37.45
<output omitted>
```

Step 3: Bypass setup mode.

When the ASA completes the reload process, it should detect that the startup-config file is missing and go into Setup mode. If it does not come up in this mode, repeat Step 2.

a. When prompted to preconfigure the firewall through interactive prompts (Setup mode), respond with **no**.

```
Pre-configure Firewall now through interactive prompts [yes]?  no
```

b. Enter privileged EXEC mode with the **enable** command. The password should be blank (no password) at this point.

```
ciscoasa> enable
Password: <enter>
```

Step 4: Configure the ASA by using the CLI script.

In this step, you use the modified running-config from Lab 10E to preconfigure basic settings, the firewall and DMZ.

a. Other than the defaults that the ASA automatically inserts, ensure that there is no previous configuration in the ASA by using the **show run** command.

b. Enter CLI global configuration mode. When prompted to enable anonymous call-home reporting, respond **no**.

```
ciscoasa# conf t
ciscoasa(config)#
```

c. Copy and paste the Pre-VPN Configuration Script commands listed below at the ASA global config mode prompt to bring it to the point where you can start configuring the SSL VPNs.

d. Observe the messages as the commands are applied to ensure that there are no warnings or errors. If prompted to replace the RSA keypair, respond **yes**.

e. After script commands have been applied, issue the **`write mem`** (or **`copy run start`**) command to save the running configuration to the startup configuration and the RSA keys to nonvolatile memory.

Lab 10G Pre-VPN Configuration Script:

```
hostname CCNAS-ASA
!
domain-name ccnasecurity.com
!
enable password class
passwd cisco
!
interface Ethernet0/0
 nameif outside
 security-level 0
 ip address 209.165.200.226 255.255.255.248
 no shut
!
interface Ethernet0/1
 nameif inside
 security-level 100
 ip address 192.168.1.1 255.255.255.0
 no shut
!
interface Ethernet0/2
 nameif dmz
 security-level 70
 ip address 192.168.2.1 255.255.255.0
 no shut
!
object network inside-net
 subnet 192.168.1.0 255.255.255.0
!
object network dmz-server
 host 192.168.2.3
!
access-list OUTSIDE-DMZ extended permit ip any host 192.168.2.3
!
object network inside-net
 nat (inside,outside) dynamic interface
!
object network dmz-server
 nat (dmz,outside) static 209.165.200.227
!
access-group OUTSIDE-DMZ in interface outside
!
route outside 0.0.0.0 0.0.0.0 209.165.200.225 1
!
username admin password cisco123
!
aaa authentication telnet console LOCAL
aaa authentication ssh console LOCAL
```

```
aaa authentication http console LOCAL
!
http server enable
http 192.168.1.0 255.255.255.0 inside
ssh 192.168.1.0 255.255.255.0 inside
telnet 192.168.1.0 255.255.255.0 inside
telnet timeout 10
ssh timeout 10
!
class-map inspection_default
 match default-inspection-traffic
policy-map type inspect dns preset_dns_map
 parameters
  message-length maximum client auto
  message-length maximum 512
policy-map global_policy
 class inspection_default
   inspect icmp
!
prompt hostname context
no call-home reporting anonymous
!
crypto key generate rsa modulus 1024
```

Step 5: Access ASDM.

a. Open a browser on PC-B and test HTTPS access to the ASA by entering **https://192.168.1.1**.

Note: Be sure to specify the HTTPS protocol in the URL.

b. After entering the URL above, you should see a security warning about the website security certificate. Click **Continue to This Website**. Click **Yes** for any other security warnings. At the ASDM welcome page, click the **Run ASDM** button. The ASDM-IDM Launcher displays. Log in as user **admin** with password **cisco123**. ASDM loads the current configuration into the GUI.

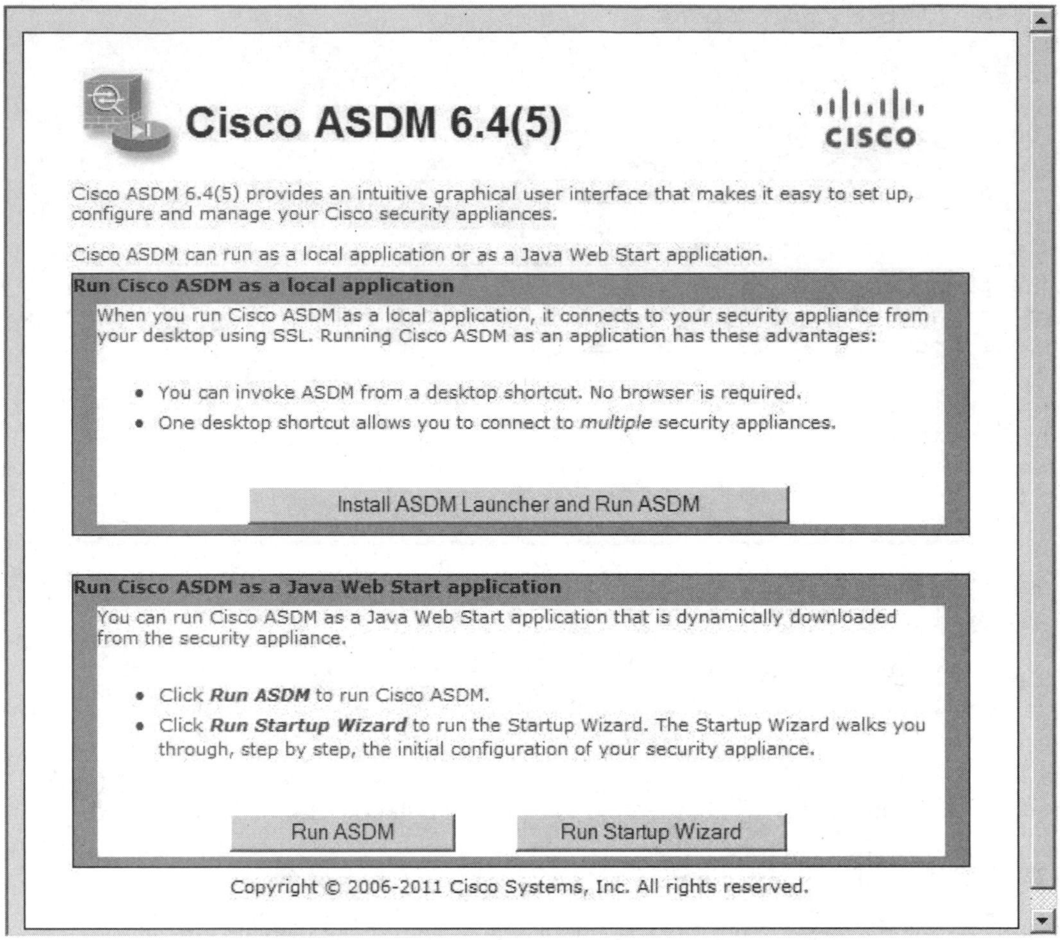
Cisco ASDM 6.4(5)
Cisco ASDM 6.4(5) provides an intuitive graphical user interface that makes it easy to set up, configure and manage your Cisco security appliances.
Cisco ASDM can run as a local application or as a Java Web Start application.
Run Cisco ASDM as a local application
When you run Cisco ASDM as a local application, it connects to your security appliance from your desktop using SSL. Running Cisco ASDM as an application has these advantages:
You can invoke ASDM from a desktop shortcut. No browser is required.
One desktop shortcut allows you to connect to multiple security appliances.
Install ASDM Launcher and Run ASDM
Run Cisco ASDM as a Java Web Start application
You can run Cisco ASDM as a Java Web Start application that is dynamically downloaded from the security appliance.
Click Run ASDM to run Cisco ASDM.
Click Run Startup Wizard to run the Startup Wizard. The Startup Wizard walks you through, step by step, the initial configuration of your security appliance.
Run ASDM
Run Startup Wizard
Copyright © 2006-2011 Cisco Systems, Inc. All rights reserved.

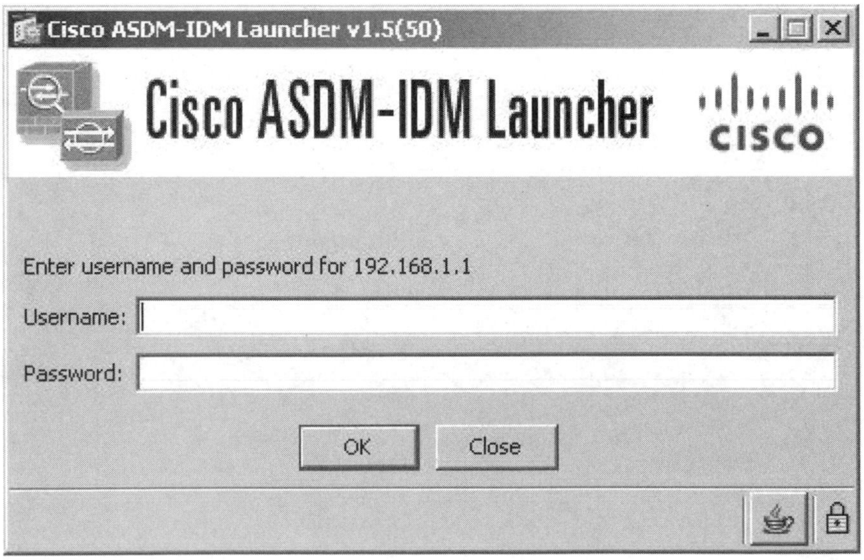
Cisco ASDM-IDM Launcher v1.5(50)
Cisco ASDM-IDM Launcher
Enter username and password for 192.168.1.1
Username:
Password:
OK
Close

Part 3: Configuring Clientless SSL VPN Remote Access Using ASDM

Step 1: Review the Remote Access VPN ASDM Assistant.

a. From the menu bar, choose the **Configuration** button and click **Remote Access VPN** to display the Introduction screen. From here, you can access information on how to create any of the three types of remote access VPNs.

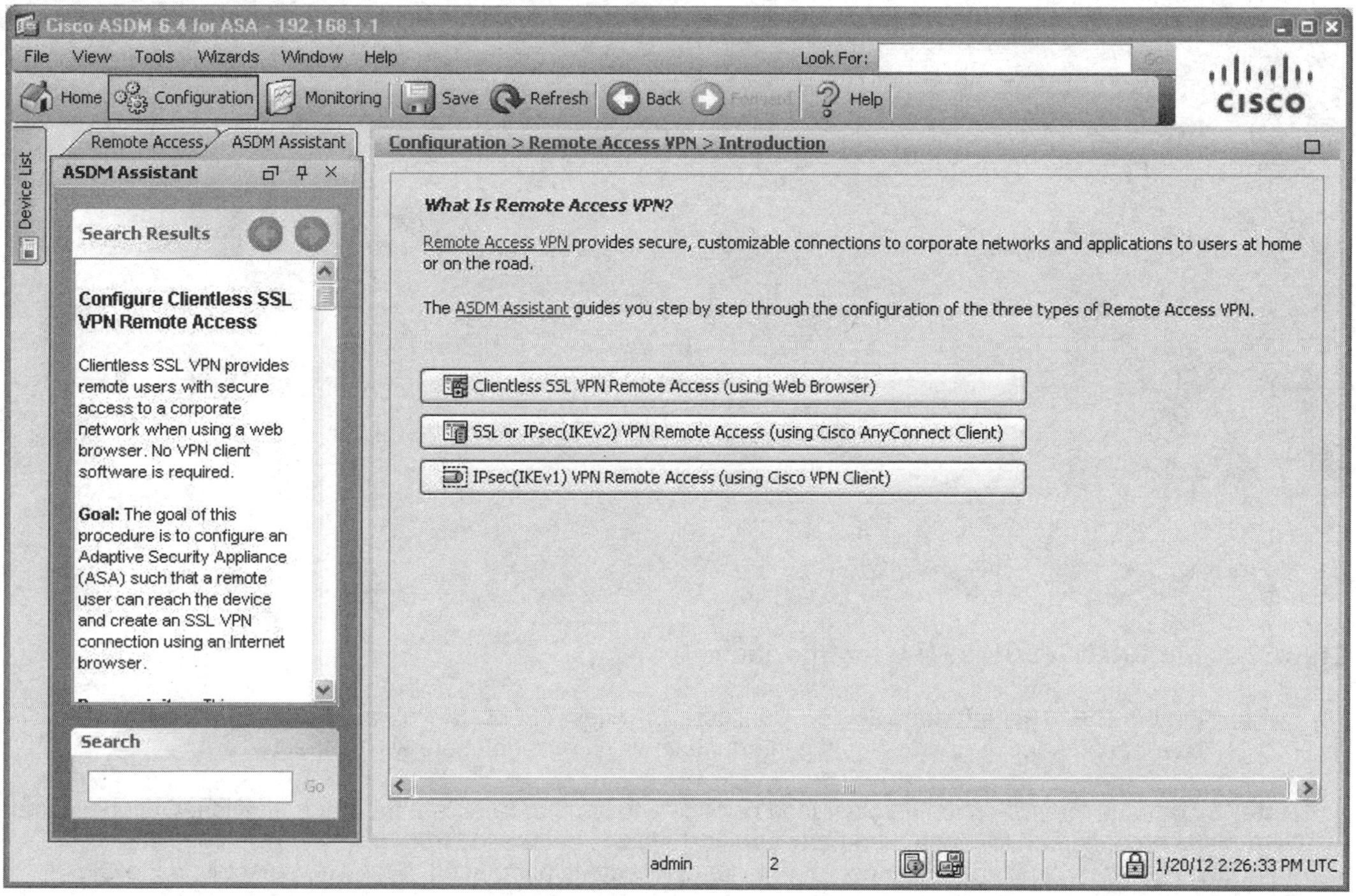

b. Click the **Clientless SSL VPN Remote Access (using Web Browser)** button to access the ASDM Assistant. Read through the information provided to get a better understanding of the process for creating this type of VPN.

Step 2: Start the VPN Wizard.

a. From the ASDM main menu at the top of the browser window, select **Wizards > VPN Wizards > Clientless SSL VPN wizard**. The SSL VPN Wizard Clientless SSL VPN Connection screen appears.

b. Review the on-screen text and topology diagram, and then click **Next** to continue.

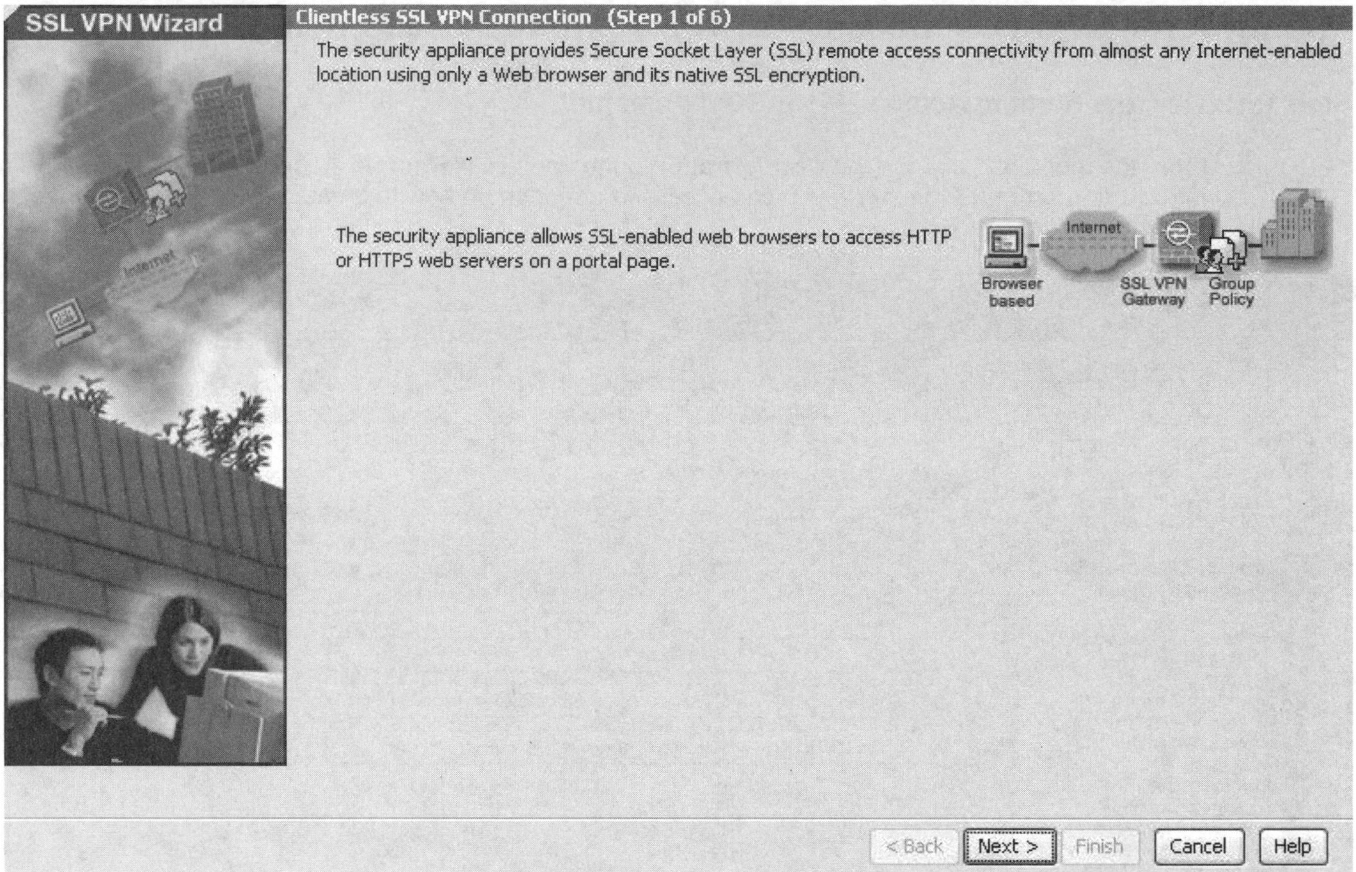

Step 3: Configure the SSL VPN user interface.

a. On the SSL VPN Interface screen, configure ClientlessVPN-Con-Prof as the Connection Profile Name, and specify **outside** as the interface to which outside users will connect.

Note: By default, the ASA uses a self-signed certificate to send to the client for authentication. Optionally, the ASA may be configured to use a third-party certificate that is purchased from a well-known certificate authority, such as VeriSign, to connect clients. If a certificate is purchased, it may be selected in the Digital Certificate drop-down menu.

The SSL VPN Interface screen provides links in the Information section. These links identify the URLs that need to be used for the SSL VPN service access (login) and for Cisco ASDM access (to access the Cisco ASDM software).

b. Click **Next** to continue.

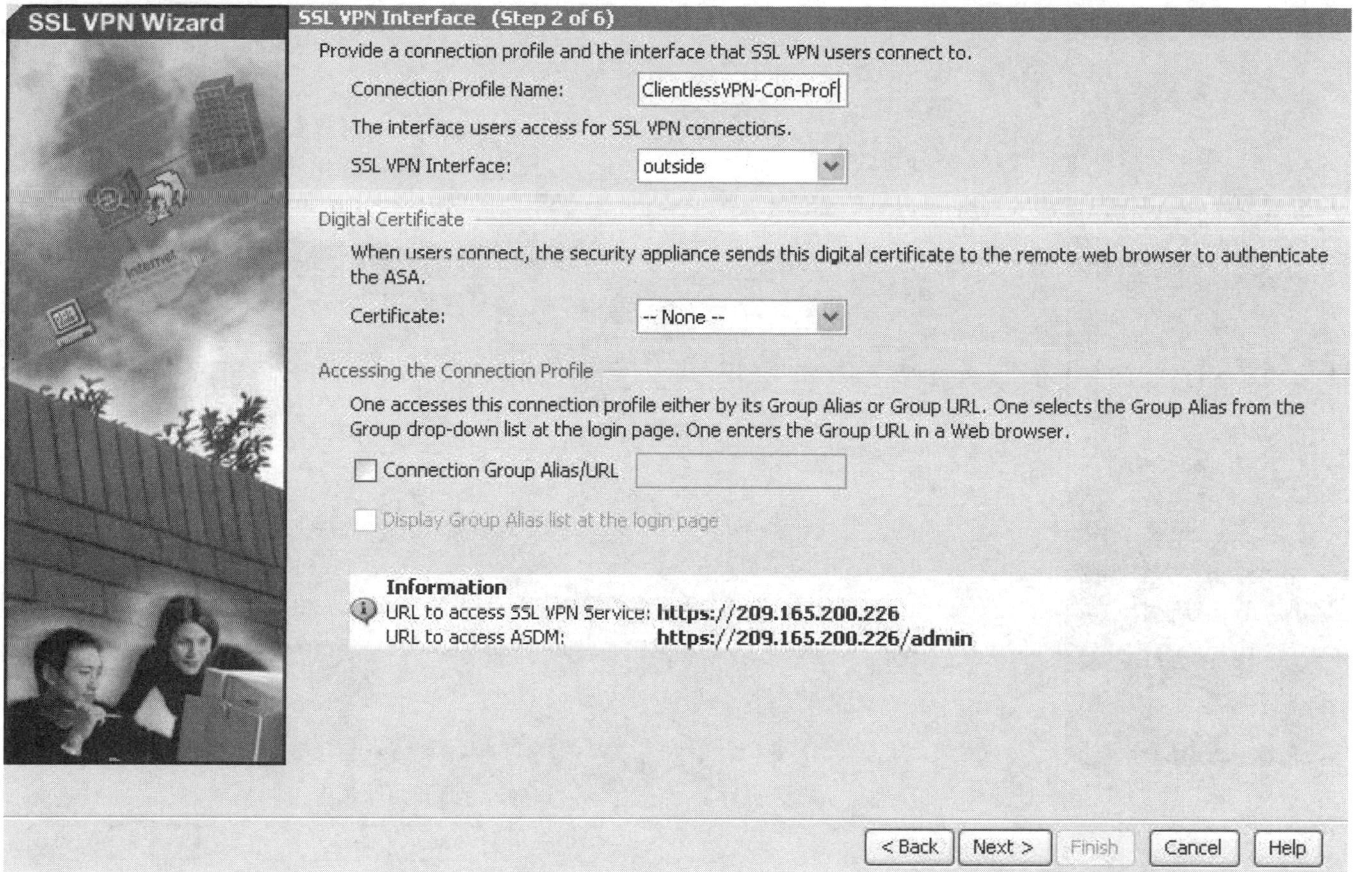

Step 4: Configure AAA user authentication.

On the User Authentication screen, click **Authenticate Using the Local User Database**, enter the username **VPN-User** with a password of **remote**. Click **Add** to create the new user, and click **Next** to continue.

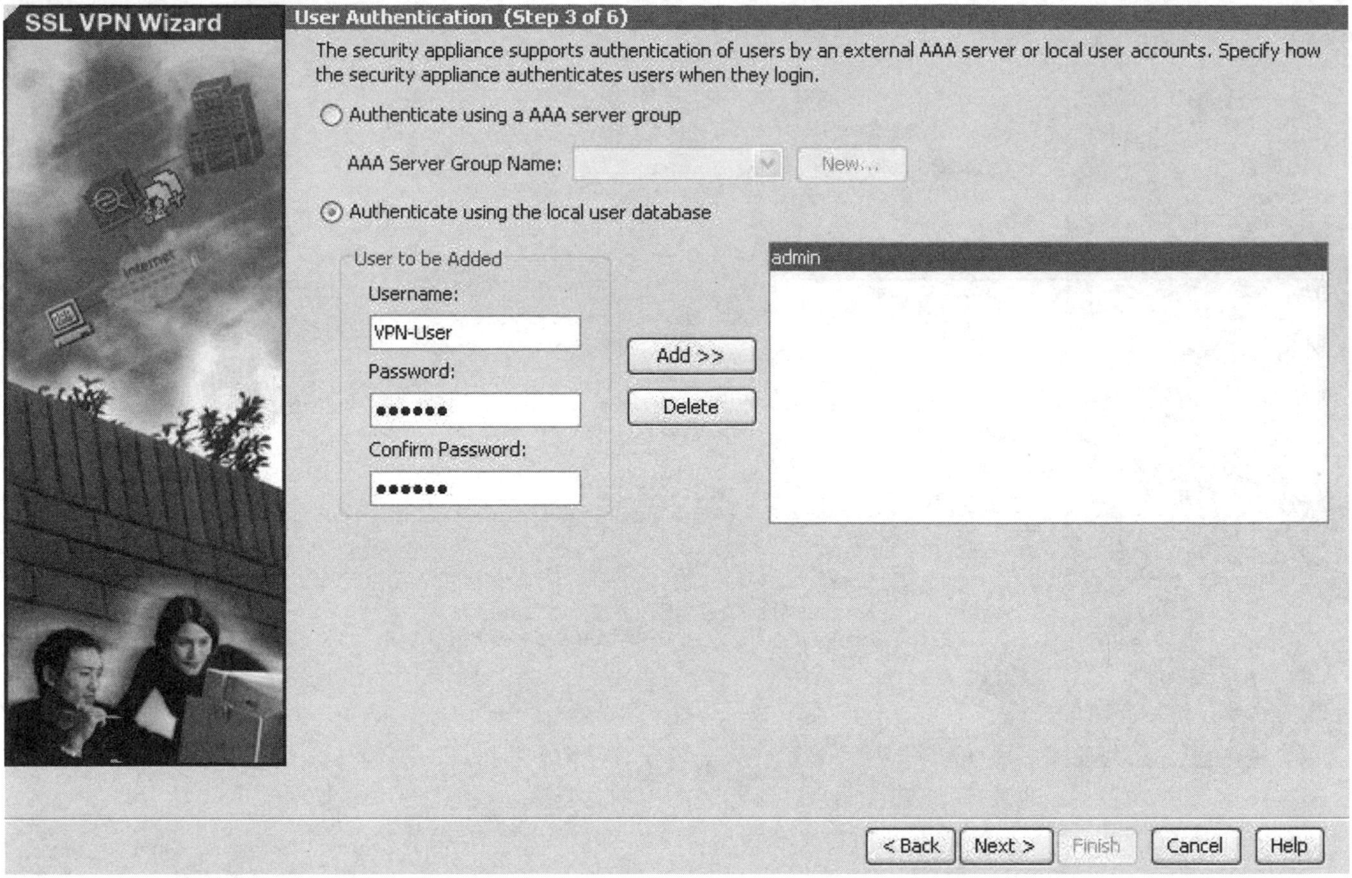

Step 5: Configure the VPN group policy.

On the Group Policy screen, create a new group policy named **ClientlessVPN-Grp-Pol**. When configuring a new policy, the policy name cannot contain any spaces. Click **Next** to continue.

Note: By default, the created user group policy will inherit its settings from DfltGrpPolicy. These settings may be modified after the wizard has been completed by navigating to the **Configuration > Remote Access VPN > Clientless SSL VPN Access > Group Policies** submenu.

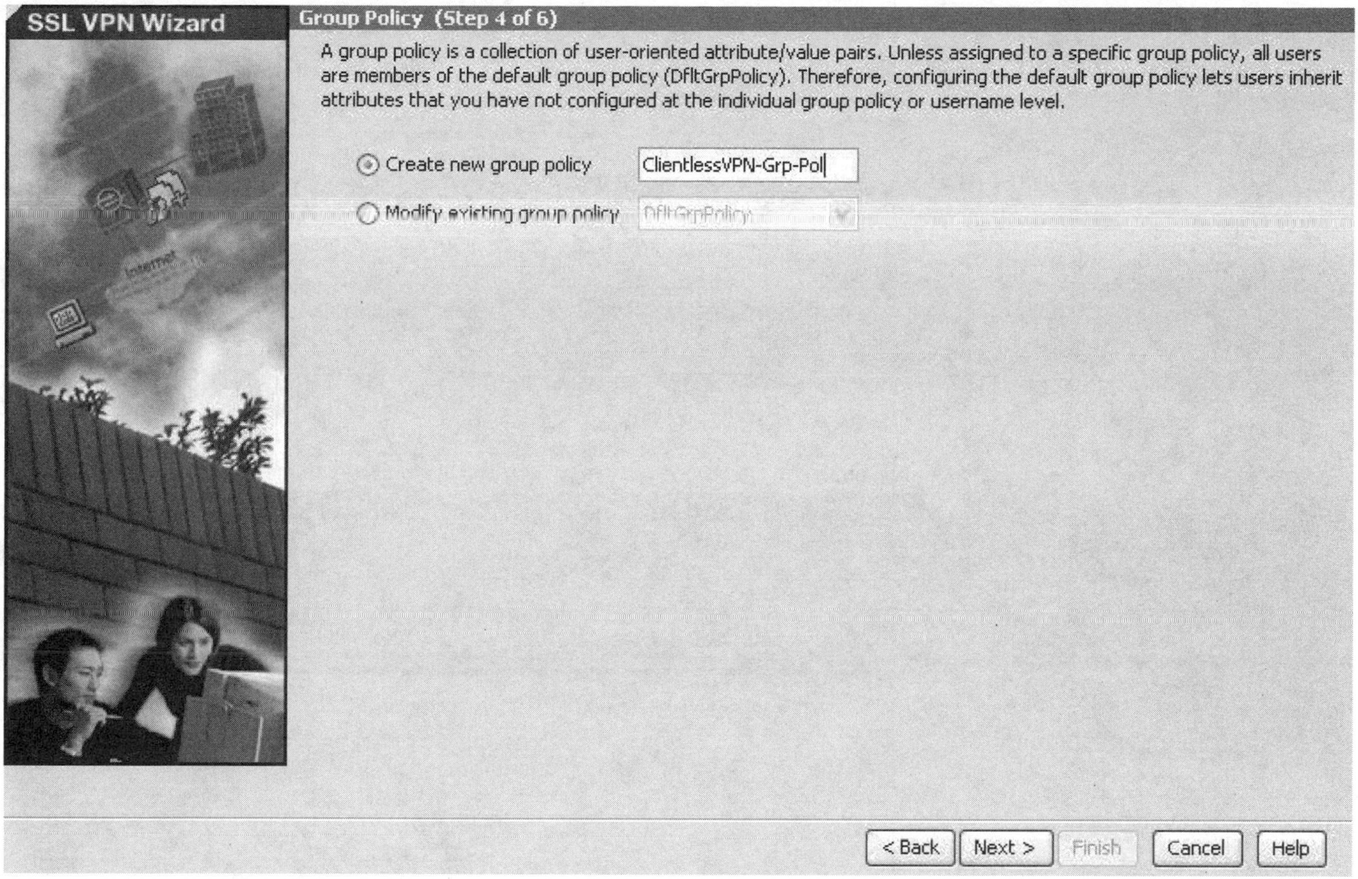

Step 6: Configure the bookmark list (clientless connections only).

A bookmark list is a set of URLs configured to be used in the clientless SSL VPN web portal. If there are bookmarks already listed, use the Bookmark List drop-down menu, select the bookmark of choice, and click **Next** to continue with the SSL VPN Wizard. However, no configured bookmark lists exist by default, and therefore they must be configured by the network administrator.

a. From the Clientless Connections Only – Bookmark List screen, click the **Manage** button to create an HTTP server bookmark in the bookmark list. In the Configure GUI Customization Objects window, click **Add** to open the Add Bookmark List window. Name the list **Web-Server**.

Note: If the Web-Server bookmark list is shown as available from a previous configuration, you can delete it in ASDM and re-create it.

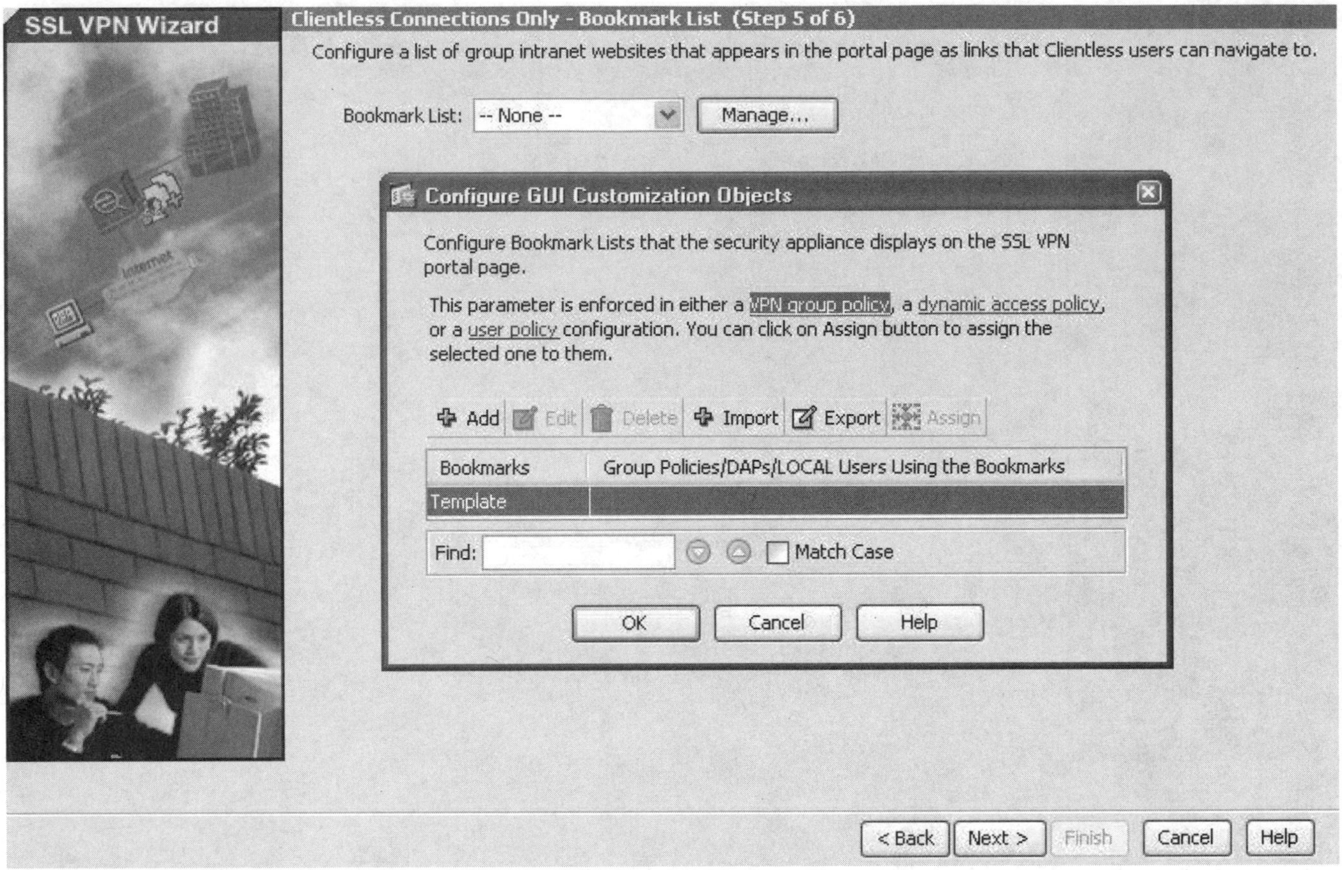
SSL VPN Wizard
Clientless Connections Only - Bookmark List (Step 5 of 6)
Configure a list of group intranet websites that appears in the portal page as links that Clientless users can navigate to.
Bookmark List: -- None --
Manage...
Configure GUI Customization Objects
Configure Bookmark Lists that the security appliance displays on the SSL VPN portal page.
This parameter is enforced in either a VPN group policy, a dynamic access policy, or a user policy configuration. You can click on Assign button to assign the selected one to them.
Add
Edit
Delete
Import
Export
Assign
Bookmarks
Group Policies/DAPs/LOCAL Users Using the Bookmarks
Template
Find:
Match Case
OK
Cancel
Help
< Back
Next >
Finish
Cancel
Help

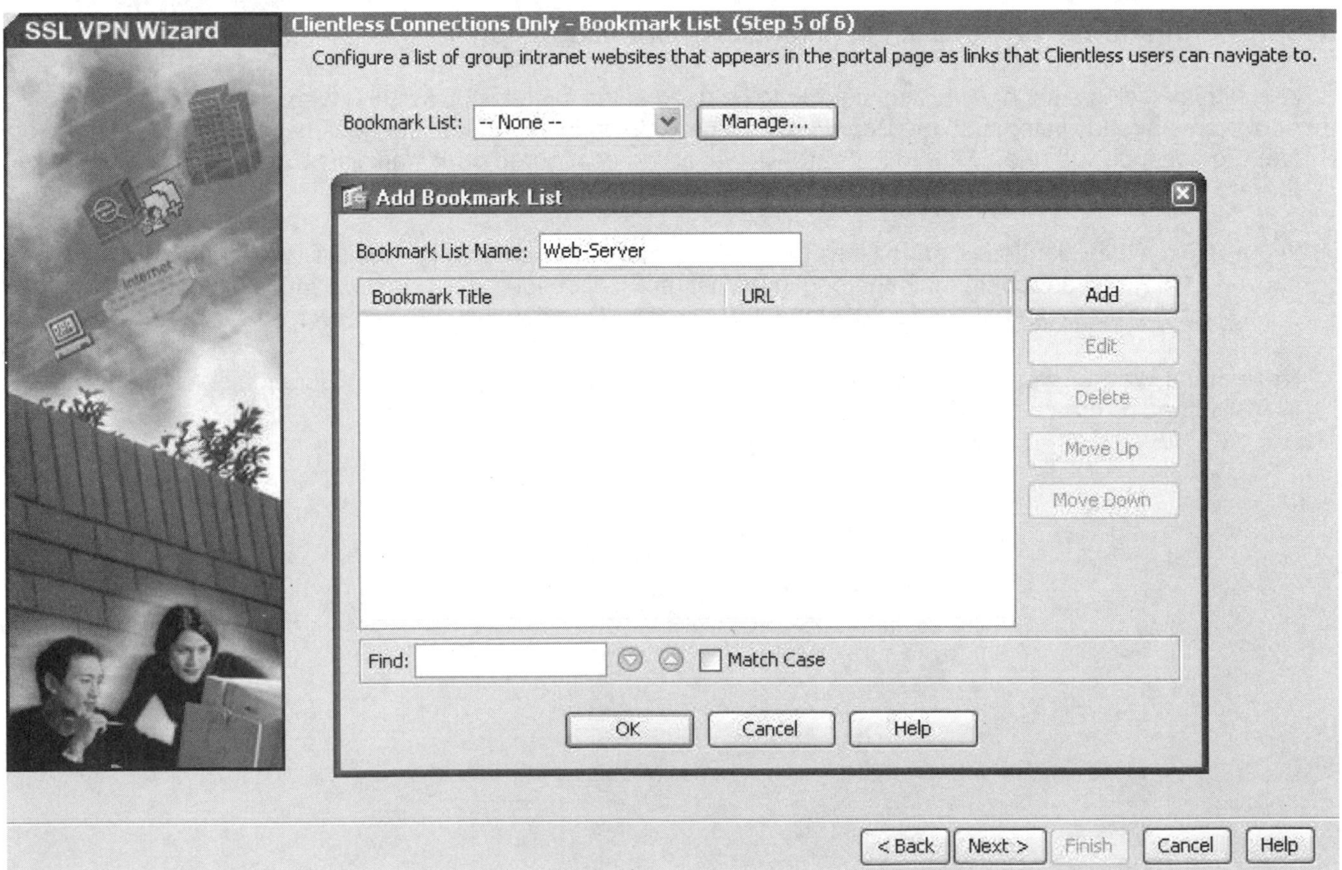
SSL VPN Wizard
Clientless Connections Only - Bookmark List (Step 5 of 6)
Configure a list of group intranet websites that appears in the portal page as links that Clientless users can navigate to.
Bookmark List: -- None --
Manage...
Add Bookmark List
Bookmark List Name: Web-Server
Bookmark Title
URL
Add
Edit
Delete
Move Up
Move Down
Find:
Match Case
OK
Cancel
Help
< Back
Next >
Finish
Cancel
Help

b. From the Add Bookmark List window, click **Add** to open the Add Bookmark window. Enter **Web-Mail** as the bookmark title. Enter the server destination IP address or hostname as the URL to be used with the bookmark entry. In this example, the internal IP address of the DMZ server is specified. If this server has HTTP web services and web mail installed and functional, the outside users will be able to access the server from the ASA portal when they connect.

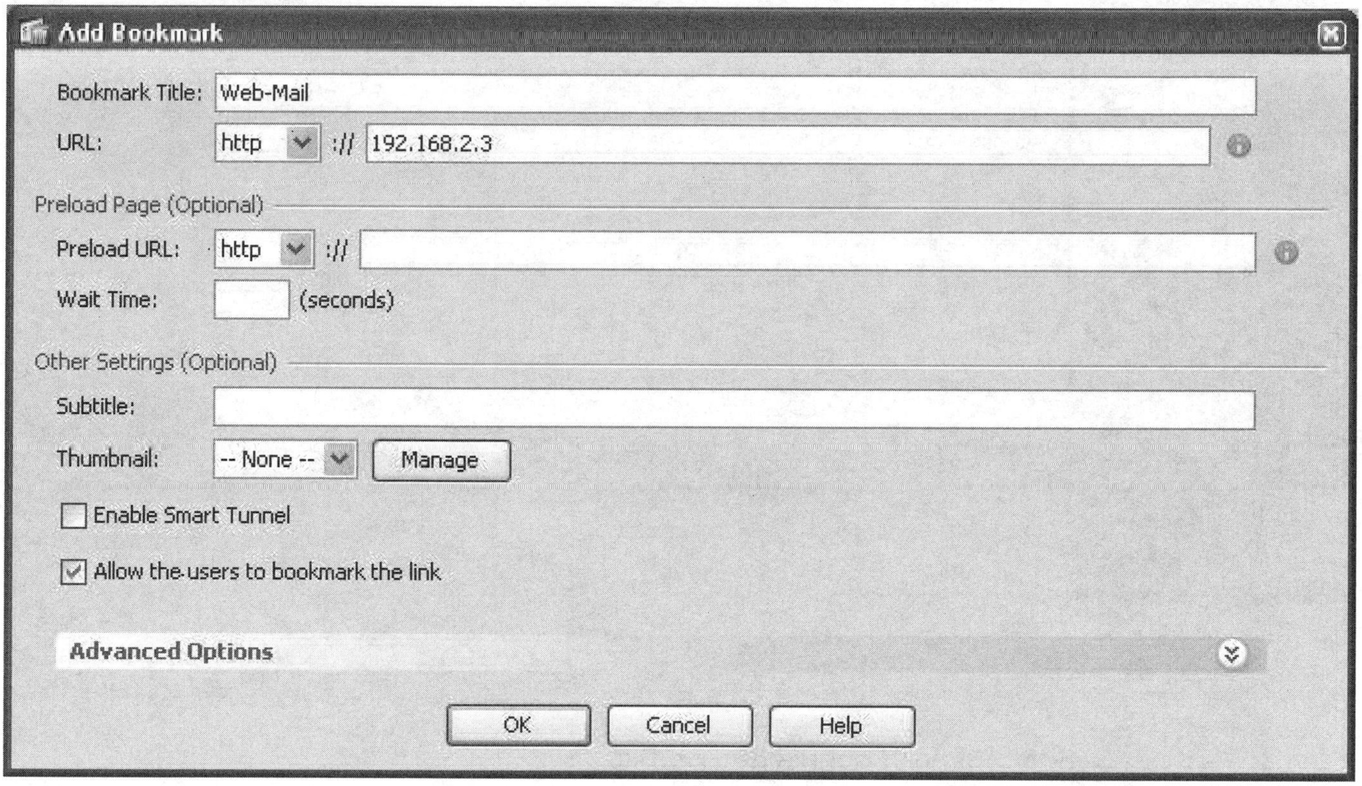

c. After you enter the bookmark title and URL, click **OK** in the Add Bookmark window to return to the Configure GUI Customization Objects window. Select the bookmark you want, and click **OK** to return to the Bookmark List window. Click **Next** to continue.

Step 7: Review the configuration summary and deliver the commands to the ASA.

a. The Summary page is displayed next. Verify that the information configured in the SSL VPN Wizard is correct. You can click the **Back** button to make changes or click **Cancel** and restart the VPN Wizard.

b. Click **Finish** to complete the process and deliver the commands to the ASA.

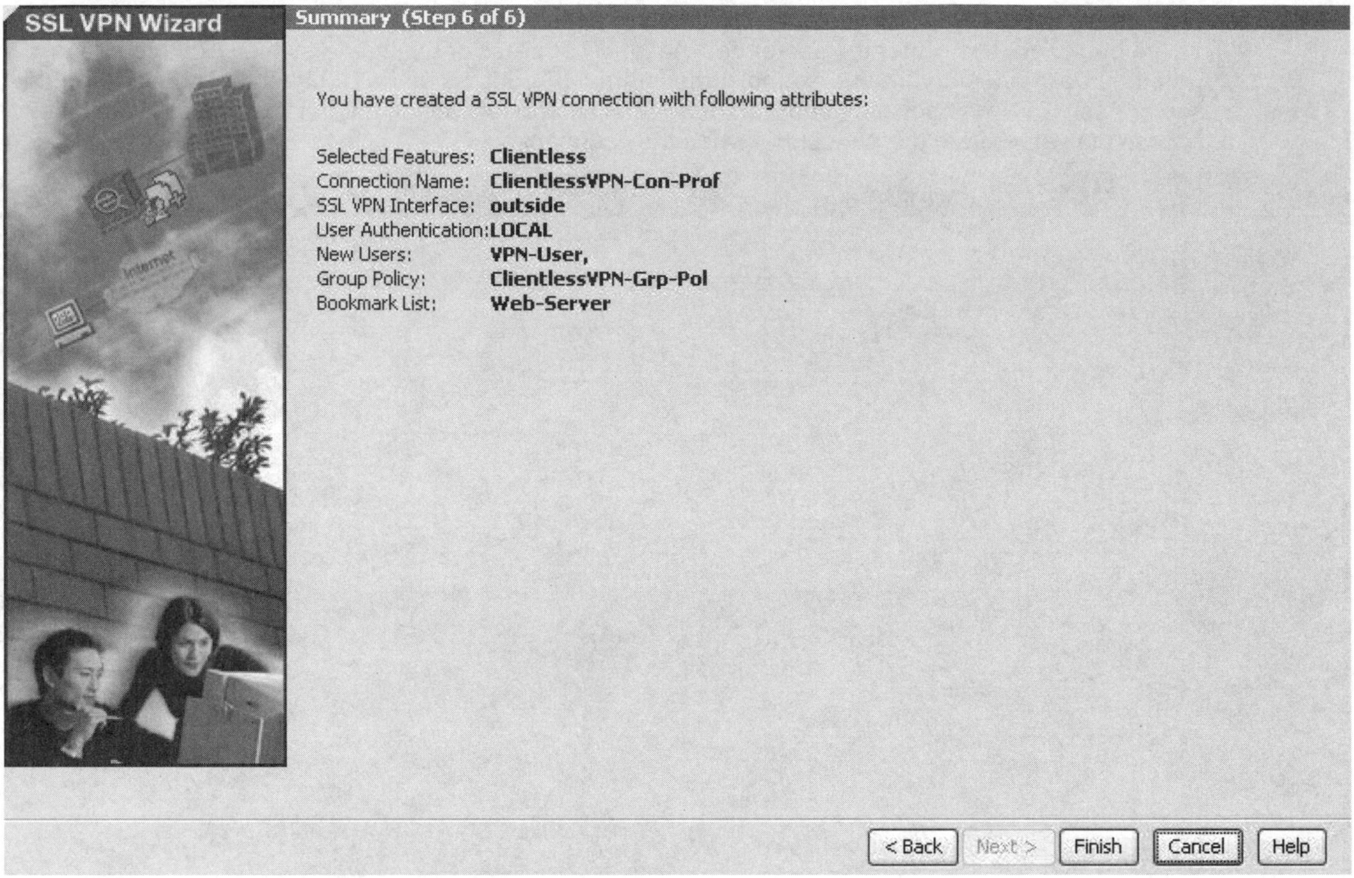

Step 8: Verify the ASDM SSL VPN connection profile.

In ASDM, choose **Configuration > Remote Access VPN > Clientless SSL VPN Access > Connection Profiles**. You can verify and edit the VPN configuration from this window.

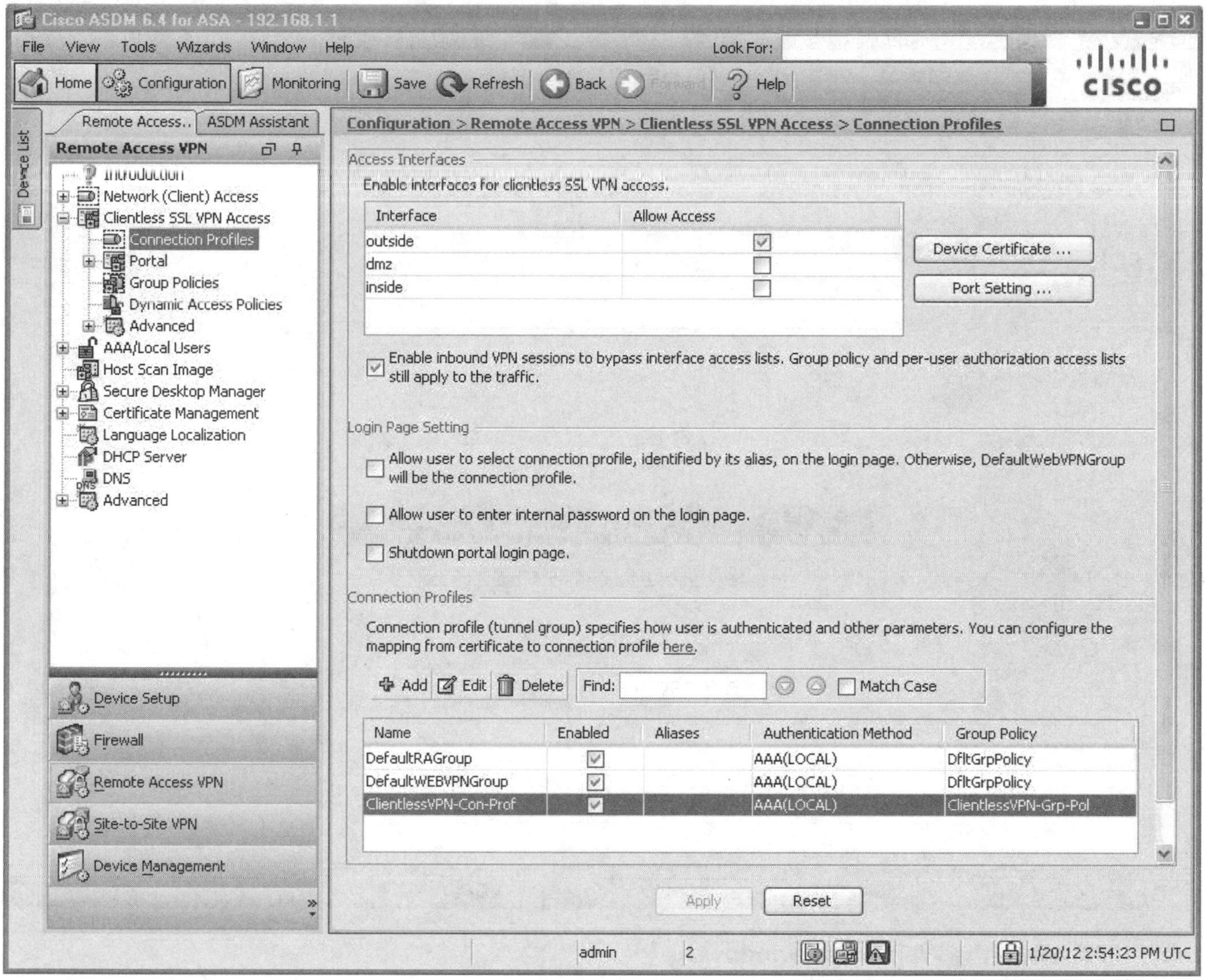

Step 9: Verify VPN access from the remote host.

a. Open the browser on PC-C and enter the login URL for the SSL VPN into the address field (https://209.165.200.226). Be sure to use secure HTTP (HTTPS) because SSL is required to connect to the ASA. After entering the URL, you should see a security warning about the website security certificate. Click **Continue to This Website**. Click **Yes** for any other security warnings.

b. The Logon window should appear. Enter the previously configured username **VPN-User** and password **remote**, and click **Login** to continue.

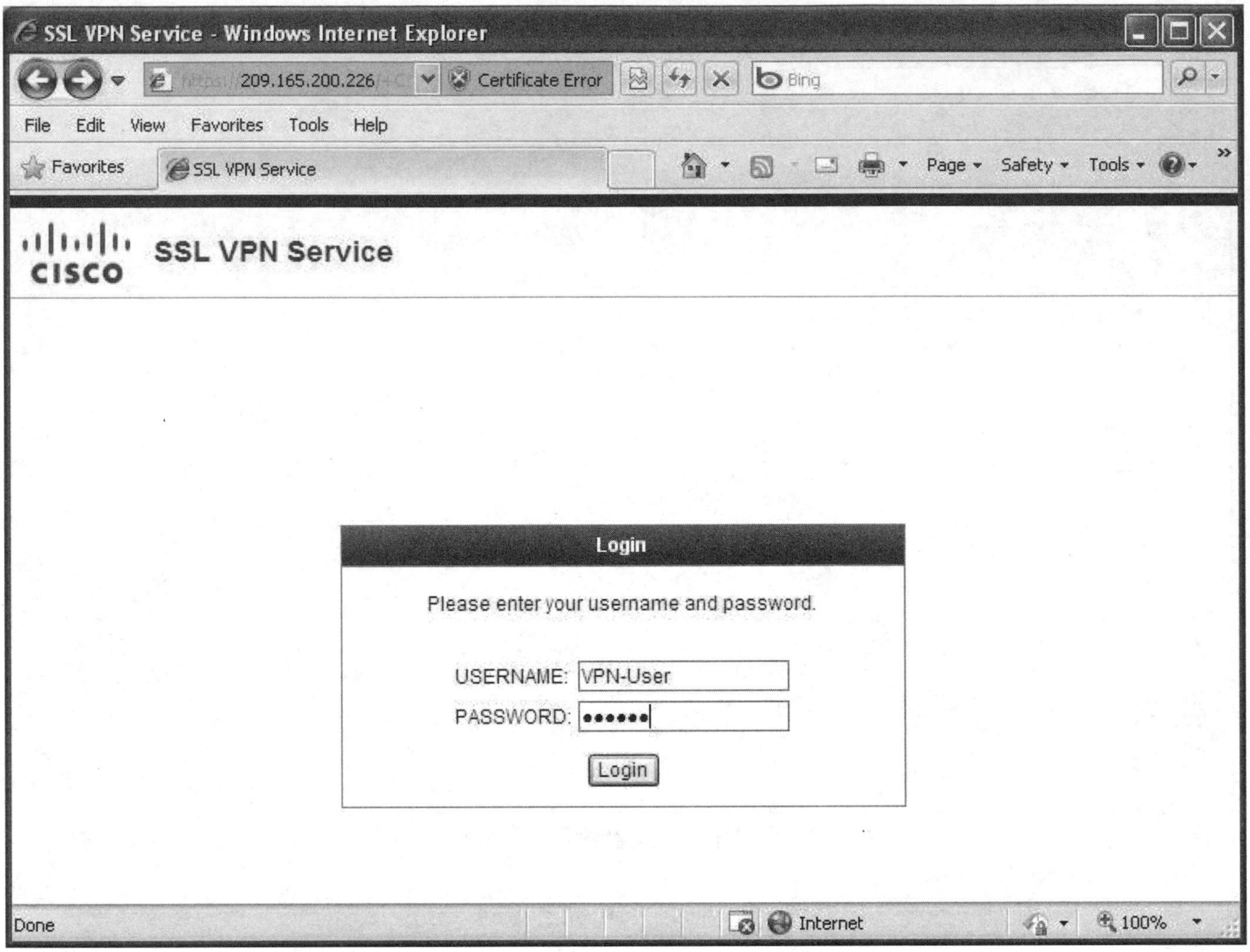

Step 10: Access the Web Portal window.

After the user authenticates, the ASA SSL Web portal web page is displayed listing the various bookmarks previously assigned to the profile. If the bookmark points to a valid server IP address or hostname that has HTTP web services installed and functional, the outside user will be able to access the server from the ASA portal. In this lab, the web mail server is not installed.

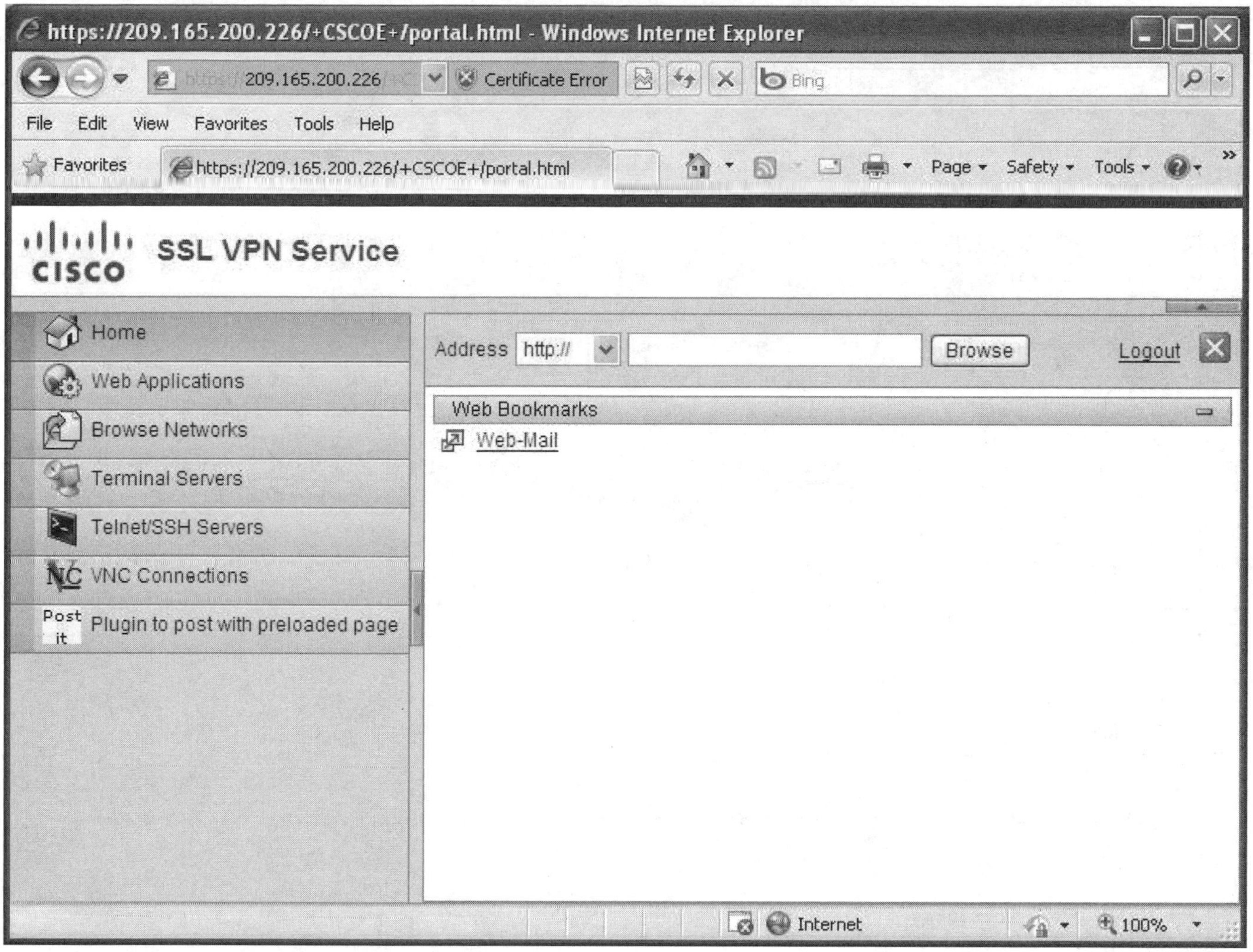

Step 11: View the clientless remote user VPN session using ASDM Monitor.

While the remote user at PC-C is still logged in and on the ASA portal page, you can view the session statistics using ASDM monitor.

From the menu bar, click the **Monitoring** button, and then choose **VPN > VPN Statistics > Sessions**. Click the **Filter By** pull-down menu and choose **Clientless SSL VPN**. You should see the VPN-User session logged in from PC-C (172.16.3.3).

Note: You might need to click the Refresh button on the menu bar to display the remote user session.

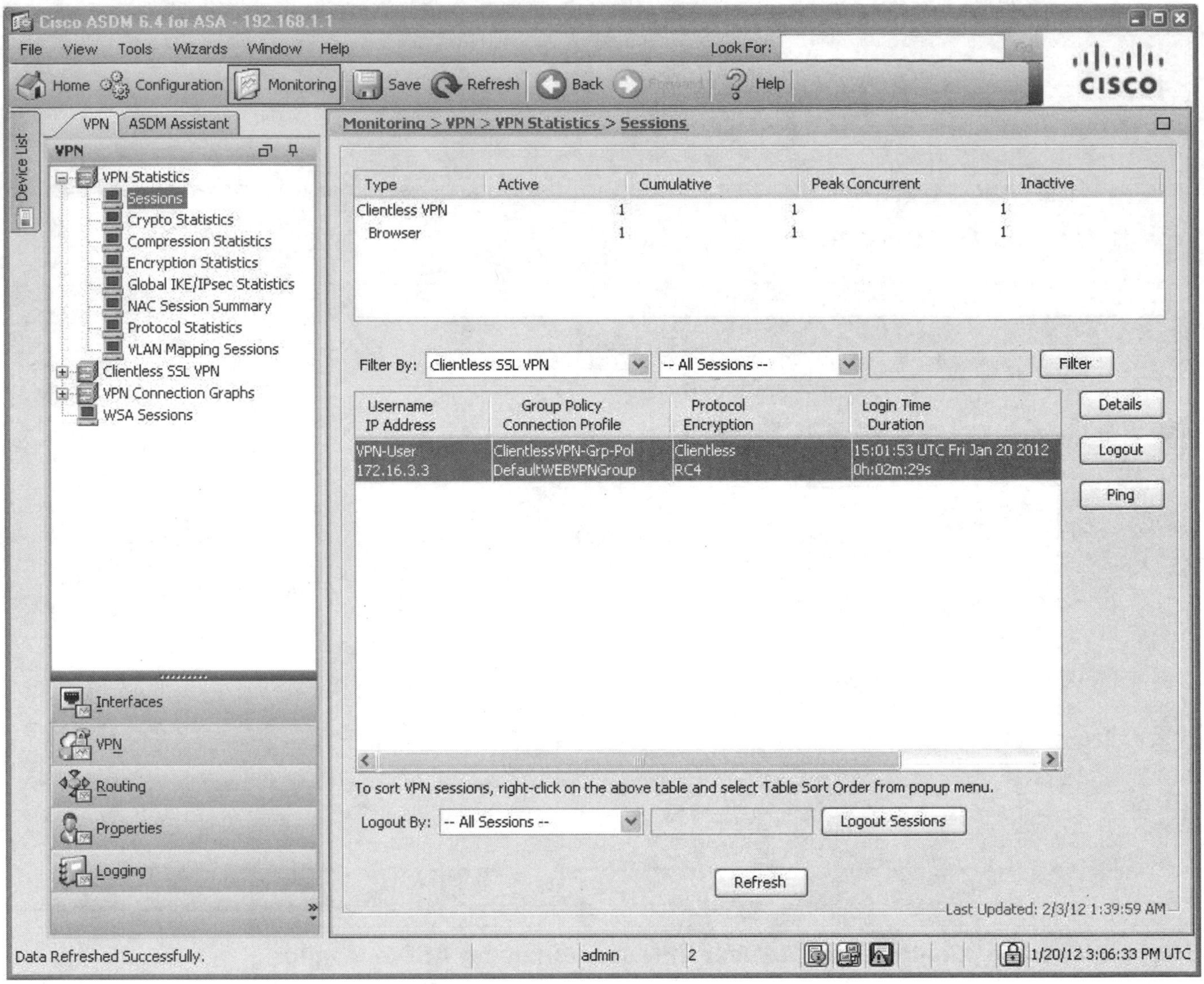

Step 12: Log out.

The user should log out of the web portal window using the **Logout** button when done (refer to Step 10). However, the web portal will also time out if there is no activity. In either case, a logout window is displayed informing users that for additional security, they should clear the browser cache, delete the downloaded files, and close the browser window.

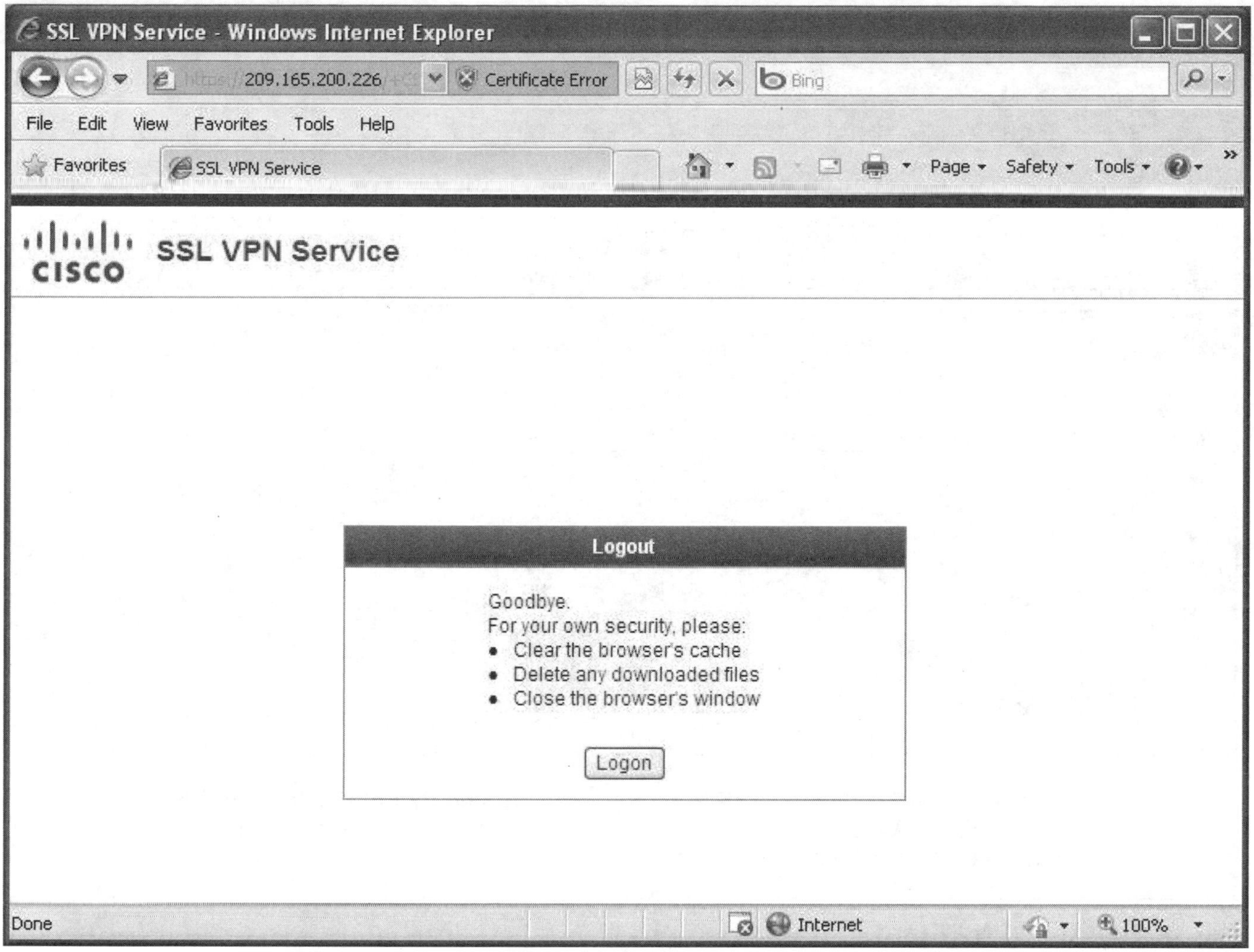

Part 4: Configuring AnyConnect SSL VPN Remote Access Using ASDM

Step 1: Clear the ASA configuration and access ASDM.

a. Before beginning Part 4 of this lab, use the procedure described in Part 2 to remove the current VPN settings, return the ASA to its base configuration, and verify ASDM access.

b. Open a browser on PC-B and test the HTTPS access to the ASA by entering **https://192.168.1.1**.

Note: Be sure to specify the HTTPS protocol in the URL.

c. After entering the URL above, you should see a security warning about the security certificate of the website. Click **Continue to This Website**. The ASDM welcome page appears. Click the **Run ASDM** button. When prompted, log in as **admin** with a password of **cisco123**.

Step 2: Review the Remote Access VPN ASDM Assistant.

a. From the ASDM menu bar, click the **Configuration** button and choose **Remote Access VPN** to display the Introduction screen. From here, you can access information on how to create each of the three types of remote access VPNs that are supported by the ASA.

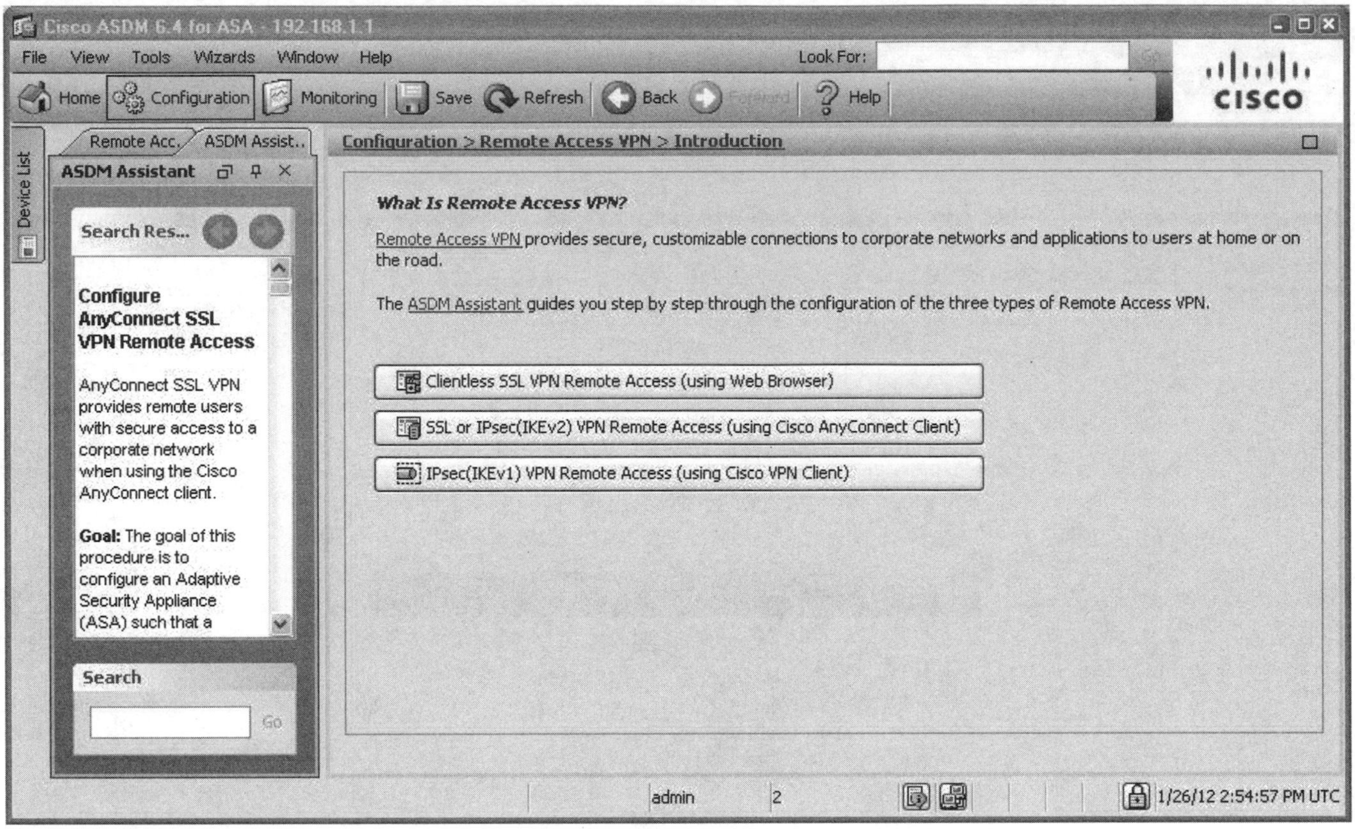

b. Click the **SSL or IPsec(IKEv2) VPN Remote Access (Using Cisco AnyConnect Client)** button to access the ASDM Assistant. Read through the information provided to get a better understanding of the process for creating this type of VPN.

Step 3: Start the VPN Wizard.

a. From the ASDM main menu, choose **Wizards > VPN Wizards > AnyConnect VPN wizard**.

b. Review the on-screen text and topology diagram, and then click **Next** to continue.

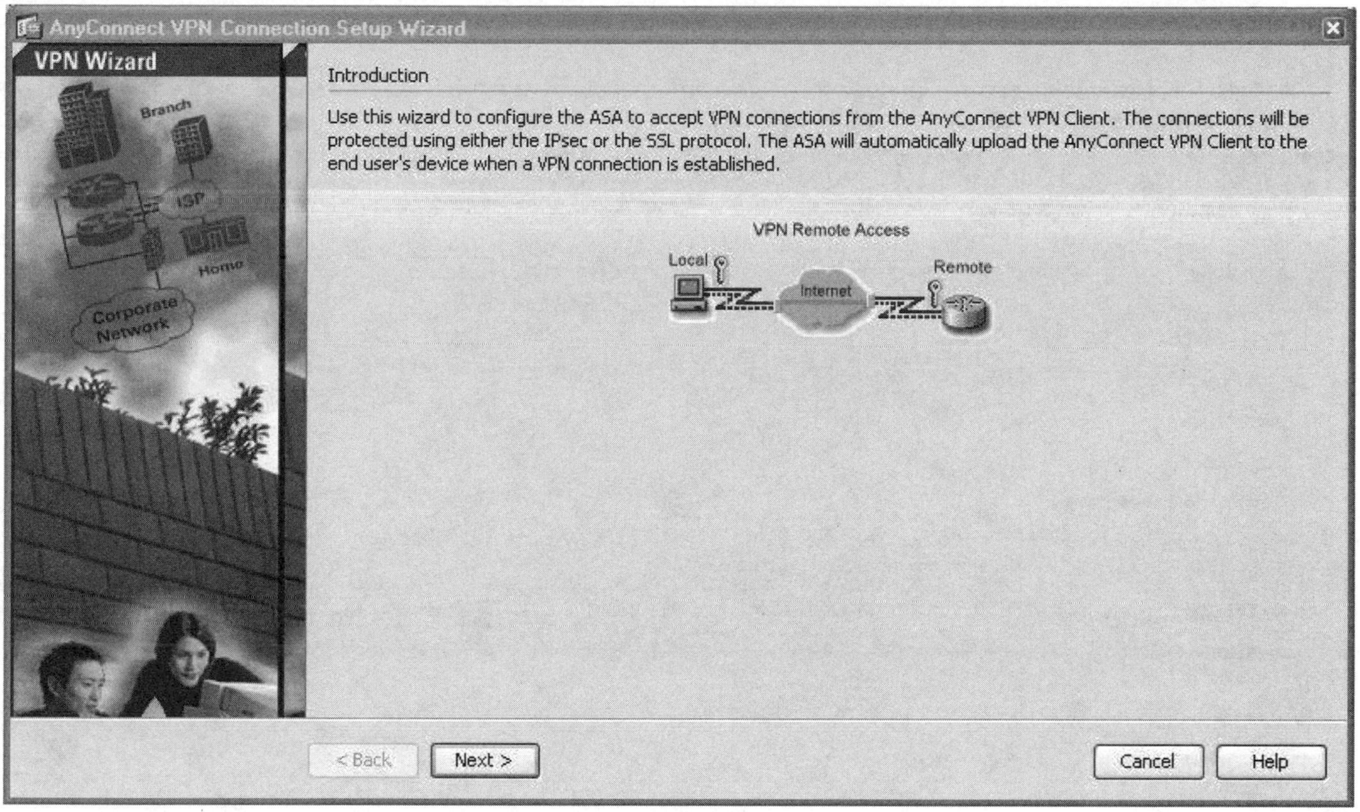

Step 4: Configure the connection profile.

On the Connection Profile Identification screen, enter **AnyC-SSL-VPN-Con-Prof** as the Connection Profile Name and specify the **outside** interface as the VPN Access Interface. Click **Next** to continue.

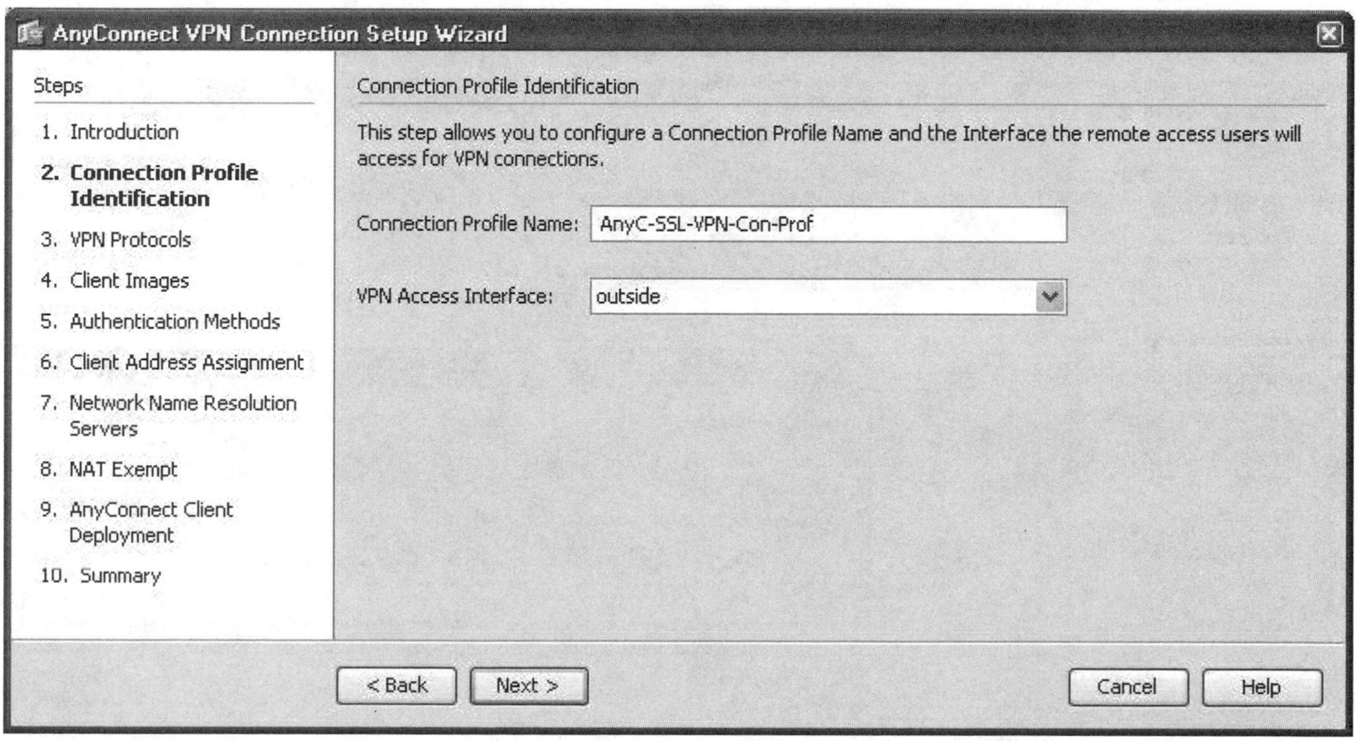

Step 5: Specify the VPN encryption protocol.

On the VPN Protocols screen, uncheck the **IPsec** protocol and leave the **SSL** check box checked. Do not specify a device certificate. Click **Next** to continue.

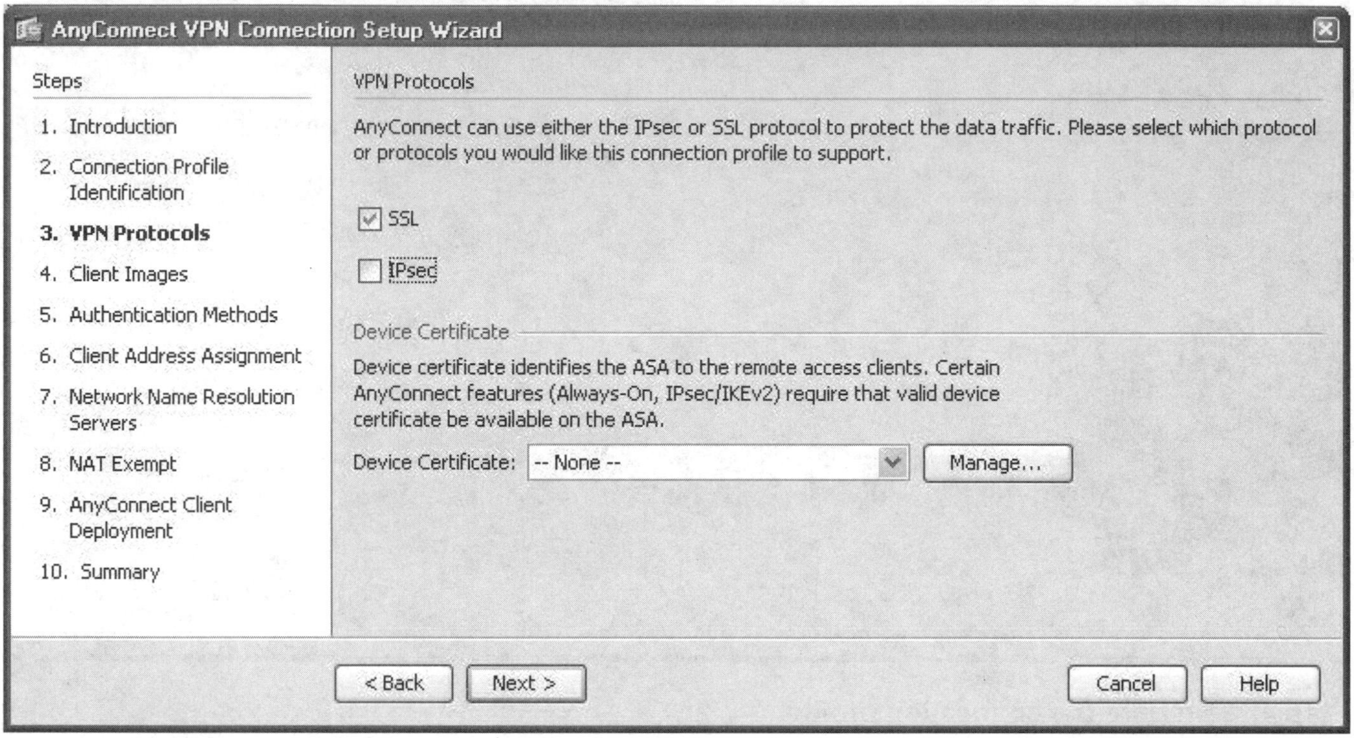

Step 6: Specify the client image to upload to AnyConnect users.

a. On the Client Images screen, click **Add** to specify the AnyConnect client image filename. In the Add AnyConnect Client Image window, click the **Browse Flash** button.

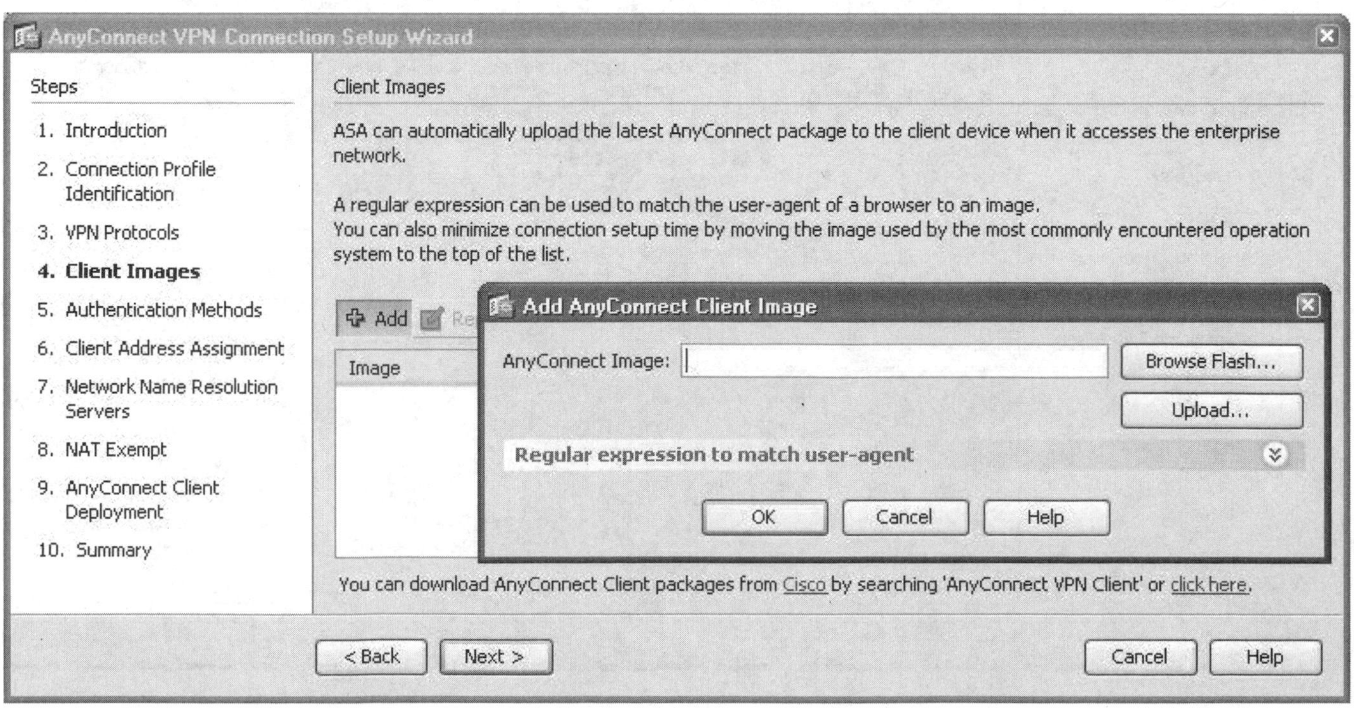

b. From the Browse Flash window, select the AnyConnect package file for Windows. Click **OK** to return to the AnyConnect Client Images window, and then click **OK** again. On the Client Images screen, click **Next** to continue.

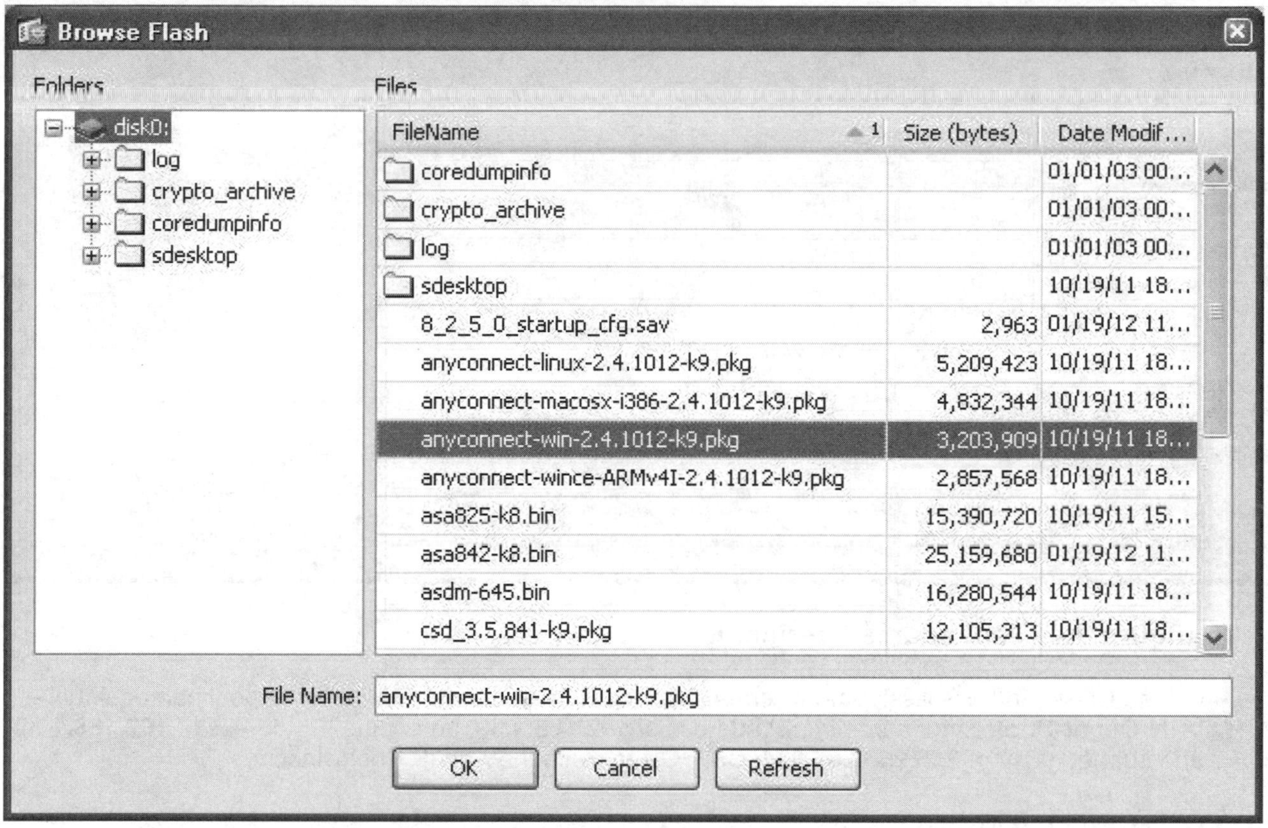

Step 7: Configure AAA local authentication.

a. On the Authentication Methods screen, ensure that the AAA Server Group is specified as LOCAL.

b. Enter a new user named **VPN-User** with a password of **remote**. Click **Add** to create the new user. Click **Next** to continue.

Step 8: Configure the client address assignment.

a. On the Client Address Assignment screen, click **New** to create an IPv4 address pool named **AnyC-VPN-Client-Pool**. Enter a starting IP address of **192.168.1.33**, an ending IP address of **192.168.1.62** and subnet mask of **255.255.255.224**. Click **OK** to close the Add IP Pool window.

b. Click **Next** to continue.

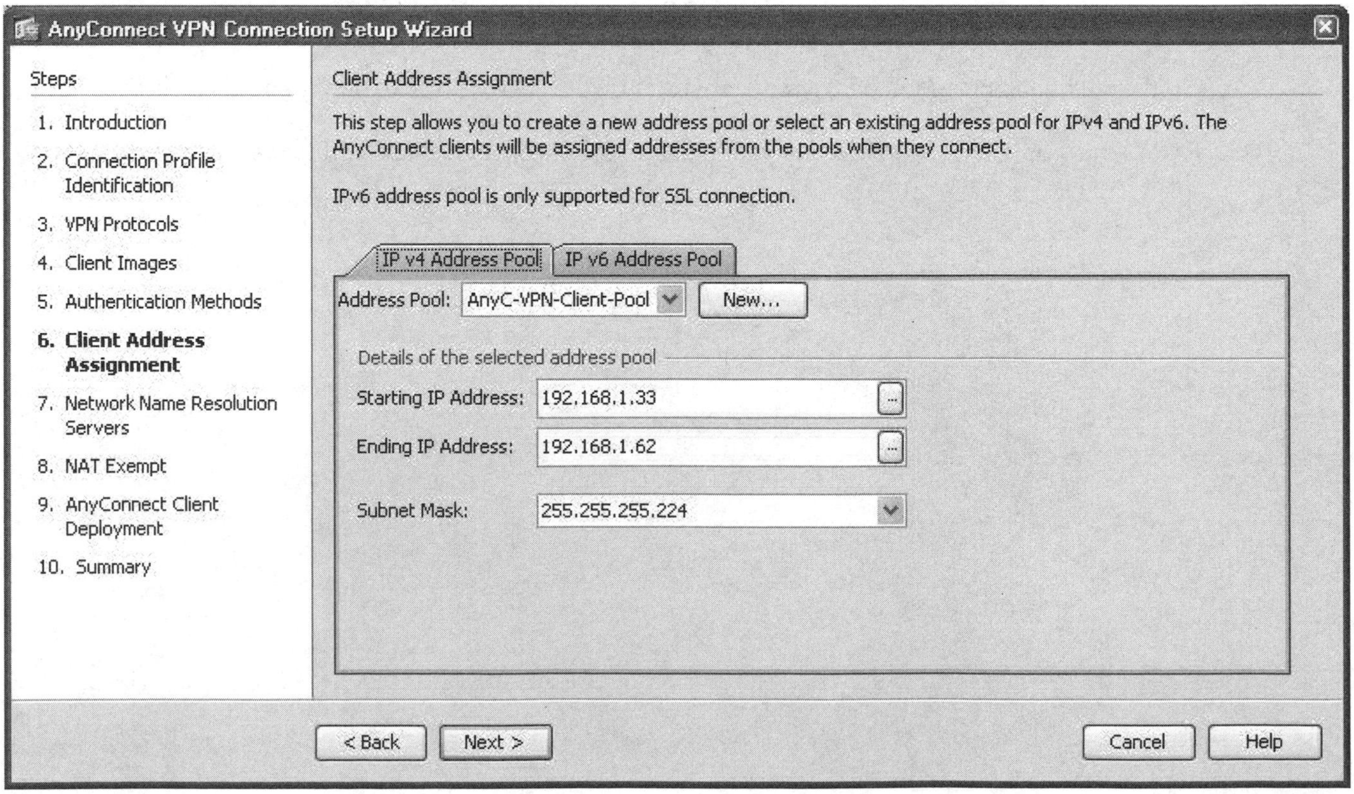

Step 9: Configure network name resolution.

On the Network Name Resolution Servers screen, enter the IP address of a DNS server. Leave the current domain name as ccnasecurity.com. Click **Next** to continue.

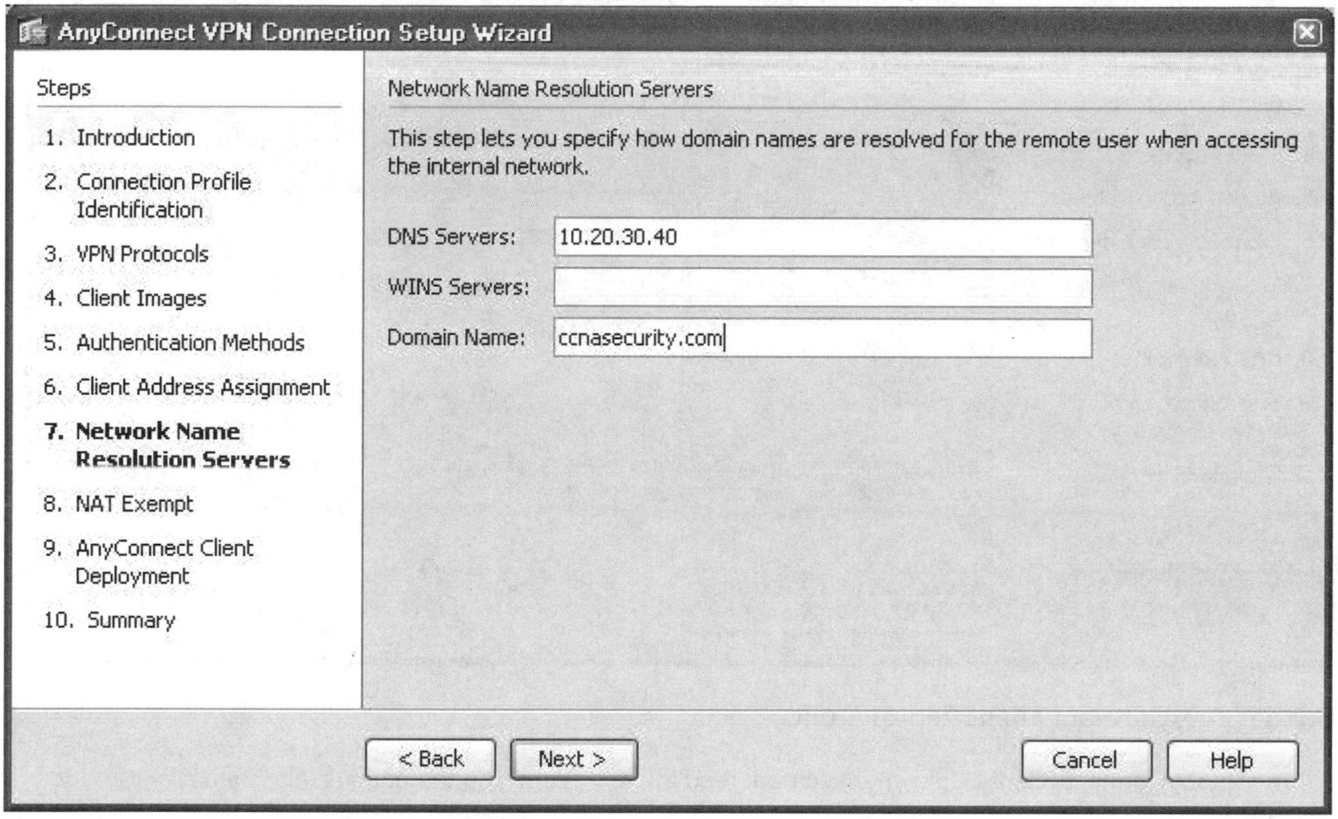

Step 10: Exempt address translation for VPN traffic.

a. On the NAT Exempt screen, select the checkbox for **Exempt VPN Traffic from Network Address Translation**.

b. Leave the default entries for the Inside Interface (inside) and the Local Network (any) as they are. Click **Next** to continue.

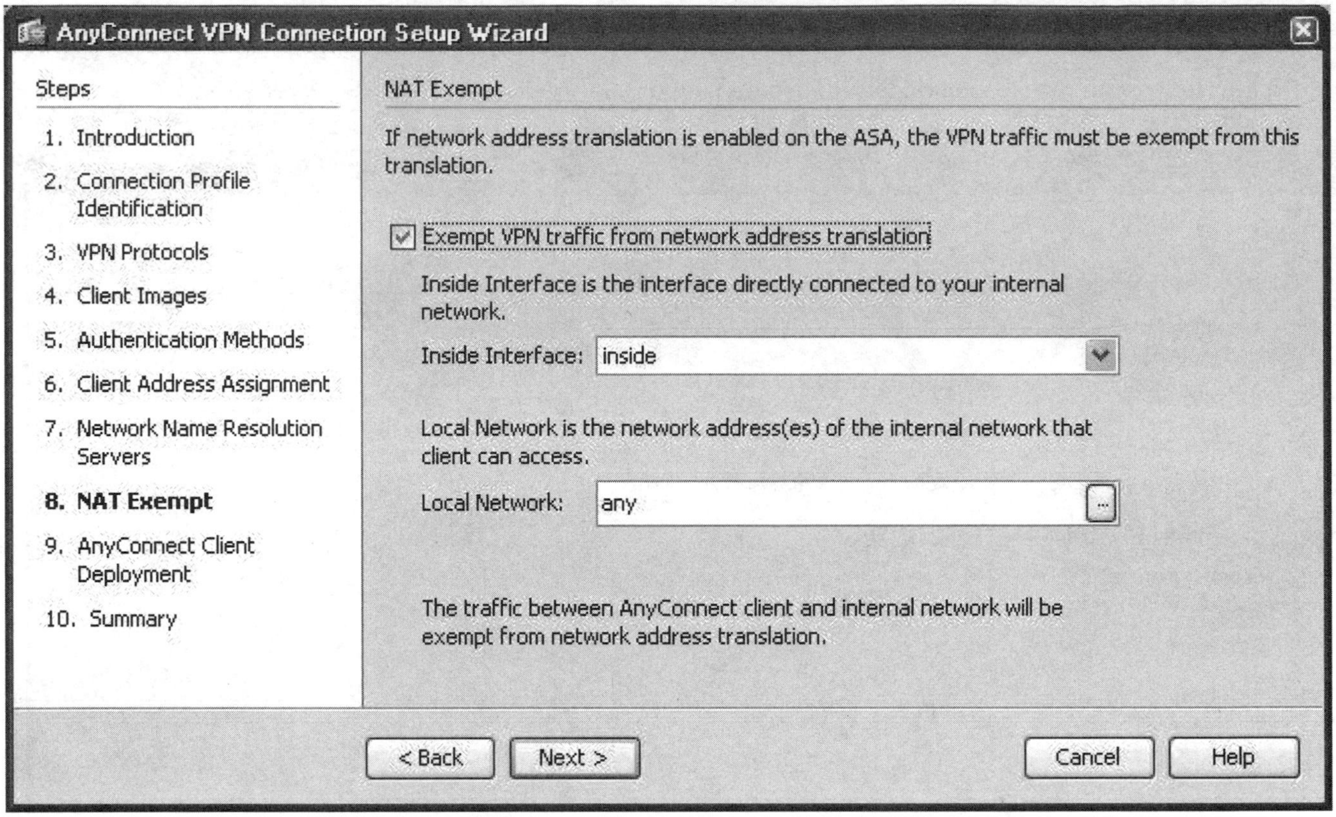

Step 11: AnyConnect client deployment.

On the AnyConnect Client Deployment screen, read the text describing the options, and then click **Next** to continue.

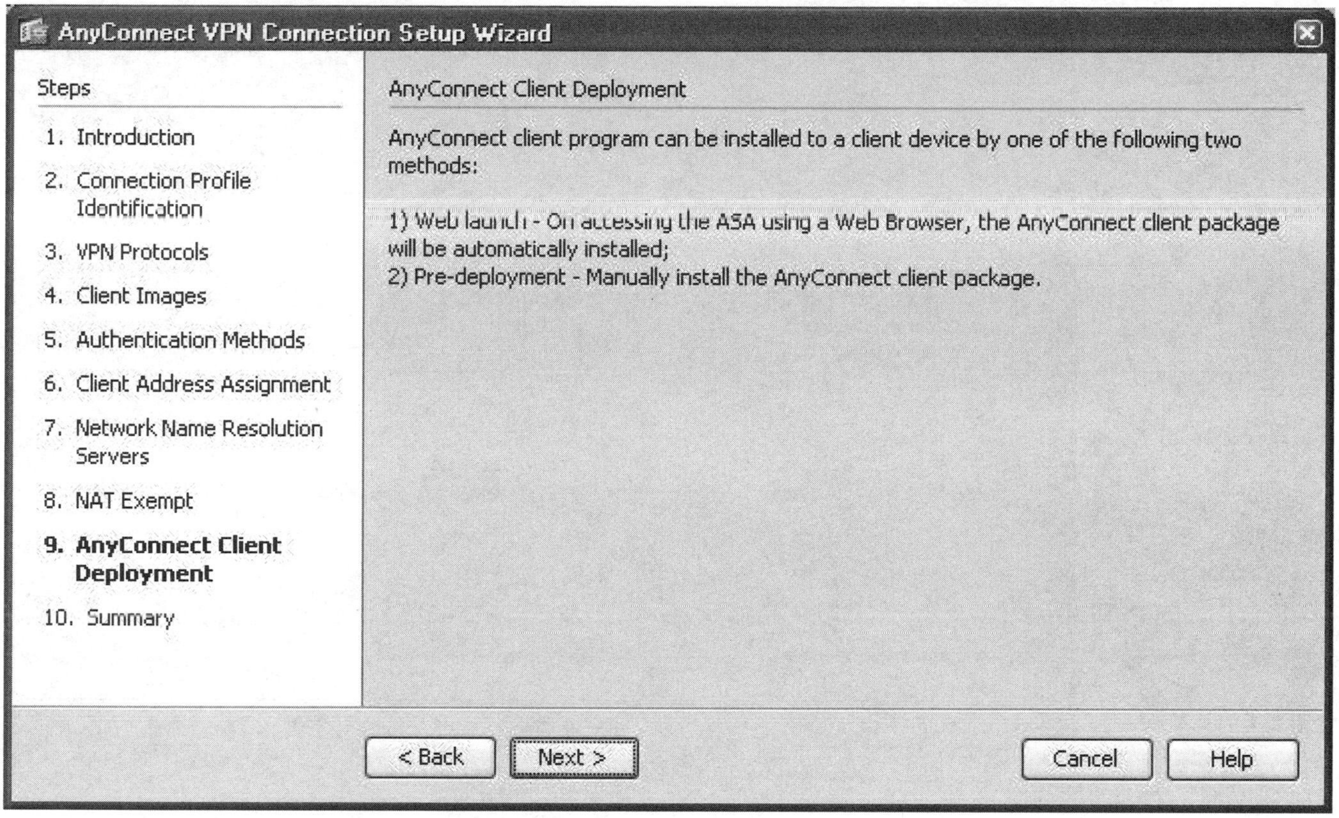

Step 12: Review the Summary screen and apply the configuration to the ASA.

On the Summary screen, review the configuration description, and then click **Finish** to send the commands to the ASA.

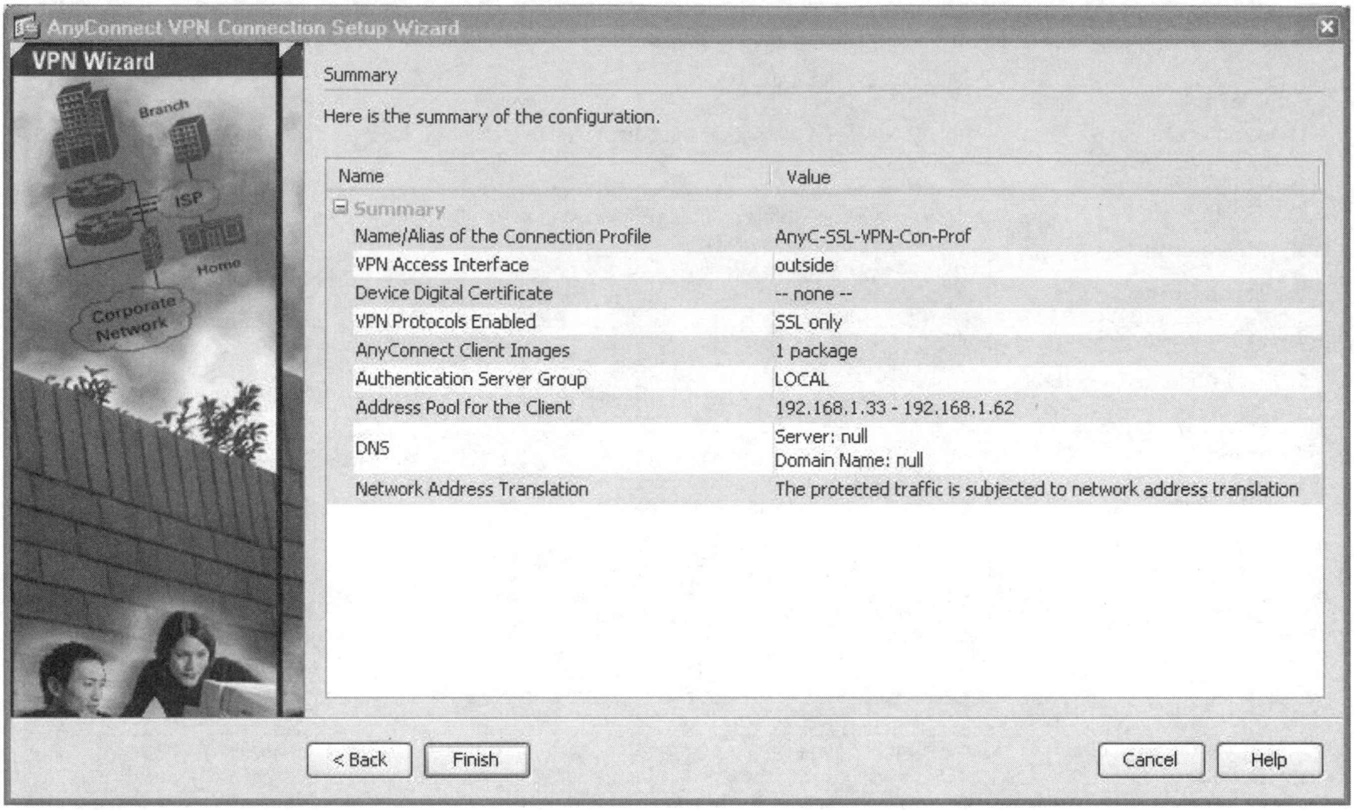

Step 13: Verify the AnyConnect client profile.

After the configuration is delivered to the ASA, the AnyConnect Connection Profiles screen is displayed.

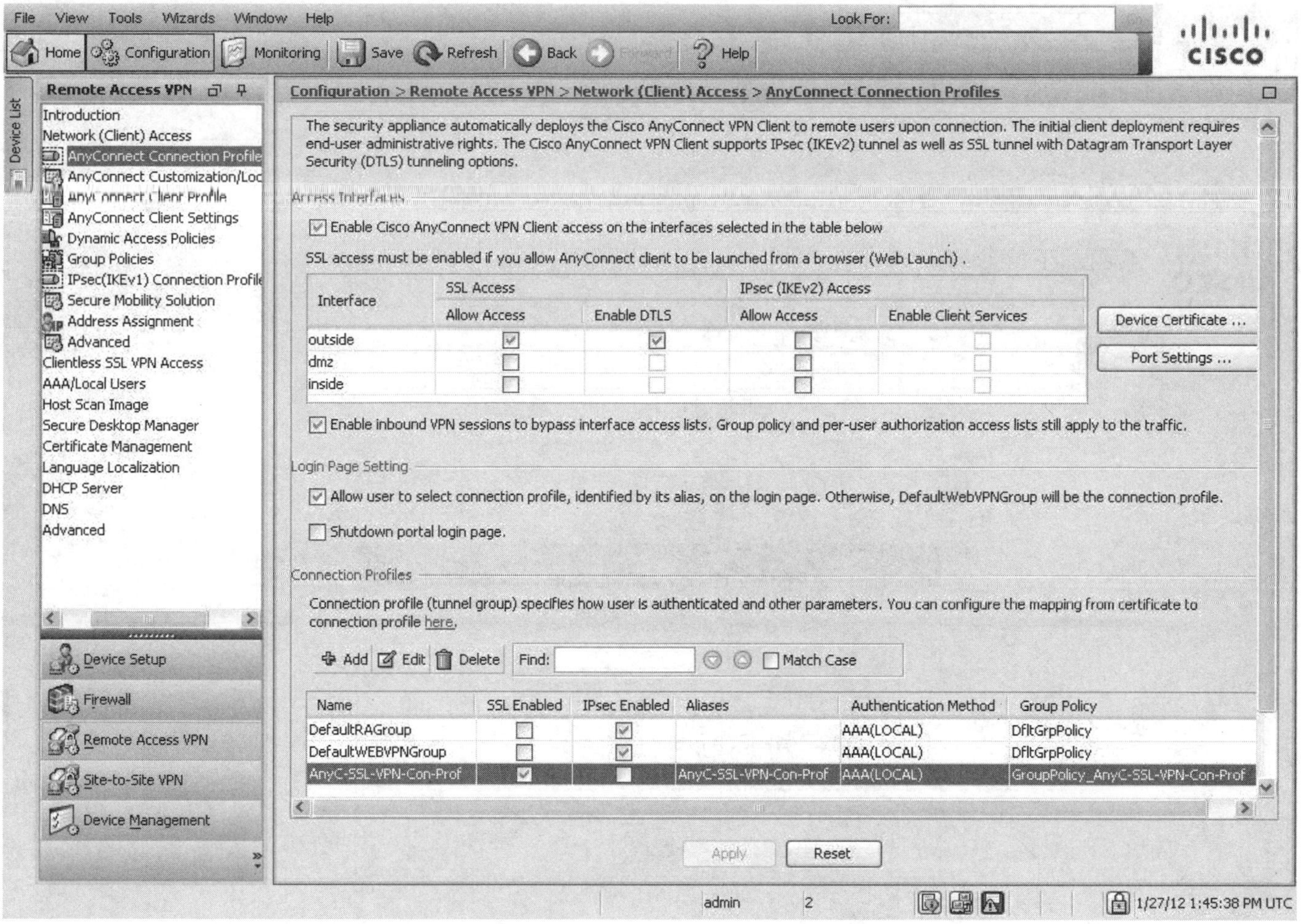

Step 14: Log in from the remote host.

Initially, you will establish a clientless SSL VPN connection to the ASA to download the AnyConnect client software.

Open a web browser on PC-C and enter the login URL **https://209.165.200.226** for the SSL VPN into the address field. Because SSL is required to connect to the ASA, be sure to use secure HTTP (HTTPS). After entering the URL, you should see a security warning about the website security certificate. Click **Continue to This Website**. Click **Yes** for any other security warnings. Enter the previously created username **VPN-User** with password **remote**, and click **Login** to continue.

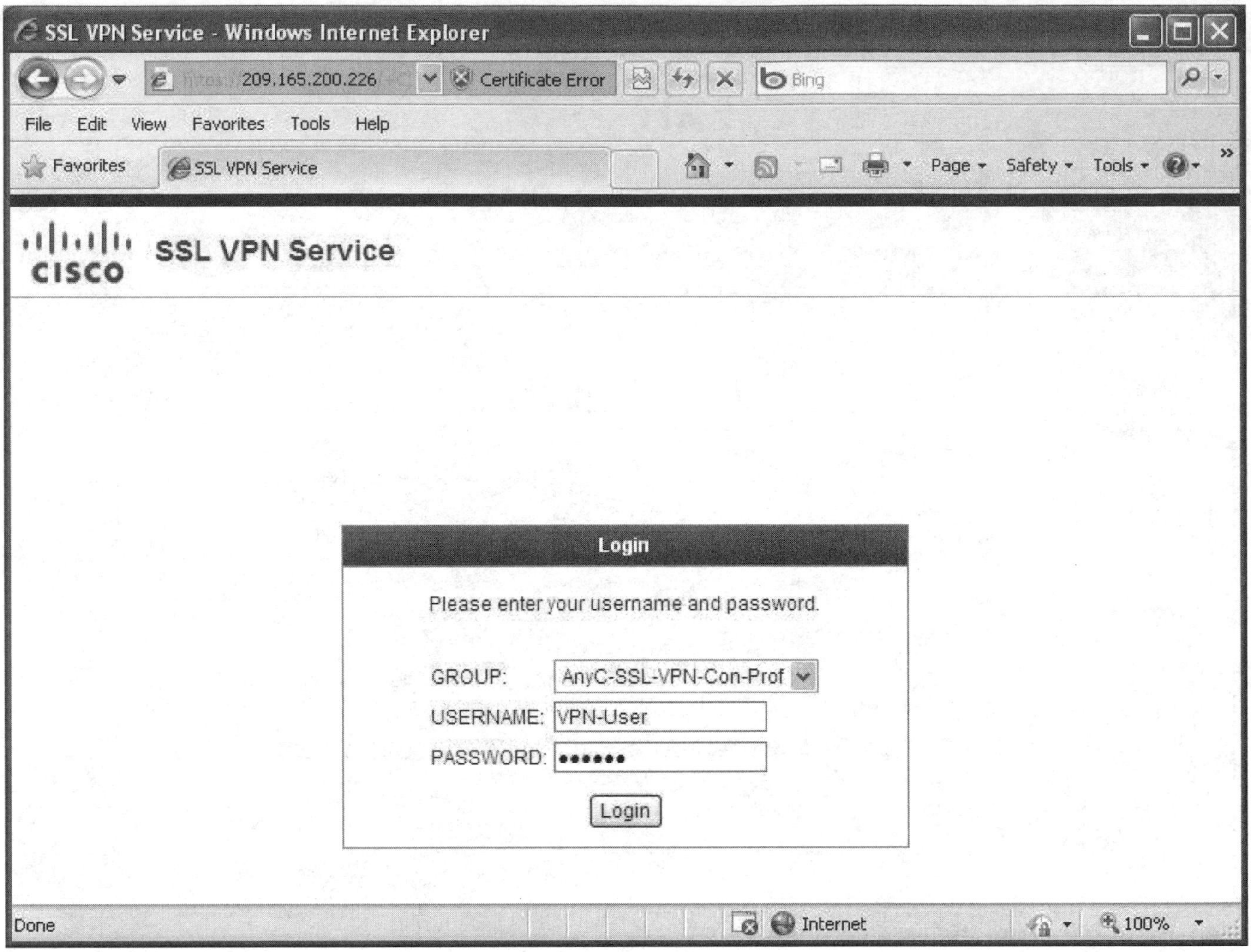

Step 15: Accept the security certificate (if required).

The ASA might request confirmation that this is a trusted site. If requested, click **Yes** to proceed.

Step 16: Perform platform detection (if required).

The ASA begins a software auto-download process consisting of a series of compliance checks for the target system. The ASA performs the platform detection by querying the client system in an attempt to identify the type of client connecting to the security appliance. Based on the platform that is identified, the proper software package may be auto-downloaded.

Step 17: Install AnyConnect (if required).

If the AnyConnect client must be downloaded, a security warning will be displayed on the remote host, and then the ASA will detect whether ActiveX is available on the host system. For ActiveX to operate properly with the Cisco ASA, it is important that the security appliance be added as a trusted network site. ActiveX will be used for client download if a web portal is not in use.

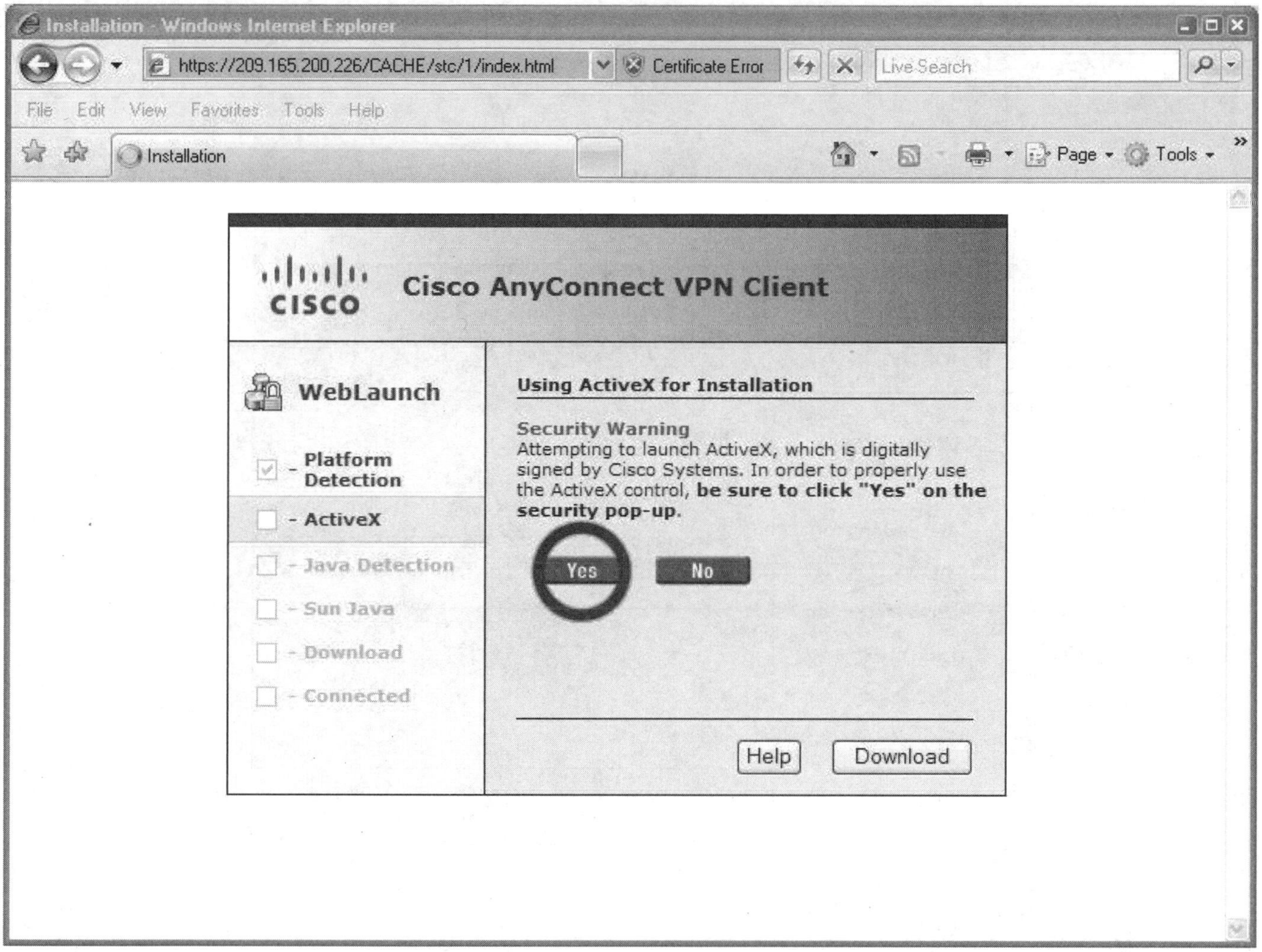

To continue, choose **Install**. If requested, click **Yes**. The VPN Client Installer begins and another security alert window might appear. If required, click **Yes** to continue and accept the security certificate.

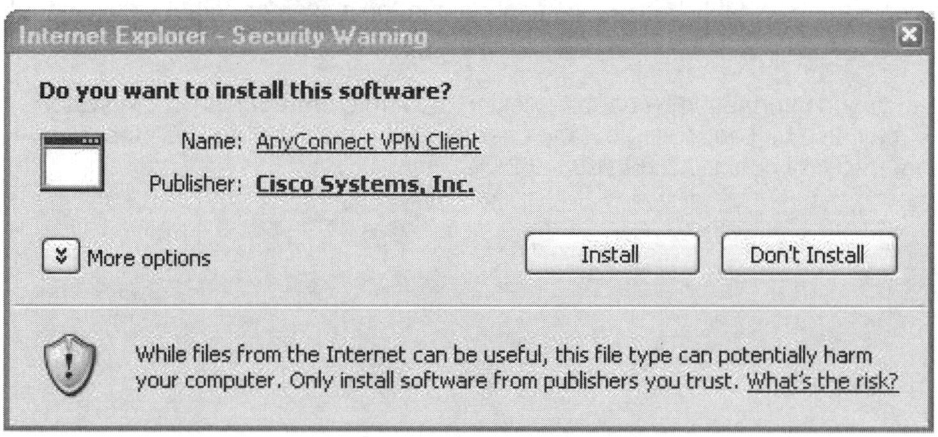

Step 18: Client connection is established with the ASA.

When the client completes the auto-download of the Cisco AnyConnect SSL VPN Client, the web session automatically launches the Cisco AnyConnect SSL VPN Client and attempts to log in the user to the network using the same credentials that are supplied when logging in to the web portal.

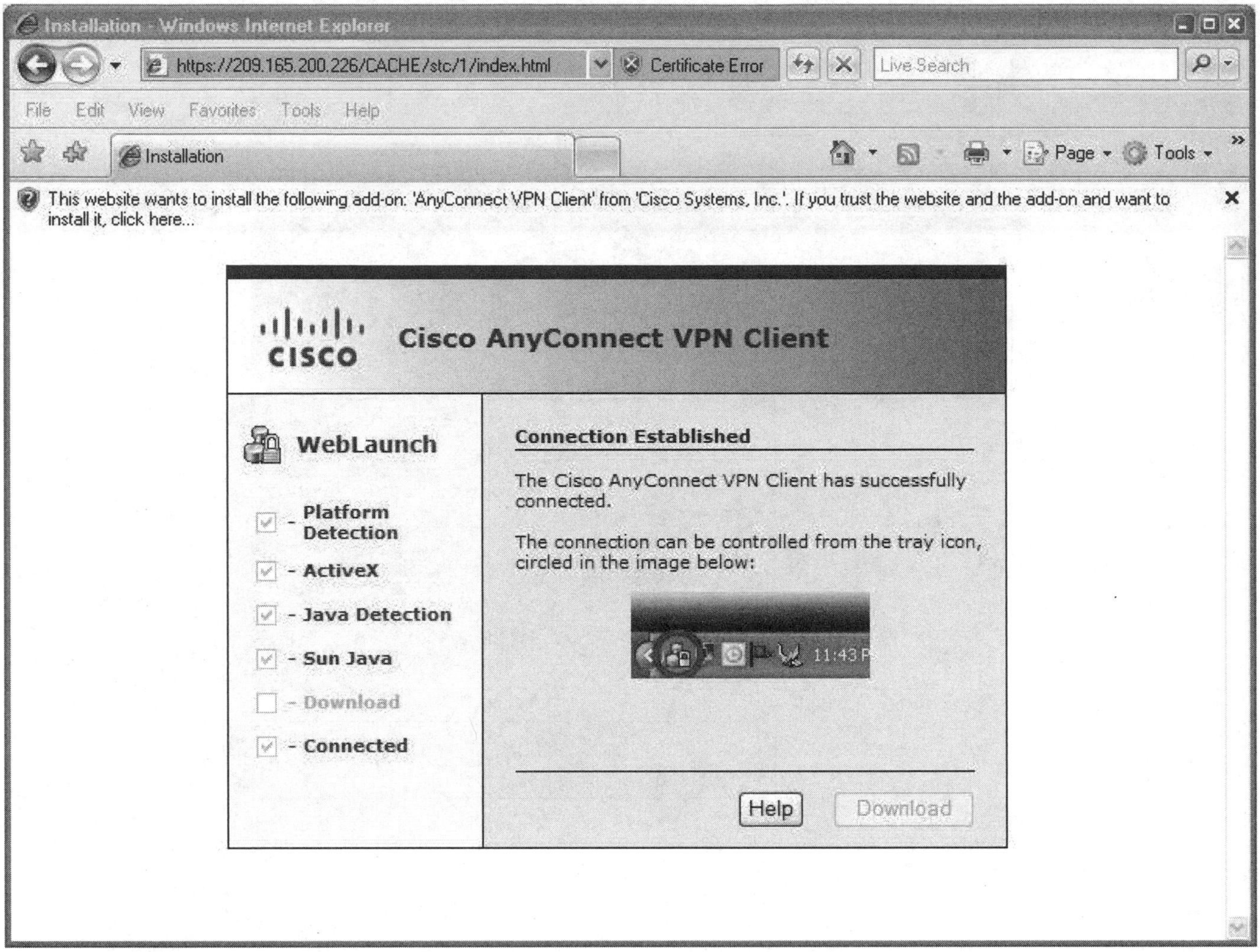

Step 19: Confirm VPN connectivity.

When the full tunnel SSL VPN connection is established, an icon appears in the system tray that signifies that the client has successfully connected to the SSL VPN network.

a. Display connection statistics and information by double-clicking the **AnyConnect** icon in the system tray. This client interface may also be used to log out the user. Note the inside IP address that is assigned to the client from the VPN pool (192.168.1.33–.62).

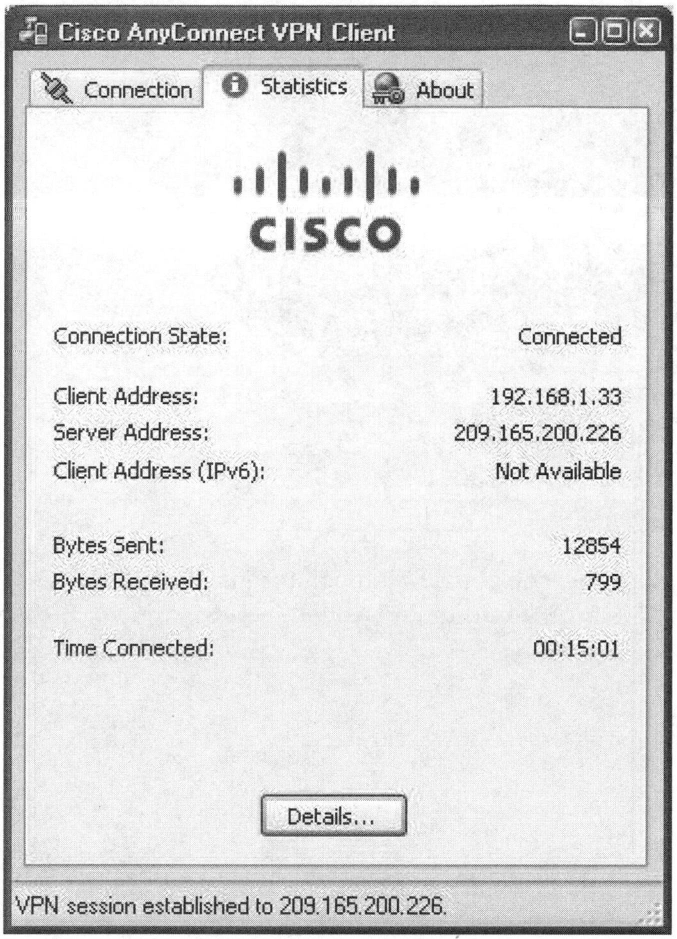

b. From a command prompt on remote host PC-C, verify the IP addressing using the **ipconfig** command. Two IP addresses should be listed—one is for the PC-C remote host local IP address (172.16.3.3) and the other is the IP address assigned by the ASA for the SSL VPN tunnel (192.168.1.33).

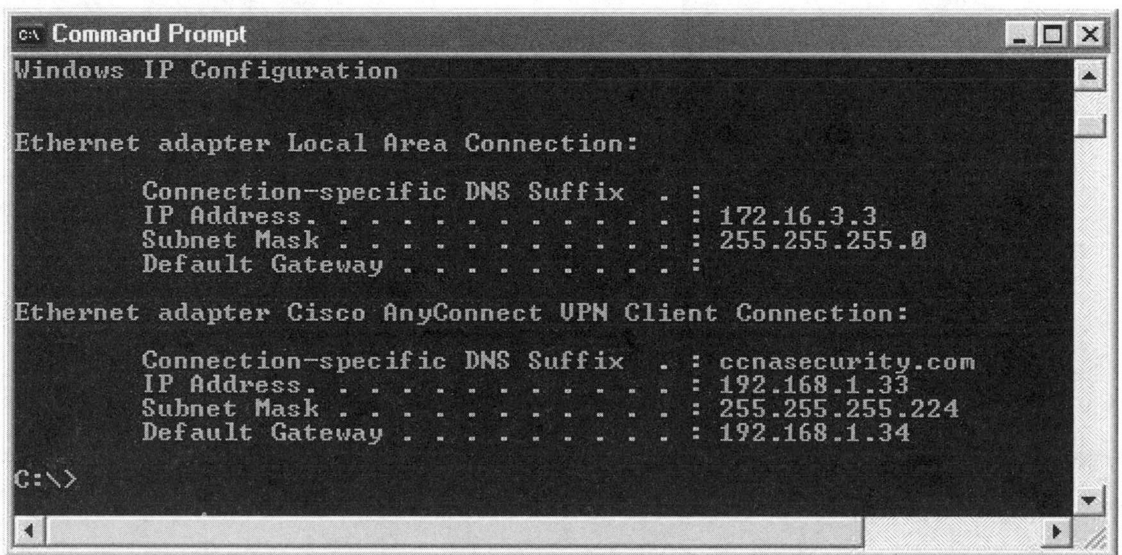

c. From remote host PC-C, ping inside host PC-B (192.168.1.3) to verify connectivity.

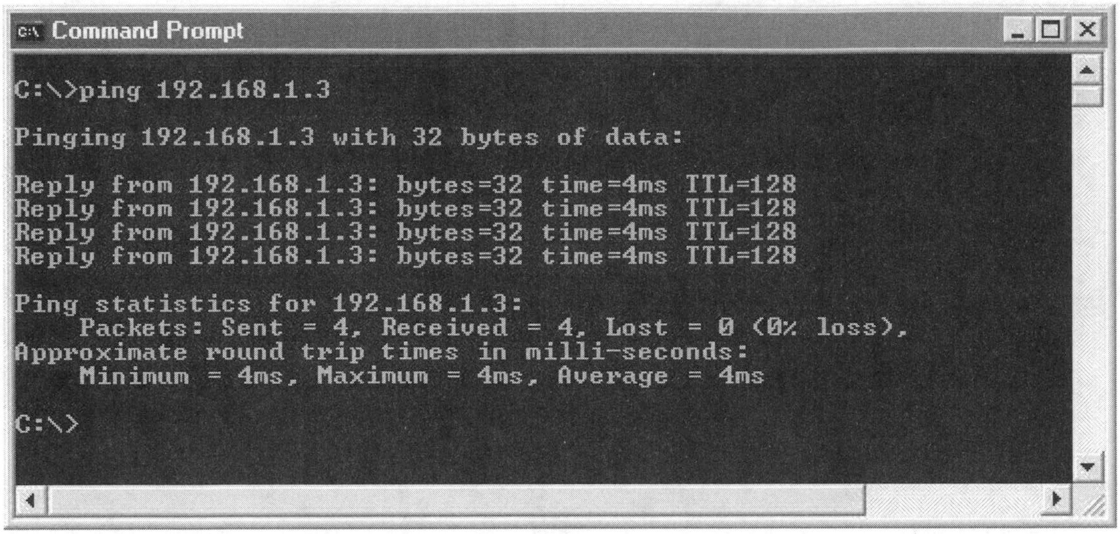

Note: Future SSL VPN sessions may be launched through the web portal or through the installed Cisco AnyConnect SSL VPN Client.

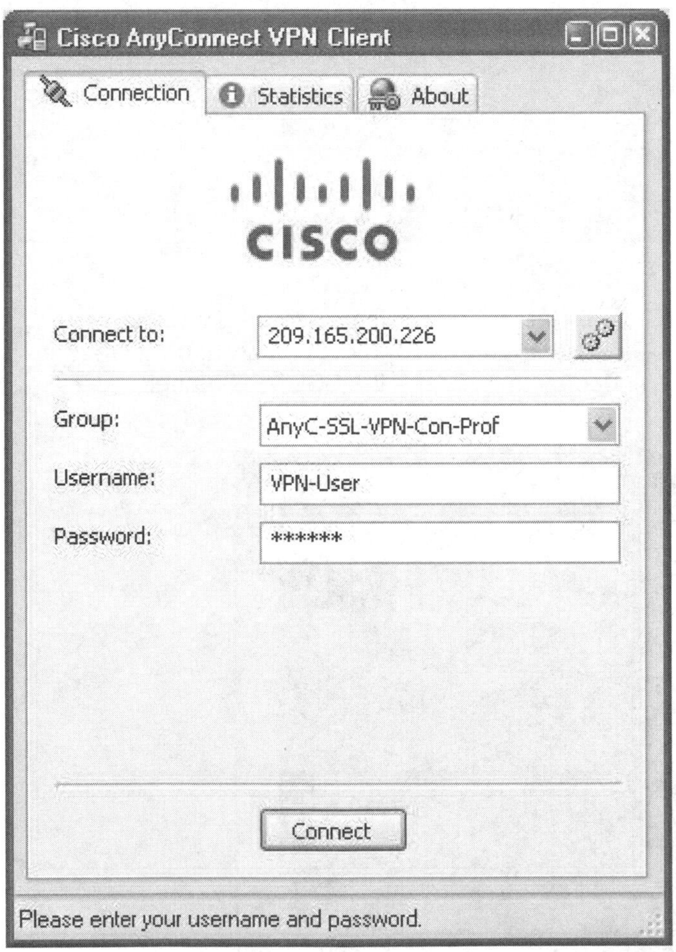

Step 20: Use the ASDM Monitor to view the AnyConnect remote user session.

While the remote user at PC-C is still logged in using the AnyConnect client, you can view the session statistics using ASDM monitor.

From the menu bar, click the **Monitoring** button and then choose **VPN > VPN Statistics > Sessions**. Click the **Filter By** pull-down menu and choose **AnyConnect Client**. You should see the VPN-User session logged in from PC-C, which has been assigned an inside network IP address of 192.168.1.33 by the ASA.

Note: You might need to click the **Refresh** button on the menu bar to display the remote user session.

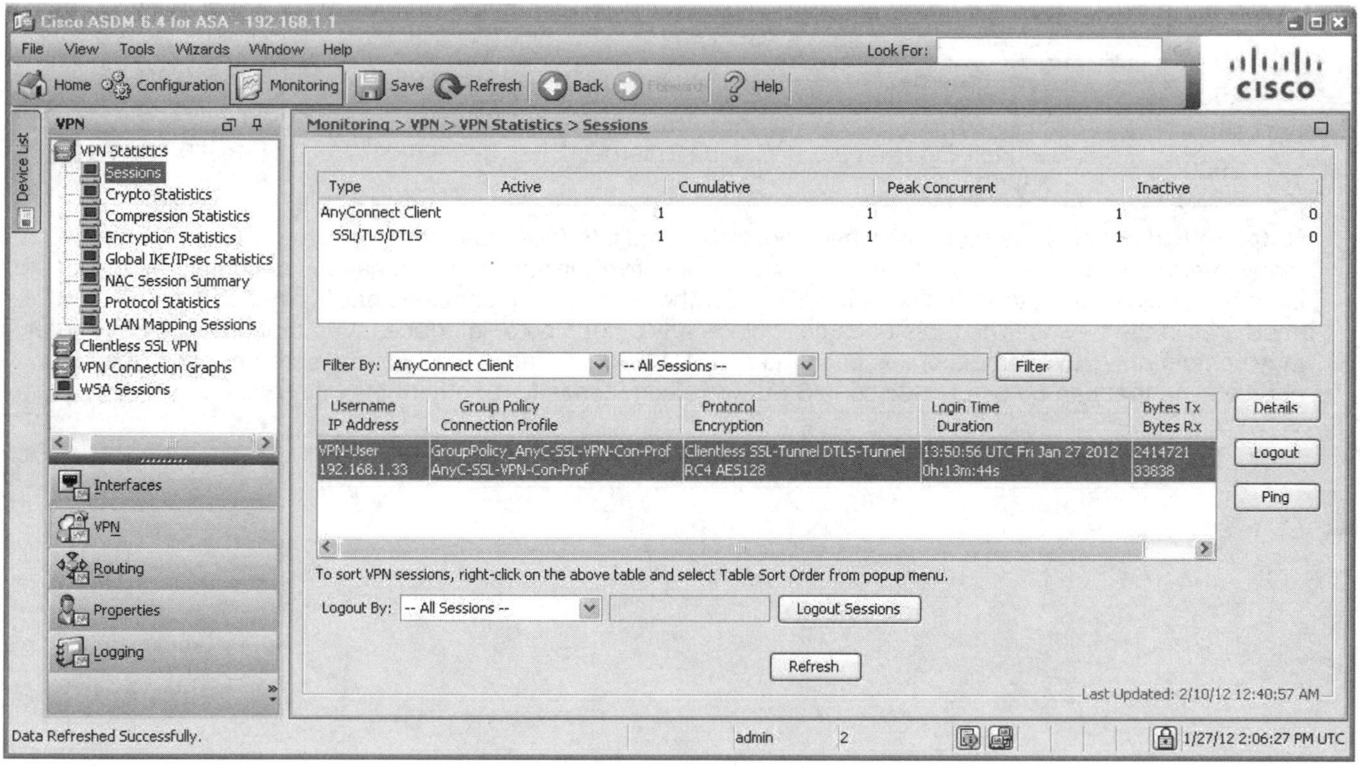

Reflection

1. What are some benefits of clientless versus client-based VPNs?

2. What are some benefits of client-based versus clientless VPNs?

3. What are some differences when using SSL compared to IPsec for remote access tunnel encryption?

Router Interface Summary Table

Router Model	Ethernet Interface 1	Ethernet Interface 2	Serial Interface 1	Serial Interface 2
1800	Fast Ethernet 0/0 (Fa0/0)	Fast Ethernet 0/1 (Fa0/1)	Serial 0/0/0 (S0/0/0)	Serial 0/0/1 (S0/0/1)
1900	Gigabit Ethernet 0/0 (G0/0)	Gigabit Ethernet 0/1 (G0/1)	Serial 0/0/0 (S0/0/0)	Serial 0/0/1 (S0/0/1)
2800	Fast Ethernet 0/0 (Fa0/0)	Fast Ethernet 0/1 (Fa0/1)	Serial 0/0/0 (S0/0/0)	Serial 0/0/1 (S0/0/1)
2900	Gigabit Ethernet 0/0 (G0/0)	Gigabit Ethernet 0/1 (G0/1)	Serial 0/0/0 (S0/0/0)	Serial 0/0/1 (S0/0/1)

Note: To find out how the router is configured, look at the interfaces to identify the type of router and how many interfaces the router has. There is no way to effectively list all the combinations of configurations for each router class. This table includes identifiers for the possible combinations of Ethernet and serial interfaces in the device. The table does not include any other type of interface, even though a specific router may contain one. An example of this might be an ISDN BRI interface. The string in parentheses is the legal abbreviation that can be used in Cisco IOS Software commands to represent the interface.

Chapter 10 Lab H: Configuring a Site-to-Site IPsec VPN Using CCP on an ISR and ASDM on an ASA 5510

Topology

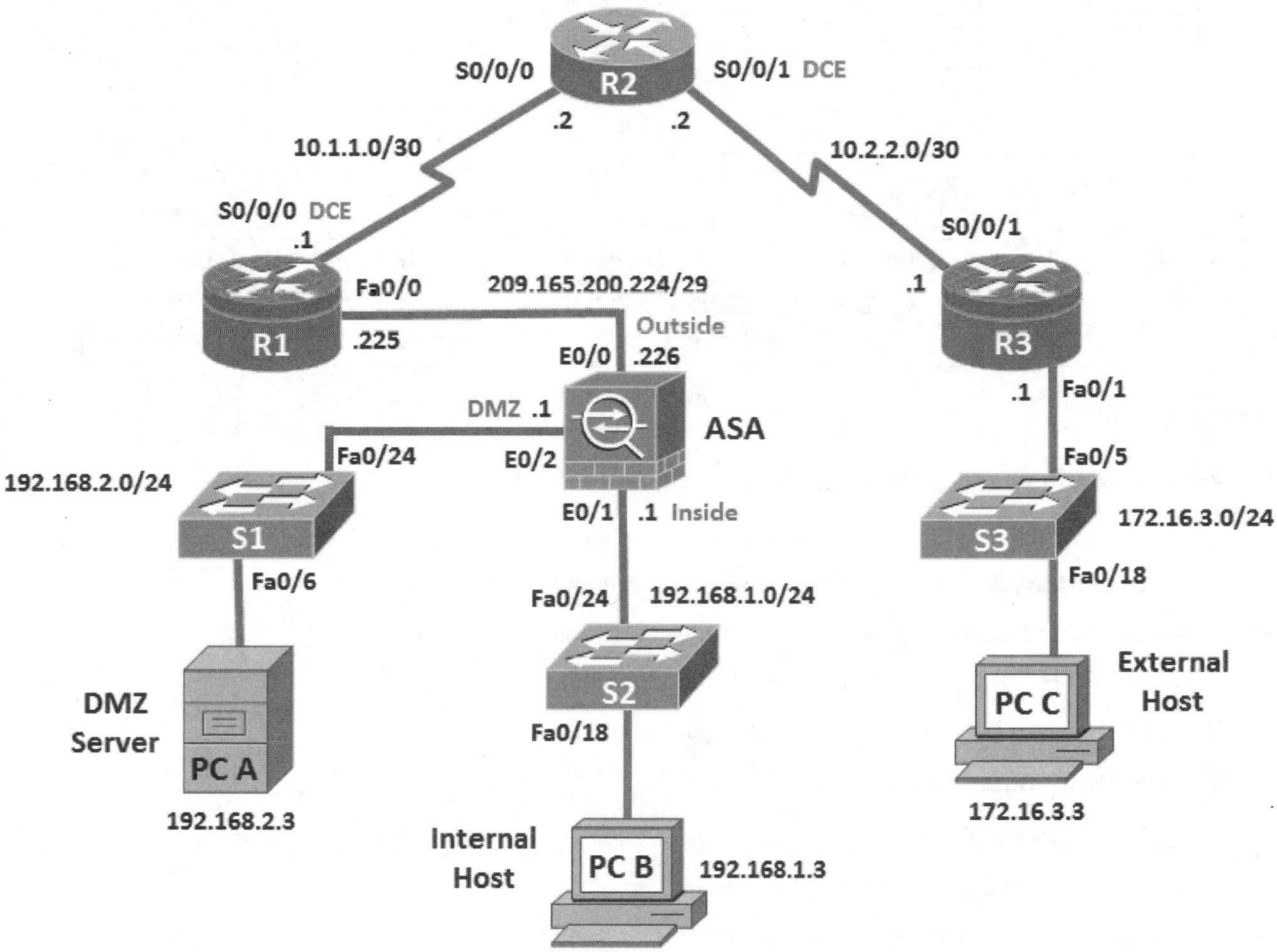

Note: ISR G2 devices have Gigabit Ethernet interfaces rathern than FastEthernet interfaces.

IP Addressing Table

Device	Interface	IP Address	Subnet Mask	Default Gateway	Switch Port
R1	Fa0/0	209.165.200.225	255.255.255.248	N/A	ASA E0/0
	S0/0/0 (DCE)	10.1.1.1	255.255.255.252	N/A	N/A
R2	S0/0/0	10.1.1.2	255.255.255.252	N/A	N/A
	S0/0/1 (DCE)	10.2.2.2	255.255.255.252	N/A	N/A
R3	Fa0/1	172.16.3.1	255.255.255.0	N/A	S3 Fa0/5
	S0/0/1	10.2.2.1	255.255.255.252	N/A	N/A
ASA	E0/0 (outside)	209.165.200.226	255.255.255.248	NA	R1 Fa0/0
	E0/1 (inside)	192.168.1.1	255.255.255.0	NA	S2 Fa0/24
	E0/2 (dmz)	192.168.2.1	255.255.255.0	NA	S1 Fa0/24
PC-A	NIC	192.168.2.3	255.255.255.0	192.168.2.1	S1 Fa0/6
PC-B	NIC	192.168.1.3	255.255.255.0	192.168.1.1	S2 Fa0/18
PC-C	NIC	172.16.3.3	255.255.255.0	172.16.3.1	S3 Fa0/18

Objectives

Part 1: Basic Router/Switch/PC Configuration

- Cable the network as shown in the topology.
- Configure hostnames, interface IP addresses for routers, switches, and PCs.
- Configure static routing, including default routes, between R1, R2, and R3.
- Configure R3 HTTP access to enable CCP management.
- Verify connectivity between hosts, switches, and routers.

Part 2: Basic ASA Configuration

- Access the ASA console.
- Clear previous configuration settings.
- Load the ASA CLI command script to configure basic settings.
- Verify access to ASA/ASDM.

Part 3: Configuring the ISR as a Site-to-Site IPsec VPN Endpoint Using CCP

- Configure basic VPN connection information settings.
- Configure IKE policy parameters.
- Configure a transform set.
- Define traffic to protect.
- Verify the VPN configuration on R3.

Part 4: Configuring the ASA as a Site-to-Site IPsec VPN Endpoint Using ASDM

- Identify peer device and access interface.

- Specify IKE version.
- Specify traffic to protect.
- Configure authentication methods.
- Specify encryption algorithm.
- Verify VPN functionality.
- Monitor the VPN connection and traffic.

Background/Scenario

In addition to acting as a remote access VPN concentrator, the ASA can provide Site-to-Site IPsec VPN tunneling. The tunnel can be configured between two ASAs or between an ASA and another IPsec VPN-capable device such as an ISR, as is the case with this lab.

Your company has two locations connected to an ISP. Router R1 represents a CPE device managed by the ISP. Router R2 represents an intermediate Internet router. Router R3 connects users at the remote branch office to the ISP. The ASA is an edge CPE security device that connects the internal corporate network and DMZ to the ISP while providing NAT services to inside hosts.

Management has asked you to provide a dedicated Site-to-Site IPsec VPN tunnel between the ISR router at the remote branch office and the ASA device at the corporate site. This tunnel will protect traffic between the branch office LAN and the corporate LAN as it passes through the Internet. The Site-to-Site VPN does not require a VPN client on the remote or corporate site host computers. Traffic from either LAN to other Internet destinations is routed by the ISP and is not protected by the VPN tunnel. The VPN tunnel will pass through R1 and R2, which are not aware of its existence.

In Part 1 of the lab, you configure the topology and non-ASA devices. In Part 2, you prepare the ASA for ASDM access. In Part 3, you use the CCP VPN Wizard to configure the R3 ISR as a Site-to-Site IPsec VPN endpoint. In Part 4, you configure the ASA as a Site-to-Site IPsec VPN endpoint using the ASDM VPN Wizard.

Note: The routers used with this lab are Cisco 1841 with Cisco IOS Software Release 12.4(20)T (advanced IP image). The switches are Cisco WS-C2960-24TT-L with Cisco IOS Software Release 12.2(46)SE (C2960-LANBASEK9-M image). Other routers, switches, and Cisco IOS versions can be used; however, results and output may vary.

The ASA used with this lab is a Cisco model 5510 with four FastEthernet routed interfaces running OS Version 8.4(2) and ASDM Version 6.4(5) and comes with a Base license that allows a maximum of 50 VLANs.

Note: Make sure the routers and switches have been erased and have no startup configurations.

Required Resources

- 3 routers (Cisco 1841 with Cisco IOS Software Release 12.4(20)T1 or comparable)
- 3 switches (Cisco 2960 or comparable)
- 1 ASA 5510 (OS Version 8.4(2) and ASDM Version 6.4(5) and Base license or comparable)
- PC-A: Windows XP, Vista, or Windows 7 with PuTTy SSH client (Web server optional)
- PC-B: Windows XP, Vista, or Windows 7 with PuTTy SSH client and Java 6 (ASDM loaded on the PC is optional)
- PC-C: Windows XP, Vista, or Windows 7 with PuTTy SSH client, Java 6, and CCP Version 2.5

- Serial and Ethernet cables as shown in the topology
- Rollover cables to configure the routers and ASA via the console

CCP Notes:

- Refer to Chapter 00 Lab A for instructions on how to install and run CCP. Hardware/software recommendations for CCP include Windows XP, Vista, or Windows 7 with Java Version 1.6.0_11 up to 1.6.0_21, Internet Explorer 6.0 or later, and Flash Player Version 10.0.12.36 and later.
- If the PC on which CCP is installed is running Windows Vista or Windows 7, it might be necessary to right-click the CCP icon or menu item and choose Run as Administrator.
- To run CCP, it might be necessary to temporarily disable antivirus programs and OS firewalls. Make sure you turn off all pop-up blockers off in the browser.

Part 1: Basic Router/Switch/PC Configuration

In Part 1 of this lab, you set up the network topology and configure basic settings on the routers, such as interface IP addresses and static routing.

Note: Do not configure any ASA settings at this time.

Step 1: Cable the network and clear previous device settings.

Attach the devices shown in the topology diagram, and cable as necessary. Make sure the routers and switches have been erased and have no startup configurations.

Step 2: Configure basic settings for routers and switches.

a. Configure hostnames as shown in the topology for each router.

b. Configure router interface IP addresses as shown in the IP addressing table.

c. Configure a clock rate for routers with a DCE serial cable attached to their serial interface. Router R1 is shown here as an example:

```
R1(config)# interface S0/0/0
R1(config-if)# clock rate 64000
```

d. Configure the hostname for the switches. Other than hostname, the switches can be left in their default configuration state. Configuring the VLAN management IP address for the switches is optional.

Step 3: Configure static routing on the routers.

a. Configure a static default route from R1 to R2 and from R3 to R2.

```
R1(config)# ip route 0.0.0.0 0.0.0.0 Serial0/0/0
R3(config)# ip route 0.0.0.0 0.0.0.0 Serial0/0/1
```

b. Configure a static route from R2 to the R1 Fa0/0 subnet (connected to ASA interface E0/0) and a static route from R2 to the R3 LAN.

```
R2(config)# ip route 209.165.200.224 255.255.255.248 Serial0/0/0
R2(config)# ip route 172.16.3.0 255.255.255.0 Serial0/0/1
```

Step 4: Configure the enable and VTY passwords on R3.

On R3, set the enable password to **class** and the console and VTY passwords to **cisco**. Configure these settings on R1 and R2. R3 is shown here as an example:

```
R3(config)# enable secret class

R3(config)# line vty 0 4
R3(config-line)# password cisco
R3(config-line)# login

R3(config)# line con 0
R3(config-line)# password cisco
R3(config-line)# login
```

Step 5: Configure HTTP access, a username, and local authentication prior to starting CCP.

a. From the CLI, enable the HTTP server and configure a username of **admin** and password of **cisco123** for use with CCP on R3:

```
R3(config)# ip http server
R3(config)# username admin privilege 15 secret cisco123
```

b. Use the local database to authenticate web sessions with CCP:

```
R3(config)# ip http authentication local
```

Step 6: Configure PC host IP settings.

Configure a static IP address, subnet mask, and default gateway for PC-A, PC-B, and PC-C as shown in the IP addressing table.

Step 7: Verify connectivity.

From PC-C, ping the R1 Fa0/0 IP address (209.165.200.225). If these pings are not successful, troubleshoot the basic device configurations before continuing.

Note: If you can ping from PC-C to R1 Fa0/0, you have demonstrated that static routing is configured and functioning correctly.

Step 8: Save the basic running configuration for each router and switch.

Part 2: Basic ASA Configuration

Step 1: Access the ASA console.

a. Accessing the ASA via the console port is the same as with a Cisco router or switch. Connect to the ASA Console port with a rollover cable.

b. Use a terminal emulation program, such as TeraTerm or HyperTerminal, to access the CLI, and use the serial port settings of 9600 baud, 8 data bits, no parity, 1 stop bit, and no flow control.

c. If prompted to enter interactive firewall configuration (Setup mode), answer **no**.

d. Enter privileged mode with the `enable` command and password (if set). By default, the password is blank, so you can just press **Enter**. If the password has been changed to that specified in this lab, the password will be **class**. In addition, the hostname and prompt will be `CCNAS-ASA>`, as shown here. The default ASA hostname and prompt is `ciscoasa>`.

```
CCNAS-ASA> enable
Password: class (or press Enter if none set)
```

Step 2: Clear the previous ASA configuration settings.

a. Use the **`write erase`** command to remove the **startup-config** file from flash memory:

```
CCNAS-ASA# write erase
Erase configuration in flash memory? [confirm]
[OK]
CCNAS-ASA#
```

Note: The IOS command **`erase startup-config`** is not supported on the ASA.

b. Use the **`reload`** command to restart the ASA. This will cause the ASA to come up in CLI Setup mode. If you see the message `System config has been modified. Save? [Y]es/[N]o:`, respond with **N**.

```
CCNAS-ASA# reload
Proceed with reload? [confirm] <enter>
CCNAS-ASA#
***
*** --- START GRACEFUL SHUTDOWN ---
Shutting down isakmp
Shutting down File system
***
*** --- SHUTDOWN NOW ---
Process shutdown finished
Rebooting.....
CISCO SYSTEMS
Embedded BIOS Version 1.0(12)13 08/28/08 15:50:37.45
<output omitted>
```

Step 3: Bypass Setup mode.

When the ASA completes the reload process, it should detect that the **startup-config** file is missing and go into Setup mode. If it does not come up in this mode, repeat Step 2.

a. When prompted to preconfigure the firewall through interactive prompts (Setup mode), respond with **no**:

```
Pre-configure Firewall now through interactive prompts [yes]?  no
```

b. Enter privileged EXEC mode with the **`enable`** command. The password should be blank (no password) at this point.

Step 4: Use the CLI script to configure the ASA.

In this step, you use the modified running-config from Lab 10E to preconfigure basic settings, the firewall, and DMZ:

a. Ensure that there is no previous configuration in the ASA, other than the defaults that the ASA automatically inserts, using the **`show run`** command.

b. Enter CLI global configuration mode. When prompted to enable anonymous call-home reporting, respond **no**.

```
ciscoasa> enable
Password: <enter>

ciscoasa# conf t
ciscoasa(config)#
```

c. Copy and paste the Pre-VPN Configuration Script commands listed below at the ASA global config mode prompt to bring it to the point where you can start configuring the SSL VPNs.

d. Observe the messages as the commands are applied to ensure that there are no warnings or errors. If prompted to replace the RSA keypair, respond **yes**.

e. After script commands have been applied, issue the **`write mem`** (or **`copy run start`**) command to save the running configuration to the startup configuration and the RSA keys to nonvolatile memory.

Lab 10H Pre-VPN ASA Configuration Script:

```
hostname CCNAS-ASA
!
domain-name ccnasecurity.com
!
enable password class
passwd cisco
!
interface Ethernet0/0
 nameif outside
 security-level 0
 ip address 209.165.200.226 255.255.255.248
 no shut
!
interface Ethernet0/1
 nameif inside
 security-level 100
 ip address 192.168.1.1 255.255.255.0
 no shut
!
interface Ethernet0/2
 nameif dmz
 security-level 70
 ip address 192.168.2.1 255.255.255.0
 no shut
!
object network inside-net
 subnet 192.168.1.0 255.255.255.0
!
object network dmz-server
 host 192.168.2.3
!
access-list OUTSIDE-DMZ extended permit ip any host 192.168.2.3
!
object network inside-net
 nat (inside,outside) dynamic interface
!
object network dmz-server
 nat (dmz,outside) static 209.165.200.227
!
```

```
access-group OUTSIDE-DMZ in interface outside
!
route outside 0.0.0.0 0.0.0.0 209.165.200.225 1
!
username admin password cisco123
!
aaa authentication telnet console LOCAL
aaa authentication ssh console LOCAL
aaa authentication http console LOCAL
!
http server enable
http 192.168.1.0 255.255.255.0 inside
ssh 192.168.1.0 255.255.255.0 inside
telnet 192.168.1.0 255.255.255.0 inside
telnet timeout 10
ssh timeout 10
!
class-map inspection_default
 match default-inspection-traffic
policy-map type inspect dns preset_dns_map
 parameters
  message-length maximum client auto
  message-length maximum 512
policy-map global_policy
 class inspection_default
   inspect icmp
!
prompt hostname context
no call-home reporting anonymous
!
crypto key generate rsa modulus 1024
```

Step 5: Verify HTTPS ASDM access.

This step is intended to verify HTTPS connectivity from PC-B to the ASA. ASDM settings are configured in Part 4 of the lab.

a. Open a browser on PC-B and test the HTTPS access to the ASA by entering **https://192.168.1.1**.

Note: Be sure to specify the HTTPS protocol in the URL.

b. After entering the URL above, you should see a security warning about the website's security certificate. Click **Continue to This Website**. The ASDM welcome page appears. From this screen, you can install ASDM on the PC, run ASDM as browser-based Java applet directly from the ASA, or run the Startup WIZARD. Click the **Run ASDM** button.

c. The ASDM-IDM Launcher appears. Log in as user **admin** with password **cisco123**. ASDM loads the current configuration into the GUI.

Note: The process can vary depending on the browser used. This example is for Internet Explorer.

Part 3: Configuring the ISR as a Site-to-Site IPsec VPN Endpoint Using CCP

In Part 3 of this lab, you configure R3 as an IPsec VPN endpoint for the tunnel between R3 and the ASA. Routers R1 and R2 are unaware of the tunnel.

Note: If the PC on which CCP is installed is running Windows 7, it might be necessary to right-click the CCP icon or menu item and choose **Run as Administrator**.

It might be necessary to temporarily disable antivirus programs and OS firewalls to run CCP. The minimum recommended Windows PC requirements to run CCP are

- Internet Explorer with Java 6 plug-in version 1.6.0-11
- Adobe Flash Player version 10
- 1 GB RAM
- Screen resolution of 1024 x 768

Note: If you receive the following Java-related error message from CCP during the VPN configuration process, perform the steps indicated in the message:

> Security component has failed. In order to work on Router or Security features, do the following. Go to **Java Control panel -> Advanced tab -> Java Plug-in** tree Entry. Uncheck the check box for **Enable next-generation Java Plug-in**. Re-launch CCP after this.

Step 1: Run the CCP application on PC-C and discover R3.

a. Run the CCP application on PC-C. In the Select/Manage Community window, enter the R3 Fa0/0 IP address **172.16.3.1**, username **admin**, and **cisco123** as the password. Click the **OK** button.

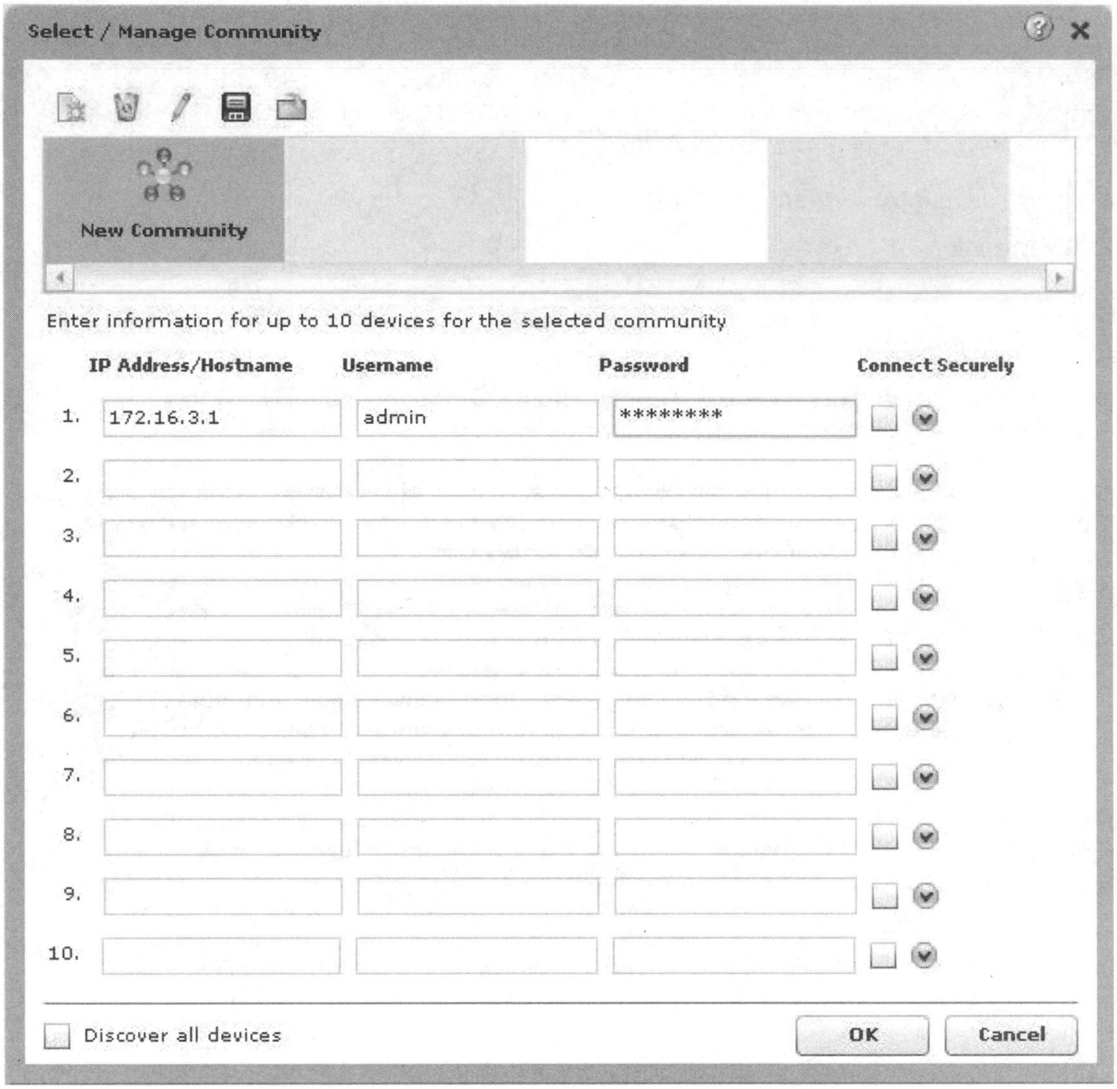

b. In the Community Information panel, click the **Discover** button to discover and connect to R3. If the PC-C CCP application can make an HTTP connection to R3, the Discovery Status will change to Discovered. If the discovery process fails, click the **Discovery Details** button to determine the problem so that you can resolve the issue.

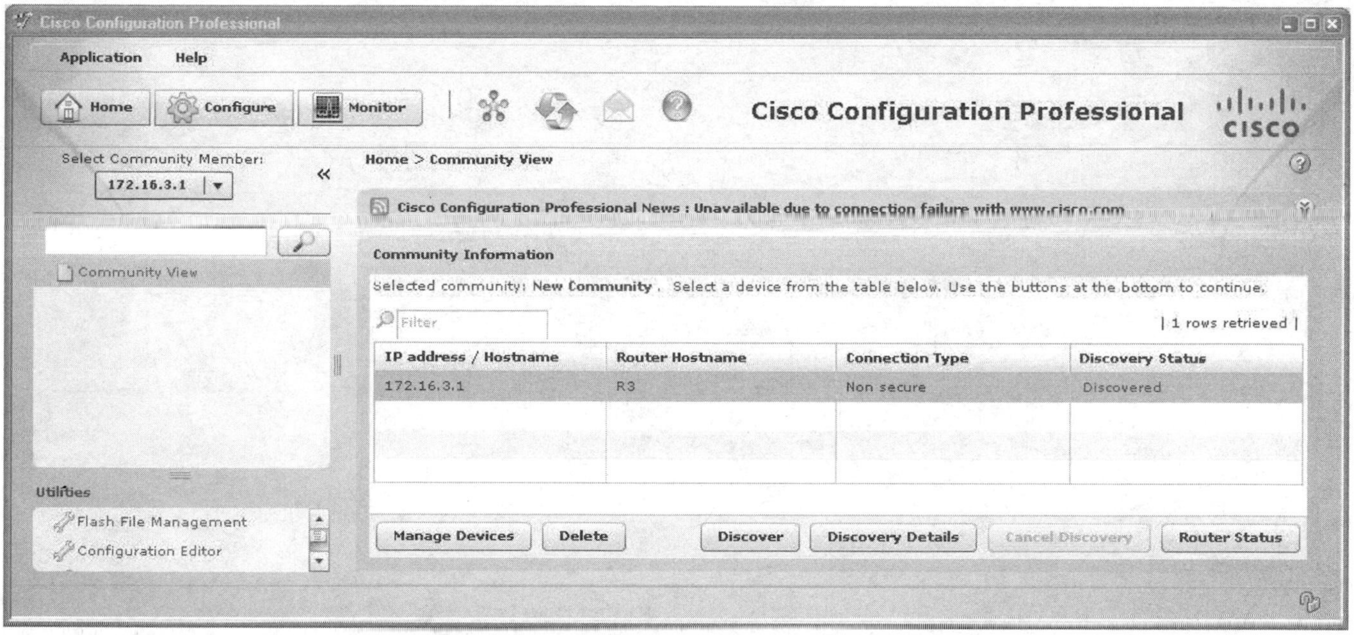

Step 2: Start the CCP VPN Wizard to configure R3.

a. Click the **Configure** button at the top of the CCP screen, and choose **Security > VPN > Site-to-Site VPN**. Read the on-screen text describing the Site-to-Site VPN.

What must you know to complete the configuration?

____

____

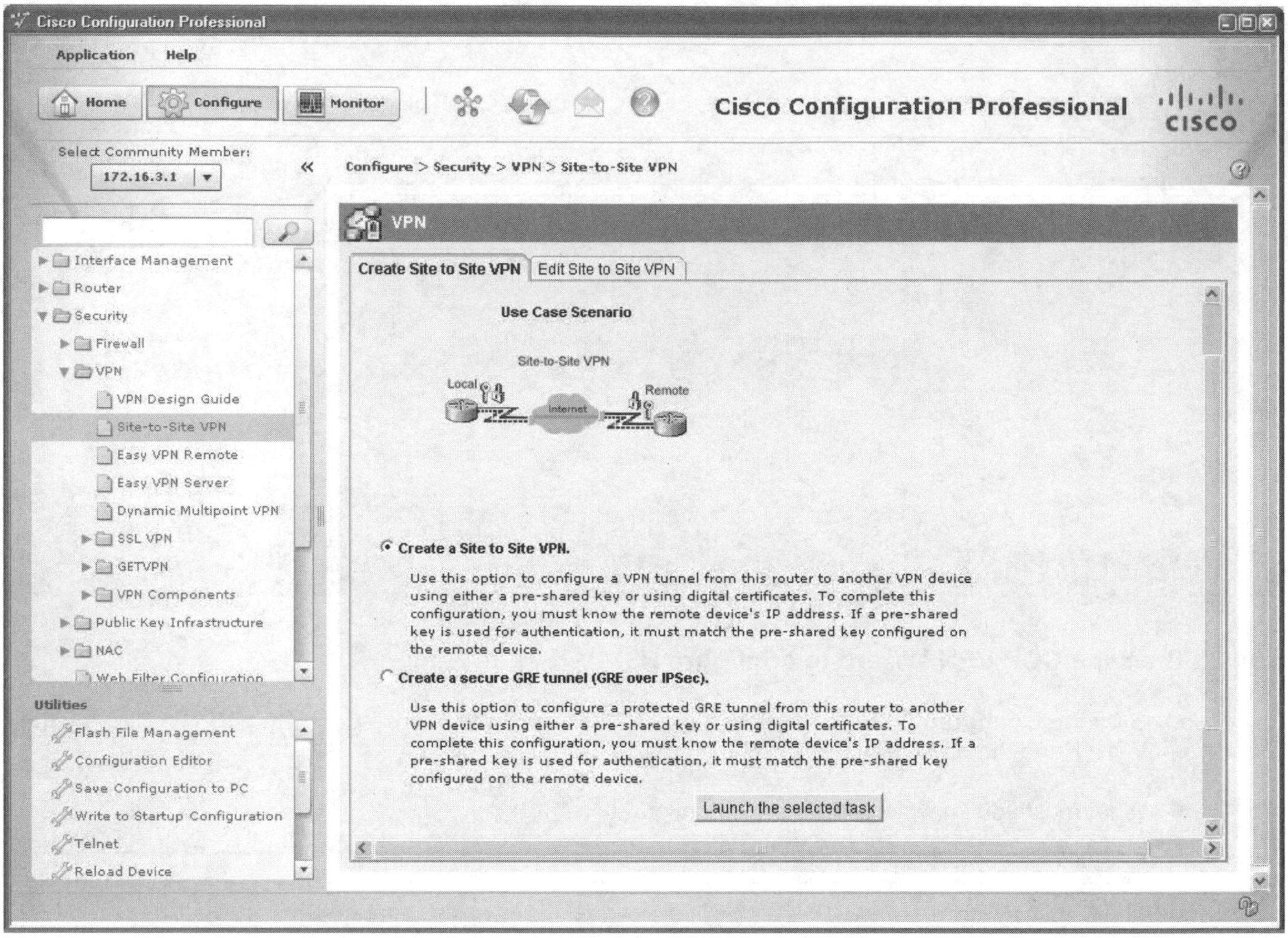

b. Click the **Launch the Selected Task** button to begin the CCP Site-to-Site VPN Wizard.

c. From the initial Site-to-Site VPN Wizard screen, choose the Step by Step Wizard, and then click **Next**.

Step 3: Configure basic VPN connection information settings.

a. On the VPN Connection Information screen, select the interface for the connection, which should be R3 Serial0/0/1.

b. In the Peer Identity section, select **Peer with Static IP Address** and enter the IP address of the remote peer, ASA interface E0/0 (209.165.200.226).

c. In the Authentication section, click **Pre-shared Keys**, and enter the pre-shared VPN key **cisco12345**. Reenter the key for confirmation. This key authenticates the initial exchange to establish the Security Association (SA) between devices. When finished, your screen should look similar to the following. After you have entered these settings correctly, click **Next**.

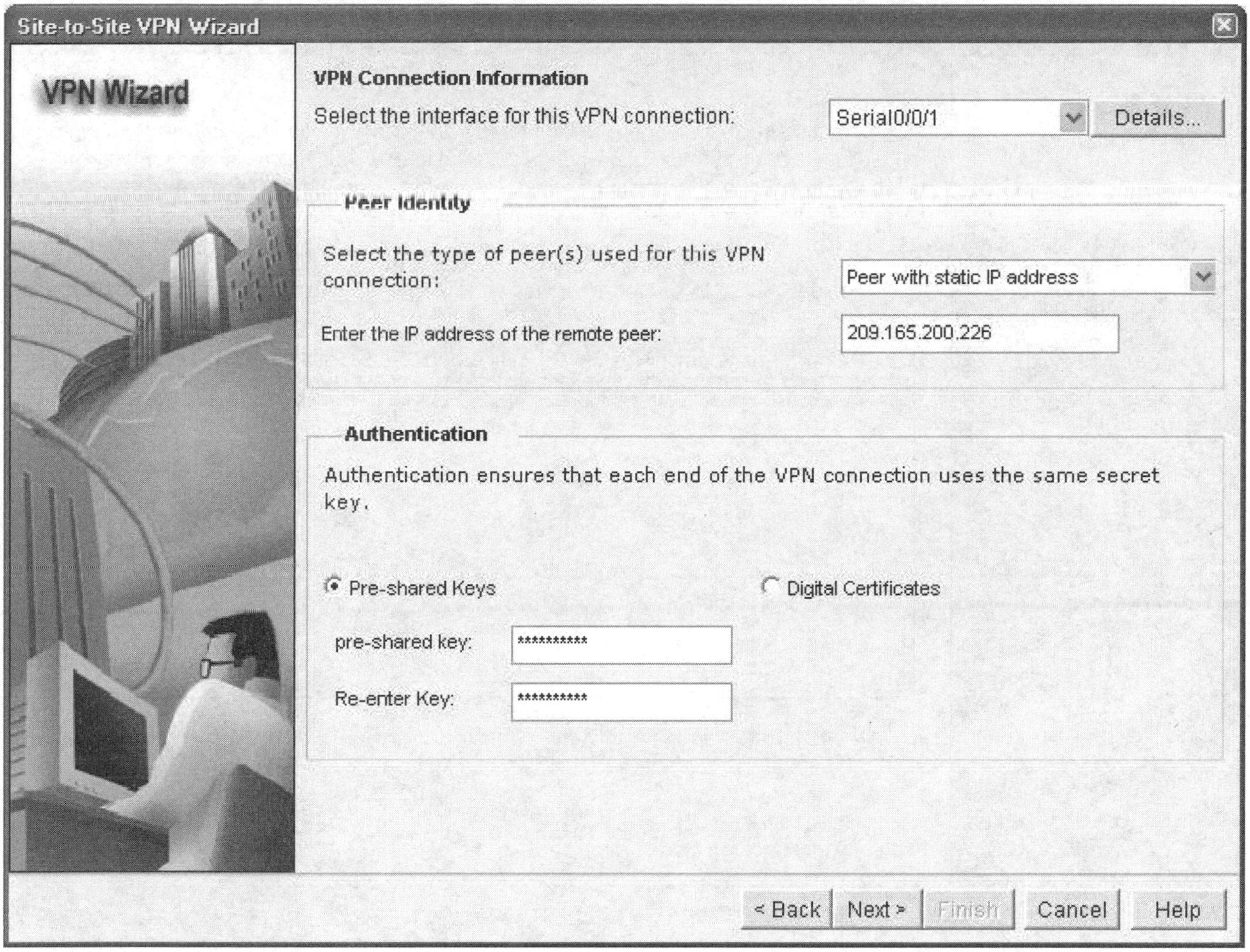

Step 4: Specify IKE policy.

IKE Phase 1 policies are used while setting up the control channel between the two VPN endpoints for key exchange. This is also referred to as the IKE secure association (SA). In contrast, the IPsec policy is used during IKE Phase 2 to negotiate an IPsec security association to pass target data traffic.

On the IKE Proposals screen, a default policy proposal is displayed with a priority of 1. You can use this one or create a new one, if necessary. In this lab, you configure the R3 end of the VPN tunnel using the default IKE proposal. Click **Next** to continue.

Settings for the CCP default IKE Phase 1 policy for this ISR are

- Priority = 1
- Encryption = 3DES
- Hash = SHA_1
- D-H Group = group2
- Authentication = PRE_SHARE

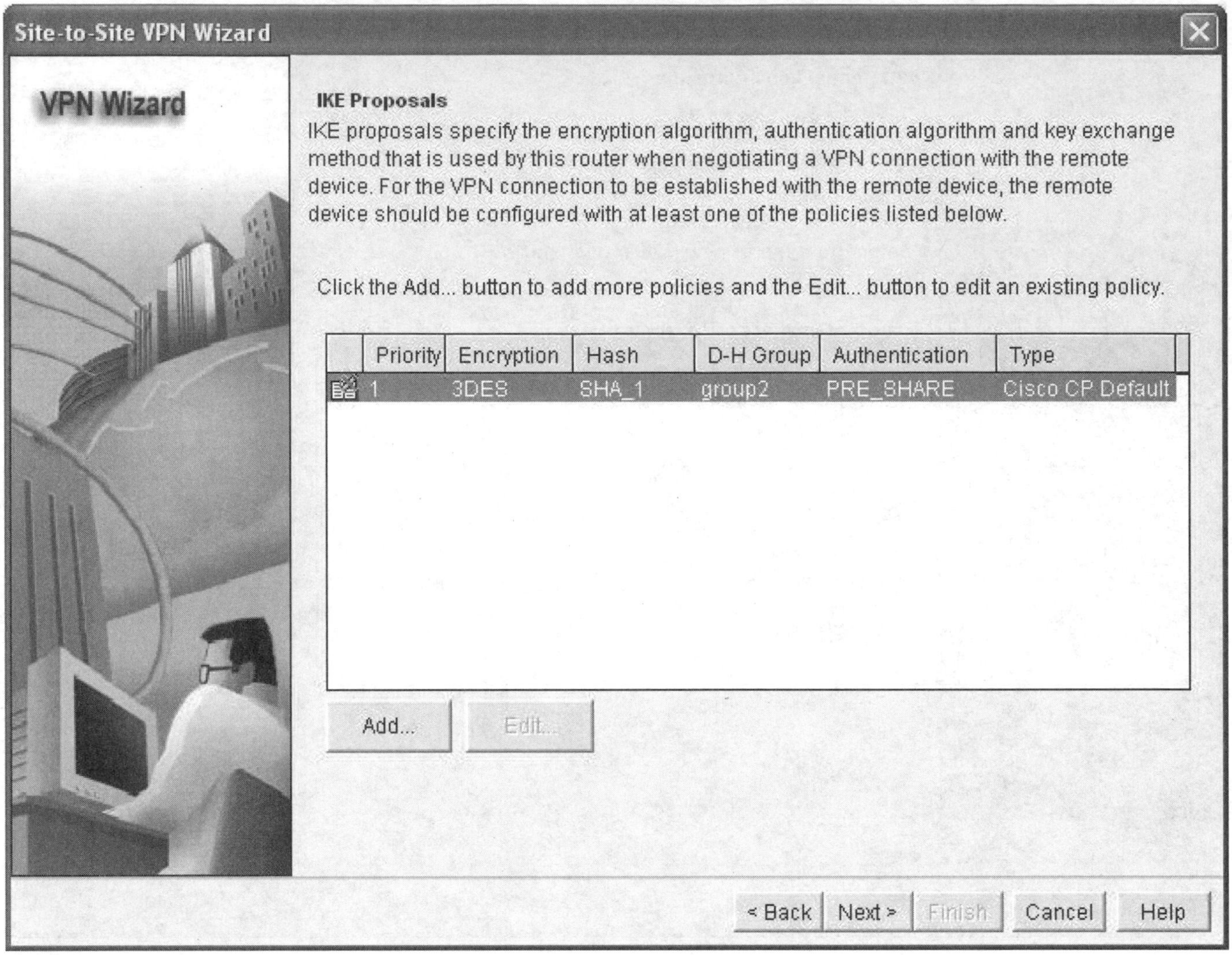

Step 5: Configure a transform set.

The transform set is the IPsec policy used to encrypt, hash, and authenticate packets that pass through the tunnel. The transform set is the IKE Phase 2 policy.

On the Transform Set screen, a default transform set is displayed. You can use this one or create a new one, if necessary. In this lab, you configure the R3 end of the VPN tunnel using the default transform set. Click **Next** to continue.

Settings for the CCP default IKE Phase 2 policy transform set for this ISR are

- Name = ESP-3DES-SHA
- ESP Encryption = ESP_3DES
- ESP Integrity = ESP_SHA_HMAC
- Mode = Tunnel

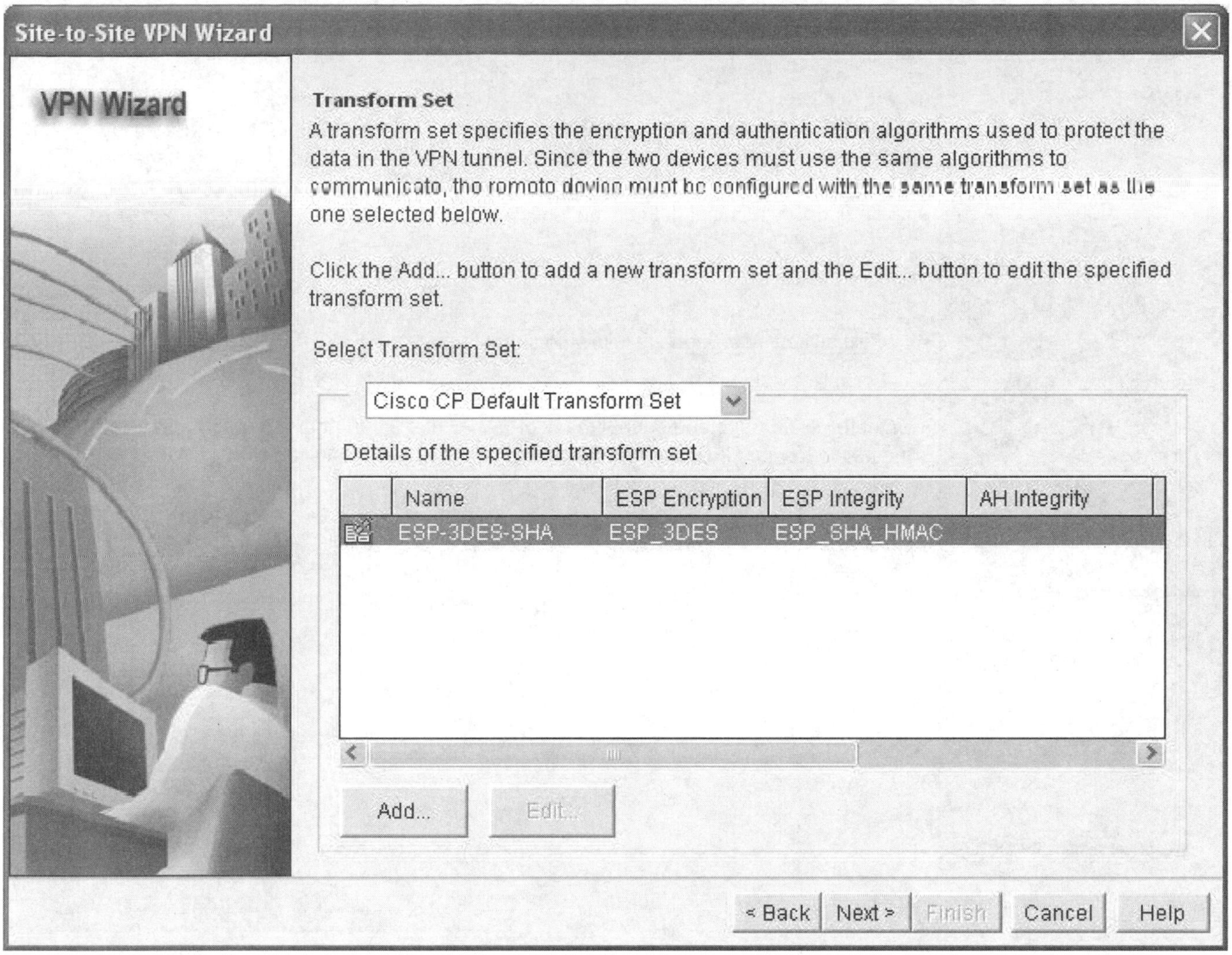

Step 6: Specify traffic to protect.

You must define "interesting" traffic to be protected through the VPN tunnel. Interesting traffic is defined through an access list that is applied to the router. By entering the source and destination subnets that you would like to protect through the VPN tunnel, CCP generates the appropriate simple access list for you.

On the Traffic to Protect screen, enter the information shown in the following figure. These are the opposite of the settings to be configured on the ASA later in the lab. When finished, click **Next**.

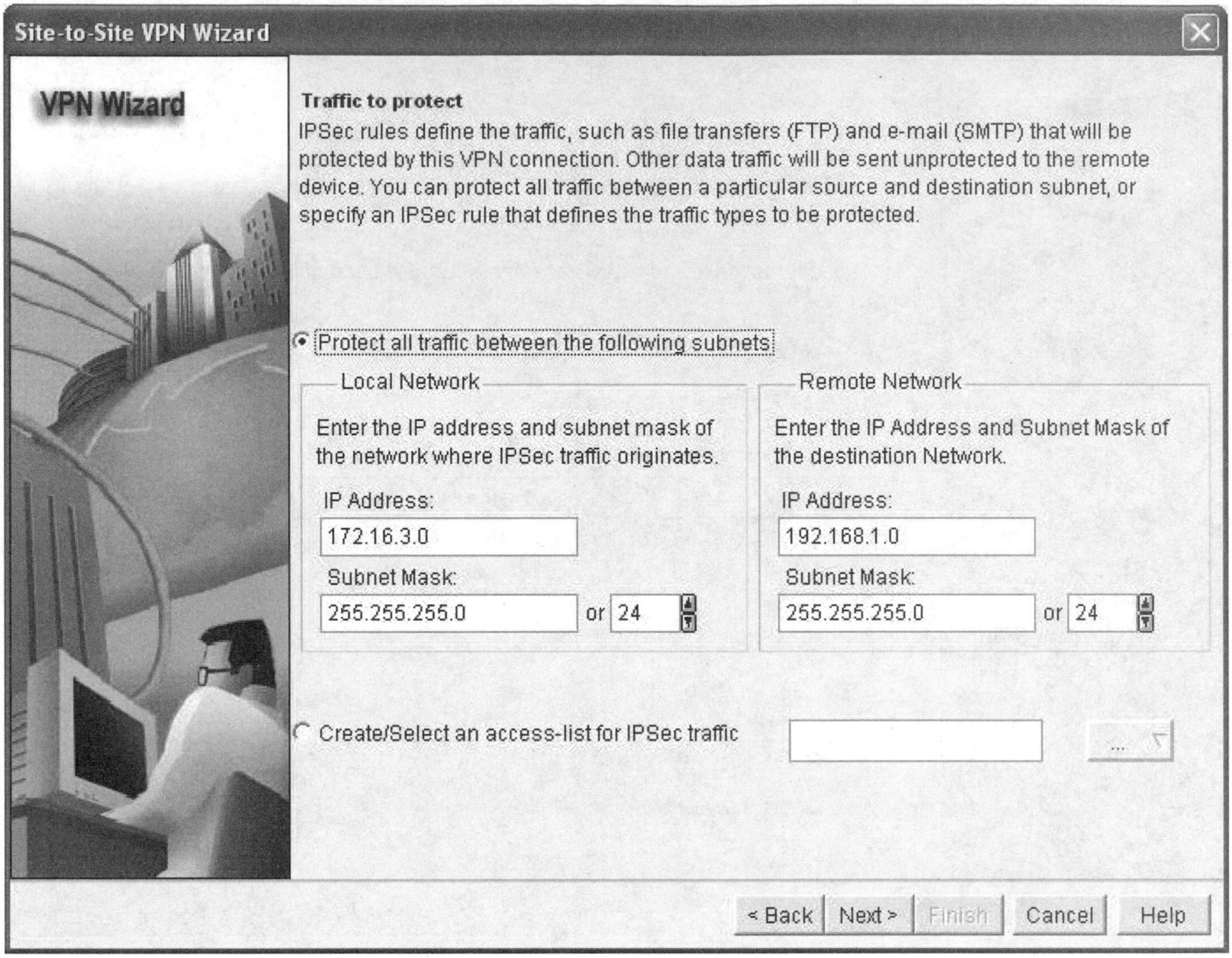

Step 7: Review the summary of the configuration.

a. Review the Summary of the Configuration screen. It should look similar to the following figure. You can scroll down to see the IPsec rule (ACL) that CCP creates for R3, which permits all traffic from network 172.16.3.0/24 to network 192.168.1.0/24.

   Do NOT select the Test VPN Connectivity After Configuring checkbox. This will be done after you configure the ASA side of the VPN tunnel.

b. Click **Finish** to go to the Deliver Configuration to Device screen.

Note: Pay particular attention to the IKE Policies and Transform Set because you will configure the ASA to match these settings in the next part of the lab.

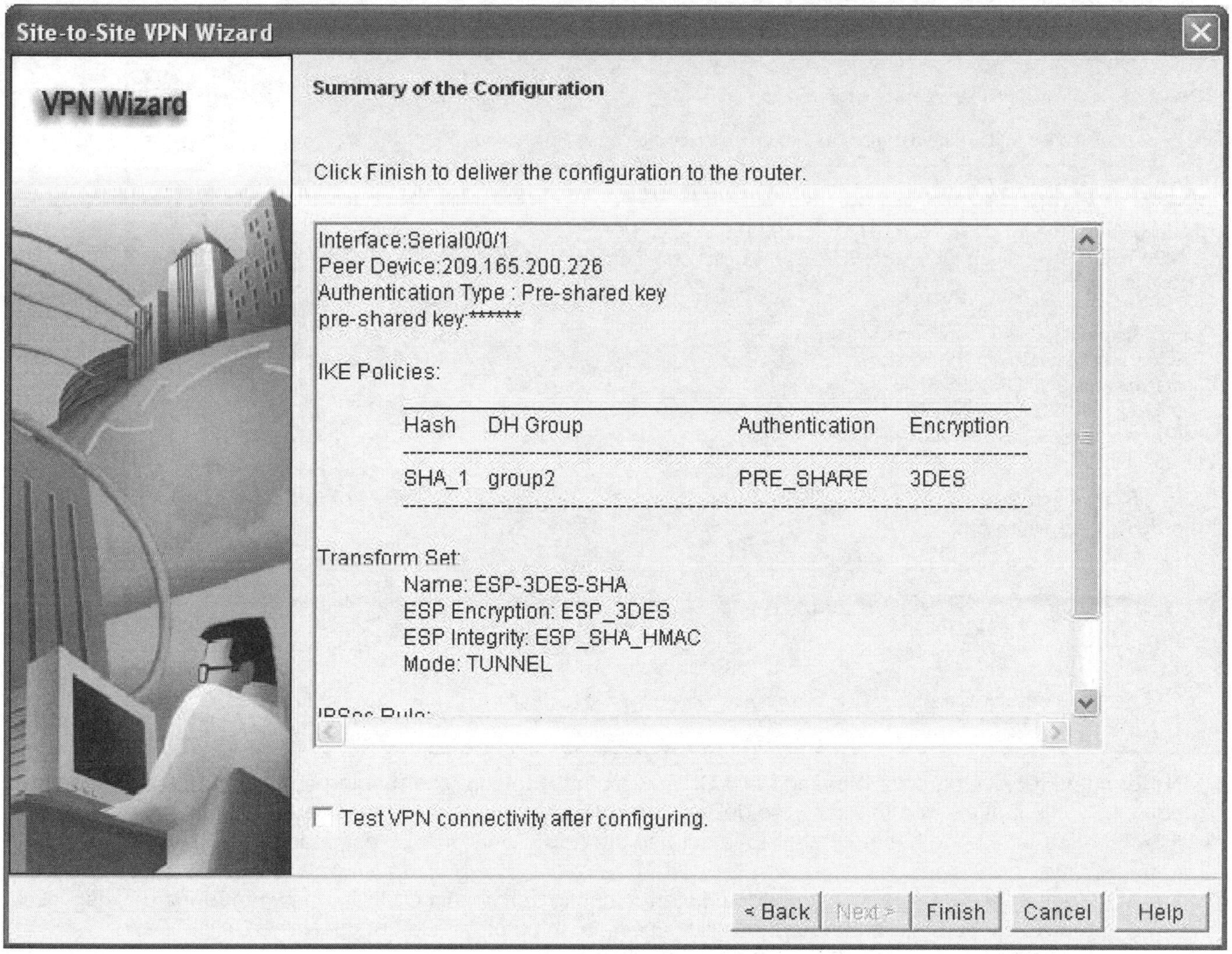

c. On the Deliver Configuration to Device screen, select **Save running config. to device's startup config** and click the **Deliver** button. After the commands have been delivered, click **OK**.

d. You can also save these configuration commands for later editing or documentation purposes by clicking the **Save to File** button.

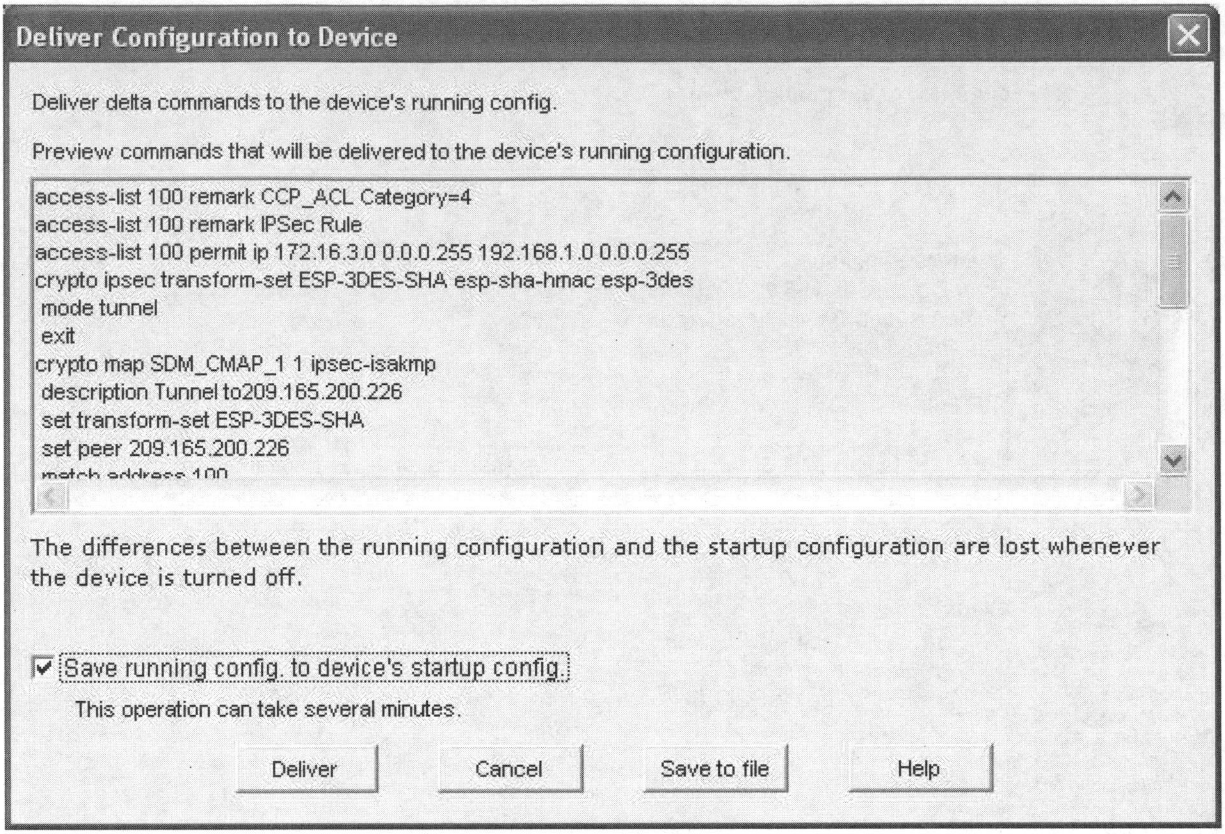

Note: If you receive an error message that CCP was unable to copy the running-config to the startup-config, you can verify that the commands were delivered by using the **`show startup-config`** CLI command on R3. If the startup-config has not been updated, use the **`copy run start`** command on R3.

e. You can view the running config and startup config from within CCP. To view the running config, click the **Home** button, and under the Utilities section at the bottom left of the screen, click **View > Running Configuration**. The running config appears.

f. To view the startup config, click **Home > Utilities > View > IOS Show Commands**. Click the pull-down menu next to the command window, select the **`show startup-config`** command. Then, click the **Show** button. The startup configuration displays.

Note: Several predefined **`show`** commands are listed in the pull-down menu but you can also enter any valid IOS command, such as **`show ip interface brief`**, and then click the **Show** button.

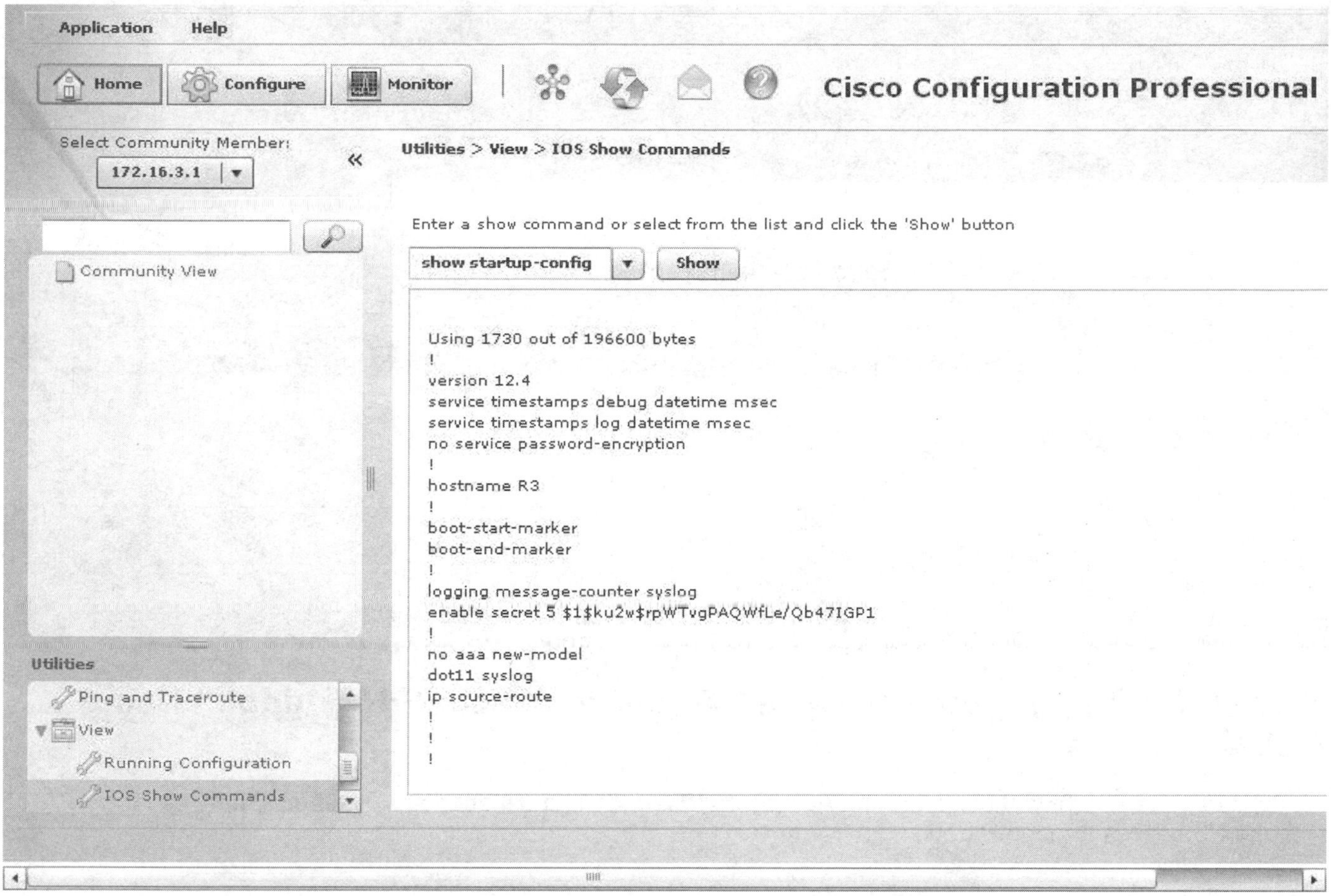

Step 8: Review the Site-to-Site VPN tunnel configuration.

The Edit Site-to-Site VPN screen is displayed after the commands are delivered. To return to this screen, choose **Configure > Security > VPN > Site-to-Site VPN** and click the **Edit Site to Site VPN** tab. Use the scroll buttons to examine the configuration. The tunnel status is down at this point because the ASA end of the tunnel is not yet configured.

Note: Leave CCP running and connected to R3 on PC-C. You will use the Test Tunnel button on this screen to verify VPN functionality after configuring the ASA end of the tunnel.

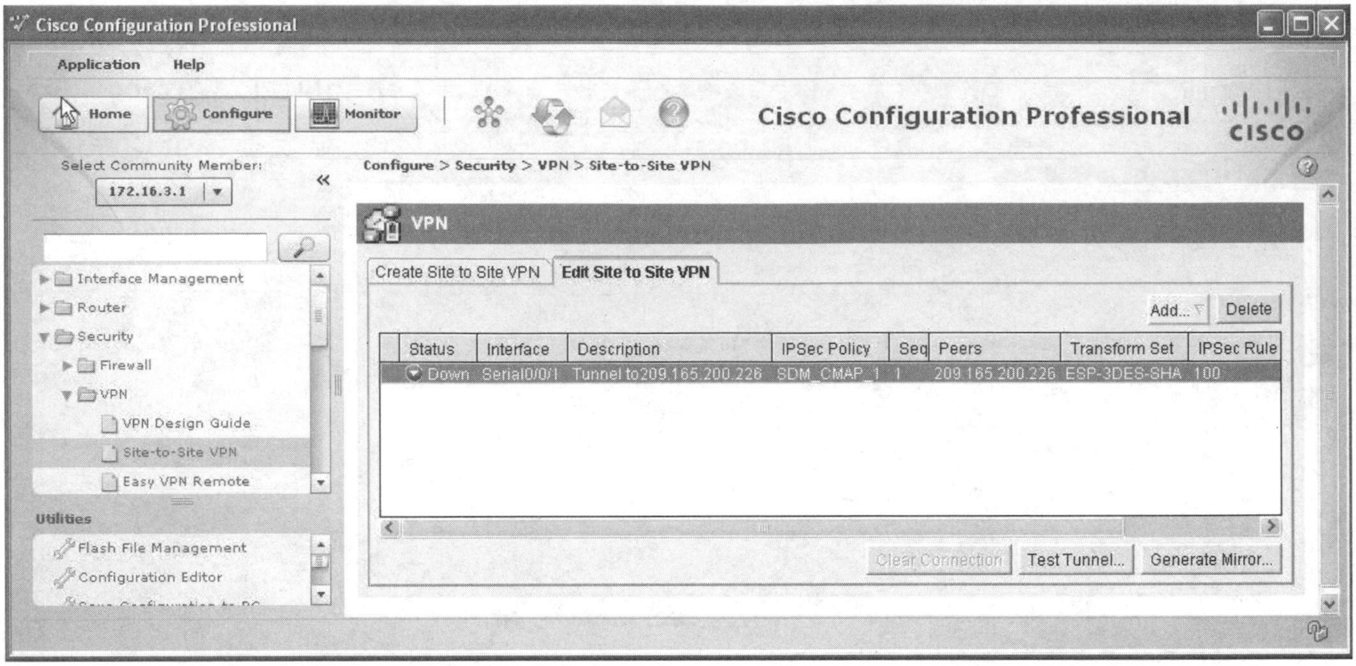

Part 4: Configuring the ASA as a Site-to-Site IPsec VPN Endpoint Using ASDM

In Part 4 of this lab, you configure the ASA as an IPsec VPN tunnel endpoint. The tunnel between the ASA and R3 passes through R1 and R2.

Step 1: Access ASDM.

a. Open a browser on PC-B and test the HTTPS access to the ASA by entering **https://192.168.1.1**.

Note: Be sure to specify the HTTPS protocol in the URL.

b. After entering the URL above, you should see a security warning about the website security certificate. Click **Continue to This Website**. Click **Yes** for any other security warnings. At the ASDM welcome page, click the **Run ASDM** button. The ASDM-IDM Launcher displays. Log in as user **admin** with password **cisco123**. ASDM will load the current configuration into the GUI.

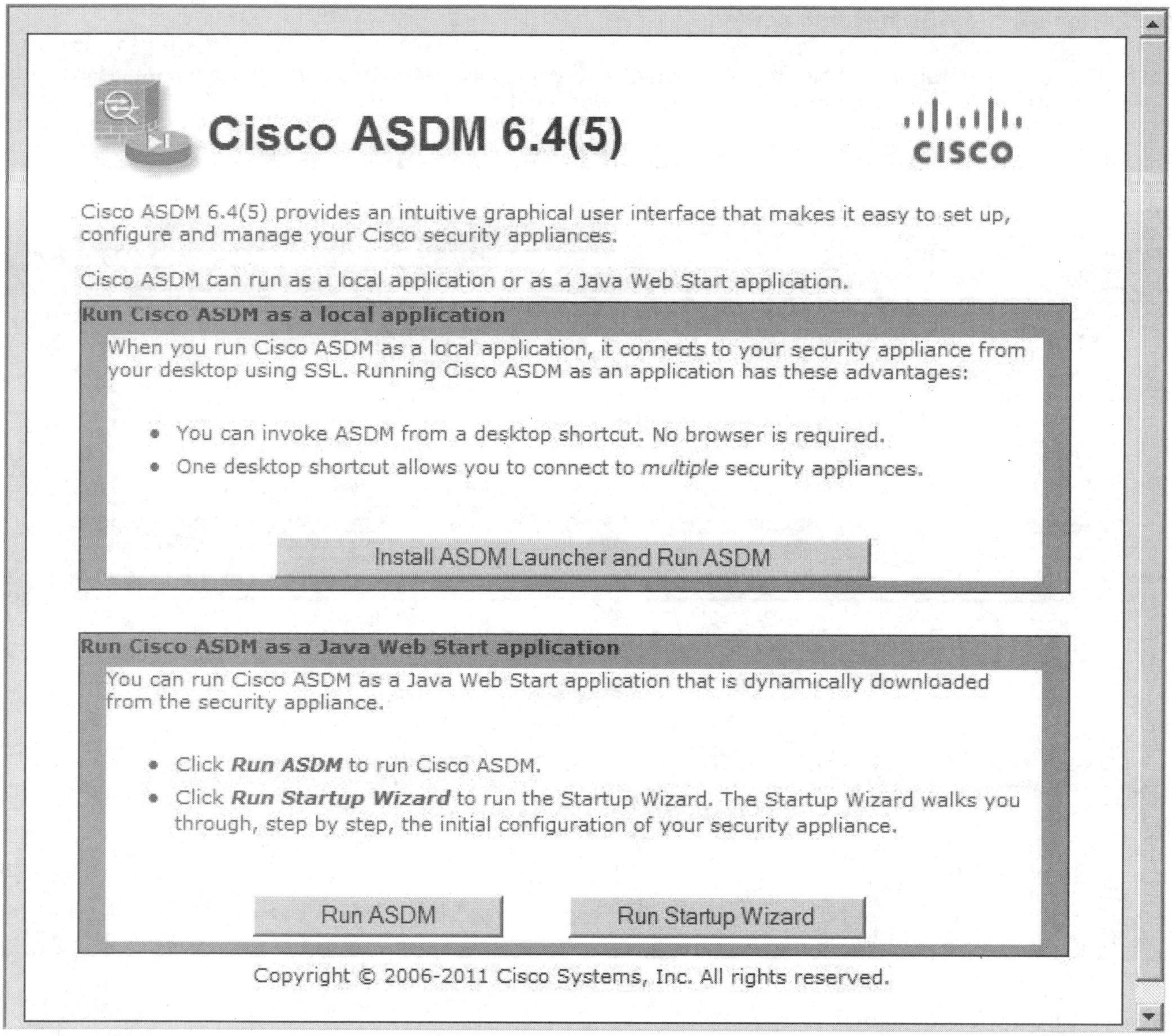
Cisco ASDM 6.4(5)
Cisco ASDM 6.4(5) provides an intuitive graphical user interface that makes it easy to set up, configure and manage your Cisco security appliances.
Cisco ASDM can run as a local application or as a Java Web Start application.
Run Cisco ASDM as a local application
When you run Cisco ASDM as a local application, it connects to your security appliance from your desktop using SSL. Running Cisco ASDM as an application has these advantages:
You can invoke ASDM from a desktop shortcut. No browser is required.
One desktop shortcut allows you to connect to multiple security appliances.
Install ASDM Launcher and Run ASDM
Run Cisco ASDM as a Java Web Start application
You can run Cisco ASDM as a Java Web Start application that is dynamically downloaded from the security appliance.
Click Run ASDM to run Cisco ASDM.
Click Run Startup Wizard to run the Startup Wizard. The Startup Wizard walks you through, step by step, the initial configuration of your security appliance.
Run ASDM
Run Startup Wizard
Copyright © 2006-2011 Cisco Systems, Inc. All rights reserved.

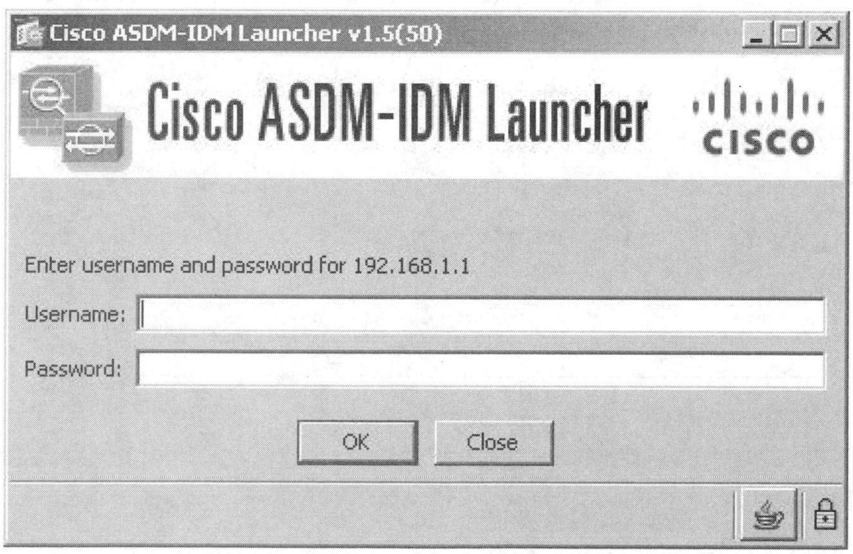
Cisco ASDM-IDM Launcher v1.5(50)
Cisco ASDM-IDM Launcher
Enter username and password for 192.168.1.1
Username:
Password:
OK
Close

Step 2: Review the ASDM Home screen.

The Home screen displays, showing the current ASA device configuration and some traffic flow statistics. Note the inside, outside, and dmz interfaces, which were configured in Part 2.

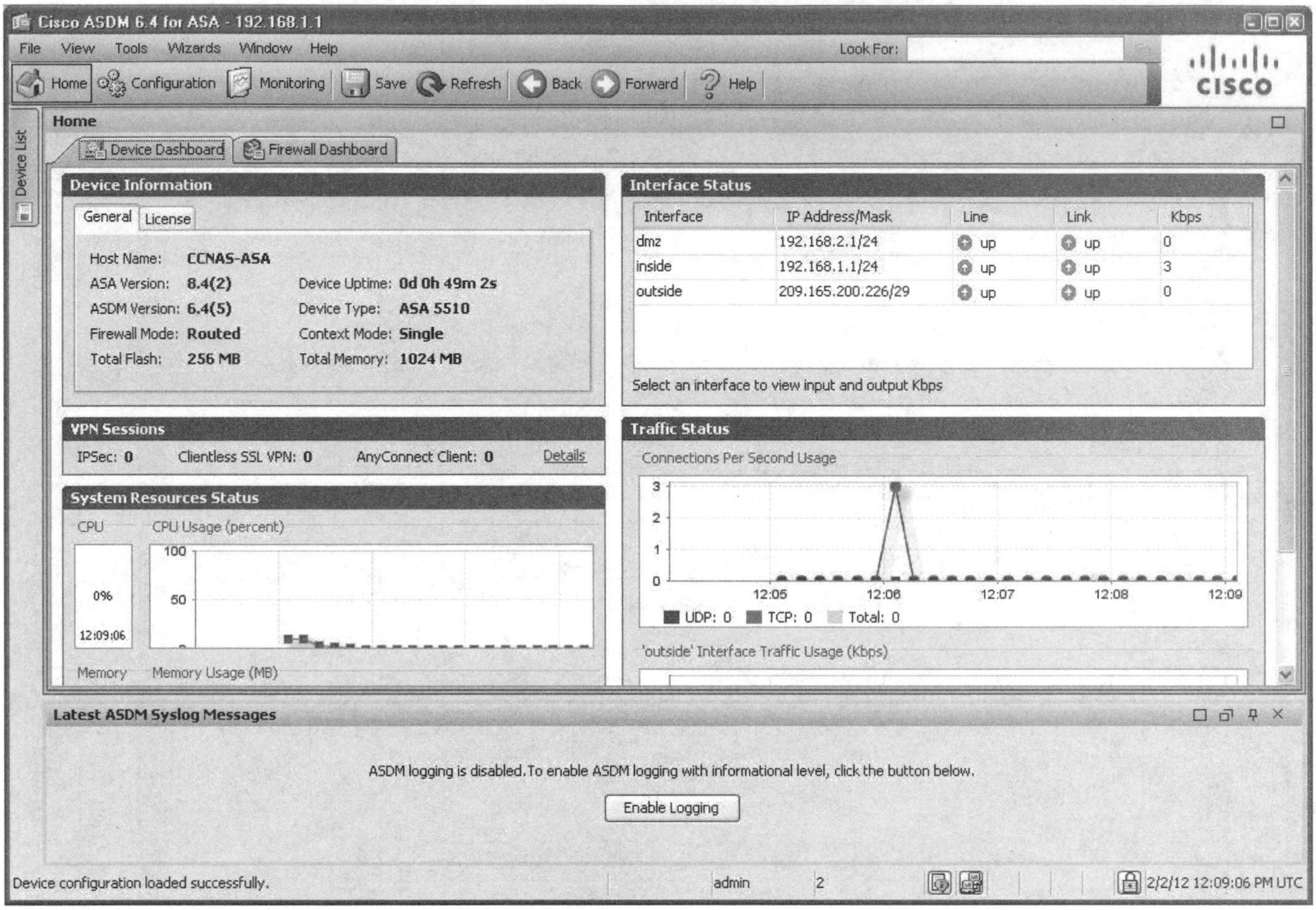

Step 3: Start the VPN Wizard.

a. From the ASDM main menu, select **Wizards > VPN Wizards > Site-to-Site VPN Wizard**. The Site-to-Site VPN Connection Setup Wizard Introduction screen is displayed.

b. Review the on-screen text and topology diagram, and then click **Next** to continue.

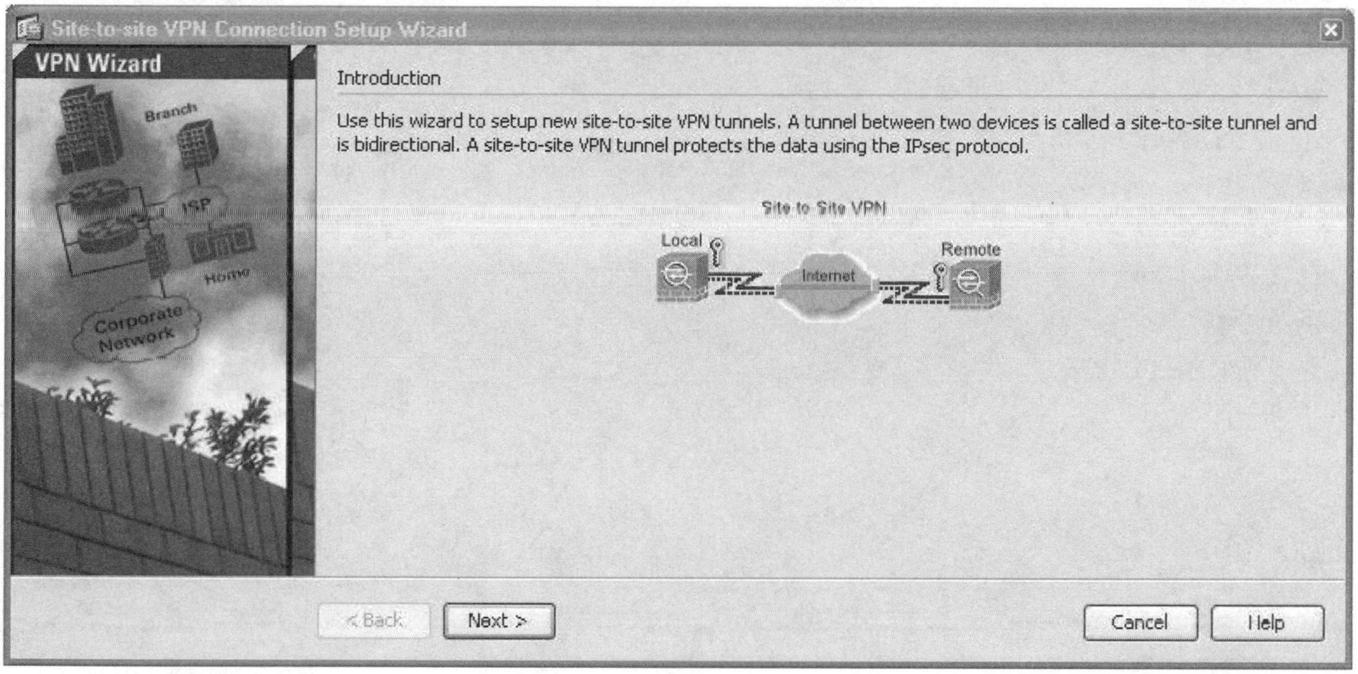

Step 4: Configure peer device identification.

On the Peer Device Identification screen, enter the IP address of the R3 Serial0/0/1 interface (**10.2.2.1**) as the Peer IP Address. Leave the default VPN Access Interface set to **outside**. The VPN tunnel will be between R3 S0/0/1 and ASA outside interface E0/0. Click **Next** to continue.

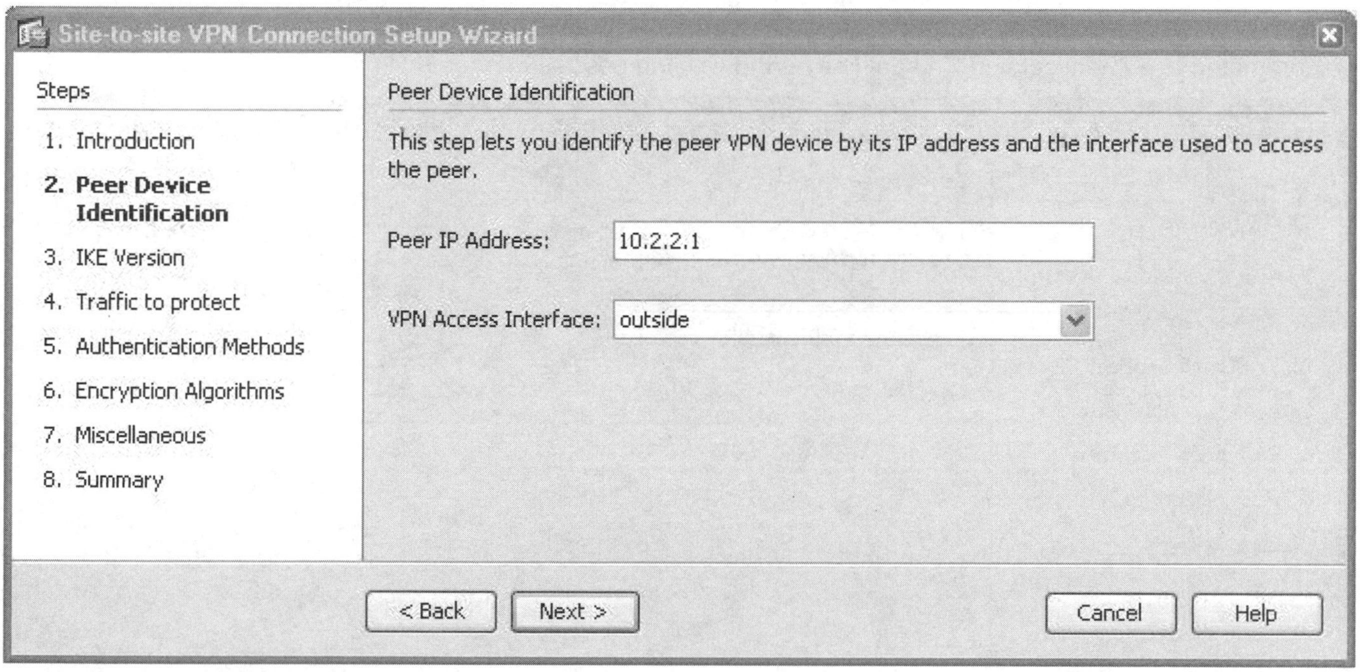

Step 5: Specify the IKE version.

IKE version 1 simple preshared keys will be used. On the IKE Version screen, uncheck the **IKE version 2** checkbox and leave **IKE version 1** checked. Click **Next** to continue.

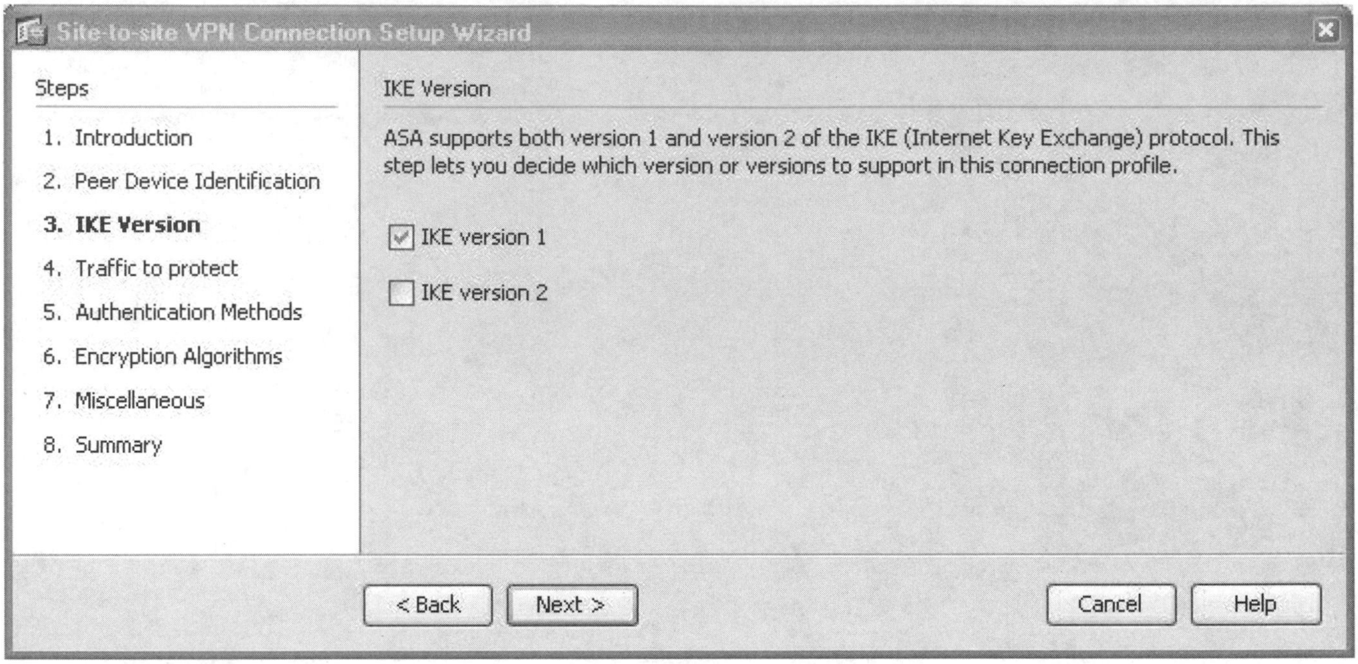

Step 6: Specify the traffic to protect.

On the Traffic to Protect screen, click **IPv4** and enter the inside network **192.168.1.0/24** as the local network and the R3 LAN **172.16.3.0/24** as the remote network. Click **Next** to continue. A message will display that the certificate information is being retrieved.

Note: If the ASA does not respond, you might need to close the window and continue to the next step. If prompted to authenticate, log in again as **admin** with the password **cisco123**.

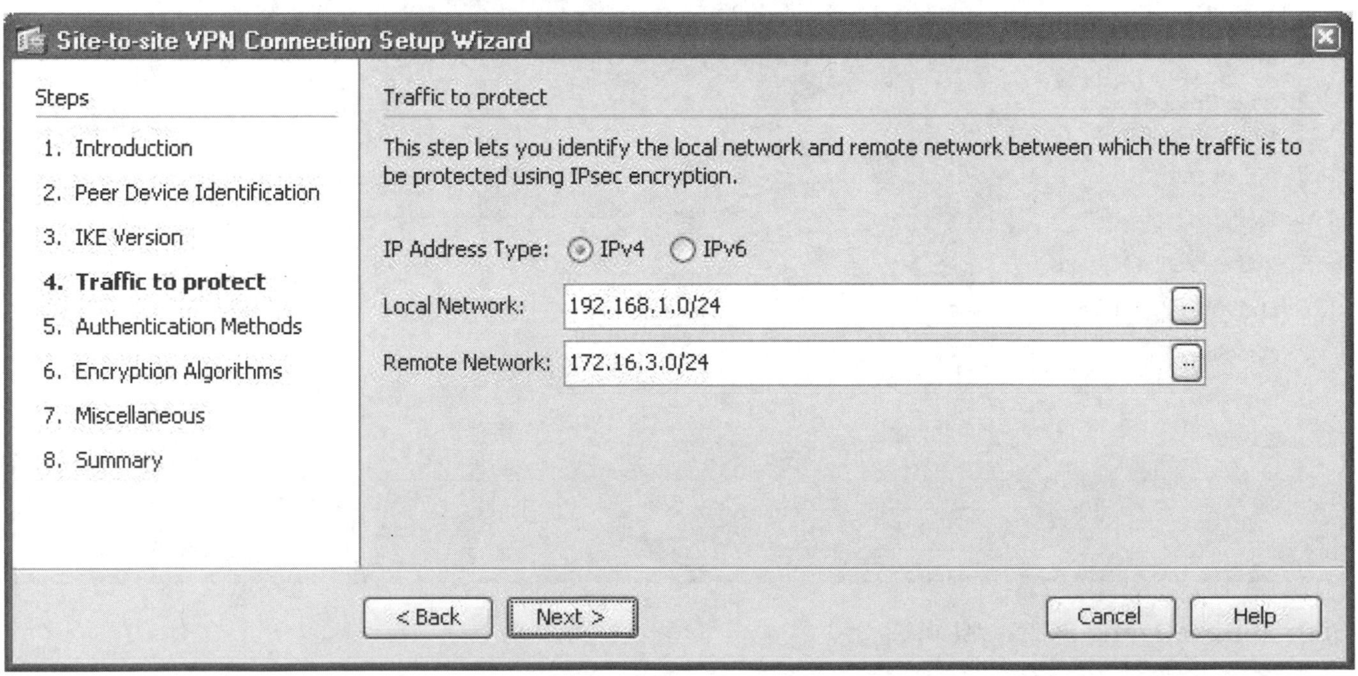

Step 7: Configure authentication.

On the Authentication Methods screen, enter a Pre-shared Key of **cisco12345**. You will not be using a device certificate, so leave it set to **None**. Click **Next** to continue.

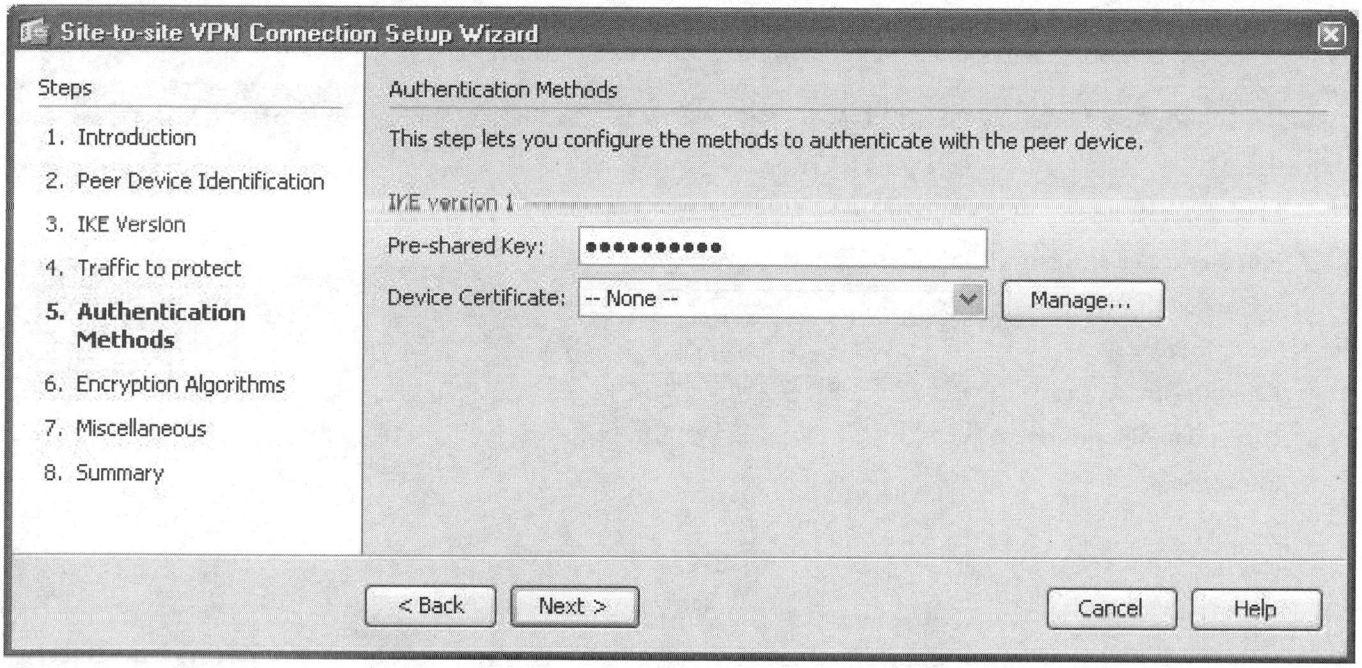

Step 8: Configure encryption algorithms (IKE policy and IPsec transform sets).

a. On the Encryption Algorithms screen, click the **Manage** button next to IKE Policy. Click **OK** to the message that IKE policy is global. On the Configure IKEv1 Policies screen, you will see many policies listed. Only IKE policy 120 is needed to establish the tunnel with R3, so you can delete all policies except 120. If you leave the others, they will become part of the ASA configuration and are unnecessary. Select and click **Delete** for all policies except 120.

Note: The entire list of policies will be repopulated in the wizard if it is run again, if it is necessary to change the IKE policy.

b. Click **OK** to accept policy **120** and return to the Encryption Algorithms screen.

- Name = pre-share-3des-sha
- Encryption = 3DES
- Hash = sha
- D-H Group = 2
- Authentication = pre-share
- Lifetime = 86400

c. On the Encryption Algorithms screen, click the **Select** button next to IPsec Proposal. On the Select IPsec Proposals (Transform Sets) screen, remove all IPsec proposal entries from the Assigned entry field, except for ESP-3DES-SHA, because this is the one R3 is using. All the transform sets listed will still be inserted into the final ASA configuration but the crypto map only draws on the specific transform-set identified.

- Name = ESP-3DES-SHA
- Mode = Tunnel
- ESP Encryption = 3DES
- ESP Authentication = SHA

d. Click **OK** to assign the IPsec proposal and return to the Encryption Algorithms screen. When finished, the screen should look like the following. Click **Next** to continue.

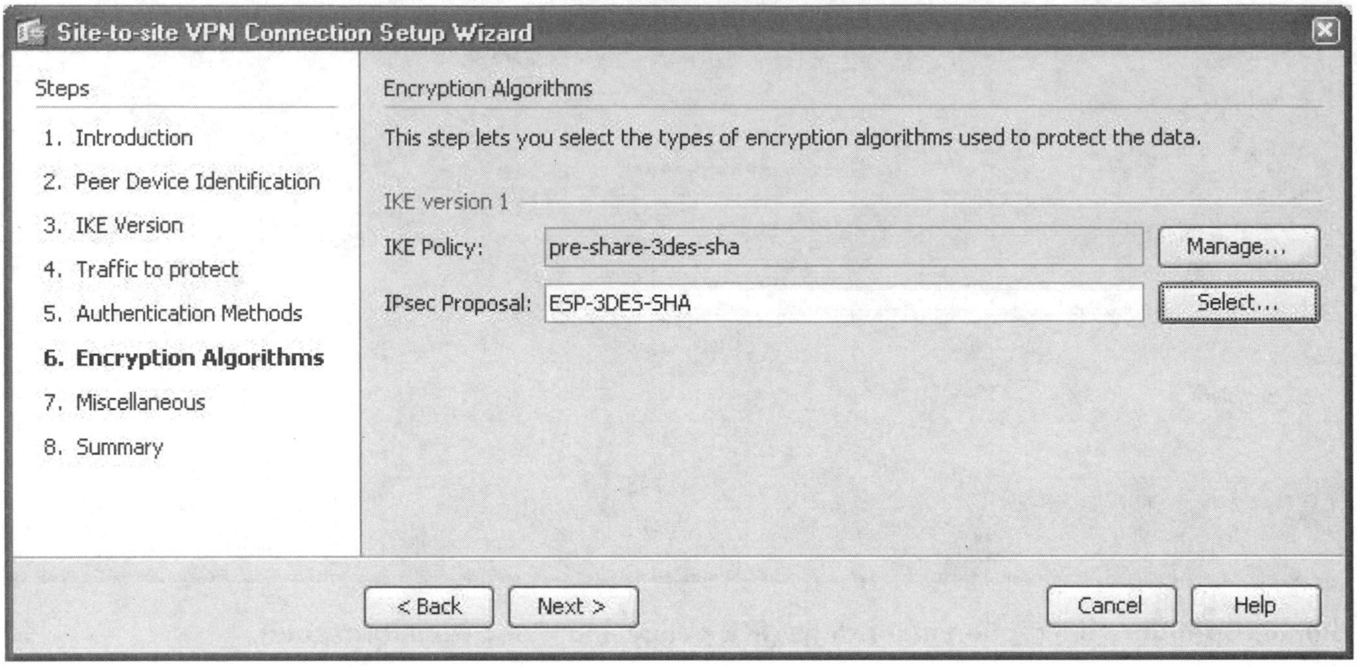

Step 9: Configure miscellaneous settings.

On the Miscellaneous screen, select the **Enable inbound IPsec sessions to bypass interface access lists** checkbox. Select the **Exempt ASA side host/network from address translation** checkbox for the inside interface. Click **Next** to continue.

Step 10: Review the configuration summary and deliver the commands to the ASA.

a. The Summary page is displayed next. Verify that the information configured in the Site-to-Site VPN Wizard is correct. You can click the **Back** button to make changes, or click **Cancel** to restart the VPN Wizard (recommended).

b. Click **Finish** to complete the process and deliver the commands to the ASA. If prompted to authenticate, log in again as admin with a password of cisco123.

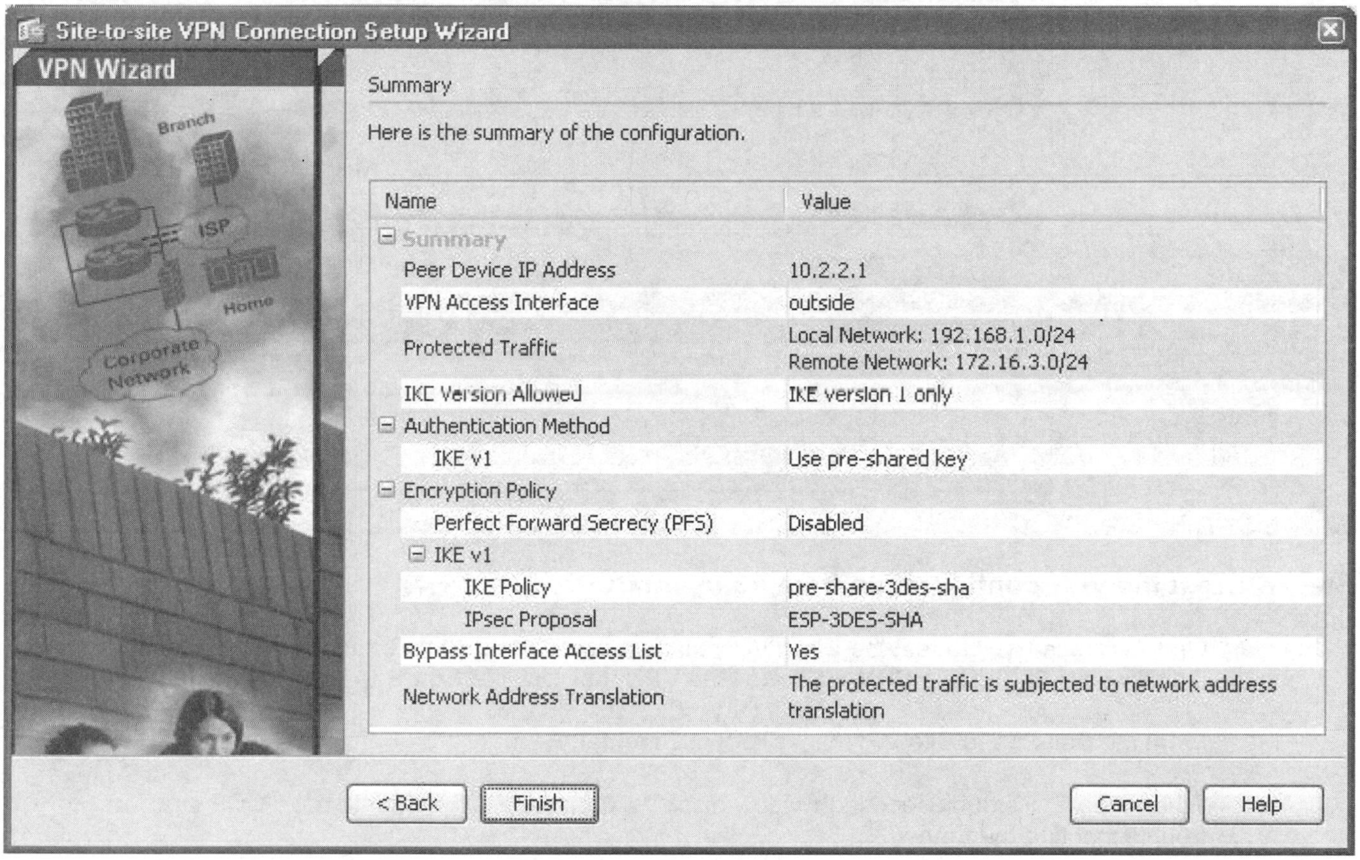

Step 11: Verify the ASA VPN connection profile.

The Configurations > Site-to-Site VPN > Connection Profiles screen will display, showing the settings you just configured. You can verify and edit the VPN configuration from this window.

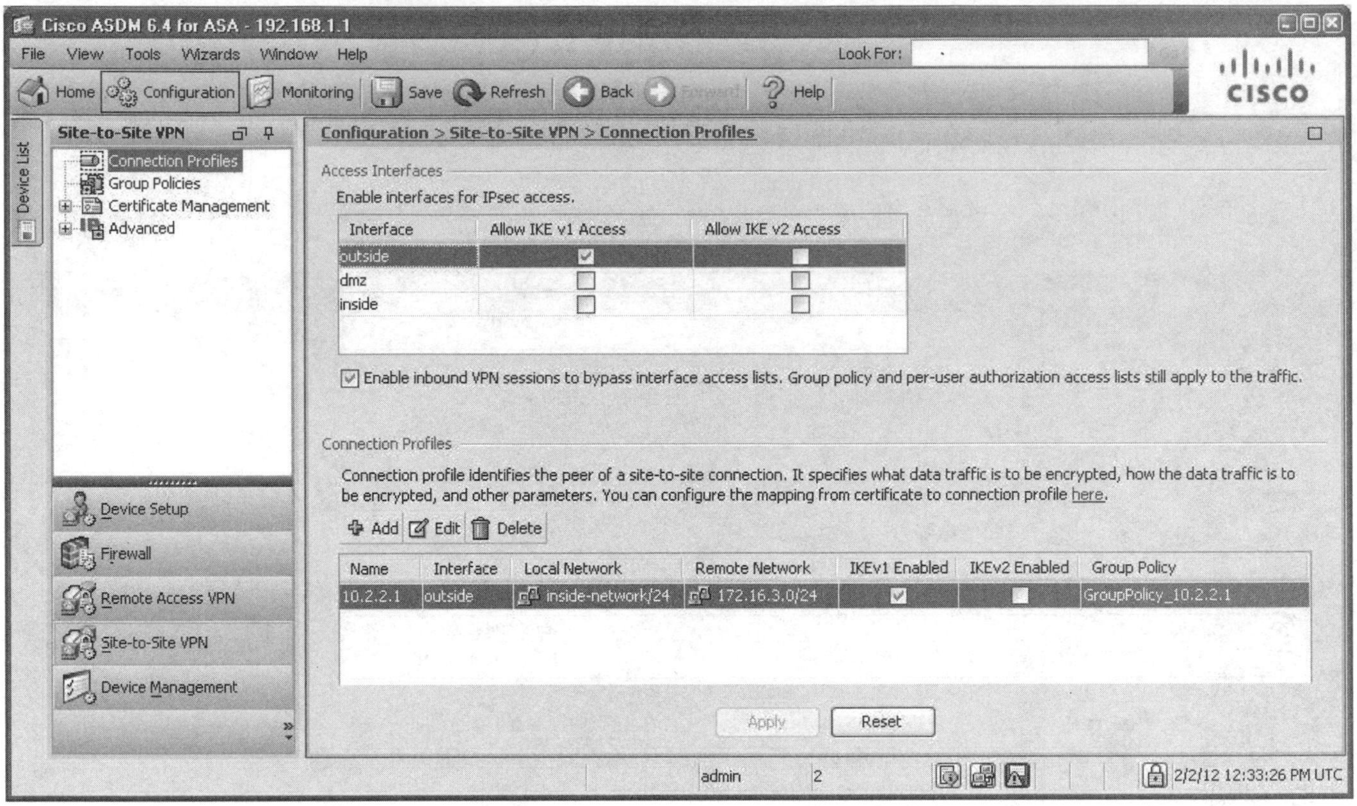

Step 12: Test the VPN configuration from R3 using CCP.

a. On PC-C, use CCP to test the IPsec VPN tunnel between the R3 ISR and the ASA. Choose **Configure > Security > VPN > Site-to-Site VPN** and click the **Edit Site to Site VPN** tab.

b. From the Edit Site to Site VPN tab, click **Test Tunnel**.

c. When the VPN Troubleshooting window displays, click the **Start** button to have CCP start troubleshooting the tunnel.

d. When the CCP warning window displays indicating that CCP will enable router debugs and generate some tunnel traffic, click **Yes** to continue.

e. On the next VPN Troubleshooting screen, the IP address of the host in the source network is displayed by default (R3 Fa0/1 = 172.16.3.1). Enter the IP address of host PC-B in the destination network field (192.168.1.3) and click **Continue** to begin the debugging process.

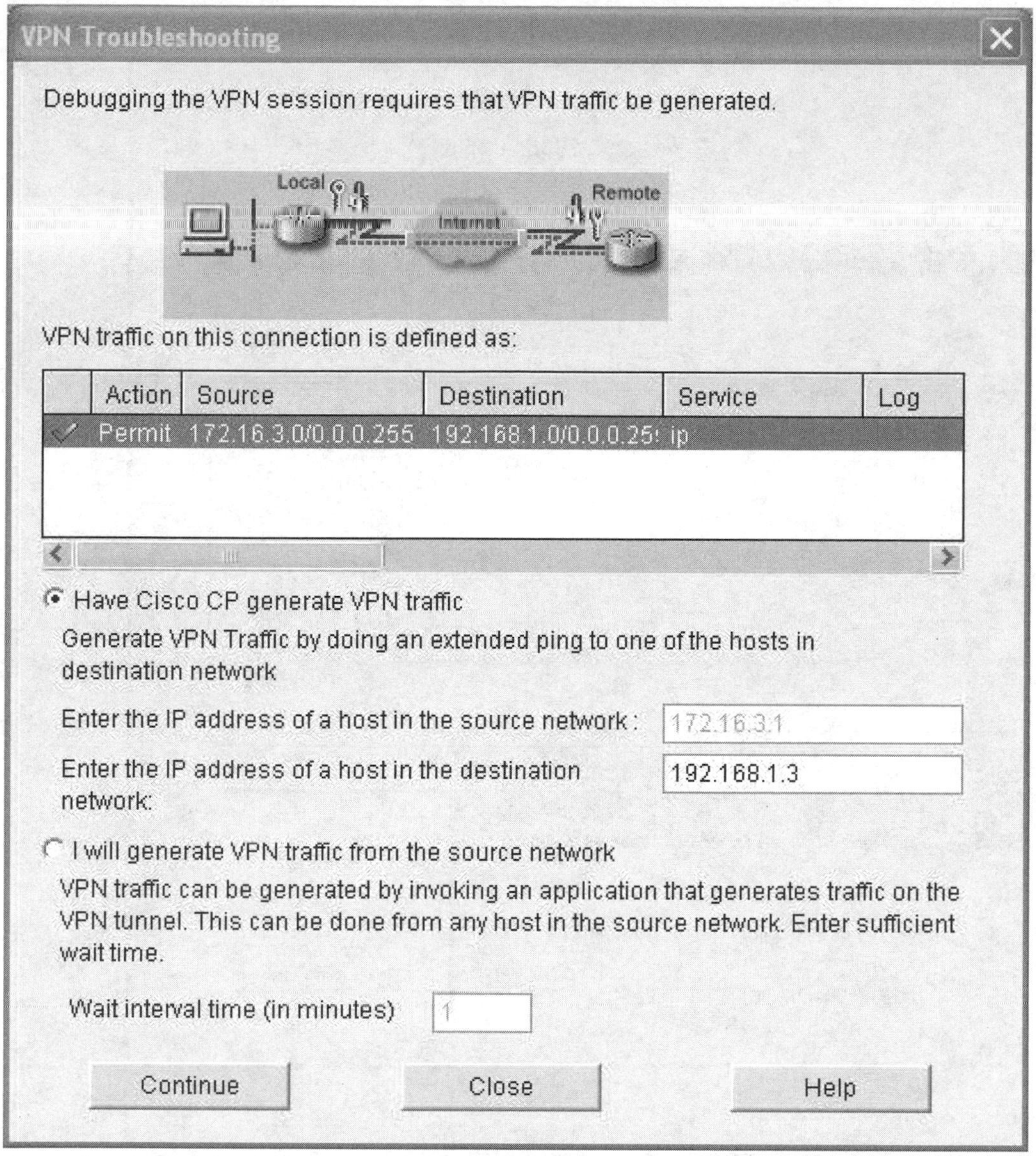

f. If the debug is successful and the tunnel is up, you should see the following figure. If the testing fails, CCP displays failure reasons and recommended actions. Click **OK** to remove the window.

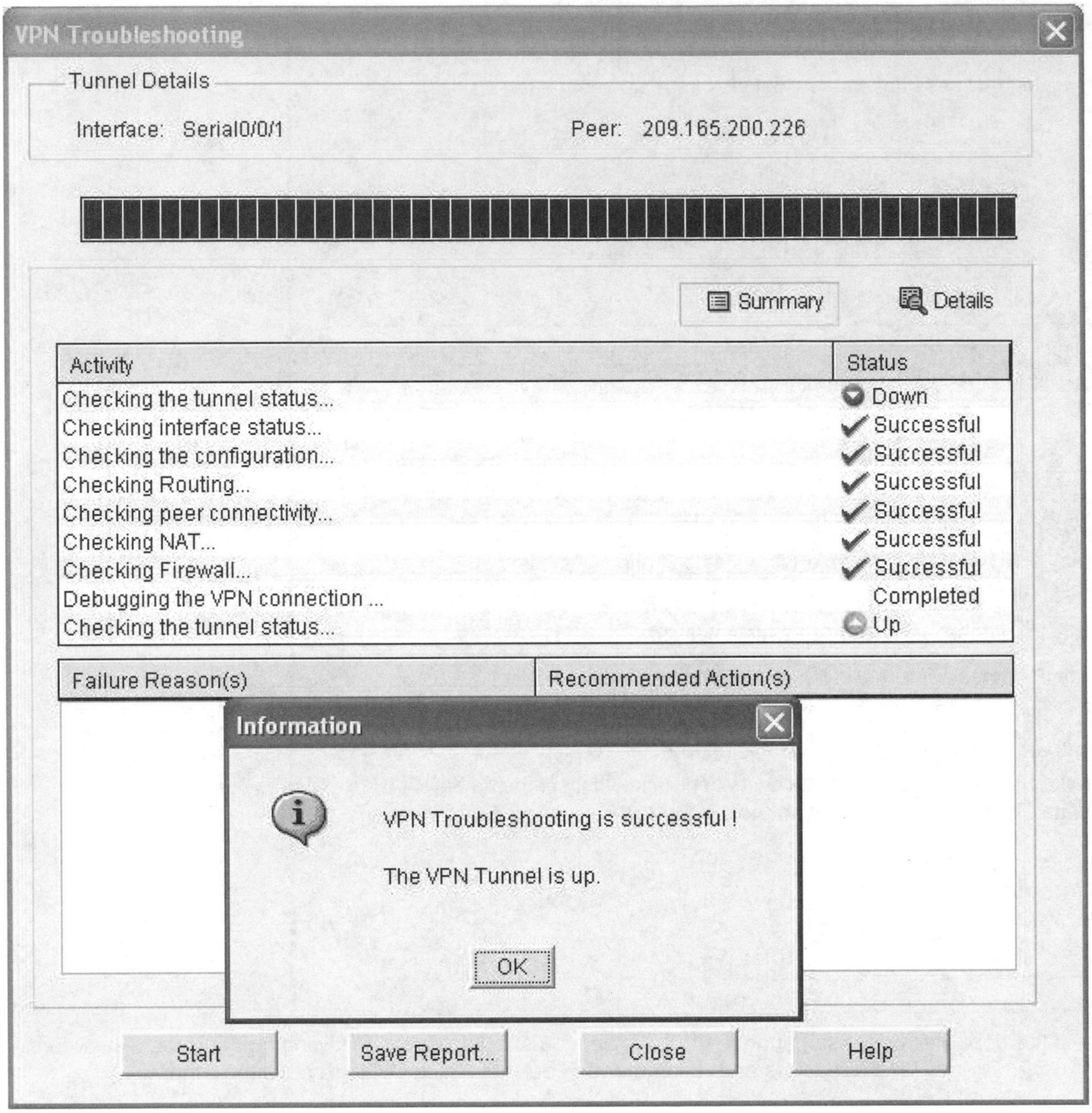

g. You can save the report if you want; otherwise, click **OK** and then **Close**.

h. On PC-C (CCP for R3), choose **Configure > Security > VPN > Site-to-Site VPN** and click the **Edit Site to Site VPN** tab. The tunnel status should now be up.

Note: If you want to reset the tunnel and test again, click the **Clear Connection** button from the Edit Site to Site VPN window.

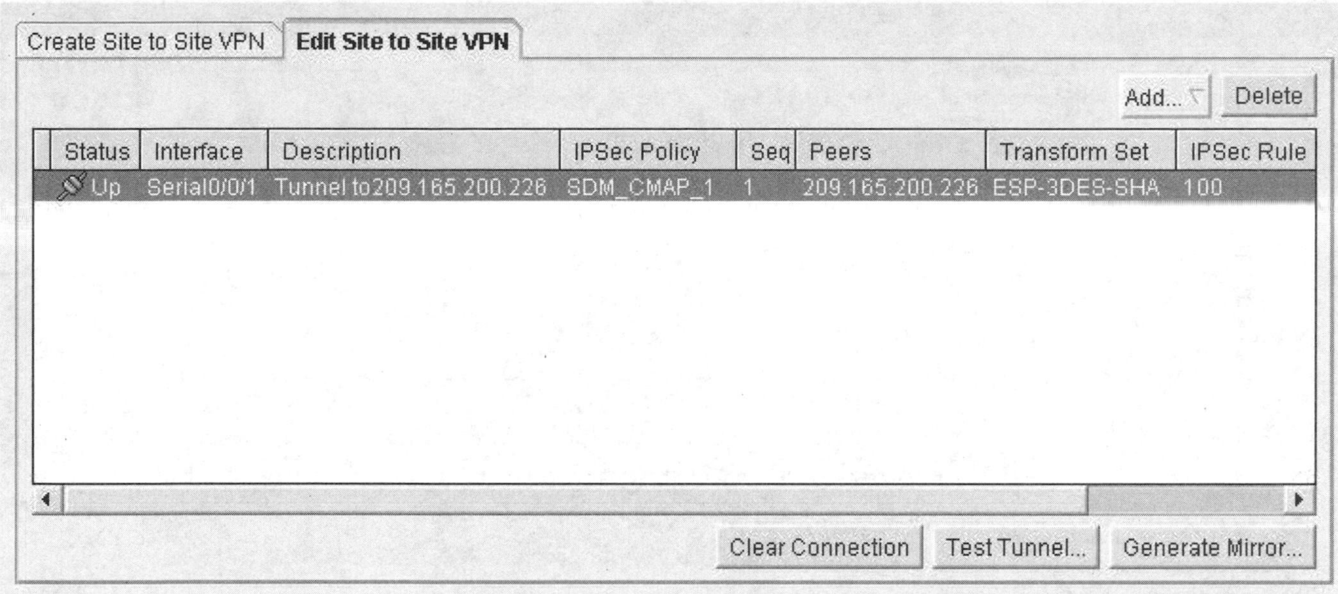

i. You can further verify tunnel functionality by pinging from branch office PC-C to PC-B on the internal network. The pings should be successful.

Note: Without the tunnel in place and bypassing NAT, it would be impossible for PC-C on the external network to ping PC-B on the private internal network.

Step 13: Use ASDM monitoring to verify the tunnel.

a. From the ASDM menu bar, select **Monitoring** and click **VPN** from the panels at the lower left of the screen. Click **VPN Statistics > Sessions**. Click the **Filter By** drop-down menu and select **IPsec Site-to-Site**. You should see the Site-to-Site IPsec VPN tunnel listed and active, as well as current VPN session information and statistics.

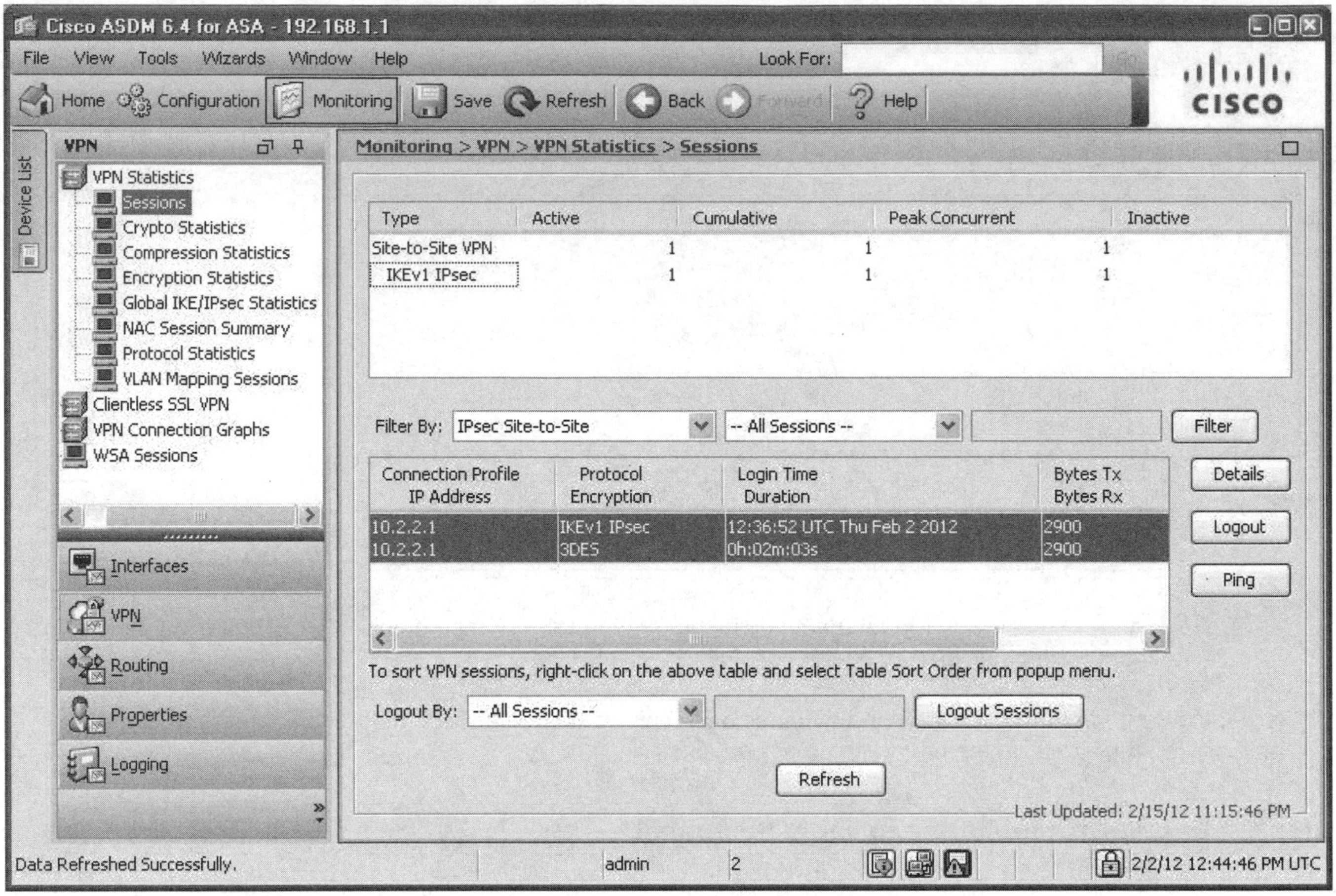

b. Click **Encryption Statistics**. You should see one or more sessions using the 3DES encryption algorithm.

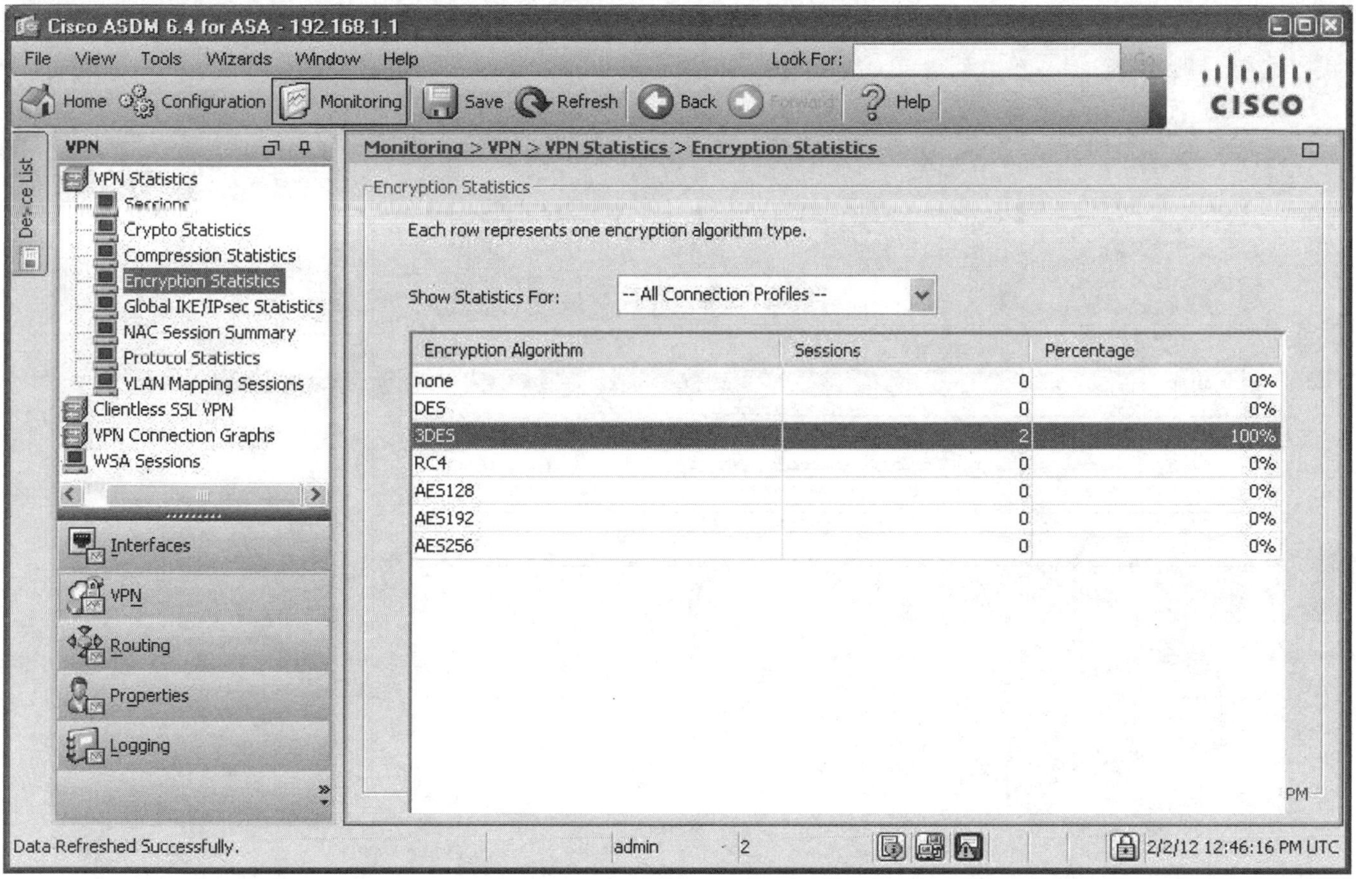

c. Click **Crypto Statistics**. You should see values for the number of packets encrypted and decrypted as well as security association (SA) requests, and so on.

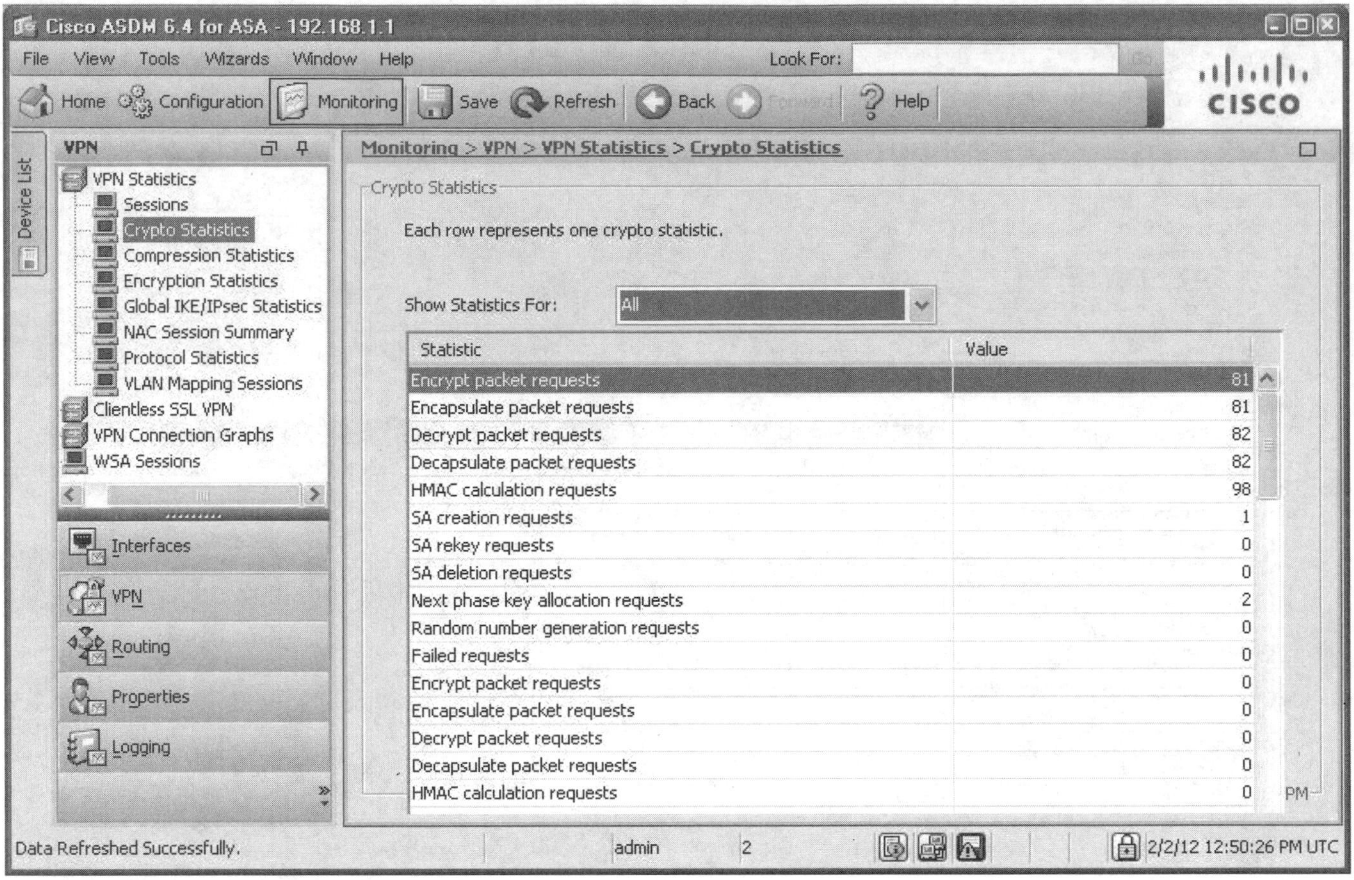

Reflection

1. What are some situations in which a site-to-site IPsec VPN would be preferable compared to a remote access SSL VPN?

____

____

____

2. What are some situations in which a remote access VPN would be preferable compared to site-to-site VPN?

____

____

____

Router Interface Summary Table

Router Model	Ethernet Interface 1	Ethernet Interface 2	Serial Interface 1	Serial Interface 2
1800	Fast Ethernet 0/0 (Fa0/0)	Fast Ethernet 0/1 (Fa0/1)	Serial 0/0/0 (S0/0/0)	Serial 0/0/1 (S0/0/1)
1900	Gigabit Ethernet 0/0 (G0/0)	Gigabit Ethernet 0/1 (G0/1)	Serial 0/0/0 (S0/0/0)	Serial 0/0/1 (S0/0/1)
2800	Fast Ethernet 0/0 (Fa0/0)	Fast Ethernet 0/1 (Fa0/1)	Serial 0/0/0 (S0/0/0)	Serial 0/0/1 (S0/0/1)
2900	Gigabit Ethernet 0/0 (G0/0)	Gigabit Ethernet 0/1 (G0/1)	Serial 0/0/0 (S0/0/0)	Serial 0/0/1 (S0/0/1)

Note: To find out how the router is configured, look at the interfaces to identify the type of router and how many interfaces the router has. There is no way to effectively list all the combinations of configurations for each router class. This table includes identifiers for the possible combinations of Ethernet and serial interfaces in the device. The table does not include any other type of interface, even though a specific router may contain one. An example of this might be an ISDN BRI interface. The string in parentheses is the legal abbreviation that can be used in Cisco IOS commands to represent the interface.